7TH EDITION

WHOSE CHOICE IS IT?

ABORTION, MEDICINE, AND THE LAW

EDITORS
DAVID F. WALBERT AND J. DOUGLAS BUTLER

AMERICAN**BAR**ASSOCIATION

ABA Publishing

Table of Contents

Chapter 3
Abortion Law in Canada   **121**

Chapter 7
A Future from the Past: Self-Managed Abortion
with Ancient Care and Modern Medicines   231

Chapter 8
Rebecca Gomperts: Providing Abortion Care
to Women Around the World   283

Chapter 9
What Lawyers Need to Know about the
Reproductive Justice Framework   309

Chapter 10
Modern Day Inquisitions   **325**

Chapter 15
The Wages of Crying Wolf: A Comment on *Roe v. Wade*   **437**

Chapter 16
Finding Abortion Rights in the Constitution   **471**

Acknowledgements and Dedication

As with our prior editions, we are fortunate in having excellent contributors who allowed us to make this book what it is. They not only provided outstanding chapters, they were a pleasure to work with. If we were going to single out one particular contributor for special thanks, it would have to be Professor Jill Morrison from Georgetown University Law Center. Not only did Professor Morrison author the chapter on reproductive justice, she "recruited" the authors of two other important chapters—one addressing abortion laws globally, and the other addressing self-managed abortion. These three chapters are essential to the book.

We would also like to dedicate this book to Dr. Alan Guttmacher and the Guttmacher Institute. Our relationship with Dr. Guttmacher began with our first book in 1973 when he graciously authored a personal retrospective on his long career in reproductive health care. He recalled medical school at Johns Hopkins in the 1920s when he was taught that an abortion was either therapeutic to save a pregnant woman's life or it was a crime. As soon as he was in his residency, he learned firsthand how that restrictive policy caused unnecessary suffering in many ways, not the least being unwanted children born into circumstances that led to a life of misery and often outright abuse. After those early experiences and throughout his life, Dr. Guttmacher was a powerful advocate for reproductive rights. The Institute which bears his name has for the last half-century been the leading research and policy organization committed to advancing sexual and reproductive health globally. It provides reliable, balanced information on sexual activity, contraception, abortion, and childbearing by identifying key questions and then collecting and analyzing the data to answer them. Both Dr. Butler and Mr. Walbert are firm believers that public policy must be based on fact if societies are to function effectively, and the Guttmacher Institute provides the evidence on which fact-based reproductive health policies can be based. Everyone should be grateful for that work no matter where their opinion might fall on issues like choice.

David F. Walbert
J. Douglas Butler

Introduction

When we undertook *Whose Choice Is It?*, our goal was to publish the most comprehensive book of the several editions of *Abortion, Medicine and the Law* we have done. We felt no less was necessary because of the continuing, and even increasing significance of the issue in the United States and globally. While the Supreme Court's 7–2 decisions in the *Roe* and *Doe* cases in 1973 were thought by most people to have resolved basic questions of reproductive choice, those questions have in fact remained prominent in political, policy, and legal debates in the United States. The intensity of the controversy has even increased in recent years as anti-choice advocates have pressed for more and more restrictive legislation by state legislatures, and Republican leadership both on the national and state levels has made restrictive legislation a core element of its political strategy.

Probably more than at any time since the Supreme Court's 1973 decisions, the continued vitality of *Roe* and *Doe* are in question. If they are overturned by the Supreme Court, legal disputes over abortion will become even more prevalent in the United States. Legislators in all 50 states will have to make a series of choices, and they will not be able to pass extreme laws for political reasons knowing they will be struck down by a federal court. Similarly, the supreme courts of all 50 states would then have the responsibility of reviewing those laws under 50 state constitutions, a responsibility that until now has fallen almost exclusively to the U.S. Supreme Court acting under the U.S. Constitution.

The ongoing abortion debate has by no means been limited to the United States. Some countries have liberalized their laws since the *Roe* decision—by judicial decision, legislation, or constitutional referendum—while others have enacted more restrictive regimes. In countries where religious objections are minimal and access to abortion care is solidly accepted, that is not likely to change. But in most countries, there is at least some debate over what the law should be and how accessible abortion care should be. That debate is not going to stop. In Argentina, intense lobbying by the Catholic church thwarted a liberalization law as recently as 2018, but an effective grassroots movement was able to reverse that decision in 2020, culminating in a dramatic 38 to 29 vote in the Senate. In spite of that victory for pro-choice advocates, one can be sure the fight over abortion will continue in Argentina.

The only indisputable fact is that the entire subject of abortion—safety, morality, legality, accessibility, human rights and freedoms, reproductive justice, and a host of other issues—is very much a present part of public policy discussions in countries around the world. That is not going to change in the foreseeable future. Because of the significance of abortion access as a subject that touches so many issues worldwide, our overriding purpose was to make this book as comprehensive as possible while maintaining the very highest quality of the work. We believe we achieved that goal and are excited by the breadth, depth, and objectivity of the work, the strength of our contributors, and the richness of each chapter. Whatever may be the future of the *Roe* and *Doe* decisions, *Whose Choice Is It?* will be an invaluable guide in the United States and globally for advocates, legislators, judges, physicians, public health officials, and anyone who wants to know more about issues related to abortion.

American and Canadian Law

Two chapters address in depth the array of legal issues that have evolved in the United States and Canada, both legislative and judicial. We felt it was important to have a particularly thorough chapter on American law not just because we are American lawyers with experience in constitutional law, but because the scope of the issues that have been addressed by American courts is unique. There are 50 separate states and any number of local jurisdictions that can pass legislation that gives rise to litigation under *Roe* and its progeny. As a result, the United States has developed a much more extensive body of law regarding different iterations of abortion restrictions than any other country.

The author of Chapter 2, Abortion Law in the United States, is Professor Edward B. Goldman from the University of Michigan Schools of Law, Public Health and Medicine. Professor Goldman is one of the nation's leading experts and a highly regarded author. He manages the University's program on sexual rights and reproductive justice in the Obstetrics and Gynecology Department and teaches reproductive justice in the law school. His chapter analyzes the entire gamut of issues that have come before the courts, and his discussion of those issues will be an excellent source and guide to anyone in the United States or elsewhere who is interested in questions about regulatory efforts to restrict access to abortion. Throughout the chapter, Professor Goldman comments on the legal implications should *Roe* be reversed, and his chapter would be especially valuable to legislators, advocates, and others should that happen. His discussion is supplemented by Appendix A, which compiles current abortion laws in every state.

Chapter 3, Abortion Law in Canada by A. Anne McLellan and Odessa M. O'Dell, is an in-depth treatment of Canadian statutory and judicial abortion issues. Ms. McLellan has served as Minister of Justice, Attorney General, and Deputy Prime Minister of Canada, and after her career in government, she was a Distinguished Scholar in Residence at the University of Alberta. No one is in a better position to address the Canadian experience. Among the reasons we felt that a thorough treatment of Canadian law was important is the unusual journey that abortion law has taken in Canada. Central to that history are the *Morgentaler* cases, a series of decisions that involved prosecutions of Dr. Henry Morgentaler, a fierce advocate of a woman's right to choose and a man with a remarkable personal history. He was a Jewish Polish-born Canadian physician who, as a youth during World War II, was imprisoned at the *Łódź* Ghetto and later at Dachau and Auschwitz. Unsurprisingly, given his personal history, Dr. Morgentaler was not cowed by the threat of prosecution by Canadian authorities, and he openly flouted Canadian legal prohibitions against abortion.

In the January 1988 *Morgentaler* case, the Canadian Supreme Court ruled the existing statutory restriction on abortion invalid under the Charter of Rights and Freedoms that had been adopted in 1982. Especially notable in that decision are the words of Justice Bertha Wilson, whose opinion (Appendix N) addressed a woman's abortion decision with exceptional sensitivity:

> [The abortion] decision is one that will have profound psychological, economic and social consequences for the pregnant woman. The circumstances giving rise to it can be complex and varied and there may be, and usually are, powerful considerations militating in opposite directions. It is a decision that deeply reflects the way the woman thinks about herself and her relationship to others and to society at large. It is not just a medical decision; it is a profound social and ethical one as well. Her response to it will be the response of the whole person.

Justice Wilson agreed that the legal right in Canada to security of the person protected both the physical and psychological integrity of a woman, but more fundamentally she found the statute offensive because it told a woman that her capacity to reproduce was not subject to her own control. She eloquently described that paradox:

[A woman] is truly being treated as a means—a means to an end which she
does not desire, but over which she has no control. She is the passive recipient of a decision made by others as to whether her body is to be used to
nurture a new life. Can there be anything that comports less with human
dignity and self-respect? How can a woman in this position have any sense
of security with respect to her person?

The authors also provide a realistic assessment of how these new rights
have actually affected women's access to abortion services as a practical matter, which varies significantly from province to province.

While it would be of limited value to include all of the American and
Canadian Supreme Court opinions that have addressed abortion issues, we
have included in the appendix excerpts from key opinions. From the *Roe* and
Doe cases, we included essential parts of Justice Blackmun's opinions (Appendices B and C, respectively); the concurrences of Justices Douglas, Burger,
and Stewart (Appendices D, E and F, respectively); and the dissents of Justices White and Rehnquist (Appendices G and H, respectively). Justice Blackmun's later opinion in *Casey* is Appendix J, where he decries Chief Justice
Rehnquist's views (Appendix K) as callous and superficial:

Even more shocking than the Chief Justice's cramped notion of individual
liberty is his complete omission of any discussion of the effects that compelled childbirth and motherhood have on women's lives. . . . [F]or the
Chief Justice, only women's *psychological* health is a concern, and only to
the extent that he assumes that every woman who decides to have an abortion does so without serious consideration of the moral implications of her
decision. In short, the Chief Justice's view of the State's compelling interest
in maternal health has less to do with health than it does with compelling
women to be maternal.

Justice Blackmun's final words in *Casey* are prescient as he describes the
politicization of the Constitution. "I am 83 years old. I cannot remain on this
Court forever, and when I do step down, the confirmation process for my
successor well may focus on the issue before us today. That, I regret, may be
exactly where the choice between the two worlds will be made." While Justice
Blackmun's prediction accurately foresaw subsequent hearings on the confirmation of Supreme Court appointees, he likely could not have imagined
just how far the process would sink where an expected vote to overrule *Roe*
became the primary qualification for nomination by Republican presidents.

Justice O'Connor's plurality opinion in *Casey* (Appendix I) is included
because of its historically significant discussion of the role of stare decisis in
landmark constitutional decisions like *Roe* and *Brown v. Board of Education*.

Other excerpted opinions in the appendix are Justice Breyer's opinion in *Whole Woman's Health* (Appendix L) and Chief Justice Roberts' 2020 concurrence in *June Medical Services* (Appendix M).

Two chapters analyze whether *Roe* and *Doe* were properly decided in 1973 when the Supreme Court ruled unconstitutional the Texas and Georgia laws that restricted a woman's access to abortion. Professor John Hart Ely in Chapter 15, The Wages of Crying Wolf: A Comment on *Roe v. Wade*, sets out the case that *Roe* was wrongly decided as a matter of constitutional law. Making the argument that *Roe* was entirely consistent with core principles of the Constitution is Chapter 16, Finding Abortion Rights in the Constitution, by Professor Laurence Tribe. Professors Ely and Tribe have been giants in the field of constitutional law, and no one has improved on their classic essays. Professor Tribe continues to be one of the leading authorities, if not the foremost authority, on constitutional law in the United States today.

Our treatment of American litigation is capped by the inclusion of two amicus curiae briefs filed with the Supreme Court. The amicus brief in Chapter 4 was filed on behalf of women lawyers in the *Whole Woman's Health* case, and each one of the more than 100 amici relates their individual story about how their own abortion changed their lives, often making their professional life as an attorney a possibility that would have been unattainable otherwise. As one put it, "To the world, I am an attorney who had an abortion; to myself, I am an attorney because I had an abortion." Their individual testimonies are personal and powerful, and some observers believe that this was the most effective of the many amicus briefs filed in the case.

The other amicus brief included in the book was filed in the *June* case by Americans United for Life, the leading anti-choice legal advocacy organization in the United States (Appendix O). It contains a comprehensive list of amicus' arguments why *Roe* should be reversed. While the brief to some extent tracks Professor Ely's analysis, it makes the additional contention that events since 1973 have revealed that *Roe* was predicated on incorrect factual assumptions.

It is no secret, as Justice Blackmun pointed out, that constitutional questions have become political ones in the United States, and we felt it important to include in the book a discussion of politics and abortion. We were fortunate that Congressman William Delahunt of Massachusetts agreed to a series of interviews with David Walbert, which became Chapter 5, Politics, Religion, and Abortion in the United States. Congressman Delahunt had an outstanding public career that included serving as district attorney, where he implemented first-in-the-nation programs to assist abused women and aggressively prosecute rape and abuse; service as a member of the state legislature; and seven terms in Congress where he was a key participant in many of the most important issues the nation faced. Congressman Delahunt is a lifelong Catholic and product of parochial schools who was taught to be anti-abortion, but later became pro-choice when he thought through the issue on his own—should it be a woman's decision whether to continue a pregnancy, or the state's? As he puts it in his interview, "It's her decision, and it is her issue to deal with the morality of it."

Congressman Delahunt was inspired to a public service career by Jack Kennedy's 1960 presidential campaign, and he notes the irony that conservative Protestants in 1960 were concerned that a Catholic president would be too subject to control by church doctrine and the Pope, but lately Justices Kennedy and Roberts—both Catholics—have been criticized by religious conservatives for the opposite reason, for *not* applying Catholic doctrine when interpreting what the Constitution means regarding anti-abortion statutes. Congressman Delahunt describes how the abortion issue has been used by many politicians who really do not care about the issue but understand how to use it to generate votes. During the course of the interviews, Congressman Delahunt mused that what happened in Germany in the 1920s and 30s could happen in the United States. Just days after his talking about the Brownshirts and the Nazis' initial attempt at a putsch, the U.S. Capitol was stormed by a right-wing mob, encouraged by the president himself.

Abortion Law around the World

We wanted the book to expand beyond North America and address the entire world, and we are grateful to Madison Glennie, Lily Milwit, and Julie Zuckerbrod—who combined practical experience with abortion issues and advocacy and their academic knowledge as lawyers—for their excellent work in Chapter 1, The World's Abortion Laws. The authors note that 67 countries permit abortion upon request, with varied gestational limits, while 26 countries prohibit abortion altogether. To provide readers with deeper insight into the variations among these laws, they describe in detail the specific laws in 31 representative countries from 12 different global regions.

The chapter is not only a comprehensive, up-to-date assessment of abortion laws around the world, it includes revealing legal history behind the laws in a number of countries. For example, the former Soviet Union and the Russian Federation are a case study in how abortion policies can be driven by considerations that have nothing to do with the interests of a pregnant woman or a fetus. The Soviet Union was the first country to permit unrestricted abortion access in 1920, but with the possibility of war with Germany looming, Joseph Stalin banned abortions in 1936 in an effort to increase the country's population. As a consequence, illegal abortions rose significantly, causing an increase in abortion-related morbidity and mortality. After World War II and Stalin's death, a 1955 decree allowed for first-trimester abortions, but the Ministry of Health fought against contraception with fabricated claims about adverse effects. That, together with bans on sex education in schools, made Russia home to one of the highest annual abortion rates in the world.

The Russian example is one of many that readers should find informative regarding the consequences of abortion regulations. Another is El Salvador, where women are prosecuted under anti-abortion laws for both miscarriages and abortions, the former because it is often difficult to distinguish between the two after the fact. More than 140 women are known to have been charged criminally in El Salvador since 1998 under the country's abortion prohibition. In Brazil, abortion is highly restricted by law, which causes 500,000 illegal abortions each year among 18- to 39-year-old women. Those illegal abortions carry a high incidence of health complications and hospitalizations. Like the experience in other countries, Brazil's legal prohibition against abortion does not stop abortions; it just causes unsafe, illegal abortions. For countries where the information is available, the authors address not just the availability of abortion as a matter of law but its practical availability in light of other barriers to access, such as economics and the refusal of providers to perform procedures.

Abortion Practices in the Past, Present, and Future

Three exceptional contributors, Dr. Rebecca Gomperts, Professor John Riddle, and Anna Reed, go beyond the law and provide a rich description of abortion practices from ancient times to the present. Readers will also gain insights from these chapters as to how abortion practices are changing now and are likely to evolve, and how those changes might impact the right to choose in the future. Professor John Riddle is the acknowledged expert on historical contraceptive and abortion practices from ancient times to today. His previous books include *Contraception and Abortion from the Ancient World to the Renaissance* and *Eve's Herbs: A History of Contraception and Abortion in the West*. We are fortunate that Professor Riddle undertook to write Chapter 6, Women's Knowledge of Abortifacients from Antiquity to the Present. It provides not only an excellent overview of abortion and contraceptive practices historically, but also includes recent historical evidence about those past practices.

While it is not widely known today, herbs were commonly used as abortifacients and contraceptives for millennia. The knowledge of the appropriate herbal regimen was passed down from one woman to another, among midwives, healers, and "wise women." Although the efficacy of herbal treatments would not have been as great as today's pharmaceuticals, they were effective and an important part of women's lives. Knowledge of contraceptives and abortifacients was suppressed at times through the persecution of midwives and "wise women" accused of witchcraft. In the United States, abortion-inducing medications and contraceptives were readily available until the middle of the 19th century. The hostility to abortions in the United States coincided with efforts by all-male medical societies advocating legislation that made it illegal for midwives, or any non-doctor, to provide such services. In short, they eliminated their competition.

Ms. Reed links the past to the present in Chapter 7, A Future from the Past: Self-Managed Abortion with Ancient Care and Modern Medicines. She explains that the historical practice of women self-aborting with herbal medicines has effectively reemerged and expanded with the advent of the medications mifepristone and misoprostol.

> Self-managed abortion (SMA) . . . encompasses a wide array of experiences, including ingesting herbs, massage, drinking tisanes, using a combination of abortion medications (mifepristone and misoprostol), using misoprostol alone, inserting objects into the vagina, using a combination of these methods, or other methods. Although there is increasing awareness about SMA, the practice is not a new phenomenon. The historical record of people self-managing extends throughout history and across cultures.

In addition to her training as a lawyer, Ms. Reed, who grew up in France, brings deep personal experience to her writing. She has been a sex education teacher and youth advocate, overseen the development of reproductive justice curricula for Georgetown University's Street Law program that is taught in high schools, and advised pregnant individuals trying to navigate the complexities of legal and health care procedures that act as de facto barriers. She is also an executive producer of *Self Managed*, a podcast dedicated to destigmatizing and demystifying the practice of self-managed abortion.

Drawing on her experience, Ms. Reed explains the widely differing access to abortion services based on people's socioeconomic, racial, gender,[1]

---

1. Our book generally uses male/female gender descriptions, not to be dismissive of the serious considerations regarding gender-affirming care, but because reported data, judicial opinions, and most other legal discussions we refer to use traditional binary pronouns.

and immigration status, among other factors. Her chapter addresses how the Trump administration stubbornly refused to make accommodations to the FDA's in-person mifepristone and misoprostol dispensing requirement during the COVID-19 pandemic, leading to litigation to the U.S. Supreme Court. Ms. Reed concludes that self-managed medication abortion will not likely replace clinical abortions entirely because of the need for late-term abortions, and some people will prefer to end their pregnancies in a clinical setting regardless. But if barriers to abortion clinics proliferate in the United States and in some other countries, she envisions self-managed abortion as a safe and promising alternative that will enable many people to bypass clinics entirely.

Once in a great while, someone does things that other people cannot even imagine. One such person is Dutch physician Rebecca Gomperts, a visionary to whom what are insurmountable barriers to others are mere hindrances to overcome. Dr. Gomperts is one of the world's foremost advocates of a woman's right of access to abortion care. David Walbert's interview with her in Amsterdam is Chapter 8. Dr. Gomperts' personal narrative of how she became interested in providing abortion services to people and what she has done in that regard is a fascinating story of how one person can change history while helping many thousands of people. It is a story that will inspire readers, even some who may oppose a woman's right to choose.

In order to care for people who live where abortion access is restricted, Dr. Gomperts outfitted a ship to travel under the Dutch flag, naming the initiative Women on Waves. She has stationed the vessel just far enough offshore to remain in international waters subject to Dutch law where abortion is legal. Women shuttle from shore to the boat to have an abortion, and the enthusiasm of women in country after country has been overwhelming. When she took the ship to Ireland where abortion was prohibited, Dr. Gomperts was told women there would not be interested, but in fact there was a huge outpouring of general support and of women specifically seeking abortions. That visit had an especially lasting impact because it triggered a public discussion of abortion that ultimately led to constitutional referenda that established a women's right to choose in Ireland.

Dr. Gomperts next initiated Women on Web, a telemedicine support service for women around the world needing abortion care. It provides medical abortions without direct in-person contact with a doctor for women where abortion clinics are nonexistent or highly restricted. In the ten years prior to her interview, over 200,000 women from more than 140 countries had had an online consultation with Women on Web, and approximately 50,000 women had received a medical abortion at home.

Dr. Gomperts' many stories about the opposition she has faced from governments and church authorities are both entertaining and deeply troubling. The Maltese government, for example, tried to brand her a persona non grata, an "outlaw" legal status that supposedly disappeared in the Middle Ages. She has been indicted in Poland and so far avoided the infamous Interpol Red Notice for arrest and extradition, but the threat is an ever-present concern. Still, Dr. Gomperts is optimistic about the future and believes that women will have access through medication to self-managed abortions, notwithstanding baseless "scare mongering that it would be dangerous." She is concerned about countries that may ban medical abortions, as Morocco had done just prior to her interview. "What will happen then is that you will have the black market, which is happening all over Latin America. And the problem with the black market is what is sold could be anything. And it's very expensive."

Whatever the future may bring, there is no doubt that Dr. Gomperts will be a major force in determining that future given her vision and personal fortitude.

The Conscience of Medical Providers

Even legislation that permits abortions often excuses medical providers from performing procedures or prescribing abortion pills if they personally oppose abortion. These "conscience clause" exceptions make abortion care unavailable as a practical matter in many places, partly because providers oppose abortion, but also just because they fear community criticism if they provide abortion care to their patients. The problem is exacerbated by conservative legislators in many countries who justify conscience clause laws by invoking the virtues of conscience, when their real objective is simply to reduce women's reproductive choices.

Professors Bernard Dickens and Rebecca Cook—two of the foremost experts in the world on reproductive and sexual health law—address these issues in Chapter 13, Conscientious Commitment to Women's Health, where they make the case that a conscientious *commitment*, the converse of conscientious objection, should be at the forefront of medical care decisions and should lead health care providers to overcome any personal reluctance to providing reproductive services to women. Conscientious commitment to providing the means of birth control has a long history that could be a precedent, but when it comes to abortion services, conscientious commitment has been largely pushed aside. The authors also discuss the analogous historical experience of social reformers who suffered religious condemnation and even imprisonment as a parallel to the opprobrium (and even assassination) directed at health care practitioners who provide abortion services today.

Abortions as a Means of Sex Selection

Cornell Professor Sital Kalantry is an expert on international human rights and is faculty director of the Cornell India Law Center. In Chapter 11, Harmful Anti-Sex-Selective Abortion Laws Are Sweeping U.S. State Legislatures: Why Do Some Pro-choice People Support Them?, she provides new insights into sex-selective abortion and its legal proscription, as well as the actual incidence of sex-selective abortions. Professor Kalantry shows how sex-selective abortions do not occur with the frequency or for the reasons that public perception assumes to be the case. She shows that that public and media misperception is rooted in stereotypes of Asian and Asian-American family views. Similarly, while even pro-choice advocates in the United States sometimes support anti-sex selection prohibitions, they do so on the erroneous assumption that sex-selective abortions are rooted in antifemale sex-selection prejudice. Professor Kalantry presents compelling evidence that that is not the case and, again, that those assumptions originate from misplaced stereotypes.

Late Abortions

Chapter 20 by Dr. Warren Hern, Late Abortion: Clinical and Ethical Issues, addresses one of the most emotionally and politically charged subjects among the complex of abortion issues. Dr. Hern specializes in very complicated medical decisions for women of reproductive age, decisions that include questions about the life and health of the woman. His work involves diagnosis of fetal development and genetic disorders, which became even more important with the Zika virus.[2] Dr. Hern learned personally of the critical need for safe abortion services as a Peace Corps physician in Brazil where he witnessed women dying from unsafe illegal abortions. He is hailed as a hero by many, including his patients, but denounced by others because he performs late abortions. While Dr. Hern has received numerous awards and recognitions, including the Carl S. Schulz Award from the American Public Health Association for his scientific contributions and

---

2. Appendix Q contains excerpts from CDC guidelines for congenital Zika viral infection and testing of pregnant women who may have been exposed to Zika.

his defense of reproductive freedom, he and other providers face constant dangers—including the threat of assassination—because they care for late-term pregnant people. Dr. Hern's life has been threatened many times, anti-abortion terrorists have shot into his clinic, and he has been on their published "hit list."

His chapter describes some of the common situations in which the need for late abortion arises, and it is impossible not to sympathize with Dr. Hern and his patients—whatever one's initial thoughts may be regarding late abortions—after taking the time to understand the actual circumstances these women face and the compelling reasons why doctors provide them with abortion care. All too often, those very real, very human, and very moral considerations are lost in the white-hot political clamor that substitutes for thoughtful discussion of the issues raised by late abortions.

Reproductive Justice

Georgetown Law Professor Jill Morrison is a passionate advocate and the author of Chapter 9, What Lawyers Need to Know about the Reproductive Justice Framework, which is a philosophy and social movement that goes well beyond the right of access to abortion. Reproductive justice encompasses the right to have a child as well as not have a child, and to be able to raise a child in an appropriate environment with access to social, health, and educational resources. Professor Morrison's views were forged when she was a young woman and watched the Religious Right become a hostile political force, Ronald Reagan fan the racist "Welfare Queen" mythology, and American prisons filled as the country waged a war not on drugs, but on drug users. As a Black woman, she is acutely aware that the generations before her could not have imagined the degree of autonomy with which she lives her life, and she is devoted to reproductive justice in the hope that everyone can one day be fully free. Her passion, commitment, and insights will give many readers a new perspective on these issues.

Thoughts from Dr. Alan Guttmacher

Dr. Guttmacher was kind enough to contribute a chapter to our first edition that described how he become an outspoken advocate for a woman's right to choose. Dr. Guttmacher's personal involvement as a leader would warrant inclusion in this volume of his original essay—*The Genesis of Liberalized Abortion in New York: A Personal Insight*—simply for its historical importance and for the personal insights of the man whose name is more associated than any other in the world with reproductive health. But with the political efforts in the United States in particular that seek to return the country to a time long ago when Dr. Guttmacher was first practicing medicine, his retrospective is especially relevant today. We have included it in this volume as Chapter 17 and are confident that readers of all views will benefit from his reflections. Lawyers will find particularly fascinating the discussion he relates between the renowned Judge Learned Hand and Professor Herbert Wechsler when the American Law Institute was preparing a model abortion law a decade before the *Roe* decision. Judge Hand unequivocally condemned the ALI "reform" law of 1962 as "a rotten law" because it was "too damned conservative." Dr. Guttmacher later realized that Judge Hand was absolutely correct.

Medical Research and Fetal Tissue

Chapter 18 by Dr. Kenneth Ryan, The Medical and Research Uses of Human Fetal Tissues, appeared in part in an earlier edition. Dr. Ryan at the time was the leading authority on the ethics of fetal tissue research and the co-chair of the panel that opposed the ban on federal financing of research using fetal tissue. In addition to being the longtime chair of OB/GYN and Reproductive Biology at Brigham and Women's Hospital at Harvard, Dr. Ryan made significant discoveries in biochemistry that included understanding how the body produces estrogen, which led to treatments for infertility and certain cancers. His chapter addressed the unique importance of human fetal tissue for medical research and explained that much of that tissue is available only as a result of induced abortions. Dr. Ryan is deceased, but the ethical, medical, and practical considerations that he addressed in his original chapter have changed little. Because of that and because of Dr. Ryan's exceptional status and expertise, we decided to republish his original chapter with an updating addendum that addresses subsequent advances in medical knowledge and technology.

When Life Begins

The debate over when "life" begins ties into the question of what constitutes a "person" under the United States Constitution. Anti-choice advocates have claimed that "human life" begins at conception, which is a religious view, not one based on biological fact. More recently, they point to a detectable "heartbeat" as the beginning of life, but again that is an argument adopted for political appeal that disregards the facts. As Dr. Charles Gardner wrote in an earlier edition of this work: "The embryo is not a child. It is not a baby. It is not yet a human being."[3] Even a solitary sperm cell and an unfertilized ovum are alive. Embryos early in gestation are equally alive, but they are no more "human persons" than either a lone sperm cell or an unfertilized ovum. As Carl Sagan wrote in addressing this question, no Western society treats all life as inviolable.[4] For Sagan the question was: When does a human embryo or fetus become so different from those of other animals as to be distinctly human? He examined the process of embryonic and fetal development and looked for the "earliest onset of human thinking" as the first point at which a human fetus should be considered meaningfully different than fetuses of other animals. He determined that does not begin even intermittently until the middle of the seventh month at the very earliest.

In Chapter 12, How Sentience Should Mediate the Right to Abortion, Cornell Professor Sherry Colb tackles the "person question" and shows that abortion of a pre-sentient fetus should not raise a moral or legal obstacle.

> Before sentience, the fetus is "something" rather than "someone." If a sperm cell disappears, we might consider that a loss to the person whose sperm cell it was, but we would not say that the sperm cell itself has lost anything. They are just cells, with no sensations or emotions that would make life "better" or "worse" for them in different circumstances. Likewise, with the non-sentient fetus. Although such a fetus looks much more like a human being than a sperm cell does, it still has no interests in avoiding pain, in feeling pleasure or warmth or in having any particular thing happen to it. [A non-sentient fetus] is a potential human being, just as the sperm cell or egg cell or zygote is. And if it never becomes a human being because pregnancy is terminated prior to sentience, it will not have lost anything that it once had—a life in which there is the experience of pleasure and pain.

---

3. C. Gardner, *Is an Embryo a Person?*, *in* ABORTION, MEDICINE AND THE LAW 437, 445 (J.D. Butler & D. Walbert eds., 1992). Similarly, the common belief that the genetic constituents of a fertilized egg comprehensively prescribe the biology of a full-term fetus is incorrect. Environmental and stochastic factors are very important in fetal development, and the gap between genetic determination and those factors is especially significant for the fetal brain. "[T]here is not enough genetic information in the approximately 20,000 genes, of which approximately half are expressed in the brain, to code for the location and connections of each of the billions of neurons and trillions of synaptic connections." T. White, *Brain Development and Stochastic Processes During Prenatal and Early Life*, 58 J. AM. ACAD. CHILD & ADOL. PSYCH. 1042, 1046 (2019).

4. C. Sagan & A. Druyan, *Is It Possible to Be Pro-Life and Pro-Choice?*, PARADE MAGAZINE, Apr. 22, 1990.

Given those facts, Professor Colb concludes that neither the reason for an abortion nor the method of an abortion should be relevant to whether an abortion should be permitted pre-sentience since an abortion can cause no harm to a being in any meaningful or moral sense at that point in a pregnancy. Only after fetal sentience is attained is there a real moral question. Professor Colb believes that that question should be resolved by the pregnant woman herself because it is her body that would be used against her will if her choice is overridden. She also explores possible scenarios that could arise if medicine were to develop an artificial womb that would permit a viable, sentient fetus to develop to maturity outside the woman if her pregnancy were terminated. Finally, Professor Colb discusses the significance of sentience in how we treat animals and cause them pain.

One cannot overstate the importance of Dr. Colb's analysis given the efforts of anti-choice legislators to ascribe personhood status to an embryo or early-stage fetus. As Dr. Charles Gardner wrote in our earlier volume, "There will always be arguments based on spiritual or ethical beliefs to convince an individual of the rightness or wrongness of abortion, but each person should first understand the biology to which those beliefs refer." Sentience may occur developmentally before human "thinking," but it still requires much more than a mass of living, functioning cells, whether those cells are acting as an early heartbeat or performing other pre-sentient activities. The fetal capacity to experience pain does not exist until well after reflexive muscle contractions occur in response to stimuli. "[P]ain perception requires cortical recognition of the stimulus as unpleasant," and the cortical connections that are necessary for that perception—in other words, for the earliest beginning of sentience—do not begin to occur until the third trimester.[5]

Anti-abortion advocates sometimes point to earlier reflexive muscle contractions in response to stimuli as fetal pain, but they are not. Perception of pain at that point is impossible because the predicate cortical connections do not exist. The spread of such misinformation about fetal pain and fetal

---

5. S. Lee et al., *Fetal Pain: A Systematic Multidisciplinary Review of the Evidence*, 294 J.A.M.A. 947, 949 (2005); H. Harcourt, J. Bering & J. Gullam, *Opposition to Abortion Related to Inaccurate Beliefs About Fetal Pain Perception in Utero*, Aust. N.Z. J. Obstet. & Gynaecol. 1 (2021), https://obgyn.onlinelibrary.wiley.com/doi/epdf/10.1111/ajo.13356 (published online ahead of print). As noted in previous editions, it is not until late in the gestational process that "individual neurons [attain] an interconnected collective" that is a prerequisite to sentience. M. Flower, *Coming into Being: The Prenatal Development of Humans*, in ABORTION, MEDICINE AND THE LAW 437, 445 (J.D. Butler & D. Walbert eds., 1992). *See also* E. Borsani et al., *Correlation Between Human Nervous System Development and Acquisition of Fetal Skills*, 41 BRAIN & DEVEL. 225 (2019).

development generally has impacted public views of abortion and, in some cases, legislative action, not to mention the adverse impact on women in need of abortion care who have been misled. According to a recent study, the false belief that "the capacity for fetal pain exists in the first and second trimesters is remarkably common. [A]nti-choice participants [in the study] had an especially accelerated view of fetal ontogeny, with 40% believing that the capacity to perceive pain exists in the first trimester."[6]

The Epidemiology of Abortion in the United States and Elsewhere

A great deal of data has been collected around the world regarding the incidence of abortion, the relation between the prevalence of abortion and a country's laws, variations among socioeconomic and ethnic groups, the relation between the incidence of abortion and unintended pregnancies, and other issues. Because of the importance of the frequency of abortion and the complex of factors that affect abortion, we have included as Appendix P, Abortion Surveillance—United States 2018, which is a November 2020 Morbidity and Mortality Report of the CDC. The report is very informative not only as to the number and rate of abortions but the variability based on a person's age, marital status, race, state of residence, gestational age, number of prior live births, and the type of abortion. Trends over time are also analyzed. After nationwide legalization of abortion in 1973, the total number of *reported* abortions increased rapidly into the 1980s before trending down, although there are large variations in the rate of abortions across various subpopulations. In 2018, a total of 620,000 abortions were reported to the CDC, which is a slight increase from the previous year but a substantial decrease from ten years earlier. A somewhat more stable number is the abortion *ratio*, that is, the number of abortions per 1,000 live births. That ratio has also decreased over the prior decade, except for adolescents less than 15 years old, but less so proportionately than did the total number of abortions or the abortion *rate* (which the CDC defines as the number of abortions per 1,000 women within a given population). Currently, approximately three-quarters of all abortions in the United States occur at nine or fewer weeks gestation, and almost 40 percent of all abortions are now medical abortions.

---

6. Harcourt, Bering & Gullam, *supra* note 5, at 3.

While more detailed in many regards than data from other countries, the CDC report does not address some important factors like socioeconomic status, nor does it evaluate the impact of governmental efforts to restrict access to abortion. Fortunately, there is a substantial amount of other data that shed light on those factors.[7] According to worldwide data over the 30 years from 1990 to 2019, the global rate of unintended pregnancy and the global abortion rate declined initially, followed by a subsequent increase in the rate, returning to the levels of the early 1990s. Unsurprisingly, there are substantial differences between low- and high-income countries in the unintended pregnancy rate. For countries with restricted access to abortion, rates of unintended pregnancies were higher than in countries where abortion was generally legal.[8] To at least some extent, the higher incidence of unintended pregnancies in restrictive countries likely relates to there being less access to sexual and reproductive education and health care, including contraception.

A significant finding of the worldwide data is that the abortion rate is not just higher, but is substantially higher in those countries where abortion access is restricted than in countries where abortion is generally permitted. The annual abortion rate for countries where abortion was restricted was 36 per 1,000 women aged 15 to 49, whereas the abortion rate in countries where abortion was broadly legal was about one-third less, 26 per 1,000 women aged 15 to 49.[9] About half of unintended pregnancies ended in abortion across the data, whether abortion was restricted or broadly legal.[10] Moreover, in the 30 years from 1990 to 2019, the abortion rate declined by 43 percent where abortion was legal, whereas the abortion rate *increased*

---

7. A recent publication is Jonathan Bearak et al., *Unintended Pregnancy and Abortion by Income, Region, and the Legal Status of Abortion: Estimates from a Comprehensive Model for 1990–2019*, 8 THE LANCET GLOBAL HEALTH e1152 (2020), https://www.thelancet.com/journals/langlo/article/PIIS2214-109X(20)30315-6/fulltext. Other articles that present substantial relevant data include Gilda Sedgh et al., *Abortion Incidence between 1990 and 2014: Global, Regional, and Subregional Levels and Trends*, 388 THE LANCET 258 (2016), https://www.thelancet.com/journals/lancet/article/PIIS0140-6736(16)30380-4/fulltext; Susheela Singh & Isaac Maddow-Zimet, *Facility-based Treatment for Medical Complications Resulting from Unsafe Pregnancy Termination in the Developing World, 2012: A Review of Evidence from 26 Countries*, 123 BJOG: AN INT. J. OF OBST. & GYN. 1489 (2016), https://obgyn.onlinelibrary.wiley.com/doi/full/10.1111/1471-0528.13552.

8. Bearak et al., *supra* note 7.

9. Bearak et al., *supra* note 7, at e1158. Data for China and India are excluded from that calculation because the practices in those countries are atypical and the populations are so large that the data from those two countries would swamp the experiences and data from the rest of the world.

10. *Id.*

by 12 percent where access to abortion was highly restricted.[11] These findings are consistent with previous studies and data from countries around the world that women continue to access abortions, regardless of legal restrictions, even though doing so subjects them to legal and physical risk.[12] While not all the result of restrictive abortion laws, an estimated 6.9 million women were reported to have been treated in 2012 for complications relating to pregnancy terminations that occurred in unsafe circumstances.[13]

Other chapters that complete the book are: (1) Professor Cook's Chapter 10, Modern Day Inquisitions, that addresses the widespread denial of reproductive healthcare and persistent gender discrimination in Central and South America, including abortion prosecutions, and draws historical parallels to past church abuses from the Inquisition to the present day; (2) Professor Paula Abrams's Chapter 14, The Bad Mother: Stigma, Abortion, and Surrogacy, which asserts that damaging stigmas attached to abortion and surrogacy derive from gender stereotyping that influences legislative and litigation outcomes and causes people to underestimate the harm caused by abortion restrictions; and (3) Megan Donovan's Chapter 19, D&E Abortion Bans: The Implications of Banning the Most Common Second-Trimester Procedure, which discusses how state bans on dilation and evacuation (D&E) procedures fall most heavily on women who are already at a socioeconomic disadvantage in obtaining abortion care.

David F. Walbert
J. Douglas Butler

---

11. *Id.* at e1159.

12. *Id.* at e1159 nn.28–31. *See also* Guttmacher Institute, *Abortion Occurs Worldwide Where It Is Broadly Legal and Where It Is Restricted,* July 28, 2020, https://www.guttmacher.org/info graphic/2020/abortion-occurs-worldwide-where-it-broadly-legal-and-where-it-restricted.

13. Singh & Maddow-Zimet, *supra* note 7. A significant number of these incidents in the developing world result from inadequate care at the time of an abortion procedure. In recent years, however, that is changing because the provision of pregnancy termination services in the developing world have changed considerably with the increased availability of misoprostol. Even with the high morbidity rates, the mortality rate has declined. WORLD HEALTH ORGANIZATION, UNSAFE ABORTION: GLOBAL AND REGIONAL ESTIMATES OF THE INCIDENCE OF UNSAFE ABORTION AND ASSOCIATED MORTALITY IN 2008 (6th ed. 2011), https://www.who.int/reproductivehealth/publications/unsafe_abortion/9789241501118/en/.

1

The World's Abortion Laws

By Madison Glennie, Lily Milwit, and Julie Zuckerbrod

I. Introduction

An abortion procedure, whether surgical or by medication, ends a pregnancy.[1] Across the globe, there is substantial divergence when it comes to how governments approach and regulate abortion. Sixty-seven countries' laws permit abortion upon request with varied gestational limits, whereas 26 countries prohibit abortion altogether.[2] To provide a detailed understanding of the worldwide variations in these laws, we describe in this chapter representative laws in 31 countries from 12 different regions.[3] We document the current laws in place and evaluate the most recent developments. In addition to cataloguing the laws on the books, we examine how

---

1. *Abortion (Termination of Pregnancy)*, HARVARD HEALTH PUB. (Jan. 2019) ("Abortion is the removal of pregnancy tissue, products of conception or the fetus and placenta (afterbirth) from the uterus."), https://www.health.harvard.edu/medical-tests-and-procedures/abortion-termination-of-pregnancy-a-to-z.

2. *The World's Abortion Laws*, CTR. FOR REPRO. RIGHTS (updated 2020), https://reproductiverights.org/worldabortionlaws#recent-developments.

3. We do not address the United States or Canada since they are treated in-depth in other chapters. The 31 countries reviewed here are Republic of Ireland *infra* at II.B.1; Northern Ireland *infra* at II.B.2; Great Britain *infra* at II.B.3; Italy *infra* at II.C.1; Portugal *infra* at II.C.2; Spain *infra* at II.C.3; France *infra* at II.D.1; Germany *infra* at II.D.2; Poland *infra* at II.E.1; Russian Federation *infra* at II.E.2; Israel *infra* at II.F.1; Saudi Arabia *infra* at II.F.2; Turkey *infra* at II.F.3; India *infra* at II.G.1; Bangladesh *infra* at II.G.2; People's Republic of China *infra* at II.H.1; Japan *infra* at II.H.2; Vietnam *infra* at II.I.1; South Africa *infra* at II.J.1; Angola *infra* at II.J.2; Egypt *infra* at II.K.1; Tunisia *infra* at II.K.2; Australia *infra* at II.L.1; New Zealand *infra* at II.L.2; Costa Rica *infra* at II.M.1; El Salvador *infra* at II.M.2; Mexico *infra* at II.M.3; Uruguay *infra* at II.N.1; Brazil *infra* at II.N.2; Peru *infra* at II.N.3; and Argentina *infra* at II.N.4.

the laws function in practice, including whether there is meaningful abortion access in the jurisdiction, the extent to which access is practicable, and the demographics and communities most likely to be burdened by uneven implementation of the laws. Abortion laws are continually changing, and this chapter captures a snapshot from late 2020. This snapshot exemplifies not only the differences among national frameworks but also the power of people in the fight for abortion access.

II. Recognition of Unequal Barriers to Access

The restrictive laws of any given state do not affect all individuals within the jurisdiction in the same way. Although we make note of the restrictive laws of certain states, these laws are inescapable for some individuals, whereas others can travel to different jurisdictions or use resources to access abortion by other methods. Low-income people, for instance, have less capability to travel to other nation-states for reproductive health services.[4] On the flip side, too, permissive laws and regulations may be limited in their reach when marginalized groups face additional barriers to access and are subject to discriminatory implementation of laws. The historical and contemporary exclusion of LGBTQIA+ people and racial minorities from medical institutions and health care creates obstacles to safe and affirming access to reproductive care, including but not limited to abortion services.[5]

These histories of marginalization are only made clearer by the COVID-19 pandemic, which, at the time of this writing, continues to cause devastation throughout the world. The pandemic has shone light on the pervasive inequality broadly, but its impacts are particularly severe in the abortion

---

4. *See, e.g.*, Mary Gilmartin & Allen White, *Interrogating Medical Tourism: Ireland, Abortion, and Mobility Rights*, 36 J. WOMEN IN CULTURE & SOC'Y 275, 277–78 (2011) ("The burden of cost is placed on the woman, who in some instances may not be able to shoulder it—some women have to resort to illegal moneylenders to pay for an abortion . . . mobility rights for pregnant women in Ireland are contingent on nationality, class, and race. The protection of (some) women's right to travel is at the expense of a more general right to medical treatment in a woman's country of residence.").

5. *See, e.g.*, S.E. James et al., *The Report of the 2015 U.S. Transgender Survey*, NAT'L CTR. FOR TRANSGENDER EQUALITY, at 3, 8 (Dec. 2016) ("The findings paint a troubling picture of the impact of stigma and discrimination on the health of many transgender people. A staggering 39% of respondents experienced serious psychological distress in the month prior to completing the survey, compared with only 5% of the U.S. population. Among the starkest findings is that 40% of respondents have attempted suicide in their lifetime—nearly nine times the attempted suicide rate in the U.S. population."); *see generally* Laetitia Zeeman et al., *A Review of Lesbian, Gay, Bisexual, Trans and Intersex (LGBTI) Health and Healthcare Inequalities*, 29 EUR. J. PUB. HEALTH 974 (Oct. 2019), doi: 10.1093/eurpub/cky226.

context as many governments have limited access to certain health services, financial resources become scarce for more individuals and families, and travel restrictions put already inaccessible abortion services even further out of reach for those for whom local abortion is unavailable. We discuss some of the implications of COVID-19 on abortion access in sections of this chapter where information was available. But the ongoing nature of the pandemic means that it may be years before we can fully understand the extent to which this global crisis affects access to abortion, and specifically the myriad ways in which the pandemic exacerbates inequality of access.

As part of our discussion of these 31 countries' formal laws and the more informal ways in which those laws operate, we include whenever possible information on the availability of medication abortion. Medication abortion, which involves taking oral medications misoprostol and mifepristone to induce a miscarriage, has been used by pregnant people as an alternative to surgical abortion when surgical abortion is legally or logistically unavailable or simply because medication abortion may allow for more privacy and control. Though extremely safe when used correctly, medication abortion is often high regulated. With the rise of telemedicine, however, medication abortion is a safe and practical option for people who, for any number of reasons, cannot obtain a surgical abortion. Because medication abortion is one way for pregnant people to preserve their bodily autonomy and potentially circumvent legal hurdles, we discuss its availability and any relevant regulations in sections where such local information was available.

We acknowledge throughout this chapter the disparities in access to abortion that exist and persist regardless of the formal laws and official practices of any given country. But one must recognize that these inequalities run deep. Despite our best efforts to do so, there is simply no adequate way to capture the extent to which racism, colorism, classism, and economics have always dictated, and will continue to dictate, meaningful and safe access to abortion. It is important that readers, advocates, and activists continue to study and analyze this area of the law through a lens of unequal access.

As a final note, we acknowledge that women are not necessarily the only gender demographic impacted by abortion laws. Nonbinary people, intersex people, transgender people, and others may indeed have the biological capacity to become pregnant and are equally subject to their countries' abortion laws. Throughout this chapter, we will tend to use the word "woman" or "women" to discuss abortion laws and access. This is meant only to be a shorthand way of connoting the vast spectrum of people who may seek to exercise or fight for their rights to abortion, and is not intended to erase people who do not identify as women but are nonetheless impacted by abortion laws and access.

A. The United Nations (UN) and Abortion

The United Nations repeatedly uplifts abortion care as a right, including in health resolutions. Most recently, the General Assembly adopted a resolution on December 11, 2019, about global health that reaffirmed the commitment to sexual and reproductive health and rights, referencing the International Conference on Population and Development (ICPD) Programme of Action.[6] The Programme discusses abortion, and it was created at the 1994 Cairo Conference in which the UN, other countries, and intergovernmental organizations participated.[7] The Programme states that "[a]ll countries should strive to make accessible through the primary health-care system, reproductive health to all individuals of appropriate ages as soon as possible and no later than the year 2015," and they include abortion services as a reproductive health care service.[8] In total, 179 countries adopted this program. Additionally, the Human Rights Committee (HRC) clarified in 2018 that the "right to life" in article 6 of the International Covenant on Civil and Political Rights (ICCPR) does not forbid abortions, and that right actually limits the regulatory authority of states. The HRC asserts that states "may not regulate pregnancy or abortion in all other cases in a manner that runs contrary to their duty to ensure that women and girls do not have to undertake unsafe abortions, and they should revise their abortion laws accordingly."[9] These statements are a few examples of the continual support of abortion rights by the majority of the UN.

However, a minority coalition of member states have advocated within the UN against abortion since 2019. On October 22, 2020, this coalition signed the Geneva Consensus Declaration. At the time of that signing, the

---

6. *See* G.A. Res. 74/20, at 3 (Dec. 11, 2019); *see also* Harry Kretchmer, *A Brief History of Racism in Healthcare*, WORLD ECON. FORUM (July 23, 2020), https://www.weforum.org /agenda/2020/07/medical-racism-history-covid-19/.

7. Forward, *Programme of Action*, UNPF, at iii (2004), https://www.unfpa.org/sites/default /files/event-pdf/PoA_en.pdf.

8. Programme of Action of the International Conference on Population and Development, at 7.6, U.N. Doc. A/CONF.171/13/Rev.1 (Sept. 5–13, 1994).

9. Human Rights Committee, General Comment No. 36 (2018) on Article 6 of the International Covenant on Civil and Political Rights, on the Right to Life, ¶ 8, U.N. Doc. CCPR/C/GC/36 (Oct. 30, 2018).

coalition included 32 countries.[10] The declaration asserted that "in no case should abortion be promoted as a method of family planning," and they claimed to "[r]eaffirm . . . that 'every human being has the inherent right to life.'"[11] This declaration is the latest action against abortion by the coalition. Their previous actions include a speech asserting that "sexual and reproductive health and rights" were "undermin[ing] the critical role of the family and promot[ing] practices like abortion in circumstances that do not enjoy international consensus and which can be misinterpreted by UN agencies."[12] Nineteen countries joined this statement during the UN General Assembly meeting in September 2019. Another anti-abortion action at the UN includes the June 2019 Joint Letter by U.S. Secretary of Health and Human Services (HHS) Alex Azar and Secretary of State Michael Pompeo.[13] That letter included a plea for support to create a joint statement against abortion rights, and it was from this appeal that the coalition was created.[14]

B. Northern Europe

1. Republic of Ireland

In May 2018, voters in Ireland chose to legalize abortion in a historic referendum. This achievement follows a series of earlier referendums in which Irish voters rejected the country's outdated and severe abortion restrictions.

Since 1983, the Eighth Amendment to the Irish Constitution had imposed a near-total abortion ban and greatly restricted maternity care by giving a pregnant person and a fetus equal legal status.[15] In addition to overriding women's right to family self-determination, that amendment

---

10. Daniel Cassady, *U.S. Signs Anti-Abortion Declaration with 32 Countries*, FORBES (Oct. 22, 2020, 5:12 PM EDT), https://www.forbes.com/sites/danielcassady/2020/10/22/us-signs-anti-abortion-declaration-with-32-countries/.

11. Press Release, *Trump Administration Marks the Signing of the Geneva Consensus Declaration*, HHS.gov (Oct. 22, 2020), https://www.hhs.gov/about/news/2020/10/22/trump-administration-marks-signing-geneva-consensus-declaration.html.

12. Sarah McCammon, *At U.N., Trump Administration Profess 'No International Right to an Abortion,'* NPR (Sept. 23, 2019, 4:32 PM ET), https://www.npr.org/2019/09/23/763496171/at-u-n-trump-administration-professes-no-international-right-to-an-abortion.

13. Joint Letter from Alex Azar, U.S. Secretary of Health and Human Services, and Michael Pompeo, U.S. Secretary of State, to International States (July 18, 2019), https://www.theguardian.com/global-development/2019/sep/23/leaked-letter-suggests-us-is-rallying-un-member-states-to-oppose-abortion.

14. *See id.*

15. IRELAND CONST. art. 40.3.3.

inflicted exceptionally harmful consequences on numerous occasions over its 35-year existence.

For example, in 1992, the Irish High Court prevented a 14-year-old girl who had been raped from leaving the country for an abortion.[16] The Irish Supreme Court overturned that decision, reasoning that there was a right to abortion under Irish law where there was "a real and substantial risk" to the pregnant woman's life. Because the pregnant girl was at risk for suicide, the Court allowed her to have an abortion.[17] This case prompted an initial referendum, which resulted in adoption of the Thirteenth Amendment to the Irish Constitution in November 1992. After that amendment, people in Ireland still could not get a legal abortion in their home country, but they were no longer forbidden from fleeing to another country in order to end a pregnancy.

A new wave of abortion activism was sparked by the 2012 death of Savita Halappanavar, a 31-year-old Indian immigrant living in Galway, Ireland, who was pregnant with her first child. At approximately 16 weeks' gestation, she had an incomplete miscarriage, but upon seeking aid, medical staff denied her request for abortion care.[18] Doctors told Halappanavar that they were unable to expedite the miscarriage because a fetal heartbeat was still present, and Ireland was a "Catholic country."[19] By the time the doctors declared that the fetus's heartbeat had stopped, Halappanavar had developed an infection.[20] She died of sepsis the following day.[21]

Partly in response to the protest movement that erupted after Savita Halappanavar's death, the Irish government introduced the Protection of Life During Pregnancy Act (PLDPA), which permitted abortions when there is a threat to the life of the mother.[22] It also legalized abortions when there is medical consensus that the expectant mother will take her own life over her pregnancy.[23] However, the PLDPA imposed a criminal penalty of

---

16. Anna Carnegie & Rachel Roth, *From the Grassroots to the Oirechtas: Abortion Law Reform in the Republic of Ireland*, HEALTH & HUMAN RIGHTS J. (Dec. 9. 2019), https://www.hhrjournal.org/2019/12/from-the-grassroots-to-the-oireachtas-abortion-law-reform-in-the-republic-of-ireland/.

17. Attorney General v. X, (1992) I.E.S.C. 1 (Ireland).

18. Megan Specia, *How Savita Halappanavar's Death Spurred Ireland's Abortion Rights Campaign*, N.Y. TIMES (May 27, 2018), https://www.nytimes.com/2018/05/27/world/europe/savita-halappanavar-ireland-abortion.html.

19. *Id.*

20. *Id.*

21. *Id.*

22. Protection of Life During Pregnancy Act, No. 35, Act of the Oireachtas, 2013 (Ireland).

23. *Id.*

up to 14 years imprisonment for anyone who either obtained an abortion in Ireland or provided an abortion outside of the law's parameters.[24]

Pro-choice activists considered this new law wholly inadequate, and they campaigned for a referendum to repeal the Eighth Amendment. The official referendum campaign launched on March 22, 2018, and it concluded with the successful vote on May 25, 2018, ratifying the Thirty-Sixth Amendment to the Irish Constitution.[25] With the repeal of the Eighth Amendment, together with the Thirteenth and Fourteenth Amendments that also addressed abortion access, the awkwardly worded Health (Regulation of Termination of Pregnancy) Act (the Health Act) became law on January 1, 2019.[26] It made abortion fully legal up to 12 weeks of pregnancy, subject to a three-day wait period between seeing a doctor and receiving the abortion.[27] However, the law continues to criminalize anyone who assists a pregnant person in obtaining an abortion outside of the act's provisions, with the possibility of a 14-year prison sentence.

Since Ireland's founding as an independent state in 1922, the Catholic Church has been a dominant political force, influencing a wide range of patriarchal social and public policies.[28] Thus, although Ireland has made abortion somewhat more accessible, the church still exerts a strong influence in when and how abortions are provided.

There is no doubt that the Health Act is a step forward. It offers a free, safe, legal abortion for most people who need it before 12 weeks' gestation. Abortion is now provided by more than 300 general practitioners and in ten out of 19 maternity hospitals in the country.[29] However, beyond 12 weeks, abortion is only available in very limited circumstances. The waiting period imposes a substantial burden on people with limited flexibility in their schedules, people who may need childcare, and those who are unable to take time off work. Additionally, the combination of the strict 12-week limit plus the three-day waiting period can push abortion out of reach for some. In 2019, the Abortion Support Network heard from 25 people in Ireland who were turned away from the abortion service less than three days past

---

24. *Id.*

25. *See* Carnegie & Roth, *supra* note 16.

26. Health (Regulation of Termination of Pregnancy) Act 2018, No. 31, Act of the Oireachtas, 2018 (Ireland).

27. *Id.*

28. *See* Carnegie & Roth, *supra* note 16.

29. Sydney Calkin, *One Year On, It's Clear That the New Irish Abortion Services Have Serious Limitations*, THE CONVERSATION (Jan. 15, 2020, 6:39 AM EST), https://theconversation.com /one-year-on-its-clear-that-the-new-irish-abortion-services-have-serious-limitations-129491.

the legal limit.[30] Without the mandatory three-day waiting period, those 25 people would have qualified for a free, legal, and local abortion in Ireland.

2. Northern Ireland

In 1861, the United Kingdom enacted the Offences Against the Person Act, which made having an abortion—or assisting someone in doing so—punishable by up to life in prison.[31] In 1967, Great Britain changed its laws to legalize abortion in certain circumstances, but this new law did not extend to Northern Ireland. Successive governments in Northern Ireland never changed the 1861 law, so this arcane and draconian abortion law remained on the books for more than a century.[32] During that time, pregnant people in Northern Ireland were forced to travel to England for abortions, even in cases of fetal abnormality.

Recently, a series of court cases declared Northern Ireland's abortion restrictions illegal under international laws. In 2015, the Belfast High Court deemed Northern Ireland's abortion law contrary to the right to respect for one's private and family life under Article 8 of the European Convention on Human Rights.[33] In 2018, the U.K. Supreme Court ruled that Northern Ireland's near-total abortion ban violated women's rights and was a breach of human rights.[34] Still, Northern Ireland's government had collapsed, leaving it politically impossible for the country to pass legislation expanding access to abortion.

As pressure mounted to revise Northern Ireland's draconian laws, Britain stepped in. During Northern Ireland's governmental turmoil in 2019, Britain's Parliament passed a measure creating an ultimatum: Britain itself would liberalize the country's abortion laws unless a restored government intervened.[35] The restored government did not intervene, however,

---

30. *Id.*

31. *Abortion in Ireland and Northern Ireland*, AMNESTY INT'L UK, https://www.amnesty.org .uk/abortion-rights-northern-ireland-timeline (last accessed Nov. 9, 2020).

32. *Id.*

33. *Timeline: NIHRC Challenge to the Law on Termination of Pregnancy in Northern Ireland*, NORTHERN IRELAND HUMAN RIGHTS COMM'N, https://www.nihrc.org/news/detail/time line-nihrc-challenge-to-the-law-on-termination-of-pregnancy-in-northern? (last accessed Nov. 9, 2020).

34. *UK Supreme Court Recognizes that Northern Ireland's Abortion Ban Contravenes Human Rights Law and Requires Radical Reconsideration*, CTR. FOR REPROD. RIGHTS (June 7, 2018), https://reproductiverights.org/press-room/uk-supreme-court-recognizes-that-northern -ireland%E2%80%99s-abortion-ban-contravenes-human-rights.

35. Benjamin Mueller, *U.K. Parliament Backs Same-Sex Marriage and Abortion Rights in Northern Ireland*, N.Y. TIMES (July 9, 2019), https://www.nytimes.com/2019/07/09/world

and as a result, in October 2019, abortion was decriminalized and became lawful in Northern Ireland by the force of U.K. law.[36] A new framework for lawful abortion services up to 12 weeks' gestation came into effect on March 31, 2020.[37]

When Northern Ireland's government was restored, the promise of abortion access seemed within reach. But even with U.K. law in place and a new government to implement it, Northern Ireland's Health Minister, Robin Swann, led the effort to delay introduction of abortion services based on his personal opposition. In recent months, Swann has been accused of using the coronavirus outbreak to further stall the process of implementing and scaling abortion services.[38]

Because of this delay in introducing abortion services, the only practical option for people seeking abortions in Northern Ireland remains traveling to England. (Abortion services are available in the Republic of Ireland, but the cost of $500 is prohibitive for many people.[39]) The coronavirus crisis in 2020 underscored the extent to which this barrier burdens Northern Irish citizens seeking abortions. Due to coronavirus-related travel restrictions in Europe, the only way to get to England from Northern Ireland is to take an eight-hour ferry ride from Belfast to Liverpool. If the person seeking an abortion is eligible for a medication abortion, they must still meet with a doctor and take the abortion pill in the doctor's presence. Additional barriers, such as the cost of overnight accommodation, difficulty securing childcare, or extra days off of work, cause many patients to immediately return on the ferry where they risk miscarrying during the trip. If they are having a surgical abortion, a pregnant person might be required to stay overnight. In these cases, the financial and logistical obstacles can be insurmountable. The current health risks associated with travel and prolonged hotel stays can force pregnant people to choose between seeking an abortion and protecting themselves from the pandemic.

/europe/uk-same-sex-marriage-abortion.html.

36. *See* Marie-Louise Connolly, *Northern Ireland Abortion Law Changes: What Do They Mean?*, BBC (Oct. 22, 2019), https://www.bbc.com/news/uk-northern-ireland-50125124.

37. Hillary Margolis, *England Leads Way in UK after U-Turn on COVID-19 Abortion Access*, HUMAN RIGHTS WATCH (Mar. 31, 2020, 1:00 AM EDT), https://www.hrw.org/news/2020/03/31/england-leads-way-uk-after-u-turn-covid-19-abortion-access#.

38. Ceylan Yeginsu, *Technically Legal in Northern Ireland, Abortions Are Still Unobtainable*, N.Y. TIMES (Apr. 9, 2020), https://www.nytimes.com/2020/04/09/world/europe/northern-ireland-abortion.html.

39. Ceylan Yeginsu, *Legal Abortion Begins in Northern Ireland*, N.Y. TIMES (Apr. 10, 2020), https://www.nytimes.com/2020/04/10/world/europe/northern-ireland-abortion-uk.html.

Additionally, when early medication abortion became available in local clinics on March 31, 2020, there was very little information about how to access these services. On April 15, a private charitable organization called Informing Choices NI launched a hotline that directed patients to sexual and reproductive health providers who were beginning to offer early medication abortion for up to ten weeks of pregnancy.[40] The fleeting hope that abortion would be accessible locally vanished on October 5 when Northern Ireland's Northern Health and Social Care Trust stopped referrals for early medical abortion services, affecting almost half of the Northern Ireland population.[41]

At this writing, the Northern Ireland Direct website still has no information about what services are available for a pregnant person seeking an abortion.[42] Much like Crisis Pregnancy Centers in the United States,[43] rogue pregnancy centers in Belfast pose as abortion clinics for the purpose of misinforming women, stating among other things that abortions cause breast cancer, and purposely delaying women's access to care.[44] These actions can cause those in need of abortion care to be pushed beyond the ten-week limit when they may have otherwise accessed an abortion.[45]

3. Great Britain

As just noted, in 1861, the Offences Against the Person Act placed abortion alongside the most serious of crimes.[46] There were no exceptions. The law remained in effect until 1967, when the Abortion Act legalized abortion in certain circumstances.[47]

---

40. Press Release, *Informing Choices NI to Provide Central Access Point to Local Abortion Services*, INFORMING CHOICES NI (Apr. 15, 2020), https://informingchoicesni.org /central-access-point-press.

41. Press Release, *Northern Trust Ceases Early Medical Abortion Service Due to Department of Health Failings*, INFORMING CHOICES NI & Amnesty Int'l UK (Oct. 2, 2020), https://inform ingchoicesni.org/wp-content/uploads/2020/10/AIUK-ICNI-PR-NHSCT-EMA-Service.pdf.

42. *See Information and Services*, NI DIRECT, https://www.nidirect.gov.uk/ (last visited Nov. 9, 2020).

43. Shari Inniss-Grant, *Crisis Pregnancy Centers Undermine the Reproductive Health of Women of Color*, NAT'L WOMEN'S L. CTR. (Mar. 28, 2013), https://nwlc.org/blog /crisis-pregnancy-centers-undermine-reproductive-health-women-color/.

44. Isabel van Brugen, *Belfast Pregnancy Clinic Said Abortion Fills Breasts with Cancer*, THE TIMES (June 2, 2018, 12:01 AM BST), https://www.thetimes.co.uk/article /belfast-pregnancy-clinic-said-abortion-fills-breasts-with-cancer-x2btsc0bz.

45. *See id.*

46. Offences Against the Person Act 1861, (24 & 25 Vict c. 100), Act of Parliament, 1861 (U.K. and Ir.).

47. The Abortion Act 1967, c. 87, Act of Parliament, 1967 (U.K.).

The Abortion Act applies only in England, Scotland, and Wales. It does not extend to Northern Ireland. The act makes it possible to have an abortion up to 24 weeks of pregnancy, but it contains a number of restrictions.[48] For example, the law states that two doctors must decide "in good faith" that a woman meets the legal requirements for an abortion, thereby bestowing upon doctors a gatekeeping power over who can have an abortion.[49]

Although the act dramatically shifted the abortion landscape in Great Britain, its guidelines did not keep up with the times. The Abortion Act was initially implemented when all abortions were performed surgically. While medication abortion has been proven as a safe, effective way to end a pregnancy at home, self-managed abortion remained illegal in Great Britain until 2018.[50] As a result, people seeking abortions were required to travel to clinics or hospitals just to take a pill.

In 2018, Claudia Craig's story exposed the harm associated with self-managed abortion bans. Claudia, who was 22 at the time, was forced to travel to a hospital to take the second of the two pills that were required to complete her medication abortion. Not knowing how quickly she would begin to feel its effects, she called a taxi home, and she began to miscarry in the car.[51] Afterward, Claudia wrote an open letter describing her experience, which spurred action to legalize self-managed medication abortion.[52] Activists were successful in their efforts: on August 25, 2018, England's Department of Health announced that it would legalize home use of medication abortion up to ten weeks' gestation.[53]

Women in Great Britain are often assumed to have access to available, acceptable, and affordable services, especially when compared to other parts of the United Kingdom and the British Isles. Although almost 200,000 abortions were carried out in Britain in 2016, some groups of people still

---

48. *Id.*

49. *Id.*

50. Sanya Burgess, *Campaign Launched to Allow Women in England and Wales to Take Abortion Pills at Home*, SKY NEWS (Mar. 30, 2018, 1:31 AM), https://news.sky.com/story/campaign -launched-to-allow-women-in-england-and-wales-to-take-abortion-pills-at-home-11308762.

51. *See* Claudia Craig, *It's Perfectly Safe So Why Can't Women Take Abortion Pills at Home?*, THE GUARDIAN (Aug. 1, 2018, 10:50 AM EDT), https://www.theguardian.com /commentisfree/2018/aug/01/abortion-pill-law-scotland-women-english.

52. *See id.*

53. Yonette Joseph, *England to Allow Women to Take Early Abortion Pill at Home*, N.Y. TIMES (Aug. 25, 2018), https://www.nytimes.com/2018/08/25/world/europe/uk-abortion-pill -england.html.

experience particularly challenging, if not impossible, circumstances when seeking abortion access.[54]

A major barrier to abortion access is the long wait times, sometimes several weeks.[55] Such waiting times can push people past the time limits for medication abortion. Another common barrier is logistical difficulties getting to a clinic due to an inability to take time off work or secure childcare in order to attend one or more appointments.[56]

Some people are eligible for free, nonemergency abortion services through Britain's National Health Service.[57] However, those who are ineligible face barriers finding and paying for abortion care on their own. Most commonly, these women are either undocumented immigrants or have been admitted under a visa program.[58]

These barriers can push people to end pregnancies outside of the formal health care setting. However, many people simply prefer not to have an in-clinic abortion. In fact, almost one-third of reasons for seeking abortion outside a clinic were due to concerns about privacy and confidentiality and preferences for at-home abortion.[59] An additional 20 percent involved a situation in which women did not feel able to seek abortion services at a clinic or hospital because of the fear or threat of partner violence or a controlling family.[60] These statistics underscore the importance of making abortion widely accessible, and allowing those seeking an abortion to choose the method that works best for them.

C. Southern Europe

1. Italy

Until 1978, abortion in Italy was labeled a "crime against the integrity and the health of the bloodline."[61] In the 1970s, Italy's feminist movement began to raise the issues of maternity, sexuality, and bodily autonomy.[62] The

---

54. *See* Abigail Aiken et al., *Barriers to Accessing Abortion Services and Perspectives on Using Mifepristone and Misoprostol at Home in Great Britain*, 97 CONTRACEPTION 177 (Feb. 2018), https://oar.princeton.edu/bitstream/88435/pr1vt95/1/Barriers.pdf.

55. *Id.*

56. *Id.*

57. *See Abortion*, NAT'L HEALTH SERVICE, https://www.nhs.uk/conditions/abortion/.

58. *See* Aiken et al., *supra* note 54.

59. *See id.*

60. *See id.*

61. C.p. arts. 545–555 (It.).

62. Elena Caruso, *Abortion in Italy: Forty Years On*, 28 FEMINIST LEGAL STUDIES 87 (Jan. 28, 2020), https://link.springer.com/article/10.1007/s10691-019-09419-w#Fn2.

movement also started to push for safe abortion access, but advocates were divided on how to get there. Some Italian feminists advocated for a legal right to abortion through legislation that would allow women to obtain abortions in public hospitals, whereas others were against such legislation and refused to call for a patriarchal law that regulated women's bodies. These feminists focused on nonreproductive sexuality and advocated full decriminalization of abortion.

Ultimately, legislation was passed. In 1978, Law 194 was enacted, which creates the right to abortion during the first 12 weeks of pregnancy.[63] But the right is not absolute: within the first 12 weeks, a person can have an abortion due to health, economic, social, or family reasons.[64] But after the twelfth week, a person can only have an abortion if there is a significant fetal abnormality, if the pregnancy poses a serious risk to the pregnant person's mental or physical health, or if the pregnancy endangers the pregnant person's life.[65]

Furthermore, a doctor is required to certify a person's reason for abortion as "urgent."[66] If a doctor deems the reason urgent, the pregnant person can get an abortion immediately. If the request is not evaluated as "urgent," the physician signs a document affirming that the woman is pregnant, is asking to terminate her pregnancy, and then "invites her to reflect for seven days."[67] Only then, with this document, may the woman obtain an abortion. Getting an abortion is even harder for people under the age of 18. The law requires that minors get permission from a parent or guardian, or alternatively, permission from a judge.[68]

In addition to all of the aforementioned abortion restrictions, there are sanctions for those who break the rules. For instance, people who self-manage their own abortions may face up to three years in prison or substantial fines.

Another big obstacle to abortion is the prevalence of conscientious objections. Because of the Catholic Church's dominant influence over Italians, many gynecologists are personally against abortion. Law 194 makes it

---

63. Legge No. 194, 2 May 1978, n. 194, G.U. May 22, 1978, n.140 (It.) [hereinafter L. 194].

64. Catherine Edwards, *The Long Road to Legal Abortion in Italy—And Why Many Women Are Still Denied It*, THE LOCAL (May 25, 2018, 5:28 PM CEST), https://www.thelocal.it/20180525 /history-abortion-laws-italy-doctors-objection-pills.

65. *See id.*

66. L. 194, *supra* note 63.

67. *Id.*

68. *Id.*

very easy for them to opt out of providing abortions. In fact, about 68.4 percent of gynecologists declare themselves conscientious objectors.[69]

Conscientious objection significantly hampers abortion access at the local level. It forces people to travel long distances to find an abortion provider willing to treat them, crowding clinics and leading to longer wait times.[70] Conscientious objection also has a disproportionate impact on women living in lower-income regions or experiencing other forms of economic disadvantage.[71]

2. Portugal

Abortion was completely illegal in Portugal until 1984. Since then, Portugal has incorporated laws that allow abortion in some narrow circumstances. The first law, passed in 1984, legalized abortion only in cases of serious maternal and fetal disease, rape, and when continuing the pregnancy would represent "a crime against the woman's freedom and sexual self-determination."[72] Portuguese hospitals and health care providers interpreted this law narrowly, and, in many cases, public hospitals simply refused to comply with it.[73] Throughout this time period, Portugal was one of the few countries that criminally prosecuted women who had abortions and the doctors who performed them.[74]

Due to the restrictiveness of the 1984 law, abortion advocates launched a campaign to decriminalize abortion in 1998. A nonbinding national referendum was held on the issue, but it narrowly failed.[75] A second referendum was held in 2007 to legalize abortion in the first ten weeks of pregnancy, and despite strong opposition from Catholic leaders and Right to Life groups claiming to protect the country from "moral decay," the pro-choice movement won with 59.3 percent of the vote.[76] Portugal's President, Ani-

69. *See* Caruso, *supra* note 62.

70. Tommaso Autorino et al., *The Impact of Gynecologists' Conscientious Objection on Abortion Access*, 87 Soc. Sci. Research 1 (Jan. 27, 2020), https://www.sciencedirect.com/science/article/pii/S0049089X20300016.

71. *Id.*

72. Lisa Ferreira Vicente, *The Woman's Choice for Abortion: The Experience in Portugal with Implementation of the National Network*, 36 Cad. Saúde Pública 1 (Apr. 6, 2020), https://www.scielo.br/scielo.php?pid=S0102-311X2020001300502&script=sci_arttext&tlng=en.

73. Tiago Villanueva, *Portugal Is Ready to Decriminalise Abortion*, 334 BMJ 332 (Feb. 17, 2007), https://www.ncbi.nlm.nih.gov/pmc/articles/PMC1801020/.

74. Tracy Wilkinson, *Legal Abortion Comes to Portugal*, L.A. Times (July 31, 2007), https://www.latimes.com/archives/la-xpm-2007-jul-31-fg-abortion31-story.html.

75. *Id.*

76. *See* Vicente, *supra* note 72.

bal Cavaco Silva, then signed a bill allowing abortion in the first ten weeks of pregnancy.[77] However, he also declared abortion "a social evil to be avoided."[78]

Rhetoric like this from Portugal's leaders further stigmatizes abortion. Such stigmatization, in combination with the Roman Catholic Church's condemnation of abortion, has a significant impact on the availability and accessibility of abortion services. Even with a law that legalizes abortion, numerous doctors refuse to perform the procedure.[79] Administrators at several public hospitals have claimed that their hospitals would not be able to offer abortions, despite legal obligations, because they lacked the doctors or necessary equipment.[80]

3. Spain

Abortion was a crime in Spain until 1985 when it became legal only in cases of rape or serious risk of physical harm to the pregnant person or the fetus. In 2010, Spain passed a law to relax restrictions on women's access to abortion.[81] The new law allowed for abortion under any circumstance up to 14 weeks of pregnancy, and it required abortions to be covered by the public national health care system.[82] It also declared abortion a woman's right.[83]

In 2014, former Spanish Prime Minister Mariano Rajoy proposed a bill that would have recriminalized abortion except in instances of rape or where the pregnant person's health was at serious risk. However, the proposal drew widespread opposition and lacked the political support needed to enact the bill into law. The proposal reignited the debate over abortion access, and it led to a "compromise" whereby 16- and 17-year-olds are now

---

77. Paul Christopher Manuel & Maurya N. Tollefsen, *The 1998 and 2007 Referenda on Abortion in Portugal: Roman Catholicism, Secularization and the Recovery of Traditional Communal Values*, 13 S. EUR. SOC'Y & POLITICS 117 (Mar. 2008), https://www.researchgate.net/pub lication/228584388_The_1998_and_2007_Referenda_on_Abortion_in_Portugal_Roman _Catholicism_Secularization_and_the_Recovery_of_Traditional_Communal_Values.

78. Wilkinson, *supra* note 74.

79. *Id.*

80. *Id.*

81. *Spain Expands Legal Access to Abortion*, GUTTMACHER INSTITUTE (Mar. 3, 2010), https://www.guttmacher.org/article/2010/03/spain-expands-legal-access-abortion.

82. Shauna Blackmon & Lucía Benavides, *Abortion Is a Protected Right in Spain. But the Govt Blocked a Website That Provides Abortion Info and Pills*, THE WORLD, (July 16, 2020, 3:30 PM EDT), https://www.pri.org/stories/2020-07-16/abortion-protected-right-spain-govt -blocked-website-provides-abortion-info-and.

83. *Id.*

required to obtain parental consent before getting an abortion.[84] While 16-
and 17-year-olds in Spain have the right to freely decide to become parents,
get married, or reject medical treatment, parental consent requirements
on abortion mean parents can force their children to carry pregnancies to
term against their will. Recognizing the incongruency of youth rights in the
country and the ways in which the parental consent law undermined bodily
autonomy for young people, Equality Minister Irene Montero announced
in October 2020 a plan to repeal the requirement.[85] Before the parental
consent law was added, approximately one in every ten persons aged 16 or
17 who terminated a pregnancy did not even have a parental guardian.

Spain has also enacted barriers to abortion by limiting access to information. In January 2020, the Spanish government banned the nonprofit
organization, Women on Web (WoW), which offers medically approved
information about abortions in 22 different languages, along with access
to contraceptives and medication abortion. Websites like WoW empower
women to make their own health care decisions, and while Spain deems
abortion a protected right, this action is a clear sign that the Spanish government does not trust pregnant people to control their own reproductive
health.

D. Western Europe

1. France

On April 5, 1971, a petition signed by 343 people was published in the magazine *Nouvel Observateur*. It read: "A million women have abortions every
year in France, in dangerous conditions. . . . I declare that I am one of them.
I declare that I have aborted. . . . We demand free abortion."[86] This petition
marked a turning point, breaking the country's long silence on abortion.

Abortion had been a crime in France since 1810. For generations,
pregnant people had to risk both their lives and their liberty in order to
get an abortion. France prosecuted abortion, and, for a brief time, it was

---

84. *Spain Abortion: Rajoy Scraps Tighter Law*, BBC (Sept. 23, 2014), https://www.bbc.com
/news/world-europe-29322561.

85. Pilar Álvarez, *Spain Seeks Law Change to Allow 16- and 17-Year-Olds to Abort without
Parental Consent*, EL PAÍS (Oct. 8, 2020, 5:17 AM EDT), https://english.elpais.com/poli
tics/2020-10-08/spain-seeks-law-change-to-allow-16-and-17-year-olds-to-abort-without-paren
tal-consent.html.

86. Jess McHugh, *How 343 Women Made French History by Talking about Their Abortions*, TIME
(Nov. 26, 2018, 12:00 PM EST), https://time.com/5459995/manifesto-343-abortion-france/.

punishable by death. The last execution for abortion, carried out by guillotine, was in 1943.[87] By the 1970s, women demanded change.

The 1971 petition was followed by a wave of momentum. A year later, Simone De Beauvoir, who helped write the manifesto, testified when a 16-year-old rape victim named Marie-Claire was tried for having an abortion.[88] The case got international attention, shining a spotlight on the inequities and harshness of France's abortion laws.[89] In 1975, abortion became legal up to 12 weeks of pregnancy,[90] but that first abortion law had significant restrictions. For example, it required a pregnant person to have two medical consultations, a week apart, before having an abortion. After 12 weeks, abortion remained a crime, punishable by six months to ten years imprisonment.[91] Many of these restrictions have since been repealed. Today, abortion is considered the right of every woman, regardless of her reasons, and it is fully reimbursed by French social security. Since April 2016, related medical expenses such as blood tests, sonograms, and painkillers have also been covered.[92]

Despite the liberalization of France's abortion laws, however, access is still limited. More than 100 French abortion clinics have closed in the past decade, mainly because they are unprofitable for doctors and nurses.[93] In 2019, a French gynecologists' union threatened to stop performing abortions in an attempt to force the country's Health Minister to meet doctors' demands.[94] Syngof, which represents about a quarter of France's gynecologists and obstetricians, published a letter protesting the lack of funding.[95]

---

87. *Id.*

88. *Id.*

89. *Abortion Battle Pushed in France*, N.Y. TIMES (Nov. 24, 1972), https://www.nytimes .com/1972/11/24/archives/abortion-battle-pushed-in-france-court-verdict-reinvigorates .html.

90. D. Gaudry & G. Sadan, *France: Late Abortion*, 18 PLAN. PARENT. EUR. 6 (1989), https:// pubmed.ncbi.nlm.nih.gov/12315825/.

91. *See Abortion Legislation in Europe*, INT'L PLANNED PARENTHOOD FED. (Jan. 2009), *available at* http://www.spdc.pt/files/publicacoes/Pub_AbortionlegislationinEuropeIPPFEN _Feb2009.pdf.

92. Lara Marlowe, *Abortion Battles Rage on in France Despite Liberal Regime*, THE IRISH TIMES (Dec. 15, 2017), https://www.irishtimes.com/news/social-affairs/abortion-battles-rage-on -in-france-despite-liberal-regime-1.3327713.

93. *Id.*

94. *Id.*

95. Kim Willsher, *French Gynaecologists' Union Threatens to Stop Performing Abortions*, THE GUARDIAN (Mar. 14, 2019, 12:43 PM EDT), https://www.theguardian.com/world/2019 /mar/14/french-gynaecologists-union-threatens-to-stop-performing-abortions.

Health Minister Agnès Buzyn and feminist organizations said the threat was "unacceptable" and amounted to "taking women hostage."[96]

The Syngof protest highlights the importance of making abortion accessible outside of a medical clinic. Not only does medication abortion allow pregnant people to manage their own abortions, it also removes obstacles that can be presented when people are forced to go into a clinic and meet with a doctor in person. During the coronavirus pandemic, the Health Authority decided to allow women to have access to medication abortion at home up to nine weeks.[97] In a statement, they said that the decision is justified by "the need to guarantee women's rights to access abortion during the COVID-19 epidemic and to avoid as much as possible that they go into a health facility."[98]

2. Germany

Under German law, anyone who terminates a pregnancy can be fined or imprisoned for up to three years.[99] However, there is no criminal liability if the abortion is necessary in order to protect the health of the pregnant person, if rape led to the pregnancy, or if the pregnant person takes part in consultation and has the abortion before the twelfth week of pregnancy.[100] Rather than making abortion legal, these exceptions simply make it possible without punishment. If a person is eligible to seek out an abortion, a waiting period of three days is required after a consultation. The counseling, called Schwangerschaftskonfliktberatung ("pregnancy-conflict counseling"), must take place at a state-approved clinic, which afterward gives the pregnant person a Beratungsschein ("certificate of counseling").

The German Criminal Code also makes it a crime for doctors to publicly advertise in any way that they perform abortions, even though they are permitted to do so in the first 12 weeks of pregnancy.[101] Although a woman can terminate a pregnancy, locating a provider and figuring out what procedures they perform are serious challenges. In 2017, Dr. Kristina Hänel, a gynecologist, was convicted of breaking the law and fined 6,000 euros, or about 6,850 U.S. dollars, for stating on her website that she provided

---

96. *Id.*

97. Sarah Elzas, *France Extends Access to Abortions during Covid-19 Pandemic,* RFI (Nov. 4, 2020),   https://www.rfi.fr/en/france/20200411-france-extends-access-to-abortions-during -covid-19-pandemic.

98. *Id.*

99. STRAFGESETZBUCH [STGB] [PENAL CODE] § 218.

100. *Id.*

101. STRAFGESETZBUCH [STGB] [PENAL CODE] § 219.

abortions and would send information on them—in German, English, or Turkish—to anyone requesting it.[102] Faced with this fine, Dr. Hänel wrote an open letter to Angela Merkel urging her to enforce the right of women to have information about abortion.[103] In 2019, Merkel announced a compromise, which still prohibited abortion providers from publicly saying much about abortion. Instead, the proposal tasked the German Medical Association, which represents physicians, with compiling and publishing a list of all doctors and clinics providing abortions, along with information about which procedures are offered.[104]

Due to the legal uncertainty, many doctors do not dare offer abortions. Even if a doctor wanted to perform abortions, many do not have the necessary training, because German medical schools often do not teach abortions. One of the biggest medical universities in Germany, the Charité in Berlin, only began offering courses on the subject in 2018.[105]

E. Eastern Europe

1. Poland

On October 22, 2020, Poland's Constitutional Tribunal eliminated one of the three exclusive legal justifications to access abortion in the country. The case reviewed a 1993 law that permitted abortion for "severe and irreversible fetal defect or incurable illness that threatens the fetus's life."[106] The court determined that the provision was unconstitutional because it killed a "conceived child" for a reason that the court deemed only for "the comfort

---

102. Melissa Eddy, *Germany Proposes to Ease, Not End, Nazi-Era Abortion Law*, N.Y. TIMES (Jan. 29, 2019), https://www.nytimes.com/2019/01/29/world/europe/germany-abortion -paragraph-219a.html.

103. Kristina Hänel, *Kristina Hänel Writes to Federal Chancellor Dr. Angela Merkel*, SOLIDARITY WITH KRISTINA (Mar. 19, 2018), https://solidaritaetfuerkristinahaenel.wordpress .com/2018/03/19/kristina-haenel-schreibt-an-bundeskanzlerin-dr-angela-merkel/#more -1512.

104. Eddy, *supra* note 102.

105. Clara Suchy, *Activists in Germany Demand Legalization of Abortion*, DW (Sept. 27, 2019), https://www.dw.com/en/activists-in-germany-demand-legalization-of-abortion/a-50613936.

106. The Family Planning, Human Embryo Protection and Conditions of Permissibility of Abortion Act of 7 January 1993, at art. 4(a), https://www.reproductiverights.org /sites/crr.civicactions.net/files/documents/Polish%20abortion%20act–English%20transla tion.pdf (English translation); *see also Poland's Constitutional Tribunal Rolls Back Reproductive Rights*, AMNESTY INT'L (Oct. 22, 2020, 6:42 PM UTC), https://www.amnesty.org/en/latest /news/2020/10/polands-constitutional-tribunal-rolls-back-reproductive-rights/.

of a woman's life."[107] The abortion, according to the court, would violate the "constitutional values respect and protection of human dignity, the legal protection of the life of every human being [and] discriminates against foetuses on the grounds of their health status."[108] A group of politicians from the conservative ruling party, Law and Justice Party (PiS), requested the tribunal to review the constitutionality of the law.[109] Only one of the tribunal's 15 judges was not appointed by the PiS.[110] The decision has been criticized as evading "social legitimacy," because it was imposed by the court and did not go through the parliament.[111]

As of November 4, 2020, Poland's government delayed the publication of the tribunal's decision.[112] The publication delay prevented the ruling and its new restriction on abortion from going into legal force.[113] The Polish Constitution required that the decision be published by November 2 for the law to be implemented, but the Polish government has evaded this restriction with other rulings.[114] This change in the government's approach was the result of two weeks of mass protests against the decision.[115] Protests were ongoing despite the fact that gatherings of more than ten people were prohibited because of the COVID-19 pandemic.[116] In one of these protests, women dressed up in outfits similar to those in *The Handmaid's Tale*, a dystopian novel and popular television show that imagines an intensely patriarchal society, and walked through church services to vocalize their

---

107. Krystyna Kacpura, *Poland's Constitutional Court Has Effectively Banned Abortion, But We Will Not Stop Fighting for Our Fundamental Rights*, TIME (Oct. 30, 2020, 5:34 PM), https://time .com/5905885/poland-abortion-ban-protest/.

108. *Attempts to Use the Non-Sovereign Constitutional Tribunal in Order to Restrict Women's Rights to Legal Abortion*, FED. FOR WOMEN & FAM. PLANNING, https://en.federa.org.pl/attempts -to-use-the-non-sovereign-constitutional-tribunal-in-order-to-restrict-womens-rights-to-legal -abortion/.

109. Adam Easton, *Poland Abortion: Top Court Bans Almost All Terminations*, BBC (Oct. 23, 2020), https://www.bbc.com/news/world-europe-54642108.

110. Monika Pronczuk, *Poland Delays a Near-Total Ban on Abortion*, N.Y. TIMES (Nov. 4, 2020, updated Jan. 28, 2021), https://www.nytimes.com/2020/11/04/world/europe /poland-abortion-law-delay.html.

111. Kacpura, *supra* note 107.

112. Pronczuk, *supra* note 110.

113. *Id.*

114. *Id.*

115. Marc Santora, Monika Pronczuk & Anatol Magdziarz, *Polish Women Lead Strike Over Abortion Ruling Amid Threats of Crackdown*, N.Y. TIMES (Oct. 28, 2020), https://www .nytimes.com/2020/10/28/world/europe/poland-women-abortion-strike.html?search ResultPosition=11.

116. *See id.*; *see also* Kacpura, *supra* note 107.

opposition to the new restrictions.[117] The Polish government deemed these peaceful protestors "criminals" seeking to "destroy the Polish nation."[118] In fact, the instances of violence that did occur were caused by right-wing extremists who had formed vigilante groups.[119]

As this book goes to press, abortion remains legal in Poland to safeguard the life or health of women, if a pregnancy results from rape or another criminal act such as incest, or if there is a "severe and irreversible fetal defect" or an "incurable illness that threatens the fetus's life."[120] Still, those exceptions are only allowed in the first 12 weeks of pregnancy.[121] Abortion is illegal in all situations beyond these three circumstances, and a doctor or anyone else who aids a person to obtain an abortion outside of these exceptions is subject to imprisonment for up to three years.[122]

The PiS party proposed a law in 2020 called the "Stop Abortion" bill, which would have amended the criminal code to forbid abortion for severe or fatal fetal anomalies.[123] The bill was sent back to committee in April 2020, but after the Constitutional Tribunal's decision in October 2020, the bill was unnecessary.[124] In addition to this effort, Poland's Parliament recently sent another bill, the "Stop Paedophilia" bill, back to committee.[125] The "Stop Paedophilia" bill would criminalize "anyone who promotes or approves the undertaking by a minor of sexual intercourse or other sexual

---

117. Kelsey Vlamis, *Protesters Storm Churches in Poland on the 4th Day of Unrest after a Court Ruling Tightened the Country's Already-Strict Abortion Laws*, INSIDER (Oct. 25, 2020, 8:17 PM), https://www.insider.com/protestors-storm-churches-in-poland-over-new-abortion-restrictions-2020-10.

118. *Id.*

119. Santora, *supra* note 115.

120. The Family Planning, Human Embryo Protection and Conditions of Permissibility of Abortion Act of 7 January 1993, at art. 4(a), https://www.reproductiverights.org/sites/crr.civicactions.net/files/documents/Polish%20abortion%20act--English%20translation.pdf (English translation).

121. Press Release, *After Massive Public Outcry, Polish Parliament Rejects Total Abortion Ban*, CTR. FOR REPROD. RIGHTS (Oct. 6, 2016), https://reproductiverights.org/press-room/after-massive-public-outcry-polish-parliament-rejects-total-abortion-ban [referred to as Polish Parliament Rejects Total Abortion Ban].

122. *Id.*

123. Jessica Bateman & Marta Kasztelan, *In Poland, Abortion Access Worsens Amid Pandemic*, FOREIGN POL'Y (May 1, 2020, 9:17 AM), https://foreignpolicy.com/2020/05/01/poland-abortion-access-worsens-coronavirus-pandemic/.

124. *Id.*

125. Rachel Savage, *Poland Mulls Law Denouncing Sex Educators as Paedophiles and Gay Activists*, REUTERS (Apr. 15, 2020, 2:44 PM), https://www.reuters.com/article/us-poland-lgbt-education-trfn/poland-mulls-law-denouncing-sex-educators-as-paedophiles-and-gay-activists-idUSKCN21X2ZA; *see also Poland: Reject New Curbs on Abortion, Sex Ed*, HUMAN RIGHTS WATCH (Apr. 14, 2020, 12:01 AM EDT), https://www.hrw.org/news/2020/04/14/poland-reject-new-curbs-abortion-sex-ed.

activity."[126] The bill poses a threat to sexual and reproductive rights education organizations and educators, especially given its three-year prison sentence.[127] This bill, if imposed by the Parliament, would cause a chilling effect and decrease youths' education about abortion as well as sexual and reproductive health and rights.

In 2016, the Polish Parliament rejected a prior attempt of the PiS to pass legislation that would have made abortion illegal in all situations and criminalized those who had the procedure.[128] Poland was condemned by the European Court of Human Rights (ECHR) on multiple occasions due to its restrictive abortion laws, and those rulings came before the Constitutional Tribunal's October 2020 decision.[129] The Constitutional Tribunal's decision is the most recent and most successful restriction on abortion in the country to date.

Even though the recent Constitutional Tribunal's ruling has not yet been implemented at the time of this writing, hospitals have already begun refusing to provide abortion procedures that were previously permissible.[130] The fetal defect or illness exception has been the most frequent justification for abortion in the country.[131]

Additionally, even before the most recent constitutional tribunal decision, there were entire regions of Poland where women who were eligible for legal abortion were unable to find a doctor or hospital willing to perform an abortion under the law.[132] These regions still exist after the decision. While only slightly more than 1,000 abortions were recorded in 2018, women's rights activists assert that up to 150,000 women accessed abortion through other avenues like ordering medication abortion pills online or traveling to another country for the procedure.[133] The most common countries that Poles travel to for abortion care are Germany, the Netherlands,

126. HUMAN RIGHTS WATCH, *supra* note 125.

127. *Id.*

128. *Polish Parliament Rejects Total Abortion Ban, supra* note 121.

129. R.R. v. Poland, App. No. 27617/04, 2011 Eur. Comm'n H.R. Dec. & Rep. (2011); *see also* P. and S. v. Poland, App. No. 57375/08, 2011 Eur. Comm'n H.R. Dec. & Rep. (2012).

130. Kacpura, *supra* note 107.

131. Adam Easton, *Poland Abortion: Top Court Bans Almost All Terminations*, BBC (Oct. 23, 2020), https://www.bbc.com/news/world-europe-54642108.

132. Human Rights Watch, *Poland: Reject New Curbs on Abortion, Sex Ed*, HRW (Apr. 14, 2020, 12:01 AM EDT), https://www.hrw.org/news/2020/04/14/poland-reject-new -curbs-abortion-sex-ed.

133. Jessica Bateman & Marta Kasztelan, *In Poland, Abortion Access Worsens Amid Pandemic*, FOREIGN POL'Y (May 1, 2020, 9:17 AM), https://foreignpolicy.com/2020/05/01 /poland-abortion-access-worsens-coronavirus-pandemic/.

and the United Kingdom.[134] Due to the shutdown of Poland's borders during the COVID-19 pandemic, the Abortion Without Borders helpline saw an immense increase from about 300 calls a month to 114 calls in the first two days after the closure.[135] This increase reveals the reliance that many Polish people have on abortion procedures in other nearby countries.

2. Russian Federation

Though the region now called the Russian Federation was the first country in the world to permit unrestricted abortion access in 1920 when it was part of the Soviet Union, the country has since devolved drastically, with a history marred by health policies motivated more by geopolitical strategy than by considerations of public welfare and bodily autonomy.[136] Soviet-era leader Joseph Stalin issued a decree in 1936 essentially banning all abortions as part of a pro-natalist effort to increase the Russian population.[137] The consequences were alarming: illegal abortions rose significantly, causing an increase in abortion-related morbidity and mortality.[138] A 1955 decree, passed discretely following Stalin's death, allowed for first-trimester abortions in hospital settings only.[139] Throughout the 1960s, however, the Russian Ministry of Health waged a war against the contraceptive revolution spreading throughout the West.[140] Fearmongering about the potential side effects of contraceptives, coupled with bans on sex education in schools, made Russia home to one of the highest abortion rates in the world at 119.6 per 1,000 women aged 15 to 49.[141]

In the decades that followed, Russia began, once again, to roll back its abortion laws. A 2003 amendment removed the social justifications that had

---

134. *Id.*

135. *Id.*

136. Alexandre Avdeev, Alain Blum & Irina Troitskaya. *The History of Abortion Statistics in Russia and the USSR from 1900 to 1991*, 7 Population: An Eng. Selection 40 (1995).

137. *Id.*

138. *Id.* at 45.

139. *Id.*; Vyacheslav Karpov & Kimmo Kääriäinen, *"Abortion Culture" in Russia: Its Origins, Scope, and Challenges to Social Development*, 22 J. Applied Soc. 13, 18 (2005–2006).

140. Olga Sobolevskaya, *A Contraceptive Revolution: How Abortion Rates Have Decreased in Russia*, Higher School of Econ. (Dec. 20, 2019), https://iq.hse.ru/en/news/325273199.html.

141. *Id.*; Chloe Arnold, *Abortion Remains Top Birth-Control Option in Russia*, Radio Free Eur. (June 28, 2008, 9:54 GMT), https://www.rferl.org/a/Abortion_Remains_Top_Birth_Control_Option_Russia/1145849.html; Victoria Sakevich & Maria Lipman, *Abortion in Russia: How Has the Situation Changed since the Soviet Era?*, Ponars Eurasia (Feb. 12, 2019), https://www.ponarseurasia.org/point-counter/article/abortion-russia-how-has-situation-changed-soviet-era.

once been allowed for abortion between 12 and 22 weeks' gestation, including poverty, number of prior children, and poor housing.[142] The amendment reduced the social justifications to only four circumstances: rape, imprisonment, death or severe disability of the husband, or a court ruling stripping the woman of her parental rights.[143] Then, a 2011 amendment established waiting periods and removed all social justifications except for rape, and in 2013, the government banned all abortion advertising.[144] As a result, between 2000 and 2013, the reported rate of abortions in Russia decreased by more than 70 percent.[145]

Today, the abortion landscape in Russia is perhaps bleaker than ever. The Russian Orthodox Church is at the helm of a movement to completely illegalize abortion, and the head of the Church endorsed an anti-abortion petition in September 2016.[146] A few months later, the Church organized a one-day ban on abortion to memorialize biblical "innocents."[147] In 2020, a member of the Russian Civic Chamber, Vladimir Lebedev, proposed a tax on childlessness.[148] This came in the wake of President Vladimir Putin's launch of his "Demographic Policy for the Russian Federation—Present to 2025," an initiative that seeks to incentivize childbearing by providing

---

142. Steven Lee Myers, *After Decades, Russia Narrows Grounds for Abortion*, N.Y. TIMES (Aug. 24, 2003), https://www.nytimes.com/2003/08/24/world/after-decades-russia-narrows-grounds-for-abortions.html.

143. *Id.*

144. Federal Law of November 21, 2011 N 323-FZ "On the Basics of Health Protection of Citizens in the Russian Federation," https://rg.ru/2011/11/23/zdorovie-dok.html; *Russia Piles on Tighter Abortion Restrictions*, CTR. FOR REPRODUCTIVE RIGHTS (Feb. 2012), https://reproductiverights.org/press-room/russia-piles-on-tighter-abortion-restrictions; Sakevich & Lipman, *supra* note 141; Ian Bateson, *Russia Bans Abortion Advertisements*, REUTERS (Nov. 25, 2013, 3 PM), https://www.reuters.com/article/us-russia-abortion/russia-bans-abortion-advertisements-idUSBRE9AO0VO20131125; Sophia Kishovsky, *Russia Enacts Law Opposing Abortion*, N.Y. TIMES (July 15, 2011), https://www.nytimes.com/2011/07/15/world/europe/15iht-russia15.html.

145. Aleksandr A. Kulkin & Yelena V. Vasilyeva, *The Welfare and Public Health of the Population of Russia: Adaptation to Economic Volatility*, 1 ELECTRONIC SCI. ECON. J. 57, 64 (2015).

146. AFP, *Russian Orthodox Patriarch Signs Petition to Putin Urging Abortion Ban*, BUSINESS INSIDER (Sept. 27, 2016, 3:41 PM), https://www.businessinsider.com/afp-russian-orthodox-patriarch-signs-petition-to-putin-urging-abortion-ban-2016-9; Ola Cichowlas, *Russia's Abortion Debate Is Back*, THE MOSCOW TIMES (Sept. 29, 2016), https://www.themoscowtimes.com/2016/09/29/russias-abortion-debate-is-back-a55545.

147. *Abortions Banned in Russian City for 1 Day in Memory of Biblical 'Massacre of Innocents,'* RUSSIA TODAY (Jan. 11, 2017, 15:57), https://www.rt.com/news/373339-abortion-ban-russia-religion/.

148. Jonny Tickle, *Reproduce or Pay Up! Controversial Russian Communist Politician Backs Childlessness Tax on Citizens Who Don't Want to Have Kids*, RT NEWS (Oct. 14, 2020, 20:47), https://www.rt.com/russia/503490-childnessness-payment-tax-russia/.

financial compensation to women for second and third children.[149] Combined with the initiatives and abortion rollbacks, the 2020 childlessness tax proposition signals further commitment to return to Stalin-era reproductive policy approaches that prioritize population boosting over health care access and human autonomy.

The COVID-19 pandemic seems to have only added fuel to the fire that is Russia's contemporary attempts to make abortion inaccessible. In Moscow, for instance, only three of the city's 44 hospitals have allowed abortion procedures during the nationwide ban on nonessential procedures.[150] Even prior to the pandemic, some medical providers were engaging in practices that effectively dissuaded women from obtaining abortions by deliberately and unnecessarily dragging out the process until later in pregnancy when more restrictions applied and the procedure would no longer be eligible for state-funded medical insurance coverage.[151] In more recent months, the consequences of these practices have been further exacerbated because providers are given more leeway to turn away patients and cite the pandemic, and because the Russian Orthodox Church continues to wage a war against abortion.[152]

F. Western Asia

1. Israel

Israel's contemporary law governing abortion stems from a 1977 law, amended in 1979.[153] That law requires that a person seeking an abortion first obtain approval from the state's Committee for Interruption of

---

149. Lyubov Vladimirovna Erofeeva, *Traditional Christian Values and Women's Reproductive Rights in Modern Russia—Is a Consensus Ever Possible?* 103 AM. J. PUB. HEALTH 1931 (2013).

150. Tatev Hovhannisyan & Inge Snip, *Hypocrite Russia Promotes Childbirth but Won't Protect Pregnant Women*, OPEN DEMOCRACY (Aug. 24, 2020), https://www.opendemocracy.net /en/5050/hypocrite-russia-promotes-childbirth-wont-protect-pregnant-women/.

151. Anna Ryzhkova, *"If You Seek the Truth, Skip All Deadlines." How Women Are Denied Abortion during a Pandemic*, CODASTORY.COM (May 26, 2020), https://www.codastory.com/ru /abortions-pandemic/; Tanya Lokshina, *Denying Women Abortion Access in Moscow: Abortion Is Essential Health Care, Even in a Pandemic*, HUMAN RIGHTS WATCH (Apr. 28 2020, 8:05 AM), https://www.hrw.org/news/2020/04/28/denying-women-abortion-access-moscow#.

152. *The Russian Orthodox Church Advocated the Introduction of a Moratorium on Abortions during the Pandemic*, RBC (May 3, 2020, 5:39), https://www.rbc.ru/society/03/05/2020/5eae2b fb9a79477f6fa63c9b.

153. The Law Library of Congress, Global Research Center, *Israel: Reproduction and Abortion: Law and Policy*, L. LIBRARY OF CONGRESS (Feb. 2012), *available at* https://www.loc.gov /law/help/il-reproduction-and-abortion/israel-reproduction-and-abortion.pdf.

Pregnancies.[154] The committee is designated by the manager of a registered hospital and must comprise one qualified medical practitioner holding the title of specialist in obstetrics and gynecology; another qualified medical practitioner practicing obstetrics and gynecology, internal medicine, psychiatry, family medicine, or public health; and a registered social worker.[155] The committee may only grant permission for the abortion if the person is under 17 or over 40 years old; the pregnancy derives from a relationship that is prohibited under the penal law, is incestuous, or is out of wedlock; the fetus may have a physical or mental disability; or continuation of the pregnancy may endanger the woman's life or cause her serious harm.[156] Initially, the committee was also permitted to consider economic circumstances, but a 1980 amendment repealed that condition.[157] Anyone who provides a woman with an abortion or otherwise assists her in terminating a pregnancy outside the bounds of the committee's procedures is subject to criminal penalties with up to five years imprisonment.[158]

Despite the facially harsh laws governing abortion, statistics paint a very different picture. In 2018, 99.2 percent of all requests to committees for abortions were approved.[159] As of 2014, abortion is covered by Israel's national health insurance system for all women aged 20 to 33 who receive committee approval for abortion.[160] But these more progressive policies cannot be understood in a vacuum, particularly when considering the region's complex histories of settler-colonialism and xenophobia. Indeed, abortion is not immune to the contentious and often violent land and power struggle that colors Israel's historical and contemporary approach to policy making.

The United Nations acknowledged this in 2008 when the Convention on the Elimination of All Forms of Discrimination Against Women (CEDAW) Committee officially expressed concern about the lack of reproductive health care access at Israeli checkpoints and in the Palestinian territories,

---

154. *Id.*

155. *Id.* at 12.

156. *Id.* at 13.

157. *Id.*

158. Penal Law, 5737-1977, LAWS OF THE STATE OF ISRAEL § 313 (Authorized Translation from the Hebrew Prepared at the Ministry of Justice) (Special Volume) (1977).

159. State of Israel Central Bureau of Statics, *Inquiries to Abortion Committees in 2018–2017* (Dec. 2019), https://www.cbs.gov.il/he/mediarelease/pages/2019/מינפ-תועדות-לההפסקת-היריו-בשנים-2017-2018.aspx.

160. Debra Kamin, *Israel's Abortion Law Now Among World's Most Liberal*, THE TIMES OF ISRAEL (Jan. 6, 2014, 4:08 AM), https://www.timesofisrael.com/israels-abortion-law-now-among-worlds-most-liberal/.

calling upon Israel to ensure that checkpoint authorities allow pregnant Palestinian women to have access to health care services, including abortion.[161] Human Rights Watch, too, submitted a report to the CEDAW Committee and voiced its disapproval of discriminatory residency and citizenship policies that "restrict[] the freedom of . . . individuals to marry and tears apart families, increasing barriers for Palestinian women to work and participate fully in public life."[162]

These barriers to participation in public life certainly include heightened restrictions on abortion, even in a territory whose disputable borders are next to, and sometimes overlapping with, a state whose abortion policies have been called "among [the] world's most liberal."[163] The Palestinian Public Health Law states that in the West Bank and Gaza, abortion is prohibited "by any means unless necessary to save the pregnant woman's life, as proven by the testimony of two specialist physicians" and also requires written approval from the woman's husband.[164] Because Palestine is not a sovereign state, there is no real enforcement mechanism for this or any other Palestinian law.[165] Due to the fragmented geography of the region and strict laws governing Palestinians' entry into Israel and their access to Israeli services, abortion is extremely inaccessible for Palestinian women.[166]

Palestinians who live in East Jerusalem are eligible to enroll in Israel's health insurance system and may, on paper, be able to access abortion through the same committee approval procedure that Israelis use.[167] In practice, however, xenophobia and colorism may dictate access: the State Central Bureau of Statistics reports that in 2018, referrals to abortion

---

161. Center for Reproductive Rights, *Bringing Rights to Bear: Preventing Maternal Mortality and Ensuring Safe Pregnancy*, CTR. FOR REPROD. RIGHTS (Oct. 2008), *available at* http://www.reproductiverights.org/sites/default/files/documents/BRB_Maternal%20Mortality_10.08.pdf.

162. Human Rights Watch, *Human Rights Watch Submission to the CEDAW Committee of Israel's Periodic Report 68th Session*, HUMAN RIGHTS WATCH (Oct. 2017), *available at* https://www.hrw.org/sites/default/files/supporting_resources/20171009_israel_cedaw_final.pdf.

163. *See* Kamin, *supra* note 160.

164. Palestinian Legislative Council Public Health Law No. 20, Article 8 (2005) (Translated into English by the World Health Organization Office for the West Bank and Gaza), *available at* http://www.hdip.org/public%20health%20law%20English.pdf.

165. *See* Sarrah Shahawy, *The Unique Landscape of Abortion Law and Access in the Occupied Palestinian Territories*, HEALTH & HUMAN RIGHTS J. (Dec. 9, 2019), https://www.hhrjournal.org/2019/12/the-unique-landscape-of-abortion-law-and-access-in-the-occupied-palestinian-territories/.

166. *Id.*; *see also* Ayesha Airifai, *Abortion as a Contested Right in Occupied Palestine*, 14 J. OF MIDDLE E. WOMEN'S STUDIES 384 (2018).

167. Yardena Schwartz, *Palestine's Abortion Problem*, FOREIGN POL'Y (Dec. 4, 2015, 4:39 PM), https://foreignpolicy.com/2015/12/04/palestines-abortion-problem/.

committees of Muslim women were substantially lower than those of Jewish women and Arab Christian women (6.5 per 1,000 versus 9.2 per 1,000).[168] As of 2013, 85 percent of people receiving abortions in Israel were members of the Jewish majority.[169]

In Gaza and the West Bank, mobility of Palestinians is extremely restricted, and the reproductive health care landscape is sparse. Because abortion is technically illegal in Palestine, there are almost no public doctors that provide abortion services, and though there are a handful of private clinics in Gaza and the West Bank where an abortion might be available, they are cost-prohibitive and, in many cases, unsafe because of a lack of meaningful regulation.[170] To make matters even more difficult, there is virtually no data on abortion in Palestine because of the region's lack of statehood.[171] Throughout the Palestinian territories, both women who receive illegal abortions and the providers who offer them are subject to up to three years' imprisonment.[172]

Recently, a Jerusalem-based nonprofit organization called the Palestinian Family Planning and Protection Association (PFPPA) has expanded into these territories to provide reproductive health services to Palestinian women lacking access.[173] In 2014, PFPPA provided abortion-related services to more than 10,000 women in the region, primarily by connecting women to clinics and doctors willing to perform confidential and legally risky abortions.[174] Even with PFPPA's important work to increase access, the abortion landscape in the region continues to mimic the multifaceted race- and religion-based inequities that plague Israel and the Occupied Palestinian Territories. In this way, the abortion analysis is perhaps an instructive microcosm of the complex struggle for identity, land, and power in the region. As the director of PFPPA, Amina Stavridis, has said of occupation, "[n]ow, it feels like we as Palestinian women are under another occupation—one of our bodies."[175]

---

168. State of Israel Central Bureau of Statistics, *supra* note 159, at clix.

169. *See* Sabreen Taha, *For Palestinian Women, Abortion Can Mean Lies, Jail or Worse*, REUTERS (Mar. 8, 2016, 8:42 AM), https://www.reuters.com/article/us-womens-day-palestinians /for-palestinian-women-abortion-can-mean-lies-jail-or-worse-idUSKCN0WA1OV.

170. Shahawy, *supra* note 165.

171. *Id.*

172. Taha, *supra* note 169.

173. Schwartz, *supra* note 167.

174. *Id.*

175. *Id.*

2. Saudi Arabia

Abortion in Saudi Arabia is almost entirely illegal unless it is required to save the life of the pregnant woman.[176] Even in that instance, the threat to the woman must be confirmed by a medical committee.[177] Because of Saudi Arabia's intolerance for abortion and its authoritarian political regime, there are no readily available data about abortion in the country. There is also little information about the realities of reproductive health care access for Saudi women. Still, after the United Nations reaffirmed its commitment to safe abortion in 2013, Saudi Arabia was one of only five member states that pressed the UN for a religious or cultural exemption to the policy recommendations, which included providing comprehensive sex education and reproductive health services as well as providing emergency contraception and safe abortion for victims of gender-based violence.[178] Saudi Arabia has also banned the website Women on Web and its telemedicine abortion services, which are specifically designed to provide abortion services and information to women living in restrictive regions.[179]

More contemporary rulings in the Saudi Arabian religious court support abortion in certain cases of rape and fetal impairment, in addition to the preexisting law allowing for abortion to preserve the health or life of the pregnant woman.[180] The World Health Organization reports that even if these conditions are met, spousal consent and parental consent for minors

176. Saudi Commission for Health Specialties, *Code of Ethics for Healthcare Practitioners* (2014), *available at* https://www.iau.edu.sa/sites/default/files/resources/5039864724.pdf (citing Royal Decree No. M/59: Law of Practicing Healthcare Professions, Article 22 (Dec. 2005), *available at* https://udh.med.sa/filespdf/english_book_small_en.pdf).

177. *Id.*

178. Press Release, *CRR Commends U.N. Commission on the Status of Women for Adopting Plan to Combat Violence Against Women and Girls*, CTR. FOR REPRO. RIGHTS (Mar. 19, 2013), https://reproductiverights.org/press-room/crr-commends-un-commission-status-women-adopting-plan-combat-violence-against-women-and.

179. Hazal Atay, *When Abortion Is "Haram," Women Find Strategies to Claim Their Rights*, SCIENCES PO, https://www.sciencespo.fr/programme-presage/en/news/when-abortion-haram-women-find-strategies-claim-their-rights.html.

180. Irene Maffi & Liv Tønnessen, *The Limits of the Law: Abortion in the Middle East and North Africa*, 21 HEALTH & HUMAN RIGHTS J. (Dec. 2019); *see also* Noga Malkin, *Alabama, Iran, or Saudi Arabia? We Checked Where Abortion Laws Are Better for Women*, HAARETZ (May 26, 2019), https://www.haaretz.com/middle-east-news/.premium.MAGAZINE-alabama-iran-or-saudi-arabia-we-checked-where-abortion-laws-are-better-for-women-1.7271623.

is still required.[181] Medication abortion (mifepristone and misoprostol) is strictly prohibited in Saudi Arabia.[182]

3. Turkey

Currently, abortion in Turkey is governed by the Law Concerning Population Planning, passed and published in May 1983.[183] Under this law, terminations of pregnancies are permitted through the tenth week of gestation with the request of the pregnant individual.[184] Parental consent is required for minors, and spousal consent is required for adults.[185] Despite the fact that current law has its roots in the 1983 statute, a comprehensive understanding of the history of abortion access in the region now called Turkey requires going back centuries.

When the Ottoman Empire collapsed and the Republic of Turkey was established, political leaders sought to build a nation that was more secular than the preceding regime, which had been based on Shar'iah law.[186] In 1858, Turkey's leaders passed Article 193, the Criminal Law, based on the Napoleonic Panel Code of 1810.[187] Article 193 made abortion punishable by imprisonment or hard labor, both for those who obtained abortions for themselves and for those who assisted others in obtaining abortions.[188] Throughout the 19th century and well into the 20th century, pro-natalist motivations drove Turkey's abortion policies.[189]

By 1965, though, decades of pro-natalist policies had led to overpopulation and Turkey was approaching economic and social collapse.[190] The government's Five Year Development Plan, published in 1963, recognized that overpopulation was also leading to adverse maternal health outcomes, and that at least 12,000 rural women were dying annually from unsafe,

---

181. World Health Organization, *Global Abortion Policies Database: Saudi Arabia*, WHO/ HUMAN REPRO. PROGRAMME (last updated May 17, 2018), https://abortion-policies.srhr .org/country/saudi-arabia/.

182. *Id.*; *see also* Mariam Nabbout, *Man Arrested for Selling Abortion Pills in Saudi Arabia, Triggering Debate*, STEPFEED.COM (Oct. 11, 2018, 9:18), https://stepfeed.com /man-arrested-for-selling-abortion-pills-in-saudi-arabia-triggering-debate-4258.

183. "NÜFUS PLANLAMASI HAKKINDA KANUN." May 24, 1983, *available at* https://abortion -policies.srhr.org/documents/countries/01-Turkey-Abortion-Law-1983.pdf.

184. *Id.*

185. *Id.*

186. Akile Gürsoy, *Abortion in Turkey: A Matter of State, Family or Individual Decision*, 42 SOC. SCI. MED 531, 532 (1996).

187. *Id.*

188. *Id.*

189. *Id.*

190. *Id.*

self-induced abortions.[191] The Population Planning Law, passed in 1965, lifted the ban on contraceptives that had been formally in place since 1930, but abortion remained illegal.[192] The decades that followed brought considerable debate and attention to the issue of abortion and population planning—a national discussion that culminated in the Law Concerning Population Planning.

Although the 1983 law signaled a shift from the country's history of complete illegalization of abortion, advocates for abortion access were largely dissatisfied with the law. They argued that the law focused more on population control than on women's health or autonomy, and many took issue with the conservative ten-week limit and the requirement of spousal consent.[193] Opposition came from all sides: religious conservatives, too, took issue with the passage of the 1983 law, but for other reasons. The Prime Ministry Family Research Institute was created in 1989 to address concerns about the breakdown of the family.[194] The Institute's committee on family health made several proposals, including a proposal to restrict the availability of legal abortion.[195]

Though that proposal was never adopted into law, it signified what could be viewed as contemporary regression in the nation's abortion policies. Today, only three hospitals in the country provide nonemergency abortions, and the current Turkish president has stated publicly that he believes abortion "is murder."[196] In 2012, the Turkish government proposed a law that would permit doctors to refuse to provide otherwise legal abortions on conscientious objection grounds.[197] The proposal was never codified, due in part to widespread protests that drew thousands of women and advocates for abortion access.[198] Three years later, some Turkish hospitals began implementing a policy requiring abortion providers to inform fathers about their daughters' pregnancies when those women sought abortions.[199]

---

191. *Id.*

192. *Id.*

193. *Id.* at 536.

194. Turkish Family Health and Planning Foundation, *in* DOGUM KONTROLU ÜZERINE DINI GURÜSSLER VE FEIVALAR (Religious Views and Proclamations on Birth Control), 1988.

195. *Id.*

196. Shena Cavallo, *Access to Abortion in Turkey: No Laughing Matter*, INT'L WOMEN'S HEALTH COALITION (Feb. 17, 2015), https://iwhc.org/2015/02/access-abortion-turkey-no-laughing-matter/.

197. *Id.*

198. Reuters Staff, *Thousands Protest at Turkey Anti-abortion Law Plan*, REUTERS (June 3, 2012), https://www.reuters.com/article/us-turkey-abortion-idUSBRE85207520120603.

199. Constanze Letsch, *Istanbul Hospitals Refuse Abortions as Government's Attitude Hardens*, THE GUARDIAN (Feb. 4, 2015), https://www.theguardian.com/world/2015/feb/04/istanbul-hospitals-refuse-abortions-government-attitude.

Again, the policy was met with harsh opposition, but nevertheless signals ongoing attacks on reproductive rights in the country.

Like other countries, Turkey's formal policies only tell part of the story when it comes to abortion access. As one of the few majority-Muslim countries where abortion is technically legal, Turkey is a hot spot for abortion tourism. Wealthy women from neighboring Saudi Arabia and Iran, where abortion is entirely illegal, travel to Turkey to obtain expensive abortions in private clinics.[200] But for Turkish women with less means, the procedure remains both out of reach and stigmatized.[201] Unable to access the 7.8 percent of public hospitals that allow abortion at the request of the pregnant woman or the high price tag that accompanies abortions performed at private hospitals, many are forced to resort to unsafe practices.[202] A safe abortion can cost hundreds of dollars in Turkey, where average household incomes are far lower than the European average and where only a third of women are in the workforce. It is notable, too, that Turkey is now home to a large population of Syrian refugees, many of whom are denied health care in public hospitals and cannot afford the cost of private abortion.[203] These women, too, are often forced to resort to illegal practices that jeopardize their health and safety.[204]

G. South-Central Asia

1. India

India's current abortion law is established by the Medical Termination of Pregnancy Act of 1971.[205] The act allows women to obtain abortions within the first 12 weeks of pregnancy in cases of severe fetal abnormality or to preserve the physical or mental health of the pregnant woman.[206] The acceptable justifications that the act designates as "mental health" reasons include several social reasons, including contraceptive failure for a married couple, trauma resulting from rape, and the woman's "actual or reasonably

---

200. Fariba Nawa, *Abortion Increasingly Hard to Access in Turkey*, THE WORLD (Oct. 5, 2020), https://www.pri.org/stories/2020-10-05/abortion-increasingly-hard-access-turkey.

201. *Id.*

202. Burcu Karakas, *Turkey's Women Face Dangerous Conditions to Obtain Legal Abortion*, DEUTSCHE WELLE (Jan. 27, 2019), https://www.dw.com/en/turkeys-women-face -dangerous-conditions-to-obtain-legal-abortion/a-47257680.

203. Nawa, *supra* note 200.

204. *Id.*

205. Medical Termination of Pregnancy Act 1971, No. 34, Acts of Parliament, 1971 (India), https://main.mohfw.gov.in/acts-rules-and-standards-health-sector/acts/mtp-act-1971.

206. *Id.*

foreseeable environment."[207] Initially, the act allowed abortions up to 20 weeks' gestation with approval of a second physician, but, in 2020, the Indian government amended the act to allow abortions up until 24 weeks' gestation.[208] Still, all abortions must be performed in a hospital or government-licensed clinic.[209]

Though India's abortion laws are relatively progressive on paper, their implementation in practice is inconsistent, with many women being denied access to abortion even though their circumstances would seemingly make them eligible under the Medical Termination of Pregnancy Act. As a result, unsafe and illegal abortions in India are common. A 2019 study found that 67 percent of all abortions in the country could be classified as unsafe, and further found that vulnerable and disadvantaged populations, including younger women aged 15 to 19, rural women, Muslim women, poor women, and lower caste women, were disproportionately more likely to have resorted to unsafe abortions.[210] Unsafe abortion is reported as the fourth leading cause of maternal death in India, a country that has historically reported extremely high rates of maternal mortality.[211]

Several women and girls have been successful in circumventing the 24-week cutoff by utilizing the Indian judiciary.[212] That India's abortion

---

207. *Id.* § 3(2)–(3).

208. *See* Chitra Subramaniam, *India's New Abortion Law Is Progressive and Has a Human Face*, OBSERVER RESEARCH FOUND. (Mar. 7, 2020), https://www.orfonline.org/expert-speak /india-new-abortion-law-progressive-human-face-62023/.

209. Medical Termination of Pregnancy Act 1971, *supra* note 205, at § 4(a).

210. Ryo Yokoe et al., *Unsafe Abortion and Abortion-Related Death among 1.8 Million Women in India*, 4 BMJ GLOB. HEALTH 1491 (May 2019).

211. *Id.*; Max Roser & Hannah Ritchie, *Maternal Mortality*, OUR WORLD IN DATA (2013), https://ourworldindata.org/maternal-mortality.

212. Press Trust of India, *High Court Allows 13-Year-Old Rape Victim to Abort 26-Week Old Fetus*, NEW DELHI TELEVISION LIMITED (Dec. 6, 2017, 7:05 AM), https://www.ndtv.com /mumbai-news/high-court-allows-13-year-old-rape-victim-to-abort-26-week-old-fotus-1784118 (reporting that the Indian bench of Justices Shantanu Kemkar and G.S. Kulkarni allowed a 13-year-old rape survivor to get an abortion at 26 weeks' gestation. Justice Kemkar is quoted as saying, "Considering that the child, if born, will suffer from life-long neurological complications, and considering the Fundamental Rights of the petitioner, we allow the plea."); Kalpesh Mhamunkar, *Bombar High Court Allows Thane Woman to Abort 22-week Feotus*, THE ASIAN AGE (Dec. 20, 2017, 6:16 AM), https://www.asianage.com/metros/mumbai/201 217/high-court-allows-thane-woman-to-abort-22-week-foetus.html (reporting that Justices Shantanu Kekar and Rajesh Ketkar approved a petition of a woman seeking to abort her pregnancy based on the fact that the fetus had various incurable neurological complications); Rosy Sequeira, *HC Lets Woman Abort 24-Week Foetus with Heart Condition*, TIMES OF INDIA (Dec. 21, 2017, 6:22), https://timesofindia.indiatimes.com/city/mumbai/hc-lets-woman-abort-24 -week-foetus-with-heart-condition/articleshow/62186619.cms (reporting that the Bombay high court approved medical termination of a 24-week fetus with cardiac anomalies);

policies can be circumscribed by the courts may provide some solace for women whose circumstances are dire enough and whose pockets are deep enough to get them their day in court. For the vast majority of Indian women, though, barriers to access remain the norm. The Guttmacher Institute reports that the country suffers from an insufficient number of facilities that offer abortion care, lack of certified staff, shortages of equipment and supplies, failures to ensure privacy and confidential care, a lack of knowledge among women that abortion is legal under certain circumstances, and widespread stigma surrounding abortion and abortion-related

---

Press Trust of India, *SC Allows Women to Abort Foetus with Arnold Chiari Syndrome*, THE HINDUSTAN TIMES (Oct. 9, 2017, 18:10 IST), https://www.hindustantimes.com/india-news /sc-allows-women-to-abort-foetus-with-arnold-chiari-syndrome/story-jtZW46R14jB c9V0gqMjVNL.html (reporting that the Supreme Court of India allowed two women, one at 29 weeks' gestation and the other at 30 weeks' gestation, to abort their pregnancies after it was detected that both fetuses had Arnold Chiari Type II syndrome, a malformation leading to underdeveloped brains and distorted spines); Press Trust of India, *Jharklhand HC Allows Abortion in 23rd Week for Minor Rape Victim; Foetus' DNA to Be Used as Evidence*, FIRSTPOST (Oct. 16, 2017, 8:19 IST), https://www.firstpost.com/india/jharkhand-hc-allows-abortion-in-23rd -week-for-minor-rape-victim-foetus-dna-to-be-used-as-evidence-4146403.html (reporting that the Jharkhand High Court allowed a young rape survivor to terminate her pregnancy at 23 weeks' gestation and directed the state government to bear the expense of the termination); Sofi Ahsan, *Punjab & Haryana High Court Allows Minor Rape Survivor to Terminate Pregnancy at 26 Weeks*, INDIAN EXPRESS (Oct. 18, 2017, 12:57 PM), https://indianexpress .com/article/india/punjab-haryana-high-court-allows-minor-rape-survivor-to-terminate -pregnancy-4896356/ (reporting that the Punjab and Haryana High Court allowed for the termination of a pregnancy at 26 weeks' gestation for a young rape survivor); Press Trust of India, *SC Allows Woman to Abort 31-Week Foetus Having Kidney Problems*, ZEE NEWS (Oct. 7, 2017, 4:54 PM), https://zeenews.india.com/india/sc-allows-woman-to-abort-31-week-foetus -having-kidney-problems-2048475.html (reporting that the Supreme Court of India allowed a woman who was 31 weeks pregnant to medically terminate her pregnancy because it had been detected that both the fetus' kidneys were not functioning and that continuation of the pregnancy would cause mental anguish to the pregnant woman); Express Web Desk, *Supreme Court Allows Pune Woman to Abort Foetus with No Skull*, THE INDIAN EXPRESS (Aug. 31, 2017, 12:56 PM), https://indianexpress.com/article/india/sc-allows-pune-woman-to-abort -24-week-foetus-with-no-skull-4821892/ (reporting that the Indian Supreme Court allowed a woman who was 24 weeks pregnant to abort her fetus that did not have any skull or brain because the survival rate was minimal and, as the bench comprised of Justices S.A. Bobde and L. Nagaswara Rao said, "We consider it appropriate and in the interest of justice to allow termination of pregnancy."); Aayushi Pratap, *Mumbai Woman Can Abort 24-Week Foetus with Brain Abnormalities as SC Gives Nod*, THE HINDUSTAN TIMES (July 28, 2017, 2:42 PM), https://www .hindustantimes.com/mumbai-news/mumbai-woman-can-abort-24-week-foetus-with-brain -abnormalities-as-sc-gives-nod/story-SVLtOAKoqfaXA2shcCCiFO.html (reporting that the Supreme Court allowed a 21-year-old woman at 24 weeks' gestation to abort her pregnancy because doctors had diagnosed the fetus with aqueductal stenosis and hydrocephalus— brain abnormalities that would cause mental disabilities).

care.[213] Moreover, challenges exist in addressing and curbing sex-selective abortion while still protecting access to abortion generally. India passed the Pre-Conception and Pre-Natal Diagnostics Techniques Act in 2003, which prohibits the misuse of prenatal diagnostic tests for the purpose of sex determination, but this legislation led to some unintended difficulties in obtaining and providing safe abortion and post-abortion care.[214] Many providers, for instance, have indicated reluctance to offer abortion services because of the real or perceived threat of authorities attempting to restrict sex-selective abortions.[215]

Because surgical abortion is largely inaccessible in India, medication abortion has become an increasingly popular means for accessing abortion. As of 2016, the prescription drugs mifepristone and misoprostol accounted for four out of every five abortions in Bihar, Gujarat, and Uttar Pradesh, three of the more densely populated states in India.[216] Although there are no national laws in India outlawing medication abortion, access is still fragmented with little regulation. In Maharashtra, for instance, only 1.2 percent of medical shops stock abortion pills.[217] In Uttar Pradesh, on the other hand, 66 percent of pharmacists said they stock the drugs.[218] In Bihar, 37.8 percent of pharmacists stock abortion drugs.[219] But even in Uttar Pradesh and Bihar, where abortion pills are more readily available, only 9 percent and 15 percent of pharmacists, respectively, report being trained on medication abortion, and 35 percent of total pharmacists surveyed could not recall the name of the medications used for abortion.[220] Throughout the

213. Susheela Singh et al., *Abortion and Unintended Pregnancy in Six Indian States: Findings and Implications for Policies and Programs*, GUTTMACHER INSTITUTE (Nov. 2018), https://www.guttmacher.org/report/abortion-unintended-pregnancy-six-states-india# [hereinafter Singh Guttmacher Article].

214. Amendment to the Pre-Conception and Pre-Natal Diagnostic Techniques (Prohibition of Sex Selectin) Act, Acts of Parliament, 2003 (India).

215. *See* V. Nidadavolu & H. Bracken, *Abortion and Sex Determination: Conflicting Messages in Information Materials in a District of Rajasthan, India*, 14 REPROD. HEALTH MATTERS 160 (2006); P.R. Shidhaye et al., *Study of Knowledge and Attitude Regarding Prenatal Diagnostic Techniques Act among the Pregnant Women at a Tertiary Care Teaching Hospital in Mumbai*, 1 J. EDUC. & HEALTH PROMOTION (2012); S. Yasmin et al., *Gender Preference and Awareness Regarding Sex Determination among Antenatal Mothers Attending a Medical College of Eastern India*, 41 SCANDINAVIAN J. PUB. HEALTH 344 (2013).

216. *See* Singh Guttmacher Article, *supra* note 213.

217. *See* Alfie Habershon, *Why Indian Pharmacies Are Reluctant to Stock Abortion Pills*, INDIA SPEND (Sept. 26, 2019), https://www.indiaspend.com/why-indian-pharmacies-are-reluctant-to-stock-abortion-pills/.

218. *Id.*

219. *Id.*

220. *Id.*

country, 43 percent of pharmacists reported that they believed abortion to
be illegal.[221]

2. Bangladesh

Bangladesh's Penal Code of 1860 continues to govern abortion law in the
country. Under section 312 of the Code,

> whoever voluntarily causes a woman with child to miscarry, shall, if such
> miscarriage be not caused in good faith for the purpose of saving the life
> of the woman, be punished with imprisonment of either description for a
> term which may extend to three years, or with fine, or with both.[222]

Although Bangladesh continues to impose criminal penalties for "causing
miscarriage," the country's contemporary abortion policies and practices
are largely dictated by the Bangladeshi national family planning program,
which allows for a procedure called menstrual regulation, or MR.[223] MR is
defined as "an interim method to establish a case of non-pregnancy in a
woman who is at risk of being pregnant" and includes manual vacuum aspiration in combination with medication abortion to regulate the menstrual
cycle and terminate early stage pregnancies.[224]

Incidence of MR has declined in recent years due to barriers such as
cost and lack of knowledge among Bangladeshi women.[225] More than half
of married women reported not knowing about the MR program, and a
quarter of women seeking MR reported refusals of care by providers.[226]
Though MR procedures are supposedly offered to women free of charge,
unauthorized charges and hidden fees are, unfortunately, commonplace.[227]
In 2014, 430,000 MR procedures were performed across the country, indi-

---

221. *Id.*

222. The Penal Code, 1860 (Act No. XLV of 1860) (Oct. 6, 1860) § 312, http://www
.oecd.org/site/adboecdanti-corruptioninitiative/46812525.pdf (Bangl.).

223. *See* Janie Benson, Kathryn Andersen & Ghazaleh Samandari, *Reductions in Abortion-
Related Mortality Following Policy Reform: Evidence from Romania, South Africa and Bangladesh*, 8
J. REPROD. HEALTH (2011), https://reproductive-health-journal.biomedcentral.com/track/
pdf/10.1186/1742-4755-8-39; *see also* Altaf Hossain et al., *Postabortion Care in Bangladesh: Evidence from a Survey of Health Facilities, 2014*, GUTTMACHER INSTITUTE (Mar. 2017), https://
www.guttmacher.org/report/menstrual-regulation-postabortion-care-bangladesh [hereinaf-
ter Guttmacher Bangladesh Report].

224. Susheela Singh et al., *The Incidence of Menstrual Regulation Procedures and Abortion in
Bangladesh, 2014*, 43 INT'L PERSP, SEXUAL & REPROD. HEALTH 1 (2017) [hereinafter Singh
Bangladesh Article].

225. *Id.*

226. *Id.*

227. *Id.*

cating a 34 percent decline since 2010.[228] In the same year, only 53 percent of public facilities permitted to provide MR services actually provided the procedure, and 92 percent of the facilities not offering MR claimed that they lacked necessary training.[229] Three in ten of these facilities lacked basic MR equipment.[230]

As MR access declined, incidences of unsafe abortions rose. In the same year that MR procedures decreased by 34 percent, 1,194,000 induced abortions were performed, many by untrained providers.[231] These barriers to MR and increases in unsafe abortions have led to some drastic health consequences for Bangladeshi women seeking abortion care. In 2014, 256,000 women were treated in facilities for complications from unsafe abortions and another 128,000 needed post-abortion care but did not obtain treatment.[232]

H. Eastern Asia

1. People's Republic of China

China's reproductive health care landscape is often defined by its notorious one-child policy, a policy in place since the 1970s aimed at controlling the national population.[233] Although the one-child policy started phasing out in favor of a two-child policy, the country's strict population control mechanisms allow for compete state control of abortion.[234] In China, a woman must get permission from the state to have a legal pregnancy.[235] For women who become pregnant outside the bounds of state permission, abortion is a mandatory, state-sponsored service, with no gestational age restrictions.[236]

The Planned Birth Rules for the Hainan Province state that "those whose pregnancies do not conform to these Regulations must promptly terminate

---

228. *See* Guttmacher Bangladesh Report, *supra* note 223.

229. *Id.*

230. *Id.*

231. Singh Bangladesh Article, *supra* note 224.

232. *Id.*

233. Jamie Jordan, Note, *Ten Years of Resistance to Coercive Population Control: Section 601 of the IIRIRA of 1996 to Section 101 of the Real Id Act of 2005*, 18 HASTINGS WOMEN'S L.J. 229, 232 (2007); *see also* XIAN FA (Constitution of the People's Republic of China), art. 25 (2004) (P.R.C.).

234. Beverly Winioff, Irving Sivin et al., *The Acceptability of Medical Abortion in China, Cuba and India*, 23 INT'L FAM. PLANNING PERSPECTIVES 73 (June 1997), *available at* http://www .guttmacher.org/pubs/journals/2307397.pdf.

235. Elina Hemminki et al., *Illegal Births and Legal Abortions—the Case of China*, 2 REPROD. HEALTH *2–3 (2005), http://www.reproductive-health-journal.com/content/2/1/5.

236. *See* Jordan, *supra* note 233, at 234.

their pregnancy. Those who still refuse to terminate their pregnancies after persuasive education will be dealt with according to the relevant provisions of these Regulations."[237] Regulations in the Hunan, Liaoning, Hubei, and Guizhou provinces have similar stipulations.[238] In almost all provinces, couples who exceed their government-mandated birth limit can be fined up to ten times their annual household income in "social compensation fees."[239]

As of October 2015, all Chinese families are allowed to have two children, but the country's coercive approach to abortion continues to affect access and perception.[240] Indeed, while China's approach to abortion may appear as a stark contrast to the oppressive regimes of many other countries' outright prohibitions, mandatory abortion policies are equally oppressive in that they still override a woman's express wishes in favor of state control. The story of one Chinese woman, Feng Jianmei, is illustrative. In 2013, she was forced to undergo an abortion while seven months pregnant with her second child.[241] She and her husband had refused to pay the mandatory social compensation fees for their second child, so the state responded by sending family planning workers to violently assault Feng Jianmei and inject her with a drug to induce abortion against her will.[242]

Despite the one-child policy rollback in 2015, the number of induced abortions has increased, with 9,626,731 reported in 2017.[243] This increase potentially evidences that abortion continues to be used as a tool of state control and violence in China. Not all Chinese women have been equally subjected to this violence. The Associated Press found that Muslim and rural Chinese families were most likely to be victims of the government's

237. Steven W. Mosher & Jonathan Abbamonte, *Forced Abortion Still Mandated under China's "Planned Birth" Laws*, POPULATION RESEARCH INST. (Jan. 2018), https://www.pop.org /forced-abortion-still-mandated-chinas-planned-birth-laws/.

238. *Id.*

239. *Id.*

240. Editor, *China to Allow Two Children for All Couples*, XINHUA ENGLISH.NEWS.CN (Beijing) (Oct. 29, 2015, 6:49 PM), http://news.xinhuanet.com/english/2015-10/29/c_134763507 .htm.

241. David Barboza, *China Suspends Family Planning Workers after Forced Abortion*, N.Y. TIMES (June 15, 2012), http://www.nytimes.com/2012/06/16/world/asia/china-suspends-family -planning-workers-after-forced-abortion.html; Edward Wong, *Forced to Abort, Chinese Woman under Pressure*, N.Y. TIMES (June 26, 2012), http://www.nytimes.com/2012/06/27/world /asia/chinese-family-in-forced-abortion-case-still-under-pressure.html?_r=0.

242. *See* Barboza, *supra* note 241.

243. Jinlin Liu, Yvon Englert & Wei-Hong Zhang, *Is Induced Abortion a Part of Family Planning in China?*, INTECHOPEN (Aug. 2019), https://www.intechopen.com/books/induced -abortion-and-spontaneous-early-pregnancy-loss-focus-on-management/is-induced-abortion -a-part-of-family-planning-in-china-.

efforts to slash birth rates, with interviews and data showing that the Han Chinese majority is largely spared forced abortions, sterilizations, and IUD insertions that ethnic minorities are forced to undergo.[244] As recently as 2019, Chinese officials threatened detention for families that did not register their children, and rewarded those who reported illegal births.[245]

2. Japan

Abortion law in Japan is governed by the Japanese Penal Code of 1907 and the 1996 Maternal Protection Law (MPL). Under Articles 212 and 213 of the Penal Code, a pregnant woman causing her own abortion may be imprisoned for up to one year, and a person who causes a woman's abortion may be punished with imprisonment of up to two years.[246] The MPL, originally called the Eugenic Protection Law, allows for abortion in instances of hereditary physical or mental illnesses or nonhereditary mental illnesses, or in cases of rape, risk of serious harm, or financial hardship.[247] The law was renamed the Maternal Protection Law in 1996 only after pressure from advocates to remove the eugenics element of the policy.[248] The MPL provides exceptions to the Japanese Penal Code, but only for women less than 22 weeks pregnant who receive abortion care from a designated physician.[249]

Though Japan's 1948 Eugenic Protection Law made it one of the first countries in the world to legalize abortion, current abortion data paint a much more complex picture. Unplanned birth rates in Japan, for instance, have been reported to be as high as 52 percent, compared to 30 percent in the United States and 19 percent in France.[250] This may be due to limited contraceptive access in Japan, with oral contraceptives only being approved by the Japanese government in 1999.[251] Additionally, abortion is not covered by the Japanese national health insurance and can cost upward

---

244. The Associated Press, *China Cuts Uighur Births with IUDs, Abortion, Sterilization*, Associated Press, (June 29, 2020), https://apnews.com/article/269b3de1af34e17c1941a514f7 8d764c.

245. *Id.*

246. Penal Code Japan (Act No. 45 of 1907), Articles 212–213, http://www.cas.go.jp/jp /seisaku/hourei/data/PC.pdf.

247. Mariko Kato, *Abortion Still Key Birth Control*, Japan Times (Oct. 20 2009), https:// www.japantimes.co.jp/news/2009/10/20/reference/abortion-still-key-birth-control/.

248. *Id.*

249. *Id.*

250. Aya Goto et al., *Abortion Trends in Japan, 1975–95*, 31 Studies in Fam. Planning 301 (Dec. 2000).

251. *Id.*

of 200,000 yen, or 1,910 U.S. dollars, a cost-prohibitive amount for many individuals.[252] Abortion pills, misoprostol and mifepristone, are not available at all in Japan, keeping abortion further out of reach for many who may not qualify for or be able to afford surgical abortion.[253]

Contemporary Japanese women are also still grappling with the fallout from the MPL's predecessor, the Eugenic Protection Law, which legalized abortion in Japan but also instituted a government policy endorsing forced sterilizations and abortions for as many as 29 million people between 1955 and 1996.[254] In 2018, two suits were filed against the Japanese government for violating plaintiffs' reproductive and constitutional rights.[255] The plaintiffs, now in their seventies and eighties, demanded compensatory damages from the Japanese government for having undergone involuntary abortion and sterilization procedures based on the presence of hereditary diseases or intellectual disabilities.[256]

I. Southeast Asia

1. Vietnam

In 1964, Vietnam's government first introduced a general population policy.[257] After the Vietnam War in 1975, women were averaging 6.1 children as the total fertility rate.[258] The government, in 1988, introduced a two-child policy to restrict the high fertility rate.[259] The policy relied on the provision of legal

---

252. Julia Mascetti, *Abortion in Japan*, SAVVY TOKYO (Oct. 23, 2018), https://savvytokyo .com/abortion-in-japan/.

253. Lily Crossley-Baxter, *Women's Health in Tokyo: White Lies, Pregnancy Tests and Pills*, TOKYO CHEAPO (Apr. 30, 2017), https://tokyocheapo.com/living/womens-health-tokyo -clinics-birth-control/.

254. International Campaign for Women's Right to Safe Abortion, *JAPAN – Government Suits over Forced Sterilisation and Abortion under Former Eugenics Law*, INT'L CAMPAIGN FOR WOMEN'S RIGHT TO SAFE ABORTION (July 23, 2018), https://www.safeabortionwomensright.org /japan-government-suits-over-forced-sterilisation-and-abortion-under-former-eugenics-law/.

255. *Id.*

256. *Id.*

257. Bang Nguyen Pham et al., *The Evolution of Population Policy in Viet Nam*, 27 ASIA-PACIFIC POP. J. 61, 63 (2013), https://www.researchgate.net/publication/255822947_The_Evolution _of_Population_Policy_in_Viet_Nam.

258. *See id.* at 63.

259. Anh P. Ngo, *Effects of Vietnam's Two-Child Policy on Fertility, Son Preference, and Female Labor Supply*, 33 J. OF POP. ECON. 751 (2020), https://link.springer.com/arti cle/10.1007/s00148-019-00766-1#:~:text=In%201988%2C%20facing%20a%20total,no%20 more%20than%20two%20children.&text=The%20policy%20reduced%20the%20 average,by%200.2%20births%20per%20woman.

abortion to married individuals with no cost.[260] The population policy resembled China's one-child policy.[261] The fertility rate rapidly declined in Vietnam when the formal policy was instituted.[262] However, in 2003, the Population Ordinance was issued and recognized reproductive rights, and it permitted couples to make family planning choices.[263] The ordinance was amended in December 2008, apparently taking away what reproductive rights and family planning abilities had been granted before and again giving the government emergency powers.[264] The 2008 law provides that

> [e]ach couple and individual has the right and responsibility to participate in the campaigns on population and family planning, reproductive health care: (i) decide time and birth spacing; (ii) have one or two children, exceptional cases to be determined by the Government.[265]

Additionally, Vietnam guarantees, through Article 44 of their Law on Protection of the People's Health, that abortion is a right.[266] The law was passed in 1989 shortly after the two-child policy.[267] Under this law, abortion is legal in the first 22 weeks of gestation, and both public and private hospitals provide the service.[268] Sex-selection abortion is banned.[269] A health care provider that performs an illegal abortion risks five years of imprisonment, and if they cause further serious consequences through the procedure, they could be imprisoned for up to ten years.[270] This law is recognized as one of

---

260. *See* Dana Fllek-Gibson, *Vietnam Tackles High Abortion Rates*, ALJAZEERA (Aug. 28, 2014), https://www.aljazeera.com/features/2014/8/28/vietnam-tackles-high-abortion-rates.

261. *See* Ngo, *supra* note 259, at 62.

262. *See id.* at 64.

263. *See id.*

264. *See id.* at 65.

265. Bang N. Pham *et al.*, *The Evolution of Population Policy in Viet Nam*, p. 9, PRINCETON (Dec. 11, 1:32 PM), *available at* https://epc2012.princeton.edu/papers/120007.

266. Law No. 21-LCT/HDNN8, art. 44(1) (1989) (Viet.), https://vanbanphapluat.co /law-no-21-lct-hdnn8-of-june-30-1989-of-people-s-health ("Women have the right of abortion according to expectations, to be served the medical examination and treatment of gynaecological diseases, to be monitored the health during pregnancy, to be served medicare as childbearing in the health facilities.").

267. *Abortion Laws in Vietnam*, HOW TO USE ABORTION PILL, https://www.howtouseabor tionpill.org/regions/asia/vietnam/ (last visited Nov. 27, 2020).

268. *Termination of Pregnancy and Abortion in Vietnam*, ANGLOINFO, https://www.angloinfo .com/how-to/vietnam/healthcare/pregnancy-birth/termination-abortion (last visited Nov. 27, 2020).

269. Implementation of the Population Policy, Gov. Decree No. 104/2003/ND-CP, art. 10 (Sept. 16, 2003) (Viet.).

270. Criminal Code of 1999, art. 243 (Viet.), *available at* https://abortion-policies.srhr .org/documents/countries/02-Vietnam-Criminal-Code-1999.pdf.

the broadest internationally. It also continues to survive attempts at restriction. For example, in 2014, members of the National Assembly attempted to amend the law to limit abortion to only health or life of the mother, but the effort failed.[271]

Vietnam has one of the highest abortion rates in the world, with an average of two and a half abortions per the life of a woman.[272] The Tu Du Hospital in Ho Chi Minh City "carried out approximately 29,000 abortions in 2015, and in the first six months of this year over 14,000 pregnancies were terminated."[273] The country also has one of the highest rates of repeat abortions.[274] A factor influencing this high abortion rate is the increased rate of adolescent and premarital sex together with a lack of sex education and contraceptive use.[275] The stigma around premarital sex correlates with increased use of abortion services, particularly in secret.[276] For instance, the director of the Institute for Reproductive and Family Health asserts that "[a]bout 70% of secret abortions are performed on teenagers aged between 13 and 19."[277] Despite the high rates of abortion since 1989, when the Law on Protection of the People's Health was passed, abortion is highly stigmatized among social groups.[278]

---

271. *Termination of Pregnancy and Abortion in Vietnam*, ANGLOINFO, https://www.angloinfo.com/how-to/vietnam/healthcare/pregnancy-birth/termination-abortion (last visited Nov. 27, 2020).

272. VnExpress, *Abortion Rate in Vietnam Highest in Asia*, VNEXPRESS INT'L (Sept. 30, 2016, 4:31 PM GMT), https://e.vnexpress.net/news/news/abortion-rate-in-vietnam-highest-in-asia-3476746.html.

273. *Id.*

274. H. Ball, *Repeat Abortions Are Common in Vietnam, May Be Linked to Son Preference*, 40 GUTTMACHER INSTITUTE (June 2014), https://www.guttmacher.org/journals/ipsrh/2014/07/repeat-abortions-are-common-vietnam-may-be-linked-son-preference.

275. *See id; see also* AFP, *Abortion Still "Used as Contraceptive" in Vietnam*, BANGKOK POST (June 8, 2020, 11:45 AM), https://www.bangkokpost.com/world/1931284/abortion-still-used-as-contraceptive-in-vietnam.

276. *See* VnExpress, *supra* note 272.

277. *See id.*

278. Son Le et al., *VIETNAM—We Did Not Talk About It (Her Abortion). It Was Not a Happy Story*, INT'L CAMPAIGN FOR WOMEN'S RIGHT TO SAFE ABORTION (June 25, 2020), https://www.safeabortionwomensright.org/news/vietnam-we-did-not-talk-about-it-her-abortion-it-was-not-a-happy-story/.

J. Southern Africa

1. South Africa

Under the apartheid regime, abortion in South Africa was governed first by common law and then by the Abortion and Sterilization Act of 1975.[279] Under the Abortion and Sterilization Act, abortion was only allowed in cases of serious threat of injury or danger of permanent damage to the fetus or the woman, and two medical practitioners had to approve of the procedure.[280] Even in cases where these rigid requirements were met, providers had no affirmative duty to provide abortions, and the costs of abortion fell to the women, leaving abortion out of reach for many people despite its legal status.[281] As with all social policies during this time, abortion policy was enforced and regulated differently across racial lines, with many white women able to circumvent the governing laws by virtue of their race and financial resources.[282]

South Africa's transition to a democracy also brought legal changes to the country's abortion infrastructure, with the Choice on Termination of Pregnancy Act of 1996 (CTOPA) decriminalizing abortion and making it available on nearly any grounds, including socioeconomic reasons, during the first 12 weeks of pregnancy.[283] The CTOPA allowed for abortions between 13 and 20 weeks' gestation for the following reasons: if a medical practitioner certifies that the pregnancy poses a risk of injury to the woman's physical or mental health; if there is a fetal anomaly; if the pregnancy is the result of rape or incest; or if the pregnancy would negatively impact the woman's socioeconomic conditions.[284] After 20 weeks' gestation, a woman can obtain an abortion if two medical practitioners certify that the pregnancy poses a serious danger to the woman's health or life or if the fetus

---

279. Sally Guttmacher et al., *Abortion Reform in South Africa: A Case Study of the 1996 Choice on Termination of Pregnancy Act*, GUTTMACHER INSTITUTE (Dec. 1998), https://www.guttmacher.org/journals/ipsrh/1998/12/abortion-reform-south-africa -case-study-1996-choice-termination-pregnancy-act.

280. Charles Ngwena, *An Appraisal of Abortion Laws in Southern Africa from a Reproductive Health Rights Perspective*, 32 J.L. MED. & ETHICS 708, 713 (2004).

281. *Id.*

282. Guttmacher et al., *supra* note 279.

283. *See* President's Office, *No. 92 of 1996: Choice on Termination of Pregnancy Act*, 1996, *available at* https://www.parliament.gov.za/storage/app/media/ProjectsAndEvents/wom ens_month_2015/docs/Act92of1996.pdf.

284. *Id.*

will be severely malformed.[285] A 2008 amendment to the CTOPA allowed for registered nurses and midwives to provide abortion services.[286]

Following the passage of the CTOPA, the South African Department of Health made maternal health a priority, which in turn led to a significant decline in abortion-related and maternal mortality rates in the country.[287] Still, the country's initial efforts to put reproductive and maternal health at the forefront of health policy have not necessarily been long-lasting. With the 2008 amendment, South Africa's provinces were each given regional control over CTOPA implementation, making access across the country inconsistent and subject to differing politics and priorities that exist across provincial lines.[288]

In addition to regional barriers, the CTOPA also allows for conscientious objections to abortion, and many providers in more rural and politically conservative areas invoke conscientious objection to obstruct access to abortion care.[289] In a survey of women in Cape Town who had previously sought abortion care, 45 percent did not receive abortions after attempting to assert their rights under the CTOPA.[290] Of those denied care, 20 percent were turned away because of advanced gestational age, 20 percent because the clinic did not have available staff to perform abortions, and 5 percent because they could not afford the procedure.[291] As of 2013, only half of the facilities in the country that were licensed to provide abortions were actually providing abortion services.[292] Another report from the Guttmacher-Lancet Commission in Johannesburg, released in 2019, indicated that only 7 percent of the country's total health facilities offered abortion services.[293]

Uneven access and high rates of conscientious objection have, unfortunately, made unsafe abortion commonplace in some parts of South

---

285. *Id.*

286. Mary Favier et al., *Safe Abortion in South Africa: "We Have Wonderful Laws but We Don't Have People to Implement Those Laws,"* 143 INT'L. J. GYNECOLOGY & OBSTETRICS 38 (2018).

287. Rachel Jewkes & Helen Rees, *Dramatic Decline in Abortion Mortality Due to the Choice on Termination of Pregnancy Act.* 95 S. AFR. MED. J. 250 (2005).

288. Favier et al., *supra* note 286.

289. *Id.*

290. Women's Health Research Unit, *Reproductive Health Research Policy Brief: Denial of Legal Abortion in South Africa,* UNIV. OF CAPE TOWN (Mar. 2016), https://www.ansirh.org /sites/default/files/publications/files/deniallegalabortionsouthafrica-march2016.pdf.

291. *Id.*

292. Karen A. Trueman & Makgoale Magwentshu, *Abortion in a Progressive Legal Environment: The Need for Vigilance in Protecting and Promoting Access to Safe Abortion Services in South Africa,* 103 AM. J. PUB. HEALTH 397 (2013).

293. Amy Green, *Abortion Access in SA: A "Disaster,"* HEALTH-E NEWS (May 11, 2018), https://health-e.org.za/2018/05/11/abortion-access-in-sa-a-disaster/.

Africa.[294] As before the CTOPA, rural, poor, black women are those most likely to be denied access and to resort to unsafe alternatives. Evidence shows that the gains in reproductive care access and maternal health from the first ten years after CTOPA's passage have since been eroded.[295] As of 2019, more than half of all abortions in South Africa are unlicensed, and as many as one-quarter of the country's total maternal deaths from miscarriages were the result of illegal abortions.[296]

In recent years, there has also been a disturbing increase in lamppost advertisements for "affordable 100% guaranteed, fast, safe and pain-free abortions."[297] Even though such advertising is illegal under the CTOPA and the Advertising Standards Authority of South Africa, and despite the likelihood that it contributes to the high rates of illegal and unsafe abortions in the country, neither the National Department of Health nor the provincial bodies responsible for providing health care services appear to have made meaningful efforts to address the troublesome trend.[298]

In 2017, the African Christian Democratic Party put forward a bill in the South African Parliament that would have further decreased abortion access.[299] The bill was ultimately defeated, but its proposal, coupled with increasing rates of unsafe abortion and decreasing rates of access to legal abortions, may signal national regression.

2. Angola

Abortion in Angola was, until 2019, almost entirely illegal, with narrow exceptions for rape, fetus malformation, or endangerment of the mother's life.[300] In September of 2017, Angola elected President João Lourenço,

---

294. Rebecca Hodes, *The Culture of Illegal Abortion in South Africa*, 42 J. S. AFR. STUDIES 79 (2016).

295. *See* Trueman & Magwentshu, *supra* note 292.

296. Anita Powell, *South Africa's Liberal Abortion Laws Hampered by Widespread Stigma*, VOA NEWS, (Mar. 22, 2019, 5:35 AM), https://www.voanews.com/africa /south-africas-liberal-abortion-laws-hampered-widespread-stigma.

297. *See* News 24, *Illegal Abortion Advertising in Focus*, NEWS 24 (Apr. 25, 2011), https:// www.news24.com/news24/illegal-abortion-advertising-in-focus-20110425.

298. *Id.*; *see also* Trueman & Magwentshu, *supra* note 292.

299. Green, *supra* note 293.

300. Efe-Epa, *Angola Decriminalizes Same-Sex Relations, Allows Abortion in Certain Cases*, EFE.COM (Jan. 24, 2019), https://www.efe.com/efe/english/life/angola-decriminalizes -same-sex-relations-allows-abortion-in-certain-cases/50000263-3877510; Rumbi Chakamba, *Shock and Anger as Angola Seeks to Ban Abortion Entirely*, THE NEW HUMANITARIAN (Apr. 26, 2017), https://deeply.thenewhumanitarian.org/womenandgirls/articles/2017/04/26/shock -and-anger-as-angola-seeks-to-ban-abortion-entirely.

ending a 38-year reign of the country's previous leader.[301] As part of the regime change, the country embarked on the process of replacing its 1886 Penal Code, which had, until that point, governed abortion and all other social policies. Prior to 2017, there were few modifications to the country's approach to abortion. In 2012, Justice Minister Guilhermina Prata proposed an abortion bill that would have expanded access to safe and legal abortions in an effort to address the high rates of clandestine abortions and related deaths in Angola.[302] The bill was swiftly defeated in parliament, due in part to the fact that 60 percent of Angolans identify as Catholic.[303]

Those actors who led the charge to defeat the 2012 bill led other efforts during the 2017 redrafting of the Angolan Penal Code.[304] They sought to make abortion completely illegal by proposing that the revived Penal Code eliminate the already narrow exceptions to the general ban on abortions.[305] Their proposal would also imprison for four to ten years anyone who performed an abortion.[306] Given that the 2017 redrafting project was expected to expand, not restrict, abortion access for Angolan women, the harsh proposal generated quick backlash from pro-choice advocates.[307] Ultimately, the general ban was defeated in Parliament, and the country updated its Penal Code to expand access to abortion.

The revised Penal Code still criminalizes abortion, stating that

> a pregnant woman who, for reasons of their own, interrupts her pregnancy, or in anyway, participates in the termination or consents that a third person terminates it [except for statutorily excepted circumstances] shall be punished with imprisonment up to three years or a fine of up to 360 days.[308]

Those who assist a pregnant woman in terminating a pregnancy may also be punished with one to four years' imprisonment.[309] The law allows for

---

301. *Angola: Events of 2017*, HUMAN RIGHTS WATCH (Jan. 2018), https://www.hrw.org/world-report/2018/country-chapters/angola.

302. *See* Gender Links for Equality and Justice, *Angola: Abortion Bill Causes Uproar*, GENDER LINKS (Feb. 5, 2012), https://genderlinks.org.za/barometer-newsletter/angola-abortion-bill-causes-uproar-2012-02-05/.

303. *Id.*

304. Chakamba, *supra* note 300.

305. *Id.*

306. *Id.*

307. *Id.*; *see also* BBC News, *Protest in Angola Against Abortion Criminalisation Law*, BBC NEWS (Mar. 19, 2017), https://www.bbc.com/news/av/world-africa-39319953.

308. Penal Code of Angola (Preliminary Draft), Article 142, June 2020, https://www.warnathgroup.com/wp-content/uploads/2020/06/Penal-Code-.pdf.

309. *Id.*

exceptions when there is serious risk of death or irreversible damage to the physical or mental health of the pregnant woman, there is strong reason to believe that the fetus is not viable, there would be lasting physical or mental damage to the pregnant woman if the pregnancy continued, the pregnancy resulted from rape or incest, or there is strong reason to expect that the fetus will suffer incurable malformation or serious illness.[310] All of the exceptions require that the abortion be performed by a doctor in an official health clinic.[311]

There is almost no data available on abortion in Angola because of the country's long-standing illegalization of abortion.[312] Accordingly, it is difficult to discern the ways in which Angolan abortion law affects women on the ground, or the extent to which the country's historically harsh approach to abortion impacted reproductive health care access and outcomes. The little information available comes from individualized studies and surveys. One such survey of 1,545 reproductive-aged women from Luanda, Angola, found that only 42 percent of respondents would "do anything to help a friend or family member who needed to have a pregnancy terminated."[313] Sixty-three percent of respondents stated that they would avoid telling other people if they, a friend, or a family member terminated a pregnancy.[314] This data, though limited, may indicate either pervasive stigma, religious or social disapproval of abortion, fear of criminalization, or some combination of these factors. Medication abortion is not registered in Angola.[315]

K. Northern Africa

1. Egypt

Human rights organizations consider Egypt's abortion laws "the most restrictive worldwide."[316] Except when the life of the pregnant person is at

---

310. *Id.* at art. 144.

311. *Id.*

312. Natalie Morris & Ndola Prata, *Abortion History and Its Association with Current Use of Modern Contraceptive Methods in Luanda, Angola,* 9 J. CONTRACEPTION 45 (2018); Madeline Blodgett et al., *Do Perceived Contraception Attitudes Influence Abortion Stigma? Evidence from Luanda, Angola,* 5 POPULATION HEALTH 38 (2018).

313. Blodgett et al., *supra* note 312.

314. *Id.*

315. *Angola: Abortion Law,* WOMEN ON WAVES, https://www.womenonwaves.org/en /page/4978/angola–abortion-law.

316. Press Release, *On the Global Day of Action for Access to Safe Abortion: The Egyptian Government Should Sign the Maputo Protocol and Take Action to Protect the Life and Health of Women,* EGYPTIAN INITIATIVE FOR PERSONAL RIGHTS (Sept. 28, 2017), https://eipr.org/en/press/2017/09 /global-day-action-access-safe-abortion-egyptian-government-should-sign-maputo-protocol.

risk, the Penal Code prohibits abortion.[317] The Physician's Code of Ethics issued by the Ministry of Health contradicts the Penal Code by including an exception for the health of the pregnant person.[318] Even this health exception requires the corroboration of two specialist physicians before an abortion can be performed.[319] The Physician's Code is included in the Ministry of Health's 2003 decree. The decree and the code within it are not enforced by the criminal law, but violating the code can result in professional consequences, such as losing one's medical license, facing clinic closures, or malpractice suits.[320] Under the code, medical providers are allowed to provide an abortion without other doctors' approval in an emergency.[321] Still, a patient may die eventually in a nonemergency circumstance that threatens their health because the provider must not only get the two other doctors' consent but also write a detailed report for the record.[322] The strong prohibition in the Penal Code on abortions also causes health care providers to be even more cautious and deny treatment to those in clear need of abortions.[323]

The Penal Code penalizes any woman found guilty of inducing an abortion with up to three years' imprisonment unless her life was at risk.[324] The courts have found a woman guilty even when she was already dead due to

---

317. Law No. 58 of 1937 (Penal Code of 1937), Aug. 1937, arts. 61, 260-64 (Egypt), https://www.refworld.org/docid/3f827fc44.html.

318. Physicians' Code of Ethics, Resolution of the Minister of Health & Population No. 238/2003, at art. 29 (Egypt), http://webcache.googleusercontent.com/search?q=cache:aZK 7J-_O_d0J:www.ems.org.eg/userfiles/file/kanon/ (English translation); *see also* Press Release, *supra* note 316.

319. Physicians' Code of Ethics, *supra* note 318.

320. Letter from Center for Reproductive Rights to the Committee on the Elimination of Discrimination against Women (CEDAW Committee) (Dec. 18, 2009), at 7, 9, https://www2.ohchr.org/english/bodies/cedaw/docs/ngos/EIPR_CRR_Egypt45.pdf (recommends that "[t]he state . . . incorporate article 29 of the physicians' Code of Ethics—which permits a physician to carry out an abortion to protect the pregnant woman's health and life—into the law, and eliminate the need for approval by two other specialists to protect the woman's health.") [hereinafter CRR Letter on Egypt].

321. Physicians' Code of Ethics, at art. 29.

322. *Id.*

323. Law No. 58 of 1937 (Penal Code of 1937), Aug. 1937, art. 260, 261, 263 (Egypt), https://www.refworld.org/docid/3f827fc44.html ("If the person causing the abortion is a physician, surgeon, pharmacist, or midwife, he or she shall be punished with a harsh prison sentence."); Aswat Masriya, *The Reality of Getting an Abortion in Egypt*, EGYPTIAN STREETS (June 1, 2014), https://egyptianstreets.com/2014/06/01/the-reality-of-getting-an-abortion-in-egypt/.

324. *See* Law No. 58 of 1937 (Penal Code of 1937), Aug. 1937, art. 262 (Egypt), https://www.refworld.org/docid/3f827fc44.html.

an unsafe abortion.[325] When women have died from unsafe abortions, some of their families have brought suit in courts against the person(s) who provided the abortion.[326]

A bill was proposed in 2008 that would have created an exception from criminalization for instances of rape or incest.[327] However, it failed to pass because the Parliament's Constitutional and Legislative Affairs Committee never debated it; also, the bill lacked support from the Ministry of Justice.[328] The lack of an incest or rape exception in current law is compounded by the prohibition of the Ministry of Health against providing the option of emergency contraception to sexual violence victims.[329] Emergency contraception is only provided at private pharmacies with narrow standards of practice for distribution.[330]

The criminalization of abortion in Egypt causes disproportionate harm to low-income and younger women.[331] Wealthier women can go to private clinics or hospitals, whereas low-income women or minors usually must go to unofficial clinics that "do not meet minimal medical standards, are unsanitary and lack blood and oxygen supplies."[332] Women in extreme poverty also must resort to traditional methods that can be ineffective and unsafe, like inserting sharp objects into their vaginas.[333] Additionally, misoprostol is available at local pharmacies, but mifepristone is not. Instructions on usage of misoprostol for abortion care are not publicized.[334] These restrictions lessen the efficacy of medication abortion even in the narrow legal abortion category.

Although there is a lack of national data on abortions, one study of 1,025 women from rural Upper Egypt found an abortion rate of 40.6 percent,

---

325. Court of Cassation, case no. 167/66, session of 4 Nov. 1998 (Egypt).

326. *See* Court of Cassation, case no. 302/40, session of 27 Dec. 1970 (Egypt); *see also* Court of Cassation, case no. 195/29, session of 23 Nov. 1959 (Egypt); *see* Court of Cassation, case no. 118/57, session of 12 May 1987 (Egypt).

327. *See* CRR Letter on Egypt, *supra* note 320, at 8–9.

328. *Id.*

329. *Id.* at 9.

330. *Id.*

331. *See id.* at 7.

332. *See id.; see also* Egyptian Initiative for Personal Rights (EIPR) & Center for Reproductive Rights (CRR), CEDAW Shadow Report, p. 7 (2009), http://www2.ohchr.org/english/bodies/cedaw/docs/ngos/EIPR_CRR_Egypt45.pdf [hereinafter CEDAW Shadow Report].

333. *See* CRR Letter on Egypt, *supra* note 320, at 8; *see also* S.D. Lane et al., Buying Safety, the Economics of Reproductive Risk and Abortion in Egypt (1998).

334. *See* CEDAW Shadow Report, *supra* note 332, at 8.

with 24.6 percent getting more than one abortion.[335] Almost 20 percent
of Egypt's obstetrical and gynecological hospital admissions were for post-
abortion care.[336] Although the available studies are older, they emphasize
the dissonance between the legality of the procedure and its commonality.

Civil society organizations and feminist movements declared September 28 the International Day of Movement for Decriminalization of Abortion, and they participated in varied activism toward decriminalization. One
example is renewing the call for the legislature to decriminalize or at least
include an exception for rape or incest.[337] Thus, there is some movement
toward widening the legal abortion options, but they face large barriers.

2. Tunisia

Abortion was legalized in Tunisia more than 40 years ago in 1973.[338] The
law permits registered physicians in medical institutions to provide abortion
care through the first trimester. After the first 12 weeks, abortion can still
be acquired if there are physical or mental health risks to the woman or a
fetal anomaly. Tunisia also was the first country in Africa to legalize mifepristone for medication abortion.[339] Minors in Tunisia are required by law
to get consent from their parents or a legal tutor. In 2013, a deputy of the
Islamist party Ennahdha in Tunisia tried to re-criminalize abortion, but she
failed.[340] Abortion has remained available in the country.

The original legalization of abortion emerged from the political elite in
the newly independent Tunisia.[341] They were concerned about the high fertility rate.[342] The law was used as an instrument of population control. Additionally, religious leaders legitimized abortion with statements that abortion

---

335. K.M. Yassin, *Incidence and Socioeconomic Determinants of Abortion in Rural Upper Egypt*,
114 Pub. Health 269 (July 2000).

336. Dale Huntington et al., *The Postabortion Caseload in Egyptian Hospitals: A Descriptive
Study*, 24 Int. Fam. Planning Persp. 25 (1998).

337. Press Release, *Egyptian Initiative for Personal Rights* (Sept. 28, 2016), https://eipr.org
/en/press/2016/09/feminist-bodies-demand-action-make-abortion-safe-women.

338. Code Penal, art. 214 (Tunis.)

339. J. Blum et al., *The Medical Abortion Experiences of Married and Unmarried Women in
Tunis*, 69 Contraception 63 (2004).

340. Irene Maffi & Malika Affes, *The Right to Abortion in Tunisia after the Revolution of 2011:
Legal, Medical, and Social Arrangements as Seen through Seven Abortion Stories*, Health & Human
Rights J. (Dec. 2019).

341. F. Sandron & B. Gastineau, *La transition de la fécondité en Tunisie* (2000).

342. *Id.*

is religiously permitted until 120 days after conception,[343] thereby avoiding in Tunisia much of the religious conflict around abortion that has occurred in some other places.

The population control reason for legalizing abortion led to the use of forced contraception and sterilization as well as other coercive practices.[344] These harms were inflicted primarily against uneducated, rural, and poor women.[345]

Abortion and contraception are provided for free in public facilities. However, in action, issues arise. In private facilities, the rules around minors are not complied with as readily. The public facilities enforce the extra obligations of parental consent for youth more rigidly. In 2010, Tunisia lowered the majority age for women from 20 to 18, but many providers still treat 18- to 20-year-olds as minors who need parents' permission for an abortion.[346] Additionally, many health care providers refuse to provide abortion care.[347] These providers often cite the International Federation of Gynecology and Obstetrics' 2006 Resolution on Conscientious Objection as their justification. The free aspect of the procedure has little tangible effect because of both the refusals of care as well as the narrow legal exceptions. Also,

> a lack of coordination between the police, the legal system, and the medical sector makes the abortion experiences of some groups of women—especially prisoners, minors, and the unmarried—very difficult. These women are subject to structural and institutional forms of violence that increases their social suffering.[348]

In general, women express that they are treated poorly by medical staff, denied services, and referred unnecessarily.[349] Tunisia is an example of wide availability in the letter of the law, but a lack of actual access.

---

343. G.K. Shapiro, *Abortion Law in Muslim-Majority Countries: An Overview of the Islamic Discourse with Policy Implications*, 29 HEALTH POL'Y & PLANNING 483 (2014).

344. *See* Maffi & Affes, *supra* note 340.

345. *Id.*

346. *Id.*

347. *Id.*

348. *Id.*

349. S. Hajri et al., *"This Is Real Misery": Experiences of Women Denied Legal Abortion in Tunisia*, 10 PLoS ONE (2015).

L. Oceania

1. Australia

Despite significant advocacy and scholarship pushing for a national standard on abortion,[350] Australia's abortion laws remain inconsistent, decided on a state-by-state basis. There is much travel between states but also a resulting lack of access for low-income women. The inconsistency of Australia's laws can cause confusion and a chilling effect. Given this extensive patchwork, Australia is analyzed by state.

a. Australia Capital Territory (ACT)

In 2018, ACT amended its abortion laws through the Health (Improving Abortion Access) Amendment Act 2018.[351] Abortions are available up to 16 gestational weeks with some distinctions on this time limit based on provider type.[352] Abortion can only be provided by registered practitioners, and if a nonregistered practitioner provides an abortion, they may face five years of imprisonment.[353] A medication abortion is not required to be performed at an approved medical facility; instead, general practitioners, telehealth providers, and a Marie Stopes provider can perform medical abortions.[354] A surgical abortion must be performed in an approved facility and is subject to higher regulation.[355] Providers have a right to refuse to provide an abortion, and no qualification exists in the statute to ensure a referral.[356]

ACT also has enacted positive laws to protect abortion patients from the actions of other individuals who attempt to harm, threaten, or scare them. It is an offense to commit "[h]arassment, hindering, intimidation, interference with, threatening or obstruction of a person, including by the capturing of visual data of the person, in the protected period that is intended to stop the person from . . . having or providing an abortion in the approved medical facility."[357] ACT's abortion regulations criminalize publishing visual

350. *See, e.g.*, Lachlan J. de Crespigny & Julian Savulescu, *Abortion: Time to Clarify Australia's Confusing Laws*, 181 MED. J. AUSTL. 201 (Aug. 2004), https://www.mja.com.au/system/files/issues/181_04_160804/dec10242_fm.pdf.

351. A2018-37 (2018) (Austl.).

352. *Frequently Asked Questions, Abortion in the ACT*, ACT GOV. HEALTH, https://www.health.act.gov.au/services-and-programs/sexual-health/abortion-access.

353. Medical Practitioners (Maternal Health) Amendment Bill 2002, sec. 55B.

354. *Frequently Asked Questions, supra* note 352.

355. Health (Improving Abortion Access) Amendment Act 2018, A2018-37, at § 82 (2018).

356. Medical Practitioners (Maternal Health) Amendment Bill 2002, sec. 55E.

357. Health (Patient Privacy) Amendment Bill 2015, sec. 85(1)(a)(ii).

data of a person entering/exiting an abortion facility with the intent of stopping the person from getting an abortion.[358] There is also a protected area around an approved medical facility that provides abortions.[359] These protections add to the newer abortion regulations, creating stronger protections for patients.

b. New South Wales (NSW)

In 2019, NSW enacted the Abortion Law Reform Act 2019 into law.[360] The act makes abortion legal up to 22 weeks into pregnancy. The legislation also allows abortions after 22 weeks if two doctors agree that the procedure is needed.[361] The two-doctor approval requirement does not apply in emergency cases.[362] The act also does not require that a patient attend counseling before receiving an abortion; however, the provider must consider whether counseling would be beneficial for the person.[363]

The act allows a right to conscientious objection, but the patient must be referred to a provider who can provide the service, and conscientious objection is not a basis for refusing to perform an abortion in an emergency.[364] The previous legislation, the Crimes Act 1900 sections 82-84 made providing an abortion "unlawfully" to oneself or another a crime with punishment of up to ten years imprisonment. The Abortion Law Reform Act 2019 also supersedes the Levine doctrine from *R v. Wald*.[365] That case interpreted the Crimes Act 1900 such that a doctor provides a "lawful" abortion when they express an honest belief that it is required for "any economic, social or medical ground or reason" to avoid danger to the life or physical or mental health of the pregnant person.[366] After the 2019 act, that doctrine is no longer needed.

---

358. *Id.* at 87(2).

359. *Id.* at (c).

360. Abortion Law Reform Act 2019 (Oct. 3, 2019), https://www.legislation.nsw.gov.au/view/whole/html/inforce/current/act-2019-011#statusinformation (hereafter, ALRA 2019).

361. *Id.* sec. 6(1); *see also Australia Abortion Laws: Terminations Now Legal in New South Wales,* BBC News (Sept. 26, 2019), https://www.bbc.com/news/world-australia-49834734.

362. ALRA 2019, sec. 6(5).

363. *Id.* at sec. 7(1).

364. *Id.* at sec. 9(3)–(4).

365. R v. Wald, [1971] 3 DCR (NSW) 25 (Aus.).

366. *Id.*

c. Northern Territory

The Termination of Pregnancy Law Reform Act 2017 makes abortion legal until 14 weeks if a medical provider agrees.[367] Abortion is legal up to 23 weeks after conception if two doctors agree the abortion is reasonable.[368] Medication abortion is also legal under the Termination of Pregnancy Law Reform Act 2017 until nine weeks' gestation. Medical providers have a right to conscientious objection but also have a duty to refer the patient to an alternate provider.[369] Prohibited behavior, like harassment or recording patients, in safe access zones is criminalized and punishable with up to 12 months' imprisonment.[370]

d. Queensland

Queensland has decriminalized abortion, allowing abortion until 22 weeks after gestation.[371] Under the Termination of Pregnancy Bill 2018, two medical practitioners in agreement can also authorize abortions after 22 weeks based on the circumstances.[372] In an emergency, a practitioner can perform the abortion without the concurrence of another provider.[373] The Termination of Pregnancy Bill 2018 also creates 150-meter safe access zones around the clinic.[374] Medication abortion is included within the Pharmaceutical Benefits Scheme, which is a nationwide program where the government subsidizes the price of medications,[375] and general practitioners can provide medication abortion as long as they are certified.[376] The certification

---

367. Termination of Pregnancy Law Reform Act 2017, sec. 7 (hereafter, "TPLA 2017") https://legislation.nt.gov.au/en/LegislationPortal/Acts/~/link.aspx?_id=4617397A1A4F42 678E8BD9A552930AE7&_z=z&format=assented *See also Termination of Pregnancy Law Reform Act of 2017 (Northern Territory)*, LEGAL INFO. INST., https://www.law.cornell.edu/women -and-justice/resource/termination_of_pregnancy_law_reform_act_of_2017_%28northern _territory%29 (last accessed Oct. 16, 2020).

368. TPLA 2017, sec. 8.

369. *Id.* at secs. 11, 12.

370. *Id.* at sec. 14.

371. Termination of Pregnancy Bill 2018, sec. 5, https://www.legislation.qld.gov.au/view /pdf/bill.first/bill-2018-089.

372. *Id.* at sec. 6.

373. *Id.* at sec. 6(3).

374. *Id.* at sec. 14.

375. *About the PBS*, THE PHARMACEUTICAL BENEFITS SCHEME, AUS. GOV. DEP'T OF HEALTH (last visited Nov. 25, 2020); *see also* Danielle Mazza et al., *Medical Abortion*, 49 AUS. J. GEN. PRACTICE 324, https://www1.racgp.org.au/ajgp/2020/june/medical-abortion.

376. *Queensland Clinical Guidelines: Termination of Pregnancy*, sec. 6(1), p. 24, https://www. health.qld.gov.au/__data/assets/pdf_file/0029/735293/g-top.pdf. *See also* Seema Deb et al., *Providing Medical Abortion in General Practice: General Practitioner Insights and Tips for Future Providers*, 49 AUS. J. GEN. PRACTICE 331, https://www1.racgp.org.au/ajgp/2020/june/medical

is required by regulations from the Pharmaceutical Benefits Advisory Committee within the Australian Government Department of Health.[377]

e. South Australia

South Australia is the only state that still has abortion offenses in their criminal statutes. The Criminal Law Consolidation Act criminalizes the attempt to procure an unlawful abortion with a possible penalty of life imprisonment with exceptions only for life and health of the pregnant person.[378] Anyone who provides a person an abortion, including the pregnant person themselves, can be liable for life imprisonment.[379] Possession of medication abortion materials, whether or not the person is pregnant, is an offense with a three-year imprisonment charge.[380] However, the act exempts any woman who "has not resided in South Australia for a period of at least two months before the termination of her pregnancy."[381]

The University of Adelaide Law School's South Australian Law Reform Institute released a report, developed independently, examining South Australia's abortion laws.[382] The Department for Health and Wellbeing issued a response, accepting 51 of the 66 recommendations and deferring the other 15 to the Crown for legal advice.[383] Specifically, in response to the recommendation to decriminalize abortion, the Department agreed in theory to repeal "sections 81, 82 and 82A of the Criminal Law Consolidation Act 1936 (SA)"—which establish the criminal sanctions just noted—but deferred "to the Crown Solicitor's Office for specific legal advice regarding

---

-abortion-in-general-practice; *Queensland Abortion Providers*, CHILDREN BY CHOICE, https://www.childrenbychoice.org.au/foryou/abortion/clinicsqld (last visited Nov. 20, 2020) (lists abortion providers with medication abortion access, including general practitioners).

377. *See Mifepristone and Misoprostol (MS-2 Step) Composite Pack: Use Extended to 63 Days' Gestation*, NPS MEDICINEWISE (Feb. 1, 2015), https://www.nps.org.au/radar/articles/mifepristone-and-misoprostol-ms-2-step-composite-pack-use-extended-to-63-days-gestation; *Mifepristone (&) Misoprostol*, THE PHARMACEUTICAL BENEFITS SCHEME, AUS. GOV. DEP'T OF HEALTH (last visited Nov. 25, 2020), https://www.pbs.gov.au/medicine/item/10211K.

378. Criminal Law Consolidation Act, secs. 81–82(A)(1). https://www.legislation.sa.gov.au/LZ/C/A/CRIMINAL%20LAW%20CONSOLIDATION%20ACT%201935/CURRENT/1935.2252.AUTH.PDF

379. *Id.* at sec. 82.

380. *Id.* at sec. 82(A).

381. *Id.* at sec. 82(A)(2).

382. John Williams et al., *Abortion: A Review of South Australian Law and Practice*, S. AUS. L. REFORM INST., Rep. 13 (Oct. 2019), https://law.adelaide.edu.au/system/files/media/documents/2019-12/Abortion%20Report%20281119.pdf.

383. *Response to SALRI Report*, DEP'T FOR HEALTH & WELLBEING (Nov. 2019), https://www.sahealth.sa.gov.au/wps/wcm/connect/edeb1d5d-a8c9-4975-94b8-e06aa4c04b69/DHW+reponse+to+SALRI+report+-+final.pdf.

the most suitable Act."[384] The Department accepted other positive recommendations, but again deferred to the Solicitor for specific implementation
steps.[385] They did clarify that prosecution could not be done against the
pregnant person or qualified provider.[386] Otherwise, the changes are still
in flux.

f. Tasmania

Abortion is lawful up to 16 weeks after conception, and it can be provided
after 16 weeks if two practitioners agree.[387] The Reproductive Health
(Access to Terminations) Act 2013 deemed that no woman who "consents
to, assists in or performs a termination on herself" is guilty of a crime.[388]
The providers have a right to conscientious objection but have a duty to
refer the patient.[389] The Reproductive Health (Access to Terminations) Act
2013, section 9 prohibits harassment and other similar behaviors within 150
meters of an abortion provider. Medication abortion is allowed until nine
weeks after conception. These provisions combine into a web of protections
in the text of the law.

Despite these written laws and promises from the government, all surgical abortion clinics have shut down.[390] The only surgical abortion clinic in
Tasmania closed in 2018, and the government only offered patient travel
assistance to the mainland.[391] Despite ongoing promises from the government that Hampton Park Women's Health Centre will open in Tasmania for
low-cost surgical abortions, the clinic has not yet opened.[392] The state also
claims that low-cost surgical abortions are temporarily available at a private
abortion provider, but Women's Health Tasmania, although acknowledging
that some women were getting access to low-cost abortions, reported that

---

384. *Id.* at Table 1.

385. *Id.* at Recommendation Nos. 4, 6, 7, 8, 10, 12, 14, 64, 65, and 66.

386. *Id.* at Recommendation Nos. 6–8.

387. Reproductive Health (Access to Terminations) Bill 2013, § 4-5.

388. *Id.* § 8.

389. *Id.* § 6; *see also* Dep't of Health & Human Services, *Pregnancy Terminations: Summary of the New Law*, POPULATION HEALTH SERVICES, https://www.dhhs.tas.gov.au/__data/assets /pdf_file/0005/151727/Summary_of_the_New_Law_Fact_Sheets.pdf.

390. Ellen Coulter, *No Timeframe for Abortion Provider to Do Terminations in Tasmania, as Women Face "Hodge-Podge" of a System*, ABC NEWS (Mar. 6, 2019, 1:10 AM), https://www.abc .net.au/news/2019-03-06/abortion-provider-still-not-operating-in-tasmania/10875438.

391. Georgie Burgess & Tamara Glumac, *Tasmania's Only Abortion Clinic Closes, Putting Pressure on Government to Find Alternative*, ABC NEWS (Jan. 12, 2018, 4:34 PM), https://www .abc.net.au/news/2018-01-13/tasmanias-only-abortion-clinic-closes/9325194.

392. *Id.*

some were still paying substantial private costs and some were flying to Melbourne for access.[393]

g. Victoria
Abortion is permitted if gestation is 24 weeks or less and a qualified medical practitioner makes the request, whereas after 24 weeks another practitioner must agree that the abortion is in the patient's best interest.[394] Registered pharmacists or registered nurses can provide medication abortion drugs to a person less than 24 weeks pregnant.[395] After 24 weeks, a registered pharmacist or registered nurse can only provide the drugs after a medical practitioner issues a recommendation.[396] A practitioner has a right to conscientious objection but must refer the patient to a provider without objection and must provide aid during an emergency.[397] Under the Public Health and Wellbeing Amendment (Safe Access Zones) Bill 2015, threatening, intimidating, or harassing behavior within 150 meters of an abortion provider is prohibited.[398]

h. Western Australia
Western Australia decriminalized abortion in Acts Amendment (Abortion) Act 1998, section 4-5. Abortion is available up to 20 gestational weeks on the condition of a referral to counseling services.[399] After 20 weeks, a panel of six doctors must convene, and two out of the six must approve the abortion under the standard that the mother or unborn child "has a severe medical condition."[400] Those under 16 years of age must notify their parents, and the parents must be offered a chance to be involved in the counseling process.[401] Medical providers have a right to conscientious objection but not a duty to refer.[402]

393. Coulter, *supra* note 390.
394. Abortion Law Reform Act 2008, sec. 4-5.
395. *Id.* at sec. 6.
396. *Id.* at sec. 7.
397. *Id.* at sec. 8.
398. Public Health and Wellbeing Amendment (Safe Access Zones) Act 2015 (No. 66 OF 2015), sec. 5, Part 9A (2015).
399. Acts Amendment (Abortion) Act 1998, sec. 7 (adding Sec. 334 to the Health Act 1911). https://www.parliament.wa.gov.au/parliament/bills.nsf/43EBDD658FC50BA148256 63400102F5D/$File/Act15.pdf.
400. *Id.*
401. *Id.*
402. *Id.* (adding sec. 334(2) to the Health Act 1911).

2. New Zealand

On March 18, 2020, New Zealand passed the Abortion Legislation Act 2020, decriminalizing abortion and allowing abortion on demand up to 20 weeks since conception.[403] After 20 weeks, abortion can be provided if a health provider deems it "appropriate."[404] The provider must consult another provider and assess "'all relevant legal, professional and ethical standards,' the woman's physical and mental health and 'overall well-being,' and the age of the fetus."[405] The bill was an omnibus bill, and in addition to decriminalizing abortion, it initiated regulating abortion like other health services.[406] The bill extensively amended the Contraception, Sterilisation, and Abortion Act 1977, which had allowed abortions prior to 12 gestational weeks since 2013, and the Crimes Act 1961.[407] Despite the Contraception, Sterilisation, and Abortion Act 1977's allowance of abortion until 12 weeks in the 2013 version, the Crimes Act criminalized anyone "who causes the death of any child that has not become a human being in such a manner that he or she would have been guilty of murder if the child had become a human being" until the Abortion Legislation Act 2020 passed.[408] The possible punishment was up to 14 years imprisonment, and the only exception was life of the mother.[409] Thus, the new legislation is a drastic positive change for abortion rights. Furthermore, a minor of any age now has full authority to consent to an abortion or to refuse an abortion.[410]

After 20 weeks, abortion access depends on a health practitioner's reasonable belief "that the abortion is clinically appropriate in the cir-

---

403. Abortion Legislation Act 2020, pt. 1, sec. 10. http://www.legislation.govt.nz/act/public/2020/0006/latest/whole.html.

404. *Id.* at sec. 11; *see also* Richard Pérez-Peña, *New Zealand Eases Abortion Restrictions*, N.Y. TIMES (Mar. 18, 2020), https://www.nytimes.com/2020/03/18/world/australia/new-zealand-abortion.html.

405. Abortion Legislation Act 2020, *supra* note 403, pt. 1, sec. 11.

406. *See id.* at pt. 2, subpt. 3, sec. 17, amending sec. 2 of Health and Disability Commissioner Act 1994.

407. *See* Contraception, Sterilisation, and Abortion Act 1977 (2013 amended version) ("Subject to the provisions of this Act, no abortion shall be performed elsewhere than in an institution licensed for the purpose in accordance with this Act. . . . Subject to the provisions of this Act, no abortion shall be performed, after the pregnancy has subsisted for at least 12 weeks, elsewhere than in an institution in respect of which a full licence is for the time being in force under this Act.").

408. Crimes Act 1961, § 182(1) (2019 version).

409. *Id.* at (1)–(2).

410. *Care of the Children Act 2004*, sec. 38, http://www.legislation.govt.nz/act/public/2004/0090/latest/DLM317472.html.

cumstances."[411] The definition of "appropriate" is not included in the statute.[412] The provider must consult another practitioner and consider other factors, like the women's health and the age of the fetus.[413] The Abortion Legislation Act 2020 also provides a right to conscientious objection for medical providers, but they also have a duty to refer and a duty to assist in an emergency.[414]

The New Zealand Ministry of Health issued the Interim Standards for Abortion Services in New Zealand to reflect the new abortion law.[415] These guidelines instruct that medication abortion should be used during the first trimester of a pregnancy.[416] However, a person still must go to a medical provider to get a prescription for the medication abortion pills.[417] Abortion providers must notify the Ministry of Health about the abortion, including details about the type of the procedure but excluding the patient's name and identifying information. The notification must be issued within a month of the abortion.[418] Despite these regulations, the change in New Zealand's law is promising.

Given that the change in the law is so recent, it is unclear at this point how it will apply in practice. New Zealand officials claim that under the prior law, despite criminalizing most abortion on paper, it was never used to prosecute anyone.[419] Pregnant persons under the previous law would either legitimately use the mental and physical health exception or feign the symptoms in order to access care.[420] Ideally, with this significant change in the law, this requirement of pregnant persons to struggle and lie for care will lessen.

---

411. Abortion Legislation Act 2020, *supra* note 403, pt. 1, sec. 11.

412. *Id.*

413. *Id.*; *see also* Pérez-Peña, *supra* note 404.

414. Abortion Legislation Act 2020, *supra* note 403, at pt. 1, sec. 14.

415. *Interim Standards for Abortion Services in New Zealand*, MINISTRY OF HEALTH (Apr. 15, 2020), https://www.health.govt.nz/publication/interim-standards-abortion-services-new -zealand; *see also* Pérez-Peña, *supra* note 404.

416. *Id.* at 17.

417. *The Law Around Abortion*, NZ FAM. PLANNING, https://www.familyplanning.org.nz /advice/abortion/the-law-around-abortion.

418. *Abortion Legislation: Information for Health Practitioners*, MINISTRY OF HEALTH, https://www.health.govt.nz/our-work/regulation-health-and-disability-system/abortion -legislation-information-health-practitioners.

419. Pérez-Peña, *supra* note 404.

420. *Id.*

M. Central America

1. Costa Rica

Costa Rica criminalizes abortion in all circumstances except a threat to the health or life of the mother when no alternative path exists to prevent the harm.[421] A person who performs an abortion can face up to ten years in prison if it is determined that they acted without consent or performed the procedure on a minor under 15 years of age.[422] With the consent of the pregnant person, the provider faces up to three years of imprisonment for performing an abortion outside what is permitted by the law.[423]

Even the health exception, which is included in the Penal Code, was not accessible in practice until 2019.[424] No regulations clarified the limitations of the health exception, so many health care providers and institutions refused to provide them even when a health risk was present.[425] A new technical norm permits abortions for the health of the mother when "there is no other medical alternative, . . . the woman gives consent, and after mandatory evaluation by three medical professionals."[426] The norm does not change the law but offers guidance for medical providers to implement the law—ideally, the providers will be more willing to provide the care with knowledge of what is classified as a legal or illegal abortion.[427] Prior to this new technical norm, fewer than 80 abortions were registered with the Social Security System over 20 years, from 1998 to 2018.[428] It is likely that many self-managed or clandestine abortions occurred during this time.

Religion has an immense influence in Costa Rica. The country's Constitution expresses that "Roman, Catholic, Apostolic Religion is that of the

---

421. Código Penal, art. 121 (Costa Rica).

422. *Id.* at art. 118(1).

423. *Id.* at art. 118(2).

424. Reuters Staff, *Costa Rica's President Says Therapeutic Abortions Will Be Allowed*, REUTERS (Dec. 12, 2019, 11:57 PM), https://www.reuters.com/article/us-costa-rica-abortion/costa -ricas-president-says-therapeutic-abortions-will-be-allowed-idUSKBN1YH0EK [hereinafter *Costa Rica's President Allows Therapeutic Abortions*].

425. *Id.*; Alejandro Zúñiga, *President Alvarado Signs Technical Norm, Essentially Legalizing Therapeutic Abortion In Costa Rica*, THE TICO TIMES (Dec. 12, 2019), https://ticotimes .net/2019/12/12/president-alvarado-signs-technical-norm-essentially-legalizing-abortion-in -costa-rica; *see also* Press Release, *Despite Country's Own Laws, Costa Rica Continues to Deny Women Legal Abortion*, CTR. FOR REPROD. RIGHTS (Aug. 23, 2013), https://reproductive rights.org/press-room/despite-countrys-own-laws-costa-rica-continues-to-deny-women-legal -abortion [hereinafter *Costa Rica Violates Its Own Law*].

426. *Costa Rica's President Allows Therapeutic Abortions*, *supra* note 424.

427. Zúñiga, *supra* note 425.

428. *Id.*

State."[429] The religious focus recently arose to counter the technical norm law. The Archbishop of San José, José Rafael Quirós, and evangelical lawmakers specifically spoke out in opposition of the 2018 technical norm.[430] Despite Costa Rica still remaining one of the most restrictive countries on abortion, even after the technical norm was implemented, these religious figures asserted that the norm permits "free abortion."[431] In opposition to the technical norm, legislators that followed the religious figures proposed an opposing norm that would limit abortion only to instances of death, not health.[432] Religious motivation also caused people to "say Yes to life" in the National Front for Life's march at the end of 2019.[433] These individuals spoke against the technical norm, but ultimately the president still signed the law.

Before the technical norm was proposed, Costa Rica faced multiple legal claims due to the repeated denials of abortion to individuals with health risks. For instance, Aurora brought an action in the Supreme Court of Costa Rica, requesting an "amparo," which would grant her an abortion. Aurora was suffering mental and physical health concerns after her fetus was diagnosed with a severe impairment that made it inviable and harmed her health.[434] Aurora endured an emergency C-section, giving birth to a stillborn as the case progressed, and the Supreme Court determined that there was no threat to Aurora's health, agreeing with the hospital.[435] Thus, the court reinforced the hospital's narrow, if not nonexistent, perception of a health threat. Aurora's case was submitted to the Inter-American Commission on Human Rights (IACHR).

Another case from Costa Rica was brought to the IACHR in 2008.[436] Two nongovernmental organizations brought the claim on behalf of "A.N.," who

---

429. COSTA RICA CONST. art. 75, https://www.constituteproject.org/constitution/Costa_Rica_2011.pdf.

430. *See* Marco Sibaja, *Therapeutic Abortion Regulation Unleashes Political Storm in Costa Rica*, THE TICO TIMES (Oct. 24, 2019), https://ticotimes.net/2019/10/24/therapeutic-abortion-regulation-unleashes-political-storm-in-costa-rica (The Archbishop asserted, "We express our rejection of the claim to promulgate that decree . . . which, far from making our country progress in true respect for human rights, would make it disrespect the most absolute of those rights in the unborn person.").

431. *Id.*

432. *Id.*

433. Javier Bolaños, *Tens of Thousands of Costa Ricans Took the Streets to Defend Life*, EVANGELICAL FOCUS (Dec. 11, 2019, 18:10 CET), https://evangelicalfocus.com/world/4959/Thousands-of-Costa-Ricans-took-the-streets-to-defend-life.

434. *Costa Rica Violates Its Own Law, supra* note 425.

435. *Id.*

436. *Id.*

was denied an abortion even though her pregnancy was not viable; no brain was developing in the embryo.[437] A.N. faced mental health issues that put her at risk for suicide.[438] Due to the hospitals' refusals to provide her with an abortion, she gave birth vaginally to a stillborn, and she endures ongoing health issues.[439] The two cases jointly were deemed admissible to the IACHR on April 21, 2020, and they are now proceeding on the merits.[440]

These two stories, despite their disturbing facts and publicity, did not motivate legal change; the president did not sign the technical norm until 2018. Despite Costa Rica's innovative social choices, like eliminating their army and redirecting military funds to education and health, the country remains highly restrictive of abortion care.[441]

2. El Salvador

El Salvador passed an abortion law in 1998 that criminalized all abortion, and it still stands.[442] Persons receiving an abortion and lay people that aid them could be imprisoned for eight years.[443] Health professionals are subject to six to 12 years imprisonment for providing an abortion.[444] Article I of the Constitution still recognizes the right to life from the moment of conception, since a 1999 amendment.[445]

In recent legislation, Johnny Wright Sol, an ARENA party member, proposed a bill that legalized abortion for the pregnant person's life or health or the rape of a minor, but the national legislature adjourned without voting on the bill.[446] "[A]n alliance of social conservatives and religious

---

437. *Id.*

438. *Id.*

439. *Id.*

440. A.N. & Aurora v. Costa Rica, Petition 1159-08, Inter-Am. Comm'n H.R., Report No. 122/20, OEA/Ser.L/V/II, VIII(1)–(3) (2020), http://www.oas.org/en/iachr/decisions/2020/crad1159-08en.pdf.

441. Ariana López Peña, *Is Costa Rica the World's Happiest, Greenest Country?*, The Conversation (Feb. 2, 2017, 2:50 AM EST), https://theconversation.com/is-costa-rica-the-worlds-happiest-greenest-country-71457.

442. *See El Salvador's Total Ban on Abortion: the Facts*, Amnesty Int'l (Nov. 5, 2015, 12:20 AM UTC), https://www.amnesty.org/en/latest/campaigns/2015/11/el-salvador-total-abortion-ban/.

443. *Id.*

444. *Id.*

445. Political Constitution of El Salvador, art. 1 (1998), https://constitution.com/constitution-of-the-republic-of-el-salvador/.

446. Elisabeth Malkin, *Supporters of El Salvador's Abortion Ban Foil Efforts to Soften It*, N.Y. Times (Apr. 26, 2018), https://www.nytimes.com/2018/04/26/world/americas/abortion-ban-salvador.html.

organizations" prevented the law's passage.[447] The bill was never even presented for vote. El Salvador's health minister, Dr. Violeta Menjívar, asked legislators "to hold a 'serene, responsible debate, removed from electoral interests'" about abortion.[448] Menjívar encouraged reflection on the damages caused by the absolute prohibition.[449] Zeid Ra'ad Al Hussein, the former UN High Commissioner for Human Rights, requested that El Salvador institute "a moratorium on laws that punish women with harsh jail terms for having an abortion" at least while the government conducts a case review to determine if anyone is wrongly incarcerated.[450] Hussein also recommended overturning the absolute prohibition on abortion all together.[451] However, no changes were made.

El Salvador continues to prosecute women for miscarriage and abortion. Although the Supreme Court overturned Evelyn Beatriz Hernández's conviction for murder, she was tried again. "Evelyn Beatriz Hernández . . . is a rape victim and had no idea she was pregnant, had already served thirty-three months of her thirty-year sentence when the Supreme Court overturned the ruling against her in February and ordered a new trial, with a new judge."[452] There was a severe delay in receiving justice in that case. After her verdict was postponed twice and the prosecution recommended a sentence of 40 years, Hernández was finally acquitted.[453] Unfortunately, Hernández's anguished experience is only one of many such cases.

In March 2019, El Salvador's Supreme Court released three women who had been jailed for 30 years after being accused of having abortions. The women said they suffered miscarriages but were convicted of aggravated homicide. The Supreme Court ordered their release after concluding that they were serving "disproportionate and immoral" sentences.[454]

---

447. *Id.*

448. *Id.*

449. Silvia Quinteros, *MINSAL a favor de la despenalización el aborto en casos de madres en riesgo de vida*, DIARIO CO LATINO (Feb. 22, 2017), http://www.diariocolatino.com /minsal-favor-la-despenalizacion-aborto-casos-madres-riesgo-vida/.

450. *U.N. Calls on El Salvador to Stop Jailing Women for Abortion*, REUTERS (Nov. 17, 2017, 7:06 PM), https://www.ohchr.org/EN/NewsEvents/Pages/DisplayNews.aspx?NewsID=22412 &LangID=E; https://br.reuters.com/article/us-el-salvador-abortion-idUSKBN1DI001.

451. *Id.*

452. Marcos Aleman, *Salvadoran Accused of Abortion Faces Retrial, Hefty Sentence*, AP NEWS (July 15, 2019), https://apnews.com/45d982cfb5814187970b2699da1627d1.

453. Karla Zabludovsky, *The Woman Who Was Tried Twice for Having a Stillbirth Has Been Acquitted*, BUZZFEED NEWS (Aug. 18, 2019, 2:55 PM ET), https://www.buzzfeednews.com /article/karlazabludovsky/evelyn-hernandez-stillbirth-murder-retrial-acquitted.

454. *El Salvador: Three Women Jailed for Abortions Freed*, BBC NEWS (Mar. 7, 2019), https:// www.bbc.com/news/world-latin-america-47487116.

"Alba Rodríguez and María del Tránsito Orellana had both served nine years, while Cinthia Rodríguez had spent more than 11 years in prison."[455] Once again, aside from the impropriety of their convictions at all, justice was gravely delayed in each instance. More than 140 women are known to have been charged criminally under the country's abortion prohibition since 1998.[456]

3. Mexico

The states of Mexico determine most of their own laws under the country's federal system, including laws pertaining to abortion.[457] That autonomy was affirmed when the Mexican Supreme Court ruled in favor of Mexico City decriminalizing abortion in the first 12 weeks after conception.[458] The result of the ruling is both positive and negative for abortion rights because Mexico City's liberal policy was upheld, but many other states' restrictive policies remain in place.

In July 2020, Mexico's Supreme Court overturned an injunction that would have required Veracruz's State Congress to remove articles 149, 150, and 154 (which criminalize abortion) from its penal code.[459] The Supreme Court rejected the opportunity to decriminalize abortion for the first 12 weeks of pregnancy, but it did rule that abortion must be permitted for the patient's health and at any point in cases of rape.[460] The Court rejected the injunction on the ground that it could not overrule Veracruz's constitutional provision, which was controlling under article 40, Mexico's Constitution of 1917.[461] Veracruz criminalized all abortions through a constitutional amendment in 2016, protecting "life from conception." Javier Duarte, the

---

455. *Id.*

456. Kate Smith & Gilad Thaler, *These Women Say They Had Miscarriages. Now They're in Jail for Abortion*, CBS NEWS (May 28, 2020, 7:02 AM), https://www.cbsnews.com/news /miscarriages-abortion-jail-el-salvador/.

457. *See* Art. 40, Mexico's Constitution of 1917, https://www.constituteproject.org/consti tution/Mexico_2015.pdf?lang=en.

458. *Mexico: Supreme Court Upholds Mexico City Abortion Law*, HUMAN RIGHTS WATCH (Aug. 28, 2008, 8:00 PM EDT), https://www.hrw.org/news/2008/08/28/mexico-supreme -court-upholds-mexico-city-abortion-law#:~:text=In%20a%20historic%20decision%20 today,came%20into%20force%20in%202007.

459. *Mexico Supreme Court Rejects State's Bid to Decriminalise Abortion*, BBC NEWS (July 29, 2020), https://www.bbc.com/news/world-latin-america-53584575.

460. *Id.*

461. *Id. See also* Art. 40, Mexico's Constitution of 1917. https://www.constituteproject .org/constitution/Mexico_2015.pdf?lang=en.

governor at the time who was responding to the state's Catholic bishops and evangelical leaders, pushed through the constitutional change.[462]

Abortion is legal in the states of Oaxaca and Mexico City only. Oaxaca decriminalized abortion for the first 12 weeks of gestation in September 2019.[463] Querétaro criminalizes abortion for any reason, even including risk to the pregnant person's life. Baja California allows abortion in three limited cases: health risk to the mother, rape, or if the fetus has serious genetic issues.[464] Many states, including Hidalgo, Durango, Colima, México, Tabasco, Veracruz, and Tamaulipas, considered abortion decriminalization legislation in recent years—all failed. Mexico's president, Andres Manuel Lopez Obrador, despite being a "left-leaning" president, did not mention abortion in his platform.[465] Thus, Mexico remains a predominately restrictive country on abortion.

Mexico City released a study that analyzed data collected from 2007 to 2017. The study assessed statistics about abortion patients from when abortion was legalized for the first 12 weeks in Mexico City.[466] This data indicate the residency of abortion patients as well as their occupations, education levels, relationship status, and so on.[467] Although most of the patients were residents of Mexico City, individuals traveled from other states to receive abortions.[468] Upon legalization, Mexico City's residents sought out the abortion services available, and those in other states would likely do the same if travel distance did not make the trip too costly.

---

462. David Agren, *Abortion Banned by Controversial Mexican State Governor*, THE GUARDIAN (July 28, 2016, 9:30 PM EDT), https://www.theguardian.com/world/2016/jul/29/abortion-banned-controversial-mexican-state-governor-veracruz.

463. David Agren, *'We Have Made History': Mexico's Oaxaca State Decriminalises Abortion*, THE GUARDIAN (Sept. 26, 2019, 4:52 PM EDT), https://www.theguardian.com/world/2019/sep/26/we-have-made-history-mexicos-oaxaca-state-decriminalises-abortion.

464. *Despenalización del aborto, olvidada en 10 estados; en 9 está congelado*, MILENIO (Sept. 26, 2019, 11:57 PM), https://mexiconewsdaily.com/news/decriminalization-of-abortion-not-on-the-agenda/.

465. Isabella Cota, *What's the Future of Abortion Rights in Mexico under AMLO?*, ALJAZEERA (Nov. 30, 2018), https://www.aljazeera.com/news/americas/2018/11/whats-future-abortion-rights-mexico-amlo-181130202340174.html.

466. Secretaría de Las Mujeres, *Interrupción Legal Del Embarazo, Estadísticas Abril 2007–20 de Abril 2017 (ILE)*, Gobierno de la Ciudad de Mexico, http://ile.salud.cdmx.gob.mx/wp-content/uploads/Interrupcion-Legal-del-Embarazo-Estadisticas-2007-2017-20-de-abril-de-2017.pdf.

467. *Id.*

468. *Id.* at 2.

Meanwhile, in the state of Sonora at least 19 people have been sentenced for having or for assisting someone with an abortion procedure, with 75 investigations as of June 2018.[469] A BBC Report from 2016 asserts that more than 600 women were facing legal proceedings for termination of pregnancy, while 700 other women are imprisoned and charged with homicide.[470] Abortions continue occurring, and they are criminalized. These women's abortions, if in the first 12 weeks, would be legal if they had traveled to Mexico City, but traveling this distance is not possible for most women.

Even if women meet the requirements for abortion in their states, many do not seek abortion care "likely due to profound stigma against abortion at the social level."[471] Some states, like Chihuahua, passed a constitutional amendment against abortion but did not change their criminal code, so confusion among residents as well as a chilling effect exists.[472] These factors further inhibit access to abortion in Mexico.

N. South America

1. Uruguay

Uruguay's abortion law, enacted in 2012, permits abortion in the first 12 weeks of gestation in any case.[473] Abortion is also permitted up to 14 weeks in cases of rape, and there are no limitations in cases where there are "fetal malformations incompatible with life" or health risk to the pregnant person.[474] The law requires a five-day reflection period after an ultrasound appointment. [475] The person must also attend a separate counseling session and then attend a third appointment to confirm the decision.[476] The law

---

469. Priscila Cárdenas, *Sentencian a 19 personas por aborto en Sonora; en 10 años se han abierto 75 investigaciones*, PROYECTO PUENTE (Sept. 28, 2018), https://proyectopuente.com.mx/2018/09/28/sentencian-a-19-personas-por-aborto-en-sonora-en-10-anos-se-han-abierto-75-investigaciones/.

470. Alberto Nájar, *"¡Bésalo, pídele perdón! ¡Tú lo mataste!": el drama de las 700 mujeres presas por aborto en México, muchas veces espontáneo*, BBC NEWS (July 25, 2016), https://www.bbc.com/mundo/noticias-america-latina-36863185.

471. Fatima Juarez et al., *Women's Abortion Seeking Behavior under Restrictive Abortion Laws in Mexico*, 14 PLoS ONE at 2 (2019), https://journals.plos.org/plosone/article?id=10.1371/journal.pone.0226522.

472. *Id.* at 2, 5.

473. Law No. 18.987 on Voluntary Termination of Pregnancy (10/22/2012), at art. 2.

474. *Id.*

475. Law No. 18.987 on Voluntary Termination of Pregnancy (10/22/2012), at art. 11.

476. *Id.*

also granted medical providers the right to conscientious objection.[477] This law was only successful after four failed attempts at passing legislation.[478]

The Ministry of Health regulates the 2012 abortion law. It requires that abortion services only be provided at Integrated National Health System (INHS) public and private facilities.[479] The Ministry of Health focuses on medication abortion due to the following factors: a perceived lack of training materials for surgical abortion, high availability of misoprostol, the specialization of the existing Iniciativas Sanitarias group in medication abortions, and the goal of less conscientious objections.[480] Thus, the form and facility is restricted.

In a 2017 case, a lower court judge held that a woman could not get an abortion over the objections of her partner.[481] The case was appealed, and the Supreme Court of Justice held that the proposed course of action by the lower court, which forced the woman to remain pregnant, was "inadmissible."[482] The Court reaffirmed Uruguay's 2012 law and granted the woman her abortion.[483]

According to the Ministry of Health, more than 40,000 safe abortions were performed from 2013 to 2017.[484] In some areas, 100 percent of available medical providers invoke conscientious objection and will not perform an abortion, and these actions make abortion effectively inaccessible.[485] The providers also do not have to refer the patient to a provider who performs

---

477. *Id.*

478. Bianca M. Stifani et al., *From Harm Reduction to Legalization: The Uruguayan Model for Safe Abortion*, 143 INT. J. GYNECOLOGY & OBSTETRICS 45, 46 (Oct. 2018), https://obgyn .onlinelibrary.wiley.com/doi/full/10.1002/ijgo.12677 [hereinafter Stifani et al., *From Harm Reduction to Legalization*].

479. *Id.*

480. *Id.* at 45, 47.

481. *Statement: Supreme Court Of Justice Ruling Declares Unconstitutionality Recourse Inadmissible Against Voluntary Termination of Pregnancy Law*, MUJUR Y SALUD EN URUGUAY (May 22, 2017), http://www.mysu.org.uy/que-hacemos/incidencia/posicionamiento-politico /statement-supreme-court-of-justice-ruling-declares-unconstitutionality-recourse-inadmissi ble-against-voluntary-termination-of-pregnancy-law/.

482. *Id.*

483. *Id.*

484. Ministerio de Salud Pública, *Indicadores De Salud Sexual Y Reproductiva: Aborto*, MUJER Y SALUD EN URUGUAY (2018), http://www.mysu.org.uy/que-hacemos/observatorio /datos-oficiales/indicador-de-salud-sexual-y-reproductiva/aborto/.

485. F. Coppola et al., *Conscientious Objection as a Barrier for Implementing Voluntary Termination of Pregnancy in Uruguay: Gynecologists' Attitudes and Behavior*, 134 INT J. GYNECOL. OBSTET. (2016), https://obgyn.onlinelibrary.wiley.com/doi/full/10.1016/j.ijgo.2016.06.005; *see* Stifani et al., *From Harm Reduction to Legalization, supra* note 478, at 45, 47.

abortion care.[486] The Uruguayan Ministry of Health reported in 2013 that the conscientious objection rate nationwide was 30 percent of providers, which placed insurmountable travel burdens of cost and time that prevented many persons seeking abortions from getting a prescription.[487]

Prior to decriminalization, Iniciativas Sanitarias, a group of physician advocates who worked for harm reduction, took an active role in aiding persons seeking abortions.[488] Harm reduction is programs that seek to "minimise negative health, social and legal impacts," and the programs originated as a way to address drug use.[489] Before the 2012 law, Iniciativas Sanitarias used a harm reduction model to train providers in the methods of clandestine abortion to inform their patients seeking an abortion about the health concerns but not facilitating their access, which would have been illegal at the time.[490] The providers would then provide care at after visits, including performing uterine aspiration if the abortion was incomplete.[491] The program reached 675 women, and there were no maternal deaths or complications.[492] After this success, Iniciativas Sanitarias then took a significant role in supporting new abortion providers and providing services once abortions were allowed in the first trimester.[493] Their efforts reduced stigma around abortion and created "an infrastructure that facilitated the provision of abortion services."[494] The model of the Iniciativas Sanitarias was replicated in poorer and more conservative counties in Uruguay, and their harm reduction approach is being considered in other countries.[495]

A new study was released in 2019 discussing the perspectives of women seeking abortions in Uruguay. The study emphasized that, despite abortion being legal, there was ongoing abortion stigma in the country.[496] Even in

---

486. Regiane Folter, *Why Uruguay Is One of the Only Latin American Countries to Legalize Abortion*, WOMEN'S MEDIA CTR. (Apr. 24, 2019), https://www.womensmediacenter.com/fbomb/why-uruguay-is-one-of-the-only-latin-american-countries-to-legalize-abortion.

487. Coppola et al., *supra* note 485; *see* Stifani et al., *From Harm Reduction to Legalization*, *supra* note 478, at 45, 47.

488. Patrick Adams, *From Uruguay, a Model for Making Abortion Safer*, N.Y. TIMES (June 28, 2016), https://www.nytimes.com/2016/06/28/opinion/from-uruguay-a-model-for-making-abortion-safer.html.

489. *What Is Harm Reduction?*, HARM REDUCTION INT'L, https://www.hri.global/what-is-harm-reduction (last accessed Dec. 1, 2020).

490. *Id.*

491. *Id.*

492. *Id.*

493. *Id.*

494. Stifani et al., *From Harm Reduction to Legalization*, *supra* note 478, at 45.

495. Adams, *supra* note 489.

496. S. Makleff et al., *Experience Obtaining Legal Abortion in Uruguay: Knowledge, Attitudes, and Stigma among Abortion Clients*, 19 BMC WOMEN'S HEALTH 155 (2019), https://doi.org/10.1186/s12905-019-0855-6.

states where the law in text permits abortion access, these factors like conscientious objections or stigma continue to inhibit care.

2. Brazil

In Brazil, abortion is only legal in cases of rape, incest, danger to the woman's life, and fetal anencephaly.[497] Providing an unlawful abortion is punishable by imprisonment of one to four years.[498] Brazil's Supreme Court considered whether those abortion restrictions were constitutional in the first 12 weeks of pregnancy after a woman, Ingriane Barbosa Carvalho, died from an unlawful abortion procedure.[499] The court declined to create an exception.

At the end of August 2020, Brazil's Health Ministry created new requirements for rape survivors seeking abortion care. The survivors would be required to look at the embryo or fetus on an ultrasound, and doctors must report the case to the police.[500] The requirements, passed by ordinance, also demand that medical providers "keep fragments of embryos or fetuses as evidence" for the police.[501] Medical professionals have condemned the ordinance and its requirements, specifically citing concerns about doctor-patient confidentiality.[502]

Brazil's Supreme Court denied the abortion exception for those infected with Zika during their pregnancy.[503] The Court heard the case in April 2020, and the majority refused to grant an exception to criminalization. Despite COVID-19's overall health threats, the Brazilian Ministry of Health "identified 579 new suspected cases of Zika between December 2019 and February 2020."[504] The Zika problem goes unaddressed due to the hesitance to create pathways to abortion.

In August 2020, a ten-year-old girl who became pregnant from rape had to fly more than 900 miles across Brazil to get her abortion when

---

497. Penal Code, Law Decree No 2.848, Art. 124, 126, 128.

498. *Id.*

499. Manuela Andreoni & Ernesto Londoño, *Brazil's Supreme Court Considers Decriminalizing Abortion*, N.Y. TIMES (Aug. 3, 2018), https://www.nytimes.com/2018/08/03/world/americas/brazil-abortion-supreme-court.html.

500. *See* Ordinance No. 2,282; Lise Alves, *Brazilian Doctors Condemn New Rules on Abortion*, 396 WORLD REP. (Sept. 2020).

501. *Id.*

502. *Id.*

503. *Direct Action on Unconstitutionality*-ADI 5581.

504. Ministério da Saúde, *Monitoramento dos casos de arboviroses urbanas transmitidas pelo Aedes (dengue, chikungunya e Zika), Semanas Epidemiológicas 1 a 7, 2020*, 51 EPIDEMIOLOGICAL BULLETIN 1, 2 (Mar. 2020), http://portalarquivos.saude.gov.br/images/pdf/2020/April/07/Boletim-epidemiologico-SVS-14.pdf.

the facilities in her state refused to provide the procedure. On the day of the procedure at the alternative hospital, anti-abortion activists and politicians had occupied the entrance, screaming abuse at the ten-year-old survivor. Extremists with associations to President Jair Bolsonaro's administration spread false information that the child was kidnapped and being forced to abort.[505] Counter-protestors arrived to support the child.[506] All of these actions and difficulties occurred despite that the Penal Code includes an exception from abortion criminalization for pregnancies that result from rape.[507]

In June 2020, the Ministry of Health dismissed two civil servants who signed a letter of support for women's sexual and reproductive health access during the pandemic. The letter, also called a technical note, supported access to contraception and maintaining the abortion procedures during COVID-19 that are allowed by law. The Ministry of Health published a response that asserted the technical note had no legitimacy or authorization. These two civil servants worked for the Ministry of Health as Coordinator for Women's Health and Coordinator for Men's Health.[508]

Five-hundred thousand illegal abortions happen each year in Brazil among 18- to 39-year-old women.[509] There is also a high incidence of health complications among these women, resulting in hospitalization.[510] As has long been the experience in other countries around the world, despite Brazil's legal prohibition of abortion, large numbers of abortions occur there regardless.

3. Peru

Peru has extremely restrictive abortion laws. Peru criminalizes abortion except in cases to protect the woman's health or life. The option for abortion due to health is only available until the 22nd week of pregnancy. In

---

505. Tom Phillips & Caio Barretto Briso, *Brazil: Outcry as Religious Extremists Harass Child Seeking Abortion*, THE GUARDIAN (Aug. 17, 2020, 4:27 PM EDT), https://www.theguardian.com/world/2020/aug/17/brazil-protest-abortion-recife-hospital#.

506. Ananda Portela (@anandaportela), TWITTER (Aug. 16, 2020, 6:46 PM) https://twitter.com/anandaportela/status/1295129720330297345?s=20.

507. Penal Code, Law Decree No 2.848, Art. 128.

508. *Brazil's Minister of Health Dismisses Two Civil Servants for Expressing Support for Women's Sexual and Reproductive Health*, SEXUALITY POL'Y WATCH (June 12, 2020), https://sxpolitics.org/brazils-minister-of-health-dismisses-two-civil-servants-for-expressing-support-for-womens-sexual-and-reproductive-health/20965.

509. Debora Diniz et al., *Understanding the Sexual and Reproductive Health Needs in Brazil's Zika-Affected Region: Placing Women at the Center of the Discussion*, 147 INT. J. GYNECOL. OBSTET. (July 2019).

510. *Id.*

addition to consent of the woman to perform the abortion, two physicians must agree that the abortion is needed.[511] Peru's health care workers must report suspected abortions to the police under a mandatory reporting law. Abortions under these exceptions were not included on the Ministry of Health's mandated free health services list.

In 2011, the United Nations Committee on the Elimination of Discrimination Against Women (CEDAW) heard the case of *L.C. v. Peru* and ruled that Peru must amend its laws to allow abortion in cases of rape and sexual assault, ensuring that there is actual availability of these services along with services access for cases that endanger the life or health of the woman.[512] L.C. was an 11-year-old girl who had become pregnant when repeatedly raped by a 34-year-old man. She attempted to commit suicide by jumping from a building. Although she survived the suicide attempt, she sustained serious injuries which required emergency surgery. The hospital declined to perform the surgery based on the risk posed to her pregnancy and refused to perform an abortion despite that the pregnancy posed a danger to her physical and mental health. As a consequence, L.C. was paralyzed from the neck down. Despite the ruling by CEDAW, abortion remains illegal in circumstances of sexual assault. Numerous attempts were made by legislators in 2014 and 2015 to add an exception for abortion in cases of rape, but these have all failed.[513] Three bills to criminalize abortion services advertisements were presented to the legislature from 2011 to 2016, but all three failed.[514] Although these anti-abortion bills did not pass, Peru instituted a Day of the Unborn Child in 2004.[515]

Activists in Peru continue to use four main arguments to advance abortion rights: "Autonomy, Maternal Morbidity and Mortality, Economic, and Pragmatism."[516] Low-income women and those in rural areas have the highest rate of complications from unsafe abortions.[517] Peru's maternal mortality has been in decline, but research is ongoing for ways to further decrease

---

511. Código Penal (1991), Ley de 3 Abril 1991, Capitulo II, Artículos 114–120.

512. Communication No. 22/2009, CEDAW/C/50/D/22/2009, https://www.repro ductiverights.org/sites/default/files/documents/CEDAW-C-50-D-22-2009%20English%20 %28clean%20copy%29.pdf.

513. Camila Gianella, *Abortion Rights Legal Mobilization in the Peruvian Media, 1990– 2015*, HEALTH & HUMAN RIGHTS J. (June 2017)., https://www.hhrjournal.org/2017/06 /abortion-rights-legal-mobilization-in-the-peruvian-media-1990-2015/.

514. *Id.*

515. Law 27654.

516. Cynthia Beavin et al., *Activist Framing of Abortion and Use for Policy Change in Peru*, 27 SEX. & REPROD. HEALTH MATTERS 160 (Apr. 2019).

517. L. Távara et al., *La planificación familiar requiere atención especial como estrategia para reducir la mortalidad materna*, 57 REV. PERU GINECOL. OBSTET. 177 (2011).

it, including by expanding access to legal abortion.[518] Peru has conducted research into medication abortion in the context of maternal mortality. A study in 2018 analyzed a harm-reduction model whereby women were given misoprostol and pre- and post-abortion care. The study found that 89 percent of the women who took misoprostol completed an abortion and reported an 81 to 89 percent satisfaction rate. In conclusion, the study determined that medication abortion and legalization would lessen the maternal mortality and morbidity rates in Peru.[519] These studies and facts are used by advocates for abortion rights.

4. Argentina

Argentina's criminal code, written in 1921, only allowed abortion for instances of rape or danger to a woman's life and health.[520] However, Argentina's provinces must all implement the law individually, and a few provinces did not permit abortions even for danger to a woman's health.[521] Although the Office of the Ombudsman instituted a resolution recommending that the provinces each institute protocols, some still did not do so.[522]

The Penal Code also included in the text a requirement that, for an abortion to be justified, the individual who was raped must also be mentally disabled. However, in 2012, the Supreme Court decided *F, A.L.*, where medical providers performed an abortion on a 15-year-old who became pregnant after a rape.[523] She did not have a mental disability, but the Supreme Court ruled that she still fulfilled the rape exception because of her age, and the Court encouraged a broad interpretation of the code.[524]

Argentina has had ongoing political action to decriminalize abortion and expand access. In 2018, Argentina's lower house passed a bill to legalize

---

518. *Peru Maternal Mortality Rate*, WORLD BANK (2000–2019), https://www.macrotrends .net/countries/PER/peru/maternal-mortality-rate.

519. Daniel Grossman et al., *A Harm-Reduction Model of Abortion Counseling about Misoprostol Use in Peru with Telephone and In-Person Follow-up: A Cohort Study*, PLOS ONE (Jan. 2018), https://doi.org/10.1371/journal.pone.0189195.

520. Cód. Pen. [Criminal Code] art. 85-88 (Arg.).

521. Ch. 4, sec. 75(12) Constitución Nacional [Const. Nac.] (Arg.); *see also* Uki Goñi, *Argentina Senate Rejects Bill to Legalise Abortion*, THE GUARDIAN (Aug. 9, 2018, 5:36 EDT), https:// www.theguardian.com/world/2018/aug/09/argentina-senate-rejects-bill-legalise-abortion.

522. Office of the National Ombudsman, Res. DPN No. 65/15 (2015), www.dpn.gob.ar /documentos/20160927_30933_556933.pdf, (Arg.).

523. Corte Suprema de Justicia de la Nación [CSJN] [National Supreme Court of Justice], 13/3/2012, "F, A.L., FSAL [the petitioner] s. /Medida Autosatisfactiva," Fallos (259) (Arg.).

524. *Id.*

abortion on demand, but the Senate rejected the bill by seven votes. Despite former President Mauricio Macri having stated that he would sign the bill if it passed, the 1921 Penal Code remained the law. The failure to pass the bill in the final moments was attributed to anti-liberalization pressure by Pope Francis, who is Argentinian, and the Catholic Church.[525] The Campaign for Legal, Safe and Free Abortion has presented a legalization bill at every session since 2008. 2018 was the first year the bill made it onto the congressional agenda, and 2019 was the second. In 2019, Alberto Fernández ran for president and included abortion legalization in his platform. He won the presidency and reaffirmed his commitment to abortion reform.[526]

On March 2, 2020, President Alberto Fernández announced that he would send an abortion legalization bill to Congress as well as a 1,000-day plan, which would create a program to support the health and vital care for pregnant women and young children.[527] The March for International Women's Day was held on March 8, 2020, with anticipation about the new legislation.[528] COVID-19 then caused a lockdown and delayed legislative action.[529] Eight months later, however, the lower house of Congress, after more than 20 hours of debate, approved a bill by a vote of 131 to 117 to broadly legalize abortion. It was expected the vote in the Senate would be more difficult, as it had been before.[530] But, on December 27, 2020, the Senate passed the liberalization bill by a wider-than-expected margin, 38 to

---

525. *Argentina Lower House Passes Legal Abortion Bill in Tight Vote*, REUTERS (June 14, 2018, 10:02 AM), https://www.reuters.com/article/us-argentina-abortion/argentina-lower-house-passes-legal-abortion-bill-in-tight-vote-idUSKBN1JA1ZT; *see also* Goñi, *supra* note 522.

526. Felipe Yapur & Victoria Ginzberg, *Alberto Fernández enviará un proyecto de legalización del aborto al Congreso*, PÁGINA 12 (Nov. 17, 2019), https://www.pagina12.com.ar/231474-alberto-fernandez-enviara-un-proyecto-de-legalizacion-del-ab.

527. *Argentina Abortion: President Alberto Fernández Proposes Legalization*, BBC NEWS (Mar. 2, 2020), https://www.bbc.com/news/world-latin-america-51701077; *see also* Mariana Carbajal, *Plan de los 1000 días: Alberto Fernández anunció la iniciativa para el cuidado de la mujer y sus hijas e hijos*, PÁGINA 12 (Mar. 2, 2020), https://www.pagina12.com.ar/250397-plan-de-los-1000-dias-alberto-fernandez-anuncio-la-iniciativ.

528. Carlos Rodríguez, *8M: la fuerza de la revolución feminista*, PÁGINA 12 (Mar. 9, 2020), https://www.pagina12.com.ar/251992-8-m-la-fuerza-de-la-revolucion-feminista.

529. Cora Fernández Anderson, *Activists Keep Argentina's Abortion Reform on the Agenda Despite Covid-19*, NACLA (July 9, 2020), https://nacla.org/news/2020/07/08/argentina-abortion-reform-covid.

530. Daniel Politi, *Argentina Moves Toward Legal Abortion Amid Push for Women's Rights*, N.Y. TIMES (Dec. 11, 2020), https://www.nytimes.com/2020/12/11/world/americas/argentina-abortion.html.

29 with one abstention, culminating intense grassroots political action over a period of years.[531]

During the pandemic, the government declared the limited legal abortion procedures to be an essential service. Although access is difficult, pro-choice health care providers made information available to patients regarding reproductive service access in the country.[532] The demand for self-managed medication abortions has increased according to Socorristas en Red, a feminist collective that provides information and support to women who want medication abortions.[533] Socorristas en Red also continues their support through telemedicine options.

III. Conclusion

Countries vary extensively in their regulation of abortion care, and the history of abortion around the world is, unfortunately, one that has too often been marked by oppression. For people seeking to exercise autonomy over their bodies and for those who support them, long-fought legal and political battles have sometimes fallen short. Although many countries have recently revised or overturned the most severe prohibitions on abortion, hostility toward free and equal access to abortion is still present in many places around the globe.

There have been slow and important improvements to abortion laws and policies that have made abortion safer and more accessible. But just as that progress is worth celebrating, it is equally if not more important to recognize those who are being further oppressed and left behind. Abortion restrictions are increasingly being implemented as a compromise to make abortion legal, while keeping it "rare." In reality, these restrictions make abortion inaccessible for those who are already marginalized due to poverty, racism, homophobia, transphobia, xenophobia, and other forms of structural oppression. Even in countries with relatively liberal abortion laws, these barriers mean that abortion may only be available to a privileged few.

---

531. Daniel Politi & Ernesto Londoño, *Argentina Legalizes Abortion, a Milestone in a Conservative Region*, N.Y. TIMES (Dec. 30, 2020), https://www.nytimes.com/2020/12/30/world /americas/argentina-legalizes-abortion.html. *See also* Richard Pérez-Peña, *How Argentina Bucked Tradition in Latin America and Legalized Abortion*, N.Y. TIMES (Dec. 30, 2020), https:// www.nytimes.com/2020/12/30/world/americas/argentina-abortion-questions-answers.html.

532. *See generally Inicio*, RED SALUD DECIDIR (last updated Oct. 18, 2020), http://www .redsaluddecidir.org/.

533. Ludmila Ferrer, *Abortar en cuarentena: el abrazo socorrista*, EL GRITO DEL SUR (May 28, 2020), https://elgritodelsur.com.ar/2020/05/abortar-cuarentena-abrazo-socorrista.html.

Religion also continues to serve as a powerful force against access to abortion. Conscience exemptions and refusals of care can overcome even the most expansive abortion policies. Abortion can be locally available, free, and legal in theory. But if no provider is willing to offer the service, the legal right to abortion means little to pregnant persons seeking to control their own reproduction.

Additionally, paternalistic attitudes and stigma toward abortion persist worldwide. Prohibitions and restrictions on self-managed abortion, requirements for waiting periods and counseling before obtaining an abortion, spousal consent requirements, and parental notification rules for young people all point to widespread perceptions among lawmakers that pregnant people are incapable of making their own decisions about their bodies, or should not be permitted to make those decisions. These attitudes serve the confounding function of simultaneously infantilizing people seeking abortions while also coercing them to carry a pregnancy to term with the expectation that they are mature enough to birth and parent a child.

Despite these troubling trends, all is certainly not lost. Just as our review of these 31 countries reveals widespread barriers to abortion access, it also shows that change and progress are possible, particularly when large-scale protests, international condemnation, and the sharing of salient stories propel societies forward, forcing them to affirm and expand the right to abortion. At this juncture, attention, acknowledgment, and action are critical in the continued effort to provide all people with meaningful opportunity to direct their own lives and self-actualize their own futures—opportunities that cannot exist when abortion is illegal and unsafe. These efforts must include renewed focus on medication abortion, particularly given the circumstances of the COVID-19 pandemic and what is likely to be a lasting decentralization and individualization of medical care, including reproductive care. Perhaps most importantly, these efforts must address the serious disparities that often exist between laws on the books and laws in practice, and in particular the compounding and cumulative barriers that exist for low-income people, rural people, and racial, religious, gender, and sexual minorities when it comes to accessing abortion care. Though progress has undoubtedly been made in many parts of the world, there remains much work to be done.

2

Abortion Law in the United States

By Edward B. Goldman, J.D.[1]

I. Introduction

This chapter discusses the legal aspects of abortion in the United States. Historical, social, cultural, and ethical issues are discussed in other chapters and other sources.[2] Abortion law in Canada and around the world is discussed in detail in other chapters in this book.

Abortion is only one issue in reproductive justice. Reproductive justice, as defined by Sister Song, also includes reproductive health (medical issues), reproductive rights (legal issues), and reproductive advocacy (a social justice movement). Sister Song argues that reproductive justice will only be attained when every woman can decide to have children, not have children, determine who will deliver her children, and raise children in a supportive society.[3]

This chapter, with its focus on legal issues around abortion, is only a small part of a much larger set of issues involving equal rights for women and human rights for all.

Generally, when the Supreme Court decides a significant case, there is some flame and dissatisfaction, but the fires soon die down. Even with

---

1. Associate Professor of Law, Medicine and Public Health in the University of Michigan Schools of Law, Public Health and Medicine (Obstetrics and Gynecology).

2. *See, e.g.*, University of San Francisco, *Research*, ADVANCING NEW STUDIES IN REPRODUCTIVE HEALTH (Nov. 14, 2020, 1:19 PM), https://womenshealth.ucsf.edu/research/advancing-new-standards-reproductive-health.

3. Sister Song is building a movement for reproductive justice (2015). See http://www.sistersong.net/.

major social issues like the desegregation of schools in the aftermath of *Brown v. Board*,[4] the reaction,[5] although significant in some states, was not as dramatic or persistent as the continued aftermath of *Roe v. Wade*.[6]

In 1973, *Roe* created a fire storm that continues to burn today.

II. Abortion Pre-*Roe*

Prior to 1973, in the United States, 17 states allowed abortion in some or most circumstances.[7] Women were having abortions, often illegally, and had a risk of mortality and morbidity significantly higher than the risk today. The world-renown Guttmacher Institute advances sexual and reproductive health through research, policy analysis, and public education, and it collects data about reproductive health. That data and data collected by others showed that the risk of death from abortion in 1965 had declined significantly as laws were liberalized before *Roe*, and morbidity and mortality continued to decrease after *Roe* was decided.[8]

The experience in Romania is a telling international example of what happens when abortion is illegal. When Nicolae Ceausescu became dictator of Romania in 1965, he wanted to increase the population, so he outlawed abortion and access to birth control. Employed women up to age 45 were asked to undergo monthly gynecological exams, and a series of other punitive actions and penalties were assessed by Ceausescu in his effort to force childbearing.[9] Prior to his decree, abortion and birth control had been inexpensive and easily accessible. Abortion became legal again in 1990. What happened in between?

When abortion was outlawed in Romania, the birth rate did increase.[10] But the rate of abortion-related deaths soared, as illegal abortions

---

4. Brown v. Board of Education of Topeka, 347 U.S. 483 (1954).

5. Exhibition (on view May 13–November 13, 2004), *The Aftermath—Brown v. Board at Fifty: "With an Even Hand,"* LIBRARY OF CONGRESS (Nov. 14, 2020, 1:33 PM), http://www.loc.gov/exhibits/brown/brown-aftermath.html.

6. For a detailed discussion of the law and politics before *Roe* was decided, see LINDA GREENHOUSE & REVA SIEGEL, BEFORE ROE V. WADE (2010).

7. Sarah Kliff, *CHARTS: How Roe v. Wade Changed Abortion Rights*, WASH. POST (Jan. 22, 2013), http://www.washingtonpost.com/blogs/wonkblog/wp/2013/01/22/charts-how-roe-v-wade-changed-abortion-rights/.

8. W. Cates, Jr., *"Abortion Myths and Realities": Who Is Misleading Whom?*, 142 AM. J. OBSTET. & GYN. 954 (1982), https://pubmed.ncbi.nlm.nih.gov/7072785/.

9. H. David, *Romania Ends Compulsory Childbearing*, 9 ENTREZ NOUS CPH DEN. 14 (1990), https://pubmed.ncbi.nlm.nih.gov/12222213/.

10. William R. Johnston, *Historical Abortion Statistics, Romania*, http://www.johnstonsarchive.net/policy/abortion/ab-romania.html (last updated Jan. 14, 2020).

proliferated. "The maternal mortality rate increased from 86 maternal deaths/100,000 live births in 1966 to 140 in 1981 and nearly 150 in 1984, when 86% of maternal deaths came from abortions."[11] The maternal death rate quickly dropped when abortion was made legal again.[12] This effect is clearly illustrated in Figure 2.1 from the Guttmacher Institute.

FIGURE 2.1 Abortion-Related Deaths per 100,000 Births (Romania)

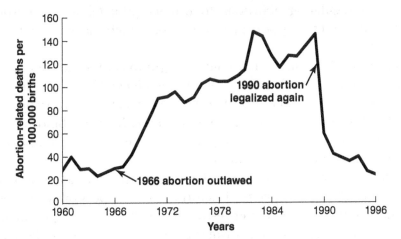

The Romanian experience indicates that women were accessing contraception and abortion services illegally, and illegal abortions were causing increased mortality rates. That is consistent with the experience in the United States and other countries around the world. Contrary to the contentions of anti-choice groups in the United States, abortion rates generally are lower where abortion is legal, as countries with lower abortion rates also tend to have meaningful family planning and contraceptive access, and it is those efforts that reduce unwanted pregnancy and therefore abortion rates. The difference between countries where abortion is legal and those where it is highly restricted is that, in the latter, maternal mortality rates are substantially higher.[13]

---

11. David, *supra* note 9.

12. *Id.*

13. Jonathan Bearak et al., *Unintended Pregnancy and Abortion by Income, Region, and the Legal Status of Abortion: Estimates from a Comprehensive Model for 1990–2019*, 8 THELAN CET.COM e1152 (2020), https://www.thelancet.com/journals/langlo/article/PIIS2214-109X (20)30315-6/fulltext; *see also New Estimates Show Worldwide Decrease in Unintended Pregnancies—Abortion Rates Fall in Regions Where It Is Broadly Legal*, GUTTMACHER INSTITUTE (Nov. 14, 2020, 4:09 PM), https://www.guttmacher.org/news-release/2020/new-estimates-show-worldwide-decrease-unintended-pregnancies.

III. *Roe v. Wade* and *Doe v. Bolton*: 1973

In *Roe*, the Court struck down a Texas statute prohibiting abortion on the theory that the right to privacy under the due process clause of the 14th Amendment extended to a woman's decision to have an abortion.[14] The right to have a legal abortion was not seen to be a fundamental right, but rather a privacy right that could be balanced against the state's legitimate interests in regulating abortions to protect prenatal life and women's health. The case created a trimester analysis, which was modified in 1992 by *Casey*.[15]

During the first trimester, a woman's right to confer with her physician and decide to have an abortion could not be blocked by a state. In the second trimester, a state could provide rules to protect the safety of the woman. In the third trimester, after the point of fetal viability (the ability to live outside the womb), the state could regulate and even ban abortion except as necessary for the health of the mother.

In *Doe*, the Court considered a Georgia statute that allowed abortion only in cases of rape, severe fetal deformity, or the possibility of severe or fatal injury to the mother. Other restrictions included the requirement that the procedure be approved in writing by three physicians and by a special committee of the staff of the hospital where the abortion was to be performed. In addition, only Georgia residents could receive abortions. The Court struck down the law, saying that it imposed too many restrictions and that any woman had a right to decide, with her physician, to terminate her pregnancy.[16]

The Court's opinion in *Doe v. Bolton* also stated that a woman may obtain an abortion after viability if necessary to protect her health. The Court defined "health" as follows:

> Whether, in the words of the Georgia statute, "an abortion is necessary" is a professional judgment that the Georgia physician will be called upon to make routinely. We agree with the District Court . . . that the medical judgment may be exercised in the light of all factors—physical, emotional, psychological, familial, and the woman's age—relevant to the well-being of the patient. All these factors may relate to health.[17]

---

14. Roe v. Wade, 410 U.S. 113 (1973).
15. Planned Parenthood of Se. Pa. v. Casey, 505 U.S. 833 (1992).
16. Doe v. Bolton, 410 U.S. 179 (1973).
17. *Id.* at 192.

Roe and *Doe* did not legalize abortion as a matter of federal law. Rather, these cases concluded, using a privacy analysis, that states cannot prohibit abortion prior to viability, but they can regulate the "safety" of the procedure during the second trimester and can prohibit abortion post-viability so long as there is a post-viability exception for the health and life of the mother. *Roe* introduced several issues that are still being argued about today. First, is a fetus a person? Second, what laws can a state pass in the name of safety of the mother? Third, what laws can a state pass to fully inform a mother of her rights? Fourth, what rights and protections can be provided to a fetus (both viable and pre-viable)? Fifth, what rights ought minors have to obtain an abortion independent of parental notice or permission? Sixth, what, if any procedures, can be prohibited post (and even prior to) viability?

The issue of regulation for the health and safety of the woman has become a significant issue in current laws that purport to regulate safety. What did *Roe* and *Doe* allow? The decisions allowed states, with a compelling reason, to pass laws during the second trimester for a woman's safety and to restrict access to abortion post-viability except as required for the life or health of the woman.

The cases could have been decided on constitutional fundamental rights grounds, making it more difficult to overturn them. Justice Ruth Bader Ginsburg believed that if *Roe* and *Doe* were decided on equal protection grounds, that would have provided women a fundamental right that could not be balanced against the state's interest in the fetus.[18] She also felt that *Roe* may have gone too far too fast, thus energizing the anti-abortion movement. "My criticism of *Roe* is that it seemed to have stopped the momentum on the side of change,"[19] Ginsburg said. She would have preferred abortion rights be secured more gradually, in a process that included state legislatures being allowed to make certain changes. Ginsburg was troubled that the focus on *Roe* was on a right to privacy, rather than on women's rights. "*Roe* isn't really about the woman's choice, is it?" Ginsburg said. "It's about the doctor's freedom to practice . . . it wasn't woman-centered, it was physician-centered."[20]

Equal protection is a fundamental legal right based in the 14th Amendment to the Constitution. An example of an equal protection analysis

---

18. Meredith Heagney, *Justice Ruth Bader Ginsburg Offers Critique of Roe v. Wade during Law School Visit*, UNIV. OF CHICAGO L. SCH. (May 15, 2013), https://www.law.uchicago.edu/news /justice-ruth-bader-ginsburg-offers-critique-roe-v-wade-during-law-school-visit.

19. *Id.*

20. *Id.* For more details about Justice Ginsburg's thoughts on these issues, see RUTH GINSBURG, MY OWN WORDS (2016).

is *United States v. Virginia*,[21] where the Court found that an all-male state school that refused to admit women was engaging in gender discrimination in violation of equal protection. The relevant language of the 14th Amendment is in Section 1:

> All persons born or naturalized in the United States, and subject to the jurisdiction thereof, are citizens of the United States and of the state wherein they reside. No state shall make or enforce any law which shall abridge the privileges or immunities of citizens of the United States; nor shall any state deprive any person of life, liberty, or property, without due process of law; nor deny to any person within its jurisdiction the equal protection of the laws.

If *Roe* had been decided on equal protection grounds (i.e., states do not have laws prohibiting males from deciding with their physicians about medical procedures and interventions including sterilization, therefore it is a violation of Equal Protection for states to have laws pertaining only to females stopping them from deciding with their physicians about medical procedures and interventions), it would have provided women fundamental legal rights that could not be easily restricted by a state asserting an interest in the fetus.

IV. Evolution of Supreme Court Law from *Roe* to *Whole Woman's Health*: The March to the "Undue Burden" Standard for Review

This section will briefly discuss the cases between *Roe v. Wade* and *Whole Woman's Health v. Hellerstedt*,[22] where states have tried a variety of approaches to narrow the holding in *Roe*.

After *Roe* and *Doe* were decided, states began passing laws designed to test the limits of those decisions. The laws were designed to convince women to carry a pregnancy to term, to limit access to abortion, and even to try to overturn the rulings in *Roe* and *Doe*. Major cases included:

1. *Bigelow v. Virginia*, 421 U.S. 809 (1975), held that abortion clinics have a first amendment right to advertise.
2. *Planned Parenthood of Central Missouri v. Danforth*, 428 U.S. 52 (1976), held that a law requiring prior written consent from parents for a

---

21. United States v. Virginia, 518 U.S. 515 (1996).
22. Whole Woman's Health v. Hellerstedt, 136 S. Ct. 2292 (2016).

minor or from the spouse of an adult woman was unconstitutional because the state could not grant a veto power to a third party.

3. *Colautti v. Franklin*, 439 U.S. 379 (1979), ruled that a Pennsylvania law requiring a physician to first make a determination of viability and to then use only those procedures that had the best chance of a live birth in performing an abortion was impermissibly vague and therefore unconstitutional.

4. *Bellotti v. Baird*, 443 U.S. 622 (1979), mandated judicial bypass for minors—a process whereby a minor could go to court and ask a court to allow an abortion without parental permission—and found bypass was legally required in order for parental notification or consent laws to be constitutional.

5. *Harris v. McRae*, 448 U.S. 297 (1980), upheld the Hyde Amendment that prohibited the use of federal Medicaid funds for abortions by holding that there was no requirement for the government to pay for an abortion.

6. *City of Akron v. Akron Center for Reproductive Health*, 462 U.S. 416 (1983), ruled that the city could not (1) require minors under 15 to obtain parental or judicial consent for an abortion; (2) require physicians to give women information designed to dissuade them from having abortions; (3) impose a 24-hour waiting period after the signing of the consent form; or (4) require that all second-trimester abortions be performed in a hospital. (Latter cases have backed away from this ruling and have allowed waiting periods and "informed consent" requirements that mandate providing certain information to women, even if that information was designed to persuade women not to have an abortion.)

7. *Thornburgh v. American College of Obstetricians & Gynecologists*, 476 U.S. 747 (1986). Pennsylvania passed a new law after the *Colautti* decision in an attempt to force doctors to try to save the life of a to-be-aborted fetus. The Supreme Court struck down this law. The law was problematic because, among other issues, it required doctors to use abortion techniques that maximized the chance of fetal survival, even when such techniques increased the medical risks to the pregnant woman's life or health.

8. *Webster v. Reproductive Health Services*, 492 U.S. 490 (1989), gave the Court an opportunity to overrule *Roe*. Although the Court did not do that, it did shift its analysis. The Missouri law said public facilities could not be used for abortions except those necessary to save a woman's life; required physicians to perform tests to determine the viability of fetuses after 20 weeks of gestation; and imposed other

restrictions. The Supreme Court upheld these provisions, thereby allowing greater state regulation of abortion.

9. *Hodgson v. Minnesota*, 497 U.S. 417 (1990), allowed parental notification and even parental consent laws, so long as there was a potential judicial bypass that allowed a minor to go to court and ask for permission to have an abortion. The ongoing issue with judicial bypass is that there are no clear standards for determining when a court ought to grant or deny permission to a minor.

10. *Rust v. Sullivan*, 500 U.S. 173 (1991), upheld federal regulations that barred abortion counseling and referral by family planning programs that received funds under Title X of the federal Public Health Service Act. This meant that doctors working in federally funded clinics could not discuss or even mention abortion with their patients. The specific regulations at issue were adopted during the Reagan administration, but were rescinded in 1993 by the Clinton administration.

11. *Planned Parenthood of Southeastern Pennsylvania v. Casey*, 505 U.S. 833 (1992). This case was a sea change for the Court. Instead of focusing on the health and safety of the woman, the Court focused on the fetus. It held that state regulations can survive constitutional review so long as they do not place a "substantial obstacle in the path of a woman seeking an abortion of a nonviable fetus." The majority also found that a state can have a legitimate compelling interest in a pre-viable fetus. This new standard did not overrule *Roe* but did replace the *Roe* analysis. It was named the "undue burden" analysis of restrictions placed on abortions. Because of the importance of this case, a more detailed analysis follows.

V. *Planned Parenthood v. Casey*

In 1988–89, Pennsylvania passed a law that required informed consent and a 24-hour waiting period prior to the pregnancy termination procedure. A minor seeking an abortion was required to obtain the consent of one parent, but the law allowed for a judicial bypass. A married woman seeking an abortion had to indicate that she had notified her husband of her intention to abort the fetus.

The Supreme Court was sharply divided (5–4) in *Casey*. It did not overrule *Roe* but instead created a new standard for review. It found that a state could have a "compelling interest" in the fetus even pre-viability, and that the standard for review of laws restricting abortion access would be whether the state's abortion regulation has the purpose or effect of imposing an "undue burden." Undue burden was defined as placing a "substantial obstacle in the path of a woman seeking an abortion before the fetus attains viability." The "compelling interest" standard is used to determine the constitutionality of a state action. Under this standard, the only provision in the *Casey* case that failed the undue burden test was the husband notification requirement.

The Court overruled holdings in prior cases like *Akron* and *Thornburgh* by saying:

> [Pennsylvania's] informed consent provision is not an undue burden on a woman's constitutional right to decide to terminate a pregnancy. To the extent *Akron I* . . . and *Thornburgh* . . . find a constitutional violation when the government requires, as it does here, the giving of truthful, non-misleading information about the nature of the abortion procedure, the attendant health risks and those of childbirth, and the "probable gestational age" of the fetus, those cases are inconsistent with *Roe's* acknowledgment of an important interest in potential life, and are overruled.[23]

Justice O'Connor's opinion went on to provide the following rationale for the Court's judgment:

> Requiring that the woman be informed of the availability of information relating to the consequences to the fetus does not interfere with a constitutional right of privacy between a pregnant woman and her physician, since the doctor-patient relation is derivative of the woman's position, and does not underlie or override the abortion right. Moreover, the physician's First Amendment rights not to speak are implicated only as part of the practice of medicine, which is licensed and regulated by the state. There is no evidence here that requiring a doctor to give the required information would amount to a substantial obstacle to a woman seeking an abortion. The premise behind *Akron I's* invalidation of a waiting period between the provision of the information deemed necessary to informed consent and the performance of an abortion . . . is also wrong. Although [Pennsylvania's] 24-hour waiting period may make some abortions more expensive and less convenient, it cannot be said that it is invalid on the present record and in the context of this facial challenge [to the statute].[24]

---

23. 505 U.S. at 838.
24. *Id.* at 838–39.

Thus, the Court ruled that states could pass laws that imposed waiting periods, required detailed informed consent that could be structured to try to convince a woman to continue her pregnancy, and could express a state policy that abortion was not favored. This type of legislation is known as "viewpoint legislation" and was specifically allowed in the decision.

> The requirement that information be provided about the availability of paternal child support and state-funded alternatives is also related to the state's informed consent interest and furthers the state's interest in preserving unborn life. That such information might create some uncertainty and persuade some women to forgo abortions only demonstrates that it might make a difference and is therefore relevant to a woman's informed choice.[25]

The Court specifically found that the state's "interest in preserving unborn life" was compelling and could be used in opposition to a woman's right to an abortion. Justice Scalia, joined by Chief Justice Rehnquist, Justice White, and Justice Thomas, concluded that a woman's decision to abort her unborn child is not a constitutionally protected "liberty" and would have overruled *Roe*, allowing each state to decide what their laws would be.

The "undue burden" standard sets no clear guidelines. If a woman has to travel 100 miles to a facility and wait two days between the process of consent and the procedure, is that an undue burden? The case offers no way to answer that question, which means each new law must be looked at to see if a majority of the Court feels it creates an undue burden for a pregnant woman.

Where did the "undue burden" idea come from? *Morgan v. Virginia*[26] and *City of Akron v. Akron Center*.[27] The undue burden concept came from civil rights law. In *Morgan*, Virginia law required the separation of "white and colored passengers" on public transportation. Morgan was on an interstate trip from Virginia to Maryland when asked to change seats. She refused and was arrested. The Court found that it would be an "undue burden" for a passenger to have to change seats. "It seems clear to us that seating arrangements for the different races in interstate motor travel require a single uniform rule to promote and protect national travel. Consequently, we hold the Virginia statute in controversy invalid."[28]

---

25. *Id.* at 841.
26. Morgan v. Virginia, 328 U.S. 373 (1946).
27. City of Akron v. Akron Ctr., 462 U.S. 416 (1983).
28. 328 U.S. at 386.

City of Akron addressed a requirement that all abortions after the first trimester be performed in a hospital. The Court there had said:

> By preventing the performance of dilatation-and-evacuation abortions in an appropriate nonhospital setting, Akron has imposed a heavy and unnecessary burden on women's access to a relatively inexpensive, otherwise accessible, and safe abortion procedure. [That requirement] has the effect of inhibiting the vast majority of abortions after the first trimester, and therefore unreasonably infringes upon a woman's constitutional right to obtain an abortion.[29]

VI. *Whole Woman's Health v. Hellerstedt,* 136 S. Ct. 2292 (2016)

The next important challenge to *Roe* came in the Supreme Court's 2015 term. Texas had passed a law requiring physicians who perform abortions to have admitting privileges at a hospital within 30 miles of the clinic, and also required clinics to have facilities that met the standards for ambulatory surgical centers. These requirements would have reduced the 42 clinics in Texas to fewer than nine, with those clinics all being in major metropolitan centers hundreds of miles away from the rural parts of Texas. Texas claimed that the law was necessary to protect the life and health of pregnant women. The plaintiffs argued that the laws did not protect women but instead were designed to restrict access to clinics in a way that unduly burdened the rights of women to seek an abortion. This case was seen as the most significant challenge to *Roe* since *Casey*.

Justice Scalia died February 13, 2016. Thus, there were only eight members on the Court to decide this case. The decision was issued June 27, 2016, on a 5–3 vote striking down the Texas requirements. Justice Breyer wrote the decision, and Justices Alito, Thomas, and Chief Justice Roberts dissented. It was the vote of Justice Kennedy that, along with Justices Ginsburg, Kagan, Sotomayor, and Breyer, decided the case. They held that the Texas law placed a substantial obstacle in the path of women seeking an abortion without any health benefit. Therefore, the law imposed an "undue burden" and violated the Constitution under the *Casey* ruling.

The importance of this case is that it is a clear application of the undue burden standard that could be used to challenge numerous state laws that

---

29. 462 U.S. at 432–39.

impose obstacles to abortion without a medically supportable health or safety rationale.

In 2019, the Court heard argument on the constitutionality of a Louisiana law that was very similar to the Texas statute the Court struck down in *Whole Woman's Health*. The Louisiana decision is *June Medical Services v. Russo*,[30] and the Court ruled the Louisiana law unconstitutional based on the precedent set in *Whole Women's Health*. In a 5 to 4 decision, Chief Justice Roberts sided with the liberal wing of the Court. The Chief Justice had dissented in *Whole Woman's Health* and said in *June* that he had not changed his position but was deferring to past precedent to support the judgment.

Thus, the Chief Justice may be receptive to other TRAP law challenges[31] that could limit *Roe*.

Since the *June* case, the Court's composition has changed drastically. Justice Ginsburg died September 18, 2020, and was swiftly replaced by Justice Barrett on October 27, 2020. There are now six very conservative members and three moderate to liberal members on the Court.

Given the composition of the Court as of 2021, it is unlikely that the Court will expand the undue burden approach. It is more likely that we will see further chipping away at *Roe*, if not an outright overruling of the case.

VII. The "Partial Birth" Cases

Another attempt to limit abortion is to portray specific procedures as gruesome or inhumane. This approach continues the shift away from safety for women to protection for the fetus. Of course, the point of any termination procedure is to terminate the fetus, so these laws are actually an attempt to move closer to personhood for a fetus.

The so-called partial birth cases were decided in 2000 and 2007 and will be reviewed here. The term "partial birth" refers to a form of abortion where the nonviable fetus is extracted intact, then terminated. Because the fetus has not yet reached the point of viability, the term "partial birth" is a fiction that has nothing to do with the actual procedure. Even if delivered intact, the fetus would not be able to breathe on its own or sustain vital bodily functions. Rather than describe an actual procedure, the term was an attempt to stir resentment against this method. The actual medical term

---

30. June Medical Services v. Russo, 514 S. Ct. 2103 (2020).

31. TRAP (Targeted Regulation of Abortion Providers) are laws that restrict abortion providers, typically under the guise of safety regulations, but are not designed for legitimate safety reasons nor do they further such purposes. Their real purpose is simply to make abortions less and less affordable and accessible as a practical matter.

is "dilation and extraction" (or D&X). D&X is a procedure that can be used after 21 weeks' gestation.[32]

In a 1997 policy statement, the American College of Obstetrics and Gynecology said the following regarding the procedure:

> [A]n intact D&X, however, may be the best or most appropriate procedure in a particular circumstance to save the life or preserve the health of a woman, and only the doctor, in consultation with the patient, based upon the woman's particular circumstances can make this decision.[33]

There was significant news and argument about the College's statement at the time.

A. *Stenberg v. Carhart*, 530 U.S. 914 (2000)

The Court was asked to invalidate Nebraska's so-called partial birth abortion ban. Sending a strong message regarding the paramount importance of women's health, the Court struck Nebraska's law down on two independent grounds: the law's failure to include an exception when the women's health was threatened, and the law's language, which encompassed the most common method of second-trimester abortion, placing a substantial obstacle in the path of women seeking abortions and thus imposing an "undue burden" on a woman's access to abortion.

Following the Court's striking down state "partial birth laws," Congress enacted the Partial-Birth Abortion Ban Act of 2003.[34] This law was similar to the state law struck down in *Carhart I*, but it had a section finding that the D&X procedure was unnecessary. Interestingly enough, in 1992, Dr. Mark Haskell presented data showing the procedure was, in certain instances, safer for the woman,[35] but this information was ignored in Congress's findings of fact. The federal law had no exception for the health or safety of a woman.

---

32. *See* http://www.religioustolerance.org/abo_pba1.htm.

33. http://cnsnews.com/news/article/american-college-obstetricians-and-gynecologists
-statement-partial-birth-abortion.

34. Codified at 18 U.S.C. § 1531.

35. Martin Haskell, *Dilation and Extraction for Late Second Trimester Abortion*, presented at the National Abortion Federation Risk Management Seminar (Sept. 13, 1992), http://oper
ationrescue.org/pdfs/NAFpaper091392.pdf.

B. *Gonzales v. Carhart*, 550 U.S. 124 (2007)

Seven years after *Carhart I*, the Court considered the federal ban and essentially overturned its decision in *Stenberg v. Carhart (Carhart I)*, even though the federal ban failed to include an exception to protect women's health and even though D&X could have been found to be a matter to be decided between the patient and her physician.

Writing for the majority, Justice Kennedy said:

> Respect for human life finds an ultimate expression in the bond of love the mother has for her child. The Act recognizes this reality as well. Whether to have an abortion requires a difficult and painful moral decision. . . . While we find no reliable data to measure the phenomenon, it seems unexceptionable to conclude some women come to regret their choice to abort the infant life they once created and sustained. . . . Severe depression and loss of esteem can follow. . . .
>
> In a decision so fraught with emotional consequence some doctors may prefer not to disclose precise details of the means that will be used, confining themselves to the required statement of risks the procedure entails. From one standpoint this ought not to be surprising. Any number of patients facing imminent surgical procedures would prefer not to hear all details, lest the usual anxiety preceding invasive medical procedures become the more intense. This is likely the case with the abortion procedures here in issue. . . .
>
> It is, however, precisely this lack of information concerning the way in which the fetus will be killed that is of legitimate concern to the state. *Casey*, at 873 (plurality opinion) ("States are free to enact laws to provide a reasonable framework for a woman to make a decision that has such profound and lasting meaning"). The State has an interest in ensuring so grave a choice is well informed. It is self-evident that a mother who comes to regret her choice to abort must struggle with grief more anguished and sorrow more profound when she learns, only after the event, what she once did not know: that she allowed a doctor to pierce the skull and vacuum the fast-developing brain of her unborn child, a child assuming the human form.[36]

This language shows clearly Justice Kennedy's (and a majority of the Justices') distaste for abortion. It is exceptional language because judges are supposed to decide only on the facts presented and not show bias. Use of language like "the way in which a fetus will be killed" or speculation not based on any facts in the record, like "While we find no reliable data to

---

36. 550 U.S. at 159–60.

measure the phenomenon, it seems unexceptionable to conclude some women come to regret their choice . . . ," shows a clear bias.

Furthermore, Kennedy wrote that, in the face of "medical uncertainty," lawmakers could overrule a doctor's medical judgment and that the "state's interest in promoting respect for human life at all stages in the pregnancy" could outweigh a woman's interest in protecting her health. This was a dramatic shift that came about because Justice O'Connor had left the Court and was replaced by Justice Alito, thereby shifting the *Carhart I* vote from 5–4 to strike down the state law to a 5–4 vote to uphold the federal law and, by implication, similar state laws.

The decision specifically states that "The Act prohibits intact D&E; and, notwithstanding respondents' arguments, it does not prohibit the D&E procedure in which the fetus is removed in parts."[37] This language is highlighted because, since 2015, some states have been considering laws to ban all D&E procedures.

Carhart II illustrates at least two important issues. First is the use of language. No physician uses the term "partial birth" because the fetus is not yet viable so it cannot be born and live. However, the term resonates and is very useful politically. In the abortion debate, each side uses language designed to evoke strong feelings. "Pro-choice" and "pro-life" are artificial distinctions. An argument over "partial birth abortion" is a political, not a medical, argument. People who oppose the language suggest that this is "partial truth abortion."[38] Clearly, language is being used for political purposes, not for clarity.

Fighting over language is seen frequently in abortion and women's rights cases. For example, in 2011, a debate occurred over a federal law its backers called the "Protect Women" Act, whereas its detractors named it the "Let Women Die" Act. The act was written to allow facilities and providers to refuse to provide services they oppose and to prevent women from purchasing health insurance with abortion coverage. The act did not pass.[39]

Second is the use of repugnance. As described, the D&X procedure is called "gruesome" because it involves extraction of the intact fetus and then termination by causing the skull to collapse. Kansas legislation seeks to use this idea of repugnance to ban most second-trimester procedures by

---

37. *Id.* at 150.

38. Miranda Kennedy, *Partial Truth Abortion Coverage*, FAIR (Mar. 1, 2000), http://fair .org/extra-online-articles/partial-truth-abortion-coverage/.

39. Jodi Jacobson, *House Passes H.R. 358, the "Let Women Die" Act of 2011*, REWIRE NEWS GROUP (Oct. 13, 2011), http://rhrealitycheck.org/article/2011/10/13/house-passes-hr-358 -the-let-women-die-act-of-2011/.

banning any D&C or D&E, which the laws describe as "knowingly dismembering a living unborn child and extracting such unborn child one piece at a time from the uterus." Note the use of "living unborn child" instead of nonviable fetus. In 2015, Kansas law banned "dismemberment abortion."[40]

Thus, laws and case holdings have moved from a focus on protecting the right of a woman to confer with her physician to a focus on preserving unborn life with laws labeling certain procedures unseemly and therefore illegal.[41]

VIII. Current Approaches to Anti-Abortion Legislation

Several states have considered "personhood" laws. Although these laws have not passed in Colorado and North Dakota,[42] discussion continues. At least one state, Tennessee, did pass a personhood law.[43] Other states are considering laws to defund Planned Parenthood facilities, and the proposed 2017 federal budget legislation would have banned Medicare or Title X funding going to Planned Parenthood, even though Planned Parenthood provides health care services to women, and their abortion services are not supported with any federal funding.[44]

Another approach to promote the "rights of fetuses" are laws making the fetus a victim.[45] In Indiana, Purvi Patel was sentenced to 20 years in prison in February 2015 after being convicted of fetal homicide for a miscarriage

---

40. Erik Eckholm & Frances Robles, *Kansas Limits Abortion Method, Opening a New Line of Attack*, N.Y, TIMES (Apr. 7, 2015), http://www.nytimes.com/2015/04/08/us/kansas-bans -common-second-trimester-abortion-procedure.html.

41. A few important articles discussing this trend in the law and how to change the discussion are L. Harris, *Second Trimester Abortion Provision: Breaking the Silence and Changing the Discourse*, 16 REPRO. HEALTH MATTERS 74 (2008); R. Charo, *The Partial Death of Abortion Rights*, 356 NEW ENGL. J. MED. 2125 (2007); R. Stahl & E. Emanuel, *Physicians, Not Conscripts-Conscientious Objection in Health Care*, 376 NEW ENG. J. MED 14 (2017).

42. Zach Schonfeld, *Fetal 'Personhood' Laws Defeated in Colorado and North Dakota*, NEWSWEEK (Nov. 5, 2014, 3:27 PM), http://www.newsweek.com/fetal-personhood-laws-defeated -colorado-and-north-dakota-282545.

43. Erika Eichelberger, *Three States Could Have Ended Legal Abortion. Only One Did,* MOTHER JONES (Nov. 5, 2014), http://www.motherjones.com/mojo/2014/11/abortion -personhood-ballot-initiatives.

44. *See* http://www.vox.com/identities/2017/3/6/14836998/obamacare-repeal-replace -bill-defund-planned-parenthood. For what Planned Parenthood provides, see https://www .plannedparenthood.org/.

45. *See, e.g.,* the federal Unborn Victims of Violence Act of 2004, Pub. L. No. 108-212, making it a crime to cause the death of a fetus. Although abortion is exempted, self-abortion is a crime under some similar state laws.

where the state argued she intended to end the pregnancy.[46] The Indiana Court of Appeals later ruled that the legislature had not "intended the feticide statute to apply to pregnant women," but affirmed her conviction under a less severe provision for "neglect of a dependent" and remanded her case for resentencing under that statute.[47]

Yet another approach is to support so-called crisis pregnancy counseling centers. These centers advertise as if they were abortion providers, but actually they try to talk women out of abortions and do not offer abortion services. These facilities were challenged by California in *National Institute of Family and Life Advocates v. Becerra*, a 2018 decision[48] where Justice Thomas wrote the majority decision. California had enacted a law requiring crisis pregnancy centers to provide full disclosures about services they do and do not provide. The law required that licensed centers post visible notices that abortions are available from state-sponsored clinics. Unlicensed centers were required to tell patrons that they were not licensed to provide medical services. The centers, typically run by Christian nonprofit groups or groups opposed to abortion, said the law violated their free speech rights. In a 5–4 decision, the Court agreed that the notices required by the California law violated the venters' First Amendment right to freedom of speech.

This means that so-called crisis counseling centers that try to counsel pregnant women to continue their pregnancy do not have to disclose that they do not provide information about how to obtain an abortion, even though that is the misleading impression they present to the public and to the women who come to them for assistance.

IX. Who Pays for an Abortion?

Although abortion is legal, there is no legal requirement that any state or federal agency pay for the procedure. In fact, as noted previously, there are laws making it clear that the state or federal government will not pay for an

---

46. Christina Cauterucci, *Court Vacates Purvi Patel's Feticide Conviction, Landing a Blow Against "Personhood" Laws*, SLATE (July 22, 2016), https://slate.com/human-interest/2016/07/court-vacates-purvi-patels-feticide-conviction-in-blow-against-personhood-laws.html. Although her sentence was eventually reduced on appeal, Patel still had to serve 18 months of time on a child neglect charge. *Id.*

47. Patel v. Indiana, Ct. of App., No. 71A04-1504-CR-166, 60 N.E.3d 1041 (2016), https://www.in.gov/judiciary/opinions/pdf/07221601tac.pdf.

48. 138 S. Ct. 2361 (2018).

abortion. (See *Harris v. McRae* earlier in the chapter.) Today, only 17 states provide low-income women funding for abortions.[49]

Title X, a federal law providing funding for facilities that provide for family planning, was amended in 2019 to prohibit Title X grantees from providing or referring patients for abortion except in cases of rape, incest, or medical emergency. As a result, Planned Parenthood has rejected Title X funding. It is estimated that Planned Parenthood serves about 40 percent of the nation's four million Title X recipients and has given up approximately $60 million a year in federal aid.[50]

X. Why the Violent Reaction?

There are a variety of reasons for the ongoing reaction to the legalization of abortion. These include Humane Vitae, a 1968 Papal Encyclical saying sterilization, contraception, and abortion violate Catholic doctrine;[51] political gain (politicians winning votes by being against abortion); the ongoing discussion about the place of women in society; the argument that abortion is murder and therefore contributes to a weakening of society; and the desire to protect the fetus.

These issues are all part of the ongoing societal debate over the legality of abortion. As just one example of the politicization of the issue—and the political hypocrisy of some prominent opponents of abortion—while he was governor of California, Ronald Reagan signed legislation liberalizing abortion law. But when he ran for president, he promised to appoint Supreme Court justices who would reverse *Roe*.

> California Governor Ronald Reagan had signed a bill liberalizing abortion laws in his state, and other states were contemplating similar measures. . . . Quite unanticipated at the time was that the growing Evangelical movement would embrace opposition to abortion as a bedrock principle and drive it into the Republican Party platform, reversing the prior position taken by the

---

49. *Public Funding for Abortion*, ACLU, https://www.aclu.org/public-funding-abortion (last visited Nov. 14, 2020).

50. Planned Parenthood provides educational programs and outreach to 1.2 million people every year and to millions more online through digital sex education programs. https://www.plannedparenthood.org/about-us/who-we-are.

51. http://w2.vatican.va/content/paul-vi/en/encyclicals/documents/hf_p-vi_enc_2507 1968_humanae-vitae.html.

party. And that Ronald Reagan would campaign for president, promising to appoint Supreme Court justices who would reverse *Roe vs. Wade.*[52]

Discussion of these topics is outside the scope of this chapter, but understanding and analysis are critical for future discussion about abortion. So far, there is no common ground in the debate.

XI. Other Supreme Court Activity

Freedom of access to clinic entrances (FACE) cases balance the free speech rights of individuals who wish to protest clinics against the privacy of patients. In general, the courts allow picketing but may place limits on how close picketers can stand to a facility so that patients and staff can have access. Federal legislation also addresses the issue.[53]

In 2014, the Supreme Court, in a 9–0 decision based on free speech, struck down a Massachusetts law that created buffer zones around abortion clinics.[54]

In 2014, the Court was going to hear *Cline v. Oklahoma Coalition for Reproductive Justice,* a case involving an Oklahoma law requiring administration of a medical abortion pursuant to the original FDA guidelines. The argument was that current research demonstrated the guidelines are outdated and too restrictive and therefore the law should be struck down. Ultimately, the Court decided not to hear the case and vacated the writ of certiorari, sending the case back to the lower court.[55] The Center for Reproductive Rights then pursued the case in state court. On August 10, 2015, an Oklahoma judge ruled that the law violated the Oklahoma State Constitution's prohibition against special laws.[56]

The Oklahoma law would have required physicians to conduct medication abortions using the recommendations of the FDA from 2000. Using those guidelines instead of current medical evidence would force a woman to take three times more medication than the American College of Obstetricians and Gynecologists recommends, require additional visits to the clinic, and limit the time for a medical abortion to seven weeks instead of

---

52. Nina Totenberg, *Tape Reveals Nixon's Views on Abortion,* NAT'L PUB. RADIO (June 23, 2009), http://www.npr.org/templates/story/story.php?storyId=105832640.

53. *See* 18 U.S.C. § 248.

54. McCullen v. Coakley, 573 U.S. 464 (2014).

55. Cline v. Oklahoma Coal. for Reprod. Justice, 571 U.S. 985 (2013) (Mem.).

56. https://rewire.news/legislative-tracker/legal-case/oklahoma-coalition-for-reproductive-justice-v-cline/.

nine weeks from conception. Figure 2.2 shows the difference between the
2000 guidelines and the latter approach.

FIGURE 2.2 Comparison of FDA and Evidence-Based Regimens

MEDICATION ABORTION REGIMENS		
	FDA-Approved	**Evidence-based alternatives**
Mifepristone dosage	600 mg	200 mg
Home administration of misoprostol	No	Yes
Number of clinic visits required	Three or more	Two or more
Gestational limit	Up to 49 days (seven weeks of pregnancy)	Up to 63 days (nine weeks of pregnancy)

Although the Oklahoma Supreme Court held the law unconstitutional
for technical reasons, it is clear that the law would have interfered with the
doctor-patient relationship, ignored existing law allowing physicians to prescribe "off label," and subjected women to an increased risk.[57]

XII. What Do We Know About Abortion?

One in four women of child-bearing age in the United States[58] will have an
abortion, but very few will talk about it. This silence helps to create a culture of shame and stigma.[59] Half of American pregnancies are unintended
and four in ten of those end in abortion. Approximately 862,000 abortions were performed in 2017, down 7 percent from 926,000 in 2014.[60]
Factors contributing to the decline in reported abortions likely include

---

57. Heather D. Boonstra, *Medication Abortion Restrictions Burden Women and Providers—
and Threaten U.S. Trend toward Very Early Abortion*, GUTTMACHER INSTITUTE (Mar. 19, 2013),
https://www.guttmacher.org/pubs/gpr/16/1/gpr160118.html.

58. *Induced Abortion in the United States*, GUTTMACHER INSTITUTE (Sept. 2019), https://
www.guttmacher.org/fact-sheet/induced-abortion-united-states.

59. Lisa Harris, *Stigma and Abortion Complications in the United States*, 120 OBST. & GYN. 1472
(2015), http://journals.lww.com/greenjournal/Fulltext/2012/12000/Stigma_and_Abortion
_Complications_in_the_United.30.aspx.

60. *Induced Abortion in the United States*, *supra* note 58.

improvements in contraceptive use and increases in the number of individuals relying on self-managed abortions outside of a clinical setting.[61]

Abortion as a medical procedure is extremely safe. Data from 1985–2005 showed that "[l]egal induced abortion is markedly safer than childbirth. The risk of death associated with childbirth is approximately 14 times higher than that with abortion. Similarly, the overall morbidity associated with childbirth exceeds that with abortion."[62]

The topic of abortion is one that divides society into pro- and anti-camps rather than allowing a woman and her physician to make medical decisions free of societal oversight.

A key issue in the debate is the question: who is the patient? If the patient is the woman, then the focus of health care can be on her. If the patient is the fetus, then the woman is relevant only as a way to nourish the fetus until delivery. If both are the patient, then the provider ought to try to provide care for both. Of course, in a termination, the goal is to end the pregnancy so the fetus cannot be seen as a patient with rights. As Justice Blackmun said in *Roe*: "[T]he unborn have never been recognized in the law as persons in the whole sense."[63] Justice Blackmun's discussion of the fetus as a person is a basis for the personhood law approach being seen today in various states. If a fetus is a person, then abortion would be murder under that argument.

XIII. State Activities

Because *Roe* allows each state to make its own laws so long as they do not overtly prohibit abortion, there is now an extremely large patchwork of legislation, with new laws being proposed and passed frequently. In many cases, there are then legal challenges to those laws and years of litigation follow. This chapter cannot list the laws and litigation in each state because they are changing so quickly. Instead, it will point out trends and focus on a few examples. For current details on the laws of each state, the reader is directed to the Guttmacher Institute. The goal of the Institute is to provide

---

61. Rachel K. Jones, Elizabeth Witwer & Jenna Jerman, *Abortion Incidence and Service Availability in the United States, 2017*, GUTTMACHER INSTITUTE (Sept. 2019), https://www.guttmacher.org/report/abortion-incidence-service-availability-us-2017.

62. Elizabeth G. Raymond & David A. Grimes, *The Comparative Safety of Legal Induced Abortion and Childbirth in the United States*, 119 OBST. GYN. 215 (2012), http://www.ncbi.nlm.nih.gov/pubmed/22270271. The actual numbers were 8.8 deaths per 100,000 live births and 0.6 deaths per 100,000 abortions.

63. 410 U.S. at 162.

research, policy analysis, and data about reproductive health. It has up-to-date information on state laws and trends about abortion and other reproductive issues.[64]

Just as one state example, in March 2016, then-Governor Pence of Indiana signed HEA 1337, which contained provisions designed to prevent women from accessing abortions. It forced women to have an ultrasound at least 18 hours before an abortion; banned abortions when a fetal anomaly was detected; mandated the burial and cremation of miscarried or aborted remains; restricted fetal tissue donation; and required doctors performing abortions to have admitting privileges at a hospital or to have an agreement with a doctor who does.

On March 31, 2017, U.S. District Judge Tanya Walton Pratt ruled that the requirement that women have an ultrasound appeared to create an "undue burden" on their right of access to an abortion, particularly for low-income women.[65] Based on that conclusion, she granted a preliminary injunction against the provision pending a trial and final ruling.

In 2018 and 2019, states passed or tried to pass hundreds of laws to restrict or even prohibit abortion. For example, the Michigan legislature passed a law saying telemedicine could not be used for medical abortions, but Governor Snyder vetoed that bill.[66] In November 2018, Ohio passed a fetal heartbeat law saying abortion was not allowed once a fetal heartbeat could be detected. A heartbeat can be detected as soon as six weeks into a pregnancy, which is well before viability and before many women even know they are pregnant.[67]

The Ohio law is clearly unconstitutional under *Roe* and is plainly intended as a challenge to *Roe.* A similar Georgia law was struck down on July 13, 2020.[68]

---

64. *See* https://www.guttmacher.org/state-policy/explore/overview-abortion-laws. Another current source is RH-Reality Check for topical articles about pending laws and litigation. https://rewirenewsgroup.com/primary-topic/abortion/.

65. https://ecf.insd.uscourts.gov/cgi-bin/show_public_doc?12016cv1807-42.

66. https://mhealthintelligence.com/news/michigan-governor-vetoes-extension-of-tele medicine-abortion-ban.

67. https://www.nytimes.com/2018/11/16/health/ohio-abortion-ban-heartbeat-bill .html.

68. https://www.fox5atlanta.com/news/judge-permanently-blocks-georgias-heartbeat -abortion-law.

XIV. Where Do These State Laws Come From?

An important source is Americans United for Life, who describe themselves as the "legal architects of the pro-life movement."[69] This organization publishes and sends to the states a yearly briefing book suggesting language for bills. AUL Model Legislation and Legislative Guides are available online.[70] The site also provides an annual legislative report.[71]

There has been a dramatic shift in how *Roe* has been attacked. Originally, the idea was to stop demand for abortion by "educating women" on why they should not have an abortion (counseling, waiting periods, viewing ultrasounds and pictures of fetuses, telling woman that abortion carried risks like an increased risk of breast cancer, etc.). These approaches did not result in any change in demand.

The shift was then to approaches that would decrease availability and access using a factually disingenuous theory of patient safety (physician must have staff privileges at a hospital within 30 miles, license facility as ambulatory facility, use the FDA "guidelines" for medical abortion, no telemedicine, no state funding for Planned Parenthood facilities, etc.) with the goal of eliminating access to facilities in the state. This was coupled with laws to increase the cost of any procedure by requiring disposal of fetal remains by burial or cremation, counseling about coercion, mandatory ultrasounds, face-to-face meetings with the physician, long waiting periods, and so on. At clinics, there is also demonization of abortion providers by calling them "abortion doctors" instead of "board certified obstetricians" and by picketing of clinics. At least 11 persons who were abortion providers or connected to abortion providers have been assassinated in the United States by "pro-life" advocates—including members of the underground "Army of God"—and the threat of further assassinations is ever present as names and home addresses of providers are distributed on the Internet by anti-choice groups. The Department of Justice considers anti-abortion extremists domestic terrorists.[72]

---

69. *AUL Welcomes Prominent Attorney and Pro-Life Advocate Ovide Lamontagne as General Counsel*, AMERICANS UNITED FOR LIFE (Apr. 17, 2013), https://aul.org/2013/04/17/aul-welcomes-prominent-attorney-and-pro-life-advocate-ovide-lamontagne-as-general-counsel/.

70. https://aul.org/what-we-do/legislation/ (last visited Nov. 14, 2020).

71. *2020 State Legislative Sessions Report: Annual Report on Government Affairs from America's Leader in Life-Affirming Law and Policy*, AMERICANS UNITED FOR LIFE https://aul.org/wp-content/uploads/2020/10/2020-State-Legislative-Sessions-Report.pdf (last visited Nov. 14, 2020).

72. *Anti-Abortion Violence*, WIKIPEDIA, https://en.wikipedia.org/wiki/Anti-abortion_violence#Murders (last visited Nov. 14, 2020).

XV. What Are Some Current Controversies and Litigation?

A. Federal Activity

The House of Representatives proposed a 20-week ban on abortion, which was stopped in January 2015 by women Republicans who felt the proposed ban needed a stronger exception for rape. Instead of the 20-week ban, Congress passed a bill forbidding any use of federal funding for abortion,[73] expanding the prohibition upheld in *Harris v. McRae*. Among other things, this bill would mean that women in the military do not have health coverage for, or on-base access to, abortions.

In January 2015, Sen. David Vitter (R-La.) introduced four bills in Congress that would bar Planned Parenthood from receiving federal family planning funds; require all abortion providers to have admitting privileges at a local hospital; ban abortions performed on the basis of gender; and allow hospitals, doctors, and nurses to refuse to provide or participate in abortion care for women, even in cases of an emergency. This approach is consistent with a current theme of legislative attacks: forbid any use of federal funding for abortion, expand conscience clause legislation, and seek ways to close existing facilities.[74]

B. State Activity

For women who seek to find a way to end their pregnancies, it has become increasingly clear that they may face prosecution and incarceration. As noted earlier, the state of Indiana convicted Purvi Patel of feticide for allegedly attempting to terminate her own pregnancy with medication. Increasingly, pregnant women—whether seeking to end a pregnancy or go to

---

73. *H.R.7—No Taxpayer Funding for Abortion and Abortion Insurance Full Disclosure Act of 2015*, Congress.Gov, https://www.congress.gov/bill/114th-congress/house-bill/7 (last visited Nov. 14, 2020).

74. Laura Bassett, *Republicans Introduce Five Anti-Abortion Bills in First Days of New Congress*, HuffPost (Jan. 15, 2015), https://www.huffpost.com/entry/republicans-abortion_n_6438522?guccounter=1&guce_referrer=aHR0cHM6Ly9zZWFyY2gueWFob28uY29tLw&g uce_referrer_sig=AQAAAK4OREG5TPFQ3r1aFcS_NZzRw5QQryRFc7qExgbpbpdNcJRoAC m9SiJTTDr2R1A2CBJfde4lKbJad_bn8xHQUgVqYDeDBIxM4N0U0e6zOPTSWmH3jJJo VNDciQd4wEWtDyjnLvQm264CKlVH_TRUbYcwGve56YaGv2-fDc9e3Zvq.

term—are finding that their rights and their own personhood are under attack.[75]

In Wisconsin, Tamara Loertscher is challenging Wisconsin's "cocaine mom" law, which is being used to prosecute pregnant women who use illegal drugs during pregnancy, whether or not their baby is injured.[76]

In New York, Rinat Drey sued based on a forced C-section where her doctor ignored her refusal to have surgery and performed a C-section over her express objection in order to give the fetus what he thought was the best chance for a good life. During the course of the procedure, he damaged Drey's bladder, and she asserted malpractice and lack of informed consent. The case shows the "two-patient" problem. Here, a doctor decided the fetus needed protection from its competent mother and therefore ignored her personhood and her legal right to refuse a surgical procedure. The starkness of the physician's decision can be seen in his note, which reads: "The woman has decisional capacity. I have decided to override her refusal to have a C-section."[77] On April 4, 2018, a mid-level New York appeals court ruled against Drey. The court wrote that "the state interest in the well-being of a viable fetus is sufficient to override a mother's objection to medical treatment, at least where there is a viable full-term fetus and the intervention presents no serious risk to the mother's well-being."[78]

As an overview of state activity, there are several different theories being used in anti-abortion laws:

First is the idea of personhood. In *Doe*, Justice Blackmun said if the fetus were a person under the Constitution, a state prohibition against abortion would be legal. Since then, there have been attempts to pass personhood laws or create personhood indirectly by laws like fetal pain, violence against fetuses, fetal heartbeat laws, and other laws providing protection to a fetus equal to child abuse and neglect laws that provide protection to born children.

Second is the idea of laws designed under the guise of protecting the safety of women. Many anti-abortion laws are written to say that they are

---

75. *See* NATIONAL ADVOCATES FOR PREGNANT WOMEN, http://www.advocatesforpregnant women.org/ (last visited Nov. 14, 2020).

76. Bruce Vielmetti, *Pregnant Woman Challenging Wisconsin Protective Custody Law*, MILWAUKEE J. SENTINEL (Jan. 2, 2015), http://archive.jsonline.com/news/wisconsin/pregnant-woman-challenging-wisconsin-protective-custody-law-b99411705z1-287395241.html.

77. *Forcing Pregnant Women to Have Cesarean Surgery Is Never Justified*, NAT'L ADVOCATES FOR PREGNANT WOMEN (May 28, 2014).

78. Dray v. Staten Island Univ. Hosp., Case No. 2015-12064 & 12068 (N.Y. Sup. Ct. App Div. Apr. 4, 2018), http://www.courts.state.ny.us/courts/ad2/Handdowns/2018/Decisions /D54973.pdf.

necessary to protect women and keep them safe but are not based on medical facts. These are the so-called Targeted Regulation of Abortion Providers (TRAP) laws.[79] Their actual approach is to make it more expensive or difficult to run clinics in the name of patient safety. For example, some state laws force any physician working in a clinic to have staff privileges at a hospital within 30 miles of the clinic. If the hospital refuses to grant privileges, then the clinic would be unable to function. The argument is that any patient at a clinic could need hospital backup. The main problem with this argument is that abortion is an extremely safe procedure, and if any patient needs to go to a hospital, treatment would be provided both by the ethical duty of providers and by the legal command of the Emergency Treatment and Active Labor Act, which requires a hospital to see them.[80]

Several laws require abortion facilities to follow the same facility construction requirements as ambulatory surgery centers. This means spending thousands of dollars to widen hallways, to change procedure rooms into surgical suites, and to make electrical and other changes, even though these levels of protection are not necessary for the procedures performed.[81]

Other laws are designed to force women to have second-trimester termination in a hospital, thereby substantially increasing the expense, or to require a patient to drive to a facility instead of using telemedicine for a medical abortion.

Laws about informed consent are based on the idea that a woman must be informed before she can decide to terminate her pregnancy. In other medical contexts, informed consent laws are designed to provide relevant truthful and medically accurate information so a patient can make an informed choice. But for abortion, states pass laws with mandatory waiting periods, or laws that tell women things that are not medically correct in an attempt to increase costs or change a woman's decision. In some cases, laws require a physician to tell a patient that abortion has an increased risk of

---

79. *Targeted Regulation of Abortion Providers (TRAP) Laws*, GUTTMACHER INSTITUTE (Jan. 2020), https://www.guttmacher.org/evidence-you-can-use/targeted-regulation-abortion-providers-trap-laws.

80. The Emergency Medical Treatment and Labor Act (EMTALA) is a federal law that requires anyone coming to an emergency department to be stabilized and treated, regardless of their insurance status or ability to pay. 42 U.S.C. § 1395dd.

81. Heather D. Boonstra & Elizabeth Nash, *A Surge of State Abortion Restrictions Puts Providers—and the Women They Serve—in the Crosshairs*, GUTTMACHER INSTITUTE (Mar. 1, 2014), https://www.guttmacher.org/gpr/2014/03/surge-state-abortion-restrictions-puts-providers-and-women-they-serve-crosshairs.

breast cancer, or that it can cause depression, or that abortion increases the rate of suicide.[82] None of these assertions are medically factual.

In Arkansas and Arizona, 2015 laws entitled "The Women's Right to Know Regarding Abortion" require doctors to tell patients that a chemical abortion may be reversed. In reviewing the science to support this law, RH-Reality Check found no credible evidence to support the claim that progesterone could reverse a medical abortion.[83]

Interestingly, a recent study by Ibis Reproductive Health and the Center for Reproductive Rights reviewed extensive evidence and prior studies and found that states with the most "safety for women" laws actually have the worst record of safety as measured by maternal mortality and morbidity.[84] As the Center summed up the findings: "States with the highest number of abortion restrictions have the poorest health outcomes and the least supportive policies for women and children."[85]

Third is the notion that taxpayer funds should never be used for abortion. On the federal level, there is the Hyde Amendment that prohibits use of federal funds for abortion.

On the state level, there are laws like Arkansas', which seek to prevent "the abortion industry from building their profit margins at the expense of taxpayers."[86] Note the use of language like "abortion industry," "profit margin," and "abortion doctors" instead of "board certified obstetricians."

Fourth is conscience clause legislation, which allows licensed health care professionals and other health care workers to refuse to be trained in or to provide any services where they have a moral objection. These services are typically abortion, contraception, or sterilization, but recent Supreme

---

82. Jessica Mason Pieklo, *When Lying to Women Is Mandated Care: Informed Consent, Abortion, and the Role Played by Justice Kennedy*, REWIRE NEWS GROUP (July 25, 2012), http://rhrealitycheck.org/article/2012/07/25/when-lying-to-women-is-mandated-care-informed-consent-and-abortion/.

83. *Id.*

84. Terri-Ann Thompson & Jane Seymour, *Measuring Women's and Children's Health and Well-being against Abortion Restrictions in the States: 2017 Research Report*, CTR. FOR REPROD. RIGHTS & IBIS REPRODUCTIVE HEALTH (Nov. 15, 2020, 12:49 AM), *available at* http://www.reproductiverights.org/sites/default/files/documents/USPA-Ibis-Evaluating-Priorities-v2.pdf.

85. *New Report Debunks Politicians' Disingenuous Claims about Protecting Women's Health and Safety in Passing Abortion Restrictions*, CTR. FOR REPROD. RIGHTS (Oct. 1, 2014), http://www.reproductiverights.org/press-room/new-report-debunks-politicians-claims-about-protecting-womens-health-safety-with-abortion-restrictions.

86. *Arkansas Uses AUL-Based Language to Protect Taxpayers from Funding Abortion*, Americans, UNITED FOR LIFE (Apr. 7, 2015), http://www.aul.org/2015/04/arkansas-uses-aul-based-language-to-protect-taxpayers-from-funding-abortion/.

Court activity (*Hobby Lobby*) and state activity around Religious Freedom Reformation Acts have tried to broaden the area where an individual can refuse to perform a service.[87]

Fifth are laws prohibiting the use of a specific technique. For instance, Iowa and initially Michigan forbid the use of telemedicine for a medical abortion. Michigan law now allows this. Some states have tried to force providers to do medical abortions as originally approved by the FDA, thereby ignoring recent research showing it is safe to use less medication. This is especially disingenuous in states that say they are passing laws for the safety of women because, in this case, the law would mandate a less safe procedure.

Sixth are laws mandating increased parental involvement so that minors cannot obtain an abortion or contraception without parental notice or consent. This ignores Supreme Court cases discussed previously that say that a minor can seek a judicial bypass.

Seventh are laws seeking to bar specific procedures on the grounds that they are gruesome. The "partial birth" cases are discussed earlier in the chapter.

To provide a further flavor of what states are doing, this section will review current Virginia law because it includes several different elements, ranging from laws designed to cause a woman to change her mind about an abortion to laws making it more expensive to obtain an abortion to laws designed to eliminate access to an abortion to laws requiring a medically un-necessary invasive "fetal trans-abdominal ultrasound."

Virginia laws, found in the Virginia Code at 18.2-71 to 76.2, include section 18.2-71, which makes any abortion a felony. This law was passed in 1950 and is unenforceable because of the *Roe v. Wade* decision. It would be effective, except as amended, if *Roe* were to be overturned.

Also included in Virginia law is section 18.2-71.1, which was enacted in 2003. It outlaws any "partial birth" procedure. The actual language is:

A. Any person who knowingly performs partial birth infanticide and thereby kills a human infant is guilty of a Class 4 felony.

B. For the purposes of this section, "partial birth infanticide" means any deliberate act that (i) is intended to kill a human infant who has been born alive, but who has not been completely extracted or expelled from its mother, and that (ii) does kill such infant, regardless of whether death occurs before or after extraction or expulsion from its mother has been completed.

---

87. Burwell v. Hobby Lobby, 573 U.S. 682 (2014).

The term "partial birth infanticide" shall not under any circumstances be construed to include any of the following procedures: (i) the suction curettage abortion procedure, (ii) the suction aspiration abortion procedure, (iii) the dilation and evacuation abortion procedure involving dismemberment of the fetus prior to removal from the body of the mother, or (iv) completing delivery of a living human infant and severing the umbilical cord of any infant who has been completely delivered.

C. For the purposes of this section, "human infant who has been born alive" means a product of human conception that has been completely or substantially expelled or extracted from its mother, regardless of the duration of pregnancy, which after such expulsion or extraction breathes or shows any other evidence of life such as beating of the heart, pulsation of the umbilical cord, or definite movement of voluntary muscles, whether or not the umbilical cord has been cut or the placenta is attached.

D. For purposes of this section, "substantially expelled or extracted from its mother" means, in the case of a headfirst presentation, the infant's entire head is outside the body of the mother, or, in the case of breech presentation, any part of the infant's trunk past the navel is outside the body of the mother.

E. This section shall not prohibit the use by a physician of any procedure that, in reasonable medical judgment, is necessary to prevent the death of the mother, so long as the physician takes every medically reasonable step, consistent with such procedure, to preserve the life and health of the infant. A procedure shall not be deemed necessary to prevent the death of the mother if completing the delivery of the living infant would prevent the death of the mother.

F. The mother may not be prosecuted for any criminal offense based on the performance of any act or procedure by a physician in violation of this section.

Note the use of terms like "infanticide" and the idea that a pre-viable fetus could live independent of its mother.

Virginia Code section 18.2-72, enacted in 2020, allows first trimester abortions performed by a physician or licensed nurse practitioner.

Compare this to California's 2013 law, which allows not just physicians but nurse practitioners, certified nurse-midwives, and physicians' assistants who complete specified training to perform abortions.[88]

Virginia Code section 18.2-73 says that any second-trimester abortion is lawful only if conducted by a physician in a licensed hospital. This law adds

---

88. CAL. HEALTH & SAFETY CODE § 123468 & CAL. BUS. & PROF. CODE § 2253.

to the costs of the procedure and, if challenged, would therefore need to be reviewed under the "undue burden" standard established in *Casey*.

Virginia Code section 18.2-74 covers third-trimester abortions, which are only legal if performed in a hospital with three physicians agreeing in writing that "continuation of the pregnancy is likely to result in the death of the woman or substantially and irremediably impair the mental or physical health of the woman." If the fetus shows any signs of viability, life support must be provided.

The Virginia Board of Health, in 2013, set forth rules that would make any clinic offering termination procedures follow the same rules as ambulatory surgical facilities. These rules and a litany of the other restrictive statutes and regulations were challenged, some successfully and others not.[89] The litigation is still going on as this treatise goes to press.

Although the Virginia laws include several different approaches, there are other proposed and existing laws for model anti-abortion laws that a state could pass.[90] The Guttmacher Institute points out the dramatic rise in abortion restriction laws in Figure 2.3.

---

89. Falls Church Medical Center, LLC v. Oliver, 412 F. Supp. 3d 668 (E.D. Va. 2019). The trial court ruled as follows: (1) surgical-center requirements governing abortion facilities posed a significant burden on the right of women to choose and served no valid state interest with respect to first-trimester procedures; (2) evidence of progressively increasing risks of complications during surgical second-trimester abortion procedures precluded a finding that the addition of safeguards of surgical-center guidelines were unduly burdensome in that context; (3) hospital-specific regulations governing record keeping, minimum staffing, and employment of only physicians licensed in Virginia were not unduly burdensome to women seeking abortions in Virginia; (4) requirement that second-trimester nonsurgical abortion procedures be performed in facilities qualifying as surgical hospitals was unduly burdensome; (5) physician-only law was valid, even as applied to first-trimester abortion procedures; (6) plaintiffs failed to satisfactorily demonstrate that Virginia's ultrasound requirement and 24-hour waiting period placed an undue burden on abortion access; and (7) plaintiffs failed to establish that consent to unannounced inspections of abortion clinics was involuntary so that a Fourth Amendment violation might have occurred.

90. *Legislation*, AMERICANS UNITED FOR LIFE, https://aul.org/what-we-do/legislation/ (last visited Nov. 15, 2020). *See also* Morgan Brinlee, *This Group You've Never Heard of Has Been Pushing TRAP Laws since before Roe V. Wade*, BUSTLE (Jan. 22, 2018), https://www.bustle.com/p /how-americans-united-for-life-has-been-pushing-trap-laws-since-before-roe-v-wade-7968168.

FIGURE 2.3 Restrictive Laws Enacted

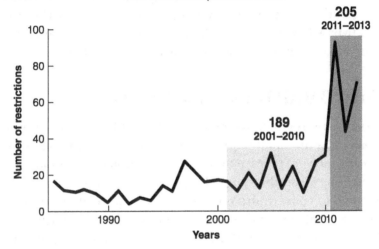

A WAVE OF RESTRICTIONS
More state abortion restrictions were enacted in 2011–2013
than in the entire previous decade

As another example of recent state activity, Alabama requires a minor who wants an abortion to have permission from a parent, and a law enacted in 2014 provides a judicial bypass alternative for minors who do not provide judicial consent.[91] Judicial bypass is meant to be swift, nonconfrontational, and strictly confidential, but that is not the case in Alabama as the law sets up procedures that will often be time-consuming, burdensome, and oppressive.

The law requires district attorneys to represent the interests of the state in opposition to the minor's bypass petition, and the district attorneys are authorized to cross-examine the minor and witnesses called on behalf of the minor, as well as call and examine other witnesses. The law also authorizes the judge to assign an attorney as a guardian ad litem to represent the fetus, though it is unclear how those lawyers will determine what their clients wish the lawyers to do. The law grants the fetus's guardian "the same rights and obligations of participation in the proceeding as given to the district attorney's office."[92] Moreover, the fetus's representative is required to "assist[] and advis[e] the court."[93]

---

91. ALA. CODE § 26-21-4.
92. *Id.* § 26-21-4 (j).
93. *Id.*

A judge can adjourn bypass hearings for long periods of time and can disclose the minor's identity to any person who "needs to know." If a minor's parents become aware of a bypass hearing—which the Supreme Court intended to be confidential—the law allows the parents to participate in the hearing and be represented by a lawyer. A U.S. District Court enjoined Alabama's bypass law because of these deficiencies.[94] Alabama responded by enacting an even more restrictive abortion law in 2019.[95]

XVI. State TRAP Laws in the Courts

TRAP laws impose regulations on abortion providers—but not other medical professionals—in an attempt to drive doctors out of practice and make abortion care more expensive and difficult to obtain. Common TRAP regulations include those that limit the provision of care only to physicians; force practices to convert into mini-hospitals; require abortion providers to get admitting privileges; and require facilities to have a transfer agreement with a local hospital, with nothing requiring hospitals to grant such privileges, thereby granting a de facto veto over qualified and willing abortion providers. In many states, abortion care is limited to hospitals or other specialized facilities, rather than physicians' offices. Anti-choice supporters of TRAP laws contend that these are necessary requirements to ensure patient health and safety. However, peer-reviewed literature shows that legal abortion is an extremely safe procedure.[96]

Although some TRAP laws have been found legally unenforceable, many TRAP laws have gone into effect and caused clinic closures or significant costs to renovate clinics into outpatient surgery centers in several states, severely limiting access to safe and legal abortion care for millions of women.[97]

---

94. Reproductive Health Services v. Marshall, 268 F. Supp. 3d 1261 (M.D. Ala. 2017).

95. *Alabama Abortion Laws*, FindLaw (May 16, 2019), https://statelaws.findlaw.com/alabama-law/alabama-abortion-laws.html.

96. Nathalie Kapp et al., *A Review of Evidence for Safe Abortion Care*, 88 Contraception 350 (2013), http://www.ncbi.nlm.nih.gov/pubmed/23261233.

97. *Targeted Regulation of Abortion Providers (Trap)*, Ctr. for Reprod. Rights (Aug. 28, 2015), http://www.reproductiverights.org/project/targeted-regulation-of-abortion-providers-trap.

A. Recent State Activity and Status: Data from the Guttmacher Institute

- Forty-four states and the District of Columbia have subjected abortion providers to restrictions not imposed on other medical professionals: AL, AK, AZ, AR, CA, CT, DE, DC, FL, GA, HI, ID, IL, IN, IA, KS, KY, LA, ME, MD, MA, MI, MN, MS, MO, NE, NV, NJ, NM, NY, NC, ND, OH, OK, PA, RI, SC, SD, TN, TX, UT, VA, WA, WI, WY.
- All of these states prohibit some qualified health care professionals from providing abortion care.
- Only six states and the District of Columbia have expanded the scope of practice of advanced-practice clinicians to include medical and/or surgical abortion services: CA, CT, DC, IL, NY, RI, WA.
- Twenty-six states have restricted the provision of abortion care—often even in the early stages of pregnancy—to hospitals or other specialized facilities: AK, AR, CT, GA, ID, IN, MA, MN, MS, MO, NV, NJ, NY, NC, ND, OH, OK, PA, RI, SC, SD, TN, TX, UT, VA, WI.
- Nineteen such laws have been found to be at least partially unenforceable: AL, AK, AZ, ID, IL, IN, KS, LA, MA, MS, MO, NY, ND, OH, OK, PA, TN, TX, WI.
- Four states enacted measures that require clinicians to be board-certified Ob-Gyns or eligible for certification: AR, LA, MS, SC.

B. Some Specific State Information

Some of the laws noted here, or parts of these laws, have been enjoined by a court. But they are still very informative for several reasons. Most importantly, they remain on the books, and it may be that they will be enforceable at some time in the future if *Roe* is further restricted, or reversed, limiting challenges to claims based on state constitutions. They also provide an indication of the kinds of restrictions that are likely to be passed by some other states if *Roe* is further restricted.

Texas requires admitting privileges and mandates doctors' offices to meet the standards of ambulatory surgical centers, including an array of rules that govern hallway widths, the presence of showers and lockers, and heating and cooling specifications. The rules also require conformance with other construction codes that can have significant costs. *Whole Women's Health v. Hellerstedt* held the Texas law had no compelling basis and was an undue burden on women and therefore was unconstitutional.[98] Louisiana then passed a very similar law, which was immediately challenged. In *June Medical Services v. Russo*,[99] the Louisiana law was held unconstitutional because it mirrored the law in *Hellerstedt*. Although he dissented in *Hellerstedt*, Chief Justice Roberts wrote a separate concurring opinion in *June* in which he explained that his vote to support the Court's majority ruling was based on deference to precedent. Because the Louisiana law was for all practical purposes the same as the Texas law, he believed it should be invalidated because of the *Hellerstedt* decision. Of course, this does not mean the Chief Justice has changed his opinion about abortion; it simply means that he was not willing to ignore valid precedent without a compelling reason. However, he would be receptive to other TRAP cases.

Indiana's federal district court ruled that a 2013 Indiana law mandating all abortion clinics meet the same architectural requirements as stand-alone surgical clinics is unconstitutional. Why? The law allows the state to arbitrarily divide medication abortion providers into two groups, "abortion clinics" and "physician's offices," and to treat those groups differently without a rational basis for doing so. Indiana required only "abortion clinics," and not "physician's offices," meet the surgical center requirements at issue.[100]

This ruling came on the heels of court decisions striking down laws in Alabama, Louisiana, Mississippi, Oklahoma, and Texas.

Alabama's regulation that doctors must have admitting privileges was overturned in a 172-page opinion.[101]

Louisiana requires that hospital admitting privileges are required for providers and any provider of five or more first-trimester surgical abortion procedures per month, and any provider of even one second-trimester abortion, including private physicians, must be classified as an "outpatient abortion facility." The abortion facility must comply with a uniquely imposed licensure scheme not required of other medical providers. Hospitals and ambulatory surgical centers are exempted.[102]

Mississippi requires administrative, professional qualifications, and admitting privileges, and requires that abortion services after the first

---

98. 136 S. Ct. 2292 (2016).

99. June Medical Services v. Russo, 514 S. Ct. 2103 (2020).

100. Planned Parenthood of Ind. & Ky., Inc. v. Comm'r, 194 F. Supp. 3d 818 (S.D. Ind. 2016), *aff'd*, 888 F.3d 300 (7th Cir. 2018), *rev'd in part on other grounds sub nom.* Box v. Planned Parenthood of Ind. & Ky., Inc. v. Comm'r, 139 S. Ct. 1780 (2019).

101. Planned Parenthood Se, Inc. v. Strange, 33 F. Supp. 3d 1330 (M.D. Ala. 2014).

102. June Medical Services LLC v. Kliebert, 158 F. Supp. 3d 473 (M.D. La. 2016), *rev'd*, 905 F.3d 787 (5th Cir. 2018), *rev'd*, 140 S. Ct. 2103 (2020).

trimester be provided in an ambulatory surgical facility, a hospital, or in a facility that has met the standards for an ambulatory surgical facility.[103] The court rejected the state's argument that the undue burden test could be met by showing that there were available facilities in an adjacent state, even though relatively nearby. A later Mississippi statute that prohibited abortions after 15 weeks' gestation, except in a medical emergency or in case of severe fetal abnormality (a "heartbeat" statute), was invalidated in 2018.[104]

Oklahoma's criminal bans on abortion, required counseling, and mandatory delays between the consent process and a procedure were temporarily enjoined by the Oklahoma Supreme Court in 2014 pending a full trial on the merits of plaintiffs' constitutional claims.[105] The Oklahoma trial court then upheld the statute, but the state Supreme Court again reversed the lower court and held the admitting privileges requirement was an unconstitutional undue burden. The Supreme Court also struck the remainder of the bill because it violated the Oklahoma constitutional prohibition against legislation having multiple subjects.[106] Oklahoma also has a choose life license plate program.

Michigan law banned the use of telemedicine for medical abortions. Why? If abortion can be done more privately, it is harder to protest and less burdensome on women. As indicated earlier, the legislature tried to extend this ban in a lame duck session, but the law was vetoed in December 2018 by then-Governor Richard Snyder.

State abortion laws are an ever-changing legal mosaic in the United States. Fortunately, there are several sources that maintain current information on the laws throughout the country.[107]

XVII. Criminal Prosecution of Pregnant Women

The National Advocates for Pregnant Women (NAPW) assists pregnant women charged with crimes against their fetuses.[108] NAPW cases include

---

103. Jackson Women's Health Org. v. Currier, 760 F.3d 448 (5th Cir. 2014).

104. Jackson Women's Health Org. v. Currier, 349 F. Supp. 3d 536 (S.D. Miss. 2018).

105. Burns v. Cline, 339 P.3d 887 (Okla. 2014).

106. Burns v. Cline, 387 P.3d 348 (Okla. 2016).

107. U.S. Supreme Court—http://www.scotusblog.com/; state laws—http://www.findlaw.com/; NARAL—http://www.prochoiceamerica.org/government-and-you/state-governments/state-profiles/oklahoma.html; Guttmacher Institute—http://www.guttmacher.org/statecenter/spibs/spib_TRAP.pdf; law professors Reproductive Justice Blog—http://lawprofessors.typepad.com/reproductive_rights/; Americans United for Life—http://www.aul.org/.

108. *See* https://www.nationaladvocatesforpregnantwomen.org/about-us/.

women charged with fetal homicide, fetal child abuse, reckless endangerment through the use of controlled (including prescribed) substances, and
self-abortion.

A few examples of criminal cases against pregnant women follow. Many
others are described on NAPW's website.[109]

1.   **Wisconsin:** *Loertscher.* NAPW and others filed a civil rights lawsuit in
     federal court on behalf of Tamara Loertscher against the Wisconsin
     Department of Children and Families and the Wisconsin Attorney
     General. The suit challenged a Wisconsin law that allows the state to
     seize control of women, detain them in jail or locked facilities, and
     subject them to numerous other deprivations of their civil rights if
     they are pregnant and use—or even admit to past use of—alcohol or
     a controlled substance. The statute allowed juvenile courts to treat
     the fetus as a child in need of protection and detain the expectant
     mother if her "habitual lack of control" with respect to use of alco-
     hol or controlled substances posed "substantial risk of harm" to the
     unborn child. The district court found the statute unconstitutionally
     vague and hence void but refused to allow any recovery of damages
     for Ms. Loertscher's incarceration.[110]

2.   **Indiana:** *Patel.* Purvi Patel was found guilty of feticide and sentenced
     to 20 years in prison. The state used its feticide law to prosecute her
     because she either (from the state's account) self-induced an abor-
     tion or (from her account) suffered a stillbirth. The original idea
     behind feticide laws was to be able to criminally prosecute someone
     who assaulted a pregnant woman and caused a miscarriage. Those
     laws are now being used against pregnant women. In the *Patel* case,
     she was required to convince a jury that her miscarriage was an acci-
     dent, not an attempt at self-abortion. A different approach to these
     cases could be to provide medical and social assistance for pregnant
     women otherwise unable to receive help with addiction or other
     problems.[111] As indicated earlier, her conviction was reversed in part
     by the appellate court. Indiana's feticide law was passed with the
     promise that it would protect pregnant women. However, it was used
     here for the opposite purpose, against a pregnant woman.

---

109. *Id.*

110. Loertscher v. Anderson, 259 F. Supp. 3d 902 (W.D. Wis. 2017), *vacating as moot* 893
F.3d 386 (7th Cir. 2018).

111. *See* National Advocates for Pregnant Women, http://www.advocatesforpreg
nantwomen.org/ (last visited Nov. 14, 2020).

3. **Alabama:** *Hicks, et al.* After 2006, more than 130 Alabama women who became pregnant and tested positive for a controlled substance were arrested under the theory that a pregnant woman's uterus is a dangerous "environment," no different from a methamphetamine lab. They were arrested under Alabama's 2006 "chemical endangerment of a child" law, which makes it illegal to expose a child to "an environment in which controlled substances are produced or distributed."[112] In 2013, the Alabama Supreme Court upheld the application of this law to pregnant women, though there is no language in the statute that suggests it should apply to a fetus rather than a living child.[113]

4. **Virginia:** *Roberts.* In March 2017, Virginia indicted Michelle Roberts on a felony charge of "producing an abortion or miscarriage" after police found fetal remains buried in her backyard. She said she had a stillbirth. Her initial defense to the criminal charge was that the statute could not be used to prosecute a woman concerning her own pregnancy. This defense was rejected by the trial court. The defense then obtained medical expert reports that said there was no medical evidence to support a claim of abortion. The prosecution was unable to obtain medical experts to support its case and finally asked the court to dismiss all charges in September 2018.[114]

XVIII. How to Reduce Abortions?

There are at least three areas to consider:

1. Improved access to birth control, including Plan B. As studies have proven, access to birth control significantly lowers the teenage abortion rate to less than half of the national average.[115]

---

112. ALA. CODE § 26-15-3.2. *See also Alabama Supreme Court Rules That Women Can Be Charged with Chemical Endangerment if They Become Pregnant and Use a Controlled Substance,* NATIONAL ADVOCATES FOR PREGNANT WOMEN (Apr. 22, 2014), https://www.nationaladvocatesforpreg nantwomen.org/alabama-supreme-court-rules-that-women-can-be-charged-with-chemical -endangerment-if-they-become-pregnant-and-use-a-controlled-substance/.

113. Ankrom v. State, 152 So. 3d 397 (Ala. 2013); Hicks v. State, 153 So. 3d 53 (Ala. 2014).

114. https://www.nationaladvocatesforpregnantwomen.org/?s=michelle+roberts.

115. Gina Secura et al., *Provision of No-Cost, Long-Acting Contraception and Teenage Pregnancy,* 371 N. ENGL. J. MED. 316 (Oct. 2, 2014), https://www.nejm.org/doi/10.1056 /NEJMoa1400506?url_ver=Z39.88-2003&rfr_id=ori%3Arid%3Acrossref.org&rfr_dat=cr _pub++0pubmed. *See also* Amanda Dennis & Daniel Grossman, *Barriers to Contraception and Interest in Over-the-Counter Access among Low-Income Women: a Qualitative Study,* 44 PERSPECT. SEX REPROD. HEALTH 84 (Mar. 30, 2012), https://pubmed.ncbi.nlm.nih.gov/22681423/.

2. Better sex education. Instead of teaching only abstinence, comprehensive sex education is known to lower pregnancy rates.[116]

3. Better support for pregnant women. Provision of care and insurance coverage for pregnant women increases the chances of a healthy pregnancy.[117]

Although this chapter covers only abortion, it is important to remember that there are other laws dealing with reproductive justice issues (violence against women, equal pay, breastfeeding, post-birth accommodations, access to birth control, access to health services, etc.) that are critical to fair and equitable treatment of women and to a full understanding of women's rights. Under the Trump administration, salutary laws providing access to contraception and birth control were challenged by the federal government.[118] While that will change with the Biden administration, state and federal policies will remain uncertain as politics change unless effective, fact-based advocacy can change the politics.

XIX. Conscience Clause Legislation

Almost every state has conscience clause legislation, giving health care professionals the right to refuse to provide certain services, such as sterilization, birth control, and abortion. Most of the laws say that students with moral or religious objections do not have to learn about these areas, and that a professional cannot be required to provide these services. The laws generally do not require that an objecting professional refer their patient to a bona fide provider.[119]

Dr. Lisa Harris, in an article in the *New England Journal of Medicine*, argues that these laws are one-sided and ought to allow for the conscience of someone who wants to assist patients by performing procedures, not just

---

116. Gina Secura et al., *Provision of No-Cost, Long-Acting Contraception and Teenage Pregnancy*, 371 N. ENGL. J. MED. 316 (Oct. 2, 2014), https://www.nejm.org /doi/10.1056/NEJMoa1400506?url_ver=Z39.88-2003&rfr_id=ori%3Arid%3Acrossref .org&rfr_dat=cr_pub++0pubmed.

117. *See Health Coverage if You're Pregnant, Plan to Get Pregnant, or Recently Gave Birth*, HEALTHCARE.GOV, https://www.healthcare.gov/what-if-im-pregnant-or-plan-to-get-pregnant /, (last visited Nov. 15, 2020).

118. *Trump-Pence Administration Takes Aim at Birth Control Access under the Nation's Reproductive Health Care Program*, PLANNED PARENTHOOD (Feb. 23, 2018), https://www .plannedparenthood.org/about-us/newsroom/press-releases/trump-pence-administration -takes-aim-at-birth-control-access-under-the-nations-reproductive-health-care-program.

119. *Refusing to Provide Health Services*, GUTTMACHER INSTITUTE (Mar. 1, 2014), https:// www.guttmacher.org/state-policy/explore/refusing-provide-health-services.

for those who wish to refrain.[120] Drs. Stahl and Emanuel argue that health care professionals "unlike conscripted soldiers . . . voluntarily choose their roles and thus become obligated to provide, perform, and refer patients for interventions according to the standards of the profession."[121] Bernard M. Dickens and Rebecca Cook argue that "conscientious commitment"—the converse of conscientious objection—should motivate health care providers to overcome barriers to delivering reproductive services to women if medical providers are going to truly respect women's health.[122]

XX. The Future

Roe was decided in 1973, so it should now be settled law backed by the power of precedent. That precedent doctrine, stare decisis, means current judges should respect prior decisions. Of course, some cases do not stand the test of time. For example, *Brown v. Board of Education*[123] overruled *Plessy v. Ferguson*, which held that racially segregated public facilities were legal so long as the facilities for blacks and whites were equal. But, in general, precedent is important in the development of the law. Justice O'Connor discussed the importance of stare decisis in the American constitutional system in her opinion in *Casey*, and she specifically explains why the Supreme Court's abortion decision in *Roe* is completely different than *Plessy*, which was rightfully overruled in *Brown*:

> [*Brown*] rested on facts, or an understanding of facts, changed from those which furnished the claimed justifications for the earlier constitutional resolutions. . . . In constitutional adjudication as elsewhere in life, changed circumstances may impose new obligations, and the thoughtful part of the Nation could accept each decision to overrule a prior case as a response to the Court's constitutional duty. . . . Because the cases before us present no such occasion it could be seen as no such response. Because neither the factual underpinnings of *Roe*'s central holding nor our understanding of it has changed (and because no other indication of weakened precedent has been shown), the Court could not pretend to be reexamining the prior law

---

120. Lisa Harris, *Divisions, New and Old—Conscience and Religious Freedom at HHS*, 378 NEW ENGL. J. MED. 1369 (2018).

121. Ronit Stahl & Ezekiel Emmanuel, *Physicians, Not Conscripts—Conscientious Objection in Health Care*, 376 NEW ENGL. J. MED. 1380 (2017).

122. Bernard M. Dickens & Rebecca J. Cook, *Conscientious Commitment to Women's Health*, 113 INT. J. GYNAECOL. OBSTET. 163 (May 2011), reprinted in this treatise as chapter 13.

123. Brown v. Board of Education, 347 U.S. 483 (1954).

with any justification beyond a present doctrinal disposition to come out
differently from the Court of 1973.[124]

In short, Justice O'Connor believed the Constitution is not supposed to
change meaning just because of politics. Justice Blackmun's separate opinion in *Casey*, now three decades old, was prescient. He discussed the role of
stare decisis and other issues and concluded with the following remark:

> I am 83 years old. I cannot remain on this Court forever, and when I do
> step down, the confirmation process for my successor well may focus on
> the issue before us today. That, I regret, may be exactly where the choice
> between the two worlds will be made.[125]

So, why are states like Ohio passing unconstitutional laws like a six-
week ban? Because sentiment against abortion remains strong, because the
nation has not yet accepted abortion the same way it has accepted same-sex
marriage, and because the composition of the Supreme Court has changed
to become more conservative. With the addition of Justices Gorsuch in
2017, Kavanagh in 2018, and Barrett in 2020, there is now a majority on the
court willing to consider overruling *Roe*. Chief Justice Roberts is no longer
the swing vote on this issue.

For the current term, the Court has not yet taken any abortion cases as
of this writing, but that could change as more states pass new anti-abortion
laws, and it will inevitably change at some point in the future, probably
the near future. There are a number of state laws now in litigation, many
designed to overrule *Roe*, while others try to substantially narrow *Roe*. If a
law like the Texas law regulating clinics and their physicians is upheld, the
number of available clinics in a state may narrow drastically or disappear
altogether, making it very difficult if not impossible for those without sufficient income and transportation to get to a facility.

What would a substantial change in the law mean?

If *Roe* is overruled, then it would be up to each state to decide its own
rules. Some states will outlaw or severely restrict abortion, others will not.
Pregnant women in states that prohibit abortion who do not have the funds
to travel will be limited to seeking care through the Internet for medical
abortions (harder to legally regulate, but states could try to outlaw access
to the medical drugs necessary for an abortion and could seek to prosecute
companies or physicians who provide drugs, and even women who try to

---

124. *Casey*, 505 U.S. at 863–64 (O'Connor, majority and plurality opinion in part,
announcing the judgment of the Court).

125. *Id.* at 943 (Blackmun, J. concurring in part, dissenting in part).

self-abort), whereas others will be left with only illegal options. Those who leave a state where abortion is illegal to go to a place where abortion is legal might face prosecution in their home state for conspiring to violate the law or for feticide. The *New York Times* recently published an informative article addressing the "tremendous inequality" that would occur because of clinics closing if *Roe* is overruled.[126]

If *Roe* gets even more limited but the central provision remains intact, some facilities will close while fewer remain open. Access will be limited.

Federal Title X money for Planned Parenthood was removed by the Trump administration but could be restored by the Biden administration.[127]

If states can outlaw abortion, they can also decide that ending a pregnancy would be a crime. This could include a pregnancy loss suspected of being an abortion attempt, something that has happened in the United States and elsewhere, notoriously so in El Salvador.[128]

Pursuant to a "feticide law," Shirley Wheeler in Florida was arrested and convicted of manslaughter in 1971 after undergoing an abortion.[129] Many states currently have feticide laws, and an unknown number of women have been prosecuted in the United States under those statutes for being suspected of attempting an abortion. That was true even when the threats to *Roe* were far more distant than they are today.[130]

States could also try to substantially limit access to contraception, which would have the contrary result of increasing unwanted pregnancies and illegal abortions.

---

126. Quoctrung Bui et al., *What Happens if Roe v. Wade Is Overturned?*, N.Y. Times (Oct. 15, 2020), https://www.nytimes.com/interactive/2020/10/15/upshot/what-happens-if-roe -is-overturned.html?searchResultPosition=1.

127. On January 28, 2021, President Biden signed an executive order that repealed the "global gag rule" that banned international groups that receive U.S. aid from performing, facilitating, or even discussing abortion. The Biden administration also announced it is considering efforts to repeal or limit the similar "domestic gag rule" that targeted Planned Parenthood by barring recipients of Title X family planning government funding from performing abortions or referring women for abortions. Ema O'Connor, *Biden Just Repealed One of Trump's Major Anti-Abortion Policies*, BuzzFeed News (Jan. 28, 2021), https://www.buzzfeed news.com/article/emaoconnor/biden-executive-order-abortion-global-gag-rule-trump.

128. *See* Kate Smith & Gilad Thaler, *These Women Say They Had Miscarriages. Now They're in Jail for Abortion*, CBS News (May 28, 2020, 7:02 AM), https://www.cbsnews.com/news /miscarriages-abortion-jail-el-salvador/.

129. Jon Nordheimer, *She's Fighting Conviction for Aborting Her Child*, N.Y. Times (Dec. 4, 1971), https://www.nytimes.com/1971/12/04/archives/shes-fighting-conviction-for-aborting -her-child.html.

130. *See* Lynn M. Paltrow and Jeanne Flavin, *Arrests of and Forced Interventions on Pregnant Women in the United States, 1973–2005: Implications for Women's Legal Status and Public Health*, 38 J. Health Pol. Pol'y & L. 299 (2013).

So, as of the end of 2020, where are we? The Supreme Court has a conservative 6–3 majority, and the Justices appointed by the Trump administration are said to be willing to overrule *Roe*, as are Justices Thomas and Alito. This would mean access would return to a state-by-state issue. The Biden administration may help women with access to care and contraception and could restore Title X funding to Planned Parenthood, but would not likely be able to pass any federal law making abortion legal—assuming such a law would be upheld as constitutional, which would be questionable for a Supreme Court so personally hostile to women's right to choose.

XXI. Conclusion

Is there an alternative to this debate? There are several approaches. One is to normalize abortion by showing that nearly one in three women have abortions and will continue to do so even if abortion is illegal. This would require women speaking out and society being willing to stop stigmatizing women who have abortions. The cycle of shame leading to silence is one important element that makes it difficult to change the conversation around abortion.

Another is to lower the rate of unwanted pregnancies by better sex education in schools, free access to the morning after pill for rape and failed contraception, and easy access to contraception for all women, including minors. If a woman does not get pregnant, she does not need to consider abortion. The data from St. Louis and New York City shows that access to contraception lowers teen pregnancy and therefore abortions.[131] When barriers to contraception were removed in Saint Louis, the abortion rate was 9.7 per 1,000, compared with 41.5 per 1,000 in 2008 for sexually active U.S. teens.

A third approach is for society to better protect women and provide assistance for pregnancy and childbirth. Many places in the world use a human rights approach and try to provide care and protection to pregnant women. The Center for Reproductive Rights has a world map showing the laws and rules throughout the world.[132] As one example, the United Nations has a treaty on the elimination of all forms of discrimination against women (CEDAW, the Convention on the Elimination of All Forms

---

131. *See supra* note 111.

132. *The World's Abortion Laws*, CTR FOR REPROD. RIGHTS (last visited Nov. 15, 2020), https://reproductiverights.org/worldabortionlaws.

of Discrimination Against Women).[133] Signatories accept a legal obligation to counteract discrimination against women.

And finally, a society that is tolerant and allows women to decide what is in their own best interests would remove much of the stigma. Of course, that would, in the view of some, ignore the rights of a fetus. There is always the argument about the needs of the fetus to be born. That argument plays out in abortion in continued "life support" after the death of the mother to allow the fetus to develop and in cases where a facility wants to force a C-section over the express objection of the mother to potentially enhance the outcome for the fetus. But, as the District of Columbia Court of Appeals said in 1990, "in virtually all cases the question of what is to be done is to be decided by the patient—the pregnant woman—on behalf of herself and the fetus."[134] The court concluded, after a detailed and thoughtful discussion: "Surely a fetus cannot have rights in this respect superior to those of a person who has already been born."[135] For an extreme literary example of what can happen when women are seen simply as delivery systems for a fetus, one may read Margaret Atwood's novel, *The Handmaid's Tale*.

If a woman-centric approach is not adopted, this is an area that will continue to see significant legislative and judicial activity for the foreseeable future.

133. *Convention on the Elimination of All Forms of Discrimination against Women*, UN WOMEN (last visited Nov. 15, 2020), http://www.un.org/womenwatch/daw/cedaw/committee.htm.
134. *In re A.C.*, 573 A.2d 1235, 1237 (D.C. App. 1990).
135. *Id.* at 1244.

3

Abortion Law in Canada

By A. Anne McLellan[1] and Odessa M. O'Dell[2]

In Canada, the legal and political context in which the issue of abortion is discussed was transformed with the adoption of the Charter of Rights and Freedoms in 1982.[3] Once considered to have a restrictive abortion law, Canada has had no law prohibiting a woman's right to an abortion[4] since the Canadian Supreme Court's 1988 decision invalidating section 251 of the Criminal Code of Canada,[5] which had contained a prohibition against abortion. That decision created a significant change in the legal and political climate in which the contentious issue of abortion has been discussed ever since.

This chapter will outline the history of the regulation of abortion in Canada before 1968, when significant changes were made to the Criminal Code prohibitions. Next will come an analysis of section 251 of the Criminal Code, followed by a discussion of the *Morgentaler* cases, including the 1988 case[6] in which the Supreme Court of Canada found that section 251 of the Criminal Code was unconstitutional. The decisions of the various members of the Supreme Court will be analyzed, their judgments reflecting deep divisions in relation to both the appropriate role for the Court in

---

1. A. Anne McLellan; Senior Advisor, Bennett Jones LLP, former Minister of Justice and Attorney General of Canada.

2. Odessa M. O'Dell; Associate, McCague Borlack LLP, former Associate, Bennett Jones LLP.

3. Enacted as schedule B of the Canada Act 1982, (U.K.) 1982, c.ll.

4. Some provinces have tried to place limitations upon a woman's right to an abortion, exercising their constitutional jurisdiction over health and hospitals. *See* discussion *infra* (The Aftermath of Morgentaler).

5. See Appendix A-I for the complete text of section 251.

6. [1988] 1 S.C.R. 30.

interpreting the Charter and in determining the extent of constitutional guarantees, if any, for a woman seeking an abortion.

Finally, the legal and political events in the post-*Morgentaler* period will be considered. This period has witnessed a marked increase in political activity from both anti-and pro-choice advocates; proposed legislation from the federal government to recriminalize abortion;[7] and attempts by provincial governments to regulate certain aspects of abortion through their constitutional jurisdiction over health care and hospitals. It also has seen continued litigation regarding questions that were not addressed by the Supreme Court of Canada, particularly clarifications around the legal status of the unborn.

I. The History of Abortion in Canada before 1968

The Constitution Act, 1867, gives the federal Parliament the exclusive jurisdiction over both criminal law and procedure.[8] It was by virtue of this power that Parliament enacted a criminal law in 1869 that prohibited abortion and punished it with a penalty of life imprisonment.[9] This law mirrored the laws of a number of provinces in pre-Confederation Canada, all of which were more or less modeled on Lord Ellenborough's Act.[10] Lord Ellenborough's Act criminalized abortion, whether procured before quickening or not, but continued to treat the fact of quickening as relevant in relation to the issue of penalty.[11] Those who procured abortions after quickening were subject to the penalty of death, and those who procured an abortion before quickening faced a lesser sentence. The basic structure of this legislation was adopted by the pre-Confederation provinces of Canada.[12] In the

---

7. Bill C-43, An Act Respecting Abortion, defeated in the Senate January 31, 1991. (See Appendix A-II for the text).

8. Section 91(27).

9. Offences Against the Person Act, 1869, 32–33 Vict., c.20, section 60.

10. 1803, 43 Geo. 111, c.58. The act placed the offence of criminal abortion on a statutory basis for the first time. For a thorough history of English abortion laws, *see* B.M. DICKENS, ABORTION AND THE LAW (1966).

11. Quickening has been defined as when a woman could feel the fetus move in her womb. Different times have been suggested as to when quickening occurs, but 14 weeks after conception is often suggested. Under common law, procuring an abortion before quickening was not a criminal offence.

12. For an excellent history of the development of Canadian abortion laws in the 19th century, see Backhouse, *Involuntary Motherhood: Abortion, Birth Control and the Law in Nineteenth Century Canada*, 3 WINDSOR Y.B. OF ACCESS TO JUST. 61 (1983).

1840s both Upper Canada[13] and New Brunswick[14] enacted legislation that abolished this distinction based upon quickening. Also, during this time, anti-abortion legislation was amended to make it clear that the prohibition against the procurement of an abortion applied to the pregnant woman herself.[15]

In 1892, the Canadian Parliament enacted the first Criminal Code,[16] which reflected the approach of earlier 19th-century legislative attempts to criminalize abortion. Section 273 made it possible to charge a woman with procuring her own abortion, whether or not pregnant. The Code also included section 179, dealing with obscenity, one of the provisions of which provided that everyone who "offers to sell, advertises, or publishes an advertisement of or has for sale or disposal, any medicine, drug or article intended or represented as a means of preventing conception or causing abortion" was guilty of an indictable offence and liable to imprisonment

---

13. An Act for Consolidating . . . Offences Against the Person, 1841 (Upper Canada) 4&5 Vict., c.27, section 13.

14. An Act Further to Amend the Law Relating to Offences Against the Person, 1842 (N.B.) 5 Vict., c.33, section 2.

15. For example, New Brunswick passed such a law in 1849 and Nova Scotia did so in 1851.

16. 1892, 55 Vict., c.29, sections 272–274 (Can.).
Section 272:

Everyone is guilty of an indictable offence and liable to imprisonment for life who, with intent to procure the miscarriage of any woman, whether she is or is not with child, unlawfully administers to her or causes to be taken by her any drug or other noxious thing, or unlawfully uses any instrument or other means whatsoever with the like intent.

Section 273:

Every woman is guilty of an indictable offence and liable to seven years' imprisonment who, whether with child or not, unlawfully administers to herself or permits to be administered to her any drug or other noxious thing, or unlawfully uses on herself or permits to be used on her any instrument or other means whatsoever with intent to procure miscarriage.

Section 274:

Everyone is guilty of an indictable offence and liable to two years imprisonment who unlawfully supplies or procures any drug or other noxious thing, or any instrument or thing whatsoever, knowing that the same is intended to be unlawfully used or employed with intent to procure the miscarriage of any woman, whether she is or is not with child.

for two years.[17] This was the first statutory prohibition against the sale, distribution, and advertisement of contraceptives as well as abortifacients. It appears that this section was modeled upon the Comstock Act in the United States,[18] and it has been suggested that the net effect of the prohibitions in sections 273 and 179(c) was "to cover all aspects of fertility control—even the efforts of individual women who were unaided and not pregnant."[19]

The prohibition in section 273 of the Code continued in force until 1954 when an amendment made it plain that only a woman who was in fact pregnant could be found guilty of the crime of procuring her own miscarriage.[20] Another change in the legislation, seemingly a small one, was the removal of the word "unlawfully" from section 272(1), thereby calling into question the assumption of both the medical and legal professions that the defense of necessity was available in Canada to a physician accused of procuring an abortion.[21]

II. The 1968 Amendments to the Criminal Code

There were no further changes in Canada's abortion law until 1968 when the Liberal government of Pierre Trudeau introduced significant amendments to the existing law.[22] The amendments created a therapeutic exception to the criminal prohibitions against doctors and women who procured

---

17. Gavigan, *"On Bringing on the Menses": The Criminal Liability of Women and the Therapeutic Exception in Canadian Abortion Law*, 1 C.J.W.L. 279, 296 (1986). It was only in 1969 that the Criminal Code was amended to make it legal to sell and advertise contraceptives.

18. Backhouse, *supra* note 12, at 119–20.

19. Gavigan, *supra* note 17, at 296. *See generally* A. McLaren & A.T. McLaren, The Bedroom and the State: The Changing Practices and Politics of Contraception and Abortion in Canada, 1880–1997 (1997) for a detailed discussion on birth control and abortion in Canada between 1880 and 1997.

20. R.S.C. 1953-54, c.51. The amended section became 237(2).

21. The amended section became 237(1) and read:

> Everyone who, with intent to procure the miscarriage of a female person, whether or not she is pregnant, uses any means for the purpose of carrying out his intention is guilty of an indictable offence arid is liable to imprisonment for life. See: Parker, Bill C-150: Abortion Reform (1968-69) 11 Crim. L.Q. 267 for a discussion of the possible implications of the removal of the word "unlawfully." The English case of R v. Bourne, [1939] 1 K.B. 687 appears to be the first case to consider the defense of necessity in the context of abortion. The prohibition against abortion, both under common law and by statute, was held to be subject to a common law defense based upon the necessity of saving the mother's life.

22. *See* Appendix I for the text. Criminal Law Amendment Act S.C. 1968–69, c.38, section 18. The abortion amendments were part of an omnibus criminal law reform package that included the legalization of homosexuality between consenting adults in private. It should

abortions. The new law, in essence, legalized the procurement of an abortion in those circumstances in which a physician believed the life or health of a woman to be endangered. The legislation put in place a mechanism by which therapeutic abortion committees could be created in accredited or approved hospitals. Upon certification by such a committee, an abortion could be performed lawfully, if, in the committee's opinion, the continuation of the pregnancy endangered the life or health of the woman.

Although the legislative reforms of 1968 were viewed by some as a liberalization of the existing criminal law,[23] practical problems arose immediately in relation to its implementation. It was believed that the new law created an unacceptable level of vagueness and uncertainty concerning the circumstances in which the therapeutic exception would be available. It must be remembered that the exception was only available when, in the opinion of a therapeutic abortion committee, the continuation of a pregnancy would, or would likely, endanger a woman's life or health. There was no definition of health contained in the legislation. Some had suggested that the definition of health should be that accepted by the World Health Organization, which defined the term as "a state of complete physical, mental, and social well-being and not merely an absence of disease or infirmity."[24] Others suggested that, in spite of the wording of section 251(4)(c) that referred to the endangerment of life or health, an abortion should only be performed

---

be remembered that Trudeau, as minister of justice, had made the now-famous, if inaccurate, comment that "the state has no place in the bedrooms of the nation."

23. This view was not shared by everyone. For example, then-Minister of Justice John Turner suggested in the House of Commons that the substance of the proposed amendments did no more than recognize what had actually been happening in a number of hospitals. House of Commons Debates, (1969) 28th Parl., 1st Sess. at 8058.

The Canadian Medical Association (C.M.A.) and the Canadian Bar Association (C.B.A.) were both instrumental in convincing the government to reform its abortion law. Both groups believed that the existing law put doctors in an untenable position, since it was not clear as to doctors' possible criminal liability when they performed abortions, believing in their medical opinion, that the life or health of a woman was endangered by the continuation of the pregnancy. All such abortions possibly were illegal under the existing law.

24. Taken from the judgment of A.C.J. Parker in *R. v. Morgentaler, Smoling and Scott* (1984), 47 O.R. (2d) 353 at 377. In the House of Commons, the debate regarding the definition of the "health" had consumed considerable time and energy. Minister of Justice John Turner had offered the following comments in support of the government's decision not to include a definition of "health":

This is a question that is left to medical judgment. Certainly it has to be taken in a global sense. You cannot isolate physical from mental health; they interact and react each upon professional judgment of medical practitioners to decide.

House of Commons Debates, (1969) 28th Parl., 1st Sess. at 8124.

where there was proof that the continuation of the pregnancy would endanger the life of the woman. It became clear that the definition of health could, and did, vary from province to province and between individual therapeutic abortion committees.[25]

Further, the therapeutic exception depended on the establishment of abortion committees in accredited or approved hospitals.[26] No provision was made for the performance of therapeutic abortions in freestanding abortion clinics. The definition of accredited and approved hospitals was found in section 251(6) of the Criminal Code, and the effect thereof was to limit the number of hospitals in a position to create such committees.[27] It has been estimated that two out of five Canadians did not live in communities served by hospitals eligible to establish therapeutic abortion committees. Neither was there any requirement in the Criminal Code that

---

25. As to the differing and arbitrary definitions of health, *see generally Canada, Report of the Committee on the Operation of the Abortion Law* (1977) (Badgley Report) [hereinafter Badgley Report]; *Report on Therapeutic Abortion Services in Ontario, A Study Commissioned by the Ministry of Health* (Toronto, 1987) (the Powell Report); and Smith & Wineberg, *A Survey of Therapeutic Abortion Committees (1968–70)*, 12 CRIM. L.Q. 279.

26. Several conditions had to be complied with under section 251 before an abortion could be lawfully performed. They were:

- The procedure must be done by a qualified medical practitioner, i.e., a person qualified to engage in the practice of medicine under the laws of the province.
- The qualified medical practitioner must be a physician other than a member of a hospital's therapeutic abortion committee.
- The abortion must be approved by a therapeutic abortion committee.
- The therapeutic abortion committee for any hospital means a committee appointed by the board of that hospital for the purpose of considering and determining questions relating to the termination of pregnancy within that hospital.
- The therapeutic abortion committee must be composed of not less than three members, each of whom is a qualified medical practitioner appointed by the board of that hospital.
- The procedure must be done in an "accredited hospital" means a hospital accredited by the Canadian Council on Hospital Accreditation in which diagnostic services and medical, surgical and obstetrical treatment is provided. An approved hospital means a hospital in a province approved for the purposes of this section by the minister of health of that province.

Provincial statutes are operative as "nothing in subsection (4) shall be construed as making unnecessary the obtaining of any authorization or consent that is or may be required, otherwise than under this Act, before any means are used for the purpose of carrying out an intention to procure the miscarriage of a female person." Badgley Report, *supra* note 25, at 85–86.

27. Of a total of 1,348 civilian hospitals in Canada in 1976, 789, or 58.5 percent, were ineligible to establish committees. Badgley Report, *supra* note 25, at 105.

approved or accredited hospitals establish committees, and therefore a significant number of hospital boards chose not to do so.[28]

The effect of the Criminal Code amendments was to require the involvement of a minimum of four doctors before a therapeutic abortion could be performed. The four doctors were the woman's physician and the three members of the therapeutic abortion committee, a majority of whom had to certify that the continuation of a woman's pregnancy would, or would be likely to, endanger her life or health. Of the 1,348 civilian hospitals in operation in Canada in 1976, at least 331, or 24 percent, of those hospitals had less than four physicians on their medical staffs.[29] Also, since the Code offered no guidance to hospital boards or committees as to whether the consent of a husband or father of the fetus was required, or, in the case of an unmarried minor, the consent of a parent or guardian, considerable variation existed in practice between provinces and hospitals within provinces.[30]

The problems in relation to the availability, accessibility, and terms on which therapeutic abortions could be procured were due almost entirely to the lack of legislative guidance from the federal Parliament. Parliament may have wished to leave such "details" to provincial legislative regulation, in a misguided attempt to respect provincial legislative jurisdiction over health care and the regulation of hospitals. The practical result for women seeking therapeutic abortions was uncertainty as to the availability of the procedure and the terms upon which an abortion would be performed. Not surprisingly, reports indicated that relatively well-off women, with a reasonably high level of education, living in urban centers, were those most likely to successfully procure therapeutic abortions.

III. The *Morgentaler* Cases

If there is one name, more than any other, that Canadians have associated with the issue of abortion, it is that of Dr. Henry Morgentaler.[31] Dr. Morgentaler's importance to the issue of abortion in Canada operates on at least two levels—the first being strictly legal and the second political. Dr. Morgentaler was a ceaseless advocate for a woman's right to choose whether

---

28. In 1976, of the 559 general hospitals that met the conditions required for the establishment of a committee, 288, or 51.5 percent, did not have committees. *Id.*

29. Badgley Report, *supra* note 25, at 30.

30. *Id.* at 32.

31. Dr. Morgentaler emigrated to Canada in 1950, after surviving Auschwitz and Dachau. For a thorough, if uncritical, history of Dr. Morgentaler's life up to 1975, *see* E.W. PERLINE, MORGENTALER: THE DOCTOR WHO COULDN'T TURN AWAY (1975).

to terminate a pregnancy and lobbied unsuccessfully in 1967, as president of the Montreal Humanist Association, to have Parliament repeal its existing abortion law. Dr. Morgentaler established a freestanding abortion clinic in Montreal as early as 1968 to provide abortions to those women who requested them. Those abortions were in violation of existing Canadian criminal law. Dr. Morgentaler dedicated his life to political activities on behalf of women and their "right to choose." Viewed as a martyr by some and as a murderous villain by others, Dr. Morgentaler kept the issue of abortion and a woman's right thereto at the forefront of the Canadian political and legal agenda for decades.

Dr. Morgentaler's importance to the issue of abortion in Canada extends well beyond the political realm. He was prosecuted four times for allegedly violating section 251 of the Criminal Code. He was charged first, in 1970, by the Attorney General of Quebec.[32] Dr. Morgentaler was acquitted by four juries, three in Quebec and one in Ontario, and proceeded with two appeals to the Supreme Court of Canada—the first of which he lost when the court rejected both his constitutional and criminal law arguments and upheld his conviction[33] and the second of which he won, when the Supreme Court of Canada declared section 251 of the Criminal Code unconstitutional, as being in violation of section 7 of the Charter of Rights and Freedoms.[34] However, to simply state these conclusions is to ignore the uniqueness and complexity of the litigation in which both the state and Dr. Morgentaler were involved.

Indeed, Dr. Morgentaler waged one of the longest and most successful campaigns of civil disobedience in Canadian history.[35] As a humanist, Dr. Morgentaler was deeply committed to the concepts of personal autonomy and equality and consistently argued these beliefs in relation to a woman's right to choose whether to terminate a pregnancy.[36] To some extent, Dr.

---

32. For a detailed account of the numerous legal proceedings in which Dr. Morgentaler was involved from 1970 to 1976, *see* Dickens, *The Morgentaler Case: Criminal Process and Abortion Law*, 14 OSGOODE H.L.J. 229 (1976).

33. [1976] 1 S.C.R. 616. For convenience, we will refer to this decision throughout the chapter as *Morgentaler* (1975).

34. [1988] 1 S.C.R. 30, at 31. We will refer to this decision throughout the chapter as *Morgentaler* (1988).

35. For a discussion of Morgentaler and civil disobedience, *see* B. Wardhaugh, *Socratic Civil Disobedience: Some Reflections on Morgentaler*, 2 CAN. J. LAW & JURISPRUDENCE 91 (1989).

36. These views informed the submission made by Dr. Morgentaler on behalf of the Humanist Fellowship of Montreal to the Parliamentary Committee on Health and Welfare in October 1967 when the committee was considering proposed reforms to Canada's abortion

Morgentaler's subsequent treatment by the legal system was due to his openly defiant violation of Canada's existing criminal laws.[37] At no time did Dr. Morgentaler deny performing abortions in apparent violation of section 251 of the Criminal Code. He ignored the law because he believed it to be morally indefensible.[38] Because Dr. Morgentaler made no secret of his willingness to perform abortions in his private clinic in Montreal, the Attorney General of Quebec soon concluded that he had no choice but to prosecute him.

A. *Morgentaler* (1975)

Dr. Morgentaler's clinic in Montreal was first raided in June 1970, and he was originally charged on a number of counts of conspiracy to commit abortion and procuring an abortion under section 251(1) of the Criminal Code. After numerous pretrial motions on the part of Dr. Morgentaler, the Attorney General preferred an indictment in relation to one count of unlawfully procuring the miscarriage of a female person.[39] Dr. Morgentaler was acquitted at trial in November 1973, but on appeal the Quebec Court of Appeal entered a conviction and returned the matter to the trial judge for sentencing. Dr. Morgentaler then applied for, and was granted, leave to appeal to the Supreme Court of Canada.

Having admitted performing the act of abortion with which he was charged, Dr. Morgentaler argued the common law concept of necessity in his defense. In addition to this argument, Dr. Morgentaler attacked the

law. The brief affirmed the inherent dignity of the individual and suggested that "this ideal should be reflected in the laws governing our society which should provide equal justice and benefits to all, rich or poor, informed or uninformed, believer or non-believer, and be continually updated in accordance with new conditions and new knowledge." (Standing Committee on Health and Welfare, *Minutes of Proceedings and Evidence*, 1967/68).

37. Perhaps most galling to Dr. Morgentaler's opponents was a nationwide television broadcast on Mother's Day 1973 in which Dr. Morgentaler permitted cameras into his clinic in Montreal and, with the consent of the patient involved, allowed the filming of an abortion being performed. In addition, in the December 15, 1973, edition of the Canadian Medical Association Journal, Dr. Morgentaler published a report on 5,641 outpatient abortions by vacuum suction curettage. This frank disclosure of the number of abortions he had performed in his clinic surprised, and shocked, many.

38. Throughout Dr. Morgentaler's numerous prosecutions by authorities, he maintained that the jury should acquit him because the law under which he was charged was "a bad law." In essence, Dr. Morgentaler was suggesting that a jury could ignore a law that it did not like.

39. By preferring an indictment against Dr. Morgentaler, the Attorney General denied Dr. Morgentaler the opportunity of a preliminary inquiry.

constitutional validity of section 251 on a number of grounds, most of which related to the Canadian Bill of Rights.[40] His main arguments were based on sections 1(a) and (b) of the bill. Section 1(a) recognized and declared the right of an individual to life, liberty, and security of the person and the right not to be deprived thereof except by due process of law, and section 1(b) spoke of the right of an individual to equality before the law and the protection of the law. Counsel for Dr. Morgentaler drew heavily on the then-recently decided U.S. cases of *Roe v. Wade*[41] and *Doe v. Bolton*[42] for support for his claim that section 251 of the Criminal Code was unconstitutional. Counsel advanced the argument that the concept of liberty protected in section 1(a) of the Canadian Bill of Rights should be defined to include a right to privacy and the "qualified right" to terminate a pregnancy. In relation to Dr. Morgentaler's claim to security of his person, he argued that the standard established in section 251(4) under which an abortion could be performed lawfully was "so vague, so uncertain and so subjective as among different physicians and as among different therapeutic abortion committees as to deny due process of law."[43]

Dr. Morgentaler's equality argument under section 1(b) of the Bill of Rights was based on the operational effect of section 251(4). The section permitted, but did not compel, hospital boards to establish therapeutic abortion committees. In addition, the section specified the number of medical practitioners who were required to serve on such committees. Counsel for Dr. Morgentaler argued that such a requirement created inequality "in respect of women in rural areas and in areas where no such committee had been established."[44] Counsel further argued that the economic status of some women denied them the mobility necessary to avail themselves of therapeutic abortion committees, where they did exist. Finally, it was alleged that the vague standards to be applied by the committees led to varying

---

40. The Canadian Bill of Rights was enacted by the federal Parliament in 1960. It was an ordinary statutory enactment that could have been repealed by Parliament at any time. It applied only to the federal Parliament, federal government and businesses, agencies, and so on, within federal legislative jurisdiction. Therefore, the Bill of Rights had no application to the provinces. The bill has been described as having "quasi-constitutional" status only, and for this reason, and others, Canadian courts assumed a posture of some hostility toward the bill, and therefore it was viewed as little more than an interpretive guide. The Supreme Court of Canada declared only one federal law invalid under the Canadian Bill of Rights, which occurred in the case of *R. v. Drybones* (1969) 9 D.L.R. (3d) 473 (S.C.C.).

41. 410 U.S. 113 (1973).

42. 410 U.S. 179 (1973). The legislative scheme struck down (in part) by the U.S. Supreme Court in *Doe* was very similar to section 251 of the Criminal Code.

43. *See* [1976] 1 S.C.R. 616, at 629.

44. *Id.* at 630.

applications and interpretations, having the effect of denying some women equal protection of the law.

Surprisingly, only in the minority judgment of the court is there any discussion of why these arguments, based on the Canadian Bill of Rights, were rejected.[45] Chief Justice Laskin provided the legal and historical context in which the Court considered these "rights" arguments. The Chief Justice commented:

> How foreign to our constitutional traditions, to our constitutional law, and to our conceptions of judicial review was any interference by a Court with the substantive content of legislation.[46]

Although recognizing the "quasi-constitutional" status of the Canadian Bill of Rights, the Chief Justice called for restraint in its application:

> [I]t cannot be forgotten that it [the Bill of Rights] is a statutory instrument, illustrative of Parliament's primacy within the limits of its assigned legislative authority, and this is a relevant consideration in determining how far the language of the Canadian Bill of Rights should be taken in assessing the quality of federal enactments which are challenged under s.1(a). There is as much a temptation here as there is on the question of ultra vires to consider the wisdom of the legislation and I think it is our duty to resist it in the former connection as in the latter.[47]

With these general comments to guide his approach to the interpretation of the Bill of Rights, it is not surprising that the Chief Justice rejected the approach adopted by the U.S. Supreme Court in *Roe v. Wade*.[48] Without clearly articulating why, he concluded that it would be unwarranted for the court to divide the normal period of pregnancy into zones of interest. The Chief Justice also rejected counsel's arguments based on the uncertainty and subjectivity of the standard upon which a lawful abortion could be performed under section 251(4) of the Code. The section required a finding on the part of a therapeutic abortion committee that the continuation of a pregnancy would, or would be likely to, endanger the life or health of the

---

45. At the conclusion of the submission by counsel for Dr. Morgentaler, the court announced that it did not need to hear from the respondent Crown on the applicability and effect of the Canadian Bill of Rights "because no case was made out on these matters which required an answer." *Id.* at 624. However, Chief Justice Laskin, on behalf of himself and fellow Justices Judson and Spence, believed it was important to state why the arguments were being rejected.

46. *See* [1976] 1 S.C.R. 616, at 632.

47. *Id.* at 632–33.

48. *See* 410 U.S. 113 (1973).

woman. Again, the Chief Justice cautioned restraint in relation to the doctrine of substantive due process and concluded:

> It is enough to say that Parliament has fixed a manageable standard because it is addressed to a professional panel, the members of which would be expected to bring a practiced judgment to the question whether "the continuation of the pregnancy . . . would or would be likely to endanger . . . health or life."[49]

In relation to the appellant's arguments based on the concept of equal protection of the law, the Chief Justice concluded that section 1(b) of the Bill of Rights did not charge the courts with supervising the administrative efficiency of legislation or with evaluating the regional or national organization of its administration. The reality that economic or geographic circumstances precluded many women from sheltering under or taking advantage of the exculpatory provisions of section 251 was constitutionally irrelevant to the Chief Justice.[50] He concluded that any unevenness in the administration of section 251(4) was for Parliament to correct, not for the courts to monitor. In summary, in keeping with its restrained, if not completely ineffectual, approach to the interpretation and application of the Canadian Bill of Rights, the Court concluded that Parliament's legislative scheme in relation to abortion was constitutionally valid.[51]

The majority of the Supreme Court of Canada resolved the case on the basis of criminal law arguments only.[52] In relation to the common law defense of necessity, the Court was divided, with the majority expressing

---

49. *See* [1976] 1 S.C.R. 616, at 634.

50. *Id.* at 636.

51. Although it is only in the judgment of Chief Justice Laskin (concurred in by Justices Spence and Judson) that there is any discussion of the Bill of Rights, it can be presumed that the remaining justices of the Court concurred in his reasoning. The Chief Justice had earlier rejected Dr. Morgentaler's argument that section 251 exceeded the legislative jurisdiction of Parliament, being a law concerning hospitals and the regulation of the profession of medicine. Chief Justice Laskin concluded that section 251 was a valid exercise of the federal Parliament's criminal law power. He commented:

> Parliament has in its judgment decreed that interference by another, or even by the pregnant woman herself, with the ordinary course of conception is socially undesirable conduct subject to punishment. I need cite no authority for the proposition that Parliament may determine what is not criminal as well as what is, and may hence introduce dispensations or compensations in its criminal legislation.

Id. at 627.

52. These arguments were primarily in relation to the common law defense of necessity and the appropriateness of the Quebec Court of Appeal's actions in entering a verdict of guilty in place of the trial jury's acquittal.

doubt as to the very existence of the defense but ultimately concluding that even if the defense was a "theoretical possibility" in the case, there was no evidence to support it.[53] Justice Dickson in reviewing the testimony of both Dr. Morgentaler and one of his patients, concluded that there was no evidence of urgency and no evidence that Dr. Morgentaler could not have complied with the law found in the Code, in relation to therapeutic abortions. Therefore, Justice Dickson concluded that the Quebec Court of Appeal had not erred in deciding that "there was on the record little evidence of real and urgent medical need."[54]

In conclusion, the majority of the Supreme Court of Canada upheld the conviction against Dr. Morgentaler entered by the Quebec Court of Appeal and sent the matter back to the trial judge for sentencing. Dr. Morgentaler was sentenced to 18 months in jail, of which he served ten months, before being released on bail, pending retrial.[55]

Dr. Morgentaler had continued to operate his clinic during this protracted court process, and new charges were laid against him as a result of the continuation of his practice. Again, he was tried and acquitted. The Attorney General of Quebec chose not to appeal this acquittal, but to simply lay additional charges against Dr. Morgentaler for which he was again acquitted. After the election of the *Parti Quebecois* in late 1976, the position of the Quebec government in relation to the availability of abortion and the continued prosecution of Dr. Morgentaler changed dramatically. Due to the difficulty of obtaining a conviction from a jury under section 251(4),

---

53. *See* [1976] 1 S.C.R. 616, at 681. Chief Justice Laskin (with J.J. Spence and Judson concurring) considered the defense of necessity and concluded that there was evidence the trial judge could have left with the jury on the issue of necessity, and hence, they would have reinstated the verdict of acquittal.

54. *Id.* at 685. Justice Dickson summarized the views of the majority of the Court on the defense of necessity in the following terms:

> On the authorities it is manifestly difficult to be categorical and state that there is a law of necessity, paramount over other laws, relieving obedience from the letter of the law. If it does exist it can go no further than to justify non-compliance in urgent situations of clear and imminent peril when compliance with the law is demonstrably impossible. No system of positive law can recognize any principle, which would entitle a person to violate the law because on his view the law conflicted with some higher social value.

Id. at 678.

55. Dr. Morgentaler applied for parole after serving six months, or one-third, of his sentence. However, his application was denied by the National Parole Board, apparently because he was viewed as a difficult prisoner and had spent some time in solitary. However, some suggest that the Parole Board's refusal of Dr. Morgentaler's application was politically motivated and an attempt to further punish him for his defiance.

the government decided that no further charges would be laid against Dr. Morgentaler nor against any other doctor performing abortions in free-standing clinics within the province. Indeed, abortions have been regularly performed in government-sponsored community clinics in Quebec since 1982. In essence, the government of Quebec decided to ignore section 251 of the Criminal Code and by so doing offered to Canadian women the prospect of readily available abortion in private clinics.

B. *Morgentaler* (1988)

Dr. Morgentaler was not satisfied with this political victory in Quebec. He believed that all women, wherever they lived in Canada, should have ready access to safe abortion procedures. His experiences had persuaded him that the requirements of section 251(4) of the Criminal Code limited or denied access to abortion for many Canadian women and that it was actually medically safer and psychologically less traumatic for women to have the procedure performed in freestanding clinics rather than in hospitals. Therefore, Dr. Morgentaler opened a new clinic in Toronto, Ontario, in 1982.[56] The Attorney General of Ontario was not nearly as accommodating of Dr. Morgentaler's plans as was his counterpart in Quebec. Police raided Dr. Morgentaler's clinic in July 1982; he was charged and tried, before a judge and jury, and acquitted. The Attorney General appealed this acquittal, and the Ontario Court of Appeal ordered a new trial. This decision was appealed by Dr. Morgentaler to the Supreme Court of Canada, and in January 1988, a majority of the Court declared section 251 of the Criminal Code unconstitutional, as being in violation of section 7 of the Charter of Rights and Freedoms.

The Attorney General of Ontario charged Dr. Morgentaler with conspiring with fellow doctors, Smoling and Scott, who performed the majority of abortions at the Toronto clinic, to procure the miscarriage of female persons. Before entering a plea, counsel for Dr. Morgentaler and his alleged fellow conspirators moved to quash the indictment on the basis that section 251 was unconstitutional. Associate Chief Justice Parker of the Ontario High Court rejected the arguments of defense counsel as to the section's unconstitutionality.[57] The arguments advanced by the defendant closely resembled those raised in *Morgentaler* (1975), with the important addition of arguments based on the Charter of Rights and Freedoms. In particular,

---

56. Dr. Morgentaler also opened a clinic in Winnipeg, Manitoba, in 1982.
57. *See supra* note 24 and 47 O.R. (2d) at 377.

counsel argued that section 251 of the Criminal Code violated section 7 of the Charter, which guarantees the right to life, liberty, and security of the person, such rights not to be denied except in accordance with the principles of fundamental justice.

The importance of the Charter of Rights and Freedoms to the ultimate outcome in *Morgentaler* (1988) cannot be underestimated. Clearly, the only thing that had changed in Canadian law since the upholding of section 251 and the conviction of Dr. Morgentaler in 1976 was the adoption of an "entrenched" charter of rights.[58] The doctrine of parliamentary supremacy, which calls for judicial restraint in reviewing laws duly enacted by Parliament was no longer the paramount and fundamental value of the Canadian political order. The Charter of Rights guaranteed certain fundamental freedoms and rights to all Canadians that the government had to respect. For the first time in Canadian history, as part of the country's constitution, there were limitations placed on lawmakers and government officials.

It is therefore somewhat surprising that Associate Chief Justice Parker drew so heavily from the Supreme Court of Canada's earlier decision in *Morgentaler* (1975). This is even more surprising in light of the fact that he recognized that "the Courts have entered a new age with the enactment of the *Charter*."[59] However, one senses in his language and approach an unease that is reflective of the long-standing judicial fear of overstepping the courts' appropriate role when asked to review legislative pronouncements.

The main argument, advanced by counsel for Dr. Morgentaler, claimed that the guarantee of "liberty and security of person" contained a right of privacy that would permit a woman to choose whether or not to have an abortion. Not surprisingly, U.S. jurisprudence was invoked to support this claim, but Associate Chief Justice Parker counseled caution in relation to the relevance of U.S. jurisprudence in the interpretation of the Charter:

> Clearly, the entrenchment of the Constitution has brought our system of laws more closely in line with that of the United States. We now have constitutional limitations imposed upon our Legislatures which were formerly omnipotent within their respective spheres of power, with the modest exception of the federal limitations on Parliament due to the Canadian

---

58. In Canada, the concept of "entrenchment" is different than that in the United States. The Charter includes section 33, which permits the federal Parliament or provincial legislatures to "opt out" of certain of the guaranteed fundamental rights and freedoms. In practice, what this means is that a province or the federal Parliament can insulate a legislative enactment from judicial review by simply including a section in the law indicating that it will operate "notwithstanding" the Charter of Rights and Freedoms.

59. 47 O.R. (2d) at 366.

Bill of Rights. This transition does not, however, mean that we must accept an American interpretation whenever the wording of the Charter is similar to that of the American Bill of Rights. Differences in wording between the two documents, the use of headings, and our traditions will often be more powerful in construing a section of the Charter than the similarities between them.[60]

In attempting to define the scope and content of the phrase "liberty and security of person," Associate Chief Justice Parker began with an inquiry into the legal rights Canadians have at common law or by statute. If the claimed right was not protected by the Canadian system of positive law, then it would be necessary to consider if it was "so deeply rooted in the traditions and conscience of our people as to be ranked as fundamental."[61] Because the claimed right to abortion was not recognized by either existing common law or statute law, Associate Chief Justice Parker focused his inquiry on whether the asserted right was one rooted in our traditions. This analysis led him to conclude that certain elements of the right to privacy, for example the decision to marry and to have children, might be granted constitutional protection. However, he also decided that the right not to have children and the attendant right to terminate a pregnancy were not similarly "rooted in our traditions and conscience of this country."[62] He asserted this conclusion after a cursory and one might suggest, selective, historical review of the development of Canadian laws prohibiting abortion.

The interpretive approach of Associate Chief Justice Parker seemed to suggest that the definition of the guaranteed rights found in the Charter would be determined by a historical inquiry into the existing laws and mores of the country, thereby in reality providing scant recognition of the fact that the adoption of the Charter of Rights and Freedoms signaled a new constitutional order in Canada.[63] By concluding that section 7 of the Charter did not contain within it a right to privacy that extended to a woman's decision to terminate an unwanted pregnancy, he did not have to consider section 1 of the Charter, which explicitly calls on the courts to balance the interests

---

60. *Id.* at 397.

61. *Id.* at 406.

62. *Id.* at 408.

63. It appears that Associate Chief Justice Parker is invoking a "frozen rights" concept in defining those rights guaranteed under the Charter. The content of Charter rights is to be determined by existing statutory and common law, such law reflecting the traditions and history of our country. Such a theory provides little flexibility or room for future expansion of the guaranteed rights. One presumes that the relevant date at which rights are "frozen" is April 1982, when the Charter was proclaimed in force.

of the applicant, who is alleging a "rights" violation, against those of the state, in limiting the asserted right.[64] This task is, of course, one of assessing ends and means and calls on the state to justify any limitation on a guaranteed right. After finding that section 251 of the Criminal Code was constitutional, Associate Chief Justice Parker proceeded to trial, at the conclusion of which the jury acquitted Dr. Morgentaler and his fellow defendants. The Attorney General appealed this acquittal.

The Ontario Court of Appeal began its judgment by sounding the same note of caution expressed by Associate Chief Justice Parker in relation to the court's task—that task not being to express an opinion on the merits or demerits of abortion but on whether Parliament had the jurisdiction to enact section 251.[65] In essence, the Court of Appeal reiterated the approach taken by Parker in reviewing Canada's history in relation to abortion and concluded that the right to procure an abortion was not "so deeply rooted in our traditions and way of life as to be fundamental."[66] It would appear that upon this finding, the Court of Appeal needed to go no further. A woman's right to liberty and security did not include the right to choose to terminate her pregnancy; therefore, there should have been no necessity for the Court of Appeal to consider whether the right had been denied in such a way that the denial violated the principles of fundamental justice. However, the Court of Appeal offered a lengthy discussion of substantive and procedural due process, before concluding that the words of section 7 included both. The Court did caution, however, that "substantive reviews should take place only in exceptional circumstances where there has been a marked departure from the norm of civil or criminal liability resulting in the infringement of liberty or in some other injustice."[67] The Court concluded that section 251 did not contain any exceptional provision that would justify submitting it to substantive review. Indeed, the Court saw section 251 as relieving against the "somewhat Draconian provisions" of earlier legislative prohibitions.[68]

With this conclusion, the Ontario Court of Appeal avoided the application of section 1 of the Charter. After dismissing Dr. Morgentaler's

---

64. Section 1 of the Charter states:

   The Canadian Charter of Rights and Freedoms guarantees the rights and freedoms set out in it subject only to such reasonable limits prescribed by law as can be demonstrably justified in a free and democratic society.

65. (1985), 11 O.A.C. 81 at 85.

66. *Id.* at 98.

67. *Id.* at 103.

68. *Id.*

constitutional arguments, the Court of Appeal concluded that the defense of necessity should not have been left with the jury because there was no evidence to support it. Due to this, and other "fundamental errors" in law at trial, the Court of Appeal set aside the verdict of acquittal and ordered a new trial.[69]

C. The Decision of the Supreme Court of Canada

In January 1988 the Supreme Court declared section 251 of the Criminal Code constitutionally invalid.[70] In a 5–2 decision, the Court determined that section 251 violated section 7 of the Charter of Rights and Freedoms and that it could not be justified under section 1. The decision surprised many in spite of the fact that the Court earlier had confessed to a lack of judicial will and enthusiasm in applying the Canadian Bill of Rights, a "mistake" the court indicated would not be repeated.[71] Further, the Court clearly felt emboldened by the fact that the Charter was part of the supreme law of the land and that Canada's latter-day founding fathers had knowingly, if not exactly willingly, provided the courts with greater jurisdiction in resolving disputes between the individual and the state. However, based on the traditions of judicial conservatism and restraint evident in the courts' earlier pronouncements on "rights issues," many presumed this deferential posture to legislative choice would continue.

If any further evidence was required that the Supreme Court of Canada believed, as of 1982, that a new constitutional order had been created in Canada, its decision in *Morgentaler* (1988) provided it. Many thought the Court would be reluctant to enter the contentious debate on abortion and

---

69. *Id.* at 143. The Criminal Code had been amended after *Morgentaler* (1975) to prevent a court of appeal from entering a conviction after an acquittal by a jury. Therefore, the Ontario Court of Appeal had no choice but to order a new trial.

70. *See* [1988] 1 S.C.R. 30.

71. Singh v. Minister of Employment and Immigration [1985] 1 S.C.R. 177 at 209 per Wilson, J.:

> I do not think this kind of analysis is acceptable in relation to the *Charter*. It seems to me rather that the recent adoption of the *Charter* by Parliament and nine of the ten provinces as part of the Canadian constitutional framework has sent a clear message to the courts that the restrictive attitude which at times characterized their approach to the Canadian Bill of Rights ought to be re-examined.

However, observers of the Court could have looked to the court's decisions in cases such as *R. v. Big M. Drug Mart Ltd.*, [1985] 1 S.C.R. 295 and *Re B.C. Motor Vehicle Act*, [1985] 2 S.C.R. 486 for some indication of the court's new approach to rights issues.

would simply maintain the status quo, as reflected in section 251 of the Criminal Code. That was not to be the case.

It is not possible to speak of "the" decision of the Court in *Morgentaler*. Seven justices participated in the hearing, and there were four separate judgments written.[72] Although five of the seven justices found the law to be unconstitutional, they did so for remarkably different reasons, and therefore the precedential value of *Morgentaler* is unclear. The following discussion will concentrate on the decisions of Chief Justice Dickson and Justice Wilson.[73]

1. The Judgment of Chief Justice Dickson

A number of grounds for appeal were raised by counsel for Dr. Morgentaler, but the discussion that follows will deal only with the challenge to section 251 of the Criminal Code on the basis of section 7 of the Charter of Rights and Freedoms. It should be reiterated that section 7 is a somewhat complicated, two-part guarantee. The opening clause of the section guarantees to everyone the right to life, liberty, and security of the person; the second clause requires that *deprivations* of those rights be in accordance with the principles of fundamental justice. Therefore, section 7 anticipates a two-stage analysis: first, prima facie proof of a violation of one or more of the three identified rights and, second, proof that the alleged violation was not in accordance with the principles of fundamental justice. It is only after an applicant has convinced the court of both of these elements that the

---

72. The four decisions were written by (1) Chief Justice Dickson with whom Justice Lamer concurred, (2) Justice Beetz with whom Justice Estey concurred, (3) Justice Wilson, and (4) Justice McIntyre, dissenting, with whom Justice LaForest concurred.

73. Justice Beetz (Justice Estey concurring) held section 251 unconstitutional but on narrower grounds than Chief Justice Dickson and Justice Wilson. However, like Chief Justice Dickson, Justice Beetz only deals with the right to security of the person, concluding that a "pregnant woman cannot be said to be secure if, when her life or health is in danger, she is faced with a rule of criminal law which precludes her from obtaining efficient and timely medical treatment. If an act of Parliament makes a woman chose between the commission of a crime to obtain timely treatment and no treatment, that act is unconstitutional." *Morgentaler* (1988), 1 S.C.R. 30, at 90.

Justice Beetz did indicate that a legislative requirement for independent verification of a physician's medical opinion that a woman's life or health was endangered was reasonable but that the present requirement for therapeutic abortion committees was unreasonable and unconstitutional. He also concluded that the requirement that all abortions be performed in accredited or approved hospitals was unconstitutional.

He made one questionable comment in the course of his judgment to the effect that section 251(4) represented a constitutional minimum so that Parliament could not adopt a more restrictive abortion law. For him, it was as if that statutory provision was read into the definition of "security of the person," upon the proclamation of the Charter.

government will be called on to justify a limitation under section 1 of the Charter.

Further, it should be noted that much controversy has surrounded the meaning of the phrase "the principles of fundamental justice." It appears that this phrase was deliberately chosen by the drafters of the Charter to avoid the jurisprudential quagmire created by the concept of "due process" in the United States.[74] It is clear that the drafters of the Charter had intended that "the principles of fundamental justice" refer only to issues of procedural justice or fairness and not to the possibility of substantive review of impugned legislation by the courts. However, the Supreme Court has stated that it is not bound by expressions of intention, whether made by government officials charged with the actual drafting of the Charter or by ministers of the Crown, such as the Attorney General of Canada.[75] Consequently, the court will interpret the necessarily general language of the Charter on the basis of a "purposive" approach, with that approach being informed by the appropriate "linguistic, philosophical and historical contexts."[76] The Chief Justice, probably feeling some necessity to distinguish his approach and conclusions in *Morgentaler* (1988) from what he had said and done in *Morgentaler* (1975), alluded to the additional responsibilities the Court had been given with the adoption of the Charter—to ensure "that the legislative initiatives pursued by our Parliament and legislatures conform to the democratic values expressed in the Charter."[77] This justified the Court taking "another look" at the validity of section 251 of the Criminal Code.

The Chief Justice concluded that "state interference with bodily integrity and serious state imposed psychological stress, at least in the criminal law context, constituted a breach of security of the person."[78] On the basis of this definition, the Chief Justice easily concluded that section 251 had violated the right to security of thousands of Canadian women who had made the decision to terminate a pregnancy. He went on to explain:

> At the most basic, physical and emotional level, every pregnant woman is told by the section that she cannot submit to a generally safe medical procedure that might be of clear benefit to her unless she meets criteria

---

74. *See, e.g.,* the comments of Barry Strayer, Assistant Deputy Minister of Justice for Canada in Canada, Minister of Proceedings and Evidence of the Special Joint Committee of the Senate and House of Commons on the Constitution of Canada, 46: 32 (27 January 1981).

75. *See, e.g.,* the judgment of Justice Lamer *In re B.C. Motor Vehicle Act, supra* note 71.

76. R. v. Big M. Drug Mart Ltd., [1985] 1 S.C.R. 295.

77. *See* [1988] 1 S.C.R. 30, at 46.

78. *Id.* at 56.

entirely unrelated to her own priorities and aspirations. Not only does the removal of decision-making power threaten women in a physical sense; the indecision of not knowing whether an abortion will be granted inflicts emotional stress. Section 251 clearly interferes with a woman's bodily integrity in both a physical and emotional sense. Forcing a woman, by threat of criminal sanction, to carry a foetus to term unless she meets certain criteria unrelated to her own priorities and aspirations, is a profound interference with a woman's body and thus a violation of security of the person.[79]

The Chief Justice identified additional violations of a woman's right to physical and psychological security in the documented delays caused by the procedures created by Parliament in section 251(4).[80] The requirement that lawful abortions be performed only in approved or accredited hospitals, after the granting of consent by a therapeutic abortion committee, led to delays that increased the health risks to women. Expert advice established that even short delays, for example, of a few weeks, led to a higher risk of complications and mortality. In addition, delay created greater psychological trauma; stress levels were increased because of the "red tape" created by section 251(4); and the committee structure created a high degree of uncertainty as to whether an abortion would be approved.

The Chief Justice went on to consider whether this violation denied the principles of fundamental justice. After documenting the limited, and uneven, accessibility to the statutorily created procedures in section 251(4), he concluded that the subsection created a criminal defense that was, for many Canadian women, nothing more than an illusion. This illusory defense violated the principles of fundamental justice, those principles being found in "the basic tenets of our legal system."[81] He stated:

> One of the basic tenets of our system of criminal justice is that when Parliament creates a defence to a criminal charge, the defence should not be illusory or so difficult to attain as to be practically illusory. . . . In the present case, the structure—the system regulating access to therapeutic abortions—is manifestly unfair. It contains so many potential barriers to its own operation that the defence it creates will in many circumstances be practically unavailable to women who would prima facie qualify for the defence, or at least would force such women to travel great distances at substantial

---

79. *Id.* at 56–57.

80. The Chief Justice draws heavily upon two expert reports to provide evidence of both delay and variations in the definition of key concepts such as health. These two reports were the Badgley Report, *supra* note 25, and the Powell Report, *supra* note 25.

81. *See* [1988] 1 S.C.R. 30, at 70.

expense and inconvenience in order to benefit from a defence that is held
out to be generally available.[82]

After finding a violation of section 7, the Chief Justice had to consider
the applicability of section 1 of the Charter, which can be used to save a legislative provision found to be in violation of a guaranteed right. In essence,
the interpretive approach adopted by the Supreme Court to section 1
requires an ends and means analysis. For a limitation to be saved under section 1, it must be in pursuit of an objective "of sufficient importance to warrant overriding a constitutionally protected right or freedom."[83] The means
chosen to achieve this sufficiently important objective must be proportional
to the legislative ends. The means must be rational, fair, and not arbitrary;
they should impair as little as possible the right or freedom under consideration; and, finally, the effects of the limitation on the relevant right should
not be out of proportion to the objectives sought to be achieved.[84]

The Chief Justice concluded that section 251 had been enacted in pursuit of an important government objective. He stated:

> I think the protection of the interests of pregnant women is a valid gov-
> ernmental objective, where life and health can be jeopardized by criminal
> sanctions. . . . I agree that protection of foetal interests by Parliament is
> also a valid governmental objective. It follows that balancing these inter-
> ests, with the lives and health of women, a major factor, is clearly an impor-
> tant governmental objective.[85]

However, the Chief Justice concluded that the means chosen by Parliament to achieve this objective were neither rational nor proportionate. He
found that the procedures and administrative structures created by section
251 were often arbitrary and unfair. Further, the procedures established to
implement the policy of section 251 impaired section 7 rights far more than
was necessary because they held out an illusory defense to many women
who would prima facie qualify under the exculpatory provisions. The effects
of the limitation upon the section 7 rights of many pregnant women were
disproportionate to the objective sought. He stated: "Indeed, to the extent

---

82. *Id.* at 70–73.
83. *Id.* at 73. In *R. v. Oakes,* [1986] 1 S.C.R. 103, the Court articulated the test to govern
the application of section 1.
84. *See* [1988] 1 S.C.R. 30, at 74.
85. *Id.* at 75.

that s.251(4) is designed to protect the life and health of women, the procedures it establishes may actually defeat that objective."[86]

The judgment of the Chief Justice provides Parliament with few clear guidelines as to what a new law on abortion should look like. Most importantly, he leaves unanswered the question of whether section 7 contains within it a right for women to control their reproductive capacity. He identifies only procedural deficiencies within section 251(4). Should we, therefore, conclude that if Parliament drafts a law that remedies these deficiencies, it will be immune from attack? He speaks of the security of the person being violated when laws force women to make choices unrelated to their own "priorities and aspirations." The sweeping implications of this statement must lead us to question its ultimate utility as a test for defining the concept of "security of the person." Further, the Chief Justice appears to suggest that his comments are limited to the criminal law context of section 251. Therefore, it is difficult to predict how his comments regarding "priorities and aspirations" will be applied in the context of provincial laws purporting to regulate the provision of health care and hospitals. He provides us with little indication as to how he would balance a claim that may be made by government on behalf of the fetus with that made on behalf of women to control their reproductive capacity. Finally, and perhaps most importantly, the Chief Justice does not inform us as to how he sees women's claims for equality within Canadian society enhancing or informing their claims for reproductive choice and control.

2. The Judgment of Justice Wilson

Justice Bertha Wilson took a dramatically different approach to the constitutional questions before her than did her fellow justices. For Justice Wilson, it was impossible to avoid answering the question of whether section 7 guaranteed to women at least a qualified right to terminate an unwanted pregnancy. The Chief Justice expressly refused to answer that question, finding it unnecessary because of his conclusion that the legislative procedures set out in section 251(4) were so arbitrary, unfair, and vague that they could not be upheld. Justice Wilson refused to take the "easy way out" in relation to this difficult issue and astutely comments:

> A consideration as to whether or not the procedural requirements for obtaining or performing an abortion comport with fundamental justice is purely academic if such requirements cannot, as a constitutional matter, be

---

86. *Id.* at 75–76.

imposed at all. If a pregnant woman cannot, as a constitutional matter, be compelled by law to carry the foetus to term against her will, a review of the procedural requirements by which she may be compelled to do so seems pointless.[87]

Justice Wilson was the only member of the Court to consider the right to liberty protected by section 7. For her, the right to individual liberty was "inextricably tied to the concept of human dignity."[88] Respect for human dignity is given meaning, at least in part, by permitting individuals to make fundamental personal decisions without interference from the state. Justice Wilson drew heavily from U.S. case law in reaching her conclusion that the right to liberty guarantees to every individual a degree of personal autonomy over important decisions intimately affecting his or her private life.[89] She then considered whether the decision of a woman to terminate her pregnancy fell within this class of protected decisions and concluded that it did. In words of unusual sensitivity and insight she described this decision:

> This decision is one that will have profound psychological, economic and social consequences for the pregnant woman. The circumstances giving rise to it can be complex and varied and there may be, and usually are, powerful considerations militating in opposite directions. It is a decision that deeply reflects the way the woman thinks about herself and her relationship to others and to society at large. It is not just a medical decision; it is a profound social and ethical one as well. Her response to it will be the response of the whole person.
>
> It is probably impossible for a man to respond, even imaginatively, to such a dilemma not just because it is outside the realm of his personal experience (although this is, of course, the case) but because he can relate to it only by objectifying it, thereby eliminating the subjective elements of the female psyche which are at the heart of the dilemma.
>
> . . . The more recent struggle for women's rights has been a struggle to eliminate discrimination, to achieve a place for women in a man's world, to develop a set of legislative reforms in order to place women in the same position as men. It has not been a struggle to define the rights of women in relation to their special place in the societal structure and in relation to the biological distinction between the two sexes. Thus, women's needs and aspirations are only now being translated into protected rights. The right to reproduce or not reproduce, which is an issue in this case, is one such

---

87. *Id.* at 161–62.
88. *Id.* at 164.
89. *Id.* at 166.

right and is properly perceived as an integral part of a modern woman's struggle to assert her dignity and worth as a human being.[90]

Based on her definition of liberty, Justice Wilson concluded that section 251 of the Criminal Code violated a woman's right to choose for herself whether or not to terminate her pregnancy. She found particularly offensive the fact that section 251 left with a committee a decision she believed rightly belonged to the woman herself.

In defining the right to security of the person, Justice Wilson agreed with the Chief Justice that the guarantee protected both the physical and psychological integrity of a woman. However, she identified an additional and more fundamental concern with the legislative scheme established in section 251(4). For Justice Wilson, the effect of the section was to tell a woman that her capacity to reproduce was not subject to her own control. She chillingly described this reality:

> She is truly being treated as a means—a means to an end which she does not desire, but over which she has no control. She is the passive recipient of a decision made by others as to whether her body is to be used to nurture a new life. Can there be anything that comports less with human dignity and self-respect? How can a woman in this position have any sense of security with respect to her person?[91]

For Justice Wilson, the principles of fundamental justice included not only the concept of procedural fairness but also any infringement of other fundamental rights and freedoms set out elsewhere in the Charter. She believed that section 251 of the Criminal Code not only infringed section 7 of the Charter but also section 2(a), which guaranteed to everyone freedom of conscience and religion. The decision whether or not to terminate a pregnancy was "essentially a moral decision, a matter of conscience. The question is: whose conscience? Is the conscience of the woman to be paramount or the conscience of the state?"[92] She ultimately concluded that for the state to take sides on the issue of abortion as it had done in the enactment of section 251(4) was to validate one conscientiously held view at the expense of another. "Legislation which treats some as a means to an end deprives them of their essential humanity and therefore violates freedom of

---

90. *Id.* at 171–72.

91. *Id.* at 173–74. The language chosen by Justice Wilson in describing a woman merely as a means to an end evokes images of the bleak and repressive world so hauntingly described by Margaret Atwood in her novel *A Handmaid's Tale* (1985).

92. *Id.* at 176.

conscience."[93] Such a violation could not be, according to Justice Wilson, in accordance with the principles of fundamental justice.

In the application of section 1, Justice Wilson disagreed with the Chief Justice as to the paramount legislative objective to be achieved by section 251. For Justice Wilson, the primary objective of the legislation was the protection of the fetus, which she considered to be a valid legislative objective. She would permit certain limitations to be placed on a woman's right to terminate her pregnancy, depending on the developmental stage of the fetus. She asked the question: "At what point does the state's interest in the protection of the foetus become compelling and justify state intervention in what is otherwise a matter of purely personal and private concern?"[94] Although Justice Wilson did allude to the viability test adopted by the U.S. Supreme Court in *Roe v. Wade*,[95] she did not expressly adopt it. Indeed, she was very careful to avoid the use of the concept of viability as the point at which the state's interest in the protection of the fetus becomes compelling.[96] She preferred to discuss this difficult and contentious issue of line-drawing or balancing in terms of a developmental progression. In her opinion, a developmental view of the fetus supported a permissive approach to abortion in the early stages of pregnancy and a restrictive approach in the later stages:

> In the early stages a woman's autonomy would be absolute; her decision reached in consultation with her physician, not to carry the foetus to term would be conclusive. . . . [H]er reasons for having an abortion would, however, be the proper subject of inquiry at the later stages of her pregnancy when the state's compelling interest in the protection of the foetus would justify it in prescribing conditions. The precise point in the development of the foetus at which the state's interest in its protection becomes "compelling," I leave to the informed judgment of the legislature which is in a position to receive guidance on the subject from all the relevant disciplines. It seems, however, that it might fall somewhere in the second trimester.[97]

Justice Wilson astutely pointed out that section 251 of the Criminal Code took the decision away from a woman at all stages of her pregnancy and reposed it in a therapeutic abortion committee. The section worked as

93. *Id.* at 179.
94. *Id.* at 181.
95. *See* 410 U.S. 113 (1973).
96. This is undoubtedly because Justice Wilson was well aware of the advances in science and technology that make it more difficult to define this point and of the jurisprudential controversy surrounding it in the United States.
97. *See* [1988] 1 S.C.R. 30, at 183.

a complete denial of a woman's constitutionally protected right, not merely as a limitation on it. Consequently, Justice Wilson concluded that it was impossible for section 251 to meet the proportionality test of *Oakes*.[98]

Therefore, for Parliament merely to remedy the procedural defects identified by the Chief Justice would not be sufficient to meet the concerns of Justice Wilson. Even if the facilities necessary to provide equal access to therapeutic abortions were available, Justice Wilson would continue to characterize the law as one that denied a woman the right to decide for herself whether or not to terminate her pregnancy. Although the state has the right to impose certain limitations upon a woman's right to an abortion, such limitations would only be constitutionally permissible later on in the "gestational process." Justice Wilson does not define the exact point in this "gestational process" at which Parliament could impose constitutionally valid limitations. Out of judicial deference to legislative choice, she leaves the definition of this crucial point to Parliament. One would presume, however, that had Justice Wilson believed it necessary to define this point, viability would be, for her, the determining factor.

IV. The Aftermath of *Morgentaler*

A. Political Activity Surrounding Abortion

Predictably, the decision of the Supreme Court of Canada in *Morgentaler* (1988) did not end the debate surrounding abortion; if anything, the Court's decision energized the competing sides of this divisive issue. For a time, there was renewed political activity, with the anti-choice movement demanding a new federal criminal law that would give supremacy to fetal rights; the pro-choice movement argued against the recriminalization of abortion.

After the defeat of Bill C-43 in the Senate in January 1991, federal governments have refrained from reopening the abortion debate; however, a number of private member bills have been tabled since that time and as recently as 2016. They have dealt with a variety of issues, including insurance for medically unnecessary abortions,[99] the protection of conscience

---

98. *Id.*

99. Bill C-242 was introduced in 2002 but did not pass the first reading in the House of Commons. It sought a referendum to determine whether Canadians wish medically unnecessary abortions to be insured under the Canada Health Act.

rights in the health care professions,[100] and the criminalization of coercion of pregnant women to abort.[101] Attempts were also made to recriminalize abortion after 20 weeks' gestation.[102] Perhaps most controversial, however, have been the multiple attempts to criminalize the abuse of pregnant women, whereby the legislature would recognize the unborn child as a victim.[103]

The only legislative initiative introduced by a federal government after the decision in Morgentaler (1988) was Bill C-43,[104] introduced by the

---

100. Bill C-537 only passed its first reading in the House of Commons in 2008. It sought to protect health care professionals from having to participate in procedures against their will, such as abortion. It would have made it a criminal offence for employers to coerce their employees into performing such procedures, or to dismiss employees who refused.

101. Sometimes referred to as Roxanne's Law, Bill C-510 sought to make it a criminal offence to coerce a pregnant woman into procuring an abortion. It was defeated at its second reading in the House of Commons in 2010. Coercion is already an offence pursuant to section 264.1 of Canada's Criminal Code, which rendered this piece of legislation redundant. However, the debate in the House also raised issues such as the fact that the text of the bill recognized the fetus as a child, as well as the fact that it implied that women were only pressured to have abortions, rather than also being pressured to carry their unborn child to term.

102. Bill C-338 sought to recriminalize abortion, but for a few exceptions, after 20 weeks' gestation. It was introduced in 2006 and only made it through its first reading.

As a practical matter, later-stage abortions remain scarce in Canada. As of this writing, only three locations in Canada offered abortions up to 23 weeks and 6 days (one in British Columbia, one in Southern Ontario, and one in Quebec). No providers in Canada offered abortion care beyond 23 weeks and 6 days. For women wanting an abortion beyond 23 weeks and 6 days, one potential option has been to travel to the United States.

103. Bill C-484 was known as the Unborn Victims of Crime Act and would have created an independent criminal offence for the injury or death of an unborn child where a pregnant woman was assaulted or killed. The proposed amendment would have recognized the fetus as a victim independent of its mother, thus granting it a legally separate status. Bill C-484 passed its second reading in the House of Commons; however, it died on the Order Paper with the dissolution of Parliament in 2008. The pro-choice community vehemently opposed it.

Bill C-543 was introduced in 2008 and passed its first reading. Many pro-life organizations, such as the Abortion Rights Coalition of Canada, preferred Bill C-543 to Bill C-484. Although similar, Bill C-543 did not recognize the fetus as victim, and its primary purpose was to require the courts to recognize pregnancy as an aggravating factor in sentencing.

Finally, Bill C-225 was introduced in 2016, but was defeated at second reading in the House of Commons. The Protection of Pregnant Women and their Preborn Children Act was viewed as almost identical to Bill C-484 as it sought to create a separate offence in the Criminal Code for injuring or killing a fetus where an offence is committed against a pregnant woman. It also sought formal recognition of the abuse of a pregnant woman as an aggravating factor in sentencing. It was defeated in its second reading in the House of Commons and drew the ire of many pro-choice organizations who, again, opposed the recognition of fetal rights, believing it could threaten a woman's constitutional and abortion rights.

104. See Appendix II for the text of Bill C-43. The impact of this proposed bill was felt immediately. It is estimated that between 60 and 100 doctors stopped performing abortions

government of Prime Minister Brian Mulroney. Its effect would have been to recriminalize abortion, punishable by up to two years in prison, unless a doctor was of the opinion that the pregnancy threatened the physical or mental health of a woman. The legislation fueled immediate controversy, once again proving to politicians that this divisive issue was one over which no government was likely to achieve consensus.

Although most proposed legislation has not addressed abortion or the rights of a fetus directly, their implications, had they been successful, would have been to reopen the debate on abortion and the reproductive rights of women in Canada, thus undermining the Supreme Court of Canada's decision in *Mortgentaler* (1988).

B. Access to Abortion

While federal governments of different political persuasions have chosen to avoid future legislative attempts to limit or overturn *Morgentaler* (1988), since the failed 1991 attempt, political attention has shifted to the provinces. It is primarily at the provincial level where the issue continues to create political controversy and division.

The provinces have constitutional jurisdiction over health care and hospitals. Therefore, much of the activity surrounds provincial regulations dealing with access to abortion services and medical insurance of the same.[105] Since *Mortgentaler* (1988), the anti-choice movement has had success in lobbying provincial governments to place restrictions on the medical procedure of abortion. Some of these restrictions have included (1) the "de-insuring" of the procedure of abortion under a province's health care

---

for fear of criminal prosecution (this was merely in anticipation of the bill becoming law) and that more than 275 doctors threatened to stop performing abortions if the bill was passed. Doctors particularly feared the prospect of third parties (e.g., anti-choice groups, disgruntled husbands, boyfriends, etc.) laying private prosecutions. Although the federal Minister of Justice, Kim Campbell, tried to allay the fears of the Canadian Medical Association and individual doctors regarding this prospect, her efforts were met with hostility and disbelief.

The government's experience with Bill C-43 again proves that compromise on the issue of abortion is impossible. By requiring that the federal Cabinet support the government initiative in Bill C-43, its passage was assured in the House of Commons. However, when the bill was considered in the Senate there was no such government discipline imposed and pro-choice forces joined with anti-choice forces to defeat the bill. The vote was a tie, with the result that the bill failed.

105. *Abortion in Canada: Twenty Years After R v. Morgentaler,* K. Richer, Law and Government Division, Sept. 2008.

system, thereby forcing women to pay for their abortions;[106] (2) requiring that the consent of at least two physicians be obtained before a provincial health care plan will authorize payment;[107] (3) requiring that abortions be performed only in hospitals;[108] and (4) requiring that doctors counsel women seeking abortions as to the stage of fetal development and alternatives to the procedure of abortion.[109] So far, these strategies have met with some political success but with no legal success.

1. Nova Scotia

In 1989, the Nova Scotia legislature passed an act to "prohibit the privatization of the provision of certain medical services in order to maintain a single high-quality health care delivery system for all Nova Scotians."[110] Doctors could perform "designated medical services" in approved hospitals only and anyone who performed such services outside an approved facility would not be reimbursed under the health insurance plan.[111] Under regulations passed by the Cabinet, abortion was one of a number of designated services that could be performed only in an approved hospital.[112]

Dr. Morgentaler was again at the center of this political and legal conflict. He opened a clinic in Halifax in 1989 and was charged quickly with 14 counts of performing abortions in contravention of section 4 of the Medical Services Act. He was acquitted by the trial judge, who found the legislation to be ultra vires or beyond the legislative authority of the province because it was, in essence, criminal law. Dr. Morgentaler's counsel argued that the legislation was unconstitutional on two main grounds: (1) that the legislation was criminal law, as it purported to prohibit abortions in all but

---

106. The government of British Columbia enacted such a provision on February 10, 1988, only 13 days after the Supreme Court's decision in *Morgentaler*. The government of Saskatchewan currently is considering such action.

107. A number of provinces adopted this requirement, including Alberta and New Brunswick. However, Alberta dropped it in 1991 and New Brunswick dropped it in 2015.

108. The Province of Nova Scotia had adopted this strategy. In addition, a number of provinces made it a condition of payment under their health care plans that an abortion be performed only in an approved hospital. These provinces are New Brunswick, Prince Edward Island, and Nova Scotia.

109. The Province of Saskatchewan adopted this strategy.

110. S.N.S. 1989, c.9, as quoted from *R. v. Morgentaler* (1991), 270 A.P.R. 293.

111. In addition, anyone performing an abortion outside an approved facility was subject to a fine of not less than $10,000 and not more than $50,000. Medical Services Act, S.N.S. 1989, c.9 section 6(1).

112. N.S. Reg. 152/89.

approved hospitals, and legislative jurisdiction over criminal law is an exclusive federal matter; and (2) that the legislation violated sections 7 and 15 of the Charter of Rights and Freedoms. Provincial Court Judge Kennedy found it unnecessary to deal with the Charter arguments as he concluded that the legislation was a colorable attempt by the province to control and prohibit abortions, an objective beyond its legislative competence.[113] This decision was upheld both by the Nova Scotia Court of Appeal and, ultimately, the Supreme Court of Canada.[114]

2. British Columbia

In British Columbia, the provincial government chose to "de-insure" the medical procedure of abortion, unless there was a significant threat to a woman's life and the abortion was performed in an approved facility.[115] The former condition would preclude payment for most abortions performed in British Columbia. Chief Justice McEachern observed that this regulation was passed "almost upon delivery of judgment in *Morgentaler*."[116] As in Nova Scotia, this issue was decided at trial, without recourse to Charter arguments, on the basis that the Cabinet had exceeded its delegated authority when it ordered that abortion was not to be considered a service that was medically required.

---

113. *Supra* note 110, at 302–03. The provincial government claimed that the legislative purposes were (1) a desire to prevent a two-tier system for the delivery of health care, one for the rich and one for the poor; (2) to provide high quality delivery of health care; and (3) to rationalize existing services to prevent duplication.

114. (1992), 283 A.P.R. 361, *aff'd* [1993] 3 SCR 463 [*Mortgentaler* (1993)].

115. B.C. Reg. 54/88, O.C. 221/88.

116. B.C. Civil Liberties Assn. v. B.C. (A.G.), [1988] 4 W.W.R. 100 at 105. Chief Justice McEachern does suggest that the Cabinet might have been acting within its authority had it simply de-insured the procedure of abortion. However, he also notes the limitations upon a province in de-insuring medical procedures. Because the federal government pays for a percentage of provincial health care costs, it has created certain national standards or objectives, including universality and accessibility, that must be maintained by the provinces. The province could therefore run the risk of being disqualified from federal funding by de-insuring the medical procedure of abortion. Section 3 of the Canada Health Act, R.S.C. 1970, c.C-6 provides:

> It is hereby declared that the primary objective in Canadian health care policy is to protect, promote and restore the physical and mental well-being of residents of Canada and to facilitate reasonable access to health services without financial or other barriers.

3. New Brunswick

In 1985, shortly after Dr. Morgentaler proposed a freestanding abortion clinic in Fredericton, the government of New Brunswick enacted amendments to the Medical Act[117] that characterized the performance of abortion outside a hospital as an act of professional misconduct. In 1994, Dr. Morgentaler attacked the validity of these provisions.[118] The Court of Queen's Bench relied on the Supreme Court of Canada's decision in *Morgentaler* (1988) and found that the provisions in question exceeded the province's jurisdiction. Specifically, the Court found that:

> The impugned sections of the Medical Act were enacted by the legislature, not with a view to controlling or ensuring the quality and nature of health care or the maintenance of professional standards, but to prohibit abortions outside hospitals with a view to suppressing or punishing what the members of the government and of the Legislative Assembly perceived to be the socially undesirable conduct of abortion.[119]

The Court of Appeal upheld this decision; however, controversy ensued. In 2002, Dr. Morgentaler launched an action that challenged the legality of a regulation under the Medical Services Payment Act.[120] Specifically, the regulation excluded abortions performed in a nonhospital setting from its definition of "entitled services." The consequences of the regulation were such that no abortion performed at Dr. Morgentaler's private clinic qualified as "entitled" services. Thus, patients paid for the procedures performed at the clinic out of pocket. Dr. Morgentaler argued that the regulation in question violated the Canada Health Act, as well as sections 7 and 16 of the Charter of Rights and Freedoms. Dr. Morgentaler died in 2013, whereupon the case was stayed and finally discontinued in 2014, more than 12 years

---

117. The Bill became SNB 1985, c.76, which stated the following at section 56 (b.1):

56 A member may be found guilty of professional misconduct if
(b.1) he has been involved in the performance or attempted performance of an act intended to procure the miscarriage of a female person outside a hospital approved by the Minister of Health.

118. Morgentaler v. New Brunswick, [1994] 152 NBR (2d) 200, 117 DLR (4th) 753 (NBQB).

119. *Id.* at 42.

120. RSNB 1973, c.M-7. The issue was specifically with reg. 84-20, which limited abortion as an "entitled" service only if (1) two medical practitioners certified in writing that the abortion was "medically required" and (2) that the abortion was performed in an approved hospital by specialists in the field of obstetrics and gynecology.

after it had begun.[121] In January of 2015, the provisions at issue in the 2003 action were addressed by the legislature. It was no longer required that two medical practitioners certify the abortion as "medically required" or that a specialist in obstetrics and gynecology perform the procedure. However, for abortions to be paid for by the province they still had to be performed in a hospital.[122]

Although these changes were welcome by some, the amended legislation failed to address access concerns. In New Brunswick, only three hospitals perform abortions. When the Morgentaler Clinic closed its doors in July 2014 due to a lack of provincial funding, it was performing the majority of abortions in New Brunswick.[123]

4. Prince Edward Island

In 1994, Dr. Morgentaler challenged a regulation under the PEI Health Services Act, whereby the province would fund abortion services only if they were performed in a public hospital and deemed medically necessary by the Health and Community Services Agency.[124] The Prince Edward Island Supreme Court, like its counterparts in other provinces, found the impugned provision to be beyond the legislative mandate of the Agency. Although the act provided the Agency with broad discretion to determine which health services would be insured and what conditions would be imposed for eligibility, the Court found that it did not give the Agency the discretion to exclude from coverage some abortion services, which were considered basic health service under the regulation.

---

121. While Dr. Morgentaler had been granted public interest standing, the clinic in Fredericton did not have standing or the means to pursue the lawsuit. *See The Canadian Press, Morgentaler's Lawsuit over New Brunswick Abortion Funding Dropped,* THE GLOBE AND MAIL (Apr. 15, 2014).

122. See A. Abdelwahab, *N.B. Provincial Government Publishes New Abortion Regulations,* CBC NEWS (Jan. 7, 2015).

123. *See Morgentaler Clinic in Fredericton Performs Last Abortions before Closure,* CBC NEWS (July 18, 2014). The clinic had been performing about 60 percent of the abortions in New Brunswick, which were not covered by the province. At the time of closure, abortions cost $700 before 14 weeks of pregnancy and $850 between 14 and 16 weeks. Due to a rally of public support and a fundraising campaign, the Morgentaler Clinic reopened as a private abortion facility, Clinic 554, in 2015. *See Morgentaler's Old Fredericton Clinic to Reopen as Private Abortion Facility,* CBC NEWS (Jan. 16, 2015).

124. Morgentaler v. Prince Edward Island (Government of), [1994] 117 NFLD & PEIR 181, 112 DLR (4th) 756.

The Court of Appeal overturned this decision in 1996.[125] Access to abortion services for women on Prince Edward Island was nonexistent. Women had to travel out of province—to Nova Scotia most often—in order to obtain an abortion. As had been the case before 1994, the cost was covered by Prince Edward Island's medical insurance scheme only where the abortion was performed in a hospital, and where a physician, who deemed the procedure to be medically necessary, referred the woman.[126]

In early 2016, Abortion Access Now P.E.I. began litigation to force the province to provide unrestricted access to publicly funded abortion services. Shortly thereafter, the government announced that the province would once again provide abortion services.[127] On January 31, 2017, the first abortion procedures, in almost 35 years, were performed on Prince Edward Island.

5. Manitoba

Two female plaintiffs who had undergone abortions in 1994 and 2001, respectively, began litigation against the province in 2004. Both had originally pursued the procedure at a local hospital; however, there were long delays in obtaining an appointment. Consequently, both women underwent their abortions at the private Morgentaler Clinic, where they had to pay a fee that could not be reimbursed under the Health Services Insurance Act.[128] Known as Jane Doe 1 and Jane Doe 2, the plaintiffs successfully argued that the legislation violated their section 7 rights under the Charter of Rights and Freedoms. The Court also found that the legislation violated sections 2(a) and 15 of the Charter. Since 2005, abortions performed at private clinics in the province have been publicly funded.

The current debate in Canada regarding abortion services centers on the "abortion pill," which made its long-awaited debut in early 2017.[129] The two-drug combination, commonly referred to as Myfegymiso, was approved by Health Canada in July 2015 after a three-year application process.[130]

---

125. PEI (Minister of Health and Social Services) v. Morgentaler, [1996] 144 NFLD & PEIR 263, 139 DLR (4th) 603.

126. *Abortion in Canada, supra* note 105.

127. *See* G. Harding, *P.E.I. Premier Wade MacLauchlan Says Abortion Lawsuit Required Timely Response*, CBC NEWS (Apr. 1, 2016).

128. Section 2(28)(a) of Manitoba Regulation 46/93 stated that therapeutic abortions had to be performed by a medical practitioner in a hospital (other than a private hospital) in order to be considered "insured services."

129. Kelly Grant, *Abortion Pill Makes Canadian Debut*, THE GLOBE AND MAIL (Jan. 21, 2017).

130. *Id.* This was considered an unusually long time for a medication that was already approved in more than 60 countries, including the United States. Some countries have had

Despite this, significant challenges remain, particularly the number of stipulations in place for prescribing the drug[131] and the fact that it is not covered by most provincial drug plans.[132] While the "abortion pill" is considered to be a welcome solution to the barriers faced by many women, particularly those who reside in rural or remote areas of the country, as well as those who are low income, the slow rollout of the treatment, coupled with the lengthy list of stipulations, remain concerns for pro-choice advocates.[133] In November 2017, Health Canada did change its product monograph from "physicians only" to "health professional," thereby extended prescribing and dispensing authority to include professionals such as pharmacists, nurse practitioners, and midwifes.

C. The Legal Status of the Unborn

One of the significant gaps in *Morgentaler* (1998) was that the Supreme Court of Canada did not directly address the legal status of the fetus. Since that time, there have been a number of legal proceedings dealing with this

---

access to the treatment since 1987. It is considered to be the "gold standard" of care as defined by the World Health Organization. *See also* M. Shkimba, *New Year, New Choices for Canadian Women?*, THE HAMILTON SPECTATOR (Jan. 9, 2017).

131. *Id.* Some of the stipulations include that doctors should give the medication directly to women and that it should not be used for pregnancies further along than seven weeks (though it should be noted that efforts are being made to allow pharmacists to dispense the drug and to extend the upper limit to nine weeks). An ultrasound is also required before doctors can distribute the pill. Women must also make a return trip to their physician to ensure the abortion is complete. Finally, in order to be able to prescribe the drug, physicians are required to undergo training.

132. In Canada, all provinces, except Quebec, work together to determine which medications are to be included in provincial drug plans. This is done through the Canadian Agency for Drugs and Technologies in Health (CADTH). Celopharma is the small Canadian drug company, which brought Myfogymiso to market. It applied to CADTH; however, withdrew its application upon learning that the agency charges $72,000 to review a new drug. Consequently, for women who don't have access through their private health insurance, the treatment comes at a $300 cost (albeit, this is cheaper than surgical abortion). Four provinces—Alberta, New Brunswick, Ontario, and Quebec—have announced that women in those provinces will be able to access the drug free of charge. See Paula Simons, *Access to Abortion Drug One Step Closer for Alberta Women*, THE EDMONTON JOURNAL (Oct. 7, 2016); Janet French, All Alberta *Women Should Have Free Abortion Pill Access, Health Minister Says*, THE EDMONTON JOURNAL (July 18, 2019). *See also New Brunswick Women Will Be Able to Get Abortion Pill Free of Charge*, CBC NEWS (Apr. 4, 2017); and *Alberta to Cover Cost of Abortion Pill*, CBC NEWS (Apr. 22, 2017).

133. *See, e.g.*, Federation of Medical Women of Canada Newsletter, Winter 2016, for an article by the Federation's President entitled "Drug Restrictions, a Violation of Canadian Women's Human Rights and Freedoms."

controversial issue, some of which provided the Supreme Court with the opportunity to provide some clarity.

1. *Tremblay v. Daigle*

One post-*Morgentaler* development was the attempted use of injunctive relief by disgruntled "boyfriends" to prevent women from terminating pregnancies. In the summer of 1990, two highly publicized incidents alerted Canadians to the possibility that those opposed to choice might employ this particularly traumatizing strategy.[134] The most troubling, and newsworthy, of these cases was that involving Chantal Daigle.

At the time, the story of Chantal Daigle was well known in Canada: her pregnancy, her failed relationship with her boyfriend, Jean-Guy Tremblay, her decision to terminate her pregnancy, Tremblay's attempts to stop the abortion, the Quebec courts' granting Tremblay's request for an injunction,[135] her decision to have an abortion in defiance of the order of the Quebec Court of Appeal,[136] and, finally, vindication from the Supreme Court of Canada when it allowed her appeal.[137]

The decision of the Supreme Court of Canada was an exercise in statutory interpretation and, in particular, the interpretation of the Quebec Charter of Rights and Freedoms. The task of the Court was to determine if the phrase "human being," as used in Quebec's Charter, included a fetus. In answering this question, the Supreme Court of Canada relied primarily on the status of the fetus under the Civil Code of Quebec.

Counsel for the respondent, Jean-Guy Tremblay, made three arguments to support the injunction: (1) that the fetus had a right to life under the

---

134. *Murphy v. Dodd* (1990), 63 D.L.R. (4th) 515; *Tremblay v. Daigle* [1989] 2 S.C.R. 530, *rev'g* [1989]. R.J.Q. 1735, *aff'g* [1989] R.J.Q. 1980.

135. An interlocutory injunction was granted against Daigle by Justice Viens of the Quebec Superior Court on July 17, 1989. An appeal from this decision was heard by the Quebec Court of Appeal on July 20, 1989. It rendered its judgment on July 26 and, in a 3–2 decision, denied the request of the appellant to vacate the injunction.

136. The Quebec Court of Appeal upheld the interlocutory injunction issued by Justice Viens. The injunction stated, in part:

> The Court grants the request for an interlocutory injunction, orders the Respondent to refrain, under threat of legal penalty, from having an abortion or taking recourse voluntarily to any method which directly or indirectly would lead to the death of the foetus which she is presently carrying.

137. Although during the summer recess, due to the urgency of the matter five justices of the Supreme Court of Canada heard the appellant's application for leave to appeal on August 1. Leave was granted the same day, and the appeal was heard on August 8 before the entire court.

Quebec Charter; (2) that the appellant, Chantal Daigle, would violate this right by having an abortion; and (3) that an injunction was an appropriate remedy by which to protect this right. The Supreme Court concluded that it needed to address only the first of these issues, because if there were no substantive rights of the fetus on which to base an injunction, it would be vacated. The Court, exercising its characteristic judicial restraint,[138] simply declared that it would answer no more questions than required to determine the appeal. Based on its decision that there were no substantive rights to justify the issuing of an injunction in the first place, the Court needed to go no further in its deliberations and, in particular, did not need to address the argument that the fetus had a constitutionally protected right to life independent of the woman carrying it.

The respondent argued that the substantive rights on which an injunction could be based were (1) that the fetus had a right to life, under the Quebec Charter; (2) that the fetus had a right to life under the Canadian Charter of Rights and Freedoms; and (3) that the respondent, as "potential father,"[139] had a right to be heard in respect of decisions regarding his potential child. The Supreme Court devoted most of its judgment to the first of these three arguments. The Quebec Charter guarantees that "[e]very human being has a right to life . . . he also possesses juridical personality."[140] There is no reference in the Quebec Charter to the fetus or fetal rights.

Counsel for the respondent made much of the linguistic interpretation of the phrase "human being," seemingly basing his argument on something akin to the "plain meaning" rule. The Court made it plain that the question it was asked to resolve was a "legal" one, not a philosophical, theological, scientific, or linguistic one,[141] although all might provide some assistance or background in resolving the "legal" issue. Indeed, the asserted linguistic approach would make strangely simple the most contentious of issues, that of the definition of a human being. Questions of when life begins, and when a "life form" becomes a human being, are deeply divisive and morally difficult issues that will not be resolved by reference to a dictionary.

---

138. *See Morgentaler* (1988); Borowski v. Canada [1989] 1 S.C.R. 342.

139. The language of "potential father" is that used by the Supreme Court.

140. Section 1 of the Quebec Charter of Rights and Freedoms, R.S.Q., c.C-12. In addition, section 2 of the Quebec Charter states: "Every human being whose life is in peril has a right to assistance."

141. The question the Supreme Court had to answer was whether the Quebec legislature had accorded the fetus personhood. The Court suggests that classifying the fetus for the purpose of a particular law or for scientific or philosophical purposes may be fundamentally different tasks. The Court describes the ascribing of personhood to the fetus, in law, as a fundamentally normative task.

Much was made of the differing uses of the words "human being" and "person" in the Quebec Charter. It is only to human beings that the right to life is guaranteed. Persons are guaranteed other, and arguably, lesser rights, such as respect for their private life and peaceful enjoyment of their property. Although the Court made no final decision on this issue, it appears likely that the choice of words was dictated by a desire on the part of the Quebec National Assembly to make clear that only natural persons or human beings possess the right to life, while artificial persons, such as corporate entities, might assert and enjoy the other rights guaranteed.

The Supreme Court of Canada quite reasonably concluded that the Quebec Charter displayed no clear intent on the issue of who was to be included within the term "human being." Indeed, as the Court pointed out, one would expect that on such a controversial issue, if the National Assembly had intended to include protection for the fetus within this term, it would have said so explicitly.

Because the language of the Quebec Charter displayed no clear intent on the meaning of the phrase "human being," the Court turned to the Civil Code to see if its provisions or its interpretation offered an answer to this definitional problem. The Court undertook a lengthy analysis of various provisions of the Code[142] and ultimately concluded that it "does not generally accord a foetus legal personality."[143] Indeed, the Court suggested that a fetus is treated as a person under the civil code only where it is necessary to do so in order to protect its interests after it is born. The Court found further confirmation for its interpretation of the civil code in Anglo-Canadian common law, in which it has been recognized generally that, to enjoy rights, a fetus must be born alive and have a separate existence from its mother.[144]

The Court quickly dealt with the remaining two "substantive rights" arguments of the respondent. The first of these was that the Charter of Rights and Freedoms provided the fetus with an independent right to life, under section 7. Again, the Supreme Court avoided answering this question.[145]

---

142. In particular, Civil Code of Lower Canada, arts. 18, 338, 345, 608, 771, 838, 945, 2543.

143. *Tremblay v. Daigle* [1989] 2 S.C.R. 530, *rev'g* [1989], at 564.

144. This view can be contrasted with that of Chief Justice Bernier of the Quebec Court of Appeal [1989], R.J.Q. 1735:

> He (the foetus) is not an inanimate object nor anyone's property but a living human entity distinct from that of the mother who bears him . . . and who from the outset has the right to life and to the protection of those who conceived him.

145. As it did in *Borowski*, [1989] 1 S.C.R. 342, and *Morgentaler* (1988).

The Court invoked its decision in *Dolphin Delivery*,[146] in which it concluded that the Charter did not apply to private disputes. It should be remembered that the facts of this case involved Jean-Guy Tremblay seeking an injunction against his former girlfriend, Chantal Daigle, a matter the Court described as a private civil dispute. There was no law to which Tremblay could point nor any government action that created the asserted violation of section 7. The Court did not consider an argument based on government "inaction." The argument would be that, by not legislating to protect the rights of the unborn, both the Quebec National Assembly and the federal Parliament were violating the right to life of the unborn.[147]

The Supreme Court concluded its assessment of the "substantive rights" arguments by briefly addressing the father's rights issue. The respondent argued that, since he had played an equal part in the conception of the potential child, he should have an equal say in what happened to it. The Court found no support for this proposition, the practical effect of which would be to provide a "potential father" with a veto over any decision made by a woman in relation to the fetus she was carrying.

The Supreme Court declined to answer many of the interesting Charter questions raised by this appeal. Some of them are (1) the rights of the fetus, if any, under section 7 of the Canadian Charter of Rights and Freedoms; (2) the balance between a woman's right to liberty and security and governmental interest in the fetus; (3) the constitutional rights, if any, of potential fathers; and (4) the possibility that the Charter may give rise to positive obligations upon the government to act, at least in certain circumstances, to protect guaranteed rights.

Ultimately this was an "easy" case for the Supreme Court of Canada.[148] Undoubtedly, it was correct in its finding that the Quebec National Assembly did not intend to extend protection to the fetus when it used the expression "human being" in section 1 of the Quebec Charter. Therefore, if there is no right to life for the fetus recognized in either Quebec human rights

---

146. R.W.D.S.U. v. Dolphin Delivery Ltd., [1986] 2 S.C.R. 573. It must be presumed that the court-ordered injunctions do not constitute "government action" for the purpose of the application of the Charter.

147. *See generally* B. Slattery, *A Theory of the Charter*, 2 Osgoode H.L.J. 701 (1987). This raises an issue of major significance in the interpretation of the Charter—namely, whether it can be construed as imposing positive obligations upon government to act.

148. The reason offered by the Court for continuing the hearing, after Daigle's counsel announced that she had had an abortion, was so that the law pertaining to "women in the position in which Ms. Daigle found herself could be clarified." Technically, the issues raised in this appeal became moot upon Daigle obtaining an abortion.

legislation or the Civil Code, then the only other source of such a right
would be the Charter of Rights and Freedoms. The Court was able to deny
the Charter's application to these facts by characterizing the dispute as a
"private" one. Further, the right of the "potential father" to assert a claim to,
or on behalf of, the fetus, over the objections of the woman carrying it, is
one that has virtually no support in English, Canadian, and U.S. law and was
dismissed with even greater certainty.

Although in *Daigle* the Supreme Court avoided dealing with the claim
that a fetus has a constitutionally protected right to life, the issue is one that
has been before the courts in Canada, in one form or another, for some
time.[149] These claims now usually involve an argument under section 7 of
the Charter. Problematic for the proponents of this view is the question of
to whom this right is granted. Section 7 rights are granted to "everyone,"
and although the Supreme Court of Canada has assiduously avoided ruling on this issue, it is predicted that the Court finally will conclude that the
term "everyone" does not include a fetus.[150] It should be remembered that
in *Morgentaler* (1988)[151] all members of the Court made a point of clearly
stating that they were not deciding whether a fetus had constitutionally protected rights under section 7. In *Daigle*,[152] the Court avoided the issue by
characterizing the dispute before it as a private one. Therefore, this important issue remains to be resolved by the Court.

2. *Borowski v. Canada*

Just as the name of Henry Morgentaler resonates with meaning for those
who believe in choice, so does the name of Joe Borowski for many who support fetal rights. Mr. Borowski, a former cabinet minister in Manitoba, cham-
pioned the rights of the fetus for over 20 years. Ironically, Mr. Borowski also
challenged the constitutional validity of section 251 of the Criminal Code
on the basis of the Canadian Bill of Rights but did so on behalf of the fetus,
arguing that the fetus was being denied the right to life guaranteed in section 1(a) of the bill.

---

149. *See, e.g.,* Dehler v. Ottawa Civic Hospital (1980), 117 D.L.R. (3d) 512 (Ont. C.A.);
Medhurst v. Medhurst (1984), 9 D.L.R. (4th) 252.

150. It is predicted that the Court will reach this conclusion on a number of grounds,
including (1) the intention of the drafters of section 7 of the Charter, (2) existing statutory
and case law, and (3) the implications of such a conclusion for women.

151. *See* [1988] 1 S.C.R. 30.

152. *See Tremblay v. Daigle* [1989] 2 S.C.R. 530, *rev'g* [1989].

Because the federal Attorney General contested the "standing" of Mr. Borowski to challenge the constitutional validity of section 251 of the Code,[153] by the time the merits of his claim were finally dealt with by the Saskatchewan Court of Queen's Bench, the Charter had come into force. Therefore, Mr. Borowski's main constitutional arguments were based on section 7 of the Charter and not section 1(a) of the Canadian Bill of Rights.[154]

Borowski lost both at trial and on appeal.[155] Counsel for Mr. Borowski had presented extensive evidence in an attempt to convince the trial judge that the term "everyone" included the fetus. Although Justice Matheson clearly, and not surprisingly, accepted the fact that the fetus is a potential person, he rejected the argument that the term "everyone" was intended to include such potential persons. Historically, the fetus had never been recognized in Canadian law as a legal person, and Justice Matheson concluded that "the Courts are not . . . endowed with the power to import into terms utilized in the *Charter* interpretations they cannot reasonably bear."[156]

The Saskatchewan Court of Appeal upheld the decision of Justice Matheson,[157] and on appeal to the Supreme Court of Canada, the Court declared Mr. Borowski's challenge moot.[158] The Court did so because Mr. Borowski's challenge to section 251 of the Code had been overtaken by the Court's decision in *Morgentaler* (1988)[159] in which section 251 had been declared null and void. Therefore, in the Court's opinion, the legal basis for Mr. Borowski's claim had disappeared.[160]

---

153. [1981] 2 S.C.R. 575. The Court granted Mr. Borowski standing on the basis that there was a serious issue as to the section's invalidity, that Mr. Borowski had a genuine interest as a citizen in the validity of the legislation and that there was no other reasonable and effective manner in which the issue might be brought before the Court. Martland, J, speaking for the majority, at 598.

154. However, Justice Matheson considered the arguments based on the Bill of Rights and for the reasons of Chief Justice Laskin, in *Morgentaler* (1975), dismissed them.

155. [1984] 1 W.W.R. 15 (Sask. Q.B.); *aff'd.* [1987] 4 W.W.R. 385 (Sask. C.A.).

156. *Id.* at 34.

157. *See* [1984] 1 W.W.R. 15 (Sask. Q.B.); *aff'd.* [1987] 4 W.W.R. 385 (Sask. C.A.).

158. [1989] 1 S.C.R. 342.

159. *See* [1988] 1 S.C.R. 30.

160. It might be argued that the issue was not moot on the basis that, if the fetus does have a constitutional right to life, then "inaction" on the part of the federal Parliament in not legislating to protect fetal life constitutes government "action" in violation of section 7 of the Charter.

It was clear from the Court's comments that it did not wish to address the complex issue of fetal rights in the abstract, that is, without a concrete legislative context in which the balancing of interests could take place.

3. *Sullivan and Lemay v. R.*

The decision of the Supreme Court in *Sullivan and Lemay v. R.*[161] may provide a further indication as to the Court's thinking in relation to a constitutionally based right to life for the fetus. Sullivan and Lemay were two midwives charged under sections 203 and 204 of the Criminal Code[162] after a full-term baby they were attempting to deliver died in the birth canal. At trial, they were convicted of criminal negligence causing death to the baby but were acquitted of criminal negligence causing bodily harm to the mother. The case raised the question of whether a fetus in the birth canal is a "person" for the purposes of section 203 of the Code.[163] In reaching its conclusion that the word "person" in section 203 did not include a fetus, the Court considered section 206 (now section 223) of the Code, which stated that a child became a human being within the meaning of the Code when it had completely proceeded, in a living state, from the body of its mother. Much was made of the fact that section 203, under which Sullivan and Lemay were charged, did not use the term "human being" but used the term "person." It was argued that the two terms were not synonymous and that the term "person" was broader than that of "human being" and, therefore, could include a fetus. The Court commented that it was not persuaded by any of the textual arguments put forward and consequently it concluded that the terms "person" and "human being" were synonymous. Therefore, Sullivan and Lemay could not be convicted of criminal negligence in causing death to another person.[164]

---

161. [1991] 1 S.C.R. 489.

162. Now sections 220 and 221.

163. Section 203 stated: "Everyone who by criminal negligence causes death of another person is guilty of an indictable offence and is liable to imprisonment for life."

164. *See* [1991] 1 S.C.R. 489, at 503. L.E.A.F. (Legal Education and Action Fund), a national organization that promotes equality for women, intervened in this case to argue that "the fetus should not be viewed as independent of a pregnant woman but as 'in her' and 'of her' in that it is interconnected with her in many intricate and intimate ways." Para. 43, p. 22 of Factum of the Intervenor Women's Legal Education Action Fund. L.E.A.F. argued that the structuring of the legal issues in the appeal improperly failed to place the pregnant woman, in whose body the fetus is, at the center of the legal analysis. *Id.* at para. 27, p. 15.

> Clothing the foetus with independent legal and constitutional rights may lead to the foetus having a right to the use of a woman's body, or a right to medical treatment that overrides the welfare of the pregnant woman—rights to be asserted over the woman by the putative father, a doctor, a self-appointed foetal curator or an arm of the State. *Id.* at para. 41, p. 22.

L.E.A.F. was seeking on interpretation of the Criminal Code "that would enhance women's equality by ensuring that the status of the foetus was not considered apart from the woman who carries it." *Id.* at para. 27, p. 15.

This case, like *Daigle*,[165] involved the interpretation of existing statutory provisions. In neither case was the Court forced to consider the more fundamental question of whether the fetus had a constitutional right to life. In all likelihood, the Court will not deal with this question unless the federal Parliament, or a provincial legislature, enacts a statutory provision that attempts to provide the fetus with rights. There would then be a concrete legislative context in which the Court could balance the state's interests in protecting fetal life with the interests of women in controlling their bodies and their reproductive capacity.[166]

4. *Winnipeg Child and Family Services (Northwest Area) v. G. (D.F.)*

The respondent, a woman known as D.F.G., was five months pregnant with her fourth child in August 1996. She was addicted to glue sniffing at the time, which had the potential to damage her unborn child's nervous system. Two of her previous children were born permanently disabled on account of her addiction and were permanent wards of the state. Winnipeg Child and Family Services successfully obtained an order from the Manitoba Court of Queen's Bench placing D.F.G. in the custody of the Director of Child and Family Services, thus detaining her in a health center for treatment until her child was born. The Court of Appeal later overturned this decision.

Ultimately, the Court concluded that it did not have to deal with the equality arguments presented by L.E.A.F., although it recognized that the result it reached was consistent with L.E.A.F.'s "equality approach."

165. *See Tremblay v. Daigle* [1989] 2 S.C.R. 530, *rev'g* [1989].

166. In an article entitled *Abortion & Democracy for Women: A Critique of Tremblay v. Daigle*, 35 McGILL L.R. 633, 662 (1989), Donna Greschner offers the following explanation for the increasing demands to recognize and protect fetal rights:

> The idea of foetal rights and personhood only entered political discourse when women began to achieve some control over our lives, when we gained a measure of freedom from the rule of fathers and husbands, when we could exercise some self-determination. With the rise of the women's movement has come, as a counter-attack, the concept of foetal personhood to guarantee women's traditional role in the patriarchal family. Abortion restrictions can no longer be overtly justified in order to ensure that women fulfill the function of mothers subject to the control of men. Hence laws are rhetorically justified as necessary to protect the foetus. Consider, for instance, that while all advocates of foetal rights state that someone must represent and speak for the foetus, they refuse to allow the mother to be that representative, proving the point that foetal rights are a method of controlling, not empowering or valuing, the women who create, nurture and deliver foetuses. Foetal personhood is the latest weapon in the battle to deny women's personhood.
> . . .

The case was heard by the Supreme Court of Canada in 1997,[167] by which time D.F.G. had completed her treatment—voluntarily—and given birth to her child. However, important legal questions remained: (1) does tort law permit (or might it be extended to permit) an order detaining a pregnant woman against her will to protect her unborn child from conduct that might harm the child; and (2) does the power of a court to make orders for the protection of children (parens patriae jurisdiction) extend to a fetus.[168]

The majority of the Supreme Court found that, under the law, a fetus is not recognized as a legal person possessing rights. Therefore, there was no legal person in this case in whose interest a court order could be made:

> Before birth the mother and child are one in the sense that "[t]he 'life' of the fetus is intimately connected and cannot be regarded in isolation from, the life of the pregnant woman." It is only after birth that the fetus assumes a separate personality. Accordingly, the law has always treated the mother and unborn child as one. To sue a pregnant woman on behalf of her unborn fetus therefore posits the anomaly of one part of a legal and physical entity suing itself.[169]

On the second issue, the majority rejected the applicability of parens patriae jurisdiction. In the case of an unborn child, the Court found that it could not make decisions for the fetus "without inevitably making decisions for the mother herself. The intrusion is therefore far greater than simply limiting the mother's choices concerning her child."[170] The majority concluded that any changes to tort law or to parens patriae were beyond the power of the Court and, ultimately, in the hands of the legislature.

The dissent in this case was also interesting. Although Justice Major (as he then was) recognized a woman's right to terminate her pregnancy, he argued that once she had decided to see her pregnancy to term, the state had an interest to ensure the child was born healthy. As such, he argued that the court should be able to exercise parens patriae jurisdiction "when there is a reasonable probability of [the mother's] conduct causing serious and irreparable harm to the fetus within her."[171]

---

167. [1997] 3 SCR 925.
168. *Id.* at 9.
169. *Id.* at 27 (citations omitted).
170. *Id.* at 56.
171. *Id.* at 93.

5. *Dobson v. Dobson*

In *Dobson v. Dobson*,[172] a woman was involved in a motor vehicle accident while 27 weeks pregnant, causing prenatal injuries to her unborn child. The child was delivered by C-section the same day, resulting in the child's permanent mental and physical impairment. The child brought an action against his mother alleging that she had been driving negligently. The central issue was whether or not a mother could be held liable in tort for damages to her child arising from a prenatal negligent act.

A majority of the Supreme Court determined that there was sufficient proximity to establish a duty of care between a mother and fetus; however, they determined that such a duty should not be imposed for public policy reasons. These reasons included "(1) the privacy and autonomy rights of women and (2) the difficulties inherent in articulating a judicial standard of conduct for pregnant women."[173]

The Court acknowledged that by seeking to recognize a duty of care, the lower courts wanted to provide children born with prenatal injuries due to their mother's neglect with a means to recover under their mother's insurance policy. However, the Court determined that a remedy to this concern was not found in tort law but rather in legislative action.

> For example, the statute might specify that this constituted an exception to the general rule of tort immunity, fix the limits of liability, and prohibit the recovery of damages above the limit fixed in the insurance policy. Legislation of this type could be socially rewarding for it could benefit the injured child, the mother and the rest of the family. Yet, if it were carefully drafted, such legislation would not constitute an undue intrusion into the privacy and autonomy rights of pregnant women in Canada.[174]

---

172. [1999] 2 S.C.R. 753. Judicial recognition of the legal duty of care was established in *City of Kamloops v. Nielsen*, [1984] 2 S.C.R. 2, as a two-part test: (1) whether the relationship between the parties in question was close enough as to impose a duty of care; and (2) whether there are public policy considerations which ought to negate or limit the scope of that duty, including the class of persons to whom the duty is owed or the damages to which a breach of it may give rise.

173. *Id.* at 21.

174. *Id.* at 70. In Alberta, the Maternal Tort Liability Act, SA 2005, c.M-7.5, limits a mother's liability for prenatal injuries caused by the mother's use of a motor vehicle if, at the time of operating the motor vehicle, the mother was insured. Moreover, the act restricts a mother's liability to the amount of money payable under the insurance policy indemnifying the mother that the child can recover as a creditor pursuant to section 579 of the Insurance Act, RSA 2000, c.I-3.

It should be noted that, although the Court did not conduct an analysis on Charter grounds, reference was made that to allow the action would be to create a gender-based tort, contrary to section 15(1).

V. Conclusion

In Canada, as elsewhere, abortion will continue to be a highly emotional and divisive issue. It is an issue upon which compromise does not seem possible. Hence, a political solution is not likely. Moreover, there remains a lack of clarity at common law on some issues that are central to the debate. Hopefully, this overview of the historical development of Canadian law dealing with abortion will be helpful and informative as part of the continuing debate regarding a woman's right to choose and access to abortion.

For many women, the struggle for reproductive choice is an important part of their ongoing battle for equality. Reproductive choice is not only about abortion, it is about effective contraception, infertility, new reproductive technologies, medical practices surrounding birth, and the development and control of all of these. The reproductive capacity of women provides a unique context within which women define themselves, their relationships, and their roles in society. Indeed, many others, including legislators, have defined women, and their appropriate roles, largely in terms of this capacity. Women have realized for a long time that control over reproduction is a starting point, from which they can take control over their lives, based on their priorities and aspirations. It is unthinkable that the control, so recently gained, over one aspect of reproduction, that of deciding whether or not to terminate a pregnancy, will be relinquished without a struggle.[175]

In terms of the present situation regarding access to abortion, the Supreme Court's decision in *Morgentaler* (1988) appears to have not had the decisive impact that one would have thought. There are many hospitals that choose not to perform abortions. It is estimated that only 16 percent of Canadian hospitals provide abortion services and a growing number of doctors refuse to participate in the procedure. This perpetuates the inequality

---

175. Women have had the support of the Canadian Medical Association in their efforts to prevent the recriminalization of abortion. In its *Brief to the House of Commons Legislative Committee on Bill C-43* (Ottawa, Feb. 6, 1990), it stated that the decision to perform an induced abortion is a medical decision made confidentially between the patient and her physician, within the context of a physician-patient relationship after conscientious examination of all other options.

that existed under section 251 of the Code. Where a woman lives, both in terms of province of residence and the site of her residence within the province, often determines her accessibility to abortion services.

There continues to be some resistance to the establishment of private clinics.[176] Even in communities where they exist, provincial health care plans may not pay for everything. Usually, they only pay part of the actual cost of the procedure, the doctor's fee, thereby forcing doctors to bill their patients directly for an amount to underwrite the operating costs of the clinic. The effect of this practice is to discriminate against women in poor economic circumstances, as well as those who reside outside of major centers.

The debate over abortion continues in Canada, although more muted than in many other countries, including the United States. The anti-choice forces will continue their efforts to have Parliament recriminalize abortion (which becomes less likely all the time), and at the provincial level, they will continue to lobby to prevent the further establishment of private clinics and will continue to harass the women who seek their services where they do exist. They will also continue to lobby provincial politicians to have abortion de-insured under provincial health care plans. The pro-choice forces will continue to place the issue of abortion in the context of a larger struggle—the realization of equality for Canadian women.

---

176. Abortion may be the only "medically necessary" procedure under the Canada Health Act that is better delivered in clinics than hospitals. As of February 2017, only 16 percent of Canadian hospitals performed abortions, and clinics were only found in major cities. Unlike hospitals, clinics offer abortions for later pregnancies, often have shorter waiting lists, provide full counseling services, and do not require a doctor's referral. See Abortion Rights Coalition of Canada, *Hospital versus Clinics: Comparisons of Abortion Care*, Position Paper #9, February 2017.

Appendix A-I

Sections of the Criminal Code of Canada Relating to Abortion as They Existed up to January 1988

Procuring miscarriage

Section 251(1)—Everyone who, with intent to procure the miscarriage of a female person, whether or not she is pregnant, uses any means for the purpose of carrying out his intention is guilty of an indictable offence and is liable to imprisonment of life.

Woman procuring her own miscarriage (2) Every female person who, being pregnant, with intent to procure her own miscarriage, uses any means or permits any means to be used for the purpose of carrying out her intention is guilty of an indictable offence and is liable to imprisonment for two years.

"Means"

(3) In this section, "means" includes
   (a) the administration of a drug or other noxious thing,
   (b) the use of an instrument, and
   (c) manipulation of any kind.

Exceptions

(4) Subsections (1) and (2) do not apply to
   (a) qualified medical practitioner, other than a member of a thera-peutic abortion committee for any hospital, who in good faith uses in an accredited or approved hospital any means for the purpose of carrying out his intention to procure the miscarriage of a female person, or
   (b) a female person who, being pregnant, permits a qualified medi-cal practitioner to use in an accredited or approved hospital any means described in paragraph (a) for the purpose of carrying

out her intention to procure her own miscarriage if, before the use of those means, the therapeutic abortion committee for that accredited or approved hospital, by a majority of the members of the committee and at a meeting of the committee at which the case of such female person has been reviewed,

(c) has by certificate in writing stated that in its opinion the continuation of the pregnancy of such female person would or would be likely to endanger her life or health, and

(d) has caused a copy of such certificate to be given to the qualified medical practitioner.

Information requirement

(5) The Minister of Health of a province may by order

(a) require a therapeutic abortion committee for any hospital in that province, or any member thereof, to furnish to him a copy of any certificate described in paragraph (4)(c) issued by that committee, together with such other information relating to the circumstances surrounding the issuance of that certificate as he may require, or

(b) require a medical practitioner who, in that province, has procured the miscarriage of any female person named in a certificate described in paragraph (4)(c), to furnish to him a copy of that certificate, together with such other information relating to the procuring of the miscarriage as he may require.

Definitions

(6) For the purposes of subsections (4) and (5) and this subsection

— "accredited hospital" means a hospital accredited by the Canadian Council on Hospital Accreditation in which diagnostic services and medical, and surgical and obstetrical treatment are provided;

— "approved hospital" means a hospital in a province approved for the purposes of this section by the Minister of Health of that province;

— "board" means the board of governors, management or directors, or the trustees, commission or other person or group of persons having the control and management of an accredited or approved hospital;

— "Minister of Health" means:

    (a) in the Provinces of Ontario, Quebec, New Brunswick, Manitoba, Alberta, Newfoundland and Prince Edward Island, the Minister of Health,

    (b) in the Province of British Columbia, the Minister of Health Services and Hospital Insurance,

    (c) in the provinces of Nova Scotia and Saskatchewan, the Minister of Public Health, and

    (d) in the Yukon Territory and the Northwest Territories, the Minister of National Health and Welfare;

— "qualified medical practitioner" means a person entitled to engage in the practice of medicine under the laws of the province in which the hospital referred to in subsection (4) is situated;
— "therapeutic abortion committee" for any hospital means a committee, comprised of not less than three members each of whom is a qualified medical practitioner, appointed by the board of that hospital for the purpose of considering and determining questions relating to terminations of pregnancy within that hospital.

(7) Nothing in subsection (4) shall be construed as making unnecessary the obtaining of any authorization or consent that is or may be required, otherwise than under this Act, before any means are used for the purpose of carrying out an intention to procure the miscarriage of a female person. 1953-54 c.51, s.237; 1968–69, c.38, s.18.

Section 252 — Everyone who unlawfully supplies or procures a drug or other noxious thing or an instrument or thing, knowing that it is intended to be used or employed to procure the miscarriage of a female person, whether or not she is pregnant, is guilty of an indictable offence and is liable to imprisonment for two years.

1953-54, c.51, s.238.

Appendix A-II

Bill C-43, An Act Respecting Abortion (2nd
Session, 34th Parliament 38 Elizabeth 11,
1989)
Introduced in the House of Commons
November 3, 1989; defeated in the Senate,
January 31, 1991

Inducing abortion

Section 287 — (1) Every person who induces an abortion on a female
person is guilty of an indictable offence and liable to imprisonment for a
term not exceeding two years, unless the abortion is induced by or under
the direction of a medical practitioner who is of the opinion that, if the
abortion were not induced, the health or life of the female person would be
likely to be threatened.

Definitions

(2) For the purposes of this section,

— "health" includes, for greater certainty, physical, mental and
psychological health;
— "medical practitioner," in respect of an abortion induced in a
province, means a person who is entitled to practice medicine under
the laws of that province;
— "opinion" means an opinion formed using general accepted
standards of the medical profession.

Interpretation

(3) For the purposes of this section and section 288, inducing an abortion does not include using a drug, device or other means on a female person that is likely to prevent implantation of a fertilized ovum.

Supplying noxious things

Section 288 — Everyone who unlawfully supplies or procures a drug or other noxious thing or an instrument or thing, knowing that it is intended to be used or employed to induce an abortion on a female person, is guilty of an indictable offence and liable to imprisonment for a term not exceeding two years.

4

Amicus Curiae *Brief in* Whole Woman's Health

Summitted to the Supreme Court on Behalf of Janice MacAvoy, Janie Schulman and 100 Other Women in the Legal Profession Who Have Exercised Their Constitutional Right to an Abortion*

Interest of *Amici*[1]

Amici are lawyers[2] who have obtained abortions and who have participated in a wide variety of different aspects of the legal profession, including at private law firms, corporations, multinational governmental organizations,

---

* Some non-substantive redactions and formatting edits have been made to the original brief filed in Whole Woman's Health v. Hellerstedt, 579 U.S. ___, 136 S. Ct. 2292 (2016).

1. A complete list of the "113 *Amici Curiae* Women in the Legal Profession" is included as an appendix to the brief as filed in the Supreme Court.

2. The terms "women in the legal profession," "lawyers," and "attorneys" are used broadly in this brief to refer to women who are or were participants in the field of law, including lawyers currently or formerly at firms or otherwise in private practice, current or former in-house lawyers, current or former government lawyers, current or former public defenders, current or former public interest lawyers, current or former law professors, retired attorneys who are no longer active members of the bar, professors who graduated from law school but were not admitted to practice law, and current or former law students. While the majority of signers are law school graduates (107 of the 113 *Amici*), six current law students have joined this brief to reflect the continuing importance of the constitutional right to abortion access to the rising generation of lawyers.

nonprofit organizations, and law schools.[3] Amici care deeply about the reproductive rights this Court has recognized—in *Roe v. Wade*, 410 U.S. 113 (1973), *Planned Parenthood v. Casey*, 505 U.S. 833 (1992), and elsewhere—as constitutional entitlements. And Amici believe that, like themselves, the next generation of lawyers should have the ability to control their reproductive lives and thus the opportunity to fully participate in the "economic and social life of the Nation," as promised in *Casey*, 505 U.S. at 856.

Amici obtained their abortions at different ages and life stages, under a variety of circumstances, and for a range of reasons both medical and personal, but they are united in their strongly-held belief that they would not have been able to achieve the personal or professional successes they have achieved were it not for their ability to obtain safe and legal abortions. They are 113 individual women but they represent many more of the past, present, and future members of the profession who have, like one in three American women, terminated a pregnancy in their lifetimes. Guttmacher Institute, *Fact Sheet: Induced Abortion in the United States* (July 2014), http://www.guttmacher .org/pubs/fb_induced_abortion.html (last visited Jan. 3, 2016).

Summary of Argument

"To the world, I am an attorney who had an abortion, and, to myself, I am an attorney because I had an abortion."

> Email received from an *Amicus*, an appellate
> court attorney, December 18, 2015.

In reaffirming a woman's right to safe and legal abortion access in *Casey*, this Court observed that "[t]he ability of women to participate equally in the economic and social life of the Nation has been facilitated by their ability to control their reproductive lives." 505 U.S. at 856. The statutory provisions at issue in this case would dramatically restrict women's ability to exercise their right to safe and legal abortions—and thus their ability to participate equally in the life of the nation—not only in Texas, but in any other state that has or will adopt similar laws. The right to terminate a pregnancy, to autonomy in decision-making and bodily integrity, should be a right in fact and not just in theory.

---

3. *Amici* submit this brief only in their capacities as private citizens. To the extent an *Amicus's* employer is named, it is solely for descriptive purposes and does not constitute the employer's endorsement of the brief or any portion of its content.

This brief is intended to inform the Court of the impact of the right this Court has recognized in *Roe, Casey*, and elsewhere on the lives of women attorneys, and, by extension, on this nation. As this Court held in *Casey*, a woman's right to terminate a pregnancy necessarily follows from her "dignity and autonomy," which are "central to the liberty protected by the Fourteenth Amendment." *Casey*, 505 U.S. at 851.

Amici live and practice across the country, including in Texas, and hail from diverse backgrounds. *Amici* are partners, counsel, and associates at private law firms; they are government attorneys, a former state legislator, and public defenders; they are members of legal service organizations and law school professors; they are counsel to corporations, universities, and foundations; and they include several attorneys who have argued before this Court or authored briefs submitted to it. Many *Amici* are former federal and state judicial clerks, and two *Amici* were judges themselves. *Amici* have achieved considerable professional success; among them are a MacArthur Fellow, published authors, former editors-in-chief of leading law journals, and former academic deans. Many are mothers, and some are grandmothers. For all *Amici*, meaningful access to reproductive choice allowed them to become, remain, or thrive as lawyers.

Amici write respectfully to urge the Court to overturn the Fifth Circuit's decision at issue here. That decision, if affirmed, would have the very real effect of preventing numerous women, including many current and future attorneys, from effectively planning their family and professional lives. The legacy of this Court's decisions, in *Roe, Casey*, and others—specifically, women's full participation in economic and social life—has enriched not just individuals like *Amici*, but this esteemed profession, and our nation itself.

Argument

I. Meaningful, Safe, and Legal Access to Abortion Is a Fundamental, Constitutionally Protected Right

The decision whether or not to give birth to a child is "central to the liberty protected by the Fourteenth Amendment" and one of "the most intimate and personal choices a person may make in a lifetime." *Casey*, at 851. "[I]mplicit in the meaning of [this] liberty" is a woman's right to "retain the ultimate control over her destiny and her body." *Id.* at 869 (plurality opinion). Consistent with these holdings, the Court has repeatedly recognized and reaffirmed women's competence and authority to decide whether to obtain an abortion, and by extension to "define one's own concept of existence, of meaning, of the universe, and of the mystery of human life." *Id.* at 851 (majority opinion). By drastically reducing (and threatening to eliminate) the number of abortion providers in Texas, and offering a model for other states to do the same, the provisions of Texas House Bill 2 ("HB2"), 83rd Leg., 2nd Called Sess. (Tex. 2013), at issue here are a direct affront to a fundamental liberty and to a woman's right to control her destiny. They should therefore be invalidated for that reason alone.

Further, and of particular concern to *Amici*, by limiting women's "ability to control their reproductive lives," the challenged provisions necessarily undermine "[t]he ability of women to participate equally in the economic and social life of the Nation." *Casey*, 505 U.S. at 856. *Amici's* experiences underscore the Court's critical observations concerning the centrality of reproductive choice to gender equality, both within the legal profession and more broadly within the nation.

The Constitution's recognition and this Court's repeated reaffirmation of the right to an abortion are explicitly linked to the longstanding "rejection" of legislation premised on the notion of "'woman . . . as the center of home and family life,' with attendant 'special responsibilities' that precluded full and independent legal status under the Constitution." *Id.* at 897 (majority opinion) (quoting *Hoyt v. Florida*, 368 U.S. 57, 62 (1961)). Consistent with that understanding, undue restrictions on abortion access like those at issue in this case implicate a woman's autonomy to determine her life's course, and thus her "personal dignity" and even her equal citizenship. *See, e.g., Casey*, 505 U.S. at 928 (Blackmun, J., concurring in part and dissenting in part) ("A State's restrictions on a woman's right to terminate her pregnancy also implicate constitutional guarantees of gender equality. . . . This assumption—that women can simply be forced to accept the 'natural' status and incidents of motherhood—appears to rest upon a conception of women's role that has triggered the protection of the Equal Protection Clause.").

As Justice Stevens has explained, the right to an abortion "is an integral part of a correct understanding of . . . the basic equality of men and women." *Casey*, 505 U.S. at 912 (Stevens, J., concurring in part and dissenting in part). This observation is borne out by *Amici's* professional successes, which merely a few generations ago could have been enjoyed only by men.

The Court in *Casey* recognized the simple fact that "for two [now four] decades of economic and social developments, people have organized intimate relationships and made choices that define their views of themselves and their places in society, in reliance on the availability of abortion in the event that contraception should fail." *Id.* at 856 (majority opinion). This remains the case. Following *Roe*, two "generation[s] ha[ve] come of age free to assume [the] concept of liberty in defining the capacity of women to act in society, and to make reproductive decisions." *Id.* at 860.

In sum, this Court has squarely and repeatedly held that the right to terminate a pregnancy is grounded in the "liberty" protected by the Fourteenth Amendment. Further, the Court has recognized in so holding that women have now come to rely on that right as a means of participating to an equal extent as men in the "economic and social life" of the Nation." *Casey*, 505 U.S. at 856. The *Amici* whose experiences are set forth below represent just a portion of the women who have come to rely on the Constitution's promise of reproductive freedom and autonomy to determine the paths of their lives and careers. Their reliance, and their participation in the nation's economic and social life, weigh strongly in favor of invalidating the provisions of the Texas law at issue here.

II. *Amici*'s Reflections on the Effects of Their Abortions on Their Careers and Lives

While *Amici* come from different regional, religious, racial, and socioeconomic backgrounds, and had their abortions for a variety of medical and personal reasons, certain themes repeat throughout their experiences, among them: that they would not have been able to graduate from high school, college, or law school but for their abortions; that abortions provided them with the freedom to escape unhealthy or abusive situations and relationships; and that abortions allowed *Amici* to delay childbearing until they could be good parents. Most of all, *Amici* share a common recognition of the critical importance to their careers and their lives of safe access to abortion and the dangers of laws that complicate that path.

Justice Blackmun observed that "[b]ecause motherhood has a dramatic impact on a woman's educational prospects, employment opportunities, and self-determination, restrictive abortion laws deprive her of basic control over her life." *Casey*, 505 U.S. at 928 (Blackmun, J., concurring in part and dissenting in part). *Amici's* experiences bear this out.

1. Abortion Access Directly Affects Educational Access

To begin with, many *Amici* reported that they would not have been able to graduate from high school, college, or law school, let alone excel as attorneys, without safe and unrestricted access to abortion.

a. Breaking the Cycle of Teenage Pregnancy

Several *Amici* described how their abortions allowed them to break a recurring family cycle of teenage pregnancy—a condition this Court has held a state has a "strong interest in preventing," *Michael M. v. Superior Court of Sonoma City*, 450 U.S. 464, 470 (1981). Instead, their abortions enabled them to finish high school and go on to higher education and law school.

One *Amicus*, a public defender, recounted:

> I am the daughter of a teenage mother who is the daughter of a teenage mother. I had an abortion when I was 16 years old and living in rural Oregon. I believe that access to a safe, legal abortion broke the familial cycle of teenage parenthood and allowed me to not only escape a very unhealthy, emotional[ly] abusive teenage relationship but to graduate from an elite college, work for one of the nation's most storied civil rights organizations, and go on to graduate from the University of Michigan Law School . . . I often tell people—and I believe it to be true—that access to a safe, legal abortion saved my life. If I had not had an abortion, I would have never been able to graduate high school, go to college, [or] escape my high-poverty rural county in Oregon. I would never have been able to fully participate in the civil and social life of the country. I have seen the effects of teenage motherhood for women in my family, my friends, and loved ones. I have seen all the dreams deferred, the plans derailed, the poverty endured.

Email received December 17, 2015.

Another *Amicus*, a litigation partner at a large law firm, described her experience:

> [A]t the age of 18, I knew that I wanted to be a lawyer and did not want to follow in the footsteps of my mother, my grandmother and my great-grandmother in becoming a mother by the age of 18. Taking control of my reproductive freedom gave me the ability to be the first person in my family to graduate from high school, the first person to graduate from college, and the first person to achieve a post-graduate degree. I do not believe that any of those accomplishments would have been possible if I had not had the ability to take control over my destiny and my body through access to safe and legal abortion.

Email received December 14, 2015.

Another *Amicus*, a senior attorney for a major legal non-profit organization, explained:

> As a young African-American woman, growing up in the Bronx, New York—one of the poorest counties in our country—the ability to decide for myself whether I would become a teenage mother was very empower-

ing. It is at least in part because of that decision that I was able to complete high school and college and fulfill my childhood goal of becoming a lawyer. America cannot be the land of equality and opportunity for all if we simultaneously place unreasonable limits on a person's ability to choose how they achieve their version of those ideals.

Email received December 23, 2015.

Another *Amicus,* a former law clerk to a federal judge and now a prominent human rights attorney, related:

> I had not considered an abortion until one day I stepped back and took an honest look at my very grim reality: I had just quit my job at a fast food restaurant where I was earning minimum wage, I took a leave of absence from school, I had no source of income to support myself and no healthcare, I had already missed a semester of eleventh grade and was behind in my studies, I was living in a three-bedroom house with nine people in an economically struggling area of town and I had no child care options available, besides dropping out of school. . . . However, once I had my abortion, I was registered back in school three weeks later and went on to earn the highest grade-point average (GPA) in my high school, earning the opportunity to speak at graduation. I attended a public university for free on a merits-based scholarship because of my grades and became a student leader active in diverse aspects of student life on campus. Later, I obtained a master's degree and a law degree. . . . My ability to have access to a low-cost abortion fundamentally altered the course of my life and my ability to fully participate not only in society, but in my life.

Email received December 17, 2015.

b. Achieving Higher Education

In the 43 years since this Court decided *Roe v. Wade,* in 1973, women's educational and professional participation in the law has increased many fold. In 1970, only 8.5% of law students enrolled at ABA-approved law schools were women. By 1980, that number had risen dramatically, to 33.6%.[4] Today, women make up nearly half of all law students: according to the ABA, women accounted for 47.3% of the law degrees awarded during the 2010–2011 academic year.[5] In 2013, women accounted for over one third of

---

4. *See* SUSAN E. MARTIN AND NANCY C. JURIK, DOING JUSTICE, DOING GENDER: WOMEN IN LEGAL AND CRIMINAL JUSTICE OCCUPATIONS 112–113 (2d ed. 2007).

5. American Bar Association, *A Current Glance at Women in the Law* 4 (July, 2014), available at http://www.americanbar.org/content/dam/aba/marketing/women/currentglance statistics_july2014.authcheckdam.pdf.

practicing attorneys.[6] These numbers are reflected in *Amici's* experiences. Many *Amici* obtained abortions during or immediately before college or law school, and directly credit their access to reproductive choice for their ability ultimately to earn their law degrees.

One *Amicus*, a current law student, described how she could not have remained in college had she been required to carry her pregnancy to term:

> I found out I was pregnant just a few weeks after moving away from home to start college. When I told my resident advisor, she told me that pregnant students were not allowed to live in the university's dormitories out of a concern for increased liability. I was on full financial aid and could not afford a place to live off-campus on top of tuition, books and food. My decision to have an abortion was essential to the freedom that allowed me to finish college while working more than one job; to move across the country two weeks after graduation to take my dream job; and to attend law school and . . . to continue to pursue my dreams.

Email received December 17, 2015.

One *Amicus*, in-house counsel to a major university, described obtaining an abortion just before starting law school:

> I was staying with my mother and readying myself for the new challenging adventure that would be law school when I learned I was unintentionally pregnant. The other participant in this pregnancy was many thousands of miles away and we had no plans for aligning our lives. Financing law school was entirely up to me. I had few possessions (warm weather clothing and I think a camera). I was heading to New England and I didn't even own a winter coat. How could I have a child? . . .
>
> Had I not had an abortion, it is entirely possible that I would not have been able to finish law school—I might not have even been able to manage starting law school. I likely would have lived with my mother for a time and found a way to support my unexpected family. And then—I have no idea. What did happen was law school, law firm, two excellent in-house counsel jobs, two children, marriage, three step-children, six grandchildren . . .

Email received December 18, 2015.

Another *Amicus*, a former clerk to a federal court of appeals judge, now a constitutional litigator, described obtaining her abortion while studying for the LSAT:

---

6. *Id.* at 2 (figured based on the 59% of the legal profession that reported gender with respect to employment).

I had an abortion when I was 22. I was three weeks pregnant after a contraception failure, single, waiting tables for a living, and studying to apply to law school. At the time, I did not have the mental, emotional, or perhaps most importantly, economic resources to have a child. Living in New York, I was fortunate to have easy access to the services I needed. However, because of the arbitrary limitations Pennsylvania put on abortion coverage in health insurance plans, my Pennsylvania-based health insurance did not cover my abortion and I had to pay for it on credit. The following spring I was admitted to Yale Law School. . . . After graduation, I served as a law clerk to [a Judge on the federal Court of Appeals for the Ninth Circuit] . . . and worked as a Skadden Fellow at a legal aid office in Los Angeles representing . . . victims of wage theft. During that time, I collected hundreds of thousands of stolen wages for individual workers and worked with litigation teams that collected millions more for low-wage workers and victims of human trafficking. Both NPR and the L.A. Times chronicled my clients' stories. I have been published in the Yale Law Journal and the University of Pennsylvania Journal of Constitutional Law. . . . The foregoing is not meant to congratulate myself for my achievements but only to highlight all that would have been impossible if I became a mother before I was ready. I cannot imagine that I would have gone to law school in that circumstance. I now look forward to the opportunity to have a family and encourage my children to follow their own dreams and work for the public good. I can lead by example. I am thankful every day for that opportunity.

Email received December 16, 2015.

2. Safe and Legal Access to Abortion Is Critical to Professional Freedom and Advancement for Women Lawyers

Research shows that the ability to control reproductive decisions, to engage in family planning and to delay childbirth has a long term impact on women's career paths, leading to increased earnings and career success.[7] *Amici's* experiences reflect that without the ability to control reproductive decisions—to choose when, how, and whether to have children—many women lawyers would not have been able to remain in the legal profession or to practice the kind of law they have chosen to practice.

One former general counsel described obtaining her abortion while serving as a federal district court law clerk:

---

7. *See, e.g.,* A. Miller, *The Effects of Motherhood Timing on Career Path,* 24 (3) J. POPULATION ECON. 1071, 1071 (2011) (finding that "[m]otherhood delay leads to a substantial increase in career earnings of 9% per year of delay").

I had an abortion when I was a young lawyer, just out of law school and clerking for one of the best known and busiest federal trial judges in the country. . . . Everything was before me, and I had made that happen; I didn't come from a family with a lot of money, or a long history of higher education, much less professional education for women. I was inventing myself and learning to control—to the perhaps limited, but still real, extent any of us can—my own destiny. . . . I found myself pregnant in the middle of my clerkship, while in a dysfunctional long-distance relationship with the man in question. Had I not had the choice to exercise control over my reproductive destiny by choosing an abortion, there is no doubt in my mind that I would not have been able to move from the clerkship to the amazing fellowship I had at the American Civil Liberties Union, which played such a significant role in forming my life in the law and my understanding of our Constitution.

Email received December 17, 2015.

One *Amicus*, a law professor, explained how obtaining an abortion allowed her to leave her abusive partner and complete her graduate studies:

I became pregnant the spring of my final year of graduate school. I had obtained my law degree two years prior, and spent the following year working on my Ph.D. My goal was to be a professor of law or legal studies. The postdoc was the next step, and my plan was to go on the job market in the fall. . . . I was in disbelief when I found out I was pregnant. I had the Paraguard IUD, a 99% effective form of contraception. . . . [My partner at the time] said that were I to keep the child, I would not be able to go to [my post-doctoral fellowship], nor would he consider following me for my career or [would he] let me raise the child away from him. I realized I was in a desperate situation. . . . My abortion provided me with the geographic freedom I needed, saved my child from having an abusive father, and allowed me to use my education for the social good.

Email received December 9, 2015.

One senior public defender wrote:

I took 6 months off of work when my son was born. I came back to work with a promotion to senior staff attorney and a specialist position. Six months after my return to work, while I was still breastfeeding, I became pregnant again, despite the fact that I had an IUD in place. My abortion made it possible for me to re-inhabit my body as an individual. After nine months of pregnancy and a year of breastfeeding, regaining whole possession of my body was essential to my autonomy and mental health. . . . My abortion also made it possible for me to continue to build my career as a public defender. The trials in the type of complex litigation that I began to specialize in after I came back from maternity leave can take months to complete, so going out on a second maternity leave so quickly after beginning my specialty would have meant giving up all of my new cases to other attorneys and probably giving up my specialty altogether.

Email received December 19, 2015.

And another *Amicus*, counsel at a large law firm, explained:

I love being a mother and I love being a lawyer. Though balancing those two roles is challenging, I am able to do both in part because my husband and I chose when to have our children. Knowing now what is involved in being a parent, if I had not been able to have an abortion in 1993, I doubt that I would have been able to attend law school or [hold] the positions that followed.

Email received December 9, 2015.

3. Safe and Unrestricted Access to Abortion Plays a Critical Role in the Lives of Women Lawyers

The Court has long recognized the many "detriment[s] that the state would impose upon" a woman denied access to an abortion, among them:

Specific and direct harm medically diagnosable even in early pregnancy may be involved. Maternity, or additional offspring, may force upon the woman a distressful life and future. Psychological harm may be imminent. Mental and physical health may be taxed by child care. There is also the distress, for all concerned, associated with the unwanted child, and there is the problem of bringing a child into a family already unable, psychologically and otherwise, to care for it. In other cases, as in this one, the additional difficulties and continuing stigma of unwed motherhood may be involved.

Roe v. Wade, 410 U.S. 113, 153 (1973).

Research fully supports the Court's findings. A recently published report, based on data from the Turnaway Study,[8] a longitudinal study from the University of California, San Francisco that aims to "describe the mental health, physical health, and socioeconomic consequences of receiving an abortion compared to carrying an unwanted pregnancy to term," compared

---

8. *See Advancing New Standards in Reproductive Health, About the Turnaway Study,* http://www.ansirh.org/research/turnaway.php (last visited Jan. 3, 2016).

the one-year plans to the outcomes of women who had abortions.[9] The study found that "ensuring women can have a wanted abortion enables them to maintain a positive future outlook and achieve their aspirational life plans."[10]

a. Negative Impact of Restrictions on Abortion Access

Amici's experiences illustrate the crucial role that safe and unrestricted access to abortions has played in their lives and their careers, as well as in the lives and wellbeing of their families. In particular, many of *Amici's* experiences demonstrate the devastating practical effects of laws that place restrictions on abortion access.

One *Amicus,* a law professor, recounted:

> When I was seventeen years old, I was pregnant and scared. And then, I was pregnant and desperate: Tennessee, where I lived, had enacted a parental consent law, and my mother had always told me that if I got pregnant, I would be expected to keep the baby. . . . [W]ith my state's law in essence forcing me to give birth against my will, the two options my frightened teenage mind kept coming back to were self-abortion by clothes hanger . . . and suicide. A decision by the Supreme Court saved my life, just in the nick of time. The Court's Webster decision, issued around the same time I was seriously considering suicide rather than being forced to give birth against my will, saved my life. The Court's holding that parental consent laws must have a judicial bypass provision ended up invalidating the Tennessee parental consent law, allowing me to have a safe and legal abortion well within the first trimester of my pregnancy. Were it not for my ability to have a safe and legal abortion that day, I could have ended up dead. If not dead, I certainly would not have been able to continue down the life path that I have taken so very seriously, a career journey of working hard to succeed in life and help others succeed along with me.

Email received December 20, 2015.

Another *Amicus,* a senior attorney at a non-profit organization, described obtaining her abortion at a Texas clinic that has subsequently closed as a result of the provisions of HB2 that are at issue in the pending case:

> Within days of accepting a full fellowship to law school, where I aspired to study women's human rights law, I discovered I was pregnant. My plan at the time was to move from Texas to New York, where my then-fiancé

---

9. U. Upadhyay, et al., *The Effect of Abortion on Having and Achieving Aspirational One-Year Plans,* 15 (1) BMC WOMEN'S HEALTH 102, 102 (2015).

10. *Id.*

and I would pursue graduate programs. A pregnancy would have made that impossible. It is overwhelming to consider the advantages I had at the time that would be unavailable to others today. . . . I was able to secure an appointment at my local Whole Woman's Health clinic within days. There was nobody at the clinic to harass me the day I went in for the procedure. That clinic has since closed because of the law being challenged in this suit . . . even then, the restrictions in place and a provider shortage made the experience more painful and frightening than it should have been. But the clinic staff did their best to ensure that the procedure was safe, compassionate, and dignified. . . . I know that my having had access to a safe, early abortion has not only permitted me to become the first person in my family to practice law, it has had a direct impact on individual women and on women's equality through my work. My story is just one of many that shows that when women have the power to decide when they are ready to parent, they have the power to achieve their goals, and even change the world.

Email received December 21, 2015.

b. Escaping Abuse

Some *Amici* explained that their abortions allowed them to escape abusive environments, which they would have brought a child into had they not obtained an abortion.

One professor related that:

[T]he decisive factor in having an abortion was not subjecting my child to the dysfunction, and likely abuse, that it would endure in its father's home. Moreover, another child would have exacerbated an already dysfunctional situation for his children, not just for me and him.

Email received December 11, 2015.

Another *Amicus*, a former clerk to a federal district court judge, now a law professor and practicing attorney, recounted:

I became pregnant at age 18, during my first year of college, due to a contraceptive failure. College was a means of escape from a family plagued with violence and alcohol and drug addiction. I had nowhere to turn for the significant financial or emotional support that raising a child would require.

Going "home" was simply not an option for me, as it was there I was subjected to physical abuse by my older brother. The legality and availability of abortion allowed me to terminate my pregnancy, stay in school and continue on to law school. I am convinced that it is only education that allowed me to break the horrific cycle of generational dysfunction that [I] can now only truly appreciate as a well-adjusted adult. I also had the good fortune to be [in] New Jersey, where I had access to a number of clinics with no waiting period to increase the cost of the procedure. . . . Abortion access was critical in allowing me to determine my life path, gain freedom from an abusive household, become a lawyer and fight for the right of others to make the same reproductive choices I did.

Email received December 18, 2015.

Another *Amicus*, general counsel of a large international consulting firm, explained:

I had an abortion at age 35, when I had an unplanned pregnancy with a man who had become emotionally abusive. Being able to choose the father of my children and knowing how important a safe and loving home is to children, I chose to have an abortion. I was firm in my belief that my happiness and that of any family I would start begins with the stability of my relationship with a partner. I also knew that the best chance a woman has to keep a successful career and to be a mother is to have an amazing partner. I eventually found that man and married him at age 42. We are blessed with two amazing sons. I went on to become general counsel of an international energy consulting firm, where I still work today, and know that my family and career would not have been as joyful and successful had I not had the option to choose when to start a family.

Email received December 25, 2015.

c. Medical Necessity

Some *Amici* obtained abortions due to certainty or likelihood of severe birth defects or medical danger posed to themselves, and described how critical their abortions were to their entire families' well-being.

One partner at a major law firm explained:

In April 2000, I was happily married with a three-year-old daughter whom I conceived without any difficulty. My husband and I wanted more children and were able to provide for them. After the birth of my daughter, however, I had three first trimester miscarriages. My husband and I were delighted when I again became pregnant in December, 1999, and safely made it past the "danger zone" of the first trimester, passing an amnio with flying colors. . . . Five weeks later, on April 24, 2000, when I was heading into the sixth month of my pregnancy, I returned to the doctor for a routine ultrasound. . . . The doctor immediately detected a problem. He suspected a heart defect and sent my husband and me off to a pediatric cardiologist. . . . After our visit to that cardiologist—as well as to two other cardiologists and my own visit to the UCLA Medical School library—the prognosis was clear. Our baby had a very rare but well-known heart defect (truncus arteriosus with a stenotic valve). It was so severe that he was already in congestive heart failure.

Under the best-case scenario, he had less than a 10 percent chance of making it to term, and, if he were born alive, he would have less than a one percent chance of seeing his first birthday. That year, moreover, held no prospect of any reasonable quality of life. I asked each of the cardiologists what he or she would do if it was her pregnancy or that of a spouse. Without hesitation, each said "terminate the pregnancy". From the looks in their eyes, I understood that these doctors had seen a degree of suffering in their tiny patients and their patients' families that I could not comprehend. . . . Knowing that the baby had virtually no chance of surviving, my husband and I finally decided that to continue the pregnancy would be selfish, and in early May, 2000, I had a late term abortion. . . . I was also fortunate that a year after my abortion, I gave birth to a son who is now a thriving high school freshman. . . . As a woman, a mother and a lawyer, I know I did the right thing. I have shared my story with my children, and hope that should my daughter ever find herself in a position similar to mine, she will enjoy the same rights that were available to me.

Email received December 18, 2015.

One former partner at a large law firm described:

I had an abortion in 1995. At the time, I was a litigation partner at a leading law firm in charge of the defense of a major consumer class-action suit, which required that I travel regularly from our home to the client in Texas. My husband, a litigation partner at another firm, also had similar professional responsibilities and time constraints. Moreover, we had three children aging in age from four to 10 years. On a more personal level, our middle child had been diagnosed with major learning deficits and was attending a special school that addressed those issues. The school was a 45-minute drive from our home and did not offer transportation to or from the campus. At that point in our lives, we were pulled as tight as we could be, both personally and professionally. We were determined to provide all three children with the family life and educations they deserved . . . [and] it was a challenge to keep all the balls in the air every day. In November of 1995, my father suffered a major setback in his battle against ALS while he was visiting us. The details are not important other than to note that while I sat with him in the ICU, a nurse came to administer a portable x-ray. She confirmed that I was not pregnant—there was no doubt in my mind, given the birth control we were using—and then permitted me to remain in the room without any protection as they took the x-ray. A month later, I discovered that my birth control had failed, that I was pregnant, and

that I had, in fact, been pregnant the day I sat with my father in the ICU.
At the time, medical experts believed that exposure to x-rays early in the
pregnancy could significantly increase the risk of birth defects, many of
which could not be determined by the available prenatal testing. I was fortunate in 1995 to be able to make this decision without interference from
the outside world. . . . I was allowed to control my future and my body, and
to choose what I thought was the best path for our family, rather than have
someone else's ideology imposed on me. . . . [T]his decision was critical to
our family. . . . I now have three wonderful adult children, each of whom
was raised in a loving home and given all the attention they needed and
deserved while their father and I pursued . . . rewarding careers. After a
number of years in that special school, our middle child transitioned to
a traditional school, attended college and graduate school, and is now a
pursuing his own career.

Email received December 22, 2015.

One appellate litigator, who has argued multiple cases before this Court,
recounted:

I have often wondered how my life might have changed if . . . my doctors
had delayed treatment [of two dangerous pregnancies] because of restrictive laws, and my reproductive capacity had been destroyed as a result. The
Court's decisions protecting my right to choose have been indispensable to
all of the opportunities I've been able to pursue, both in my professional
career as an attorney and in my personal life as a wife and mother.

Email received December 21, 2015.
* * *

Amici's experiences demonstrate the real world effects of abortion
access on the lives and careers of women attorneys, and underscore the
truth of the Court's observation in Casey that reproductive choice facilitates women's ability "to participate in the economic and social life of the
Nation." 505 U.S. at 856.

Amici are credits to the legal profession. They are public interest attorneys, lawyers for the government, professors of law, partners at major firms,
and counsel to corporations and institutions. They are the classmates, co-
clerks, and colleagues of the Justices and clerks of this Court. They firmly
believe that they could not have been the attorneys they have been or done
the fine work that they have, were it not for their access to reproductive
choice.

Amici write as attorneys who care deeply about the Constitution and its protections, as women who have exercised their rights—recognized and reaffirmed by this Court—to liberty, dignity, and autonomy over their bodies and destinies, and on behalf of future generations of women lawyers, whose meaningful access to reproductive choice are in jeopardy if the provisions of HB2 at issue here are allowed to stand.

Conclusion

For all of the foregoing reasons, the Fifth Circuit's decision should be reversed.

Respectfully submitted,

Allan J. Arffa COUNSEL OF RECORD
Alexia D. Korberg
Brian K. Steinwascher
Rebecca L. Orel
PAUL, WEISS, RIFKIND, WHARTON & GARRISON LLP
1285 Avenue of the Americas
New York, New York 10019
(212) 373-3000
aarffa@paulweiss.com
January 4, 2016.

5

Politics, Religion, and Abortion in the United States

An Interview with Congressman William D. Delahunt[1]

By David F. Walbert

WALBERT. Thank you, Congressman, for taking the time to talk about what has been one of the most contentious issues in the country.

CONGRESSMAN DELAHUNT. Glad to. Abortion has been an important issue for many people personally and as a political and public policy issue.

WALBERT. It is an area where religion, and Catholicism in particular, has played an important role. Your life experience is especially significant as we address these issues in this book. You are a Catholic, and you have had an illustrious public career. Back when you were District Attorney, you initiated groundbreaking programs to protect women. You then served in the Massachusetts House of Representatives and for seven terms in the United States Congress where you were a key participant in some of the most important issues the country faced.

Before we get into your observations about the political process, could you share with us your religious background?

---

1. Congressman Delahunt was elected to Massachusetts' 10th congressional district in 1996. He won reelection six times by at least 32 points over his challenger and served until January 2011, when he declined to run for reelection for an eighth term.

CONGRESSMAN DELAHUNT.   I was a product of parochial schools. The first eight grades I had the Nuns, God bless them. I didn't reach my beliefs then by my own independent logic, I was just accepting of what I was told and taught. I was an only child, and my parents were both religious, but they weren't over the top. When I look back and think of those grammar school years, even then when I saw injustice—whether it was racism, for example, let's use that—even then I could never reconcile an individual describing himself as a Catholic or a Christian and having that kind of disparaging view of others.

Ted Kennedy and I were very close, and Ted often said that what motivated him in his faith was based on the Beatitudes, and that was where I was as well. We didn't need a lot of what you might call the "BS" that came from the Church. For us, and for many other Catholics I knew in public life, it was enough to remember just to "love they neighbor as thyself." If you did that, everything else falls into place.

Believe me, I was no saint, but the basic view of the Beatitudes is deep in my DNA. One can review religious doctrine and have questions or what have you, but many of the key questions about religion can't be answered. They come down to your own personal belief about such things. I never challenged myself to be logical about it, it was just an acceptance that that was part of my life, part of my culture. But for me, the Beatitudes were a pretty good roadmap. If you embraced them, they gave you a life of value, simple as that. And they have served as a guide for me all along.

WALBERT.   Could you share with us how you became interested in politics and public service?

CONGRESSMAN DELAHUNT.   I was brought up in the Boston area and always had an inclination towards public service, but I was one of those who were specifically motivated by Jack Kennedy and what he was doing. A lot of people in my generation shared that story. Back in the 1960 presidential election, I was at Middlebury College and was one of the co-chairs of Students for Kennedy in the State of Vermont. I met him as he was flying down to Boston the night before the election, election eve, and he made a stop in Burlington. So that provided me an opportunity to meet him personally and talk with him when I was 18 or 19.

Another co-chair was a dear friend and my Big Brother in our fraternity, Ron Brown, who later was Secretary of Commerce and Chairman of the Democratic National committee. Ron was the first African-American to hold either of those positions, and his tragic death in that plane crash was a big loss for the country.

Kennedy had a special charisma. Everybody wanted to be Jack Kennedy, not just for what he espoused, but for his style, too. And you had a particular connection with him if you were from Boston and were Irish—my paternal grandmother's family was Irish—as well as the religious issue being a Roman Catholic. It was a breakthrough, if you will, at that point in time, his being a Catholic and running for President. That was a huge thing.

You remember his address to the Baptist ministers down in Houston? Where they applauded him, and we nudged history a little bit forward with his election?

WALBERT.   I remember that vaguely, but please remind me about it. What happened at the Baptist Convention?

CONGRESSMAN DELAHUNT.   He assured the convention and the American people that he was able to separate his religious beliefs from what his role would be as president. That was a very big deal because some people were saying that a Catholic president would be under the control of the Pope. Jack said a distinction could be made between your religious beliefs and your public service, and that was a distinction he would have no trouble making as president. I think he invoked the biblical maxim, "Render unto Caesar what is Caesar's, render unto God what is God's."

So he made that distinction, and he had a huge influence on a whole generation. When you look back and if you could take a roll call of those who were in government who are my age—and they would have different versions of their own experience and how they got into public service—but a lot of them would echo my own experience. We were inspired by Jack Kennedy as to what we could do for the country and for the public good. Public service was not a cynical expression then. Jack really moved people. Before that, I had been dropping leaflets for local candidates, but he really motivated me to have a career in public service, and I'm very glad I did. It was very rewarding and very gratifying.

WALBERT.   I'm jumping ahead, but I can't help but think of the irony of Jack Kennedy being attacked by religious conservatives for possibly being "too Catholic" and under the "Pope's control." I say that because religious conservatives in recent years have attacked Justices Kennedy and Roberts, both Catholics, for the opposite—*not* strictly following Catholic doctrine in their votes on the Supreme Court in abortion cases. A bit inconsistent there, if not outright hypocritical!

CONGRESSMAN DELAHUNT.   Inconsistent for sure. When Jack was running for President, Baptists, Evangelicals, and conservative Protestants generally wanted guarantees that his public actions would be completely separate from his religious views and from church doctrine.

WALBERT. And I interrupted as you were talking about the Beatitudes being good governing principles for your life. You could pretty well apply those to all things in life, couldn't you?

CONGRESSMAN DELAHUNT. Exactly. So it was easy for me with that set of underlying beliefs, or principles, to then take on what could be perceived as liberal causes or progressive causes even when I was relatively young. In law school, I was active writing briefs and what have you. That was the Civil Rights era, and that meant a lot to me in an emotional way because, at that moment in time, we were beginning to slay a dragon that had been festering for 400 years in this country, and continues to fester to this day. But one thing I think you learn from a life in politics is that things rarely change overnight in a democracy. So you are constantly nudging things forward.

WALBERT. Congressman, were there other things, aside from abortion, where your progressivism conflicted with church doctrine? For example, where was the Catholic church on Civil Rights?

CONGRESSMAN DELAHUNT. They were usually pretty progressive, really. Sometimes they wouldn't take a stand, but it was really the abortion issue that created discomfort for many of us who were legislators and been brought up in the Catholic church. Initially, I was a pro-life Catholic, as I had been taught, but then I made what I would call the "Mario Cuomo distinction." Maybe looking for a way out of a difficult political and personal situation.

WALBERT. What is the Mario Cuomo distinction, Congressman?

CONGRESSMAN DELAHUNT. In a couple of words, the biblical philosophy "Render unto Caesar." Early on in his tenure as Governor of New York, Mario openly defied the church in a speech—maybe not as famous as Jack Kennedy's at the Baptist convention, but similar—at the University of Notre Dame. He said that Roman Catholic politicians who personally opposed abortion, as he did, could still support the right of a woman to have an abortion and could vote for pro-choice legislation consistent with being a Catholic. "Render unto Caesar what is Caesar's and unto God what is God's." He believed that decisions about legislation should not be dictated by church doctrine.

He was heavily criticized by some in the Church for saying that. But his taking that very public position was philosophically and personally helpful to many Catholic legislators who were wrestling with the issue, including myself.

Acknowledging in a society that is diverse with different opinions, there comes a point when you have to recognize that rights evolve, and in the case of a woman, are we really going to send doctors to jail for performing an abortion? Are we going to penalize women for making those decisions? And the answer is clearly, "No." And that works into a choice position. It's her decision, and it is her issue to deal with the morality of it.

Mario was a leading voice and a brilliant person, and when he said what he did, it made it a lot easier for many other Catholics to support a woman's right to choose.

WALBERT. There is a lot of irony here again because Mario Cuomo's son, New York governor Andrew Cuomo, was attacked recently for signing New York's liberalized abortion law. Some Catholic leaders called for his excommunication, and he said something like, "I know the Catholic Church doesn't believe in a woman's right to choose, but I'm not here to legislate religion." And he referred to the fact that his father had been attacked in much the same way 30 or 40 years before! Déjà vu all over again, as they say.[2]

CONGRESSMAN DELAHUNT. For sure. As I said earlier, things can change pretty slowly. Speaking of Mario Cuomo, it's a shame he never became president. He would been outstanding! He was very smart, had great values, and understood what government should be doing for people.

WALBERT. I knew a lot of people who thought the same way about him. Congressman, when you were young and receiving a Catholic education, was abortion an issue then? Did it even come up then?

CONGRESSMAN DELAHUNT. Not really. I've actually learned something talking with you and from what's in the book about ancient practices and attitudes, how herbs were used for contraceptive and abortion for centuries. But as to the church and my education, I don't really remember it being discussed when I was young. It just wasn't a debated or discussed issue then. It wasn't until later that it became a public issue.

And when I did deal with it and decided what was right as a matter of public policy, I think I was helped at least somewhat by knowing of the foibles of the Church historically. It had made mistakes before,

---

2. Andrew Cuomo reportedly replied as follows when asked about the Church's criticism of his support for New York's new law: "Bishops attacking Governor Cuomo? . . . Let's pull that headline up from about 30 years ago." Caleb Parke, *Cuomo Brushes Off Criticism of New York Abortion Law: "I'm Not Here to Legislate Religion,"* Fox News (Jan. 30, 2019), https://www.foxnews.com/politics/cuomo-defies-catholic-church-with-new-york-abortion-law-im-not-here-to-legislate-religion.

and the immoral nature of the church at times has to be acknowledged. We've seen that with the abuse of children. And there were popes and priests having children, and moving the papacy from Rome to Avignon, and all of that. I can certainly understand the outrage that people have had over church doctrine on the one hand and the conduct of church leaders on the other. So I didn't see church views as necessarily above reproach, which I'm sure made it easier to go from a pro-life Catholic to pro-choice when I really had to decide the question as a matter of public policy.

WALBERT. Could it be that some of your early involvement in other "women's issues" may have influenced your thinking about abortion? One of the things you're well known for, long before you were elected to Congress, is your work as District Attorney that focused on protecting women. You were a leader in that regard.

CONGRESSMAN DELAHUNT. It's been interesting as I look back. I created the first program in the nation on sexual assault in the DA's office as well as a domestic violence program. When I started what we called the "Rape Unit," Norfolk County where I was DA reported only a small number of rapes. I felt that crime was abhorrent and deserved to be treated in a particularly sensitive way.

When we created the Unit, I was surprised how much the number of reported rapes increased because we were treating the crime appropriately and sensitively. We also discovered that the majority of sexual assaults occurred within families—brothers, fathers, or someone not necessarily blood kin, but people that they knew. Molestation, we had assumed it was rare, but it was much more commonplace. It's devastating to the women affected, and to society. I remember getting a call about having a priest arrested, and there was no special treatment.

WALBERT. How did you happen to start that initiative, Congressman? Did something specific occur? Or maybe women you were working with got you focused on the issue?

CONGRESSMAN DELAHUNT. Not really. I remember just noting the statistics on sexual assault and said, "boy, these are really low." I couldn't believe that that was the extent of it. It seemed like there had to be a different order of magnitude. And once we pierced that, all hell broke loose.

I was just going through all of that information recently for historical reasons because they passed legislation naming the Superior courthouse after me. . . . Incidentally, it's the same courthouse where Sacco and Vanzetti were tried and convicted.

WALBERT. That's quite a piece of history!

CONGRESSMAN DELAHUNT. Yeah, I'm in good company—Sacco, Vanzetti and Delahunt (laughing). But seriously, we did a lot of good things in that office when I was DA. Those were the Camelot years, when criminal justice was reformed, and what we did went beyond the traditional role of a prosecutor's office. We were really into the community, and we tried to deal with intolerance and racism. We created programs in the schools, and I had advocates there.

I had few talents, but one was the ability to attract and retain really good people. Assistant DA's who worked for me went on to the Massachusetts Supreme Court, to the federal district court, to be U.S. attorneys and what have you. And they made our office, I would like to think, a real force for change.

When I created the domestic violence program, the first one in the nation, we had each police department in our jurisdiction designate a "DOVE" officer—"domestic violence ended". They really took it to heart and did a lot of training. We created a women's shelter, and we had advocates that helped in terms of housing and supporting women who found themselves in intolerable situations. So it went well beyond the "go to court and prosecute" role. The power of the DA's office is immense. If it's abused, it is horrible, but it can be used in what I believe can be a very positive force.

WALBERT. It's especially gratifying to hear that, Congressman, because there are so many bad stories about the abuse of prosecutorial and police power.

CONGRESSMAN DELAHUNT. I think particularly in the federal government. I had some problems with the FBI. And in fact there is an FBI agent we had issues with who has now been incarcerated for about 18 or 19 years for murder down in Florida. But the abuse of power is the most dangerous thing to American values.

WALBERT. I had one case where FBI agents spent *10 years* trying different schemes to entrap an outspoken African-American public figure in Atlanta. There's no way in the world, of course, that kind of effort would have been spent to entrap a white man.

CONGRESSMAN DELAHUNT. Prosecutorial power is very dangerous when it is abused. The positive use of the power of a DA, on the other hand, is a real tool for constructive change in my judgement. And I'd like to think that, whoever delivers my eulogy will make a point that I tried to do that, and I think we succeeded. With the police we designated, first of all to deal with domestic violence, and we also had a civil rights office in each of the 30 police departments in the jurisdiction. I had my own investigators, my own advocates for outreach to the community, and once they were assigned either to deal with domestic violence or civil rights, they really became the agents of change. They set an example for why we need police, not in terms of how you shoot a gun, but to understand the community that they are dealing with. And the irony is that the police in these units became true believers.

A lot of what I see now in terms of the whole issue of police brutality etc., at least in my jurisdiction the opposite was true. They were social workers, they really were, and they were the catalyst for change. Maybe the direction came from the DA's office, and there were cases where we sent strong messages in terms of dealing with minorities. In my city, Quincy, I have a daughter we adopted from Vietnam, and she was probably one of 50 Asians in the entire community—now there are about thirty-five thousand. On my watch, there wasn't going to be any nonsense. We got right into the community, and the changes that have occurred have been peaceful, and they have been very positive.

WALBERT. This is somewhat off our subject, but was that model one that could be replicated today, or have things disintegrated too much?

CONGRESSMAN DELAHUNT. It absolutely can be replicated. If you have some time, the history of what we did that was put together for the courthouse naming is about 40 pages. A lot of it is the staff being overly generous about my role, but again, working the way we did, it really was the Camelot era.

WALBERT. It's interesting you say this, Congressman, because when I think of the Boston area back then, I think of it being pretty raw on race. So when you start talking about being aggressive as the DA on civil rights, I imagine you had quite a challenge?

CONGRESSMAN DELAHUNT. It was, but they knew me. I was "one of them," and that helped me push things forward.

WALBERT. That's a key isn't it? Personal credibility.

CONGRESSMAN DELAHUNT. "He's one of those crazies, but he is still our guy." I had no problems walking into any meeting, or any bar room, and having candid conversations because they knew I was "them." I came from the same soil, and I could easily say, "cut the bull."

And that's when your Catholicism came into play. Because I remember even being in Congress, and when I would hear some of the other Congressmen spouting nonsense, I would say "What would Jesus do?" And that was effective.

WALBERT.   In that era too, politically, I assume you wouldn't have had what we have in the South now, which is domination of the Republican party by the most extreme right-wing. So if you were progressive on race or women's rights, you wouldn't be subject to being politically "outflanked" by a conservative Republican backlash?

CONGRESSMAN DELAHUNT.   No. In my time, where I was, and even now, a Republican can't win. It's really blue. There is some really bad element in every society in every community, of course. I was saying to Julia while watching news about the militia that was going to take out the Michigan Governor, that you could see from listening to them that there were a lot of people in that group that had serious mental health, maybe even retardation issues. They couldn't have put together a sophisticated conspiracy in any way, shape, or form.

WALBERT.   You sound like you are ready to be a defense lawyer?

CONGRESSMAN DELAHUNT.   I really am. (Laughing).

WALBERT.   Sounds like you were having a lot of fun as DA, which can be a great job, while you were also having a very positive impact on the community.

CONGRESSMAN DELAHUNT.   I was enjoying it a lot, but I knew it was time to leave because we were doing all kinds of innovative things, and finally everyone else was replicating what we were doing, so it was time. I didn't know what I was going to do. I always saw Congress as a possibility, and I always had an inclination towards foreign policy. And ironically, again going back to the Catholicism, there was a particular kinship, I don't know how it evolved, between the Archdiocese of Boston and Latin America.

We had missions from Boston to there. Joe Moakley, who was a beloved congressman here, and Jim McGovern, were very much involved in Central America. Again, it was that Catholicism that was a motivator, and we were very concerned about the rampant injustice and pervasive poverty that afflicted the people in Central America. And we were very bothered by what happened to the Jesuits and the nuns down there. There had been massacres. There was a Bishop Romero in El Salvador who was very outspoken about poverty, social injustice, assassinations, and torture that was commonplace. He was shot and assassinated on the altar because of what he was saying. That motivated us even more to do something. And I was always fascinated with Cuba.

What happened was, I was ready to move on when my representative, Gary Studds—who was one of the first openly gay members of

Congress—decided not to run for reelection. I ran a real knock-'em-out campaign for his seat. I had to go to court to win, but finally did by like 140 votes. After that it was a safe seat. I was involved in a lot of foreign policy, sat on the judiciary committee my first term—and in the Clinton impeachment I had a significant role because of my background as DA.

That was my first encounter with Lindsey Graham, incidentally. I was working with Asa Hutchinson, now the Governor of Arkansas, and a Democrat named Howard Berman. We were working together on an alternative to impeachment to get the country moving forward. Then the election came. Gingrich thought he was going to pick up an additional 15 seats, but he lost 6 or 7 and that was the end of our efforts. I think it was *Time* magazine that called us "The Breakfast Club." Barney Frank quipped that the one thing that came out of it was that everyone's cholesterol level increased. (Laughter).

WALBERT. You mention Lindsey Graham, and I had lunch with him years ago with a mutual friend, Paul Coverdell, who was a Georgia State Senator and then U.S Senator. I was underwhelmed to be honest. How did you find him when you served together?

CONGRESSMAN DELAHUNT.   He was a chameleon and not to be underestimated. He was very much aware. He felt that if he was going to achieve any kind of national stature, he had to show that he could work with the other side. And he did that rather skillfully until he was so back and forth all the time he lost credibility. He became really vituperative in the aftermath of Clinton's impeachment, even though he had demonstrated he was willing to avoid impeachment and a trial in the Senate. If you watched him, you could almost predict on an issue where he was going to be because he assessed it in terms of giving him some status or stature that he was looking for. The merits of an issue were not foremost to his decision.

WALBERT. Was Newt Gingrich already speaker then?

CONGRESSMAN DELAHUNT. Yes, he was already speaker.

WALBERT. I would like to ask you more about Gingrich, Congressmen, because of how destructive his career seems to have been to the entire political process in this country, including how his methods have further inflamed, and really impeded, reasonable and rational discussion about abortion. There was a recent book written about Gingrich—Burning Down the House—and one reviewer said that, to advance the Republican party, Gingrich "tied American politics to a rock and threw it down a well." He is described as ground zero for the destruction of decency in American politics, telling his party not to "disagree" with Democrats, but to call them liars, evil, the enemy and so on. How would you describe him based on your time together in Congress?

CONGRESSMAN DELAHUNT. I would say "spot on" with that description. I think he doesn't get the "credit" he deserves—if credit is the right term—for poisoning American Democracy. He was smart, articulate and he saw things. I imagine he was frustrated when the Democrats had such a huge majority in Congress, but when the Republicans finally won, the venom he used to attack Democrats got even worse.

WALBERT. Some say he pushed us down a fork in the road, one we may not be able to return from. Before him, there had always been partisan politics, of course, but there was a greater good, a national interest, that was a big part of the political formula too. Did Gingrich really have that much effect in reducing us to the lowest "cutthroat" politics where the truth and the national interest be damned?

CONGRESSMAN DELAHUNT. Absolutely. That was the Republican play-book. It was Lee Atwater. It was that kind of era. And it was effective, politically, in terms of winning offices and raw political power. Put it in terms of—I doubt whether Gingrich had any genuine feelings one way or another about abortion—I'm sure he may have said "I'm Pro-Life"—but in my judgment he knew what appealed to that base, Evangelicals, Conservative Catholics, what have you, and that's the reason he and many other Republicans took that position. Gingrich knew that was something that energized that base. And he was very effective at it. There may be a Pope Pius VI parallel there.

I don't know this, but leading up to *Roe v. Wade*, I don't know what his position was then because I wasn't focused on it. But it would be interesting to see where Gingrich was on the issue early on in his career and compare that to how abortion and a woman's right to choose was used as a political weapon. The use of extreme language like "they kill babies," "they kill babies coming out of the womb," which doesn't happen. If it is a life or death situation in terms of the mother's health or whatever, but the use of that kind of language by Republicans—who may or may not even care about the issue—has been very effective to energize their base. And we've all seen cases of extreme pro-life legislators who insist that their girlfriends or mistresses have an abortion when that comes up.

WALBERT. Was Gingrich one of the first Republicans who politicized abortion?

CONGRESSMAN DELAHUNT. I don't specifically remember whether he was upfront on it, but he would have had others, a Chris Smith from

New Jersey who was Mr. Pro-Life, and I think he was more genuine in terms of his belief, but Gingrich knew how to manipulate the electorate. And how often was it utilized to energize their base? There are a lot of people who genuinely believe their position, I'm sure, and you have to respect that, but for a Gingrich it was another tool in the political toolbox. He was a master of using language that worked, regardless of what the truth was and regardless of how much destruction that extreme language caused.

WALBERT.   Another theme political scientists talk about is that many in the Republican hierarchy don't care about the issue one way or another, but they understand they can exploit abortion politically to win votes for Republicans to get what they really want, like low taxes for the rich and laissez-faire business regulation.

CONGRESSMAN DELAHUNT.   Donald Trump, what a perfect example of that! You think he cares one way or another about whether abortion is right or wrong, moral or immoral? It doesn't even enter his mind. But he knew he had to go into Indiana, Iowa, that world, and he exploited it there without the slightest regard for what's right and wrong. The incredible things he's done since the election show what has always been obvious about his character—he will say anything to advance his own personal interests. There isn't anything more to him than that.

When it came to abortion, that meant catering to the most conservative religious voters by being very anti-choice, even though he never once indicated that was his belief before. And he went so far as to make it the central issue when it came to appointing Supreme Court Justices.

WALBERT.   Congressman, I would like to ask you to expand a bit more on your own personal evolution on the issue of abortion.

CONGRESSMAN DELAHUNT.   Well, like I said, I was raised a traditional Catholic and was taught to be pro-life, or anti-choice, but when I really had to think it through and take a public policy position, I evolved and from then on I supported a woman's right to choose. There were a fair number of people like me in Congress, men or mostly men who were Democrats, fairy liberal, and raised Catholic. And the question of abortion and the right to choose, was really one that most of us would rather not have had to decide. When someone like Mario Cuomo said what he did, that made it a lot easier, politically and personally.

From a purely religious point of view, I don't pretend to know any ultimate answers. It's very difficult to explain religious emotions, religious doctrines, and ultimate questions of life, god or religion. I think those kinds of questions are beyond the limits of our understanding. I don't know the answers. Is there an afterlife? I don't know, but I hope there is, and I hope that I've done enough good things on this earth that whatever afterlife I get is a good one. But the fact that I don't know the answer to these questions doesn't mean that religious considerations aren't in our DNA. They are for me, and those religious considerations are summed up in the Beatitudes, which are really Catholic social doctrine.

When you got down to the ultimate decision—whose choice is it, a pregnant woman's or a legislature making the decision for her—that's a pretty easy question to answer. As a matter of legislative policy, it's extremely presumptuous to tell a woman who is pregnant that she has to stay pregnant and give birth. There aren't many more intrusive personal decisions the government could force on a person than that. And just because we might be of Catholic lineage, that doesn't mean we can make those choices for others. Even from a religious point of view, isn't free will why we suffer? If there were no free will, we wouldn't suffer, would we? Our deity would step in and resolve our problems.

Questions of life after death, a soul, the idea that there is human life at conception, and questions like that, those are religious questions. I pray more now than I used to. But these are not questions a legislature should be legislating, as Mario and Andrew Cuomo said. They are very personal questions.

When I served in the legislature, we didn't talk a lot about the question of abortion or a woman's right to choose. It's a difficult issue to address, personally and emotionally. As close as I was to Ted Kennedy, and even with our similar Catholic backgrounds, we never really had a deep discussion about the issue of abortion, as important as it was. He was certainly pro-choice, as I was, but our generation, especially among men and Catholic men in particular, we just didn't discuss it if we didn't have to.

I was fortunate in Congress that the issue did not come up that often. It was more an issue in the state legislatures, and I was only there two years. That's been particularly true in recent years as anti-abortion advocates have pushed some states to more and more restrictive laws. But abortion didn't become a particularly big wedge issue when I was in Congress.

WALBERT. Sometimes I wonder if the Supreme Court doesn't feel that same way, wishing they did not have to address the issue.

CONGRESSMAN DELAHUNT. I don't have any special insight into the Supreme Court's future rulings, but I don't think it's as obvious as some how the Court will rule on abortion in the future. A number of justices have evolved during their career—they've come from more extreme positions towards the center. I think Justice Roberts is an example of that, and maybe Justice Kavanaugh will be as well, although he is so new that you can't say he's defined yet.

For the Court, stare decisis may be a way for a justice to avoid a difficult personal decision. It's not unlike what we did in Congress. You could file a bill on something but never have a hearing on it. That was a way of finessing tough issues, and it's sort of like deciding an abortion case based on stare decisis. That can save you from having to personally make a very difficult decision.

WALBERT. Congressman, you have shared with us some important insights about how you and others worked through the issue of abortion from a legislative point of view in light of your theology, and how the politicization of abortion became part of Republican politics. Before we close, are there other thoughts you might share concerning the state of our politics?

CONGRESSMAN DELAHUNT. As you know from our previous conversations—even before the extraordinary events concerning this presidential election—I have been worried about the direction of our country. People are so consumed doing things, and the pace of life is so fast they miss everything. Life has become more and more superficial in my opinion. I think all of that ties in with the deterioration of our political process. If you haven't seen it, take a look at the Netflix documentary Social Dilemma, which is very disturbing but very enlightening in terms of the manipulative impact of social media.

This is an area where the right and the left should come to agreement. Both sides *should* want the facts presented fairly and accurately, rather than being driven by computer programs that manipulate people's perceptions for the benefit of the people who pay for them.

WALBERT. I tried a case some years ago with a cast of witnesses that included an ex-governor, a Supreme Court Justice, and Eugene Patterson, the Pulitzer Prize winning newspaperman. Gene said something that is like what you're saying, that a democracy cannot survive unless people have a shared perception of the facts. We can have different values, but not fabricated "alternative truths" about events. It goes back to the problem you talked about that started with Gingrich and "matured" into the constant stream of lies Trump puts out with no regard for the truth.

CONGRESSMAN DELAHUNT.   That's exactly right, and I think it really puts our democracy at risk. With the speed of things, the problem is worse, and we are really losing our fundamental values. If you look at how the Nazis gained power, you can see how that could happen here. The Proud boys are like the early Brownshirts in Germany. You can dismiss them, but when they storm the Capitol, you have more reason to see parallels to what happened in Germany.

What is so disheartening is that these people were being misled by the President himself for his own interests, together with help from people like Ted Cruz. Cruz knows that Trump's election claims are baseless, but he doesn't care. He repeats them because he thinks that's in his political interest. Before Trump, it would have been difficult to imagine we could sink to this level so fast.

I believe very deeply in what this country stands for. With all the history of the Founding Fathers that is tied to Boston, and how much of the American Revolution is tied to Boston, it's hard not to have that kind of respect for our country. But I worry that it is at risk, and I worry that the election of Trump—and his lies about his election loss—show that our democratic institutions are not guaranteed to be as safe and sound as we thought.

WALBERT.   Thank you, Congressman Delahunt, for sharing your thoughts on religion, politics, and abortion, as well as on the broader political world we live in.

6

Women's Knowledge of Abortifacients from Antiquity to the Present

By John M. Riddle[1]

"[She] had driven her child away from her through plants" [3rd century]

In 1946, an Australian veterinary medicine journal article unwittingly linked modern science to the distant past in a way its journal authors could not imagine. Sheep grazing on a species of clover had sharply reduced fertility. Investigators discovered that this clover's particular isoflavonoids induced estrogenic activity in these sheep. Could plants affect fertility in higher mammals?[2]

Following the Australian veterinarian article, numerous researchers disclosed how plants are affecting fertility in various ways hormonally.[3] The

---

1. Professor Riddle is an Alumni Distinguished Professor Emeritus of History at North Carolina State University and a specialist in the history of medicine. He would like to thank Anne van Arsdall for her expert editorial advice and assistance in preparing this chapter.

2. H.W. Bennets et al., *A Specific Breeding Problem of Sheep on Subterranean Clover Pastures in Western Australia*, 22 AUST. VET. J. 2–12 (1946).

3. Norman Farnsworth studied plants as fertility agents and collected vast data published as *Potential Value of Plants as Sources of New Antifertility Agents*, 64 J. PHARM. SCI. 535–98 (1975); more recently, *see* Gamal Mohammed et al., *A Review of Natural Contraceptive Agents*, 4 AM. J. PHARMTECH RESEARCH 124 (2014). A new field was founded called zoopharmacognosy that studies nonhuman animals apparent self-medicating themselves by selecting and ingesting or topically applying plants and other substances to prevent or treat afflictions. *See* Rajasekar

Australian sheep did not know how the plants were affecting them, but humans made the association long ago when it was about their bodies.

A pregnant woman ingests a particular plant; later she has a miscarriage. She makes an association of cause-and-effect, especially after repeated action. She would speak to other women with something like this: "If you want a baby, don't take plant X." If the recipient knew what to avoid, she would also know what to take for the effect. Ancient Egyptian, Mesopotamian, Greek, and Roman medical records contain notices of contraceptives and abortifacients. The written notice came after untold, sometimes untellable, personal experiences with birth control plants. The chain of orally transmitted experiences went back centuries, perhaps millennia before writing. Whereas the placebo effect is a powerful factor in judging a drug's efficacy, a contraceptive or abortifacient is unlikely to be a placebo. If a woman wants an abortion, she may take a plant about which she learned from other women. If it "works," she may not know whether the plant was an active agent. If her purpose was the termination of her pregnancy, she would know all too well that it was ineffective for her intended purpose.

Plants can stimulate or inhibit the production of hormones that include estrogen and progesterone, the same ones in the "pill" we thought we discovered. About 380 C.E., Sulpicius Severus described a woman who "had driven her child away from her through plants (*gramen*)."[4] Sulpicius' observation is just one among many through the centuries and millennia before and thereafter.

Sulpicius did not name the plant or plants—probably he did not know them. Before, during, and after Sulpicius' time, medical, anecdotal, and pharmaceutical sources record many plants that we know to be effective abortifacients through scientific studies. Before discussing some of the more prominent plants, we first discuss ancient and medieval peoples' understanding of the biology and physiology of pregnancy, miscarriage, and abortion. Second, we relate the actions of some specific plants about birth control. The third and final sections trace attitudes and religious principles from pagan to Judaic, Christian, and Muslim.

Raman & Sripathi Kandula, *Zoopharmacgonosy: Self-Medication in Wild Animals*, RESONANCE 245–53 (Mar. 2008).

4. SULPICIUS SEVERUS, 2 CHRONICA 1330–31 (P. Parroni ed. 2017).

I. Meaning of Pregnancy in Antiquity and Medieval Periods

From the time of the ancient Egyptians and Babylonians, the male head of a household possessed not only the power of life and death over neonatal children but also even over an unmarried daughter.[5] This convention, dastardly to us, extended into the Christian medieval period until the 20th century in rare instances, albeit illegally. Without direct contradiction to the former, laws protected the lives of families, tribes, ethnic groups, or what we call "nations," for example, Egyptians, Sumerians, and city-states, namely, Attica, Rome, and Corinth. To ancient peoples, a fetus was not a separate human being, and thus was not protected by laws governing homicide.

An understanding of abortion necessitates an understanding of basic biology concepts. Ancient peoples knew that coitus between males and females was necessary for pregnancy. The male seed (the Greek word is *semen*) was thought to live as a seed within the female body for an unknowable period, weeks even months. The womb would then either reject or accept the seed. If accepted, the condition was pregnancy because a *conceptus* or *fetus* formed (to use a couple of frequently used Latin terms; less frequently the Greek term, *embryo*). Some ancient sources thought that a woman's body formed a female fetus earlier than a male fetus, and the concept may have been widely held.[6] Aristotle took his clues from the birds and animals, if not also the bees. The male was the fullest expression of each species, noting, for example, the plumage of male birds in comparison with females and the male lion's mane. Males produced seed (*semen*) and female bodies attempted the same action, monthly for humans. When the female body failed to purify the nascent seed, her body menstruated and tried again the following month. Conventional wisdom envisioned the interval between coitus and pregnancy as analogous to the experience with agriculture: the soil receives the seed in a variable interval before it germinates into a plant. Just as the ground accepts the seed that germinates after an indefinite time, the womb accepts the seed and supplies nourishment. Times vary just as plant seed germinations do.[7]

---

5. Stephen Krason & William Holberg *The Law and History of Abortion: The Supreme Court Refuted, in* ABORTION, MEDICINE AND THE LAW 196–98 (3d ed., J. Douglas Butler and David F. Walbert eds. 1986); JOHN M. RIDDLE, CONTRACEPTION AND ABORTION FROM THE ANCIENT WORLD TO THE RENAISSANCE 14–24 (1992).

6. *E.g.,* LEVITICUS 12:1-5.

7. Ann Elis Hanson, *The Gradualist View of Fetal Development, in* L'EMBRON: FORMATION ET ANIMATION ANTIGUÉ GRECQUE ET LATINE TRADITION HÉBRAIQUE, CHRÉTIENNE ET

Women's menstrual cycles can be whimsically irregular for any number of reasons, among them being pregnancy. Help may come from phytostimulators, as we shall specifically discuss later in the chapter. The difference between a miscarriage and abortion is intention. A physician in antiquity could not determine an early pregnancy. As a rule, pregnancy was either a woman's declaration or when her outward appearances were obvious. Aristotle, as had observers much earlier, knew that events could cause a pregnant woman to bring forth a live child, whether through trauma, high stress, post-mortem Caesarian, or unknown causes. At what point in fetal development was there independent "life"? Aristotle said the dividing line was between an unformed fetus and a formed fetus, with the implication that a formed fetus had a capacity for independent life.[8]

During antiquity and, for the most part the medieval ages, a fetus was considered property and was protected as such. Convention was widely based on the Biblical account in Exodus 21:22: "If a person hurts a woman with child, so that there is a miscarriage, and, yet no harm follows," her husband receives a fine paid by the assaulter if judges so decide. Implicit is that a miscarriage itself does not rise to the level of "harm." If harm follows "life is given for life" (21:23), interpreted as a woman's life is taken, then the assaulter pays with his life. Hebrew scholars translated the Hebrew *nefesh*, the word meaning harm, with the Greek word ψυχῆ (*psyche*) in the translation known as Septuagint (3rd century B.C.E.). Jews living in Egypt, especially Alexandria, no longer knew Hebrew; thus, they were cut off from their own Torah.

Depending on time, the meaning in Greek has different connotations than did the Hebrew word for "harm." During the third century B.C.E. when Jewish scholars translated the Hebrew Torah into Greek, the meaning of *psyche* was changing from roughly "life" or "breath" to "soul," especially as used by the Stoic philosophers of the period. The Stoics, however, never gave human qualities to a prenatal existence, and the Stoics were not Christians (although some Christians incorporated some Stoic teachings). Christian theologians selected from their philosophy those precepts they cherished. An interpretation of "soul for a soul" could lead to distinguishing between unformed and formed fetuses; thus, a fetal life is a life or a

---

ISLAMIQUE 95–108 (Luc Brisson et al. eds. 2006). Hanson demonstrates that some Greek and Latin medical writers saw hints of incremental fetal development, but such ideas were not codified and seemingly did not reach their common cultures.

8. Aristotle, HISTORY OF ANIMALS, 7. 3. 588b (Bekker ed. 5 vols. 1960–87); GENERATION OF ANIMALS 736a-b (Bekker ed.), and *Quaestionum* in HEPTATEUCHUM 2. 80. See other references in Michael Boylan, *The Galenic and Hippocratic Challenges to Aristotle's Conception Theory,* 17 J. HIST. BIOLOGY 83–112 (1984).

soul that could be lost in the assault. In contrast, the Old Latin Biblical translation relied on Greek, not Hebrew, with a *possible* interpretation that the assault took a fetal life or soul. Using the Hebrew text, St. Jerome (d. 420 C.E.) made a better translation (called the Vulgate) with the implication of causing harm, but not implying taking fetal life. St. Jerome was an excellent linguist. St. Augustine and most of the Latin and Greek Church Fathers accepted the meaning of formed and unformed fetus as a dividing line in Christian thought until the late 18th and 19th centuries of our era. Notable exceptions were Sts. Jerome and Basil.[9] Many Christian theologians regarded the formed fetus as the point when god delivers the soul, an act called ensoulment. The human couple form the body, god the soul.

Lacking the means to determine early pregnancy, the period between coitus and pregnancy was essentially within the discretion of a woman whether she wanted or needed a menstrual restoration. Physicians had no means of diagnosing an early-term pregnancy. For that matter, most physicians were not concerned with pregnancy unless there was a complication. What we call gynecology and obstetrics was within the responsibility of experienced women and midwives, not physicians. Birth control medicines can include contraceptives, abortifacients, and emmenagogues, the latter to bring on menstruation.[10] In modern medicine, the latter condition is amenorrhea, but the distinction between abortifacient and emmenagogue blurred in practice.

II. The Hippocratic Oath on Abortion

Modern culture stresses the importance of the Hippocratic Oath. Today the oath exists in a few Greek manuscripts as well as subsequent Latin or other translations, plus many modern revisions and adaptations. Various versions have the famous prohibition forbidding a physician to administer an abortion. A single, short line is variously translated into English, for example: "Similarly I will not give to a woman an abortive remedy"; "Neither will I give a woman means to procure an abortion."[11] The literal translation of

---

9. RIDDLE, *supra* note 5, at 19, 21.

10. ETIENNE VAN DE WALLE & ELISHA P. RENNE, REGULATING MENSTRUATION, BELIEFS, PRACTICES, INTERPRETATIONS (2001); BARBARA EHRENREICH, WITCHES, MIDWIVES & NURSES: A HISTORY OF WOMEN HEALERS (2010).

11. Ludwig Edelstein, *The Hippocratic Oath: Text, Translation and Interpretation, in* 6 ANCIENT MEDICINE: SELECTION PAPERS OF LUDWIG EDELSTEIN (1967); see other translations in RIDDLE, *supra* note 5, at 7; an older study, reprinted, is by Keith Hopkins, in SOCIOLOGICAL STUDIES IN ROMAN HISTORY 55–80 (2017). Hopkins' focus is on the strategies of Roman upper classes to regulate their reproductions, including with abortifacients.

the Greek is "Similarly I will not give a suppository [or "pessary"] to cause an abortion."[12] Émile Littré (1801–1891), the famous French physician and translator of the "complete" works of Hippocrates, assumed that the Greeks disapproved of abortion and supplied a general prohibition for doctor-assisted abortion as what he took to be the intended meaning. Likely, Littré's interpretation was because of his belief that doctors would not assist in abortions.[13] Even though he understood that Greek culture accepted infanticide, in the case of the Hippocratic Oath he thought physicians would not perform an abortion. But the oath attributed to Hippocrates was taken neither as an oath by rank-and-file Greco-Roman physicians nor by physicians in Judaic, Christian, or Muslim societies. Even so, many Greek and Roman physicians, as well as those in the medieval periods, were aware of its ethics as goals, not rules.[14] Not all physicians were aware of the oath and probably fewer felt bound to its tenets.[15] Although the oath contains many principles largely accepted in modern law codes,[16] there was in fact no prohibition of physician-assisted abortion. Women's sexuality and reproductive practices were largely unobserved by physicians, and the oath was a distant whisper.

---

12. RIDDLE, *supra* note 5, at 7; supported by STEVEN H. MILES, THE HIPPOCRATIC OATH AND THE ETHICS OF MEDICINE 81–90 (2004). ZUBIN MISTRY, ABORTION IN THE EARLY MIDDLE AGES C. 500–900 28 (2015) characterizes my (Riddle) translation as "an improbable and overly literalistic interpretation." But the Greek word for pessary is unambiguous, without alternative meaning. This meaning is also supported by Soranus, a Roman writer on gynecology, who cautioned that pessaries were less reliable and caused secondary problems. All classical Greek manuscripts have no alternative reading other than "pessary." *Also see* Olivia De Brabandere, *The "Hippocratic" Stance on Abortion: The Translation, Interpretation and Use of the Hippocratic Oath, in* ABORTION DEBATED FROM THE ANCIENT WORLD TO PRESENT-DAY, master's thesis, Queen's University, Kingston, Ontario (2018).

13. JOHN RIDDLE, EVE'S HERBS. A HISTORY OF ABORTION IN THE WEST 2–3 (1997).

14. Heinrich von Staden, *"In a Pure and Holy Way": Personal and Professional Conduct in the Hippocratic Oath?*, 51 J. HIST. MED. ALLIED SCI. 404–17 (1996).

15. Another frequent misapplication of history is that the Hippocratic Oath contained the phrase "Above all, do no harm"—in Latin, *Primum non nocere*. Such a phrase is embedded in *Epidemics* (1. 12), attributed to Hippocrates, but the attribution comes from Thomas Sydenham (d. 1689) who ostensibly was quoting Hippocrates. *See* Cedric Smith, *Origin and Uses of Primum Non Nocere—"Above All, Do No Harm,"* 45 CAN. J. CLIN. PHARMACOL. 371-5 (2005).

16. *See* Robert Orr et al., *Use of the Hippocratic Oath: A Review of Twentieth-Century Practice and a Content Analysis of Oaths Administered in Medical Schools in the U. S. and Canada in 1993*, 8 J. CLINICAL ETHICS 377–88 (1997).

III. Summary of Ancient and Medieval Views

Surgical abortion and other manipulative procedures were always available in ancient and medieval cultures, especially in densely populated areas, as is evidenced by surviving surgical instruments.[17] Abundant evidence leads to this conclusion: women relied on herbal abortifacients as more reliable, convenient, and less dangerous than surgery.[18] When taken early in what we—not pre-modern peoples—call early-term pregnancy, there was little restraint in employing menstrual restorative drugs. John Noonan's research traces religious and legal concepts about contraception and abortion in Western cultures.[19] Christian theologians condemned birth control as a sin because they considered it thwarting God's will. Muslim cultures were more tolerant of contraception (acceptable) and abortion (nearly acceptable). Hanafi jurists allowed a woman to decide on an abortion, but they added she ought to have a good reason.[20] Even Rabbinic opinion in antiquity allowed the use of menstrual regulators and, in some instances, even explicitly for an abortion.[21] The concept of an unformed/formed fetus as the dividing line between fetus and "life" was too abstract and too undeterminable by observation. The English called the last stage "quickening," which is perceived as fetal movement in the womb. A slow change occurred during the medieval period as a response to the Christian Church's doctrine that sin was interference with God's plans to create a person with a soul.

IV. Some Abortifacient Herbs

Cato said that gardens heal as well as nourish. A single plant species has many variables. How to use herbs is the cumulative knowledge of many generations; few old, wise women are alive today who have the necessary

17. Ralph Jackson, *Roman Doctors and Their Instruments: Recent Research into Ancient Practice*, 3 J. ROMAN ARCHAEOLOGY 5 (1990); LARRY BLIQUEZ, THE TOOLS OF ASCLEPIUS: SURGICAL INSTRUMENTS IN GREEK AND ROMAN TIMES (2015); VIVIAN NUTTON, ANCIENT MEDICINE (2012).

18. While accepting that some contraceptive and abortifacients may have been effective, Plinio Prioreschi concludes that the they could have had only a limited impact on population in Antiquity. Plinio Prioreschi, *Contraception and Abortion in the Greco-Roman World*, 1 VESALIUS 77 (1995). I contend that, while effectiveness and degree of usage cannot be proven with certainty, neither can the impact on the population production rate be disproven either.

19. JOHN T. NOONAN, JR., CONTRACEPTION: A HISTORY OF ITS TREATMENT BY THE CATHOLIC THEOLOGIANS AND CANONISTS (Enlarge ed. 1986).

20. RIDDLE, *supra* note 13, at 101.

21. John Riddle, *Women's Medicines in Ancient Jewish Sources: Fertility Enhancers and Inhibiters*, *in* DISEASE IN BABYLONIA 200–04 (I.L. Finkel & M.J. Geller eds. 2007).

information about identification, morphology, preparation, amounts, and frequencies. The information, moreover, can be imperfectly transmitted. For example, in 1972, a pregnant Colorado woman fatally took pennyroyal for an abortion. But she imbibed pennyroyal *oil,* which is a very high concentration, the equivalent of about 7,000 cups of tea. She should have used a mild tea (infusion), which, historically, women drank. In American pharmacy stores, the oil was sold to prevent fleas on animals. Herbal medicine requires more knowledge than take-this-for-that. Following are some of the more important herbal menstrual or abortifacient herbs in history.

A. Pennyroyal (*Mentha pulegium* L.)

Theatergoers in the fifth century B.C.E., more than 2,500 years ago, knew what pennyroyal did. In Aristophanes' play *Peace,* Trigatius wants to have sex with a woman, but he asks what about the danger of his being hurt with her pregnancy. "Not if you add a dose of pennyroyal," was the reply, a play on a similar Greek word for "fruit."[22] In another play, *Lysistrata,* a very noticeably pregnant Athenian woman comes on stage with a nonpregnant woman from Boeotia, a place described as "a very lovely land, well cropped and trimmed, and spruced with pennyroyal."[23] The audience would understand that the Boeotian woman was not pregnant because Boeotia was associated with pennyroyal.

In the works attributed to Hippocrates, written about the same time as Aristophanes, pennyroyal was known as an abortifacient.[24] Medical, pharmaceutical, and literary sources from the classical to modern periods frequently identify pennyroyal's birth control quality, but sometimes implicitly; it was done in code. In 1671, Mrs. Jane Sharp published a popular guide to midwifery and included at least four menstrual stimulators, one being pennyroyal. She added: "But do none of these things to women with a child for that will be murder."[25] Where drugs were sold in the 19th century, pennyroyal pills were sold under such brand names as Colchester's Pennyroyal and Tansy or just Colchester's Pennyroyal pills (Figure 6.1), as well as other brands that had names with cleverly worded guides, such as "restores female regulatory" and "removing from the system every impurity." A single issue of small-town Dunn, North Carolina, newspaper *Central Times* (Feb. 25, 1891)

---

22. ARISTOPHANES, PEACE 706–12.
23. *Lysistrata,* 87–9.
24. *See* discussion in RIDDLE, *supra* note 5, at 59.
25. JANE SHARP, THE COMPLEAT MIDWIFE'S COMPANION 182 (1725, 2018 ed.).

advertised three brands of pennyroyal pills, each box costing four cents.[26] A Buffalo newspaper in 1859 observed that "nearly every newspaper in our land" has small advertisements for women's medicines.[27] Carachipita® is sold over-the-counter today, and it includes pennyroyal as one of four herbs for abortion, each herb being an abortifacient.[28]

FIGURE 6.1 Typical Pennyroyal Advertisement

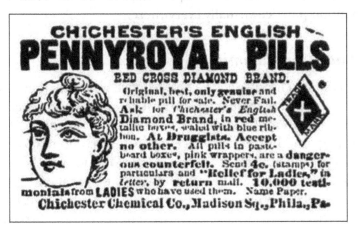

B. *Ecballium elaterium* L. A. Rich

This plant is unambiguously for abortion. The name in Greek, Ἔκβλειον, means "abortion." Thus, *ecballium* is literally the "abortion plant." The modern scientific name is *Ecballium elaterium* L. A. Rich. Pedanius Dioscorides (fl. ca. 50 C.E.), the Greek herbalist, writes that it "kills embryos/fetuses."[29] Despite its scientific name meaning abortion, the English common name is "Squirting cucumber." There is no Freudian connotation with the English name. The fruit squirts out its seed as the plant matures. Dioscorides gave careful, explicit instructions on how the medicine was to be processed and prepared. People wanting the drug need not go in the fields to collect the plant because vendors in the streets sold the abortion wine, as well as other prepared drugs. Dioscorides knew that a compounded drug was the

---

26. RIDDLE, *supra* note 13, at 235; JOHN D'EMILIO & ESTELLO FREEDMAN, INTIMATE MATTER: A HISTORY OF SEXUALITY IN AMERICA 63–66 (2d ed. 1997).

27. *Id.*

28. Julian Gold & Willard Cates, Jr., *Herbal Abortifacients*, 243 J.A.M.A. 1365–66 (1980); Anilia Banfi Vique et al., *El veto del ejecutivo Uruguayo a la despenalizaci del aborto: deconstruyendo sus fundamento*, Montevideo: Mujer y Saluden, Uruguay (2010), https://issuu.com /mujerysaludenuruguay/docs/_2010_veto_aborto (Dec. 3, 2020, 11:41 AM).

29. PEDANIUS DIOSCORIDES, 4 DE MATERIA MEDICA 150 (Max Wellmann ed. 2005, p. 307).

sum of its parts.[30] Various vendors sold the abortion wine and explained that his or her formula was unique and the best. Laws neither protected intellectual property nor customers in ancient times. Dioscorides disclosed that a woman taking the abortion wine had to fast, vomit, and drink eight cups of wine mixed with water. Squirting cucumber, or the "abortion plant," is indigenous to the Mediterranean and would not be readily available to those in central and northern Europe. Pharmaceuticals delivered in wine were a common practice virtually everywhere.

C. *Silphium* (*Ferula antiqua*)

Silphium was so much valued as a contraceptive and sometimes as an abortifacient that it became extinct by the fifth century, its existence destroyed by human exploitation. Cyrene (a Greek colony in northern Africa; today in Libya) languished economically until they discovered *silphium* on the hills facing the Mediterranean. A sixth-century B.C.E. vase shows Arkesilas, the Cyrenian king, supervising the packaging, weighing, and shipping of the plant. The plant's value was enhanced significantly because of its resistance to transplantation. Attempts to grow it in Greece and Syria failed. The city's reputation rested on the plant so much so that it became the symbol of Cyrenian coins (Figure 6.2). Ancient cities employed visual symbols for their identity, such as the owl for Athens and the pomegranate for Israel. By the late fifth century, Aristophanes exclaimed: "Don't you remember when a stalk of *silphium* sold so cheap?"

FIGURE 6.2 Cyrenian Coin (6th–5th century B.C.E. showing a seated woman touching *silphium* with one hand and the other touching her womb)

---

30. John Riddle, Dioscorides on Pharmacy and Medicine 146 (ed. 1985, 2011).

Catullus (d. ca. 54 B.C.E.), the famous Latin poet, disclosed that he would smother Lesbia, his love, with thousands of kisses. How many? As many as there are grains of sand on Cyrene's *silphium* shores. By Pliny's time (d. 79 C.E.), *silphium* was worth its weight in silver. In Pliny's memory, he had seen only a single stalk. The last reported sighting was in the fourth century when a bishop received a letter from his brother in which he disclosed that he found *silphium* growing on his farmland near Cyrene.[31]

Because the plant is extinct, how can we verify its birth control qualities? Medieval tracts called *Quid Pro Quo*—"This-for-That"—listed plant substitutes. For *silphium* the tracts list plants we classify as being in the *Ferula* family. Medieval and early modern sources name *Ferula* plants, especially *Ferula asafetida* L., that act as contraceptives and abortifacients (or were disguised as menstrual regulators). One of *Ferula*'s actions is the stimulation of progesterone. In the records of the Inquisition held at Montaillou (early 14th century), ferula was a pessary before sexual intercourse, probably for its spermicidal activity.

D. Birthwort (*Aristolochia spp.*)

A vase in Pharaonic Egypt of the New Kingdom depicts a woman nursing a baby, and prominently beside her are the twining vines of the *Aristolochia* plant (Figure 6.3). Its English common name, birthwort, connects the two. As befits its common name, birthwort was employed in medicine from ancient Egypt down to the 21st century for dual purposes, beneficially assisting childbirth and for late-term abortion. Seemingly, these actions are contradictory but, medicinally, they are understandable. The suffix "*-wort*" is the Old English word for "plant." Women took birthwort for difficult childbirth and abortion, depending on the amount, preparation, and appropriate time in a pregnancy. As late as the 19th century, professional physicians employed it to assist in complicated births; whereas, today its abortifacient qualities are used in traditional medicine. For example, the medicinal use of birthwort is "to remove the placenta, abortion, and menstrual pain," reported as recently as 2006 in Trinidad and Tobago.[32]

---

31. John Riddle & J. Worth Estes, *Oral Contraceptives in Ancient and Medieval Times*, 80 Am. Scientist 226–33 (1992).

32. Cheryl Lans, *Ethnomedicines Used in Trinidad and Tobago for Reproductive Problems*, 3 J. Ethnology & Ethnomedecine 5 (2007); (Aneeha Gurib-Fakim, *Medicinal Plants: Traditions of Yesterday and Drugs of the Tomorrow*, 27 Molecular Aspect of Medicine 1–93 (2006); Michael Heinrich et al., *Local Uses of Aristolochia Species and the Content of Nephrotoxic Aristolochia*

FIGURE 6.3 On the right, a scene from a vase found in the Egyptian city of Thebes showing a nursing mother with birthwort (Aristolochia) leaves in the background. The drawing on the left is taken from a Theban tomb that shows the plant was used to assist in childbirth and also was taken for an abortion. (From tomb n. 217, courtesy of Lise Manniche.)

E. Juniper (also known in England as *savin*) (*Juniperus communis* L.)

A leading historian of abortion in America, James Mohr, wrote: "There can be but little doubt that juniper extract was the single most commonly employed folk abortifacient in the United States during the early decades of the nineteenth century."[33] The Egyptian Ebers Papyrus dated between 1550 and 1500 B.C.E. names juniper for "loosening a child in the belly of a woman."[34] Ancient and medieval authorities wrote that juniper was both a contraceptive and an abortifacient. Published in 1761 by Dr. Jean Astruc, who was regarded in his time as the leading authority on gynecology, called

---

Acid 1 and 2—A Global Assessment Based on Bibliographic Studies, 125 J. ETHNOPHARMACOLOGY 108 (2009) (although focuses on kidney disease, references are included for abortion).

33. JAMES C. MOHR, ABORTION IN AMERICA. THE ORIGINS AND EVOLUTION OF NATIONAL POLICY 1800–1900, 8 (1978).

34. Ebers Papyrus 806, in HERMANN GRAPOW ET AL., 4 GRUNDRISS DER MEDIZIN DER ALTEN ÄGYPTER, pt.1, pp. 278–79; *see also* RIDDLE, *supra* note 5, at 70–71.

Oil of Savin (i.e., juniper) "un secret admirable." Astruc named juniper as a menstrual stimulant without explicitly writing "abortion" as a possible outcome. Earlier in the medieval era, Peter of Spain (13th century) made a similar, albeit more definitive, claim about its medicinal activities. Peter wrote an immensely popular work called *Treasure of the Poor* to advise the poor on how to administer health care and pharmaceuticals cheaply. He bemoaned that poor women were relying on drug vendors when the remedies grew in gardens and the countryside around them. Peter named specific menstrual stimulators, including a separate chapter on abortion (*De abortu*) where he imparted information on how to prevent one, not produce one. Later, Peter became Pope John XXI in the year 1276.

One who knew what not to take for the effect, naturally would know what to take for the desired effect. A woman in Modena in 1499 said it succinctly: "Who knows how to heal knows how to destroy."[35] A practicing physician in London in 1694, John Peachey, wrote a medical guide in which he named juniper (*savin*) to provoke the "Courses," "causes Miscarriage," and expel "a Dead Child." Nowhere did he say "abortion," but he noted that also witches used this formula. Witches allegedly did many things, such as killing babies before they could be baptized. Allegedly, most witches were concerned about birth control and infanticide, as will be discussed later.

F. Pomegranate (*Punica granatum* L.)

Adam and Eve ate the fruit of the tree of knowledge because the snake suggested it. God severely punished man and woman (Genesis 2:8-3:7) for directly disobeying his command not to eat the fruit. Most modern depictions and accounts suggest the fruit was an apple. But the fruit of the tree of knowledge was not an apple. First, the Hebrew word in Genesis means "golden" or "rust" colored fruit, and apples do not grow in Palestine. The fruit was the pomegranate. Baskets filled with pomegranates were on top of the two columns at the front of Solomon's Temple in Jerusalem, and the fruit was Israel's icon on its coins, as well as on many other surviving artifacts. Genesis was written approximately in the seventh century B.C.E. Roots of the history of the fruit of the tree of knowledge are traced back to ancient Sumer (remember Abraham came from Ur) and the story about Inanna, the goddess of fertility (Figure 6.4). She disobeyed the gods and, accompanied by the god of knowledge, went to the Underworld where an unnamed woman gave her the *huluppu* tree, which gave her sexuality and

---

35. RIDDLE, *supra* note 13, at 128.

power. Then she became happy and ultimately returned to the Upper World with the other gods. Inanna became the top deity in early ancient Sumer. Vases and other Sumerian evidence shows that this tree was the pomegranate. Pomegranates in early records were birth control agents.

Greek medicine tracts, attributed to Hippocrates, record the use of pomegranates for fertility control. In Greek mythology, Hades, the god of the Underworld, wanted progeny; Zeus wanted harmony. Zeus ordered Persephone, daughter of Demeter, to wed Hades, and he warned her not to eat pomegranates. As a reluctant bride, Persephone went to the Underworld but, once there, she ate pomegranates and thwarted Hades' will. Hades was robbed of children because of pomegranates' action. Zeus sentenced Persephone to dwell in the Underworld half of each year, returning to the Upper World for spring and summer. A fifth-century B.C.E. plate

FIGURE 6.4 Found in a pit near Inanna's temple in Uruk (lower Mesopotamia), the Inanna vase (dating ca. 3100 B.C.E.) has Inanna standing by the door of a storehouse. The lowest panel has figures of pomegranates (identified by three calyxes on top) interspersed with stalks of grain. Grain symbolizes fertility, and pomegranates its control. The vase was shattered during the American occupation of Baghdad in 2002 by looters. (Art Resource)

shows Demeter, Persephone's mother, seated and holding branches of grain stalks and pomegranate in a similar relief as on the Inanna vase, approximately 2,500 years before the Demeter plate. The lower border on the Uruk vase (3100 B.C.E.) shows pomegranates alternating with grain stalks. Grain represented a wish for fertility; pomegranates were for its control.[36]

Why would this birth control plant be so central historically in the ancient world and so relatively unmentioned in medical and anecdotal records in the late classical, medieval, and early modern periods? Purely as speculation, I suggest that millennia of breeding for tastes gradually reduced pomegranate's estrogenic activity so that other plants were relatively more potent. Even so, pomegranates for abortion continue, albeit in lessening frequency, in records up to the present.[37] In today's Iran, customs persist for a mother to give a pomegranate to her daughter on her wedding day.[38] Pomegranates are indigenous to the region that is now modern Iran and Turkey.

G. Other Birth Control Plants

Many more plants were employed for birth control, ranging from suppression of sexual desire (e.g., plaster of hemlock on the testicles before coitus) to late-term abortion. Among the most popular, judged by frequency of notices in medical sources, were Artemisia, including southernwood (*Artemisia spp.*), rue (*Ruta gravoellens L.*), Queen Anne's Lace (*Daucus carota L.*), myrrh (*Commiphora spp.*), asarum (*A. europaeum L.*), and chaste tree (*Vitex agnus-castus L.*). The "chaste tree" was employed primarily as a male contraceptive but also acted as an abortive. The Greek word *agnus castus* meant the same as the English common name, "chaste." Primarily its action was to reduce spermatogenesis, as well as the libido, when taken orally. Gladiators took it so their strength would be directed to the arena, not the bed. During the Middle Ages, it was called "monk's pepper" because its bark was sprinkled on food for much the same reasons.

---

36. JOHN RIDDLE, GODDESSES, ELIXIRS, AND WITCHES: PLANTS AND SEXUALITY THROUGH-OUT HISTORY 33–54 (2010), for references about Persephone and pomegranate.

37. For examples of modern notice, see E. Ernst, *Herbal Medicinal Products during Pregnancy: Are They Safe?*, 109 BJOG: INTERN. J. OBSTETRICS & GYNAECOLGY 227, 232 (2002).

38. *See id.*

V. Roman Empire

Neither law nor societal conventions provided restrictions on sexual activities. Child rearing was left to the individual and/or the head of the family. If a married woman thought that she might be pregnant, she could take a menstrual stimulator, essentially an early-term abortifacient in modern conceptualization, without the approval or even knowledge of her husband. Some of the salad plants, such as rue and some of the mints, have this action. They could be in the same bowl from which the woman and man ate and only the woman knew its purpose other than culinary. E.R. Boak (1955) attributed the fall of Rome to a crisis because of a gradual, long-term population decrease.[39] Demographer John C. Caldwell (2004) accepts that Rome had a slow decrease in population in part because of deliberate conduct through contraception, infanticide, and child exposure. Abortion was not a prominent factor, he thought, because of "the dangers of physically induced abortion." Caldwell questions the general effectiveness of abortifacients (he uses broadly the term "contraceptives") to "have caused a societal fertility decline."[40] But considering that abortifacient usage is well attested in documents from the second millennium B.C.E. to the present, it is not reasonable to believe that multiple generations used herbal substances for birth control while somehow not noticing that they were ineffective. Proof to the contrary would have been too obvious.

VI. From the Middle Ages to 1900

When discussing things medieval, generalizations are difficult; the period lasted many centuries with an amalgamation of different and evolving cultures. Church canons and penitentials denounced virtually any form of birth control, from contraception and abortion to infanticide, as a sin. Laws of Germanic states were based increasingly on the Exodus principle of a perpetrator assaulting a pregnant woman (explained earlier). Later, German feudal states and towns considered the act of assaulting a pregnant woman to be a crime if fetal death occurred, an interpretation a step beyond the protection of the woman assaulted, not the fetus. Secular courts

---

39. ARTHUR E.R. BOAK, MANPOWER SHORTAGE AND THE FALL OF THE ROMAN EMPIRE IN THE WEST (1955).

40. John C. Caldwell, *Fertility Control in the Classical World: Was There an Ancient Fertility Transition?* 21 J. POPULATION RESEARCH 7–8 (2004). *See also* Bruce Frier, *Natural Fertility and Family Limitation in Roman Marriage*, 89 CLASSICAL PHILOLOGY 318–33 (1994).

(feudal and town, royal) were inspired by this principle, giving indictments and inconsistent decrees in their applications. Ecclesiastical canons and courts had similar hurdles applying the principles to reality. The formal study of law in universities (beginning in roughly the 12th century) led to law distinguishing, albeit vaguely, between an unformed and formed fetus. In legal proceedings, the abstract principle had little application: if rational, human "life" began with formation how could an inquiry know when the fetal homicide occurred?[41] Directed by juries, English assize courts consistently refused convictions for assaults leading to a miscarriage.

Surprisingly, as discussed earlier, Peter of Spain, later Pope John XXI, was a major source for late medieval birth control information. Herbalists, vendors, and druggists increasingly supplied pharmaceuticals, and he wanted common people to know what their ancestors knew about herbal and other remedies freely available in nature around their homes. His *Thesaurus pauperum* ("Treasury of the Poor") included a large collection of birth control plants, though not explicitly for abortion—usually for stimulation of menstruation. Explicitly, however, as noted earlier, one chapter was "*De arbortu.*"[42] Albertus Magnus (d. 1280) denounced abortion and contraception, but in his works on nature he conveyed specific advice to women on how to prevent conception and how to produce a miscarriage, both implicitly and explicitly.[43] The modern mind sees a contradiction between a pope and a saint denouncing abortion and at the same time giving specific information on how to procure one. I cannot place myself within their minds but, after studying the Middle Ages, I suspect that Peter and Albert were not hypocrites. They believed birth control was in some way wrong, but they also knew that god gave some herbs (and minerals) these qualities for a purpose. They merely described the herbs' actions as god's design without adding their own advocacy.

In its courts, the Christian church treated birth control as a sin, notably, but not exclusively, regarding the use of abortifacients. Whereas ecclesiastical courts could not impose corporal punishment, they had a variety of prohibitions such as receiving the sacraments. Alternatively, secular courts increasingly had difficulty with administering corporal punishment for fetal death. For example, Clara, a servant in a Venetian home, hid her dead fetus

---

41. WOLKGANG P. MÜLLER, THE CRIMINALIZATION OF ABORTION IN THE WEST: ITS ORIGINS IN MEDIEVAL LAW (2012), especially, pp. 116–22.

42. RIDDLE, *supra* note 5, at 138.

43. John Riddle, *Albert on Stones and Minerals, in* ALBERTUS MAGNUS AND THE SCIENCES, COMMENORATIVE ESSAYS 209 (James Weisheipl ed. 1980).

for some five or six months following a miscarriage/abortion. A jury found her guilty of hiding her fetus (three undecideds; seven against). She was given lashes and three months imprisonment, following which she had to wear a pointed hat in public.[44] Wearing a hat was the community's way of shaming guilty persons. Prosecutions against women for abortions were comparably rare. Many punishments were for the use of poisons. When Justinian rewrote Roman law (sixth century) to prohibit divorces, the wag was that a lot of poisonings would occur.

VII. Poisons and Witches

Midwives and "wise women" were primary targets of the persecutions. Numerous names for witches become somewhat muddled. An estimated one-half million, predominantly women (roughly 80 percent), died horribly and unjustly in the three and half centuries of suppression in virulent witch-hunts. Most "witches" had knowledge of herbal medicine for women.[45] One result of this tragic period was that chains of knowledge were broken. "Poisoning" is the term often used in the trials indirectly, while the focus was on sexuality, infanticide, and abortion. Large-scale witchcraft suppression (ca. 1450–1700) to combat heresies evolved, beginning about the twelfth century in Europe. Many virulent witch hunts arose as extra-legal actions separate from secular or ecclesiastical controls. In 1467, two Jesuits published an invective against witches that specified that witches engaged in seven acts:

1. Inclining the minds of men to inordinate passion
2. Obstructing the generative force
3. Removing "the member" [i.e., penis]
4. Changing men into beasts by their magic art
5. Destroying the generative force in women
6. Procuring abortions
7. Offering children to the devils[46]

Six of the seven are related to sexuality, four directly to reproduction and infanticide. A long chapter could be written about each, including removing the penis, which seems connected to the chaste plant. The action described was tying a ligature (i.e., string) around the penis that prevented

---

44. MÜLLER, *supra* note 41, at 205–06.

45. RIDDLE, *supra* note 36, at 129–48.

46. HEINRICH KRAMER & JAMES SPRENGER, MALLEUS MALEFICARUM 1. 6. (Orig. 1487; Montague Summers, trans. 1971), p. 47.

erections. In fact, the chaste plant did prevent erections, the opposite of Viagra. Item number 7, offering children to the devil, connotes the oft-repeated charge that witches wished to destroy children before baptism. Related to this charge was the application of a witch's ointment consisting of fat from infant bodies. Item number 1 may relate to a major ingredient in the ointment with atropine-producing herbs, atropine being a mind-altering substance. Common law (*Jus commune*) focused more on poisons, increasingly pointing to poisons related to abortion.

When the records named a witch, usually no occupation was listed, but when named, most women were midwives or "wise women." Virtually all adult women would have feared for their lives. Quoted earlier was the woman from Modena who said: "Who knows how to heal knows how to destroy."[47] One woman telling another about birth control plants could be deadly risky. A perceived decline in populations was a motivating concern for businessmen. Towns that had growing populations prospered; where there was population loss, businesses receded. Women were blamed for not having babies. Some German town councils blamed economic recessions on women unwilling to have babies. German towns forbade the growing or possession of juniper, and town policy enforced the ordinances. Static, or declining, population concerned a few European intellectuals who looked at the advance of Turkish Muslims. Some called for Christianity to abandon its monogamy doctrine. That trial balloon suggestion did not lift off.[48]

VIII. Science and the Fetus

The impeachment of the Aristotelian-Augustan doctrine of unformed/formed fetus was a slow process taking many centuries to unfold. Researches by Ulisse Aldrovandi (d. 1605), William Harvey (d. 1657), and Marcello Malpighi (ca. 1694) disclosed that embryonic development was incremental and not in discernably distinct stages. Anton von Leeuwenhoek (d. 1675) saw sperm cells for the first time—actually, it was his young assistant—with the news that sperm life was short and could not have lived in the womb for extended times. Théophile-René-Hyacinthe Laennec announced the invention of the stethoscope in 1818; by the 1840s–50s, people expected a physician to have one around his neck. The instrument allowed a country and town physician to hear a fetal heartbeat and pronounce pregnancy. Caspar Wolf's studies of chicken embryos in 1768 disclosed that rudiments of each

---

47. RIDDLE, *supra* note 13, at 128.

48. *See* PETER BILLER, THE MEASURE OF MULTITUDE: POPULATION IN MEDIEVAL THOUGHT (2003), for an excellent study of early modern demographic thought.

new organism were present in both the female egg and male sperm. By the late 1800s, physicians and biologists understood that Aristotle was incorrect about the presence of a strict dividing line between the unformed and formed fetus (or unviable and viable fetus). Lawmakers and theologians followed the changes in medical science, but they were way behind.

IX. Drug-Induced Abortion and the Law

Lawmakers of the early nation-states began to write laws concerning birth control, but they were only vaguely aware of how to write the laws because they were only vaguely aware of what was happening. Generally, town laws became national laws. The Laws of Caroline (Charles V of the Holy Roman Empire), promulgated in 1532, declared as punishment "as for homicide" anyone who assaults a female thereby causing a miscarriage, specifically, to give her "food or drink to abort a living child." The German was "*essen oder drincken*" ("food or drink")—without specificity. The Emperor's words came from Bamberg's municipal laws. Note that the German for "food and drink" did not use the word *Drogen* for drug, because they did not consider birth control agents as "drugs." Those things that women took (and some men sold) were unspecified.

In the United States, lawmakers sought to apply the newly found understanding that there was no discernable stage in fetal development when viable life began. How could they find words to protect the fetus's "potential for life" with words that could measure whether there was intentionality in taking substances that many regarded as foods? Similar to the late Roman Empire, American lawmakers preferred to use the term "poisons" rather than drugs or abortifacients, generally the same as Romans did in the late Roman Empire.

In 1821, Connecticut passed a law that became a model for other states, declaring that a crime was committed when "any deadly poison or other noxious and destructive substance" was given with the intent to cause a miscarriage of any women "then being quick with child." By 1850, U.S. states rewrote or, in some cases, wrote laws to broaden pregnancy to "conception," a word used in Wisconsin's 1858 law. The wording in most laws refers to poisons but in various ways: "poison" (Arizona territory, 1865); "any poison or other noxious thing" (Rhode Island, 1956); "killing poison" (Illinois, 1833); "any poison, drug or substance" (Pennsylvania, 1945); "any instrument, medicine or drug or other means" (District of Columbia, 1960, and Mississippi, 1956); "recipes or prescriptions for drops, pills, tincture, or other compounds, designed to prevent inceptions, or tending to produce miscarriage or abortion" (Colorado, 1921; similar Kansas). Iowa's law

(1924) specified a few familiar plants, including juniper, and ended the shortlist with "or derivatives." Louisiana lawmakers were clever in getting at the heart of the issue. In 1924, state law prohibited any "sale or advertisement of . . . any secret drug or nostrums purporting to be *exclusively for the use of females* for preventing conception or for procuring abortion or miscarriage" (emphasis added).[49]

Throughout the 19th and early 20th centuries, advertisements, usually in newspapers, continued to promote thinly disguised "women's drugs." Knowing little about such things, law enforcement officers were hard-pressed to determine actions and intentions. In the 19th and 20th centuries, Ireland's secular laws and Catholic religious dogma restricted contraception and abortion, but both practices prevailed, many women employing the same plants as those used by their medieval ancestors.[50] Irish women learned both from networking with friends and from advertising in newspapers.

The modern state began the regulation and licensing of drugs, a new pathway in pharmacy history. The U.S. Federal Food and Drug Act in 1906 was written primarily in response to some public scandals about drug quality and was not specifically to control birth control drugs. With it, the era of substance regulation began. Vendors of birth control drugs sold the same drugs, mostly plants, and specified other beneficially therapeutic usages. The terms oft used were "Female Remedy" or "Women's Tonic" or "Female Hygiene." Public opinion, largely female, objected strenuously to government regulation. Support was militantly strenuous for widely popular Lydia Pinkham's Vegetable Compound (Figure 6.5), a formula first sold in 1875 and revised many times thereafter. Lydia Pinkham's Vegetable Compound is still sold, though not as originally compounded.

FIGURE 6.5 Lydia Pinkham's Vegetable Compound as it is currently sold, employing much the same presentation, including Pinkham's picture, but no longer using the original formula.

---

49. For references to these laws, see Riddle, *supra* note 13, at 248–50.

50. Cara Delay, *Pills, Potions, and Purgatives, Women and Abortion Methods in Ireland, 1900–1950*, 30 Women's Hist. Rev. 22–34 (2018); cf. Sally Sheldon, *How Can a State Control Swallowing? The Home Use of Abortion Pills in Ireland*, 24 Reprod. Health Matters 90–101 (2016). *See also* Ali Isaac, *Abortion and Birth Control in Ancient Ireland* (Aug. 6, 2018), https://www.aliisaacstoryteller.com/post/abortion-and-birth-control-in-ancient-ireland.

Its explicit use was for dysmenorrhea, but some vague labels said the tonic was a "Blood Purifier," "dissolves and expels tumors," and "cures irregularity." Women wrote their congressional representatives not to outlaw their tonic.[51] Indeed, legislatures were warned to make no laws forbidding use by women of what nature provided. What did these women know and how did they use what they knew? In 1936, the American Medical Association asserted: "The facts are, practically none of these preparations will reestablish the menstrual flow when its cessation has been due to pregnancy."[52] But if these plants did not work, why were lawmakers so devoted to writing a law that would prohibit them? Why did women take them for millennia, if they did not work? The birth of St. Germanus provides an insightful answer.

X. The Birth of St. Germanus, Bishop of Paris (Germain d'Autun)

In or about the year 496, Germanus' parents lived near Autun in the east-central part of modern France. Germanus' mother was pregnant in what she regarded as too short an interval since her previous child. Venantius Fortunatus, who knew Germanus personally, wrote a biography of Germanus. To better space her children, his mother took "with wine a potion to throw out an abortion." As related in a Carolingian retelling (late ninth century), Germanus' mother suffered mightily in her abdomen because the "infant was resisting from the womb." A "fight" ensued

> between the woman and her insides . . . as the bundle was struggling so that the mother would not become a parricide. So it happened that protected he emerged safe and sound and rendered his mother innocent. Here was a prophecy of the future, to have performed a miracle before he even reached birth.[53]

As a fetus, Germanus was victorious over the poison. This was the miracle: the abortifacient or "poison" (whatever it was) did not work despite the best efforts of the poison and the mother's intentions. The unborn fetus

51. SARAH STAGE, FEMALE COMPLAINTS: LYDIA PINKHAM AND THE BUSINESS OF WOMEN'S MEDICINE (1979).

52. ARTHUR CRAMP, 3 NOSTRUMS AND QUACKERY AND PSEUDO-MEDICINE 62 (3 vols., 1936).

53. ZUBIN MISTRY, ABORTION IN THE EARLY MIDDLE AGES c. 500–900 (2015), p. 296; based on *Vita Germani brevior Germani* 1, MGH SRM 7, p. 372, as quoted by Mistry (note 8), pp. 79, 296.

had the miraculous power to thwart the poison's power. Germanus became bishop of Paris long after the fetial feat. The expectation was the "poison" would accomplish its intended purpose, but for the miracle. If women in Sumerian times, when writing began and likely much before, had bad or no results from what they took for birth controls, would they have persisted in using them down to our day? As the Germanus miracle informs us: the potions worked, not all surely, but enough that women had confidence in their power to control their fertility.

7

A Future from the Past: Self-Managed Abortion with Ancient Care and Modern Medicines

By Anna Reed

> "We've been self-managing our abortions for thousands of years. Methods have changed and become very very safe—but criminalization still remains."[1]

These are the words of Renee Bracey Sherman, a movement leader in the fight for bodily autonomy and freedom from state violence. Lack of access to clinical abortion care long predates the pandemic, as does organizing for greater access to self-managed abortion (SMA). For years, anti-choice initiatives have been strategically eroding access to clinical care, which, even when available, often fails to meet people's needs. Grassroots networks of advocates, organizers, abortion funds, midwives, doulas, and other providers, have centuries-old practices of helping people navigate these barriers.

In 2020, these ancient forms of care are now equipped with new technology and new medicines that make managing abortions outside of clinics extraordinarily safe. But however settled the medical safety is behind SMA, the legal status of the practice is not quite so clear. Dozens if not hundreds

---

1. Renee Bracey Sherman (@RBraceySherman), Twitter (Oct. 24, 2020, 1:01 PM), https://twitter.com/RBraceySherman/status/1320047656035622916.

of people have been criminally charged for self-managing their abortions in the U.S., even though SMA is not illegal in most places in the United States.[2] The pandemic has created unprecedented barriers to clinical care, and the recent confirmation of Justice Amy Barrett casts the future of clinic access into even greater doubt. This chapter will explore the potential, and the pitfalls, of SMA as a safe and effective alternative to dwindling clinic access and will explore the legal landscape of SMA today and in a post-pandemic world.

I. What Is Self-Managed Abortion?

A. Defining Self-Managed Abortion

Self-managed abortion, sometimes called home abortion or self-induced abortion, refers to the practice of ending one's own pregnancy outside of a medical setting.[3] SMA encompasses a wide array of experiences—ingesting herbs, massage, drinking tisanes, using a combination of abortion medications (mifepristone and misoprostol), using misoprostol alone, inserting objects into the vagina, using a combination of these methods, and other methods.[4] Although there is increasing awareness about SMA, the practice

---

2. Only five states have explicit bans on self-managed abortion: Arizona, Delaware, Idaho, Oklahoma, and South Carolina. *See* Farah Diaz-Tello, Melissa Mikesell & Jill Adams, *Roe's Unfinished Promise: Decriminalizing Abortion Once and for All,* IF/WHEN/How (Nov. 28, 2017), https://ssrn.com/abstract=3082643 [hereinafter If/When/How, *Roe's Unfinished Promise*]; *see also* If/When/How Staff, *Fulfilling Roe's Promise: 2019 Update,* IF/WHEN/How (2019), https://www.ifwhenhow.org/resources/roes-unfinished-promise-2019-update/ [hereinafter If/When/How, *Fulfilling Roe's Promise: 2019 Update*] (explaining that New York's SMA ban was repealed); *See* also Sarah Ruiz-Grossman, *Nevada State Legislature Passes Pro-Choice Abortion Bill,* HUFFINGTON POST (May 21, 2019, 6:25 PM), https://tinyurl.com/y658ox76 (covering the passage of Nevada's We Trust Women Act, which removed criminal penalties for people who end their own pregnancies). For more information about contemporary SMA bans, *see* section II.B. *infra.* On February 22, 2021, the House of Delegates of the American Bar Association passed a resolution opposing criminal prosecution of self-managed abortions. The proponents of the resolution reported that "since *Roe v. Wade* was decided in 1973, hundreds of people have been criminalized for allegedly having a self-managed abortion." Amanda Robert, *Women Shouldn't Face Criminal Prosecution after Abortion or Miscarriage, ABA House Says,* ABA JOURNAL (Feb. 22. 2021, 7:10 PM CST), https://www.abajournal.com/news/article/women-shouldnt-face-criminal-prosecution-after-abortion-or-miscarriage-aba-house-says.

3. *See* Heidi Moseson, *Self-Managed Abortion: A Systematic Scoping Review,* 63 BEST PRACTICE & RESEARCH CLINICAL OBSTET. & GYNAEC. 87, 87 (2020) [hereinafter, Moseson, *Self-Managed Abortion: A Systematic Scoping Review*].

4. *See id.*

is not a new phenomenon. The historical record of people self-managing extends throughout history and across cultures. For centuries, herbal abortifacients were widely used by women in many cultures. That history is documented in the exhaustively researched writings of Professor John Riddle,[5] who also authors a chapter in this treatise addressing that history and the latest research findings.

Although some people self-manage without involving any health care professionals in the process, others seek out doctors, midwives, doulas, or other care providers to understand the process, procure pills, or for other forms of support. There is an important distinction to be made here between telemedical abortion and self-managed abortion. Although a telemedical abortion may take place without ever entering an abortion clinic, telemedical abortion refers to a medical abortion that is prescribed via a virtual abortion consultation and is supervised by an authorized health care professional. Self-managed abortion, on the other hand, refers to a person ending their own pregnancy without a doctor's prescription or supervision. Telemedical abortion does not carry the same risks of prosecution that SMA does. Although I will discuss telemedical abortion at several points throughout this chapter, I will focus primarily on the practice of self-managed abortion with self-sourced abortion pills (mifepristone and misoprostol) and will address legal issues that arise for abortion seekers who self-manage and for the people who assist them.

1. Why Do People Self-Manage?

Before discussing how the pills work and their significance for abortion access, it is important to understand the reasons why people decide to self-manage. While the pandemic and Justice Barrett's recent appointment to the Supreme Court have generated new momentum and media attention around SMA, people have been self-managing for thousands of years and have been self-managing with pills for decades—long before COVID-19 shuttered clinics around the world. This section will discuss some of the reasons why a person might self-manage rather than seek a clinical abortion.

---

5. Professor Riddle is an Alumni Distinguished Professor Emeritus of History at North Carolina State University and a specialist in the history of medicine. Two of his books that address this history are CONTRACEPTION AND ABORTION FROM THE ANCIENT WORLD TO THE RENAISSANCE (1992) and EVE'S HERBS: A HISTORY OF CONTRACEPTION AND ABORTION IN THE WEST (1997).

a. Personal Preference

Several studies addressed in the next section reveal that logistical barriers or a lack of clinic access are the primary reasons why people self-manage, but some people simply prefer to end their pregnancies at home. SMA, unlike clinical abortions, allows people to manage their care on their own schedules and in a place that feels comfortable and private for them.

A recent research review synthesized findings from studies of experiences with SMA from around the world. Ten of those studies indicated that the comparative ease of using and procuring abortion pills was a primary cause of respondents' self-managing.[6] Other studies found that it was the perception that SMA is safer or more acceptable than a surgical abortion.[7] Still others highlighted the comfort, privacy, and autonomy that is possible when self-managing one's care.[8] Other reasons for pursuing SMA

---

6. These studies, cited in Moseson's *Self-Managed Abortion: A Systematic Scoping Review, supra* note 3, at 101, include Abigail Aiken et al., *The Impact of Northern Ireland's Abortion Laws on Women's Abortion Decision-Making and Experiences*, 45 BMJ SEXUAL & REPROD. HEALTH 3, 3–9 (2019); Silvina Ramos et al., *Women's Experiences With the Use of Medical Abortion in a Legally Restricted Context: The Case of Argentina*, 22 REPROD. HEALTH MATTERS 4, 4–15 (2015); Abigail Aiken et al., *Experiences of Women in Ireland Who Accessed Abortion by Travelling Abroad or By Using Abortion Medication at Home: a Qualitative Study*, 44 BMJ SEXUAL & REPROD. HEALTH 181–86 (2018); Abigail Aiken, *Experiences and Characteristics of Women Seeking and Completing At-Home Medical Termination of Pregnancy Through Online Telemedicine in Ireland and Northern Ireland: a Population-Based Analysis*, 124 BJOG 1208–15 (2017); Lucila Szwarc & Sandra Salomé Fernández Vázquez, *"Lo Quería Hacer Rápido, Lo Quería Hacer Ya": Tiempos e Intervalos Durante el Proceso de Aborto*, SEX SALUD SOC., 90–115 (2018); Shivali Bhalla et al., *Self Administered Medical Abortion Pills: Evaluation of the Clinical Outcome and Complications Among Women Presenting with Unsupervised Pill Intake to a Tertiary Care Hospital in Malwa Region of Punjab, India*, 7 INT. J. REPROD., CONTRACEPTION, OBSTET. & GYNEC. 1537–42 (2018); Sharifa Alsibiani, *Use of Misoprostol for Self-Induced Medical Abortions Among Saudi Women: A Call for Attention*, 78 GYNECOLOGIC & OBSTETRIC INVESTIGATION 88–93 (2014); Nano Nimo Appiah-Agyekum, *Abortions in Ghana: Experiences of University Students*, 8 HEALTH SCI. J. 531–40 (2014); E. Tousaw et al., *"It Is Just Like Having a Period with Back Pain": Exploring Women's Experiences with Community-Based Distribution of Misoprostol for Early Abortion on the Thailand-Burma Border*, 97 CONTRACEPTION 122–29 (2017); M.A. Rosing & C.D. Archbald, *The Knowledge, Acceptability, and Use of Misoprostol for Self-Induced Medical Abortion in an Urban US Population*, 55 J. AM. MED. WOMEN'S ASS'N 183–85 (2000).

7. *See* Moseson, *Self-Managed Abortion: A Systematic Scoping Review, supra* note 3, at 101, citing Aiken et al., *The Impact of Northern Ireland's Abortion Laws on Women's Abortion Decision-Making and Experiences*, 45 BMJ SEXUAL & REPROD. HEALTH 3–9 (2019); Cara Delay, *Pills, Potions, and Purgatives: Women and Abortion Methods in Ireland, 1900–1950*, J. WOMEN'S HISTORY REV. 1–21 (2018); Rebecca Gomperts et al., *Regional Differences in Surgical Intervention Following Medical Termination of Pregnancy Provided by Telemedicine*, 91 ACTA OBSTET. GYNECOL. SCAND. 226–31 (2012).

8. *See* Moseson, *Self-Managed Abortion: A Systematic Scoping Review, supra* note 3, at 101, citing Aiken et al., *The Impact of Northern Ireland's Abortion Laws on Women's Abortion Decision-Making and Experiences*, 45 BMJ SEX. REPROD. HEALTH 3–9 (2019); C. Delay, *Pills, Potions, and*

included (1) explicitly not wanting a surgical abortion;[9] (2) being able to
have a support person (or people) with them during the abortion;[10] (3) a
previous successful self-managed abortion;[11] (4) the perception that SMA
is more affordable than a facility-based (and often surgical) abortion;[12] or
(5) that self-managed abortion is not even abortion but, rather, bringing on

---

Purgatives: Women and Abortion Methods in Ireland, 1900–1950, J. WOMEN'S HISTORY REV. 1,
1–21 (2018); A. Foster, *Exploring Polish Women's Experiences Using a Medication Abortion Telemedicine Service: A Qualitative Study*, 23 EUR. J. CONTRACEPTION REPROD. HEALTHCARE 59, 59–60;
Silvina Ramos et al., *Women's Experiences with the Use of Medical Abortion in a Legally Restricted
Context: the Case of Argentina*, 22 REPROD. HEALTH MATTERS 4–15 (2015); Abigail Aiken et
al., *Motivations and Experiences of People Seeking Medication Abortion Online in the United States*,
50 PERSPECTIVES ON SEXUAL & REPROD. HEALTH 157–63 (2018); Abigail Aiken, *Experiences
of Women in Ireland Who Accessed Abortion by Travelling Abroad or By Using Abortion Medica-
tion at Home: a Qualitative Study*, 44 BMJ SEXUAL & REPROD. HEALTH 181–86 (2018); Nano
Nimo Appiah-Agyekum, *Medical Abortions Among University Students in Ghana: Implications for
Reproductive Health Education and Management*, 10 INT. J. WOMENS HEALTH 515–22 (2018);
Rachel Jewkes et al., *Why Are Women Still Aborting Outside Designated Facilities in Metropolitan
South Africa?*, 112 BJOG: INT. J. OBSTETRICS & GYNAEC. 1236–42 (2005); Dolorès Pourette
et al., *Complications with Use of Misoprostol for Abortion in Madagascar: Between Ease of Access
and Lack of Information*, 97 CONTRACEPT. 116–21 (2018); Abigail Aiken et al., *Experiences and
Characteristics of Women Seeking and Completing At-Home Medical Termination of Pregnancy through
Online Telemedicine in Ireland and Northern Ireland: a Population-Based Analysis*, BJOG: INT. J.
OBSTETRICS & GYNAECOLOGY 1208–15 (2017); Abigail Aiken, *Barriers to Accessing Abortion
Services and Perspectives on Using Mifepristone and Misoprostol at Home in Great Britain*, 97 CON-
TRACEPT. 177–83 (2018).

9. *See* Moseson, *Self-Managed Abortion: A Systematic Scoping Review*, *supra* note 3, at 102,
citing Ann. Jilozian & Victor Agadjanian, *Is Induced Abortion Really Declining in Armenia?*, 47
STUDIES IN FAMILY PLANNING 163–78 (2016).

10. *See* Moseson, *Self-Managed Abortion: A Systematic Scoping Review*, *supra* note 3, at 102,
citing Cara Delay, *Pills, Potions, and Purgatives: Women and Abortion Methods in Ireland, 1900–
1950*, J. WOMEN'S HISTORY REVIEW 1–21 (2018); S. Ramos et al., *Women's Experiences With the
Use of Medical Abortion in a Legally Restricted Context: the Case of Argentina*, 22 REPROD. HEALTH
MATTERS 4–15 (2015); Nano Nimo Appiah-Agyekum, *Medical Abortions Among University
Students in Ghana: Implications for Reproductive Health Education and Management*, 10 INT. J.
WOMENS HEALTH 515–22 (2018); Irma Palma Manriquez et al., *Experience of Clandestine Use
of Medical Abortion Among University Students in Chile: a Qualitative Study*, 97 CONTRACEPTION
100–07 (2018).

11. *See* Moseson, *Self-Managed Abortion: A Systematic Scoping Review*, *supra* note 3, citing
M.A. Rosing & C.D. Archbald, *The Knowledge, Acceptability, and Use of Misoprostol for Self-Induced
Medical Abortion in an Urban US Population*, 55 J. AM. MED. WOMEN'S ASS'N 183–85 (2000).

12. *See* Moseson, *Self-Managed Abortion: A Systematic Scoping Review*, *supra* note 3, at 102, citing A.R.A. Aiken et al., *Motivations and Experiences of People Seeking Medication Abortion Online in
the United States*, 50 PERSPECTIVES ON SEXUAL & REPROD. HEALTH 157–63 (2018); D. Webb,
Attitudes to 'Kaponya Mafumo': The Terminators of Pregnancy in Urban Zambia, 15 HEALTH POL-
ICY PLAN, 186–93 (2000); Daniel Grossman et al., *Lifetime Prevalence of Self-Induced Abortion
Among a Nationally Representative Sample of US Women*, 97 CONTRACEPTION 460 (2018); A. Jilo-
zian & V. Agadjanian, *Is Induced Abortion Really Declining in Armenia?*, 47 STUDIES IN FAMILY
PLANNING 163–78 (2016).

a miscarriage.[13] Although most people who self-manage do so because of a lack of access to clinical care, it is important to stress that SMA is not just a measure of last resort but an alternative care model that many people find works better for them.

b. Lack of Access to Care
Barriers to clinical abortion care are the primary reason why people self-manage, and those barriers vary enormously depending on one's environment and experiences. This section will analyze barriers to abortion care in the United States specifically. These include cost, transportation, police presence at clinics, administrative barriers, a lack of gender-affirming care, and COVID-19.

i. Cost
Many people self-manage because they cannot afford the cost of clinical abortion care.[14] Abortion pills can be purchased on a sliding pay scale online and typically cost about $90, meaning that they are not nearly as costly as clinical abortions, which typically cost upwards of $500.[15] A 2017 study found that a $500 surprise expense would put most Americans into debt.[16] That means that the average American cannot afford an abortion if they need one. Low-income individuals are doubly impacted. They are both the least able to prevent unwanted pregnancy and the least able to end them when they occur.

---

13. *See* Moseson, *Self-Managed Abortion: A Systematic Scoping Review*, *supra* note 3, citing A. Jilozian & V. Agadjanian, *Is Induced Abortion Really Declining in Armenia?*, 47 STUDIES IN FAMILY PLANNING 163–78 (2016).

14. IF/WHEN/HOW, *Roe's Unfinished Promise*, *supra* note 2, at 31.

15. *See* Guttmacher Inst. Staff, *The Cost of Abortion, When Providers Offer Services and Harassment of Abortion Providers All Remained Stable between 2008 and 2012*, GUTTMACHER INST. (July 2, 2014), https://www.guttmacher.org/news-release/2014/cost-abortion-when-providers -offer-services-and-harassment-abortion-providers-all ("the median cost of a surgical abortion at 10 weeks' gestation was $495, and an early medication abortion cost $500."); *see also* Plan C Staff, *A Research-Based Review of Online Abortion Pill Suppliers*, https://plancpills.org/report card (abortion pills are available on a sliding pay scale). *See also* Anna North, *America's First Generic Abortion Pill, Explained*, Vox (Aug. 20, 2019, 9:33 AM), https://tinyurl.com/y4l74clk (abortion pills cost $90 on average).

16. *See, e.g.*, Maggie McGrath, *63% of Americans Don't Have Enough Savings to Cover a $500 Emergency*, FORBES (Jan. 6, 2016, 6:42 PM), https://www.forbes.com/sites /maggiemcgrath/2016/01/06/63-of-americans-dont-have-enough-savings-to-cover-a-500 -emergency/#94eb1d4e0d97; Aimee Picchi, *A $500 Surprise Expense Would Put Most Americans Into Debt*, CBS NEWS (Jan. 12, 2017, 11:39 AM), https://www.cbsnews.com/news/most -americans-cant-afford-a-500-emergency-expense/; Jill Cornfield, *Bankrate Survey: Just 4 in 10 Americans Have Savings They'd Rely on in an Emergency*, BANKRATE (Jan. 12, 2017), https:// www.bankrate.com/finance/consumer-index/money-pulse-0117.aspx.

A higher percentage of abortion seekers are low-income now than was true 20 years ago, and 75 percent of all U.S. abortion patients today are poor or low income.[17] This is because access to the resources and information necessary to avoid pregnancy are, increasingly, privileges reserved for the wealthy in the United States. Students living in poor and urban school districts receive less health education than their counterparts in more affluent school districts[18] and are therefore less informed about how to prevent unwanted pregnancy. This problem was exacerbated when public sex education programming largely abandoned the comprehensive sex education programs of the Obama era and reverted back to a less effective, and less accurate, abstinence-only approach under the Trump administration.[19] Anti-choice and religious freedom advocates have also centered much of their recent efforts around limiting access to contraception coverage.[20] Allowing employers to deny contraception coverage forces people to pay for it out of pocket, which is not an option for many low-income individuals.[21] Because Medicaid funding cannot be used for abortion, those who are least able to afford abortions out-of-pocket are also those who are least likely to have insurance that would cover them.[22] For all of these reasons and others, cost barriers are one of the leading reasons why people self-manage.

---

17. Guttmacher Inst. Staff, *U.S. Abortion Patients: Infographic*, GUTTMACHER INST. (May 9, 2016), https://www.guttmacher.org/infographic/2016/us-abortion-patients ("75% of U.S. abortion patients are poor or low income"); *see also* Jenna Jerman, Rachel Jones & Tsuyoshi Onda, *Characteristics of U.S. Abortion Patients in 2014 and Changes Since 2008*, GUTTMACHER INST. (May, 2016), https://www.guttmacher.org/report/characteristics-us-abortion-patients-2014 ("In 2014, three fourths of abortion patients were low-income—49% living at less than the federal poverty level, and 26% living at 100-199% of the poverty level.").

18. *See* Robert Atkins et al., *The Effects of School Poverty on Adolescent's Sexual Health Knowledge*, 35 RES. NURSE HEALTH 231, 233 (2012).

19. *See* Hildie Leung, *Development of Contextually Relevant Sexuality Education: Lessons from a Comprehensive Review of Adolescent Sexuality Education Across Cultures*, 16 INT. J. ENVTL. RESEARCH & PUB. HEALTH 621, 645 (2019); *see also* Leah H. Keller & Laura D. Lindberg, *Expanding the Scope of Sex Education and the Teen Pregnancy Prevention Program: A Work in Progress*, GUTTMACHER INST. (Feb. 2020), https://www.guttmacher.org/article/2020/02/expanding-scope-sex-education-and-teen-pregnancy-prevention-program-work-progress.

20. *See* Adam Sonfield, *Seeing the Whole Pattern: Coordinated Federal Attacks on Birth Control and Access*, GUTTMACHER INST. (June 26, 2020), https://www.guttmacher.org/print/article/2020/06/seeing-whole-pattern-coordinated-federal-attacks-birth-control-coverage-and-access.

21. *See* Nat'l Women's Law Ctr. Staff, *The Affordable Care Act's Birth Control Benefit: Too Important to Lose*, NAT'L. WOMEN'S LAW CTR. at 2 (May 2017), https://nwlc.org/wp-content/uploads/2017/05/BC-Benefit-Whats-At-Stake.pdf (analyzing the detrimental impact of removing insurance coverage for contraception for low income people).

22. *See generally* Heather Boonstra, *Abortion in the Lives of Women Struggling Financially: Why Insurance Coverage Matters*, 19 GUTTMACHER POLICY REV. (July 14, 2016), https://www.guttmacher.org/gpr/2016/07/abortion-lives-women-struggling-financially-why-insurance-coverage-matters.

ii. Transportation

Abortion pills, when procured online or via telemedicine, also eliminate transportation costs and logistical challenges—a significant barrier to care in many states. Ninety percent of all U.S. counties do not have an abortion clinic,[23] meaning that the vast majority of abortion seekers in America need to find some form of transportation in order to reach a clinic. This is a significant barrier to care, especially for those living in rural areas or in states that have enacted so many TRAP (targeted regulation of abortion providers) laws that only one or two clinics remain. A recent study found that nearly one-fifth of U.S. abortion patients have to travel more than 50 miles (each way) to reach their nearest abortion provider.[24] For those who do not have a car, do not have a license (or are too young to procure one), or who cannot access or afford public transportation, SMA eliminates a significant, if not insurmountable, barrier to care.

iii. Police Presence

People may also self-manage because of the police presence that is outside many abortion clinics in the United States. Fear of being picked up for outstanding fines and fees, immigration status, or generalized mistrust of police due to the overly aggressive policing of low-income neighborhoods can deter patients from getting the care they need.[25] The presence of anti-choice protesters outside clinics presents a series of risks that disproportionately impact communities that experience heightened levels of police surveillance and harassment. Not only is there a risk that protesters will cause a confrontation that leads to a police interaction, but the presence of police itself creates a hostile environment for those who have experienced police harassment, those who are undocumented, and anyone who may have a reason to mistrust the police.[26] Nnennaya Amuchie is a reproductive justice attorney and Black Lives Matter organizer. They described this problem in a recent interview with ReproJobs:

---

23. Rachel K. Jones & Jenna Jerman, *Abortion Incidence and Service Availability in the United States*, 49 PERSPECTIVES ON SEXUAL & REPROD. HEALTH 17, 21 (2017).

24. Liza Fuentes & Jenna Jerman, *Distance Traveled to Obtain Clinical Abortion Care in the United States and Reasons for Clinic Choice*, 28 GUTTMACHER J. WOMEN'S HEALTH 1623, 1623 (2019); *see also* Nancy Brener et al., *Variation in School Health Policies and Programs by Demographic Characteristics of US Schools*, 73 J. SCH. HEALTH, 143–49 (2003).

25. *See* Shara Crookston, *Navigating TRAP Laws, Protesters, and Police Presence at a Midwestern Abortion Clinic in the United States*, 4 FEMINIST ENCOUNTERS 35, 43 (2020).

26. *See id.*

[T]o center Black women and gender oppressed people is to understand that policing is a tool of oppression and is an off-shoot of slave patrols. [. . .] How can we rely on police officers to "protect" Black, brown and indigenous clients when they routinely target, harass, sexually assault, and kill us in both private and public? We can create networks of support without relying on the state or police.[27]

In addition to deterring abortion seekers who have had negative experiences with over-policing and surveillance, police presence outside clinics imbues abortion care with an aura of criminality that contributes to stigma-related reasons why people do not seek out clinical care. Abortion pills, when obtained online or via telemedicine, allow abortion seekers to bypass the clinic and the risks they entail. They are one way in which individuals and communities can care for themselves and create the independent "networks of support" that Amuchie describes.

iv. Administrative Requirements

Administrative requirements, such as requiring patients to provide a state-issued ID or parental consent for minors, also prevent many from accessing clinical abortions. Since the Supreme Court's decisions in *Planned Parenthood of Central Missouri v. Danforth* in 1976 and *Bellotti v. Baird* in 1979, states may give parents a veto on their child's reproductive decision making, provided that there is an alternative approval mechanism such as a judicial bypass procedure.[28] Over the years, an increasing number of states have instituted such requirements. As of 2020, 37 states have parental involvement laws in effect.[29] These laws create substantial barriers to clinical abortion that are substantially reduced—though not eliminated—in the SMA context.

Contrary to what advocates for parental consent laws argue, research shows that these requirements have almost no effect on a young person's decision to talk with their parent or guardian about their decision to seek an abortion. Instead, "the chief factor determining whether a teen consulted their parent was not legislation, but the quality of the teen's relationship

---

27. ReproJobs Team, *Nnennaya Amuchie on Defunding the Police to Fund a Reproductively Just World*, REPROJOBS (June 30, 2020), https://www.reprojobs.org/blog/defundthepolice.

28. *See* Amanda Dennis et al. *The Impact of Laws Requiring Parental Involvement for Abortion: A Literature Review*, GUTTMACHER INST. (Mar. 2009), https://tinyurl.com/y67ns3e7.

29. *See* IF/WHEN/HOW, *Judicial Bypass Wiki*, https://judicialbypasswiki.ifwhenhow.org/ (last accessed Nov. 6, 2020).

with their parent."[30] Youth who have no reason to fear that notifying their parents about their abortion will prevent them from obtaining one, notify their parents freely about their decision. Minors who decide not to tell their parents almost always do so because they feel that informing their parents about their decision might be harmful, physically dangerous, or restrict their ability to obtain an abortion.[31] "I couldn't get parental consent at the time because my dad was homeless, and my mom was on the run, about to be incarcerated," said H.K. Gray, a member of Youth Testify, a Washington D.C. program developed by We Testify and Advocates for Youth.[32] Gray is one of the many youth organizers around the country who are speaking out against parental consent laws for abortion.[33] "All these tiny things come into a bigger picture of us not being able to take control over our reproductive rights."[34] Gray was eventually able to exercise her constitutional right to end her pregnancy.[35] However, every year that "bigger picture of tiny things" she describes forces many young people in America to give birth.[36] Obtaining parental consent for abortion, for many, is simply not an option. For young people living in unstable housing situations or foster care, for example, disclosing a pregnancy could threaten the very roof over their head.[37] In fact, one-third of all female-identifying youth who are experiencing homelessness are, or have been, pregnant.[38] Young people are routinely kicked out of their homes when their parents discover that they have

---

30. Sonja Adjroud, *Abortion and Parental Involvement Laws: Policy Brief*, ADVOCATES FOR YOUTH, at 1 (2019), https://advocatesforyouth.org/wp-content/uploads/2013/12/Parental-Involvement-Policy-Brief-2019.pdf.

31. *See* Lee Hasselbacher et al., *Factors Influencing Parental Involvement Among Minors Seeking an Abortion: A Qualitative Study*, 104 AM. J. PUB. HEALTH 2207, 2207–11 (2014).

32. H.K. Gray, *Young People Are Leading the Fight for Abortion Access*, on YOUTH TESTIFY (recording of H.K. interview is available at https://youthtestify.org/).

33. *Id.*

34. *Id.*

35. *Id.*

36. *See* Amanda Dennis et al. *The Impact of Laws Requiring Parental Involvement for Abortion: A Literature Review*, GUTTMACHER INST. (Mar. 2009), https://tinyurl.com/y67ns3e7 (articulating the ways in which parental consent and notification laws prevent youth from accessing abortion); *see also* M.D. Greenberger & K. Connor, *Parental Notice and Consent for Abortion: Out of Step with Family Law Principles and Policies*, 23 FAM. PLAN. PERSPECTIVES 31, 31–35 (1991) (arguing that parental consent laws are antithetical to many of the core principles laid out in family law that protect the best interests of the young person).

37. *See* Bob Reeg et al., *Families on the Edge: Young Homeless Parents and Their Welfare Experiences: A Survey of Homeless Youth and Service Providers*, CTR. FOR LAW & SOC. POL'Y & NAT. NETWORK FOR YOUTH (2002), https://tinyurl.com/y2y677ej.

38. *See* National Network for Youth, *Pregnant and Parenting Unaccompanied Youth Factsheet*, NAT. NETWORK FOR YOUTH, https://www.nn4youth.org/wp-content/uploads/IssueBrief_Pregnancy_and_parenting.pdf.

become sexually active—something that was painfully clear when I worked at the Illinois Caucus for Adolescent Health and at the National Network for Youth. Returning to parents who have made it clear that you are unwelcome because of your pregnancy status is often unsafe, physically and emotionally. Parental consent laws force young people into these situations and grant adults (whether parents, guardians, or judges) the authority to force youth into continued pregnancy and then parenting.

Parental consent laws, as well as ID requirements generally, disproportionately impact undocumented immigrants and the children of undocumented immigrants. Ten states require a parent to either appear in person and provide government issued identification at the abortion clinic or to sign notarized parental consent documentation.[39] This poses a barrier to undocumented youth, immigrant youth with undocumented parents, and youth whose parents have been detained or deported.[40] Four states require proof of parenthood in the form of a birth certificate to prove parental consent, posing another barrier to youth whose parents are undocumented, and also to any young person who may not have access to their birth certificate.[41]

Judicial bypass proceedings are not a workable alternative to parental consent for many young people. If a young person seeks a judicial bypass, a judge must reach a determination about whether an adolescent is "mature enough" to make the decision about an abortion, and whether or not it is in their "best interest" to inform their parents.[42] This process not only delays the abortion procedure, it subjects youth to "extremely burdensome, humiliating, and stressful" court proceedings.[43] Young people are often required to divulge private details of their life to a judge who typically has "no training in counseling adolescents."[44] This aspect of the procedure impacts those who are pregnant as the result of sexual assault especially harshly because re-telling their experience with sexual assault can be a triggering

---

39. *See* Sonja Adjroud, *Abortion and Parental Involvement Laws: Policy Brief*, ADVOCATES FOR YOUTH (2019), https://advocatesforyouth.org/wp-content/uploads/2013/12/Parental-Involve ment-Policy-Brief-2019.pdf.

40. *See* Nat'l Latina Inst. for Reprod. Health, *Immigrant Latin@s & Abortion: The Fight for Access to Comprehensive Coverage and Care*, NAT'L LATINA INST. FOR REPROD. HEALTH (Mar. 2015), https://latinainstitute.org/sites/default/files/ NLIRH_ImmWmnAbrtn_FactSheet _Eng_R6.pdf.

41. *See* Guttmacher Inst., *Parental Involvement in Minor's Abortions*, GUTTMACHER INST. (Nov. 1, 2020), https://www.guttmacher.org/state-policy/explore/parental-involvement-minors -abortions.

42. *See* Molly Walker, *AAP: Abortion Parental Consent Laws Do More Harm than Good* (Jan. 23, 2017), MEDPAGE TODAY, https://www.medpagetoday.com/obgyn/pregnancy/62682.

43. Am. Acad. of Pediatrics, *The Adolescent's Right to Confidential Care When Considering Abortion*, 139 PEDIATRICS 1, 7 (2017).

44. *Id.* at 8.

and retraumatizing experience. Even if a judge has no intention of inquiring into the circumstances leading up to the minor's pregnancy, the mere fear of being asked these questions can deter a minor from seeking judicial bypass. Bypass laws also impose disproportionate barriers to undocumented youth who fear immigration enforcement and to youth from mixed status households who fear attracting attention to their undocumented parents.[45] These disparate effects further entrench inequalities in abortion access and increase the rates of forced parenthood nationwide.

SMA allows people to find alternative channels to abortion access that do not require them to first obtain their parent's consent or to provide state-issued identification. That said, some (not all) of the primary online providers that will ship abortion pills directly to people's homes do require sending a form of identification documentation to confirm the age of the abortion seeker.[46] The administrative burdens of accessing abortion care are therefore partially—though not entirely—alleviated with SMA.

v. A Lack of Gender-Affirming Care

Transgender (trans*) and gender nonconforming (GNC) people are more likely than the general U.S. population to be uninsured, to experience discrimination and mistreatment in health care settings, and to be adversely affected by limited clinician knowledge or refusal to provide care.[47] Many trans* and GNC people do not seek needed health care as a result of experiences with discrimination and lower quality care related directly to gender identity.[48] These barriers are compounded in the abortion care context, where highly gendered environments contribute to negative, stigmatizing

---

45. *See* Nat'l Latina Inst. for Reprod. Health, *Immigrant Latin@s & Abortion: The Fight for Access to Comprehensive Coverage and Care, supra* note 40.

46. This is true for AidAccess, for example—one of the largest providers that will ship abortion pills directly to people's homes. After filling out the online intake form, the organization sends the patient an email requesting a copy of a form of identification that verifies their age.

47. *See* Alexis Hoffkling, Juno Obedin-Maliver & Jaw Sevelius, *From Erasure to Opportunity: a Qualitative Study of the Experiences of Transgender Men around Pregnancy and Recommendations for Providers,* J. BMC Pregnancy & Childbirth 1491, 1491 (2017); *see also* Amanda Rodriguez, *Self-Reported Discrimination in Health-Care Settings Based on Recognizability as Transgender: A Cross-Sectional Study Among Transgender U.S. Citizens,* 47 Arch. Sex. Behav. 973, 973 (2018); *see also* S.E. James et al., *Executive Summary of the Report of the 2015 U.S. Transgender Survey,* Nat'l Ctr. For Transgender Equal. (Dec. 2016), https://www.transequality.org/sites/default/files/docs/USTS-Executive-Summary-FINAL.PDF.

48. *See* Heidi Moseson, et al., *The Imperative for Transgender and Gender Nonbinary Inclusion: Beyond Women's Health,* 135 Obstet. & Gynecol. 1059, 1061 (2020); *see also* S.E. James et al., *Executive Summary of the Report of the 2015 U.S. Transgender Survey,* Nat'l Ctr. For Transgender Equal. (Dec. 2016), https://www.transequality.org/sites/default/files/docs/USTS-Executive-Summary-FINAL.PDF.

experiences among gender minorities.[49] A recent study on trans*, nonbinary and gender-expansive people's experiences with sexual and reproductive health care documented how gendered health care environments, misgendering, discrimination, and provider knowledge gaps negatively affect the quality of care that participants received and deterred them from care.[50] SMA allows trans* and GNC people to bypass the clinic altogether, thereby minimizing their exposure to care settings that have failed to uphold their dignity in the past.

vi. Impact of COVID-19 on Abortion Access in the U.S.

On top of all the barriers just enumerated, COVID-19 added the risk of a deadly infection to the reasons why people may be deterred from clinical care. Not only do people risk their health and that of their families by attending a clinical appointment, fewer appointments are available.[51] Clinics are seeing fewer patients because of social distancing requirements. Transportation barriers are particularly difficult to overcome in the COVID era when one risks infection just by going to a clinic.

As if this were not enough, several states used COVID-19 as an excuse to shutter abortion clinics, deeming it a "non-essential" health

---

49. *See* Moseson et al., *supra* note 48.

50. *See* Laura Fix et al., *Stakeholder Perceptions and Experiences Regarding Access to Contraception and Abortion for Transgender, Non-Binary, and Gender-Expansive Individuals Assigned Female at Birth in the U.S.*, 49 ARCH. SEX. BEHAV. 2683–2702 (2020).

51. *See* Molly Hennessy-Fiske, *Abortion during Coronavirus: State Bans, Closed Clinics, Self-Induced Miscarriages*, LOS ANGELES TIMES (Apr. 16, 2020, 3:00 AM), https://www .latimes.com/world-nation/story/2020-04-16/abortion-during-coronavirus-state-bans -canceled-appointments-travel.

care service.[52] These included Alabama,[53] Alaska,[54] Arkansas,[55] Iowa,[56]

---

52. *See* Laurie Sobel et al., *State Action to Limit Abortion Access during the COVID-19 Pandemic*, KAISER FAMILY FOUND. (Aug. 10, 2020), https://www.kff.org/coronavirus-covid-19/issue-brief/state-action-to-limit-abortion-access-during-the-covid-19-pandemic/.

53. On April 12, 2020, an Alabama federal district court issued a preliminary injunction allowing providers to determine whether an abortion is necessary on a "case by case basis" to avoid additional risk, expense, or legal barriers. On April 23rd, the 11th Circuit Court of Appeals denied a stay pending the State's appeal of the preliminary injunction, thus allowing doctors to decide whether an abortion is necessary to avoid additional risk or whether a patient would lose the legal right to an abortion if delayed. Robinson v. Attorney Gen., 957 F.3d 1171 (11th Cir. 2020). Effective April 30th, abortion procedures were allowed to proceed in Alabama unless the State Health Officer or his designee determines that performing these procedures would reduce access to PPE or other resources necessary to diagnose and treat COVID-19. *See* Sobel et al., *supra* note 52.

54. Alaska's governor, Department of Health and Social Services, and Chief Medical Officer updated their health mandate on April 7, 2020, to specify that "healthcare providers are to postpone surgical abortion," without specifying whether medication abortion would be subject to parallel restrictions. On May 4th, "non-urgent/non-emergent elective surgeries and procedures" were able to resume. *See* Sobel et al., *supra* note 52.

55. Arkansas' Department of Health ordered Little Rock Family Planning (the state's only clinic providing surgical abortions), to immediately cease and desist the performance of surgical abortions, except where immediately necessary to protect the life or health of the patient. On April 13, 2020, the ACLU sought a preliminary injunction to prevent enforcement of the abortion suspension during COVID-19, and on April 14th, the federal district court granted a temporary restraining order allowing abortion services to resume. However, on April 22nd, the 8th Circuit Court of Appeals reversed the lower court's ruling. *In re Rutledge*, 956 F.3d 1018 (8th Cir. 2020). The ACLU filed emergency legal action requesting an exemption for patients approaching the state's legal limit for abortion care. Before a hearing was held, the Arkansas Department of Health released a new directive on resuming elective surgeries. This directive allowed patients to obtain abortions, if they "have at least one negative COVID-19 NAAT test within 48 hours prior to the beginning of the procedure." Given the shortage of tests and the time it takes to obtain a result, some abortion seekers were not able to satisfy this requirement. On May 1, 202, the ACLU filed a new request with the district court for a preliminary injunction for three patients approaching the legal limit to obtain an abortion. On May 7th, the court denied that request, insisting on compliance with the COVD-19 test requirement. Effective May 18, 2020, the Arkansas Department of Health modified the directive, extending the timeframe for a negative test to within 72 hours prior to the procedure. Effective August 1st, the Arkansas Department of Health released another directive rescinding the requirement for a negative COVID-19 NAAT test prior to abortion procedures. *See* Sobel et al., *supra* note 52.

56. In Iowa, state officials and the American Civil Liberties Union who challenged the policy settled out of court that abortion services could continue. *See* Sobel et al., *supra* note 52.

Kentucky,[57] Louisiana,[58] Mississippi,[59] Ohio,[60] Oklahoma,[61] Tennessee,[62]

---

57. Despite the request of Kentucky's attorney general, Kentucky's Cabinet for Health and Family Services did not declare abortion a non-essential procedure. On April 16, 2020, the Kentucky State legislature passed Senate Bill 9, which would provide the Attorney General power to seek injunctive relief against and impose criminal and civil penalties against abortion providers during the public health emergency. On April 24, 2020, the Governor vetoed that bill, allowing the only abortion clinic remaining in Kentucky to continue providing abortion services. *See* Laurie Sobel et al., *State Action to Limit Abortion Access During the COVID-19 Pandemic*, KAISER FAMILY FOUND. (Aug. 10, 2020), https://www.kff.org/coronavirus-covid-19/issue-brief/state-action-to-limit-abortion-access-during-the-covid-19-pandemic/.

58. On March 21, 2020, Louisiana's Department of Health issued a directive postponing medical and surgical procedures for 30 days, except those (1) "to treat an emergency medical condition" or (2) "to avoid further harms from underlying condition or disease," but leaves that determination to the provider's "best medical judgment." The Attorney General sent state representatives to the clinics to observe compliance with the order and requested confidential patient files. He threatened to shut down the clinics claiming they violated the state directive, in spite of a lack of evidence supporting his allegations of noncompliance. On April 13, 2020, the clinics challenged the suspension of abortion services in Louisiana in federal court. On May 1st, the clinics settled with the state, permitting abortions to continue. *See* Sobel et al., *supra* note 52.

59. On April 10, 2020, the governor of Mississippi issued an executive order requiring the delay of all non-essential adult elective surgeries and medical procedures, and deemed abortion a non-essential service. Mississippi's executive order expired on May 11th, allowing "non-emergent, elective medical procedures and surgeries" to resume. *See* Sobel et al., *supra* note 52.

60. On April 23, 2020, an Ohio federal district court issued a preliminary injunction allowing physicians in Ohio to determine whether a surgical abortion is essential on a case-by-case basis. Abortions were to be deemed essential when the "procedure is necessary because of the timing vis-à-vis pre-viability; to protect the patient's health or life; and due to medical reasons. . . ." On May 1st, the Ohio Department of Health's Stay Safe Ohio Order allowed non-essential surgeries and procedures to resume. *See* Sobel et al., *supra* note 52.

61. On March 24, 2020, Oklahoma Governor Kevin Stitt issued an executive order in response to the coronavirus (COVID-19) pandemic that required all "elective" medical and surgical procedures be postponed. In a press release issued March 27, Governor Stitt singled out abortion care, claiming the order prohibited all abortions in the state. The Center for Reproductive Rights and other advocates sought a temporary restraining order, preventing enforcement of the ban, which was granted on April 6th. *See* Center for Reproductive Rights, *Court Blocks Oklahoma's COVID-19 Abortion Ban*, CTR. FOR REPROD. RIGHTS (Apr. 6, 2020), https://reproductiverights.org/press-room/court-blocks-oklahomas-covid-19-abortion-ban.

62. On April 17, 2020, Tennessee's federal district court blocked the governor's executive order to suspend abortions, allowing providers to resume procedures. This decision was upheld by the 6th Circuit Court of Appeals on April 20th, and the order expired on April 30th, allowing elective and non-urgent procedures to resume starting May 1st. *See* Sobel et al., *supra* note 52.

Texas,[63] and West Virginia.[64] Although none of these bans remained in effect because of successful legal challenges brought by abortion provider groups and reproductive justice advocates, or were lifted by settlements outside of court, these bans had a dramatic impact on care access across the country. While some people overcame clinic closures by travelling to other states (sometimes over-burdening these providers with a new influx of patients),[65] some others had recourse to SMA.

Using data from Aid Access, the sole online abortion telemedicine service in the United States, a recent study found that demand for self-managed medication abortion increased as in-clinic access became more

---

63. On March 22, 2020, the Texas governor issued an executive order directing all licensed health care professionals and facilities to postpone all surgeries and procedures that were not immediately medically necessary until 11:59 PM on April 21st. During the period in which this executive order was in place, some abortion services were suspended. On April 22nd, the Attorney General filed a response at the 5th Circuit Court of Appeals stating that abortion services were allowed to resume under the new executive order. After a month of contentious litigation, abortion services resumed in Texas. *See* Sobel et al., *supra* note 52.

64. On March 31, 2020, West Virginia's governor issued an executive order prohibiting all elective medical procedures not immediately medically necessary to preserve the patient's life or long-term health. West Virginia's Attorney General stated that most, if not all, abortion services are impermissible under this executive order. On April 24th, Women's Health Center of West Virginia, the only abortion clinic in West Virginia, filed a complaint requesting a stay on the ban of elective medical procedures, stating that they had only been able to provide medication abortions to patients at or near 11 weeks LMP and procedural abortions to patients at or near 16 weeks LMP, the latest point at which the clinic can provide these services. The Governor issued another executive order lifting the suspension of all elective procedures, including abortions, on April 30th. *See* Sobel et al., *supra* note 52.

65. *See* Sarah McCammon, *After Texas Abortion Ban, Clinics in Other Southwest States See Influx of Patients*, NPR (Apr. 17, 2020, 2:02 PM), https://www.npr.org/sections/corona virus-live-updates/2020/04/17/837153529/after-texas-abortion-ban-clinics-in-neighboring -states-see-influx-of-patients; *see also* Steph Black, *Even in Places with Accessible Abortion Care, the Coronavirus Is Drastically Affecting Services*, REWIRE NEWS GROUP (May 19, 2020, 2:47 PM), https://rewirenewsgroup.com/article/2020/03/19/even-in-places-with-accessible-abortion-care-the-coronavirus-is-drastically-affecting-services/; *see also* Claire Cleveland, *Colorado's Abortion Providers See More Out-Of-State Patients During the Coronavirus Pandemic*, CPR NEWS (Apr. 15, 2020), https://www.cpr.org/2020/04/15/colorado-abortion-providers-are-seeing-more -out-of-state-patients-during-the-coronavirus-pandemic/.

challenging.[66] From March 20, 2020, to April 11, 2020 (the period with the greatest number of clinics closed due to COVID-19 restrictions), the study found that there was a 27 percent increase in the rate of requests for abortion pills across the United States.[67] Larger increases in requests arose in states with the most severe and longest-lasting restrictions.[68] Texas, the state with the most restrictive measures, showed the largest increase in requests for abortion pills.[69] Although it is impossible (and unethical) to track all of the avenues through which people manage their own abortions, it is reasonable to assume that greater recourse to SMA correlates with the increased barriers to care that the pandemic created.

The World Health Organization recommended telemedicine and self-managed care for abortion care during the pandemic.[70] The United Kingdom temporarily—and successfully—implemented fully remote provision of abortion medications.[71] In the United States, such services depended on sustained changes to the U.S. Food and Drug Administration's Risk Evaluation and Mitigation Strategy, which initially required patients to collect mifepristone at a hospital or medical facility (discussed later), as well as changes to state-specific laws that prohibit remote provider consultation.[72] Although providers in certain American states began to offer telemedical abortion care, many states did not authorize telemedical abortion,[73] meaning that if

---

66. Abigail Aiken et al., *Demand for Self-Managed Online Telemedicine Abortion in the United States During the Coronavirus Disease 2019 (COVID-19) Pandemic*, 136 OBSTET. & GYNEC. 835, 835 (2020).

67. *See id.*

68. *See id.* at 836.

69. *Id.*

70. *See* World Health Org., *Maintaining Essential Health Services: Operational Guidance for the COVID-19 Context: Interim Guidance*, WHO (June 1, 2020), https://apps.who.int/iris/bit stream/handle/10665/332240/WHO-2019-nCoV-essential_health_services-2020.2-eng .pdf?sequence=1&isAllowed=y.

71. *See* U.K. Dep't of Health and Social Care & Matt Hancock, *Temporary Approval of Home Use for Both Stages of Early Medical Abortion* (Mar. 30, 2020), https://www.gov.uk/government /publications/temporary-approval-of-home-use-for-both-stages-of-early-medical-abortion-2.

72. *See* Abigail Aiken et al., *supra* note 66.

73. According to the Kaiser Family Foundation, 18 states have prohibited telemedical abortion; 5 states explicitly ban telemedicine for medication abortion, and 13 states require the prescribing clinician be physically present with the patient. The "no-test" model is also not an option in the 14 states requiring patients receive an ultrasound before an abortion, and in the 13 states with in-person counseling requirements. This leaves 23 states in which the "no-test" model could be used to provide medication abortion. *See* Amrutha Ramaswamy et al., *Medication Abortion and Telemedicine. Innovations and Barriers During the COVID-19 Emergency*, KAISER FAMILY FOUND. (June 8, 2020), https://www.kff.org/policy-watch /medication-abortion-telemedicine-innovations-and-barriers-during-the-covid-19-emer gency/. Currently, only 13 of these states have providers offering telemedical abortion

a person wants to avoid an in-person consultation, their only option is often to procure the pills themselves and take on the legal risks that that entails. In order to understand the potential of SMA both now and in a potential post-*Roe* context, it is important to first understand how SMA methods came to be and how they have been restricted in the past. The following section will provide a brief overview of abortion pills, their history, and regulatory opposition towards them in the U.S. context.

B. What Are Abortion Pills?

Two primary medications are used to induce abortions. The first drug, mifepristone, blocks the effects of progesterone, a hormone without which the lining of the uterus begins to break down. A second drug, misoprostol, taken 24 to 48 hours later, causes the uterus to contract and expel its contents. When taken together, they are a safe and effective way to end a pregnancy 97.7 percent of the time.[74] In spite of the overwhelming evidence supporting the medical safety of abortion pills, achieving access to them has been a lengthy and obstacle-ridden path.

1. Abortion Pills: A Brief History

a. History of Misoprostol

Misoprostol was not supposed to be an abortion medication. These little pills that are now on the World Health Organization's list of essential medications were, initially, designed to treat ulcers.[75] They were sold over the counter throughout South and Latin America.[76] It was not until the 1980s when people in Brazil noticed the fine print on the back of the box and unlocked their full potential. *"May cause a miscarriage, premature birth or birth defects."*[77] As it turns out, in seven out of ten cases, misoprostol will cause

---

services. *See* Gynuity Health Projects, *Telabortion Study: Project States*, GYNUITY, https://telabortion.org/get-started (last accessed Nov. 6, 2020).

74. Mary Gatter et al., *Efficacy and Safety of Medical Abortion Using Mifepristone and Buccal Misoprostol Through 63 Days*, 91 CONTRACEPT., 267, 270 (2016). Note that misoprostol alone can also be used to safely and effectively induce abortions in 79 percent of cases in the first trimester. *See* Elizabeth Raymond et al., *Efficacy of Misoprostol Alone for First Trimester Medical Abortion: A Systematic Review*, 133 OBSTET. & GYNEC. 137, 147 (2020).

75. *See* James Brooke, *Ulcer Drug Tied to Numerous Abortions in Brazil*, N.Y. TIMES (May 19, 1993), https://www.nytimes.com/1993/05/19/health/ulcer-drug-tied-to-numerous-abortions-in-brazil.html.

76. *See* Nina Zamberlin, *Latin American Women's Experiences with Medical Abortion in Settings Where Abortion Is Legally Restricted*, 9 REPROD. HEALTH 34, 43 (2012).

77. Food & Drug Admin., *Cytotec: Misoprostol Tablets*, FOOD & DRUG ADMIN. (2009), https://tinyurl.com/y32zh5oj.

a person's uterus to contract and release the pregnancy if taken during the first trimester.[78] A recent systematic review found that about 78 percent of people had complete misoprostol abortions without recourse to surgery, and viable pregnancy was terminated more than 93 percent of the time.[79] Information about how to use the pills to induce abortion traveled through South and Latin America by word of mouth. When at a dinner party, my partner's childhood friend—born and raised in Colombia— chuckled when I said that I was writing a piece about access to abortion pill information. She explained that back home, there wouldn't be a need or readership for it; the utility of the pills was common knowledge—"everyone just knows about them." When I asked how, she shrugged and answered, "It's the kind of thing you just hear about from your friends or older siblings." Though it took longer for information about misoprostol to spread in the United States, grassroots networks have rendered it more widely available than ever before through train-the-trainer models of information sharing and community-based interventions.[80]

b. History of Mifepristone

The same decade that information about misoprostol began its journey across Brazil, the French company, Roussell-Uclaf, developed the first medication designed to induce abortions.[81] Mifepristone, sometimes called RU-486, stops a pregnancy from progressing by blocking the flow of progesterone to the uterus. As noted earlier, when followed with misoprostol to expel the pregnancy, it is effective in inducing complete abortions 97.7 percent of the time.[82] In spite of the fact that over ten countries had already authorized the use of mifepristone to end unwanted pregnancies,[83] the U.S. Food and Drug Administration (FDA), delayed approval of mifepristone

---

78. *See* Wendy Sheldon et al., *Early Abortion with Buccal versus Sublingual Misoprostol Alone: A Multicenter, Randomized Trial*, 99 CONTRACEPTION, 272, 277 (2019); *see also* Helena von Hertzen et al., *Efficacy of Two Intervals and Two Routes of Administration of Misoprostol for Termination of Early Pregnancy: a Randomised Controlled Equivalence Trial*, 369 LANCET 1938, 1945 (2007).

79. Elizabeth Raymond et al., *Efficacy of Misoprostol Alone for First Trimester Medical Abortion: A Systematic Review*, 133 OBSTET. & GYNEC. 137, 147 (2020).

80. *See* Mariana Prandini Assis & Sara Larrea, *Why Self-Managed Abortion Is So Much More than a Provisional Solution for Times of a Pandemic*, 28 SEXUAL & REPROD. HEALTH MATTERS 1, 2 (2020).

81. *See* R. Alta Charo, *A Political History of RU-486*, BIOMEDICAL POLITICS 43, 44 (1991).

82. Gatter et al., *supra* note 74.

83. Mifepristone has been available in Great Britain since 1991; China and Sweden since 1992; and Austria, Belgium, Denmark, Finland, Germany, Greece, the Netherlands, and Spain since 1999. *See* Julie A. Hogan, *The Life of the Abortion Pill in the United States*, HARV. DASH REPOSITORY 80, 80 (2000), http://nrs.harvard.edu/urn-3:HUL.InstRepos:8852153.

until 2000—two decades after its invention.[84] Although the FDA initially insisted that it could not release the drug because "certain questions about the manufacturing and distribution" needed to be answered,[85] the inordinate delay in authorizing the pill was clearly caused by political, rather than medical, concerns. From its inception, anti-choice organizations such as the National Right to Life Committee (NLRC) have campaigned to prevent the introduction of mifepristone on the U.S. market.[86]

Fearing that the introduction of mifepristone in the United States might undermine their entire campaign against abortion, the NLRC brought together a broad constellation of anti-choice groups behind a campaign to prevent mifepristone from entering the U.S. market. Not only would medical abortion make the procedure available in locations outside of abortion clinics (the great majority of anti-choice organizing had focused on cutting off clinic access through TRAP laws and in-person intimidation tactics), those opposed to abortion were also concerned that the simple taking of a pill, mifepristone, would eliminate or seriously diminish the moral significance of abortion because of the ease with which people can take the pills.[87] Congressman Robert K. Dornan (R-Cal) claimed in 1986 that the "death pill," as he mislabeled it for political effect, would render "the taking of a pre-born life [. . .] as easy and as trivial as taking aspirin."[88] Fearing that the release of the pills might cause American boycotts of their other medical products, the German company that manufactured the pills—Hoechst—refused to license the pill in the United States for years.[89] The FDA did nothing to assuage these anxieties and refused to authorize the pills until there had been new clinical trials in the United States (even though clinical trials in France and Germany had already established their safety and effectiveness).[90] It wasn't until the New York-based nonprofit, the Population Council, completed a series of clinical trials proving the safety and effectiveness of the pills, that progress began to be made in the United States, and the FDA began its approval process.[91]

---

84. *See* Heather D. Boonstra, *Mifepristone in the United States: Status and Future*, 5 GUTTMACHER POLICY REV. 4, 4 (2002).

85. *See* WebMD, *Brief History of the Abortion Pill*, WEB M.D. (Sept. 28, 2000), https://www.webmd.com/women/news/20000928/brief-history-of-abortion-pill-in-us#1.

86. *See* Hogan, *supra* note 83.

87. *See id.*

88. Csilla Muhl, *RU-486: Legal and Policy Issues Confronting the Food and Drug Administration*, 14 J. LEGAL MED. 319, 339 (1993).

89. *See* R. Alta Charo, *A Political History of RU-486*, BIOMEDICAL POLITICS 43, 49 (1991).

90. *See* Hogan, *supra* note 83.

91. *See id.*

2. Abortion Pills: Current Practice

In spite of the fact that mifepristone *is* safer than Tylenol, Dornan's prediction that it would become as easy to find as aspirin has yet to become reality. Although misoprostol continues to be widely available, regulatory opposition to mifepristone lives on in the form of a special set of burdensome FDA restrictions known as a Risk Evaluation and Mitigation Strategy (REMS). In general, the FDA can impose REMS restrictions on certain medications to decrease the risk of adverse drug-related outcomes.[92] Examples of REMS include limiting the settings in which health care providers can dispense or administer a certain drug. These can be seen in Table 7.1, taken from the FDA's website.[93]

TABLE 7.1 TYPES OF REMS REQUIREMENTS

Element to Assure Safe Use	Example
Health care providers who prescribe the drug have specific training/experience or be specialty certified.	Prescribers may be required to become certified and/or take training prior to prescribing the REMS drug. As part of the certification, prescribers may need to enroll in the REMS and agree to carry out certain activities for safe drug use. For example, a prescriber may be required to counsel their patients about the particular risk or agree to enroll and/or monitor patients throughout the treatment course.
Pharmacies, practitioners, or health care settings that dispense the drug may be specially certified.	Pharmacies, practitioners, or other health care settings that may dispense REMS medications may be required to take the training, train staff, and oversee all processes and procedures needed to implement the REMS requirements. For example, a pharmacy may need to put a process in place that includes that the prescriber of a REMS drug is certified, patients are enrolled, and that the laboratory testing or other certain safe use conditions have been carried out prior to dispensing the drug.
Drug be dispensed only in certain health care settings such as hospitals	FDA may require that a REMS drug be dispensed or administered only in a particular setting. For example, a drug may need to be administered or dispensed only in health care settings that have immediate access on-site to supplies and personal trained to manage a particular adverse effect.

---

92. *See* Food & Drug Admin., *Risk Evaluation and Mitigation Strategies*, FDA (Aug. 8, 2019), https://www.fda.gov/drugs/drug-safety-and-availability/risk-evaluation-and-mitigation -strategies-rems.

93. *See* Food & Drug Admin., *What's in a REMS?*, FDA (Jan. 26, 2018), https://www.fda .gov/drugs/risk-evaluation-and-mitigation-strategies-rems/whats-rems.

The FDA's REMS for mifepristone imposes three separate restrictions: (1) the drug can only be dispensed in clinics, medical offices, and hospitals by or under the supervision of a certified prescriber; (2) health care providers who want to prescribe the drug must become "certified" by completing and sending a form to the drug distributor; and (3) the patient must be given an FDA-approved medication guide and sign a patient agreement.[94] The mifepristone REMS provides no indication as to how such restrictions might decrease the risk of complication or infection.[95] Moreover, in the unlikely event that a person were to experience an infection-related complication, they would only experience symptoms after taking the misoprostol, which has no REMS requirements and is consumed at home (not in a clinical setting).[96]

Not only do these restrictions make mifepristone harder to procure— for example, by prohibiting its sale by retail or mail-order pharmacies— they also make it unnecessarily difficult to prescribe. When a drug is subject to REMS restrictions, eligible prescribers must jump through extra hoops.[97] As a result, some providers are dissuaded from prescribing the drug, disproportionately hindering access for abortion seekers in areas with severe provider shortages.

The evidence is clear that mifepristone is just as safe as many other drugs and procedures that the FDA does not similarly regulate or restrict.[98] More than three million people have successfully used mifepristone in the 16 years since the FDA approved it, and its most common side effects are shared by other less regulated drugs and procedures.[99] In the words of Susan Yanow, co-founder of Women Help Women (an international organization that provides abortion and contraception services), the pills are "safer than penicillin. They're certainly safer than Viagra and are

---

94. *See* Food & Drug Admin., *Highlights of Prescribing Information*, FDA (Mar. 2016), https://www.accessdata.fda.gov/drugsatfda_docs/label/2016/020687s020lbl.pdf; *see also* Isabel Blalock, *Removing the Mifeprex REMS Was Long Overdue. Then a Global Pandemic Began*, NARAL PRO-CHOICE M.D. (May 7, 2020), https://prochoicemd.medium.com/removing-the-mifeprex-rems-was-long-overdue-then-a-global-pandemic-began-ab4c002bd72#_edn1.

95. *See* Mifeprex REMS Study Group, *Sixteen Years of Overregulation: Time to Unburden Mifeprex*, 376 NEW ENGL. J. MED. 790 (2017).

96. *See* Blalock, *supra* note 94.

97. *See* Daniel Grossman, *Overregulation Is Forcing Women to Have Late-Term Abortions*, LOS ANGELES TIMES (Feb. 28, 2017), https://www.latimes.com/opinion/op-ed/la-oe-grossman-remove-restrictions-on-medication-abortion-20170228-story.html.

98. *See* Bixby Center Staff, *A Call to End the Excessive Regulation of Mifepristone*, BIXBY CTR. FOR REPROD. HEALTH (Mar. 2017), https://bixbycenter.ucsf.edu/news/call-end-excessive-regulation-mifepristone.

99. *Id.*

over-regulated only because of the politics of abortion. If this was simply about the safety of the medicines, they would be over the counter."[100] In short, the FDA has ignored its own standards for approving new drugs[101]—as well as the recommendations of its former commissioner and calls from providers around the country[102]—by refusing to lift the REMS restrictions on mifepristone.

The FDA tried to maintain its REMS during the pandemic, even though doing so and requiring in-person visits would force patients and providers to risk unnecessary exposure to COVID-19. They were sued by the American College of Obstetricians and Gynecologists (ACOG) and other groups to suspend the in-person requirement during the pandemic.[103] The case, discussed in more depth later in the chapter, was successful until the Supreme Court stayed the trial court's injunction pending appeal.[104]

Although the federal district court's decision to suspend mifepristone's in-person requirement alleviated some of the obstacles that people face when obtaining the pill, it was neither a sufficient nor sustainable measure to assure meaningful access. Even if there is no legal requirement imposing an in-person visit for a person to take mifepristone, the other elements of the REMS make it so that only licensed providers can distribute the pills. Regular pharmacies cannot fill prescriptions, and only some licensed providers in certain states are offering telemedical abortion services. These providers are largely located in states that already have comparatively widespread access to abortion, and none of them provide these services across

---

100. *A Story to Introduce Self-Managed Abortion*, SELF MANAGED: AN ABORTION STORY (May, 2020), https://www.dropbox.com/s/z5spswe6ijjzc3r/Part%201%20-%20Transcript%20%28ENGLISH_SPANISH%29.docx?dl=0.

101. The standards that must be satisfied in order to secure FDA approval of a new drug are "safety for its indicated use and substantial evidence of efficacy." 21 U.S.C. § 355(d) (setting efficacy standards); *see also* 21 C.F.R. §§ 312.20–312.130; *see also* Sarah Ricks, *The New French Abortion Pill: The Moral Property of Women*, 75 YALE J. L. & FEMINISM 75, 77 (1989).

102. The former FDA Commissioner Dr. Jane Henney argued that the agency should re-evaluate whether REMS measures are still necessary, taking into consideration recent studies that show mifepristone is effective and safe. *See* Jane E. Henney & Helene D. Gayle, *Time to Reevaluate U.S. Mifepristone Restrictions*, 381 NEW ENGL. J. MED. 597, 597 (2019); *see also* Grossman, *supra* note 97 (arguing that REMS restrictions prevent providers from assisting people in obtaining early abortions).

103. *See* Adam Liptak, *Supreme Court Won't Immediately Revive Abortion-Pill Restriction*, N.Y TIMES (Oct. 8, 2020), https://www.nytimes.com/2020/10/08/us/politics/supreme-court-abortion-pill-restriction.html.

104. *See* Amy Howe, *Justices Delay Action on FDA Request to Reinstate Abortion-Pill Restrictions*, SCOTUS BLOG (Oct. 8, 2020, 9:30 PM), https://www.scotusblog.com/2020/10/justices-delay-action-on-fda-request-to-reinstate-abortion-pill-restrictions/. See *infra* notes 214–20 and accompanying text.

state lines.[105] That means that, if you live in a state where there are no abortion providers offering telemedical abortion care, you still have to travel to a clinic for an in-person visit, at least if you want to comply with the FDA's legal requirements. There are other ways to procure the pills that are just as medically safe, but that do present some legal risks.

II. The Legal Landscape of Self-Managed Abortion

To understand contemporary criminalization of SMA, one must first understand the history that led up to it. Integral to that history are the efforts of anti-choice groups to disseminate false accounts of the legal history of abortion bans. Contrary to what many anti-choice groups suggest, legal restrictions on abortion access are a modern phenomenon that emerged as a consequence of the push to institutionalize reproductive medicine. This section will provide a brief overview of this history, connecting it to contemporary trends in the criminalization of SMA.

A. Background: A Brief History of Criminalizing Abortion in the United States

1. Early American Abortion Law

Anti-choice groups such as the National Right to Life[106] and the Life Network[107] have carefully crafted and disseminated a narrative that frames legal abortion as a historical anomaly. On the National Right to Life's website, for example, a page titled "Abortion History Timeline" describes "a few rogue doctors and midwives" performing abortions in early America, only "as far back as the 1850s."[108] In reality, trusted midwives and health care providers performed legal abortions from the beginning of American colonial life.

Abortion was not just legal, it was a "safe, condoned, and widespread practice in colonial America and common enough to appear in the legal

---

105. *See* Gynuity Health Projects, *Telabortion Study: Project States*, GYNUITY, https://telabortion.org/get-started (last accessed Nov. 6, 2020).

106. *See* NAT'L RIGHT TO LIFE, NRLC, https://www.nrlc.org (last accessed Nov. 10, 2020).

107. *See* Life Network Staff, *A Brief History of Abortion and Life in America*, LIFE NETWORK (Jan. 11, 2019), https://www.elifenetwork.com/history-abortion-life-america/.

108. *See* National Right to Life, *Abortion History Timeline*, NAT'L RIGHT TO LIFE, http://www.nrlc.org/archive/abortion/facts/abortiontimeline.html (last accessed Nov. 10, 2020).

and medical records of the period."[109] Abortion laws did not appear on the books anywhere in the United States until 1821, and abortion before quickening did not first become illegal anywhere in the United States until the 1860s.[110] According to writer and religious scholar Ranana Dine, "If a New Englander wanted an abortion in the 17th or 18th centuries, no legal, social, or religious force would have stopped them." The same was true in the UK, where the first abortion law appeared in 1861.[111] In her book *When Abortion Was a Crime*, Leslie Reagan explains that there was only about a 100-year period (which she sets between 1867 and 1973) when abortion was illegal in the United States.[112]

Although there are certain Catholic countries, like France, that had a long religious history of prohibiting abortion, faith was not the primary motivation behind abortion bans in the United States. Instead, the roots of contemporary criminalization of SMA originate with systematic efforts to eradicate American midwives who were, at that point in time, a predominantly Black and indigenous group of providers who drew patients away from the growing numbers of men pursuing careers in obstetrics at the time.[113] In order to understand today's legal landscape of SMA, one must first understand the racist history of midwifery bans.

2. Institutionalizing Obstetrics and Criminalizing Midwives

Prior to the Civil War, abortion and contraception were legal in the United States and primarily provided by midwives.[114] The great majority of midwives at the time were Black or indigenous women.[115] When slavery ended, skilled Black midwives—sometimes referred to as "granny midwives"—presented serious competition to white men who sought to enter the practice

---

109. Ranana Dine, *Scarlet Letters: Getting the History of Abortion and Contraception Right*, Ctr. for Am. Progress, (Aug. 8, 2013, 1:29 PM), https://tinyurl.com/o88fclh; *see also* Z. Acevedo, *Abortion in Early America*, 4 Women's Health 159, 159 (1979).

110. *See* Dine, *supra* note 109.

111. *See* Rosie Dutch, *The Globalisation of Punitive Abortion Laws: The Colonial Legacy of the Offences Against the Person Act 1861*, Ctr. for Feminist Foreign Policy (Mar. 9, 2020), https://tinyurl.com/y3lx2yn6.

112. Leslie Reagan, When Abortion Was a Crime: Women, Medicine and Law in the United States, 1867–1973 (1998).

113. *See* Phyllis L. Brodsky, *Where Have All the Midwives Gone?* 17 J. Perinat. Educ. 48–51 (2008).

114. *Id.* at 48.

115. *See* Keisha La'Nesha Goode, *Birthing, Blackness, and the Body: Black Midwives & Experiential Continuities of Institutional Racism*, 10 CUNY Acad. Works (2014), https://tinyurl.com/y5eyqozw.

of family medicine and obstetrics.[116] As the field of obstetrics gained popularity within the medical profession in the second half of the 19th century, physicians sought to eliminate preexisting networks for obstetric care.[117] Medical journals from the time make it clear that physicians viewed granny midwives as "unwelcome interlopers" in their field.[118] Smear campaigns were used in order to push them out of the profession. Some of these proliferated racist messages about the "barbaric" and "primitive" practitioners.[119] Others focused on abortion, reframing it, and the midwives who provided it, as criminal.[120]

The professionalization of medicine, beginning in the late 1800s and continuing into the 1900s, allowed licensed health professionals to claim authority over obstetric care, both through American law and within the field of medicine, by erecting a legal monopoly.[121] Physicians and other health care lobbyists advocated for medical practice regulation and criminalization of other healers with whom they competed—like midwives.[122]

The passage and promotion of medical practice acts and licensure laws positioned doctors as the only legitimate source of obstetric care.[123] These laws criminalized providers who could not obtain licenses, without which their work was illegal. Professor and sociologist, Alicia Bonaparte, has shown through her research that the proliferation of medical licensure laws was a strategic and effective way to eliminate granny midwives and abortion providers. In her doctoral thesis, *The Persecution & Prosecution of*

---

116. *See* Michele Goodwin, *The Racist History of Abortion and Midwifery Bans*, AM. CIVIL LIBERTIES UNION (July 1, 2020), https://www.aclu.org/news/racial-justice/the-racist-history -of-abortion-and-midwifery-bans/.

117. *See id.*

118. *See* Alicia D. Bonaparte, The Persecution & Prosecution of Granny Midwives 1900–1940, at 129 (July 3, 2007) (unpublished PhD dissertation, Vanderbilt University) (on file with Vanderbilt University Institutional Repository), https://ir.vanderbilt.edu /handle/1803/13563. [Hereinafter Bonaparte, The Persecution & Prosecution of Granny Midwives].

119. *Id.*

120. *Id.* at 17.

121. *See id.* at 130, citing *e.g.* PAUL STARR, THE SOCIAL TRANSFORMATION OF MEDICINE (New York: Basic Books 1982); JUDITH PENCE ROOKS, MIDWIFERY AND CHILDBIRTH IN AMERICA (Temple University Press 1985); Judith Walzer Leavitt, *The Growth of Medical Authority: Technology and Morals in Turn-of-the-Century Obstetrics*, 1 MED. ANTHROPOLOGY QUARTERLY 230–55 (1987); Alyson Reed & Joyce E. Roberts, *State Regulation of Midwives: Issues and Options*, 45 J. MIDWIFERY & WOMEN'S Health 130–49 (2000).

122. *See* Bonaparte, The Persecution & Prosecution of Granny Midwives, *supra* note 118, at 130.

123. *See id; see also* Alicia Bonaparte, *The Satisfactory Midwife Bag: Midwifery Regulation in South Carolina, Past and Present Considerations*, 38 SOC. SCI. HISTORY 155–82 (2014).

Granny Midwives, she explains that, initially, these acts ensured that practitioners had attended socially sanctioned schools of medical instruction.[124] Over time, however, they began to require that those individuals practicing medicine were under the auspices of a governing body, such as the State Board of Medical Examiners, which explicitly excluded people of color, and implicitly excluded women, from membership at the time.[125] The following excerpt from a 1905 issue of the *Journal of American Medicine* discusses the recent passage of the 1905 Construction of Practice Act:

> The statutes do not attempt to discriminate between different schools of medicine or systems for the cure of disease. No method of attempting to heal the sick, however occult, is prohibited. All that the law exacts is that, whatever the system, the practitioner shall be possessed of a certificate from the State Board of Medical Examiners, and shall exercise such reasonable skill and care as are usually possessed by practitioners in good standing of that system in the vicinity where they practice.[126]

As the passage reveals, the purpose of the act was not to prescribe safer or better care nor "to make any particular mode of effecting a cure unlawful" but to delegitimize (and deauthorize) healers who did not, or could not, obtain certification by state boards.[127] It reserved the practice of medicine exclusively to practitioners who "possessed a certificate from the State Board of Medical Examiners."[128] Requiring licensure to establish one's professional legitimacy gravely affected community healers like midwives.[129] Many state and local medical associations refused to accept Black applicants until the 1960s, and state medical boards were similarly hostile.[130] As a result, licensure laws, though neutral on their face, effectively prohibited birth work by Black midwives and other providers of color. Through these licensure laws, states were able to impose fines, fees, and, in some cases,

---

124. *See id.* at 132.

125. *See* Robert B. Baker, *The American Medical Association and Race*, 16 AM. MED. ASS'N J. OF ETHICS 479–88 (2014).

126. *See* Bonaparte, The Persecution & Prosecution of Granny Midwives, *supra* note 118, at 133.

127. *Id.*

128. *See id.*

129. *Id.*

130. *See* Robert Baker et. al., *African American Physicians and Organized Medicine, 1846–1968: Origins of a Racial Divide*, 300 J. AM. MED. ASS'N 306, 312 (2008); *see also* Jonathan Sidhu, *Exploring the AMA's History of Discrimination*, PROPUBLICA (July 16, 2008, 10:22 AM), https://www.propublica.org/article/exploring-the-amas-history-of-discrimination-716.

incarceration, upon providers of color, thereby establishing near total dominance over the field of obstetrics.[131]

These laws would eventually be accompanied by outright bans on the practice of midwifery and prohibitions on abortion.[132] Outlawing abortion was an effective proxy for criminalizing midwives, the physicians' competition, while cloaking the eradication of that qualified class of medical practitioners in a religious and moral crusade. Beginning with the American Medical Association in 1859, organized medical societies strongly opposed legal abortion and campaigned for restrictive laws that would leave the decision about whether to provide any women with an abortion strictly in physicians' hands.[133] By 1910, all but one state in America had criminalized abortion, except in cases when the judgment of a doctor deemed it necessary to save a woman's life, thus transforming legal abortion into a "physicians-only" practice.[134] These same sorts of licensure laws are used to criminalize midwives today,[135] and they are further misused to criminalize people who self-manage their abortions.

3. Criminalizing Self-Managed Abortion

Abortion law has historically centered around criminalizing abortion providers generally, and then criminalizing abortion providers who did not adhere to increasing numbers of requirements and TRAP law provisions. In the SMA context, new questions arise because the role of patient and provider become one and the same. Ill-fitting laws never intended for SMA have nevertheless been used by some prosecutors to bring charges against

131. *See* Bonaparte, The Persecution & Prosecution of Granny Midwives, *supra* note 118, at 133.

132. *See* Goodwin, *supra* note 116.

133. *See* Nat'l Inst. Rep. Health, *When Self-Abortion Is a Crime: Laws That Put Women At Risk*, NAT'L INST. REP. HEALTH (June 2017), https://www.nirhealth.org/wp-content/uploads/2017/06/Self-Abortion-White-Paper-Final.pdf, citing ROSALIND P. PETCHESKY, ABORTION & WOMAN'S CHOICE: THE STATE, SEXUALITY & REPRODUCTIVE FREEDOM 80 (1985); ALEXANDER SANGER, BEYOND CHOICE: REPRODUCTIVE FREEDOM IN THE 21ST CENTURY 28–29 (Public Affairs 2004).

134. *See* Harmon Leon, *Abortion Ban in Alabama: A Brief History of How America Got Here*, OBSERVER (May 15, 2019, 3:55 PM), https://observer.com/2019/05/abortion-ban-alabama-american-reproductive-rights-history/.

135. *See* Jennifer Block, *The Criminalization of the American Midwife*, LONGREADS (Mar. 10, 2020), https://longreads.com/2020/03/10/criminalization-of-the-american-midwife/#:~:text=New%20York%20midwife%20Elizabeth%20Catlin,counts%20at%20her%20upcoming%20trial.&text=Politics%20and%20patriarchy%20make%20the,of%20women%20and%20underserved%20communities.

people who end their own pregnancies. This history, too, is marred by institutionalized racism and biomedical patriarchy.

In 1973, the United States Supreme Court outlawed complete bans on abortion in its landmark decision, *Roe v. Wade*, that held that people have a constitutional right to seek an abortion without fear of government prohibitions, much less criminal charges. The recent appointment of Justice Barrett to the Supreme Court has caused many to contemplate, and fear, its reversal. However, in this moment of uncertainty, it is worth noting *Roe* has not stopped a number of people from being arrested—and some even jailed—for ending their own pregnancies. This is due, in part, to the fact that many of the criminal abortion laws that were enacted during the period described above have remained on the books.

B. Contemporary Criminalization of SMA

Describing the legal status of SMA throughout the country is challenging because it is often not an abortion law, but prosecutorial overreach, that drives arrests for SMA. It is not possible to establish a fixed, definitive answer to the question of whether SMA is illegal or not. That said, reproductive justice lawyers, legal scholars, and advocates have developed valuable frameworks for understanding the law surrounding SMA. Groups like If/When/How, National Advocates for Pregnant Women, Southwest Women's Law Center, Legal Voice, the Center for Reproductive Rights and Justice, and many others have laid the groundwork for understanding the legal risk that people take on when they self-manage. Here is a brief overview of some key principles.

1. Criminalization of SMA Is Linked to Broader Systems of Structural Oppression

A person's degree of risk for being arrested for SMA depends on how exposed they already are to state surveillance and criminalization. In their 2017 report, *Roe's Unfinished Promise*, the SIA legal team (now If/When/How) explained how the criminalization of SMA is intrinsically linked to larger systems of discriminatory policing and surveillance. They note that recent prosecutions have disproportionately targeted people living in poverty and people of color.[136] A survey of more than 400 cases of arrests and forced interventions on pregnant people in the United States, including people arrested for self-managed abortion, found that pregnant "low-income

---

136. *See* IF/WHEN/HOW, *Roe's Unfinished Promise, supra* note 2, at 35.

women and pregnant African American women are significantly more likely to be arrested, reported by hospital staff, and subjected to felony charges."[137] It stated that "these findings are consistent with [. . .] well-documented racially disproportionate application of criminal laws to African American communities in general and to pregnant African American women in particular."[138] The same forms of state-sanctioned abuse (hyper-surveillance, prosecutorial overreach, incarceration) that are driven by racist animus in other contexts appear within SMA. Crackdowns on abortion access therefore can—and should—be read alongside, and in relationship to, immigration crackdowns, the "war on drugs," and civil child welfare penalties.[139] Criminalizing SMA fits into a broader system of laws and policies that are used to control and violate people in general, but Black, brown, and indigenous communities in particular.[140]

2. Criminalization of SMA Is a Dynamic Endeavor that Relies on Outmoded Legislation and Prosecutorial Overreach

To date, no one has been prosecuted for ordering abortion pills, obtaining a prescription online, or trying to get a prescription filled at a pharmacy.[141] Nonetheless, evidence of having purchased abortion pills online has been used against people charged with other SMA-related crimes.[142] While the law does not provide a clear answer to the question of whether it is legal to purchase abortion pills, it does (sometimes) criminalize the act of ending one's own pregnancy.

---

137. Lynn M. Paltrow & Jeanne Flavin, *Arrests of and Forced Interventions on Pregnant Women in the United States, 1973-2005: Implications for Women's Legal Status and Public Health*, 38 J. OF HEALTH POLITICS, POLICY & LAW 299, 333 (2013).

138. *See id.*

139. IF/WHEN/HOW, *Roe's Unfinished Promise*, *supra* note 2, at 25.

140. *See id.*

141. *See* IF/WHEN/HOW, *Self-Managed Abortion, the Law and COVID-19 Factsheet*, IF/WHEN/How (Apr. 20, 2020), at 1, https://tinyurl.com/y8gfvfbx [hereinafter IF/WHEN/How, *Self-Managed Abortion, the Law, and COVID-19 Factsheet*].

142. *See* Philip J. Murphy, *How Online Searches & Texting Has Landed Some Seeking Abortions in Jail*, PHILIP J. MURPHY: ATTORNEY AT LAW (Feb. 28, 2020), https://www.phillipmurphylawyer.com/how-online-searches-texting-has-landed-some-seeking-abortions-in-jail/; *see also* Ryan Phillips, *Infant Death Case Heading Back to Grand Jury*, STARKVILLE DAILY NEWS (May 8, 2019), https://www.starkvilledailynews.com/infant-death-case-heading-back-to-grand-jury/article_cf99bcb0-71cc-11e9-963a-eb5dc5052c92.html.

Five states (Arizona,[143] Delaware,[144] Idaho,[145] Oklahoma,[146] and South Carolina[147]) do have explicit SMA bans. That is one "category" of laws that

---

143. Arizona's SMA statute, ARIZ. REV. STAT. 13-2640, reads: "A woman who solicits from any person any medicine, drug, or substance whatever, and takes it, or who submits to an operation, or to the use of any means whatever, with the intent to procure a miscarriage, unless it is necessary to preserve her own life, shall be punished by imprisonment in the state prison for not less than one nor more than five years." *See* IF/WHEN/HOW, *Roe's Unfinished Promise, supra* note 2, at 10.

144. Delaware's SMA statute, 11 DEL. CODE § 652, reads: "A female is guilty of self-abortion when she, being pregnant, commits or submits to an abortion upon herself which causes her abortion, unless the abortion is a therapeutic abortion." In 1977, the state attorney general issued a statement of policy opining that the self-abortion law is unconstitutional and declaring that it would not be enforced. *See* IF/WHEN/HOW, *Roe's Unfinished Promise, supra* note 2, at 10, citing Statement of Policy, Attorney General of Delaware (Mar. 24, 1977); Delaware Women's Health Org. v. Wier, 441 F. Supp. 497, 499 n.9 (D. Del. 1977).

145. Idaho's SMA statute, IDAHO CODE ANN. § 18-606(2), reads: "Every woman who knowingly submits to an abortion or solicits of another, for herself, the production of an abortion, or who purposely terminates her own pregnancy otherwise than by a live birth, shall be deemed guilty of a felony . . ." According to If/When/How's *Roe's Unfinished Promise* report, an Idaho mother named Jennie McCormack was "arrested in 2011 after having ended a pregnancy with medication she obtained online. Ms. McCormack safely ended her pregnancy with abortion pills, but was reported to police by a family friend who told police about fetal remains on her property. She was charged with a crime that makes it a felony for women to 'purposely terminates her own pregnancy.' A magistrate judge dismissed the charge on evidentiary grounds, and Ms. McCormack filed a lawsuit challenging the constitutionality of the law. The Ninth Circuit concluded a portion of this statute facially unconstitutional in *McCormack v. Hiedeman*, 788 F.3d 1017 (9th Cir. 2015)." *See* IF/WHEN/HOW, *Roe's Unfinished Promise, supra* note 2, at 10.

146. Oklahoma has two statutes (63 OKLA. STAT. § 1-733 and 21 OKLA. STAT. § 862) that read respectively: "No woman shall perform or induce an abortion upon herself, except under the supervision of a duly licensed physician. Any physician who supervises a woman in performing or inducing an abortion upon herself shall fulfill all the requirements of this article which apply to a physician performing or inducing an abortion." (63 OKLA. STAT. § 1-733) and "Every woman who solicits of any person any medicine, drug, or substance whatever, and takes the same, or who submits to any operation, or to the use of any means whatever, with intent thereby to procure a miscarriage, unless the same is necessary to preserve her life, is punishable by imprisonment." (21 OKLA. STAT. § 862). According to If/When/How's *Roe's Unfinished Promise* report, while this statute was declared unconstitutional in *Henrie v. Derryberry*, 358 F. Supp. 719 (N.D. Okla. 1973), its application was not enjoined and the statute was not repealed. Additionally, later legislative acts and jurisprudence leave that finding of unconstitutionality unstable in the face of increased prosecutorial hostility toward women believed to have self-induced an abortion. IF/WHEN/HOW, *Roe's Unfinished Promise, supra* note 2, at 10.

147. South Carolina's SMA statute, S.C. CODE ANN. § 44-41-80(b), reads: "[A]ny woman who solicits of any person or otherwise procures any drug, medicine, prescription or substance and administers it to herself or who submits to any operation or procedure or who uses or employs any device or any instrument or other means with intent to produce an abortion, unless it is necessary to preserve her own life, shall be deemed guilty of a misdemeanor. . . ." IF/WHEN/HOW, *Roe's Unfinished Promise, supra* note 2, at 10.

can be used to criminalize those who end their own pregnancies. However, relatively few of the recent prosecutions for SMA have been brought under these statutes. According to If/When/How, "the bigger threat stems from roughly 40 other different types of laws that politically motivated prosecutors wield as weapons against people who end their own pregnancies."[148] Even with *Roe* in place, many people[149] who allegedly induced their own abortion have been charged with crimes including murder, homicide, feticide, failure to report a death or properly dispose of remains, child endangerment or negligence, and practicing medicine without a license.[150]

Fetal harm laws—the second "category" of laws that have been used to criminalize SMA—were originally designed to protect pregnant people from physical assault and violence by others. The Federal Unborn Victims of Violence Law, for example, was passed in memory of Laci Peterson, who was murdered at a late stage of pregnancy by her abuser.[151] The act, subtitled "Laci and Connor's Law," does include specific exemptions for abortion and clearly was designed to protect pregnant people from physical violence.[152] However, state statutes that mirror that act to protect pregnant people from violence fail to include abortion exceptions. Although it is often unclear whether the drafters of a given fetal harm law intentionally failed to include an abortion exception, in certain states like Utah, for example, the feticide statute explicitly *includes* a loophole that can be used to prosecute people who self-manage. It reads: "a woman is not guilty of criminal homicide of her own unborn child if the death of her unborn child [...] is not caused by an intentionally or knowing act of the woman."[153] This provision seems to be designed as a loophole for criminalizing those who self-manage.

In 2015, Georgia prosecutors charged Kenlissa Jones with attempted murder after she took misoprostol pills to end her own pregnancy.[154] That

---

148. *See* IF/WHEN/HOW, *Fulfilling Roe's Promise: 2019 Update, supra* note 2, at 1.

149. *See* Molly Redden, *Jailed for Ending a Pregnancy: How Prosecutors Get Inventive on Abortion*, THE GUARDIAN (Nov. 22, 2016, 7:30 AM), https://www.theguardian.com/us -news/2016/nov/22/abortion-pregnancy-law-prosecute-trump. See also *supra* note 2.

150. *See* IF/WHEN/HOW, *Roe's Unfinished Promise, supra* note 2, 5–19.

151. *Criminalizing Pregnant People*, SELF MANAGED: AN ABORTION STORY at 4 (May 2020), https://www.dropbox.com/sh/kwern9euvpdi7q8/AADCw3UpMXGjFa9SroIrZ22Ea?dl=0& preview=Part%204-%20Transcript%20%28ENGLISH%3ASPANISH%29.docx.

152. *See* Laci & Connor's Law, H.R. Rep. No. 108-420, at 1 (2004), codified at 18 U.S.C. §§ 1841 *et seq.*

153. *See* IF/WHEN/HOW, *Roe's Unfinished Promise, supra* note 2, at 15, citing Utah Code § 76-5-201(3)(b) & (4)(b).

154. *See* Molly Redden, *Purvi Patel Has 20-Year Sentence for Inducing Own Abortion Reduced*, THE GUARDIAN (July 22, 2016, 2:59 PM), https://www.theguardian.com/us-news/2016 /jul/22/purvi-patel-abortion-sentence-reduced.

same year, similar charges were brought against Purvi Patel, who was sentenced to 20 years in prison under Indiana's feticide statute.[155] Although her sentence was eventually reduced on appeal, Patel still had to serve 18 months of time on a child neglect charge.[156] In both the *Jones* and *Patel* cases, the court found that the fetal harm laws did not contemplate, and were not applicable to, pregnant people performing their own abortions. However, what Purvi Patel's case demonstrates is that fetal personhood laws, and the increasingly common perception among judges that fetuses are children, will be manipulated to criminalize those who self-manage.

Even when charges are dropped, the investigation and court proceedings themselves can be long and arduous and leave long-lasting trauma both for the individual charged and for their families and communities. Even misdemeanor charges can cause a person to lose their job. This is particularly true in the care sector, where people providing childcare and home medical assistance are often terminated because of any criminal charge, or simply for missing work to attend a court date.[157] In many states, record searches used by employers will show an arrest and what the arrest was for, even if the person was never formally charged.[158] There is often no way to get this mark off one's record.[159] Simply because a person was not sentenced to prison does not mean that serious harm was not done.

In addition to SMA bans, fetal harm laws, and criminal abortion laws, there is a category that Farah Diaz-Tello, senior counsel at If/When/How, describes as "the last category of literally anything else" in her interview on the podcast, *Self-Managed: An Abortion Story*. She says that while "common themes include very antiquated laws around concealment of a birth, sometimes improper disposal of human remains, there are no clear categories when it comes to prosecutions."[160] Prosecutors will get "creative" when they want to press charges against someone who self-managed. Anne Bynum, for

---

155. *See* Ava B., *When Miscarriage Is a Crime*, PLANNED PARENTHOOD ADVOCATES OF ARIZONA (July 29, 2019, 12:00 PM), https://www.plannedparenthoodaction.org /planned-parenthood-advocates-arizona/blog/when-miscarriage-is-a-crime.

156. *Id.*

157. *See* IF/WHEN/HOW, *Making Abortion a Crime (Again): How Extreme Prosecutors Attempt to Punish People for Abortions in the U.S.*, IF/WHEN/HOW at 1, https://www.ifwhenhow.org /resources/making-abortion-a-crime-again/ (last accessed Mar. 8, 2021) [hereinafter IF/ WHEN/HOW, *Making Abortion a Crime Again*].

158. *See id.*

159. *See id.*

160. *See Criminalizing Pregnant People, supra* note 151.

example, was charged by an Arkansas prosecutor for "concealing and abuse of a corpse" after she took misoprostol to end her own pregnancy.[161] Such laws, like criminal abortion laws, can easily be misapplied to any pregnant person who experiences a miscarriage, stillbirth, or a self-managed abortion.

3. Criminalizing SMA Endangers All Pregnant People

There was no medical evidence that Purvi Patel had taken abortion pills.[162] In fact, there *is* no medical test that can scientifically distinguish a self-managed abortion from a spontaneous miscarriage.[163] Therefore, the criminalization of SMA inevitably invites the criminalization of other obstetric emergencies such as stillbirth and miscarriage. This reality has played out in countries where SMA is subject to complete criminal prohibition. In Ecuador, for example, where SMA is illegal, prosecutors have reportedly investigated over 378 obstetric emergencies since 2015 under the suspicion that that the person had attempted to self-manage.[164] Health clinics have reported individuals seeking relief for miscarriages to Ecuadorian authorities, and, in some cases, patients have been interrogated in their hospital rooms and placed in detention immediately upon medical release.[165]

Unfortunately, there is every reason to fear the possibility of a similar regime in the United States, because these forms of criminalization have already begun. The majority of people who have been criminalized for self-managing were reported when they sought medical care.[166] This is true in

---

161. *See* New York Times Editorial Board, *How My Stillbirth Became a Crime*, N.Y. Times (Dec. 28, 2018), https://www.nytimes.com/interactive/2018/12/28/opinion/stillborn-murder-charge.html.

162. *See* Christina Cauterucci, *Court Vacates Purvi Patel's Feticide Conviction, Landing a Blow Against "Personhood Laws,"* Slate (July 22, 2016, 4:58 PM), https://slate.com/human-interest/2016/07/court-vacates-purvi-patels-feticide-conviction-in-blow-against-personhood-laws.html.

163. *See* Andrew Moscrop, *"Miscarriage or Abortion?" Understanding the Medical Language of Pregnancy Loss in Britain; a Historical Perspective*, 39 Med. Humanities 98, 98 (2013).

164. *See* Zoe Carpenter, *Ecuador's Crackdown on Abortion Is Putting Women in Jail*, The Nation (May 7, 2019), https://www.thenation.com/article/ecuador-abortion-miscarriage-prosecution/; *see also* Human Rights Watch Staff, *Ecuador: Adopt UN Recommendations on Abortion Law*, Human Rights Watch (Apr. 22, 2015, 12:00 AM), https://www.hrw.org/news/2015/04/22/ecuador-adopt-un-recommendations-abortion-law.

165. *Id.*

166. *See* If/When/How, *Making Abortion a Crime Again*, *supra* note 157, at 3.

spite of the fact that providers are under no legal obligation to report people who self-manage.[167] To the contrary, providers have a legal responsibility to keep their patient's medical information private, unless they have reason to believe that the patient is a safety threat to themselves or others.[168] Moreover, medical authorities have explicitly condemned the practice of reporting people suspected of SMA.[169] Not only does it deter patients from seeking (sometimes life-saving) obstetric care, it "violate[s] long-established principles of patient privacy, and endanger[s] the foundation of trust patient-provider relationships are built upon."[170] Although providers are under legal and ethical obligations to protect their patients' privacy, that unfortunately does not stop some providers from acting in clear disregard of those responsibilities.

In 2016, Katherine Dellis gave birth to a stillborn baby in her home.[171] When she went to seek medical care, her doctor found that the fetus had died several weeks earlier in utero.[172] Instead of treating her with the

---

167. *See* IF/WHEN/HOW, *Self-Managed Abortion, the Law, and COVID-19 Factsheet, supra* note 141; *see also* Am. Coll. of Obstetricians & Gynecologists, *Joint Statement on Abortion Access during the COVID-19 Outbreak*, AM. COLL. OF OBSTETS. & GYNECOL. (Mar. 18, 2020), https://www.acog.org/news/news-releases/2020/03/joint-statement-on-abortion-access -during-the-covid-19-outbreak.

168. *See, e.g.,* Am. Coll. of Obstetricians & Gynecologists, *Criminalization of Self-Induced Abortion Intimidates and Shames Women Unnecessarily*, AM. COLL. OF OBSTET. & GYNECOL. (Jan. 3, 2018), https://www.acog.org/news/news-releases/2018/01/criminalization-of-self -induced-abortion-intimidates-and-shames-women-unnecessarily; Am. Coll. Of Obstetricians & Gynecologists, *Decriminalization of Self-Induced Abortion: Position Statement*, ACOG (Dec. 2017), https://www.acog.org/clinical-information/policy-and-position-statements/position -statements/2017/decriminalization-of-self-induced-abortion; Am. Coll. of Obstetricians and Gynecologists, *Substance Abuse Reporting and Pregnancy: The Role of the Obstetrician-Gynecologist*, ACOG Practice Bulletin 473, 117 OBSTET. & GYNECOL. 200, 201 (2011).

169. *See* Am. Coll. of Obstetricians and Gynecologists, *Criminalization of Self-Induced Abortion Intimidates and Shames Women Unnecessarily, supra* note 168.

170. *See* Am. Coll. of Obstetricians and Gynecologists, *Decriminalization of Self-Induced Abortion: Position Statement, supra* note 168.

171. *See* Christina Cauterucci, *Virginia Woman Given a Jail Sentence for "Concealing a Dead Body" After Her Stillbirth*, SLATE (May 10, 2018, 5:17 PM), https://slate.com/news-and-poli tics/2018/05/virginia-woman-given-a-jail-sentence-for-concealing-a-dead-body-after-her-still birth.html.

172. Justin Jouvenal, *After Disposing of the Remains of Her Stillborn Child, She Was Charged with a Crime*, WASHINGTON POST (May 8, 2018, 4:03 PM), https://www.washingtonpost.com /local/public-safety/after-disposing-of-the-remains-of-her-stillborn-child-she-was-charged -with-a-crime/2018/05/08/905d173e-5217-11e8-abd8-265bd07a9859_story.html.

dignity and tenderness that one might expect from a medical professional who was trained to care for people who had experienced pregnancy loss, he reported Dellis to the police.[173] She was sentenced to five months in prison for concealing a dead body.[174] Dellis is not alone—people have been arrested after falling down the stairs while pregnant,[175] being in a car accident while pregnant,[176] and even being shot in the stomach while pregnant.[177]

Black, Latinx, and Native American people are not only more likely to be targeted for their obstetric emergencies because of systemic racism in policing and state surveillance structures, they also have higher rates of miscarriage and stillbirth than non-Hispanic white women.[178] This disparity is due to a number of reasons, including the fact that (1) people of color tend to have less access to prenatal care,[179] (2) racial bias on the part of providers can lead to inaccurate or untimely diagnoses,[180] and (3) "weathering," the biological effects of cumulative exposure to racism throughout a lifetime

---

173. *See* Cauterucci, *supra* note 171.

174. *See* Jouvenal, *supra* note 172.

175. Christine Taylor was a 22-year-old mother of two who was wrongfully charged with "attempted feticide" after falling down the stairs of her home. *See* Amie Newman, *Help for Christine Taylor: Victim of Iowa's Feticide Law*, REWIRE (Feb. 25, 2020, 1:50 PM), https://rewire newsgroup.com/article/2010/02/25/help-christine-taylor-victim-iowas-feticide/.

176. Jennifer Jorgensen was in a car accident and was charged with second degree manslaughter when her baby died from injuries sustained in the crash six days after the accident. *See* Eugene Volokh, *Woman, 8 Months Pregnant, Drives Recklessly, Crashes; Baby is Born but Dies of Injuries Caused by Crash—Manslaughter?* WASHINGTON POST (Oct. 23, 2015, 1:45 PM), https://www.washingtonpost.com/news/volokh-conspiracy/wp/2015/10/23/woman -8-months-pregnant-drives-recklessly-crashes-baby-is-born-but-dies-of-injuries-caused-by -crash-manslaughter/.

177. Marshae Jones was charged for manslaughter when she miscarried after being shot in the stomach. *See* Michael Brice-Saddler & Alex Horton, *A Pregnant Alabama Woman Who Was Shot in the Stomach Was Charged in Her Baby's Death*, PHILADELPHIA INQUIRER (June 27, 2019), https://www.inquirer.com/news/nation-world/alabama-woman-shooting-death-unborn -child-manslaughter-20190628.html.

178. *See* Ctr. For Disease Control & Prevention, *Stillbirth*, CTR. FOR DISEASE CONTROL & PREVENTION (Aug. 13, 2020), https://www.cdc.gov/ncbddd/stillbirth/data.html.

179. *See* Shannon M. Pruitt et al., *Racial and Ethnic Disparities in Fetal Deaths—United States, 2015–2017*, 69 CTR. FOR DISEASE CONTROL & PREVENTION: MORBIDITY & MORTALITY WEEKLY REPORT 1277, 1280 (2020), https://www.cdc.gov/mmwr/volumes/69/wr/mm6937a1.htm.

180. *See* Swapna Venugopal Ramaswamy, *Without "An Ounce of Empathy:" Their Stories Show the Dangers of Being Black and Pregnant*, LOHUD (Sept. 9, 2020, 1:55 PM), https://www.lohud.com/in-depth/news/2020/09/08/as-black-woman-when-youre -pregnant-your-own-advocate/5442487002/; *see also* Am. Heart. Ass'n News Staff, *Why Are Black Women at Such High Risk of Dying from Pregnancy Complications*, AM. HEART ASS'N (Feb. 20, 2019), https://www.heart.org/en/news/2019/02/20/why-are-black-women-at-such-high -risk-of-dying-from-pregnancy-complications.

that medical experts have linked to negative birth outcomes.[181] Criminalization of SMA thus poses a threat to all pregnant people—and pregnant people of color in particular—regardless of whether they want to carry to term or not.

4. Criminalizing SMA Endangers Providers and Other Support People

Self-managed does not have to mean alone. These are the words of Antonia Piccone, one of the executive producers of *Self-Managed: An Abortion Story.* She is right. For as long as people have had abortions, there have been people supporting them. Today, there is a vibrant, global network of advocates, midwives, doulas, abortion funds, online abortion pill providers, and activists working to help people navigate SMA. They, too, are harmed by the criminalization of SMA. This section will explain some of the ways in which people take on legal risk when they assist people in self-managing abortions.

a. Counseling Someone about SMA

The First Amendment provides robust protections for freedom of speech that encompass speech about SMA.[182] Advocates, doulas, providers, and other support people are therefore protected when they decide to share information about self-managed abortion. However, there is a difference between sharing information about SMA (protected speech) and giving someone individualized legal or medical advice about their particular case.[183] The law does prohibit the practice of law and medicine without a license (described earlier in the chapter). Offering legal advice or recommending a course of treatment could be considered a violation of these laws.

b. Helping Someone Procure Abortion Pills

Even though abortion pills are safer than Tylenol,[184] providing them to someone entails some real legal risks. Thirty-nine states require that

---

181. *See* Kyle Simone Nisbeth, *State of Maternal Mortality: The Inequitable Burden on Black Mothers,* Univ. Mich. Sch. of Pub. Health (Feb. 28, 2020), https://sph.umich.edu/pursuit/2020posts/state-of-maternal-mortality-the-inequitable-burden-on-black-mothers.html.

182. *See* If/When/How, *Self-Managed Abortion, the Law, and COVID-19 Factsheet, supra* note 141.

183. *See id.*

184. *See* Farah Diaz-Tello, *The Law Protected Marshae Jones; Her Prosecutor Didn't,* If/When/How (Aug. 15, 2019), https://www.ifwhenhow.org/the-law-protected-marshae-jones-her-prosecutor-didnt/.

abortions be performed by a licensed physician, 18 states require an abortion to be performed in a hospital after a specified point in the pregnancy, and 18 states require the involvement of a second physician after a specified point.[185] These laws have not only been used against people who have self-managed[186] but have been used against those who have helped them procure pills. Parents have been arrested for practicing medicine without a license when purchasing pills for their children, for example.[187] These cases further illustrate the harm caused by the FDA's REMS restrictions, as well as TRAP laws that place additional requirements on abortion providers more generally.

5. Prosecutors Cannot Prosecute if the Law Forbids It

The final key principle that is important to stress here is that, while prosecutorial overreach is behind many of the prosecutions of SMA, and many other instances of reproductive oppression for that matter, a prosecutor may not press charges where the law forbids it. In her article, *The Law Protected Marshae Jones; Her Prosecutor Didn't*, Farah Diaz-Tello cautions against exaggerating the power of prosecutors to misapply, or refuse to apply, ill-fitting laws to SMA cases.[188] A primary feature of the cases where charges have been dropped against people who have self-managed is the realization that the law explicitly forbids a given statute from applying to pregnant people.

This was true in the case of Marshae Jones, for example. She was indicted by an Alabama grand jury on manslaughter charges when she lost her five-month-old fetus after being shot.[189] The person who shot Jones, whom the police claimed was acting in self-defense, was never charged for the harm he caused to Jones or her fetus.[190] Jones, however, was charged with being in a fight while pregnant and faced up to 20 years in prison for the alleged murder of her unborn child.[191] One week after her indictment, the charges were dropped because the fetal harm statute under which the

---

185. *See* IF/WHEN/HOW, *Regulation of Pregnancy: Issue Brief*, IF/WHEN/HOW, at 6 (2017), https://www.ifwhenhow.org/resources/regulation-of-pregnant-women/.

186. McCormack v. Hiedeman, 694 F.3d 1004, 1012 (9th Cir. 2012).

187. *See* Emily Bazelon, *A Mother in Jail for Helping Her Daughter Have an Abortion*, N.Y. TIMES (Sept. 22, 2014), https://www.nytimes.com/2014/09/22/magazine/a-mother-in-jail -for-helping-her-daughter-have-an-abortion.html.

188. *See* Diaz-Tello, *supra* note 184.

189. Sarah Mervosh, *Alabama Woman Who Was Shot While Pregnant Is Charged In Fetus' Death*, N.Y. TIMES (June 27, 2019), https://www.nytimes.com/2019/06/27/us/pregnant-woman -shot-marshae-jones.html.

190. *See id.*

191. *See id.*

jury indicted her explicitly excluded acts by "any woman with respect to her unborn child" from its purview.[192] It did not matter how hostile her state (Alabama), her jury, and her prosecutor were to abortion. At the end of the day, since the law prevented her from being prosecuted under the relevant statute, the case could not proceed. Jones' case illustrates Diaz-Tello's point. While prosecutorial overreach in the criminalization of SMA is an important factor, it is inaccurate (and dangerous) to conflate that with the belief that a prosecutor may bring charges where the law prohibits it. The following section addresses some of the ways in which organizers, advocates, and lawyers have been working to prevent the misuse and misapplication of the law to pregnant people who are criminalized for their pregnancy losses (wanted and unwanted).

III. SMA during the Pandemic and Beyond

The law matters. When people have been prosecuted for SMA under ill-fitting provisions, state authorities have, more often than not, dropped the charges because the law could not be reasonably read to apply. For this reason, repealing antiquated laws that could get misapplied in the SMA context is a promising strategy to reduce the criminalization of pregnant people. This section will review some of the advocacy efforts to increase legal access to SMA and anticipate what we may be able to expect in a post-pandemic (and, possibly, a post-*Roe*) world.

A. Pre-Pandemic Success Stories: A Multi-Pronged Approach

Before examining legislative strategies that have focused on decriminalizing SMA, one must understand how they relate to broader movement-building efforts to reduce state violence and over-criminalization. Because criminalizing abortion and pregnancy loss is often driven by similar racist and classist animus that motivates over-policing and hyper-surveillance generally, efforts to advance racial and immigrant justice have also advanced reproductive justice for those who self-manage.

---

192. *See* Diaz-Tello, *supra* note 184.

1. Legislative Initiatives to Decriminalize SMA

This section will provide an overview of some of the more targeted initiatives that have improved legal protections for pregnant people and close dangerous loopholes that were vulnerable to prosecutorial misuse. I will group these efforts into three categories: initiatives to (1) repeal antiquated laws, (2) reinforce protections for pregnant people and their right to autonomous decision making, and (3) authorize and legalize a wider range of abortion providers.

a. Repealing Antiquated Laws

Advocates have been working to expand access to abortion pills through a series of efforts to decriminalize them at the state level. The Massachusetts N.A.S.T.Y. Women's Act (Negating Antiquated Statutes Targeting Young Women Act), for example, is an inspiring piece of state legislation that repealed outmoded and ill-fitting statutes so that they could not be misapplied to people who self-manage (or those who assist them).[193]

Nevada and New York also took steps in 2019 to prevent antiquated laws from being applied to those who self-manage.[194] Prior to 2019, New York and Nevada were two of the few states that had SMA bans on the books.[195] New York also had several provisions criminalizing people who perform abortions after 24 weeks' gestation.[196] In 2011, New York's SMA law was applied to someone who drank an herbal tea in an attempt to induce an abortion.[197] In response, advocates began work to pass the Reproductive Health Act,[198] which would repeal all provisions criminalizing both the people who have abortions and those who provide them in New York state, removing abortion from the Penal Law entirely.[199] That legislation passed

---

193. *See* Negating Archaic Statutes Targeting Young Women Act, S. 784, 190th Gen. Ct. (Mass. 2017).

194. *See* Elizabeth Nash et al., *State Policy Trends 2019: A Wave of Abortion Bans, But Some States Are Fighting Back*, GUTTMACHER INST. (Dec. 10, 2019), https://www.guttmacher.org/article/2019/12/state-policy-trends-2019-wave-abortion-bans-some-states-are-fighting-back.

195. *See* IF/WHEN/HOW, *Roe's Unfinished Promise, supra* note 2, at 12.

196. *See* IF/WHEN/HOW, *Fulfilling Roe's Promise: 2019 Update, supra* note 2, at 2.

197. *See* Amanda Marcotte, *Herbal Remedies Unlikely to Terminate 24-Week Pregnancies*, SLATE (Dec. 21, 2011, 3:19 PM), https://slate.com/human-interest/2011/12/a-woman-is-charged-with-self-abortion-for-drinking-herbal-tea-at-24-weeks.html.

198. *See* ACLU of New York Staff, *What You Need to Know About the Reproductive Health Act*, N.Y. CIVIL LIBERTIES UNION (Jan. 23, 2019), https://www.nyclu.org/en/legislation/legislative-memo-reproductive-health-act.

199. *See id.*

in 2019, ensuring that abortion would no longer be treated like a crime in the state of New York.[200]

In Nevada, advocates worked to pass Senate Bill 179, otherwise known as the Trust Women Act, which repealed the prohibition on SMA and several other provisions that were not evidence based and perpetuated paternalism in abortion consultations.[201] Those repealed provisions included a requirement that physicians inform patients of the "emotional implications" of an abortion, and the requirement that physicians inquire about the marital status of the abortion seeker.[202] Efforts like those in Massachusetts, Nevada, and New York make it significantly harder to prosecute pregnant people under ill-fitting or outdated laws.

b. New Protections for Autonomous Decision Making in Pregnancy
In addition to advocacy that aims to repeal antiquated and harmful criminal provisions, certain states like Vermont[203] and Illinois[204] have taken steps to increase the protections that pregnant people have when it comes to their rights to bodily autonomy and self-sovereignty. Illinois' Reproductive Health Act, for example, spells out that pregnant people not only have a fundamental right to terminate a pregnancy, but to "make autonomous decisions about how to exercise that right."[205] It also defines abortion as "the use of any instrument, medicine, drug, or any other substance or device to terminate [a] pregnancy."[206] These clarifications matter. They ensure that people who self-manage are entitled to the same fundamental right to autonomous decision making as any other pregnant person.

---

200. *See* Jia Tolentino, *How Abortion Law in New York Will Change, and How It Won't*, NEW YORKER (Jan. 19, 2019), https://www.newyorker.com/news/news-desk/how-abortion-law-in-new-york-will-change-and-how-it-wont.

201. *See* Caroline Kelly, *Nevada Passes Bill to No Longer Require Doctors to Tell Women the 'Emotional Implications' of an Abortion*, CNN (May 22, 2019, 1:00 AM), https://www.cnn.com/2019/05/22/politics/nevada-bill-emotional-implications-abortion/index.html.

202. *See* Trust Women Act of 2019, SB-179, 6300, 80th Sess. (2019).

203. Passed on June 10, 2019, Vermont's Freedom of Choice Act declared a person's ability to make autonomous choices surrounding pregnancy and abortion "fundamental." *See* Elizabeth Nash, Lizamarie Mohammed & Olivia Cappello, *Illinois Steps Up as Other States Decimate Abortion Rights*, GUTTMACHER INST. (June 5, 2019), https://www.guttmacher.org/article/2019/06/illinois-steps-other-states-decimate-abortion-rights.

204. *See id.*

205. *See* Ill. Reprod. Health Act, 775 I.L.C.S. 55/1-15, at 1 (West 2019).

206. *Id.* at 2.

c. Widening the Spectrum of Authorized Abortion Providers

In order to ensure everyone has access to "pregnancy-related care that meets their needs, supports their health, and respects their dignity," it is not enough to simply ensure people do not go to jail for their abortions.[207] People must also have the practical support to have the abortion experience that feels right for them. Advocacy should be, and has been, carried out at the state level to ensure the legal safety of midwives, health providers, doulas, and other healers who offer SMA support. California and Maine passed legislation in 2013 and 2019, respectively, authorizing nurse-practitioners, certified nurse-midwives, and physicians' assistants to provide abortion care (including medical abortions) in the first trimester.[208] They are now two of the sixteen American states where nurse practitioners, certified nurse midwives, and physician assistants are authorized to provide medication abortions.[209] When these laws are paired with telemedical abortion support provisions, they have enormous potential to expand legal access to telemedical abortion, which could have the positive consequence of destigmatizing, and decriminalizing, SMA because people will understand the safety and value of no-touch abortions. Only 13 states are currently offering telemedical abortion care.[210] But that number may grow as a result of the temporary suspension of the in-person requirement, and the fact that in January 2021 a new, pro-choice administration was ushered in.

2. Democratizing Access to SMA Information

Although legal reform is a crucial component of the fight to decriminalize SMA, expanding access to accurate information about abortion pills is

---

207. *See* If/When/How, *Roe's Unfinished Promise, supra* note 2, at 1.

208. *See* Elizabeth Nash, *Ensuring Access to Abortion at the State Level: Selected Examples and Lessons*, 22 Guttmacher Pol'y Rev. 1, 5 (2019), https://www.guttmacher.org/gpr/2019/01/ensuring-access-abortion-state-level-selected-examples-and-lessons (discussing California's AB-154, which expanded the pool of providers who can perform abortions); *see also* Jacey Fortin, *Maine Abortion Law Lets Nurse Practitioners and Others Perform Procedure*, N.Y. Times (June 10, 2019), https://www.nytimes.com/2019/06/10/us/maine-abortion-bill.html (discussing the passage of Maine's Act To Authorize Certain Health Care Professionals To Perform Abortions, L.D. 1261, 129th Leg. Sess. (Me. 2019)).

209. *See* Abortion Provider Toolkit Staff, *State Abortion Laws and their Relationship to Scope of Practice*, Abortion Provider Toolkit (last accessed Apr. 14, 2021), https://aptoolkit.org/advancing-scope-of-practice-to-include-abortion-care/state-abortion-laws-and-their-relationship-to-scope-of-practice/.

210. These include Colorado, Georgia, Hawaii, Illinois, Iowa, Maine, Maryland and DC, Minnesota, Montana, New Mexico, New York, Oregon, and Washington. *See* Gynuity Health Projects Staff, *Telabortion Study: Project States*, Gynuity Health Projects, https://telabortion.org/get-started (last accessed Nov. 6, 2020).

equally important. As information about SMA becomes more widely available and accessible, the practice becomes normalized and destigmatized. Increasingly, people's associations with SMA will move them away from dangerous practices that they can more readily understand being prohibiting (such as inserting sharp objects into the uterus), and toward a shared view that SMA can be a safe and socially accepted practice. This generates support for, and momentum behind, legislative activism like that which has just been described.

In addition to driving cultural change in the perception of SMA, expanding access to information about abortion pills renders the FDA's restrictions on them increasingly less tenable. The FDA's standard for approving new medications evaluates the "safety for its indicated use and *substantial evidence of efficacy.*"[211] The more evidence there is about the efficacy and safety of abortion pills, the harder it becomes to justify REMS restrictions on mifepristone. This argument was recently made by the former FDA Commissioner, Dr. Jane Henney, who called on the agency to re-evaluate its REMS restrictions on mifepristone in light of the number of recent studies demonstrating its safety and effectiveness.[212]

Finally, efforts to democratize information about SMA advance not only the legal battle for SMA access but the actual availability of the drugs themselves. One cannot access the pills if one does not know they exist. Work to spread information about abortion pills must be creatively and widely disseminated so that it is equally accessible to all who need it. Many groups have used a creative and interdisciplinary approach for disseminating information about abortion and abortion pills. We Testify, the Illinois Caucus for Adolescent Health's For Youth Inquiry (FYI) performance company, Advocates for Youth's Abortion Out Loud campaign, Women Help Women, The Abortion Diary, The Stigma Toolkit, Voices of Courage, My Abortion, My Life, Self-Managed: An Abortion Podcast, and others, have mobilized art-making and storytelling in their work to advance abortion access. Rather than limiting SMA information to more traditional learning platforms, these groups have incorporated visual and auditory initiatives, available both online and in print, in multilingual and nonverbal formats that can be self-taught and facilitator led. Activists have also worked to ensure that

---

211. *See* 21 U.S.C. § 355(d) (1994) (setting efficacy standards); *see also* 21 C.F.R. §§ 312.20–212.130 (1999); Sarah Ricks, *The New French Abortion Pill: The Moral Property of Women*, 75 YALE J. LAW & FEMINISM 75, 77 (1989).

212. *See* Jane E. Henney & Helene D. Gayle, *Time to Reevaluate U.S. Mifepristone Restrictions*, 381 N. ENGL. J. MED. 597, 597 (2019). *See also* Grossman, *supra* note 97 (arguing that REMS restrictions prevent providers from assisting people in obtaining early abortions).

SMA information exists in a wide variety of different platforms (online and in-person workshops, online op-eds and articles, academic research, film, television, radio, etc.). By adopting a multidisciplinary and multi-platform approach for disseminating information about SMA, we can democratize information about the pills and progressively decriminalize them.

3. Destigmatizing SMA

For meaningful legal access to SMA to be realized, abortion itself must be destigmatized. Otherwise, efforts to decriminalize SMA will be hindered by a lack of public support for people who have had abortions, or who are perceived to have contributed to their obstetric emergencies. Story sharing is a widely used and powerful method of communication to change hearts and minds about abortion. Renee Bracey Sherman, founder and executive director of We Testify, describes storytelling as "a way in which people who have had abortions can talk about the nuances of their decision-making with those who have not had abortions, in hope of finding common ground, creating understanding, and building compassion around abortion experiences."[213]

Initiatives to decriminalize SMA should create platforms to lift up the stories of those who have experienced it. In particular, movement stakeholders must ensure that the voices and interests of those who are most likely to be impacted by the criminalization of abortion are centered in their work. Until the stories and needs of people of color, low-income people, undocumented immigrants, LGBTQQIA+ people, and minors are at the core of work to destigmatize SMA, the movement risks leaving them behind. It also places unnecessary limitations on how "much" justice can be achieved. If SMA is rendered legal, accessible, and affirming for those facing the greatest number of structural obstacles, it will be legal, accessible, and affirming to everyone facing fewer obstacles.

B. Pandemic-era Success Stories

The COVID-19 pandemic has shed new light on the racism that pervades our carceral and health care systems. It has also inspired a global reckoning with the role of the provider and with power imbalances in reproductive

---

213. *See* Renee Bracey-Sherman, *Saying Abortion Aloud: Research and Recommendations for Public Abortion Storytellers and Organizations*, SEA CHANGE, at 2 (May 2015), https://www.reneebraceysherman.com/wp-content/uploads/2015/05/Saying-Abortion-Aloud-Executive-Summary.pdf.

health care—in particular power imbalances that are rooted in white supremacy. It is in this context of abolition politics and community resistance that we must locate the future of SMA. There is ample reason to believe that pandemic-era organizing will have long-lasting effects on the availability, and the geography, of abortion care. This section will provide a brief overview of some of the legislative and legal decisions that have arisen in the pandemic context that reflect support for the idea that in-person requirements are unreasonable for abortion pills.

1. New Awareness about Obstacles to Clinical Care

Requiring people to attend a clinic during the pandemic is an undue burden and should be deemed unconstitutional under current abortion law principles. Recent legislative and legal decisions reflect support for this idea. On July 13, 2020, United States District Judge Chuang in Maryland preliminarily enjoined the FDA's in-person requirement, finding that "the In-Person Requirements, combined with the COVID-19 pandemic, place a substantial obstacle in the path of women seeking a medication abortion and that may delay or preclude a medication abortion and thus may necessitate a more invasive procedure. Particularly in light of the limited time-frame during which a medication abortion or any abortion must occur, such infringement on the right to an abortion would constitute irreparable harm."[214] The Trump administration then applied to the Supreme Court for a stay of Judge Chuang's injunction. Although initially denying the application, the Supreme Court stated that "a more comprehensive record would aid this court's review" and remanded the case to the trial judge to take a fresh look at the current facts and to rule again.[215] The disputed requirement remained suspended in the interim,[216] and Judge Chuang denied the

---

214. Am. Coll. of Obstetricians & Gynecologists v. U.S. Food & Drug Admin., 472 F. Supp. 3d 183, 227 (D. Md. 2020).

215. The Supreme Court ordered the district court, on remand, to rule within 40 days of receiving "a motion by the Government to dissolve, modify, or stay the injunction, including on the ground that relevant circumstances have changed." *See* Food and Drug Admin et al. v. Am. Coll. Of Obstetricians and Gynecologists, No. 20A34 slip op. at 1 (U.S. Oct. 8, 2020), https://www.supremecourt.gov/opinions/20pdf/20a34_nmjp.pdf. On October 30, 2020, the government filed a second motion requesting that Judge Chuang stay or dissolve the injunction, meaning that the lower court had until December 10 to reach its decision. *See* Mot. to Stay, Am. Coll. Of Obstetricians & Gynecologists v. U.S. Food & Drug Admin, No. 8:20-cv-01320-TDC (D. Md.).

216. *See Food and Drug Admin et al.*, No. 20A34 slip op. at 1.

government's renewed motion for a stay on December 9, 2020.[217] That triggered the Supreme Court's review of the district court's latest order, and this time the Court granted the Trump administration's request for a stay.[218] Notably, the Court's stay order was extremely perfunctory and provided no analysis of the issues, legal or factual.[219] That leaves the case on the merits before the Fourth Circuit Court of Appeals. Whether there will ever be a further ruling on the merits before the case becomes moot is an open question.[220]

While the original injunction in the FDA case is a positive step, it is clearly neither a sufficient nor sustainable measure to ensure long-lasting decriminalization of non-clinical abortions. It is also proof that efforts to shift American cultural perceptions of abortion and no-touch abortion are working. Judge Chuang used a reproductive justice framework in his evaluation of abortion access. He cited directly to Monica Simpson, the Executive Director of Sister Song—the largest national reproductive justice collective—in an opinion that demonstrates a nuanced and cumulative understanding of obstacles to abortion care.[221] This understanding was made possible by years of storytelling campaigns and reproductive justice organizing that have elucidated the intersectional and interwoven structures that limit access to abortion care. The following excerpt from Judge Chuang's order reveals the power, and the increasing acceptance, of this approach:

> Even if healthcare facilities are open, abortion patients face particular challenges in traveling to them for in-person appointments during the pandemic, many of which arise because 60 percent of women obtaining abortion care are people of color and 75 percent are poor or low-income. [. . .] The health risks from exposure are particularly amplified in communities of color, where individuals are suffering higher rates of serious illness and death from COVID-19. One study has shown that African Americans have three and a half times the risk of death as whites. These same communities are also more likely to be working in essential jobs that require inter-

---

217. Am. Coll. of Obstetricians & Gynecologists v. U.S. Food & Drug Admin., No.8:20-cv-01320-TDC, 2020 WL 7240396 (D. Md. Dec. 9, 2020).

218. Food & Drug Admin. v. Am. Coll. of Obstetricians & Gynecologists, No. 20A34, 2021 WL 99362 (U.S. Jan. 12, 2021).

219. *Id.*

220. Oral argument in the Fourth Circuit was scheduled for May 2021. Am. Coll. of Obstetricians & Gynecologists v. FDA, No. 20-1784, Dkt.Entry 64 (4th Cir. Feb. 26, 2021). Whether the new administration will continue the appeal is an initial question, but even if it does, whether the case would remain an ongoing controversy, rather than become moot, may mean there will not be another decision on the merits beyond Judge Chuang's.

221. *Am. Coll. of Obstetricians & Gynecologists*, 472 F. Supp. 3d at 196.

action with the public and to live in crowded or multigenerational housing in which the risk of viral spread, and the risk to more vulnerable elderly relatives, is increased.[222]

This cumulative approach to understanding the undue burden standard first arose in *Whole Women's Health v. Hellerstedt*[223] and resurfaced in *June Medical v. Russo*.[224] Increasingly, courts—even the Supreme Court—are not atomizing abortion restrictions, but rather, reading them in conversation with broader systems of reproductive oppression. This is a clear sign of progress that may very well be sustained after the pandemic comes under control.

2. Global Coalitions for Abortion Access

Even if more states use the pandemic as an excuse to pass additional abortion restrictions, there is reason to believe that these efforts will be ineffective in cutting off access to SMA. This is because of a growing global consensus that SMA is safe and ought to be widely accessible. France, the UK, Sweden, and several other countries not only legalized no-touch abortion but moved their early abortion services entirely online during the pandemic.[225] The UK's Pills by Post Program, for example, allows patients to simply request a telemedical appointment and then abortion pills are shipped directly to them from their providers.[226] In France, the legalization of telemedical abortion care has been accompanied by measures that authorize a wider range of health care providers than ever before to prescribe abortion pills so that a person wanting to self-manage can call their family doctor or a midwife to procure the pills if that is preferable to

---

222. *Id.*

223. *See* Marlow Svatek, *Seeing the Forest for the Trees: Why Courts Should Consider Cumulative Effects in the Undue Burden Analysis*, IF/WHEN/HOW (Dec. 14, 2016), https://www.ifwhenhow.org/seeing-the-forest-for-the-trees-why-courts-should-consider-cumulative-effects-in-the-undue-burden-analysis/.

224. *See* June Medical Services L.L.C. v. Russo Interim Secretary, Louisiana Dep't of Health and Hospitals, No. 18-1323 slip op. at 1 (U.S. June 29, 2020); *see also* Rachel Rebouche, *Abortion Restrictions After June Medical Services*, REGULATORY REV. (Aug. 4, 2020), https://www.the regreview.org/2020/08/04/rebouche-abortion-restrictions-june-medical/.

225. *See* European Parliamentary Forum for Sexual and Reproductive Rights & International Planned Parenthood Fund, *Sexual and Reproductive Health and Rights During the COVID-19 Pandemic: A Joint Report*, INT'L PLANNED PARENTHOOD FED'N 1, 7 (Apr. 22, 2020), https://www.ippfen.org/sites/ippfen/files/2020-04/Sexual%20and%20Reproductive%20Health%20during%20the%20COVID-19%20pandemic.pdf.

226. *See* British Pregnancy Advisory Serv. Staff, *Pills by Post: Abortion Pill Treatment at Home*, BRITISH PREGNANCY ADVISORY SERV. (Mar. 2020), https://www.bpas.org/abortion-care/abortion-treatments/the-abortion-pill/remote-treatment/.

talking to an OBGYN.[227] The following section will explore the potential of these networks to serve people living in countries where abortion is heavily restricted (like the United States), and seriously reduce the potency of abortion restrictions as a tool for cutting off access to care.

C. SMA in a Post-Pandemic (and Possibly Post-*Roe*) America

Although efforts to restrict abortion in the United States will likely continue, and those efforts will deter people from pursuing SMA because of the reasons just discussed, the increasing availability of abortion pills and telemedical abortion care abroad does make SMA an option for people even in places where it is heavily criminalized. Moreover, widespread international access to telemedical abortion could lead countries to liberalize access to abortion generally.

Texas was the most heavily restricted state when it came to abortion access during the pandemic.[228] Not only did the state enact the longest-lasting abortion ban, but even without the ban, the average Texan resident must travel far to get care when the state's six clinics *are* up and running.[229] However, thanks to grassroots networks that assist people through SMA, many Texan residents were able to get the care they needed. In fact, they were able to get care in record numbers.[230] More Texans received abortion pills during the period when abortion was banned than ever before.[231] Perhaps there is a lesson here: Times of crisis show us what is possible. Necessity is indeed the mother of invention. "While anti-abortion politicians have exploited this crisis by attempting to shutter clinics, we're making the

---

227. *See* Olivier Véran, *Pilule Contraceptive et IVG*, MINISTERE DES SOLIDARITES ET DE LA SANTE (Mar. 23, 2020), https://solidarites-sante.gouv.fr/actualites/presse/communiques -de-presse/article/pilule-contraceptive-et-ivg# (authorizing home abortion); *see also* Ordre des Sages-Femmes, *Fiche Covid-19 CNSF-ONSSF-ANSFL – Organisation des activités pour les sages-femmes libérales du 25/03/2020*, ORDRE DES SAGES-FEMMES (Mar. 25, 2020), http://www .ordre-sages-femmes-bdr.fr/fiche-covid-19-cnsf-onssf-ansfl-organisation-des-activites-pour-les -sages-femmes-liberales-du-25-03-2020 (announcing authorization for midwives to offer tele-medical abortion care).

228. *See* Abigail Aiken et al., *supra* note 66, at 840.

229. *See* Jonathan Bearak et al., *COVID-19 Abortion Bans Would Greatly Increase Driving Distances for Those Seeking Care*, GUTTMACHER INST. (Apr. 2, 2020), https://www.guttmacher.org /article/2020/04/covid-19-abortion-bans-would-greatly-increase-driving-distances-those -seeking-care.

230. *See id.*

231. *See id.*

Repro Legal Helpline more accessible than ever to address people's concerns about their legal rights and self-managed abortion," said Sara Ainsworth, Senior Legal and Policy Director at If/When/How.[232] Her words came in response to the twofold increase in inquiries to the organization's legal helpline during the first weeks of the pandemic.[233] The recent uptick in information about, and recourse to, abortion pills is evidence that when the going gets tough, people don't abstain from care. They get creative. They find ways to take care of themselves, and their communities, when the state refuses to play its part. Not only do these forms of resilience and resistance build strength within communities and among individuals, they place real pressure on governments too.

Ireland and Northern Ireland legalized abortion in 2019 and 2020, respectively.[234] While many factors contributed to these momentous legislative changes, one significant driver behind the changes was likely the transformation of abortion care to something that could be administered remotely.[235] Although abortion seekers in both countries risked prosecution by doing so, thousands of people imported abortion pills from England before legalization.[236] Grassroots efforts to disseminate information about abortion pills and to send abortion pills from abroad, laid the groundwork for the reforms that ultimately liberalized abortion access. Groups like Women on Web, Women on Waves, and the British Pregnancy Advisory Service refused to deny assistance to Irish and Northern Irish patients.[237] By

---

232. If/When/How Staff, *Repro Legal Helpline Mobilizes Relaunch to Address Increased Calls About Self-Managed Abortion During COVID-19 Pandemic,* IF/WHEN/HOW (May 4, 2020), https://www.ifwhenhow.org/repro-legal-helpline-covid19-coronavirus-launch/.

233. *Id.*

234. *See* SYDNEY CALKIN, AFTER REPEAL: RETHINKING ABORTION POLITICS 74–89 (Kath Browne & Sydney Calkin eds. 2019); *see also* Anna Carnegie & Rachel Roth, *From the Grassroots to the Oireachtas: Abortion Law Reform in the Republic of Ireland,* HEALTH & HUMAN RIGHTS J. (Dec. 19, 2019), https://www.hhrjournal.org/2019/12/from-the-grassroots-to-the-oireachtas-abortion-law-reform-in-the-republic-of-ireland/; *see also* Jillian Deutsch, *The Doctor Who Brought Abortion Out of the Shadows in Ireland,* POLITICO (Mar. 20, 2018, 6:47 PM), https://www.politico.eu/article/ireland-referendum-abortion-rebecca-gomperts-a-hard-pill-to-swallow-in-ireland/.

235. *See* Deutsch, *supra* note 234.

236. *Id.*

237. *See* Alexandra Sifferlin, *How Irish Women Are Getting Around Abortion Laws,* TIME (Oct. 18, 2016, 11:35 AM), https://time.com/4531429/medication-abortion-ireland/; *see also* Amanda Ferguson, *British Provider to Post Abortion Pills to Ensure N. Irish Women Have Access,* REUTERS (Apr. 9, 2020, 1:12 PM), https://www.reuters.com/article/britain-nireland-abortion/british-provider-to-post-abortion-pills-to-ensure-n-irish-women-have-access-idUSL5N2BX5QR.

2019, cultural perceptions of abortion had changed drastically and generated more widely accepted beliefs that abortion should be legal.[238]

Widespread access to medical abortion transforms the public's imagination of what an abortion is. Rather than associating it with a clinic that has been the target of so much anti-choice rhetoric and iconography, it can be something infinitely more relatable—taking pills at home, something nearly everyone has done at some point in their life. As mentioned earlier, some people do not even imagine SMA as an abortion but rather as "bringing on a miscarriage" or "bringing on a period."[239] This echoes early narratives about abortion, which described them as "restoring the menses."[240] The inability on the part of the state to effectively control access played a role in the eventual decriminalization of abortion in Ireland and Northern Ireland. There was no way, absent unacceptable intrusions into a person's personal affairs (via mail inspections and online surveillance for example), to prevent people from getting the pills and managing their care themselves.

This is a revolutionary change that removes power from the hands of the state and places it directly in the hands of the individual. If *Roe* is reversed, similar cross-border initiatives may develop. Although some states would doubtlessly try to clamp down on them, those efforts would likely be unsuccessful. In a post-pandemic world, where the infrastructure for telemedical abortion care has already been established, and cultural acceptance of SMA is more widespread than ever before, efforts to criminalize long-distance care will likely be unfruitful.

IV. Conclusion

SMA cannot replace clinical care. Not only will there always be a need for clinical abortions later in pregnancy, people who prefer to end their pregnancies in a clinical setting should be able to do so. As barriers to abortion clinics proliferate, however, SMA seems to be a safe and promising workaround. Legal access to abortion pills online allows abortion seekers worldwide to bypass the clinic (and all its requirements) entirely. A multipronged approach to decriminalize, democratize, and destigmatize SMA is called for in response to dwindling clinic access. The pandemic created a ripe

---

238. *See* CALKIN, *supra* note 234, at 87–88.

239. *See* Moseson, *Self-Managed Abortion: A Systematic Scoping Review*, *supra* note 3, citing A. Jilozian & V. Agadjanian, *Is Induced Abortion Really Declining in Armenia?*, 47 STUDIES IN FAM. PLAN. 163–78 (2016).

240. *See* REAGAN, *supra* note 112.

environment for this work, building public awareness about, and global coalitions behind, SMA, while increasing access to telemedical support for abortion around the world. These new support systems join forces with, and exist because of, care networks and providers who have been offering this essential care for centuries.

As we contemplate the future of abortion care, we must engage with—and derive strength from—those who came before us. Generations of story-tellers, advocates, midwives, doulas, activists, and community healers paved the way for today's conversation about SMA. They, too, had to navigate a system of unjust laws and overzealous prosecution in order to receive and administer care. From their work and their stories, we can find a future from the past.

8

Rebecca Gomperts: Providing Abortion Care to Women Around the World

An interview[1] with David F. Walbert

WALBERT. Dr. Gomperts, you are here in Amsterdam, but you're recognized across the globe as one of the true leaders not just in providing abortion access to women around the world, but in changing the way people think about the issue, and even changing the politics of abortion. And, of course, you're famous for Women on Waves and your extraordinary efforts to provide direct abortion access to women in restrictive countries by bringing your Dutch-flagged ship to them while staying in international waters. How did you first become interested in abortion? Was it through feminism initially?

DR. GOMPERTS. No, I don't come from a feminist background. I was a medical student, and I grew up in a family where things like social justice were very important. And so, quite young, I was involved in protesting against nuclear weapons and things like that when it happened here in the Netherlands. But I think abortion, there's a couple of moments in my life where I was confronted with it before I was really engaged or becoming an abortion fighter. Of course, when I was young abortion was legalized here. But I didn't really realize it at that point. I just remember that my mother was always very strict about it in that you had to prevent an unwanted pregnancy. That was the worst thing that could happen to you.

---

1. The interview took place in Amsterdam, the Netherlands.

And that was also because she had no history of abortions being legal. She grew up in a country where abortion was illegal.

WALBERT. Where was that?

DR. GOMPERTS. In the Netherlands. But that was in the 60s so she didn't have access here, and that was still very much part of her thinking. I remember that was one thing that I was always really afraid of when I started having boyfriends. I didn't want to end up with an unwanted pregnancy, that was something that was ingrained in your thinking then.

And then I remember it again from when I was in medical school. One of my friends there told me that she had an abortion in Paris. I thought that was a very serious thing, right. To think about that—in Paris in a hospital. I just remembered that moment, it was stuck in my mind. And then I went to work—and this was still not part of my dedication to make sure that there is enough access to safe abortions—but when I was working in Africa, I went there to visit my father. I remember times there when women were brought in severely bleeding, almost to death. And one of them did die in fact.

At that time, I knew it was because of a botched abortion, but I thought it was because of the healthcare system there. I didn't have this very strong realization that it was illegal. Actually, I did my first abortion in Africa because the doctor that I worked with—he was a French gynecologist—he helped women in his practice, which was located at the factory where my father worked. He taught me how to do abortions, but he said, you can't talk about this here. He actually used a method that we now say is outdated, but at that time it was the only thing that he had. So he was actually helping women there.

I think that was the first time that I really started to understand a little bit about the implications of unsafe abortions and what it means to do something that you're not allowed to do as a doctor. But only afterwards did I realize how brave he was. There were very few doctors at that time that would do that.

When I went to medical school, I also did art school and I was interested in a lot of other things, and I started writing a book. I didn't feel very much at home in this medical field. I had to start deciding what I was going to do, while still allowing me to do all of my other things.

At that time, there was an abortion clinic around the house where I lived. They had a vacancy, so I just started working there. It was one of the most rewarding things that I had ever done because people were coming in and they had this huge problem in their lives. It's such a small thing that you can do as a doctor to help solve their problem for them. All of the stories, the people's stories, were amazing. That is where I first started working, and then I went to work for Greenpeace, and that is when this idea of the ships came about. We can have boats, and we can take women out into international waters, and we can do abortions there. That is where I started.

WALBERT. What were you doing with Greenpeace?

DR. GOMPERTS. I was looking for ways to make my life useful. As a kid I had been at a Greenpeace ship when I was 8 or 9, and it made such an impression on me. The people there and what they were doing, and that they were fighting for a better world, it left such a positive impression. It became one of those things that I always dreamt of doing—to go with Greenpeace—and the headquarters are actually here in Amsterdam. So I wrote a letter to Greenpeace, and they needed a doctor. I was just a deckhand, but as a deckhand if there was a medical problem, you had to solve it. There was not a lot of medical work, but it was an amazing experience working with them.

WALBERT. Were you exposed then to women in other countries who needed abortions?

DR. GOMPERTS. When I was sailing for Greenpeace we went to Mexico. I had a day off and I decided to go to a hospital there because I was really interested. I asked them about abortions, and they said no, you cannot talk about that here. It's done, but you cannot talk about it.

I got more interested, and I started asking the volunteers from Mexico who were on the boat. Tell me how abortion is here in Mexico, and I heard the most horrendous stories from the girls. One girl told me that her mother had died because of an illegal abortion. She was the oldest child in the family and had to grow up taking care of her younger siblings because of her mother's unnecessary death. It had been maybe her fourteenth pregnancy. So I started getting these real life stories from the Mexican people who were working for Greenpeace.

I was more politicized because of my experience with Greenpeace, and I suddenly also understood more about the political issues of abortion. It's a topic that the more you know about it, the more it's going to get under your skin.

WALBERT. Because you saw the impact on the women?

DR. GOMPERTS. Well, it's a combination of things. It was such a taboo, and I didn't understand that because I didn't have that taboo. At that time, medical schools didn't teach you this. They don't teach you the health effects of an illegal abortion—it's not part of our medical training. Abortion is one of the most frequently performed medical interventions in the world. It's the highest public health problem for women.

But the moment you start thinking like that, there is this disconnect. Why are we never taught about it in medical school? I'm a doctor. We're supposed to know this. And that compared with the sexual abuse of women as well. Like a girl that wants an abortion. She has found somebody who will do it, and she did get the abortion, but she was raped. You can't help but be affected by the total sensibility that they are put in that position when they are confronted with an unwanted pregnancy, the health effect that it had, the social inequality. When women have money, they just travel to other places, and it's not a problem. It's when they are poor that they suffer the effects of a restrictive law.

When I started thinking about this project with the ship, I needed to have data. You have to get professional. As a medical student, you don't know about projects and proposals. You just learn how to treat patients. You don't learn to think about—okay, when I do this, what outcome do I expect? How do I get money for the project?

The data is mind blowing. At that time, the maternal mortality was so high—I think it was like 80,000 women per year that were reported to die from unsafe abortions, and fortunately that has declined over the years. According to data from the Guttmacher Institute, on average 56 million induced abortions—safe and unsafe—occurred annually, worldwide, during the years 2010–2014. Of those, it is estimated that around 25 million abortions were unsafe, almost all of those occurring in developing countries. Maternal mortality fell by almost half between 1990 and 2015, from 385 deaths to 216 deaths per 100,000 live births. According to recent estimates, eight percent of maternal deaths worldwide are from unsafe abortion, but that rate used to be 13 percent. It is estimated that 22,800 women die each year from complications of unsafe abortion.

There has been positive development if I look back to when I started 20 years ago to now. First of all, medication abortion was not that widely available 20 years ago. When we started, the pills had only just been registered in the Netherlands. So the first campaign that we did was to build a mobile clinic to be able to do surgical abortions. In that year already, we would hear that it would be useless because the pills are so much—you know, so much more convenient—and it's not safe to do the surgical procedure on a ship, which is nonsense. On a ship you can also brush your teeth, and doing a surgical abortion is not much more complicated than doing that. But, you know, this perception of people of doing surgical abortions on a ship was a bigger challenge, so the pills for me made it possible. In that sense also, kind of logistically, practically, it also changed the perception of people. So, the pills changed the world in 20 years, and that led to much lower maternal mortality rates and safer abortions, even though they are illegal.

WALBERT. Why have the rate of abortions been coming down in the world, Dr. Gomperts?

DR. GOMPERTS. First of all, the rate of unsafe abortions has come down. The rate of abortions has also gone down because there are more contraceptives available today. And I've seen a lot of work in the last 20 years to make contraceptives available. You have more contraceptives, you have the pills, there are IUDs, and they are available for much lower costs. There are huge efforts to make contraceptives available. As of 2010–2014, the global annual rate of abortion for all women of reproductive age (15–44) is estimated to be 35 per 1,000, which is down from the 1990–1994 rate of 40 per 1,000.

The problem is there are many places where there's no sex education. If you don't have sex education, you won't know about contraceptives either. But the internet has helped people get access to that information. So everything together has made it possible to prevent unwanted pregnancies more so than in the past. And of course, it depends on the region. Some countries are more ahead than others.

WALBERT. Dr. Gomperts, let's talk about some of the Women on Waves initiatives.

DR. GOMPERTS. We have done eight campaigns with the boat so far. The first one was in Ireland. And for me that's really interesting because I can now look back because of the changes that happened. Not only because of the boat, but because of all of our other work that we did in Ireland. It's a cumulative experience there. And Portugal was really interesting because the changes went so quickly.

WALBERT. How difficult was it to get the whole project set up in the Netherlands in the beginning? Was the government supporting you or opposing you?

DR. GOMPERTS. It was an almost impossible project to set up. For many reasons, but I think most of all the problem was ignorance and naiveté.

When the idea of the ship was there—of course, one of the main things was to try to find money to do it and to find a place for us to do it. Initially there was this idea to buy a ship. And then you start talking with a lot of people in the field, and that's how other things happen. Then there was a suggestion of, "why don't you do a pilot project, and then you can rent a boat." There were so many little pieces that came together. What happened, too, when this idea came about, I was finishing a book, and I was interviewed by a journalist about the book. And he asked about my next plan, and I said "Well, I'm working on this project with the boat." And he said "Wow, that is really interesting." He called the Minister of Development in the Netherlands and said, "I met this woman, a feminist, what do you think of this idea?" And he said, "Oh, great idea."

There were questions in the Dutch parliament, but . . .

WALBERT. It sounds so fortuitous as to how it got started. That's a great story!

DR. GOMPERTS. What is so interesting to me is that sometimes the idea itself, without anything else happening, creates a discussion. In this instance the story was picked up by other media, and at some point, it was in the Daily Telegraph. A Maltese newspaper called me as a result of that, and a Maltese journalist wanted to do a story, and I said sure. The whole idea blew up because in the Maltese Parliament they tried to make me a persona non-grata, which doesn't happen much over the last few centuries, to say the least. So there was the Archbishop of Malta declaring me a persona non-grata, and then that was on the front page of the International Herald Tribune.

It was fascinating to see how an idea, just by itself, could create so much interest and attention.

WALBERT. And you hadn't really done anything concrete yet?

DR. GOMPERTS. We hadn't done anything yet. But that in time led to, first, people who were interested and other people began to start giving some money. Then in the first campaign—I mean there was so much going on—when you think about the treatment room, asking for help which was really good because we got an art grant for that. Otherwise, we would have never been able to fund it, and then finding somebody who would rent the ship to us. Then there were some inconsistencies in the Dutch laws—but we just decided to go ahead and not be deterred by what seemed like petty barriers.

Then, of course, the Dutch government backed off, and said, "Ah, you don't have a license. You can't do it." But there is an exception in the law called "overtime treatment" which is 16 days after the woman missed her period, for this treatment a clinic license is not required

When we were in the harbor about to leave, there was so much media as a result of all this controversy. The whole boat crew was standing there, and the owner of the ship that was rented to us—he wanted to stop the ship. He was scared.

WALBERT. Was he opposed to what you were doing, or was he just scared, worried that "I don't need the trouble."

DR. GOMPERTS. Yeah, he was under pressure. He was in business and was worried about possible repercussions, but in the end, he just let the ship go, and we were off and running. That was in 2001.

And then when we were halfway to our destination, we got a fax from the Dutch government that we had to return immediately. They claimed that the certificates of the ship were not valid anymore because there was a clinic on the boat and that created an "extra accommodation" under the law. But the clinic was built by an artist, Joep van Lieshout. He answered by fax and simply said that it was a functional artwork and not an extra accommodation. So we were able to say to the government "no, it's art," and our certificates are good. That got us over that problem. All along, we were constantly trying to solve obstacles put in our way.

What was interesting to me as an experience was the opinion of local organizations at that time, organizations that were supportive of women's abortion rights. They said, realistically, no women in their right mind would ever come to the ship. Going on a ship to international waters to have an abortion? That's not going to happen. They would have gone to England or Scandinavia. There's no way they're going to come to your boat.

But we had a hotline set up, and when women heard that the ship was coming, we were inundated with calls. Hundreds were calling. What I learned at that point was that the abortion-rights movement really did not understand what was happening on the ground. They did not anticipate at all that there was this big, unrecognized need and interest by so many women. When the ship was there, many, many women came to the ship. They wanted the pill. "Please give it to me." To me, it was such a wakeup call to realize that the public perception of abortion is absolutely not what was truly happening, and I hope that that discrepancy and inaccuracy in the public perception was affected by what we were doing.

WALBERT. You mentioned Ireland and the changes there. Tell me about that Dr. Gomperts.

DR. GOMPERTS. Yes, the perception of people was so important. We had to fight the government to get permission to do what we did because they couldn't do any abortions there at the time. There had been a case where a girl was raped and became pregnant—a 14-year-old girl—and she tried to go to England for an abortion. She was stopped, and there was a public debate about these cases. Really desperate cases where women wanted to have an abortion and couldn't access it. But the idea that an abortion is something that women should be able to decide by themselves—without any of these restrictions—it was not much a part of the public debates at the time. It had never been addressed in depth before our initiative, so much of the media coverage that came from what we did was all about that, creating a real discussion.

And also, what we did on the boat, for example, we had brought together a group of lawyers and a group of doctors. One was called "Doctors for Choice" and the other "Lawyers for Choice." They were founded and connected on the boat. We mobilized a lot of people in civil society. We had some socialist politicians coming to the boat as well.

WALBERT. You've also mentioned the whole image presented by what you were doing. The physical presence of the boat and the fact that it's run by women. It's not a group of old OB/Gyns—guys—talking about these issues. You've discussed the fact that women took the initiative to do all this with this boat, and that alone helps stimulating discussion of the issue. And I've heard you say that that big, distinct physical presence, the boat, created interest that would be hard to generate just by posting discussions on the internet.

DR. GOMPERTS. No, you cannot do the same thing on the internet. I think there is something about the image of the ship which is very powerful. It was first associated with piracy. But also, boats are seen as a man's world. And then here we come with these women—female doctors—that are on the boat, so I think it really caught the imagination. In that sense it had become kind of a mythology, and that imagery drove interest and discussions.

After that, we started getting calls. How many boats do you have? When is your boat going to be here? And there was this perception that we have a whole fleet of ships going around the world. And, of course, that's not true. But it's really powerful. That story, it's really powerful. And I think also, we weren't defensive, it was not a defensive strategy. We are always very positive. Women have the right to do this. We are here to support these women's rights, and we were not at all timid about that fact and that what we were doing was right.

Then all of these calls started coming in from all of these women that needed help that nobody foresaw. I think it changed the discussion in the sense that people generally, as well as women's advocates, suddenly realized how wrong their perception had been. I think it was a very important moment in Ireland where they were capitalizing on events.

And then, we started Women on Web in 2005. I went to visit Irish groups again in 2006 to tell them about the fact that this was now a possibility for Irish women.

WALBERT. How were you delivering the drugs into Ireland at that time?

DR. GOMPERTS. At that point, we were just sending it by mail. The pharmacy that we worked with in India mailed the medicine.

WALBERT. Has it always been from India?

DR. GOMPERTS. It was always from India, because that is where it's possible to do it. It's legal to do it from there. The medicines are available. It's not so expensive, and it's not so difficult to get the medicines. You just need a doctor's prescription. In many other places, you need to be in a clinic in order to get access to the pills, or women have to take the pills there physically.

WALBERT. How many women have you helped in Ireland from 2001 until now?

DR. GOMPERTS. It's hard to say. From 2005, because we really started—I think now it's around 1,000 to 1,100 per year. But that's also including Northern Ireland. Okay, let's count back. It's now 2018, but it was less.

WALBERT. Maybe 10,000?

DR. GOMPERTS. Yeah. It's a lot of women helped. And then at some point we were contacted in 2014 by a parliamentarian, Ruth Coppinger, whose main agenda was to try to change the Constitution, to repeal the anti-abortion amendment. That was our goal in 2014. We started working with her on a campaign. What they did first—the first action that they organized—was to go to Northern Ireland because the abortion pills, at that time, they couldn't ship them to Ireland anymore.

In Ireland, customs began to stop the packages, so women were traveling to Northern Ireland and took the pills back. But it's a two-hour train ride, and that was very difficult or impossible for many women. So we created this public performance together. I said, the problem we have is that people say taking the pills is dangerous, and we need to educate them that that's not true because that misinformation was a big factor. So you need to swallow the pills in public. That way you totally undermine this idea that it's so dangerous. Because if a politician swallows an abortion pill publicly before the press, then suddenly you can't say anymore it's dangerous. She did that at the train station, and 30 women all took the abortions pills that we had sent to Northern Ireland that they picked up.

WALBERT. Visual image is so important on getting the message out, isn't it?

DR. GOMPERTS. Yes, it's very important. And since then, we worked with her very closely. She was presenting a legal proposal, and that is when we decided to publish the data on Ireland. Because, we said, there is not enough information here. People don't know what they are talking about. And so, we had this research here from Texas, from a law professor at the University of Texas, in 2016.

She published this paper and it was big news—how many women in Ireland everyday were doing their own abortions. There were three a day. I mean, nobody knew. So that totally changed the debates around abortion in Ireland. And from that moment on, there has been a big change in public opinion.

WALBERT. Everything I've ever read or heard is that restrictions in the laws don't really change the frequency of abortion. It just changes the methods and the legality. Is that consistent with your experience around the world—that abortions are as common where they are prohibited as where they are permitted?

DR. GOMPERTS. Yes, but I depend on research there. And all of the research that has been done—and it's very fundamental, good research by the World Health Organization—it shows that, whether it's legal or illegal, the abortion rate is the same. There is no difference. The only difference is safety and who has access to a safe abortion.

We talked about poverty. Abortion is fundamentally about social justice. Because it's the poor women—always the poor women that are suffering. In Ireland, women who have money, they could easily travel to the UK. They have money to have a babysitter, whatever they need. It's women that have to work and are in controlling situations who suffer. It's awful with abusive boyfriends. And women that have never left Ireland. So there is a very disproportionate effect of these laws where poor women are at a much greater disadvantage.

WALBERT. You took the boat to Poland once didn't you?

DR. GOMPERTS. Yes. From Poland and a year later to Portugal.

WALBERT. How was that experience in Poland?

DR. GOMPERTS. What was interesting for us in Poland, very contrary to Ireland, was that we could not find even one doctor there who was willing to be publicly supportive of the project. Poland is interesting because abortion used to be legal there.

WALBERT. What year were you there?

DR. GOMPERTS. We were there in 2003. And in 1993, abortion was made illegal. So we were there 10 years after abortion was made illegal. But in reality, many abortions were still taking place. All the gynecologists were doing it, but they weren't advertising it. In Ireland, no gynecologist was doing it. It was a very different situation in Poland than in Ireland where it had always been illegal. There were no doctors that were ever doing it in Ireland. In Poland, it hasn't always been illegal, but many doctors were still doing it, and that is why they didn't want to be publicly supporting it. They were afraid it might affect everything for the worse.

In Poland, we worked with women's groups rather than doctors.

WALBERT. Were the obstetricians in Poland overwhelming male?

DR. GOMPERTS. Mostly male. But now it has changed. It's been changing. But the impact of 10 years already by the time we were there—no sex education in school—the Catholic Church teaching in the schools, it was having a very distinct impact. The reason abortion was made illegal was because Pope John Paul had been very involved in the opposition to communism. After communism was overthrown, in 1993 as a thank you to the Pope, sterilization was made illegal and so was abortion.

And the schools were now teaching the Catholic doctrine concerning abstinence only. All of the kids that we worked with had been shown this video of the right to life, or whatever. And there was a very fundamentalist, very aggressive neo-fascist group that's now actually in the government that was protesting against us.

WALBERT. Protesting against *you*?

DR. GOMPERTS. Yes, with eggs and paint, and they were threatening to photograph the women who were seeking an abortion to intimidate them. There was huge tension. It was very aggressive. It was very different in that sense than in Ireland because of the aggressiveness. But we were able to sail there and work there. We were able to help women in international waters, and we were able to overcome the obstacles that they had put up to stop us. They chained the ship first because they said that we came in there illegally. And we had to pay a huge fine, which we did, and then we could set out again. And then we got the fine back because we appealed to the court and won. There was always crisis management the whole time.

But after the ship came to Poland—there had been an opinion poll before we were there and after we were there—we saw a shift in opinion that more people were supporting the legalization of abortion. And the socialist party at that point—there were elections coming and they were afraid to put it up for a vote in the parliament. And then the right-wing party won the election. So that was the end of any advance in women's abortions rights in Poland. It was really a missed opportunity, and now it's worse.

WALBERT. It has gotten more restrictive in Poland, hasn't it?

DR. GOMPERTS. Yes. It's getting more restrictive, and there are still efforts to restrict it more. But the problem in Poland is not just abortion. The rule of law and freedom of the press are undermined by the current political party in power. Poland is really bleak in that regard.

WALBERT. That is a clear example of the arrest of progress and society regressing. Can you describe, Dr. Gomperts, how you have observed those trends in the world in your experience? Can you characterize how attitudes in the world overall are changing? Are they stagnant? Regressing? Or progressing overall towards women's rights and women's right to self-control?

DR. GOMPERTS. Well, I think there are different tendencies in different states. I think that states that are undermining their democratic basics—that are becoming more authoritarian—they are also undermining women's rights. That's what we see everywhere. We see it in Poland, in Hungary, in Turkey, in Russia and in the U.S. But also states that are more corrupt than others. They tend to undermine women's rights. I think that when you look at the index of democratization of countries—like Ireland is clearly a state where the democratic process has advanced—and where the influence of the Catholic Church has diminished, there we see there that there is more progress. Gay rights have been put in place. They can get married now in Ireland since 2015. Same-sex people can marry, and abortion is legalized now.

It is the same in Portugal where the state has improved enormously in the sense of a more democratic state, and that is also why abortion was legalized there. I think that is one of the things that we can do with the ship as well as we did in Portugal. When the ship visited Portugal, there was a right-wing government—very corrupt, very much leaning to the Catholic Church. They sent warships to stop our boat from coming in. That created such an outcry in society because it made the repressiveness very visible, very easy to see and what they were doing looked really awful to many people. It made visible what was happening in the government.

The President at that time did not agree as well with the hostile actions taken against us, so there was a whole debate in the parliament, and also in the European parliament because a boat under one country's flag was stopped by two warships from another European country. So that conflict led to whole debates about abortions rights. Many people were supportive of the ship—more than 60%. Again, what happened to us is what made it visible. People thought before then that abortion was so taboo. There had just been a court case against a nurse that had assisted an abortion, and she had been sentenced to 16 years in prison! Then suddenly what you see is huge public support for legal abortion, and her prosecution looked ridiculous.

The government fell only two months after the ship had been there. Then there were new elections, and the reaction of the government to us was one of the factors in that election. The socialist party won, and abortion was legalized within the next two years. I think that that is a big strength with the ship. It can capitalize on change that is already happening in society, and we can make visible the contradiction between oppressiveness and democracy and what happens to women where abortion access is restricted.

WALBERT. Could you share some specific stories of women over the years, Dr. Gomperts, either on the boat or not, who really affected you—touched you personally because of the impact you had on them?

DR. GOMPERTS. What I think, for example, with the ship—what is interesting for the women in Poland that we helped—these women were so brave because they were very convinced of their right to have this abortion. They wanted to come to the ship. That was their way to make a statement as well. And I think the women that come to the ship are a special kind. What was funny is that my father always came to help. He was the one that was driving the women from the train station to the boat by car, and they were surprised because they didn't expect an old guy to do that.

WALBERT. Your father doing that, that's a wonderful story. It says a lot about him.

DR. GOMPERTS. And then what happened, the last time that we sailed out, there was a special unit of the customs that came aboard. Because the anti-abortion groups had said that we were illegally carrying contraband, they body searched all of the women and their bags. And what the women did, they just—they had pills. The second pill they need to take at home. They were just handing over the pills to each other so when one was called, they just gave their pills to the next one, and then they had nothing. There was super solidarity. They were not scared. That's really a special category of women as well.

And that's also what we saw from some of the women when we were in Mexico. There was this young woman who came with her boyfriend. And we said, we can help you in another way, with pills. You can choose. We can help you with pills here if you want to, or you can go with the boat. And she says, "I want to go with the boat because I want to have a legal abortion. I think that this is really my right, and I want to have a legal abortion." And for me, that was really a significant statement.

WALBERT. Very human, and very intense when she's been living under such a repressive legal regime.

DR. GOMPERTS. I think that is how women feel. All of the women feel like that. They actually—women that have a normal pregnancy, they are not questioning themselves, whether they have a right to have a baby. It's only other people that are questioning that.

Strangely enough, I think the stories of the women in the U.S., for me, are in many ways the most tragic. Because when women live in a country where it's illegal, it's illegal for everybody. And then they try to find help, it's part of their reality. "We are not allowed to do it, so I will find a way to find help."

There are women that are being raped which, of course, is always very sad. Especially a girl in the Middle East who would be killed if they find out about her being pregnant. It's such an enormous relief when she got the medicine. We really saved her life.

WALBERT. Who was threatening her?

DR. GOMPERTS. Her family. She was not married. That was the problem, she was not married.

But in the U.S., a woman would send me a picture of her face, totally beaten up, and she said, "I am trying to get out of this abusive relationship. I have been unable to leave. Now I found out I'm pregnant. I was raped by this guy. I cannot afford a clinic in the U.S. I don't have $600, and it's far away. This is my only chance to get out of this. If I get a child, I will be at the end of my rope." Or another saying "I'm living in my car with a suitcase. I was put out of my house a few months ago, and I can hardly survive. I don't have any food for my children." And what makes it so sad for me is that these women, in the U.S., there is no way they can go to a clinic with this story and get a free abortion.

WALBERT. Economics in the U.S. are a pervasive determinant of your well-being for even the most basic needs and issues. The poor suffer in so many ways, and the well-off are very often ignorant, or don't care, or both.

DR. GOMPERTS. I know. Why cannot people in the U.S. just say, this woman really, really needs help? She doesn't have the money. We have to help her. It isn't the case in the U.S., this idea that you can get an abortion for free.

WALBERT. And there's the so-called Hyde Amendment, named after the congressional sponsor.

DR. GOMPERTS. I know. Government money cannot be used. But the doctor can decide. Right? If I was working in a clinic, and a woman spoke to me with that story, I would do something for her. If I was working the front desk as a receptionist, I would go to the doctor and say, "Hey man, we have a problem here." We don't register it. We just don't tell anybody. Let's just help this woman. It's 10 minutes. I mean, why is that not possible?

I know that there are abortion funds in the U.S. These funds raise money to help women in trouble. But they don't pay for it, or as part of the fee, women still have to come up usually with another $600 or $700. Which is impossible. It's impossible.

WALBERT. That's a lot of money for a lot of people in the U.S., an amount they just can't come up with.

DR. GOMPERTS. So, it's impossible for them to have an abortion. A person that has been raped or is in an abusive relationship, they're desperate. I think this is where the biggest act of resistance is with our work, that we make abortion available regardless of your financial status. We help women for free. And that is unprecedented.

What we do—and that was part of how we were set up—we want to be self-sustainable. But we don't think any women should be denied having access to an abortion because she doesn't have any money. We ask women for a donation. Most of them can afford it. Some women can even afford more. The women that cannot afford it, we ask them how much they can donate. The women that don't have anything get it for free. And the rate of people that cannot give anything is about 10%.

WALBERT. Is that in the U.S., or where is that Dr. Gomperts?

DR. GOMPERTS. No, no. That analysis for the U.S. doesn't exist yet. That's the analysis for other countries in the world. And in a sense, it's usually the women from the north that are able to pay. Women from the south, like Africa or South America, they usually can't pay, or some people can, but I think that is where we really do change things. None of the internet pharmacies will ever send medicines without having somebody pay. There are some other abortion websites as well, but they couldn't do it differently because that's the standard that we set.

And that is why I feel so good about Women on Web because I really feel it creates access where it would otherwise be denied.

WALBERT. You indicated when we were talking earlier that you're doing the U.S. on your own and that your board doesn't want to expand to the U.S. Is that because abortion is perceived to be available there?

DR. GOMPERTS. No, it's not because it is perceived to be available. It's really because most people are kind of concerned because the U.S. is such a—they have a long reach and their legal system, when you get caught up in it, it's very expensive. And it's complicated.

WALBERT. There are 50 state laws—federal law and then state law.

DR. GOMPERTS. Yes. And also because Women on Web is based in Canada. It's too close to the U.S., they felt. And I understand that, but I . . .

WALBERT. You couldn't let it go . . .

DR. GOMPERTS. Nobody else is doing it for the U.S. So yeah, let's see what happens. And I think I did a good legal analysis, and I think it can be done. I think it can be done safely and legally. So let's see.

WALBERT. What kind of problems do Women on Web run into in the different jurisdictions throughout the world?

DR. GOMPERTS. In some countries they stop all of the packages—which is happening now in Brazil and the Philippines. When the medicines are sent, they are confiscated by customs. So we cannot help women anymore in these countries. And in Ireland, before, we could help because we have a connection to Northern Ireland.

Some countries have censors that block our website. The website is not available in Turkey or Saudi Arabia, for example. Women there cannot access the service unless they have a work-around. And we are being censored by YouTube, by Facebook, all the time, and it's constantly going on, so we are constantly fighting the censorship.

WALBERT. You are being censored on YouTube and Google in these countries or . . .

DR. GOMPERTS. Everywhere.

WALBERT. Is YouTube censoring you?

DR. GOMPERTS. Yes. They will remove our channel. And then we have to write a letter saying that they are violating women's rights, etc., and they don't respond. And now with YouTube—which is also Google—we have a contact. We then email them, "hey, we're blocked again," and then he puts it back online. But it's ridiculous, just ridiculous. And I think that is one of the biggest censors. The problem is—people don't know what's censored. The people rely so much on the internet, but they have no idea anymore about what information is being censored.

These are animations, animations of how women can use abortion pills. That's what's being censored. It's not anything else.

WALBERT. It's not the URL, just the information?

DR. GOMPERTS. Just the information. The animations, the films that we made. It's amazing.

WALBERT. And so the government can close down the website too. Have governments tried to stop you more aggressively?

DR. GOMPERTS. Yes. In Ireland, they filed a complaint because I practice medicine from Austria. My medical practice is from Austria, which is because of legal reasons. I registered there, so then I can practice. And they wrote to the Dutch government saying that they have to stop us, but we're not really "here." I mean, I'm sitting here in Amsterdam, but legally, there is nothing happening here. At the time I was the only doctor prescribing, but that's not the case anymore. And I don't do the prescriptions anymore. We found other doctors.

And then they wrote to the Austrian government, and there was an investigation against me. I was convicted—but there was no criminal law, it was administrative law, where I guess there was some rule that as a doctor you have to treat your patients directly in person. But that's open for interpretation. Because if you do a phone call, many doctors do consultations by phone. So how can you complain? The internet is not different.

WALBERT. Telemedicine is everywhere now.

DR. GOMPERTS. Yes, but it's regulated. In the Netherlands, you cannot prescribe when you can't see a patient. They are trying to regulate it. And there's also exceptions for emergencies, and these are all emergencies. These women don't have access otherwise. Finally, there was a court case in Austria, and I won that.

WALBERT. It sounds like every day you go to work and wonder, what's the obstacle of the day going to be.

DR. GOMPERTS. That's true. For example, recently I was in Poland. And the polish government had requested me for questioning. I was first in the courts in the Netherlands in respect to the polish government trying to extradite me to Poland for prosecution.

What was scary about that, which I didn't realize at first, is that Poland can actually send out, if they really think I'm a suspect, they can ask for an international . . .

WALBERT. A Red Notice with Interpol?

DR. GOMPERTS. Yes. When I realized that, I was like, okay, so it means that whenever I travel somewhere, across a border, I could get arrested and extradited to Poland. So it's not over. I mean that feeling is not over, but . . .

WALBERT. The issuance of a Red Notice can be very arbitrary from what I understand. If some country really wanted to shut down Rebecca Gomperts, you are then locked into the Netherlands. You can't cross the border.

DR. GOMPERTS. Yeah. But it hasn't happened yet.

WALBERT. But it's got to be a fear.

DR. GOMPERTS. They still have to make a point where I broke the law.

WALBERT. Do they?

DR. GOMPERTS. Yes. You can be arrested under a Red Notice, but after that, you can only be extradited to another country if there is double criminality.

WALBERT. What if they said you are breaking the law here, in Poland, by aiding and abetting the commission of an illegal abortion in our country because it's illegal what you are doing?

DR. GOMPERTS. No, because there has to be double criminality. In order to have extradition—it has to be illegal in both countries. If it's not illegal in both countries, you cannot do that.

WALBERT. I didn't know that.

DR. GOMPERTS. It may be illegal in the U.S., but where I am doing it from, it is not a crime. If it's not a crime where they are trying to extradite you from, they cannot extradite you. And that is how we have set up all of what we're doing. There are crimes where you have extradition agreements, for murder, all those kinds of things. But this is not one of them.

WALBERT. You've mentioned before how you see things changing over time where women will have control of their own lives—doctors are going to be out of it. Women will have access to the medications and so on. How do you see that changing over the next 20 or 30 years?

DR. GOMPERTS. There will be a lot of changes. The U.S. is a special country in this sense, as well. Things are going back with more restrictions on abortion access in a lot of the states, so there's a whole movement in the U.S. now about self-induced abortions. It's happening. People know about it, women get the medicine from abroad, and they are doing their own abortions. There have been a couple of court cases against women in the U.S. in those situations.

If you look at international human rights, that is not acceptable. It's a violation of their human rights for women to be criminalized for inducing their own abortion. There's a whole movement about that now too.

WALBERT. Where do you see that in the future?

DR. GOMPERTS. I think the future will be self-induced abortion by women.

WALBERT. And do you envision a lot of resistance to that from medical professionals—as opposed to philosophical opposition?

DR. GOMPERTS. There is that kind of resistance because doctors are used to keeping control. They like to keep control of the patient. But I think the research is showing that self-induced abortion is possible, and it's safe. If you look at the medical research, there is no reason why not. If we look at contraceptives, it used to also be available only on prescription by doctors. The same with the morning after pill. It was also only on prescription. So I think abortions will move to self-induced abortions, but it will take time. I think women are going to do it anyway, so the doctors won't have any control anymore. Women are taking control over this by themselves.

WALBERT. Do you think that that is the future, that women will ultimately have control so that the law becomes an anachronism, and the medical profession also kind of an anachronism in this context? They'll be there in the case of an unusual complication, but that will be it?

DR. GOMPERTS. Yes, that's going to happen.

WALBERT. Do you think that is inevitable?

DR. GOMPERTS. I think it is inevitable. Ironically, I think maybe the countries where abortion is more restricted are even more advanced insofar as self-abortion is concerned. In the Netherlands where the law was made in order to have abortions happening only in the clinics, there it's going to happen less. But what our research is showing in the U.K., for example, and we have a lot of data there, is increasing self-abortion. We can really see what's happening on the ground because the women that don't have access to the regular clinics, they are the ones that find us.

We have data about women who cannot access regular abortion services, even in the U.K. where it is supposed to be for free. Real access is not so available. Why not? Because some women are in controlling situations, or the distance to a clinic is 2 or 3 hours away and they cannot get there. We have this whole research that was recently published, and that's already led to some legal change in the U.K. so that women can now take the second pill at home as well.

But there will be more change and some countries will be quicker to do it than others. I think the countries that are going to legalize abortion from now on, they will take that aspect more into consideration. Ireland is interesting because in a sense now women are self-taking care of their abortions, although it is with supervision and guidance of the help desk. But when the new law will be implemented, it will become more restrictive actually than it is now because then women will have to go to their general physician and get a prescription. In a sense what Ireland did in legalizing abortion is trying to take control of it again.

The Irish law will be the most advanced law in Europe—together with France, where women can actually go to their family doctor and get a prescription and be able to get an abortion that way. And there's very few other places.

WALBERT. I assume you'll still hear from women in Ireland who cannot use a clinic because of privacy issues or control issues?

DR. GOMPERTS. We'll see. It will be very interesting to see what kind of situations we still get. We will use those data to inform the Irish government again so that they can adapt. That is why we are publishing the data so the governments that are willing to adapt their practices when they know that they are not properly serving women.

WALBERT. I hadn't thought about how your data is so unique. You hear from the women who are really adversely affected by the law or by their circumstances.

DR. GOMPERTS. Yes. And of course, even we don't get all those because women have to have access to the internet and have to be educated. But we see many women that people would normally think would have access to an abortion.

WALBERT. I started thinking about Professor John Riddle and the extent to which we are really getting back to the past when it comes to self-administered abortions. In a sense, we're trying to get back to the middle ages when, as I understand the history, women had reasonably decent control over both contraception and abortion through herbal medicine compared to the last 200 years.

DR. GOMPERTS. The medicines now are better.

WALBERT. That's what I was going to ask you. What was the relative efficacy of herbal contraceptives and abortifacients?

DR. GOMPERTS. I don't think we know because there was no research then. There's no way to—there's definitely herbal medicines that work, but there's just no research on *how* effective they were. And of course, one of the problems with plants is that the amount of the effective ingredient is not consistent. There would have to be a whole new set of research into the plants that were used before to see how effective they actually are. One of the problems is that if you search for how to abort at home, or self-abortion in Google, the first website you will find is that women are advised to take Vitamin C to do an abortion. That is ridiculous. We get emails from women that say they swallowed 70 Vitamin C pills to try to induce their abortion and it didn't work. There's a lot of misinformation.

WALBERT. Do you think there might be some good herbal concoction that could be found that would be very efficacious? Or is that unlikely?

DR. GOMPERTS. I don't think it's highly likely. People over the centuries have used plants and herbs to cure illness and disease, but I'm very scientific, and I think that if you would want to know, you would have to do research to see if it wasn't just a coincidence that she had a miscarriage. Because 20% of pregnancies end in miscarriage. It could be that an herb didn't have any effect, it was a natural miscarriage where the woman used herbs and thought she had a miscarriage because of the herbs. You would have to do scientific research to determine the real effect. And there is no money for this kind of scientific research. No willingness.

WALBERT. No pharmaceutical company is going to do it since it won't make them money, no matter how good it might be for women.

DR. GOMPERTS. No pharmaceutical company is going to do it, so who is going to fund it? And again, the problem with herbs is it is kind of difficult to really measure the active ingredients because the active ingredients in the plants vary so much. It's not a reliable amount that you have . . .

WALBERT. So, 200 milligrams could be totally different from one plant of the same species to another.

DR. GOMPERTS. Yes. How much plant do you need? That is a problem with herbal medicine.

WALBERT. So you really end up having to process it anyhow to know you are getting the right amount.

DR. GOMPERTS. Yes, exactly. That is why they started making medicines. In order to know exactly how much people got so it wouldn't be toxic. People wouldn't die and that it would cure.

WALBERT. You're an extremely focused, energetic, and capable person, Doctor Gomperts. How frustrating is it to you that the problem you are dealing with even exists, that there are so many legal and extra-legal obstacles to a woman's self-determination over their own body? You would probably prefer that policies and practices around the world were set by compassionate, informed people and women had full real access to abortions so that you wouldn't have to do all that you do.

DR. GOMPERTS. That would be so nice.

WALBERT. And maybe you could go to the beach then.

DR. GOMPERTS. I enjoy overcoming obstacles, and it's empowering. But yes, it should be taken care of, and I really want to have a more just world where people can live their lives decently.

WALBERT. On balance, has what you are doing been more fulfilling than frustrating?

DR. GOMPERTS. It depends. But most of the time—of course, it's really frustrating with countries like Brazil where the need is so big, and we can't get anything in there. We tried everything through all kinds of ways, and that is really sad. There's so much poverty there and women are so desperate—that's so frustrating for all of us. You have no idea the emails that we get from women that have been helped. It is so amazing. They are so grateful. Women are so grateful. So, there's that and that's the other part—where they are totally powerless, but we help them when they are desperate and have no one else to turn to.

WALBERT. To be absolutely mired in poverty and then have another child that you can't possibly sustain has got to be profoundly depressing.

DR. GOMPERTS. Yes. And for example, I was a witness at a Supreme Court case in Brazil. In June there was a court case—the Supreme Court heard the request of the socialist party and some other groups that the abortion law is violating the constitutional rights and the human rights of the women. They called for a couple of expert witnesses, and I was one of them. I shared with them our experience, and in one of the cases that I talked about, we had the whole email communication with a girl who was able to find Cytotec. She was all alone, she was using the medication, and she had complications. She went to the doctor and the doctor totally ignored her. We have that happening under our nose, and there is nothing we can do. Her mother emailed us later and told us she had died.

WALBERT. She went to the doctor and they gave her no treatment at all?

DR. GOMPERTS. He didn't even look at her. She said, I have a problem with my belly, and he just put his hand on her belly and said go on home. And that's also part of this inequality where if you are a poor woman who goes to a doctor, you are not taken seriously.

WALBERT. When you talk about pregnancy, the number of problem pregnancies or unwanted pregnancies, it really is a huge portion of women's need for healthcare, isn't it?

DR. GOMPERTS. Yes. Abortion is the most common medical procedure that exists.

WALBERT. And if you go back again to Professor Riddle's expertise with classical and medieval history, all of this was outside of the medical profession then.

DR. GOMPERTS. Yes, of course, because there was no medical profession. And then the medical professionals killed off all of the knowledge of the midwives and all of the women that were helping women with herbs and helping them control their own lives because the doctors wanted to be in control.

WALBERT. And as you've said, when you went to medical school, there was nothing that addressed women's health? No discussion about abortion—that wasn't part of the curriculum, even though it's a massive issue as a practical matter.

DR. GOMPERTS. And another thing is, it's not considered a medical issue. Like giving birth and having a miscarriage, having an abortion is also just a normal part of women's lives. And usually they can deal with it all themselves. It's just in cases when giving birth doesn't work that a doctor is needed. That's one of the other problems that's happening now everywhere in the world, where giving birth is being medicalized, abortion is being medicalized, contraception is being medicalized. And it doesn't have to be. Most women can give birth by themselves. Only when there is a problem, or a complication, do they need help. And now all of the women—like, one of the things we are seeing in the U.S. is the increasing rate of caesarean sections. That's also happening in Brazil by the way, where women are forced to have a caesarean section where they could have given birth naturally. That's the same with miscarriages, women don't need medical treatment. An abortion pill is like a miscarriage. Miscarriages, women deal with by themselves, and if there is a complication, they go to the doctor.

WALBERT. Why is all that happening? Is that just desire for control by the medical profession?

DR. GOMPERTS. I think there is financial incentive. A lot of it is about money. You can charge a lot for doing a caesarean section even if there is no medical indication to do one. But it's not based on medical evidence that it's required and actually needed. To the contrary, it is very harmful for women to have a caesarean section because it means that they have to have one in the future and it's causing a lot of medical complications.

But in the U.S. people are medicalized anyway. Right? All the antidepressant medication that is being prescribed. The pain medication that is being prescribed. There is huge over-medicalization.

WALBERT. Overall, though, you sound pretty optimistic that, ultimately, women will have control for themselves with self-induced abortions.

DR. GOMPERTS. Yes, I do think so, and I think one of the obstacles there is that there is a lot of scare mongering that women couldn't do that—that it would be dangerous. I think that is also why our research is so important. We can show that's not true. People will say that it's dangerous, but it's not.

WALBERT. You talk about generational change—attitudes changing. We're not talking about five years, but as long as the future is good, I'm glad to hear your perspective on that. Like you were saying earlier, a lower index of democratization correlates very much to oppressive abortion laws. Where that index may be headed today is troubling around the world, not just in the U.S.

DR. GOMPERTS. Yeah, we just don't know where it's going to go overall.

WALBERT. But if women can take control by being outside the system, that's very good on the issue of abortion.

DR. GOMPERTS. The only obstacle on that I see now is that many countries are banning—for example, the access to misoprostol which is one of the medicines that they use. Morocco just did it. They banned the sale of Arthrotec, which is one of the medicines that women can use to do their own abortion. But what will happen is that you will have the black market, which is happening all over Latin America. And the problem with the black market is what is sold could be anything. And it's very expensive.

WALBERT. Can be good, bad, fake . . .

DR. GOMPERTS. So that is the problem. The problem is not that women cannot do it themselves. The problem is the black market that is being created by controlling access to the medication. Then it becomes like any substance that people need—and the quality can't be controlled anymore in the black market. There is still a lot of work to be done there so that the medications are not overly restricted, or made illegal.

WALBERT. That's very troubling as to the illegalization of the drug. Right now, you really can't do that because Cytotec is also needed for other medical reasons, but presumably medical research could find an alternative medicine for those purposes. I'm sure the anti-abortion forces would want to have an alternative that satisfies the other therapeutic uses of Cytotec, but that doesn't have the abortion effect.

DR. GOMPERTS. Exactly. It's a real problem.

WALBERT. Again, you have a unique perspective on all of these things throughout the world. Is there any particular advice that you would give to women's advocates—men or women—who are advocating for women's rights and women's access to abortion based on your experiences?

DR. GOMPERTS. I think that part of progress starts sometimes very small, which means talking in your own community with people about this. And one of the problems that I see within the abortion rights movement is that people talk too much with each other and not with the outside world. Real mobilization and changing people's opinions happens outside our own normal environment. That's why I like so much the socialist movement because they do that. Because they understand that you need to have a conversation with people that think differently than you. That's what happened with the government in Ireland—women learned how to have a conversation like that. Don't just stick in your own social role. Go out.

WALBERT. Has misinformation been a problem with the internet and social media like Facebook? Has that been more of a positive thing in terms of reaching out to people, or has misinformation from abortion opponents been a bigger problem than the benefits?

DR. GOMPERTS. What I think has already been proven with research is that people tend to only—that the communities get to become more extreme because everybody is always drifting off in their own group. All the things that you receive reinforce the opinion that you already have. There is very little space for exchange with other opinions. That has been proven to be a problem now with social media. People don't talk to each other anymore. They are just sending messages through Facebook. People are only communicating among their own community that already thinks like they do. So I think there is a big issue there. This polarization—and that's also I think what the election of Trump showed—I think why people were so shocked. They had no idea—they were not aware of how many people would vote for him.

I think that is something small that everybody can do—if you become well informed, well prepared to go and talk about this topic, and talk about it—to everybody. I always talk with the taxi drivers because they know a lot. And they have a very close connection with the rest of the world. Whenever I'm in a taxi, I talk with the taxi driver. But you can also do it when you take public transportation. Talk with the people next to you. And say hey, there's an issue I've just been really looking into.

It is also interesting that there is a lot of money going to the abortion rights movement, but then, for example, this year there have been already three international conferences on abortion, and it's the same people that go to the same conferences talking about the same things. These are people that are flown in from all over the world. And I think it's probably a waste of money, plus the impact on the environment, because nobody is talking to anyone outside their group, and their group is pro-choice already.

WALBERT. It makes no difference, no impact.

DR. GOMPERTS. Write a blog. That is one of the things that we always tell people, is that people don't have good information. You can help—help women find the services that are there, so write on blogs, post things— you can go to all of these websites where people are asking for help. Try to see if you can find women that are looking for safe abortions. Tell them where to go to. That's a really direct form of helping where you try to find women that need help. You might not know where to go, but you can help them try to find the resources.

WALBERT. And that's local?

DR. GOMPERTS. It can be local. It can also be international. If you speak Spanish, you can go to Spanish language sites and inform women about what they should do.

WALBERT. Is there anything you would like to say, Dr. Gomperts, that we haven't already touched on today?

DR. GOMPERTS. I don't think I have anything more to say specifically. It's such a rich topic. I think for the future what is really important is that you cannot see this topic separately from other problems affecting healthcare. The same problem applies for people that have other healthcare issues that don't have the money to get help in the U.S. In the end it has to do with our society that has to change in a basic way.

WALBERT. Thank you Dr. Gomperts. Your clarity of purpose, your vision, and your personal fortitude are truly exceptional. I join many, many women and men in saying that you are a powerful inspiration to everyone who strives for a better world.

9

What Lawyers Need to Know about the Reproductive Justice Framework

By Jill C. Morrison*

I. Introduction

The theory of Reproductive Justice (RJ) was developed in the mid-1990s. Although it is an achievement for the movement that this phrase has gained some popular usage, very often it is misused interchangeably with reproductive rights or reproductive health.[1] This erases the important history of the term, its explicit goal of responding to structural racism, and avoids hard conversations about very different visions of how the world should be. No one knows better than lawyers that words matter.

This chapter provides a brief background for lawyers who are interested in reproductive health and rights with how these terms are distinguished from Reproductive Justice. A much deeper understanding can be obtained from the sources cited in the endnotes, and I hope that readers will be motivated to explore this issue further. Having this background also will help those who are allies to the RJ movement further the vision of its founding mothers.

---

*Visiting Professor of Law, Georgetown University Law Center and Executive Director of Women's Law & Public Policy and Leadership & Advocacy for Women in Africa Fellowship Programs.

1. For an analysis of how these frameworks differ in both theory and practice, see Asian Communities for Reproductive Justice, *Forward Together, A New Vision for Advancing our Movement for Reproductive Health, Reproductive Rights and Reproductive Justice* (2005) [hereinafter *A New Vision*].

Section I describes the creation of the Reproductive Justice framework as a response to the inadequacies of the Reproductive Rights framework, especially its reliance on the right to privacy. Section II identifies how the grounding of Reproductive Justice in human rights secures the full range of parenting options. Finally, Section III provides some guidance on how to advance Reproductive Justice.

II. The Reproductive Justice Framework Responded to the Inadequacy of the Reproductive Rights Framework in Addressing Reproductive Oppression

The theory of Reproductive Justice was developed in 1994. In Chicago, 12 Black women activists met before the International Conference on Population and Development to be held in Cairo, Egypt. These women identified a critical gap in how reproductive health issues are approached in the United States.[2] Their discussion was sparked by President Bill Clinton's plan for health care reform. He would not commit to the inclusion of reproductive health care, and abortion was a nonstarter.[3]

The women considered how reproductive issues had been treated in isolation from the totality of women's[4] health care, and indeed their lives. Their experiences and work within their communities made clear that all social justice issues—gender-based violence, housing, employment, and immigration, among others—were central to reproduction.[5] These women were also dismayed by how the discussion of reproductive health had been limited to abortion and contraception, when they had all experienced attacks on their ability to have children, as well as raise them.[6]

To address their concerns with how the reproductive rights issues were being framed, these women combined the concepts of reproductive rights with social justice to create Reproductive Justice. It is most simply defined as the right to *not* have a child, the right *to* have a child, and the right to

---

2. LORETTA J. ROSS & RICKIE SOLINGER, REPRODUCTIVE JUSTICE: AN INTRODUCTION (2017) [hereinafter Ross].

3. *Id.* at 63.

4. I recognize that everyone who is capable of becoming pregnant and giving birth does not necessarily identify as a woman. The term is not used in an attempt to erase the experiences of individuals who identify as male or nonbinary, but to reflect the history of efforts to control a specific category of people based on their sex characteristics.

5. *Id.*

6. *Id.*

parent in a safe and healthy environment.[7] Most importantly, in defining what is meant by the term "right," the women advocated for a system that supported the choices of each individual by providing everything they might need to effectuate that choice.

The primary goal of those 12 women in Chicago was to build a more inclusive movement that spoke to the concerns of the women with whom they worked every day. This more inclusive framework acknowledges the history of oppressive reproductive practices against Women of Color, calls for a more conscious remediation of these harms, and begins the work of reforming the entrenched systems of reproductive oppression that impact women's day-to-day lives.

A. Defining "Reproductive Oppression"

Asian Communities for Reproductive Justice defines Reproductive Oppression as "systematic denial of women and girls' self determination and control over our bodies and limiting our reproductive choices," and "control and exploitation of women and girls through our bodies, sexuality and reproduction by families, communities, institutions and society."[8] It is important to recognize that reproductive oppression can take the form of restrictions on childbearing, forced childbearing, or prohibitions on raising children.

The clearest example of this is chattel slavery in the United States. During enslavement, owners would sometimes force enslaved women to become pregnant by certain men whom they deemed especially productive in order to give birth to a child with particular qualities.[9] This child would often then be sold by the owner, denying the parents any physical or emotional connection.[10] Removing the choice of partner from the enslaved woman and man, the forced pregnancy, and the sale of the child were the most extreme forms of reproductive oppression.

Currently, laws and policies work to force childbirth on those who do not wish to remain pregnant, as well as restrict childbearing and limit the ability to raise children among those who wish to do so. While it might seem somewhat contradictory that very often these are the same individuals, it is

---

7. *Id.* at 65.

8. *A New Vision, supra* note 1, at 6.

9. Margaret A. Burnham, *An Impossible Marriage: Slave Law and Family Law,* 5 Law & Ineq. 187, 195 (1987); Dacia Green, *Ain't I . . . ?: The Dehumanizing Effect of the Regulation of Slave Womanhood and Family Life,* 25 Duke J. Gender L. & Pol'y 191 (2018).

10. Burnham, *id. at* 201–02.

the continuum of coercion and control that defines Reproductive Oppression. Scholar Dorothy Roberts notes that the goal is "to limit indigent women's control over their own bodies by making it more difficult to realize their reproductive decisions," ultimately forcing them to take extreme measures to avoid pregnancy.[11]

B. The Reproductive Rights Movement in the U.S. was Focused Primarily on Legal Access to Abortion and Contraception and Did Not Address the Unique Concerns of Women of Color

The RJ framework encompasses all aspects of reproduction, resonating with a broader set of women. Accessing abortion and contraception are important to the vast majority of women, regardless of their race, ethnicity, income, or social status. Nonetheless, the mainstream Reproductive Rights movement did not recognize the long history of Women of Color being subjected to limits on their childbearing and childrearing. The use of abortion and contraception as tools of oppression rendered suspect a movement that focused solely on the prevention of pregnancy.

1. This limited focus failed to recognize how abortion and contraception were and still are used to oppress Black and Brown women

Killing the Black Body: Race, Reproduction and the Meaning of Liberty, by Professor Dorothy Roberts, charts the history of reproductive oppression of women of African descent from our arrival on the shores of what would become the United States until present day.[12] It is widely considered one of the most important pieces of scholarship in Reproductive Justice. *Undivided Rights* chronicles the advocates who identified and organized to challenge abusive practices against Black, Latina, Asian and Pacific Islander, and Native American women.

Undivided Rights and *Killing the Black Body* cite numerous examples of practices to limit childbearing among Women of Color. These include the "Mississippi Appendectomy,"[13] the practice of sterilizing Black women when they entered the hospital for any reason. Civil rights organizer Fannie Lou

---

11. DOROTHY ROBERTS, KILLING THE BLACK BODY: RACE REPRODUCTION AND THE MEANING OF LIBERTY 235 (2d ed. 2017) [hereinafter ROBERTS].

12. *See generally, id.*

13. *Id.* at 90.

Hamer testified in 1965 that 60 percent of the Black women in her county had been sterilized without their permission at the public hospital, confirming this with examinations from physicians.[14]

Puerto Rican women were similarly subjected to systemic nonconsensual sterilization procedures.[15] They were also used in mass medical experiments to develop the birth control pill, resulting in the deaths of some unwitting participants.[16]

Native American women were sterilized by the Indian Health Service through the 1960s and 1970s, which continues to have a devastating impact on the community.[17] The practice of removing Native American children from their families of origin and placing them in boarding schools is now widely recognized as a violation of the right to parent, stemming from the deeply racist notion that Native parents were presumably unfit.[18]

Controlling the fertility of Black and Brown women was a centerpiece of the 1996 Welfare Reform bill.[19] This included the promotion of so-called "family caps," which allowed states to deny additional assistance to families who had "extra" children while receiving cash benefits.[20] Many states have since abolished family caps, finding that they did not actually

---

14. *Id.* at 91.

15. Helen Rodriguez-Trias MD, *Sterilization Abuse*, 3 WOMEN & HEALTH 10 (1978). Dr. Rodriguez-Trias is widely considered the mother of the movement for reproductive autonomy for Puerto Rican women, in addition to having been a tireless advocate for health equity. American Public Health Association, Helen Rodriguez-Trias Award, https://www.apha.org /about-apha/apha-awards/helen-rodriguez-trias-award.

16. Ray Quintanilla, *Puerto Ricans Recall Being Guinea Pigs for "Magic Pill"*, CHI. TRIBUNE, Apr. 11, 2004.

17. Jane Lawrence, *The Indian Health Service and the Sterilization of Native American Women*, 24 AM. INDIAN Q. 400 (Summer 2000).

18. Mary Annette Pember, Death by Civilization, THE ATLANTIC, Mar. 8, 2019. The express goal of these schools was to "civilize" children by stripping them of their customs and language through abuse and shaming.

19. JAEL SILLIMAN, MARLENE GERBER FRIED, LORETTA J. ROSS & ELENA GUTIERREZ, UNDIVIDED RIGHTS: WOMEN OF COLOR ORGANIZING FOR REPRODUCTIVE JUSTICE 8 (2004) [hereinafter SILLIMAN].

20. Ctr. on Reproductive Rts. & Just., *Bringing Families out of 'Cap'tivity: the Path Toward Abolishing Welfare Family Caps* 2 (Aug. 2016) [hereinafter *Family Caps*]. *available at* https:// www.law.berkeley.edu/wp-content/uploads/2015/04/2016-Caps_FA2.pdf.

reduce birthrates, and only served to deepen poverty.[21] Some evidence also indicated that they increased abortion.[22] Thirteen states still have these policies.[23]

A 2020 documentary, *Belly of the Beast*, identified the practice within the California Prison System between the years of 1997 and 2013 of sterilizing imprisoned Black women both immediately after childbirth and during supposedly diagnostic surgeries.[24] As recently as March 2020, women being held in detention by U.S. Immigration and Customs Enforcement claimed that they were subjected to hysterectomies without their consent.[25]

Low-income women and Women of Color are also sometimes pressured to use long-acting reversible contraceptives (LARCs), even when these contraceptives are not their preferred method or are even contraindicated.[26] Some state governments have conditioned the receipt of welfare benefits on their use.[27] When methods such as the contraceptive injection and implant were developed in the 1990s, judges imposed the use of LARCs on women as a condition of probation or parole.[28]

Any movement that promoted contraception and abortion without this awareness alienated those who were the subjects of these oppressive actions. As discussed next, the rhetoric of "choice" did not resonate with those who so often were given no choice.

2. The framing of abortion as a choice didn't acknowledge that sometimes abortion was not an actual choice for women

The Reproductive Justice framework advances protecting the right to parent and raise children for those who wish to do so. It advocates for the social and economic supports that so often make parenting challenging, if not

---

21. Teresa Wiltz, *Family Welfare Caps Lose Favor in More States*, May 3, 2019 STATELINE PEW CHARITABLE TRUST, citing Urban Institute (Arizona, Arkansas, Connecticut, Delaware, Florida, Georgia, Indiana, Mississippi, North Carolina, North Dakota, South Carolina, Tennessee, and Virginia).

22. *Family Caps* 3.

23. *Id.*

24. Belly of the Beast (Independent Lens 2020), https://www.pbs.org/independentlens/films/belly-of-the-beast/.

25. Caitlin Dickerson, Seth Freed Wessler & Miriam Jordan, *Immigrants Say They Were Pressured into Unneeded Surgeries*, N.Y. TIMES (Sept. 29, 2020), https://www.nytimes.com/2020/09/29/us/ice-hysterectomies-surgeries-georgia.html.

26. Ross, *supra* note 2, at 156–57.

27. Rachel Benson Gold, *Guarding Against Coercion While Ensuring Access: A Delicate Balance*, 17 GUTTMACHER POL'Y REV. 8, 10 (Summer 2014).

28. *Id.* at 12.

impossible. Most importantly, the framework interrogates the very concept of "choice" which is elevated in much of the rhetoric in support of abortion rights.

> "Choice" implies a marketplace of options, in which women's right to determine what happens to their bodies is legally protected, ignoring the fact that for women of color, economic and institutional constraints often restrict their choices. For example, a woman who decides to have an abortion out of economic necessity does not experience her decision as a "choice."[29]

While Reproductive Justice fully supports access to safe, legal and affordable abortion services, it also wishes to address the circumstances of women's lives that very often lead them to make that decision. If a full-time, minimum-wage worker has an abortion only because she knows that she will be fired if she takes too many sick days, and the additional expense of a baby would leave her unable to make rent, she is experiencing reproductive oppression. The solution lies in changing the social circumstances to enable this woman to carry her pregnancy to term and raise her child.

As most recently highlighted in *The Turnaway Study: Ten Years, A Thousand Women, and the Consequences of Having—or Being Denied—an Abortion*,[30] women's decisions to terminate a pregnancy are often due to factors like an inability to continue their education if they have a child, and escaping the birth of a child that would forever tie them to a violent partner. Reproductive Justice envisions a society where every institution provides childcare, and where all women feel safe in their homes.

3. The focus on the right to not have children did not address attacks on the right to parent faced by Women of Color

The founders of the theory of Reproductive Justice also sought to develop a framework that would advance protections for those who wished to raise children. They identified many systems that seek to sever the bond between Women of Color and their children, including the criminal justice and child welfare systems.

In the wake of the exponential growth of those incarcerated due to the so-called War on Drugs, in 1997 Congress passed the Adoption and Safe

---

29. SILLIMAN, *supra* note 19, at 5–6.

30. DIANA GREENE FOSTER, PhD, THE TURNAWAY STUDY: TEN YEARS, A THOUSAND WOMEN, AND THE CONSEQUENCES OF HAVING—OR BEING DENIED—AN ABORTION (2020).

Families Act. This act severed custody rights for parents of children who were in foster care for 15 out of the past 22 months. This had a devastating effect on a disproportionate number of Black and Brown women serving long sentences for minor drug offenses.[31]

The child welfare system is also a major factor in limiting Black and Brown women's ability to parent.[32] Most cases involve neglect and not abuse. This neglect is often directly tied to the mother's impoverishment: the school reports to social services that a child seems hungry all the time; a water bill went unpaid so a child shows up to school with dirty clothes; or the family has lost their housing altogether. Moreover, it is often only poverty that has the state involved in the family's life to begin with, thus making them vulnerable to involvement in the child welfare system.[33]

More recently, we can see limitations on the right to parent in immigration policies. It was an express policy of the Trump administration to separate undocumented parents and children when detained at the border.[34] Then-Attorney General Jeff Sessions, identified as the architect of the policy, intended to dissuade parents from attempting entry into the United States with the explicit threat that they would lose their children.[35] Officials are currently unable to identify at parents for at least 545 children who were taken from their parents by the federal government.[36]

---

31. The War on Drugs gave also rise to a national wave of prosecutions against who were pregnant and addicted, a disproportionate number against Women of Color. Rather than treat substance use as a public health issue, women were charged with child abuse or neglect, delivery of controlled substances to a minor, and even homicide. Lynn M. Paltrow & Jeanne Flavin, *Arrests of and Forced Interventions on Pregnant Women in the United States, 1973-2005: Implications for Women's Legal Status and Public Health*, 38 HEALTH POL., POL'Y & L. 299, 323 (2013).

32. DOROTHY ROBERTS, SHATTERED BONDS: THE COLOR OF CHILD WELFARE (2002).

33. KHIARA M. BRIDGES, THE POVERTY OF PRIVACY RIGHTS (2017).

34. Michael D. Shear, Katie Benner & Michael S. Schmidt *"We Need to Take Away Children," No Matter How Young, Justice Dept. Officials Said*, N.Y. TIMES, Oct. 6, 2020.

35. *Id.*

36. Caitlin Dickerson, *Parents of 545 Children Separated at the Border Cannot Be Found*, N.Y. TIMES, Oct. 21, 2020. Other sources have put this number even higher. Daniel Cassady, *The Number of Separated Migrant Kids Has Grown To 666*, FORBES, Nov. 9, 2020.

C. Reproductive Rights Are Grounded in the Right to Privacy, Which Fails to Guarantee Everyone the Ability to Make Meaningful Reproductive Choices

1. *Roe v. Wade* and the right to privacy

I frequently guest lecture on Reproductive Justice, typically to undergraduates or master's students in public health. I direct the students to a PowerPoint slide with the question: "What did *Roe v. Wade*[37] do?" More often than not, the answer I get back is some variation of "it guaranteed a right to abortion." This is a common but inaccurate understanding of *Roe*. It is more precise to say that *Roe* limited the extent to which a government could interfere with a woman's access to abortion. *Roe* did nothing to actually secure that right.[38]

The right to privacy, while critically important, is not enough to create meaningful access to abortion. While I will always smile when I see a bumper sticker proclaiming "US Out of My Uterus," the fact is that some people need the government to help them carry out their choice. This reality was made clear in the cases addressing Medicaid funding for abortion.

2. *Harris v. McRae* and abortion as a negative right

Henry Hyde was the architect of the Hyde Amendment, which barred states from using Medicaid funds to pay for abortions.[39] He made his intent clear during the 1976 floor debate, acknowledging that his appropriations rider was singling out the most vulnerable: "I would certainly like to prevent, if I could legally, anybody having an abortion, a rich woman, a middle class woman, or a poor woman. Unfortunately, the only vehicle available is the HEW Medicaid bill."[40] *Harris v. McRae* held that the Hyde Amendment was

---

37. Roe v. Wade, 410 U.S. 113 (1973).

38. Many commentators have made additional critiques of *Roe*, most notably the late Justice Ruth Bader Ginsburg, who would have much preferred that abortion access be framed as an issue of the right to equality. Ruth Bader Ginsburg, *Some Thoughts on Autonomy and Equality in Relation to* Roe v. Wade, 63 N.C. L. Rev. 375 (1985).

39. The reach of the Hyde Amendment goes far beyond those receiving Medicaid. It includes those receiving health care through Indian Health Services, Federal Employee Benefits Program, Peace Corps. See, Alina Salganicoff, Laurie Sobel & Amrutha Ramaswamy, *The Hyde Amendment and Coverage for Abortion Services*, Kaiser Family Found. (Sept. 10, 2020), https://www.kff.org/womens-health-policy/issue-brief/the-hyde-amendment-and-coverage-for-abortion-services/.

40. Ross, *supra* note 2, at 82.

constitutional.[41] The reasoning behind the decision is at the heart of why the Reproductive Justice framework was needed.

> [A]lthough government may not place obstacles in the path of a woman's exercise of her freedom of choice, it need not remove those not of its own creation. Indigency falls in the latter category.[42]

Then I ask the students to make the argument that the government actually *does* play a role in a woman's impoverished status and her unintended pregnancy. They are able to name the ways that structural racism, sex discrimination, and corporate exploitation make parenting extremely challenging and leave women living paycheck-to-paycheck. Students also identify the government's "contribution" to her pregnancy as well. Many of them come from states where there is abstinence-only sexuality education and where religious employers are exempt from laws requiring that insurance plans cover contraceptives.

This is the best illustration of the concept of negative rights, and how a meaningful framework to advance reproductive health must encompass all social justice issues. I press my students to think about the social structures that impact reproductive decisions. Once they see how the issues are interconnected, they begin to understand the full scope and power of the Reproductive Justice frame.

III. Reproductive Justice: Applying Human Rights Principles to Actualize Reproductive Rights and Health

As the preceding analysis of *Roe* and *Harris v. McRae* shows, the status of abortion as a negative right can leave those without means in the same situation they would be in if abortion was illegal. In adopting the human rights framework[43] of positive rights, Reproductive Justice ensures that the most vulnerable are entitled to the same rights as those who are wealthy.

---

41. Harris v. McRae, 448 U.S. 297 (1980).

42. *Id.* at 316 (1980), citing Maher v. Roe, 432 U.S. 464 (1977).

43. Of course, the United States has not ratified many of the Conventions cited below, and these Conventions are not binding. The purpose of identifying these aspirational rights is to illustrate how the human rights framework shifts the conversation from negative rights to positive rights.

A. Reproductive Justice Considers How Access to Other Social Rights Impacts Reproductive Decision Making

An important component of adopting the human rights framework is that the international conventions enshrining human rights are far more expansive in their protections than the U.S. Constitution. Under international law, adequate housing,[44] health care,[45] and having a family[46] are human rights. These rights are perceived as commodities in the United States. You have access only if you can afford them.[47]

The human rights framework also focuses on the conditions in which children are raised. Reproductive Justice intersects with movements for environmental justice, the fight against climate change, freedom from state violence and police brutality, protection from domestic violence, and the ability to live one's life free from discrimination regardless of race, gender identity, sexual orientation, or ability.[48] Lack of adequate housing, a poor education system, and barriers to health care access are all primary factors in decision making about whether to have a child, and the conditions in which that child is raised.[49]

While there is no country that can be said to have achieved Reproductive Justice, it is clear that of the wealthier countries, the United States is the furthest away from this goal.[50] This is evidenced by paltry social support for parenting like the lack of paid maternity leave,[51] and child care costs

---

44. ICESCR, Article 11 (1966). The right to housing is also a component of the right to health under the Universal Declaration of Human Rights, Article 25 (1) 1948.

45. ICESCR, Article 12 (1966); Universal Declaration of Human Rights, Article 25 (1), 1948. The Convention on the Elimination of all forms of Discrimination Against Women explicitly protects reproductive health care as a human right. CEDAW, General Recommendation 24, U.N. Doc. A/54/38 at 5 (1999).

46. UDHR Article 16; ICCPR Article 23.

47. As one commentator observed, the passage of the Affordable Care Act in 2010 increased the number of Americans who receive health insurance but did little to shift our conversation about health care as a human right. Health care is still perceived as a commodity. Mary Gerisch, *Health Care as a Human Right*, 43 HUM. RTS. MAG. 2 (2018).

48. Ross, *supra* note 2, at 212–37.

49. *Id.*

50. Raising a Family Index: The Best for Raising a Family in 2020, *available at* https://www.asherfergusson.com/raising-a-family-index/ (ranking the US among the five worst countries out of 35 in which to raise a family).

51. Gretchen Livingston & Deja Thomas, *Among 41 Countries, Only U.S. Lacks Paid Parental Leave*, PEW RESEARCH CENTER (Dec. 16, 2019), Https://Www.Pewresearch.Org/Fact-Tank/2019/12/16/U-S-Lacks-Mandated-Paid-Parental-Leave/#:~:Text=In%2020%20of%2041%20countries,Or%20care%20of%20a%20child (analysis of the members of the The Organisation for Economic Co-Operation and Development (OECD)).

that leave even middle-income families struggling.[52] The U.S. also has the highest maternal mortality of 11 high-income nations, with Black women being three times more likely than white women to die as a result of child-birth.[53] Of course, this lack of support for childbearing and families also highlights the hypocrisy of those who wish to limit access to contraception and abortion.[54]

B. Reproductive Justice Promotes Positive Rights; the Affirmative Duty of the State to Help Individuals Actualize Rights

As important as the broad scope of rights that are protected, is the manner in which international law protect those rights. Unlike the negative right to be free from government intrusion established in *Roe v. Wade*, the principle of positive rights in international law requires the government to take steps to ensure that individuals have rights.[55]

> Reproductive justice demands that the state (that is, the government) not unduly interfere with women's reproductive decision making, but it also insists that the state has an obligation to help create the conditions for women to exercise their decisions without coercion and with social supports.[56]

This presents a drastic expansion of the scope of "rights" as defined in *Roe v. Wade*. The application of the principle would certainly have meant

---

52. Simon Workman & Steven Jessen-Howard, *Understanding the True Cost of Child Care for Infants and Toddlers*, CENTER FOR AMERICAN PROGRESS (Nov. 15, 2018), available at https://www.americanprogress.org/issues/early-childhood/reports/2018/11/15/460970 /understanding-true-cost-child-care-infants-toddlers/#:~:text=Key%20findings%20from%20 this%20analysis,cost%20is%20%24800%20per%20month.

53. Munira Z. Gunja, *What Is the Status of Women's Health and Health Care in the U.S. Compared to Ten Other Countries?* THE COMMONWEALTH FUND SURVEY BRIEF (Dec. 2018), 16, *available at* https://www.commonwealthfund.org/sites/default/files/2018-12/Gunja_status_womens _health_sb.pdf.

54. National Partnership for Women and Families, A Double Bind (Sept. 2016) (showing that the states with the most restrictive abortion laws also provide the least workplace protections for pregnancy and parenting).

55. "The obligation to fulfil means that States must take positive action to facilitate the enjoyment of basic human rights." *International Human Rights Law*, UNITED NATIONS, OFFICE OF THE HIGH COMMISSIONER, *available at* https://www.ohchr.org/en/professionalinterest /pages/internationallaw.aspx.

56. Ross, *supra* note 2, at 169.

a different outcome in *Harris v. McRae*. But beyond support for the actual reproductive health services that would allow individuals to not have, or have and raise children, the application of positive rights requires governments to address all systemic inequality that impacts reproductive choices.

IV. What Reproductive Justice Looks Like in Practice: Acting Locally, Thinking Intersectionally

My hope is that after reading this chapter, readers will have the same response as many of the students in my Reproductive Justice course: that you see Reproductive Justice (or its opposite, Reproductive Oppression) present in your everyday life. Perhaps you will consider how laws and policies that might appear to be unrelated to reproduction are actually working to influence individuals' decisions about whether to bear children, and how they will be raised.

You do not have to work in the reproductive health, rights, or justice fields to advance Reproductive Justice. You can review the parental leave policies in your own workplace. Do they discriminate against those who choose to parent through adoption or fostering? Even if the policy is good, are there unspoken rules that keep employees from utilizing them? What are the policies for the workers around you who are not lawyers—does the company your firm contracts with to clean the building pay a living wage, and provide paid sick leave and health insurance benefits?

A. RJ Every Day: Identifying and Addressing Structural Inequality and Barriers to Reproductive Choices

Reproductive Justice advocacy also requires you to question what appear to be immutable facts, especially about life in the United States. My students are uniformly thoughtful and socially aware, and most would describe themselves as extremely progressive. Nonetheless, they have still absorbed the message that having a child is a luxury. They are challenged by the notion that is at the core of the Reproductive Justice framework: that there is a human right to have and raise a child, regardless of your means.

I ask them to think about whether they are currently in the position to have a child. Due to the exorbitant cost of law school and their six-figure debt, most answer no. Then I ask them to think about how their perception of their own readiness may result in some unconscious bias against younger parents, low income parents, or parents that do not have even one-quarter of the earning potential of a soon-to-be Georgetown Law graduate. Many admit that prior to the class, they gave little thought to what it would take to change the systems that drive this perception.

There has never been a more important time to have these conversations in the United States. The Supreme Court is hostile to abortion rights, while many political leaders both in the federal government and in the states are actively working to shrink the social safety net that keeps so many impoverished families' heads slightly above water. Hopefully this framework gives you the language to advance the argument that having children and raising them are human rights, and not luxuries to be commodified.

B. Thinking Intersectionally and Practicing Anti-Racism

Another goal for those who wish to advance Reproductive Justice is intersectional thinking. Intersectionality, a concept developed by Professor Kimberlé Williams Crenshaw, posits that oppression based on race and gender interact in ways that are unique and independent from either oppression experienced singularly.[57]

Reproductive Justice was necessitated by a Reproductive Rights movement that viewed reproduction from the lens of white, middle-class women. For those who did not face persistent attacks on their right to have children and to parent those children, it is not surprising at all that their focus would be limited to addressing threats to abortion and contraceptive access. As we move forward in advancing a vision of Reproductive Justice, intersectionality must be a core principle.

Because racism is at the center of reproductive oppression, practicing anti-racism is also an essential component to advancing Reproductive Justice. This means identifying and challenging racism in all its forms.[58] The murder of George Floyd in May 2020 and subsequent uprisings across the country have sparked an interest in learning about race and privilege.[59] This horrific episode also presents an opportunity to examine how laws and

---

57. Kimberlé Crenshaw, *Demarginalizing the Intersection of Race and Sex: A Black Feminist Critique of Antidiscrimination Doctrine, Feminist Theory and Antiracist Politics*, 1989 U. OF CHI. LEGAL F. 139 (1989).

58. Forms of racism include individualized, interpersonal, institutional and structural. *See* Annie E. Casey Foundation, *Equity vs. Equality and Other Racial Justice Definitions*, Aug. 24, 2020.

59. A quick Google search will produce dozens of reading lists for those who are interested, but in addition to the books cited within, I also recommend *The New Jim Crow: Mass Incarceration in the Age of Colorblindness* by Michelle Alexander, and *Caste: The Origins of Our Discontent* by Isabelle Wilkerson and *How to Be An Antiracist* by Ibram X. Kendi.

policies regulating reproduction and families in the United States have and continue to be deeply racialized.

V. Conclusion

The creation of the Reproductive Justice framework presented a new way of thinking about what should be included in the scope of rights regarding reproduction. The movement's founders were responding to persistent attacks on Black and other marginalized women's right to have and raise children. Advancing a theory of social justice and applying the human rights concept of positive rights, Reproductive Justice envisions a world where every individual has all of the resources needed to actualize their reproductive decisions. Everyone has a role to play in advancing these efforts.

10

Modern Day Inquisitions*

By Rebecca J. Cook**

I. Introduction

Thanks and ever thanks to the organizers for giving us this remarkable opportunity to:

- celebrate our past achievements in applying human rights and constitutional provisions to protect the dignity of different sexualities, reduce violence, and promote reproductive and sexual health,
- explore some of the lessons learned in applying human rights and constitutional provisions to these issues: why we won, why we failed and how we missed opportunities, and finally,
- think together about our strategic plans to face the challenges ahead and strengthen our networks to create better synergies in our research, teaching, and advocacy to improve gender justice in the Americas.

Like the Inquisition in the 1600s, particularly its trials that took place in Lima, Peru; Cartagena, Colombia; and Mexico City,[1] and the trial of Galileo

---

* This chapter originally appeared in volume 65 of the University of Miami Law Review and is reprinted here with the permission of the Law Review. It was presented as the Keynote Address for the Gender Justice and Human Rights in the Americas Conference at the University of Miami School of Law February 23–25, 2011.

** Professor Emerita & Co-Director, International Reproductive and Sexual Health Law Program, Faculty of Law, University of Toronto, Canada. For more information on the goals, research, and advocacy work of the International Reproductive and Sexual Health Law

for defying the scripture that took place in Rome,[2] the modern day inquisitions are attempts to secure the supremacy of fundamentalist religions and their hierarchies in matters of gender, sexuality, and reproduction. The modern day inquisitions jeopardize academic freedoms of researchers, such as those whose scholarship focuses on reproductive health law and ethics,[3] and use hostile stereotypes and social condemnation, among other mechanisms, to control sexuality and reproduction and to privilege male dominance. In this sense the overarching barriers to achieving gender justice in this hemisphere are the modern day inquisitions.[4]

As we take stock, explore lessons learned, and face the challenges ahead, we need to recognize that each of us does so from particular perspectives. My perspective is that public universities are created as trusts to generate knowledge and make it universal in order to benefit societies. As a result of that perspective, I am constantly testing research questions about gender justice, exploring whether those questions are relevant, and determining how best to do the research in ways that resonate with those who might use it. I also have a perspective on the nature of the legal research. Domestic legal research is essential, but transnational research is increasingly

---

Program, *see International Reproductive and Sexual Health Law Program*, UNIV. OF TORONTO FACULTY OF LAW, http://www.law.utoronto.ca/programs/reprohealth.html (last visited Nov. 30, 2020).

1. BOLESLAO LEWIN, LA INQUISICIÓN EN MÉXICO: IMPRESIONANTES RELATOS DEL SIGLO XVII (J.M. Cajica Jr. ed., 1967); BOLESLAO LEWIN, LA INQUISICIÓN EN MÉXICO: RACISMO INQUISITORIAL (EL SINGULAR CASO DE MARÍA DE ZÁRATE) (1971).

2. DAVA SOBEL, GALILEO'S DAUGHTER 7 (1999) ("In 1616, a pope and a cardinal inquisitor reprimanded Galileo, warning him to curtail his forays into the supernal realms.").

3. *See, e.g.*, Debora Diniz Rodrigues v. Brazilian Union of Culture & Educ., Processo: 0019900-12.2007.5.10.0101 (Vara do Trabalho de Taguatinga do Tribunal Regional do Trabalho da 10 Regi file Feb. 13, 2007). *See also* DEBORA DINIZ, SAMANTHA BUGLIONE & ROGER RAUPP RIOS, ENTRE A DÚ VIDA E O DOGMA: LIBERDADE DE CÁTEDRA E UNIVERSIDADES CONFESSIONAIS (2006); VICTORIA BAXTER, AM. ASS'N FOR THE ADVANCEMENT OF SCI., DIRECTORY OF PERSECUTED SCIENTISTS, ENGINEERS, AND HEALTH PROFESSIONALS (2003), *available at* http://shr.aaas.org/aaashran/directory_2003.pdf; *AAAS Science and Human Rights Program*, AM. ASS'N FOR THE ADVANCEMENT OF SCI. (Oct. 21, 2002), (discussing firing of Brazilian bioethicist "in retaliation for her participation in a public debate about abortion"); Mariana Carbajal, *Metodos para Interrumpir un Debate Pendiente*, PAGINA 12 (Oct. 19, 2009), http://www.pagina12.com.ar/diario/elpais/1-133700-2009-10-19.html (explaining the expulsion of law professors from Catholic universities in Argentina for their work on behalf of pregnant women).

4. *See* Juan Marco Vaggione, *Evangelium Vitae Today: How Conservative Forces Are Using the 1995 Papal Encyclical to Reshape Public Policy in Latin America*, 31:3 CONSCIENCE 23 (2010), *available at* http://viewer.zmags.com/publication/f1f99f2e#/f1f99f2d/24 (stating that "the manner in which these [Catholic] activists work has been transformed," though "the content of their beliefs" remains the same).

important as our world globalizes. Transnational research is not about privileging one kind of knowledge. It is, for example, about learning from successes in the South and the mistakes of the North.

* * *

With my perspectives clear, let me proceed by taking stock, exploring lessons learned, and facing the challenges ahead.

II. Taking Stock

We often forget to take stock of our achievements: add them up, examine their importance, and assess how they can contribute to longer-term victories within countries and within the Western Hemisphere. Acknowledging our achievements is critical to understanding how to build on them. We might start by doing a mapping of significant legislative reforms, important domestic court decisions, and significant decisions of the Inter-American Commission on Human Rights[5] and the Inter-American Court of Human Rights[6] within our respective fields. We might find important synergies,

---

5. *See, e.g.*, Ramírez Jacinto v. Mexico, Petition 161-02, Inter-Am. Comm'n H.R., Report No. 21/07, OEA/Ser.L/V/II.130, doc. 22 rev. 1 ¶¶ 24–27 (2007), *available at* http://www .cidh.oas.org/annualrep/2007eng/Mexico161.02eng.htm (friendly settlement between girl and Government of Baja California where rape of girl caused unwanted pregnancy and authorities denied abortion); Mamérita Mestanza Chávez v. Peru, Case 12.191, Inter-Am. Comm'n H.R., Report No. 71/03, OEA/Ser.L/V/II.118, doc. 70 rev. 2 ¶¶ 9–12, 14, 17 (2003), *available at* http://www.cidh.oas.org/annualrep/2003eng/Peru.12191.htm (friendly settlement between various women's rights nongovernmental organizations and Peruvian State where coerced sterilization of 33-year-old rural mother of seven caused death); "Baby Boy" v. United States, Case 2141, Inter-Am. Comm'n H.R., Res. No. 23/81, OEA/Ser.L./V/ II.54, doc. 9 rev. 1 ¶¶ 30–31 (1981), *available at* http://www.cidh.org/annualrep/80.81eng /usa2141.htm (permitting abortion); Ann Farmer, *Luisa Cabal: Turning National Wrongs into International Rights*, VOICES UNABRIDGED (Sept. 26, 2003) (Peruvian government paid reparations for rape of a street vendor by her examining physician and the subsequent denial of remedies.).

6. *See, e.g.*, Xákmok Kásek Indigenous Cmty. v. Paraguay, Merits, Reparations, & Costs, Judgment, Inter-Am. Ct. H.R. (ser. C) No. 214, ¶¶ 217, 232, 234, 275, 301–03, 306 (Aug. 24, 2010) (State of Paraguay responsible for failing to prevent a maternal death of a woman in the Xákmok Kásek indigenous community); Gonzalez v. Mexico, Preliminary Objection, Merits, Reparations, & Costs, Judgment, Inter Am. Ct. H.R. (ser. C) No. 205, ¶¶ 1–2, 20–30 (Nov. 16, 2009) (Mexican State accepted partial international responsibility for disappearances and deaths of three women later found in a cotton field, where State had knowledge of gender-related violence yet failed to prevent deaths); De La Cruz-Flores v. Peru, Merits, Reparations, & Costs, Judgment, Inter-Am. Ct. H.R. (ser. C) No. 115, ¶¶ 73(8), 74, 90, 94–102 (Nov. 18, 2004) (criminal prosecution of doctor for providing care to terrorists impermissible). *See also* Patricia Palacios Zuloaga, *The Path to Gender Justice in the Inter-American Court of Human Rights*, 17 TEX. J. WOMEN & L. 227, 232–46, 286–87 (2008) (discussing six

or troubling divergences in these reforms and court decisions. One right
might be applied in one way in one context and another way in another sector, or the criminal law might be used advantageously in one sector and not
in another.

A. Gender Identities

Legislators and judges have begun to grasp the importance of respecting
different gender norms and identities. Laws permitting same sex marriage
have been passed in Argentina,[7] Canada, and Mexico City, and those laws in
Canada[8] and Mexico City[9] have been affirmed as constitutionally compliant.
These legal reforms have helped to reframe the way we think about sexuality[10] and sexual health.[11] Sexual intimacy is an important part of everyone's
lives and should not be compromised, especially on grounds of one's sexual
preference.[12]

A particular sexuality can no longer be privileged over another. The
meaning of sexual citizenship is expanding,[13] most recently as gays and les-
bians are being allowed increasingly to openly serve in the various militar-
ies of the region, such as the U.S.[14] Degrading stereotypes of a person or
groups of persons with one orientation is increasingly prohibited legally
and socially. Individuals cannot be stereotyped in ways that deny them a

---

Inter-American Court of Human Rights gender-related cases and prescribing strategies for
"a more gender-friendly Court jurisprudence" in the future).

7. Law No. 26.618, July 21, 2010, [CXVIII] B.O. 31.949 (Arg.).

8. Reference re Same Sex Marriage, [2004] 3 S.C.R. 698, ¶ 5 (Can.), *available at* http://
scc.lexum.org/en/2004/2004scc79/2004scc79.pdf (holding that "the Proposed Act, which
defines marriage as the union of two persons, is consistent with the Canadian Charter of
Rights and Freedoms.").

9. Acción de Inconstitucionalidad 2/2010, Promovente: Procurador General de la
República. Suprema Corte de Justicia de la Nación [SCJN] [Supreme Court], Novena Época,
Agosto de 2010 (Mex.).

10. *See generally* Jeffrey A. Redding, *Dignity, Legal Pluralism, and Same-Sex Marriage*, 75
BROOK. L. REV. 791, 863 (2010) ("re-discovery [of gay and lesbian dignity] may have to
happen by traveling to very unfamiliar places.").

11. *See generally* Esteban Restrepo-Saldarriaga, *Advancing Sexual Health through Human
Rights in Latin America and the Caribbean* (Int'l Council on Human Rights Pol'y, Working
Paper, 2011).

12. Alice M. Miller, Int'l Council on Human Rights Pol'y, *Sexuality and Human Rights*, at 8
(2009) ("Sexual rights make a strong claim to universality, since they relate to an element of
the self which is common to all humans: their sexuality.").

13. *See* BRENDA COSSMAN, SEXUAL CITIZENS: THE LEGAL AND CULTURAL REGULATION OF
SEX AND BELONGING (2007).

14. Don't Ask, Don't Tell Repeal Act of 2010, Pub. L. No. 111-321, 124 Stat. 3515 (2010).

benefit or impose a burden.[15] Debates and literature now explore the importance of masculinities,[16] enabling a fuller sense of the meanings of gender identities.

B. Freedom from Violence

There have been many important advances in norms that protect us from violence,[17] the most recent of which was the decision of the Inter-American Court of Human Rights in *Gonzalez v. Mexico* (the "Algodonero" decision).[18] That decision held Mexico responsible under the American Convention on Human Rights (the "Convention") and the Convention on Prevention, Punishment and Eradication of Violence against Women (the "Convention Belém do Pará") for failing to investigate the gendered disappearances and murders of three poor, migrant women, two of whom were minors.[19] The bodies of these three women, Claudia Ivette Gonzalez, Esmeralda Herrera Monreal and Laura Berenice Ramos Monarrez, were found in the cotton field near Juarez, a Mexican town bordering El Paso, Texas, in the Mexican state of Chihuahua.[20]

The decision is important for a number of reasons including that, for the first time, the Court ruled that states have positive obligations to respond to violence against women by private actors, looked at the murders of these three women in the context of mass violence against women and structural discrimination, and found that gender-based violence constitutes gender discrimination.[21] The Court decided that the State violated the obligation not to discriminate contained in Article 1(1) of the Convention, in connection with the obligation to guarantee the rights embodied in Articles 4(1) (life), 5(1) (physical, mental and moral integrity), 5(2)

---

15. *See* REBECCA COOK & SIMONE CUSACK, GENDER STEREOTYPING: TRANSNATIONAL LEGAL PERSPECTIVES 3, 85–89 (2010) (available in Spanish).

16. *See, e.g.,* Nancy E. Dowd, *Asking the Man Question: Masculinities Analysis and Feminist Theory,* 33 HARV. J. L. & GENDER 415, 417–24 (2010); NANCY E. DOWD, THE MAN QUESTION—MALE SUBORDINATION AND PRIVILEGE (2010).

17. *See* Inter-American Convention on the Prevention, Punishment and Eradication of Violence against Women, June 9, 1994, 33 I.L.M. 1534, *available at* http://www1.umn.edu/humanrts/instree/brazil1994.html. *See also* LILIANA TOJO, CTR. FOR JUSTICE AND INT'L LAW, SUMMARIES OF JURISPRUDENCE: GENDER-BASED VIOLENCE 355–56 (2010).

18. Gonzalez v. Mexico, Preliminary Objection, Merits, Reparations, and Costs, Judgment, Inter-Am. Ct. H.R. (ser. C) No. 205 (Nov. 16, 2009) (also known informally as the "Algodonero" or the "cotton field" decision).

19. *Id.* ¶¶ 1–2, 20–30.

20. *Id.* ¶ 2.

21. *Id.* ¶¶ 164, 402.

(torture or cruel, inhuman, or degrading punishment or treatment) and 7(1) (personal liberty and security) of the Convention to the detriment of the three victims; as well as in relation to the right of access to justice established in Articles 8(1) (right to a fair trial) and 25(1) (simple, prompt, effective recourse) of the Convention, to the detriment of the victims' next of kin.[22]

In presenting the facts of the case, the Court included a section, *Stereotyping allegedly manifested by officials to the victims' next of kin.*[23] It referenced the testimony of the victims' mothers to show how state officials had generated hostile stereotypes of the victims' roles, attributes, and characteristics, in part to justify their avoidance of their obligations to investigate.[24] For example, the Court cited testimony of Esmeralda Herrera's mother saying that when she reported her daughter's disappearance, the authorities told her that she "had not disappeared, but was out with her boyfriends or wandering around with friends" and "that if anything happened to her, it was because she was looking for it, because a good girl, a good woman, stays at home."[25] Importantly, the Court concluded that "the comments made by officials that the victims had gone off with a boyfriend or that they led a disreputable life . . . constitute stereotyping."[26]

In the section of its judgment, *Obligation not to discriminate: violence against women as discrimination,* the Court took judicial notice of the phenomenon of gender stereotyping: "the Tribunal finds that gender stereotyping refers to a preconception of personal attributes, characteristics or roles that correspond or should correspond to either men or women."[27] The Court then went on to refer to the statements made by the State agents, to identify how hostile stereotypes are perpetuated in the particular context of the police authorities: "Bearing in mind the statements made by the State, the subordination of women can be associated with practices based on persistent socially-dominant gender stereotypes, a situation that is exacerbated when the stereotypes are reflected, implicitly or explicitly, in policies and practices and, particularly, in the reasoning and language of the judicial police authorities, as in this case."[28]

---

22. *Id.* ¶¶ 402, 602.
23. *Id.* ¶¶ 196–208.
24. *Id.*
25. *Id.* ¶¶ 197–98.
26. *Id.* ¶ 208.
27. *Id.* ¶ 401.
28. *Id.* (internal cross-reference omitted).

Significantly, the Court concluded this section by saying that "[t]he creation and use of stereotypes becomes one of the causes and consequences of gender-based violence against women."[29] In short, the Court recognized the structural nature of violence against women, reframed it as a form of discrimination, and acknowledged the contribution of stereotypical thinking to violence.

C. Reproductive Dignity and Equality

Important achievements have been made transnationally in characterizing reproductive choice as a component of dignity and to holding a state accountable for failing to respect that dignity.

1. Reproductive Dignity

In 2005, the United Nations Human Rights Committee held Peru responsible when a governmental hospital denied an adolescent girl, pregnant with an anencephalic fetus, a fetus without an upper brain, access to abortion services to which she was legally entitled.[30] In order to protect prenatal life at any cost, the adolescent girl was forced to carry her pregnancy with an anencephalic fetus to term and to breast feed the child for a few days after birth, knowing that newborn infant would die a few days after birth.[31] The Committee found that the treatment forced upon this young girl constituted a violation of her rights to be free from inhuman and degrading treatment, to private life, to such measures of protection as are required by her status as a minor, and to her right to an effective legal remedy for violation of such rights.[32]

Dignity is a foundational concept in the 2006 Colombian Constitutional Court decision liberalizing the abortion law.[33] The Court explained its meaning as follows:

29. *Id.*

30. U.N. Human Rights Comm., Noelia Llantoy Huamán v. Peru, ¶¶ 2.1–2.3, 6.4–6.6, 7, U.N. Doc. CCPR/C/85/D/1153/2003 (Oct. 24, 2005), http://www1.umn.edu/humanrts/undocs/1153-2003.html.

31. *Id.* ¶ 2.6.

32. *Id.* ¶¶ 6.4–6.6, 7. *See also* Rebecca J. Cook, Joanna N. Erdman, Martin Hevia & Bernard M. Dickens, *Prenatal Management of Anencephaly*, 102 INT'L J. GYNECOLOGY & OBSTETRICS 304, 304–08 (2008), *available at* http://ssrn.com/abstract=1263905 (discussing legal and ethical implications of abortion of anencephalic fetuses in South America).

33. Colombian Constitutional Court Decision C-355/2006; Rebecca J. Cook, *Foreword to* WOMEN'S LINK WORLDWIDE, C-355/2006: EXCERPTS OF THE CONSTITUTIONAL COURT'S RULING THAT LIBERALIZED ABORTION IN COLOMBIA 7 (2007), *available at* https://www

[T]he rules which flow from the concept of human dignity—both the constitutional principle and the fundamental right to dignity—coincide in protecting the same type of conduct. This Court has held that in those cases where dignity is used as a criterion in a judicial decision, it must be understood that dignity protects the following: (i) autonomy, or the possibility of designing one's life plan and living in accordance with it (to live life as one wishes); (ii) certain material conditions of existence (to live well); and (iii) intangible goods such as physical integrity and moral integrity (to live free of humiliation). . . .[34]

As a result of this foundational concept of human dignity, the Court explained that

when the legislature enacts criminal laws, it cannot ignore that a woman is a human being entitled to dignity and that she must be treated as such, as opposed to being treated as a reproductive instrument for the human race. The legislature must not impose the role of procreator on a woman against her will.[35]

2. Reproductive Equality

The Inter-American Court of Human Rights, in the case of *Xákmok Kásek Indigenous Community v. Paraguay,* held Paraguay responsible for the lack of guarantee of the right of the members of the Xákmok Kásek Indigenous Community to their ancestral property.[36] This case is historic for many reasons, including for purposes of reproductive health. The Court ruled that the failure of the government to guarantee for the Xákmok Kásek indigenous peoples the possession of their property kept this community in a vulnerable state regarding their health and welfare.[37]

Specifically with regard to one member, Remigia Ruíz, a 38 year-old woman who died in childbirth because she did not receive appropriate medical attention, the Court declared that the circumstances of her death manifested "many of the signs relevant to maternal deaths, namely: death

.womenslinkworldwide.org/en/files/1353/c355-2006-english-version.pdf. *See also* ISABEL CRISTINA JARAMILLO SIERRA & TATIANA ALFONSO SIERRA, MUJERES, CORTES Y MEDIOS: LA REFORMA JUDICIAL DEL ABORTO (2008); Verónica Undurraga & Rebecca J. Cook, *Constitutional Incorporation of International and Comparative Human Rights Law: The Colombian Constitutional Court Decision C-355/2006, in* CONSTITUTING EQUALITY: GENDER EQUALITY AND COMPARATIVE LAW 215 (Susan H. Williams ed., 2009).

34. WOMEN'S LINK WORLDWIDE, *id.* at 35 (initial alteration in original).
35. WOMEN'S LINK WORLDWIDE, *id.* at 37.
36. Xákmok Kásek Indigenous Cmty. v. Paraguay, *supra* note 6, ¶¶ 2, 337(2).
37. *Id.* ¶¶ 214, 273.

while giving birth without adequate medical care, a situation of exclusion or extreme poverty, lack of access to adequate health services, and a lack of documentation on cause of death, among others."[38]

The Court emphasized that

> extreme poverty and the lack of adequate medical care for pregnant women or women who have recently given birth result in a high maternal mortality rate. Because of this, States must put in place adequate health-care policies that allow it to offer care through personnel who are adequately trained to handle births, policies to prevent maternal mortality with adequate prenatal and postpartum care, and legal and administrative instruments regarding healthcare policy that allow for the adequate documentation of cases of maternal mortality.
>
> All this is because pregnant women need special measures of protection.[39]

The Court found that the State violated her right to life (Article 4(1)) and the right to exercise that right without discrimination (Article 1(1)) of the American Convention, because Paraguay "did not take the positive measures necessary within the realm of its responsibilities, which would be reasonably expected to include preventing or avoiding risk to the right to life. As a consequence, the deaths of the following individuals are attributed to the State: . . . Remigia Ruiz, who died in 2005 at 38 years of age from complications while giving birth and did not receive medical care . . . ."[40]

In the finding on discrimination, the Court went beyond the discrimination that can be found in the letter of the law and looked at *de facto* discrimination against the members of the community based on: their marginalization in the enjoyments of the rights that the Court declared were violated, the lack of positive measures taken by the State to reverse this exclusion and, in general, their situation of extreme and special vulnerability with the consequent "lack of adequate and effective remedies that protect the rights of the indigenous in practice and not just formally . . . ."[41]

The Court decided the State discriminated by not complying with their obligation "to provide goods and services to the Community, particularly in regard to food, water, healthcare, and education; and to the preeminence of a view of property that grants greater protection to private property

---

38. *Id.* ¶ 232.
39. *Id.* ¶ 233.
40. *Id.* ¶ 234.
41. *Id.* ¶¶ 272–73.

owners over indigenous territorial claims, thereby failing to recognize their cultural identity and threatening their physical subsistence."[42]

In the order of reparations, the Court ordered the State to take measures which are immediate and permanent while the land is in the process of being handed over to the community: "provision of special medical care for the pregnant women, both pre- and post-natal and during the first few months of the baby's life . . . ."[43]

To assure that the provision of basic goods and services are adequate, the State must provide a study, within six months of the notification of the judgment, "regarding the medical and psycho-social care, as well as the delivery of medication: 1) the necessary regularity of medical personnel's visits to the Community; 2) the principal ailments and illnesses suffered by the members of the Community; 3) the medications and treatments necessary for those ailments and illnesses; 4) the necessary pre- and post-natal care; and 5) the manner and regularity with which the vaccinations and deparasitizations should be carried out. . . ."[44]

Finally, the State must provide a healthcare center in the settlement where the community is temporarily located "with the medications and supplies necessary to provide adequate healthcare. To do this, the State has six months as of the notification of this Judgment. Likewise, it must immediately establish a system of communication in the settlement that allows the victims to contact the relevant healthcare authorities for care in the event of an emergency. Should it be necessary, the State will provide transportation to the individuals who need it. Later, the State shall also ensure that the healthcare center and communication system are moved to the place where the Community settles permanently."[45]

* * *

These victories regarding gender identities, freedom from violence, and reproductive dignity and equality are fragile and backlash is inevitable, but significant beginnings have been made, and we must think strategically about how best to build on them.

---

42. *Id.* ¶ 273.
43. *Id.* ¶ 301.
44. *Id.* ¶ 303.
45. *Id.* ¶ 306.

III. Lessons Learned

What are the lessons learned from the last decade for achieving gender justice? Learning lessons is an evolving process: what should we build on from past experiences, and what should we change in our programs, polices, and advocacy moving forward to secure gender justice? Answers to these questions will depend on one's perspective. Some of the lessons that I have learned include the need to

- redefine religious space,
- understand technology as transformation, and
- build on the constitutive role of the law.

A. Redefining Religious Space

If one steps back from the particular fights on sexuality and reproduction in the past decade, a lesson learned is that there has been an undeniable expansion of religious space to the detriment of gender justice. This can be seen in the unaccountable nature of religious hierarchies, as evidenced by the clerical sexual abuse scandal, and the abuse of the right of conscience.

1. Unaccountable Nature of Church Hierarchies

I want to talk specifically about the unaccountable nature of the hierarchy of the Catholic Church, but I recognize that other religious have challenges in failing to hold themselves accountable for abusive acts. What might we learn from how the sexual abuse scandal has put the Catholic Church on the defensive? The recently published book *The Case of the Pope: Vatican Accountability for Human Rights Abuse*, carefully, one might say forensically, documents the widespread practice of clerical sexual abuse, the systematic way the Vatican has covered it up, and how it has consistently failed to report the abuse, no matter how heinous, to the police.[46] The book lays out the case for considering the widespread and systematic cover up of clerical sexual abuse, as a crime against humanity, such crimes not being confined to times of war.[47] The book raises the possibility of convicting the current

---

46. Geoffrey Robertson, The Case of the Pope: Vatican Accountability for Human Rights Abuse 6 (2010) ("[S]exual abuse of children by priests in the Catholic Church . . . has been covered up by many bishops with the support and at the direction of the Vatican. The cover-up has included an almost visceral refusal to call in the police. . . .").

47. *Id.* at 149–50 (stating "[i]t must be hoped that, in due course, international law will develop its very real potential to threaten heads of state with accountability if they oppress

Pope Benedict XVI for aiding and abetting the international crime of systematic child abuse through his previous position as head of the Office of
the Doctrine of the Faith, formerly known as the Office of the Inquisition.[48]

The Church has begun,[49] but has a long way to go, to remedy the abuses
and to prevent their repetition. The Church has been shamed into acknowledging the devastating impact of its cover-up of clerical sexual abuse on the
well-being of children and the adults they become. Now it has to be shamed
into recognizing the harmful impact, on women and their reproductive and
sexual health, of its policies on contraception, abortion and its expansion
of the abuse of conscience on sexual and reproductive health. What lessons
might be drawn from how the clerical sexual abuse scandal was exposed for
holding the Church accountable for its policies on the spread of HIV or for
stigmatizing different sexualities for its opposition to same-sex marriage?

2. The Abuse of the Right of Conscience

The right of conscience is being invoked in the reproductive and sexual
health field by pharmacists not to fill prescriptions for contraception,[50] by
doctors not to treat ectopic pregnancies until the tube ruptures,[51] not to
perform abortions in emergencies,[52] not to perform lawful abortions,[53] and

---

their own people or their own faithful, or turn their eyes, blinded with a mote, to crimes that
their own agents are committing[,]" noting the Vatican is responsible under international
law due to its "decision to opt for statehood," and hoping for a new "stage in the struggle for
global justice.").

48. *Id.* at 121–33.

49. Alexei Barrionuevo & Pascale Bonnefoy, *Chilean Priest Found Guilty of Abusing Minors*, N.Y. TIMES (Feb 18, 2011), https://www.nytimes.com/2011/02/19/world
/americas/19chile.html.

50. Pichon & Sajous v. France, Eur. Ct. H.R. (Third Section), Appl. No. 49853/99 (2001)
(claim of pharmacists to object on grounds of conscience to selling contraceptives held inadmissible, but limitations on conscience permissible when necessary for women's health).

51. *See, e.g.,* Susan Berke Fogel & Lourdes A. Rivera, *Saving* Roe *Is Not Enough: When Religion Controls Healthcare*, 31 FORDHAM URB. L.J. 725, 733 (2004).

52. *See, e.g.,* Katharina Wecker, *Doctors Refuse to Perform Abortion on 13-Year-Old Rape Victim*, COLOMBIA REPORTS (July 1, 2009), https://colombiareports.com/doctors-refuse-to
-perform-abortion-on-13-year-old-rape-victim/.

53. Decision T-209 of 2008 20-21 and 45 (Constitutional Court of Colombia) (objecting
providers are obligated to refer women to non-objecting providers and that hospitals, clinics
and other institutions have no rights of conscience); *see also* Rebecca J. Cook, Monica Arango
Olaya & Bernard M. Dickens, *Health Care Responsibilities and Conscientious Objection*, 104 INT'L
J. GYNECOLOGY & OBSTETRICS 249–52 (2009).

by anesthesiologists not to provide anesthesia, leaving pregnant women to endure the pain of undergoing lawful abortions,[54] or early induction of labor of an anencephalic fetus, without the benefit of anesthesia.[55]

The right of conscience is an important right and should be accommodated to the extent possible. However, when providers object on grounds of conscience to providing such services and refuse to refer patients to a willing provider or fail to provide these services in the case of emergency, this refusal infringes the rights of women to receive lawful services.

Health care providers are professionals and have professional and ethical duties to consider first the well-being of the patient. Why is it that firefighters are not allowed to choose the burning houses they rescue, while health care providers may choose the patients they treat? Why is it that the right of conscience in the context of a burning building will not be accommodated, while the right of conscience of health care providers is accommodated when women's lives are at stake? Why is it that the rights of women to their own conscience, to live their lives according to their own moral codes, get lost in the equation?

Is there a contagion in the abuse of the rights of conscience? In Canada, at least, the spread of this contagion was limited by the Saskatchewan Court of Appeal that ruled that public officers cannot discriminate on grounds, for instance of sexual orientation, in rendering lawful public services, such as the celebration of non-religious marriages.[56]

* * *

Last year, the Vatican lost credibility in publishing the so-called New Norms that issued no instructions to report clerical sexual abusers to the

---

54. Laurie Michelle Denyer, Call Me "At-Risk": Maternal Health in Sao Paulo's Public Health Clinics and the Desire for Cesarean Technology, at 9 (Aug. 19, 2009) (unpublished M.S. thesis, Massachusetts Institute of Technology), *available at* https://dspace.mit.edu/bit stream/handle/1721.1/55107/589272652-MIT.pdf;sequence=2 (noting that racially marginalized women are often denied anesthesia).

55. *Brazil: Severina's Story (Uma História Severina)*, THE HUB (Aug. 20, 2008); Debora Diniz, *Research Ethics in Social Sciences: The Severina's Story Documentary*, 1 INT'L J. FEMINIST APPROACHES TO BIOETHICS 23–35 (Fall 2008). *See also* Imagines Lives, *Severina's Story*, YOU-TUBE (June 27, 2012), https://www.youtube.com/watch?v=JW1aBeVCC7Y.

56. *In re* Marriage Commissioners Appointed under *The Marriage Act*, 1995, S.S. 1995, c. M-4.1 (2011), 2011 SKCA 3 (Can. Sask. C.A.), *available at* http://www.lawsociety.sk.ca /judgments/2011skca3.pdf.

civil authorities and announced that attempts to ordain women are as serious as sexually abusing a child.[57] In claiming immunity from human rights, the church hierarchy has defied criminal laws on sexual abuse and child protection. In hiding behind the right of conscience, the hierarchy has ignored the rights of women to reproductive and sexual health care.

A lesson is that our field has not been sufficiently adept at taking on the religious opposition, in part because no one wants to be considered as anti-religious. Religious faith plays an important role in people's lives, and religious institutions run hospitals and schools that are essential to societies. However, religious space has grown well beyond its religious purpose, to abuse the rights of children and women, and to offend the dignity of those of the same-sex who want to marry.

What might we change moving forward to achieve gender justice, given this expansion of religious space? We need to be more effective in challenging the practices of religious hierarchies that offend human rights, being clear that it is not religious faith behind these practices that is the issue. People are entitled to believe what they want, but they are not free to impose those beliefs on others to the detriment of their rights, or pursue practices that offend the rights of others.

B. Technology as Transformation

The last decade has seen the introduction of methods to treat HIV/ AIDS, HPV vaccines to reduce liability to cervical cancer,[58] improved in-vitro fertilization techniques to accommodate infertility ("IVF"),[59] the introduction of

---

57. *Modifications Made in the Normae de Gravioribus Delictis*, VIS NEWS (July 15, 2010), http://visnews-en.blogspot.com/2010/07/modifications-made-in-normae-de.html; *see also* Nicole Winfield, *Female Ordination and Sex Abuse of Minors*, THE GLOBE AND MAIL, July 16, 2010, at A9; Maureen Dowd, Op-Ed, *Rome Fiddles, We Burn*, N.Y. TIMES (July 17, 2010), https://www.nytimes.com/2010/07/18/opinion/18dowd.html.

58. Joanna N. Erdman, *Human Rights in Health Equity: Cervical Cancer and HPV Vaccines*, 35 AM. J.L. & MED. 365, 377 (2009) (describing the HPV vaccine as "a particularly promising remedial measure for cervical cancer inequity").

59. *See* Sanchez Villalobos v. Costa Rica, Case 12.361, Inter-Am. Comm'n H.R., Report No. 25/04, OEA/Ser.L/V/II.122, doc. 5 rev. ¶¶ 1, 16–17 (2004), *available at* http://www.cidh .org/annualrep/2004eng/CostaRica.12361eng.htm (noting that President of Costa Rica authorized IVF and Supreme Court of Justice subsequently declared authorization

Viagra, the expanded use of improved emergency contraception ("EC"),[60] the expanded use of Misoprostol for purposes of preventing hemorrhage in child birth and the post-partum period, causing abortion or treating post-abortion complications,[61] and the abortion pill combination of Mifepristone/Misoprostol.

With many of the initiatives to introduce new methods or initiatives for expanded use, clinical protocols have been elaborated to ensure safe and effective use.[62] These initiatives are essential to meeting the practical needs of women and men in accessing medicines and methods essential to their reproductive and sexual health and well-being.

But with many of these initiatives, there have been and will be innumerable fights in the region. Some have turned to the court decisions for resolution, some have been resolved by new regulatory guidelines, and some have resulted in outright bans.

There are current attempts in El Salvador to control the distribution of Misoprostol for post abortion care by requiring its registration as a narcotic; that is the class of drugs which requires special prescription, thus limiting its distribution and use.

---

unconstitutional due to high aggregate loss of embryos associated with the procedure at the time); Brief for Sanchez Villalobos as Amici Curiae Supporting Petitioners, Sanchez Villalobos v. Costa Rica, Case 12.361, Inter-Am. Comm'n H.R., Report No. 25/04, OEA/Ser.L/V/II.122, doc. 5 rev. ¶ II.C.3 (2009) (explaining that scientific and technological development of IVF procedures renders concern about embryo loss unjustified).

60. *See Welcome to ICEC: The International Consortium for Emergency Contraception*, INT'L CONSORTIUM FOR EMERGENCY CONTRACEPTION, http://www.cecinfo.org/ (last visited Mar. 22, 2011) ("Now women in over 140 countries can buy emergency contraception. . . .").

61. *See* GYNUITY HEALTH PROJECTS, http://gynuity.org/ (last visited Mar. 22, 2011) (offering information on how to use Misoprostol and Misoprostol's intersection with law).

62. *Sexual and Reproductive Health*, WORLD HEALTH ORGANIZATION, https://www.who.int/reproductivehealth/about_us/en/ (last visited Mar. 10, 2021) (listing initiatives).

Another example is emergency contraception ("EC").[63] The highest courts in Argentina,[64] Chile,[65] and, for example, Ecuador[66] have prohibited the use of EC because of its alleged action after the union of the sperm and the egg, thus running afoul of the view that "human life" begins at conception. Ignoring the science, the Supreme Court of Argentina based its reasoning on religious doctrines expressed in the national constitution that state that life has to be protected from conception.

The reproductive and sexual health field is constantly searching for a better technological fix, a better contraceptive, a more effective health intervention, without regard to the need to change norms and values to ensure women are empowered to make choices, and to ensure that technologies are distributed fairly. My fear is that in focusing on the technological fix without regard to the impact of prohibiting EC on the rights of women and their rights to equal access to medicines, we are missing important opportunities to promote gender justice and health equity.

Have the transformative roles of technology to promote gender justice and health equity been overlooked in these battles to introduce new methods? Has the discourse been changed? Do communities understand that neglecting medicines that only women need is a form of discrimination

---

63. *See* Maria Alejandra Cardenas, *Banning Emergency Contraception in Latin America: Constitutional Courts Granting an Absolute* Right to Life *to the Zygote*, 3 HOUMBOLT AM. COMP. L. REV., no. 6 (2009). *available at* https://www.scribd.com/document/89065139 /Banning-Emergency-Contraception-in-Latin-America.

64. Corte Suprema de Justicia de la Nación [CSJN] [National Supreme Court of Justice], 5/3/2002, "Portal del Belén—Asociación Civil sin Fines de Lucro c. Ministerio de Salud y Acción Social de la Nación / recurso de amparo", La Ley [L.L.] (2002-P-709) (Arg.) (the use of emergency contraception prohibited as the fertilized egg has full legal protection prior to implantation due to the national constitution which states that life begins at conception). *See also* Fiorella Melzi, *The Supreme Court of Argentina: Ruling against Women's Equality*, 4 J.L. & EQUALITY 261, 263 (2005).

65. Corte Suprema de Justicia [C.S.J.] [Supreme Court], 30 agosto 2001, "Sara Philippi Izquierdo y otros c. Minesterio de Salud y otros," Rol de la causa: 2186-2001, civiles, REVISTA DE DERECHO Y JURISPRUDENCIA [R.D.J.] No. 98 p.199 (Chile) (emergency contraception violates constitutional protection of life "from conception" because of its possible action after the union of sperm and egg); Tribunal Constitucional [T.C] [Constitutional Court], 18 Abril 2008, "José Antonio Kast Rist c. Ministerio de Salud," Rol de la causa: 740-07-CDS, Sentencia (Chile). *See also* Angela Castellanos, *Chile: The Struggle over Emergency Contraception*, REWIRE NEWS GRP. (Oct. 19, 2009, 6:00 AM), https://rewirenewsgroup.com/article/2009/10/19 /chile-the-struggle-over-emergency-contraception/.

66. *In re* Access to Emergency Contraception in Ecuador / Amici (Constitutional Tribunal of Ecuador), CTR. FOR REPROD. RIGHTS (Dec. 10, 2008), https://reproductiverights.org/case /in-re-access-to-emergency-contraception-in-ecuador-amici-constitutional-tribunal-of-ecua dor (noting the distribution of emergency contraception was declared unconstitutional as a violation of the right to life established in the Ecuadorian Constitution).

against them? Has the fact that Viagra gets covered by health insurance plans, and not contraceptives, been sufficiently characterized, debated, and advocated both in the court of public opinion and the courts of law as an offense to gender justice?

C. The Constitutive Role of the Law

Another lesson learned is that we have to underscore the importance of evidence-based policies and laws, and to hold governments accountable for basing their policies on pseudo-science, junk science, fraudulent science, or what might be called theo-physiology. In particular, we need more systematically to expose judicial reasoning that is not evidence-based, and show how such judicial thinking migrates from one religiously motivated judge to another.

Where ministries of health and therapeutic drug approval agencies have been motivated by factors other than scientific evidence of safety and efficacy of emergency contraception, some courts in Colombia[67] and the U.S.[68] have generally considered their actions to be arbitrary.

While recognizing the transcending importance of religious and theological questions to some people, judges often emphasize that their obligations are to apply the law.[69] For instance, in *Smeaton v. Secretary of State for Health*, addressing whether the distribution of emergency contraception constitutes an offense under the country's abortion laws, Justice Munby explained that the "days are past when the business of the judges was the

---

67. *See* Consejo de Estado [C.E.] [State Council], First Section, junio 5, 2008, Counselor Ostau de Lafont Pianeta (Colom.). *See also In re* Access to Emergency Contraception in Colombia (amicus brief) (Colombian Council of State), CTR. FOR REPROD. RIGHTS (Dec. 10, 2008), http://reproductiverights.org/en/case/in-re-access-to-emergency-contraception -in-colombia-amicus-brief-colombian-council-of-state (noting decision held EC "is a contraceptive method and not an abortifacient, and therefore, access to emergency contraception is in accordance with the right to life as established in the Colombian Constitution").

68. *See* Tummino v. Torti, 603 F. Supp. 2d 519, 523 (E.D.N.Y. 2009) ("The FDA repeatedly and unreasonably delayed issuing a decision on Plan B for suspect reasons. . . . [T]he record is clear that the FDA's course of conduct regarding Plan B departed in significant ways from the agency's normal procedures regarding similar applications to switch a drug product from prescription to non-prescription use . . .").

69. *See* Smeaton v. Sec'y of State for Health, [2002] EWHC 610 (Admin) (Eng.); *see also* Rebecca J. Cook, Bernard M. Dickens & Joanna N. Erdman, *Emergency Contraception, Abortion and Evidence-Based Law*, 95 INT'L J. GYNECOLOGY & OBSTETRICS 191 (2006) (courts and legal tribunals increasingly decline to serve as religious or moral guardians, and require social evidence to support access to emergency contraception and abortion).

enforcement of morals or religious belief."[70] This particular English *Smeaton* decision was so meticulous in its analysis of scientific evidence that a translation into Spanish and publication in *Revista Mexicana de Bioéthica* was arranged by a Mexican lawyer, Pedro Morales.[71]

* * *

Exposing the deficiencies of judicial reasoning is important, but it is also essential to examine our own advocacy, why it succeeded and how it might be improved. We might start by examining our briefs or amicus briefs, determining which briefs worked, which briefs did not work and why, and what are the implications for our advocacy moving forward? Have our briefs sufficiently emphasized the constitutive role of the law, the role of the law in constituting new conceptions of gender justice? Why do courts rule on equality grounds in cases of violence against women, and resist such claims when it comes to reproductive rights?

The team at the University of Toronto has tried under our director of the Health Equity and Law Clinic, Joanna Erdman, to select cases where we could file amicus briefs promoting equality arguments. We have filed amicus briefs in eight cases, but have failed to convince the courts of the discriminatory dimensions of neglecting health care that only women need. Some courts, such as the Colombian Constitutional Court in the 2006 abortion decision, have nodded to the importance of equality, but none have held on that ground. Are we not sufficiently adept at arguing equality in the context of reproductive health, do we do it at too high a level of abstraction? What can we learn from the cases on violence against women, like *Algodonero*, that hold governments accountable for the structural nature of discrimination?

IV. Challenges Ahead

There are many ways to think about challenges: practical challenges, strategic challenges, and intellectual challenges. There are challenges of ensuring the implementation of cases that have been decided by different tribunals, the challenges of advocacy around cases that are pending before domestic courts, the Inter-American Commission on Human Rights,[72] the

---

70. *Id.* ¶ 48.

71. *See* Smeaton v. Sec'y of State for Health, 1 Revista Mexicana de Bioethica 87, 87–123 (2003) (Spanish translation of the English case).

72. *See, e.g.,* F.S. v. Chile, Inter-Am. Comm'n H.R. (filed Feb., 2009) (forced sterilization of HIV-positive woman); *Forcibly Sterilized Woman Files International Case against Chile,* Ctr. for Reprod. Rights (Feb. 3, 2009), http://reproductiverights.org/en/press-room

Inter-American Court of Human Rights, and, for example, the Committee on the Elimination of Discrimination against Women.[73] For purposes of this talk, I want to focus on the following challenges:

- Protection of Life Provisions,
- Health Disparities,
- Networks.

A. Protection of Life Provisions

Like the various inquisitions in the 1600s, such as the inquisition of Galileo for defying scripture, the modern day inquisitions are attempts to ensure the supremacy of the Catholic Church in matters of sexuality and reproduction. There are many dimensions of the modern day inquisitions, but perhaps the one that is the most pressing is the constitutional provisions attempting to protect life from the moment of conception.

Constitutional provisions protecting prenatal life exist in many countries of the world, such as Dominican Republic,[74] Chile,[75] Ireland,[76] Mexico,[77]

/forcibly-sterilized-woman-files-international-case-against-chile. *See also* A.N. v. Costa Rica, Inter-Am. Comm'n H.R. (filed Oct., 2008) (denial of lawful abortion for a high risk pregnancy of a fetus with severe brain abnormality); Del Rosario Guzmán Albarracín v. Ecuador, Petition 1055–06, Inter-Am. Comm'n H.R., Report No. 76/08 (2008), *available at* http://www.cidh.oas.org/annualrep/2008eng/Ecuador1055-06eng.htm (violence against adolescents in public educational institutions); Sanchez Villalobos v. Costa Rica, Case 12.361, Inter-Am. Comm'n H.R., Report No. 25/04, OEA/Ser.L/V/II.122, doc. 5 rev. ¶¶ 1, 16–17 (2004), *available at* http://www.cidh.org/annualrep/2004eng/CostaRica.12361eng.htm (prohibition of IVF treatment).

73. *See, e.g.*, Comm. on the Elimination of Discrimination against Women, Alyne da Silva Pimentel v. Brazil (filed Nov. 30, 2007) (avoidable maternal death).

74. Dom. Rep. Const., Jan. 6, 2010, art. 8, para. 1, art. 37, para. 8, *available at* http://pdba.georgetown.edu/constitutions/domrep/domrep02.html.

75. Constitución Política de la República de Chile [C.P.] [Constitution] Article 19, paragraph 1 of the Chilean Constitution states, "[t]he law protects the life of those about to be born." *Id.*

76. Eighth Amendment to the Constitution Act 1983 (Amendment No. 8/1983) (Ir.), *available at* http://www.irishstatutebook.ie/1983/en/act/cam/0008/print.html. Article 40, paragraph 3(3) of the Irish Constitution guarantees to defend and vindicate the "right to life of the unborn . . . with due regard to the equal right to life of the mother." *Id.*

77. *A Backlash that Has Gone Viral*, GIRE: Info. Grp. on Reprod. Choice (July 29, 2009), http://www.gire.org.mx/contenido.php?informacion=187 ("So far fourteen Mexican states have approved constitutional reforms that protect life from the moment of fertilization"); Alejandro Madrazo, Abortion in Mexico: A Brief Description of Its Current Regulation and Recent History 1 (May 2010) (unpublished presentation, Yale Law School Workshop on Comparative & Transnational Perspectives on Reproductive Rights) (on file with author)

and the Philippines.[78] A growing number of Mexican states now have constitutional amendments that protect life from the moment of conception. These provisions are part of a backlash strategy to attempt to limit the influence and spread of liberal abortion laws, such as the legislative reform in Mexico City, and the subsequent decision of the Supreme Court of Mexico to uphold the reform.[79] They are variously worded: one stating, "[t]he law protects the life of those about to be born,"[80] another requiring the vindication of the "right to life of the unborn . . . with due regard to the equal right to life of the mother."[81] The American Convention states that "[e]very person has the right to have his life respected. This right shall be protected by law and, in general, from the moment of conception."[82]

These provisions present many questions that need research, for example: Do these provisions have only symbolic value, or do they have actual legal and material consequences for how pregnant women are treated and how pregnancies are managed? What negative and positive obligations are implicated by the protection of unborn life as a constitutional norm?[83] Do they express rights, norms, or values concerning pre-natal life? How do these rights, norms, or values interact with the rights of pregnant women?

The Spanish Constitutional Court upheld a proposed 1985 bill extending grounds for abortion,[84] and explained that the fetus cannot be holder of rights, because the right to life provision,[85] in conjunction with the

---

("sixteen out of thirty-two States have amended their Constitutions to expressly establish the right to life.").

78. CONST. (1987), art. II, sec. 12 (Phil.). The Filipino Constitution requires the State to "equally protect the life of the mother and the life of the unborn from conception."). *Id.*

79. Alejandro Madrazo, *The Evolution of Mexico City's Abortion Laws: From Public Morality to Women's Autonomy*, 106 INT'L J. GYNECOLOGY & OBSTETRICS 266 (2009), *available at* http://www.ijgo.org/article/S0020-7292(09)00256-2/abstract.

80. *See supra* note 75.

81. Eighth Amendment to the Constitution Act 1983 (Amendment No. 8/1983) (Ir.), *available at* http://www.irishstatutebook.ie/1983/en/act/cam/0008/print.html (memorialized at Article 40, paragraph 3(3) of the Irish Constitution).

82. Organization of American States, American Convention on Human Rights art. 4(1), Nov. 22, 1969, O.A.S.T.S. No. 36, 1144 U.N.T.S. 123, *available at* http://www.oas.org/juridico/english/Treaties/b-32.html; "Baby Boy" v. United States, Case 2141, Inter-Am. Comm'n H.R., Res. No. 23/81, OEA/Ser.L/V/II.54, doc. 9 rev. 1 ¶ 14 (1981).

83. Verónica Undurraga, *Propuesta Interpretativa del Mandato de Protección del que está por Nacer Bajo la Constitución Chilena en el Contexto de la Regulación Jurídica del Aborto* (forthcoming 2011) (PhD thesis, University of Chile) (on file with author) (interpretative proposal of the duty to protect the unborn under the Chilean Constitution in the context of the legal regulation of abortion).

84. This bill became Criminal Code art. 417 (C.P. 1985) (Spain).

85. CONSTITUCIÓN ESPAÑOLA, sec. 15, B.O.E n. 311, Dec. 29, 1978 (Spain).

provision protecting human dignity,[86] of the Spanish Constitution does elaborate a general norm to protect prenatal life.[87] What is the meaning of the 1985 decision of the Spanish Constitutional Court which ruled that the "fetus is not the holder of the right to life; yet, on the other hand, there exists a right (although it is nobody's right) to the protection of the unborn life as a constitutional norm[?]"[88]

Consistently with the Spanish 1985 decision, the Costa Rica Supreme Court in 2004 held that notwithstanding the fact that the unborn is protected by the right to life, therapeutic abortion is permitted.[89]

In 2006, the Colombian Constitutional Court, in declaring the criminal prohibition of all abortions unconstitutional, recognized the constitutional value of life, including fetal life. However, the Court distinguished between the value of life and the claimed legal right to life. The legal right to life was ruled to be limited to a born human being, while the constitutional value of life can be protected before a fetus has been born. The Court explained that the state can protect pre-natal life, but it may do so only in a way that is compatible with the rights of women: "A woman's right to dignity prohibits her treatment as a mere instrument for reproduction. Her consent is essential to the fundamental life changing decision of giving birth to another person."[90]

Most recently in 2010, the Portuguese Constitutional Court[91] upheld the constitutionality of a 2007 law that enables a woman to decide to terminate a pregnancy during the first ten weeks of pregnancy, provided she

86. *Id.* at sec. 10.

87. S.T.C., Apr. 11, 1985 (B.O.E., No. 53) (Spain), *available at* https://www.tribunalconsti tucional.es/ResolucionesTraducidas/53-1985,%20of%20April%2011.pdf .

88. Blanca Rodriquez Ruiz & Ruth Rubio Marin, Abortion in Spain 6 (May 2010) (unpublished presentation, Yale Law School Workshop on Comparative & Transnational Perspectives on Reproductive Rights) (internal reference omitted) (on file with author) (discussing the Spanish Constitutional Court decision S.T.C., Apr. 11, 1985 (B.O.E., No. 53) (Spain), opinion *available at* https://www.tribunalconstitucional.es/ResolucionesTraduci-das/53-1985,%20of%20April%2011.pdf.

89. Tribunal Supremo de Costa Rica, 17 marzo 2004, Sentencia No. 2004-02792.

90. Corte Constitucional [C.C.] [Constitutional Court], mayo 10, 2006, Sentencia C-355/06 (Colom.), *available at* https://www.minsalud.gov.co/sites/rid/Lists/BibliotecaDig-ital/RIDE/INEC/IGUB/sentencia-c-355-de-2006.pdf. *See* Martha I. Morgan, *Emancipatory Equality: Gender Jurisprudence under the Colombian Constitution, in* THE GENDER OF CONSTITU-TIONAL JURISPRUDENCE 75, 93–97 (Beverly Baines & Ruth Rubio-Marin eds., 2005) for an analysis of the Colombian Constitution's treatment of fetuses as people prior to this 2006 decision.

91. S.T.C., Feb. 23, 2010 (Acórdáo No. 75/2010) (Port.), *available at* https://dre.pt/appli cation/dir/pdf2sdip/2010/03/060000000/1556615605.pdf. *See also* https://www.law.utoron to.ca/documents/reprohealth/LS056_Portugal_abortion_law.pdf.

undergoes counseling and a three-day reflection period.[92] No doubt draw-ing from the reasoning of the 1985 decision of the Spanish Constitutional Court, the Portuguese Constitutional Court explained that the unborn is not a rights holder under the right to life provision of the Portuguese Constitution,[93] but that the unborn is to be protected as an objective value.[94]

Research is needed on the meaning of constitutional provisions and court decisions to determine what kinds of protection of prenatal life are in fact required. A case is now pending in the Supreme Court of Justice of Nicaragua that might provide some illumination in the context of that country.[95] In the context of France, the 1975 decision of the French Con-stitutional Court, upholding the liberal law allowing abortion on extended grounds, required "respect for all human beings from the inception of life."[96] Respect for "human beings from inception of life" is met in part by the reflection delay requirement in the laws of France,[97] Portugal,[98] Spain,[99] and the U.S.[100]

---

92. Law No. 16/2007 art. II, CXLII (2007) (Port.).

93. Constituição da República Portuguesa [C.R.P.] Apr. 2, 1976, art. 24.

94. Ruth Rubio Marin, Constitutional Framing: Abortion and Symbolism in Constitutional Law 35 (on file with author).

95. *See* Sentencia [S.] No. 38-2008, 15 July 2008 [Supreme Court of Justice] p. 143, 144–49 Cons. I (Nicar.). *See also* Ley No. 641, 9 May 2008, Título Preliminar Sobre Las Garantías Penales y de la Aplicación de la Ley Penal [Preliminary Title About the Penal Guarantees and the Application of the Penal Law], LA GACETA, DIARIO OFICIAL [L.G.] 9 May 2008 (Nicar.), *available at* http://legislacion.asamblea.gob.ni/Normaweb.nsf/($All)/1F5B59264A8F00F906257540005EF77E?OpenDocument.

96. Conseil constitutionnel [CC] [Constitutional Court] decision No. 74-54DC, Jan. 15, 1975, J.O. 671 (Fr.), *available at* http://www.conseil-constitutionnel.fr/conseil-constitutionnel/francais/les-decisions/acces-par-date/decisions-depuis-1959/1975/74-54-dc/decision-n-74-54-dc-du-15-janvier-1975.7423.html.

97. Loi 75-17 du 17 janvier 1975 relative á l'interruption volontaire de la grossesse [Law 75-17 of January 17, 1975 on the Voluntary Interruption of Pregnancy], Journal Officiel de la République Francaise [J.O.] [Official Gazette of France], Jan. 18, 1975, p. 739, *as amended by* Loi 79-1204 du 31 décembre 1979 relative á l'interruption volontaire de la grossesse [Law 79-1204 of December 31, 1979 on the Voluntary Interruption of Pregnancy], J.O., Dec. 31, 1979, p. 3, *available at* http://www.legifrance.gouv.fr/jopdf/common/jo_pdf.jsp?numJO=0&dateJO=19750118&numTexte=&pageDebut=00739&pa.

98. Law No. 16/2007 art. II, CXLII (2007) (Port.).

99. Organic Law 2/2010 art. XIV (B.O.E. 2010, 3514) (Spain), *available at* https://www.reproductiverights.org/sites/crr.civicactions.net/files/documents/Organic%20law%202-2010%20on%20SRH%20and%20voluntary%20pregnancy%20termination%20-%20English%20Translation.pdf (three days).

100. *Biased Counseling & Mandatory Delays*, NARAL Pro-Choice America, https://www.prochoiceamerica.org/issue/biased-counseling-mandatory-delays/ (last visited Mar. 10, 2021) (typically twenty-four hours).

Other ways of protecting prenatal life have evolved in other countries, such as Germany, which requires counseling of pregnant women.[101] Debates exist as to whether such approaches undermine women's rights and their moral agency.[102]

Research is needed to help shift the debate beyond the dichotomous thinking of either protecting women's rights or protecting prenatal interests, to address how best to promote human dignity by protecting prenatal life in ways that are consistent with women's rights.[103]

Some law reforms, such as the new 2010 Spanish Statute on Sexual and Reproductive Health and Voluntary Interruption of Pregnancy, states clearly that its purpose is to protect women's sexual and reproductive health as an aspect of their equality.[104] The statute protects prenatal life, consistently with women's rights, by informing women with unwanted pregnancies about assistance for them as mothers.[105] However, Spanish legal scholars question "whether the obligation to protect the unborn life from the very moment of conception is sufficiently served by a system informing women of the social and legal possibilities at their disposal if they decide to bring pregnancy to term and to assist them as mothers."[106] It also needs to be asked whether a system of informing women of such possibilities better protects their rights to substantive equality.

Means of protecting prenatal life in ways that are consistent with women's rights include addressing the preventable causes of maternal death[107] (death to a woman while pregnant or within forty-two days of pregnancy)

---

101. Mary Anne Case, *Perfectionism and Fundamentalism in the Application of the German Abortion Laws, in* CONSTITUTING EQUALITY: GENDER EQUALITY AND COMPARATIVE CONSTITUTIONAL LAW 93, 97 (Susan H. Williams ed., 2009). *Accord* D.A. Jeremy Telman, *Abortion and Women's Legal Personhood in Germany: A Contribution to the Feminist Theory of the State,* 24 N.Y.U. REV. L. & SOC. CHANGE 91, 91 (1998).

102. Case, *supra* note 101, at 101–04; Telman, *supra* note 101, at 135.

103. *See* Rebecca J. Cook & Susannah Howard, *Accommodating Women's Differences under the Women's Anti-Discrimination Convention,* 56 EMORY L.J. 1039, 1087–90 (2007).

104. Organic Law 2/2010 Preamble (B.O.E. 2010, 3514) (Spain), *available at* https://www.reproductiverights.org/sites/crr.civicactions.net/files/documents/Organic%20law%202-2010%20on%20SRH%20and%20voluntary%20pregnancy%20termination%20-%20English%20Translation.pdf.

105. Blanca Rodriquez Ruiz & Ruth Rubio Marin, Abortion in Spain 4 (May 2010) (unpublished presentation, Yale Law School Workshop on Comparative & Transnational Perspectives on Reproductive Rights) (on file with author).

106. *Id.* at 8.

107. *See generally* Oona M. R. Campbell & Wendy J. Graham, *Strategies for Reducing Maternal Mortality: Getting on with What Works,* 368 LANCET 1284 (2006).

now estimated around 358,000 annually,[108] which can result in the death of the fetus during birth, or the baby soon after birth. It also requires addressing socioeconomic and sociocultural conditions, such as reduction of economic and social vulnerabilities of pregnant women.[109] In addition, protecting prenatal life consistently with women's rights necessitates addressing the social determinants of poor birth outcomes, such as poor nutrition during pregnancy, including the lack of folic acid supplements during pregnancy, and intimate partner violence against pregnant women.[110]

Clinical measures for protecting prenatal life consistently with women's rights include:

- decreasing miscarriages, including recurrent miscarriages, of wanted pregnancies;[111]
- decreasing perinatal deaths (fetal or early neonatal deaths that occur during late pregnancy—at 22 completed weeks gestation and over— during childbirth and up to seven completed days of life), now estimated around 5.9 million annually;[112] and
- reducing intrapartum (during labor and childbirth) stillbirths and neonatal deaths (death in the first twenty-eight days of life), now estimated around two million annually.[113]

These policies go much further in protecting life than restrictive abortion policies because they increase the resources available for care of pregnant women and their newborns. Moreover, they serve women's and men's interests in healthy birth outcomes, rather than merely seeking to assure

---

108. World Health Org. [WHO], *Trends in Maternal Mortality: 1990 to 2008*, at 17 (2010), http://whqlibdoc.who.int/publications/2010/9789241500265_eng.pdf.

109. Véronique Filippi et al., *Maternal Health in Poor Countries: The Broader Context and a Call for Action*, 368 LANCET 1535, 1535–36 (2006), *available at* http://www.ncbi.nlm.nih .gov/pubmed/17071287 (discussing, *inter alia*, fear of costs, time spent looking for funds to pay costs, and costs themselves as contributing to vulnerability).

110. Joanna Cook & Susan Bewley, *Acknowledging a Persistent Truth: Domestic Violence in Pregnancy*, 101 J. ROYAL SOC'Y MED. 358, 362 (2008) ("Further work needs to be concentrated on establishing which interventions consistently reduce the incidence of violence in pregnancy. . . .").

111. I.A. Greer, *Antithrombotic Therapy for Recurrent Miscarriage?*, 362 NEW ENG. J. MED. 1630, 1630–31 (2010); Raj Rai & Lesley Regan, *Recurrent Miscarriage*, 368 LANCET 601, 601 (2006).

112. WHO, Dep't of Making Pregnancy Safer, *Neonatal and Perinatal Mortality: Country, Regional, and Global Estimates 2004*, at 2–4 (2007), http://whqlibdoc.who.int/publica tions/2007/9789241596145_eng.pdf.

113. Joy E. Lawn et al., *Two Million Intrapartum-related Stillbirths and Deaths: Where, Why, and What Can Be Done?*, 107 INT'L J. GYNECOLOGY & OBSTETRICS S5, S5–S19 (2009).

the birth of children, irrespective of their condition and their prospects for survival.

Research is needed to move the discourse beyond a myopic focus on protection of prenatal life to a broader focus on developing public policy that serve women's and men's interests in family life,[114] and on developing public policies "on gender, work and family that distributes the cost of child bearing and caring evenly among mothers, fathers and the State."[115] Does equitable family policy require more than a new legal framework for abortion? Does it require the State develop a new sensitivity towards the deeper social problems surrounding abortion?[116]

B. Health Disparities

Gender, as with race, ethnicity, class, and sexual orientation, has an effect on health status, how services are provided and used, and health-seeking behaviors and risk factors, to name but a few. In addition, reducing gender health inequities is essential to achieving all the Millennium Development Goals, and is not limited to the sole issues of maternal mortality and HIV.

Gender is a social determinant of health[117] as are restrictive laws and policies. Research shows that the burden of restrictive sexual and reproductive health laws is borne disproportionately by different sub-groups of women,[118] for example by adolescents,[119] by rural residents,[120] or racial

---

114. *See generally* Priscilla J. Smith, *Responsibility for Life: How Abortion Serves Women's Interests in Motherhood*, 17 J.L. & POL'Y 97 (2009).

115. Blanca Rodriquez Ruiz & Ruth Rubio Marin, Abortion in Spain 11 (May 2010) (unpublished presentation, Yale Law School Workshop on Comparative & Transnational Perspectives on Reproductive Rights) (on file with author).

116. *Id.* (arguing states must "develop a new sensitivity towards the deeper social problems surrounding" abortion if abortion is to be made more widely available).

117. WHO, Comm. on Social Determinants of Health, *Closing the Gap in a Generation: Health Equity through Action on the Social Determinants of Health*, at 2 (2008), *available at* http://whqlibdoc.who.int/publications/2008/9789241563703_eng.pdf ("In order to address health inequities, and inequitable conditions of daily living, it is necessary to address inequities—such as those between men and women—in the way society is organized.").

118. *Access to Abortion Reports: An Annotated Bibliography of Reports and Scholarship*, INT'L REPROD. & SEXUAL HEALTH LAW PROGRAM (2d Ed. Apr. 1, 2020), https://www.law.utoronto.ca/documents/reprohealth/abortionbib.pdf.

119. *See, e.g.*, WHO, *Women and Health: Today's Evidence, Tomorrow's Agenda*, at 31 (2009), *available at* http://whqlibdoc.who.int/publications/2009/9789241563857_eng.pdf.

120. *See, e.g.*, Antonio Bernabé-Ortiz et al., *Clandestine Induced Abortion: Prevalence, Incidence and Risk Factors among Women in a Latin American Country*, 180 CAN. MED. ASS'N J. 298, 302–03 (2009).

groups.[121] The report of the Inter-American Commission on Human Rights, *Access to Maternal Health Services from a Human Rights Perspective*,[122] explained that improving access to appropriate care includes at least ensuring

- access to information necessary in appropriate languages to make health care decisions and obtain health care services, often referred to as information access;[123]
- transparent access to ensure that the terms and conditions of delivery of health care services are clear to the provider and the patient;[124]
- dignified access to ensure service provision is free of dignity-denying treatment; such as forced pregnancy,[125] coercive sterilization,[126] and,

121. When the U.S. reported national developments to the UN Committee on the Elimination of Racial Discrimination (CERD), the Center for Reproductive Rights filed a shadow letter with CERD showing that in the U.S., African-American women are almost four times more likely to die from pregnancy-related causes than white women. Letter from Nancy Northup, Pres., Ctr. for Reprod. Rights, to Nathalie Prouvez, Sec'y, Comm. on the Elimination of Racial Discrimination (Dec. 19, 2007); *cf.* Dorothy E. Roberts, *Punishing Drug Addicts Who Have Babies: Women of Color, Equality, and the Right of Privacy*, 104 HARV. L. REV. 1419, 1446 & n.141 (1991) (discussing black infant mortality rates in the U.S.).

122. Inter-American Commission on Human Rights [IACHR], *Access to Maternal Health Services from a Human Rights Perspective*, OEA/Ser.L/V/II. Doc 69 (June 7, 2010), *available at* http://cidh.org/women/SaludMaterna10Eng/MaternalHealth2010.pdf.

123. *Id.* ¶ 20; *see also* Open Door Counselling, Ltd. v. Ireland, App. Nos. 14234/88, 14253/88, 15 Eur. H.R. Rep. 244 (1993); Comm. on Econ., Soc., & Cultural Rights, Gen. Comment No. 14: The Right to the Highest Attainable Standard of Health, 22nd Sess., Apr. 25–May 12, 2000, ¶ 12(b), U.N. Doc. E/C. 12/2000/4, Apr. 25, 2000–May 12, 2000; Joanna N. Erdman, *Access to Information on Safe Abortion: A Harm Reduction and Human Rights*, 34 HARV. J. L. & GENDER (2011); Letter from Rebecca Gomperts, Founder, Women on Waves, to Joanna Erdman, Dir., Univ. of Toronto Health Equity & Law Clinic & Susan Newell, Univ. of Toronto Health Equity & Law Clinic, to Google Inc. Legal Department (June 30, 2009), *available at* https://www.womenonwaves.org/en/media/inline/2012/4/4/090630_final _google_advocacy_letter_wo_sig.pdf.

124. IACHR, *supra* note 122, ¶ 28. *See also* R. v. Morgentaler, [1988] 1 S.C.R. 30 (Can.); Smeaton v. Sec'y of State for Health, [2002] EWHC 610 (Admin) (Eng.); Family Planning Ass'n of N. Ir. v. Minister for Health, Soc. Servs. & Pub. Safety, [2005] NICA (Civ) 37, N.I. 188, CA (N. Ir.); Tysiaç v. Poland, App. No. 5410/03, 45 Eur. Ct. H.R. 42 (2007); U.N. Human Rights Comm., Noelia Llantoy Huamán v. Peru, ¶¶ 2.1–2.3, U.N. Doc. CCPR/C/85/D/1153/2003 (Oct. 24, 2005), at http://www1.umn.edu/humanrts/undocs/1153-2003.html.

125. *See, e.g.*, Ramírez Jacinto v. Mexico, Petition 161-02, Inter-Am. Comm'n H.R., Report No. 21/07, OEA/Ser.L/V/II.130, doc. 22 rev. 1 ¶¶ 9–16 (2007); U.N. Human Rights Comm., Noelia Llantoy Huamán v. Peru, ¶¶ 2.1–2.3, U.N. Doc. CCPR/C/85/D/1153/2003 (Oct. 24, 2005), at http://www1.umn.edu/humanrts/undocs/1153-2003.html.

126. *See, e.g.*, IACHR, *supra* note 122, ¶ 45; *see also* Mamérita Mestanza Chávez v. Peru, Case 12.191, Inter-Am. Comm'n H.R., Report No. 71/03, OEA/Ser.L/V/II.118, doc. 70 rev. 2 ¶¶ 9–12, 14, 17 (2003) (holding case alleging compulsory sterilization that caused death admissible); Ann Farmer, *Luisa Cabal: Turning National Wrongs into International Rights*, VOICES

for example, breaches of their confidentiality.[127] Terrible breaches of confidentiality continue to exist in some countries of the region,[128] despite the important decision of the Inter-American Court of Human Rights, which decided that physicians have "an obligation to protect the confidentiality of the information to which, as physicians, they have access,"[129] and norms elaborated by the Committee on the Elimination of Discrimination against Women,[130] the Committee on the Rights of the Child,[131] and the Committee against Torture.[132]

- nondiscriminatory access to ensure that services are provided to all, irrespective of gender, race, ethnicity, and class in public health services. This might require that health insurance schemes cover services in ways that are proportionate to the health needs of individuals and groups of individuals.[133] Nondiscriminatory access might also

UNABRIDGED (Sept. 26, 2003) (case settled for the rape of a young Peruvian woman by a public health doctor and for the victim's subsequent denial of justice).

127. IACHR, *supra* note 122, ¶¶ 37, 98, 105; *see also* María Mercedes Cavallo, Law as a Social Determinant of Unsafe Abortion in Argentina 36–44 (2009) (unpublished LL.M. thesis, University of Toronto) (on file with author).

128. Cavallo, *supra* note 127.

129. De La Cruz-Flores v. Peru, Merits, Reparations, and Costs, Judgment, Inter-Am. Ct. H.R. (ser. C) No. 115, ¶ 101 (Nov. 18, 2004).

130. *See* Comm. on the Elimination of Discrimination against Women, *CEDAW General Recommendation 24: Women and Health*, ¶ 12(d), U.N. Doc. A/54/38 (Pt. 1); GAOR, 54th Sess., Supp. No. 38 (May 4, 1999) ("lack of respect for the confidentiality of patients . . . may deter women from seeking advice and treatment and thereby adversely affect their health and well- being.").

131. *See* Office of the High Comm'r for Human Rights, *CRC General Comment No. 4: Adolescent Health and Development in the Context of the Convention on the Rights of the Child*, ¶¶ 7, 29, 35–37, U.N. Doc. CRC/GC/2003/4 (July 2003).

132. The Committee Against Torture took Chile to task for breaches of confidentiality of women seeking post-abortion care. Comm. Against Torture, Consideration of Reps. Submitted by States Parties Under Article 19 of the Convention, 32nd Sess., May 3–21, 2004, U.N. Doc. CAT/ C/CR/32/5 (June 14, 2004). Responding to these recommendations, the Chilean Ministry of Health instructed the directors of health services not to condition the treatment of women with post-abortion complications to the confession of the crime of abortion, explaining that this would offend Article 15 of the Convention Against Torture, among other legal obligations. Daniela Estrada, *Activists Demand Humane Treatment for Women Who Abort*, IPS (Aug. 28, 2009), http://www.ipsnews.net/2009/08 /chile-activists-demand-humane-treatment-for-women-who-abort/.

133. WHO, *Safe Abortion: Technical and Policy Guidance for Health Systems*, at 92 (2003), *available at* http://whqlibdoc.who.int/publications/2003/9241590343.pdf. The Superior Court of Quebec has ordered the Quebec government to reimburse a total of $13 million to nearly 45,000 women who paid out-of-pocket expenses for abortion services in private clinics. The Court decided the case on the basis of a duty imposed on the government by statute and regulation because abortion services are covered under the Quebec Health Insurance Act. *Ass'n pour l'accès á l'avortement c. Procureur Gen. du Que.* [*Ass'n for Access to Abortion v. Att'y*

require that States ensure that medicines, such as Misoprostol, are
registered in national essential drug list to maximize availability and
facilitate cost containment.[134]

The elimination of *de facto* discrimination to achieve substantive equality "requires paying sufficient attention to groups of individuals which suffer
historical or persistent prejudice instead of merely comparing the formal
treatment of individuals in similar situations."[135] In thinking about how
human rights have helped to constitute notions of gender justice in the
Americas, it is important to understand how the social practices of gender
generate and perpetuate prejudice against women and different subgroups
of women.

The elimination of structural discrimination requires understanding
how health systems perpetuate negative stereotypes of women and how that
perpetuation inhibits women's access to health care services. A gender stereotype is a generalized view or preconception of qualities or characteristics
possessed by, or the roles that are or should be performed by, men and
women, respectively.[136]

A pervasive and persistent stereotype that inhibits women's equal
access to health care services is that women are incompetent decision-mak-
ers. This stereotype implies that women are irrational in their decisions,
lack the capacity for moral agency and self-determination, and, therefore,
should be denied access to health care services of their choice.[137] This stereotype is compounded by prejudices about poor ethnically marginalized
women who are denied information to make informed decisions about
their health care.[138]

The elimination of *de facto* discrimination in order to realize substantive
equality requires, among other measures, reforming law, policies, and practices that are sex-neutral but in practice disproportionately negatively affect

---

Gen. of Que.] [2006] C.S. 8654 (Can.), *available at* http://www.jugements.qc.ca/php/deci
sion.php?liste=51846250&doc=40B3D66F1DCD753D52C38E24737ADACAAE302A7529389
71B8BD1CBA0AFA5853C&page=1.

134. *Id.* at 62–64.

135. Comm. on Econ., Soc. & Cultural Rights, *Gen. Comment No. 20*, 42nd Sess., May 4–22,
2009, ¶ 8(b), U.N. Doc. E/C.12/GC/20 (July 2, 2009).

136. COOK & CUSACK, *supra* note 15, at 9.

137. *Id.* at 85–86.

138. *See* Views of the Comm. on the Elimination of Discrimination against Women, A.S.
v. Hungary, ¶¶ 1.1, 2.2, U.N. Doc. CEDAW/C/36/D/4/2004 (Aug. 29, 2006) (coerced sterilization of Roma woman after receiving signature on permission form she could not understand presented to her while she was in a state of shock).

women or specific groups of women. In an effort to achieve substantive equality, courts rely on statistics produced by claimants to establish a difference in treatment between two groups (men and women) in similar situations. The European Court of Human Rights has explained that "where an applicant is able to show, on the basis of undisputed official statistics, the existence of a prima facie indication that a specific rule—although formulated in neutral manner—in fact affects a clearly higher percentage of women than men,"[139] it shifts the burden to the government to explain why a sex-neutral policy disproportionately affects women.

Governments will have to show that there are legitimate objectives for the sex-neutral rule despite the fact that it disproportionately prejudices the health of women, or a subgroup of women. In the field of health care, governments often try to justify policies that have disproportionate impact on certain groups by pointing to cost considerations[140] or to the nature of the circumstances.[141]

C. Networks

Our field is filled with examples of strong partnerships, networks, and other types of collaboration,[142] but how can we think anew to strengthen the collective impact of our collaborations to address the challenges of the modern day inquisitions? How can our networks collaborate with associations of universities and colleges to ensure that they hold academic institutions accountable for infringements of academic freedoms?[143]

---

139. Hoogendijk v. Netherlands, App. No. 58641/00, 40 Eur. Ct. H.R. at 22 (2005). *Accord* D.H. v. Czech Republic, App. No. 57325/00, 47 Eur. H.R. Rep. 3, ¶¶ 188–89 (2007) (stating that statistics are sufficient to constitute the prima facie evidence the applicant is required to produce).

140. *See* T.C., 6 agosto 2010, "Constitucionalidad del artículo 38 ter de la Ley No. 18.933," Rol de la causa: 1710–10, ¶¶ 103, 155–56 (Chile).

141. CEDAW was concerned about a law that forces victims of sexual violence to report to police immediately, prior to seeking health care, as it may cause some victims to choose not to seek health or psychological support. Since most victims of sexual violence are women, this law may have a disproportionate effect upon women's health. Comm. on the Elimination of Discrimination against Women, Concluding Observations, Myanmar, 42nd Sess., Oct. 20–Nov. 7, 2008, ¶¶ 22–23, U.N. Doc. CEDAW/C/MMR/CO/3 (Nov. 7, 2008).

142. *See, e.g.,* Reprod. Health Matters & Asian-Pacific Res. & Research Ctr. for Women, Repoliticizing Sexual and Reproductive Health and Rights: Report of A Global Meeting 1 (2010).

143. *See generally* Matthew W. Finkin & Robert C. Post, For the Common Good: Principles of American Academic Freedom (2009).

What can be learned from the network literature to improve the collective impact of our political and legal advocacy? That literature explains that "large-scale social change comes from better cross-sector coordination rather than from the isolated intervention of individual organizations."[144]

How might we strengthen our networks to build on the historic Paraguay decision to apply the necessary norms to ensure that each woman in indigenous communities can access the care that she needs to survive pregnancy and childbirth and to have a healthy infant? How can we hold other governments accountable for preventable causes of high rates of maternal mortality? It is worth repeating that the Inter-American Court ruled that states have positive obligations, not just negative ones, to address preventable maternal deaths in the Xákmok Kásek indigenous community by ensuring access to appropriate services.[145]

What can be learned from the knowledge translation methodologies, which have emerged primarily in the health sciences,[146] to ensure that greater attention is given to maximize utilization and impact of research undertaken in the legal academy? Might the same be asked of court decisions?

What can be learned from the 2008 Commission for the Legal Empowerment of the Poor[147] ("LEP"), a group of developing and developed countries' experts, chaired by Madeleine Albright and Hernando de Soto, to empower more indigenous communities to advocate and ensure that the health disparities that they face are removed?

One of the main arguments of the LEP Commission Report is that over 4 billion people are "robbed of the chance to better their lives and climb out of poverty, because they are excluded from the rule of law."[148] LEP, conceptualised broadly in terms of access to justice, property rights, labour rights, and business rights is thus thought to provide the opportunity for those living in poverty to improve their conditions.

---

144. John Kania & Mark Kramer, *Collective Impact*, STAN. SOC. INNOVATION REV., Winter 2011, at 36, 38, *available at* http://www.ssireview.org/pdf/2011_WI_Feature_Kania.pdf.

145. Xákmok Kásek Indigenous Cmty. v. Paraguay, *supra* note 6, at ¶¶ 217, 232, 234, 275, 301–03, 306.

146. KNOWLEDGE TRANSLATION IN HEALTH CARE: MOVING FROM EVIDENCE TO PRACTICE (Sharon Straus et al. eds., 2009); WORLD HEALTH ORG., BRIDGING THE "KNOW-DO" GAP: MEETING ON KNOWLEDGE TRANSLATION IN GLOBAL HEALTH (2006); WORLD HEALTH ORG., WORLD REPORT ON KNOWLEDGE FOR BETTER HEALTH 97–128 (2004).

147. COMM'N ON LEGAL EMPOWERMENT OF THE POOR & UNITED NATIONS DEV. PROGRAMME, MAKING THE LAW WORK FOR EVERYONE (LEP) (2008).

148. *Id.* at 1.

The LEP Commission Report explains that existing political, administrative, and judicial institutions are not geared to protect the rights of the poor. A broad international framework in terms of human rights protections does already exist, but what is "lacking are the myriad national and local rules of the game and policies that give substance to" these rights.[149] The Report notes that LEP must not be bound by processes that are stalled or dysfunctional. Problems cannot be solved using the same processes that created them. Solutions must be bottom-up, affordable, realistic, liberating, and risk-aware.[150]

What needs to happen in the next few years to ensure that the legal wrong of these failures to address gender health disparities becomes more broadly understood within the indigenous communities of the region? Do we need to think beyond law as a way of ordering the world, law as policy, to law as culture, as a way of belonging with one another in the world?[151]

We cannot take one kind of law, in our case human rights law, and assume that it is the whole law.[152] We need to be more cognizant of the range of different models of how human rights universals are internalized domestically.[153] One model is norm internationalization, a top-down approach whereby norm dissemination happens through trickle-down mechanisms where universal norms are internalized.[154] "[T]his model assumes that people will internalize human rights norms once states legislate their commitments to these principles."[155]

Another model, articulated by legal anthropologists, is more bottom-up. It examines the process of rendering human rights meaningful according to local languages and values. This has been called the process of vernacularization of human rights norms with local conceptions of justice. It interrogates the gaps between global visions of justice and specific visions in local contexts, the vernacular, and examines how the vernacular might

---

149. *Id.* at 76.

150. Following the report, the United Nations General Assembly acknowledged the importance of the LEP Commission in terms of its poverty eradication goals and initiatives. G.A. Res. 64/57, U.N. GAOR, 64th Sess., U.N. Doc. A/C.2/64/L.4/Rev.2, at 2 (Dec. 3, 2009).

151. Shai Lavi, *Turning the Tables on "Law and . . .": A Jurisprudential Inquiry into Contemporary Legal Theory*, 96 CORNELL L. REV. 811 (2011).

152. *Id.*

153. KAMARI MAXINE CLARKE, FICTIONS OF JUSTICE: THE INTERNATIONAL CRIMINAL COURT AND THE CHALLENGE OF LEGAL PLURALISM IN SUB-SAHARAN AFRICA 30 (2009).

154. *Id.* at 30–31.

155. *Id.* at 31.

move beyond the notions of justice from which it emerged.[156] Important work has been done by legal anthropologists to examine this phenomenon in the context of violence against women. This suggests that we need to work with social scientists to determine the conditions under which human rights become valid for and used by different communities.[157]

* * *

Yes, we are skilled at networking among like-minded groups, but we need to push ourselves to network beyond our disciplinary, programmatic, and geographic borders to work with differently-minded groups that can expand our visions in order to more adequately address the challenges of the Modern Day Inquisitions to secure gender justice in the region.

---

156. *Id. See also* SALLY ENGLE MERRY, HUMAN RIGHTS AND GENDER VIOLENCE: TRANSLATING INTERNATIONAL LAW INTO LOCAL JUSTICE 219–23 (2006) (discussing vernacularization).

157. *See generally* MERRY, *supra* note 156; Kamari Clarke, *Constituting Terms for International Change: Reflecting on Strategies for Women's Rights*, 104 ASIL PROC. 561 (2010), *available at* http://www.kamariclarke.com/wp-content/uploads/2013/09/ClarkeK_ASIL2010.pdf.

11

Harmful Anti-Sex-Selective Abortion Laws Are Sweeping U.S. State Legislatures: Why Do Some Pro-Choice People Support Them?

By Sital Kalantry[1]

Anti-sex selective abortion laws punish medical professionals for performing abortions if they know that the patient's motive for the abortion relates to the predicted biological sex of the fetus. Since 2009, nearly half of all state legislatures have considered bills to prohibit sex-selective abortion.[2] The majority of the U.S. House of Representatives voted in favor of a similar ban in 2012.[3] That same year, anti-sex-selective legislation was the second most proposed anti-abortion prohibition in the United States.[4] Today, laws

---

1. Clinical Professor of Law, Cornell Law School. Full CV available at https://www.lawschool.cornell.edu/faculty/bio_sital_kalantry.cfm. I would like to thank Maithli Pradhan and Rachel Skene for their excellent research work on this chapter.

2. SITAL KALANTRY, WOMEN'S HUMAN RIGHTS AND MIGRATION: SEX-SELECTIVE ABORTION LAWS IN THE UNITED STATES AND INDIA 74 (2017).

3. Ed O'Keefe, *Bill Banning 'Sex-Selective Abortions' Fails in the House*, WASHINGTON POST (May 31, 2012), https://www.washingtonpost.com/blogs/2chambers/post/bill -banning-sex-selective-abortions-fails-in-the-house/2012/05/31/gJQAgCYn4U_blog .html?utm_term=.45f2f7c1faf9.

4. Lydia O'Connor, *San Francisco May Be First City to Oppose Sex-Selective Abortion Bans*, HUFFINGTON POST, (Sept. 10, 2014), https://www.huffingtonpost.com/2014/09/10/san -francisco-sex-selective-abortion_n_5800840.html.

prohibiting women from terminating their pregnancies because of the sex of the fetus are effective in nine states.[5]

The laws stigmatize and stereotype Asian Americans, restrict women's access to non-selective abortion, and are likely to be adjudicated by the U.S. Supreme Court in the near future. Yet, elected officials who are pro-choice have voted in favor of the bans. Liberal media sources wrongly report that Asian Americans are aborting female fetuses at rates similar to people in India and China. Pro-choice people appear to be torn about how to react to these particular abortion restrictions.

I attempt to explain this puzzling state of affairs here. I show that pro-choice legislators and other people have been misled to support sex-selective abortion bans by misinterpretations of demographic data in a way that aligns with stereotypes about Asians and Asian Americans. In Section I, I explain how legislation banning sex-selective abortion was driven by misinterpretation of information in a 2008 academic article suggesting that sex-selective abortion was widespread among Asian Americans. Next, in Section II, I explain why the laws are harmful to all women's right to choose. Through an analysis of the voting records of legislative representatives in Oklahoma and in the U.S. House of Representatives, I conclude that many pro-choice legislators voted in favor of sex-selective abortion restrictions in Section III. Then, in Section IV, I analyze the findings of the 2008 article to demonstrate that their conclusions were misinterpreted to suggest that sex-selective abortion is widespread among Asian Americans when that is not the case. In Section V, I show how stereotypes about Asians and Asian Americans contributed to those misinterpretations of the data. I analyze census data

---

5. The nine states that prohibit women from terminating their pregnancies because of the sex of a fetus are: Arizona, Arkansas, Kansas, Mississippi, North Carolina, North Dakota, Oklahoma, Pennsylvania, and South Dakota. *See* Ariz. Rev. Stat. Ann. § 13-3603.02(A)(1) (Westlaw through the Second Regular Session of the Fifty-Fourth Legislature (2020)); Ark. Code Ann. § 20-16-1904(a) (LexisNexis through all legislation of the 2020 First Extraordinary Session and the 2020 Fiscal Session); Kan. Stat. Ann. § 65-6726(a) (Westlaw through laws enacted during the 2020 Regular and Special Sessions of the Kansas Legislature effective on or before July 1, 2020); H.B. 1295, 2020 Reg. Sess. (Miss. 2020); N.C. Gen. Stat. § 90-21.121(a) (LexisNexis through Session Laws 2020-94 of the 2020 Regular Session); N.D. Cent. Code § 14-02.1-04.1(1)(a) (LexisNexis through all acts approved by the governor through the end of the 2019 Regular Legislative Session); Okla. Stat. tit. 63, § 1-731.2(B) (Westlaw through enacted legislation of the Second Regular Session of the 57th Legislature (2020)); 18 Pa. Stat. and Cons. Stat. Ann. § 3204(c) (Westlaw through 2020 Regular Session Act 78); S.D. Codified Laws § 34-23A-64 (Westlaw through 2020 Session Laws). Illinois adopted a ban in 1975, but repealed the law in 2019. *See* Illinois Abortion Law of 1975, Pub. Act No. 79-1126, 1975 Ill. Laws 3462, *repealed by* Reproductive Health Act, Pub. Act No. 101-0013, 2019 Ill. Laws (codified at scattered chapters of the Ill. Comp. Stat.).

in Section VI that is more recent than the data that was used in the 2008 article and that challenges the dominant assumptions about the motives of the behavior of Asian Americans. Finally, in Section VII, I discuss the significance of sex-selective abortion bans for the future of U.S. Supreme Court jurisprudence on reproductive rights.

I. The Genesis and Justifications for Sex-Selective Abortion Bans

A two-page article published in 2008 by Douglas Almond and Lena Edlund, entitled "Son-Biased Sex Ratios in the 2000 United States Census," started a legislative firestorm to ban sex-selective abortion.[6] The article was published in the *Proceedings of the National Academy of Sciences*, an influential multidisciplinary science journal. By examining the ratio of boys to girls born to Asian Americans, they suggested that Asian Americans abort female fetuses at the same rates as people living in Asia. Specifically, the authors stated that "the magnitude of the deviations ... for second and third children of Chinese, Indian, and Korean Americans is comparable to that documented for India, China and South Korea."[7] In Section IV, I explain why this statement is inaccurate.

Bills began to be introduced in state legislatures almost immediately after the study was released, and they continue to be proposed today. In 2009, five state legislatures considered sex-selective abortion bans; in 2010 eight state legislatures considered the bans; in 2011, five state legislatures considered the ban; in 2012, nine states considered the bill; and in 2013, 16 states considered the bill. In 2014, ten states considered the ban (one state enacted it).

Illinois[8] and Pennsylvania were the only states that enacted sex-selective abortion bans prior to the publication of Almond and Edlund's article. In examining the transcripts of discussions of the bills in those state legislatures, I found that there was never any mention of the purported behavior of Asian Americans as a justification for the bills in those two states. The focus of the legislative discussion in those states was broadly on the

---

6. Douglas Almond & Lena Edlund, *Son-biased Sex Ratios in the 2000 United States Census*, 105 Proc. Nat'l Acad. Sci. 5681, 5681 (2008).

7. *Id.*

8. The sex-selective abortion prohibition has now been repealed in Indiana. *See* Illinois Abortion Law of 1975, Pub. Act No. 79-1126, 1975 Ill. Laws 3462, *repealed by* Reproductive Health Act, Pub. Act No. 101-0013, 2019 Ill. Laws (codified at scattered chapters of the Ill. Comp. Stat.).

sex-selective behavior of all Americans.[9] The only time Asia was referred to in the legislative debates is when a pro-choice Pennsylvania senator pointed out that sex-selection occurs in parts of Asia but not in the United States.[10]

But since 2009, the bills that have been introduced specifically cite Almond and Edlund's article and claim that bans are necessary to prevent widespread discriminatory abortions of female fetuses. For example, the preamble of the bill proposed in the U.S. Congress in 2017, the Prenatal Nondiscrimination Act (PRENDA) of 2017 states:

> In a March 2008 report published in the Proceedings of the National Academy of Sciences, Columbia University economists Douglas Almond and Lena Edlund examined the sex ratio of United States-born children and found "evidence of sex selection, most likely at the prenatal stage."[11]

PRENDA further suggests that the data in Almond and Edlund's article "reveal[s] obvious 'son preference' . . . within . . . segments of the United States population . . . tracing their origins to countries where sex-selection abortion is prevalent."[12]

The preambles of bills introduced in state legislatures also contain the same language just quoted.[13] The political rhetoric of politicians that support the bills further refer to Asian immigration as a justification for the bans.[14] For example, Don Hagger, a Republican state representative in South Dakota, stated:

> Let me tell you, our population in South Dakota is a lot more diverse than it ever was. There are cultures that look at a sex-selection abortion as being

---

9. *See* Sital Kalantry, *Sex Selection in the United States and India: A Contextualist Feminist Approach*, 18 UCLA J. INT'L L. & FOREIGN AFFS. (2013). *See also* State of Ill. Gen. Assemb., S. Transcripts Discussing H.B. 1399, 83d Gen. Assemb., at 36–38 (June 25, 1983); State of Ill. Gen. Assemb., S. Transcripts Discussing H.B. 1399, 83d Gen. Assemb., at 222–23 (June 29, 1983); State of Ill. Gen. Assemb., S. Transcripts Discussing H.B. 1399, 83d Gen. Assemb., at 17–33 (Apr. 30, 1984); State of Ill. Gen. Assemb., S. Transcripts Discussing H.B. 1399, 83d Gen. Assemb., at 142–51 (June 30, 1984); State of Ill. Gen. Assemb., H. Transcripts Discussing H.B. 1399, 83d Gen. Assemb., at 175–79 (May 27, 1983); State of Ill. Gen. Assemb., H. Transcripts Discussing H.B. 1399, 83d Gen. Assemb., at 81–86 (Apr. 26, 1984); State of Ill. Gen. Assemb., H. Transcripts Discussing H.B. 1399, 83d Gen. Assemb., at 50–64 (June 29, 1984); H.R. 173-65, 1989 Sess., at 1743–44 (Pa. 1989), http://www.legis.state.pa.us/WU01 /LI/HJ/1989/0/19891024.pdf (last visited Mar. 12, 2021).
10. H.R. 173-65, 1989 Sess. at 1749 (Pa. 1989), http://www.legis.state.pa.us/WU01/LI /HJ/1989/0/19891024.pdf (last visited Nov. 8, 2020).
11. Prenatal Nondiscrimination Act (PRENDA) of 2017, H.R. 147, 115th Cong. § 2(a)(1)(F).
12. *Id.*
13. H.B. 845, 2013 Leg., Reg. Sess. (Fla. 2013)
14. CLIFFORD GEERTZ, THE INTERPRETATION OF CULTURE 44 (1973).

culturally okay. And I will suggest to you that we are embracing individuals from some of those cultures in this country, or in this state. And I think that's a good thing that we invite them to come, but I think it's also important that we send a message that this is a state that values life, regardless of its sex.[15]

The narrative used to justify the laws can be summarized as follows: (1) people in Asia prefer sons and that is why they abort female fetuses, (2) Asians have emigrated to the United States and many of them obtain sex-selective abortions, (3) Asian Americans obtain these abortions because (like Asians) they have a sexist preference for sons and an aversion to daughters, and (4) sex selection in both the United States and Asia is discriminatory. Later in the chapter, I explain why these assumptions are inaccurate.

II. The Bans Impact Every Woman's Right to Choose

Medical professionals are required to enforce bans on sex-selective abortion. A doctor who has knowledge that a woman is seeking an abortion due to the sex of the fetus will face criminal liability in most of the states that ban sex-selective abortion.[16] But what if an abortion seeker does not volunteer her motive, how will a medical professional know about them? Because the rhetoric around the bills targets Asian Americans, it is possible that doctors will inquire about the motives of Asian American women or deny them reproductive care altogether for fear of their own liability. But this inquiry will be made of every woman in some states.

Many states require medical professionals to inquire about the motives of all abortion seekers. For example, South Dakota's law banning sex-selective abortion requires medical professionals to "[i]nquire into whether the pregnant mother knows the sex of her unborn child and if so, whether the mother is seeking an abortion due to the sex of the unborn child."[17] Oklahoma requires medical professionals to complete a form for each abortion, which includes a section on the reasons a woman obtained the abortion.[18] In Arizona, while the law does not require inquiry, it motivates the medical professional to ask questions about the motive for any abortion because he or she must sign an affidavit certifying that he or she "is not

---

15. Molly Redden, *GOP Lawmaker: We Need to Ban Sex-Selective Abortions Because of Asian Immigrants*, MOTHER JONES (Feb. 25, 2014), http://www.motherjones.com/politics/2014/02/south-dakota-stace-nelson-ban-sex-based-abortions-because-asian-immigrants.

16. *See, e.g.*, ARIZ. REV. STAT. § 13-3603.02 (2013).

17. S.D. CODIFIED LAWS § 34-23A-56 (4A) (2014).

18. OKLA. STAT. ANN. tit. 63, § 1-738k (2013).

aborting the child because of the child's sex or race and has no knowledge
that the child to be aborted is being aborted because of the child's sex or
race."[19] Arizona also requires health care professionals to report "known
violations . . . to appropriate law enforcement authorities."[20] This kind of
inquiry can be humiliating and invasive for a woman who is already embarking upon what is likely a difficult decision.

The most recent state to adopt a ban, Arkansas, went further than any
other state. It requires medical professionals to ask each patient whether
she knows the predicted future sex of the fetus, and if she answers in the
affirmative, then the professional must spend "time and effort" seeking
her entire pregnancy-related history (including prior pregnancies).[21] This
means that any woman who is aware of the predicted biological sex of the
fetus may suffer long delays in receiving reproductive care.

Sex-selective abortion bans create a wedge in the patient-doctor relationship because they require medical professionals to enforce them. This
may lead to doctors denying Asian American women reproductive care. But
it is not just Asian American women who are impacted; all women in some
states that have adopted such bans must now be subjected to inquiry about
their motives for seeking an abortion to rule out sex selection as the motive.
One state adds a time delay in receiving an abortion for any woman who
happens to know the predicted biological sex of her fetus. Laws that interfere with the patient-doctor relationship in such a way jeopardize the quality of health care services.

III. Some Pro-Choice Legislators Support
the Harmful Abortion Restrictions

Despite the fact that sex-selective abortion legislation will restrict even non-
selective abortion and the scale and reality of gender-biased sex selection
among Asian Americans is grossly exaggerated (as discussed in Sections
IV–VI), several pro-choice national and state legislative representatives have
supported the harmful legislation. In 2012, when the majority of the U.S.
House of Representatives voted in favor of a federal law prohibiting sex-
selective abortion, 20 Democrats voted with the majority.[22]

---

19. ARIZ. REV. STAT. ANN. § 36-2157 (2011).

20. ARIZ. REV. STAT. § 13-3603.02 (2013).

21. H.B. 1434, 91st Leg., Reg. sess (Act 733).

22. Kate Sheppard, *House GOP's 'Prenatal Nondiscrimination' Bill Fails*, MOTHER JONES (May
31, 2012), www.motherjones.com/politics/2012/05/house-gop-abortion-sex-selection/.

Most people assume that Republicans are pro-life and Democrats are pro-choice, but that is not always the case. Consider the prior voting records of the Democrats in the U.S. House of Representatives who voted in favor of the federal ban as a proxy for their political position on the right to choose. The prior voting records of the Democrats that voted for the federal ban show that some of them generally voted in favor of abortion restrictions. Thus, many of them were likely pro-life and would vote in favor of any abortion restrictions. Their vote in favor of banning sex-selective abortion is not particularly surprising.

However, eight of the Democrats who voted in favor of sex-selective abortion bans had mixed voting records—they sometimes voted against anti-abortion legislation and sometimes voted in favor of it.[23] Two of those Democrats were avowedly pro-choice.[24] One of the Democrats, Representative Garamendi, stated: "I am a strong pro-choice feminist and a proud father of 5 daughters and 3 granddaughters! My daughters and wife are my closest advisors and confidants and all of my decisions are heavily weighed by their influence."[25] Thus, it appears that Democrats who never voted in favor of abortion restrictions but did vote in favor of restricting sex-selective abortion accepted the narrative about Asian Americans put forward by pro-life advocates.

Even in state legislatures that enacted bans on sex-selective abortion, some pro-choice Democrats voted in favor of them. We see the largest number of pro-choice Democrats voting for the bans in Oklahoma, the first state to adopt the restriction after Almond and Edlund's article was published. In Oklahoma, nearly 90 percent of Democrats in both the House and Senate voted for the ban, which is a total of 61 Democrats. Of these Democrats

---

23. *John Barrow on Abortion*, ONTHEISSUES, www.ontheissues.org/GA/John_Barrow .htm (last visited October 30, 2017); *Dan Boren on Abortion*, ONTHEISSUES, http://www .ontheissues.org/House/Dan_Boren.htm (last visited Nov. 8, 2020); *Henry Cuellar on Abortion*, ONTHEISSUES, http://www.ontheissues.org/TX/Henry_Cuellar.htm (last visited Nov. 8, 2020); *Mike Ross on Abortion*, ONTHEISSUES, www.ontheissues.org/House/Mike_Ross .htm (last visited Nov. 8, 2020); *Roy Cooper on Abortion*, ONTHEISSUES, http://www.onthe issues.org/Roy_Cooper.htm (last visited Nov. 8, 2020); *Steve Lynch on Abortion*, ONTHEISSUES, http://www.ontheissues.org/MA/Steve_Lynch.htm (last visited Nov. 8, 2020); *Jim Matheson on Abortion*, ONTHEISSUES, http://www.ontheissues.org/House/Jim_Matheson.htm (last visited Nov. 8, 2020); *Silvestre Reyes on Abortion*, ONTHEISSUES, http://www.ontheissues.org /TX/Silvestre_Reyes.htm (last visited Nov. 8, 2020).

24. Franco Ordonez, *In Congress, Democrat Kissell Is Stuck in the Middle*, MIAMI HERALD (Nov. 1, 2012, 4:35 PM), www.miamiherald.com/latest-news/article1944175.html; *John Garamendi on Abortion*, ONTHEISSUES, www.ontheissues.org/CA/John_Garamendi.htm (last visited Nov. 8, 2020).

25. *Garamendi on Abortion, supra* note 24.

voting to ban sex-selective abortion, 28 consistently vote to limit abortion
access. However, 17 consistently vote against bills that limit abortion access
and eight have a mixed voting record. Thus, 25 pro-choice Democrats and
on-the-fence Democrats voted in favor of adopting restriction on sex-selective abortion in Oklahoma.[26]

IV. Misinterpretations of Demographic Data about Asian Americans

Many people in the United States who otherwise support access to abortion may be conflicted about how to react to sex-selective abortion bans
because women's equality is implicated by both its practice and its prohibition. Sex-selective abortion appears to be discriminatory (at least in some
situations), and prohibition of such abortion restricts reproductive rights.[27]
One person commenting on a story in the *Atlantic* on sex-selective abortion
stated, "I lean pro-choice, but I doff my hat to the pro-life camp for this deft
maneuver. They have demonstrated that it is logically impossible to be both
'pro-choice' and 'anti-discrimination.'"[28] I argue that pro-choice legislators
and others have been misled into supporting sex-selective abortion bans
through misinterpretations of demographic data to align with stereotypes
about Asians and Asian Americans.

As described earlier, Almond and Edlund's article sparked the enactment of laws across the American states to ban sex-selective abortion. The
authors analyzed the genders of children born in the United States to parents that were born in China, Korea, and India. They obtained this data
from the publicly released sample of the 2000 U.S. Census, which is only
5 percent of the overall census data. They came up with a ratio of boys
to girls of the first child of Chinese, Koreans, and Indians, then the ratio
for the second child and for the third child for these groups. They found
that the first child born to Chinese, Indian, and Korean parents was just
as likely to be a male as the first child born to Caucasian families: the sex

---

26. *See* KALANTRY, WOMEN'S HUMAN RIGHTS AND MIGRATION, *supra* note 2 at 85–87.

27. *See, e.g.*, Noah Berlatsky, *Neither Pro-Life Nor Pro-Choice Can Solve the Selective Abortion Crisis*, THE ATLANTIC, (Mar. 6, 2013), https://www.theatlantic.com/sexes/archive/2013/03/neither-pro-life-nor-pro-choice-can-solve-the-selective-abortion-crisis/273704/.

28. Chris Bodenner, *The Gendercide Crisis in Asia*, ATLANTIC (May 23, 2016, 12:25 PM), http://www.theatlantic.com/notes/2016/05/abortion/483866/.

ratio of both groups was 1.05, which was considered to be the biologically normal sex ratio.[29]

However, the authors found that the sex ratio of second children of Asian American families that had one prior girl child was more male-biased (1.17) than the sex ratio of second children of Caucasian Americans who had one prior girl child (1.05).[30] For the third child, the ratio of boys to girls was even more male-biased in those Asian American families that had two prior girl children. The sex ratio of the third child for these parents who had two prior girl children was 1.51.[31] The sex ratio at the second and third births was considered abnormal because it deviated from the sex ratio of Caucasian American families at this level, which was again 1.05.[32]

The same day Almond and Edlund's findings were published, National Public Radio (NPR) aired an interview with Professor Almond. When asked to provide an explanation of their findings, Professor Almond stated:

> To us, given the context that in certain Asian countries there's a traditional preference for sons, that desire of sons is being exercised not only in Asia but in the United States, and that the technologies for prenatal sex determination, there's now evidence that those are being used to generate male birth.[33]

Numerous media stories also claimed that the findings of the article suggested that Asian Americans prefer to have sons. For example, the headline in a story in the *International Herald Tribune* states "Asians Show Bias for Boys; Census Data on Births Also Reflects Embrace of Sex Selection."[34] Even authors that provided a more careful analysis than the sensationalism of daily newspapers accepted the view that sex selection was occurring among the Asian American community at crisis proportions.[35]

---

29. The sex ratio is the ratio of males to females in any given population (males per 100 females).

30. Douglas Almond & Lena Edlund, *Son-Biased Sex Ratios in the 2000 United States Census*, 105 Proc. Nat'l Acad. Sci. 5681, 5681 (2008), *available at* https://www.pnas.org/content/pnas/105/15/5681.full.pdf.

31. *Id.*

32. *Id.*

33. *Male Birth Rate Among Asian Americans Studied*, NPR (Apr. 1, 2008), http://www.npr.org/templates/story/story.php?storyId=89284549.

34. *See* Sam Roberts, *U.S. Asians Show Bias for Boys; Census Data on Births Also Reflects Embrace of Sex Selection, Experts Say*, Int'l Herald Trib., June 16, 2009, at 2; *See also* Sam Roberts, *U.S. Births Hint at Bias for Boys in Some Asians*, NY Times (June 14, 2009), www.nytimes.com/2009/06/15/nyregion/15babies.html.

35. *See* William Saletan, *Fetal Subtraction*, Slate (Apr. 3, 2008), https://slate.com/technology/2008/04/abortion-and-sex-selection-in-the-united-states.html.

But simply by looking at the sex ratios that Almond and Edlund reported, it is not obvious how many cases of sex selection the authors are actually claiming occur. The authors never revealed that number. Instead, they noted that that "the magnitude of the deviations . . . for second and third children of Chinese, Indian, and Korean Americans is comparable to that documented for India, China and South Korea."[36] This statement is part of the reason reporters concluded that there was a sex selection crisis in the United States similar to the one occurring in Asia. For example, a story in *Slate* entitled "Fetal Subtraction: Sex Selection in the United States" suggested that technological advancements could contribute to long-lasting cultural traditions of sex selection such as those in the Almond and Edlund study.[37] But this prevailing understanding of a sex selection crisis in the United States is not accurate.

Recall that Almond and Edlund's analysis found that the sex ratio of the third child of Chinese, Indian, and Korean Americans is 1.51 (i.e., the number of male children born for every female child).[38] They then argue that this figure is similar to the sex ratio in India. They point out that "[a]s a comparison, for India, the corresponding figure was found to be 1.39:1."[39] They are correct that the third births of Asian Americans and Indians seem to have a very similar sex ratio (1.51 for Asian Americans and 1.39 for Indians). But this comparison of only the third births of the children of Asian Americans and people living in India is misleading because it only shows part of the picture.

The full picture comes from comparing the second births of Asian Americans with the second births of people living in India. The sex ratio for second births of Asian Americans is 1.17 when parents have previously had a girl.[40] On the other hand, the sex ratio for the second birth of Indians is 1.32 when parents have previously had a girl.[41] Thus, the sex ratio of Indians at the second birth is far more male-skewed than that of Asian Americans. A significant amount of sex selection occurs at the second birth in India when there is one prior girl child, but sex selection is rarer in the United States at the second birth in the three Asian American communities.

---

36. Almond & Edlund, *supra* note 30.

37. *See* Saletan, *supra* note 35 ("Sex selection of this magnitude has previously been documented in China, South Korea, and India, but not in the United States.").

38. Almond & Edlund, *supra* note 30, at 5681.

39. *Id.*

40. *Id.*

41. *Id.*

The conclusion Almond and Edlund draw from the comparison of the Asian American sex ratios to the sex ratio in China is also inaccurate. They point out that the overall sex ratio in China is 2.25:1.[42] But this sex ratio is significantly more male-skewed than the sex ratio for Asian Americans that they articulated (which was 1.51).

The comparison to Asian American sex ratios and the sex ratio in South Korea is inaccurate for another reason—the sex ratio was actually balanced in South Korea at the time of their article (and continues to be so today).[43] South Korea is often cited as a sex ratio success story in Asia for eradicating sex selection.[44] Yet, while ratios were balanced in South Korea, the ratios among Korean Americans (when combined with Indian and Chinese Americans) were male-skewed. Consequently, unlike what Almond and Edlund stated, the magnitude of sex selection was hardly the same among Asian Americans as that of people living in China, India, and South Korea at the time they published their article. It was far more male-skewed in India and China and far less in South Korea.

Although the economists never reported the number in their article, from simple calculation we can determine that they found that there were about 2,500 "missing" Asian American girls. Similarly, Jason Abrevaya, a professor in the economics department at the University of Texas, reports that he thinks there were "2,000 'missing girls' in the United States between 1991 and 2004."[45] In 2011, James Egan, with his coauthors, estimated that there were 1,000 missing girls per year across the entire United States from 1983 to 2002.[46] This is a small fraction of the total Asian American population in the United States, which, according to the latest U.S. Census, is more than 17 million people.[47] By way of comparison, there are over 60 million girls "missing" just in India.[48]

---

42. *Id.*

43. Jae Woo Lim, *The Changing Trends in Live Birth Statistics in Korea, 1970 to 2010*, 54 Korean J. Pediatric 429 (2011), http://www.ncbi.nlm.nih.gov/pmc/articles/PMC3254888/.

44. *See* Woojin Chung & Monica Das Gupta, *Why Is Son Preference Declining in South Korea? The Role of Development and Public Policy, and the Implications for China and India* (World Bank, Working Paper No. 4373, 2007), https://ssrn.com/abstract=1020841.

45. *See, e.g.,* Jason Abrevaya, *Are There Missing Girls in the United States? Evidence from Birth Data*, 1 Am. Econ. J. Applied Econ. 1, 23 (2009).

46. James F.X. Egan et al., *Distortions of Sex Ratios at Birth in the United States: Evidence for Prenatal Gender Selection*, 31 Prenatal Diagnosis 560, 565 (2011).

47. Elizabeth M. Hoeffel et al., *The Asian Population: 2010, in 2012 Census Briefs*, U.S. Census Bureau 1, 14 (2012), http://www.census.gov/prod/cen2010/briefs/c2010br-11.pdf.

48. Sunny Hundal, *India's 60 Million Women That Never Were*, Al Jazeera (Aug. 8, 2013), www.aljazeera.com/indepth/opinion/2013/07/201372814110570679.html.

Moreover, based on their research, Almond and Edlund can only find deviations in sex ratios, but cannot explain at all how they are occurring. People in the United States can sex-select using pre-implantation means such as sperm-sorting and in vitro fertilization combined with Preimplantation Genetic Diagnosis (PGD).[49]

Cutting the data a different way to compare the overall sex ratios across all children of Asian Americans to people in China and India, we can see even more clearly that sex ratios in China and India are significantly male-biased, but they are in the normal range among foreign-born Indian and Chinese people living in the United States.

FIGURE 11.1 SEX RATIOS OF ASIAN AMERICAN AND ASIANS (STANDARD RANGE SHOWN HORIZONTALLY)

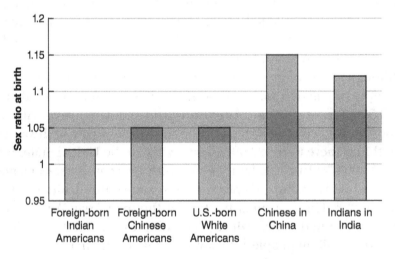

Source: Sital Kalantry & Miriam Yeung, *Replacing Myths with Facts: Sex-Selective Abortion Laws in the United States*, University of Chicago Law School International Human Rights Clinic, National Asian Pacific Women's Forum, Advancing New Standards for Reproductive Justice (2014), available at https://chicagounbound.uchicago.edu/ihrc/7/.

There is a general perception that data is neutral. However, the methodology researchers use, the questions they ask, and the conclusions they reach from the data are influenced by their own and society's biases.[50] How

49. *See* Molina B. Dayal et al., *Preimplantation Genetic Diagnosis*, MEDSCAPE (Dec. 30, 2015), https://emedicine.medscape.com/article/273415-overview.

50. *See* Tufuku Zuberi & Eduardo Bonilla-Silva, *Towards a Definition of White Logic and White Methods, in* WHITE LOGIC, WHITE METHODS: RACISM AND METHODOLOGY 3 (Tufuku Zuberi & Eduardo Bonilla-Silva eds., 2008).

researchers themselves and readers of the research interpret data is also influenced by their own previously held views.

V. Stereotypes about Asians and Asian Americans

A number of misperceptions about Asians, Asian Americans, and the motives for sex selection in Asia has led to a widespread misunderstanding of narrow demographic data to conclude that there is a sex ratio crisis in the United States among Asian Americans. First, some people may have assumed that just because people who come from Asia and live in the United States look the same as people who live in their countries of origin, they share the same behavioral traits. The argument goes that if people widely abort female fetuses in Asia, they must also be doing so in the United States once they move to that country. Of course, while some behaviors of immigrants may be similar to people in their countries of origin, it is a form of stereotyping to assume that Asian Americans act in the same way as Asians. Moreover, the longer immigrants remain in the United States, the more their traits and behaviors may begin to deviate from people in their country of origin.

Second, some people may have readily accepted the view that sex selection both in parts of Asia and the United States is caused by sexism. There is a general perception that foreign cultures are inherently sexist and this view finds some support in feminist thought.[51] When a certain practice occurs in immigrant cultures, it is seen to be motivated by a misogynist culture, but that same practice, when it appears among the majority group, does not lead people to make broad conclusions about that culture. Rather it is seen as an exception.[52]

A closer examination of the trends in India,[53] however, paints a more nuanced picture of the reasons for sex selection and women's motives. In India, sex selection started on a significant scale only when American ultrasound machines were shipped to India in the 1980s.[54] Although against the

---

51. *See, e.g.,* Susan Moller Okin, *Is Multiculturalism Bad for Women?, in* Is MULTICULTURALISM BAD FOR WOMEN? 7 (Martha Nussbaum ed.1999), in which Okin lists many practices and ways in which minority and immigrant cultures are repressive to women.

52. *See, e.g.,* Leti Volpp, *Blaming Culture for Bad Behavior,* 12 YALE J.L. & HUMAN. 89 (2000).

53. While gender-biased sex selection also occurs in China, given my knowledge, I include only a detailed examination of the factors that lead to sex selection in India.

54. *See* MARA HVISTENDAHL, UNNATURAL SELECTION 80 (2011); Christophe Z. Guilmoto, *Characteristics of Sex-Ratio Imbalance in India, and Future Scenarios* 4–8, 4TH ASIA PACIFIC CONFERENCE ON REPRODUCTIVE AND SEXUAL HEALTH AND RIGHTS (2007), http://www.unfpa.org/gender/docs/studies/india.pdf.

common presumptions, sex ratio data as well as survey data suggests that there is not widespread "daughter-aversion," but that what many (but not all) Indian families want to have is at least one boy. Some families want to have at least one son for economic support during old age, to carry on the family name, and to perform certain death rituals for their parents.

For people living in poverty, a daughter can be expensive: she must be clothed and fed, but is less likely to contribute to the financial welfare of the family and may instead require significant expense in the form of a dowry or payment to the family of the man she marries. Technology, combined with the desire to have fewer children, and the cultural preference to have at least one son, leads many women each year to illegally learn the sex of their fetuses and abort female fetuses if they already have one or two prior girl children.

Third, there is a failure to recognize that a practice, discriminatory in one context, may not be discriminatory in another. In addition, it is often assumed that the behavior of immigrants (unlike the majority community) is driven by deep-seated cultural beliefs rather than the product of the social and economic context in which they are living.

To illustrate my point, I compare two scenarios. Take the case of an Indian woman living in India, who takes steps to have a boy child after she has had a girl child, with the case of a woman of Indian descent in the United States, who takes steps to have a boy after she has a girl. The first scenario in India raises different concerns than the second one. Social institutions such as dowry, patrilocal forms of marriage, and fewer economic opportunities for girls are some reasons why families may want to have at least one boy child in India. When families play into this tradition, they further perpetuate and reinforce those patriarchal customs. What is more troubling is that emerging empirical studies have found that the male surplus is harming women in other ways. Studies suggest that there are higher levels of sexual harassment, rape, and early child marriage in districts where there is greater sex selection.[55]

---

55. *See* Ravinder Kaur, *Mapping the Adverse Consequences of Sex Selection and Gender Imbalance in India and China*, ECONOMIC & POLITICAL WEEKLY, August 2013, at 37; RAVINDER KAUR, TOO MANY MEN TOO FEW WOMEN: SOCIAL CONSEQUENCES OF GENDER IMBALANCE IN INDIA AND CHINA (2016); Scott J. South et al., *Skewed Sex Ratios and Criminal Victimization in India*, DEMOGRAPHY, 1019 (2014); Sofia Amaral & Sonia Bhalotra, *Population Sex Ratios and Violence Against Women: the Long-Run Effects of Sex Selection in India*, INSTITUTE FOR SOCIAL & ECONOMIC RESEARCH (2017), https://www.iser.essex.ac.uk/research/publications/working -papers/iser/2017-12.pdf .

In the case of an immigrant woman in the United States, the context in which her act occurs is different. She will not likely be required to pay money to a groom to marry her daughter, she can rely on social security and other state support rather than relying solely on her son for economic support in old age, and there is no prevailing custom against daughters providing economic support. Her daughter born in the United States may have more economic opportunities for self-sufficiency than one born in India. Furthermore, large numbers of people in the United States are not systematically selecting in favor of boys. Given that there is no male surplus in the United States, there are no consequences that relate to imbalanced sex ratios (such as increased sexual harassment and rape) that occur. Moreover, as I discuss later, the few Asian American people who might be intervening to obtain the family composition they desire are not necessarily doing so for the same motives as people living in Asia.

In this section, I have outlined some of the views about Asians and Asian Americans and culture and context that may have primed some Americans to more readily accept misrepresentations of academic studies to fit comfortably into certain stereotypes. I elaborate on this point elsewhere.[56] In the next section, using newer demographic data as well as survey data, I argue that the reasons for the behavior of some Asian Americans may be very different than the actions of some Asians.

VI. Beyond "Son Preference"

The data used in Almond and Edlund's study is from the U.S. Census of 2000. In 2014, I worked with an interdisciplinary team to conduct an empirical analysis on sex ratios based on U.S. Census data from 2008 to 2012 and found something that had not been previously observed.[57]

Like Almond and Edlund, we found that when foreign-born Chinese, Korean, and Indian parents have two girls, the sex ratio of the third child shows a male-bias (1.33). However, unlike Almond and Edlund's study, we found that in more recent data, the sex ratio of the third child of Chinese, Korean, and Indian parents in the United States is female-biased after they

---

56. *See* KALANTRY, WOMEN'S HUMAN RIGHTS AND MIGRATION, *supra* note 2 at 12–46, 152–75.

57. The data grows out of work I have done with Miriam Yeung, Executive Director of the National Asian Pacific Women's Forum, Shivana Jorawar, Reproductive Justice Program Director, National Asian Pacific Women's Forum, Sujatha Jesudason, Director of CoreAlign at the University of California, San Francisco, and Brian Citro, Clinical Lecturer in Law, University of Chicago Law School.

have had two boys (0.89) (see Figure 11.2). This suggests that a very small number of Chinese-, Korean-, and Indian-American families are taking measures to ensure that they have both boy children and girl children in their families.

FIGURE 11.2 COMPARISON OF SEX RATIOS OF CHINESE, INDIAN, AND KOREAN CHILDREN AND U.S.-BORN CAUCASIAN CHILDREN (2008–2012 ACS).

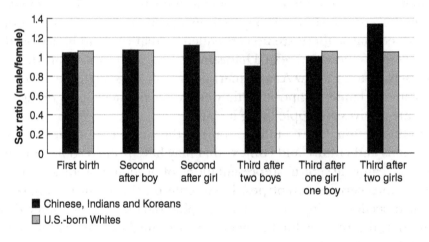

Source: Analysis of pooled American Community Survey data from 2008–2012.

Sex ratio research has certain limitations. As noted earlier, even where researchers find imbalanced sex ratios, those ratios do not tell us what methods are being used for sex-selection—pre-implantation methods or abortion. In addition, from demographic data, we cannot determine the motivations for people's behavior. To ascertain what motivates the behavior of Asian Americans, I included two questions in an annual national survey conducted by the Cornell Survey Research Institute (Cornell SRI). In total, 1,000 households were surveyed. By way of comparison, the most recent Gallup Poll survey on gender preferences surveyed 1,020 people nationally using a similar methodology.[58] In these two questions, I asked respondents their gender preference if they could only have one child, and if they could have only two children.

Consistently across each racial and ethnic group, more respondents said they would prefer to have a son than a daughter if they could have only one child as can be observed in Table 11.1. In the Cornell SRI poll, only

---

58. See Frank Newport, *Americans Prefer Boys to Girls, Just as They Did in 1941*, GALLUP (June 23, 2011), http://www.gallup.com/poll/148187/americans-prefer-boys-girls-1941.aspx.

18.8 percent of the Asian Americans surveyed said they would want to have a boy if they could only have one child. Similarly, 16.8 percent of Caucasian Americans said they would want a boy if they could have only one child. On the other hand, a significantly greater percentage of Native Americans (28.6 percent) and African Americans (32.7 percent) indicated they would want a boy if they could have a boy. Across all groups, fewer numbers wanted to have a girl if they could have only one child. Thus, when asked about their attitudes, Asian Americans do not manifest a greater preference for sons than any other racial group in the United States.

When the respondents are told they can have two children, 5 percent of Caucasian Americans want two boys and 2.7 percent want only girls. If this disparity were observed among Asian Americans, some might see this as proof of "son preference," but few would interpret this to mean "son preference" among Caucasian Americans. Contrary to the dominant narrative of "son preference" among Asian Americans, 6.3 percent of Asian Americans want only boys and an equal percentage—6.3 percent—want only girls when they are told they can have only two children.

The most important finding is that 60.4 percent of Asian Americans want to have one boy and one girl if they could have only two children. The desire for gender balance is greater among Asian Americans than any other group. Approximately 58 percent of African Americans desire a gender-balanced family, whereas only 49.4 percent of Caucasian Americans desire a gender-balanced family. Still, a quarter of the Asian Americans surveyed stated that they have no preference for the gender composition of their children. These results are consistent with another poll conducted by the Cornell Survey Research Institute in 2015 among New York State residents only, the state with the second largest Asian American population.[59]

An analysis of new demographic data combined with survey data contradicts the Almond-Edlund misconception about Asian American reproductive patterns. One plausible interpretation of the sex ratio and survey data is that Asian Americans desire both boy children and girl children. A few Asian families who have three children may have intervened to achieve balanced families. While there may be a small number of Asian Americans who still desire to have at least one son out of their "cultural" preference, this is a small group of people. It is not necessary to pass legislation that has a negative impact on all women just to attempt to prevent the behavior of a small minority of people who may not even be acting because of "sexist" motives.

---

59. Hoeffel et al., *supra* note 47, at 7.

TABLE 11.1 RESULTS OF A POLL OF U.S. RESIDENTS ON GENDER PREFERENCES

	Caucasian Americans	Asian Americans	African Americans	Native Americans	Other
If you could have only one child:					
Boy Only	16.8%	18.8%	32.7%	28.6%	19.0%
Girl Only	11.2%	10.4%	15.0%	8.2%	4.8%
Don't Care	66.1%	66.7%	47.8%	59.2%	66.7%
Don't Want Children	5.9%	4.2%	4.4%	4.1%	9.5%
If you could have only two children:					
Only Boys	5.0%	6.3%	8.0%	18.4%	0.0%
Only Girls	2.7%	6.3%	6.2%	2.0%	0.0%
One Boy/ One Girl	49.4%	60.4%	58.4%	44.9%	52.4%
Don't Care	38.2%	25.0%	24.8%	34.7%	42.9%
Don't Want Children	4.7%	2.1%	2.7%	0.0%	4.8%
Total Respondents	**768**	**48**	**113**	**49**	**21**

Source: Poll conducted by Cornell Survey Research Institute 2015.

Some pro-choice people may find sex selection for both girls and boys problematic. First, people informed by postmodern and queer theories may oppose sex selection because it supports the idea of gender as a binary category—male or female.[60] Another possible argument against sex selection is that people who sex-select are more likely to force their children to conform to traditional gender expectations and roles.[61] Yet another possible argument against sex selection posits that by sex selecting, parents make a statement that one sex is superior to another. Although people who are uneasy with sex-selective abortion may not necessarily support sex-selective abortion bans, their ambivalence about the practice of sex selection may weaken their opposition to such bans.

---

60. *See generally* JUDITH BUTLER, GENDER TROUBLE: FEMINISM AND THE SUBVERSION OF IDENTITY (2006).

61. *See* Jonathan M. Berkowitz & Jack W. Snyder, *Racism and Sexism in Medically Assisted Conception*, 12 BIOETHICS 25 (1998). Others have argued that the concept of family balancing creates this idea that an appropriate family has at least one boy and one girl. Soren Holm, *Like a Frog in Boiling Water: The Public, the HFEA, and Sex Selection*, 12 HEALTH CARE ANALYSIS, 27 (2004).

In the prior section, I have shown that the scale of sex-selective abortion among Asian Americans has been widely exaggerated in popular discourse. It was assumed this behavior was driven by misogyny and daughter aversion. The data presented in this section adds a very different layer to the dominant narrative. If Asian Americans are sex selecting (which we cannot know for certain and also cannot know what methods they are using), their motives may relate to balancing their families with both genders. In the next section, I explain how sex-selective abortion statutes could impact the future of abortion jurisprudence of the U.S. Supreme Court.

VII. Sex-Selective Abortion Statutes and the U.S. Supreme Court

A decision by the U.S. Supreme Court on the constitutionality of sex-selective abortion statutes could have a significant impact on reproductive rights in the United States. Indeed, a case involving the constitutionality of sex-selective abortion bans reached the U.S. Supreme Court in the 2018 term.[62] A U.S. District Court judge declared Indiana's sex-selective abortion statute unconstitutional, to the extent it applies to pre-viability of the fetus.[63] The U.S. Court of Appeals for the Seventh Circuit granted *en banc* review of a portion of the opinion unrelated to the sex-selective abortion ban, but then vacated that order when one of the participating judges recused themselves.[64] By vacating its order granting *en banc* review, the Seventh Circuit thereby reinstated the original panel decision finding that the statute was unconstitutional. Seventh Circuit Judge Barrett (now Justice Barrett) joined a dissenting opinion that analogized the practice of sex selection as akin to eugenics.[65] The U.S. Supreme Court refused to review the Seventh Circuit's ruling that the statute in question was unconstitutional, but in an unusual move, went on to give a reason for why it denied certiorari.[66] The Court indicated that it wanted to give more appeals courts the opportunity

---

62. Box v. Planned Parenthood of Ind. & Ky., 139 S. Ct. 1780 (2019).
63. Planned Parenthood of Ind. & Ky. v. Comm'r, 265 F. Supp. 3d 859 (S.D. Ind. 2017).
64. Planned Parenthood of Ind. & Ky. v. Comm'r, 727 Fed. App'x. 208 (7th Cir. 2018).
65. Planned Parenthood of Ind. & Ky. v. Comm'r, 917 F.3d 532, 536 (7th Cir. 2018).
66. *Box*, 139 S. Ct. at 1782.

to review similar statutes.[67] In his concurring opinion, Justice Thomas made
it clear that he did not agree with the lower court's opinion.[68]

U.S. jurisprudence on abortion forms a complicated web of decisions.
Given this complexity, we cannot be certain what legal test the Supreme
Court will use in evaluating the constitutionality of the prohibitions on
sex-selective abortion. The composition of the justices will also drive what
test is used and what conclusion is reached. There is no consensus among
legal scholars about what legal test the Court will use let alone how they
will rule.[69]

---

67. *Id.* ("Only the Seventh Circuit has thus far addressed this kind of law. We follow our
ordinary practice of denying petitions insofar as they raise legal issues that have not been
considered by additional Courts of Appeals.").

68. *Id.* at 1792 (Thomas, J., concurring) ("The Court's decision to allow further percola-
tion should not be interpreted as agreement with the decisions below.").

69. *See* Annie Moskovia, *Bans on Sex-Selective Abortions: How Far Is Too Far?*, 40 HASTINGS
CONST. L. Q. 423 (2013) (arguing that sex-selective bans infringe on women's constitutional
right to privacy and liberty, fail *Casey's* undue burden test because they completely ban abortion based on sex, and differ from *Gonzales* as there are no alternative methods of abortion; in addition, there is no precedent of the court having limited a woman's reasons for
seeking an abortion); Justin Gillette, *Pregnant and Prejudiced: The Constitutionality of Sex- and
Race-Selective Abortion Restrictions*, 88 WASH. L. REV. 645 (arguing that motive-based abortion
restrictions, such as sex-selective abortion bans, are unconstitutional because they violate
a woman's constitutional liberty rights—although Gillette notes that the Supreme Court
has allowed increasingly restrictive abortion laws since *Roe*); Jaime Staples King, *Not This
Child: Constitutional Questions in Regulating Noninvasive Prenatal Genetic Diagnosis And Selective
Abortion*, 60 UCLA L. REV. 2 (2012) (arguing that the right to choose abortion for any reason should be grounded in the principles of liberty and autonomy, rather than sex equality and that sex-selective abortion bans would fail the undue burden test because women
would need to withhold information from their doctors or opt not to have abortions); Mary
Kanowsky, *A Hidden Gendercide: Discrepancies Between Embryo Destruction and Sex Selective Abortion
Laws*, 14 AVE MARIA L. REV. 163 (2016) (arguing that using a gender equality framework, it
remains unclear whether sex-selective abortion bans would be constitutional because it is
unclear what standard of scrutiny would apply, that under a right to privacy argument such
bans fail the undue burden test prior to viability, and that under Case, post-viability bans
would be unconstitutional because they not leave exceptions for the health of the mother);
Krissa Webb, *Gender Mis-Conception: The Prenatal Nondiscrimination Act as A Remix of the Abortion Debate*, 11 GEO. J. L. & PUB. POL'Y 257 (2013) (arguing that federal regulations on sex-
selective abortion should be constitutional and would likely be justifiable if imposed on
state-run medical centers or as an issue of private discrimination by the medical industry that
has a substantial effect on interstate commerce); Jason C. Greaves, *Sex-Selective Abortion in the
U.S.: Does* Roe v. Wade *Protect Arbitrary Gender Discrimination?*, 23 GEO. MASON U. CIV. RTS. L.
J. 333, 363 (2013) (concluding that current jurisprudence does not seem to allow for sex-
selective abortion bans under the fundamental right to privacy, but that public opinion may
influence the court's decision); Thomas J. Molony, *Roe, Casey, and Sex-Selection Abortion Bans*,
71 WASH. & LEE L. REV. 1089 (2014) (differentiating between narrow bans that ban abortion
based solely on sex, and broader bans that proscribe abortions when sex selection is one of
other reasons and that do not contain a life or health exception and arguing that in light of

One approach the Court might take is to distinguish between pre-viability and post-viability sex-selective abortion bans.[70] While it would prohibit all pre-viability restrictions, it would evaluate post-viability bans using the approach articulated in *Whole Woman's Health v. Hellerstedt*.[71] In *Whole Woman's Health*, in determining whether the abortion restrictions in question were an "undue burden," the Court used a cost/benefit analysis test.[72] The cost/benefit test to evaluate "undue burden" in *Whole Woman's Health* was applied again in *June Medical Services v. Russo*; however, Chief Justice Roberts, wrote a separate concurring opinion stating that he would dispense with the cost/benefit analysis and instead focus only on what burdens the abortion restriction creates.[73]

Assuming that when the Court reviews the constitutionality of sex-selective abortion statutes that it uses the cost/benefit test as articulated in *Whole Woman's Health*, then whether it decides that the benefits of such a ban exceeds the costs depends on which narrative it believes—the one I have just articulated or the one advanced by pro-life groups and accepted by some pro-choice people based on the misinterpretation of narrow data provided in the Almond and Edlund study.

The foundational decision that established the right to choose was *Roe v. Wade*.[74] It established different legal tests based on the number of weeks of gestation.[75] The U.S. District Judge in Indiana interpreted *Roe* to mean a state was not permitted to restrict pre-viability abortion in any way. She stated that "[t]he woman's right to choose to terminate a pregnancy pre-viability is categorical: 'a State may not prohibit any woman from making the ultimate decision to terminate her pregnancy before viability.'"[76]

Gonzales, a narrowly drafted sex-selective abortion ban that does not include life or health exceptions could survive a challenge despite the Casey ruling). *See also* Greer Donley, *Does the Constitution Protect Abortions Based on Fetal Anomaly?: Examining the Potential for Disability-selective Abortion Bans in the Age of Prenatal Whole Genome Sequencing*, 20 MICH. J. GENDER & L. 291 (2013) (presenting an analysis of the unconstitutionality of disability-selective abortion bans under the Commerce Clause and the Equal Protection Clause and highlighting the slippery slope argument that may be illuminating when considering sex-selective abortion bans).

70. The sex of a fetus could be determined using blood tests of the pregnant woman's blood as early as seven weeks of gestation or as early as 12 weeks using an ultrasound.

71. Whole Woman's Health v. Hellerstedt, 136 S. Ct. 2292 (2016).

72. *Id.* at 2309–10.

73. June Medical Services v. Russo, 140 S. Ct. 2103, 2133–43 (2020).

74. Roe v. Wade, 410 U.S. 113 (1973).

75. *Id.* at 164–65.

76. Planned Parenthood of Ind. & Ky v. Comm'r, 265 F. Supp. 3d 859, 866 (S.D. Ind. 2017).

Nearly a quarter of a century before the Indiana decision, the State of Illinois had settled a similar suit against its ban on sex-selective abortion. Illinois agreed that the statute should only apply post-viability after the Supreme Court's *Roe* decision.[77] In rejecting an objection to this settlement, the U.S. District Court for the Northern District of Illinois stated that "[t]he Casey court made it clear that any pre-viability regulation which imposes a palpable restriction on a women's right to elect abortion would be prohibited."[78] Thus, at least one other court has suggested that pre-viability sex-selective bans are unconstitutional. The Ninth Circuit Court of Appeals has also found that pre-viability bans on abortion generally are unconstitutional.[79]

Even if it decides that pre-viability restrictions are categorically impermissible under *Roe v. Wade*, the Court might treat post-viability abortions differently. In *Whole Woman's Health v. Hellerstedt*, the Court evaluated two Texas regulations to determine whether the costs of the prohibition exceed its benefits.[80] The first regulation required medical professionals who perform abortions to have admitting privileges at a hospital within 100 miles of the abortion site.[81] The other regulation required abortion clinics to satisfy the state requirements imposed on surgical centers.[82] As noted earlier, the Court framed the "undue burden" test as a cost/benefit analysis.[83]

Supporters of the legislation argued that strict health regulations were needed to protect the health of abortion seekers. However, the Court found that the Texas restrictions had no benefits since abortions are already very safe procedures in Texas.[84] On the other hand, they impose significant costs on women's access to abortion given that scores of clinics had already closed in Texas as a result of the statute.[85] The Court emphasized the need to consider factual findings, rather than merely the law's purported benefits, when engaging in this analysis.[86] Applying a cost/benefit test, the Court found that the Texas restrictions imposed an undue burden on abortion access and were therefore unconstitutional.[87]

---

77. Herbst v. O'Malley, No. 84 C 5602, 1993 WL 59142 (N.D. Ill. Mar. 2, 1993).

78. *Id.* at 9.

79. Isaacson v. Horne, 716 F.3d 1213, 1231 (9th Cir. 2013).

80. Whole Woman's Health v. Hellerstedt, 136 S. Ct. 2292, 2300, 2309–10 (2016).

81. *Id.* at 2300.

82. *Id.*

83. *Id.* at 2309–10.

84. *Id.* at 2311.

85. *Id.* at 2312.

86. *Id.* at 2310–11.

87. *Id.* at 2309–20.

If it follows *Whole Woman's Health*, the Court will likely undertake a cost/benefit analysis if it applies the "undue burden" test to post-viability sex-selective abortion bans. I have described the costs of the ban in Section II. To recap: sex-selective abortion bans will create a tension in the relationship between a medical professional and her patient, could lead to racial profiling by medical professionals, and will burden the rights of women who desire to obtain non-selective abortions.

According to pro-life advocates, there are two key benefits of bans on sex-selective abortion. First, a ban will address a widespread practice (targeted abortion of female fetuses). As discussed in Sections IV and V, by relying on stereotypes about the behavior of Asian Americans and drawing on misinformation about foreign countries and misunderstandings of empirical data, some people argue that gender-biased abortion occurs in crisis proportions in the United States. The truth is that, at most, sex ratio data suggests that a few thousand Asian Americans sex selected because they wanted boy children when they already had one or two girl children. Even if we assume that every single one of these people selected against a girl, it is possible that each of these people used sperm-sorting or IVF and PGD to manipulate the gender of their children rather than abortion. A small number of other Asian Americans may also be selecting in favor of girl children.

Second, some people argue that the aborting of female fetuses in the United States is problematic because the motives of the people who do it are discriminatory. This conclusion draws on information about what is believed to motivate gender-biased abortion in foreign countries. In Section VI, I explain using more recent data on Asian American childbirths that there are a small number of people who select in favor of girls when they have prior boy children. This challenges the notion that those Asian Americans who sex select are manifesting sex discrimination—rather, it suggests that they desire families with both genders. A survey of Americans confirms that Asian Americans are the group that is most likely to want a family with at least one boy and one girl. One could morally object to family balancing, but that practice does not manifest discrimination against women and girls in the same way as in parts of Asia.

In part, what makes gender-biased selection problematic in India is defined by the context in which it occurs. A practice gains meaning as discriminatory in the context in which it occurs. In India, sex selection may be discriminatory because it occurs in the context of gender inequalities such as son preference, dowry, a patrilocal system wherein the daughter physically leaves her parents' family and joins her husband's family after marriage, and inheritance traditions that favor sons. Those contextual societal motivations for sex selection are not present in the United States. If one accepts the facts that I have presented, it seems clear that the costs of the sex-selective abortion prohibitions are not justified.

There are several other approaches that the Court could take. It might not distinguish between pre-viability and post-viability sex selective abortion bans and instead apply the same legal test to both periods. It could categorically reject sex-selective abortion bans at all times during the pregnancy. Unlike the abortion prohibitions that the Court has previously considered, the sex-selective abortion laws are complete bans rather than "obstacles" to obtaining abortions. For example, the state legislation at issue in *Casey* merely created obstacles to a woman's path to an abortion.[88] The sex-selective bans do more than that—they prohibit abortion altogether for a specific reason. Alternatively, the Court could apply the "undue burden" test to both the pre-viability and post-viability period.

Another issue that the Court might consider is whether a fetus *should* have a legal right to be free from discrimination. No American court has found that a state has an interest in protecting a fetus from discrimination. Indeed, in a concurring opinion, Justice Stevens has noted that "no member of [the Supreme Court] has ever suggested that a fetus is a 'person' within the meaning of the Fourteenth Amendment," which would entitle the fetus to equal protection of the law.[89] If the Court were to extend this protection to a fetus, it would mean granting the fetus full personhood. To grant the fetus full personhood would open the door to a host of other abortion restrictions.

Bans on sex-selective abortion may seem harmless. After all, most people do not approve of the practice. Very few women want to have an abortion for that purpose. But the right to choose could hinge on how the U.S. Supreme Court rules on sex-selective abortion bans if the issue ever reaches the Court. If the Supreme Court rules that sex-selective abortion bans are constitutional, this will invite more states to adopt a host of other reason-based pre-viability prohibitions. For example, states could prohibit a woman from terminating her pregnancy if her reason is that she does not want to have a child born with a disability (assuming the fetus was diagnosed with a disability).

On the other hand, if the U.S. Supreme Court does not accept decontextualized arguments about the practice and instead relies on evidence-based

---

88. Planned Parenthood of Southeastern Pennsylvania v. Casey, 505 U.S. 833 (1992).
89. Thornburgh v. American College of Obstetricians & Gynecologists, 476 U.S. 747, 779 n.8 (1986).

research about sex-selective abortions in the United States, then they are more likely to find them unconstitutional. When the costs of sex-selective abortion bans are placed against an evidence-based and contextualized understanding of the benefits of such bans, it is clear that the costs far outweigh the benefits. However, the Supreme Court might apply a different standard to the case and, even if it applies the cost/benefits analysis, it might consider different costs/benefits and weigh them differently. Given the current composition of the Court, inclusive of Justice Barrett, any case in which it adjudicates the constitutionality of sex-selective abortion bans will have a significant impact on reproductive rights for years to come.

VIII. Conclusion

In recent years, there has been a spate of anti-abortion legislation targeting sex-selective abortions. The strategic framing by pro-life advocates of such legislation in women's equality terms has created a situation where some pro-choice supporters of a woman's right to choose find themselves supporting (or at least, not strongly opposing) these bans. The dominant public narrative has centered on exploiting false assumptions about Asian Americans and exaggerating empirical data to fit those stereotypes. The dominant narrative is wrong. The practice of sex-selective abortion is not widespread in the United States among Asian Americans. Moreover, even if some women do abort to sex-select (which we do not have persuasive evidence for), we cannot attribute the same motives to Asian women in the United States as we might attribute to women living in Asia. Sex-selective abortion bans should be found unconstitutional if and when the question reaches the U.S Supreme Court, but this decision will no doubt turn on what set of facts the Court believes—the narrative that has gained popularity in the United States or the more nuanced approach I have suggested here. The story of sex-selective abortion laws is a reminder about the importance of carefully interrogating empirical data and challenging our own assumptions about minority and foreign peoples.

12

How Sentience Should Mediate the Right to Abortion

By Sherry F. Colb[1]

When politicians and pundits talk about the right to abortion, they often speak of it as though it were one thing, as though abortion were one particular type of act that either is or is not worthy of protection and either is or is not an act of violence. But the reality is otherwise. Abortions are not all the same, and people's intuitive reactions to different kinds of abortions are properly distinct from one another. When I say "different kinds of abortion," let me specify what I do not mean. I do not mean to refer to different types of medical procedures, such as dilation and evacuation versus dilation and extraction, the latter of which some call "partial-birth abortion" and which a federal law that the Supreme Court upheld in *Gonzales v. Carhart*, prohibits.[2] I also do not mean to refer to abortions motivated by different sorts of situations, such as financial pressures versus a profound birth defect discovered on ultrasound. For reasons I will explain later in this chapter, I do not regard the foregoing differences as very relevant to our consideration of which abortions give rise to the greatest moral dilemmas.

What I mean by "different kinds of abortions" is abortions that take place at different stages of pregnancy. Such differences matter to people expressing their gut intuitions about the procedure and therefore to legislatures

1. C.S. Wong Professor of Law, Cornell Law School. The author thanks Grace Brosofsky, Rebecca Duncan, and Doug Wagner, who provided excellent research assistance, and Michael C. Dorf, who gave terrific feedback and suggestions. The author also expresses gratitude to Dean Eduardo Peñalver of Cornell Law School for providing generous summer research support.
2. Gonzales v. Carhart, 550 U.S. 124 (2007).

expressing the public will to regulate some but not all abortions. I will argue here that the stage at which a termination takes place is the main factor to consider in determining whether and when to give the strongest protection to the right to terminate a pregnancy.

I. Why the Method of Abortion Doesn't Matter

The first distinction just noted, between procedures such as dilation and evacuation versus dilation and extraction, is irrelevant, even though federal law currently embraces it. The different methods of terminating a pregnancy all aim for and result in the same outcome: the death of the fetus and the corresponding termination of the pregnancy. Unless some methods cause more fetal distress than others, they are all morally equivalent.

To be sure, there could be valid grounds for distinguishing among methods of abortion. For example, if one posed substantially greater health risks to the mother than another, without compensating benefits, the law could bar the riskier procedure.[3] However, legal and political fights over abortion do not tend to focus on laws that address genuine health risks.[4]

Charles Camosy would distinguish between what could be called an active abortion (where the provider actively and intentionally kills the fetus)

---

3. The Supreme Court would likely uphold against a constitutional challenge such laws barring unnecessarily dangerous abortion methods, so long as the laws left open other, accessible methods. In *Whole Woman's Health v. Hellerstedt*, the Court performed a benefits–burdens balancing test to determine the constitutionality of laws restricting abortion access. Whole Woman's Health v. Hellerstedt, 136 S. Ct. 2292, 2309 (2016), *as revised* (June 27, 2016) (finding that courts must "consider the burdens a law imposes on abortion access together with the benefits those laws confer" to determine whether a law unduly burdens women's substantive due process right to seek pre-viability abortions). Under this test, if a law conferred the legitimate benefit of protecting the health of women by proscribing a dangerous method of abortion and imposed minimal burdens because it still allowed women to obtain an abortion through safe and accessible methods, courts would likely uphold it as constitutional. Recently, in *June Medical Services L.L.C. v. Russo*, the Supreme Court reaffirmed *Whole Woman's Health* and purported to apply the same test but instead of balancing benefits against burdens, assessed whether a law posed a "substantial obstacle" to abortion. 140 S. Ct. 2103, 2120 (2020). Under this "substantial obstacle" test, a law banning a dangerous method of abortion but allowing other safer, accessible methods would likely still pass constitutional muster. Such a law would not place a "substantial obstacle in the path of women seeking an abortion," *id.* at 2112, since it would leave open the door to relatively safe abortions.

4. *E.g., Whole Woman's Health*, 136 S. Ct. at 2311 (upholding, in spite of the legislature's contention that the law protected women's health, the district court's finding that "there was no significant health-related problem that the [Texas admitting-privileges law at issue] helped to cure,"); *June Med. Servs.*, 140 S. Ct. at 2130 (similarly upholding the district court's finding that there was "no significant health-related problem that the [Louisiana admitting-privileges law] helped to cure," in spite of the legislature's arguments to the contrary).

and a passive abortion (where the provider supports the woman's decision not to give aid to the fetus).[5] The distinction rests on the proposition that killing is a culpable act in a way that letting die might not be.

Some terminations of pregnancy would qualify as merely letting die. For example (assuming that the goal is not to kill the fetus), inducing labor in a woman whose fetus is not yet viable could be a form of passive abortion under Camosy's definition, because the woman does not actively kill her fetus (or hire someone else to do so) but instead fails to provide aid to her fetus, in the form of the nourishment that her body would have provided were labor not induced. Although Camosy does not condone most passive abortions,[6] he does regard some as justified under conditions in which an active abortion would not be. For example, if a woman becomes pregnant due to rape, Camosy would support her right to terminate the pregnancy through an indirect method, even though he would not permit her to actively kill the fetus (through one of the common abortion methods that do so).[7]

Camosy's distinction between killing and letting die will no doubt resonate with many readers. Both morality and law frequently distinguish acts from omissions, after all. However, the distinction does not quite work as applied to pregnancy.

A passive abortion is not the same as a bystander passing an endangered stranger (or even friend or family member) and failing to provide aid. That is because a pregnant woman is uniquely situated relative to her fetus. If she "does nothing" about the pregnancy, then the fetus lives, but not because she is truly doing nothing. She is bearing the burden of literally carrying the

---

5. CHARLES C. CAMOSY, BEYOND THE ABORTION WARS: A WAY FORWARD FOR A NEW GEN-ERATION 64 (2015) ("Direct abortions . . . are examples where death is either the goal of the act or the means by which the goal is accomplished. But not all abortions are like this. *Indirect* abortions of pregnancy that do not aim at the death of the child are different. Indeed, even the Catholic Church allows this kind of abortion for a proportionately serious reason. Suppose a pregnant woman is given the devastating diagnosis of cancer of the uterus. According to Catholic teaching, she may abort her pregnancy by having her uterus removed if the goal of her action . . . does not involve the death of the prenatal child.").

6. *Id.* at 69, 71 (noting that "[t]he cases that require direct abortion to defend a mother's life are extremely rare," and that "even if [indirect abortion] doesn't aim at death, one needs a proportionately serious reason to refuse aid to a child that will die without such aid").

7. *Id.* at 148 (explaining that due to the "increased burden, and [the] decreased sense of what is owed the child" in pregnancies caused by rape, Camosy "believe[s] the law should respect a mother's choice to refuse to aid a child via indirect abortion in the case of rape"). However, Camosy's proposed legislation would not allow a direct abortion, even in the case of rape. *Id.* ("[I]t is always wrong to aim at the death of an innocent person ([Camosy's proposed legislation] would not permit direct abortion in the case of rape).").

fetus wherever she goes and also supplying all of its needs through her own blood supply, thus potentially compromising her own health and burdening her various organ systems. In other words, merely *remaining pregnant* is activity in a way that typical omissions are not. If you hate your neighbor but decide nonetheless to allow him to live, this decision does not require you to do anything to support his continued living. But as Judith Jarvis Thomson argued in her landmark article,[8] being pregnant requires active support of the developing fetus that should not be demanded of anyone against her will, even to save the life of a full person. Thomson makes this point with a provocative analogy to a person involuntarily attached to a famous violinist who will die if the first person cuts off the connection between the two.[9]

Because pregnancy is an active supplying of life support, terminating a pregnancy—in whatever manner one chooses—represents a failure to help, at least in part.[10] Whether the fetus is actively killed or simply removed from the woman's body, it will die, and its not being viable means that it will necessarily die because of its removal. Therefore, whether it is killed first (by whatever method) or is allowed to emerge alive and then die for a lack of oxygen would not seem to matter very much. Indeed, one could even say that removing a nonviable fetus from one's body is comparable to removing a fish from water, which no one would characterize as a mere "failure to aid" the fish. Thus, inducing abortion amounts to a failure to aid only because pregnancy itself is a process of aiding (the termination of which is thus necessarily a failure to aid), not because removing a being from an area where it can absorb oxygen to an area where it cannot is necessarily something other than active killing.

---

8. Judith Jarvis Thomson, *A Defense of Abortion*, 1 PHIL. & PUB. AFF. 47, 48–49 (1971), https://eclass.uoa.gr/modules/document/file.php/PPP475/Thomson%20Judith%20Jarvis%2C%20A%20defense%20of%20abortion.pdf (last visited Mar. 7, 2021) (analogizing a pregnant woman to a person who has been involuntarily connected to a famous violinist in kidney failure and faces the choice whether to continue to be attached to him for nine months or whether to disconnect him and thereby end his life).

9. *Id.*

10. *See* SHERRY F. COLB, MIND IF I ORDER THE CHEESEBURGER? AND OTHER QUESTIONS PEOPLE ASK VEGANS 89 (2013) [hereinafter CHEESEBURGER] ("If the pregnant woman does not kill her fetus, then she will have to carry and gestate that fetus inside her body and then undergo either labor and delivery or a major surgery at the end. She must therefore select between committing affirmative violence, on the one hand, and acting as a Good Samaritan, on the other. These are the only alternatives."); *see also* SHERRY F. COLB & MICHAEL C. DORF, BEATING HEARTS: ABORTION AND ANIMAL RIGHTS 79 (2016) [hereinafter BEATING HEARTS] (noting that having an abortion allows a woman to "restor[e] the physical state in which her bodily processes are no longer involuntarily diverted to the task of providing life support to another living thing . . . thereby reestablish[ing] her bodily integrity").

II. Why the Reason for the Abortion Doesn't Matter

Many people believe that the reason for an abortion bears on whether it ought to be legal. Opinion polls show strong support for permitting abortion where the pregnancy results from rape or incest.[11] By contrast, if a woman wants to terminate because she lacks the funds to take care of a baby (or perhaps another baby, if she already has children), people are less sympathetic to her decision to terminate her pregnancy.[12] Why? Some would say that if she cannot afford to care for a baby, then she can take the pregnancy to term and give up her child for adoption.[13]

Yet adoption is not always a plausible substitute for abortion. A woman who endures an entire pregnancy and labor is likely to experience strong emotional bonds with her baby and will suffer if she is required to give him

---

11. CAMOSY, *supra* note 5, at 29 (noting that a CNN poll from 2012 found that 83 percent of Americans believe that abortion should be legal when the pregnancy was the product of rape or incest).

12. *See* SCOTT B. RAE & PAUL M. COX, BIOETHICS: A CHRISTIAN APPROACH IN A PLURALISTIC AGE 122 (1999) ("Though [the burden of having a disabled child] should not be underestimated, the hardship on the parents does not justify ending the pregnancy, any more than the financial hardship of a poor woman justifies her ending her pregnancy."); *Common Abortion Fallacies*, ABORT 73 (Feb. 8, 2017), http://abort73.com/abortion/common_objec tions/ ("Has anyone ever heard someone argue that the mothers of these born-children should have the right to kill them, since they can't afford to raise them? No one makes such an absurd and heartless argument because we all know that no amount of financial hardship is sufficient rationale for killing another human being, particularly an innocent child."); Larry L. Bumpass, *The Measurement of Public Opinion on Abortion: The Effects of Survey Design*, 29 FAM. PLANNING PERSP. 177, 177–78 (1997) ("[According to four surveys conducted between 1975 and 1994,] 41–46% [of Americans] approve [of abortions] . . . if the woman desires an abortion because she wants no more children, has financial constraints or is unmarried.") According to a public opinion survey conducted by the University of Michigan every two years between 1980 and 2008, 27–32% of Americans believe that abortion should only be allowed in cases of rape, incest, or danger to the life of the woman. Karlyn Bowman & Heather Sims, ATTITUDES ABOUT ABORTION 19 (2016) https://www.aei.org/wp-content /uploads/2016/01/ABORTION1.pdf. In a similar study conducted by *Time Magazine* and CNN, conducted eighteen times between 1987 and 2001, only 34–49% of Americans believe that a woman should be able to get an abortion if she decides she wants one, no matter the reason. *Id.* at 20. In a 2005 study, which included 1,147 women who had obtained an abortion, more than 60% of all respondents cited financial hardship as a reason for their abortion. Lawrence B. Finer, Lori F. Frohwirth, Lindsay A. Dauphinee, Susheela Singh & Ann M. Moore, *Reasons U.S. Women Have Abortions: Quantitative and Qualitative Perspectives*, 37 PERSP. ON SEXUAL & REPROD. HEALTH 115 (2005).

13. Kristi Burton Brown, *Abortion vs. Adoption: Why So Many Choose the First and What We Can Do*, LIVEACTION (May 15, 2012, 2:13 PM), https://www.liveaction.org/news/abortion-vs -adoption-why-so-many-choose-the-first-and-what-we-can-do/ ("I firmly believe that one of the best things the pro-life movement can do is promote adoption.").

up for adoption.[14] After all, even women who keep their babies sometimes suffer post-partum depression. Giving up a baby can only exacerbate such feelings. Accordingly, adoption may not be a "win-win" proposition from the perspective of many women who cannot afford to have another child. An abortion in that situation spares the woman the emotional pain of having to give up her child once he is born.

Meanwhile, the public acceptance of rape as a justification for abortion tacitly endorses a logic that extends to other abortions. When people support the right of women to terminate pregnancies caused by a rape, what they are supporting is the woman's interest in killing the product of the rape. The idea appears to be that no one should have to carry to term a pregnancy that was entered into involuntarily through rape. The rapist's attack on the woman's bodily integrity is continuous with the fetus's intrusion on the woman's physical boundaries. The fetus is thus an extension of its father, and the woman has the right to kill that extension in a sort of self-defense against the extension of the rape. Of course, not everyone agrees that women should be able to end a pregnancy that results from rape.[15] But those who do believe in this right are plainly distinguishing between pregnancy and other states of being, because no one would say that a woman may kill a born child because the child was originally conceived in rape. The rape exception is accordingly an acknowledgment that pregnancy is a special condition in which a woman is required to provide life support with her body and thus play the role of a Good Samaritan if she takes her pregnancy to term, a role that many believe she should not be required to take upon herself.

To be sure, many people who think rape justifies abortion regard rape as a special case. But is it? Pregnancy itself is always a profound intrusion on the pregnant woman's bodily integrity, as people who believe in a rape exception acknowledge, at least in that subset of cases.

---

14. *See* Sherry F. Colb, *"Never Having Loved at All": An Overlooked Interest That Grounds the Abortion Right*, 48 CONN. L. REV. 933, 945 (2016) ("When a woman carries a pregnancy to term and endures labor and delivery—by contrast to when she terminates her pregnancy at an early stage (and perhaps even at a later stage)—she is likely to experience a sense of tremendous attachment to the infant to whom she has given birth. There are a number of reasons for this, but one is biological: mammals produce hormones during labor, including oxytocin, which—like a drug that activates our neural networks—induce feelings of love and bonding in both the woman and her young infant.") (citations omitted).

15. Serrin M. Foster, *Pro-Woman Answers to Pro-Choice Questions*, FEMINISTS FOR LIFE, https://www.feministsforlife.org/what-about-rape/ (last visited Mar. 12, 2021) ("Abortion after rape is misdirected anger. It doesn't punish the perpetrator of the crime or prevent further assaults against other women.").

Indeed, the rape exception is more telling still, because—even apart from what it reveals regarding what people believe about pregnancy—pregnancy can be analogized to rape.[16] The analogy works even when a woman has a morally repugnant reason for wanting an abortion. Suppose that a man wants to have sexual intercourse with a woman, and the woman refuses the man's advances for a bad reason (such as his race). The man nonetheless proceeds to force the woman to have sex against her will. That act is a rape, no matter how offensive or inappropriate the woman's reasons for saying no.

Just like the woman who does not wish to experience the bodily intrusion of sexual intercourse with a particular man, the pregnant woman who does not want to be pregnant does not wish to suffer the bodily intrusion of pregnancy. In both cases, the woman in question may have a good reason or a bad reason for refusing the bodily intrusion. She may want to terminate her pregnancy because it was the product of rape, or she may wish to abort because she wants to avoid stretch marks on her body. It should not matter, because, like the woman who refuses sex for a bad reason, a woman should have the right to stop being pregnant for a bad reason as well, and that right—like the right to self-defense against rape—should perhaps come with the option of using lethal force to put an end to her condition of being internally occupied against her will.

The analogy here is not perfect, of course. A rapist is a culpable perpetrator of a violent crime, while a fetus is not guilty of doing anything wrong to have brought about its own existence. The woman also (ordinarily) has no special obligation to the rapist to save or spare his life, while the woman is arguably bound by her role as the mother of the fetus to take care of it in the way that parents generally have a special relationship creating duties to their children. Finally, the rape victim did not do anything consensual to bring about the rape, but the woman—at least outside the case of rape—did do something consensual to bring about the existence of the fetus, by

---

16. *See* BEATING HEARTS, *supra* note 10, at 88–89; *see also* Sherry F. Colb, *Acting for the Wrong Reasons: Abortion versus Other Choices*, DORF ON LAW (July 29, 2016), http://www.dorf onlaw.org/2016/07/acting-for-wrong-reasons-abortion.html; Sherry F. Colb, *The Man's Role in Abortion and Paternity*, DORF ON LAW (Mar. 1, 2017), http://www.dorfonlaw.org/2017/03 /the-mans-role-in-abortion-and-paternity.html; Sherry F. Colb, *The Logic of Trump's Comment Endorsing Punishment for Abortion*, VERDICT (Apr. 5, 2016), https://verdict.justia .com/2016/04/05/the-logic-of-trumps-comment-endorsing-punishment-for-abortion.

having consensual intercourse or embarking consensually on a course of IVF (in vitro fertilization) or donor insemination.[17]

Yet these distinctions are less important than they might seem. Even if a rapist were insane and thus not responsible for his actions, a woman would still be entitled to protect her bodily integrity, despite his lack of culpability.[18] So culpability does not matter that much to the right to restore one's bodily integrity from an unwanted intrusion. As for a special obligation, until the fetus reaches some critical stage in the pregnancy (which I will argue later is sentience), it has not yet come to occupy the status of the woman's child such that she owes it special obligations. And finally, one act of consensual sex is not very likely to yield a pregnancy,[19] a reality that makes it difficult to argue that consent to sex is the equivalent of consent to pregnancy. Arguably, people take the risk of getting raped when they leave their homes, but that does not in any way mean that they have consented to the attack. The same arguably holds true for those who engage in consensual sexual activity without the wish to become pregnant.[20]

The most compelling argument for the right to an abortion lies in the physical intrusion that an unwanted pregnancy represents, regardless of the method of termination and regardless of the woman's reason for seeking to terminate. So what ought to matter in distinguishing between abortions

---

17. *See* BEATING HEARTS, *supra* note 10, at 90 ("[I]f the pregnancy was the result of consensual sex, then the pregnant woman has played an active role in creating the circumstances in which the innocent sentient being grows inside her.").

18. George P. Fletcher & Luis E. Chiesa, *Self-Defense and the Psychotic Aggressor, in* CRIMINAL LAW CONVERSATIONS 372 (Paul H. Robinson, Stephen Garvey & Kimberly Kessler Ferzan, eds., 2008) ("The fact that the psychotic actor would be acquitted on grounds of insanity if he were tried for his aggression is beside the point, for excuses such as insanity do not negate the wrongfulness of the act. Ultimately, the roots of the right to use defensive force are not in the culpability of the aggressor, but in the unjustifiable invasion of the defender's autonomy.").

19. David Spiegelhalter, *Sex: What Are the Chances?*, BBC.COM (Mar. 15, 2012), http://www .bbc.com/future/story/20120313-sex-in-the-city-or-elsewhere (noting that "a single act of [unprotected] intercourse between a young couple has on average a one in 20 chance of pregnancy").

20. Judith Jarvis Thomson provides a useful analogy for unwanted children conceived through consensual sex. Thomson, *supra* note 8 ("[P]eople-seeds drift about in the air like pollen, and if you open your windows, one may drift in and take root in your carpets or upholstery. You don't want children, so you fix up your windows with fine mesh screens, the very best you can buy. As can happen, however, and on very, very rare occasions does happen, one of the screens is defective, and a seed drifts in and takes root. Does the person-plant who now develops have a right to the use of your house? Surely not—despite the fact that you voluntarily opened your windows, you knowingly kept carpets and upholstered furniture, and you knew that screens were sometimes defective.").

that "count" as harms (that might perhaps be legally prohibited) and those that do not count? In a word, the answer is sentience.

III. Sentience

As we have seen, not all distinctions among abortions withstand critical scrutiny. One that may fare better is stage of pregnancy. Most Americans regard early termination as more justifiable than late-term abortion.[21] Why? The answer seems straightforward enough. In the very early stages of pregnancy (such as when the so-called morning-after pill works), it is unclear that abortion kills a human organism.[22] Moral intuitions scale with time. People tend to feel less and less comfortable with an abortion the later in pregnancy that it occurs. Fortunately, most abortions take place during the first trimester,[23] when people (including, presumably, the women who have the procedure) are most ethically comfortable with abortion.

But why are people increasingly uncomfortable with abortion as a pregnancy progresses? What changes? Plainly, the fetus develops. Early on in pregnancy, there are just cells with potential. As pregnancy continues, the cells become more specialized and the fetus begins to look more like a human. This appearance may play some role in people's feelings about later abortions, but the moral intuition need not rest simply on what the fetus looks like. In addition to the fetus appearing more humanlike, its brain develops in the course of pregnancy. At some point the fetus acquires the capacity to experience pain and pleasure. In other words, the fetus at some stage becomes sentient.

Fetal sentience marks a crucial divide. Before sentience, the fetus is "something" rather than "someone," because to be someone, a being has to have interests—desires for such things as warmth and comfort and for

---

21. CAMOSY, *supra* note 5, at 28 (noting that 61 percent of Americans believe abortion should be legal in the first three months of pregnancy).

22. *Id.* at 152–53 (noting that Camosy's proposed act purposefully does not address "the moral status of the early embryo" and "says nothing about possible abortifacients such as Ella or the morning-after pill" because of the ambiguity surrounding the moral status of the early embryo, observing, "[s]ome argue that, because of the early embryo's ability to 'twin' and 'recombine,' the embryo cannot be an individual person or even an individual member of the species Homo sapiens," and "[o]thers argue that the early embryo constitutes a transition stage between gametes and human beings").

23. *Induced Abortion in the United States*, GUTTMACHER INSTITUTE, https://www.gutt macher.org/fact-sheet/induced-abortion-united-states (last visited Nov. 2, 2020) [hereinafter GUTTMACHER, *Induced Abortion*] (noting that 88 percent of abortions in 2016 took place within the first 12 weeks of pregnancy).

avoiding the sensation of cold or pain. Until a being has interests, it is unreasonable to speak of things going well or ill for that being except as a loose metaphor. Metaphorically, we can say that it is in the interest of the sperm to meet with an egg and fertilize that egg so that it can grow into a baby, but sperm cells do not in fact have interests. They are just cells, with no sensations or emotions that would make life "better" or "worse" for them in different circumstances. If a sperm cell disappears, we might consider that event a loss to the person whose sperm cell it was, but we would not say that the sperm cell itself has lost anything.

Likewise, with a non-sentient fetus. Although such a fetus looks much more like a human being than a sperm cell does, it still has no interests in avoiding pain, in feeling pleasure or warmth or in having any particular thing happen to it. Other beings—especially the parents of a wanted pregnancy—of course have interests in its further development. That interest is one reason why everyone—regardless of whether they are pro-choice or pro-life—opposes forced abortion, even very early in pregnancy. However, and importantly, the interests of the parents or others *regarding the fetus* are not interests *of the fetus*.

To be sure, as with sperm cells, we can metaphorically speak of the interest of the fetus in becoming a sentient being, but from the perspective of the fetus, there is no such interest because it has no perspective. It lacks interests altogether, just as the sperm cell does. It is a potential human being, just as the sperm cell or egg cell or zygote is. Until the fetus achieves sentience, nothing that happens to it harms it in the present. And if it never becomes a human being because pregnancy is terminated prior to sentience, it will not have lost something that it once had—a life in which there is the experience of pleasure and pain.

IV. The Law Post-Sentience

By saying that pre-sentience abortions do not raise serious moral concerns (because the fetus has yet to evolve from "something" into "someone") but post-sentience abortions do, am I saying that it would be legitimate for states to ban abortion after fetal sentience? Some states have passed laws that seem premised on this assumption, calling their targets "pain capable abortion."[24] Do I endorse such legislation?

---

24. *State Bans on Abortion Throughout Pregnancy*, GUTTMACHER INSTITUTE, https://www .guttmacher.org/state-policy/explore/state-policies-later-abortions (last updated Mar. 1, 2021) (noting that "17 states ban abortion at 22 weeks [after the woman's last menstrual

The short answer is no. Post-sentience abortions raise moral concerns in a way that pre-sentience abortions do not; however, the woman rather than the government ought to be making the choice of how to resolve those moral concerns. Why? Once a baby is born, we do not leave it up to parents to decide whether or not to allow the baby to live, based on their own conscience and belief system. We quite appropriately ban infanticide. So why the difference when it comes to a sentient fetus?

The difference has less to do with the status of the fetus than it does with the fact that a sentient fetus, no less than a non-sentient one, physically occupies and intrudes upon the bodily functions of a second person, the pregnant woman. Post-sentience, an unwanted pregnancy presents a conflict between two persons: the sentient fetus and the woman.

So what? Why isn't this an easy conflict to resolve in favor of the fetus? After all, one of the people in the conflict simply wants to live, while the other person in the conflict asserts an interest in killing the first person. How could it be just to resolve the conflict in any way other than by requiring the woman to take her pregnancy to term?

The answer turns on the burden that a pregnancy places on a woman. Pregnancy imposes physical burdens on all pregnant women, but those burdens fall hardest on women who do not want to be pregnant. What the fetus asks of the woman is not simply to be left alone or not to be killed, as would be the case if the two persons were truly separate beings (i.e., if the fetus were already a born baby). It asks as well that she sacrifice her internal bodily integrity for an extended period of time, during which her health might suffer and she would experience internal discomfort, culminating in an extremely painful prolonged process (labor) or in invasive surgery (a C-section). Even someone who is undisputedly a full person does not ordinarily have the right to demand this sort of sacrifice of another person, however much the first person might need the sacrifice in order to continue living.

Post-sentience abortions raise the hard case that Thomson meant to pose—that of the full person demanding that another full person remain physically invaded against her will. However generous it would be for the target of the demand to permit the invasive process to continue, and however much we might believe the right decision from her perspective is to

period] (20 weeks postfertilization in state law) on the unscientific grounds that a fetus can feel pain at that point."); *see, e.g.,* Pain-Capable Unborn Child Protection Act, 40 LA. STAT. ANN. § 1061.1 (2015) ("It is the purpose of the state to assert a compelling state interest in protecting the lives of unborn children from the stage at which substantial medical evidence indicates that they are capable of feeling pain.").

nurture the sentient fetus (or to support Thomson's hypothetical violinist), it would be wrong for others—including the society in general acting through the law—to demand such a sacrifice against her will. That is the rationale for recognizing a right to abortion even in the tragic case of a sentient fetus.

V. The Other Side

The foregoing section closely tracks what the literature sometimes calls a "feminist" argument for abortion, regardless of the moral status of the fetus. The argument is persuasive to the extent that one appreciates pregnancy as a rendering of affirmative aid rather than as a passive activity that lets nature take its course. But is the former a fair characterization?

True, a woman must actively "help" the fetus by remaining pregnant (and is therefore forced to do something rather than simply to refrain from doing something when she is refused an abortion). When she aborts, she refuses to aid. But she does not *only* refuse to aid; she also commits an affirmative act of violence against the fetus. This is particularly true if the fetus is sentient, because in that case the fetus is probably also viable—that is, capable of survival outside of the womb—by this stage and therefore could in theory be delivered alive rather than killed. To the extent that we focus our attention on the affirmative act of violence involved in an abortion rather than simply on the failure to help, the right to abortion begins to look more like a right to kill than a right to be free of an internal occupation.

The preceding may well be a fair response to a post-viability abortion but only because viability, as we use the term in abortion jurisprudence, is not truly viability. That is, although a fetus at 23 or 24 weeks may be able to survive outside the womb with heroic interventions and potentially lifelong disabilities to follow, we cannot reasonably be hoping that a woman who no longer wants to be pregnant will deliver her fetus extremely prematurely and subject him or her to the risk of a life of great suffering. The better outcome is that she either take the pregnancy to term and give birth to a child with a chance to survive and thrive in the world or that she have an abortion.

If, however, we define viability in a different way, we might legislate a requirement that a woman with a viable and sentient fetus terminate the pregnancy without killing the fetus, if she can do so without causing substantial harm to herself. This would be the case if modern medicine were to develop an artificial womb that could gestate the premature fetus to maturity such that it would have the same chance at life as a baby delivered by a woman at term. It would also be the case if the woman decided she wanted to terminate her pregnancy at a point at which the fetus truly was viable, in the robust sense of the word.

Say, for instance, that a woman decided at 34 weeks' gestation that she no longer wanted to be pregnant. As explained in the prior section, even if she lacks a good moral reason for that decision from her perspective, it ought to be her choice to make because of the bodily intrusion involved in refusing her this right. However, terminating a pregnancy at this stage need not mean having an abortion. The 34-week pregnant woman might be required to deliver the fetus alive rather than killing it inside (or outside) her body. At bottom, a right to abortion is—or at least should be—a right to end a pregnancy rather than a right to kill an unwanted fetus. The two are, of course, inseparable prior to viability, so it is difficult to tell the difference between the two putative rights, functionally, at earlier stages (when an overwhelming majority of abortions take place).[25] True viability is where the proverbial rubber hits the road. The feminist argument for a right to abortion fails—to the extent that it includes a right to kill the fetus—when the fetus is both sentient and robustly viable, and it can be delivered alive without causing great harm to the woman.[26]

VI. Coda: Implications for Animal Rights

Talk about sentience as the morally relevant line between a mere "something" and an inherently valuable "someone" invokes a quality that extends well beyond humans. Animals, including those whose flesh and bodily secretions people consume and whose skins people wear and use for handbags and wallets, are sentient just as we are. Cows, pigs, chickens, and even fishes (whom some consider the equivalent of vegetables when defining "vegetarian") are all sentient, all capable of experiencing pain and pleasure.[27] If

---

25. *See* GUTTMACHER, *Induced Abortion, supra* note 23 (noting that 88 percent of abortions happen in the first 12 weeks and only 1.3 percent of abortions take place after 21 weeks).

26. To be sure, if a woman is legally required to give birth rather than killing her viable fetus, and she cannot keep her baby, she is likely to experience the emotional pain of separation from the baby to whom she has given birth, a violation of her interest described earlier in Colb, *"Never Having Loved at All," supra* note 14, at 945–47. When we are dealing with a sentient being, however, and the woman can successfully terminate her internal intrusion without killing the fetus in the process, the interest of the fetus in life arguably trumps his or her mother's interest in never having loved at all.

27. JONATHAN BALCOMBE, WHAT A FISH KNOWS: THE INNER LIVES OF OUR UNDERWATER COUSINS 96, 98, 104–05, 138–41 (2017) ("Fishes show the hallmarks of pain both physiologically and behaviorally. . . . Not only is scientific consensus squarely behind consciousness and

a human organism becomes worthy of moral consideration at the point of sentience, then it follows that every sentient being is worthy of moral consideration, as there is nothing specifically human about sentience.

What should this mean, in practice? I have contended that even after fetal sentience, a woman should have the right to terminate her pregnancy, that is, to kill her fetus (so long as the fetus is not yet robustly viable, at which point the woman should have the right to remove the fetus from her body but not necessarily to kill it). How much, then, does it benefit a being to be granted moral consideration, if it does not even mean that the being has the right to live?

This is a fair question, but the answer will by now be a familiar one. In the case of pregnancy, the reason that the woman has the right to terminate (and therefore, ordinarily, to kill the fetus) is that compelled pregnancy is such a profound intrusion upon her bodily integrity. A woman has the right to terminate a pregnancy, even when the fetus is sentient, because the state should not be forcing the intrusiveness of pregnancy onto any individual. This does not mean, however, that it is morally blameless to terminate; it can be immoral to terminate a pregnancy when the fetus is sentient, but that immorality should not translate into illegality because of the bodily intrusion that such a translation would demand.

Contrast forced pregnancy with what would be required of people if they were compelled to stop harming sentient animals (or paying for their

---

pain in fishes, consciousness probably evolved first in fishes.") ("When Blackie [a deformed black moor goldfish] was transferred into a tank containing a larger oranda goldfish named Big Red, Big Red took an immediate interest in his disabled tankmate. He also began to provide assistance by placing himself just beneath Blackie. Together they would swim around the tank as a tandem, Big Red providing the propulsion that aided Blackie's mobility and access to food after it was sprinkled on the surface. The pet store owner attributed Big Red's behavior to compassion.") ("When rats play, their brains release large amounts of dopamine and opiates. . . . Fishes also have a dopamine system. If you give a goldfish a compound that stimulates the release of dopamine from his brain—such as amphetamine or apomorphine—the goldfish engages in rewarding behavior: he wants more of the compound. . . . Amphetamine produces a rewarding effect in monkeys, rats, and humans, and this happens by increasing the availability of dopamine receptors in the central reward system. Since the goldfish brain has cells containing dopamine, the same mechanism is thought to be responsible for amphetamine's rewarding effects on goldfishes.") (reviewing an experiment which tested animals' ability to solve a space-time puzzle involving a food reward in which cleaner wrasse fish outperformed capuchin monkeys, orangutans, and chimpanzees; "When fishes outperform primates on a mental task, it is another reminder of how brain size, body size, presence of fur or scales, and evolutionary proximity to humans are wobbly criteria for gauging intelligence.").

harm) for flesh, dairy, and eggs[28]—foods that we do not need to survive and thrive.[29] Unlike compelled pregnancy, which would forcibly exploit the reproductive capacities of a woman on behalf of another individual (the fetus), a prohibition against animal consumption would bar the exploitation of the reproductive[30] and other capacities of nonhuman animals. People would not have to suffer an intrusion upon their bodily integrity in order to stop using animals; they would simply have to stop intruding upon the bodily integrity of their fellow sentient earthlings. They would still have plenty to eat, wear, and enjoy in the world.

While abortion poses a very difficult case when a fetus is sentient, the question of animal rights poses a very easy case. This may be difficult to

---

28. Dairy and eggs may appear to be harmless products. The reality, however, is that dairy cows suffer within the industry because mother cows are separated from their infants, whom they want to nurse, and because the cows are eventually slaughtered at a young age. *See* CHEESEBURGER, *supra* note 10, at xix ("After several rounds of subjecting a cow to inseminations, pregnancies, births, and the taking of her children, when the cow's milk production drops off, the farmer sends her to slaughter as well, to become some variant on hamburger meat or dog food."); *see also Happy Cows: Behind the Myth*, HUMANEMYTH, http://www.humane myth.org/happycows.htm (last visited Nov. 2, 2020) ("Cows and calves cry out for each other as they are separated."). Male calves born to dairy cows, moreover, become veal while still babies. *See* CHEESEBURGER, *supra* note 10, at 44. Chickens within the egg industry suffer because the females have been bred to lay many times more eggs than their wild cousins do and thus suffer uterine prolapse and other maladies and because the males of the laying breed are worthless to the farmer and are therefore killed shortly after hatching by being ground to death, suffocated, or gassed. *See id.* at 45–46 (noting that chickens within the egg industry lay about fifteen times more eggs than their wild cousins, and that "the production of so many eggs also leads layer hens to suffer extreme osteoporosis at a young age.") (citing other sources); *see also Cage Free Eggs: Behind the Myth*, HUMANEMYTH, http://www.humane myth.org/cagefree.htm (last visited Nov. 2, 2020).
29. T. COLIN CAMPBELL & THOMAS M. CAMPBELL II, THE CHINA STUDY 230 (2005) ("There are virtually no nutrients in animal-based foods that are not better provided by plants."); *see also* JOEL FUHRMAN, DISEASE-PROOF YOUR CHILD: FEEDING KIDS RIGHT 148 (2005) ("[F]or optimal health you must get the majority of calories from unrefined plant food with a minimal amount of animal products [if any at all]."); NEAL BARNARD, FOOD FOR LIFE xvi (1993) ("The plan in this book is a simple one, but it has the power to bring health and vigor to a new level, and add years to life. The New Four Food Groups program recommends that your diet be based on grains, legumes, vegetables, and fruits. . . . [M]eat and dairy lose their food-group status.").
30. To produce milk, a cow must first be pregnant and give birth, like other mammals. CHEESEBURGER, *supra* note 10, at 42. Inseminating the cow, as farmers do in the dairy industry, *id.*, and then taking the milk that was intended for her calf, exploits the cow's reproductive capacities. *Id.* at 46–47 ("[One disturbing aspect of the egg and dairy industries is] the use of female animals as reproductive slaves."). Laying hens have been bred to lay hundreds of eggs a year. *Id.* at 45 ("the contemporary layer hens lay close to 300 eggs every year."). To breed more of these animals into existence and then take their eggs amplifies the exploitation of the hens' reproductive capacities.

believe because most human societies treat the consumption of animal products as normal and natural, despite the grotesque violence that such consumption demands.[31] If one talks to a vegan, however, one learns that refraining from violence against animals demands very little of us.

This detour into animal rights issues shows that recognizing sentience as a key moral dividing line has powerful implications, even though it does not imply that all abortions of sentient fetuses ought to be legally prohibited.[32] Meanwhile, the fact that one can be pro-choice with respect to sentient but not yet truly viable fetuses, even after recognizing that abortion of a sentient fetus may be an immoral act, shows that pregnancy is a unique condition. We uncritically apply to pregnancy moral intuitions derived from other contexts at our peril.

---

31. *See* MELANIE JOY, WHY WE LOVE DOGS, EAT PIGS, AND WEAR COWS 96 (2010) ("In order to consume the meat of the very species we had caressed but minutes before, we must believe so fully in the justness of eating animals that we are spared the consciousness of what we are doing. To this end, we are taught to accept a series of myths that maintain the carnistic system and to ignore the inconsistencies in the stories we tell ourselves. Violent ideologies rely on promoting fiction as fact and discouraging any critical thinking that threatens to expose this truth. There is a vast mythology surrounding meat, but all the myths are in one way or another related to what I refer to as the Three Ns of Justification: eating meat is *normal, natural,* and *necessary.*"); GAIL A. EISNITZ, SLAUGHTERHOUSE: THE SHOCKING STORY OF GREED, NEGLECT, AND INHUMANE TREATMENT INSIDE THE U.S. MEAT INDUSTRY 29 (2006) ("'A lot of times the skinner finds out an animal is still conscious when he slices the side of its head and it starts kicking wildly. If that happens, or if a cow is already kicking when it arrives at their station, the skinners shove a knife into the back of its head to cut the spinal cord.' This practice paralyzes the cow from the neck down but doesn't deaden the pain of head skinning or render the animal unconscious. . . . Sometimes animals would break free of their shackles and come crashing down headfirst to the floor fifteen feet below, where other men worked.").

32. *See* BEATING HEARTS, *supra* note 10, at 5 ("We are pro-choice with respect to abortion, even though we regard some abortions as immoral, because we think that ultimate authority for deciding whether to have an abortion ought to rest with each individual woman."); *see also* CHEESEBURGER, *supra* note 10, at 91 ("Despite the violence entailed in abortion, the person who has an abortion is not comparable to the person who consumes animal products, for a number of reasons. First, someone who faces the dilemma of whether or not to consume an animal product will not play the role of the Good Samaritan, either way. Ethical vegans are not Good Samaritans any more than [a person who refrains from murdering another despite temptation] is a Good Samaritan. Both vegans and [those who refrain from murdering others] are simply refraining from participating in violence. Neither is acting affirmatively to save anyone.").

13

Conscientious Commitment to Women's Health*

By Bernard M. Dickens and Rebecca J. Cook**

I. Introduction

The right to live according to one's conscience is a key human right. The United Nations (UN) International Covenant on Civil and Political Rights, giving legal effect to the UN's 1948 Universal Declaration of Human Rights, provides in Article 18(1) that "[e]veryone shall have the right to freedom of thought, conscience and religion. This right shall include [an individual's] freedom . . . in public or private, to manifest his religion or belief in worship, observance, practice and teaching." To preserve everyone's freedom of conscience against religious or other oppression, Article 18(3) provides that "[f]reedom to manifest one's religion or beliefs may be subject only to such limitations as are prescribed by law and are necessary to protect public safety, order, health or morals or the fundamental rights and freedoms of others."

Recognition that the law may limit manifestations of conscience when "necessary to protect public . . . morals" was the basis on which laws in many countries historically prohibited many practices seen today as contributing

---

*This chapter is reprinted here with kind permission from the *International Journal of Gynecology and Obstetrics* (FIGO). It originally appeared in volume 113 of the *Journal*.

**Rebecca Cook is Professor Emerita & Co-Director, International Reproductive and Sexual Health Law Program, Faculty of Law, University of Toronto, Canada. Bernard Dickens is Professor Emeritus of Health Law and Policy & Co-Director, International Reproductive and Sexual Health Law Program, Faculty of Law, University of Toronto.

to reproductive health, which includes the health of women liable to suffer unwanted burdens of repeated pregnancy and childbearing. Health care practitioners once almost uniformly faced legal constraints and punishments, instituted or supported by religious authorities, for advising and providing contraception, contraceptive sterilization, and abortion.[1] In the course of the twentieth century, these laws were challenged and eventually considerably liberalized, particularly in westernized, democratic countries. However, some laws, particularly regarding abortion, are retained by independent countries in which they were introduced under European colonization, such as in Sub-Saharan Africa and Latin America.

The progressive relaxation of restrictive laws affecting women's reproductive health has generated a reaction, particularly among healthcare practitioners who hold conservative religious beliefs, of invoking rights of conscience to object to participation in such practices as prescribing or dispensing contraceptive products and undertaking contraceptive sterilization procedures and elective abortions. Their modern claims to conscientious objection, which may be required and/or channeled by religious institutions, reflect an earlier history of conscientious commitment to challenge the restrictive laws in regard to these practices and procedures that previously prevailed.

II. Historical Conscientious Commitment

Conscientious commitment to advocacy for means of birth control has a distinguished history.[2] The English philosopher and social reformer Jeremy Bentham advocated means of birth control as long ago as 1797, and in 1824 his follower and colleague the philosopher John Stuart Mill was arrested and briefly imprisoned for distributing birth control literature to the poor in London. Similarly, in 1886, the English secular politician Charles Bradlaugh was prosecuted, with the socialist activist Annie Besant, for republishing a pamphlet advocating birth control—the conviction subsequently being annulled on appeal.

Religious and conservative opposition to the promotion of birth control fueled the prosecution of proponents of family planning well into the twentieth century. In 1914, Margaret Sanger, an American nurse working in the impoverished and overcrowded ghettos of New York, published a magazine that provided advice on contraception, and in 1916 founded the first

---

1. G. WILLIAMS, THE SANCTITY OF LIFE AND THE CRIMINAL LAW (1958).
2. B. Dickens, *Conscientious Commitment*, 371(9620) LANCET 1240–01 (2008).

American birth-control clinic in Brooklyn, New York City, for which she was prosecuted and imprisoned. The previous year, to forestall prosecution, she had travelled to England, where she met and motivated the botanist Marie Stopes. Appalled at the marital unhappiness caused by ignorance about sex and contraception, Marie Stopes began to disseminate information about these subjects. In 1918, she published her book Married Love, which caused great controversy and was banned in the USA.

The momentum toward public and political acceptance of family planning generated by these courageous pioneers, who defied the authority of organized religion, conservative convention, and at first the medical establishment, rewarded their conscientious commitment to serve women's health and reproductive self-determination. Nevertheless, until 1969, the Canadian Criminal Code reflected the history of earlier times in penalizing the spread of knowledge of contraceptive means as a "crime against morality." The courts had previously approved so many exceptions that the prohibition was effectively nullified, but family-planning initiatives remain under attack wherever they are proposed, particularly from the Roman Catholic Church hierarchy.

Voluntary sterilization was historically similarly contentious, although opposition declined with acceptance of contraceptive means. Involuntary, punitive sterilization, by castration of vanquished foes and later of sexual offenders, has a long history,[3] and non-consensual eugenic sterilization has been approved by legislatures and courts since the 1920s, with continuing effect. The leading US Supreme Court decision of 1927 in *Buck v. Bell*,[4] approving sterilization without her consent of an 18-year-old woman—the daughter of a mentally impaired mother and herself the mother of an allegedly impaired child—has never been reversed. However, the case remains highly controversial, and it is commonly believed that it would not now be followed. In modern times, the legality of voluntary sterilization of mentally competent adult individuals is not generally doubted. An echo of earlier conservatism was heard in England in 1954, however, when a judge in a divorce case considering matrimonial cruelty described voluntary male sterilization as "degrading to the man himself and injurious to his wife and any woman whom he may marry."[5] The other 2 judges in the case rejected

---

3. J.K. Mason, Medico-legal Aspects of Reproduction and Parenthood 67–84 (1998).

4. 274 U.S. 200 (1927).

5. Bravery v. Bravery, [1954] 3 All England Reports 59 (Court of Appeal), Lord Denning at 67–68.

this view, which was widely regarded as anachronistic at the time it was expressed.

Considerably greater conscientious commitment was required to liberalize restrictive abortion laws than to undertake voluntary sterilization. The incidence of deaths and injuries due to unskilled abortion among English families caused great concern in the mid-1930s, perhaps associated with economic depression and child-rearing costs. In 1938, the Ministry of Health and the Home Office, responsible for criminal law and its enforcement, setup the Interdepartmental (Birkett) Committee on Abortion to plan "the reduction of maternal mortality and morbidity arising from this cause."

A consultant obstetrician at a London hospital, Aleck Bourne, had terminated the early pregnancy of a 14-year-old gang-rape victim, to save her from becoming "a mental wreck," and informed the Birkett Committee of the realities of therapeutic abortion. For admitting to deliberately terminating a pregnancy, he was prosecuted for the crime of criminal abortion. The judge instructed the jury on the legal difference between the secretive actions of an unqualified person and a physician acting in a public hospital in good faith to preserve a patient's physical and/or mental health. This statement of the law in the *Bourne* case,[6] distinguishing between criminal and lawful abortion, resulted in acquittal and remains an influential landmark in the laws of many countries inheriting English criminal law, establishing the legality of therapeutic abortion to preserve women's physical or mental health.

Conscientious commitment to the health of pregnant women is illustrated in the largely parallel careers of two physicians: the American William Harrison in Arkansas; and the Canadian Henry Morgentaler in Quebec and later Ontario. Both were motivated by the plight of usually poor, vulnerable women who sought their help in the late 1960s. Dr. Harrison explained that he was affected by seeing in his hospital emergency room "girls and women with raging fevers, extraordinary uterine and pelvic infections, enormous blood loss and a multitude of serious injuries of the pelvic and intra-abdominal organs as a result of illegal and self-induced abortions."[7] He set up the Fayetteville Women's Clinic in Arkansas in 1972, a year before the US Supreme Court recognized abortion as a constitutional right. Nevertheless, for many years, he faced fury, fire-bombing, and death threats from anti-abortion activists for providing safe, legal abortion care.

---

6. R v. Bourne, [1938] 3 All England Reports 615 (Central Criminal Court).

7. S. Boseley, *Obituary: William Harrison,* 376(9751) LANCET 1460 (2010).

Henry Morgentaler, whose abortion clinic in Toronto was picketed and also fire-bombed, began his abortion practice in Montreal when, after speaking out against Canada's restrictive criminal abortion law, he felt conscientiously bound to assist the often desperate, disadvantaged women who then flocked to him for treatment. He opened his abortion clinic in 1969 but acted outside the restrictively demanding requirements for lawful performance of abortion. He was prosecuted in 1973 but his acquittal by jury was exceptionally reversed by the Quebec Court of Appeal, and in 1975 he was imprisoned for 10 months of an 18-month sentence. On relocating his clinic to Toronto, he was further prosecuted in 1984. When his case was decided by the Supreme Court of Canada in 1988, the Court accepted his argument that the criminal abortion law was unconstitutional. The Chief Justice of Canada condemned the provisions that made lawful abortion often inaccessible and observed that "[f]orcing a woman, by threat of criminal sanction, to carry a foetus to term unless she meets certain criteria unrelated to her own priorities and aspirations, is a profound interference with a woman's body and thus a violation of security of the person," which failed to conform to principles of fundamental justice.[8] Modern governments in Canada express no interest in recriminalizing abortion. In 2008, Dr. Morgentaler was awarded the Order of Canada, the country's highest honor.

III. Modern Conscientious Commitment

The call for healthcare practitioners' conscientious commitment to undertake procedures to protect women's health often arises in response to other practitioners' failures or refusals to provide care. Refusals of care may be based on explicit claims of conscientious objection or on reasoning that affords priority to the perceived interests of embryos and/or fetuses over the rights and interests of the pregnant women who bear them. For instance, early in 2010, the Inter-American Commission on Human Rights required Nicaragua to act on a complaint arising from denial of indicated care to a 27-year-old, 10-week-pregnant woman, given the disguised name of Amelia. She suffered from life-endangering cancer, but physicians and the state-run hospital denied indicated cancer treatment such as chemotherapy and radiotherapy, for fear of causing spontaneous abortion and being accused of violating Nicaragua's extremely repressive abortion law.[9]

---

8. R. v. Morgentaler (1988), 44 Dominion Law Reports (4th) 385, Dickson CJC at 402, 417.
9. R. Carroll, *Nicaragua Prevents Treatment of Pregnant Cancer Patient*, THE GUARDIAN (UK), Feb. 23, 2010.

Practitioners conscientiously committed to promoting the health of pregnant women would recognize that the women, rather than the fetuses, are
their patients.[10] Accordingly, as patients, the women rather than their care-
givers determine whether or not they receive available treatment indicated
for their care, unrelated to pregnancy itself, that may affect the fetuses they
bear or may bear in the future.

A similar concern has been observed regarding the treatment of women
who experience spontaneous abortion. In hospitals owned or operated by
Roman Catholic authorities, religious doctrines may be applied to prevent
uterine evacuation in the event of threatened spontaneous abortion while
a fetal heartbeat is detected. In a 2008 review of practice in the USA, cases
were observed in which:

> *Catholic-owned hospital ethics committees denied approval of uterine evacuation
> while fetal heart tones were still present, forcing physicians to delay care or transport
> miscarrying patients to non-Catholic-owned facilities. Some physicians intentionally
> violated protocol because they felt patient safety was compromised.*[11]

Protocols, ethics committee decisions on clinical cases, and rulings in
such cases by religious office-holders that deny patients the available care
their physicians consider to be in their best interests or that result in injury
by delay of care or because of transportation of patients to other facilities
raise serious concerns in law and in healthcare providers' professional ethics. Treating threatened spontaneous abortion via uterine evacuation is
legally distinguishable from deliberately inducing abortion. Legal concerns
about denying or delaying treatment involve liability for negligence, particularly due to failure to satisfy professional standards of timely care, possibly
for breach of physician–patient contracts and breach of physicians' fidu-
ciary duties to their patients, and criminal liability for negligence, reaching
even as far as manslaughter liability, including criminal liability, may attach
not only to individual physicians but also to third parties who intervene
to obstruct indicated care, in addition to hospital institutions. Concerns
in professional ethics include whether conscientious physicians can allow
compromise of their judgment, and of their provision of best care to their
patients, by third-party doctrinal intervention. Conscientious commitment

---

10. B.M. Dickens & R.J. Cook, *Ethical and Legal Approaches to the Fetal Patient*, 83(1) INT'L J.
GYNECOL. & OBSTET. 85–91 (2003).

11. L.R. Freedman, U. Landy & J. Steinauer, *When There's a Heartbeat: Miscarriage Management in Catholic-Owned Hospitals*, 98(10) AM. J. PUBLIC HEALTH 1774–78 (2008).

to patients' safest care and healthcare providers' own safety from legal liability and professional censure may coincide.

Comparable concerns arise in the treatment of ectopic or "tubal" pregnancy. This is the leading cause of pregnancy-related death during the first
trimester in the USA, and accounts for an estimated nine percent of all
pregnancy-related deaths. It also accounts for considerable morbidity in
survivors, whose future ability to have children may be lost or severely compromised.[12] Treatment of this condition in the USA is aided by advances
in anesthesia, antibiotics, and blood transfusion. In countries and regions
where these means are not easily accessible or of a high standard, surgical interventions may be unavailable or unsuccessful. Fetal survival occurs
rarely, if ever, and gestation to the point of rupture of the fallopian tube
is hazardous to women's survival and to survivors' future health. After one
ectopic pregnancy, evidence shows that a woman has a 7 to 13-fold increase
in the likelihood of having another ectopic pregnancy.[13]

Care guidelines for women with ectopic pregnancies are established
by several specialist medical associations such as the American College (or
Congress) of Obstetricians and Gynecologists[14] and the UK Royal College
of Obstetricians and Gynaecologists.[15] In addition, the Cochrane Collaboration's review of evidence provides a synopsis of randomized controlled
trials of treatment for tubal pregnancy and assessments of short-term and
long-term outcome measures.[16] The range of treatment and management
options for non-ruptured ectopic pregnancy includes salpingectomy, salpingostomy, medical treatment, and expectant management. Selection is based
on the patient's clinical circumstances and future fertility intentions.[17]

Surgical and non-surgical management options are determined as a
medical matter, directed to the woman's condition and taking account of
her informed choice. By contrast, religious hierarchies, particularly those
not including and explicitly excluding women, may direct their attention
to the embryo or fetus, and whether its removal constitutes abortion. The

---

12. V.P. Sepilian & E. Wood, *Ectopic Pregnancy.* eMEDICINE OBSTET. & GYNECOL., *available
at* http://emedicine.medscape.com/article/258768-overview (last updated Sept. 28, 2017).

13. *Id.*

14. American College of Obstetricians and Gynecologists, *ACOG Practice Bulletin No. 94:
Medical Management of Ectopic Pregnancy*, 111(6) OBSTET. GYNECOL. 1479–85 (2008).

15. Royal College of Obstetricians and Gynaecologists, *The Management of Tubal Pregnancy.
Guideline No. 21* (May 2004).

16. P.J. Hajenius et al., *Interventions for Tubal Ectopic Pregnancy*, COCHRANE DATABASE SYST.
REV. 2007; 1 CD000324.

17. S.B. Fogel & T.A. Weitz, *Health Care Refusals: Undermining Quality Care for Women* at
56–57, Los Angeles: National Health Law Program (NHeLP), 2010.

Ethical and Religious Directives for Catholic Health Care Services, issued by the US Conference of Catholic Bishops, are ambivalent. Directive 48 provides that:

> *In case of extrauterine pregnancy, no intervention is morally licit which constitutes a direct abortion.*[18]

This is consistent with long-standing Catholic teaching, but it follows a directive that appears more accommodating of physicians' conscientious commitment to women's health. Directive 47 provides that:

> *Operations, treatment, and medications that have as their direct purpose the cure of a proportionately serious pathological condition of a pregnant woman are permitted when they cannot be safely postponed until the unborn child is viable, even if they will result in the death of the unborn child.*[19]

From a medical perspective, the ectopic embryo or fetus may never be considered viable, but much turns on how the purpose of a treatment is characterized (e.g., whether by an attending physician, a hospital committee or chaplain, or a more senior church official such as a bishop) and by whom decision makers are influenced.

For instance, a leading Catholic healthcare theologian, Thomas O'Donnell, claims that no intervention is permissible unless, or until, the fallopian tube is so pathologically affected that ending the tubal pregnancy is justified. Further, he finds that removal of a non-viable fetus from the fallopian tube is not theologically different from its removal from the uterus, which is condemned as abortion.[20] However, the Catholic bioethicist Kevin O'Rourke claims that all treatment options are permissible. Removing the affected fallopian tube (salpingectomy) is justified because the direct intention is to save the mother's life—the fetal death being an unintended but unpreventable effect. Salpingostomy, in which the tube is not removed, is similarly defensible because the intention is to remove the woman's damaged tubal tissue and the damaging trophoblastic tissue (e.g., by use of methotrexate), not to kill or destroy the embryo.[21]

Theologic analysis and debate are governed by their own principles, but what constitutes abortion is also a matter of law. This is shown in the

---

18. *Id.* at 58.
19. *Id.*
20. T.J. O'DONNELL, MEDICINE AND CHRISTIAN MORALITY 180 (3d ed. 2002).
21. K.D. O'Rourke, *Applying the Directives. The Ethical and Religious Directives Concerning Three Medical Situations Require Some Elucidation,* 79(4) HEALTH PROG. 64–69 (1998).

context of emergency contraception,[22] which allows conscientiously committed physicians scope to enjoy legal protection when they provide care (e.g., to women who have been raped) contrary to religious directives.[23] A judgment of the California Court of Appeal concerned a rape victim treated at a Catholic hospital, where she was not informed about emergency contraception. She sued, not for compensation, but for 2 judicial declarations. The first was that the hospital's failure "to provide information about and access to estrogen pregnancy prophylaxis to rape victims . . . constitutes a failure to provide optimal emergency treatment of rape victims in accordance with the [local] standard of good medical practice." The second was that the hospital must "provide rape victims with information and access to estrogen Pregnancy prophylaxis, including the morning-after pill," or discontinue treatment and transport patients to the nearest facility that, within 72 hours of the sexual assault, would provide complete emergency medical treatment, including emergency contraception.[24]

The hospital's defense was that these forms of emergency treatment would constitute abortion had fertilization occurred and that, as a nonprofit religious institution, the hospital had legal protection against having to undertake such a procedure. However, the Court found that, as a matter of law, emergency contraception as described in the requested declarations does not constitute abortion because its purpose and effect are not to terminate but rather to avoid pregnancy by preventing fertilization or implantation. The Court followed earlier judgments that abortion, as it is commonly and legally understood, does not include intrauterine devices, the morning-after pill, or birth-control pills. The Court agreed with the contention that the rape victim's right to control her treatment must prevail over the moral and religious convictions under which a hospital is conducted and that, whether or not the hospital would transfer her care to another facility, failure to provide her with information of the emergency contraception option constitutes medical malpractice. Accordingly, even in a religiously run hospital, a conscientious physician is entitled, and perhaps obliged, to inform the patient about emergency contraception and, at her request, to administer such treatment if it is not feasible to transfer the patient to another facility in time for the treatment to be effective.

---

22. R.J. Cook et al., *The Legal Status of Emergency Contraception*, 75(2) INT'L J. GYNECOL. OBSTET. 185–91 (2001).

23. R.J. Cook, B.M. Dickens & J.N. Erdman, *Emergency Contraception, Abortion and Evidence-Based Law*, 93(2) INT'L J. GYNECOL. OBSTET. 191–97 (2006).

24. Brownfield v. Daniel Freeman Marina Hosp., 256 Cal. Rptr. 240 (Ct. App., 2d Dist., Div. 4 1989).

In view of the assertiveness of Roman Catholic leaders that treatments the law does not consider to be abortion remain condemned as such in their teachings, it is perhaps not surprising that they react strongly regarding treatments that laws clearly do characterize as abortion. This creates the danger, however, of reacting too aggressively, even in ways that senior church officials themselves find excessive. This occurred in Recife, Brazil, in early 2009, when physicians conscientiously terminated the life-endangering twin pregnancy of a nine-year-old rape victim. The young girl's stepfather reportedly admitted sexually abusing her repeatedly since she was six years old and was taken into police custody. The police had no interest in the abortion because this is lawful in Brazil when rape is proven.[25]

However, Archbishop Sobrinho of Recife made public pronouncement of the resultant excommunication of the doctors involved in procuring the abortion and of the girl's mother, who requested it. The girl herself, being a minor, was not liable to excommunication and the church announced no ecclesiastic penalty regarding the stepfather. The Archbishop's requirement that this 9-year-old girl, whose pelvis was too small to accommodate even a single fetus, should continue a pregnancy imposed by rape and risk her life to become the mother of twins sadly reflects the insensitivity to the needs and feelings of children shown more widely in the inadequate, self-protective initial response of the church leadership to sexual depredations against children committed by their own priests.

Support for the physicians who were conscientiously committed to the young girl's survival, health, and wellbeing came from a bioethicist within the Vatican, Archbishop Fisichella, who was subsequently removed from his position as President of the Pontifical Academy for Life. Writing in the Vatican's newspaper *L'Osservatore Romano* on March 15, 2009, to express his dismay at the reaction of the Archbishop of Recife, he stressed that abortion is always bad but that the local prelate's apparent lack of compassion for the young girl's plight "hurts the credibility of our teaching, which appears in the eyes of many as insensitive, incomprehensible and lacking mercy."[26] This marks the contrast with the compassion, sensitivity, and care shown by the physicians who lawfully terminated the pregnancy. Archbishop Fisichella's view proved controversial within the church, but political and popular sentiment in Brazil was that the physicians had acted conscientiously and humanely.

---

25. *"Mercy" Needed in Brazil Abortion Case: Fisichella*, INT'L HERALD TRIBUNE, Mar. 16, 2009.
26. *Id.*

Conscientious commitment to assist infertile patients has been internationally acclaimed via the award of the 2010 Nobel Prize in Physiology or Medicine to Robert Edwards. His pioneering work with the late Patrick Steptoe resulted, in 1978, in the birth of the world's first infant from in vitro fertilization (IVF). He persevered to surmount the disappointments of denial of UK governmental research-funding support and of the lack of enthusiasm of peers in his commitment to overcome the childlessness of infertile patients. He also faced condemnation on some ethical and religious doctrinal grounds that continues to this day. Edwards himself was deeply involved in advancing the ethical analysis of IVF research and practice, however, and—as long ago as 1971—co-authored an important paper that initiated debate on many of the complex ethics and legal concerns to which IVF has given rise.[27] He proposed strict ethical guidelines for embryo research, acted with keen regard for the ethical propriety of IVF research and clinical practice, and ensured that an ethics committee for IVF was established at the clinic he founded with Steptoe at Bourne Hall, Cambridge, UK, which was the world's first IVF clinic.[28]

IV. Conclusion

The need has grown for physicians' and other healthcare providers' conscientious commitment to delivery of women's reproductive health services, to counter the rise of providers' religiously based claims to deny services on grounds of their conscientious objection. Conservative legislatures in many countries have enacted laws to protect such objection, publicly invoking the virtues of conscience to pursue the sometimes less visible aim of reduction of women's reproductive choices. In the USA, for instance, the 2010 report of the National Health Law Program, entitled Health Care Refusals: Undermining Quality Care for Women,[29] covers the spectrum of reproductive health services to show how women's care is denied or obstructed.

Respect for conscience requires accommodation of both objection to participation in services and commitment to their delivery. Conscientious commitment may call for courage when treatment is provided that contradicts non-medical directives such as those by religious institutions and

---

27. R.G. Edwards & D.J. Sharpe, *Social Values and Research in Human Embryology*, 231(5298) Nature 87–91 (1971).

28. T. Kirby, *Robert Edwards: Nobel Prize for Father of In-vitro Fertilisation*, 376(9749) Lancet 1293 (2010).

29. S.B. Fogel & T.A. Weitz, *supra* note 17.

officers. Healthcare providers' professional ethics require mutual tolerance and accommodation, however, and resistance to forces of intolerance. The FIGO Ethical Guidelines on Conscientious Objection provide, in Guideline 4, that "[p]ractitioners have a right to respect for their conscientious convictions in respect both of undertaking and not undertaking the delivery of lawful procedures, and not suffer discrimination on the basis of their convictions."[30] Institutions that would apply punitive sanctions against those whose exercising of their rights to conscience the institutions disapprove weaken the justification for protection of the exercise of conscience they require or approve.

---

30. FIGO Committee for the Study of Ethical Aspects of Human Reproduction and Women's Health, ETHICAL ISSUES IN OBSTETRICS AND GYNECOLOGY (FIGO 2009).

14

The Bad Mother: Stigma, Abortion and Surrogacy[1]

By Paula Abrams[2]

Introduction

Surrogacy and abortion represent two facets of procreative liberty, the right to reproduce and the right to avoid reproducing. Research on stigma associated with abortion and surrogacy illuminates how these very different experiences carry similar stigmatic harm. Why do certain decisions about reproduction engender social support, other decisions social disapproval? Restrictions on surrogacy and abortion derive from a common legal paradigm—state regulation on the pregnant body—that is rooted in traditional gender roles. Not all laws restricting abortion and surrogacy evince gender stereotyping. Abortion and surrogacy pose complex moral and social dilemmas. But research of stigma associated with abortion and surrogacy suggests that gender stereotypes play a role in the creation of stigma.

This stigma reflects complex cultural disagreements about the meaning of maternity. The debate is framed by medical advancements that have transformed our understanding of reproduction. Despite the fact that modern birth control has been available for over 50 years, the separation of sexual intercourse from reproduction continues to generate social controversy.[3]

---

1. Published with the permission of the *Journal of Law, Medicine, and Ethics* where this chapter first appeared.

2. Paula Abrams, JD, is the Edward Brunet Professor of Law, Lewis & Clark Law School.

3. H. Ragoné, *Chasing the Blood Tie: Surrogate Mothers, Adoptive Mothers and Fathers*, 23(2) AMERICAN ETHNOLOGIST 352–65, 353 (1996).

Advances in assisted reproductive technologies and reproductive medicine have altered the social construct of motherhood, fracturing the cultural understanding that motherhood is biological and inevitable.[4] Prior to these advances, pregnancy was the expected outcome of sexual intercourse and motherhood was understood to begin with pregnancy.

Surrogacy and abortion disrupt traditional expectations regarding pregnancy by separating gestation from maternity. A pregnant woman who bears a child for another or who chooses abortion embodies the archetype of the bad mother by "abandoning" her child.[5] She transgresses the social understanding that "respect for human life finds an ultimate expression in the bond of love the mother has for her child."[6] Stigma attached to these reproductive decisions reflects a legacy of gendered roles and disapproval of women who fail to conform to social expectations of motherhood.

This article examines how stigma attached to abortion and surrogacy reveals similar patterns of gender stereotyping. It argues that evidence of stigma is relevant to determining whether laws regulating abortion or surrogacy are based on impermissible stereotyping. Evidence of stigma is probative of two significant issues, whether gender stereotypes influenced legislative purpose, and the degree of harm imposed by a regulation, for stigma may adversely impact reproductive decisions.

I. Good Mother/Bad Mother

Maternity is widely understood as biological.[7] Society deems the attachment between a woman and the fetus she is carrying as innate and genetically ordained, despite evidence to the contrary.[8] Conception is assumed to begin a process that inevitably leads to gestation and nurturance; the social identity of women has been shaped by the expectation that women are "natural" nurturers.[9] To the extent both abortion and surrogacy suggest that maternal bonds are a function of choice, they are at odds with this assumption.[10]

---

4. *Id.* at 353.

5. For the distinction between traditional surrogacy and gestational surrogacy, see note 48, *infra*, and related text. The bad mother moniker may attach to either arrangement.

6. Gonzales v. Carhart, 550 U.S. 159 (2007).

7. C.E. Miall, Community *Constructs of Involuntary Childlessness: Sympathy, Stigma, and Social Support*, 31(4) CAN. REV. SOCIOLOGY & ANTHROPOLOGY 392–21 (1996).

8. O.B.A. van den Akker, *Psychosocial Aspects of Surrogate Motherhood*, 13(1) HUMAN REPRODUCTION UPDATE 53–62, at 56 (2007) [hereinafter *Psychosocial Aspects*].

9. *See* Ragoné, *supra* note 3, at 360.

10. Both practices also challenge the traditional conception of family. *See, e.g.,* M.A. FIELD, SURROGATE MOTHERHOOD 33 (1988) (arguing that surrogacy raises fears about our understanding of family).

Surrogacy and abortion challenge the socially constructed understanding of maternity, separating conception and pregnancy from parenting, and disrupting the unity of reproductive work.[11] Social changes that challenge cultural norms are likely to be met with resistance and dissonance; stigma is one manifestation of the social dissonance surrounding gender roles.[12]

Social perceptions of maternity are shaped in part by pronatalist values, which are foundational to social organization and religion.[13] The state historically has asserted its interest in assuring healthy offspring; women bear the primary responsibility for raising and socializing each new generation of citizens.[14] Thus, private decisions about reproduction are drawn into the public arena. The social value placed on fertility is pervasive across gender, age, race, religious, and class distinctions.[15] These norms are exceedingly resistant to change.[16]

The controversies over abortion and surrogacy evoke two archetypes—the good mother and the bad mother. Popular culture frames these archetypes in various ways, lionizing the "supermom" and demonizing women

---

11. *See* Ragoné, *supra* note 3, at 360.

12. *See Psychosocial Aspects, supra* note 8, at 55.

13. *See* Muller v. Oregon, 208 U.S. 412, 422 (1908) (referring to the importance of maternal function to the "well-being of the race").

14. *See, e.g., Muller,* 208 U.S. at 421 (describing that her physical structure and a proper discharge of her maternal functions—having in view not merely her own health, but the wellbeing of the race—justify legislation to protect her from the greed, as well as the passion, of man).

15. C.E. Miall, *The Stigma of Involuntary Childlessness,* 33(4) SOCIAL PROBLEMS 268–82, 270 (1986). Infertility is not solely a biological condition; individuals may be socially infertile for a variety of reasons, including lack of affordable access to infertility treatments, or, in the case of single individuals or same sex couples, because they must rely on means other than sexual intercourse with a partner. *See* M.M. Shultz, *Reproductive Technology and Intent-Based Parenthood: An Opportunity for Gender Neutrality,* 2 WIS. L. REV. 297–398 (1990); O.B.A. van den Akker, *The Acceptable Face of Parenthood: The Relative Status of Biological and Cultural Interpretations of Offspring in Infertility Treatment,* 3.2 PSYCHOLOGY, EVOLUTION & GENDER 137–53, 138 (2001); J. Daar, *Accessing Reproductive Technologies: Invisible Barriers, Indelible Harms,* 23(1) BERKELEY J. GENDER, LAW & JUSTICE 18–82, 24 (2008). Regardless of the source, infertility is stigmatized and this stigma shapes social attitudes toward personal identity, family, sexuality, and reproduction. *See* Miall at 270. *See generally* Miall, *supra* note 5 (studying stigma and infertility). Research has correlated the reaction to infertility with grief. *See* A. E. Poote & O.B.A. van den Akker, *British Women's Attitudes to Surrogacy,* 24(1) HUMAN REPRODUCTION 139–45 (2009).

16. *See* Miall, *supra* note 15, at 270; A.S. Rossi & B. Sitaraman, *Abortion in Context: Historical Trends and Future Changes,* 20(6) FAMILY PLANNING PERSPECTIVES 273–81+381, 275 (1988). Issues of race and class attach to social incentives to reproduce. *See generally* K.M. Franke, *Theorizing Yes: An Essay on Feminism, Law, and Desire,* 101(1) COLUM. L. REV. 186–95, 181 (2001) (defining assumptions regarding reproduction as "repronormativity").

who delay or reject childbearing for personal or professional reasons.[17] The good mother embraces her maternal role, accepting the social link between conception, gestation, and maternal bonds. She is self-sacrificing, putting the demands of her maternal role before other personal choices. The bad mother, by contrast, acts in ways that reject the inevitability of maternal bonds.[18] Thus a woman who terminates a pregnancy or becomes a surrogate is by definition a bad mother. The bad mother manifests two similar moral failings common to perceptions of abortion and surrogacy. First, by rejecting her maternal role she abandons her child. Second, a bad mother is one who puts personal concerns before motherhood.[19] Social movements opposing surrogacy and abortion share overlapping identities and narratives. Surrogacy emerged as a contentious issue in conjunction with the media frenzy surrounding the Baby M case in 1986. The visibility of the "pro-life" movement increased during this same period.[20] The coalition of social conservatives and religious groups that opposed surrogacy also has played a significant role in opposing legal abortion.[21] Unlike abortion, controversy over surrogacy has been episodic, but moral disgust has been a prevalent theme invoked by opponents of both practices.[22]

Public discourse about abortion and surrogacy tracks the extent to which maternal identity issues dominate. Negative political framings of abortion and surrogacy rely on the bad mother archetype, drawing on embedded social taboos, such as identifying abortion with murder. Pro-life social movements have effectively connected abortion to broader social themes of family values, emphasizing the significance of traditional maternal roles to family stability.[23] Surrogacy is defined as baby selling; the surrogate is portrayed as a breeder for hire.[24] The moral disgust frequently attached to surrogacy extends beyond objections concerned with the potential for

---

17. The social value of mothering may also be deeply impacted by racial politics. *See, e.g.,* S. MARKENS, SURROGATE MOTHERHOOD AND THE POLITICS OF REPRODUCTION 12–13 (2007).

18. *Id.* at 11.

19. C. Sanger, *Separating from Children,* 96(2) COLUM. L. REV. 375–517, 424, 453 (1996).

20. R.B. Siegel, *The New Politics of Abortion: An Equality Analysis of Woman-Protective Abortion Restrictions,* 3 U. ILL. L. REV. 991–1054, 1029 (2007).

21. *See* MARKENS, *supra* note 17, at 163–65.

22. R. Macklin, *Is There Anything Wrong with Surrogate Motherhood, in* SURROGATE MOTHERHOOD, POLITICS AND PRIVACY 136 (L. Goslin, 1990); C. Cahill, *Abortion and Disgust,* 48 HARV. C.R.-C.L. L. REV. 409–56 (2013).

23. J. Strickler & N.L. Danigelis, *Changing Frameworks in Attitudes toward Abortion,* 17(2) SOCIOLOGICAL FORUM 187–201, 200 (2002).

24. *See* MARKENS, *supra* note 17, at 83.

exploitation of economic disparities.[25] Surrogacy and abortion engender dissonance that society may resolve by labeling women who select abortion or surrogacy within the familiar construct of the bad mother. If we examine the effects of this social censure on women who choose abortion or decide to become a surrogate, the links emerge between social disapproval, stigma, and gender stereotyping.

II. Stigma and Stereotyping

Influential sociologist Erving Goffman describes stigma as an "attribute that is deeply discrediting," that reduces the bearer "from a whole and usual person to a tainted, discounted one."[26] Most researchers agree that stigma (1) concerns an attribute that marks an individual as different or "other" and (2) is socially constructed.[27] Stigma is particularly associated with identity norms and deviations from group identity may give rise to stigma.[28]

Stigma may be experienced in several ways. Internalized stigma occurs when the individual accepts and incorporates a negative cultural judgment as part of her identity.[29] Stigma also may be "felt" when an individual perceives negative attitudes from others.[30] Finally, "enacted" stigma occurs when the individual encounters prejudice or discrimination.[31] Individuals who experience stigma may suffer psychological harm or chronic physiological stress responses.[32]

Not all forms of differentiation generate stigma, nor do negative public attitudes alone create stigma. Researchers Bruce Link and Jo Phelan theorize that stigma occurs when a number of interrelated components converge; the dominant culture acts to label and stereotype undesirable

---

25. *See, e.g.,* S. Saravanan, *An Ethnomethodological Approach to Examine Exploitation in the Context of Capacity, Trust and Experience of Commercial Surrogacy in India,* 8(1) PHILOSOPHY, ETHICS & HUMANITIES IN MEDICINE 10 (Aug. 20, 2013).

26. E. GOFFMAN, STIGMA: NOTES ON THE MANAGEMENT OF SPOILED IDENTITY 3 (1963).

27. K.M. Shellenberg, Abortion Stigma in the United States: Quantitative and Qualitative Perspectives from Women Seeking an Abortion, at 11 (Apr. 2010) (unpublished PhD dissertation, Johns Hopkins University) (on file with Milton S. Eisenhower Library, Johns Hopkins University).

28. GOFFMAN, *supra* note 26, at 4–5. Goffman also describes stigma associated with visible physical traits. *Id.*

29. K. Cockrill & A. Nack, *"I'm Not That Type of Person": Managing the Stigma of Having an Abortion,* 34(12) DEVIANT BEHAVIOR 973–90, 974 (2013).

30. *Id.* at 974.

31. *Id.*

32. See GOFFMAN, *supra* note 26, at 128; R.J. Cook & B.M. Dickens, *Reducing Stigma in Reproductive Health,* 125(11) INT'L J. GYNECOLOGY & OBSTETRICS 89–92, 90 (2014).

behavior or characteristics and these actions lead to isolation and status loss or discrimination for those identified as "other."[33]

Social inequalities contribute to the creation and experience of stigma.[34] Economic disparities particularly influence public perceptions of abortion and surrogacy. Restrictions on access to abortion are especially burdensome to low-income women who rely on abortion clinics.[35] They are apt to encounter challenges in arranging time off from work and family and are likely to face harassment from clinic protests.[36] Economic disparities play a large role in perceptions of surrogacy as well.[37] The Baby M case embodied the stereotypes associated with surrogacy—the wealthy, educated, white intended parents contracting with the socially and economically disadvantaged surrogate. Negative public attitudes toward surrogacy are shaped in part by the view that surrogates are desperately poor women forced to sell their bodies or their babies, despite the fact that surrogates in the United States typically are working-class women.[38]

Link and Phelan argue that certain differentiations carry substantial social power, particularly distinctions based on race and gender.[39] Stereotyping based on these traits may be automatic and preconscious.[40] Abortion and surrogacy, experienced only by women, are particularly susceptible to gender-based stigma.[41] "Bad mother" stigma is constructed through a multifaceted framework of messages and experiences that include the beliefs of the individual and her interactions with friends, family, the community, and

---

33. B.G. Link & J.C. Phelan, *Conceptualizing Stigma*, 27(1) ANN. REV. SOCIOLOGY 363–85, 367 (2001).

34. *See id.* at 375.

35. *See* T.J. JOYCE ET AL., THE IMPACT OF STATE MANDATORY COUNSELING AND WAITING PERIOD LAWS ON ABORTION: A LITERATURE REVIEW 11 (2009) (citing one survey that showed costs for low-income women increased by 48% when a second visit to the provider was required).

36. K. Kimport, K. Cockrill & T. Weitz, *Analyzing the Impacts of Abortion Clinic Structures and Processes: A Qualitative Analysis of Women's Negative Experience of Abortion Clinics*, 85(2) CONTRACEPTION 204–10, 207 (2012).

37. J.C. Ciccarelli & L.J. Beckman, *Navigating Rough Waters: An Overview of Psychological Aspects of Surrogacy*, 61(1) J. SOCIAL ISSUES 21–43, 29 (2005).

38. *Id.* at 30–31; P. Laufer-Ukeles, *Mothering for Money: Regulating Commercial Intimacy*, 88(4) IND. L.J. 1223–79, 1234 (2013).

39. *Id.*

40. *Id.*

41. *See, e.g.*, Cockrill & Nack, *supra* note 29, at 979; A. Kumar et al., *Conceptualising Abortion Stigma*, 11(6) CULTURE, HEALTH & SEXUALITY 625–39, 629 (2009); P.C. Dunn, I.J. Ryan & K. O'Brien, *College Students' Acceptance of Adoption and Five Alternative Fertilization Techniques*, 24(1) J. SEX RES. 282–87 (1988); Poote & van den Akker, *supra* note 15.

society.[42] It labels women who seek abortions as "promiscuous, sinful, selfish, dirty, irresponsible, heartless or murderous."[43] Likewise, the surrogate is deemed a coldhearted baby-seller or a fool.[44] Women who experience stigma learn these negative stereotypes and frequently internalize poor self-judgments.[45]

When reproductive decisions are stigmatized, both the women who make these decisions and the procedures become marginalized. Marginalization leads to further stigma and isolation that may encourage additional legal restrictions; stigma thus becomes normalized.[46] If we examine public attitudes toward surrogacy and abortion and the experiences of women who become surrogates or terminate a pregnancy, common patterns emerge. First, public attitudes toward these decisions evince similar demarcations of moral approval and disapproval. Second, the perceptions and experiences of stigma that attach to surrogacy and abortion reveal shared themes reflecting gender stereotyping.

III. Surrogacy and Stigma

Discourse surrounding surrogacy often reflects the good mother/bad mother binary. On one hand, surrogacy is extolled as a reproductive decision that allows an otherwise infertile couple to have a child with a genetic connection to one or both of the intended parents.[47] In contrast, surrogacy is decried as exploitation of a woman's body, as classist and sexist, and the marketing of babies.[48] Surrogacy divides feminists; some argue surrogacy recognizes a woman's moral agency, others condemn surrogacy for reinforcing the association of woman with womb.[49] These widely divergent analyses address a common normative question—how to distinguish between the social and biological attributes of maternity. This question informs the analysis of surrogacy and stigma.

Surrogacy may involve one of two types of biological arrangements. Traditional surrogacy relies on artificial insemination of the surrogate's eggs with the intended father's sperm. Thus, the surrogate is the genetic

---

42. *See* Shellenberg, *supra* note 27, at 39.
43. *See* Kumar et al., *supra* note 41, at 629.
44. *See* Ciccarelli & Beckman, *supra* note 37, at 22–23.
45. *See* Cockrill & Nack, *supra* note 29, at 979; *Psychosocial Aspects*, *supra* note 8, at 57.
46. Kumar et al., *supra* note 41, at 629.
47. *See, e.g.*, van den Akker, *supra* note 15, at 149.
48. *See, e.g.*, Ciccarelli & Beckman, *supra* note 37, at 23.
49. *See* MARKENS, *supra* note 17, at 17–18.

mother.[50] The second form of surrogacy, gestational surrogacy, involves the implantation in the surrogate of an embryo that contains the sperm and egg of the intended parents, or their donors. The gestational surrogate carries no genetic connection to the baby.[51] Gestational surrogacy is now the preferred and dominant approach, with 95% of surrogacy contracts based on IVF.[52] Its dominance is due, at least in part, to the perceived moral differences between traditional and gestational surrogacy, discussed, below.[53] Strong preferences of parents to have a child with a genetic connection to one or both of the parents provide some insight into why a woman who terminates a pregnancy may be stigmatized.[54] Similarly, research suggests that the significance attached to genetic relatedness explains why genetic surrogates are perceived less favorably than gestational surrogates.[55]

An early and influential assessment of surrogacy, the British Warnock Report published in 1984, offers harsh moral criticism of surrogacy: "To deliberately become pregnant with the intention of giving up the child distorts the relationship between mother and child."[56] The report explains that an arrangement where the woman who deliberately becomes pregnant with the intention of giving up the child at birth is the "wrong way" to approach pregnancy.[57] It also describes significant social objections to surrogacy for undermining the value of the marital relationship. The Warnock Report expresses no doubt that courts faced with surrogacy disputes should find the arrangement void as against public policy.[58] It assumes that the best interests of the child lie with the surrogate and recommends that the woman who gives birth be considered the legal mother for all purposes, even in a gestational surrogacy arrangement.[59] The report concludes that surrogacy for "convenience" was "morally unacceptable," and questionable in "compelling" medical circumstances because it is exploitive to treat other

---

50. E. Scott, *Surrogacy and the Politics of Commodification*, 72(3) LAW & CONTEMP. PROBS. 109–46, 112 n.14 (2009).

51. *Id.*

52. *Id.* at 139.

53. *See* G. Bernstein, *Unintended Consequences*, 10(2) IND. HEALTH L. REV. 291–324, 311–18 (2013).

54. *See Psychosocial Aspects*, *supra* note 8, at 55.

55. *See* van den Akker, *supra* note 15, at 138.

56. M. Warnock et al., *Report of the Committee of Inquiry into Human Fertilisation and Embryology* (1984) [hereinafter Warnock Report].

57. *Id.* at 45.

58. *Id.* at 43.

59. *Id.* at 44.

humans as a means to one's own ends.[60] Britain embraced this moral critique by banning commercial surrogacy arrangements.[61]

The Baby M case had a significant impact on the public perception of surrogacy in America.[62] The controversy surrounding Baby M, which involved a traditional surrogacy agreement, produced a negative framing of surrogacy, depicting it as baby selling and exploitive of low-income women. The New Jersey Supreme Court's repeated descriptions of surrogacy as "baby-bartering" or "baby-buying" and "selling" became part of the public discourse about surrogacy.[63] The case led to a flurry of legislative action throughout the states seeking to ban surrogacy as against public policy.[64] The moral revulsion that widely greeted Baby M may, in part, be a reflection of the discomfort associated with new reproductive technologies. But the tenor of the debate, particularly the focus on the moral assessment of the women involved, suggests the case challenged traditional norms of maternity. The narrative generated by Baby M insisted that motherhood was the inescapable consequence of pregnancy. Surrogates could not be expected to negate this biological identity; they were destined to regret their decision and thus were incapable of informed consent.

Public opposition to surrogacy coalesced after the Baby M case.[65] Decades later, surrogacy is still considered the least acceptable way to have a child.[66] Only a minority of states directly regulates surrogacy; most jurisdictions resolve disputes through contract and family law principles, leaving the decision to enter into a surrogacy arrangement a risky legal undertaking.[67]

One recent study of British women's attitudes suggests that stigma is widely associated with surrogacy.[68] This data is consistent with results in the United States and Canada.[69] Surrogates widely report experience of

---

60. *Id.* at 46.

61. Surrogacy Arrangements Act, 1985; Human Fertilization and Embryology Authority Act, 1990.

62. *In re* Baby M, 537 A.2d 1227 (N.J. 1988).

63. *Id.* at 1241–42.

64. *See* Scott, *supra* note 50, at 117.

65. *Id.* at 135.

66. *See* Ciccarelli & Beckman, *supra* note 37; Poote & van den Akker, *supra* note 15, at 140; *Psychosocial Aspects, supra* note 8, at 58.

67. M. Hansen, *As Surrogacy Becomes More Popular, Legal Problems Proliferate*, ABA JOURNAL—LAW NEWS NOW (Mar. 1, 2011), https://www.abajournal.com/magazine/article/as_surrogacy_becomes_more_popular_legal_problems_proliferate/. By contrast, surrogacy is highly regulated in most other industrial nations. *See* MARKENS, *supra* note 17, at 23.

68. *See* Poote & van den Akker, *supra* note 15, at 140–44.

69. *See* Ciccarelli & Beckman, *supra* note 37, at 29.

stigma.[70] Stigma may impact personal relationships: some surrogates report significant lack of social support from partners and families, particularly at two critical and symbolic stages of the pregnancy: early in the pregnancy when the success of the pregnancy is established and post-delivery when the surrogate relinquishes the baby.[71] A 2005 survey of research on the psychological and social aspects of surrogacy in the United States and Great Britain reported that while husbands and partners were generally supportive, more than half of the surrogates surveyed experienced increased conflict in their extended family relationships as a result of their decision to become a surrogate; 40% reported loss of a significant relationship.[72]

Religion appears to be a relevant factor, in surrogacy as with abortion, with those who identify as religious less inclined to find these practices acceptable.[73] The Catholic Church opposes reproductive technologies, including surrogacy.[74] A brief filed in the Baby M case by the New Jersey Catholic Conference, describes surrogacy this way: "In surrogacy, a child is conceived precisely in order to be abandoned to others . . ."[75] This statement gets to the heart of the moral disapproval of surrogacy. Not all actions that result in relinquishing a child are perceived as objectionable. Adoption tends to be perceived as a morally appropriate response to untenable circumstances, presumably with the best interest of the child the foremost concern. In that sense the abandonment is "excused." Surrogacy by contrast is labeled offensive because it involves the intention both

---

70. *See Psychosocial Aspects, supra* note 8, at 57. Some commentators argue that a surrogate's contentment with her decision is no more than an "ironic self-deception" because it may be reinforcing oppressive gender roles. *See* M.J. Radin, *Market-Inalienability*, 100(8) HARV. L. REV. 1849–1937, 1930 (1987).

71. O.B.A. van den Akker, *Psychological Trait and State Characteristics, Social Support and Attitudes to the Surrogate Pregnancy and Baby*, 22(8) HUMAN REPRODUCTION 2287–95, 2293–94 (2007) [hereinafter *Psychological Trait*].

72. *See* Ciccarelli & Beckman, *supra* note 37, at 33.

73. *See Psychosocial Aspects, supra* note 8, 53–62; Poote & van den Akker, *supra* note 15, at 140.

74. Cardinal W. Levada, Prefect of the Congregation for the Doctrine of the Faith, "Dignitas Personae" (May 16, 2009). *Catechism of the Catholic Church* § 2376 states:

Techniques that entail the dissociation of husband and wife, by the intrusion of a person other than the couple (donation of sperm or ovum, surrogate uterus), are gravely immoral.

Catechism of the Catholic Church § 2376 (New York: Doubleday, 2d ed. 1997) (citing CDF, Donum vitae II, 1).

75. J.F. Sullivan, *Bishops File Brief Against Surrogate Motherhood*, N.Y. TIMES, July 19, 1987, at 28, https://www.nytimes.com/1987/07/19/nyregion/bishops-file-brief-against-surrogate-motherhood.html.

to conceive and abandon. This purposeful bypass, not of conception or gestation, but of motherhood, is at odds with social norms linking gestation to maternal bonding.

Surrogates and surrogacy programs take measures to reduce stigma, characterizing surrogacy in terms that are consistent with social expectations of motherhood and reproduction. Financial remuneration is de-emphasized; compensation in fact may be intentionally low.[76] Few surrogates, particularly gestational surrogates, regret their decisions; they typically view their role as participating in the "gift of life."[77] The casting of surrogacy as the gift of a child rather than a business transaction brings the practice more in line with traditional views of self-sacrificing mothers. This emphasis on altruism over remuneration has been critical to legislative recognition of noncommercial surrogacy.[78] The "gift of life" cannot be sold, but the law may recognize a woman's selfless desire to help a childless couple.[79] Altruism is deemed incompatible with remuneration; this dichotomy allows commercial surrogacy to be condemned as the prostitution of maternity.[80] The moral disgust associated with commercial surrogacy correlates to social disapproval of abortion for economic reasons; both create dissonance with the model of altruistic maternity. Popular culture reinforces stereotypes of commercial surrogates as greedy, uneducated, and dishonest.[81]

The shift to gestational surrogacy has engendered a change in the social discourse, and, to some extent, the stigma associated with surrogacy. Surrogates are now described as "gestational carriers" rather than mothers.[82] The altered social framing has generated greater public acceptance of gestational surrogacy.[83] This development suggests that the constructed meaning of maternity is grounded in the correlation between genetic and maternal identity. The pregnancy per se is not the source of the maternal obligation; the stigma of abandonment attaches with genetic relation. The absence of

76. *See* Ragoné, *supra* note 3, at 354.

77. *See Psychosocial Aspects, supra* note 8, at 56.

78. *See* Ragoné, *supra* note 3, at 356.

79. *Id.* Testimony of altruistic motives helped sway a 1989 California state legislative committee to authorize noncommercial surrogacy.

80. *See Psychosocial Aspects, supra* note 8, at 56.

81. "Baby Mama" is one example of a highly popular film that depicted the commercial surrogate as unemployed, uneducated, and scheming.

82. *See* Scott, *supra* note 50, at 140.

83. The use of surrogacy is increasing, particularly among same-sex couples. A. Hartocollis, *And Surrogacy Makes 3*, N.Y. TIMES (Feb. 19, 2014), *available at* http://www.nytimes.com/2014/02/20/fashion/In-New-York-Some-Couples-Push-for-Legalization-of-Compensated-Surrogacy.html?hp.

genetic relationship allows gestational surrogacy to more easily be characterized as a medical response to infertility.

The divergent framing of traditional surrogacy and gestational surrogacy expresses the relative moral comfort culture attaches to one practice and not the other. Gestational surrogacy does not threaten the genetic-based theory of maternity to the same extent as traditional surrogacy; the traditional surrogate and the woman who chooses abortion are stigmatized for challenging the inevitability of genetic attachment.[84] Despite this distinction, gestational surrogacy is not free of gendered stigma; common law presumed the birth mother was the legal mother, and the maxim *mater est quam gestation demonstrate* (by gestation the mother is demonstrated) remains a common legal basis for establishing maternity.[85] Further, the biochemical and hormonal relationship that nurtures the fetus during pregnancy may satisfy social and legal definitions of maternity.[86]

IV. Abortion and Stigma

If the bad mother is defined primarily as a woman who abandons her genetic relation, the woman who terminates a pregnancy is likely to encounter stigma. Unlike the planned pregnancies of surrogacy, most abortions occur as the result of unintended pregnancies.[87] While the intent to conceive may not be present, the decision to terminate a pregnancy may be perceived as the ultimate abandonment of the life in being, a rejection of maternity and of the "essential nature" of woman.[88] Negative social framing of abortion frequently reflects strong moral disapproval.[89] This disapproval,

---

84. Certainly some scholars argue that maternal identity is established through pregnancy, not through the genetic link. Research on adoption suggests maternal identity can be formed through nurturance. *See generally* B. KATZ ROTHMAN, RECREATING MOTHERHOOD: IDEOLOGY AND TECHNOLOGY IN A PATRIARCHAL SOCIETY (1990).

85. *See, e.g., In re* C.K.G., 173 S.W.3d 714, 729 (2005), Belsito v. Clark, 644 N.E.2d 760, 763 (1994).

86. R.F. Kandel, *Which Came First: The Mother or the Egg? A Kinship Solution to Gestational Surrogacy*, 47(1) RUTGERS L. REV. 165–239, 188 (1994).

87. R.K. JONES, L.B. FINER & S. SINGH, CHARACTERISTICS OF U.S ABORTION PATIENTS, 2008, at 12 (2010).

88. A. Norris et al., *Abortion Stigma: A Reconceptualization of Constituents, Causes, and Consequences*, 21 Supp. WOMEN'S HEALTH ISSUES S49–S54, S51(2011).

89. *See, e.g.,* B. Major et al., *Abortion and Mental Health: Evaluating the Evidence*, 64(9) AMERICAN PSYCHOLOGIST 863–90, 867 (2009); L.L. Littman et al., *Introducing Abortion Patients to a Culture of Support: A Pilot Study*, 12(6) ARCHIVES OF WOMEN'S MENTAL HEALTH 419–31, 421 (2009); B. Major & R. H. Gramzow, *Abortion as Stigma: Cognitive and Emotional Implications of Concealment*, 77(4) J. PERSONALITY & SOC. PSYCHOL. 735–45, 735.

influenced in part by the lack of public awareness about the commonness of abortion, highly polarized political discourse, and public ambivalence about acceptable circumstances for abortion, can contribute to stigma and the experience of isolation and social denigration associated with stigma.[90]

Abortion stigma has deep historical roots in negative social attitudes toward women who decline maternity; abortion often was associated with out-of-wedlock sex, promiscuity, and prostitution.[91] Women who terminated pregnancies typically were depicted as impoverished and desperate.[92] By the late 19th century, abortion became part of a larger cultural debate; concerns that white, middle class women were rejecting their "roles" as child bearers and raisers led to a nationwide movement to criminalize abortion.[93] Women who supported abortion were berated as frivolous and self-indulgent.[94] Pre-*Roe*, the procedure was identified with the unsafe reality of "back alley" abortions.[95] The post-*Roe* political backlash against abortion demonstrates how stigma can be used to discredit legally protected conduct.[96]

Public support of abortion has remained generally consistent since *Roe v. Wade* was decided in 1973.[97] A majority of Americans favor the legality of abortion, although that majority has decreased in recent years.[98] Approval deviates sharply however when the reasons for the abortion are considered.[99] Abortion is widely accepted as a response to significant health risks, rape, or serious fetal anomalies but acceptance drops below 50% when abortion is chosen for reasons of social, economic or personal hardship.[100] Public opposition to abortion in the absence of rape or medical risk has increased since 1992 when the Supreme Court opened the door to greater

---

90. *See* Cockrill & Nack, *supra* note 29, at 973.

91. R.W. Bourne, *Abortion in 1938 and Today: Plus Ça Change, Plus C'est La Même Chose*, 12(2) S. CAL. REV. L. & WOMEN'S STUDIES 229–75, 247 (2003).

92. J.C. MOHR, ABORTION IN AMERICA: THE ORIGINS AND EVOLUTION OF NATIONAL POL-ICY, 1800–1900, at 241–44 (1978).

93. *Id.* at 104–08.

94. *Id.* at 108.

95. *See* Norris et al., *supra* note 88, at S52.

96. *Id.*

97. *See* T.W. Smith & J. Son, *Trends in Public Attitudes towards Abortion* (2013), NORC Final Report.

98. *Id.* at 6, 7.

99. *Id.*

100. *Id.* at 2, 6. Abortion is approved where there is a serious health risk (87%), rape (78.3%), or serious fetal abnormality (77.1%). *Id.* at 2. Inability to afford a child (40.6%), married, wants no more children (43.2%), any reason (41.7%). *Id.* at 2, 6–7.

regulation of abortion in *Planned Parenthood of Southeastern Pennsylvania v. Casey*,[101] and rekindled a high profile national debate.[102]

These demarcations in approval are consistent with the good mother/ bad mother binary. Abortion is more acceptable to many when the woman is perceived as a victim of circumstances beyond her control, whether the acts of another or medical happenstance. The woman who decides to terminate her pregnancy for personal or economic reasons is less deserving of respect because she is rejecting motherhood for selfish reasons. The woman who chooses abortion in order to better provide for children she already has receives little sympathy.

Abortion stigma was common during the pre-*Roe* era of criminalized abortion.[103] Current data showing high rates of underreporting of abortions, active concealment, and fear of social rejection suggests that legalization has not eliminated the stigma.[104] Multiple studies conclude most women experience abortion as a stigmatizing event.[105] Socio-economic factors play a significant role in mediating abortion stigma including racial and ethnic identity, economic status, geography, and religion.[106] As with surrogacy, stigma is most commonly experienced as external disapproval.[107]

A recent study of women who terminated pregnancies concludes that 67% perceived or experienced disapproval from others, including friends and family.[108] Abortion stigma derives from social disapproval as well; in one study women identified sources of stigma from how society "discusses abortion" or "talks about women who have had an abortion."[109] Negative

---

101. 505 U.S. 833 (1992).

102. *See* Smith & Son, *supra* note 97, at 7; T.G. Jelen & C. Wilcox, *Causes and Consequences of Public Attitudes toward Abortion: A Review and Research Agenda*, 56(4) POL. RES. Q. 489–500, 491 (2003).

103. *See* Bourne, *supra* note 91, at 229, 273.

104. *See* Kumar et al., *supra* note 41, at 629.

105. *See* Shellenberg, *supra* note 27, at 16.

106. *See id.*, at 19, 183, 194–99; Major et al., *supra* note 89, at 885 (noting that abortion is often hallmarked by ambivalence); Jones, Finer & Singh, *supra* note 87, at 11 (discussing health insurance coverage and payment for abortion services); Littman et al., *supra* note 89, at 421–22 (discussing common types of abortion misinformation).

107. *See* Shellenberg, *supra* note 27, at 183–84, 192–93. *See* B. Major et al., APA Task Force on Mental Health and Abortion *Report of the APA Task Force on Mental Health and Abortion* 90 (2008) (noting that at least one study showed that a majority of women experienced no regret upon deciding to abort for fetal abnormality, and that generally, the evidence supports the assertion that the mental health risks are no greater among adult women who experience unplanned pregnancies who decide to abort than those who decide to deliver that pregnancy).

108. *See* Shellenberg, *supra* note 27, at 192.

109. *See* Littman et al., *supra* note 89, at 428.

female stereotypes influence a woman's experience of stigma; respondents expected others to perceive them as immoral or sinful, a "slut" or a bad mother.[110] As one woman explains, "[Y]ou're supposed to feel totally ashamed . . . and you're supposed to feel like you murdered someone and you're supposed to punish yourself."[111]

Abortion stigma is considered "concealable"; the stigmatizing trait is visible to others only upon disclosure.[112] A woman who terminates a pregnancy must decide whether and how to disclose her experience.[113] Secretive behavior, such as a desire to conceal the abortion or allow only selective disclosure, is a common response to real or perceived stigma.[114] Stigma can contribute to delays in scheduling the procedure, increasing the risk of medical or legal complications.[115] Stigma, and the desire to maintain secrecy, may also influence women to choose unsafe procedures, including self-induction or the use of untrained personnel.[116] Abortion stigma may be experienced as episodic or intermittent, often arising during events or experience where there is an option for disclosure.[117] The psychological consequences of abortion stigma vary, depending on the relationship of the stigma to self-identity.[118] Stigma and concealment are positively associated with psychological distress following first-trimester abortion in the United States.[119] Psychological repercussions of stigma may be "profound."[120] Social psychologist Brenda Major writes, "Women who come to internalize stigma associated with abortion (e.g., who see themselves as tainted, flawed,

---

110. *See* Shellenberg, *supra* note 27, at 183.

111. K. Kimport, *(Mis)understanding Abortion Regret*, 35(2) SYMBOLIC INTERACTION 105–22, 111 (2012).

112. *See* Norris et al., *supra* note 88, at S50. Stigma need not be attached to a visible trait. GOFFMAN, *supra* note 26, at 48–51.

113. *Id. See* Kumar et al., *supra* note 41, at 632 (noting that stigma and the associated status loss "is most often articulated at the community and social network levels").

114. K. Cockrill et al., *The Stigma of Having an Abortion: Development of a Scale and Characteristics of Women Experiencing Abortion Stigma*, 45(2) PERSPECTIVES ON SEXUAL & REPRODUCTIVE HEALTH 79–88, 80 (2013).

115. *See* Shellenberg, *supra* note 27, at 200.

116. *Id.*

117. *See* Cockrill & Nack, *supra* note 29, at 975.

118. *See* Major et al., *supra* note 89, at 867.

119. *See* Major & Gramzow, *supra* note 89, at 741–42. Other factors include the extent to which a woman wanted and felt committed to her pregnancy, perceived self-efficacy for coping with the abortion, low actual or anticipated social support for the abortion decision, and use of avoidance and denial coping strategies. *Id.*

120. *See* Major et al., *supra* note 89, at 867.

or morally deficient) are likely to be particularly vulnerable to later psychological distress."[121]

Abortion stigma is normalized through a "prevalence paradox.[122] Most women conceal their abortions, fearing stigma and lack of support.[123] Concealment creates a false perception that abortion is uncommon.[124] This misperception transforms into a social norm that labels abortion, and the women who have them, as deviant, furthering a cycle of secrecy and stigma.[125] Secrecy carries multiple risks: women who conceal abortions report insomnia, panic attacks, and anxiety.[126]

Like regulation of surrogacy, laws restricting abortion reflect a profound social disquiet about the separation of sex from procreation and women from motherhood. The woman who terminates a pregnancy is stigmatized for the ultimate, irrevocable "abandonment" of the child.

The surrogate or the woman who has an abortion may experience stigma differently depending on her personal circumstances and on the type of stigma she encounters. Because abortion is a concealable act, the stigma experienced is more likely to be felt or perceived than enacted. The surrogate, who cannot conceal the fact of pregnancy, is thus more likely to face enacted stigma. She may choose to manage stigma by concealing the circumstances of her pregnancy from all but family and close friends. Psychological stress relating to disclosure and concealment thus may be present with both abortion and surrogacy.

V. Gender Stereotypes in the Regulation of Abortion and Surrogacy

The socio-legal arguments against abortion and surrogacy bear notable similarities. Decisions that challenge the social construction of maternity are considered unreliable or immoral, in large part because of traditional stereotypes that deny women moral agency. Laws regulating abortion and surrogacy often reinforce these stigmatizing stereotypes.

---

121. *Id.*
122. *See* Kumar et al., *supra* note 11, at 629; *see* Norris et al., *supra* note 88, at S50 (noting that stigma may be episodic for some abortion patients who experience the reemergence of their stigma when prompted).
123. *See* Kimport, *supra* note 111, at 107.
124. *See* Kumar et al., *supra* note 41, at 634.
125. *Id.* at 629.
126. *See* Kimport, *supra* note 111, at 128.

A. Distrust of Judgment

Laws that question the moral agency of women perpetuate stereotypes that women lack the capacity for rational decision-making.[127] The widely held perception that women frequently decide to terminate a pregnancy or use a surrogate for purposes of reproductive "convenience" is one visible example of how culture may devalue women's judgment.[128]

Informed consent, a capacity credited to adults from common law, is suspect when a woman decides to become a surrogate or terminate a pregnancy.[129] The debate over whether informed consent is possible underlies the legal and ethical treatment of abortion and surrogacy. The assumption in both circumstances is that a rational woman would not voluntarily disrupt the connection between pregnancy and maternity. As the New Jersey Supreme Court concluded regarding informed consent by the surrogate in the Baby M case, "[Q]uite clearly any decision prior to the baby's birth is, in the most important sense, uninformed."[130] The court assumes the inevitability of the maternal bond, presuming that the uniqueness of gestation results in a type of diminished capacity to make decisions concerning the pregnancy. Baby M may not fully reflect current case law; subsequent decisions are less dismissive of the surrogate's authority but many courts still remain reluctant to give full recognition to the surrogate's consent, including one court that rejected an intent-based analysis because it relies on the "whims" of personal agreement.[131] The pre-*Roe* laws allowing abortion only when the woman's life or health was endangered denied women moral authority. In modern abortion legislation, this distrust emerges in

---

127. P. Abrams, *The Tradition of Reproduction*, 37(2) ARIZ. L. REV. 453–70, 463–70 (1995).

128. Consideration of the stigma experienced by the Intended Mother (IM) is beyond the scope of this chapter but a few points are worth noting. The stigma that attaches to the practice of surrogacy is likely a common experience for both the surrogate and the IM. An IM may also have to confront stigma associated with infertility. On the other hand, IMs may benefit from greater social support than surrogates. *See Psychological Trait, supra* note 71, at 2293.

129. *See, e.g.*, M. Manian, *Irrational Women: Informed Consent and Abortion Regret, in* FEMINIST LEGAL HISTORY: ESSAYS ON WOMEN AND LAW 118 (T.A. Thomas & T. Jean Boisseau, eds., 2011).

130. *In re* Baby M, 537 A.2d 1227, 1248 (N.J. 1988).

131. *See, e.g.*, Johnson v. Calvert, 851 P.2d 776, 785 (1993), applying an intent-based test, "The argument that a woman cannot knowingly and intelligently agree to gestate and deliver a baby for intending parents carries overtones of the reasoning that . . . prevented women from obtaining equal economic rights and professional status under the law." *But see* Belsito v. Clark, 644 N.E.2d 760, 766 (1994), refusing to apply *Johnson*. *See also In re* Marriage of Moschetta, 30 Cal. Rptr. 2d 893 (1994), refusing to apply *Johnson* to a traditional surrogacy dispute.

biased informed consent laws and laws mandating waiting periods.[132] *Casey* describes the informed consent requirement at issue as a legitimate attempt "to ensure that a woman apprehend the full consequences of her decision," so that she will not "discover later, with devastating psychological consequences, that her decision was not fully informed."[133] *Casey* also approves a 24-hour waiting period, and a gendered stereotype, with this language: "[t]he idea that important decisions will be more informed and deliberate if they follow some period of reflection does not strike us as unreasonable. . . ."[134]

These cases treat a woman's decision to abort or become a surrogate with gendered skepticism; a woman may be deemed capable of informed consent to all other major medical procedures but her decision not to become a mother justifies state intervention.

B. Expectation of Regret

A woman who cannot be trusted to make a moral and rational decision is likely to experience regret once she learns the "truth." The decision in *Gonzalez v. Carhart*, upholding the Federal Partial-Birth Abortion Ban Act, embraces the theory of regret when it opines, "While we find no reliable data to measure the phenomenon, it seems unexceptional to conclude some women come to regret their choice to abort the infant life they once created and sustained. . . . Severe depression and loss of esteem can follow."[135] The expectation of regret derives from the same presumptions that attach stigma to abortion and surrogacy; (1) the biological fact of pregnancy ordains motherhood, and (2) it is unnatural for a mother to give up a child.[136] This supposition may lead to laws that question a woman's decision or shift authority from the woman to the government.[137] Expectation of regret may lead to the imposition of waiting periods, with surrogacy a post-birth limbo when the surrogate can change her mind, with abortion, a pre-procedure state-mandated reflection.[138]

---

132. *See, e.g.*, MISS. CODE ANN. § 41–41–33 (West 1996); 18 PA. CONS. STAT. ANN. § 3205 (West 1989); WIS. STAT. ANN. § 253.10(3)(a)–(c) (West 2011).

133. *Casey*, 505 U.S. at 882.

134. *Id.* at 885.

135. Gonzales v. Carhart, 550 U.S. 124, 159 (2007).

136. L. Andrews, *Surrogate Motherhood: The Challenge for Feminists, in* SURROGATE MOTHERHOOD: POLITICS AND PRIVACY 167, 171 (L. Gostin, ed., 1990).

137. *Id.* at 172.

138. *See, e.g.*, A.H.W. v. G.H.B., 772 A.2d 948 (2000) (mandating 72-hour period after birth for gestational surrogate to decide whether to surrender the baby), R.R. v. M.H., 426

Laws that deny women the capacity to give informed consent and antic-ipate profound female regret reflect a set of stereotypes that presumes the state has a role in protecting women from the consequences of their decisions.

C. Protection of Women

The woman protective rationale supposes that the decision not to become a mother is the result of poor judgment or duress. The expectation of emo-tional harm is tied, with abortion, to thoroughly discredited data concern-ing the existence of "post-abortion distress syndrome."[139] With surrogacy, the distraught images of the Baby M surrogate, Mary Beth Whitehead, widely published in the media, convinced an entire generation of lawmak-ers and the public of the need to protect women from becoming surrogates.

The woman protective strategy is a familiar and still prevalent approach to controlling women's reproduction. By assuming that maternity is the ordained and desirable consequence of pregnancy, the state shoulders the role of protecting the woman from the harmful consequences of her deci-sion. *Carhart*, describing the abortion decision as one "fraught with emo-tional consequences," concludes, "The State has an interest in ensuring so grave a choice is well informed."[140] The report of an abortion task force in South Dakota concluded the state should limit abortion for the protec-tion of the woman because"[it] is so far outside the normal conduct of a

---

Mass. 501 (1998) (holding traditional surrogacy agreement unenforceable because it did not allow the surrogate four days after birth to change her mind). *See also* 168-B:25 N.H. Rev. Stat. Ann. (2008), requiring minimum 72-hour period after birth for surrogate to recon-sider her agreement. *See, e.g.*, Gonzales v. Carhart, 550 U.S. 124, 159–60 (2007) ("It is self-evident that a mother who comes to regret her choice to abort must struggle with grief more anguished and sorrow more profound when she learns, only after the event, what she once did not know: that she allowed a doctor to pierce the skull and vacuum the fast-developing brain of her unborn child, a child assuming the human form.").

139. Brief for Amicus Curiae Am. Psychological Ass'n in Support of Appellees at 14, Web-ster v. Reprod. Health Servs., 492 U.S. 490 (1989) (No. 88–605), 1989 WL 1127695, at *14. *See also* L. Greenhouse, *How the Supreme Court Talks about Abortion: The Implications of a Shifting Discourse*, 42(1) Suffolk U. L. Rev. 41–59, 47–48 (2008). The Carhart majority opinion thus adopts the discredited theory of a "postabortion syndrome" that inflicts lasting emotional damage on women who have had abortions. Although embraced by such organizations as Feminists for Life of America, where Jane Sullivan Roberts, the wife of Chief Justice Roberts, once served as executive vice president of the board of directors and currently as pro bono legal counsel, the theory has been widely debunked in the medical literature. *Id.* at 56 (cit-ing K.-A. Kinorski, *The Aftermath of Abortion*, 5(1) American Feminist 6–7 (1998).

140. *Carhart*, 550 U.S. at 159.

mother to implicate herself in the killing of her own child."[141] The state's interference in reproductive decisions is described as protecting the "fundamental right [of a mother to have a] relationship with her child."[142] Similarly, one of the primary arguments against surrogacy is the assumption that the arrangement exploits surrogates. In one case, a Michigan appeals court rejected a constitutional "right to procreate" challenge to the state's surrogacy law, concluding that government intrusion into private procreative choices was warranted because the state has a compelling interest in preventing the exploitation of women.[143]

VI. Stigma and the Court

Stigma is a social construct; thus the question of the interplay between stigma and law necessarily implicates the broader question of the relationship between law and culture. Although that topic is beyond the scope of this paper, a few observations are useful. Law may mediate stigma in a variety of ways. Law may reinforce the social construction of stigma by converting moral disapproval into public policy through criminalization. Outside the criminal law, legal standards that differentiate individuals may reinforce stereotypes. Laws also may serve an expressive function, sending messages about behavior, identity, and moral value that reinforce stigma.[144] Conversely, stigmatizing laws that reflect discrimination or animus against certain minority groups may be evidence of constitutional harm.

The Supreme Court has considered the role of stigma in cases involving racial discrimination, criminal convictions, government employment, paternity determinations, and involuntary commitments.[145] Evidence of stigma may be relevant to determining constitutional harm under both the due process and equal protection clauses.[146] State reinforcement of negative ste-

---

141. S. D. Task Force to Study Abortion, *Report of the South Dakota Task Force to Study Abortion* (2005), at 56 [hereinafter Task Force Report].

142. *Id.* at 65.

143. Doe v. Attorney General, 487 N.W.2d 484, 487 (1992). *See also* Andrews, *supra* note 136, at 171.

144. S. Burris, *Disease Stigma in U.S. Public Health Law*, 30(2) J. Law, Medicine & Ethics 179–90, 184 (2002).

145. *See, e.g.*, Brown v. Bd. of Educ. of Topeka, 347 U.S. 483 (1954) (racial discrimination); Bd. of Regents of State Coll. v. Roth, 408 U.S. 564 (1972) (employment); Parents Involved in Cmty. Sch. v. Seattle Sch. Dist. No. 1, 551 U.S. 701 (2007); Addington v. Texas, 441 U.S. 418 (1979) (involuntary commitment); Codd v. Velger, 429 U.S. 624 (1977) (employment).

146. *See, e.g.*, Bd. of Regents of State Coll., 408 U.S. at 573 (discussing potential due process issues). *See, e.g., id.* at 573–75; Rivera v. Minnich, 483 U.S. 574 (1987); *Addington*, 441 U.S. at 426; Beard v. Stahr, 370 U.S. 41, 42–45 (1962) (Douglas, J., dissenting).

reotypes is particularly relevant to anti-subordination concerns under equal protection.[147] Several landmark cases focus on the harm caused by state-generated stigma.

In *Lawrence v. Texas*, the Court, in an opinion by Justice Kennedy, expressed concern about the stigma created by a law that criminalized homosexual sodomy.[148] The Court observed how moral disapproval embodied in law contributes to stigma and discrimination: "When homosexual conduct is made criminal by the law of the State, that declaration in and of itself is an invitation to subject homosexual persons to discrimination both in the public and in the private spheres."[149] Concluding that adult, consenting homosexuals have a constitutionally protected liberty interest in intimate relationships, the Court found that laws criminalizing same sex sodomy generate stigma irrespective of whether the laws are enforced: "[i]f protected conduct is made criminal and the law which does so remains unexamined for its substantive validity, its stigma might remain even if it were not enforceable as drawn for equal protection reasons."[150]

The decision in *U.S. v. Windsor*[151] highlights how stigmatic harm may result from civil laws that express moral disapproval of protected constitutional interests. The Court, in an opinion once again written by Justice Kennedy, finds that Section 3 of the Federal Defense of Marriage Act (DOMA) is an unconstitutional deprivation of equality. The Court concludes that DOMA stigmatizes homosexuals through moral disapproval and animus: "[t]he avowed purpose and practical effect of the law here in question are to impose a disadvantage, a separate status, and so a stigma upon all who enter into same-sex marriages made lawful by the unquestioned authority of the States."[152] This "differentiation," characteristic of stigma, demeans those "whose moral and sexual choices the Constitution protects."[153] The Court finds that the "principal purpose and the necessary effect" of DOMA are to "demean," "disparage," and "injure" individuals who are in a lawful same-sex marriage.[154]

---

147. *See, e.g.*, Rivera v. Minnich, 483 U.S. 574, 585 (1987) (Brennan, J., dissenting); Lawrence v. Texas, 539 U.S. 558, 575 (2003).

148. *Lawrence*, 539 U.S. at 575–76.

149. *Id.*

150. *Id.* at 575. *See id.* at 571 ("The issue is whether the majority may use the power of the State to enforce these views on the whole society through operation of the criminal law."); *see also id.*, at 586–605 (Scalia, J., dissenting).

151. *United States v. Windsor*, 133 S. Ct. 2675 (2013).

152. *Windsor*, 133 S. Ct. at 2693.

153. *Id.* at 2694.

154. *Id.* at 2695–96.

The Court's description of stigma in *Windsor* reflects the pattern of disapproval, differentiation, and loss of status identified by Link and Phelan. *Windsor* articulates the relationship between moral disapproval, stigma, and constitutional harm. *Carhart*, in contrast, serves as an example of how judicial opinions can reinforce stereotypes and stigma. *Carhart* relies on stigmatizing language, describing physicians as "abortionists," fetal life as a "child," and an abortion as a "killing."[155] The Court's assumption, without "reliable data," that women may regret a decision to terminate a pregnancy relies on the same use of stereotyping that *Windsor* rejects.[156] Unlike *Lawrence* and *Windsor* and, indeed, *Casey, Carhart* accepts moral disapproval as a basis for regulation of abortion.[157]

The Court has also addressed the relationship between stigma and negative stereotyping. The decision in *Brown v. Board of* Education[158] relies substantially on the Court's conclusion that racially segregated schools stigmatized black children.[159] Other cases recognize that stigma may have a "very significant impact on the individual," including personal and social harm.[160] The Court at times has criticized affirmative action laws for stigmatizing individuals through stereotyping.[161]

Laws that perpetuate negative stereotypes are a central concern in the Court's analysis of gender discrimination.[162] In *Nevada Dept. of Human*

---

155. *Carhart*, 550 U.S. at 159.

156. *Id.*

157. *Id.* at 158 ("Congress could . . . conclude . . . the Act . . . implicates . . . ethical and moral concerns that justify a special prohibition."). *But see Casey*, 505 U.S. at 850 ("Our obligation is to define the liberty of all, not to mandate our own moral code.").

158. 347 U.S. 483 (1954).

159. *Brown*, 347 U.S. at 494 (1954). *See also* R.A. Lenhardt, *Understanding the Mark: Race, Stigma, and Equality in Context*, 79(3) N.Y.U. L. REV. 803–931 (2004) (arguing that racial stigma, not intentional discrimination, is the source of racial injury).

160. Addington v. Texas, 441 U.S. 418, 426 (1979); *see also* Patterson v. New York, 432 U.S. 197, 226 (1977) (Powell, J., dissenting); Beard v. Stahr, 370 U.S. 41, 42–45 (1962) (Douglas, J., dissenting).

161. *See* City of Richmond v. J.A. Croson Co., 488 U.S. 469, 491 (1989) ("Classifications based on race carry a danger of stigmatic harm."); City of Richmond v. J.A. Croson Co., 488 U.S. 469, 516 (1989) (Stevens, J., concurring) ("There is a special irony in the stereotypical thinking that prompts legislation of this kind. Although it stigmatizes the disadvantaged class with the unproven charge of past racial discrimination, it actually imposes a greater stigma on its supposed beneficiaries."); Grutter v. Bollinger, 539 U.S. 306, 349–78 (2003) (Thomas, J., concurring in part, dissenting in part); Parents Involved in Cmty. Sch. v. Seattle Sch. Dist. No. 1, 551 U.S. 701, 748–82 (2007) (Thomas, J., concurring).

162. United States v. Virginia, 518 U.S. 515, 533 (1996); *see also* Frontiero v. Richardson 411 U.S. 677 (1973).

Resources v. Hibbs,[163] the Court, upholding the constitutionality of the mandatory leave provision of the *Family and Medical Leave Act,* cites congressional findings of widespread employment discrimination against women based on "pervasive presumptions that women are mothers first."[164] *Hibbs* recognizes that laws regulating pregnancy are particularly susceptible to stereotyping.[165] *Casey* acknowledges deeply embedded stereotypes associated with maternity when it concludes, "[h]er suffering is too intimate and personal for the State to insist, without more, upon its own vision of the woman's role, however dominant that vision has been in the course of our history and our culture."[166]

These cases recognize the relationship between stereotyping and stigma. When the state generates stigma or enforces social stigma, it participates in creating a pariah group that is likely to suffer loss of status or discrimination.

VII. Stigma and Laws Regulating Abortion and Surrogacy

Stigma is a particularly pervasive mechanism for regulating sexual conduct and reproduction.[167] Reproduction is not solely a private matter; state intrusion into reproductive decisions has a long history and derives from public concerns about population, protection of the family unit, and morality. The cultural shame associated with infertility and unwed motherhood has deep roots and continuing influence on public attitudes towards reproduction. Abortion has been socially stigmatized on moral and religious grounds for many years; not infrequently, conservative opponents of abortion condemn surrogacy because it relies on birth outside the marriage relationship. The bad mother stigma identified with abortion and surrogacy reveals the prevalence and durability of gendered stereotypes. Controversies surrounding abortion and surrogacy serve as highly visible platforms for social debate about the roles of women.

Law serves as one medium for that dispute; in matters of sexual conduct and reproduction, law often serves to control morality through criminalization and stigma. The increasing separation and marginalization of abortion

---

163. 538 U.S. 721 (2003).

164. *Id.* at 736.

165. *Id.*

166. *Casey,* 505 U.S. at 852.

167. *See* Cook & Dickens, *supra* note 32, at 91. *See also* Lawrence v. Texas, discussed, *supra* note 150.

from other medical and reproductive health procedures reflect the process of stigmatization described by Link and Phelan. These laws designate women who choose abortion as "other." Gender stereotypes underlie abortion restrictions that contain exceptions for rape, incest, or serious medical risks for the woman.[168] These exceptions belie the state's claim that protection of prenatal life must always prevail. This good abortion/bad abortion binary, like the good mother/bad mother duality, reflects social judgment about when a woman may be "excused" from fulfilling the maternal role.[169] Similarly, laws that ban surrogacy or refuse to enforce surrogacy agreements directly stigmatize and also send powerful social messages that surrogacy is "bad" and the surrogate, the most visible manifestation of the arrangement, is aberrant.

The role of law in the generation of stigma is complex, but in matters of reproductive decisions, the risk is high that restrictions imposed on women who terminate a pregnancy or become surrogates reflect gendered stereotypes of motherhood. That risk is particularly problematic given the constitutional significance of reproductive decision making. The solution in part is to assure that the relationship between stigma and gender stereotyping informs judicial consideration of laws regulating abortion and surrogacy. Evidence of stigma is probative both of how gender stereotypes may influence legislative purpose and assessment of the harm imposed by a regulation, for stigma may impact reproductive decisions and behavior.[170]

VIII. Conclusion

The harm of stigma to an individual is multi-faceted; physical and psychological stress is likely and those who internalize stigma suffer negative self-images. But regulating reproductive decisions through stigma harms not just the individual but also society. The state should not be a participant

---

168. *See, e.g.*, Dep't of Labor, Health and Human Services, and Education, and related Agencies Appropriations Act, 1994, Pub. L. No. 103-112, (107 Stat. 1082) [hereinafter Hyde Amendment].

169. *See* Smith & Son, *supra* note 97, at 6–7.

170. Stigma evidence thus bears particularly on application of *Planned Parenthood of Southeastern Pennsylvania v. Casey*, which requires inquiry into both the purpose and burden of a law regulating abortion. Planned Parenthood Southeast v. Strange, 33 F.Supp.3d 1330 (M.D. Ala. 2014 is the first case to require consideration of stigma in assessing the burden imposed by restrictions on abortion. The Court has yet to consider whether the constitutional protection accorded the decision whether to bear or beget a child extends to noncoital conception such as surrogacy or other forms of ART. *See* J.A. ROBERTSON, CHILDREN OF CHOICE: FREEDOM AND THE NEW REPRODUCTIVE TECHNOLOGIES 22–42 (1994).

in the process of shaming women for their reproductive decisions; such actions deny women moral agency. Law instead should be a means for contesting stigma associated with gendered stereotypes, particularly those stereotypes that under- mine reproductive decision making. Martha Nussbaum, in her analysis of the role of shame and disgust in the law, rejects the use of public laws to stigmatize individuals, "for the state to participate in this humiliation . . . is profoundly subversive of the ideas of equality and dignity on which a liberal society is based."[171]

Acknowledgements

I am grateful to the participants in the Intersections in Reproduction Conference for their thoughtful insights. Thanks also to Michelle Enfield for research assistance.

---

171. M. Nussbaum, Hiding from Humanity: Disgust, Shame, and the Law 232 (2004).

15

The Wages of Crying Wolf:
A Comment on Roe v. Wade[1]

By John Hart Ely[2]

The interests of the mother and the fetus are opposed. On which side should the State throw its weight? The issue is volatile; and it is resolved by the moral code which an individual has.[3]

In *Roe v. Wade,*[4] decided January 22, 1973, the Supreme Court—Justice Blackmun speaking for everyone but Justices White and Rehnquist[5]—held unconstitutional Texas's (and virtually every other state's[6]) criminal abortion statute. The broad outlines of its argument are not difficult to make out:

1. The right to privacy, though not explicitly mentioned in the Constitution, is protected by the Due Process Clause of the Fourteenth Amendment.[7]
2. This right "is broad enough to encompass a woman's decision whether or not to terminate her pregnancy."[8]

---

1. This chapter originally appeared in volume 82 of the *Yale Law Journal* and is reprinted here with the permission of the *Journal.*

2. John Hart Ely was Professor of Law, Yale Law School, when the chapter was first published.

3. United States v. Vuitch, 402 U.S. 62, 80 (1971) (Douglas, J., dissenting in part).

4. 410 U.S. 113 (1973).

5. Were the dissents adequate, this comment would be unnecessary. But each is so brief as to signal no particular conviction that *Roe* represents an important, or unusually dangerous, constitutional development.

6. *See* 410 U.S. at 118 n.2. *See also* Doe v. Bolton, 410 U.S. 179, 181–82 (1973).

7. 410 U.S. at 153–54. *But cf.* note 60 *infra.*

8. *Id.*

3. This right to an abortion is "fundamental" and can therefore be regulated only on the basis of a "compelling" state interest.[9]

4. The state does have two "important and legitimate" interests here,[10]
   the first in protecting maternal health, the second in protecting the
   life (or potential life[11]) of the fetus.[12] But neither can be counted
   "compelling" throughout the entire pregnancy: Each matures with
   the unborn child. These interests are separate and distinct. Each
   grows in substantiality as the woman approaches term and, at a point
   during pregnancy, each becomes "compelling."[13]

5. During the first trimester of pregnancy, neither interest is sufficiently compelling to justify any interference with the decision of
   the woman and her physician. Appellants have referred the Court to
   medical data indicating that mortality rates for women undergoing
   early abortions, where abortion is legal, "appear to be as low as or
   lower than the rates for normal childbirth."[14] Thus the state's interest in protecting maternal health is not compelling during the first
   trimester. Since the interest in protecting the fetus is not yet compelling either,[15] during the first trimester the state can neither prohibit an abortion nor regulate the conditions under which one is
   performed.[16]

6. As we move into the second trimester, the interest in protecting the
   fetus remains less than compelling, and the decision to have an abortion thus continues to control. However, at this point the health risks
   of abortion begin to exceed those of childbirth. "It follows that, from
   and after this point, a State may regulate the abortion procedure to
   the extent that the regulation reasonably relates to the preservation

---

9. *Id.* at 155–56.

10. *Id.* at 161–62.

11. The Court indicates that the constitutional issue is not to be solved by attempting to
answer "the difficult question of when life begins." *Id.* at 159. *See also id.* at 149–51. *But see*
discussion *infra.*

12. The suggestion that the interest in protecting prenatal life should not be considered
because the original legislative history of most laws restricting abortion concerned itself with
maternal health, *see id.* at 149–52, is rightly rejected—by clear implication in *Roe* and rather
explicitly in *Doe. Id.* at 190–91.

13. *Id.* at 731.

14. *Id.* at 725. *But cf.* note 119 *infra.*

15. *See* discussion *infra.*

16. *See* 410 U.S. at 163–64. *But see* note 119 *infra.*

and protection of maternal health."[17] Abortion may not be prohibited during the second trimester, however.[18]

7. At the point at which the fetus becomes viable[19] the interest in protecting it becomes compelling,[20] and therefore from that point on the state can prohibit abortions *except*—and this limitation is also apparently a constitutional command, though it receives no justification in the opinion—when they are necessary to protect maternal life or health.[21]

I

A number of fairly standard criticisms can be made of *Roe*. A plausible narrower basis of decision, that of vagueness, is brushed aside in the rush toward broader ground.[22] The opinion strikes the reader initially as a sort of guidebook, addressing questions not before the Court and drawing lines with an apparent precision one generally associates with a commissioner's regulations.[23] On closer examination, however, the precision proves largely illusory. Confusing signals are emitted, particularly with respect to the

---

17. *See* 410 U.S. at 163–64. *But see* note 119 *infra.*

18. *Id.* at 732

19. This, the Court tells us, is somewhere between the twenty-fourth and twenty-eighth weeks. *Id.* at 160. *But cf.* discussion *infra.*

20. *See* discussion *infra.*

21. *Id.* at 163–64. (Thus the statutes of most states must be unconstitutional *even as applied to the final trimester,* since they permit abortion only for the purpose of saving the mother's life. *See id.* at 118.) This holding—that even after viability the mother's life *or health* (which presumably is to be defined very broadly indeed, so as to include what many might regard as the mother's convenience, *see* 410 U.S. at 179 (Burger, C.J., concurring)); *United States v. Vuitch,* 402 U.S. 62 (1971), must, as a matter of constitutional law, take precedence over what the Court seems prepared to grant at this point has become the fetus's *life, see* discussion *infra*—seems to me at least as controversial as its holding respecting the period prior to viability. (Typically, of course, one is not privileged even statutorily, let alone constitutionally, to take another's life in order to save his own life, much less his health.) Since, however, the Court does not see fit to defend this aspect of its decision at all, there is not a great deal that can be said by way of criticism.

22. The Court's theory seems to be that narrow grounds need not be considered when there is a broad one that will do the trick: "This conclusion makes it unnecessary for us to consider the additional challenge to the Texas *statute asserted on grounds of vagueness.*" 410 U.S. at 164. *Compare id.* at 119 n.3, 120–22; Doe v. Bolton, 410 U.S. at 191–92; Roe v. Wade, 314 F. Supp. 1217, 1223 (N.D. Tex. 1970); cases cited 410 U.S. at 154–55; and United States v. Vuitch, 402 U.S. 62 (1971), bearing in mind that the Supreme Court lacks jurisdiction to "construe" a state statute so as to save it from the vice of vagueness.

23. *See also* Doe v. Bolton, 410 U.S. 179 (1973).

nature of the doctor's responsibilities[24] and the permissible scope of health regulations after the first trimester.[25] The Court seems, moreover, to get carried away on the subject of remedies: Even assuming the case can be made for an unusually protected constitutional right to an abortion, it hardly seems necessary to have banned during the first trimester *all* state regulation of the conditions under which abortions can be performed.[26]

By terming such criticisms "standard," I do not mean to suggest they are unimportant, for they are not. But if they were all that was wrong with *Roe*, it would not merit special comment.[27]

II

Let us not underestimate what is at stake: Having an unwanted child can go a long way toward ruining a woman's life.[28] And at bottom *Roe* signals

---

24. Apparently doctors are expected, or at least can be required despite the decisions, to exercise their best "medical" or "clinical" judgment (and presumably can be prosecuted if they perform abortions conflicting with that judgment). 410 U.S. at 190–91, 199–200. *But cf.* United States v. Vuitch, 402 U.S. 62, 97 (Stewart, J., dissenting in part). But if it is unconstitutional to limit the justifications for an abortion to considerations of maternal life and health, what kind of "medical" judgment does the Court have in mind? *See* A. STONE, ABORTION AND THE SUPREME COURT (1973): "[T]here are no clear medical indications for abortion in the vast majority of cases. Where there are no indications, there is no room for clinical judgment."

25. *Compare* 410 U.S. at 163–64 *with id.* at 194–200. An additional element of confusion may have been injected by Justice Douglas's indication in his concurrence that "quickening" is the point at which the interest in protecting the fetus becomes compelling. *Id.* at 160. *But see id.* at 160, where the Court distinguishes quickening from viability and holds the latter to be the crucial point. *See also id.* at 163–64 and discussion *infra*.

26. The state *can* require that the abortion be performed by a doctor, but that is all. *But see* note 119 *infra*. Even after the first trimester, the limits on state regulation of the conditions under which an abortion can be performed arc extremely stringent. *See* Doe v. Bolton, 410 U.S. 179 (1973).

27. With respect to the capital punishment litigation too, the Court rejected a narrow ground of invalidation one term only to come back with a *coup de main* the next. *Compare* McGautha v. California, 402 U.S. 183 (1971) *with* Furman v. Georgia, 408 U.S. 238 (1972). Miranda v. Arizona, 384 U.S. 436 (1966), has something of a "guidebook" quality about it. *See* A. Dershowitz & J. Ely, *Harris v. New York: Some Anxious Observations on the Candor and Logic of the Emerging Nixon Majority,* 80 YALE L.J. 1198, 1210 (1971). United States v. Wade, 388 U.S. 218 (1967), to take but one example, has always struck me as a case where the Court, starting from the entirely valid realization that trials cannot be fair if lineups are not, went a bit far in limiting the appropriate remedies. And of course, many opinions have emitted confusing signals respecting what is henceforth permissible. *See, e.g.,* discussion *infra*.

28. The child may not fare so well either. Of course, the Court requires of the mother neither sort of showing, though it may be hoping the doctors will do so. *But cf.* note 24 *supra.* It is also probably the case, although this is the sort of issue where reliable statistics

the Court's judgment that this result cannot be justified by any good that anti-abortion legislation accomplishes. This surely is an understandable conclusion—indeed it is one with which I agree[29]— but ordinarily the Court claims no mandate to second-guess legislative balances, at least not when the Constitution has designated neither of the values in conflict as entitled to special protection.[30] But even assuming it would be a good idea for the Court to assume this function, *Roe* seems a curious place to have begun. Laws prohibiting the use of "soft" drugs or, even more obviously, homosexual acts between consenting adults can stunt "the preferred life styles"[31] of those against whom enforcement is threatened in very serious ways. It is clear such acts harm no one besides the participants, and indeed the case that the participants are harmed is a rather shaky one.[32] Yet such laws survive,[33] on the theory that there exists a societal consensus that the behavior involved is revolting or at any rate immoral.[34] Of course the consensus is not universal but it is sufficient, and this is what is counted crucial, to get the laws passed and keep them on the books. Whether anti-abortion legislation cramps the life style of an unwilling mother more significantly than anti-homosexuality legislation cramps the life style of a homosexual is a close question. But even granting that it does, the *other* side of the

---

and comparisons are largely unobtainable, that a number of women have died from illegal abortions who would have lived had they been able to secure legal abortions. It is a strange argument for the unconstitutionality of a law that those who evade it suffer, but it is one that must nevertheless be weighed in the balance as a cost of anti-abortion legislation. The Court does not mention it, however; and given the severe restrictions it places on state regulation of the conditions under which an abortion can be performed, it apparently did not appreciably inform its judgment.

29. *See* discussion *infra.*

30. *See* discussion *infra.* Even where the Constitution does single out one of the values for special protection, the Court has shown an increasing tendency to avoid balancing, or at least to talk as though it were. *See* Brandenburg v. Ohio, 395 U.S. 444 (1969). *See also* United States v. Robel, 389 U.S. 258, 268 n.20 (1967); *but see* Note, *Less Drastic Means and the First Amendment,* 78 YALE L.J. 464, 467–08 (1969). *See also* United States v. O'Brien, 391 U.S. 367, 376–77 (1908); *but cf.* J. Ely, *Legislative and Administrative Motivation in Constitutional Law,* 79 YALE L.J. 1205, 1340–41 (1970).

31. 410 U.S. at 209 (Douglas, J., concurring).

32. The claim that the participants are injuring their health seems at least as plausible respecting abortion. *Cf.* note 119 *infra.* To the extent that the use of soft drugs and homosexual activities interfere with the lives of those other than the participants, those interferences can be dealt with discretely.

33. *Cf.* Poe v. Ullman, 367 U.S. 497, 551–53 (1961) (Harlan, J., dissenting), quoted in part in Griswold v. Connecticut, 381 U.S. 479, 499 (1965) (Goldberg, J., concurring), distinguishing laws proscribing homosexual acts (even those performed in the home) as not involving the "right" at stake in those cases.

34. *See, e.g.,* Poe v. Ullman, 367 U.S. 497, 545–46 (Harlan, J., dissenting).

balance looks very different. For there is more than simple societal revulsion to support legislation restricting abortion:[35] Abortion ends (or if it makes a difference, prevents) the life of a human being other than the one making the choice.

The Court's response here is simply not adequate. It agrees, indeed it holds, that after the point of viability (a concept it fails to note will become even less clear than it is now as the technology of birth continues to develop[36]) the interest in protecting the fetus is compelling.[37] Exactly why that is the magic moment is not made clear: Viability, as the Court defines it,[38] is achieved some six to twelve weeks after quickening.[39] (Quickening is the point at which the fetus begins discernibly to move independently of the mother[40] and the point that has historically been deemed crucial—to the extent *any* point between conception and birth has been focused on.[41]) But no, it is *viability* that is constitutionally critical: the Court's defense seems to mistake a definition for a syllogism.

With respect to the State's important and legitimate interest in potential life, the "compelling" point is at viability. This is so because the fetus then presumably has the capacity of meaningful life outside the mother's womb.[42]

---

35. Nor is the Court's conclusion that early abortion does not present serious physical risk to the woman involved shared by all doctors. *Cf.* note 119 *infra.*

36. It defines viability so as not to exclude the possibility of artificial support, 410 U.S. at 159–60, and later indicates its awareness of the continuing development of artificial wombs. *Id.* at 161–62. It gives no sign of having considered the implications of that combination for the trimester program the Constitution is held to mandate, however.

37. Albeit not so compelling that a state is permitted to honor it at the expense of the mother's health. *See* note 21 *supra.*

38. Note 19 *supra.*

39. 410 U.S. at 131–32.

40. *Id.*

41. *Id.* at 131–42.

42. *Id.* at 163-64. *See also id.* at 160:

> Physicians and their scientific colleagues have regarded [quickening] with less interest and have tended to focus either upon conception or upon live birth or upon the interim point at which the fetus becomes "viable," . . .

The relevance of this observation is not explained. It is, moreover, of questionable validity:

> This line is drawn beyond quickening, beyond the point where any religion has assumed that life begins, beyond the time when abortion is a simple procedure, and beyond the point when most physicians and nurses will feel the procedure is victimless. It is also beyond the point which would have satisfied many who, like myself, were long term supporters of the right to abortion.

A. Stone, *supra* note 24.

With regard to why the state cannot consider this "important and legitimate interest" prior to viability, the opinion is even less satisfactory. The discussion begins sensibly enough: The interest asserted is not necessarily tied to the question whether the fetus is "alive," for whether or not one calls it a living being, it is an entity with the potential for (and indeed the likelihood of) life.[43] But all of arguable relevance that follows[44] are arguments that fetuses (a) are not recognized as "persons in the whole sense" by legal doctrine generally[45] and (b) are not "persons" protected by the Fourteenth Amendment.[46]

To the extent they are not entirely inconclusive, the bodies of doctrine to which the Court adverts respecting the protection of fetuses under general legal doctrine tend to undercut rather than support its conclusion.[47]

---

43. Logically, of course, a legitimate state interest in this area need not stand or fall on acceptance of the belief that life begins at conception or at some other point prior to live birth. In assessing the State's interest, recognition may be given to the less rigid claim that as long as at least *potential* life is involved, the State may assert interests beyond the protection of the pregnant woman alone. 410 U.S. at 150.

> We need not resolve the difficult question of when life begins. When those trained in the respective disciplines of medicine, philosophy, and theology arc unable to arrive at any consensus, the judiciary, at this point [sic] in the development of man's knowledge, is not in a position to speculate as to the answer. The Texas statute, like those of many states, had declared fetuses to be living beings.

Id. at 159. *See id.* at 117 n.1, 119 n.3; *cf. id.* at 141–42, 146 n.40, 158 n.55.

44. The opinion does contain a lengthy survey of "historical attitudes" toward abortion, culminating in a discussion of the positions of the American Medical Association, the American Public Health Association, and the American Bar Association. *Id.* at 129–50. (The discussion's high point is probably reached where the Court explains away the Hippocratic Oath's prohibition of abortion on the grounds that Hippocrates was a Pythagorean, and Pythagoreans were a minority. *Id.* at 129–32.) The Court does not seem entirely clear as to what this discussion has to do with the legal argument, *id.* at 117, 129–30, and the reader is left in much the same quandary. It surely does not seem to support the Court's position, unless a record of serious historical and contemporary dispute is somehow thought to generate a constitutional mandate.

45. *Id.* at 160–62.

46. *Id.* at 155–60.

47.

> [T]he traditional rule of tort law had denied recovery for prenatal injuries even though the child was born alive. That rule has been changed in almost every jurisdiction. In most States recovery is said to be permitted only if the fetus was viable, or at least quick, when the injuries were sustained, though few courts have squarely so held. In a recent development, generally opposed by the commentators, some States permit the parents of a stillborn child to maintain an action for wrongful death because of prenatal injuries. Such an action, however, would appear to be one to vindicate the parents' interest and is thus consistent with the view that the fetus, at most, represents only the potentiality of life. Similarly, unborn children

And the argument that fetuses (unlike, say, corporations) are not "persons" under the Fourteenth Amendment fares little better. The Court notes that most constitutional clauses using the word "persons"—such as the one outlining the qualifications for the Presidency—appear to have been drafted with postnatal beings in mind. (It might have added that most of them were plainly drafted with *adults* in mind, but I suppose that wouldn't have helped.) In addition, "the appellee conceded on reargument that no case can be cited that holds that a fetus is a person within the meaning of the Fourteenth Amendment."[48] (The other legal contexts in which the question could have arisen are not enumerated.)

The canons of construction employed here are perhaps most intriguing when they are contrasted with those invoked to derive the constitutional right to an abortion.[49] But in any event, the argument that fetuses lack constitutional rights is simply irrelevant. For it has never been held or even asserted that the state interest needed to justify forcing a person to refrain from an activity, *whether or not that activity is constitutionally protected,* must implicate either the life or the constitutional rights of another person.[50] Dogs are not "persons in the whole sense" nor have they constitutional rights, but that does not mean the state cannot prohibit killing them: It does not even mean the state cannot prohibit killing them in the exercise

---

have been recognized as acquiring rights or interests by way of inheritance or other devolution of property, and have been represented by guardians *ad litem.* Perfection of the interests involved, again, has generally been contingent upon live birth. In short, the unborn have never been recognized in the law as persons in the whole sense.

Id. at 161–62 (footnotes omitted). *See also, e.g.,* W. PROSSER, HANDBOOK OF THE LAW OF TORTS 355 (3d ed. 1964).

48. *Id.* at 157 (footnote omitted).

49. *See* discussion *infra.*

50. Indeed, it is difficult to think of a single instance where the justification given for upholding a governmental limitation of a protected right has involved the constitutional rights of others. A "free press-fair trial" situation might provide the basis for such an order, hut thus far the Court has refused to approve one. *See* J. Ely, *Trial by Newspaper & Its Cures,* ENCOUNTER 80–92 (Mar. 1967).

In the Court's defense it should he noted that it leans in the other direction as well, by suggesting that if a fetus *were* a person protected by the Fourteenth Amendment, it would necessarily follow that appellants would lose. 410 U.S. at 156–57. Yet in fact all that would thereby be established is that one light granted special protection by the Fourteenth Amendment was in conflict with what the Court felt was another; it would not tell us which must prevail.

of the First Amendment right of political protest. Come to think of it, draft cards aren't persons either.[51]

Thus even assuming the Court ought generally to get into the business of second-guessing legislative balances, it has picked a strange case with which to begin. Its purported evaluation of the balance that produced anti-abortion legislation simply does not meet the issue: That the life plans of the mother must, not simply may, prevail over the state's desire to protect the fetus simply does not follow from the judgment that the fetus is not a person. Beyond all that, however, the Court has no business getting into that business.

III

Were I a legislator I would vote for a statute very much like the one the Court ends up drafting.[52] I hope this reaction reflects more than the psychological phenomenon that keeps bombardiers sane—the fact that it is somehow easier to "terminate" those you cannot see—and am inclined to think it does: that the mother, unlike the unborn child, has begun to imagine a future for herself strikes me as morally quite significant. But God knows I'm not *happy* with that resolution. Abortion is too much like infanticide on the one hand, and too much like contraception on the other, to leave one comfortable with any answer; and the moral issue it poses is as fiendish as any philosopher's hypothetical.[53]

Of course, the Court often resolves difficult moral questions, and difficult questions yield controversial answers. I doubt, for example, that most people would agree that letting a drug peddler go unapprehended is morally preferable to letting the police kick down his door without probable cause. The difference, of course, is that the Constitution, which legitimates and theoretically controls judicial intervention, has some rather pointed things to say about this choice. There will of course be difficult questions about the applicability of its language to specific facts, but at least the

---

51. *See* United States v. O'Brien, 391 U.S. 367, 376–77 (1968). And if you don't like that example, substitute post offices for draft cards.

52. I would, however, omit the serious restrictions the Court puts on slate health regulation of the conditions under which an abortion can be performed, and give serious thought—though the practical difference here is not likely to be great—to placing the critical line at quickening rather than viability. *See* note 42 *supra*.

53. Some of us who fought for the right to abortion did so with a divided spirit. We have always felt that the decision to abort was a human tragedy to be accepted only because an unwanted pregnancy was even more tragic. A. STONE, *supra* note 24.

document's special concern with one of the values in conflict is manifest. It simply says nothing, clear or fuzzy, about abortion.[54]

The matter cannot end there, however. The Burger Court, like the Warren Court before it, has been especially solicitous of the right to travel from state to state, demanding a compelling state interest if it is to be inhibited.[55] Yet nowhere in the Constitution is such a right mentioned. It is, however, as clear as such things can be that this right was one the framers intended to protect, most specifically[56] by the Privileges and Immunities Clause of Article IV.[57] The right is, moreover, plausibly inferable from the system of government, and the citizen's role therein, contemplated by the Constitution.[58] The Court in *Roe* suggests an inference of neither sort—from the intent of the framers,[59] or from the governmental system contemplated by the Constitution—in support of the constitutional right to an abortion.

What the Court does assert is that there is a general right of privacy granted special protection—that is, protection above and beyond the baseline requirement of "rationality"—by the Fourteenth Amendment,[60] and that that right "is broad enough to encompass" the right to an abortion.

---

54. Of course, the opportunity to have an abortion should be considered part of the "liberty" protected by the Fourteenth Amendment.

55. *See, e.g.,* Dunn v. Blumstein, 405 U.S. 330 (1972); Shapiro v. Thompson, 394 U.S. 018 (1969).

56. *See also* Edwards v. California, 314 U.S. 160 (1941).

57. *See* United States v. Wheeler, 254 U.S. 281, 294 (1920); Slaughterhouse Cases, 83 U.S. (16 Wall.) 36, 75 (1872); U.S. CONST. art. IV; 3 M. FARRAND, THE RECORDS OF THE FEDERAL CONVENTION OF 1787, at 112 (1911); *cf.* The Federalist, No. 42, at 307 (Wright ed. 1961).

58. *See* Crandall v. Nevada, 73 U.S. (6 Wall.) 35 (1867); C. BLACK, STRUCTURE AND RELATIONSHIP IN CONSTITUTIONAL LAW (1969). The Court seems to regard the opportunity to travel *outside* the United States as merely an aspect of the "liberty" that under the Fifth and Fourteenth Amendments cannot he denied without due process. *See* Zemel v. Rusk, 381 U.S. 1, 14 (1965).

59. Abortions had, of course, been performed, and intermittently proscribed, for centuries prior to the framing of the Constitution. That alone, however, need not be dispositive. *See infra* note 99.

60. The Court does not seem entirely certain about which provision protects the right to privacy and its included right to an abortion. "Appellant would discover this right in the concept of personal "liberty" embodied in the Fourteenth Amendment's Due Process Clause; or in personal, marital, familial, and sexual privacy said to be protected by the Bill of Rights or its penumbras . . . or among those rights reserved to the people by the Ninth Amendment. . . ." 410 U.S. at 129.

> This right of privacy, whether it be founded in the Fourteenth Amendment's concept of personal liberty and restrictions upon state action, as we feel it is, or, as the District Court determined, in the Ninth Amendment's reservation of rights to the people, is broad enough to encompass a woman's decision whether or not to terminate her pregnancy.

The general right of privacy is inferred, as it was in *Griswold v. Connecticut*,[61] from various provisions of the Bill of Rights manifesting a concern with privacy, notably the Fourth Amendment's guarantee against unreasonable searches, the Fifth Amendment's privilege against self-incrimination, and the right, inferred from the First Amendment, to keep one's political associations secret.[62]

One possible response is that all this proves is that the things explicitly mentioned are forbidden, if indeed it does not actually demonstrate a disposition *not* to enshrine anything that might be called a general right of privacy.[63] In fact the Court takes this view when it suits its purposes. (On the *same day* it decided *Roe*, the Court held that a showing of reasonableness was not needed to force someone to provide a grand jury with a voice exemplar, reasoning that the Fifth Amendment was not implicated because the evidence was not "testimonial" and that the Fourth Amendment did not apply because there was no "seizure."[64]) But this approach is unduly crabbed. Surely the Court is entitled, indeed I think it is obligated, to seek out the sorts of evils the framers meant to combat and to move against their twentieth century counterparts.[65]

Id. at 153. This inability to pigeonhole confidently the right involved is not important in and of itself. It might, however, have alerted the Court to what is an important question: whether the Constitution speaks to the matter at all.

61. 381 U.S. 479 (1965).

62. *See* NAACP v. Alabama, 357 U.S. 449 (1958), relied on in *Griswold*, 381 U.S. at 483. The *Roe* Court's reference to Justice Goldberg's concurrence in Griswold for the proposition that "the roots of" the right of privacy can be found in the Ninth Amendment, 410 U.S. at 152, misconceives the use the earlier opinion made of that Amendment. *See* 381 U.S. at 492–93. A reference to "the penumbras of the Bill of Rights," 93 S. Ct. at 726, can have no content independent of a description of some general value or values inferable from the provisions involved (and therefore assignable to their penumbras). *See* San Antonio Independent School Dist. v. Rodriguez, 411 U.S. 1, 69 (1973) (Marshall, J., dissenting).

63. *See* Katz v. United States, 389 U.S. 347, 364 (1967) (Black, J., dissenting); Griswold v. Connecticut, 381 U.S. 479, 529 (Stewart, J., dissenting).

64. United States v. Dionisio, 410 U.S. 1 (1973). *See also* United States v. Mara, 410 U.S. 19 (1973) (handwriting exemplars), also decided the same day as *Roe*, and Couch v. United States, 409 U.S. 322 (1973) finding no privacy interest in records a taxpayer had turned over to her accountant) decided thirteen days earlier.

65. "[T]he proper scope of [a constitutional provision], and its relevance to contemporary problems, must ultimately be sought by attempting to discern the reasons for its inclusion in the Constitution, and the evils it was designed to eliminate." United States v. Brown, 381 U.S. 437, 442 (1965). *See also* Weems v. United States, 217 U.S. 349, 373 (1910); C. Reich, *Mr. Justice Black and the Living Constitution*, 76 HARV. L. REV. 673 (1963); Note, *The Bounds of Legislative Specification: A Suggested Approach to the Bill of Attainder Clause*, 72 YALE L.J. 330 (1962).

Thus it seems to me entirely proper to infer a general right of privacy, *so long as some care is taken in defining the sort of right the inference will support.* Those aspects of the First, Fourth and Fifth Amendments to which the Court refers all limit the ways in which, and the circumstances under which, the government can go about gathering information about a person he would rather it did not have.[66] *Katz v. United States,*[67] limiting governmental tapping of telephones, may not involve what the framers would have called a "search," but it plainly involves this general concern with privacy.[68] *Griswold* is a long step, even a leap, beyond this, but at least the connection is discernible. Had it been a case that purported to discover in the Constitution a "right to contraception," it would have been *Roe's* strongest precedent.[69] But the Court in *Roe* gives no evidence of so regarding it,[70] and rightly not.[71] Commentators tend to forget, though the Court plainly has not,[72] that the Court in *Griswold* stressed that it was invalidating only that portion of the Connecticut law that proscribed the *use,* as opposed to the manufacture, sale, or other distribution of contraceptives. That distinction (which would be silly were the right to contraception being constitutionally enshrined) makes sense if the case is rationalized on the ground that the section of the law whose constitutionality was in issue was such that *its enforcement would have been virtually impossible without* the most outrageous sort of

---

66. *Cf.* C. Fried, *Privacy,* 77 YALE L.J. 475 (1968). The Third Amendment, mentioned in *Griswold* though not in *Roe,* surely has this aspect to it as well, though it probably grew in even larger measure out of a general concern with the pervasiveness of military power.

67. 389 U.S. 347 (1967).

68. *Cf.* Schmerber v. California, 384 U.S. 757 (1966).

69. Contraception and at least early abortion obviously have much in common. *See* A. STONE, *supra* note 24.

70. The *Roe* opinion docs not rely on the obvious contraception-abortion comparison and indeed gives no sign that it finds *Griswold* stronger precedent than a number of other cases. *See* note 81 infra. In fact, it seems to go out of its way to characterize *Griswold* and *Eisenstadt v. Baird,* 405 U.S. 438 (1972), as cases concerned with the privacy of the bedroom. *See* note 81 *infra.* It is true that in *Eisenstadt* the Court at one point characterized *Griswold* as protecting the "decision whether to bear and beget a child," 405 U.S. at 453, but it also, mysteriously in light of that characterization, pointedly refused to decide whether the earlier case extended beyond use, to the distribution of contraceptives. *Id.* at 452–53. Nor is there any possibility the refusal to extend Griswold in this way was ill-considered; such an extension would have obviated the Eisenstadt Court's obviously strained performance respecting the Equal Protection Clause.

71. Admittedly the *Griswold* opinion is vague and open ended, but the language quoted in the text at note 74 *infra* seems plainly inconsistent with the view that it is a case not about likely invasions of the privacy of the bedroom but rather directly enshrining a right to contraception.

72. *See* Eisenstadt v. Baird, 405 U.S. 438, 443 (1972). *Cf.* 410 U.S. at 159–60; note 81 *infra.*

governmental prying into the privacy of the home.[73] And this, indeed, is the theory on which the Court appeared rather explicitly to settle:

> The present case, then, concerns a relationship lying within the zone of privacy created by several fundamental constitutional guarantees. And it concerns a law which, in forbidding the *use* of contraceptives rather than regulating their manufacture or sale, seeks to achieve its goals by means having a maximum destructive impact upon that relationship. Such a law cannot stand in light of the familiar principle, so often applied by this Court, that "a governmental purpose to control or prevent activities constitutionally subject to state regulation may not be achieved by means which sweep unnecessarily broadly and thereby invade the area of protected freedoms." *NAACP v. Alabama*, 377 U.S. 288, 307. Would we allow the police to search the sacred precincts of marital bedrooms for telltale signs of the use of contraceptives? The very idea is repulsive to the notions of privacy surrounding the marriage relationship.[74]

Thus even assuming (as the Court surely seemed to) that a state can constitutionally seek to minimize or eliminate the circulation and use of contraceptives, Connecticut had acted unconstitutionally by selecting a means, that is a direct ban on use, that would generate intolerably intrusive modes of data-gathering.[75] No such rationalization is attempted by the Court in *Roe*—and understandably not, for whatever else may be involved, it is not a case about governmental snooping.[76]

The Court reports that some amici curiae argued for an unlimited right to do as one wishes with one's body. This theory holds, for me at any rate, much appeal. However, there would have been serious problems with its invocation in this case. In the first place, more than the mother's own body

---

73. Stanley v. Georgia, 394 U.S. 557 (1969), cited by the Court in *Roe*, might also be rationalized on such a theory, though it reads more like a "pure" First Amendment case concerned with governmental attempts at thought control.

74. 381 U.S. at 485–86 (emphasis in original).

75. *See also* Poe v. Ullman, 367 U.S. 497, 548–49, 553–54 (1961) (Harlan, J., dissenting). That the Court in *Griswold* saw fit to quote *Boyd v. United States*, 116 U.S. 616, 630 (1886), is also significant. *See* 381 U.S. at 484–85. *See also* United States v. Grunewald, 233 F.2d 556, 581–82 (2d Cir. 1956) (Frank, J., dissenting). The theory suggested in Poe v. Ullman, 367 U.S. at 551–52 (Harlan, J., dissenting), extending heightened protection to activities (though it turns out to be *some* activities, note 33 *supra*) customarily performed in the home, is also inapplicable to *Roe*.

76. Of course, in individual cases the government might seek to enforce legislation restricting abortion, as indeed it might seek to enforce any law, in ways that violate the Fourth Amendment or otherwise intrude upon the general privacy interest the Bill of Rights suggests. The Court does not suggest, however, that the laws at issue in *Roe* are in any sense unusually calculated to generate such intrusions.

is involved in a decision to have an abortion; a fetus may not be a "person in the whole sense," but it is certainly not nothing.[77] Second, it is difficult to find a basis for thinking that the theory was meant to be given constitutional sanction: Surely it is no part of the "privacy" interest the Bill of Rights suggests.[78]

> [I]t is not clear to us that the claim . . . that one has an unlimited right to do with one's body as one pleases bears a close relationship to the right of privacy. . . .[79]

Unfortunately, having thus rejected the amici's attempt to define the bounds of the general constitutional right of which the right to an abortion is a part,[80] on the theory that the general right described has little to do with privacy, the Court provides neither an alternative definition[81] nor

---

77. *See* discussion *supra.*

78. *See* discussion *supra.*

79. 410 U.S. at 153–54.

80. The Court's rejection of the "non-paternalism" argument is of course underlined by the health regulations it is prepared to allow during the second trimester, before the interest in protecting the fetus is cognizable.

81. The Court does assert that only personal rights that can be deemed "fundamental" or "implicit in the concept of ordered liberty," Palko v. Connecticut, 302 U.S. 319, 325 (1937), are included in this guarantee of personal privacy. They also make it clear that the right has some extension to activities relating to marriage, Loving v. Virginia, 388 U.S. 1, 12 (1967), procreation, Skinner v. Oklahoma, 316 U.S. 535, 541–42 (1942), contraception, Eisenstadt v. Baird, 105 U.S. 438, 453–54 (1972); *id.* at 460, 463–65 (White, J., concurring), family relationships, Prince v. Massachusetts, 321 U.S. 158, 166 (1944), and child rearing and education, Pierce v. Society of Sisters, 268 U.S. 510, 535 (1925), Meyer v. Nebraska, [262 U.S. 390, 399 (1923)]. 410 U.S. at 152–56.

The *Palko* test was stated and has heretofore been taken as a definition (of questionable contemporary vitality) of due process generally, not of privacy. *Loving* was a case involving explicit racial discrimination and therefore decidable (and decided) by a rather straightforward application of the Equal Protection Clause. *See* Ely, *supra* note 30, at 1230. And while the *Loving* Court did, inexplicably, append a reference to due process, it did not mention privacy. *Skinner* invalidated the Oklahoma criminal sterilization act's distinction between larcenists and embezzlers. Although it too did not allude to privacy, it did suggest it was applying a higher equal protection standard than usual. Why it did so is unclear. "Faced with the possibility of a finding of cruel and unusual punishment and the virtual certainty of invalidation under the clause proscribing ex post facto laws, the stale declined to argue the case on the theory that the . . . Act was a penal statute, and therefore tried to justify the distinction in 'regulatory' terms." Ely, *supra* note 30, at 1235 n.101. That being so, the state was unable to come up with even a plausible justification for the distinction. *Eisenstadt* was a case applying "traditional" equal protection standards, albeit in a less than satisfactory way. *See* Note, *Legislative Purpose, Rationality, and Equal Protection,* 82 YALE L.J. 123 (1972).

The passage cited by the Court in Roe reiterated *Griswold's* conclusion that privacy interests are threatened by a ban on the use of contraceptives, but declined to decide whether its rationale should he extended to restrictions on distribution. *Prince* upheld the application

an account of why *it* thinks privacy is involved. It simply announces that the right to privacy "is broad enough to encompass a woman's decision whether or not to terminate her pregnancy." Apparently this conclusion is thought to derive from the passage that immediately follows it:

> The detriment that the State would impose upon the pregnant woman by denying this choice altogether is apparent. Specific and direct harm medically diagnosable even in early pregnancy may be involved. Maternity, or additional offspring, may force upon the woman a distressful life and future. Psychological harm may be imminent. Mental and physical health may be taxed by childcare. There is also the distress, for all concerned, associated with the unwanted child, and there is the problem of bringing a child into a family already unable, psychologically and otherwise, to care for it. In other cases, as in this one, the additional difficulties and continuing stigma of unwed motherhood may be involved.[82]

All of this is true and ought to be taken very seriously. But it has nothing to do with privacy in the Bill of Rights sense or any other the Constitution suggests.[83] I suppose there is nothing to prevent one from using the word "privacy" to mean the freedom to live one's life without governmental

---

of a child labor law to Jehovah's Witness children distributing religious literature. It did, however, reiterate the conclusion of *Pierce* and *Meyer* that family relationships arc entitled to special protection. Those two cases are products of "the *Lochner* era." The vitality of the theory on which they rested has been questioned, Epperson v. Arkansas, 393 U.S. 97, 105–06 (1968), and the Court has attempted to recast them as First Amendment cases. Griswold v. Connecticut, 381 U.S. 479, 482 (1965); *cf.* Poe v. Ullman, 367 U.S. 497, 533–34 (1961) (Harlan, J., dissenting). Even reading the cases cited "for all that they are worth," it is difficult to isolate the "privacy" factor (or any other factor that seems constitutionally relevant) that unites them with each other and with *Roe.* So the Court seems to admit by indicating that privacy has "some extension" to the activities involved, and so it seems later to grant even more explicitly.

> The pregnant woman cannot be isolated in her privacy. She carries an embryo and, later, a fetus. . . . The situation therefore is inherently different from marital intimacy, or bedroom possession of obscene material, or marriage, or procreation, or education, with which *Eisenstadt, Griswold, Stanley, Loving, Skinner, Pierce,* and *Meyer* were respectively concerned.

410 U.S. at 159.

82. *Id.* at 153–54. *See also id.* at 209 (Douglas, J., concurring).

83. It might be noted that most of the factors enumerated also apply to the inconvenience of having an unwanted two-year-old, or a senile parent, around. Would the Court find the constitutional right of privacy invaded in those situations too? I find it hard to believe it would; even if it did, of course, it would not find a constitutional right to "terminate" the annoyance—presumably because "real" persons are now involved. *But cf.* note 50 *supra* and accompanying text. But what about ways of removing the annoyance that do not involve "termination"? Can they really be matters of constitutional entitlement?

interference. But the Court obviously does not so use the term.[84] Nor could it, for such a right is at stake in *every* case. Our life styles are constantly limited, often seriously, by governmental regulation; and while many of us would prefer less direction, granting that desire the status of a preferred constitutional right would yield a system of "government" virtually unrecognizable to us and only slightly more recognizable to our forefathers.[85] The Court's observations concerning the serious, life-shaping costs of having a child prove what might to the thoughtless have seemed unprovable: That even though a human life, or a potential human life, hangs in the balance, the moral dilemma abortion poses is so difficult as to be heartbreaking. What they fail to do is even begin to resolve that dilemma so far as our governmental system is concerned by associating either side of the balance with a value inferable from the Constitution.

But perhaps the inquiry should not end even there. In his famous *Carolene Products* footnote, Justice Stone suggested that the interests to which the Court can responsibly give extraordinary constitutional protection include not only those expressed in the Constitution but also those that are unlikely to receive adequate consideration in the political process, specifically the interests of "discrete and insular minorities" unable to form effective political alliances.[86] There can be little doubt that such considerations have influenced the direction, if only occasionally the rhetoric, of the recent Courts. My repeated efforts to convince my students that sex should be treated as a "suspect classification" have convinced me it is no easy matter to state such considerations in a "principled" way. But passing that problem, *Roe* is not an appropriate case for their invocation.

Compared with men, very few women sit in our legislatures, a fact I believe should bear some relevance—even without an Equal Rights Amendment—to the appropriate standard of review for legislation that favors men over women.[87] But *no* fetuses sit in our legislatures. Of course they have

---

84. *But cf.* 410 U.S. at 209 (Douglas, J., concurring).

85. *Cf.* Katz v. United States, 389 U.S. 347, 350–51 (1967).

86. United Slates v. Carolene Products Co., 304 U.S. 144, 152 n.4 (1938).

87. This is not the place for a full treatment of the subject, but the general idea is this: Classifications by sex, like classifications by race, differ from the usual classification—to which the traditional "reasonable generalization" standard is properly applied—in that they rest on "we-they" generalizations as opposed to a "they-they" generalization. Take a familiar example of the usual approach, *Williamson v. Lee Optical Co.*, 348 U.S. 483 (1955). Of course, few legislators are opticians. But few are optometrists either. Thus while a decision to distinguish opticians from optometrists will incorporate a stereotypical comparison of two classes of people, it is a comparison of two "they" stereotypes, viz. "They [opticians] are generally inferior to or not so well qualified as they [optometrists] are in the following respect(s),

their champions, but so have women. The two interests have clashed repeatedly in the political arena, and had continued to do so up to the date of the opinion, generating quite a wide variety of accommodations.[88] By the Court's lights virtually all of the legislative accommodations had unduly favored fetuses; by its definition of victory, women had lost. Yet in every legislative balance one of the competing interests loses to some extent; indeed usually, as here, they both do. On some occasions the Constitution

---

which we find sufficient to justify the classification: . . ." However, legislators traditionally have not only not been black (or female); they have been white (and male). A decision to distinguish blacks from whites (or women from men) will therefore have its roots in a comparison between a "we" stereotype and a "they" stereotype, viz. "They [blacks or women] are generally inferior to or not so well qualified as we [whites or men] are in the following respect(s), which we find sufficient to justify the classification. . . ."

The choice between classifying on the basis of a comparative generalization and attempting to come up with a more discriminating formula always involves balancing the increase in fairness which greater individualization will produce against the added costs it will entail. It is no startling psychological insight, however, that most of us are delighted to hear and prone to accept comparative characterizations of groups that suggest that the groups to which we belong are in some way superior to others. (I would be inclined to exclude most situations where the "we's" used to be "they's," *cf.* Ferguson v. Skrupa, 372 U.S. 726 (1963), and would therefore agree that the unchangeability of the distinguishing characteristic is indeed relevant, though it is only part of the story.) The danger is therefore greater in we-they situations that we will overestimate the validity of the proposed stereotypical classification by seizing upon the positive myths about our own class and the negative myths about theirs—or indeed the realities respecting some or most members of the two classes—and too readily assuming that virtually the entire membership of the two classes fit the stereotypes and therefore that not many of "them" will be unfairly deprived, nor many of "us" unfairly benefitted, by the proposed classification. In short, I trust your generalizations about the differences between my gang and Wilfred's more than I do your generalizations about the differences between my gang and yours.

Of course, most judges, like most legislators, are white males, and there is no particular reason to suppose they are any more immune to the conscious and unconscious temptations that inhere in we-they generalizations. Obviously the factors mentioned can distort the evaluation of a classification fully as much as they can distort its formation. But all this is only to suggest that the Court has chosen the right course in reviewing classifications it has decided are suspicious—a course not of restriking or second-guessing the legislative cost-benefit balance but rather of demanding a congruence between the classification and its goal as perfect as practicable. When in a given situation you can't be trusted to generalize and I can't be trusted to generalize, the answer is not to generalize—so long as a bearable alternative exists. And here, the Court has recognized, one does—the alternative of forcing the system to absorb the additional cost that case by case determinations of qualification will entail. Legislatures incur this cost voluntarily in a great many situations, and courts have on other occasions forced them to do so where constitutionally protected interests will be threatened by an imperfectly fitting classification. The unusual dangers of distortion that inhere in a we-they process of comparative generalization, the Court seems to have been telling us in the racial classification cases, also demand that we bear the increased cost of individual justice.

88. *See* 410 U.S. at 116–20, 139–47, 181–83, 201–07.

throws its weight on the side of one of them, indicating the balance must be restruck. And on others—and this is Justice Stone's suggestion—it is at least arguable that, constitutional directive or not, the Court should throw *its* weight on the side of a minority demanding in court more than it was able to achieve politically. But even assuming this suggestion can be given principled content, it was clearly intended and should be reserved for those interests which, *as compared with the interests to which they have been subordinated,* constitute minorities unusually incapable of protecting themselves.[89] Compared with men, women may constitute such a "minority"; compared with the unborn, they do not.[90] I'm not sure I'd know a discrete and insular minority if I saw one, but confronted with a multiple choice question requiring me to designate (a) women or (b) fetuses as one, I'd expect no credit for the former answer.[91]

---

89. If the mere fact that the classification in issue disadvantages a minority whose viewpoint was not appreciated by a majority of the legislature that enacted it were sufficient to render it suspect, *all* classifications would be suspect.

90. Even if the case could be made that abortion is an issue that pits the interests of men against those of women, that alone would not bring it within a theory that renders suspect classifications based on generalizations about the characteristics of men and women. And even if there were some way to expand the theory (and I confess I cannot see what judicial remedy would be appropriate were the theory so expanded, *but see* note 87 *supra*) to cover all "interests of men versus interests of women" situations, it will take some proving to establish that this is one:

> Decisions in society are made by those who have power and not by those who have rights. Husbands and boyfriends may in the end wield the power and make the abortion decision. Many women may be forced to have abortions not because it is their right, but because they are forced by egocentric men to submit to this procedure to avoid an unwanted inconvenience to men.

A. STONE, *supra* note 24.

91. It might be suggested that legislation restricting abortion had been kept on the books by the efforts of an intense minority and did not represent the will of most legislative majorities. Though I am aware of no basis for inferring this is any truer here than it is with respect to other sorts of legislation, *see also* note 87 *supra*, it is the sort of claim that is hard to disprove. (The phenomenon described *infra*, one of relief that the issue has been taken out of the political arena, is a very different matter.) In any event it is not the Court's job to repeal such legislation. In the first place there is nothing unusual, and I was not aware there was anything wrong, with an intense minority's compromising on issues about which it feels less strongly in order to garner support on those it cares most about. Moreover, precisely because the claims involved are difficult to evaluate, I would not want to entrust to the judiciary authority to guess about them— certainly not under the guise of enforcing the Constitution. Leaving aside the arguable case of a law that has been neither legislatively considered *nor enforced* for decades, *see* A. BICKEL, THE LEAST DANGEROUS BRANCH 143–56 (1962), the Court should rest its declaration of unconstitutionality, if any, on more than a guess about how widespread and intense the support for the law "really" is.

Of course, a woman's freedom to choose an abortion is part of the "liberty" the Fourteenth Amendment says shall not be denied without due process of law, as indeed is anyone's freedom to do what he wants. But "due process" generally guarantees only that the inhibition be procedurally fair and that it have some "rational" connection—though plausible is probably a better word[92]— with a permissible governmental goal.[93] What is unusual about *Roe* is that the liberty involved is accorded a far more stringent protection, so stringent that a desire to preserve the fetus's existence is unable to overcome it—a protection more stringent, I think it fair to say, than that the present Court accords the freedom of the press explicitly guaranteed by the First Amendment.[94] What is frightening about *Roe* is that this super-protected right is not inferable from the language of the Constitution, the framers' thinking respecting the specific problem in issue, any general value derivable from the provisions they included,[95] or the nation's governmental structure. Nor is it explainable in terms of the unusual political impotence of the group judicially protected vis a-vis the interest that legislatively prevailed over it.[96] And that, I believe—the predictable[97] early reaction to *Roe* notwithstanding ("more of the same Warren-type activism"[98])—is a charge that can responsibly be leveled at no other decision of the past

---

92. The claimed connection is often empirical, causal or normative. About all that does *not* seem to become involved is formal logic. *See* discussion *infra;* Ely, *supra* note 30, at 1237–49.

93. Even this statement of the demands of "substantive due process" is too strong for many Justices and commentators, who deny that any such doctrine should exist.

94. *See* Branzburg v. Hayes, 408 U.S. 665 (1972).

95. Necessarily, a claim of this sort can never be established beyond doubt; one can only proceed by examining the claims of those values he thinks, or others have suggested, are traceable to the Constitution. It is always possible, however, that someone will develop a general theory of entitlements that encompasses a given case and plausibly demonstrate its constitutional connections. It is also possible that had the constitutional right to an abortion been developed as constitutional doctrines usually are—that is incrementally, rather than by the quantum jump of *Roe*—the connection of the first step with the Constitution, and that of each succeeding step with its predecessor, would have seemed more plausible. I cannot bring myself to believe, however, that any amount of gradualism could serve to make anything approaching the entire inference convincing.

96. The thing about permitting disparity among slate laws regulating abortion that I find most troubling is not mentioned by the Court, and that is that some people can afford the fare to a neighboring state and others cannot. Of course, this situation prevails with respect to divorce and a host of other sorts of laws as well. I wish someone could develop a theory that would enable the Court to take account of this concern without implying a complete obliteration of the federal system that is so obviously at the heart of the Constitution's plan. I have not been able to do so. *See* note 89 *supra*.

97. *See* discussion *infra.*

98. *See, e.g., Abortion,* The New Republic, Feb. 10, 1973, at 9; A. Stone, *supra* note 24.

twenty years.[99] At times the inferences the Court has drawn from the values

---

99. Of course one can disagree with the lengths to which the inferences have been taken; my point is that the prior decisions, including those that have drawn the most fire, at least started from a value singled out by, or fairly inferable from, the Constitution as entitled to special protection. Whatever one may think of the code of conduct laid down in *Miranda v. Arizona*, 384 U.S. 436 (1966), the Constitution does talk about the right to counsel and the privilege against self-incrimination. Whatever one may think of the strictness of the scrutiny exercised in *Furman v. Georgia*, 408 U.S. 238 (1972), the Eighth Amendment surely does indicate in a general way that punishments are to be scrutinized for erratic imposition ("unusual") and severity disproportionate to any good they can be expected to accomplish ("cruel").

Note that the claim in the text has to do with the capacity of the earlier decisions to be rationalized in terms of some value highlighted by the Constitution, not with the skill with which they were in fact rendered. It is now pretty generally recognized, for example, that the various "wealth discrimination" cases could better have been defended in terms of the constitutional attention paid explicitly or implicitly to the "goods" whose distribution was in issue—the right to vote and the assurance of fair judicial procedures. *See, e.g.*, Michelman, *Foreword: On Protecting the Poor Through the Fourteenth Amendment*, 83 HARV. L. REV. 7 (1969). *Reynolds v. Sims*, 377 U.S. 533 (1964), is a badly articulated opinion. Its only response to the argument made by Justice Stewart—that since an equal protection claim was involved, a rational defense of a disparity among the "weights" of votes should suffice—was simply to announce that the goals Justice Stewart had in mind were off limits. *See* Ely, *supra* note 30, at 1226–27. But even Justice Stewart could not take the equal protection mold too seriously, for he added he would not approve a plan that permitted "the systematic frustration of the will of a majority of the electorate of the State." Lucas v. Colorado Gen. Assembly, 377 U.S. 713, 753–54 (1964) (footnote omitted). Such a plan, however, could be quite "rational" in terms of the sort of goals Justice Stewart had in mind, goals that in other contexts would count as legitimate. Obviously Justice Stewart was moved to some extent by the notion that a system whereby a minority could perpetuate its control of the government was out of accord with the system of government envisioned by the framers. *See also* Kramer v. Union Free School District No. 15, 395 U.S. 621, 628 (1969) (Warren, C.J., for the Court). This was what moved the Court too, though much further. And though the Court did not give the reason, there is one: a fear that by attempting to apply Justice Stewart's "in between" standard it would become embroiled in unseemly "political" inquiries into the power alignments prevalent in the various states. *See* Deutsch, *Neutrality, Legitimacy, and the Supreme Court: Some Intersections Between Law and Political Science*, 20 STAN. L. REV. 169, 246–47 (1968); *cf.* note 91 *supra; but cf.* Mahan v. Howell, 410 U.S. 315 (1973). Though the point is surely debatable, the impulse is understandable, and the fight in *Reynolds*, like that in *Miranda*, turns out to be not so much over the underlying values as over the need for a "clean" prophylactic rule that will keep the courts out of messy factual disputes.

In his concurrence in *Roe*, Justice Stewart lists ten cases to prove that "the Due Process Clause of the Fourteenth Amendment covers more than those freedoms explicitly named in the Bill of Rights." 410 U.S. at 168. His point is obviously that the freedoms involved were given protection above and beyond the ordinary demand for a "rational" defense and therefore *Roe* is just more of the same. It is not. Schware v. Bd. of Bar Examiners, 353 U.S. 232 (1957); Aptheker v. Secretary of State, 378 U.S. 500 (1964); and Kent v. Dulles, 357 U.S. 116 (1958), are all obviously rationalizable as First Amendment cases and indeed have since been so rationalized. Concerning *Schware, see* Griswold v. Connecticut, 381 U.S. 479, 483 (1965); *cf.* United States v. Brown, 381 U.S. 437, 456 (1965). As to *Aptheker* and *Kent, see*

the Constitution marks for special protection have been controversial, even shaky, but never before has its sense of an obligation to draw one been so obviously lacking.

IV

Not in the last thirty-five years at any rate. For, as the received learning has it, this sort of thing did happen before, repeatedly. From its 1905 decision in *Lochner v. New York*[100] into the 1930's the Court, frequently though not always under the rubric of "liberty of contract," employed the Due Process Clauses of the Fourteenth and Fifth Amendments to invalidate a good deal of legislation. According to the dissenters at the time and virtually all the commentators since, the Court had simply manufactured a constitutional right out of whole cloth and used it to superimpose its own view of wise social policy on those of the legislatures. So indeed the Court itself came to see the matter, and its reaction was complete:

> There was a time when the Due Process Clause was used by this Court to strike down laws which were thought unreasonable, that is, unwise or incompatible with some particular economic or social philosophy. In this manner the Due Process Clause was used, for example, to nullify laws prescribing maximum hours for work in bakeries, *Lochner v. New York*, 198 U.S. 45 (1905), outlawing "yellow dog" contracts, *Coppage v. Kansas*, 236 U.S. 1 (1915), setting minimum wages for women, *Adkins v. Children's Hospital*, 261 U.S. 525 (1923), and fixing the weight of loaves of bread, *Jay Burns Baking Co. v. Bryan*, 264 U.S. 504 (1924). This intrusion by the judiciary into the realm of legislative value judgments was strongly objected to at the time. . . . Mr. Justice Holmes said, "I think the proper course is to recognize that a state legislature can do whatever it sees fit to do unless it is restrained by some express prohibition in the Constitution of the United States or of the State, and that Courts should be careful not to extend such prohibitions beyond their obvious meaning by reading into them conceptions of public policy that the particular Court may happen to entertain." . . . The

---

Zemel v. Rusk, 381 U.S. 1, 16 (1965); United States v. Brown, 381 U.S. at 456. Concerning Pierce v. Society of Sisters and Meyer v. Nebraska, *see* note 81 *supra.* As to Shapiro v. Thompson, 394 U.S. 618 (1969), and United States v. Guest, 383 U.S. 745 (1966), *see* discussion *supra.* With respect to Carrington v. Rash, 380 U.S. 89 (1965), *see* the preceding paragraph of this footnote and C. BLACK, *supra* note 58. Concerning Bolling v. Sharpe, 347 U.S. 497 (1954), *see* note 81 *supra; but cf.* H. Linde, *Judges, Critics, and the Realist Tradition*, 82 YALE L.J. 227, 233–35 (1972). And compare Truax v. Raich, 239 U.S. 33 (1915), *with* Graham v. Richardson, 403 U.S. 365 (1971), and note 87 *supra.*

100. 198 U.S. 45 (1905).

doctrine that prevailed in *Lochner, Coppage, Adkins, Burns,* and like cases—
that due process authorizes courts to hold laws unconstitutional when they
believe the legislature has acted unwisely—has long since been discarded.
We have returned to the original constitutional proposition that courts do
not substitute their social and economic beliefs for the judgment of legislative bodies, who are elected to pass laws.[101]

It may be objected that *Lochner et al.* protected the "economic rights"
of businessmen whereas *Roe* protects a "human right." It should be noted,
however, that not all of the *Lochner* series involved economic regulation;[102]
that even those that did resist the "big business" stereotype with which
the commentators tend to associate them; and that in some of them the
employer's "liberty of contract" claim was joined by the employee, who
knew that if he had to be employed on the terms set by the law in question,
he could not be employed at all.[103] This is a predicament that is economic
to be sure, but is not without its "human" dimension. Similarly "human"
seems the predicament of the appellees in the 1970 case of *Dandridge v.
Williams,*[104] who challenged the Maryland Welfare Department's practice
of limiting AFDC grants to $250 regardless of family size or need. Yet in
language that remains among its favored points of reference,[105] the Court,
speaking through Justice Stewart,[106] dismissed the complaint as "social and
economic" and therefore essentially Lochneresque.

> [W]e deal with state regulation in the social and economic field, not affect-
> ing freedoms guaranteed by the Bill of Rights. . . . For this Court to approve
> the invalidation of state economic or social regulation as "overreaching"
> would be far too reminiscent of an era when the Court thought the Four-
> teenth Amendment gave it power to strike down state laws "because they
> may be unwise, improvident, or out of harmony with a particular school of
> thought." . . . That era long ago passed into history. . . .
>   To be sure, the cases cited . . . have in the main involved state regulation
> of business or industry. The administration of public welfare assistance, by
> contrast, involves the most basic economic needs of impoverished human

---

101. Ferguson v. Skrupa, 372 U.S. 726, 729–30 (1963) (footnotes omitted). *See also* Lin-
coln Federal Labor Union v. Northwestern Iron & Metal Co., 335 U.S. 525, 533–37 (1949).

102. *See* Pierce v. Society of Sisters, 268 U.S. 510 (1925); Meyer v. Nebraska, 262 U.S. 390
(1923).

103. *E.g.,* Adkins v. Children's Hospital, 261 U.S. 525, 542–43 (1923). *See also* Adair v.
United States, 208 U.S. 161, 172–73 (1908). *Cf.* Hammer v. Dagenhart, 247 U.S. 251 (1918).

104. 397 U.S. 471 (1970).

105. *See, e.g.,* San Antonio Independent School Dist. v. Rodriguez, 411 U.S. 1 (1973) ; Ort-
wein v. Schwab, 410 U.S. 656 (1973); United States v. Kras, 409 U.S. 434 (1973).

106. *But cf.* note 111 *infra.*

beings. We recognize the dramatically real factual difference between the cited cases and this one, but we can find no basis for applying a different constitutional standard. . . . [I]t is a standard . . . that is true to the principle that the Fourteenth Amendment gives the federal courts no power to impose upon the States their views of wise economic or social policy.[107]

It may be, however—at least it is not the sort of claim one can disprove—that the "right to an abortion," or noneconomic rights generally, accord more closely with "this generation's idealization of America"[108] than the "rights" asserted in either *Lochner* or *Dandridge*. But that attitude, of course, is *precisely* the point of the *Lochner* philosophy, which would grant unusual protection to those "rights" that somehow *seem* most pressing, regardless of whether the Constitution suggests any special solicitude for them. The Constitution has little to say about contract,[109] less about abortion, and those who would speculate about which the framers would have been more likely to protect may not be pleased with the answer. The Court continues to disavow the philosophy of *Lochner*.[110] Yet as Justice Stewart's concurrence admits, it is impossible candidly to regard *Roe* as the product of anything else.[111]

That alone should be enough to damn it. Criticism of the *Lochner* philosophy has been virtually universal and will not be rehearsed here. I would, however, like to suggest briefly that although *Lochner* and *Roe* are twins to be sure, they are not identical. While I would hesitate to argue that one is more defensible than the other in terms of judicial style, there *are*

---

107. 397 U.S. at 484–86.

108. Karst & Horowitz, *Reitman v. Mulkey: A Telophase of Substantive Equal Protection*, 1967 SUP. CT. REV. 39, 57–58; *cf.* 2 L. POLLAK, THE CONSTITUTION AND THE SUPREME COURT: A DOCUMENTARY HISTORY 266–67 (1966).

109. *But see* U.S. CONST. art. I, § 10; Calder v. Bull, 3 U.S. (3 Dall.) 386 (1798).

110. *See* note 105 *supra*.

111. 410 U.S. at 167–68. The only "*Lochner* era" cases Justice Stewart cites are *Meyer* and *Pierce*. It therefore may be he intends to pursue some sort of "economic-noneconomic" line in selecting rights entitled to special protection. *But see* text at note 107 *supra*. The general philosophy of constitutional adjudication, however, is the same. *See* text at notes 108–09 *supra*. Justice Stewart rather clearly intends his Roe opinion as a repudiation of his Griswold dissent, and not simply as an acquiescence in what the Court did in the earlier case. *See* 410 U.S. at 169–70.

Having established to his present satisfaction that the Due Process Clause extends unusual substantive protection to interests the Constitution nowhere marks as special, *but see* note 99 *supra*, he provides no further assistance respecting the difficult questions before the Court, but rather defers to the Court's "thorough demonstration" that the interests in protecting the mother and preserving the fetus cannot support the legislation involved. *But see* discussion *supra*.

differences in that regard that suggest *Roe* may turn out to be the more dangerous precedent.

All the "superimposition of the Court's own value choices" talk is, of course, the characterization of others and not the language of *Lochner* or its progeny. Indeed, those cases did not argue that "liberty of contract" was a preferred constitutional freedom, but rather represented it as merely one among the numerous aspects of "liberty" the Fourteenth Amendment protects, therefore requiring of its inhibitors a "rational" defense.

> In our opinion that section . . . is an invasion of the personal liberty, as well as of the right of property, guaranteed by that Amendment. Such liberty and right embraces the right to make contracts for the purchase of the labor of others and equally the right to make contracts for the sale of one's own labor; each right, however, being subject to the fundamental condition that no contract, whatever its subject matter, can be sustained which the law, upon reasonable grounds, forbids as inconsistent with the public interests or as hurtful to the public order or as detrimental to the common good.[112]
>
> Undoubtedly, the police power of the State may be exerted to protect purchasers from imposition by sale of short weight loaves. . . . Constitutional protection having been invoked, it is the duty of the court to determine whether the challenged provision has reasonable relation to the protection of purchasers of bread against fraud by short weights and really tends to accomplish the purpose for which it was enacted.[113]

Thus the test *Lochner* and its progeny purported to apply is that which would theoretically control the same questions today: whether a plausible argument can be made that the legislative action furthers some permissible governmental goal.[114] The trouble, of course, is they misapplied it. *Roe*, on the other hand, is quite explicit that the right to an abortion is a "fundamental" one, requiring not merely a "rational" defense for its inhibition but rather a "compelling" one.

A second difference between *Lochner et al.* and *Roe* has to do with the nature of the legislative judgments being second-guessed. In the main, the "refutations" tendered by the *Lochner* series were of two sorts. The first took the form of declarations that the goals in terms of which the legislatures'

---

112. Adair v. United States, 208 U.S. 161, 172 (1908). *See also id.* at 174.

113. Jay Burns Baking Co. v. Bryan, 264 U.S. 504, 513 (1924). *See also id.* at 517; Meyer v. Nebraska, 262 U.S. 390, 399–400, 403 (1923); Adkins v. Children's Hospital, 261 U.S. 525, 529 (1923); Coppage v. Kansas, 236 U.S. I, 14 (1915); Lochner v. New York, 198 U.S. 45, 53, 54, 56, 57 (1905); *id.* at 68 (Harlan, J., dissenting).

114. *But cf.* note 93 *supra*.

actions were defended were impermissible. Thus, for example, the equalization of unequal bargaining power and the strengthening of the labor movement are simply ends the legislature had no business pursuing, and consequently its actions cannot thereby be justified.[115]

The second form of "refutation" took the form not of denying the legitimacy of the goal relied on but rather of denying the plausibility of the legislature's empirical judgment that its action would *promote* that goal.

> In our judgment it is not possible in fact to discover the connection between the number of hours a baker may work in the bakery and the healthful quality of the bread made by the workman.[116]
>
> There is no evidence in support of the thought that purchasers have been or are likely to be induced to take a nine and a half or a ten ounce loaf for a pound (16 ounce) loaf, or an eighteen and a half or a 19 ounce loaf for a pound and a half (24 ounce) loaf; and it is contrary to common experience and unreasonable to assume that there could be any danger of such deception.[117]

The *Roe* opinion's "refutation" of the legislative judgment that anti-abortion statutes can be justified in terms of the protection of the fetus takes neither of these forms. The Court grants that protecting the fetus is an "important and legitimate" governmental goal,[118] and of course it does not deny that restricting abortion promotes it.[119] What it does, instead,

---

115. Coppage v. Kansas, 236 U.S. 1, 16–17, 17–18 (1915). *See also* Meyer v. Nebraska, 262 U.S. 390, 403 (1923); Adair v. United States, 208 U.S. 161, 174–75 (1908); Lochner v. New York, 198 U.S. 45, 57–58 (1905).

116. Lochner v. New York, 198 U.S. 45, 62 (1905). *See also id.* at 57, 58, 59, 64.

117. Jay Burns Baking Co. v. Bryan, 264 U.S. 504, 517 (1924). *See also* Coppage v. Kansas, 236 U.S. 1, 15–16 (1915).

118. Note 10 *supra.*

119. The *Lochner* approach to factual claims is, however, suggested by the Court's ready acceptance—by way of nullifying the state's health interest during the first trimester—of the data adduced by appellants and certain amici to the effect that abortions per formed during the first trimester are safer than childbirth. 410 U.S. 149. This is not in fact agreed to by all doctors—the data are of course severely limited—and the Court's view of the matter is plainly not the only one that is "rational" under the usual standards. *See* San Antonio Independent School Dist. v. Rodriguez, 411 U.S. 1 (1973); Eisenstadt v. Baird, 405 U.S. 438, 470 (1972) (Burger, C.J. dissenting):

> The actual hazards of introducing a particular foreign substance into the human body arc frequently controverted, and I cannot believe the unanimity of expert opinion is a prerequisite to a State's exercise of its police power, no matter what the subject matter of the regulation. Even assuming no present dispute among medical authorities, we cannot ignore that it has become commonplace for a drug or food additive to be universally regarded as harmless on one day and to

is simply announce that that goal is not important enough to sustain the restriction. There is little doubt that judgments of this sort were involved in *Lochner et al.*,[120] but what the Court *said* in those cases was not that the legislature had incorrectly balanced two legitimate but competing goals, but rather that the goal it had favored was impermissible or the legislation involved did not really promote it.[121]

Perhaps this is merely a rhetorical difference, but it could prove to be important. *Lochner et al.* were thoroughly disreputable decisions, but at least they did us the favor of sowing the seeds of their own destruction. To say that the equalization of bargaining power or the fostering of the labor movement is a goal outside the ambit of a "police power" broad enough to forbid all contracts the state legislature can reasonably regard "as inconsistent with the public interests or as hurtful to the public order or as detrimental to the common good"[122] is to say something that is, in a word, wrong.[123] And it is just as obviously wrong to declare, for example, that restrictions on long working hours cannot reasonably be said to promote health and safety.[124]

---

be condemned as perilous the next. It is inappropriate for this Court to overrule a legislative classification by relying on the present consensus among leading authorities. The commands of the Constitution cannot fluctuate with the shifting tides of scientific opinion.

I suppose the Court's defense of its unusual reaction to the scientific data would be that the case is unusual, in that it involves a "fundamental" interest. It should be noted, however, that even a sure sense that abortion during the first trimester is safer than childbirth would serve only to blunt a state's claim that it is, for reasons relating to maternal health, entitled to proscribe abortion; it would not support the inference the Court draws, that regulations designed to make the abortion procedure safer during the first trimester are impermissible. *See* 410 U.S at 163–64.

120. *Cf.* Meyer v. Nebraska, 262 U.S. 390 (1923); Adkins v. Children's Hospital, 261 U.S. 525, 546 (1923); Lochner v. New York, 198 U.S. 45, 53–54, 57 (1905).

121. And even those cases that interlaced such claims with indications of a balancing test, *see* note 120 *supra*, sowed the seeds of their own reversal. *See* text at notes 122–23 *infra*. A claim that X weighs more than Y will have little persuasive or precedential value if it is bracketed with an indefensible assertion that Y is nothing.

122. Adair v. United States, 208 U.S. 161, 172 (1908). *See also, e.g.,* Lochner v. New York, 198 U.S. 45, 54 (1905).

123. Wrong, that is, if one assigns to the words anything resembling their ordinary meanings. *See, e.g.,* Daniel v. Family Insurance Co., 336 U.S. 220, 224 (1949). One can of course argue that states should also have governments of few and defined powers, that they should not be vested with broad authority to go after whatever they regard as evils. But the Federal Constitution imposes no such restraint, and according to the test accepted even at the time of Lochner such authority, at least as a matter of federal constitutional law, does exist.

124. It is possible, of course, that I am here time-bound, and that the wrongness of Lochner et al., is obvious only because a half century of commentary has made it so. While I cannot rebut this, I am inclined to doubt it. In those decisions the Court stated the applicable

Roe's "refutation" of the legislative judgment, on the other, is *not* obviously wrong, for the substitution of one nonrational judgment for another concerning the relative importance of a mother's opportunity to live the life she has planned and a fetus's opportunity to live at all, can be labeled neither wrong nor right. The problem with *Roe* is not so much that it bungles the question it sets itself,[125] but rather that it sets itself a question the Constitution has not made the Court's business. It *looks* different from *Lochner*—it has the shape if not the substance of a judgment that is very much the Court's business, one vindicating an interest the Constitution marks as special—and it is for that reason perhaps more dangerous. Of course in a sense it is more candid than *Lochner.*[126] But the employment of a higher standard of judicial review, no matter how candid the recognition that it is indeed higher, loses some of its admirability when it is accompanied by neither a coherent account of why such a standard is appropriate nor any indication of why it has not been satisfied.

V

I do wish "Wolf!" hadn't been cried so often. When I suggest to my students that *Roe* lacks even colorable support in the constitutional text, history, or any other appropriate source of constitutional doctrine, they tell me they've heard all that before. When I point out they haven't heard it before from *me,* I can't really blame them for smiling.

But at least crying "Wolf!" doesn't influence the wolves; crying "Lochner!" may. Of course the Warren Court was aggressive in enforcing its ideals of liberty and equality. *But by and large, it attempted to defend its decisions in terms of inferences from values the Constitution marks as special.*[127] Its inferences

---

tests in language much the same as would be used today—language the dissents cogently demonstrated could not be reconciled with the results. That views with which one disagrees can be reasonable nonetheless was a concept hardly new to lawyers even in 1900.

125. *But compare* 410 U.S. at 163–64 with Doe v. Bolton, 410 U.S. 179 (1973).

126. With respect to the Equal Protection Clause, by way of contrast, the Court has taken to claiming it is simply applying the traditional rationality standard, whether it is or not. For a more optimistic view of the development, *see* G. Gunther, *Foreword: In Search of Evolving Doctrine on a Changing Court: A Model for a Newer Equal Protection,* 86 Harv. L. Rev. 1 (1972).

127. *See* note 99 *supra.* The "footnote 4" argument suggested in note 87 *supra* responds not so much to any clear constitutional concern with equality for women (but see U.S. Const. amend. XIX) as to the unavoidable obligation to give "principled" content to the facially inscrutable Equal Protection Clause. Virtually everyone agrees that classifications by race were intended to be and should be tested by a higher than usual standard, and that at least some others—though the nature and length of the list are seriously disputed—are sufficiently "racelike" to merit comparable treatment. *See, e.g.,* Graham v. Richardson, 403 U.S.

were often controversial, but just as often our profession's prominent criticism deigned not to address them on their terms and contented itself with assertions that the Court was indulging in sheer acts of will, ramming its personal preferences down the country's throat—that it was, in a word, Lochnering. One possible judicial response to this style of criticism would be to conclude that one might as well be hanged for a sheep as a goat: So long as you're going to be told, no matter what you say, that all you do is Lochner, you might as well Lochner. Another, perhaps more likely in a new appointee, might be to reason that since Lochnering has so long been standard procedure, "just one more" (in a good cause, of course) can hardly matter. Actual reactions, of course, are not likely to be this self-conscious, but the critical style of offhand dismissal may have taken its toll, nonetheless.

Of course the Court has been aware that criticism of much that it has done has been widespread in academic as well as popular circles. But when it looks to the past decade's most prominent academic criticism, it will often find little there to distinguish it from the popular. Disagreements with the chain of inference by which the Court got from the Constitution to its result, if mentioned at all, have tended to be announced in the most conclusory terms, and the impression has often been left that the real quarrel of the Academy, like that of the laity, is with the results the Court has been reaching and perhaps with judicial "activism" in general.[128] Naturally the Court is sensitive to criticism of this sort, but these are issues on which it will, when push comes to shove, trust its own judgment. (And it has no reason not to: Law professors do not agree on what results are "good," and even if they did, there is no reason to assume their judgment is any better on *that* issue than the Court's.) And academic criticism of the sort that might (because it should) have some effect—criticism suggesting misperceptions in the Court's reading of the value structure set forth in the document from which it derives its authority, or unjustifiable inferences it has drawn from that value structure— has seemed for a time somehow out of fashion, the voguish course being simply to dismiss the process by which a disfavored result was reached as Lochnering pure and simple. But if the critics cannot trouble themselves with such details, it is difficult to expect the Court to worry much about them either.

---

365 (1971). The problem thus becomes one of identifying those features of racial classifications that validly compel the deviation from the usual standard, and in turn those classifications that share those features.

128. *See, e.g.,* P. Kurland, *Foreword: Equal in Origin and Equal in Title to the Legislative and Executive Branches of Government,* 78 HARV. L. REV. 143, 144–45, 149, 163, 175 (1964).

This tendency of commentators to substitute snappy dismissal for careful evaluation of the Court's constitutional inferences—and of course it is simply a tendency, never universally shared and hopefully on the wane—may include among its causes simple laziness, boredom and a natural reluctance to get out of step with the high-steppers. But in part it has also reflected a considered rejection of the view of constitutional adjudication from which my remarks have proceeded. There is a powerful body of opinion that would dismiss the call for substantive criticism—and its underlying assumption that some constitutional inferences are responsible while others are not—as naive. For, the theory goes, except as to the most trivial and least controversial questions (such as the length of a Senator's term), the Constitution speaks in the vaguest and most general terms;[129] the most its clauses can provide are "more or less suitable pegs on which judicial policy choices are hung."[130] Thus anyone who suggests the Constitution can provide significant guidance for today's difficult questions either deludes himself or seeks to delude the Court. Essentially all the Court *can* do is honor the value preferences it sees fit, and it should be graded according to the judgment and skill with which it does so.[131]

One version of this view appears to be held by President Nixon. It is true that in announcing the appointment of Justices Powell and Rehnquist, he described a "judicial conservative"—his kind of Justice—as one who does not "twist or bend the Constitution in order to perpetuate his personal political and social views."[132] But the example he then gave bore witness that he was not so "naive" after all.

> As a judicial conservative, I believe some court decisions have gone too far in the past in weakening the peace forces as against the criminal forces in our society. . . . [T]he peace forces must not be denied the legal tools they need to protect the innocent from criminal elements.[133]

---

129. *See, e.g.,* A. Bickel, *supra* note 91, at 84–92; A. BICKEL, THE SUPREME COURT AND THE IDEA OF PROGRESS 177 (1970); W. Mendelson, *On the Meaning of the First Amendment: Absolutes in the Balance,* 50 CAL. L. REV. 821 (1962).

130. H. Linde, *supra* note 99, at 254.

131. The Court will continue to play the role of the omniscient and strive toward omnipotence. And the law reviews will continue to play the game of evaluating the Court's work in light of the fictions of the law, legal reasoning, and legal history rather than deal with the realities of politics and statesmanship. P. Kurland, *supra* note 128, at 175.

132. 7 Weekly Comp. of Presidential Documents 1431 (Oct. 25, 1971).

133. *Id.* at 1432.

That this sort of invitation, to get in there and Lochner for the right goals, can contribute to opinions like *Roe* is obvious. In terms of process, it is just what the President ordered.

The academic version of this general view is considerably more subtle. It agrees that the Court will find little help in the Constitution and therefore has no real choice other than to decide for itself which value preferences to honor, but denies that it should necessarily opt for the preferences favored by the Justices themselves or the President who appointed them. To the extent "progress" is to concern the Justices at all, it should be defined not in terms of what they would like it to be but rather in terms of their best estimate of what over time the American people will make it[134]—that is, they should seek "durable" decisions.[135] This, however, is no easy task, and the goals that receive practically all the critics' attention, and presumably are supposed to receive practically all the Court's, are its own institutional survival and effectiveness.[136]

Whatever the other merits or demerits of this sort of criticism, it plainly is not what it is meant to be—an effective argument for judicial self-restraint. For a Governor Warren or a Senator Black will rightly see no reason to defer to law professors on the probable direction of progress; even less do they need the Academy's advice on what is politically feasible; and they know that despite the Court's history of frequent immersion in hot water,[137] its "institutional position" has been getting stronger for 200 years.

Roe is a case in point. Certainly, many will view it as social progress. (Surely that is the Court's view, and indeed the legislatures had been moving perceptibly, albeit too slowly for many of us, toward relaxing their

---

134. *See generally* A. BICKEL, THE SUPREME COURT AND THE IDEA OF PROGRESS (1970). Professor Bickel's thought is of course much richer than it is here reported. But the catchier aspects of a person's work have a tendency to develop a life of their own and on occasion to function, particularly in the thinking of others and perhaps to an extent even in the author's own, without the background against which they were originally presented. *Cf.* note 140 *infra.*

135. *See* H. Hart, *Foreword: The Time Chart of the Justices,* 73 HARV. L. REV. 84, 99 (1959). *See also* A. Bickel, *supra* note 129, at 99; P. Kurland, *Earl Warren, the "Warren Court," and the Warren Myths,* 67 U. MICH. L. REV. 353, 357 (1968). *Cf.* K. Karst, *Invidious Discrimination: Justice Douglas and the Return of the "Natural-Law—Due-Process" Formula,* 16 U.C.L.A. L. REV. 716, 746–48 (1969); Karst & Horowitz, *supra* note 108, at 79.

136. *E.g.,* A. Bickel, *supra* note 127, at 95; P. Kurland, *Toward a Political Supreme Court,* 32 U. CHI. L. REV. 19, 20, 22 (1969).

137. *See generally* W. MURPHY, CONGRESS AND THE COURT (1962); C. WARREN, THE SUPREME COURT IN UNITED STATES HISTORY (rev. ed. 1932).

anti-abortion legislation.)[138] And it is difficult to see how it will weaken the Court's position. Fears of official disobedience are obviously ground-less when it is a criminal statute that has been invalidated.[139] To the pub-lic the *Roe* decision must look very much like the New York Legislature's recent liberalization of its abortion law.[140] Even in the unlikely event some-one should catch the public's ear long enough to charge that the wrong institution did the repealing, they have heard that "legalism" before without taking to the streets. Nor are the political branches, and this of course is what really counts, likely to take up the cry very strenuously: The sighs of relief as this particular albatross was cut from the legislative and executive necks seemed to me audible. Perhaps I heard wrong—I live in the North-east, indeed not so very far from Hyannis Port. It is even possible that a con-stitutional amendment will emerge, though that too has happened before without serious impairment of the Position of the Institution. But I doubt one will: *Roe v. Wade* seems like a durable decision.

It is, nevertheless, a very bad decision. Not because it will perceptibly weaken the Court—it won't; and not because it conflicts with either my idea of progress[141] or what the evidence suggests is society's[142]—it doesn't. It is bad because it is bad constitutional law, or rather because it is *not*

---

138. "In the past several years, however, a trend toward liberalization of abortion statutes has resulted in adoption, by about one-third of the States, of less stringent laws, most of them patterned after the ALI Model Penal Code. . . ." 410 U.S. at 139–40. "By the end of 1970, four other States had repealed criminal penalties for abortions performed in early pregnancy by a licensed physician, subject to stated procedural and health requirements. ALASKA STAT. § 11.15.000 (1970); HAWAII REV. STAT. § 453-16 (Supp. 1971); N.Y. PENAL CODE § 125.05 (McKinney Supp. 1972-1973); WASH. REV. CODE §§ 9.02.060 to 9.02.080 (Supp. 1972). . . ." *Id.* at 140 n.37.

139. As opposed to the invalidation of a police practice. *Cf.* Miranda v. Arizona, 384 U.S. 436 (1966). *See also, e.g.,* Engel v. Vitale, 370 U.S. 421 (1962).

140. Even the headline in *The New York Times* announced: "High Court Rules Abortions Legal [sic] the First 3 Months." N.Y. TIMES, Jan. 23, 1973, p. 1, cols. 1-8.

141. Of course there are some possible uses of the decision that scare me, particularly when it is considered in conjunction (a) with some of this Court's notions relating to a moth-er's "waiver" of AFDC assistance, *see* Wyman v. James, 400 U.S. 309 (1971), and (b) with Buck v. Bell, 274 U.S. 200 (1927), which was indeed relied on by the Court in *Roe*, 410 U.S. at 154, and cited without apparent disapproval in Justice Douglas's concurrence, *id.* at 209. But those are quite different cases I'm conjuring up.

142. *See* note 138 *supra. But cf. Abortion,* THE NEW REPUBLIC, Feb. 10, 1973, at 9:

> [I]f the Court's guess concerning the probable and desirable direction of prog-ress is wrong, it will nevertheless have been imposed on all 50 states, and imposed permanently, unless the Court itself should in the future change its mind. Normal legislation, enacted by legislatures rather than judges, is happily not so rigid, and not so presumptuous in its claims to universality and permanence.

constitutional law and gives almost no sense of an obligation to try to be.[143] I am aware the Court cannot simply "lay the Article of the Constitution which is invoked beside the statute which is challenged and . . . decide whether the latter squares with the former."[144] That is precisely the reason commentators are needed.

> [P]recisely because it is the Constitution alone which warrants judicial interference in sovereign operations of the State, the basis of judgment as to the Constitutionality of state action must be a rational one, approaching the text which is the only commission for our power not in a literalistic way, as if we had a tax statute before us, but as the basic charter of our society, setting out in spare but meaningful terms the principles of government.[145]
>
> No matter how imprecise in application to specific modern fact situations, the constitutional guarantees do provide a direction, a goal, an ideal citizen-government relationship. They rule out many alternative directions, goals, and ideals.[146]
>
> And they fail to support the ruling out of others.

Of course, that only begins the inquiry. Identification and definition of the values with which the Constitution is concerned will often fall short of indicating with anything resembling clarity the deference to be given those values when they conflict with others society finds important. (Though even here the process is sometimes more helpful than the commentators would allow.) Nor is it often likely to generate, full blown, the "neutral" principle that will avoid embarrassment in future cases.[147] But though the identification of a constitutional connection is only the beginning of analysis, it is a

---

143. In judicial review, the line between the "juridical" and the "legislative" mode does not run between "strict constructionists" and competing theorists of constitutional interpretation. Rather, it divides constructionists and non-constructionists, those who do and those who do not see judicial review as a task of construing the living meaning of past political decisions—a division in which the alternating libertarianism and conservatism of the late Justices Black and Harlan were on the same side. H. Linde, *supra* note 99, at 254–55 (footnote omitted).

144. United States v. Butler, 297 U.S. 1, 62 (1936).

145. Poe v. Ullman, 367 U.S. 497, 539–40 (1961) (Harlan, J., dissenting).

146. J.S. Wright, *Professor Bickel, The Scholarly Tradition, and the Supreme Court*, 84 HARV. L. REV. 769, 785 (1971) (footnote omitted).

147. *See generally* J. Ely, *supra* note 30.

> Starting from a clearly unconstitutional course of action—and I have trouble seeing the unconstitutionality of a tax exemption for only Caucasian children as a controversial assumption—and attempting to explain why it is unconstitutional in terms of a theory capable of acceptable and consistent application to other areas, is a perfectly sensible way of developing constitutional doctrine.

necessary beginning. The point that often gets lost in the commentary, and obviously got lost in *Roe,* is that *before* the Court can get to the "balancing" stage, *before* it can worry about the next case and the case after that (or even about its institutional position) it is under an obligation to trace its premises to the charter from which it derives its authority. A neutral and durable principle may be a thing of beauty and a joy forever. But if it lacks connection with any value the Constitution marks as special, it is not a constitutional principle and the Court has no business imposing it.[148] I hope that will seem obvious to the point of banality. Yet those of us to whom it does seem obvious have seldom troubled to say so.[149] And because we have not, we must share in the blame for this decision.

Id. at 1262. I might have made (even more) explicit that the action around which the search for the "principled" approach is to be centered should be one—and, to paraphrase myself, I have trouble seeing the example I chose as controversial in this regard—whose impermissibility is established by values traceable to the Constitution.

148. *But see, e.g.,* H. Hart, *supra* note 135, at 99, quoted in part in A. Bickel, *Foreword: The Passive Virtues,* 75 HARV. L. Rev. 40, 41 (1961):

> [T]he Court is predestined . . . to be a voice of reason, charged with the creative function of discerning afresh and of articulating and developing impersonal and durable principles. . . .
>
> But discerning constitutional principles afresh is one thing; developing them, no matter how neutral and durable, is quite another. An institution charged with looking after a set of values the rest of us have entrusted to it is significantly different from one with authority to amend the set.

149. *But see, e.g.,* H. Linde, *supra* note 99. *Cf.* R. Bork, *Neutral Principles and Some First Amendment Problems,* 47 IND. L.J. 1, 6–11 (1971), espousing the general view of constitutional adjudication espoused here, but characterizing *Griswold* as a typical Warren Court product, *id.* at 7, in order to buttress the more general claim—equally unfair in my view—that one cannot accept that general view and at the same time generally approve the work of that Court. *Id.* at 6. *See* Griswold v. Connecticut, 381 U.S. 479, 527 n.23 (1965) (Black, J., dissenting).

16

Finding Abortion Rights in the Constitution[1]

Laurence H. Tribe

Because the abortion question is so difficult and may be approached in so many ways, it should be no surprise that the approach taken by the U.S. Supreme Court generates continuing controversy. It would be foolish to expect any judicial approach to the abortion question to be uncontroversial; if that test were applied, every answer to the question would be wrong. But neither difficulty nor controversy can justify letting the Court's decision in *Roe* escape critical examination. Was that decision legally defensible? We address that issue next, exploring some of the implications of deciding the constitutional question in different ways.

We should be clear at the outset that the abortion issues poses constitutional problems not simply for judges but for every federal, state, or local official who must at some point address the issue. Each such official is required to take an oath to uphold the Constitution of the United States. Even if the Supreme Court were someday to conclude that judges have no business enforcing constitutional limitations in the abortion area, that conclusion would not relieve other public officials of the burden of deciding what they believe those limitations are. In deciding what laws to vote for or against or what enforcement measures to take, public officials cannot properly avoid considering what they believe the Constitution allows or requires them to do.

---

1. © Laurence H. Tribe. This chapter first appeared in LAURENCE TRIBE, ABORTION: THE CLASH OF ABSOLUTES (1990), and is reprinted here with his permission. Professor Tribe is the Carl M. Loeb University Professor, Emeritus, Harvard Law School.

Those who either defend or attack the constitutional analysis contained
in *Roe v. Wade* purely in terms of the role judges should or should not play
in our system of government are therefore missing much of what is at stake.
Of course, *Roe v. Wade* involved, in part, the question of what the judicial
role should be. But that is only part of what it involved. It involved as well
the question of what protection, if any, the Constitution, as a document
addressed to all officials, extends either to a woman who wishes to terminate
her pregnancy or to the fetus, or to both. To say that the abortion question
should be resolved, in whole or in part, by officials other than judges tells us
nothing about how those officials should resolve it.

In addition, it is an illusion to imagine that all aspects of the abortion
issue could possibly be left to officials outside the judicial system. However
tempting it might be for judges to throw up their hands and say that the
whole matter should be resolved "politically," a little thought should make
clear that judges must, at a minimum, set the outer boundaries of political
power in this area.

Suppose, for example, that the Constitution is interpreted so as to give
each state broad latitude in deciding which abortions to permit and which
to prohibit. Judges would still have to decide whether or not a state could
pass a law that would force a woman to save a viable fetus when that would
require delivery by caesarean section. Judges would still have to decide
whether or not a state could constitutionally force a woman to abort one
fetus in order to save its twin if the medical circumstances were such that
only one could live. Judges would still have to decide whether or not a state
could impose financial pressures designed to force a woman on welfare to
abort a fetus that would be born with severe genetic defects and whose survival after birth would require a large commitment of public resources.

Whatever a court might conclude about government's power over normal pregnancy, it could hardly avoid determining the limits of government
power over an ovum that has been fertilized in a test tube. May the government require that such a fertilized ovum be preserved for future implantation? May the government require that such an ovum be frozen until its fate
has been agreed upon? May the sperm donor be given an enforceable veto
over the woman's decision to discard the ovum after its test tube fertilization? May the government enforce her promise to have the fertilized ovum
implanted in her uterus? May it enforce her promise to have it implanted in
another woman? If state officials refuse to enforce such promises, are they
violating any rights of the persons to whom those promises were made?

Courts simply cannot avoid deciding, in the multitude of cases
spawned by the newest technologies and the oldest human desires, *who*

will be permitted to decide *what*: the woman, the man, a doctor, a hospital, or the state?

I. Was *Roe* Rightly Decided?

For all the talk of possible future compromises, it must not be forgotten that *Roe* itself represented a compromise. The Supreme Court in *Roe v. Wade* had heard arguments that the woman's right to decide for herself whether, when, and why to terminate a pregnancy is absolute. The Court's conclusion was unequivocal: "With this we do not agree."[2] Thus, the Court in *Roe* and in the decisions that followed it upheld the validity of government regulations requiring that all abortions be performed by licensed physicians, government regulations to protect the health of women in second-trimester abortions and beyond, and government regulations to protect the unborn from abortions that are not needed to protect the woman's life or health once the fetus is "viable" (i.e., can survive outside the woman).

Still, no judicial ruling since segregated public schools were held unconstitutional by *Brown v. Board of Education*[3] has generated anything resembling the degree of criticism and even outright violence triggered by *Roe v. Wade*. Criticism of the decision, and particularly of its result, has led to a revolution in constitutional law that may have profound consequences for all Americans, a revolution touching the full range of our rights. It has already led to a radical transformation in the role of the American judiciary.

II. The "Judicial Restraint" Objection

One unexpected consequence of *Roe v. Wade* was the growth of a veritable cottage industry promoting judicial restraint. The epithet "judicial activism," the foe of supposed champions of restraint, is most often used to describe the work of the Supreme Court of the 1950s and 1960s under Chief Justice Earl Warren. But *Roe*, sometimes derided as an example of unparalleled judicial activism, was decided by the Court under the leadership of conservative Chief Justice Warren Burger. Indeed, the decision in *Roe* was written by Nixon appointee Harry Blackmun and was joined by conservative jurists Potter Stewart and Lewis Powell as well as by Chief Justice Burger, who was appointed by President Nixon precisely to fulfill a campaign promise to change the activist complexion of the federal judiciary.

---

2. 410 U.S. 113, 153 (1973).
3. 349 U.S. 294 (1954).

People have undertaken to criticize *Roe*, in every aspect and from every angle, as *illegitimate* judicial activism, and the sheer volume of the attack seems to have lent it legitimacy. Are these criticisms convincing?

III. "Legislators and Not Judges Should Decide"

The simplest argument against *Roe*, an argument that has gained considerable credence and that has great resonance in a nation devoted to principles of democracy, criticizes *Roe* as antidemocratic. The issue of abortion rights, the reasoning goes, should be returned to Congress and to state and local legislators for decision in a democratic way by the legislative process. How sound is that argument?

Our system of government, of course, neither offers us nor threatens us with *absolute* democracy, in the style, say, of ancient Athens, where it is said that each citizen cast one vote on all matters, or in the style of the New England town meeting. Ours is a republican form of government, in which the votes of citizens are used primarily to select legislatures and executives, which themselves select judges whose role it is to ensure that the government does not violate basic rights or otherwise upset the fundamental agreements underlying our governmental institutions. The whole *point* of an independent judiciary is to be "antidemocratic," to preserve from transient majorities those human rights and other principles to which our legal and political system is committed. Without this role there would be nothing to stop a bare majority of our citizens from deciding tomorrow that the minority should be enslaved or required to give up its belongings for the greater good of the greater number. This elementary civics lesson is forgotten or ignored by those who would leave *every* issue of individual rights that was a matter of moral controversy to be decided *solely* by the legislative and executive branches. And in the end, most of these critics do not seriously attempt to deny that the federal judiciary, and ultimately the Supreme Court of the United States, is empowered to invalidate legislation, although duly enacted by the democratically elected representatives of the people, if it runs afoul of the Constitution.

In particular, the protections of the first eight amendments to the Constitution—the "Bill of Rights" (guaranteeing freedom of speech and of religion, the right to bear arms, and so forth)—and of the Fourteenth Amendment, adopted after the Civil War, which guarantees all persons equal protection of the laws and prohibits deprivations of life, liberty, or property without due process of law, insulate certain aspects of individual behavior from governmental intrusion and provide norms for government action that no legislature can contravene, although the exact bounds of these rights may be open to debate.

Should a legislature, through the democratic process, enact a law that transgresses the guarantees contained in the Constitution, the federal courts have not merely the power but the obligation to strike that law down. Indeed, the Constitution provides for unelected judges, appointed by the President and confirmed by the Senate, who serve for life and whose salary cannot be diminished, precisely to prevent them from making decisions based on the popular will, however formally and democratically expressed.

This power of judicial review and invalidation was first exercised by the Supreme Court to strike down an act of Congress in an opinion written by the great chief justice John Marshall in the case of *Marbury v. Madison*[4] in 1803. There a disappointed office seeker named William Marbury, who had been named to a federal post by President John Adams, sued Secretary of State James Madison for refusing to deliver his commission of office when the administration of President Adams was replaced by that of President Thomas Jefferson. The Supreme Court, after saying that Madison and the new President were acting lawlessly, pronounced itself powerless to award Marbury the judicial relief he sought, explaining that the act of Congress which supposedly empowered it to hear Marbury's suit against Madison violated the Constitution's provision defining the Court's jurisdiction to try cases. Writing for the Court, Chief Justice Marshall held that much as the Court would like to rely on that act of Congress, its duty to obey the Constitution required it to strike that act down. Striking down a law as unconstitutional is "undemocratic," in the sense that no simple majority acting through the legislative process can overcome a ruling of the Supreme Court holding a law invalid. But it is a cornerstone of our system of government.

As Justice Robert Jackson wrote in 1943 in an opinion for the Court holding that children cannot be punished by public authorities for refusing to take part in a school's compulsory flag salute ceremony, the "very purpose of a Bill of Rights was to withdraw certain subjects from the vicissitudes of political controversy, to place them beyond the reach of majorities and officials and to establish them as legal principles to be applied by the courts. One's right to life, liberty, and property, to free speech, a free press, freedom of worship and assembly, and other fundamental rights may not be submitted to vote; they depend on the outcome of no elections."[5]

---

4. 5 U.S. (Cranch) 137 (1803).
5. West Virginia State Bd. of Educ. v. Barnette, 319 U.S. 624, 638 (1943).

Every time a court holds that a duly enacted law violates the Constitution, it behaves in what might be described as an antidemocratic way. But this does not make the court's action a usurpation of power. The antidemocratic nature of *Roe* provides no decisive evidence of its illegitimacy—provided we agree, as nearly everyone does, that the Constitution itself has sufficiently democratic roots to count as an enduring basis for a government of, by and for the people. The question remains, though: Can *Roe* find support in the Constitution?

IV. "The Right to Privacy Is Not in the Constitution's Text"

A second basis for objection to *Roe* is that it protects a right, the right to privacy, that appears nowhere in the text of the Constitution. The Court, it is said, in a naked power grab and on the strength of nothing more than personal disagreement with the outcome of the legislative process, illegitimately carved out an area and put it beyond the reach of the democratic, political branches of government. If true, the charge would be grave indeed; the Supreme Court's only warrant to override the outcome of politically democratic processes is the agreement of "We the People," as the Constitution's preamble calls those in whose name it is ordained.

Judge Robert Bork, in his 1989 book *The Tempting of America,* could find in the Court's opinion "not one line of explanation, not one sentence that qualifies as legal argument."[6] In the years since *Roe,* according to Bork, "no one, however pro-abortion, has ever thought of an argument that even remotely begins to justify *Roe v. Wade* as a constitutional decision. . . . There is no room for argument," writes Bork, "about the conclusion that the decision was the assumption of illegitimate judicial power and usurpation of the democratic authority of the American people."[7]

What may surprise some, given the certitude with which Judge Bork and a number of others pronounce that *Roe v. Wade* was constitutionally illegitimate, is how many lawyers and law professors throughout the country believe the Supreme Court's decision in that case was entirely correct as a legal matter. For example, a friend of the court brief was filed in the *Webster* case "on behalf of 885 American law professors . . . who believe that the right of a woman to choose whether or not to bear a child, as delineated . . . in *Roe v. Wade,* is an essential component of constitutional

---

6. ROBERT BORK, THE TEMPTING OF AMERICA 112 (1989).

7. *Id.* 115–16.

liberty and privacy commanding reaffirmation by [the Supreme] Court."[8] Similarly, the American Bar Association in February 1990 approved a resolution expressing the ABA's recognition that "the fundamental rights of privacy and equality guaranteed by the United States Constitution" encompass "the decision to terminate [a] pregnancy."[9]

Now, of course, nearly a thousand law professors and the nation's leading organization of lawyers could certainly be wrong on a matter of law. But how plausible is it that all of them would fail to recognize as blatant a legal blunder as some say that Court made in *Roe*? To understand what separates the vast majority of lawyers and legal scholars from those who continue to insist that no honest and professionally competent attorney or academic could possibly agree with *Roe*, we need to look more closely at what *Roe*'s most strident critics claim.

On the most simplistic level, of course, the critics are correct. The word "privacy" is not in the text of the Constitution. But the guarantees of the Constitution are not like itemized deductions. The Constitution contains broad provisions whose meaning requires judicial interpretation. Interpretation, in turn, requires judgment.

One of the most important of these broad provisions, contained in the Fourteenth Amendment, reads: "No State shall . . . deprive any person of life, liberty, or property, without due process of law." It is the guarantee of "liberty" contained in the due process clause, sometimes also called the liberty clause, of the Fourteenth Amendment that provides protection of our rights from infringement by the state governments. And the word "liberty" simply is not self-defining.

V. The Meaning of the Liberty Clause

Some commentators believe, or at least argue, that the liberty clause does not give special protection to *any* of our rights. This position has been rejected by every sitting Supreme Court justice and, indeed, by every Supreme Court justice of the last half century, including such conservative jurists as John Marshall Harlan, Felix Frankfurter, William Rehnquist, and Antonin Scalia. Still, it is valuable to understand this argument and to understand why, though touted as "conservative," it is actually revolutionary.

---

8. Brief for a Group of American Law Professors as Amicus Curiae Supporting Appellees, in *Webster v. Reproductive Health Services*, 492 U.S. 490 (1989), at 1.

9. *A.B.A. Policy Group Backs Right of Women to Decide on Abortion*, N.Y. TIMES, Feb. 14, 1990, at A23. The vote in the ABA's House of delegates was 238 to 106.

A modern reader of the words of the Fourteenth Amendment might well conclude that they provide only *procedural* protection for "life," "liberty," and "property." Put another way, the amendment appears to authorize deprivations of life, liberty, and property as long as those deprivations are accompanied by "due process" of law. As Judge Bork describes it, the due process clause of the Fourteenth Amendment "was designed *only* to require fair procedures in implementing laws."[10]

And the due process clause *does* provide us with procedural protection for our lives, our liberty, and our property. It has been held by the Supreme Court to mandate hearings and other procedures before a state government can take certain actions that affect a variety of our interests.

However, from its earliest days this clause has also stood for the substantive protection of individual rights from intrusion by the government. During the nineteenth century, and even before, it was widely believed that the people retained certain "natural rights." Legislatures could not enact legislation that intruded upon these rights. Any such attempt would be of no operative effect because it would be outside the sphere of legislative authority. It would not, by definition, be "law."

Consistent with this view, the word "law" in the phrase "due process of law" was employed by courts to limit state legislatures to those areas in which they could *legitimately* operate. As the nineteenth-century Supreme Court explained, "[i]t is not every act, legislative in form, that is law. Law is something more than mere will exerted as an act of power."[11] In a phrase, the Constitution's ideal of "law" rejects the proposition that might makes right. Certain legislative acts that infringed on protected areas of liberty, acts beyond the scope of the legislature's power, therefore were not considered "due process of law." Within a quarter century of the Fourteenth Amendment's adoption in 1868 the Supreme Court began striking down state laws on the basis of that amendment's due process clause because of particular substantive rights those laws infringed.[12] By 1937 the Court had invalidated almost two hundred state laws on this ground.[13]

The most striking aspect of this early foray by the Supreme Court into "substantive due process" was its disastrous result. For the right in whose name the Supreme Court wielded the due process clause was not a right

---

10. Bork, *supra* note 6, at 43 (emphasis added).

11. Hurtado v. California, 110 U.S. 516, 535–36 (1884).

12. *See* Allgeyer v. Louisiana, 165 U.S. 578 (1897).

13. *See* Benjamin Wright, The Growth of American Constitutional Law 154, 175–76 & n.96 (1942).

familiar to the law today. It was, rather, an economic right: the "freedom to contract."

During this era—dubbed the *Lochner* era after the 1905 decision in *Lochner v. New York*[14] invalidating New York's sixty-hour limit on a bakery employee's workweek—a majority of the Court imported into the due process clause then-fashionable economic and social theories, most notably the views of Darwin as bastardized by Herbert Spencer in his 1851 book *Social Statics*. It was believed that legislation meant to redress imbalances in economic bargaining power or to redistribute wealth or income was not law enacted for the "general welfare" but power exercised "purely for the promotion of private interests."[15] Such use of government power to readjust the "natural" inequalities arising from the ordinary workings of the common law rules of property and contract was beyond the implicit boundary of legislative authority.

In the name of liberty of contract during this period, social and economic legislation that we now consider routine, even if not always wise, and the enactment of which nearly everyone takes for granted as falling within the legitimate power of legislative bodies, was repeatedly struck down by the Supreme Court. Minimum-wage laws, child labor laws, limitations on the hours of work, laws regulating labor-management relations—indeed, all regulations of the employment relationship except those the Court found to be directly in aid of the *public* health and welfare—were struck down as meddlesome interferences with the worker's liberty to contract and with the employer's freedom to use his property in traditional ways. Any attempt to improve the position of the employee vis-a-vis the employer, or of the buyer vis-a-vis the seller, was invalid. Inequality in bargaining power was, the Court said, "but the normal and inevitable result" of the exercise of the right to contract.[16]

From its inception the doctrine of *Lochner* was criticized. Justice Oliver Wendell Holmes, dissenting in the *Lochner* case, wrote that "a Constitution is not intended to embody a particular economic theory, whether of paternalism and the organic relation of the citizen to the state or of *laissez faire*. It is made for people of fundamentally differing views, and the accident of our finding certain opinions natural and familiar, or novel, and even shocking, ought not to conclude our judgment upon the question whether statutes

---

14. 198 U.S. 45 (1905).

15. Thomas Cooley, A Treatise on the Constitutional Limitations Which Rest upon the Legislative Power of the States of the American Union 1227–28 n.2 (8th ed. 1927).

16. Coppage v. Kansas, 236 U.S. 1, 17–18 (1915).

embodying them conflict with the Constitution of the United States."[17] As he put it most famously, "[t]he 14th Amendment does not enact Mr. Herbert Spencer's Social Statics."

Ultimately the economic realities of the Great Depression graphically undermined *Lochner's* premise. The belief that the "invisible hand" of economics was functioning both to protect individual rights and to maximize the social good was no longer tenable. The idea of a "natural" economic order that could be restored by striking down the laws that had artificially upset it was no longer believable.

Criticism of the Court grew as the depression deepened and the Court continued to strike down social and economic regulation in the name of what one commentator poignantly described as "the legal right to starve."[18] As Franklin D. Roosevelt's enormously popular New Deal policies were overturned one after another, pressure on the Court increased.

This culminated in Roosevelt's infamous Court-packing plan in 1937. Roosevelt proposed a law to expand the membership of the Supreme Court, a law that would have been most unwise but one that Congress clearly had authority to enact under the Constitution. The bill would have given Roosevelt the right to make six immediate appointments to the Court with which he could easily overcome the already narrow five to four majority that then supported *Lochner* and the liberty to contract.

This state of affairs came to an end only when Justice Owen Roberts, a member of the pro-*Lochner* majority since his appointment to the Court by Herbert Hoover in 1930, in what some saw as a response to the political pressure and the threat to both the prestige and the integrity of the Court, switched his vote in the minimum-wage and maximum-hour case of *West Coast Hotel v. Parrish*,[19] a reversal still described in certain legal circles as "the switch in time that saved nine."[20] Justice Roberts's switch in time was in fact based on a vote he had cast during the Court's confidential deliberations even before FDR's Court-packing scheme had been unveiled. In any event, it laid to rest any residual congressional support for that scheme and permitted the New Deal reforms and, really, most now-familiar state and federal social and economic legislation, to go forward. It also spelled the end of the protection of the liberty of contract from state interference under the due process clause of the Fourteenth Amendment.

---

17. 198 U.S. 45, 75–76 (Holmes, J., dissenting).

18. "The Legal Right to Starve," 34 *New Republic* 254 (May 2, 1923).

19. 300 U.S. 379 (1937).

20. *See* WRIGHT, *supra* note 13, at 202; LEO PFEFFER, THIS HONORABLE COURT 295–320 (1965).

The *Lochner* era haunts judges and legal scholars to this day. The damage it did to both Court and country and its invalidation of the democratically enacted will of the people must give us pause. The Court's usurpation of the powers of democratically elected legislatures in the name of the liberty clause animates the concerns of many of the advocates of judicial restraint who oppose judicial protection of abortion rights today. Indeed, it is largely in reaction to *Lochner* that Judge Bork claims that the due process clause is entirely a procedural guarantee.

But the fault with *Lochner* lay not in judicial intervention to protect "liberty"—including the "liberty" of workers and of businesses—but in a misguided understanding of what "liberty" required. The protection of substantive liberties under the Constitution is not, as some have argued, an illegitimate departure from the text. The text of the Fourteenth Amendment, both during and after the *Lochner* era, continues to provide real protection for liberty. The question is how to give this broad guarantee *content.*

VI. "Incorporation" of the Bill of Rights

A simple case proves the point. It may surprise some, but the protections of the Bill of Rights do not apply in any direct way to actions by the state governments. For example, the First Amendment reads: "Congress shall make no law . . . abridging the freedom of speech, or of the press. . . ." *Congress,* not the state legislatures, is prohibited from abridging free speech, perhaps our most cherished freedom.

In a series of decisions beginning as long ago as 1897 but accelerating rapidly in the 1960s, the Supreme Court held that the protection of "liberty" contained in the Fourteenth Amendment's due process clause prevents the states from enacting laws that, if enacted by Congress, would be invalid under the protections of individual rights contained in the Bill of Rights. It is only because of these decisions, decisions that treat the Fourteenth Amendment's liberty clause as protecting substantive rights, that the protections enumerated in the Bill of Rights are relevant to the states at all.

To this day, when we say that a state law violates the First Amendment's protection of free speech or its prohibition on the establishment of religion (the separation of church and state), what we mean is that the state law violates that protection as applied to the states through the liberty clause of the Fourteenth Amendment.

The idea that the liberty clause applies the Bill of Rights to the states, called the doctrine of incorporation of the Bill of Rights into the Fourteenth Amendment, was not fully implemented until the 1960s. Even now the application of the Bill of Rights to the states is not complete. Some of its provisions, for example the Seventh Amendment's guarantee of a jury trial in civil cases, have been held not to apply to the states. Nearly all of the others have been held to apply—for example, the First Amendment freedoms of speech, press, assembly, petition, and free exercise of religion and the prohibition on the establishment of religion; the Fourth Amendment rights to be free of unreasonable search and seizure and to exclude from criminal trials evidence seized illegally; the Fifth Amendment rights to be free of compelled self-incrimination and double jeopardy; the Sixth Amendment rights to counsel, to a speedy and public trial before a jury, to an opportunity to confront opposing witnesses, and to the use of subpoena power for the purpose of obtaining favorable witnesses; the Eighth Amendment right to be free of cruel and unusual punishment. All have been held to be protected from state infringement, based on the due process clause of the Fourteenth Amendment.

The application of the Bill of Rights to the states, although not specifically intended by the framers of the Fourteenth Amendment and although once highly controversial, is now common ground. No sitting justice questions it. History has made it the place from which any discussion of the liberty clause of the Fourteenth Amendment must depart. Indeed, without incorporation of the Bill of Rights, we would have a world in which, although the federal government could not censor an antigovernment newspaper, the state of Illinois could. In which, although the federal government could not take a person's property without providing compensation for it, the state of Kansas could. Or in which, though there could be no official church of the United States, the state of New York could declare Presbyterianism the official state religion, with the governor as its head.

For this reason, the claim that the liberty clause is "entirely" procedural is unsustainable. The liberty clause protects us from infringements of certain rights, although the exact character of these rights is often open to debate.

Judge Bork, one of the few proponents of the claim that the liberty clause has *no* substantive effect, appears to recognize that this position stakes out a Maginot Line. Indeed, in *The Tempting of America* he insists that the clause is purely procedural, "*aside from* incorporating the Bill of Rights."[21] Whether or not there is any basis for limiting the meaning of "liberty" *only* to rights specifically mentioned in the Bill of Rights is therefore plainly the real issue.

---

21. BORK, *supra* note 6, at 236 (emphasis added).

VII. The Question of "Unenumerated" Rights

While the incorporation against the states of the Bill of Rights through the Fourteenth Amendment's liberty clause is now universally accepted, opponents of *Roe v. Wade* argue that the Bill of Rights should be an outer limit to the liberty protected by the Fourteenth Amendment. We are told that only those rights *specifically enumerated* in the Bill of Rights—freedom of speech, the freedom of religion, and so forth—apply against the states so as to create areas in which the states cannot enact laws. We are told that the *Roe* decision erred in defending an "unenumerated" right—namely, the right to privacy. This is hardly a principled objection to the Supreme Court's invalidation of legislative enactments under the broad protection of "liberty" in the Constitution. Indeed, by accepting incorporation, this argument implicitly acknowledges the validity of that judicial enterprise.

Neither is it a principled objection on the grounds of the text of the Constitution. For the text of the Constitution no more explicitly protects, against infringement *by the states*, the right of free speech than it does the right of privacy. Indeed, the very description of this objection is something of a misnomer since *all* individual rights are "unenumerated" with respect to the power of the state governments. The liberty clause of the Fourteenth Amendment simply does not enumerate *any* specific rights.

In any event, the fact that a right is not mentioned in so many words anywhere in the Constitution is not, and cannot be, a decisive objection. For the Constitution tells us that it was not constructed with an exhaustive list of enumerated rights. The Constitution's Ninth Amendment expressly states: "The enumeration in the Constitution, of certain rights, shall not be construed to deny or disparage others retained by the people." That is the one constitutional provision expressly designed to instruct all of us, as readers of the document, how we are *not* to construe, or interpret, what it may fail to list explicitly.

Still, one can formulate an argument, unprincipled though it may be, that only those protection explicitly listed elsewhere in the Constitution apply through the liberty clause of the Fourteenth Amendment. This was the position taken by Justice Hugo Black. This reverse incorporation view, however, never garnered a majority of the votes on the Supreme Court. Indeed, every member of the Court, both in the 1973 *Roe* decision and since, has accepted the Court's role in giving the liberty clause of the Fourteenth Amendment the vitality to protect more than the freedoms expressly listed in the Bill of Rights.

Here is just one example among many of an unenumerated right vindicated by the Supreme Court. Inez Moore lived in East Cleveland, Ohio, with her two grandsons, Dale and John. The boys were not brothers, but cousins; John's mother had died when he was an infant, and he had been raised since then by Mrs. Moore. She lived in a neighborhood that had been zoned for "single family dwelling units." In 1973 she received a notice from the city that since her grandsons were cousins rather than brothers, her household did not meet the city's definition of a "family." She was told that John, who was then ten and had lived with her his whole life, was an "illegal occupant" and that he must be removed. When she refused, East Cleveland fined this sixty-three-year-old grandmother and sentenced her to five days in jail.

The Supreme Court did not let the city of East Cleveland's narrow view of what was an acceptable family interfere with Mrs. Moore's right, her "liberty," to create a household with her grandchildren. This right is nowhere mentioned in the Bill of Rights, yet the Court held that because it is fundamental, it is protected by the liberty clause of the Fourteenth Amendment to the Constitution.[22]

The word "liberty," which appears both in the Fifth Amendment as a limit on federal power and in the Fourteenth Amendment as a limit on state power, does not in any obvious sense mean "those rights specifically listed in the first eight amendments to the Constitution." To limit the meaning of "liberty" only to these listed rights, apart from seeming to violate the command of the Ninth Amendment, would adopt a radical understanding of the Constitution itself. To say that *only* these rights exist is to say that when the framers wrote the Constitution, and the people of the United States ratified it in 1789, they thereby surrendered to government all the fundamental rights they regarded themselves as possessing the rights that the Revolutionary War had been fought to preserve—with the sole exception of whatever specific rights were to be mentioned in a Bill of Rights that had been promised but that had not yet been written (and was not to be ratified until 1791).

No understanding of the Constitution could be further from the central premises of those who wrote and ratified the Constitution and the Bill of Rights. From the very beginning of our Republic, the Supreme Court has consistently recognized that in adopting the Constitution the people did *not* mean to place the bulk of their hard-won liberty in the hands of government save only for those rights specifically mentioned in the Bill of Rights or elsewhere in the document.

---

22. Moore v. City of East Cleveland, 431 U.S. 494 (1977).

The Supreme Court has, accordingly, never limited the substantive protection of either the Fifth Amendment's or the Fourteenth Amendment's liberty clauses to those rights enumerated in the Bill of Rights. And if the Court were ever to do so, we would live in a nation in which any state or local government would be free to control our lives in innumerable ways, ranging from a federal abolition of birth control to a local imposition of detailed rules like those of East Cleveland about which family members could live together in their grandmother's household.

VIII. Deciding Which Rights Are Specially Protected

If the enumeration of certain rights in the Constitution is not to become an exhaustive list of our protected liberties, the Supreme Court must have some principle for deciding what rights (such as the right to live with one's grandchildren) are fundamental and what rights (such as the right to burn trash in one's backyard) are not.

The Court's duty to protect certain unenumerated rights makes some judicial conservatives anxious. Judge Bork, for example, argues that judges unconstrained by an enumeration of rights in the text of the Constitution will be free simply to invalidate democratically enacted laws "in accordance with their own philosophies."[23]

While it makes sense to proceed with caution, the answer to questions about our liberty simply cannot be found by denying the existence of fundamental rights that are not listed in the Bill of Rights. Nor can there be any precise formula to define fundamental rights because the text of the Constitution offers us only general guidance.

Judges certainly should not feel free simply to import into the Constitution their own personal moral views. They must *interpret* the provisions of the Constitution. Judges, and others sworn to uphold the Constitution, may differ on whether a certain sphere of activity is protected. Indeed, they may differ on what principles should inform that decision. But interpreting the Constitution is the essential role of the judge in our system of government.

There are also checks on the ability of any single Supreme Court justice to impose upon the country some extremist vision. To begin with, each justice—indeed, every federal judge—must be selected by the President and confirmed by the Senate. History shows that while one cannot predict with certainty a justice's vote in a particular case, the judicial philosophy of a Supreme Court nominee rarely changes drastically after his

---

23. BORK, *supra* note 6, at 220.

or her appointment. The President has enormous latitude in his selection of justices, and the Senate has at times exercised a responsibility to satisfy itself about the constitutional vision of a nominee whose name it is sent for confirmation. Indeed, the Senate has rejected almost one out of every five nominees to the Court. Most recently the Senate in 1987 rejected the nomination of Judge Robert Bork, citing objections to his constitutional philosophy.

In addition, no single justice of the Court has the power to transform our nation. The Court is a nine-member body, and the requirement of a majority vote necessarily acts as a restraint on any extreme or outlandish position. For this reason, no one judge's personal philosophy could ever be imposed as the law of the land.

Though some might prefer a system in which the human element, a judge's "temperament," as Judge Bork puts it,[24] would play no role—perhaps a system in which a "justice machine" could predictably resolve constitutional cases—such a world of perfectly defined rights could be achieved only by denying the existence of *any* rights protected from the states under the Fourteenth Amendment.

We are left then with the question of what principles to use to define the content of the Fourteenth Amendment's protection of liberty. What principles should judges use in deciding whether a right is so "fundamental" that it is specially protected by the liberty clause? This is a question about the meaning of America.

The enterprise of answering that question began even as the *Lochner* era crashed to an end. In 1937, the year *Lochner* fell, Justice Benjamin Cardozo wrote for the Court that the due process clause would invalidate legislation that trod upon interests "so rooted in the traditions and conscience of our people as to be ranked as fundamental." As conceived by Justice Cardozo, the interests protected were those "implicit in the concept of ordered liberty."[25]

The hypothetical inquiry Justice Cardozo suggested—could one imagine a civilized system without this or that protection?—was ultimately rejected, and the Court began to define the protection of individual rights less hypothetically and thus more broadly. As it applied more and more of the Bill of Rights to the states in the 1960s, the Court, in an opinion by Justice White, suggested that the rights that are protected are those that are

---

24. *Id.*
25. Palko v. Connecticut, 302 U.S. 319, 325 (1937).

fundamental to the "Anglo-American regime of ordered liberty."[26] More recently the Court explained that it seeks to protect certain areas against state intrusion because they are "deeply rooted in this Nation's history and tradition."[27]

In 1989 Justice Scalia wrote for the four youngest conservative members of the Court (himself, Chief Justice Rehnquist, and Justices O'Connor and Kennedy):

> [I]t is an established part of our constitutional jurisprudence that the term "liberty" in the Due Process Clause extends beyond freedom from physical restraint. . . . In an attempt to limit and guide interpretation of the Clause, we have insisted not merely that the interest denominated as a "liberty" be "fundamental" (a concept that, in isolation, is hard to objectify), but also that it be an interest traditionally protected by our society. As we have put it, the Due Process Clause affords only those protections "so rooted in the traditions and conscience of our people as to be ranked as fundamental." Our cases reflect "continual insistence upon respect for the teachings of history [and] solid recognition of the basic value that underlie our society."[28]

IX. A "Right of Privacy"?

Under such formulations, the Court has protected the constitutional right of privacy, conceived, most famously, in Justice Louis Brandeis's words, as "the right to be let alone—the most comprehensive of rights and the right most valued by civilized men."[29] This right is not some recent invention. It did not spring full-blown like Athena from the head of Justice Harry Blackmun in his opinion in the case of *Roe v. Wade*.

Indeed, the first Supreme Court case decided on this ground came in 1923. In that year the Supreme Court held that the states could not forbid the teaching of modern foreign languages before the eighth grade. Two years later it held that states could not compel all students to attend public schools.

---

26. Duncan v. Louisiana, 391 U.S. 145, 150 n.14 (1968).
27. *Moore*, 431 U.S. at 503 (plurality opinion).
28. Michael H. v. Gerald D., 491 U.S. 110, 122–23 (1989) (citations omitted).
29. Olmstead v. United States, 277 U.S. 438, 478 (1928) (Brandeis, J., dissenting).

These twin rulings, *Meyer v. Nebraska*[30] and *Pierce v. Society of Sisters*,[31] stand as bulwarks in our legal system. The state law that the Supreme Court struck down in *Meyer* had been passed amid the tension of the nation's struggle with Germany in World War I. It was rooted in suspicion and aimed at suppressing the culture and heritage of Nebraska's German minority. If parents wanted their children to learn German, the Court said, the state had no right to dictate otherwise, even if the United States and Germany were at war. The law that the Court struck down in *Pierce*, which would have shut down both parochial and secular private schools as alternatives to Oregon's public school system, had been aimed at the state's Catholic minority, although it was successfully challenged by the Hill Military Academy as well as by the Society of Sisters. Government has no power, the Court said in these cases, "to standardize its children"[32] or to "foster a homogenous people."[33] Parents have a right to "direct the upbringing and education of children under their control."[34] This, of course, is now beyond challenge. From these now quite ancient roots has developed the "right of privacy," which, Justice Blackmun wrote in *Roe*, is "broad enough to encompass a woman's decision whether or not to terminate her pregnancy." These decisions of the 1920s are immediate ancestors of the very liberty invoked by women when they insist upon a right not to be made mothers against their will.

In 1942 the Court first recognized the fundamental character of decisions concerning reproduction. In the landmark right-of-privacy case of *Skinner v. Oklahoma*, on which the Court later relied in *Roe*, the Court invalidated a state statute providing for the sterilization of persons convicted two or more times of "felonies involving moral turpitude."[35] The Court in *Skinner* characterized the right to reproduce as "one of the basic civil rights of man" and observed, against the implicit background of Nazi policies to eradicate supposedly inferior genetic types, that "[t]he power to sterilize, if exercised . . . [i]n evil or reckless hands . . . can cause races or types which are inimical to the dominant group to wither and disappear."[36] In *Skinner* the Court recognized the grotesque disempowerment that could occur if

---

30. 262 U.S. 390 (1923).
31. 268 U.S. 510 (1925).
32. *Pierce*, 268 U.S. at 535.
33. *Meyer*, 262 U.S. at 402.
34. *Pierce*, 268 U.S. at 534–35.
35. 316 U.S. 535, 536 (1942).
36. *Id.* at 541.

the choice of whether to beget a child were transferred from the individual to the state.

The privacy right was also found to include decisions about marriage in the aptly named case of *Loving v. Virginia,* in which the Court recognized the fundamental nature of the unenumerated right to marry and struck down Virginia's law against interracial marriage. This added to the list of fundamental rights "the right to choose one's spouse."[37]

In 1965, in *Griswold v. Connecticut,* the Supreme Court recognized that the liberty clause protects the right of a married couple to decide whether or not to use contraceptives. The Court struck down a Connecticut law that made the use of contraceptives by married persons a crime. It overturned the aiding and abetting conviction of someone who had provided a married person with contraceptives and with information regarding their use. In a majority opinion by Justice William O. Douglas the state's regulation was condemned as invading "the area of protected freedoms," which included "the zone of privacy created by several fundamental constitutional guarantees."[38] Although Justice Byron White was later one of the two dissenters in *Roe,* he wrote a concurring opinion in *Griswold* separately explaining his conclusion that the Connecticut anticontraceptive law failed to serve the purposes the state's lawyers claimed for it (deterring illicit sexual relationships) and impermissibly deprived married persons of "liberty without due process of law."[39]

The Court in 1972 addressed a Massachusetts law that made contraceptives more difficult for unmarried people to obtain than for those who were married. Justice Brennan, writing for the majority, observed that if "the right of privacy means anything, it is the right of the individual, married or single, to be free from unwarranted governmental intrusion into matters so fundamentally affecting a person as the decision whether to bear or beget a child."[40] Again, Justice White concurred in the majority's action in reversing the criminal conviction that was at issue, but his separate opinion, which was joined by Justice Blackmun, did not include anything like the majority's sweeping language about each individual's right of privacy.[41]

Although, in its decision the following year in *Roe,* the Court characterized these contraception decisions as cases about the right not to have to

---

37. *See* Turner v. Safley, 482 U.S. 78 (1987); Zablocki v. Redhail, 434 U.S. 374 (1978); Loving v. Virginia, 388 U.S. 1 (1967).

38. 381 U.S. 479, 485 (1965).

39. *Id.* at 507 (concurring opinion).

40. Eisenstadt v. Baird, 405 U.S. 438, 453 (1972).

41. *Id.* at 460–65 (concurring opinion).

bear and beget children, *that* right could, of course, be vindicated without
need for contraception—people could simply refrain from sexual intercourse. What is really protected as a fundamental right in the contraception
cases is the right to engage in sexual intercourse without having a child. It
was on the basis of these precedents that *Roe* was decided. Interestingly, of
the four justices who would apparently vote to overrule *Roe* (Chief Justice
Rehnquist and Justices White, Scalia, and Kennedy), none has expressed
any disagreement with *Griswold.*

Most people would probably agree that among those liberties that
must be deemed "fundamental" in our society, in addition to the freedoms
embodied in the Bill of Rights, we must include the right to be free from
at least some sorts of state interference in the intimacies of our bedrooms.
As Professor Charles Black of Yale Law School put it, describing the Connecticut criminal ban on the use of contraceptives: "If our constitutional
law could permit such a thing to happen, then we might almost as well not
have any law of constitutional limitations, partly because the thing is so outrageous in itself, and partly because a constitutional law inadequate to deal
with such an outrage would be too feeble, in method and doctrine, to deal
with a very great amount of equally outrageous material."[42]

When the Court revisited the question of abortion in the *Webster* case
in 1989, and when it strongly signaled that it was retreating from the principles of *Roe v. Wade*, Justice Scalia's separate opinion expressed his impa-
tience with most of the other Justices. He thought it too plain to require
extended discussion that the constitutional "mansion" of abortion rights
that he claimed was "constructed overnight in *Roe v. Wade*" should be dis-
mantled as soon as possible.[43]

He was unclear, however, about just how far the demolition project he
had in mind would go. Would it, for example, leave in place the Supreme
Court's decisions upholding the right to birth control? Harvard Law Professor Charles Fried, arguing for the Bush administration in *Webster,* went out of
his way to emphasize that unlike Judge Robert Bork, he thought the Court
had been correct in upholding the birth control right and would not want
to see it undone. But if women have no significant "liberty" at stake in the
abortion context, how can they possess a fundamental liberty to use birth
control? The contradiction becomes clearest when we recognize that some
of the most commonly used methods of birth control, such as the IUD and

---

42. Charles Black, *The Unfinished Business of the Warren Court*, 56 WASH. L. REV. 3, 32
(1970).

43. 492 U.S. at 537 (Scalia, J., dissenting).

even at times the pill, operate as abortifacients, or abortion-causing agents. That is, they do not invariably prevent conception so much as arrest the embryo's development and implantation in the uterine wall at a very early stage in pregnancy. Although Professor Fried told the Court that *Roe* was merely a "thread" that could be pulled without "unravel[ing]" the "fabric" of the Court's privacy decisions, Frank Sussman, counsel for Reproductive Health Services in the *Webster* case, may have been closer to the mark when he replied, "It has always been my personal experience that when I pull a thread, my sleeve falls off."[44]

The threat of government regulation of these kinds of intimate personal choices cannot lightly be dismissed. At the time of the *Griswold* decision, as recently as 1965, the existence of the law prohibiting the use of contraception had prevented the establishment of family planning clinics in Connecticut. Predictably the poor and uneducated suffered disproportionately.

Even after *Griswold* the state of Massachusetts amended its law to prohibit the distribution of contraceptives to unmarried persons for the prevention of pregnancy.[45] Some have argued that even without the protection of the constitutional right to privacy, laws like this simply would not be enacted. But they have been enacted! Others have described them, dismissively, as "uncommonly silly."[46] Such dismissive remarks only cloud the real point: Those who deny the existence of a constitutionally protected right of privacy would abdicate judicial responsibility in protecting individuals from this threat.

X. Does the Presence of a Fetus Automatically Negate the "Private" Character of the Abortion Decision?

And so we come to yet another and a considerably more plausible attack on *Roe*. This attack accepts the woman's right of privacy yet argues that the *abortion* right in particular was invented by the justices in *Roe*.

It may seem strange in this regard even to discuss the woman's right to abortion before considering the rights of the fetus. It may seem a case of staging *Hamlet* without the prince. Yet the Supreme Court has had good reasons for its long tradition of asking *first* about the right that is asserted, to see whether it is a fundamental liberty, and only *then* turning to the reasons,

---

44. *Transcript of Oral arguments Before Court on Abortion Case*, N.Y. Times, Apr. 27, 1989, at B12.

45. Mass. G.L. c. 272 § 21 (1966).

46. Griswold v. Connecticut, 382 U.S. at 527 (Stewart, J., dissenting).

such as protection of the fetus's right to life, that might nonetheless justify that liberty's abridgment. Putting the cart before the horse by inquiring from the outset about government's *justifications* for abridging a liberty would leave us without guidance in deciding how strong a justification to demand. Even the right to free speech can be abridged for a reason that is sufficiently compelling—for example, to prevent the publication of the sailing dates of troopships in time of war. But without first assessing how fundamental the liberty of publication is, we would find ourselves at sea.

Justice White in a dissent from a 1986 abortion ruling suggested that because the decision to terminate a pregnancy affects a fetus, the liberty involved is unlike that involved in the question of whether an individual has a right to use contraception. Unlike the latter case, he argued, the woman deciding to end a pregnancy is not "isolated in her privacy." He argued that because of their effect on others, particular *exercises* of otherwise concededly fundamental liberties, "by their very nature, should be viewed as outside the scope of the fundamental liberty interest."[47]

In a more recent case, one dealing with a biological father's alleged right to receive a hearing on issues of paternity and visitation, Justice Scalia has also criticized the Court's traditional method of examining a right in isolation and then seeing what opposing reason the state puts forward to justify its abridgment. Writing for himself and for fellow conservative Justices Rehnquist, O'Connor, and Kennedy in the 1989 case *Michael H. v. Gerald D.,* he said, in language broader than that previously used by Justice White: "We cannot imagine what compels this strange procedure of looking at the act which is assertedly the subject of a liberty interest in isolation from its effect *upon other people*—rather like inquiring whether there is a liberty interest in firing a gun where the case at hand happens to involve its discharge into another person's body."[48]

Although he was writing to explain why he was ruling against the adulterous biological father in a love triangle, Justice Scalia appears to have been talking, indirectly, about abortion. Justice Scalia's immediate objective was to explain why a man who fathers a child through a sexual liaison with another man's wife has no specially protected "liberty" interest in his parental connection with that child despite the existence of parental "liberties" in general. The Scalia approach would link the existence of a parental interest, such as the one urged by this biological father, with an asserted "right"

---

47. Thornburgh v. American Coll. of Obstetricians & Gynecologists, 476 U.S. 747, 792 n.2 (1986) (White, J., dissenting).
48. *Michael H.,* 491 U.S. at 124 n.4 (plurality opinion) (emphasis added).

to interfere with a marital relationship and would deny that any such right merits recognition.

In the setting of an abortion case, the method that Justices Scalia and White propose would similarly link the existence of a woman's liberty interest in deciding whether to continue her pregnancy with an asserted "right" to end the fetus's life and would deny the existence of any such right at the threshold. That is, their method would simply deny a woman, in the first instance, even a hard look at the reasons why her ability to choose abortion was being restricted by government. Their method would apparently be to define the *woman*'s liberty in terms of the *fetus*—a great rhetorical advantage, since a "right to kill a fetus" wouldn't be fundamental by anyone's definition—and not in terms of the dignity or autonomy of the woman herself. The state would need no special justification to abridge this right as Justice White and Justice Scalia would define it. Of course, it is in requiring a more serious reason, a "compelling" reason, for a restriction of a fundamental liberty or privacy interest and in closely examining the state law to find such a reason that the Court provides protection against the excesses of a temporary majority.

The approach suggested by Justices Scalia and White, which seems almost tailor-made as a way to overrule *Roe v. Wade*, would do violence to all our rights. If it were applied faithfully, it would give the state nearly absolute power over us all. Take, for example, the state's power of military conscription. Obviously that is a complete restriction on a fundamental right. It completely denies a young person's physical liberty. Yet equally obviously, *some* reasons are sufficiently compelling to permit conscription. Conscription, for example, can be justified by the compelling needs of national security. Other reasons will not be compelling. Conscription surely could not be justified, for example, by the state's desire to have a cadre of youngsters available as chauffeurs for state officials or by its wish to have a crew of garbage collectors or oil-spill fighters.

But Justices White and Scalia, at least as they expressed their views in these two opinions, would define the right in terms of the state's interest. Under this approach, of course, conscription for the military is still permissible since there is surely no fundamental liberty interest in endangering the national security. But neither is there a fundamental liberty interest in inhibiting efficient chauffeur-driven travel by state of officials or in preventing the collection of trash or the cleanup of an oil spill. So if the justices' system of analysis were faithfully followed, a state should be as free to conscript a cadre of crack trash collectors or even chauffeurs as it is to draft men for military service in wartime. If we incorporate the state's reason for its regulation into the initial definition of the liberty, in other words, the fundamental nature of that liberty *inevitably vanishes*. We don't even look to the strength of the state's reason for its intrusive action.

If we were to take this approach seriously, then *no right would be fundamental*. And if we do *not* take it at face value—if we assume that Justices White and Scalia would not really have the Court apply so harsh a test in all circumstances—then this method gives judges *more* power to choose whether or not to protect rights than they hold under the Court's current approach. The approach put forward by Justices White and Scalia could not be consistently applied by a majority of the Court without truly radical consequences. So it seems safe to proceed by examining first the asserted liberty—in this case the right of the woman *not to be forced to remain pregnant*—and only then turning to the fetus on the other side of the constitutional equation.

In the context of abortion, the attempt to distinguish the *right not to remain pregnant* from a *right to destroy one's fetus* may seem strange. We must recognize that, in view of today's technology, until the time of fetal "viability" it is (by definition) impossible to perform an abortion—to permit a woman freedom from the sacrifice of pregnancy and childbirth—without killing the fetus from which the woman is separated.

But this is not something that is inherent in nature. One can imagine a time when it will be possible for a woman to decide to terminate her pregnancy but when it will be possible to save the life of the fetus by removing it from the womb and incubating it either in a volunteer "surrogate" mother or in some kind of artificial womb. Of course, if such procedures are developed, society will then have to balance the presumably higher medical risk for the woman posed by those procedures against the increased chance of fetal survival.

As we shall see, the liberty that is most plainly vindicated by the right to end one's pregnancy is the woman's liberty not to be made unwillingly into a mother, the freedom to say no to the unique sacrifice inherent in the processes of pregnancy and childbirth. A "right" not to have a biological child in existence—the right during pregnancy, for example, to *destroy* one's fetus rather than simply being *unburdened* of it—is analytically distinct, and seems harder to support. No one has such a right *after* a child is born; there is certainly no "right" to commit infanticide. Men certainly have no right to destroy a fetus once pregnancy begins, for while the Constitution protects a man's right to engage in nonprocreative sexual activity, it does not give him the power to insist on abortion of a fetus for which he is partially responsible. While there may be arguments in favor of recognizing a woman's right, early in pregnancy, to destroy the fetus growing within her for the very purpose of preventing a living child of hers from coming into being, this is not the liberty the Court undertook to protect in *Roe.*

Judge Bork says that "the right to abort, whatever one thinks of it, is not to be found in the Constitution."[49] In a sense this is obviously right. Indeed, not one of the words "abortion," "pregnancy," "reproduction," "sex," "privacy," "bodily integrity," and "procreation" appears anywhere in the United States Constitution. But neither do such phrases as "freedom of thought," "rights of parenthood," "liberty of association," "family self-determination," and "freedom of marital choice." Yet nearly everyone supposes that at least some of these dimensions of personal autonomy and independence are aspects of the "liberty" which the Fourteenth Amendment says no state may deny to any person "without due process of law."

The "right to abortion" was first *announced,* it's true, in *Roe v. Wade.* But as we have seen, the "right to privacy," whatever its outer bounds, was suggested as early as 1923 in the case of *Meyer v. Nebraska. Roe* was simply the first case in which the general question of state regulation of abortion was squarely considered by the Supreme Court. To argue that for this reason, the Constitution does not protect the right to abortion, or that it did not do so until January 22, 1973, is no better than to argue that it does not protect the "right to contribute money to a political campaign." Although that right was not *announced* until the Supreme Court's 1976 decision in *Buckley v. Valeo,*[50] it is beyond doubt that this right is, and has long been, a right protected by the free speech guarantee of the First Amendment. For that matter, the Supreme Court has never had occasion to declare that young lovers have a fundamental constitutional right to embrace one another lustily as they dance the night away. But that right, too, is there waiting to be proclaimed against any state or locality so prudish as to insist that the young couple conduct themselves with greater decorum.

XI. At How Specific a Level Must "Rights" Be Defined?

This, however, is not a completely satisfactory response to Judge Bork's criticism. The question remains: Even if we admit that certain fundamental rights are protected from infringement by the states, how are we to tell what

---

49. BORK, *supra* note 6, at 112.

50. 424 U.S. 1 (1976) (per curiam).

the "right" in question is? By defining the right broadly or narrowly, one can apparently reach whatever result one desires. The "right to abortion" is a narrow way of describing the right protected in *Roe v. Wade.* Its very specifically makes it seem illegitimate.

By contrast, defining it broadly—for example, as "the right to make such intimate decisions as the decision whether to have a child"—makes it sound more like a right whose recognition is consistent with American tradition.

It seems that this may be the judicial battleground in coming years over the right of privacy. It is a question that has captured the attention of Justice Scalia in particular. Addressing this question in the 1989 parental rights case we have discussed, Justice Scalia argued that the proper approach was to "refer to the most specific level at which a relevant tradition protecting, or denying protection to, the asserted right can be identified."[51]

Not surprisingly, Justice Scalia's approach would do away with the right to choose abortion. But quite apart from that result, which some would welcome, his approach presents grave difficulty. To begin with, while Justice Scalia's test has a nice scientific ring to it, it does not tell us upon what axis we are to determine "specificity." In the case of abortion, for example, are we to look to the most specific tradition with regard to reproduction? Or surgery? Or women? Or children? Is the abortion question about a woman's right not to remain pregnant? About a person's right not to have a child? About a fetus's right not to be mistreated by others, as in assaults upon pregnant women? For that matter, why don't we look to see if there are traditions with respect to particular medical techniques? Justice Scalia cannot tell us.

In almost every case, of course, no matter what axis we examine, Justice Scalia's test will mandate a conclusion that there is no tradition protecting the asserted right. There is no more a tradition protecting the *particular* right to nonprocreative heterosexual intercourse or the *particular* right to live with two grandchildren who are not siblings than there is a tradition protecting the *particular* right to choose an abortion. Justice Scalia's formulation of a test to determine whether a right is fundamental would deny protection even to specific examples of the most historically familiar rights.

Most rights for which people seek vindication in the courts are going to be, at their most *specific* level, *new* rights. America has no long tradition of permitting interracial marriage; the history is just the opposite. But because the Court found a tradition protecting the *broader* right to choose whom to

---

51. 491 U.S. at 127 n.6 (plurality opinion).

marry, it struck down Virginia's antimiscegenation laws in the 1967 case of *Loving v. Virginia.*

It would be a radical transformation indeed if the Constitution were the straitjacket Justice Scalia would make of it—able to protect only those specific practices that existed and were legally approved in the past. The Constitution is, and must be, a living document, not a history book. President Wilson said of the Constitution: "As the life of the nation changes so must the interpretation of the document which contains it change, by a nice adjustment, determined, not by the original intention of those who drew the paper, but by the exigencies and the new aspects of life itself."[52]

Two justices who joined the rest of Justice Scalia's opinion in *Michael H.* (Justices O'Connor and Kennedy) pointedly declined to join him in his strikingly narrow view of the traditions protected by the Constitution. Only Chief Justice Rehnquist agreed completely. Indeed, Justice Scalia's view of the Constitution or at least of its liberty clause drew an emotional dissent from eighty-three-year-old Justice William J. Brennan, Jr., who had served on the Court for thirty-three years as a jurist universally respected for his intellect and integrity. He writes:

> The document that the plurality construes today is unfamiliar to me. It is not the living charter that I have taken to be our Constitution; it is instead a stagnant, archaic, hidebound document steeped in the prejudices and superstitions of a time long past. *This* Constitution does not recognize that times change, does not see that sometimes a practice or rule outlives its foundations. I cannot accept an interpretive method that does such violence to the charter that I am bound by oath to uphold.[53]

XII. Privacy: Who Decides Whether to Terminate a Pregnancy?

So does the right of privacy encompass the right to decide whether to terminate a pregnancy or doesn't it? Is that a fundamental right protected by the Fourteenth Amendment? Is it protected by the tradition and conscience of our people?

Professor Charles Fried, who was solicitor general under President Ronald Reagan, understood that the Supreme Court's line of decisions on the

---

52. WOODROW WILSON, CONSTITUTIONAL GOVERNMENT IN THE UNITED STATES 192 (1908), quoted in MICHAEL KAMMEN, SOVEREIGNTY AND LIBERTY 141 (1988).

53. 491 U.S. at 141 (Brennan, J., dissenting) (emphasis in original).

subject of personal privacy rested squarely on "the moral fact that a person belongs to himself and not others nor to society as a whole."[54] In his book *Right and Wrong* Fried acknowledges that to say, "[M]y body can be used," is to say, "*I* can be used."[55] And there can be no doubt that forcing a woman into continued pregnancy does entail using her body. Although the fetus at some point develops an independent identity and eventually even an independent consciousness, it begins as a living part of the woman's body, growing from a single cell supplied by her and sustained solely by nutrients carried to it through her uterine wall. Fetal cells even circulate in the woman's bloodstream as her pregnancy progresses. To say that the fetus might have rights of its own does not demonstrate that it is somehow a being separate and distinct from its mother, at least in the beginning. It is not a lodger or prisoner or guest, nor is its mother a mere home or incubator. The fetus is, after all, her "flesh and blood."

Some people apparently believe that acknowledging the fetus to be part of the woman's body somehow sacrifices any moral claim on its behalf—as though the fetus would be more secure and its value would be enhanced if we were to pretend that it is an entirely separate or alien being. That assumption rests on a strange view of the psychology and morality of women.

It seems a serious mistake to think that a woman who regards a developing fetus as a part of her body will, as a result of that view, feel freer to injure or destroy it than she would if she were to regard the fetus as some sort of intruder temporarily housed within her womb. On the contrary, it is precisely a woman's identification with the fetus as an aspect of herself, her love for the new life within her as flesh of her flesh and blood of her blood, that makes it seem so strange for the law to intervene between her and that life. If the fetus is a part of its mother, it is certainly a unique part, one infinitely more valued by nearly every mother than, say, her arm or her kidney. To recognize the fetus as part of its mother in deciding what her rights are is not to denigrate the moral value of its life or to deny the possibility that it might be entitled to the protection and concern of society as a whole. At the very least, it cannot fairly be denied that telling a woman what to do or not to do with the fetus within her entails telling her what to do or not to do with her own body.

Beyond this basic point about whose body is being used, the privacy cases recognize that the liberty clause of the Fourteenth Amendment guarantees each of us the right not to have the state shackle us with self-defining

---

54. Correspondence, 6 Philosophy & Public Affairs 288 (1977).
55. Charles Fried, Right and Wrong 121 n.* (1978) (emphasis in original).

decisions. It is fundamental that we remain free of the power of total regi-
mentation held invalid more than sixty-five years ago in *Pierce v. Society of
Sisters*. This requires a zone that is protected by respect for individual autonomy and reverence for the privacy of intimate human relations. It cannot
be denied that this is traditionally central among the values for whose protection the United States, and its Constitution, stands.

The liberty involved in deciding whether to terminate a pregnancy is, in
part, the interest in being able to avoid pregnancy without abstaining from
sex, the liberty recognized as fundamental in the contraception decisions.
But it is much more. Indeed, the right to decide whether to end a pregnancy lies at the very intersection of several liberties that must be deemed
fundamental.

Certainly it is a significant restriction of a woman's physical liberty to
force her to carry a pregnancy to term. Some have dismissed the burden
as mere inconvenience. Whatever the reason some people take that view,
it is not sustainable. Pregnancy entails unique physical invasion and risk.
As Chief Justice Rehnquist has observed in another context, any pregnancy
entails "profound physical, emotional, and psychological consequences."[56]

Over the nine-month term, the size of a pregnant woman's uterus
increases five hundred to a thousand times. Her body weight increases by
twenty-five pounds or more. Even a healthy pregnancy may be accompanied by frequent urination, water retention, nausea, and vomiting, as well
as labored breathing, back pain, and fatigue.[57]

Every pregnancy also entails substantial medical risk. As many as 30
percent of pregnant women have major medical complications, and 60
percent have some kind of medical complication. Labor and vaginal delivery represent unique and painful physical demands that can last for many
hours or even days. Caesarean section (required, under current medical
practice, in one out of four live births) involves invasive surgery, including an abdominal incision and general anesthesia. Continued pregnancy
significantly increases the risk of fatality. Early abortion, of course, is statistically a far safer procedure for a pregnant woman than carrying her pregnancy to term.[58]

Even if one stresses the potential independence of the fetus from the
woman's body, forcing her to continue a pregnancy to term and to deliver

---

56. Michael M. v. Superior Court of Sonoma County, 450 U.S. 464, 471 (1981).

57. *See* Susan Estrich & Kathleen Sullivan, *Abortion Politics: Writing for an Audience of One*,
138 U. Pa. L. Rev. 119, 126–27 (1989).

58. *Id.*

an unwanted baby obviously intrudes into the integrity of her body far more profoundly than do the other invasions for which the Supreme Court has routinely required extremely strong justification—for example, the stomach pumping for evidence invalidated by the Supreme Court in 1952[59] or the surgical removal of a bullet lodged in a suspect's shoulder invalidated by the Supreme Court in 1985.[60]

Being forced to proceed to childbirth also does extreme and unique psychological violence to a woman. The permanent psychological bond created between mother and child has been well documented. Pregnancy is not in this sense a minor and temporary imposition whose burdens are limited by the availability of adoption. The fact is that in 1986, the most recent year for which data are available, only 3 percent of unwed mothers in the United States, whatever their initial disposition to putting an unwanted child up for adoption, actually did so.[61]

As Dr. Harold Rosen, a psychiatrist, described in his 1967 article about abortion, "A Case Study in Social Hypocrisy," many of his pregnant patients told him the same thing: "Do you think I could give my baby away after carrying it for nine months . . . ? [Y]ou can't turn me into the kind of animal that would give my baby away!"[62] Pregnancy does not merely "inconvenience" the woman for a time; it gradually turns her into a mother and makes her one for all time.

Even more dramatically than laws telling one how to bring up one's children or with which family members one may live or laws saying that one has no right to nonprocreative sex, laws telling a woman she must remain pregnant deprive her of the very core of liberty and privacy. It would be quite unthinkable if a liberty broad enough to encompass intimate decisions about the bearing of children, the formation of a family, and the preservation of one's own body were somehow to *exclude* a woman's decision about whether her body is to carry a baby until she becomes a parent— either a parent who thereafter raises her own child or one who undergoes the trauma of giving it up for adoption.

Attorney Jed Rubenfeld, in a 1989 essay entitled "The Right of Privacy," underscores perhaps the deepest sense in which laws restricting abortion

---

59. Rochin v. California, 342 U.S. 165 (1952).

60. Winston v. Lee, 470 U.S. 753 (1985).

61. McNamara, "Choice Wasn't Abortion: Maternity Homes a Refuge for Some," *Boston Globe*, Nov. 26, 1989, Metro/Region, at 1.

62. Harold Rosen, *A Case Study in Social Hypocrisy, in* ABORTION IN AMERICA 310 (Harold Rosen, ed.) (1967).

reduce women to "mere instrumentalities of the state."[63] Such laws "take diverse women with every variety of career, life-plan, and so on, and make mothers of them all."[64]

If the constitutional protection of our individual rights and human dignity mean much of anything, then the freedom to decide whether or not to endure pregnancy *must* be deemed a fundamental aspect of personal privacy. Even if the introduction of the fetus into the picture makes abortion a close question, the right to decide whether or not to carry a pregnancy to term is not a marginal case in terms of whether or not a fundamental liberty of the woman at least is at stake. Pregnancy is a burden that cannot be imposed by the state without the most serious justification.

XIII. Equality: Abortion Rights and Sex Discrimination

There is a further reason why the decision whether or not to end a pregnancy should not be subject to infringement without a compelling reason. Although the Court in *Roe* relied solely on the liberty clause of the Fourteenth Amendment, any restriction that prohibits women from exercising the right to decide whether to end a pregnancy would, in the absence of a truly compelling justification, deny them the "equal protection of the laws" also guaranteed by the Fourteenth Amendment.

In *Skinner v. Oklahoma*, as we saw earlier, the Court recognized the fundamental nature of the right to control one's own reproduction. It did so in part because, in that case, forced sterilizations were being carried out only against those habitual criminals who were guilty of working-class crimes. The statute at issue applied to those convicted of "felonies involving moral turpitude," but it exempted such white-collar offenses as embezzlement and tax violations. As the Court wrote, "[s]terilization of those who have thrice committed grand larceny with immunity for those who are embezzlers is a clear, pointed, unmistakable discrimination."[65]

Laws restricting abortion so dramatically shape the lives of women, and only of women, that their denial of equality hardly needs detailed elaboration. While men retain the right to sexual and reproductive autonomy, restrictions on abortion deny that autonomy to women. Laws restricting access to abortion thereby place a real and substantial burden on women's ability to participate in society as equals. Even a woman who is not pregnant

---

63. Jed Rubenfeld, *The Right of Privacy*, 102 HARV. L. REV. 737, 790 (1989).
64. *Id.* at 788.
65. *Skinner*, 316 U.S. at 541.

is inevitably affected by her knowledge of the power relationships created by a ban on abortion.

It is true that not all women are burdened by restrictions on abortion, although certainly all fertile women of childbearing age are. Laws that disadvantage women disproportionately but that also disadvantage many men—laws favoring war veterans, for example—have sometimes been upheld by the Supreme Court without close scrutiny.[66] But laws restricting abortion do not merely burden women disproportionately; they directly burden *women alone*.

A law that discriminates in such a forceful way against an entire group of people and that poses such an obvious danger of majoritarian oppression and enduring subjugation must not be permitted unless it is needed to serve the most compelling public interest. Otherwise its victims are, in the most fundamental sense imaginable, denied the equal protection of the laws. This is the lesson of *Skinner v. Oklahoma*.

XIV. The "Original Understanding" of the Framers

Notwithstanding all this, foes of the right to choose abortion have a further line of attack they advance even before expressly introducing the fetus into the picture. It was put most succinctly by William Rehnquist in his *Roe* dissent: "By the time of the adoption of the Fourteenth Amendment in 1868, there were at least 36 laws enacted by state or territorial legislatures limiting abortion. . . . [Twenty-one] of the laws on the books in 1868 remain in effect today. . . . The only conclusion possible from this history is that the drafters did not intend to have the Fourteenth Amendment withdraw from the States the power to legislate with respect to this matter."[67]

Obviously, in the interpretation of any written document it is important to examine the intention of those who chose the words. So it is with the Constitution. But the suggestion, almost elevated to a fetish by some in the post-*Roe* new wave of conservative legal scholars, that we must look *only* to the understanding of the Framers with regard to each *particular* situation that comes before a court, is outlandish.[68]

To begin with, in a wide variety of circumstances there will be no correct answer. To ask, for example, "What did Thomas Jefferson think (or what would he have thought) about drug testing in the workplace?" is essentially

66. Personnel Adm'r of Massachusetts v. Feeney, 422 U.S. 256 (1979).
67. Roe v. Wade, 410 U.S. at 174–77 (Rehnquist, J., dissenting).
68. *See* RONALD DWORKIN, A MATTER OF PRINCIPLE 33–71 (1985).

meaningless. The truth is that the framers and the many who voted to ratify the Fourteenth Amendment will have thought and intended many often inconsistent things. In fairness, it must be said that conservatives are frequently as quick to concede all this as liberals and that bogus invocation of "original intent" has by no means been confined to any one part of the ideological spectrum.

We must certainly look at the intent of the framers, but at a much more general level. The Constitution, particularly in its open-ended provisions such as those guaranteeing liberty, equality, and due process, lays down broad principles. It is these principles that courts must apply to particular situations.[69] In the context of the Eighth Amendment's prohibition on cruel and unusual punishments, for example, the Supreme Court has held that what is "cruel" cannot be determined by what practices would have been so considered at the time of the framers. Rather, "[t]he Amendment must draw its meaning from the evolving standards of decency that mark the progress of a maturing society."[70]

As the great chief justice John Marshall put it more generally, "we must never forget that it is a *constitution* we are expounding."[71] Even in situations with which the framers of a particular constitutional provision would have been familiar, therefore, the provisions of the Constitution may have consequences that would have surprised them.

The interpretive method put forward by some of those who view the original understanding as a rigid talisman would plunge our nation into a deep freeze in which, in the absence of a new constitutional amendment for each occasion on which the judiciary has heard a case presenting an arguably new right, only the very rights anticipated in 1791, when the Bill of Rights was ratified, or in 1868, when the Fourteenth Amendment was adopted, would be protected.

For this precise reason one of the principal architects of the Constitution, James Madison, insisted that his notes from the Constitutional Convention not be published until after his death. The United States was not to be bound by the particular vision of the small group of men who, in the late eighteenth century, drafted its fundamental charter. As Madison wrote, "[a]s a guide in expounding and applying the provisions of the Constitution, the debates and incidental decisions of the Convention can have no authoritative character." Indeed, Madison stated that his knowledge of the

---

69. *See* Ronald Dworkin, Law's Empire 70–72, 355–99 (1986).
70. Trop v. Dulles, 356 U.S. 86, 101 (1959) (plurality opinion).
71. McCulloch v. Maryland, 17 US. (Four Wheat) 316, 407 (1989) (emphasis in original).

views expressed by delegates to the Constitutional Convention were a possible source of "bias" in his own interpretation of the Constitution.[72]

A world in which we focused upon the subjective and narrow intent of selected framers in deciding the meaning of various constitutional provisions would be a strange one indeed. For one thing, each constitutional provision has many authors, and there is the problem of which framer's intent should count as decisive. For another thing, constitutional provisions become law not when they are proposed by the authors but when they are duly ratified. Needless to say, the assumptions and intentions of the individuals who vote to ratify a provision may differ from one ratifier to another, and it may be that the ratifiers' intent differs significantly from that of the proposers. However we were to resolve these many differences, the results would be peculiar and often unacceptable. For starters, the Bill of Rights would not apply to protect us from any of the actions of state government, however outrageous.

Or consider this example: If specific "original intent" alone governed, we would live in a world in which although the schools run by the states and their subdivisions (the cities and towns) would have to be racially integrated (this is the command of the equal protection clause of the Fourteenth Amendment as interpreted by the Supreme Court in *Brown v. Board of Education*), the schools run by the federal government—for example, in the District of Columbia—*could* be segregated by law.

The equal protection clause of the Fourteenth Amendment reads: "No State shall . . . deny to any person within its jurisdiction the equal protection of the laws." As its words make clear, it applies only to the states. While there is a second due process clause that applies to the federal government, contained in the Bill of Rights, in the Fifth Amendment to the Constitution, there is no textual guarantee that the *federal* government must guarantee *equal protection* of the law. Indeed, the same Congress that adopted the Fourteenth Amendment subsequently operated a segregated school system in the District of Columbia.[73] At this specific level we know that the original understanding of the guarantee of equality in the Fourteenth Amendment must have been that it did *not* prohibit the federal government from running segregated schools in the nation's capital. And on a more general level, it would be hard indeed to attribute to those who wrote or ratified the

---

72. H. Jefferson Powell, *The Original Understanding of Original Intent*, 98 Harv. L. Rev. 885, 936 (1985), quoting 3 Letters and Other Writings of James Madison 53, 54, 228 (1865).

73. Brief for Respondents, Bolling v. Sharpe, 347 U.S. 497 (1954), at 12–13.

Fifth Amendment in the late eighteenth century even a broad equality principle that could one day embrace a ban on segregation by race.

Nonetheless, the Supreme Court—on the day in 1954 that it handed down *Brown*—decided in the companion case of *Bolling v. Sharpe*[74] that the public schools of Washington, D.C., must be desegregated. While the Court recognized that the Fourteenth Amendment's equal protection clause does not apply to the federal government, it observed that "[i]n view of our decision that the Constitution prohibits the states from maintaining racially segregated public schools, it would be unthinkable that the same Constitution would impose a lesser duty on the Federal Government."[75] The Court held that the federal law segregating the District's schools violated the due process clause of the Fifth Amendment, which it saw as informed by, and embodying, the equality principle adopted many decades later in the equal protection of the Fourteenth.

Strict adherence to a jurisprudence of original intent simply would not have permitted this result. And indeed Judge Bork, who has long been a vocal advocate of "originalism," continues to condemn emphatically the *Bolling* decision that invalidated the school segregation laws of Washington, D.C., as a "clear rewriting of the Constitution by the Warren Court." He calls it "social engineering from the bench."[76] Although Judge Bork often tries to come up with reasons why politically popular decisions that he considers illegitimate should have come out the same way under some different provision of the Constitution—he argues, for example, that *Meyer v. Nebraska* and *Pierce v. Society of Sisters,* the early child-rearing cases, could have been decided the same way under the First Amendment[77]—here he doesn't even try.

XV. Judicial Legislation?

Another criticism of *Roe,* and one that must be addressed because of its apparently powerful hold on many opponents of abortion rights, is that it was an essentially legislative act because the elaborate scheme announced in *Roe,* with its delineation of trimesters and its emphasis on the significance of viability, is not suitably "judicial." This is different from the argument that our democratic system somehow requires that abortion be left to legislatures, but it seems no more convincing.

---

74. 347 U.S. 497 (1954).

75. *Id.* at 500.

76. BORK, *supra* note 6, at 83, 84.

77. *Id.* at 47–49.

In *Webster,* Chief Justice Rehnquist wrote that the trimester framework is "hardly consistent with the notion of a Constitution cast in general terms, as ours is. . . . The key elements of the *Roe* framework . . . are not found in the text of the Constitution." He went on to argue that *Roe* has engendered "a web of legal rules that have become increasingly intricate, resembling a code of regulations rather than a body of constitutional doctrine."[78]

This is remarkable argument for a judge to make. As Justice Blackmun stated powerfully in his *Webster* dissent, much of our constitutional doctrine is made up of judge-made rules that give detailed, operational content to broad constitutional guarantees. For example, the Supreme Court has announced a complicated standard for deciding whether speech is obscene, in order to determine whether it is outside the protective reach of the First Amendment. Even Judge Bork, when sitting on the U.S. Court of Appeals for the District of Columbia Circuit, won praise from free speech advocates when he insisted that First Amendment rules dealing with libel suits must take account of a "rich variety of factors" so that those rules might properly reflect "how the framers' values, defined in the context of the world they knew, apply to the world we know."[79] Equal protection cases, too, are decided by reference to a complex series of judicially created tests whose texts cannot be found in the Constitution.

Neither is the complexity of the rules about what abortion restrictions will and will not pass constitutional muster a hallmark of illegitimately "legislative" judicial decisionmaking. Indeed, it is in areas in which there has been significant adjudication that such lines appear, marking the outer bounds of a well-considered constitutional doctrine. For example, the Fourth Amendment's ban on unreasonable searches and seizures has been held to permit the police, when arresting the driver of a car, to search without a warrant the passenger compartment of the car, any luggage in the car and its glove compartment, but not the car's trunk or any luggage it contains.

The argument that *Roe* is legislative in character retains some vitality and credibility because of the method by which the rules enunciated in *Roe* were handed down. Ordinarily the Court will not, in Justice Brandeis's words, "formulate a rule of constitutional law broader than is required by the precise facts to which it is to be applied."[80] This is a rule of judicial prudence with roots in the policies underlying the constitutional limits on the

---

78. 492 U.S. at 518 (plurality opinion).

79. Ollman v. Evans, 750 F.2d 970, 993–95 (D.C. Cir. 1984) (concurring opinion), *cert. denied,* 471 U.S. 1127 (1985).

80. Ashwander v. TVA, 297 U.S. 288, 347 (1936) (Brandeis, J., concurring), quoting Liverpool & Philadelphia Steamship Co. v. Comm'r of Emigration, 113 U.S. 33, 39 (1885).

power of the judiciary, included in Article III of the Constitution, to decide only "cases" or "controversies."

The result of this principle is a system of case-by-case adjudication in which areas of the law evolve gradually as each new situation, with its unique implications, is presented to the Court. The Court can thus consider carefully, in one concrete situation after another, the application of the reasoning of its previous decisions to new circumstances.

Roe v. Wade, of course, did far more than that! Rather than simply strike down the Texas statute that prohibited abortion except to save the life of the woman, leaving the exact contours of the constitutional right to privacy for later cases that presented less intrusive abortion regulations, the Court spelled out at one breath much of a complex constitutional doctrine. This obviously was not required by the "precise facts" of the case.

This approach is not necessarily illegitimate. The Court is under no duty to announce Delphic rules or to leave the country guessing about its intentions. On the contrary, it has some responsibility to give lower courts guidance and to permit the American people to order their affairs with confidence in the lay of the legal land and to seek a constitutional amendment if there is overwhelming consensus that the Court is wrong. Indeed, many judges have argued that the general rule about the breadth of constitutional pronouncements should be overridden when good cause exists.

Still, the sensitivity of the abortion question counseled more restraint than the Court exhibited in *Roe.* A gradual enunciation and articulation of the line that separated permissible state laws from laws that violated the constitutional right to privacy might have permitted the nation gradually to become acclimated to each piece of the abortion right and to have understood why each new piece of the framework that protected a woman's right to reproductive choice was put in place. This approach would have been more judicious, and it might also have given those who oppose abortion less of a shock, one that even today informs the arguments of some that *Roe* was a brazen act of judicial fiat.

XVI. What's at Stake?

Why is it so important whether the abortion right, although nowhere mentioned in the Constitution by name, is a fundamental right protected by that document so that any governmental restriction of the right requires special justification? The answer is that much more is at stake in this battle, a battle being fought out in the Supreme Court today, than abortion rights alone.

A world with *only* enumerated rights would be a vastly different one from the world we know today. If women were held not to have a fundamental liberty interest in control over their own bodies simply because that right is not expressly stated in the Constitution, not only could abortion be *prohibited*, but abortion as well as sterilization could be *mandated* by the state. If a person had no specially protected "liberty" interest in privacy or in decisions about reproduction, the state could make a rational decision, for reasons of population control or eugenics, for example, to require abortions in certain circumstances, on pain of criminal punishment or imposition of a tax or other penalty. The courts would be unable to interfere in the name of the Constitution.

But if there *is* a fundamental right to decide whether or not to terminate a pregnancy, then before the Supreme Court could uphold laws of this sort, it would have to decide that the reasons supporting them were exceptionally strong (or, as the Court usually puts it, "compelling"). That is a decision very rarely made. Even if the Court found protection of the fetus a compelling reason for restricting abortions, one would hope it would not find population control a compelling enough reason to abridge reproductive freedom. Thus, the Court could strike down laws requiring abortion or sterilization even while upholding laws banning abortion.

This may seem an unlikely area for concern, but in China, of course, such policies are now in effect. As we saw in the preceding chapter, a policy of forced abortion is utilized by the Chinese government, and has been used by other governments in the past, as a means of population control.

In addition, in the Gansu Province of China, a law mandates that moderately to severely mentally retarded people must be sterilized if they are or plan to become married, even to people of normal intelligence. This law is being strictly enforced. If the woman becomes pregnant anyway, whether she herself is retarded or not, she is forced to have an abortion. An official of the Gansu Province Family Planning Association was quoted in the *New York Times* as saying that the "purpose of the law is to raise the quality of our population and our nation."[81] Similar sentiments animated the policy of Nazi Germany, also described in the preceding chapter. Between 1933 and 1940 more than five hundred thousand people were ordered sterilized against their will by the eugenic health courts in Germany.

Most of us would probably like to believe that such a thing could never happen in the United States. But our states have a long and gruesome

---

81. Nicholas Kristoff, *Chinese Region Uses New Law to Sterilize Mentally Retarded*, N.Y. TIMES, Nov. 21, 1989, at A1.

history of forced sterilization. Many, many thousands of Americans were sterilized in this century by the states on eugenic grounds. Indeed, the Supreme Court upheld the involuntary sterilization of a woman named Carrie Buck by the state of Virginia in the 1927 case of *Buck v. Bell,* in which Justice Holmes wrote, in words that now seem ominously totalitarian, "society can prevent those who are manifestly unfit from continuing their kind. . . . Three generations of imbeciles are enough."[82]

Stephen J. Gould has written that by today's standards, Carrie Buck, who was sterilized with the Supreme Court's blessing, would not be considered mentally deficient.[83] Under the law upheld by the Supreme Court in 1927, the state of Virginia continued to perform forced, involuntary sterilizations *until 1972.*

This did not violate any right protected by the Bill of Rights. The right to be free of this kind of invasion is nowhere explicitly mentioned in the Constitution. Only the constitutional protection of unenumerated rights under the liberty clause could protect us from a legislative decision to sterilize some of us or to force some of us to have abortions. And if women may be forced to use their bodies to develop and nurture children against their will without even a compelling public justification, who can guess what other bodily invasions and indignities could be imposed upon any of us without any special showing of necessity? The threat of such invasions is as real as the history of the twentieth century.

---

82. Buck v. Bell, 274 U.S. 200, 207 (1927).
83. Steven J Gould, The Mismeasure of Man 336 (1981 paperback ed.).

17

The Genesis of Liberalized Abortion in New York: A Personal Insight[1]

By Alan F. Guttmacher, M.D.

Since my debut as an Aesculapian antedates those of other physician contributors to this volume, I thought it valuable to relate medical practices and attitudes toward induced abortion three-quarters of a century ago and to analyze the genesis, direction, and magnitude of the change in those attitudes and practices and its reflection in the legal position on abortion.

I was taught obstetrics at the Johns Hopkins Medical School by Dr. J. Whitridge Williams, one of the great medical figures of the 1920s. He was forceful, confident and didactic. To him, and therefore to us, induced abortion was either therapeutic or "criminal." He told us therapeutic abortion was performed to save the life of the pregnant woman and that the primary threats involved dysfunction by three organs: the heart, the lung, and the kidney. To these hazards he begrudgingly added toxic vomiting of pregnancy. I say "begrudgingly" because I remember full well the drastic treatment meted out to hyperemetic gravidae: isolation, submammary infusions, rectal clyses, and feeding by stomach tube. To resort to therapeutic abortion in these cases was admission of medical failure. No medical sanction was then given to abortion on socioeconomic or psychological grounds.

The experiences I encountered during my residency from 1925 to 1929 made me question the wisdom of such a restrictive medical policy. In a short period, I witnessed three deaths from illegal abortions: a 16-year-old

---

1. Dr. Guttmacher wrote this retrospective for the 1973 edition of ABORTION, MEDICINE AND THE LAW, and it has been included in subsequent editions because of his unique historical role in the struggle for a woman's right to choose. It is reprinted here with permission of Dr. J. Douglas Butler.

with a multiperforated uterus, a mother of four who died of sepsis rejecting
another child, and a patient in early menopause who fatally misinterpreted
amenorrhea. My skepticism of the wisdom of existing abortion laws was further reinforced by an incident involving Dr. Williams. A social worker came
to me seeking abortion services for a 12-year-old black child who had been
impregnated by her father. Dr. Williams was a court of one to validate abortion requests, so I sought his permission to perform the operation. He was
sympathetic but reminded me that Maryland prohibited abortion except
where necessary to preserve the life of the mother,[2] and he did not believe
that continuation of pregnancy in this case would endanger the girl's life.
When I brought up the social injustice of compelling a child to bear her
father's bastard, Dr. Williams compromised, saying that if I could obtain a
letter from the district attorney granting special permission to the Johns
Hopkins Hospital, then I could perform the abortion.[3] I failed to get this
permission and delivered the baby seven months later. At about the same
time, one of the residents at a neighboring hospital showed me a child, the
daughter of an army colonel, who had been hysterotomized to eliminate
pregnancy conceived through "rape." Experiences such as this made me
question the possibilities for social injustice and disparate treatment, ever
present under a restrictive policy which gave one man the sole power to
determine the validity and permissibility of abortion services.

Such a restrictive policy could lead to reliance on those who would go
outside the law to provide the desired services. Indeed, during the same
period there were two competent physician-abortionists in Baltimore who
practiced for many years relatively unmolested by the police. They were
so well-known that an inquiry addressed to either a traffic policeman or
a salesgirl would have elicited their names with equal ease. They were not
partners, but close collaborators, occasionally preparing death certificates
for each other. One, while attending a public national meeting in Washington, rose to defend the service provided by illegal medical abortionists who
had been defamed by a speaker. He stated openly that there had been but
four deaths in the 7,000 abortions with which he had been associated. This
was before the first use of antibiotics, "salting out," and other precaution-
ary procedures. Finally, years later when a complaint was filed, the district

---

2. *Cf.* MD. ANN. CODE art. 43. § 137(a) (1971). The present statute is patterned after the
Model Penal Code. See notes 11–12 *infra* and accompanying text.

3. Presently, California follows a similar procedure in cases of incest. CAL. HEALTH &
SAFETY CODE § 25952 (West Supp. 1971) (permitting abortion where the district attorney
is satisfied that there is probable cause to believe that the pregnancy resulted from rape or
incest and this validation is transmitted to the Committee of the Medical Staff).

attorney was compelled to take official cognizance of the existence of one of the two abortionists. At the trial, the abortionist offered to produce, in his defense, a list of 300 reputable physicians who had referred cases to him. I assume my name was among them.

On one occasion, the nestor of American gynecologists, Dr. Robert L. Dickinson, called me from New York requesting that I arrange a meeting in Baltimore with Dr. T. We lunched at a hotel, and Dr. T. produced a roster of his patients, duration of pregnancy, parity, city of residence, fees, source of referral, etc. On another occasion Dr. T met with a few of the senior medical faculty of Johns Hopkins to disclose his technique. To minimize infection, he had invented a boilable rubber perineal shield with a rubber sleeve that fitted into the vagina and through which he worked. His technique was to pack one-inch gauze strips into the cervix and lower uterine segment the night before he was to evacuate the conceptas. After 12 hours of packing, the cervix was wide open, and he was able to empty the uterus with an ovum forceps, followed by curettage without anesthesia. In advanced pregnancies he inserted intrauterine bougies, held in place by a vaginal pack until strong contractions commenced, which not infrequently took several days.

These early medical experiences with the unavailability of abortions in reputable hospitals and the incidence of illegal abortion convinced me that permitting abortion only "to preserve the life of the mother"[4] was undesirable and unenforceable. I thus sought changes which would both curb the morbidity and mortality of illegal abortion and eliminate the ethnic and social discrimination which was inherent to all induced abortions, whether legal or illegal.

I found in my hospital contacts that obstetricians and gynecologists were the most conservative medical group in regard to abortion. Internists and psychiatrists were constantly berating us for our low incidence of legal pregnancy terminations. Indeed, there had developed a feeling of prideful accomplishment among the ob-gyn staff if one's hospital had a low therapeutic abortion rate and a feeling of disgrace if the rate was relatively high compared to similar institutions. I shared this viewpoint, no doubt swayed by the writings and addresses of obstetrical leaders such as Drs. George Kosmak and Samuel Cosgrove. My sentiment was that as long as the law was as restrictive as it was, doctors should not breach it, but work to change the law—a position which I forthrightly espoused in the classroom. Despite the fact that it was not a radical notion, this position had few adherents. Members of the medical profession were content to leave things as they were;

---

4. *See, e.g.,* TENN. CODE ANN. § 39-301 (1955), which restricted abortions to such cases of necessity.

they would frequently perform a therapeutic abortion for a favored patient because of her important social position, or at least refer her to a safe, illegal medical operator. But acceptance of generally available legal abortion was still far in the future. In the early 1930s, I was invited to present a paper on abortion reform before the New Jersey Obstetrical and Gynecological Society. One participant, Dr. Cosgrove, tore into me like a tank. I can still recall my discomfiture and frustration at the unyielding establishment.

Until 1940, the decision to permit or to deny therapeutic abortion in the individual case was made solely by the chief of the obstetrical service. The physician handling the case presented the patient's history, physical examination, and laboratory findings to the chief who, in turn, made an immediate decision. Through personal observations, I learned that it was impossible to predict how the chief would decide, for such decisions seemed to turn on his mood and on the latest article he had read on the subject.

It was in recognition of the inadequacies of such a procedure that, when I became chief of obstetrics at Baltimore's Sinai Hospital in 1942, I decided to have a staff committee of five make decisions about abortion.[5] This committee consisted of representatives from medicine, surgery, pediatrics, psychiatry, and obstetrics, with the obstetrician as chairman. As far as I knew, such a plan had never been tried, although I have since learned that it had been in force in a few other hospitals. The abortion committee system functioned well. Among other things it added medical expertise in special areas beyond obstetrics. Moreover, greater consistency was attained through adherence to guidelines adopted in cases with similar factual patterns. I do not believe that the committee system significantly affected the hospital's incidence of legal abortion, but at least all applicants were treated on an equal basis.

When I became director of obstetrics and gynecology at the Mount Sinai Hospital in New York in 1952, I learned that the department of gynecology (there had been no department of obstetrics previous to my arrival) had performed 30 abortions in the previous six months. I was told that if a private patient was denied abortion in another institution, she frequently sought abortion at Mount Sinai because of its well-known, relatively liberal policy. I recall resenting this reputation. Forthwith we introduced the

---

5. The committee method of decisions regarding abortions is prevalent and is codified in many states. CAL. HEALTH & SAFETY CODE § 25951 (b) (West Supp. 1971), for example, requires the consent of an approved hospital committee before an abortion can be performed. The statute requires that the committee be composed of not less than three licensed physicians and requires that the decision to permit an abortion be unanimous.

committee system, the results of which have been reported in three publications.[6] The committee met each Wednesday afternoon if any case was to be heard. Forty-eight hours prior to that meeting, the staff obstetrician who wished to carry out an abortion would have provided each member a summary of the case together with recommendations from consultants, if any had examined the patient. The staff obstetrician and frequently a consultant from a medical discipline germane to the problem (for example, a cardiologist for a cardiac case or a neurologist for the mother who had borne a child with muscular dystrophy) presented their findings or views. The committee always voted in executive session, and a unanimous vote was required to authorize abortion. This requirement was not as forbidding as it sounds, for in almost every instance the other members of the committee would agree with the opinion of the member within whose discipline the problem lay.

Statistics on the number of abortions performed at Mount Sinai and at other New York hospitals over generally contemporaneous time periods are illuminating. At Mount Sinai Hospital, 207 therapeutic abortions were performed between 1953 and 1960, yielding an incidence of 5.7 abortions per 1,000 live births. Partly because of my efforts to eliminate discrimination, the rate was 6.3 per 1,000 live births on the private service and 4.6 per 1,000 births on the ward service.[7] One commentator, in reporting figures from another large New York voluntary hospital for the years 1951 to 1954, showed an incidence of 8.1 abortions per 1,000 live births on the private service and a rate of 2.4 on the ward service.[8] Statistics were also available for two New York municipal hospitals: Metropolitan Hospital (1959-61) and Kings County Hospital (1958-60). In the former, the abortion incidence was 0.077 per 1,000 live births, and in the latter the incidence was 0.37 per 1,000 live births.[9] Gold published a study of abortion incidence for all New York hospitals for the period 1960-62.[10] The incidence in proprietary institutions was shown to be 3.9 per 1,000 live births; and in the voluntary hospitals the incidence was 2.4 on the private services and 0.7 on the ward services.

---

6. Alan Guttmacher, *Therapeutic Abortion: The Doctor's Dilemma*, 21 J. Mt. Sinai Hospital 111 (1954); Alan Guttmacher, *Therapeutic Abortion in a Large General Hospital*, 37 Surgical Clinics of N. America 459 (1957); Alan Guttmacher, *The Legal and Moral Status of Therapeutic Abortion*, in IV Progress in Gynecology 279 (J. Meigs & S. Sturgis, eds. 1963).

7. A. Guttmacher, The Legal and Moral Status of Therapeutic Abortion, in IV Progress in Gynecology 289 (J. Meigs & S. Sturgis eds. 1963).

8. C. McLane, Abortion in the United States (Calderone ed. 1958).

9. Guttmacher, *supra* note 6.

10. Edwin Gold et al., *Therapeutic Abortions in New York City: A 20 Year Review*, 55 Am. J. of Public Health 964 (1965).

Municipal hospitals showed a rate of 0.1 per 1,000 live births. There was also a marked ethnic differential: the ratio of therapeutic abortions per 1,000 live births was 2.6 for Whites, 0.5 for Negroes, and 0.1 for Puerto Ricans.

Not only was there great disparity in the incidence rates among various hospitals but, in addition, the abortion policies and rules established by hospitals were confusingly different. Mount Sinai, for example, validated abortion for well-documented rubella (German measles), whereas Columbia-Presbyterian did not. Mount Sinai did not permit abortion for rape, whereas St. Johns in Brooklyn did. The marked differences among hospitals in regard to incidence and standards as well as patient discrimination—discrimination between ward and private patients and between ethnic groups—served to aggravate my dissatisfaction with the status quo and led to my desire for the enactment of a new law.

The question was, what should be the content of an ideal law? Because my twin brother, the late Dr. Manfred Guttmacher, a forensic psychiatrist, was a member of the American Law Institute (ALI), which was then engaged in writing a revised penal code, I was present on a Sunday afternoon in December 1959 when Mr. Herbert Wechsler (professor of law at Columbia) unveiled his model abortion statute now called the ALI bill.[11] The recommended statute provided that a doctor would be permitted to perform an abortion: (1) if continuation of pregnancy "would gravely impair the physical or mental health of the mother"; (2) if the doctor believed "that the child would be born with grave physical or mental defects"; or (3) if the pregnancy resulted from rape or incest.[12]

When Professor Wechsler had finished presenting his suggested statute, an elderly gentleman sitting at the large, felt-covered table inaudibly mumbled some comment. Mr. Wechsler said, "What did you say, Judge Hand?" The eminent federal jurist, Learned Hand said, "It is a rotten law." Mr. Wechsler asked why, and Judge Hand responded, "It's too damned conservative." How right he was. Yet most of those present, including myself, disagreed with him. The Wechsler abortion bill was passed by the institute as part of the total revised penal code revealed to the public in 1962. Many, including myself, hailed it as the answer to the legal problems surrounding abortion, which had always been the doctor's dilemma.

Even though the ALI Code had not yet been adopted by any state, its mere promulgation opened the medical profession's eyes to the preservation of health as being a justification for abortion. The most difficult health hazard to document (but equally difficult to refute) was significant trauma

---

11. MODEL PENAL CODE § 230.3(2) (Proposed Official Draft, 1962).
12. *Id.*

to the psychic stability of the pregnant individual. "Psychiatric" indications for abortion rapidly increased in importance. Tietze's figures demonstrate that in 1963 psychiatric indications accounted for 0.57 legal abortions per 1,000 live births in the United States; in 1965 the rate was 0.76 per 1,000, and in 1967 it was 1.50 per 1,000.[13] The increasing frequency of psychiatric justifications for abortion caused concern for many. Because the psychiatric indications were so ill-defined and pliable, it was feared that they might become an upper-class ticket for legal abortion, thus increasing discrimination and doing little to lower the morbidity and mortality rates in the population at large. In 1967, Colorado, California, and North Carolina,[14] and in 1968, Maryland and Georgia,[15] all modified their respective statutes, using the ALI bill as the prototype. Between 1967 and 1968 the incidence of legal abortions in the United States increased from 2.59 to 5.19 per 1,000 live births, and abortions for psychiatric indications increased from 1.50 to 3.61 per 1,000 live births.[16]

In December 1968, I was appointed to Governor Rockefeller's 11-member commission which had been formed to examine the abortion statute of New York State and to make recommendations for change. When the governor convened the commission, he said, "I am not asking whether New York's abortion law should be changed. I am asking how it should be changed." The commission was made up of a minister, a priest, a rabbi, three professors of law, three physicians, a poetess, and the president of a large black woman's organization. There were four Catholics, four Protestants, and three Jews. The commission met every two weeks for more than three months. It was apparent that three members wanted no change in the old law despite the governor's charge, two wished abortion removed entirely from the criminal code, and six advocated the enactment of the ALI model with further liberalization: the majority report—approved 8-3—added legal abortion on request for any mother of four children. My proposal of adding a clause to permit abortion on request for any woman 40 years or older was voted down—this was April 1969.

---

13. Christopher Tietze, *United Slates: Therapeutic Abortions, 1963 to 1968*, 59 STUDIES IN FAMILY PLANNING 5 (1970). Tietze's figures were based on hospitals reporting to The Professional Activities Survey in Ann Arbor, Michigan.

14. *See* COLO. REV. STAT. ANN. § 40-6-101(3)(a) (1971); CAL. HEALTH & SAFETY CODE § 25951 (West Supp. 1971); N.C. GEN. STAT. § 14-45.1 (supp. 1971).

15. *See* MD. ANN. CODE art. 43, § 137(a) (1971); GA. CODE ANN. § 26-1202 (1971). *See also* GA. CODE ANN. § 26-9925a(a) (1971) (worded identically to section 26-1202) (a prefatory note preceding section 26-992la indicates that there is some doubt as to which statute is in effect).

16. Tietze, *supra* note 13, at 7.

The more I studied early results from the five states which had been the first to liberalize their laws, the more I began to espouse the opinion that abortion statutes should be entirely removed from the criminal code. The number of legal abortions being undertaken under the new liberalized laws, when contrasted with the figures for the previously undertaken illegal abortions, was far too low. In 1968, for example, California reported only about 5,000 abortions under the new law.[17] It is true that this number has steadily increased to a present rate of over 100,000 per year, but that increase stems in large part from an increase in the number of abortions legitimized on psychiatric grounds: Over 90 percent of current abortions are performed on that ground.[18] In actuality it places the psychiatrist in the untenable situation of being an authority in socio-economics. I examined the situation personally in Colorado and discovered that two Denver hospitals were doing virtually all of the pregnancy interruptions and these were being performed primarily on the private sector. This clearly implied that the state-imposed requirement of two psychiatric consultations was causing an effective discrimination against ward patients: private consultations were too expensive as to be available only to the wealthier patients, and psychiatric appointments in public facilities were booked solid for three months—far beyond the time limitation on obtaining an abortion. From these experiences, I reluctantly concluded that abortion on request— necessitating removal of "abortion" from the penal codes—was the only way to truly democratize legal abortion and to sufficiently increase the numbers performed of legal abortion so as to decrease the incidence of illegal abortions. I came to this conclusion in 1969, 47 years after abortion first came to my medical attention when I was a third-year medical student. Abortion on request, a position which I now support after having been converted by years of medical practice and observation, was soon to have its trial in New York, the state in which I reside. This gave me the opportunity to observe firsthand how effectively it would function. The three criteria to be used for evaluation were straightforward. Did abortion on request save lives? Did it minimize socioethnic discrimination? Did it reduce the incidence of illegal abortions?

---

17. California's Therapeutic Abortion Act became operative November 8, 1967. During the first calendar year under the new law, legal abortions reported from the entire state were 5,030. *See* E. Overstreet, *California's Abortion Law—A Second Look, in* ABORTION AND THE UNWANTED CHILD 16 (Carl Reiterman, ed. 1971).

18. See Bureau of Maternal and Child Health, 4th Annual Report on the Implementation of the California Therapeutic Abortion Act (1971).

18

The Medical and Research Uses of Human Fetal Tissues[1]

By Kenneth J. Ryan, M.D.

I. Research and Transplantation Involving Human Fetal Tissue

Human fetal tissue has been used in research studies to advance general biological knowledge and for specific application to human medical needs. In one of the most notable cases, kidney tissue obtained from a human fetal source was used to culture the polio virus in the development of the polio vaccine. Since some viruses infect only human cells, human fetal cells in culture provide a way to study viruses outside the body. Human fetal tissue also allows detailed study of the factors controlling the normal growth and development of the fetus as well as those factors causing fetal disease and disability. Actually, the bulk of research performed with fetal tissue is for the ultimate benefit of the fetus as a class in terms of better management of normal pregnancy and better diagnostics and therapy for problem cases. Amniocentesis to determine fetal lung maturity as a marker of the ability to survive outside the womb is a good case in point. Study of fetal lung cells and their excretory products provided the basis for this life-saving diagnostic test.[2]

---

1. This chapter appeared in an earlier edition of ABORTION, MEDICINE AND THE LAW. It has been updated and is reprinted here with permission of Dr. J. Douglas Butler.

2. Association of American Medical Colleges, *Summary, Fetal Research and Fetal Tissue Research* (June 1988).

Another form of research has involved the use of fetal tissue for transplantation to human recipients to correct a disease process. In the most promising cases, the human subject has a disease caused by the absence of a substance that the fetal tissue can provide after transplantation. An example is a diabetic lacking insulin who is now treated by daily injections of the hormone. That individual might benefit from a transplant of pancreatic cells that could produce insulin. If the transplant is successful, the diabetic would essentially be cured of the disease.

The diseases and conditions for which fetal tissue transplantation have been considered include not only diabetes but Parkinson's disease, immune deficiency diseases, disorders of the blood cells including leukemia, Alzheimer's disease, spinal cord injuries and a range of other conditions.[3]

II. Clinical Experience with Fetal Tissue Transplantation

Human deficiency diseases have been treated since the early part of the 20th century with extracts of animal organs, as in the case of thyroid extract for hypothyroidism and pancreatic extracts of insulin for diabetes. In each case the animal hormone is similar or identical to the human form and can make up for the body's inability to secrete the hormone. With modern science, human hormones are synthesized chemically or by recombinant technology as, for example, insulin of recombinant DNA origin. In any case, rather than inject hormone extracts or pure hormones, it is preferable to substitute the diseased hormonal tissue with tissue transplants and thus "cure" the deficiency. Animal tissues (xenografts) cannot ordinarily be transplanted to humans because of the body's immune rejection response. Even tissue of human origin is rejected as a transplant unless immune suppressive drugs are used or the tissue is typed for compatibility. Some of these problems can be overcome by the use of fetal tissue, which may elicit less of an immune rejection response and which contains fewer cells that can attack the tissue recipient with a graft versus host reaction.

III. Fetal Transplants to Replace the Thymus

Transplantation of the thymus is perhaps the only example in which fetal transplantation might reasonably be considered a form of therapy rather

---

3. Council Report, *Medical Applications of Fetal Tissue Transplantation*, 263 J. AM. MED. ASSN. 565–70 (1990).

than simply a research maneuver. One defect of the relatively rare congenital disease called DiGeorge's Syndrome is an inadequate immune system due to the absence of the thymus gland. Without a thymus the infant cannot fight off infections and generally dies in the first year of life from overwhelming sepsis. More than 20 years ago, the first successful fetal thymus transplant was performed, followed by at least 27 more cases with nine infants surviving. The fetal thymus has been obtained from fetuses at 12 to 20 weeks gestation with the earlier tissue being more immunologically compatible. An alternative to thymus transplantation is donation of bone marrow cells from compatible tissue of a sibling. Otherwise fetal tissue transplantation is the only life-saving option for infants with DiGeorge's syndrome.[4]

IV. Transplantation of Fetal Pancreatic Tissue

Diabetes is a common disease affecting at least one million juvenile diabetics in the United States who require insulin for most of their lives. The disease results in the inability to metabolize sugar unless insulin is provided and, if inadequately treated, is complicated by shortened life span, risks of blindness, heart and kidney disease as well as loss of limbs from poor circulation. The use of pancreatic transplants for this condition is still largely experimental and has yet to be perfected. Such questions as the ideal tissue preparation for transplantation, the mode and site of transplanting, the regulation of the grafted tissue and its survival all need to be worked out. Human fetal pancreatic tissue has been injected into animals with experimental diabetes and has reversed the metabolic defect. Fetal pancreatic tissue can be transplanted under the capsule of the kidney in conjunction with an otherwise needed kidney transplant. Under these circumstances the fetal pancreatic graft will grow, differentiate and secrete insulin. The use of fetal tissue is generally more successful than tissue obtained from adult cadavers. Although very promising, much work remains to be done to perfect the transplanting of fetal pancreatic cells in treating the diabetic.[5]

---

4. R.H. Buckley, *Fetal Thymus Transplantation for the Correction of Congenital Absence of the Thymus (DiGeorge's Syndrome)*, 2 REPORT OF THE HUMAN FETAL TRANSPLANTATION RESEARCH PANEL D50-D57 (Dec. 1988).

5. K.J. Lafferty, *Diabetic Islet Cell Transplant Research: Basic Science*, 2 REPORT OF THE HUMAN FETAL TISSUE TRANSPLANTATION RESEARCH PANEL D142-D144 (Dec. 1988).

V. Transplantation of Fetal Neural Tissue

The use of fetal transplants to treat neurological conditions such as Alzheimer's disease, Huntington's chorea, spinal cord injury and Parkinson's disease has been proposed but only in the case of Parkinson's disease have promising results recently been obtained. Parkinson's disease is a chronic human ailment that afflicts about 400,000 patients in the United States. It is typified by uncontrollable tremors, loss of posture, muscle rigidity and extreme slowness and difficulty with purposeful motion. It is a progressive and crippling disease. The cause of the disease is believed to be the loss of cells from the central nervous system that secrete a neurotransmitter substance, dopamine, that is responsible for normal function. The loss of cells is believed to be due to a combination of genetic predisposition and environmental toxins. The objective of transplantation is to replace those cells and their secretory product. Current forms of therapy are limited. The disease can be treated with the drug L-Dopa, but the response is variable, the drug has side effects and its beneficial action may be lost over time.

Transplantation of fetal nerve cells in animals such as rats and the rhesus monkey has been successful. The cells divide, undergo differentiation and integrate themselves into existing nerve networks. In addition, there are drugs that can artificially induce a Parkinson-like disease in animals that can in turn be ameliorated by fetal tissue grafts. Fetal tissue transplantation into the brains of patients with Parkinsonism has occurred worldwide, but there have been few carefully documented studies to demonstrate its true efficacy. In 1990 two very promising reports from Stockholm and Denver demonstrated that the fetal nerve cells transferred to the brain of patients actually function to produce the missing substance, dopamine. The patients demonstrated measurable and documented improvement.[6, 7] Much remains to be learned in terms of the wider applicability of the technique and of course whether the improvement is permanent or transient.

---

6. O. Lindval, P. Brundin & H. Widner et al., *Grafts of Fetal Dopamine Neurons Survive and Improve Motor Function in Parkinson's Disease*, 247 SCIENCE 574–77 (1990).

7. C.R. Freed, et al., *Transplantation of Human Fetal Dopamine Cells for Parkinson's Disease: Results at One Year*, 47 ARCH. NEUROLOGY 505–12 (1990).

VI. Special Properties, Advantages and Alternatives to the Use of Fetal Tissue

Fetal tissue has special properties that make its transplantation advantageous. In contrast to completely differentiated adult cells, fetal cells have "plasticity," which allows them to adapt to new environments, to change in shape and migrate and to integrate functionally in the transplant recipient. Fetal cells also "proliferate" more readily than adult cells, dividing more rapidly through cell cycles. Fetal cells can induce an "angiogenic" response inducing new blood vessel growth and vascularization. Fetal cells are more immunologically compatible because they are less inherently antigenic than adult cells and have fewer immune attack cells among them to attack the host.[8] Fetal tissue research allows access to human cells to study conditions peculiar to the human. Fetal cells behave metabolically like cancer cells, making the study of them applicable to the vexing problem of malignancy. Fetal tissue is available after pregnancy terminations and would under other circumstances simply be discarded. The association of fetal tissue with induced abortion makes fetal research unacceptable to many who oppose abortion. As noted below, the use of fetal material from spontaneous abortion does not arouse as much controversy but it is much less suitable for research and medical use. Alternatives to the use of fetal tissue are to immortalize cells by tissue culture, to try to research the problems with adult or animal grafts or to seek alternative drug delivery systems and therapies.

VII. Other Research Involving the Fetus

Research on the living *fetus ex utero* was the type of investigation that first prompted societal concern. The controversial studies involved perfusion of the intact fetus in order to study metabolic pathways or to develop perfusion apparatus that would allow extrauterine development and help treat extreme prematurity at the margins of viability. The living previable fetuses for these studies were obtained at abortion and were kept functioning by perfusion during the course of studies which were terminated by discontinuation of the perfusion apparatus. There were objections to the research

---

8. R. Auerbach, *Qualities of Fetal Cells and Tissues*, 2 REPORT OF THE HUMAN FETAL TISSUE TRANSPLANTATION RESEARCH PANEL D27-D31 (Dec. 1988).

technique itself and not just to the association with abortion.[9] These types of *ex utero* studies are noteworthy in that they represented the exception to most fetal research, which was and is performed on the living *fetus in utero* on desired pregnancies going to term. Such *in utero* studies are largely observational and involve potential diagnostic and therapeutic modalities intended to develop improved care of the pregnant woman and fetuses for conditions such as diabetes, pregnancy-induced hypertension, blood group incompatability, use of anesthetic agents, inducing or stopping labor, fetal diagnosis and fetal surgery. The importance of this research required that ethically and socially acceptable methods be developed to allow them to continue. In most instances of fetal research, abortion is not involved, and the concerns about the protection of research subjects could focus on the similarity of the fetus with that of the newborn in terms of matters of risk and parental consent.

VIII. Social and Political Issues in Fetal Tissue Research

Use of the human fetus or fetal tissues for research is fraught with controversy largely because of the common association of the fetus as a product of an induced abortion. In fact, abortion is now a more contentious issue than the research itself. Human fetal tissue was not available to any significant degree for medical or research purposes until pregnancy terminations became openly practiced in the middle of the 20th century. This availability and use of fetal tissue from induced abortion took place first in Scandinavia and England before becoming common in the United States, since abortion laws were liberalized in Europe before similar changes in abortion law crossed the Atlantic Ocean. On the other hand, there is essentially no controversy over the use of fetal material from a spontaneous abortion for research. However, tissue from this source has limitations. With a spontaneous loss the fetus is often not recovered, and when it is, the event is sporadic and unpredictable and the infectious, genetic and other causes of the spontaneous loss of pregnancy could confound experimental observations.

Fetal tissue from pregnancy terminations also became available for research in the 1960s and thereafter, when rapid progress was being made in the biological sciences. As a consequence, major medical advances have been made from research using fetal tissue that can be applied for human benefit.

---

9. M.J. Mahoney, *Research on the Fetus, The Nature and Extent of Research Involving Living Human Fetuses*, Appendix, National Commission for the Protection of Human Subjects of Biomedical and Behavioral Research 1-1 to 1-48 (1975).

IX. Filling a Moral Vacuum

On January 7, 1991, the American College of Obstetricians and Gynecologists and the American Fertility Society announced that they would sponsor a National Advisory Board in Ethics of Reproduction to oversee both fetal transplantation research and studies in reproductive technologies on a voluntary basis. Congressman Waxman commented that private initiatives are welcome, but they cannot substitute for federal activity. "The Federal Government should be conducting this life-saving research, not ignoring it. Additionally, the Federal Government should be leading the way in the establishment of ethical guidelines."[10] Meanwhile, the promising reports on the outcome of fetal brain transplants into patients with Parkinson's disease will make keeping up with medical application difficult, and the technological imperative will have the last word.

X. The Future

The use of fetal tissues, along with stem cell therapy, have been encouraging for many conditions, especially in diabetes and young patients with Parkinson's disease. Fetal dopamine cells have been successfully transplanted into the brains of patients with Parkinson's disease. Finally, there is an important use of fetal tissue for vaccine development, including chickenpox, rubella, shingles, and polio.

XI. Editors' Note and Update

Sadly, Kenneth Ryan died, at a comparatively young age, after he wrote the foregoing chapter, which was published in an earlier edition of *Abortion, Medicine, and the Law.* As we prepared this latest edition, we discussed at length who might author a comparable analysis of these issues for inclusion in the current book. We ultimately decided that the best course was not to discard Dr. Ryan's earlier chapter but to retain it in full with this update. There are several reasons for that decision. For one thing, Dr. Ryan was a person of such extraordinary character, qualifications, and achievements that his comments on the multifaceted issues of medical treatments and research involving fetal tissue are as valuable today—to say nothing of their historical value—as they were when they appeared in the earlier edition. Before his distinguished career at Harvard, Dr. Ryan had been chair of

---

10. P.J. Hilts, *Groups Set Up Panel on Use of Fetal Tissue*, N.Y. TIMES, Jan. 8, 1991, at C3.

Obstetrics and Gynecology at Western Reserve University and was the first professor and chair at the newly established medical school of the University of California at San Diego. Subsequently, he was professor of obstetrics, gynecology and reproductive medicine at Harvard Medical School, and chief of staff of the Boston Hospital for Women, where he was instrumental in the merger that led to the present Brigham and Women's Hospital.[11]

But it is Dr. Ryan's work and prominence on ethical issues, specifically the use of fetal tissue for medical research and treatments, that make his views as relevant today as when he first wrote them. As a scholar of ethics, he was a leading voice regarding the issues of research ethics and reproductive bioethics. At the Harvard Medical School, he was a founding senior fellow of the Ethics Center and played a major role in creating the Division of Medical Ethics at the School. In the public arena, he served as chair of the National Commission for the Protection of Human Subjects of Biomedical and Behavioral Research, and he was elected to the Institute of Medicine of the National Academy of Sciences.

As chair of the National Commission, Dr. Ryan was instrumental in developing the 1988 recommendations on the propriety of using fetal tissue from abortions for developing disease treatments. That issue had taken on particular significance during the Reagan administration because of the ban on federal financing of research that used fetal tissue, an action that President Reagan saw as politically advantageous, notwithstanding that as governor of California he had favored a woman's right to choose. The same politics played out again under President Trump, who had never been opposed to abortion before his well-publicized commitment to conservative religious groups in exchange for their supporting his presidential

---

11. The Harvard Medical Faculty published a memorial tribute to Dr. Ryan that summarized his life and his work, https://fa.hms.harvard.edu/files/hmsofa/files/memorial minute_ryan_kenneth_j.pdf. *See also* Eric Nagourney, *Kenneth Ryan, 75, Obstetrician and Leader in Medical Ethics*, N.Y. TIMES, Jan. 28, 2002, at Sec. B, p. 7, https://www.nytimes.com /2002/01/28/us/kenneth-ryan-75-obstetrician-and-leader-in-medical-ethics.html.

campaign. Pursuant to that agenda, the Trump administration sought to further restrict medical research related to fetal tissue in 2018[12] and 2019.[13]

The criticisms of the Trump administration's actions reflect the same considerations addressed by Dr. Ryan and expressed in the findings of the National Commission that he chaired. As one reporter put it after the announcement in 2019: "Doctors and scientists are denouncing the Trump administration's decision to cut funding for research that uses fetal tissue, saying that the material is essential for life-saving medical research."[14] Dr. Elias Zambidis, a pediatric oncologist at Johns Hopkins who uses stem cells in his research, called the new limitations on fetal tissue research "catastrophic." He was adamant that that research has saved patients' lives without causing any harm to any living being.[15] Lawrence Goldstein, PhD, is distinguished professor at University of California, San Diego, School of Medicine, and founder of the Sanford Stem Cell Clinical Center at UC San Diego. He summed up the impact of the Trump restrictions as follows:

12. The Department of Health and Human Services announced on September 24, 2018, that it had cancelled a contract between Advanced Bioscience Resources, Inc. and the Food and Drug Administration to provide human fetal tissue to develop testing protocols, ostensibly because HHS was not "sufficiently assured that the contract included the appropriate protections applicable to fetal tissue research or met all other procurement requirements." Statement from the Department of Health and Human Services, Sept. 24, 2018, https://www.hhs.gov/about/news/2018/09/24/statement-from-the-department-of-health-and-human-services.html.

13. The Department of Health and Human Services announced on June 9, 2019, that it was refusing to extend an existing contract with the University of California, San Francisco, regarding research involving human fetal tissue from elective abortions. HHS justified its action with the following explanation:

Promoting the dignity of human life from conception to natural death is one of the very top priorities of President Trump's administration. The audit and review helped inform the policy process that led to the administration's decision to let the contract with UCSF expire and to discontinue intramural research—research conducted within the National Institutes of Health (NIH)—involving the use of human fetal tissue from elective abortion. Intramural research that requires new acquisition of fetal tissue from elective abortions will not be conducted.

. . .

HHS will also undertake changes to its regulations and NIH grants policy to adopt or strengthen safeguards and program integrity requirements applicable to extramural research involving human fetal tissue.

Statement from the Department of Health and Human Services, June 9, 2019, https://www.hhs.gov/about/news/2019/06/05/statement-from-the-department-of-health-and-human-services.html.

14. Erika Edwards, *What Is Fetal Tissue Research? And Why Is It Important to Medicine?*, NBC News, June 9, 2019, https://www.nbcnews.com/health/health-news/what-fetal-tissue-research-why-it-important-medicine-n1014481.

15. *Id.*

A very important goal of biomedical research is to develop new medical therapies as rapidly as possible for patients who suffer from terrible diseases. When we place these restrictions on important areas of research, we slow down the hunt for understanding and the development of new therapies for the patients of physicians, both in academic health centers and out in the regular community.[16]

The COVID–19 pandemic again brought the issue into the news because of the role of fetal tissue in vaccine development. Even some groups the most steadfast in their opposition to abortion modified their position regarding the use of fetal tissue for developing COVID–19 vaccines, as illustrated by the U.S. Conference of Catholic Bishops' approval of vaccines that had used fetal tissue in some way in their development.[17]

Finally, in deciding to include Dr. Ryan's original chapter, we took into account that medical treatment and research issues concerning fetal tissue remain surprisingly similar today to what they were when he discussed them at that time. There is abundant opinion from leading scientists that cells derived from fetal tissue are essential in vaccine development and research seeking treatment for a range of diseases, including HIV, hereditary blood diseases, Parkinson's disease, Alzheimer's and other neurodegenerative diseases, and spinal cord injury, to name a few.[18]

It is true, however, that successful disease treatments related to fetal tissue usage remain largely aspirational. For example, when Dr. Ryan authored his chapter, at least some researchers expected that more progress would have been made by now in treating Parkinson's disease with fetal tissue transplants. Parkinson's disease is a tremendous individual and societal problem and is the second most common progressive neurodegenerative disease, affecting one to two percent of persons over 65 years of age. Two groundbreaking articles in the late 1970s had shown that fetal mesencephalic grafts rich in dopaminergic neurons reduced Parkinson's

---

16. Julia Haskins, *New Restrictions Put Fetal Tissue Research in the Balance*, AAMC NEWS, Sept. 24, 2019, https://www.aamc.org/news-insights/new-restrictions-put-fetal-tissue-research-balance.

17. "The United States bishops' conference has said that Catholics can take two of the three available COVID-19 vaccines, even though they were developed with a 'remote connection' to 'morally compromised' cell lines." CNA Staff, *Catholic US Bishops Approve Use of Coronavirus Vaccines with "Remote Connection" to Abortion*, CATHOLIC NEWS AGENCY, Dec. 14, 2020, https://www.catholicnewsagency.com/news/catholic-bishops-approve-use-of-coronavirus-vaccines-with-remote-connection-to-abortion-54693.

18. Haskins, *supra* note 16; Edwards, *supra* note 14; James Harris et al., *Emerging Regenerative Medicine and Tissue Engineering Strategies for Parkinson's Disease*, 6 NPJ PARKINSON'S DISEASE 1 (2020), https://www.ncbi.nlm.nih.gov/pmc/articles/PMC6949278/.

symptoms in an animal model.[19] Subsequent studies produced mixed results, however. Tissue graft longevity was generally good, and some studies evidenced improvement in motor symptoms, but some patients showed no significant improvements and others had side effects. Study results were sufficiently limited that clinical treatment with tissue grafts did not become widespread. Treatment was further complicated by the fact that multiple fetal donors are required to produce enough cells for a single patient's treatment. There were also immunosuppression issues because of the non-native origin of the grafts.

It was thought by some that the variability in patient outcomes might have resulted from the lack of homogeneity in patients' tissue grafts. It was hoped that some of these issues could be resolved by more rigorous study, which led to the European Union funded study (TRANSEURO), which was designed to rigorously examine patient selection, tissue dissection, preparation and storage, grafting technique, and other variables. That study did not complete enrollment, however, because of the lack of available fetal tissue.[20]

Some researchers today point to the possibility of alternative cell sources that might obviate the need for fetal tissue,[21] and opponents of abortion argue that such developments support a ban on any use of fetal tissue. Regenerative medicine therapies are being considered and developed that use neurons derived from autologous stem cells, which—if successful—could have a number of benefits, including minimization or elimination of immunosuppression and tumorgenicity problems. One such approach uses induced pluripotent stem cells (iPSCs), which potentially could provide an unlimited source of any cell type.[22]

---

19. S. Bjorklund & U. Stenevi, *Reconstruction of the Nigrostriatal Dopamine Pathway by Intracerebral Nigral Transplants*, 177 BRAIN RES. 555 (1979), https://pubmed.ncbi.nlm.nih.gov/574053/; M. Perlow, et al., *Brain Grafts Reduce Motor Abnormalities Produced by Destruction of Nigrostriatal Dopamine System*, 204 SCI. 643 (1979), https://pubmed.ncbi.nlm.nih.gov/571147/.

20. Harris et al., *supra* note 18, at 4.

21. Yong Fan et al., *Replacing What's Lost: A New Era of Stem Cell Therapy for Parkinson's Disease*, 9 TRANSLATIONAL NEURODEGENERATION 1 (2020), https://www.ncbi.nlm.nih.gov/pmc/articles/PMC6945567/.

22. Harris et al., *supra* note 18. *See also* Malin Parmar et al., *Cell-Based Therapy for Parkinson's Disease: A Journey through Decades toward the Light Side of the Force*, 49 EUR. J. NEUROSCI. 463 (2019), https://pubmed.ncbi.nlm.nih.gov/30099795/; Tiago Cardoso et al., *Target-Specific Forebrain Projections and Appropriate Synaptic Inputs of hESC-Derived Dopamine Neurons Grafted to the Midbrain of Parkinsonian Rats*, 526 J. COMP. NEUROL. 2133 (2018), https://www.ncbi.nlm.nih.gov/pmc/articles/PMC6175216/.

Genetic medicine is another potentially powerful technology, and gene discovery methods and sequencing technologies have evolved significantly in recent years. CRISPR gene editing is an especially interesting approach that some see as a potential pathway to treatment of neurodegenerative disorders, including Huntington's disease, Alzheimer's, Parkinson's, and Amyotrophic lateral sclerosis.[23] One feature of CRISPR is that targeting the disease-causing gene may yield a medical solution even if we do not fully understand its biological function. Possibly, that will allow CRISPR to avoid some of the limitations of RNA-targeted therapies. But the technology remains early-stage, involving preclinical applications of CRISPR in models of neurodegenerative disorders.[24] Diabetes is another disease where fetal tissue has been used that has received attention from CRISPR researchers, but again, research efforts are early-stage.[25]

To be sure, regenerative medicine and other new approaches like CRISPR are extremely exciting fields that may provide new disease treatments in the future, but a long, arduous, and expensive path of research, development, and clinical experimentation lies ahead before the possibility that fetal tissue might be adequately replaced by these, or any other, new approach. In the time being, all of the issues that Dr. Ryan spent years addressing concerning the propriety and ethics of using fetal tissue for research and for treatment remain with us, undiminished.

---

23. Jun Wan Shin & Jong-Min Lee, *The Prospects of CRISPR-Based Genome Engineering in the Treatment of Neurodegenerative Disorders*, 11 THER. ADV. NEUROL. DISORD. 1 (2018), https://www.ncbi.nlm.nih.gov/pmc/articles/PMC5784517/.

24. *Id.*

25. *See, e.g.*, Eun Yi Cho et al., *Lecithin Nano-liposomal Particle as a CRISPR/Cas9 Complex Delivery System for Treating Type 2 Diabetes*, 17 J. NANOBIOTECHNOLOGY 1 (2019), https://www.ncbi.nlm.nih.gov/pmc/articles/PMC6350399/pdf/12951_2019_Article_452.pdf; Lauren Coombe et al., *Current Approaches in Regenerative Medicine for the Treatment of Diabetes: Introducing CRISPR/CAS9 Technology and the Case for Non-embryonic Stem Cell Therapy*, 7 AM. J. STEM CELLS 104 (2018), https://www.ncbi.nlm.nih.gov/pmc/articles/PMC6334205/; Dario Gerace et al., *CRISPR-Targeted Genome Editing of Mesenchymal Stem Cell-Derived Therapies for Type 1 Diabetes: A Path to Clinical Success?*, 8 STEM CELL RES. THER. 62 (2017), https://www.ncbi.nlm.nih.gov/pmc/articles/PMC5345178/.

19

D&E Abortion Bans: The Implications of Banning the Most Common Second-Trimester Procedure[*]

By Megan K. Donovan, J.D.

Since 2015, state lawmakers have begun to target the abortion method most commonly used in the second trimester, dilation and evacuation (D&E). Banning D&E is one of several trends to emerge from among the recent onslaught of state abortion restrictions, and the idea is rooted in a long history of efforts to limit access to abortion after the first trimester by enacting restrictions on specific abortion methods. Legislation to create a nationwide D&E ban was introduced in the 114th Congress, and antiabortion members of Congress—emboldened by the 2016 elections—may seize upon this tactic as part of an expansive new agenda to roll back abortion rights.

By restricting the most common method of second-trimester abortion, policymakers hostile to abortion would take a significant step forward in their campaign to eliminate abortion access in the United States. As with most abortion restrictions, the consequences would fall hardest on those already struggling to obtain access to abortion.

D&E is a safe and common method of second-trimester abortion. Dilation and evacuation is a surgical abortion procedure that takes place after the first trimester of pregnancy.[1] Similar to a first-trimester surgical proce-

---

[*] Published with permission of the Guttmacher Institute; first appeared online February 21, 2017, https://www.guttmacher.org/gpr/2017/02/de-abortion-bans-implications-banning-most -common-second-trimester-procedure.

dure, the patient's cervix is dilated and suction is used to remove the fetus.[2] Depending on a variety of factors (including gestational age, the extent of dilation, and providers' training and preference), the provider might also use surgical instruments as a primary or secondary part of the procedure.[1,2] Eleven percent of abortions in the United States take place after the first trimester, and national estimates suggest that D&E accounts for roughly 95% of these procedures.[3,4]

The safety of the D&E method was documented by the late 1970s.[5] According to the American College of Obstetricians and Gynecologists (ACOG), D&E is the "predominant approach to abortion after 13 weeks," and it is "evidence-based and medically preferred because it results in the fewest complications for women compared to alternative procedures."[6]

Unable to ban abortion outright, abortion foes are trying to ban it method by method. Since *Roe v. Wade* legalized abortion nationwide in 1973, state and federal policymakers have pursued numerous strategies to restrict access. One such strategy has focused on eliminating access to abortion after the first trimester by banning one method at a time.

Missouri enacted the first method ban in 1974, the year after *Roe v. Wade* was decided. Missouri's law banned what was then the most common and safest method for second-trimester abortion, saline amniocentesis. The U.S. Supreme Court ultimately struck down Missouri's law in *Planned Parenthood of Central Missouri v. Danforth* in 1976, identifying it as an "arbitrary

---

1. P. Stubblefield et al., *Methods for Induced Abortion*, 104 OBSTET. & GYNECOL. 2004 174–85 (2004).

2. C. Hammond & S. Chasen, *Dilation and Evacuation, in* MANAGEMENT OF UNINTENDED AND ABNORMAL PREGNANCY: COMPREHENSIVE ABORTION CARE 157–77 (M. Paul et al., eds. 2009).

3. T. Jatlaoui et al., *Abortion Surveillance—United States, 2013*, 65 MORBIDITY AND MORTALITY WEEKLY REPORT: SURVEILLANCE SUMMARIES, No. SS-12 (2016), https://www.cdc.gov /mmwr/volumes/65/ss/ss6512a1.htm.

4. K. O'Connell et al., *Second-Trimester Surgical Abortion Practices: A Survey of National Abortion Federation Members*, 78 CONTRACEPTION 492–99 (2008).

5. American College of Obstetricians and Gynecologists (ACOG), *Second-Trimester Abortion, Practice Bulletin No. 135*, 121 OBSTET. & GYNECOL. 1394–1406 (2013).

6. ACOG, ACOG statement regarding abortion procedure bans, Oct. 9, 2015. [Ed. Note: ACOG has updated its statements on access to abortion. *See* ACOG, *ACOG Committee Opinion No. 815: Increasing Access to Abortion*, 136 OBSTET. & GYNECOL. e107 (Dec. 2020), https:// www.acog.org/-/media/project/acog/acogorg/clinical/files/committee-opinion/arti cles/2020/12/increasing-access-to-abortion.pdf. The update addresses ongoing legislative and extra-legislative efforts to restrict access to abortion care and "opposes such interference with the patient–clinician relationship, affirming the importance of this relationship in the provision of high-quality medical care. This revision includes updates based on new restrictions and litigation related to abortion."]

regulation designed to prevent the vast majority of abortions after the first 12 weeks." Nonetheless, as medicine and technology evolved and other abortion procedures were developed in the years following *Roe v. Wade*, antiabortion policymakers revived their focus on specific methods.

In the 1990s and early 2000s, state efforts to restrict access to abortion after the first trimester coalesced around bans on "partial-birth" abortion— an inflammatory term, coined by the antiabortion group National Right to Life, that has no precise medical definition. Many, but not all, of these state-level restrictions were struck down by courts, until the Supreme Court upheld a federal version in *Gonzales v. Carhart* in 2007. That law bans "partial-birth" abortion except when the woman's life is endangered. The Court found the provocatively worded, but medically imprecise definition of the procedure sufficient to pass constitutional muster and applied it to the dilation and extraction (D&X) abortion method. In doing so, a majority on the Court reasoned that women would still have access to the safe and effective D&E method. In response to the decision, ACOG stated that the Supreme Court disregarded medical consensus that the D&X method is "safest and offers significant benefits for women suffering from certain conditions" and further noted that the ban "diminishes the doctor-patient relationship by preventing physicians from using their clinical experience and judgment."[7]

Current efforts to restrict D&E adhere closely to the "partial-birth" abortion ban playbook. As of mid-February, seven states have enacted laws essentially banning D&E; four of the bans are currently not in effect while litigation against them proceeds and a fifth is scheduled to go into effect in August.[8] The bills enacted so far, as well as the federal bill introduced in 2015, follow model legislation crafted by National Right to Life. They include only very limited exceptions. In addition, while they appear to target procedures in which surgical instruments are used prior to suction, the bills do not use precise medical terminology. Rather, they employ inflammatory rhetoric designed to arouse antiabortion sentiment (for example, referring to the banned procedure as "dismemberment abortion") and leave providers with the difficult task of figuring out how to amend their practice to comply with ideological restrictions that are not grounded in science.

---

7. ACOG, ACOG statement on the US Supreme Court decision upholding the Partial-Birth Abortion Ban Act of 2003, Apr. 18, 2007. [Ed. Note: As stated in note 6 *supra*, ACOG subsequently updated its statements on access to abortion in December 2020. Among other things, the updated statement reaffirmed ACOG's criticism of the Supreme Court's *Carhart* decision.]

8. E. Nash, Guttmacher Institute, *Special Analysis of State D&E Bans* (2017).

D&E bans interfere with providers' medical judgment and limit options for patients. Because D&E bans are in effect in only two states and affect very few abortion providers, the impact of these policies is not yet clear. Medical groups argue that if faced with one of these bans, providers would be forced to base clinical decisions on fear of prosecution rather than on their professional medical judgment or the preferences of their patients. According to ACOG, such restrictions "limit the ability of physicians to provide women with the medically appropriate care they need, and will likely result in worsened outcomes and increased complications."[6] In sum, "doctors will be forced, by ill-advised, unscientifically motivated policy, to provide lesser care to patients."

One potential modification to the procedure would require women to undergo an additional, invasive step before a D&E to induce fetal demise, such as an injection through the woman's abdomen or cervix. Although some providers take this step when they believe it will make an abortion easier to perform in a specific case or when a patient requests it, leading authorities such as ACOG and the Society of Family Planning have concluded that the available evidence does not support induction of fetal demise as a general practice to increase patient safety.[5,9]

Although rarely used in the United States, another potential option is to induce labor using medication instead of performing a D&E. According to leading authorities, induction is a safe and effective method of second-trimester abortion and is sometimes preferred over D&E in specific instances, such as when burial or an autopsy is desired.[5,9,10] Overall, however, induction is less common than D&E for a variety of reasons. Perhaps most significantly, induction requires a woman to experience contractions and go through labor; in addition to the emotional toll this can take, it can also be associated with greater pain and an increased risk of complications.[5] And typically, induction takes longer than D&E, is more expensive, and is performed in a hospital setting.[2,5] Although a patient undergoing a second-trimester abortion may not be able to choose the method used, most women select D&E when given the option between D&E and induction in research settings.[5,11]

9. Society of Family Planning (SFP), *Induction of Fetal Demise before Abortion, SFP Guideline 20101*, 81 CONTRACEPTION 462–73 (2010), https://www.societyfp.org/_documents/resources/InductionofFetalDemise.pdf.

10. National Abortion Federation, *2016 Clinical Policy Guidelines* (2016), https://prochoice.org/wp-content/uploads/2016-CPGs-web.pdf.

11. D. Grimes, *The Choice of Second Trimester Abortion Method: Evolution, Evidence and Ethics*, 31 REPRODUCTIVE HEALTH MATTERS, Supp. 183–88 (2008).

A D&E ban would compound other obstacles to abortion care. Research indicates that the vast majority of women obtaining an abortion during the second trimester would have preferred to have had it earlier.[12] State abortion restrictions are one increasingly common reason women encounter delays receiving abortion care, and D&E bans must be considered in the context of such restrictions.

Restrictions that force women to delay abortion care have a disproportionate impact on low-income women, women of color and young women—which is one reason why these groups are overrepresented among women who obtain abortions during the second trimester.[13] And as a woman struggles to overcome legal, financial and logistical obstacles to obtaining abortion care, the passage of time can push that care further out of reach. The further along a pregnancy is, the higher the cost and the fewer the providers who offer abortion services.[14] A recent Guttmacher analysis found that needing financial assistance to pay for an abortion and living 25 miles or more from the facility both increased the likelihood of obtaining a second-trimester abortion.[15]

In addition to women who are disadvantaged in ways that limit access to services, women who receive diagnoses of fetal anomalies or maternal health complications would be disproportionately impacted by D&E bans because many of these diagnoses are received during the second trimester.

Thus, many of the women most likely to be impacted by D&E bans are already facing challenging circumstances, such as pregnancy complications or obstacles to earlier abortion care. In this way, targeting D&E could be particularly harmful as part of antiabortion activists' larger, strategic campaign to reduce access to abortion in the United States.

---

12. L. Finer et al., *Timing of Steps and Reasons for Delays in Obtaining Abortions in the United States,* 74 CONTRACEPTION 334 (2006), https://www.guttmacher.org/sites/default/files/pdfs/pubs/2006/10/17/Contraception74-4-334_Finer.pdf.

13. R. Jones & L. Finer, *Who Has Second-Trimester Abortions in the United States?,* 85 CONTRACEPTION 544 (2012), http://www.contraceptionjournal.org/article/S0010-7824(11)00625-1/fulltext.

14. J. Jerman & R. Jones, *Secondary Measures of Access to Abortion Services in the United States, 2011 and 2012: Gestational Age Limits, Cost, and Harassment,* 24 WOMEN'S HEALTH ISSUES e419–e424 (2014), http://www.whijournal.com/article/S1049-3867(14)00058-9/fulltext.

15. R. Jones & J. Jerman, *Characteristics and Circumstances of U.S. Women Who Obtain Very Early and Second-Trimester Abortions,* PLoS ONE, Jan. 25, 2017, http://dx.doi.org/10.1371/journal.pone.0169969.

20

Late Abortion:
Clinical and Ethical Issues

By Warren M. Hern, M.D., M.P.H., Ph.D.

Although abortion has become one of the most difficult and controversial issues in Western society during the past 50 years, the performance of late abortion—after 20 weeks of pregnancy, to use one definition—is the most controversial. Even those who claim to be "pro-choice" and support women's reproductive freedom often disagree with the performance of late abortion for any reason. For those opposed to the availability of any kind of abortion services, late abortion is the most abhorrent and should not be permitted for any reason, including rape, incest, fetal abnormality, or saving the woman's life.

People who question the need for late abortion services ask: Why would any woman want to end a pregnancy at such a late stage? Why do women wait? What is the possible justification for late abortion?

Medical technology over the past 50 years has not only made abortion safer, it has increased the chance for survival of fetuses born alive well before the normally expected length of pregnancy. Abortions are now routinely performed at stages of pregnancy that would have constituted "viability" in earlier times such as at 26 to 28 weeks of pregnancy. This does not account for the high risk of severe handicaps and increased risk of death suffered by severely immature infants born alive so early in gestation. The costs of caring for severely impaired infants can range up to $1,000 per day for decades, and this is not a cost that can be carried by individual families.

These are extremely complicated circumstances for medical decisions about the woman's life and health, and the life and health of the fetus or immature infant, and they are increasingly fraught with social, political, legal, and emotional conflicts. People with no direct or personal interest, knowledge of, or stake in the outcome of such decisions but with political goals are increasingly inclined to interfere with these decisions being considered by anguished individuals and families.

Abortion is a global phenomenon known to all societies and known to have been practiced from the earliest historical times, and it is known to have been practiced by tribal societies of all kinds.[1] Although the number of abortions performed on women or by women on themselves cannot be known with any accuracy, there may be as many as 50,000 deaths annually among women due to unsafe abortion, and they account for from 9 to 15 percent of all maternal mortality worldwide.[2,3] Meanwhile, deaths from illegal, unsafe abortion have become almost nonexistent in the United States since 1973, when the U.S. Supreme Court issued its *Roe v. Wade* decision legalizing the operation. In the United States, deaths due to abortion fell from 40 per million live births in 1970 to eight per million in 1976.[4] The immediate consequence of the liberalization of the New York state abortion law in 1970 was the elimination of deaths in New York City due to illegal abortion, a decline in the number of deaths associated with childbirth, and a reduction in deaths following legally performed abortion. There was also a decline in births, particularly among high-risk women, a decline in infant mortality, and a decline in the number of deaths associated with pregnancy. From 1973 to 1975, there were no deaths from abortion performed before 12 weeks of pregnancy for the first time in the city's history.[5]

From 1973 until the present, almost 60 million abortions have been performed in the United States. Of these, about 1 percent have been what could be defined as "late abortion." Of these, most are performed before the 24th week of pregnancy.[6]

---

1. GEORGE DEVEREUX, A STUDY OF ABORTION IN PRIMITIVE SOCIETIES: A TYPOLOGICAL, DISTRIBUTIONAL, AND DYNAMIC ANALYSIS OF THE PREVENTION OF BIRTH IN 400 PREINDUSTRIAL SOCIETIES (1976).

2. N.J. Kassebaum et al., *Global, Regional, and National Levels and Causes of Maternal Mortality During 1990–2013: A Systematic Analysis for the Global Burden of Disease Study*, 384 THE LANCET 980–1004 (2014).

3. L. Say et al., *Global Causes of Maternal Death: A WHO Systematic Analysis*, 2 THE LANCET GLOBAL HEALTH e323–e333 (2014).

4. L.D. Elam-Evans et al., *Abortion Surveillance—United States 2000*, CDC MORTALITY AND MORBIDITY WEEKLY REPORT: SURVEILLANCE SUMMARIES 52(SS12):1–32 (2003).

5. J. Pakter, *National Trends in the Health Impact of Abortion*, *in* ABORTION IN THE SEVENTIES 69–76 (W.M. Hern & B. Andrikopoulos, Eds. 1977).

6. Guttmacher Institute, *Fact Sheet* (Sept. 2019), https://www.guttmacher.org/fact-sheet/induced-abortion-united-states#.

Abortion after the first trimester of pregnancy has historically been more dangerous than early abortion, and the procedure increases in complexity and risk with each week of pregnancy.[7] The risk of death in early second trimester abortion is 15 times the risk of death in early first trimester abortion, 30 times greater at 16 to 20 weeks, and more than 77 times the risk at 21 weeks or more.[8] The relative risk of death in abortion increases 38 percent per week with each week of gestation compared to abortion up to eight weeks of pregnancy. The risk of death of abortion at eight weeks is about three per million procedures.[9]

Why do women seek late abortion? Here are some of the reasons:

- Ignorance—lack of awareness of signs and symptoms of pregnancy (especially adolescents, who are more likely to delay seeking an abortion until 15 weeks or more of gestation)
- Fear, shame, guilt; afraid to tell parents or abusive intimate partner
- Denial ("I thought it would go away.")
- Lack of money, transportation, support for early abortion
- Misinformation by a patient's doctor ("you're too [old, young, fat, skinny, etc.] to get pregnant")
- Misinformation, often deliberate ("Abortion is illegal after 12 weeks.")
- Missed diagnosis (three months testing for pituitary tumor by an endocrinologist without a physical exam or pregnancy test)
- Fetal anomaly or genetic disorder
- Physician deception/withholding of information concerning fetal diagnosis
- Threats by intimate partner or relative of violence including murder if woman seeks an abortion, especially in highly conservative cultures
- Fear of loss of intimate or protective relationship
- Frightening propaganda in an anti-abortion "pregnancy alternative" "clinic"
- False belief: "I thought abortion became illegal when Trump was elected."

A typical example is the appearance of a very young adolescent 13–15 years old accompanied by a parent who has observed that the girl is visibly

---

7. W. Cates et al., *The Effect of Delay and Method Choice on the Risk of Abortion Morbidity*, 9 FAMILY PLANNING PERSPECTIVES 266–68, 273 (1977).

8. L. Bartlett et al., *Risk Factors for Legal Induced Abortion-Related Mortality in the United States*, 103 OBSTET. & GYNECOL. 729–37 (2004).

9. S. Zane et al., *Abortion-Related Mortality in the United States 1998–2010*, 126 OBSTET. & GYNECOL. 258–65 (2015).

pregnant. The girl has had one sexual experience with her boyfriend without contraception, may have suspected that she was pregnant, but she was afraid to tell her parents and perhaps not sure what she was experiencing. By the time the parent (usually her mother) sees the signs of pregnancy, the girl is 24 to 26 weeks pregnant or later. These cases are sometimes tragically associated with sexual abuse by a close relative such as a stepbrother or stepfather and concealment by the young woman who has been abused. Termination of the pregnancy is then accompanied by even more concern for the adolescent's mental health, requirement for counseling support both before and after the pregnancy termination, and notification of law enforcement and/or social services authorities for dealing with the family crisis and criminal investigation. The pregnancy is a threat to the young woman's life, especially because of her extreme youth, which carries higher risks of maternal morbidity and mortality. Pregnancy means interruption for normal adolescent life including schooling, and there is a need for specialized abortion care in the case of very advanced pregnancy.

Another typical situation is the young adolescent or young woman in her early 20s who is extremely athletic, in otherwise excellent physical health with irregular or scanty menses, who discovers that she is inexorably and inexplicably gaining weight, is in denial about her risk of pregnancy, and whose pregnancy is finally recognized by her mother.

At the other end of the reproductive spectrum is the woman in her late 30s or early 40s who has a deeply desired pregnancy that has been found to be afflicted by a severe fetal abnormality. Her obstetrician did a fetal anatomy scan at 20 weeks and found no abnormality, but a much later visit to the emergency room for gastrointestinal or other minor medical problem prompted an ultrasound evaluation of the pregnancy at which time the catastrophic fetal abnormality was discovered. The woman and her partner or husband make the difficult decision to terminate the pregnancy. This situation is made much more painful when the physician decides to withhold information about an early diagnosis of fetal abnormality because the physician is opposed to abortion and does not tell the patient of the diagnosis until it is too late to terminate the pregnancy under the local laws. It is quite common for anti-abortion physicians to withhold such diagnostic information so that the patient cannot obtain an abortion. This is one of the principal causes of delay in the case of a fetal diagnosis of genetic disorder or other fetal abnormality.

Then there is the case of the woman who is menopausal and thinks that she cannot conceive or who has been told by her physician that pregnancy is no longer possible. Amenorrhea is not perceived as a sign of pregnancy, and this contributes to a delay in the diagnosis of pregnancy.

Women with high-risk pregnancies often seek late abortion. These include:

- Very young girls (11–15) who are often victims of rape and/or incest
- Women who are impaired physically or mentally by substance abuse
- Women with a history of physical or sexual abuse
- Older primigravidas (35–45 y/o) with fetal anomalies
- Older women with long histories of serious illness (diabetes, hypertension, obesity, metabolic or endocrine diseases, neurologic disease, myomas)

I. Methods of Performing Late Abortion

Access to late abortion services depends on many factors, the first of which is the availability of physicians who are capable and willing to perform this procedure. A second critical factor is the patient's length of pregnancy at the time she presents for a termination. This often determines whether the procedure is available at all and, if so, the skill and experience of the physician and whether the physician is operating in a clinical environment that supports the increasingly complex procedure. A third critical factor is the cost. Late abortion is far more complex than early abortion, requires a much greater range of equipment and support, and requires a specialized medical staff that is highly experienced as well as committed to offering this service. Fees are therefore higher than for early abortion. Except for some university teaching hospitals, late abortion services are not available in most private and community hospitals because the administration and leadership is opposed to this service. A fourth factor is the presence of legal obstacles. Restricting access to abortion by legislation has become the major political appeal of the Republican party in the United States during the past 45 years.

There are three principal methods for pregnancy termination in gestations advanced beyond 20 weeks. One is induction of labor as is done at term in an uncomplicated desired pregnancy. Another is the "D&E," or "dilation and evacuation," abortion, in which the physician uses instruments to dilate the cervix and empty the uterus. A third method, the one that I have developed and use, is an eclectic procedure that begins with the induction of fetal demise by means of an intrauterine fetal injection of a medication that

causes the fetal heart to stop.[10] The second step is the insertion, either at
the time of fetal injection or the next day, of a single *Laminaria* stick into
the uterine cervix to begin the process of gentle cervical dilation by means
of this hygroscopic material. *Laminaria japonicum* is a seaweed that grows in
the sea of Japan; the stalk is cut to specific lengths and sterilized for medical
use by submersion in absolute alcohol, by a sterilizing gas, or by radiation.
It acts by absorbing water from the woman's body, expanding physically and
thereby dilating the cervix overnight, and by causing the release of endog-
enous prostaglandins from the woman's tissues. These prostaglandins cause
softening and further dilation of the woman's cervix. One day following the
initial insertion of the first *laminaria*, that *laminaria* is removed and replaced
under paracervical block with five or six new *laminaria*. On the day of the
procedure, these *laminaria* are removed, and the membranes are ruptured
to release the amniotic fluid, thereby minimizing the risk of amniotic fluid
embolism and increasing the likelihood of uterine contractions.

In my procedure, the amniotomy and removal of the amniotic fluid is
followed by intrauterine placement of misoprostol, a synthetic prostaglan-
din. If the patient has not had a prior cesarean delivery, a slow oxytocin
infusion is begun intravenously. At that time, the patient is placed in a
recovery room to await progress. When there is a presenting fetal part in the
patient's vagina, or if there is some other reason to progress to an operative
phase, the fetus and placenta are removed, and the uterus is explored with
instruments to assure complete uterine emptying. All these procedures are
performed under real-time ultrasound visualization to assure, to the extent
possible, the complete removal of all products of conception. The patient
receives medications to cause her uterus to contract, and she is observed in
the recovery room for a period of approximately two hours. At the end of
this time, she is examined again in the procedure room to confirm that the
uterus is empty and that there is no evidence of uterine trauma. After that,
she is discharged to her own private physician or other physician who is willing to see the patient for a follow-up exam one month after the abortion.

The major complication rate in my office in 5,000 of these procedures
is 0.3%, which includes in the definition "operative hemorrhage requiring
transfusion."

---

10. W. Hern, *Second-Trimester Surgical Abortion*, ch. 25 in GYNECOLOGY AND OBSTETRICS
(J. Sciarra, Ed. 2002) (Updated version: *Global Library of Women's Medicine* (ISSN: 1756-2228)
2016; DOI: 10.3843/GLOWM.10442).

II. Fetal Abnormality or Genetic Disorder

Among the most tragic aspects of obstetrics practice is the discovery that a desired pregnancy carries a fetal diagnosis of serious developmental abnormality or genetic disorder. Spontaneous fetal death is another painful development in a desired pregnancy. A cruel dilemma is presented in a twin pregnancy in which one twin is healthy and the other is stricken with a catastrophic diagnosis. In all these cases, the woman must decide whether to continue the pregnancy to term and have a child with a serious disorder, risk premature delivery or stillbirth, or decide to terminate the pregnancy in the safest manner possible. A twin pregnancy with a single affected fetus presents the choice of selective termination of the fetus with a poor prognosis to improve the outcome for the normal one.

Unfortunately, for a variety of reasons, the diagnosis of a significant abnormality may not be made, communicated, or accepted until relatively late in pregnancy. In most of the United States, such patients then have no local, legal options for termination of the pregnancy. Although we perform pregnancy terminations for many reasons, we have served as a referral point for such patients with fetal abnormalities for 35 years. In 2014, we reported the experiences of women coming to my office over a period of 20 years to end pregnancies because of an adverse fetal diagnosis.[11]

During the period of observation, 1,005 women requested termination of pregnancy for reasons of fetal disorder. Most of these patients were seen during the last 15 years of the observation period. The proportion of all patients seeking pregnancy termination for fetal disorder increased over time from 2.5 to 30 percent. For example, of the 7,587 patients seen at my office from 4/1/92 through 8/31/97, 189 (2.5 percent) of the patients sought termination of pregnancy for reasons of fetal abnormality. But from 9/1/2007 to 8/31/2012, 1,251 patients were seen for pregnancy termination, of whom 375, or 30 percent, were requesting termination for reason of fetal abnormality. This increase reflected a gradual change in clinic policy to accept patients with more advanced gestations, more requests for late termination of pregnancy because of fewer options being available elsewhere, and advances in fetal diagnosis.

More than 95 percent of patients in this series of 1,005 patients had uncomplicated pregnancy terminations with complete evacuation of the

---

11. W. Hern, *Fetal Diagnostic Indications for Second and Third Trimester Outpatient Pregnancy Termination*, 34 PRENATAL DIAGNOSIS 438–44 (2014), https://obgyn.onlinelibrary.wiley.com /doi/full/10.1002/pd.4324 (preoperative fetal diagnoses in 1005 women requesting pregnancy termination over a period of 20 years 1992–2012).

uterus. Twenty-six patients presenting with a spontaneous fetal demise were managed by a straightforward D&E procedure following serial multiple *laminaria* dilation of the cervix. In nine patients carrying a twin pregnancy with one healthy twin, a selective termination procedure was performed in which fetal demise was induced in the twin with a poor prognosis. For 12 patients with a single live abnormal fetus, fetal demise was induced at the patient's request followed by management of the delivery by the patient's own obstetrician.

The median age of all patients in this series was 32 years, with a range of from 14 to 47 years. The median length of gestation for all patients was 24 menstrual weeks with a range of from 12 to 39 menstrual weeks (Figure 20.1), with older women being seen at either end of the spectrum of gestational age. Patients seeking selective termination or induced fetal demise tended to be older (median ages 34 and 35, respectively) and requesting these procedures later in pregnancy (median gestations 33 and 36 weeks, respectively).

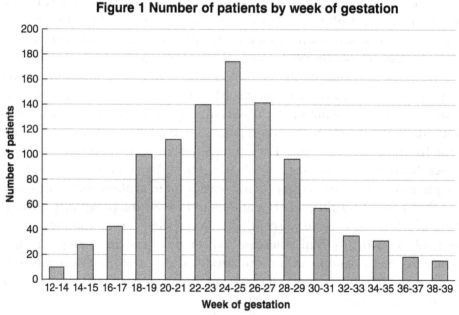

Figure 1 Number of patients by week of gestation

Genetic disorders were seen in approximately 40 percent of all patients. About one-fourth of all patients had a fetus with a neural tube defect or neurological abnormality, and approximately 9 percent of all fetuses had a skeletal dysplasia. In this series, 2.6 percent of all patients presented for termination of the pregnancy because of a previously diagnosed spontaneous intrauterine fetal demise occurring late in pregnancy. Nine patients, diagnosed too late for the procedure to be done elsewhere, requested selective termination in a twin pregnancy that was dizygotic, diamniotic, and dichorionic because one twin had a severe abnormality. In 12 patients with a very advanced pregnancy and a single abnormal fetus, for various medical, emotional, and religious reasons, patients requested an induced fetal demise with subsequent delivery by their personal obstetrician.

There were 160 diagnostic categories of fetal abnormality, including spontaneous intrauterine fetal demise, among these 1,005 patients. Although some preoperative diagnoses provided by referral sources and patients were unequivocal and highly specific, others were referred with less specific information (e.g., "cerebral abnormalities," "neural tube defect"). In nearly all cases, multiple abnormalities affecting various systems were present.

The proportions of preoperative diagnosis of fetal disorder changed over time and by week of gestation, with chromosomal disorders being discovered earlier in pregnancy and other problems such as CNS abnormalities or skeletal dysplasia being discovered later in pregnancy.

In numerous cases, the patient requesting termination of the pregnancy for reasons of fetal abnormality concomitantly had a severe and sometimes life-threatening medical condition such as pre-eclampsia, multiple sclerosis, lupus erythematosis, severe hyperemesis gravidarum, massive uterine fibroids, morbid obesity, coagulation disorder, placenta previa, or diabetes exacerbated by pregnancy. Many of these conditions precluded termination of the pregnancy by labor induction alone.

III. Zika

In 2016, there was an outbreak of Zika virus in Brazil.[12] This was discovered when there suddenly appeared many children being born in northeast Brazil with catastrophic abnormalities, principally microcephaly.[13] Abortion is illegal in Brazil and in most of South America. Most of the families confronted with this tragedy were too poor to have had prenatal care that could have given the diagnosis early enough in pregnancy for a termination to have been performed, but the lack of availability of this service made the point moot.

---

12. P. Brasil et al., *Zika Virus Infection in Pregnant Women in Rio De Janeiro*, 375 N. Eng. J. Med. 2321–34 (2016), https://www.nejm.org/doi/full/10.1056/NEJMoa1602412.

13. M. Johansson et al., *Zika and the Risk of Microcephaly*, 375 N. Eng. J. Med. 1–4 (2016), DOI: 10.1056/NEJMp1605367, http://www.nejm.org/doi/full/10.1056/NEJMp1605367#t=article.

In Brazil, over 2,000 cases of babies permanently damaged by Zika have been identified, and hundreds have been identified in Colombia. The number of cases that have occurred in other countries is unknown. Most of the families in South America who have been struck by this tragedy have had neither access to adequate prenatal diagnosis of Zika nor means of seeking a pregnancy termination outside of South America if it had been discovered.[14]

One couple that we saw in my office recently, however, was found to have a diagnosis of Zika by a local laboratory where they lived in South America. The couple did not live in Brazil, but the husband had work that took him close to Brazil. On discovering that she was pregnant following in vitro fertilization, her physicians advised her to be tested for Zika. She was positive, and he was also found to be seropositive for Zika. He apparently transmitted this to his wife via sexual contact, and her desired pregnancy was afflicted by this virus. They were advised to go to the United States for further testing, where it was found that both fetuses in her twin pregnancy showed major abnormalities that could be ascribed to Zika. I helped them terminate their desired pregnancy at 30 weeks. Tragic as this was, they were among the fortunate ones who had the diagnosis in time and the resources to seek assistance in terminating the pregnancy.

Public health officials in the United States have been concerned that women infected with Zika in Latin America will need diagnosis and treatment once they have arrived in or returned to the United States. Some cases have been identified, and women living in the United States have access to abortion that women in Latin America generally do not have. For those who do not get the diagnosis during pregnancy or cannot afford to have an abortion, the Centers for Disease Control estimates that a Zika baby with the kinds of catastrophic neurological damage that are common will have expenses of $10 million or more during its lifetime. This is a cost that is beyond the reach of nearly every family. Families living under conditions of extreme poverty, poor sanitation, and daily exposure to mosquito-borne diseases are the families whose children are mostly likely to be infected with and permanently damaged by the Zika virus, and they are the least likely to have the resources to deal with this devastating illness.

---

14. L. Sun, *Lifelong Care, Heartaches Ahead for Babies Born with Zika in the U.S.*, WASH. POST, June 24, 2016, https://www.washingtonpost.com/national/health-science/lifelong-care-heartaches-ahead-for-babies-born-with-zika-in-the-us/2016/07/24/2cc5e360-42d6-11e6-bc99-7d269f8719b1_story.html.

IV. Abortion Denied

What happens to a woman when she is denied an abortion that she seeks? This is a new question in recent history, at least in the United States, because prior to 1967, when Colorado passed the first abortion reform law in the nation, women could not hope or expect to have an abortion if they requested one. There were no options except illegal abortions, most of which were unsafe or self-induced. Many abortions were performed more or less safely by physicians, some with the best motives, or safely by skilled lay practitioners, or unsafely by unskilled and/or unscrupulous persons with no experience. Illegal abortion resulted in uncounted numbers of "back-alley" abortions that resulted in thousands of deaths per year among women who had them. With the advent of legal abortion in many states prior to the *Roe v. Wade* decision legalizing abortion nationally, and throughout the nation after that decision in 1973, it became possible for women with modest means and access to obtain relatively safe abortions. But it still meant that many women could not satisfy that goal. What were the consequences for them?

In Europe, where attitudes toward abortion were more relaxed and even supportive, restrictions on abortion availability were local and unpredictable. From the early 1960s, a team of European and American psychologists and psychiatrists began a long-term study in several European countries to determine the effects of denial of abortion for women seeking to end their pregnancies. The researchers published their work over a period of several decades, with the final volume, edited by Henry P. David, published in Czechoslovakia under the title *Born Unwanted: Developmental Effects of Denied Abortion.*[15]

Comparing children whose mothers had sought abortion with identical numbers of children for whom the pregnancy had been desired in Sweden, Finland, and Czechoslovakia, the investigators found the children whose mothers had been denied an abortion had significantly more physical, psychological, and social problems than those in the control groups. These deleterious effects were apparent from birth on through the rest of their lives into adulthood. The unwanted children had more physical disabilities, more trouble in school, more trouble with relationships of all kinds as youth, and even had more problems with marriage and parenthood. The young women were more likely to have unwanted pregnancies and to have less satisfactory relationships with their own children. There was a circular effect of unwantedness that persisted in their lives.

---

15. BORN UNWANTED: DEVELOPMENTAL EFFECTS OF DENIED ABORTION (H.P. David, Ed. 1988).

A more recent study in the United States comparing the psychological effects of having or being denied an abortion for an unwanted pregnancy showed that the women "turned away" from the abortion services for various reasons, such as the pregnancy was too far advanced, had more emotional stress and disturbances than the women who had received the abortion they sought.[16,17,18]

But what are the long-term consequences for their lives for women who have unwanted pregnancies and are unable to obtain a safe abortion? Even with more information, it would be difficult to generalize about this, but one constant dilemma that often leads to tragedy is found in the situation of young adolescent women who are pregnant as the result of their first sexual experience or with minimal life experience of any kind, sometimes against their will. These young women historically have been forced into motherhood well before they are prepared emotionally, socially, or financially, and the course of their lives is permanently shaped in a negative way. The younger the woman, the higher the risk of a fatal or seriously complicated result for her and for the baby she is forced to carry to term. From the standpoint of the human evolutionary perspective of the past several million or hundreds of thousands of years, most human reproduction has taken place at this stage of a woman's life, and most young women have survived, but we know that the risks for both mother and child are also greater the younger the woman. In modern society, it often means the interruption of education and the loss of social and economic opportunities. It makes a young woman less able to cope with the challenges of a complex industrial or post-industrial society.

Older women who find themselves pregnant in the later reproductive years may be happy only to find that the fetus they are carrying has a catastrophic abnormality or genetic disorder from which there is no hope of improvement. Older women also face higher risks of maternal morbidity and mortality as well as higher risks of infant morbidity and mortality. A woman who cannot find access to safe termination of such a pregnancy may be condemned to death if she has a major illness made worse by pregnancy, or she and her family may be burdened with unlimited expenses of caring

16. U.D. Upadhyay et al., *Denial of Abortion Because of Provider Gestational Age Limits in the United States*, 104 AM. J. PUB. HEALTH 1687–94 (2014), https://ajph.aphapublications.org /doi/full/10.2105/AJPH.2013.301378.

17. D. Foster et al., *Denial of Abortion Care Due to Gestational Age Limits*, 87 CONTRACEPTION 3–5 (2013).

18. A. Biggs et al., *Women's Mental Health and Well-being 5 Years After Receiving or Being Denied an Abortion:* A Prospective, Longitudinal Cohort Study, 24 J.A.M.A. PSYCHIATRY 169–78 (2017).

for a severely impaired child. When I was a medical student more than 50 years ago, one of our field trips was to a facility that cared for such children for families that could afford the care. It was an enormous building the size of an athletic field house, and there were hundreds of children suffering in various degrees of vegetative or incapacitated state being kept alive until they died of some major complication or other illness. It was tragic beyond words. One of the main questions was: who pays for this care?

In other countries, women being denied abortions are often subject to catastrophic results. A young Indian woman in Ireland, a 31-year-old dentist with her first pregnancy, experienced ruptured membranes at 17 weeks. Learning that there was no hope for fetal survival and delivery of a healthy baby, she asked physicians to help her end the pregnancy. She was refused because of the Irish laws against abortion. She received inadequate medical treatment, delivered a stillborn two days later, and died in septic shock two days after that. With the most basic medical and surgical procedures available in the United States and a few hours from her in England, she could have had a prompt treatment of this dangerous condition with full recovery. Her terrible suffering and shocking death were both unnecessary, but they were the clear consequence of medieval laws and attitudes in Ireland.

In India, an impoverished young woman who had been raped on the street in Patna was found to be pregnant and infected with HIV as the result. She was denied an abortion. In another part of India, a woman learned at the 26th week of pregnancy that her fetus had a catastrophic neurological disorder that caused hydrocephaly, among other things, and threatened her life if she carried the pregnancy to term, but Indian law prohibited abortion after 20 weeks. The baby had no hope for a meaningful life, was at risk of immediate death due to infection or other complication, and the couple had no means of caring for it at home.

There are countless thousands of cases of women and families who face these circumstances.

V. Ethical Issues in Late Abortion

Any woman who is pregnant is at risk of losing her life because of the pregnancy.[19] The closest measure of this is the "maternal mortality ratio" expressed as the proportion of women dying during pregnancy, during

---

19. N. Martin & R. Montagne, *The Last Person You'd Expect to Die in Childbirth*, PROPUBLICA, May 12, 2017, https://www.propublica.org/article/die-in-childbirth-maternal-death-rate-health-care-system.

delivery, or during the immediate period (30 days) after the delivery. The maternal mortality ratio in the United States at this time is 17 per 100,000 live births.[20] By comparison, in 1920, prior to the development of modern surgery, blood transfusions, antibiotics, and drugs for managing conditions such as pre-eclampsia, the maternal mortality ratio was 680 per 100,000 live births. In 1987, the maternal mortality ratio in the U.S. was 7.2 per 100,000 live births.[20] This ratio has increased due to the increasing number of women who are becoming pregnant in their later reproductive years when they already have serious intercurrent medical conditions such as heart disease, kidney disease, diabetes, or auto-immune disease such as lupus.

The risk of death in term delivery depends on many factors, but it is about 14 times higher than the risk of death with abortion. A study of comparative mortality rates in the United States from 1998 to 2005 found that the pregnancy-associated mortality rate among women who delivered live neonates was 8.8 deaths per 100,000 live births, but the mortality rate due to induced abortion was 0.6 deaths per 100,000 abortions.[21]

Another measure of risk or maternal health in pregnancy is the major complication rate. One part of the definition of "major complication rate" in pregnancy and abortion is "major unintended surgery." About 30 percent of all U.S. deliveries are performed by cesarean delivery, which means that the major complication rate for pregnancy is 30 percent or more. This becomes important in comparing the safety of term delivery with the risks of late abortion.

In my practice, there have been no deaths due to late abortion in over 5,000 cases, and the major complication rate is approximately 0.3 percent. This is important for the woman weighing the decision of whether to carry the pregnancy to term or to end the pregnancy. It is seldom the most important or determining factor, which is almost always whether the woman wants to have a baby or to end the pregnancy, and it is critically important to the woman who is already a mother of small children but who is considering ending a pregnancy that is complicated with a condition such as severe fetal abnormality or genetic disorder.

What of the very young adolescent woman who is healthy and who has a healthy fetus but, at the age of 12 or 13, has been impregnated by her father, her stepfather, her stepbrother, or some other member of the family? The

---

20. Centers for Disease Control and Prevention, *Pregnancy Mortality Surveillance System, Trends in Pregnancy-Related Deaths,* https://www.cdc.gov/reproductivehealth/maternal-mortality/pregnancy-mortality-surveillance-system.htm (last accessed Mar. 27, 2021).

21. E. Raymond & D. Grimes, *The Comparative Safety of Legal Induced Abortion and Childbirth in the United States,* 119 OBSTET. & GYNECOL. 215–19 (2012).

fetus may be viable by some definition at 30 or 32 weeks, but what about the risk to her health and to her life itself? What is the justification for denying an abortion and forcing her to carry the pregnancy to term? Is she prepared to be a parent? At that age, emphatically she is not. Moreover, her risks of dying in childbirth or having a severe pre-eclampsia are greatly increased over those of a woman who is ten years older. For the adolescent, terminating the pregnancy is a life-saving operation in many ways.

What about the young woman who is addicted to any one or a variety of street drugs or alcohol or some combination thereof, and, partly due to her impaired mental function, finds herself seeking an abortion at 26, 28, or 30 weeks of pregnancy? If she does not terminate the pregnancy, she is sure to have a baby that is severely impaired and/or addicted to one of the drugs. She is herself at higher risk of death due to the pregnancy than an otherwise healthy woman. She is less prepared than most to be a mother and manage the responsibilities of parenthood. Her child is more likely to suffer from inadequate care. Should she have an abortion? Should she be denied an abortion? A major problem for her obtaining a safe abortion is that, if she is on drugs at the time she presents for treatment, she cannot legally sign a consent form. Her signature, because she is impaired, is worthless.

How about the young woman who has been raped and who has suffered such severe depression and anxiety since the sexual assault that she has been unable to seek help until she is 30 weeks pregnant? Should she be permitted to have an abortion? Should she be required to carry her pregnancy to term and give birth to the rapist's child? What are the consequences for her and for the child? Who pays for the child's care if she abandons it because she is so horrified by her experience?

What about the terrified young adolescent woman who conceals her pregnancy until it is too late and finally delivers a baby that she does not want and places it, dead or alive, in a dumpster? Should she have been able to terminate the pregnancy when she discovered that she was pregnant, or should she have been forced to continue the unwanted pregnancy to term? In days past, there was no choice, but now there is.

These are some of the kinds of ethical dilemmas that occur in late abortion practice.

VI. Limited Availability of Late Abortion Services

In March 1988, five shots were fired through the front windows of my office, narrowly missing a member of my staff, and I had just walked through the space. This occurred soon after the publication of my textbook, *Abortion Practice*, and other publications of mine in which I described the techniques and instruments for the performance of late abortions.[22] The national networks of anti-abortion fanatics who were violently opposed to these services focused on me as well as some other physicians. The 1988 shooting was a clear sign of their fanaticism.

The availability of late abortion services by any means has increasingly diminished during the past 30 years due to legal restrictions, anti-abortion violence directed toward physicians and clinics offering late abortion services, and a declining willingness among physicians to be at risk of assassination. Dr. David Gunn was assassinated in 1993, Dr. John Britton was assassinated in 1994, the physician who owned the clinic where both of these physicians worked was assassinated in 1994, and Dr. Bernard Slepian was fatally shot through his kitchen window in October 1998 by a well-known anti-abortion fanatic. On May 31, 2009, Dr. George Tiller was assassinated in his Lutheran church lobby in Wichita, Kansas, by an anti-abortion fanatic who had stalked him for years for that purpose.[23,24] Dr. Tiller was one of two physicians in the United States at that time (the other one being this author) who offered late abortion services on an outpatient basis. Dr. Tiller was shot in both arms in 1994 by Shelley Shannon, who wrote to me from Kansas State prison later, telling me, "you're next." Beginning with Dr. Gunn's murder in 1993, these five physicians specializing in abortion services have been assassinated in the United States along with increasing attacks on physicians who perform late abortions. Other clinic workers and an off-duty policeman have been assassinated, and several other clinic workers have been grievously injured with life-threatening wounds. Twenty-four-hour protection of physicians, patients, and all others who work in and around abortion clinics and private physicians' offices have become constant major concerns.

On January 22, 1995, the "American Coalition of Life [sic] Activists" held a national press conference to announce the names of the first 13 physicians they wanted assassinated for performing abortions. I was on this list, and so was Dr. Tiller. The group also posted a website with the names and detailed personal information of dozens of physicians known for performing abortions with lines drawn through the names of those who had been assassinated. These actions were clearly designed to identify targets for potential anti-abortion assassins. The group was successfully sued in federal

---

22. WARREN HERN, ABORTION PRACTICE (1990).

23. STEPHEN SINGULAR, THE WICHITA DIVIDE: THE MURDER OF DR. GEORGE TILLER AND THE BATTLE OVER ABORTION (2011).

24. W. Hern, *Dr. George Tiller's Political Assassination Is Result of Rabid Anti-abortion Harassment*, THE COLORADO STATESMAN, June 19, 2009.

court by a group of plaintiffs, including the author, who were threatened by this incitement of anti-abortion violence.

Political attacks on abortion services in the United States have steadily increased since 1974, and as of this writing, more than half of all states have enacted laws restricting the performance of abortion after 19 weeks or later.[25] Women and couples in these states being suddenly faced with the unexpected diagnosis of fetal abnormality and choosing to terminate the pregnancy must now find a physician who is willing to perform an abortion late in pregnancy and is capable of doing so. Since many public and community hospitals have been taken over by sectarian religious groups that do not permit abortion, choices are limited to a few private physicians operating in private clinics prepared to perform these procedures.

In addition to these problems, few physicians are willing to perform late abortion, even if they have experience and training in this area of medicine. Performing abortions, particularly late in pregnancy, is the lowest status activity in medicine, notwithstanding its very beneficial impact on patients. It is highly stigmatized in the medical community, particularly among young women obstetrician/gynecologists, who actively work to destroy the careers and professional standing of physicians who perform late abortions. Physicians with training in obstetrics and gynecology have many high-status and more financially rewarding, as well as professionally interesting, opportunities that are far more attractive than that of performing late abortions, which has the added undesirability of being dangerous because of the constant risk of assassination by anti-abortion fanatics. The altruistic appeal of helping desperate women suffers in the context of these other factors, and so does the altruistic appeal of death and martyrdom for a good cause. Life is short, and performing abortions, especially late abortions, has proven to be a tragic way of making it shorter for physicians who do that work.

Outpatient termination for fetal disorder in a specialized private facility offers many advantages over hospital care. In a specialized clinic such as mine, medical care is completely oriented toward assisting and supporting women who have decided to terminate a pregnancy and to giving each woman and her family individual attention. All clinic personnel have a positive attitude toward the patients who have made this decision including those with desired but complicated pregnancies. Staff members are employed specifically because of supportive attitudes in addition to professional competence. Patients having questions, complaints or complications who call after discharge speak with the same physician and staff members

---

25. *See* Appendix 1 *infra* at 559.

who took care of them at the clinic. Continuity of care is a basic principle. Disadvantages of outpatient care consist primarily of increasingly heightened security concerns, needs and costs due to anti-abortion harassment and violence directed toward patients, staff, the physician, and support personnel. Response to these issues includes the provision of secure private transportation to and from the clinic for patients staying at local hotels, especially during anti-abortion demonstrations.

Except for some university hospitals with abortion training programs that will see patients up to 24 weeks' gestation, choices of hospital access for abortion patients after 16 weeks' gestation and for physicians are increasingly restricted by the acquisition of private hospitals by agencies that are officially opposed to abortion and by aggressive legislative restriction of access to abortion in various states. For women seeking termination of an advanced pregnancy for reasons of a fetal abnormality, this means that there are fewer choices for individual care among a diminishingly small number of experienced private physicians specializing in this service.

VII. Conclusion

Women seeking late abortion at an advanced stage of pregnancy are frequently among the most desperate because of severe medical complications of the pregnancy; intercurrent medical conditions that threaten the patient's life immediately; severe social and mental health problems such as a history of rape, incest, intimate partner violence, extreme poverty; and complex combinations of these various problems. Some or all these factors have contributed to the delay in seeking an abortion.

Their choices and chances for medical treatment that could save their lives is increasingly limited by widespread sectarian hospital prohibition of abortion, repressive anti-abortion legislation throughout the United States and in many other countries, especially limiting abortion after 20 weeks of pregnancy, and lack of interest among physicians and other health care practitioners in performing late abortions.

Performing late abortions exposes the physician to constant legal, political, and legislative attacks; extremely negative public scrutiny; ostracism in the medical community; interminable threats of violence; and the daily threat of assassination by anti-abortion fanatics. The costs of security are astronomical.

The consequences for women and their families of not being able to terminate a pregnancy after late diagnosis of fetal anomalies or late diagnosis of the pregnancy itself are often catastrophic, including prolonged suffering for severely impaired infants born alive and insupportable costs of palliative medical care over periods of decades. Safe, supportive, and humane medical care for women seeking late termination of pregnancy is available, but few physicians are willing to offer this service, and few women have access to it for the reasons just stated.

About the Editors

David F. Walbert received degrees in physics from Stanford and the University of Michigan before he returned home to law school at Case Western Reserve University, where he graduated with honors and was selected as Editor in Chief of the Law Review. After a clerkship in Oregon with a federal district court judge who played a significant role in the country's legal and political history, he moved to Atlanta where he has practiced law since. He has also taught Constitutional Law and Constitutional Litigation at the Emory University School of Law, spoken frequently at legal education seminars, and published articles in various legal journals. In addition to more traditional litigation, Mr. Walbert has represented clients in many constitutional cases, including before the U.S. Supreme Court where he has argued several times. Notable clients include past governors of Georgia, the Judiciary of the State of Georgia, the U.S. Senate as special counsel when the U.S. Attorney General was the opposing party, and civil rights groups asserting voting rights and other claims. His litigation practice has included cases involving medical practice standards and regulatory issues that overlap with the many medical issues that are addressed in *Whose Choice Is It?* He has tried to judgment and argued appeals of a wide variety of civil and criminal cases in state and federal courts.

Dr. J. Douglas Butler studied at Case Western Reserve University's joint program with the schools of medicine and law. Upon completion of his studies, he left the United States for several years to practice and further study medicine in other countries. Those experiences took him to Ecuador where he served as a medical missionary and then to Portugal where he studied pediatric orthopedics. While Dr. Butler was not an OB/GYN delivering babies, he became keenly aware of the appalling practices in Latin America regarding reproductive medical care. The shocking state of family planning and contraception, abortion access, and what passed for medical care for newborns with physical deficiencies reinforced Dr. Butler's views about morality and medicine. He practiced medicine in Maryland after returning to the United States from Portugal and was inducted into the American College of Legal Medicine, where he continues to be a member.

The editors collaborated on their first edition of *Abortion Medicine and the Law* while in law school, and it was published in 1973 when the original 1965 edition had been largely superseded by events, both legal and medical. One or both of them then served as editors of four subsequent editions, leading up to this latest seventh edition. They have received excellent support and contributions from the academic community, and the schools of medicine and law at the University of Michigan have been especially supportive. While prior editions received various awards, the editors are hopeful that the present edition is the best of the series in its comprehensiveness, depth, and quality, as well as in the number of chapters that will bring important new information to readers no matter how great their prior expertise may be.

Appendix A

An Overview of State Abortion Laws

By the Guttmacher Institute[1]

Background

Since the Supreme Court handed down its 1973 decisions in *Roe v. Wade* and *Doe v. Bolton*, states have constructed a lattice work of abortion law, codifying, regulating and limiting whether, when and under what circumstances a woman may obtain an abortion. The following table highlights the major provisions of these state laws. More detailed information can be found by selecting the table column headings in blue. Except where noted, the laws are in effect, although they may not always be enforced.

Highlights

- *Physician and Hospital Requirements*: 38 states require an abortion to be performed by a licensed physician. 19 states require an abortion to be performed in a hospital after a specified point in the pregnancy, and 17 states require the involvement of a second physician after a specified point.
- *Gestational Limits*: 43 states prohibit abortions, generally except when necessary to protect the woman's life or health, after a specified point in pregnancy.

---

1. © 2021 by the Guttmacher Institute and printed with permission. Updated versions of this information are available from time to time at https://www.guttmacher.org/print /state-policy/explore/overview-abortion-laws.

- *"Partial-Birth" Abortion*: 21 states have laws in effect that prohibit "partial-birth" abortion. 3 of these laws apply only to postviability abortions.
- *Public Funding*: 16 states use their own funds to pay for all or most medically necessary abortions for Medicaid enrollees in the state. 33 states and the District of Columbia prohibit the use of state funds except in those cases when federal funds are available: where the woman's life is in danger or the pregnancy is the result of rape or incest. In defiance of federal requirements, South Dakota limits funding to cases of life endangerment only.
- *Coverage by Private Insurance*: 12 states restrict coverage of abortion in private insurance plans, most often limiting coverage only to when the woman's life would be endangered if the pregnancy were carried to term. Most states allow the purchase of additional abortion coverage at an additional cost.
- *Refusal*: 45 states allow individual health care providers to refuse to participate in an abortion. 42 states allow institutions to refuse to perform abortions, 16 of which limit refusal to private or religious institutions.
- *State-Mandated Counseling*: 18 states mandate that women be given counseling before an abortion that includes information on at least one of the following: the purported link between abortion and breast cancer (5 states), the ability of a fetus to feel pain (13 states) or long-term mental health consequences for the woman (8 states).
- *Waiting Periods*: 25 states require a woman seeking an abortion to wait a specified period of time, usually 24 hours, between when she receives counseling and the procedure is performed. 12 of these states have laws that effectively require the woman make two separate trips to the clinic to obtain the procedure.
- *Parental Involvement*: 37 states require some type of parental involvement in a minor's decision to have an abortion. 27 states require one or both parents to consent to the procedure, while 10 require that one or both parents be notified.

Overview of State Abortion Law (Table 1 of 2)

STATE	MUST BE PERFORMED BY A LICENSED PHYSICIAN	MUST BE PERFORMED IN A HOSPITAL IF AT:	SECOND PHYSICIAN MUST PARTICIPATE IF AT:	PROHIBITED EXCEPT IN CASES OF LIFE OR HEALTH ENDANGERMENT IF AT:	"PARTIAL-BIRTH" ABORTION BANNED	PUBLIC FUNDING OF ABORTION — Funds All or Most Medically Necessary Abortions	PUBLIC FUNDING OF ABORTION — Funds Limited to Life Endangerment, Rape and Incest	PRIVATE INSURANCE COVERAGE LIMITED
AL	X	Viability	Viability	20 weeks*	▶		X	
AK	X	Viability	Viability	Viability	▶	X	θ	
AZ	X		Viability	20 weeks†	X		X	X
AR	X		Viability	Viability	X	X		
CA						X		
CO								
CT		Viability		Viability		X	X	
DE	X			Viability^Ω			X	
DC							X	
FL	X	Viability	24 weeks	24 weeks	▶		X	
GA	X			20 weeks*	Postviability		X	
HI	X^ξ			Viability		X		
ID	X	Viability	3rd trimester	Viability	▶	X	X	X
IL				Viability		X		
IN	X	20 weeks	20 weeks	20 weeks*	X		X*	X
IA	X			20 weeks*	▶		X	
KS	X		Viability	20 weeks*	X		X	X
KY	X	2nd trimester		20 weeks*	▶		X	X
LA	X		Viability	20 weeks*	X		X	
ME				Viability		X		
MD	X			Viability^Ω		X		
MA				24 weeks		X	X	X
MI	X			Viability†	X	X		
MN	X		20 weeks	Viability			X	
MS	X^Φ			20 weeks*, €	X	X	X^Ω	X
MO	X	Viability	Viability	Viability*	X		X	X
MT			Viability	Viability*	Postviability	X		
NE	X			20 weeks*	▶		X	X
NV	X	24 weeks		24 weeks			X	
NH					X	X	X	
NJ	X^ξ				▶	X	X	
NM	X^ξ	14 weeks			Postviability	X		

Overview of State Abortion Law (Table 1 of 2)

STATE	MUST BE PERFORMED BY A LICENSED PHYSICIAN	MUST BE PERFORMED IN A HOSPITAL IF AT:	SECOND PHYSICIAN MUST PARTICIPATE IF AT:	PROHIBITED EXCEPT IN CASES OF LIFE OR HEALTH ENDANGERMENT IF AT:	"PARTIAL-BIRTH" ABORTION BANNED	PUBLIC FUNDING OF ABORTION — Funds All or Most Medically Necessary Abortions	PUBLIC FUNDING OF ABORTION — Funds Limited to Life Endangerment, Rape and Incest	PRIVATE INSURANCE COVERAGE LIMITED
NY	X^ξ			Viability^Ω		X		
NC	X	20 weeks		Viability*			X	
ND	X			20 weeks*	X		X	X
OH	X	20 weeks	20 weeks	20 weeks*	X		X	
OK	X	2nd trimester	Viability	20 weeks*	X		X	X
OR	X					X		
PA	X	Viability	Viability	24 weeks*	▶		X	
RI	X^ξ			Viability	X		X	
SC	X	3rd trimester	3rd trimester	20 weeks*	X		X	
SD	X	24 weeks		20 weeks*	X		Life Only	
TN	X	Viability	Viability	Viability*	X		X	
TX	X			20 weeks*	X		X*	X
UT	X			Viability†,Ω	X		X*	X
VT								
VA	X	2nd trimester	Viability	3rd trimester	X	X	X^θ	
WA				Viability		X		
WV				20 weeks*	▶		X*,Φ	
WI	X	Viability		20 weeks*	▶		X*	
WY	X			Viability			X	
TOTAL	38	19	17	43	21	16	33+DC	12

▶ Permanently enjoined; law not in effect.

* Exception in case of threat to the woman's physical health.

† Exception in case of rape or incest.

†† Exception in case of life endangerment only. A 2016 New York Attorney General opinion determined that the state's law conflicts with U.S. Supreme Court rulings on abortion, and that abortion care is permissible under the U.S. Constitution to protect a woman's health, or when the fetus is not viable.

Ω Exception in case of fetal abnormality.

θ Despite a court order, the state Medicaid program does not pay for medically necessary abortions.

ξ Only applies to surgical abortion. In New Mexico, some but not all advanced practice clinicians may provide medication abortion.

Φ Law limits abortion provision to OB/GYNs.

€ A court has temporarily blocked enforcement of a Mississippi law that would have banned abortion at 15 weeks after the patient's last menstrual period.

Overview of State Abortion Law (Table 2 of 2)

STATE	PROVIDERS MAY REFUSE TO PARTICIPATE		MANDATED COUNSELING INCLUDES INFORMATION ON:			WAITING PERIOD (in Hours) AFTER COUNSELING	PARENTAL INVOLVEMENT REQUIRED FOR MINORS
	Individual	Institution	Breast Cancer Link	Fetal Pain	Negative Psychological Effects		
AL						48	Consent
AK	X	Private	X	X			▶
AZ	X	X				24	Consent
AR	X	X		X^{Φ}		72	Consent
CA	X	Religious					▶
CO							Notice
CT	X						
DE	X	X					Notice$^{\xi}$
DC							
FL	X	X				▶	Consent and Notice
GA	X	X		X		24	Notice
HI	X	X					
ID	X	X				24	Consent
IL	X	Private					Notice

Overview of State Abortion Law (Table 2 of 2)

STATE	PROVIDERS MAY REFUSE TO PARTICIPATE		MANDATED COUNSELING INCLUDES INFORMATION ON:			WAITING PERIOD (in Hours) AFTER COUNSELING	PARENTAL INVOLVEMENT REQUIRED FOR MINORS
	Individual	Institution	Breast Cancer Link	Fetal Pain	Negative Psychological Effects		
IN	X	Private		X		18	Consent
IA	X	Private				§	Notice
KS	X	X	X	X	X	24	Consent
KY	X	X				24	Consent
LA	X	X		X	X	24	Consent
ME	X	X					
MD	X	X					Notice[ξ]
MA	X	X				▶	Consent[β]
MI	X	X			X	24	Consent
MN	X	Private		X[Φ]		24	Notice[b]
MS	X	X	X			24	Consent[b]
MO	X	X		X[Φ]		72	Consent
MT	X	Private				▶	▶
NE	X	X			X	24	Consent
NV	X	Private					▶

Overview of State Abortion Law (Table 2 of 2)

STATE	PROVIDERS MAY REFUSE TO PARTICIPATE		MANDATED COUNSELING INCLUDES INFORMATION ON:			WAITING PERIOD (in Hours) AFTER COUNSELING	PARENTAL INVOLVEMENT REQUIRED FOR MINORS
	Individual	Institution	Breast Cancer Link	Fetal Pain	Negative Psychological Effects		
NH							Notice
NJ	X	Private					▶
NM	X	X					▶
NY	X						
NC	X	X			X	72	Consent
ND	X	X				24	Consent[b]
OH	X	X				24	Consent
OK	X	Private	X	X[Φ]		72	Consent and Notice
OR	X	Private					
PA	X	Private				24	Consent
RI	X						Consent
SC	X	Private				24	Consent
SD	X	X		X	X	72[◊]	Notice
TN	X	X				▶	Consent
TX	X	Private	X	X	X	24	Consent and Notice

Overview of State Abortion Law (Table 2 of 2)

STATE	PROVIDERS MAY REFUSE TO PARTICIPATE		MANDATED COUNSELING INCLUDES INFORMATION ON:			WAITING PERIOD (in Hours) AFTER COUNSELING	PARENTAL INVOLVEMENT REQUIRED FOR MINORS
	Individual	Institution	Breast Cancer Link	Fetal Pain	Negative Psychological Effects		
UT	X	Private		X^{Φ}		$72^{\Diamond}$	Consent and Notice
VT							
VA	X	X					Consent and Notice
WA	X	X					
WV					X	24	Notice$^{\xi}$
WI	X	X		X		24	Consent$^{\xi}$
WY	X	Private					Consent and Notice
TOTAL	45	42	5	13	8	25	37

▶ Permanently enjoined; law not in effect.
§ Enforcement temporarily enjoined by court order; policy not in effect.
Φ Fetal pain information is given only to women who are at least 20 weeks gestation; in Missouri at 22 weeks gestation.
þ Both parents must consent to the abortion.
ξ Specified health professionals may waive parental involvement in certain circumstances.
◊ In South Dakota, the waiting period excludes weekends or annual holidays and in Utah the waiting period is waived in cases of rape, incest, fetal defect or if the patient is younger than 15.
β Parental consent required for minors under the age of 16.

Appendix B

Opinion of Justice Blackmun for the Court[1]

— Roe v. Wade (1973) —

This Texas federal appeal and its Georgia companion, *Doe v. Bolton, post,* p. 179, present constitutional challenges to state criminal abortion legislation. The Texas statutes under attack here are typical of those that have been in effect in many States for approximately a century. The Georgia statutes, in contrast, have a modern cast, and are a legislative product that, to an extent at least, obviously reflects the influences of recent attitudinal change, of advancing medical knowledge and techniques, and of new thinking about an old issue.

We forthwith acknowledge our awareness of the sensitive and emotional nature of the abortion controversy, of the vigorous opposing views, even among physicians, and of the deep and seemingly absolute convictions that the subject inspires. One's philosophy, one's experiences, one's exposure to the raw edges of human existence, one's religious training, one's attitudes toward life and family and their values, and the moral standards one establishes and seeks to observe, are all likely to influence and to color one's thinking and conclusions about abortion.

In addition, population growth, pollution, poverty, and racial overtones tend to complicate and not to simplify the problem.

Our task, of course, is to resolve the issue by constitutional measurement, free of emotion and of predilection. We seek earnestly to do this, and, because we do, we have inquired into, and in this opinion place some emphasis upon, medical and medical-legal history and what that history reveals about man's attitudes toward the abortion procedure over the centuries. We bear in mind, too, Mr. Justice Holmes' admonition in his now-vindicated dissent in *Lochner v. New York,* 198 U.S. 45, 76 (1905):

---

1. Some parts redacted; the full opinion is available at 410 U.S. 113 (1973).

"[The Constitution] is made for people of fundamentally differing views, and the accident of our finding certain opinions natural and familiar or novel and even shocking ought not to conclude our judgment upon the question whether statutes embodying them conflict with the Constitution of the United States."

I

The Texas statutes that concern us here are Arts. 1191-1194 and 1196 of the State's Penal Code.[2] These make it a crime to "procure an abortion," as therein defined, or to attempt one, except with respect to "an abortion procured or attempted by medical advice for the purpose of saving the life of the mother." Similar statutes are in existence in a majority of the States.[3]

---

2. "Article 1191. Abortion"

"If any person shall designedly administer to a pregnant woman or knowingly procure to be administered with her consent any drug or medicine, or shall use towards her any violence or means whatever externally or internally applied, and thereby procure an abortion, he shall be confined in the penitentiary not less than two nor more than five years; if it be done without her consent, the punishment shall be doubled. By 'abortion' is meant that the life of the fetus or embryo shall be destroyed in the woman's womb or that a premature birth thereof be caused."

"Art. 1192. Furnishing the means"

"Whoever furnishes the means for procuring an abortion knowing the purpose intended is guilty as an accomplice."

"Art. 1193. Attempt at abortion"

"If the means used shall fail to produce an abortion, the offender is nevertheless guilty of an attempt to produce abortion, provided it be shown that such means were calculated to produce that result, and shall be fined not less than one hundred nor more than one thousand dollars."

"Art. 1194. Murder in producing abortion"

"If the death of the mother is occasioned by an abortion so produced or by an attempt to effect the same it is murder."

"Art. 1196. By medical advice"

"Nothing in this chapter applies to an abortion procured or attempted by medical advice for the purpose of saving the life of the mother."

The foregoing Articles, together with Art. 1195, compose Chapter 9 of Title 15 of the Penal Code. Article 1195, not attacked here, reads:

"Art. 1195. Destroying unborn child"

"Whoever shall during parturition of the mother destroy the vitality or life in a child in a state of being born and before actual birth, which child would otherwise have been born alive, shall be confined in the penitentiary for life or for not less than five years."

3. Ariz. Rev. Stat. Ann. § 13-211 (1956); Conn. Pub. Act No. 1 (May 1972 special session) (in 4 Conn. Leg. Serv. 677 (1972)), and Conn. Gen. Stat. Rev. §§ 53-29, 53-30 (1968) (or unborn child); Idaho Code § 18-601 (1948); Ill. Rev. Stat., c. 38, § 23-1 (1971); Ind. Code § 35-1-58-1 (1971); Iowa Code § 701.1 (1971); Ky. Rev. Stat. § 436.020 (1962); La.

Texas first enacted a criminal abortion statute in 1854. Texas Laws 1854, c. 49, § 1, set forth in 3 H. Gammel, Laws of Texas 1502 (1898). This was soon modified into language that has remained substantially unchanged to the present time. *See* Texas Penal Code of 1857, c. 7, Arts. 531-536; G. Paschal, Laws of Texas, Arts. 2192-2197 (1866); Texas Rev.Stat., c. 8, Arts. 536-541 (1879); Texas Rev.Crim.Stat., Arts. 1071-1076 (1911). The final article in each of these compilations provided the same exception, as does the present Article 1196, for an abortion by "medical advice for the purpose of saving the life of the mother."[4]

Rev. Stat. § 37: 1285(6) (1964) (loss of medical license) (*but see* § 14:87 (Supp. 1972) containing no exception for the life of the mother under the criminal statute); Me. Rev. Stat. Ann, tit. 17, § 51 (1964); Mass. Gen. Laws Ann., c. 272, § 19 (1970) (using the term "unlawfully," construed to exclude an abortion to save the mother's life, Kudish v. Bd. of Registration, 356 Mass. 98, 248 N.E.2d 264 (1969)); Mich. Comp. Laws § 750.14 (1948); Minn. Stat. § 617.18 (1971); Mo. Rev. Stat. § 559.100 (1969); Mont. Rev. Codes Ann. § 94-401 (1969); Neb. Rev. Stat. § 28-405 (1964); Nev. Rev. Stat. § 200.220 (1967); N.H. Rev. Stat. Ann. § 585: 13 (1955); N.J. Stat. Ann. § 2A:87-1 (1969) ("without lawful justification"); N.D. Cent. Code §§ 12-25-01, 12-25-02 (1960); Ohio Rev. Code Ann. § 2901.16 (1953); Okla. Stat. Ann. tit. 21, § 861 (1972-1973 Supp.); Pa. Stat. Ann. tit. 18, §§ 4718, 4719 (1963) ("unlawful"); R.I. Gen. Laws Ann. § 11-3-1 (1969); S.D. Comp. Laws Ann. § 22-17-1 (1967); Tenn. Code Ann. §§ 39-301, 39-302 (1956); Utah Code Ann. §§ 76-2-1, 76-2-2 (1953); Vt. Stat. Ann. tit. 13, § 101 (1958); W. Va. Code Ann. § 61-2-8 (1966); Wis. Stat. § 940.04 (1969); Wyo. Stat. Ann. §§ 6-77, 6-78 (1957).

4. Long ago, a suggestion was made that the Texas statutes were unconstitutionally vague because of definitional deficiencies. The Texas Court of Criminal Appeals disposed of that suggestion peremptorily, saying only,

> "It is also insisted in the motion in arrest of judgment that the statute is unconstitutional and void in that it does not sufficiently define or describe the offense of abortion. We do not concur in respect to this question."

Jackson v. State, 55 Tex. Cr. R. 79, 89, 115 S.W. 262, 268 (1908). The same court recently has held again that the State's abortion statutes are not unconstitutionally vague or overbroad. *Thompson v. State* (Ct. Crim. App. Tex.1971), *appeal docketed*, No. 71-1200. The court held that "the State of Texas has a compelling interest to protect fetal life"; that Art. 1191 "is designed to protect fetal life"; that the Texas homicide statutes, particularly Art. 1205 of the Penal Code, are intended to protect a person "in existence by actual birth," and thereby implicitly recognize other human life that is not "in existence by actual birth"; that the definition of human life is for the legislature and not the courts; that Art. 1196 "is more definite than the District of Columbia statute upheld in *[402 U.S.] Vuitch*" (402 U.S. 62); and that the Texas statute "is not vague and indefinite or overbroad." A physician's abortion conviction was affirmed.

In *Thompson*, n.2, the court observed that any issue as to the burden of proof under the exemption of Art. 1196 "is not before us." *But see* Veevers v. State, 172 Tex. Cr. R. 162, 168–69, 354 S.W.2d 161, 166–67 (1962). *Cf.* United States v. Vuitch, 402 U.S. 62, 69–71 (1971).

II

Jane Roe,[5] a single woman who was residing in Dallas County, Texas, instituted this federal action in March 1970 against the District Attorney of the county. She sought a declaratory judgment that the Texas criminal abortion statutes were unconstitutional on their face, and an injunction restraining the defendant from enforcing the statutes.

Roe alleged that she was unmarried and pregnant; that she wished to terminate her pregnancy by an abortion "performed by a competent, licensed physician, under safe, clinical conditions"; that she was unable to get a "legal" abortion in Texas because her life did not appear to be threatened by the continuation of her pregnancy; and that she could not afford to travel to another jurisdiction in order to secure a legal abortion under safe conditions. She claimed that the Texas statutes were unconstitutionally vague and that they abridged her right of personal privacy, protected by the First, Fourth, Fifth, Ninth, and Fourteenth Amendments. By an amendment to her complaint, Roe purported to sue "on behalf of herself and all other women" similarly situated.

James Hubert Hallford, a licensed physician, sought and was granted leave to intervene in Roe's action. In his complaint, he alleged that he had been arrested previously for violations of the Texas abortion statutes, and that two such prosecutions were pending against him. He described conditions of patients who came to him seeking abortions, and he claimed that for many cases he, as a physician, was unable to determine whether they fell within or outside the exception recognized by Article 1196. He alleged that, as a consequence, the statutes were vague and uncertain, in violation of the Fourteenth Amendment, and that they violated his own and his patients' rights to privacy in the doctor-patient relationship and his own right to practice medicine, rights he claimed were guaranteed by the First, Fourth, Fifth, Ninth, and Fourteenth Amendments.

John and Mary Doe,[6] a married couple, filed a companion complaint to that of Roe. They also named the District Attorney as defendant, claimed like constitutional deprivations, and sought declaratory and injunctive relief. The Does alleged that they were a childless couple; that Mrs. Doe was suffering from a "neural-chemical" disorder; that her physician had "advised her to avoid pregnancy until such time as her condition has materially improved" (although a pregnancy at the present time would not pres-

---

5. The name is a pseudonym.
6. These names are pseudonyms.

ent "a serious risk" to her life); that, pursuant to medical advice, she had discontinued use of birth control pills; and that, if she should become pregnant, she would want to terminate the pregnancy by an abortion performed by a competent, licensed physician under safe, clinical conditions. By an amendment to their complaint, the Does purported to sue "on behalf of themselves and all couples similarly situated."

The two actions were consolidated and heard together by a duly convened three-judge district court. The suits thus presented the situations of the pregnant single woman, the childless couple, with the wife not pregnant, and the licensed practicing physician, all joining in the attack on the Texas criminal abortion statutes. Upon the filing of affidavits, motions were made for dismissal and for summary judgment. The court held that Roe and members of her class, and Dr. Hallford, had standing to sue and presented justiciable controversies, but that the Does had failed to allege facts sufficient to state a present controversy, and did not have standing. It concluded that, with respect to the requests for a declaratory judgment, abstention was not warranted. On the merits, the District Court held that the

> "fundamental right of single women and married persons to choose whether to have children is protected by the Ninth Amendment, through the Fourteenth Amendment,"

and that the Texas criminal abortion statutes were void on their face because they were both unconstitutionally vague and constituted an overbroad infringement of the plaintiffs' Ninth Amendment rights. The court then held that abstention was warranted with respect to the requests for an injunction. It therefore dismissed the Does' complaint, declared the abortion statutes void, and dismissed the application for injunctive relief. 314 F. Supp. 1217, 1225 (ND Tex.1970).

The plaintiffs Roe and Doe and the intervenor Hallford, pursuant to 28 U.S.C. § 1253, have appealed to this Court from that part of the District Court's judgment denying the injunction. The defendant District Attorney has purported to cross-appeal, pursuant to the same statute, from the court's grant of declaratory relief to Roe and Hallford. Both sides also have taken protective appeals to the United States Court of Appeals for the Fifth Circuit. That court ordered the appeals held in abeyance pending decision here. We postponed decision on jurisdiction to the hearing on the merits. 402 U.S. 941 (1971).

[Sections III and IV relate to peripheral legal issues of procedure, standing, justiciability, and abstention and have been redacted].

V

The principal thrust of appellant's attack on the Texas statutes is that they improperly invade a right, said to be possessed by the pregnant woman, to choose to terminate her pregnancy. Appellant would discover this right in the concept of personal "liberty" embodied in the Fourteenth Amendment's Due Process Clause; or in personal, marital, familial, and sexual privacy said to be protected by the Bill of Rights or its penumbras, *see Griswold v. Connecticut*, 381 U.S. 479 (1965); *Eisenstadt v. Baird*, 405 U.S. 438 (1972); *id.* at 460 (WHITE, J., concurring in result); or among those rights reserved to the people by the Ninth Amendment, *Griswold v. Connecticut*, 381 U.S. at 486 (Goldberg, J., concurring). Before addressing this claim, we feel it desirable briefly to survey, in several aspects, the history of abortion, for such insight as that history may afford us, and then to examine the state purposes and interests behind the criminal abortion laws.

VI

It perhaps is not generally appreciated that the restrictive criminal abortion laws in effect in a majority of States today are of relatively recent vintage. Those laws, generally proscribing abortion or its attempt at any time during pregnancy except when necessary to preserve the pregnant woman's life, are not of ancient or even of common law origin. Instead, they derive from statutory changes effected, for the most part, in the latter half of the 19th century.

   1. *Ancient attitudes.* These are not capable of precise determination. We are told that, at the time of the Persian Empire, abortifacients were known, and that criminal abortions were severely punished.[7] We are also told, however, that abortion was practiced in Greek times as well as in the Roman Era,[8] and that "it was resorted to without scruple."[9] The Ephesian, Soranos,

---

   7. Castiglioni, A History of Medicine 84 (2d ed. 1947), E. Krumbhaar, translator and editor [hereinafter Castiglioni].

   8. J. Ricci, The Genealogy of Gynaecology 52, 84, 113, 149 (2d ed.1950) [hereinafter Ricci]; L. Lader, Abortion 75–77 (1966) [hereinafter Lader], K. Niswander, *Medical Abortion Practices in the United States, in* Abortion and the Law 37, 38–40 (D. Smith ed. 1967); G. Williams, The Sanctity of Life and the Criminal Law 148 (1957) [hereinafter Williams]; J. Noonan, *An Almost Absolute Value in History, in* The Morality of Abortion 1, 3–7 (J. Noonan ed. 1970) [hereinafter Noonan]; Quay, *Justifiable Abortion—Medical and Legal Foundations* (pt. 2), 49 Geo. L.J. 395, 40622 (1961) [hereinafter Quay].

   9. L. Edelstein, The Hippocratic Oath 10 (1943) [hereinafter Edelstein]. *But see* Castiglioni 227.

often described as the greatest of the ancient gynecologists, appears to have been generally opposed to Rome's prevailing free-abortion practices. He found it necessary to think first of the life of the mother, and he resorted to abortion when, upon this standard, he felt the procedure advisable.[10] Greek and Roman law afforded little protection to the unborn. If abortion was prosecuted in some places, it seems to have been based on a concept of a violation of the father's right to his offspring. Ancient religion did not bar abortion.[11]

2. *The Hippocratic Oath.* What then of the famous Oath that has stood so long as the ethical guide of the medical profession and that bears the name of the great Greek (460(?)–377(?) B.C.), who has been described as the Father of Medicine, the "wisest and the greatest practitioner of his art," and the "most important and most complete medical personality of antiquity," who dominated the medical schools of his time, and who typified the sum of the medical knowledge of the past?[12] The Oath varies somewhat according to the particular translation, but in any translation the content is clear:

> "I will give no deadly medicine to anyone if asked, nor suggest any such counsel; and in like manner, I will not give to a woman a pessary to produce abortion,[13]"

or

> "I will neither give a deadly drug to anybody if asked for it, nor will I make a suggestion to this effect. Similarly, I will not give to a woman an abortive remedy.[14]"

Although the Oath is not mentioned in any of the principal briefs in this case or in *Doe v. Bolton, post,* p. 179, it represents the apex of the development of strict ethical concepts in medicine, and its influence endures to this day. Why did not the authority of Hippocrates dissuade abortion practice in his time and that of Rome? The late Dr. Edelstein provides us with a theory:[15] The Oath was not uncontested even in Hippocrates' day; only the Pythagorean school of philosophers frowned upon the related act of suicide. Most Greek thinkers, on the other hand, commended abortion, at least prior to viability. *See* Plato, Republic, V, 461; Aristotle, Politics, VII,

---

10. Edelstein 12; Ricci 113–14, 118–19; Noonan 5.
11. Edelstein 13–14.
12. Castiglioni 148.
13. *Id.* at 154.
14. Edelstein 3.
15. *Id.* at 12, 15–18.

1335b 25. For the Pythagoreans, however, it was a matter of dogma. For them, the embryo was animate from the moment of conception, and abortion meant destruction of a living being. The abortion clause of the Oath, therefore, "echoes Pythagorean doctrines," and "[i]n no other stratum of Greek opinion were such views held or proposed in the same spirit of uncompromising austerity."[16]

Dr. Edelstein then concludes that the Oath originated in a group representing only a small segment of Greek opinion, and that it certainly was not accepted by all ancient physicians. He points out that medical writings down to Galen (A.D. 130-200) "give evidence of the violation of almost every one of its injunctions."[17] But with the end of antiquity, a decided change took place. Resistance against suicide and against abortion became common. The Oath came to be popular. The emerging teachings of Christianity were in agreement with the Pythagorean ethic. The Oath "became the nucleus of all medical ethics," and "was applauded as the embodiment of truth." Thus, suggests Dr. Edelstein, it is "a Pythagorean manifesto, and not the expression of an absolute standard of medical conduct."[18]

This, it seems to us, is a satisfactory and acceptable explanation of the Hippocratic Oath's apparent rigidity. It enables us to understand, in historical context, a long-accepted and revered statement of medical ethics.

3. *The common law.* It is undisputed that, at common law, abortion performed before "quickening"—the first recognizable movement of the fetus *in utero*, appearing usually from the 16th to the 18th week of pregnancy[19]— was not an indictable offense.[20] The absence of a common law crime for pre-quickening abortion appears to have developed from a confluence of earlier philosophical, theological, and civil and canon law concepts of when life begins. These disciplines variously approached the question in terms of the point at which the embryo or fetus became "formed" or recognizably human, or in terms of when a "person" came into being, that is, infused with a "soul" or "animated." A loose consensus evolved in early English law that

---

16. *Id.* at 18; Lader 76.

17. Edelstein 63.

18. *Id.* at 64.

19. Dorand's Illustrated Medical Dictionary 1261 (24th ed.1965).

20. E. Coke, Institutes III *50; 1 W. Hawkins, Pleas of the Crown, c. 31, § 16 (4th ed. 1762); 1 W. Blackstone, Commentaries *129–30; M. Hale, Pleas of the Crown 433 (1st Amer. ed. 1847). For discussions of the role of the quickening concept in English common law, *see* Lader 78; Noonan 223–26; Means, *The Law of New York Concerning Abortion and the Status of the Foetus*, 1664–68: A Case of Cessation of Constitutionality (pt. 1), 14 N.Y.L.F. 411, 418–28 (1968) [hereinafter Means I]; Stern, *Abortion: Reform and the Law*, 59 J. Crim. L.C. & P.S. 84 (1968) [hereinafter Stern]; Quay 430–32; Williams 152.

these events occurred at some point between conception and live birth.[21] This was "mediate animation." Although Christian theology and the canon law came to fix the point of animation at 40 days for a male and 80 days for a female, a view that persisted until the 19th century, there was otherwise little agreement about the precise time of formation or animation. There was agreement, however, that, prior to this point, the fetus was to be regarded as part of the mother, and its destruction, therefore, was not homicide. Due to continued uncertainty about the precise time when animation occurred, to the lack of any empirical basis for the 40-80-day view, and perhaps to Aquinas' definition of movement as one of the two first principles of life, Bracton focused upon quickening as the critical point. The significance of quickening was echoed by later common law scholars, and found its way into the received common law in this country.

Whether abortion of a quick fetus was a felony at common law, or even a lesser crime, is still disputed. Bracton, writing early in the 13th century, thought it homicide.[22] But the later and predominant view, following the

---

21. Early philosophers believed that the embryo or fetus did not become formed and begin to live until at least 40 days after conception for a male and 80 to 90 days for a female. *See, e.g.,* Aristotle, Hist. Anim. 7.3.583b; Gen. Anim. 2.3.736, 2.5.741; Hippocrates, Lib. de Nat. Puer., No. 10. Aristotle's thinking derived from his three-stage theory of life: vegetable, animal, rational. The vegetable stage was reached at conception, the animal at "animation," and the rational soon after live birth. This theory, together with the 40/80 day view, came to be accepted by early Christian thinkers.

The theological debate was reflected in the writings of St. Augustine, who made a distinction between *embryo inanimatus,* not yet endowed with a soul, and *embryo animatus.* He may have drawn upon Exodus 21:22. At one point, however, he expressed the view that human powers cannot determine the point during fetal development at which the critical change occurs. *See* Augustine, De Origine Animae 4.4 (Pub. Law 44.527). *See also* W. Reany, The Creation of the Human Soul, c. 2 and 83–86 (1932); Huser, The Crime of Abortion in Canon Law 15 (Catholic Univ. of America, Canon Law Studies No. 162, Washington, D.C.1942).

Galen, in three treatises related to embryology, accepted the thinking of Aristotle and his followers. Quay 426–27. Later, Augustine on abortion was incorporated by Gratian into the Decretum, published about 1140. Decretum Magistri Gratiani 2.32.2.7 to 2.32.2.10, in 1 Corpus Juris Canonici 1122, 1123 (A. Friedburg, 2d ed. 1879). This Decretal and the Decretals that followed were recognized as the definitive body of canon law until the new Code of 1917.

For discussions of the canon law treatment, *see* Means I, pp. 411–12; Noonan 20–26; Quay 426–30; *see also* J. Noonan, Contraception: A History of Its Treatment by the Catholic Theologians and Canonists 18–29 (1965).

22. Bracton took the position that abortion by blow or poison was homicide "if the foetus be already formed and animated, and particularly if it be animated." 2 H. Bracton, De Legibus et Consuetudinibus Angliae 279 (T. Twiss ed. 1879), or, as a later translation puts it, "if the foetus is already formed or quickened, especially if it is quickened," 2 H. Bracton, On the Laws and Customs of England 341 (S. Thorne ed.1968). *See* Quay 431; *see also* 2 Fleta 661 (Book 1, c. 23) (Selden Society ed.1955).

great common law scholars, has been that it was, at most, a lesser offense. In a frequently cited passage, Coke took the position that abortion of a woman "quick with childe" is "a great misprision, and no murder."[23] Blackstone followed, saying that, while abortion after quickening had once been considered manslaughter (though not murder), "modern law" took a less severe view.[24] A recent review of the common law precedents argues, however, that those precedents contradict Coke, and that even post-quickening abortion was never established as a common law crime.[25] This is of some importance, because, while most American courts ruled, in holding or dictum, that abortion of an unquickened fetus was not criminal under their received common law,[26] others followed Coke in stating that abortion of a quick fetus was a "misprision," a term they translated to mean "misdemeanor."[27] That their reliance on Coke on this aspect of the law was uncritical and, apparently in all the reported cases, dictum (due probably to the paucity of common law prosecutions for post-quickening abortion), makes it now appear doubtful that abortion was ever firmly established as a common law crime even with respect to the destruction of a quick fetus.

---

23. E. COKE, INSTITUTES III *50.

24. 1 W. Blackstone, Commentaries *129–30.

25. Means, *The Phoenix of Abortional Freedom: Is a Penumbral or Ninth-Amendment Right About to Arise from the Nineteenth Century Legislative Ashes of a Fourteenth Century Common Law Liberty?*, 17 N.Y.L.F. 335 (1971) (hereinafter Means II). The author examines the two principal precedents cited marginally by Coke, both contrary to his dictum, and traces the treatment of these and other cases by earlier commentators. He concludes that Coke, who himself participated as an advocate in an abortion case in 1601, may have intentionally misstated the law. The author even suggests a reason: Coke's strong feelings against abortion, coupled with his determination to assert common law (secular) jurisdiction to assess penalties for an offense that traditionally had been an exclusively ecclesiastical or canon law crime. *See also* Lader 78–79, who notes that some scholars doubt that the common law ever was applied to abortion; that the English ecclesiastical courts seem to have lost interest in the problem after 1527; and that the preamble to the English legislation of 1803, 43 Geo. 3, c. 58, § 1, referred to in the text, *infra* at 136, states that "no adequate means have been hitherto provided for the prevention and punishment of such offenses."

26. Commonwealth v. Bangs, 9 Mass. 387, 388 (1812); Commonwealth v. Parker, 50 Mass. (9 Metc.) 263, 265–66 (1845); State v. Cooper, 22 N.J.L. 52, 58 (1849); Abrams v. Foshee, 3 Iowa 274, 278-280 (1856); Smith v. Gaffard, 31 Ala. 45, 51 (1857); Mitchell v. Commonwealth, 78 Ky. 204, 210 (1879); Eggart v. State, 40 Fla. 527, 532, 25 So. 144, 145 (1898); State v. Alcorn, 7 Idaho 599, 606, 64 P. 1014, 1016 (1901); Edwards v. State, 79 Neb. 251, 252, 112 N.W. 611, 612 (1907); Gray v. State, 77 Tex. Cr. R. 221, 224, 178 S.W. 337, 338 (1915); Miller v. Bennett, 190 Va. 162, 169, 56 S.E.2d 217, 221 (1949). *Contra*, Mills v. Commonwealth, 13 Pa. 631, 633 (1850); State v. Slagle, 83 N.C. 630, 632 (1880).

27. *See* Smith v. State, 33 Me. 48, 55 (1851); Evans v. People, 49 N.Y. 86, 88 (1872); Lamb v. State, 67 Md. 524, 533, 10 A. 208 (1887).

4. *The English statutory law.* England's first criminal abortion statute, Lord Ellenborough's Act, 43 Geo. 3, c. 58, came in 1803. It made abortion of a quick fetus, § 1, a capital crime, but, in § 2, it provided lesser penalties for the felony of abortion before quickening, and thus preserved the "quickening" distinction. This contrast was continued in the general revision of 1828, 9 Geo. 4, c. 31, § 13. It disappeared, however, together with the death penalty, in 1837, 7 Will. 4 & 1 Vict., c. 85. § 6, and did not reappear in the Offenses Against the Person Act of 1861, 24 & 25 Vict., c. 100, § 59, that formed the core of English anti-abortion law until the liberalizing reforms of 1967. In 1929, the Infant Life (Preservation) Act, 19 & 20 Geo. 5, c. 34, came into being. Its emphasis was upon the destruction of "the life of a child capable of being born alive." It made a willful act performed with the necessary intent a felony. It contained a proviso that one was not to be found guilty of the offense

> "unless it is proved that the act which caused the death of the child was not done in good faith for the purpose only of preserving the life of the mother."

A seemingly notable development in the English law was the case of *Rex v. Bourne*, [1939] 1 K.B. 687. This case apparently answered in the affirmative the question whether an abortion necessary to preserve the life of the pregnant woman was excepted from the criminal penalties of the 1861 Act. In his instructions to the jury, Judge Macnaghten referred to the 1929 Act, and observed that that Act related to "the case where a child is killed by a willful act at the time when it is being delivered in the ordinary course of nature." *Id.* at 691. He concluded that the 1861 Act's use of the word "unlawfully," imported the same meaning expressed by the specific proviso in the 1929 Act, even though there was no mention of preserving the mother's life in the 1861 Act. He then construed the phrase "preserving the life of the mother" broadly, that is, "in a reasonable sense," to include a serious and permanent threat to the mother's health, and instructed the jury to acquit Dr. Bourne if it found he had acted in a good faith belief that the abortion was necessary for this purpose. *Id.* at 693-694. The jury did acquit.

Recently, Parliament enacted a new abortion law. This is the Abortion Act of 1967, 15 & 16 Eliz. 2, c. 87. The Act permits a licensed physician to perform an abortion where two other licensed physicians agree (a)

> "that the continuance of the pregnancy would involve risk to the life of the pregnant woman, or of injury to the physical or mental health of the

pregnant woman or any existing children of her family, greater than if the pregnancy were terminated,"

or (b)

"that there is a substantial risk that, if the child were born it would suffer from such physical or mental abnormalities as to be seriously handicapped."

The Act also provides that, in making this determination, "account may be taken of the pregnant woman's actual or reasonably foreseeable environment." It also permits a physician, without the concurrence of others, to terminate a pregnancy where he is of the good faith opinion that the abortion "is immediately necessary to save the life or to prevent grave permanent injury to the physical or mental health of the pregnant woman."

5. *The American law.* In this country, the law in effect in all but a few States until mid-19th century was the preexisting English common law. Connecticut, the first State to enact abortion legislation, adopted in 1821 that part of Lord Ellenborough's Act that related to a woman "quick with child."[28] The death penalty was not imposed. Abortion before quickening was made a crime in that State only in 1860.[29] In 1828, New York enacted legislation[30] that, in two respects, was to serve as a model for early anti-abortion statutes. First, while barring destruction of an unquickened fetus as well as a quick fetus, it made the former only a misdemeanor, but the latter second-degree manslaughter. Second, it incorporated a concept of therapeutic abortion by providing that an abortion was excused if it

"shall have been necessary to preserve the life of such mother, or shall have been advised by two physicians to be necessary for such purpose."

By 1840, when Texas had received the common law,[31] only eight American States had statutes dealing with abortion.[32] It was not until after the War Between the States that legislation began generally to replace the common law. Most of these initial statutes dealt severely with abortion after quickening, but were lenient with it before quickening. Most punished attempts equally with completed abortions. While many statutes included the excep-

---

28. Conn. Stat., tit. 20, § 14 (1821).

29. Conn. Pub. Acts, c. 71, § 1 (1860).

30. N.Y. Rev. Stat., pt. 4, c. 1, tit. 2, Art. 1, § 9, p. 661, and tit. 6, § 21, p. 694 (1829).

31. Act of Jan. 20, 1840, § 1, set forth in 2 H. Gammel, Laws of Texas 177–78 (1898); *see* Grigsby v. Reib, 105 Tex. 597, 600, 153 S.W. 1124, 1125 (1913).

32. The early statutes are discussed in Quay 435–38. *See also Lader* 85–88; *Stern* 85–86; and Means II 37376.

tion for an abortion thought by one or more physicians to be necessary to save the mother's life, that provision soon disappeared, and the typical law required that the procedure actually be necessary for that purpose. Gradually, in the middle and late 19th century, the quickening distinction disappeared from the statutory law of most States and the degree of the offense and the penalties were increased. By the end of the 1950s, a large majority of the jurisdictions banned abortion, however and whenever performed, unless done to save or preserve the life of the mother.[33] The exceptions, Alabama and the District of Columbia, permitted abortion to preserve the mother's health.[34] Three States permitted abortions that were not "unlawfully" performed or that were not "without lawful justification," leaving interpretation of those standards to the courts.[35] In the past several years, however, a trend toward liberalization of abortion statutes has resulted in adoption, by about one-third of the States, of less stringent laws, most of them patterned after the ALI Model Penal Code, § 230.3,[36] set forth as Appendix B to the opinion in *Doe v. Bolton, post,* p. 205.

---

33. Criminal abortion statutes in effect in the States as of 1961, together with historical statutory development and important judicial interpretations of the state statutes, are cited and quoted in Quay 447–520. *See* Comment, *A Survey of the Present Statutory and Case Law on Abortion: The Contradictions and the Problems,* 1972 U. ILL. L.F. 177, 179, classifying the abortion statutes and listing 25 States as permitting abortion only if necessary to save or preserve the mother's life.

34. ALA. CODE, tit. 14, § 9 (1958); D.C. CODE ANN. § 22-201 (1967).

35. MASS. GEN. LAWS ANN., c. 272, § 19 (1970); N.J. STAT. ANN. § 2A: 87-1 (1969); PA. STAT. ANN., tit. 18, §§ 4718, 4719 (1963).

36. Fourteen States have adopted some form of the ALI statute. *See* ARK. STAT. ANN. §§ 41-303 to 41-310 (Supp. 1971); CALIF. HEALTH & SAFETY CODE §§ 25950–25955.5 (Supp. 1972); COLO. REV. STAT. ANN. §§ 40-2-50 to 40-2-53 (Cum. Supp. 1967); DEL. CODE ANN., tit. 24, §§ 1790–1793 (Supp. 1972); Florida Law of Apr. 13, 1972, c. 72-196, 1972 FLA. SESS. LAW SERV., pp. 380–82; GA. CODE §§ 26-1201 to 26-1203 (1972); KAN. STAT. ANN. § 21-3407 (Supp. 1971); MD. ANN. CODE, Art. 43, §§ 137–139 (1971); MISS. CODE ANN. § 2223 (Supp. 1972); N.M. STAT. ANN. §§ 40A-5-1 to 40A-5-3 (1972); N.C. GEN. STAT. § 14-45.1 (Supp. 1971); ORE. REV. STAT. §§ 435.405 to 435.495 (1971); S.C. CODE ANN. §§ 16-82 to 16-89 (1962 and Supp. 1971); VA. CODE ANN. §§ 18.1-62 to 18.1-62.3 (Supp. 1972). Mr. Justice Clark described some of these States as having "led the way." *Religion, Morality, and Abortion: A Constitutional Appraisal,* 2 LOY. L.A. L. REV. 1, 11 (1969).

By the end of 1970, four other States had repealed criminal penalties for abortions performed in early pregnancy by a licensed physician, subject to stated procedural and health requirements. ALASKA STAT. § 11.15.060 (1970); HAW. REV. STAT. § 453-16 (Supp. 1971); N.Y. PENAL CODE § 125.05, subd. 3 (Supp. 1972-1973); WASH. REV. CODE §§ 9.02.060 to 9.02.080 (Supp. 1972). The precise status of criminal abortion laws in some States is made unclear by recent decisions in state and federal courts striking down existing state laws, in whole or in part.

It is thus apparent that, at common law, at the time of the adoption of our Constitution, and throughout the major portion of the 19th century, abortion was viewed with less disfavor than under most American statutes currently in effect. Phrasing it another way, a woman enjoyed a substantially broader right to terminate a pregnancy than she does in most States today. At least with respect to the early stage of pregnancy, and very possibly without such a limitation, the opportunity to make this choice was present in this country well into the 19th century. Even later, the law continued for some time to treat less punitively an abortion procured in early pregnancy.

6. *The position of the American Medical Association.* The anti-abortion mood prevalent in this country in the late 19th century was shared by the medical profession. Indeed, the attitude of the profession may have played a significant role in the enactment of stringent criminal abortion legislation during that period.

An AMA Committee on Criminal Abortion was appointed in May, 1857. It presented its report, 12 Trans. of the Am.Med.Assn. 778 (1859), to the Twelfth Annual Meeting. That report observed that the Committee had been appointed to investigate criminal abortion "with a view to its general suppression." It deplored abortion and its frequency and it listed three causes of "this general demoralization":

> "The first of these causes is a widespread popular ignorance of the true character of the crime—a belief, even among mothers themselves, that the foetus is not alive till after the period of quickening."
>
> "The second of the agents alluded to is the fact that the profession themselves are frequently supposed careless of foetal life. . . ."
>
> "The third reason of the frightful extent of this crime is found in the grave defects of our laws, both common and statute, as regards the independent and actual existence of the child before birth, as a living being. These errors, which are sufficient in most instances to prevent conviction, are based, and only based, upon mistaken and exploded medical dogmas. With strange inconsistency, the law fully acknowledges the foetus *in utero* and its inherent rights, for civil purposes; while personally and as criminally affected, it fails to recognize it, and to its life as yet denies all protection."

Id. at 776. The Committee then offered, and the Association adopted, resolutions protesting "against such unwarrantable destruction of human life," calling upon state legislatures to revise their abortion laws, and requesting the cooperation of state medical societies "in pressing the subject." *Id.* at 28, 78.

In 1871, a long and vivid report was submitted by the Committee on Criminal Abortion. It ended with the observation,

> "We had to deal with human life. In a matter of less importance, we could entertain no compromise. An honest judge on the bench would call things by their proper names. We could do no less."

22 Trans. of the Am.Med.Assn. 268 (1871). It proffered resolutions, adopted by the Association, *id.* at 38-39, recommending, among other things, that it

> "be unlawful and unprofessional for any physician to induce abortion or premature labor without the concurrent opinion of at least one respectable consulting physician, and then always with a view to the safety of the child—if that be possible,"

and calling

> "the attention of the clergy of all denominations to the perverted views of morality entertained by a large class of females—aye, and men also, on this important question."

Except for periodic condemnation of the criminal abortionist, no further formal AMA action took place until 1967. In that year, the Committee on Human Reproduction urged the adoption of a stated policy of opposition to induced abortion except when there is "documented medical evidence" of a threat to the health or life of the mother, or that the child "may be born with incapacitating physical deformity or mental deficiency," or that a pregnancy "resulting from legally established statutory or forcible rape or incest may constitute a threat to the mental or physical health of the patient," two other physicians "chosen because of their recognized professional competence have examined the patient and have concurred in writing," and the procedure "is performed in a hospital accredited by the Joint Commission on Accreditation of Hospitals." The providing of medical information by physicians to state legislatures in their consideration of legislation regarding therapeutic abortion was "to be considered consistent with the principles of ethics of the American Medical Association." This recommendation was adopted by the House of Delegates. Proceedings of the AMA House of Delegates 40-51 (June 1967).

In 1970, after the introduction of a variety of proposed resolutions and of a report from its Board of Trustees, a reference committee noted "polarization of the medical profession on this controversial issue"; division among those who had testified; a difference of opinion among AMA councils and committees; "the remarkable shift in testimony" in six months, felt to be influenced "by the rapid changes in state laws and by the judicial decisions which tend to make abortion more freely available;" and a feeling "that this trend will continue." On June 25, 1970, the House of Delegates adopted preambles and most of the resolutions proposed by the reference committee. The preambles emphasized "the best interests of the patient," "sound clinical judgment," and "informed patient consent," in contrast to "mere acquiescence to the patient's demand." The resolutions asserted that abortion is a medical procedure that should be performed by a licensed physician in an accredited hospital only after consultation with two other physicians and in conformity with state law, and that no party to the procedure should be required to violate personally held moral principles.[37] Proceedings of the AMA House of Delegates 220 (June 1970). The AMA Judicial Council rendered a complementary opinion.[38]

---

37. "Whereas, Abortion, like any other medical procedure, should not be performed when contrary to the best interests of the patient since good medical practice requires due consideration for the patient's welfare, and not mere acquiescence to the patient's demand; and"

"Whereas, The standards of sound clinical judgment, which, together with informed patient consent, should be determinative according to the merits of each individual case; therefore be it"

"RESOLVED, That abortion is a medical procedure and should be performed only by a duly licensed physician and surgeon in an accredited hospital acting only after consultation with two other physicians chosen because of their professional competency and in conformance with standards of good medical practice and the Medical Practice Act of his State; and be it further"

"RESOLVED, That no physician or other professional personnel shall be compelled to perform any act which violates his good medical judgment. Neither physician, hospital, nor hospital personnel shall be required to perform any act violative of personally held moral principles. In these circumstances, good medical practice requires only that the physician or other professional personnel withdraw from the case so long as the withdrawal is consistent with good medical practice."

Proceedings of the AMA House of Delegates 220 (June 1970).

38. "The Principles of Medical Ethics of the AMA do not prohibit a physician from performing an abortion that is performed in accordance with good medical practice and under circumstances that do not violate the laws of the community in which he practices."

"In the matter of abortions, as of any other medical procedure, the Judicial Council becomes involved whenever there is alleged violation of the Principles of Medical Ethics as established by the House of Delegates."

7. *The position of the American Public Health Association.* In October, 1970, the Executive Board of the APHA adopted Standards for Abortion Services. These were five in number:

> "a. Rapid and simple abortion referral must be readily available through state and local public health departments, medical societies, or other non-profit organizations."
>
> "b. An important function of counseling should be to simplify and expedite the provision of abortion services; it should not delay the obtaining of these services."
>
> "c. Psychiatric consultation should not be mandatory. As in the case of other specialized medical services, psychiatric consultation should be sought for definite indications, and not on a routine basis."
>
> "d. A wide range of individuals from appropriately trained, sympathetic volunteers to highly skilled physicians may qualify as abortion counselors."
>
> "e. Contraception and/or sterilization should be discussed with each abortion patient."

"Recommended Standards for Abortion Services, 61 Am.J.Pub.Health 396 (1971). Among factors pertinent to life and health risks associated with abortion were three that 'are recognized as important":

> "a. the skill of the physician,"
>
> "b. the environment in which the abortion is performed, and above all"
>
> "c. the duration of pregnancy, as determined by uterine size and confirmed by menstrual history."

Id. at 397.
It was said that "a well-equipped hospital" offers more protection

> "to cope with unforeseen difficulties than an office or clinic without such resources. . . . The factor of gestational age is of overriding importance."

Thus, it was recommended that abortions in the second trimester and early abortions in the presence of existing medical complications be performed in hospitals as inpatient procedures. For pregnancies in the first trimester, abortion in the hospital with or without overnight stay "is probably the safest practice." An abortion in an extramural facility, however, is an acceptable alternative "provided arrangements exist in advance to admit patients promptly if unforeseen complications develop." Standards for an abortion facility were listed. It was said that, at present, abortions should be performed by physicians or osteopaths who are licensed to practice and who have "adequate training." *Id.* at 398.

8. *The position of the American Bar Association.* At its meeting in February, 1972, the ABA House of Delegates approved, with 17 opposing votes, the Uniform Abortion Act that had been drafted and approved the preceding August by the Conference of Commissioners on Uniform State Laws. 58 A.B.A.J. 380 (1972). We set forth the Act in full in the margin.[39] The Opinion of the Court Conference has appended an enlightening Prefatory Note.[40]

---

39. "UNIFORM ABORTION ACT"

"SECTION 1. [Abortion Defined; When Authorized.]"

"(a) 'Abortion' means the termination of human pregnancy with an intention other than to produce a live birth or to remove a dead fetus."

"(b) An abortion may be performed in this state only if it is performed:"

"(1) by a physician licensed to practice medicine [or osteopathy] in this state or by a physician practicing medicine [or osteopathy] in the employ of the government of the United States or of this state, [and the abortion is performed] [in the physician's office or in a medical clinic, or] in a hospital approved by the [Department of Health] or operated by the United States, this state, or any department, agency, [or political subdivision of either;] or by a female upon herself upon the advice of the physician; and"

"(2) within [20] weeks after the commencement of the pregnancy [or after [20] weeks only if the physician has reasonable cause to believe (i) there is a substantial risk that continuance of the pregnancy would endanger the life of the mother or would gravely impair the physical or mental health of the mother, (ii) that the child would be born with grave physical or mental defect, or (iii) that the pregnancy resulted from rape or incest, or illicit intercourse with a girl under the age of 16 years]."

"SECTION 2. [Penalty.] Any person who performs or procures an abortion other than authorized by this Act is guilty of a [felony] and, upon conviction thereof, may be sentenced to pay a fine not exceeding [$1,000] or to imprisonment [in the state penitentiary] not exceeding [5 years], or both."

"SECTION 3. [Uniformity of Interpretation.] This Act shall be construed to effectuate its general purpose to make uniform the law with respect to the subject of this Act among those states which enact it."

"SECTION 4. [Short Title.] This Act may be cited as the Uniform Abortion Act."

"SECTION 5. [Severability.] If any provision of this Act or the application thereof to any person or circumstance is held invalid, the invalidity does not affect other provisions or applications of this Act which can be given effect without the invalid provision or application, and to this end the provisions of this Act are severable."

"SECTION 6. [Repeal.] The following acts and parts of acts are repealed: "

"(1)"

"(2)"

"(3)"

"SECTION 7. [*Time of Taking Effect.*] This Act shall take effect _____."

40. "This Act is based largely upon the New York abortion act following a review of the more recent laws on abortion in several states and upon recognition of a more liberal trend in laws on this subject. Recognition was given also to the several decisions in state and federal courts which show a further trend toward liberalization of abortion laws, especially during the first trimester of pregnancy."

VII

Three reasons have been advanced to explain historically the enactment of criminal abortion laws in the 19th century and to justify their continued existence. It has been argued occasionally that these laws were the product of a Victorian social concern to discourage illicit sexual conduct. Texas, however, does not advance this justification in the present case, and it appears that no court or commentator has taken the argument seriously.[41] The appellants and *amici* contend, moreover, that this is not a proper state purpose, at all and suggest that, if it were, the Texas statutes are overbroad in protecting it, since the law fails to distinguish between married and unwed mothers.

A second reason is concerned with abortion as a medical procedure. When most criminal abortion laws were first enacted, the procedure was a hazardous one for the woman.[42] This was particularly true prior to the development of antisepsis. Antiseptic techniques, of course, were based on discoveries by Lister, Pasteur, and others first announced in 1867, but were not generally accepted and employed until about the turn of the century. Abortion mortality was high. Even after 1900, and perhaps until as late as the development of antibiotics in the 1940s, standard modern techniques such as dilation and curettage were not nearly so safe as they are today. Thus, it has been argued that a State's real concern in enacting a criminal abortion law was to protect the pregnant woman, that is, to restrain her from submitting to a procedure that placed her life in serious jeopardy.

"Recognizing that a number of problems appeared in New York, a shorter time period for 'unlimited' abortions was advisable. The time period was bracketed to permit the various states to insert a figure more in keeping with the different conditions that might exist among the states. Likewise, the language limiting the place or places in which abortions may be performed was also bracketed to account for different conditions among the states. In addition, limitations on abortions after the initial 'unlimited' period were placed in brackets so that individual states may adopt all or any of these reasons, or place further restrictions upon abortions after the initial period."

"This Act does not contain any provision relating to medical review committees or prohibitions against sanctions imposed upon medical personnel refusing to participate in abortions because of religious or other similar reasons, or the like. Such provisions, while related, do not directly pertain to when, where, or by whom abortions may be performed; however, the Act is not drafted to exclude such a provision by a state wishing to enact the same."

41. *See, e.g.*, YWCA v. Kugler, 342 F. Supp. 1048, 1074 (N.J. 1972); Abele v. Markle, 342 F. Supp. 800, 805–06 (Conn.1972) (Newman, J., concurring in result), *appeal docketed*, No. 72-56; Walsingham v. State, 250 So. 2d 857, 863 (Ervin, J., concurring) (Fla. 1971); State v. Gedicke, 43 N.J.L. 86, 90 (1881); Means II 381–82.

42. *See* C. HAAGENSEN & W. LLOYD, A HUNDRED YEARS OF MEDICINE 19 (1943).

Modern medical techniques have altered this situation. Appellants and various *amici* refer to medical data indicating that abortion in early pregnancy, that is, prior to the end of the first trimester, although not without its risk, is now relatively safe. Mortality rates for women undergoing early abortions, where the procedure is legal, appear to be as low as or lower than the rates for normal childbirth.[43] Consequently, any interest of the State in protecting the woman from an inherently hazardous procedure, except when it would be equally dangerous for her to forgo it, has largely disappeared. Of course, important state interests in the areas of health and medical standards do remain. The State has a legitimate interest in seeing to it that abortion, like any other medical procedure, is performed under circumstances that insure maximum safety for the patient. This interest obviously extends at least to the performing physician and his staff, to the facilities involved, to the availability of after-care, and to adequate provision for any complication or emergency that might arise. The prevalence of high mortality rates at illegal "abortion mills" strengthens, rather than weakens, the State's interest in regulating the conditions under which abortions are performed. Moreover, the risk to the woman increases as her pregnancy continues. Thus, the State retains a definite interest in protecting the woman's own health and safety when an abortion is proposed at a late stage of pregnancy.

The third reason is the State's interest—some phrase it in terms of duty—in protecting prenatal life. Some of the argument for this justification rests on the theory that a new human life is present from the moment of conception.[44] The State's interest and general obligation to protect life then extends, it is argued, to prenatal life. Only when the life of the pregnant mother herself is at stake, balanced against the life she carries within her, should the interest of the embryo or fetus not prevail. Logically, of course, a legitimate state interest in this area need not stand or fall on acceptance of the belief that life begins at conception or at some other point prior to live birth. In assessing the State's interest, recognition may be

---

43. Potts, *Postconceptive Control of Fertility,* 8 Int'l J. of G. & O. 957, 967 (1970) (England and Wales); Abortion Mortality, 20 Morbidity and Mortality 208, 209 (June 12, 1971) (U.S. Dept. of HEW, Public Health Service) (New York City); Tietze, *United States: Therapeutic Abortions, 1963–1968,* 59 Studies in Family Planning 5, 7 (1970); Tietze, *Mortality with Contraception and Induced Abortion,* 45 Studies in Family Planning 6 (1969) (Japan, Czechoslovakia, Hungary); Tietze Lehfeldt, *Legal Abortion in Eastern Europe,* 175 J.A.M.A. 1149, 1152 (April 1961). Other sources are discussed in *Lader,* 17–23.

44. *See* Brief of *Amicus* National Right to Life Committee; R. Drinan, The Inviolability of the Right to Be Born, in Abortion and the Law 107 (D. Smith ed.1967); Louisell, *Abortion, The Practice of Medicine and the Due Process of Law,* 16 U.C.L.A. L. Rev. 233 (1969); Noonan 1.

given to the less rigid claim that as long as at least potential life is involved, the State may assert interests beyond the protection of the pregnant woman alone. Parties challenging state abortion laws have sharply disputed in some courts the contention that a purpose of these laws, when enacted, was to protect prenatal life.[45] Pointing to the absence of legislative history to support the contention, they claim that most state laws were designed solely to protect the woman. Because medical advances have lessened this concern, at least with respect to abortion in early pregnancy, they argue that with respect to such abortions the laws can no longer be justified by any state interest. There is some scholarly support for this view of original purpose.[46] The few state courts called upon to interpret their laws in the late 19th and early 20th centuries did focus on the State's interest in protecting the woman's health, rather than in preserving the embryo and fetus.[47] Proponents of this view point out that in many States, including Texas,[48] by statute or judicial interpretation, the pregnant woman herself could not be prosecuted for self-abortion or for cooperating in an abortion performed upon her by another.[49] They claim that adoption of the "quickening" distinction through received common law and state statutes tacitly recognizes the greater health hazards inherent in late abortion and impliedly repudiates the theory that life begins at conception.

It is with these interests, and the weight to be attached to them, that this case is concerned.

VIII

The Constitution does not explicitly mention any right of privacy. In a line of decisions, however, going back perhaps as far as *Union Pacific R. Co. v. Botsford,* 141 U. S. 250, 251 (1891), the Court has recognized that a right of personal privacy, or a guarantee of certain areas or zones of privacy,

---

45. *See, e.g.,* Abele v. Markle, 342 F. Supp. 800 (Conn.1972), *appeal docketed,* No. 72-56.

46. *See* discussions in Means I and Means II.

47. *See, e.g.,* State v. Murphy, 27 N.J.L. 112, 114 (1858).

48. Watson v. State, 9 Tex. App. 237, 244–45 (1880); Moore v. State, 37 Tex. Cr. R. 552, 561, 40 S.W. 287, 290 (1897); Shaw v. State, 73 Tex. Cr. R. 337, 339, 165 S.W. 930, 931 (1914); Fondren v. State, 74 Tex. Cr. R. 552, 557, 169 S.W. 411, 414 (1914); Gray v. State, 77 Tex. Cr. R. 221, 229, 178 S.W. 337, 341 (1915). There is no immunity in Texas for the father who is not married to the mother. Hammett v. State, 84 Tex. Cr. R. 635, 209 S.W. 661 (1919); Thompson v. State (Ct. Crim. App. Tex. 1971), *appeal docketed,* No. 71-1200.

49. *See* Smith v. State, 33 Me. at 55; *In re* Vince, 2 N.J. 443, 450, 67 A.2d 141, 144 (1949). A short discussion of the modern law on this issue is contained in the Comment to the ALI's MODEL PENAL CODE § 207.11, at 158 and nn.35–37 (Tent. Draft No. 9, 1959).

does exist under the Constitution. In varying contexts, the Court or individual Justices have, indeed, found at least the roots of that right in the First Amendment, *Stanley v. Georgia*, 394 U. S. 557, 564 (1969); in the Fourth and Fifth Amendments, *Terry v. Ohio*, 392 U. S. 1, 8-9 (1968), *Katz v. United States*, 389 U. S. 347, 350 (1967), *Boyd v. United States*, 116 U. S. 616 (1886), *see Olmstead v. United States*, 277 U. S. 438, 478 (1928) (Brandeis, J., dissenting); in the penumbras of the Bill of Rights, *Griswold v. Connecticut*, 381 U.S. at 484-485; in the Ninth Amendment, *id.* at 486 (Goldberg, J., concurring); or in the concept of liberty guaranteed by the first section of the Fourteenth Amendment, *see Meyer v. Nebraska*, 262 U. S. 390, 399 (1923). These decisions make it clear that only personal rights that can be deemed "fundamental" or "implicit in the concept of ordered liberty," *Palko v. Connecticut*, 302 U. S. 319, 325 (1937), are included in this guarantee of personal privacy. They also make it clear that the right has some extension to activities relating to marriage, *Loving v. Virginia*, 388 U. S. 1, 12 (1967); procreation, *Skinner v. Oklahoma*, 316 U. S. 535, 541-542 (1942); contraception, *Eisenstadt v. Baird*, 405 U.S. at 453-454; *id.* at 460, 463-465 (WHITE, J., concurring in result); family relationships, *Prince v. Massachusetts*, 321 U. S. 158, 166 (1944); and childrearing and education, *Pierce v. Society of Sisters*, 268 U. S. 510, 535 (1925), *Meyer v. Nebraska, supra.*

This right of privacy, whether it be founded in the Fourteenth Amendment's concept of personal liberty and restrictions upon state action, as we feel it is, or, as the District Court determined, in the Ninth Amendment's reservation of rights to the people, is broad enough to encompass a woman's decision whether or not to terminate her pregnancy. The detriment that the State would impose upon the pregnant woman by denying this choice altogether is apparent. Specific and direct harm medically diagnosable even in early pregnancy may be involved. Maternity, or additional offspring, may force upon the woman a distressful life and future. Psychological harm may be imminent. Mental and physical health may be taxed by child care. There is also the distress, for all concerned, associated with the unwanted child, and there is the problem of bringing a child into a family already unable, psychologically and otherwise, to care for it. In other cases, as in this one, the additional difficulties and continuing stigma of unwed motherhood may be involved. All these are factors the woman and her responsible physician necessarily will consider in consultation.

On the basis of elements such as these, appellant and some *amici* argue that the woman's right is absolute and that she is entitled to terminate her pregnancy at whatever time, in whatever way, and for whatever reason she alone chooses. With this we do not agree. Appellant's arguments that Texas either has no valid interest at all in regulating the abortion decision, or no interest strong enough to support any limitation upon the woman's sole determination, are unpersuasive. The Court's decisions recognizing a right of privacy also acknowledge that some state regulation in areas protected by that right is appropriate. As noted above, a State may properly assert important interests in safeguarding health, in maintaining medical standards, and in protecting potential life. At some point in pregnancy, these respective interests become sufficiently compelling to sustain regulation of the factors that govern the abortion decision. The privacy right involved, therefore, cannot be said to be absolute. In fact, it is not clear to us that the claim asserted by some *amici* that one has an unlimited right to do with one's body as one pleases bears a close relationship to the right of privacy previously articulated in the Court's decisions. The Court has refused to recognize an unlimited right of this kind in the past. *Jacobson v. Massachusetts*, 197 U. S. 11 (1905) (vaccination); *Buck v. Bell*, 274 U. S. 200 (1927) (sterilization).

We, therefore, conclude that the right of personal privacy includes the abortion decision, but that this right is not unqualified, and must be considered against important state interests in regulation.

We note that those federal and state courts that have recently considered abortion law challenges have reached the same conclusion. A majority, in addition to the District Court in the present case, have held state laws unconstitutional, at least in part, because of vagueness or because of overbreadth and abridgment of rights. *Abele v. Markle*, 342 F. Supp. 800 (Conn.1972), *appeal docketed*, No. 72-56; *Abele v. Markle*, 351 F. Supp. 224 (Conn.1972), *appeal docketed*, No. 72-730; *Doe v. Bolton*, 319 F. Supp. 1048 (ND Ga.1970), *appeal decided today, post*, p. 179; *Doe v. Scott*, 321 F. Supp. 1385 (ND Ill.1971), *appeal docketed*, No. 70-105; *Poe v. Menghini*, 339 F. Supp. 986 (Kan.1972); *YWCA v. Kuler*, 342 F. Supp. 1048 (NJ 1972); *Babbitz v. McCann*, 310 F. Supp. 293 (ED Wis.1970), *appeal dismissed*, 400 U. S. 1 (1970); *People v. Belous*, 71 Cal. 2d 954, 458 P.2d 194 (1969), *cert. denied*, 397 U.S. 915 (1970); *State v. Barquet*, 262 So. 2d 431 (Fla.1972).

Others have sustained state statutes. *Crossen v. Attorney General*, 344 F. Supp. 587 (ED Ky.1972), *appeal docketed*, No. 72-256; *Rosen v. Louisiana State Board of Medical Examiners*, 318 F. Supp. 1217 (ED La.1970), *appeal docketed*, No. 70-42; *Corkey v. Edwards*, 322 F. Supp. 1248 (WDNC 1971), *appeal docketed*, No. 71-92; *Steinberg v. Brown*, 321 F. Supp. 741 (ND Ohio 1970); *Doe v. Rampton* (Utah 1971), *appeal docketed*, No. 71-5666; *Cheaney v. State*, 259 Ind. 138, 285 N.E.2d 265 (1972); *Spears v. State*, 257 So. 2d 876 (Miss. 1972); *State v. Munson*, 86 S.D. 663, 201 N.W.2d 123 (1972), *appeal docketed*, No. 72-631.

Although the results are divided, most of these courts have agreed that the right of privacy, however based, is broad enough to cover the abortion decision; that the right, nonetheless, is not absolute, and is subject to some limitations; and that, at some point, the state interests as to protection of health, medical standards, and prenatal life, become dominant. We agree with this approach.

Where certain "fundamental rights" are involved, the Court has held that regulation limiting these rights may be justified only by a "compelling state interest," *Kramer v. Union Free School District*, 395 U. S. 621, 627 (1969); *Shapiro v. Thompson*, 394 U. S. 618, 634 (1969), *Sherbert v. Verner*, 374 U. S. 398, 406 (1963), and that legislative enactments must be narrowly drawn to express only the legitimate state interests at stake. *Griswold v. Connecticut*, 381 U.S. at 485; *Aptheker v. Secretary of State*, 378 U. S. 500, 508 (1964); *Cantwell v. Connecticut*, 310 U. S. 296, 307-308 (1940); see *Eisenstadt v. Baird*, 405 U.S. at 460, 463-464 (WHITE, J., concurring in result).

In the recent abortion cases cited above, courts have recognized these principles. Those striking down state laws have generally scrutinized the State's interests in protecting health and potential life, and have concluded that neither interest justified broad limitations on the reasons for which a physician and his pregnant patient might decide that she should have an abortion in the early stages of pregnancy. Courts sustaining state laws have held that the State's determinations to protect health or prenatal life are dominant and constitutionally justifiable.

IX

The District Court held that the appellee failed to meet his burden of demonstrating that the Texas statute's infringement upon Roe's rights was necessary to support a compelling state interest, and that, although the appellee presented "several compelling justifications for state presence in the area of abortions," the statutes outstripped these justifications and swept "far beyond any areas of compelling state interest." 314 F. Supp. at 1222-1223. Appellant and appellee both contest that holding. Appellant, as has been indicated, claims an absolute right that bars any state imposition of criminal penalties in the area. Appellee argues that the State's determination to recognize and protect prenatal life from and after conception constitutes a compelling state interest. As noted above, we do not agree fully with either formulation.

A. The appellee and certain *amici* argue that the fetus is a "person" within the language and meaning of the Fourteenth Amendment. In support of this, they outline at length and in detail the well known facts of fetal development. If this suggestion of personhood is established, the appellant's case, of course, collapses, for the fetus' right to life would then be guaranteed specifically by the Amendment. The appellant conceded as much on reargument.[50] On the other hand, the appellee conceded on reargument[51] that no case could be cited that holds that a fetus is a person within the meaning of the Fourteenth Amendment.

The Constitution does not define "person" in so many words. Section 1 of the Fourteenth Amendment contains three references to "person." The first, in defining "citizens," speaks of "persons born or naturalized in the United States." The word also appears both in the Due Process Clause and in the Equal Protection Clause. "Person" is used in other places in the Constitution: in the listing of qualifications for Representatives and Senators, Art. I, § 2, cl. 2, and § 3, cl. 3; in the Apportionment Clause, Art. I, § 2, cl. 3;[52] in the Migration and Importation provision, Art. I, § 9, cl. 1; in the Emolument Clause, Art. I, § 9, cl. 8; in the Electors provisions, Art. II, § 1, cl. 2, and the superseded cl. 3; in the provision outlining qualifications for the office of President, Art. II, § 1, cl. 5; in the Extradition provisions, Art. IV, § 2, cl. 2, and the superseded Fugitive Slave Clause 3; and in the Fifth, Twelfth, and Twenty-second Amendments, as well as in §§ 2 and 3 of the Fourteenth Amendment. But in nearly all these instances, the use of the word is such that it has application only postnatally. None indicates, with any assurance, that it has any possible pre-natal application.[53] All this, together with our observation, *supra*, that, throughout the major portion of the 19th century,

50. Tr. of Oral Rearg. 20–21.

51. Tr. of Oral Rearg. 24.

52. We are not aware that in the taking of any census under this clause, a fetus has ever been counted.

53. When Texas urges that a fetus is entitled to Fourteenth Amendment protection as a person, it faces a dilemma. Neither in Texas nor in any other State are all abortions prohibited. Despite broad proscription, an exception always exists. The exception contained in Art. 1196, for an abortion procured or attempted by medical advice for the purpose of saving the life of the mother, is typical. But if the fetus is a person who is not to be deprived of life without due process of law, and if the mother's condition is the sole determinant, does not the Texas exception appear to be out of line with the Amendment's command?

There are other inconsistencies between Fourteenth Amendment status and the typical abortion statute. It has already been pointed out, n.49, *supra*, that, in Texas, the woman is not a principal or an accomplice with respect to an abortion upon her. If the fetus is a person, why is the woman not a principal or an accomplice? Further, the penalty for criminal abortion specified by Art. 1195 is significantly less than the maximum penalty for murder prescribed by Art. 1257 of the Texas Penal Code. If the fetus is a person, may the penalties be different?

prevailing legal abortion practices were far freer than they are today, persuades us that the word "person," as used in the Fourteenth Amendment, does not include the unborn.[54] This is in accord with the results reached in those few cases where the issue has been squarely presented. *McGarvey v. Magee-Womens Hospital,* 340 F. Supp. 751 (WD Pa.1972); *Byrn v. New York City Health & Hospitals Corp.,* 31 N.Y.2d 194, 286 N.E.2d 887 (1972), *appeal docketed,* No. 72-434; *Abele v. Markle,* 351 F. Supp. 224 (Conn.1972), *appeal docketed,* No. 72-730. *Cf. Cheaney v. State,* 259 Ind. at 149, 285 N.E.2d at 270; *Montana v. Rogers,* 278 F.2d 68, 72 (CA7 1960), *aff'd sub nom. Montana v. Kennedy,* 366 U. S. 308 (1961); *Keeler v. Superior Court,* 2 Cal. 3d 619, 470 P.2d 617 (1970); *State v. Dickinson,* 28 Ohio St.2d 65, 275 N.E.2d 599 (1971). Indeed, our decision in *United States v. Vuitch,* 402 U. S. 62 (1971), inferentially is to the same effect, for we there would not have indulged in statutory interpretation favorable to abortion in specified circumstances if the necessary consequence was the termination of life entitled to Fourteenth Amendment protection.

This conclusion, however, does not of itself fully answer the contentions raised by Texas, and we pass on to other considerations.

B. The pregnant woman cannot be isolated in her privacy. She carries an embryo and, later, a fetus, if one accepts the medical definitions of the developing young in the human uterus. *See* Dorland's Illustrated Medical Dictionary 478-479, 547 (24th ed.1965). The situation therefore is inherently different from marital intimacy, or bedroom possession of obscene material, or marriage, or procreation, or education, with which Eisenstadt and Griswold, Stanley, Loving, Skinner, and Pierce and Meyer were respectively concerned. As we have intimated above, it is reasonable and appropriate for a State to decide that, at some point in time another interest, that of health of the mother or that of potential human life, becomes significantly involved. The woman's privacy is no longer sole and any right of privacy she possesses must be measured accordingly.

Texas urges that, apart from the Fourteenth Amendment, life begins at conception and is present throughout pregnancy, and that, therefore, the State has a compelling interest in protecting that life from and after conception. We need not resolve the difficult question of when life begins. When those trained in the respective disciplines of medicine, philosophy,

---

54. *Cf.* the Wisconsin abortion statute, defining "unborn child" to mean "a human being from the time of conception until it is born alive," WIS. STAT. § 940.04(6) (1969), and the new Connecticut statute, Pub. Act No. 1 (May 1972 special session), declaring it to be the public policy of the State and the legislative intent "to protect and preserve human life from the moment of conception."

and theology are unable to arrive at any consensus, the judiciary, at this point in the development of man's knowledge, is not in a position to speculate as to the answer. It should be sufficient to note briefly the wide divergence of thinking on this most sensitive and difficult question. There has always been strong support for the view that life does not begin until live birth. This was the belief of the Stoics.[55] It appears to be the predominant, though not the unanimous, attitude of the Jewish faith.[56] It may be taken to represent also the position of a large segment of the Protestant community, insofar as that can be ascertained; organized groups that have taken a formal position on the abortion issue have generally regarded abortion as a matter for the conscience of the individual and her family.[57] As we have noted, the common law found greater significance in quickening. Physician and their scientific colleagues have regarded that event with less interest and have tended to focus either upon conception, upon live birth, or upon the interim point at which the fetus becomes "viable," that is, potentially able to live outside the mother's womb, albeit with artificial aid.[58] Viability is usually placed at about seven months (28 weeks) but may occur earlier, even at 24 weeks.[59] The Aristotelian theory of "mediate animation," that held sway throughout the Middle Ages and the Renaissance in Europe, continued to be official Roman Catholic dogma until the 19th century, despite opposition to this "ensoulment" theory from those in the Church who would recognize the existence of life from the moment of conception.[60] The latter is now, of course, the official belief of the Catholic Church. As one brief *amicus* discloses, this is a view strongly held by many non-Catholics as well, and by many physicians. Substantial problems for precise definition of this view are posed, however, by new embryological data that purport to indicate that conception is a "process" over time, rather than an event, and by new medical techniques such as menstrual extraction, the

---

55. Edelstein 16.

56. *Lader*, 97–99; D. FELDMAN, BIRTH CONTROL IN JEWISH LAW 251–94 (1968). For a stricter view, *see* I. JAKOBOVITS, JEWISH VIEWS ON ABORTION, IN ABORTION AND THE LAW 124 (D. Smith ed.1967).

57. Amicus Brief for the American Ethical Union *et al.* For the position of the National Council of Churches and of other denominations, *see Lader*, 99–101.

58. Hellman & J. Pritchard, Williams Obstetrics 493 (14th ed.1971); Dorland's Illustrated Medical Dictionary 1689 (24th ed.1965).

59. Hellman & Pritchard, *supra*, note 58, at 493.

60. For discussions of the development of the Roman Catholic position, *see* D. CALLAHAN, ABORTION: LAW, CHOICE, AND MORALITY 409–47 (1970); Noonan 1.

"morning-after" pill, implantation of embryos, artificial insemination, and even artificial wombs.[61]

In areas other than criminal abortion, the law has been reluctant to endorse any theory that life, as we recognize it, begins before live birth, or to accord legal rights to the unborn except in narrowly defined situations and except when the rights are contingent upon live birth. For example, the traditional rule of tort law denied recovery for prenatal injuries even though the child was born alive.[62] That rule has been changed in almost every jurisdiction. In most States, recovery is said to be permitted only if the fetus was viable, or at least quick, when the injuries were sustained, though few courts have squarely so held.[63] In a recent development, generally opposed by the commentators, some States permit the parents of a stillborn child to maintain an action for wrongful death because of prenatal injuries.[64] Such an action, however, would appear to be one to vindicate the parents' interest and is thus consistent with the view that the fetus, at most, represents only the potentiality of life. Similarly, unborn children have been recognized as acquiring rights or interests by way of inheritance or other devolution of property, and have been represented by guardians *ad litem.*[65] Perfection of the interests involved, again, has generally been contingent upon live birth. In short, the unborn have never been recognized in the law as persons in the whole sense.

X

In view of all this, we do not agree that, by adopting one theory of life, Texas may override the rights of the pregnant woman that are at stake. We repeat,

---

61. *See* Brodie, *The New Biology and the Prenatal Child,* 9 J. FAMILY L. 391, 397 (1970); Gorney, *The New Biology and the Future of Man,* 15 U.C.L.A. L. REV. 273 (1968); Note, *Criminal Law—Abortion—The "Morning-After Pill" and Other Pre-Implantation Birth-Control Methods and the Law,* 46 ORE. L. REV. 211 (1967); G. TAYLOR, THE BIOLOGICAL TIME BOMB 32 (1968); A. ROSENFELD, THE SECOND GENESIS 138–39 (1969); Smith, *Through a Test Tube Darkly: Artificial Insemination and the Law,* 67 MICH. L. REV. 127 (1968); Note, *Artificial Insemination and the Law,* 1968 U. ILL. L. F. 203.

62. W. PROSSER, THE LAW OF TORTS 335–38 (4th ed.1971); 2 F. Harper & F. James, *The Law of Torts 1028–31 (1956);* Note, 63 HARV. L. REV. 173 (1949).

63. *See* cases cited in Prosser, *supra,* n.62, at 336–38; Annotation, *Action for Death of Unborn Child,* 15 A.L.R.3d 992 (1967).

64. Prosser, *supra* n.62 at 338; Note, *The Law and the Unborn Child: The Legal and Logical Inconsistencies,* 46 NOTRE DAME LAW. 349, 354–60 (1971).

65. Louisell, Abortion, *The Practice of Medicine and the Due Process of Law,* 16 U.C.L.A. L. REV. 233, 235–38 (1969); Note, 56 IOWA L. REV. 994, 999–1000 (1971); Note, *The Law and the Unborn Child,* 46 NOTRE DAME LAW. 349, 351–54 (1971).

however, that the State does have an important and legitimate interest in preserving and protecting the health of the pregnant woman, whether she be a resident of the State or a nonresident who seeks medical consultation and treatment there, and that it has still *another* important and legitimate interest in protecting the potentiality of human life. These interests are separate and distinct. Each grows in substantiality as the woman approaches term and, at a point during pregnancy, each becomes "compelling."

With respect to the State's important and legitimate interest in the health of the mother, the "compelling" point, in the light of present medical knowledge, is at approximately the end of the first trimester. This is so because of the now-established medical fact, referred to above at 149, that, until the end of the first trimester mortality in abortion may be less than mortality in normal childbirth. It follows that, from and after this point, a State may regulate the abortion procedure to the extent that the regulation reasonably relates to the preservation and protection of maternal health. Examples of permissible state regulation in this area are requirements as to the qualifications of the person who is to perform the abortion; as to the licensure of that person; as to the facility in which the procedure is to be performed, that is, whether it must be a hospital or may be a clinic or some other place of less-than-hospital status; as to the licensing of the facility; and the like.

This means, on the other hand, that, for the period of pregnancy prior to this "compelling" point, the attending physician, in consultation with his patient, is free to determine, without regulation by the State, that, in his medical judgment, the patient's pregnancy should be terminated. If that decision is reached, the judgment may be effectuated by an abortion free of interference by the State.

With respect to the State's important and legitimate interest in potential life, the "compelling" point is at viability. This is so because the fetus then presumably has the capability of meaningful life outside the mother's womb. State regulation protective of fetal life after viability thus has both logical and biological justifications. If the State is interested in protecting fetal life after viability, it may go so far as to proscribe abortion during that period, except when it is necessary to preserve the life or health of the mother.

Measured against these standards, Art. 1196 of the Texas Penal Code, in restricting legal abortions to those "procured or attempted by medical advice for the purpose of saving the life of the mother," sweeps too broadly. The statute makes no distinction between abortions performed early in pregnancy and those performed later, and it limits to a single reason, "saving" the mother's life, the legal justification for the procedure. The statute, therefore, cannot survive the constitutional attack made upon it here.

This conclusion makes it unnecessary for us to consider the additional challenge to the Texas statute asserted on grounds of vagueness. *See United States v. Vuitch*, 402 U.S. at 67–72.

XI

To summarize and to repeat:

1. A state criminal abortion statute of the current Texas type, that excepts from criminality only a lifesaving procedure on behalf of the mother, without regard to pregnancy stage and without recognition of the other interests involved, is violative of the Due Process Clause of the Fourteenth Amendment.

(a) For the stage prior to approximately the end of the first trimester, the abortion decision and its effectuation must be left to the medical judgment of the pregnant woman's attending physician.

(b) For the stage subsequent to approximately the end of the first trimester, the State, in promoting its interest in the health of the mother, may, if it chooses, regulate the abortion procedure in ways that are reasonably related to maternal health.

(c) For the stage subsequent to viability, the State in promoting its interest in the potentiality of human life may, if it chooses, regulate, and even proscribe, abortion except where it is necessary, in appropriate medical judgment, for the preservation of the life or health of the mother.

2. The State may define the term "physician," as it has been employed in the preceding paragraphs of this Part XI of this opinion, to mean only a physician currently licensed by the State, and may proscribe any abortion by a person who is not a physician as so defined.

In *Doe v. Bolton, post,* p. 179, procedural requirements contained in one of the modern abortion statutes are considered. That opinion and this one, of course, are to be read together.[66]

---

66. Neither in this opinion nor in *Doe v. Bolton, post,* p. 179, do we discuss the father's rights, if any exist in the constitutional context, in the abortion decision. No paternal right has been asserted in either of the cases, and the Texas and the Georgia statutes on their face take no cognizance of the father. We are aware that some statutes recognize the father under certain circumstances. North Carolina, for example, N.C. GEN. STAT. § 14-45.1 (Supp. 1971), requires written permission for the abortion from the husband when the woman is a married minor, that is, when she is less than 18 years of age, 41 N.C.A.G. 489 (1971); if the woman

This holding, we feel, is consistent with the relative weights of the respective interests involved, with the lessons and examples of medical and legal history, with the lenity of the common law, and with the demands of the profound problems of the present day. The decision leaves the State free to place increasing restrictions on abortion as the period of pregnancy lengthens, so long as those restrictions are tailored to the recognized state interests. The decision vindicates the right of the physician to administer medical treatment according to his professional judgment up to the points where important state interests provide compelling justifications for intervention. Up to those points, the abortion decision in all its aspects is inherently, and primarily, a medical decision, and basic responsibility for it must rest with the physician. If an individual practitioner abuses the privilege of exercising proper medical judgment, the usual remedies, judicial and intra-professional, are available.

[Section XII relates to procedural questions and has been redacted].

The judgment of the District Court as to intervenor Hallford is reversed, and Dr. Hallford's complaint in intervention is dismissed. In all other respects, the judgment of the District Court is affirmed. Costs are allowed to the appellee.

It is so ordered.

Affirmed in part and reversed in part.

---

is an unmarried minor, written permission from the parents is required. We need not now decide whether provisions of this kind are constitutional.

Appendix C

Opinion of Justice Blackmun for the Court[1]

— *Doe v. Bolton* (1973) —

In this appeal, the criminal abortion statutes recently enacted in Georgia are challenged on constitutional grounds. The statutes are §§ 26-1201 through 26-1203 of the State's Criminal Code, formulated by Georgia Laws, 1968 Session, pp. 1249, 1277-1280. In *Roe v. Wade, ante* p. 410 U.S. 113, we today have struck down, as constitutionally defective, the Texas criminal abortion statutes that are representative of provisions long in effect in a majority of our States. The Georgia legislation, however, is different and merits separate consideration.

I

The statutes in question are reproduced as Appendix A, *post,* p. 410 U.S. at 202.[2] As the appellants acknowledge,[3] the 1968 statutes are patterned upon the American Law Institute's Model Penal Code, § 230.3 (Proposed Official Draft, 1962), reproduced as Appendix B, *post,* p. 410 U.S. at 205. The ALI proposal has served as the model for recent legislation in approximately one-fourth of our States.[4] The new Georgia provisions replaced statutory law that had been in effect for more than 90 years. Georgia Laws 1876, No. 130, § 2, at 113.[5] The predecessor statute paralleled the Texas legislation

---

1. Some parts redacted; the full opinion is available at 410 U.S. 179 (1973).

2. The portions italicized in Appendix A are those held unconstitutional by the District Court.

3. Brief for Appellants 25 n.5; Tr. of Oral Arg. 9.

4. *See* Roe v. Wade, *ante* p. 410 U.S. 113, at 140 n.37.

5. The pertinent provisions of the 1876 statute were:

"Section I. *Be it enacted, etc.,* That from and after the passage of this Act, the willful killing of an unborn child, so far developed as to be ordinarily called 'quick,' by any injury to the mother of such child, which would be murder if it resulted in

considered in *Roe v. Wade, supra,* and made all abortions criminal except those necessary "to preserve the life" of the pregnant woman. The new statutes have not been tested on constitutional grounds in the Georgia state courts.

Section 26-1201, with a referenced exception, makes abortion a crime, and § 26-1203 provides that a person convicted of that crime shall be punished by imprisonment for not less than one nor more than 10 years. Section 21202(a) states the exception and removes from § 1201's definition of criminal abortion, and thus makes noncriminal, an abortion "performed by a physician duly licensed" in Georgia when,

> based upon his best clinical judgment . . . an abortion is necessary because:
> "(1) A continuation of the pregnancy would endanger the life of the pregnant woman or would seriously and permanently injure her health; or"
> "(2) The fetus would very likely be born with a grave, permanent, and irremediable mental or physical defect; or"
> "(3) The pregnancy resulted from forcible or statutory rape."[6]

Section 26-1202 also requires, by numbered subdivisions of its subsection (b), that, for an abortion to be authorized or performed as a noncriminal procedure, additional conditions must be fulfilled. These are

---

the death of such mother, shall be guilty of a felony, and punishable by death or imprisonment for life, as the jury trying the case may recommend."

"Sec. II. *Be it further enacted,* That every person who shall administer to any woman pregnant with a child, any medicine, drug, or substance whatever, or shall use or employ any instrument or other means, with intent thereby to destroy such child, unless the same shall have been necessary to preserve the life of such mother, or shall have been advised by two physicians to be necessary for such purpose, shall, in case the death of such child or mother be thereby produced, be declared guilty of an assault with intent to murder."

"Sec. III. *Be it further enacted,* That any person who shall willfully administer to any pregnant woman any medicine, drug or substance, or anything whatever, or shall employ any instrument or means whatever, with intent thereby to procure the miscarriage or abortion of any such woman, unless the same shall have been necessary to preserve the life of such woman, or shall have been advised by two physicians to be necessary for that purpose, shall, upon conviction, be punished as prescribed in section 4310 of the Revised Code of Georgia."

It should be noted that the second section, in contrast to the first, made no specific reference to quickening. The section was construed, however, to possess this line of demarcation. Taylor v. State, 105 Ga. 846, 33 S.E. 190 (1899).

6. In contrast with the ALI model, the Georgia statute makes no specific reference to pregnancy resulting from incest. We were assured by the State at reargument that this was because the statute's reference to "rape" was intended to include incest. Tr. of Oral Rearg. 32.

(1) and (2) residence of the woman in Georgia; (3) reduction to writing of the performing physician's medical judgment that an abortion is justified for one or more of the reasons specified by § 26-1202(a), with written concurrence in that judgment by at least two other Georgia-licensed physicians, based upon their separate personal medical examinations of the woman; (4) performance of the abortion in a hospital licensed by the State Board of Health and also accredited by the Joint Commission on Accreditation of Hospitals; (5) advance approval by an abortion committee of not less than three members of the hospital's staff; (6) certifications in a rape situation; and (7), (8), and (9) maintenance and confidentiality of records. There is a provision (subsection (c)) for judicial determination of the legality of a proposed abortion on petition of the judicial circuit law officer or of a close relative, as therein defined, of the unborn child, and for expeditious hearing of that petition. There is also a provision (subsection (e)) giving a hospital the right not to admit an abortion patient and giving any physician and any hospital employee or staff member the right, on moral or religious grounds, not to participate in the procedure.

II

On April 16, 1970, Mary Doe,[7] 23 other individuals (nine described as Georgia-licensed physicians, seven as nurses registered in the State, five as clergymen, and two as social workers), and two nonprofit Georgia corporations that advocate abortion reform instituted this federal action in the Northern District of Georgia against the State's attorney general, the district attorney of Fulton County, and the chief of police of the city of Atlanta. The plaintiffs sought a declaratory judgment that the Georgia abortion statutes were unconstitutional in their entirety. They also sought injunctive relief restraining the defendants and their successors from enforcing the statutes.

Mary Doe alleged:

(1) She was a 22-year-old Georgia citizen, married, and nine weeks pregnant. She had three living children. The two older ones had been placed in a foster home because of Doe's poverty and inability to care for them. The youngest, born July 19, 1969, had been placed for adoption. Her husband had recently abandoned her, and she was forced to live with her indigent parents and their eight children. She and her husband, however, had become reconciled. He was a construction worker employed only sporadically. She had been a mental patient at the State Hospital. She had been

---

7. Appellants by their complaint, App. 7, allege that the name is a pseudonym.

advised that an abortion could be performed on her with less danger to her health than if she gave birth to the child she was carrying. She would be unable to care for or support the new child.

(2) On March 25, 1970, she applied to the Abortion Committee of Grady Memorial Hospital, Atlanta, for a therapeutic abortion under § 26-1202. Her application was denied 16 days later, on April 10, when she was eight weeks pregnant, on the ground that her situation was not one described in § 26-1202(a).[8]

(3) Because her application was denied, she was forced either to relinquish "her right to decide when and how many children she will bear" or to seek an abortion that was illegal under the Georgia statutes. This invaded her rights of privacy and liberty in matters related to family, marriage, and sex, and deprived her of the right to choose whether to bear children. This was a violation of rights guaranteed her by the First, Fourth, Fifth, Ninth, and Fourteenth Amendments. The statutes also denied her equal protection and procedural due process and, because they were unconstitutionally vague, deterred hospitals and doctors from performing abortions. She sued "on her own behalf and on behalf of all others similarly situated."

The other plaintiffs alleged that the Georgia statutes "chilled and deterred" them from practicing their respective professions and deprived them of rights guaranteed by the First, Fourth, and Fourteenth Amendments. These plaintiffs also purported to sue on their own behalf and on behalf of others similarly situated.

A three-judge district court was convened. An offer of proof as to Doe's identity was made, but the court deemed it unnecessary to receive that proof. The case was then tried on the pleadings and interrogatories.

The District Court, per curiam, 319 F. Supp. 1048 (ND Ga.1970), held that all the plaintiffs had standing, but that only Doe presented a justiciable controversy. On the merits, the court concluded that the limitation in the Georgia statute of the "number of reasons for which an abortion may be sought," *id.* at 1056, improperly restricted Doe's rights of privacy articulated in *Griswold v. Connecticut,* 381 U.S. 479 (1965), and of "personal liberty," both of which it thought "broad enough to include the decision to abort a pregnancy," 319 F. Supp. at 1055. As a consequence, the court held invalid those portions of §§ 26-1202(a) and (b)(3) limiting legal abortions to the three situations specified; § 26-1202(b)(6) relating to certifications in a

---

8. In answers to interrogatories, Doe stated that her application for an abortion was approved at Georgia Baptist Hospital on May 5, 1970, but that she was not approved as a charity patient there, and had no money to pay for an abortion. App. 64.

rape situation; and § 26-1202(c) authorizing a court test. Declaratory relief was granted accordingly. The court, however, held that Georgia's interest in protection of health, and the existence of a "*potential* of independent human existence" (emphasis in original), *id.* at 1055, justified state regulation of "the manner of performance as well as the quality of the final decision to abort," *id.* at 1056, and it refused to strike down the other provisions of the statutes. It denied the request for an injunction, *id.* at 1057.

Claiming that they were entitled to an injunction and to broader relief, the plaintiffs took a direct appeal pursuant to 28 U.S.C. § 1253. We postponed decision on jurisdiction to the hearing on the merits. 402 U.S. 941 (1971). The defendants also purported to appeal, pursuant to § 1253, but their appeal was dismissed for want of jurisdiction. 402 U.S. 936 (1971). We are advised by the appellees, Brief 42, that an alternative appeal on their part is pending in the United States Court of Appeals for the Fifth Circuit. The extent, therefore, to which the District Court decision was adverse to the defendants, that is, the extent to which portions of the Georgia statutes were held to be unconstitutional, technically is not now before us.[9] *Swarb v. Lennox,* 405 U.S. 191, 201 (1972).

[Section III addresses standing issues and has been redacted].

IV

The appellants attack on several grounds those portions of the Georgia abortion statutes that remain after the District Court decision: undue restriction of a right to personal and marital privacy; vagueness; deprivation of substantive and procedural due process; improper restriction to Georgia residents; and denial of equal protection.

A. *Roe v. Wade, supra,* sets forth our conclusion that a pregnant woman does not have an absolute constitutional right to an abortion on her demand. What is said there is applicable here, and need not be repeated.

B. The appellants go on to argue, however, that the present Georgia statutes must be viewed historically, that is, from the fact that, prior to the 1968 Act, an abortion in Georgia was not criminal if performed to "preserve the life" of the mother. It is suggested that the present statute, as well, has this emphasis on the mother's rights, not on those of the fetus. Appellants contend that it is thus clear that Georgia has given little, and certainly not first, consideration to the unborn child. Yet it is the unborn child's rights

---

9. What we decide today obviously has implications for the issues raised in the defendants' appeal pending in the Fifth Circuit.

that Georgia asserts in justification of the statute. Appellants assert that this justification cannot be advanced at this late date.

Appellants then argue that the statutes do not adequately protect the woman's right. This is so because it would be physically and emotionally damaging to Doe to bring a child into her poor, "fatherless"[10] family, and because advances in medicine and medical techniques have made it safer for a woman to have a medically induced abortion than for her to bear a child. Thus,

> "a statute that requires a woman to carry an unwanted pregnancy to term infringes not only on a fundamental right of privacy, but on the right to life itself."

Brief 27.

The appellants recognize that, a century ago, medical knowledge was not so advanced as it is today, that the techniques of antisepsis were not known, and that any abortion procedure was dangerous for the woman. To restrict the legality of the abortion to the situation where it was deemed necessary, in medical judgment, for the preservation of the woman's life was only a natural conclusion in the exercise of the legislative judgment of that time. A State is not to be reproached, however, for a past judgmental determination made in the light of then-existing medical knowledge. It is perhaps unfair to argue, as the appellants do, that, because the early focus was on the preservation of the woman's life, the State's present professed interest in the protection of embryonic and fetal life is to be downgraded. That argument denies the State the right to readjust its views and emphases in the light of the advanced knowledge and techniques of the day.

C. Appellants argue that § 26-1202(a) of the Georgia statutes, as it has been left by the District Court's decision, is unconstitutionally vague. This argument centers on the proposition that, with the District Court's having struck down the statutorily specified reasons, it still remains a crime for a physician to perform an abortion except when, as § 26-1202(a) reads, it is "based upon his best clinical judgment that an abortion is necessary." The appellants contend that the word "necessary" does not warn the physician of what conduct is proscribed; that the statute is wholly without objective standards and is subject to diverse interpretation; and that doctors will choose to err on the side of caution and will be arbitrary.

The net result of the District Court's decision is that the abortion determination, so far as the physician is concerned, is made in the exercise

---

10. Brief for Appellants 25.

of his professional, that is, his "best clinical," judgment in the light of all the attendant circumstances. He is not now restricted to the three situations originally specified. Instead, he may range farther afield wherever his medical judgment, properly and professionally exercised, so dictates and directs him.

The vagueness argument is set at rest by the decision in *United States v. Vuitch*, 402 U.S. 62, 71-72 (1971), where the issue was raised with respect to a District of Columbia statute making abortions criminal

> "unless the same were done as necessary for the preservation of the mother's life or health and under the direction of a competent licensed practitioner of medicine."

That statute has been construed to bear upon psychological as well as physical wellbeing. This being so, the Court concluded that the term "health" presented no problem of vagueness.

> "Indeed, whether a particular operation is necessary for a patient's physical or mental health is a judgment that physicians are obviously called upon to make routinely whenever surgery is considered."

Id. at 402 U.S. at 72. This conclusion is equally applicable here. Whether, in the words of the Georgia statute, "an abortion is necessary" is a professional judgment that the Georgia physician will be called upon to make routinely.

We agree with the District Court, 319 F. Supp. at 1058, that the medical judgment may be exercised in the light of all factors—physical, emotional, psychological, familial, and the woman's age—relevant to the wellbeing of the patient. All these factors may relate to health. This allows the attending physician the room he needs to make his best medical judgment. And it is room that operates for the benefit, not the disadvantage, of the pregnant woman.

D. The appellants next argue that the District Court should have declared unconstitutional three procedural demand of the Georgia statute: (1) that the abortion be performed in a hospital accredited by the Joint Commission on Accreditation of Hospitals:[11] (2) that the procedure be approved by the hospital staff abortion committee; and (3) that the performing physician's judgment be confirmed by the independent examinations of the patient by two other licensed physicians. The appellants attack

---

11. We were advised at reargument, Tr. of Oral Rearg. 10, that only 54 of Georgia's 159 counties have a JCAH-accredited hospital.

these provisions not only on the ground that they unduly restrict the woman's right of privacy, but also on procedural due process and equal protection grounds. The physician appellants also argue that, by subjecting a doctor's individual medical judgment to committee approval and to confirming consultations, the statute impermissibly restricts the physician's right to practice his profession and deprives him of due process.

1. *JCAH accreditation.* The Joint Commission on Accreditation of Hospitals is an organization without governmental sponsorship or overtones. No question whatever is raised concerning the integrity of the organization or the high purpose of the accreditation process.[12] That process, however, has to do with hospital standards generally and has no present particularized concern with abortion as a medical or surgical procedure.[13] In Georgia, there is no restriction on the performance of nonabortion surgery in a hospital not yet accredited by the JCAH so long as other requirements imposed by the State, such as licensing of the hospital and of the operating surgeon, are met. *See* Georgia Code §§ 88-1901(a) and 88-1905 (1971) and 84-907 (Supp. 1971). Furthermore, accreditation by the Commission is not granted until a hospital has been in operation at least one year. The Model Penal Code, § 230.3, Appendix B hereto, contains no requirement for JCAH accreditation. And the Uniform Abortion Act (Final Draft, Aug.1971),[14] approved by the American Bar Association in February, 1972, contains no JCAH-accredited hospital specification.[15] Some courts have

---

12. Since its founding, JCAH has pursued the "elusive goal" of defining the "optimal setting" for "quality of service in hospitals." JCAH, Accreditation Manual for Hospitals, Foreword (Dec.1970). The Manual's Introduction states the organization's purpose to establish standards and conduct accreditation programs that will afford quality medical care "to give patients the optimal benefits that medical science has to offer." This ambitious and admirable goal is illustrated by JCAH's decision in 1966 "[t]o raise and strengthen the standards from their present level of minimum essential to the level of optimum achievable. . . ." Some of these "optimum achievable" standards required are: disclosure of hospital ownership and control; a dietetic service and written dietetic policies; a written disaster plan for mass emergencies; a nuclear medical services program; facilities for hematology, chemistry, microbiology, clinical microscopy, and sero-immunology; a professional library and document delivery service; a radiology program; a social services plan administered by a qualified social worker; and a special care unit.

13. "The Joint Commission neither advocates nor opposes any particular position with respect to elective abortions." Letter dated July 9, 1971, from John I. Brewer, M.D., Commissioner, JCAH, to the Rockefeller Foundation. Brief for *amici curiae*, American College of Obstetricians and Gynecologists et al., p. A-3.

14. *See* Roe v. Wade, *ante* at 410 U.S. at 146-147, n.40.

15. Some state statutes do not have the JCAH accreditation requirement. ALASKA STAT. § 11.15.060 (1970); HAWAII REV. STAT. § 453-16 (Supp. 1971); N.Y. PENAL CODE § 125.05, subd. 3 (Supp. 1972-1973). Washington has the requirement, but couples it with the

held that a JCAH accreditation requirement is an overbroad infringement of fundamental rights because it does not relate to the particular medical problems and dangers of the abortion operation. *E.g., Poe v. Menghini,* 339 F. Supp. at 993-994.

We hold that the JCAH accreditation requirement does not withstand constitutional scrutiny in the present context. It is a requirement that simply is not "based on differences that are reasonably related to the purposes of the Act in which its found." *Morey v. Doud,* 354 U.S. 457, 465 (1957).

This is not to say that Georgia may not or should not from and after the end of the first trimester, adopt standards for licensing all facilities where abortions may be performed so long as those standards are legitimately related to the objective the State seeks to accomplish. The appellants contend that such a relationship would be lacking even in a lesser requirement that an abortion be performed in a licensed hospital, as opposed to a facility, such as a clinic, that may be required by the State to possess all the staffing and services necessary to perform an abortion safely (including those adequate to handle serious complications or other emergency, or arrangements with a nearby hospital to provide such services). Appellants and various *amici* have presented us with a mass of data purporting to demonstrate that some facilities other than hospitals are entirely adequate to perform abortions if they possess these qualifications. The State, on the other hand, has not presented persuasive data to show that only hospitals meet its acknowledged interest in insuring the quality of the operation and the full protection of the patient. We feel compelled to agree with appellants that the State must show more than it has in order to prove that only the full resources of a licensed hospital, rather than those of some other appropriately licensed institution, satisfy these health interests. We hold that the hospital requirement of the Georgia law, because it fails to exclude the first trimester of pregnancy, *see Roe v. Wade, ante* at 410 U.S. at 163, is also invalid. In so holding we naturally express no opinion on the medical judgment involved in any particular case, that is, whether the patient's

---

alternative of "a medical facility approved . . . by the state board of health." WASH. REV. CODE § 9.02.070 (Supp. 1972). Florida's new statute has a similar provision. Law of Apr. 13, 1972, c. 72-196, § 1(2). Others contain the specification. ARK. STAT. ANN. §§ 41-303 to 41-310 (Supp. 1971); CALIF. HEALTH & SAFETY CODE §§ 25950-25955.5 (Supp. 1972); COLO. REV. STAT. ANN. §§ 40-2-50 to 40-2-53 (Cum. Supp. 1967); KAN. STAT. ANN. § 21-3407 (Supp. 1971); MD. ANN. CODE, Art. 43, §§ 137–139 (1971). *Cf.* DEL. CODE ANN., Tit. 24, §§ 1790–1793 (Supp. 1972), specifying "a nationally recognized medical or hospital accreditation authority," § 1790(a).

situation is such that an abortion should be performed in a hospital, rather than in some other facility.

2. *Committee approval.* The second aspect of the appellants' procedural attack relates to the hospital abortion committee and to the pregnant woman's asserted lack of access to that committee. Relying primarily on *Goldberg v. Kelly,* 397 U.S. 254 (1970), concerning the termination of welfare benefits, and *Wisconsin v. Constantineau,* 400 U.S. 433 (1971), concerning the posting of an alcoholic's name, Doe first argues that she was denied due process because she could not make a presentation to the committee. It is not clear from the record, however, whether Doe's own consulting physician was or was not a member of the committee or did or did not present her case, or, indeed whether she herself was or was not there. We see nothing in the Georgia statute that explicitly denies access to the committee by or on behalf of the woman. If the access point alone were involved, we would not be persuaded to strike down the committee provision on the unsupported assumption that access is not provided.

Appellants attack the discretion the statute leaves to the committee. The most concrete argument they advance is their suggestion that it is still a badge of infamy "in many minds" to bear an illegitimate child, and that the Georgia system enables the committee members' personal views as to extramarital sex relations, and punishment therefor, to govern their decisions. This approach obviously is one founded on suspicion, and one that discloses a lack of confidence in the integrity of physicians. To say that physicians will be guided in their hospital committee decisions by their predilections on extramarital sex unduly narrows the issue to pregnancy outside marriage. (Doe's own situation did not involve extramarital sex and its product.) The appellants' suggestion is necessarily somewhat degrading to the conscientious physician, particularly the obstetrician, whose professional activity is concerned with the physical and mental welfare, the woes, the emotions, and the concern of his female patients. He, perhaps more than anyone else, is knowledgeable in this area of patient care, and he is aware of human frailty, so-called "error," and needs. The good physician—despite the presence of rascals in the medical profession, as in all others, we trust that most physicians are "good"—will have sympathy and understanding for the pregnant patient that probably are not exceeded by those who participate in other areas of professional counseling.

It is perhaps worth noting that the abortion committee has a function of its own. It is a committee of the hospital, and it is composed of members of the institution's medical staff. The membership usually is a changing one. In this way, its work burden is shared and is more readily accepted. The committee's function is protective. It enables the hospital appropriately to be advised that its posture and activities are in accord with legal requirements. It is to be remembered that the hospital is an entity, and that it, too, has legal rights and legal obligations.

Saying all this, however, does not settle the issue of the constitutional propriety of the committee requirement. Viewing the Georgia statute as a whole, we see no constitutionally justifiable pertinence in the structure for the advance approval by the abortion committee. With regard to the protection of potential life, the medical judgment is already completed prior to the committee stage, and review by a committee once removed from diagnosis is basically redundant. We are not cited to any other surgical procedure made subject to committee approval as a matter of state criminal law. The woman's right to receive medical care in accordance with her licensed physician's best judgment and the physician's right to administer it are substantially limited by this statutorily imposed overview. And the hospital itself is otherwise fully protected. Under § 26-1202(e), the hospital is free not to admit a patient for an abortion. It is even free not to have an abortion committee. Further, a physician or any other employee has the right to refrain, for moral or religious reasons, from participating in the abortion procedure. These provisions obviously are in the statute in order to afford appropriate protection to the individual and to the denominational hospital. Section 21202(e) affords adequate protection to the hospital, and little more is provided by the committee prescribed by § 26-1202(b)(5).

We conclude that the interposition of the hospital abortion committee is unduly restrictive of the patient's rights and needs that, at this point, have already been medically delineated and substantiated by her personal physician. To ask more serves neither the hospital nor the State.

3. *Two-doctor concurrence.* The third aspect of the appellants' attack centers on the "time and availability of adequate medical facilities and personnel." It is said that the system imposes substantial and irrational roadblocks and "is patently unsuited" to prompt determination of the abortion decision. Time, of course, is critical in abortion. Risks during the first trimester of pregnancy are admittedly lower than during later months.

The appellants purport to show by a local study[16] of Grady Memorial Hospital (serving indigent residents in Fulton and DeKalb Counties) that the "mechanics of the system itself forced . . . discontinuance of the abortion process" because the median time for the workup was 15 days. The same study

---

16. L. Baker & M. Freeman, Abortion Surveillance at Grady Memorial Hospital Center for Disease Control (June and July 1971) (U.S. Dept. of HEW, Public Health Service).

shows, however, that 27% of the candidates for abortion were already 13 or more weeks pregnant at the time of application, that is, they were at the end of or beyond the first trimester when they made their applications. It is too much to say, as appellants do, that these particular persons "were victims of a system over which they [had] no control." If higher risk was incurred because of abortions in the second, rather than the first, trimester, much of that risk was due to delay in application, and not to the alleged cumbersomeness of the system. We note, in passing, that appellant Doe had no delay problem herself; the decision in her case was made well within the first trimester.

It should be manifest that our rejection of the accredited hospital requirement and, more important, of the abortion committee's advance approval eliminates the major grounds of the attack based on the system's delay and the lack of facilities. There remains, however, the required confirmation by two Georgia-licensed physicians in addition to the recommendation of the pregnant woman's own consultant (making under the statute, a total of six physicians involved, including the three on the hospital's abortion committee). We conclude that this provision, too, must fall.

The statute's emphasis, as has been repetitively noted, is on the attending physician's "best clinical judgment that an abortion is necessary." That should be sufficient. The reasons for the presence of the confirmation step in the statute are perhaps apparent, but they are insufficient to withstand constitutional challenge. Again, no other voluntary medical or surgical procedure for which Georgia requires confirmation by two other physicians has been cited to us. If a physician is licensed by the State, he is recognized by the State as capable of exercising acceptable clinical judgment. If he fails in this, professional censure and deprivation of his license are available remedies. Required acquiescence by co-practitioners has no rational connection with a patient's needs, and unduly infringes on the physician's right to practice. The attending physician will know when a consultation is advisable—the doubtful situation, the need for assurance when the medical decision is a delicate one, and the like. Physicians have followed this routine historically, and know its usefulness and benefit for all concerned. It is still true today that

> "[r]eliance must be placed upon the assurance given by his license, issued by an authority competent to judge in that respect, that he [the physician] possesses the requisite qualifications."

Dent v. West Virginia, 129 U.S. 114, 122-23 (1889). *See United States v. Vuitch,* 402 U.S. at 71.

E. The appellants attack the residency requirement of the Georgia law, §§ 26-1202(b)(1) and (b)(2), as violative of the right to travel stressed in

Shapiro v. Thompson, 394 U.S. 618, 629-31 (1969), and other cases. A requirement of this kind, of course, could be deemed to have some relationship to the availability of post-procedure medical care for the aborted patient.

Nevertheless, we do not uphold the constitutionality of the residence requirement. It is not based on any policy of preserving state supported facilities for Georgia residents, for the bar also applies to private hospitals and to privately retained physicians. There is no intimation, either, that Georgia facilities are utilized to capacity in caring for Georgia residents. Just as the Privileges and Immunities Clause, Const. Art. IV, § 2, protects persons who enter other States to ply their trade, *Ward v. Maryland,* 12 Wall. 418, 79 U.S. 430 (1871); *Blake v. McClung,* 172 U.S. 239, 248-56 (1898), so must it protect persons who enter Georgia seeking the medical services that are available there. *See Toomer v. Witsell,* 334 U.S. 385, 396-97 (1948). A contrary holding would mean that a State could limit to its own residents the general medical care available within its borders. This we could not approve.

F. The last argument on this phase of the case is one that often is made, namely, that the Georgia system is violative of equal protection because it discriminates against the poor. The appellants do not urge that abortions should be performed by persons other than licensed physicians, so we have no argument that, because the wealthy can better afford physicians, the poor should have nonphysicians made available to them. The appellants acknowledged that the procedures are "nondiscriminatory in . . . express terms," but they suggest that they have produced invidious discriminations. The District Court rejected this approach out of hand. 319 F. Supp. at 1056. It rests primarily on the accreditation and approval and confirmation requirements, discussed above, and on the assertion that most of Georgia's counties have no accredited hospital. We have set aside the accreditation, approval, and confirmation requirements, however, and with that, the discrimination argument collapses in all significant aspects.

[Section V addresses peripheral issues of relief and has been redacted].

In summary, we hold that the JCAH-accredited hospital provision and the requirements as to approval by the hospital abortion committee, as to confirmation by two independent physicians, and as to residence in Georgia are all violative of the Fourteenth Amendment. Specifically, the following portions of § 26-1202(b), remaining after the District Court's judgment, are invalid:

(1) Subsections (1) and (2).

(2) That portion of Subsection (3) following the words "[s]uch physician's judgment is reduced to writing."

(3) Subsections (4) and (5).

The judgment of the District Court is modified accordingly and, as so modified, is affirmed. Costs are allowed to the appellants.

APPENDIX A TO OPINION OF THE COURT

Criminal Code of Georgia

(The italicized portions are those held unconstitutional by the District Court)

CHAPTER 26-12. ABORTION.

26-1201. Criminal Abortion. Except as otherwise provided in section 26-1202, a person commits criminal abortion when he administers any medicine, drug or other substance whatever to any woman or when he uses any instrument or other means whatever upon any woman with intent to produce a miscarriage or abortion.

26-1202. Exception. (a) Section 26-1201 shall not apply to an abortion performed by a physician duly licensed to practice medicine and surgery pursuant to Chapter 84-9 or 84-12 of the Code of Georgia of 1933, as amended, based upon his best clinical judgment that an abortion is necessary because:

"*(1) A continuation of the pregnancy would endanger the life of the pregnant woman or would seriously and permanently injure her health; or*"

"*(2) The fetus would very likely be born with a grave, permanent, and irremediable mental or physical defect; or*"

"*(3) The pregnancy resulted from forcible or statutory rape.*"

"(b) No abortion is authorized or shall be performed under this section unless each of the following conditions is met: "

"(1) The pregnant woman requesting the abortion certifies in writing under oath and subject to the penalties of false swearing to the physician who proposes to perform the abortion that she is a bona fide legal resident of the State of Georgia."

"(2) The physician certifies that he believes the woman is a bona fide resident of this State and that he has no information which should lead him to believe otherwise."

"(3) Such physician's judgment is reduced to writing and concurred in by at least two other physicians duly licensed to practice medicine and surgery pursuant to Chapter 84-9 of the Code of Georgia of 1933, as amended, who certify in writing that, based upon their separate personal medical examinations of the pregnant woman, the abortion is, in their judgment, necessary because of one or more of the reasons enumerated above."

"(4) Such abortion is performed in a hospital licensed by the State Board of Health and accredited by the Joint Commission on Accreditation of Hospitals."

"(5) The performance of the abortion has been approved in advance by a committee of the medical staff of the hospital in which the operation is to be performed. This committee must be one established and maintained in accordance with the standards promulgated by the Joint Commission on the Accreditation of Hospitals, and its approval must be by a majority vote of a membership of not less than three members of the hospital's staff; the physician proposing to perform the operation may not be counted as a member of the committee for this purpose."

"*(6) If the proposed abortion is considered necessary because the woman has been raped, the woman makes a written statement under oath, and subject to the penalties of false swearing, of the date, time and place of the rape and the name of the rapist, if known. There must be attached to this statement a certified copy of any report of the rape made by any law enforcement officer or agency and a statement by the solicitor general of the judicial circuit where the rape occurred or allegedly occurred that, according to his best information, there is probable cause to believe that the rape did occur.*"

"(7) Such written opinions, statements, certificates, and concurrences are maintained in the permanent files of such hospital and are available at all reasonable times to the solicitor general of the judicial circuit in which the hospital is located."

"(8) A copy of such written opinions, statements, certificates, and concurrences is filed with the Director of the State Department of Public Health within 10 days after such operation is performed."

"(9) All written opinions, statements, certificates, and concurrences filed and maintained pursuant to paragraphs (7) and (8) of this subsection shall be confidential record and shall not be made available for public inspection at any time."

"*(c) Any solicitor General of the judicial circuit in which an abortion is to be performed under this section, or any person who would be a relative of the child within the second degree of consanguinity, may petition the superior court of the county in which the abortion is to be performed for a declaratory judgment whether the performance of such abortion would violate any constitutional or other legal rights of the fetus. Such solicitor General may also petition such court for the purpose of taking issue with compliance with the requirements of this section. The physician who proposes to perform the abortion and the pregnant woman shall be respondents. The petition shall be heard expeditiously, and if the court adjudges that such abortion would*" *violate the constitutional or other legal rights of the fetus, the court shall so declare and shall restrain the physician from performing the abortion."*

(d) If an abortion is performed in compliance with this section, the death of the fetus shall not give rise to any claim for wrongful death.

(e) Nothing in this section shall require a hospital to admit any patient under the provisions hereof for the purpose of performing an abortion, nor shall any hospital be required to appoint a committee such as contemplated under subsection (b)(5). A physician, or any other person who is a member of or associated with the staff of a hospital, or any employee of a hospital in which an abortion has been authorized, who shall state in writing an objection to such abortion on moral or religious grounds shall not be required to participate in the medical procedures which will result in the abortion, and the refusal of any such person to participate therein shall not form the basis of any claim for damages on account of such refusal or for any disciplinary or recriminatory action against such person.

26-1203. Punishment. A person convicted of criminal abortion shall be punished by imprisonment for not less than one nor more than 10 years.

APPENDIX B TO OPINION OF THE COURT

American Law Institute, MODEL PENAL CODE
Section 230.3. Abortion.

(1) *Unjustified Abortion.* A person who purposely and unjustifiably terminates the pregnancy of another otherwise than by a live birth commits a felony of the third degree or, where the pregnancy has continued beyond the twenty-sixth week, a felony of the second degree.

(2) *Justifiable Abortion.* A licensed physician is justified in terminating a pregnancy if he believes there is substantial risk that continuance of the pregnancy would gravely impair the physical or mental health of the mother or that the child would be born with grave physical or mental defect, or that the pregnancy resulted from rape, incest, or other felonious intercourse. All illicit intercourse with a girl below the age of 16 shall be deemed felonious for purposes of this subsection. Justifiable abortions shall be performed only in a licensed hospital except in case of emergency when hospital facilities are unavailable. [Additional exceptions from the requirement of hospitalization may be incorporated here to take account of situations in sparsely settled areas where hospitals are not generally accessible.]

(3) *Physicians' Certificates; Presumption from Non-Compliance.* No abortion shall be performed unless two physicians, one of whom may be the person performing the abortion, shall have certified in writing the circumstances

which they believe to justify the abortion. Such certificate shall be submitted before the abortion to the hospital where it is to be performed and, in the case of abortion following felonious intercourse, to the prosecuting attorney or the police. Failure to comply with any of the requirements of this Subsection gives rise to a presumption that the abortion was unjustified.

(4) *Self-Abortion.* A woman whose pregnancy has continued beyond the twenty-sixth week commits a felony of the third degree if she purposely terminates her own pregnancy otherwise than by a live birth, or if she uses instruments, drugs or violence upon herself for that purpose. Except as justified under Subsection (2), a person who induces or knowingly aids a woman to use instruments, drugs or violence upon herself for the purpose of terminating her pregnancy otherwise than by a live birth commits a felony of the third degree whether or not the pregnancy has continued beyond the twenty-sixth week.

(5) *Pretended Abortion.* A person commits a felony of the third degree if, representing that it is his purpose to perform an abortion, he does an act adapted to cause abortion in a pregnant woman although the woman is in fact, not pregnant, or the actor does not believe she is. A person charged with unjustified abortion under Subsection (1) or an attempt to commit that offense may be convicted thereof upon proof of conduct prohibited by this Subsection.

(6) *Distribution of Abortifacients.* A person who sells, offers to sell, possesses with intent to sell, advertises, or displays for sale anything specially designed to terminate a pregnancy, or held out by the actor as useful for that purpose, commits a misdemeanor, unless:

(a) the sale, offer or display is to a physician or druggist or to an intermediary in a chain of distribution to physicians or druggists; or

(b) the sale is made upon prescription or order of a physician; or

(c) the possession is with intent to sell as authorized in paragraphs (a) and (b); or

(d) the advertising is addressed to persons named in paragraph (a) and confined to trade or professional channels not likely to reach the general public.

(7) *Section Inapplicable to Prevention of Pregnancy.* Nothing in this Section shall be deemed applicable to the prescription, administration or distribution of drugs or other substances for avoiding pregnancy, whether by preventing implantation of a fertilized ovum or by any other method that operates before, at or immediately after fertilization.

Appendix D

Concurring Opinion of
Justice Douglas[1]
— Doe v. Bolton (1973) —

While I join the opinion of the Court,[2] I add a few words.

I

The questions presented in the present cases go far beyond the issues of vagueness, which we considered in *United States v. Vuitch*, 402 U. S. 62. They involve the right of privacy, one aspect of which we considered in *Griswold v. Connecticut*, 381 U. S. 479, 484, when we held that various guarantees in the Bill of Rights create zones of privacy.[3] The *Griswold* case involved a law

---

1. Some parts redacted; the full opinion is available at 410 U.S. 179, 209 (1973). Justice Douglas' opinion in *Doe* applied also to *Roe v. Wade*.

2. I disagree with the dismissal of Dr. Hallford's complaint in intervention in *Roe v. Wade*, *ante* p. 410 U.S. 113, because my disagreement with *Younger v. Harris*, 401 U.S. 37, revealed in my dissent in that case, still persists and extends to the progeny of that case.

3. There is no mention of privacy in our Bill of Rights, but our decisions have recognized it as one of the fundamental values those amendments were designed to protect. The fountainhead case is *Boyd v. United States*, 116 U.S. 616, holding that a federal statute which authorized a court in tax cases to require a taxpayer to produce his records or to concede the Government's allegations offended the Fourth and Fifth Amendments. Mr. Justice Bradley, for the Court, found that the measure unduly intruded into the "sanctity of a man's home and the privacies of life." *Id.* at 116 U.S. 630. Prior to *Boyd*, in *Kilbourn v. Thompson*, 103 U.S. 168, 190, Mr. Justice Miller held for the Court that neither House of Congress "possesses the general power of making inquiry into the private affairs of the citizen." Of *Kilbourn*, Mr. Justice Field later said,

> "This case will stand for all time as a bulwark against the invasion of the right of the citizen to protection in his private affairs against the unlimited scrutiny of investigation by a congressional committee."

In re Pacific Railway Comm'n, 32 F. 241, 253 (cited with approval in *Sinclair v. United States*, 279 U.S. 263, 293). Mr. Justice Harlan, also speaking for the Court in *ICC v. Brimson*, 154 U.S. 447, 478, thought the same was true of administrative inquiries, saying that the Constitution

forbidding the use of contraceptives. We held that law as applied to married people unconstitutional:

> "We deal with a right of privacy older than the Bill of Rights—older than our political parties, older than our school system. Marriage is a coming together for better or for worse, hopefully enduring, and intimate to the degree of being sacred."

Id. at 486.

The District Court in *Doe* held that *Griswold* and related cases

> "establish a Constitutional right to privacy broad enough to encompass the right of a woman to terminate an unwanted pregnancy in its early stages, by obtaining an abortion."

319 F. Supp. 1048, 1054.

The Supreme Court of California expressed the same view in *People v. Belous*,[4] 71 Cal. 2d 954, 963, 458 P.2d 194, 199.

The Ninth Amendment obviously does not create federally enforceable rights. It merely says, "The enumeration in the Constitution, of certain rights, shall not be construed to deny or disparage others retained by the people." But a catalogue of these rights includes customary, traditional, and time-honored rights, amenities, privileges, and immunities that come within the sweep of "the Blessings of Liberty" mentioned in the preamble to the Constitution. Many of them, in my view, come within the meaning of the term "liberty" as used in the Fourteenth Amendment.

First is the autonomous control over the development and expression of one's intellect, interests, tastes, and personality.

These are rights protected by the First Amendment and, in my view, they are absolute, permitting of no exceptions. *See Terminiello v. Chicago*, 337 U. S. 1; *Roth v. United States*, 354 U. S. 476, 508 (dissent); *Kingsley Pictures Corp. v. Regents*, 360 U. S. 684, 697 (concurring); *New York Times Co. v. Sullivan*, 376 U. S. 254, 293 (Black, J., concurring, in which I joined). The Free Exercise Clause of the First Amendment is one facet of this constitutional right. The right to remain silent as respects one's own beliefs, *Watkins v. United States*, 354 U. S. 178, 196-99, is protected by the First and the Fifth. The First

---

did not permit a "general power of making inquiry into the private affairs of the citizen." In a similar vein were *Harriman v. ICC*, 211 U.S. 407; *United States v. Louisville & Nashville R. Co.*, 236 U.S. 318, 335; and *FTC v. American Tobacco Co.*, 264 U.S. 298.

4. The California abortion statute, held unconstitutional in the *Belous* case, made it a crime to perform or help perform an abortion "unless the same is necessary to preserve [the mother's] life." 71 Cal. 2d at 959, 458 P.2d at 197.

Amendment grants the privacy of first-class mail, *United States v. Van Leeuwen*, 397 U. S. 249, 253. All of these aspects of the right of privacy are rights "retained by the people" in the meaning of the Ninth Amendment.

Second is freedom of choice in the basic decisions of one's life respecting marriage, divorce, procreation, contraception, and the education and upbringing of children.

These rights, unlike those protected by the First Amendment, are subject to some control by the police power. Thus, the Fourth Amendment speaks only of "unreasonable searches and seizures" and of "probable cause." These rights are "fundamental," and we have held that, in order to support legislative action, the statute must be narrowly and precisely drawn, and that a "compelling state interest" must be shown in support of the limitation. *E.g., Kramer v. Union Free School District*, 395 U. S. 621; *Shapiro v. Thompson*, 394 U. S. 618; *Carrington v. Rash*, 380 U. S. 89; *Sherbert v. Verner*, 374 U. S. 398; *NAACP v. Alabama*, 357 U. S. 449.

The liberty to marry a person of one's own choosing, *Loving v. Virginia*, 388 U. S. 1; the right of procreation, *Skinner v. Oklahoma*, 316 U. S. 535; the liberty to direct the education of one's children, *Pierce v. Society of Sisters*, 268 U. S. 510, and the privacy of the marital relation, *Griswold v. Connecticut, supra*, are in this category.[5] Only last Term, in *Eisenstadt v. Baird*, 405 U. S. 438, another contraceptive case, we expanded the concept of *Griswold* by saying:

---

5. My Brother STEWART, writing in *Roe v. Wade, supra*, says that our decision in *Griswold* reintroduced substantive due process that had been rejected in *Ferguson v. Skrupa*, 372 U.S. 726. *Skrupa* involved legislation governing a business enterprise; and the Court in that case, as had Mr. Justice Holmes on earlier occasions, rejected the idea that "liberty" within the meaning of the Due Process Clause of the Fourteenth Amendment was a vessel to be filled with one's personal choices of values, whether drawn from the *laissez faire* school, from the socialistic school, or from the technocrats. *Griswold* involved legislation touching on the marital relation and involving the conviction of a licensed physician for giving married people information concerning contraception. There is nothing specific in the Bill of Rights that covers that item. Nor is there anything in the Bill of Rights that, in terms, protects the right of association or the privacy in one's association. Yet we found those rights in the periphery of the First Amendment. *NAACP v. Alabama*, 357 U.S. 449, 462. Other peripheral rights are the right to educate one's children as one chooses, *Pierce v. Society of Sisters*, 268 U.S. 510, and the right to study the German language, *Meyer v. Nebraska*, 262 U.S. 390. These decisions, with all respect, have nothing to do with substantive due process. One may think they are not peripheral to other rights that are expressed in the Bill of Rights. But that is not enough to bring into play the protection of substantive due process.

There are, of course, those who have believed that the reach of due process in the Fourteenth Amendment included all of the Bill of Rights but went further. Such was the view of Mr. Justice Murphy and Mr. Justice Rutledge. *See Adamson v. California*, 332 U.S. 46, 123–24 (dissenting opinion). Perhaps they were right, but it is a bridge that neither I nor those who joined the Court's opinion in *Griswold* crossed.

"It is true that, in *Griswold*, the right of privacy in question inhered in the marital relationship. Yet the marital couple is not an independent entity, with a mind and heart of its own, but an association of two individuals, each with a separate intellectual and emotional makeup. If the right of privacy means anything, it is the right of the individual, married or single, to be free from unwarranted governmental intrusion into matters so fundamentally affecting a person as the decision whether to bear or beget a child."

Id. at 405 U. S. 453.

This right of privacy was called by Mr. Justice Brandeis the right "to be let alone." *Olmstead v. United States,* 277 U. S. 438, 478 (dissenting opinion). That right includes the privilege of an individual to plan his own affairs, for,

"outside areas of plainly harmful conduct, every American is left to shape his own life as he thinks best, do what he pleases, go where he pleases."

Kent v. Dulles, 357 U. S. 116, 126.

Third is the freedom to care for one's health and person, freedom from bodily restraint or compulsion, freedom to walk, stroll, or loaf.

These rights, though fundamental, are likewise subject to regulation on a showing of "compelling state interest." We stated in *Papachristou v. City of Jacksonville,* 405 U. S. 156, 164, that walking, strolling, and wandering "are historically part of the amenities of life as we have known them." As stated in *Jacobson v. Massachusetts,* 197 U. S. 11, 29:

"There is, of course, a sphere within which the individual may assert the supremacy of his own will and rightfully dispute the authority of any human government, especially of any free government existing under a written constitution, to interfere with the exercise of that will."

In *Union Pacific R. Co. v. Botsford,* 141 U. S. 250, 252, the Court said, "The inviolability of the person is as much invaded by a compulsory stripping and exposure as by a blow."

In *Terry v. Ohio,* 392 U. S. 1, 8-9, the Court, in speaking of the Fourth Amendment stated,

"This inestimable right of personal security belongs as much to the citizen on the streets of our cities as to the homeowner closeted in his study to dispose of his secret affairs."

Katz v. United States, 389 U. S. 347, 350, emphasizes that the Fourth Amendment "protects individual privacy against certain kinds of governmental intrusion."

In *Meyer v. Nebraska,* 262 U. S. 390, 399, the Court said:

"Without doubt, [liberty] denotes not merely freedom from bodily restraint, but also the right of the individual to contract, to engage in any of the common occupations of life, to acquire useful knowledge, to marry, establish a home and bring up children, to worship God according to the dictates of his own conscience, and generally to enjoy those privileges long recognized at common law as essential to the orderly pursuit of happiness by free men."

The Georgia statute is at war with the clear message of these cases—that a woman is free to make the basic decision whether to bear an unwanted child. Elaborate argument is hardly necessary to demonstrate that child-birth may deprive a woman of her preferred lifestyle and force upon her a radically different and undesired future. For example, rejected applicants under the Georgia statute are required to endure the discomforts of preg-nancy; to incur the pain, higher mortality rate, and after-effects of child-birth; to abandon educational plans; to sustain loss of income; to forgo the satisfactions of careers; to tax further mental and physical health in provid-ing child care; and, in some cases, to bear the lifelong stigma of unwed motherhood, a badge which may haunt, if not deter, later legitimate family relationships.

II

Such reasoning is, however, only the beginning of the problem. The State has interests to protect. Vaccinations to prevent epidemics are one example, as *Jacobson, supra,* holds. The Court held that compulsory sterilization of imbeciles afflicted with hereditary forms of insanity or imbecility is another. *Buck v. Bell,* 274 U. S. 200. Abortion affects another. While childbirth endan-gers the lives of some women, voluntary abortion at any time and place regardless of medical standards would impinge on a rightful concern of society. The woman's health is part of that concern; as is the life of the fetus after quickening. These concerns justify the State in treating the procedure as a medical one.

One difficulty is that this statute as construed, and applied apparently does not give full sweep to the "psychological, as well as physical wellbeing" of women patients which saved the concept "health" from being void for vagueness in *United States v. Vuitch,* 402 U.S. at 402 U. S. 72. But, apart from that, Georgia's enactment has a constitutional infirmity because, as stated by the District Court, it "limits the number of reasons for which an abortion may be sought." I agree with the holding of the District Court, "This the State may not do, because such action unduly restricts a decision sheltered by the Constitutional right to privacy." 319 F. Supp. at 1056.

The vicissitudes of life produce pregnancies which may be unwanted, or which may impair "health" in the broad *Vuitch* sense of the term, or which may imperil the life of the mother, or which, in the full setting of the case, may create such suffering, dislocations, misery, or tragedy as to make an early abortion the only civilized step to take. These hardships may be properly embraced in the "health" factor of the mother as appraised by a person of insight. Or they may be part of a broader medical judgment based on what is "appropriate" in a given case, though perhaps not "necessary" in a strict sense.

The "liberty" of the mother, though rooted as it is in the Constitution, may be qualified by the State for the reasons we have stated. But where fundamental personal rights and liberties are involved, the corrective legislation must be "narrowly drawn to prevent the supposed evil," *Cantwell v. Connecticut,* 310 U. S. 296, 307, and not be dealt with in an "unlimited and indiscriminate" manner. *Shelton v. Tucker,* 364 U. S. 479, 490. *And see Talley v. California,* 362 U. S. 60. Unless regulatory measures are so confined and are addressed to the specific areas of compelling legislative concern, the police power would become the great leveler of constitutional rights and liberties.

There is no doubt that the State may require abortions to be performed by qualified medical personnel. The legitimate objective of preserving the mother's health clearly supports such laws. Their impact upon the woman's privacy is minimal. But the Georgia statute outlaws virtually all such operations—even in the earliest stages of pregnancy. In light of modern medical evidence suggesting that an early abortion is safer healthwise than childbirth itself, it cannot be seriously urged that so comprehensive a ban is aimed at protecting the woman's health. Rather, this expansive proscription of all abortions along the temporal spectrum can rest only on a public goal of preserving both embryonic and fetal life.

The present statute has struck the balance between the woman's and the State's interests wholly in favor of the latter. I am not prepared to hold that a State may equate, as Georgia has done, all phases of maturation preceding birth. We held in *Griswold* that the States may not preclude spouses from attempting to avoid the joinder of sperm and egg. If this is true, it is difficult to perceive any overriding public necessity which might attach precisely at the moment of conception. As Mr. Justice Clark has said:[6]

---

6. Many studies show that it is safer for a woman to have a medically induced abortion than to bear a child. In the first 11 months of operation of the New York abortion law, the

"To say that life is present at conception is to give recognition to the potential, rather than the actual. The unfertilized egg has life, and if fertilized, it takes on human proportions. But the law deals in reality, not obscurity—the known, rather than the unknown. When sperm meets egg, life may eventually form, but quite often it does not. The law does not deal in speculation. The phenomenon of life takes time to develop, and, until it is actually present, it cannot be destroyed. Its interruption prior to formation would hardly be homicide, and as we have seen, society does not regard it as such. The rites of Baptism are not performed and death certificates are not required when a miscarriage occurs. No prosecutor has ever returned a murder indictment charging the taking of the life of a fetus.[7] This would not be the case if the fetus constituted human life."

In summary, the enactment is overbroad. It is not closely correlated to the aim of preserving prenatal life. In fact, it permits its destruction in several cases, including pregnancies resulting from sex acts in which unmarried females are below the statutory age of consent. At the same time, however, the measure broadly proscribes aborting other pregnancies which may cause severe mental disorders. Additionally, the statute is overbroad because it equates the value of embryonic life immediately after conception with the worth of life immediately before birth.

III

Under the Georgia Act, the mother's physician is not the sole judge as to whether the abortion should be performed. Two other licensed physicians must concur in his judgment.[8] Moreover, the abortion must be performed

---

mortality rate associated with such operations was six per 100,000 operations. Abortion Mortality, 20 Morbidity and Mortality 208, 209 (June 1971) (U.S. Dept. of HEW, Public Health Service). On the other hand, the maternal mortality rate associated with childbirths other than abortions was 18 per 100,000 live births. Tietze, *Mortality with Contraception and Induced Abortion*, 45 STUDIES IN FAMILY PLANNING 6 (1969). *See also* Tietze & Lehfeldt, *Legal Abortion in Eastern Europe*, 175 J.A.M.A. 1149, 1152 (Apr.1961); Kolblova, *Legal Abortion in Czechoslovakia*, 196 J.A.M.A. 371 (Apr. 1968); Mehland, *Combating Illegal Abortion in the Socialist Countries of Europe*, 13 WORLD MED. J. 84 (1966).

7. *Religion, Morality, and Abortion: A Constitutional Appraisal*, 2 LOYOLA L.A. L. REV. 1, 9–10 (1969).

8. In *Keeler v. Superior Court*, 2 Cal. 3d 619, 470 P.2d 617, the California Supreme Court held in 1970 that the California murder statute did not cover the killing of an unborn fetus, even though the fetus be "viable," and that it was beyond judicial power to extend the statute to the killing of an unborn. It held that the child must be "born alive before a charge of homicide can be sustained." *Id.* at 639, 470 P.2d at 630.

in a licensed hospital;[9] and the abortion must be approved in advance by a committee of the medical staff of that hospital.[10]

Physicians, who speak to us in Doe through an *amicus* brief, complain of the Georgia Act's interference with their practice of their profession.

The right of privacy has no more conspicuous place than in the physician-patient relationship, unless it be in the priest-penitent relationship.

It is one thing for a patient to agree that her physician may consult with another physician about her case. It is quite a different matter for the State compulsorily to impose on that physician-patient relationship another layer or, as in this case, still a third layer of physicians. The right of privacy—the right to care for one's health and person and to seek out a physician of one's own choice protected by the Fourteenth Amendment—becomes only a matter of theory, not a reality, when a "multiple physician approval" system is mandated by the State.

The State licenses a physician. If he is derelict or faithless, the procedures available to punish him or to deprive him of his license are well known. He is entitled to procedural due process before professional disciplinary sanctions may be imposed. *See In re Ruffalo*, 390 U. S. 544. Crucial here, however, is state-imposed control over the medical decision whether pregnancy should be interrupted. The good faith decision of the patient's chosen physician is overridden and the final decision passed on to others in whose selection the patient has no part. This is a total destruction of the right of privacy between physician and patient and the intimacy of relation which that entails.

The right to seek advice on one's health and the right to place reliance on the physician of one's choice are basic to Fourteenth Amendment values. We deal with fundamental rights and liberties, which, as already noted, can be contained or controlled only by discretely drawn legislation that preserves the "liberty" and regulates only those phases of the problem of compelling legislative concern. The imposition by the State of group controls over the physician-patient relationship is not made on any medical procedure apart from abortion, no matter how dangerous the medical step may be. The oversight imposed on the physician and patient in abortion cases denies them their "liberty," *viz.*, their right of privacy, without any compelling, discernible state interest.

Georgia has constitutional warrant in treating abortion as a medical problem. To protect the woman's right of privacy, however, the control

---

9. *See* GA. CODE ANN. § 26-1202(b)(3).

10. *See id.* § 26-1202(b)(4).

must be through the physician of her choice and the standards set for his performance.

The protection of the fetus when it has acquired life is a legitimate concern of the State. Georgia's law makes no rational, discernible decision on that score.[11] For under the Code, the developmental stage of the fetus is irrelevant when pregnancy is the result of rape, when the fetus will very likely be born with a permanent defect, or when a continuation of the pregnancy will endanger the life of the mother or permanently injure her health. When life is present is a question we do not try to resolve. While basically a question for medical experts, as stated by Mr. Justice Clark,[12] it is, of course, caught up in matters of religion and morality.

In short, I agree with the Court that endangering the life of the woman or seriously and permanently injuring her health are standards too narrow for the right of privacy that is at stake.

I also agree that the superstructure of medical supervision which Georgia has erected violates the patient's right of privacy inherent in her choice of her own physician.

---

11. *Id.* § 26-1202(b)(5).

12. *See* Rochat, Tyler, & Schoenbucher, An Epidemiological Analysis of Abortion in Georgia, 61 AM. J. OF PUBLIC HEALTH 543 (1971).

Appendix E

Concurring Opinion of Chief Justice Burger[1]
— Doe v. Bolton (1973) —

I agree that, under the Fourteenth Amendment to the Constitution, the abortion statutes of Georgia and Texas impermissibly limit the performance of abortions necessary to protect the health of pregnant women, using the term health in its broadest medical context. *See United States v. Vuitch,* 402 U. S. 62, 71-72 (1971). I am somewhat troubled that the Court has taken notice of various scientific and medical data in reaching its conclusion; however, I do not believe that the Court has exceeded the scope of judicial notice accepted in other contexts.

In oral argument, counsel for the State of Texas informed the Court that early abortion procedures were routinely permitted in certain exceptional cases, such as nonconsensual pregnancies resulting from rape and incest. In the face of a rigid and narrow statute, such as that of Texas, no one in these circumstances should be placed in a posture of dependence on a prosecutorial policy or prosecutorial discretion. Of course, States must have broad power, within the limits indicated in the opinions, to regulate the subject of abortions, but where the consequences of state intervention are so severe, uncertainty must be avoided as much as possible. For my part, I would be inclined to allow a State to require the certification of two physicians to support an abortion, but the Court holds otherwise. I do not believe that such a procedure is unduly burdensome, as are the complex steps of the Georgia statute, which require as many as six doctors and the use of a hospital certified by the JCAH.

---

1. The opinion is available at 410 U.S. 179, 207 (1973). Justice Burger's opinion in *Doe* also applied to *Roe v. Wade.*

I do not read the Court's holdings today as having the sweeping consequences attributed to them by the dissenting Justices; the dissenting views
discount the reality that the vast majority of physicians observe the standards
of their profession, and act only on the basis of carefully deliberated medical judgments relating to life and health. Plainly, the Court today rejects any
claim that the Constitution requires abortions on demand.

Appendix F

Concurring Opinion of Justice Stewart[1]
— *Roe v. Wade* (1973) —

In 1963, this Court, in *Ferguson v. Skrupa*, 372 U.S. 726, purported to sound the death knell for the doctrine of substantive due process, a doctrine under which many state laws had in the past been held to violate the Fourteenth Amendment. As Mr. Justice Black's opinion for the Court in *Skrupa* put it:

> "We have returned to the original constitutional proposition that courts do not substitute their social and economic beliefs for the judgment of legislative bodies, who are elected to pass laws."

Id. at 730.[2]

Barely two years later, in *Griswold v. Connecticut*, 381 U.S. 479, the Court held a Connecticut birth control law unconstitutional. In view of what had been so recently said in *Skrupa*, the Court's opinion in *Griswold* understandably did its best to avoid reliance on the Due Process Clause of the Fourteenth Amendment as the ground for decision. Yet the Connecticut law did not violate any provision of the Bill of Rights, nor any other specific provision of the Constitution.[3] So it was clear to me then, and it is equally clear

---

1. The opinion is available at 410 U.S. 113, 167 (1973).
2. Only Mr. Justice Harlan failed to join the Court's opinion, 372 U.S. 733.
3. There is no constitutional right of privacy, as such.

> "[The Fourth] Amendment protects individual privacy against certain kinds of governmental intrusion, but its protections go further, and often have nothing to do with privacy at all. Other provisions of the Constitution protect personal privacy from other forms of governmental invasion. But the protection of a person's General right to privacy—his right to be let alone by other people—is, like the protection of his property and of his very life, left largely to the law of the individual States."

Katz v. United States, 389 U.S. 347, 350–51 (footnotes omitted).

to me now, that the *Griswold* decision can be rationally understood only as a holding that the Connecticut statute substantively invaded the "liberty" that is protected by the Due Process Clause of the Fourteenth Amendment.[4] As so understood, *Griswold* stands as one in a long line of pre-*Skrupa* cases decided under the doctrine of substantive due process, and I now accept it as such.

"In a Constitution for a free people, there can be no doubt that the meaning of *liberty' must be broad indeed."* *Board of Regents v. Roth,* 408 U.S. 564, *572. The Constitution nowhere mentions a specific right of personal choice in matters of marriage and family life, but the "liberty" protected by the Due Process Clause of the Fourteenth Amendment covers more than those freedoms explicitly named in the Bill of Rights. See Schware v. Board of Bar Examiners,* 353 U.S. 232, *238-239; Pierce v. Society of Sisters,* 268 U.S. 510, *534-535; Meyer v. Nebraska,* 262 U.S. 390, *399-400. Cf. Shapiro v. Thompson,* 394 U.S. 618, *629-630; United States v. Guest,* 383 U.S. 745, *757-758; Carrington v. Rash,* 380 U.S. 89, *96; Aptheker v. Secretary of State,* 378 U.S. 500, *505; Kent v. Dulles,* 357 U.S. 116, *127; Bolling v. Sharpe,* 347 U.S. 497, *499-500; Truax v. Raich,* 239 U.S. 33, *41.*

As Mr. Justice Harlan once wrote:

"[T]he full scope of the liberty guaranteed by the Due Process Clause cannot be found in or limited by the precise terms of the specific guarantees elsewhere provided in the Constitution. This 'liberty' is not a series of isolated points pricked out in terms of the taking of property; the freedom of speech, press, and religion; the right to keep and bear arms; the freedom from unreasonable searches and seizures; and so on. It is a rational continuum which, broadly speaking, includes a freedom from all substantial arbitrary impositions and purposeless restraints . . . and which also recognizes, what a reasonable and sensitive judgment must, that certain interests require particularly careful scrutiny of the state needs asserted to justify their abridgment."

Poe v. Ullman, 367 U.S. 497, 543 (opinion dissenting from dismissal of appeal) (citations omitted). In the words of Mr. Justice Frankfurter,

---

4. This was also clear to Mr. Justice Black, 381 U.S. at 507 (dissenting opinion); to Mr. Justice Harlan, 381 U.S. at 499 (opinion concurring in the judgment); and to MR. JUSTICE WHITE, 381 U.S. at 502 (opinion concurring in the judgment). *See also* Mr. Justice Harlan's thorough and thoughtful opinion dissenting from dismissal of the appeal in *Poe v. Ullman,* 367 U.S. 497, 522.

"Great concepts like . . . 'liberty' . . . were purposely left to gather meaning from experience. For they relate to the whole domain of social and economic fact, and the statesmen who founded this Nation knew too well that only a stagnant society remains unchanged."

National Mutual Ins. Co. v. Tidewater Transfer Co., 337 U.S. 582, 646 (dissenting opinion).

Several decisions of this Court make clear that freedom of personal choice in matters of marriage and family life is one of the liberties protected by the Due Process Clause of the Fourteenth Amendment. *Loving v. Virginia*, 388 U.S. 1, 12; *Griswold v. Connecticut, supra; Pierce v. Society of Sisters, supra; Meyer v. Nebraska, supra. See also Prince v. Massachusetts*, 321 U.S. 158, 166; *Skinner v. Oklahoma*, 316 U.S. 535, 541. As recently as last Term, in *Eisenstadt v. Baird*, 405 U.S. 438, 453, we recognized

"the right of the *individual*, married or single, to be free from unwarranted governmental intrusion into matters so fundamentally affecting a person as the decision whether to bear or beget a child."

That right necessarily includes the right of a woman to decide whether or not to terminate her pregnancy.

"Certainly the interests of a woman in giving of her physical and emotional self during pregnancy and the interests that will be affected throughout her life by the birth and raising of a child are of a far greater degree of significance and personal intimacy than the right to send a child to private school protected in *Pierce v. Society of Sisters*, 268 U.S. 510 (1925), or the right to teach a foreign language protected in *Meyer v. Nebraska*, 262 U.S. 390 (1923)."

Abele v. Markle, 351 F. Supp. 224, 227 (Conn.1972).

Clearly, therefore, the Court today is correct in holding that the right asserted by Jane Roe is embraced within the personal liberty protected by the Due Process Clause of the Fourteenth Amendment.

It is evident that the Texas abortion statute infringes that right directly. Indeed, it is difficult to imagine a more complete abridgment of a constitutional freedom than that worked by the inflexible criminal statute now in force in Texas. The question then becomes whether the state interests advanced to justify this abridgment can survive the "particularly careful scrutiny" that the Fourteenth Amendment here requires.

The asserted state interests are protection of the health and safety of the pregnant woman, and protection of the potential future human life within her. These are legitimate objectives, amply sufficient to permit a State to regulate abortions as it does other surgical procedures, and perhaps sufficient to permit a State to regulate abortions more stringently, or even to prohibit them in the late stages of pregnancy. But such legislation is not before us, and I think the Court today has thoroughly demonstrated that these state interests cannot constitutionally support the broad abridgment of personal liberty worked by the existing Texas law. Accordingly, I join the Court's opinion holding that that law is invalid under the Due Process Clause of the Fourteenth Amendment.

Appendix G

Dissenting Opinion of Justice White[1]
— *Doe v. Bolton* (1973) —

At the heart of the controversy in these cases are those recurring pregnancies that pose no danger whatsoever to the life or health of the mother but are, nevertheless, unwanted for any one or more of a variety of reasons—convenience, family planning, economics, dislike of children, the embarrassment of illegitimacy, etc. The common claim before us is that for any one of such reasons, or for no reason at all, and without asserting or claiming any threat to life or health, any woman is entitled to an abortion at her request if she is able to find a medical advisor willing to undertake the procedure.

The Court for the most part sustains this position: During the period prior to the time the fetus becomes viable, the Constitution of the United States values the convenience, whim, or caprice of the pregnant woman more than the life or potential life of the fetus; the Constitution, therefore, guarantees the right to an abortion as against any state law or policy seeking to protect the fetus from an abortion not prompted by more compelling reasons of the mother.

With all due respect, I dissent. I find nothing in the language or history of the Constitution to support the Court's judgments. The Court simply fashions and announces a new constitutional right for pregnant women and, with scarcely any reason or authority for its action, invests that right with sufficient substance to override most existing state abortion statutes. The upshot is that the people and the legislatures of the 50 States are constitutionally disentitled to weigh the relative importance of the continued existence and development of the fetus, on the one hand, against a spectrum of possible impacts on the mother, on the other hand.

---

1. The opinion is available at 410 U.S. 179, 221 (1973). Justice White's opinion in *Doe* applied also to *Roe v. Wade.*

As an exercise of raw judicial power, the Court perhaps has authority to do what it does today; but in my view its judgment is an improvident and extravagant exercise of the power of judicial review that the Constitution extends to this Court.

The Court apparently values the convenience of the pregnant woman more than the continued existence and development of the life or potential life that she carries. Whether or not I might agree with that marshaling of values, I can in no event join the Court's judgment because I find no constitutional warrant for imposing such an order of priorities on the people and legislatures of the States. In a sensitive area such as this, involving as it does issues over which reasonable men may easily and heatedly differ, I cannot accept the Court's exercise of its clear power of choice by interposing a constitutional barrier to state efforts to protect human life and by investing women and doctors with the constitutionally protected right to exterminate it. This issue, for the most part, should be left with the people and to the political processes the people have devised to govern their affairs.

It is my view, therefore, that the Texas statute is not constitutionally infirm because it denies abortions to those who seek to serve only their convenience rather than to protect their life or health. Nor is this plaintiff, who claims no threat to her mental or physical health, entitled to assert the possible rights of those women whose pregnancy assertedly implicates their health. This, together with *United States v. Vuitch*, 402 U.S. 62 (1971), dictates reversal of the judgment of the District Court.

Likewise, because Georgia may constitutionally forbid abortions to pregnant women who, like the plaintiff in this case, do not fall within the reach of s 26—1202(a) of its criminal code, I have no occasion, and the District Court had none, to consider the constitutionality of the procedural requirements of the Georgia statute as applied to those pregnancies posing substantial hazards to either life or health. I would reverse the judgment of the District Court in the Georgia case.

Appendix H

Dissenting Opinion of Justice Rehnquist[1]
— *Roe v. Wade* (1973) —

The Court's opinion brings to the decision of this troubling question both extensive historical fact and a wealth of legal scholarship. While the opinion thus commands my respect, I find myself nonetheless in fundamental disagreement with those parts of it that invalidate the Texas statute in question, and therefore dissent.

[Section I addresses standing and has been redacted]

II

. . . I have difficulty in concluding, as the Court does, that the right of "privacy" is involved in this case. Texas, by the statute here challenged, bars the performance of a medical abortion by a licensed physician on a plaintiff such as Roe. A transaction resulting in an operation such as this is not "private" in the ordinary usage of that word. Nor is the "privacy" that the Court finds here even a distant relative of the freedom from searches and seizures protected by the Fourth Amendment to the Constitution, which the Court has referred to as embodying a right to privacy. *Katz v. United States*, 389 U.S. 347 (1967).

If the Court means by the term "privacy" no more than that the claim of a person to be free from unwanted state regulation of consensual transactions may be a form of "liberty" protected by the Fourteenth Amendment, there is no doubt that similar claims have been upheld in our earlier decisions on the basis of that liberty. I agree with the statement of MR. JUSTICE STEWART in his concurring opinion that the "liberty," against deprivation of which without due process the Fourteenth Amendment protects, embraces more than the rights found in the Bill of Rights. But that liberty is not guaranteed absolutely against deprivation, only against deprivation

---

1. The full opinion is available at 410 U.S. 113, 171 (1973).

without due process of law. The test traditionally applied in the area of social and economic legislation is whether or not a law such as that challenged has a rational relation to a valid state objective. *Williamson v. Lee Optical Co.*, 348 U.S. 483, 491 (1955). The Due Process Clause of the Fourteenth Amendment undoubtedly does place a limit, albeit a broad one, on legislative power to enact laws such as this. If the Texas statute were to prohibit an abortion even where the mother's life is in jeopardy, I have little doubt that such a statute would lack a rational relation to a valid state objective under the test stated in *Williamson, supra.* But the Court's sweeping invalidation of any restrictions on abortion during the first trimester is impossible to justify under that standard, and the conscious weighing of competing factors that the Court's opinion apparently substitutes for the established test is far more appropriate to a legislative judgment than to a judicial one.

The Court eschews the history of the Fourteenth Amendment in its reliance on the "compelling state interest" test. *See Weber v. Aetna Casualty & Surety Co.*, 406 U.S. 164, 179 (1972) (dissenting opinion). But the Court adds a new wrinkle to this test by transposing it from the legal considerations associated with the Equal Protection Clause of the Fourteenth Amendment to this case arising under the Due Process Clause of the Fourteenth Amendment. Unless I misapprehend the consequences of this transplanting of the "compelling state interest test," the Court's opinion will accomplish the seemingly impossible feat of leaving this area of the law more confused than it found it. While the Court's opinion quotes from the dissent of Mr. Justice Holmes in *Lochner v. New York*, 198 U.S. 45, 74 (1905), the result it reaches is more closely attuned to the majority opinion of Mr. Justice Peckham in that case. As in *Lochner* and similar cases applying substantive due process standards to economic and social welfare legislation, the adoption of the compelling state interest standard will inevitably require this Court to examine the legislative policies and pass on the wisdom of these policies in the very process of deciding whether a particular state interest put forward may or may not be "compelling." The decision here to break pregnancy into three distinct terms and to outline the permissible restrictions the State may impose in each one, for example, partakes more of judicial legislation than it does of a determination of the intent of the drafters of the Fourteenth Amendment.

The fact that a majority of the States reflecting, after all, the majority sentiment in those States, have had restrictions on abortions for at least a century is a strong indication, it seems to me, that the asserted right to an abortion is not "so rooted in the traditions and conscience of our people as to be ranked as fundamental," *Snyder v. Massachusetts*, 291 U.S. 97, 105

(1934). Even today, when society's views on abortion are changing, the very existence of the debate is evidence that the "right" to an abortion is not so universally accepted as the appellant would have us believe.

To reach its result, the Court necessarily has had to find within the scope of the Fourteenth Amendment a right that was apparently completely unknown to the drafters of the Amendment. As early as 1821, the first state law dealing directly with abortion was enacted by the Connecticut Legislature. Conn.Stat., Tit. 22, §§ 14, 16. By the time of the adoption of the Fourteenth Amendment in 1868, there were at least 36 laws enacted by state or territorial legislatures limiting abortion.[2] While many States have amended

---

2. Jurisdictions having enacted abortion laws prior to the adoption of the Fourteenth Amendment in 1868:

1. Alabama—Ala. Acts, c. 6, § 2 (1840).
2. Arizona—Howell Code, c. 10, § 45 (1865).
3. Arkansas—Ark.Rev.Stat., c. 44, div. III, Art. II, § 6 (1838).
4. California—Cal.Sess.Laws, c. 99, § 45, p. 233 (1849-1850).
5. Colorado (Terr.)—Colo. Gen.Laws of Terr. of Colo. 1st Sess., § 42, pp 296–297 (1861).
6. Connecticut—Conn.Stat., Tit. 20, §§ 14, 16 (1821). By 1868, this statute had been replaced by another abortion law. Conn.Pub. Acts, c. 71, §§ 1, 2, p. 65 (1860).
7. Florida—Fla.Acts 1st Sess., c. 1637, subc. 3, §§ 10, 11, subc. 8, §§ 9, 10, 11 (1868), as amended, now Fla.Stat.Ann. §§ 782.09, 782.10, 797.01, 797.02, 782.16 (1965).
8. Georgia Pen.Code, 4th Div., § 20 (1833).
9. Kingdom of Hawaii—Hawaii Pen.Code, c. 12, §§ 1, 2, 3 (1850).
10. Idaho (Terr.)—Idaho (Terr.) Laws, Crimes and Punishments §§ 33, 34, 42, pp. 441, 443 (1863).
11. Illinois—Ill.Rev. Criminal Code §§ 40, 41, 46, pp. 130, 131 (1827). By 1868, this statute had been replaced by a subsequent enactment. Ill.Pub.Laws §§ 1, 2, 3, p. 89 (1867).
12. Indiana—Ind.Rev.Stat. §§ 1, 3, p. 224 (1838). By 1868, this statute had been superseded by a subsequent enactment. Ind.Laws, c. LXXXI, § 2 (1859).
13. Iowa (Terr.)—Iowa (Terr.) Stat., 1st Legis., 1st Sess., § 18, p. 145 (1838). By 1868, this statute had been superseded by a subsequent enactment. Iowa (Terr.) Rev.Stat., c. 49, §§ 10, 13 (1843).
14. Kansas (Terr.)—Kan. (Terr.) Stat., c. 48, §§ 9, 10, 39 (1855). By 1868, this statute had been superseded by a subsequent enactment. Kan. (Terr.) Laws, c. 28, §§ 9, 10, 37 (1859).
15. Louisiana—La.Rev.Stat., Crimes and Offenses § 24, p. 138 (1856).
16. Maine—Me.Rev.Stat., c. 160, §§ 11, 12, 13, 14 (1840).
17. Maryland—Md.Laws, c. 179, § 2, p. 315 (1868).
18. Massachusetts—Mass. Acts & Resolves, c. 27 (1845).
19. Michigan—Mich.Rev.Stat., c. 153, §§ 32, 33, 34, p. 662 (1846).
20. Minnesota (Terr.)—Minn. (Terr.) Rev.Stat., c. 100, § 10, 11, p. 493 (1851).
21. Mississippi—Miss.Code, c. 64, §§ 8, 9, p. 958 (1848).

or updated their laws, 21 of the laws on the books in 1868 remain in effect today.[3] Indeed, the Texas statute struck down today was, as the majority notes, first enacted in 1857, and "has remained substantially unchanged to the present time." *Ante* at 119.

---

22. Missouri—Mo.Rev.Stat., Art. II, §§ 9, 10, 36, pp. 168, 172 (1835).
23. Montana (Terr.)—Mont. (Terr.) Laws, Criminal Practice Acts § 41, p. 184 (1864).
24. Nevada (Terr.)—Nev. (Terr.) Laws, c. 28, § 42, p. 63 (1861).
25. New Hampshire—N.H.Laws, c. 743, § 1, p. 708 (1848).
26. New Jersey—N.J.Laws, p. 266 (1849).
27. New York—N.Y.Rev.Stat., pt. 4, c. 1, Tit 2, §§ 8, 9, pp. 12-13 (1828). By 1868, this statute had been superseded. N.Y.Laws, c. 260, §§ 1, pp. 285-286 (1845); N.Y.Laws, c. 22, § 1, p. 19 (1846).
28. Ohio—Ohio Gen.Stat. §§ 111(1), 112(2), p. 252 (1841).
29. Oregon—Ore. Gen.Laws, Crim.Code, c. 43, § 509, p. 528 (1845-1864).
30. Pennsylvania—Pa.Laws No. 374, §§ 87, 88, 89 (1860).
31. Texas—Tex. Gen.Stat. Dig., c. VII, Arts. 531–536, p. 524 (Oldham & White 1859).
32. Vermont—Vt. Acts No. 33, § 1 (1846). By 1868, this statute had been amended. Vt.Acts No. 57, §§ 1, 3 (1867).
33. Virginia—Va.Acts, Tit. II, c. 3, § 9, p. 96 (1848).
34. Washington (Terr.)—Wash. (Terr.) Stats., c. II, §§ 37, 38, p. 81 (1854).
35. West Virginia—*See* Va. Acts., Tit. II, c. 3, § 9, p. 96 (1848); W.Va.Const., Art. XI, par. 8 (1863).
36. Wisconsin—Wis.Rev.Stat., c. 133, §§ 10, 11 (1849). By 1868, this statute had been superseded. Wis.Rev.Stat., c. 164, §§ 10, 11; c. 169, §§ 58, 59 (1858).
3. Abortion laws in effect in 1868 and still applicable as of August, 1970:

1. Arizona (1865).
2. Connecticut (1860).
3. Florida (1868).
4. Idaho (1863).
5. Indiana (1838).
6. Iowa (1843)
7. Maine (1840).
8. Massachusetts (1845).
9. Michigan (1846).
10. Minnesota (1851).
11. Missouri (1835).
12. Montana (1864).
13. Nevada (1861).
14. New Hampshire (1848).
15. New Jersey (1849).
16. Ohio (1841).
17. Pennsylvania (1860).
18. Texas (1859).
19. Vermont (1867).
20. West Virginia (1863).
21. Wisconsin (1858).

There apparently was no question concerning the validity of this provision or of any of the other state statutes when the Fourteenth Amendment was adopted. The only conclusion possible from this history is that the drafters did not intend to have the Fourteenth Amendment withdraw from the States the power to legislate with respect to this matter.

III

Even if one were to agree that the case that the Court decides were here, and that the enunciation of the substantive constitutional law in the Court's opinion were proper, the actual disposition of the case by the Court is still difficult to justify. The Texas statute is struck down *in toto*, even though the Court apparently concedes that, at later periods of pregnancy Texas might impose these self-same statutory limitations on abortion. My understanding of past practice is that a statute found to be invalid as applied to a particular plaintiff, but not unconstitutional as a whole, is not simply "struck down" but is, instead, declared unconstitutional as applied to the fact situation before the Court. *Yick Wo v. Hopkins*, 118 U.S. 356 (1886); *Street v. New York*, 394 U.S. 576 (1969).

For all of the foregoing reasons, I respectfully dissent.

Appendix I

Opinion of Justice O'Connor[1]
— *Planned Parenthood of Southeastern Pa. v. Casey* (1992) —

I

Liberty finds no refuge in a jurisprudence of doubt. Yet 19 years after our holding that the Constitution protects a woman's right to terminate her pregnancy in its early stages, *Roe v. Wade*, 410 U.S. 113 (1973), that definition of liberty is still questioned. Joining the respondents as *amicus curiae*, the United States, as it has done in five other cases in the last decade, again asks us to overrule *Roe*. See Brief for Respondents 104-117; Brief for United States as *Amicus Curiae* 8.

At issue in these cases are five provisions of the Pennsylvania Abortion Control Act of 1982, as amended in 1988 and 1989. 18 Pa. Cons. Stat. §§ 3203-3220 (1990). Relevant portions of the Act are set forth in the Appendix. *Infra*, at 902. The Act requires that a woman seeking an abortion give her informed consent prior to the abortion procedure, and specifies that she be provided with certain information at least 24 hours before the abortion is performed. § 3205. For a minor to obtain an abortion, the Act requires the informed consent of one of her parents, but provides for a judicial bypass option if the minor does not wish to or cannot obtain a parent's consent. § 3206. Another provision of the Act requires that, unless certain exceptions apply, a married woman seeking an abortion must sign a statement indicating that she has notified her husband of her intended abortion. § 3209. The Act exempts compliance with these three requirements in

---

1. Justice O'Connor, joined by Justices Kennedy and Souter, announced the judgment of the Court and delivered the opinion of the Court with respect to Parts I, II, III, V-A,V-C, and VI; an opinion with respect to Part V-E, in which Justice Stevens joined; and an opinion with respect to Parts IV, V-B, and V-D. Portions of the opinion have been redacted for brevity. The full opinion is available at 505 U.S. 833 (1992).

the event of a "medical emergency," which is defined in § 3203 of the Act. See §§ 3203, 3205(a), 3206(a), 3209(c). In addition to the above provisions regulating the performance of abortions, the Act imposes certain reporting requirements on facilities that provide abortion services. §§ 3207(b), 3214(a), 3214(f).

[Discussion of proceedings in the court of appeals redacted.]

After considering the fundamental constitutional questions resolved by *Roe*, principles of institutional integrity, and the rule of *stare decisis*, we are led to conclude this: the essential holding of *Roe v. Wade* should be retained and once again reaffirmed.

It must be stated at the outset and with clarity that *Roe*'s essential holding, the holding we reaffirm, has three parts. First is a recognition of the right of the woman to choose to have an abortion before viability and to obtain it without undue interference from the State. Before viability, the State's interests are not strong enough to support a prohibition of abortion or the imposition of a substantial obstacle to the woman's effective right to elect the procedure. Second is a confirmation of the State's power to restrict abortions after fetal viability, if the law contains exceptions for pregnancies which endanger the woman's life or health. And third is the principle that the State has legitimate interests from the outset of the pregnancy in protecting the health of the woman and the life of the fetus that may become a child. These principles do not contradict one another; and we adhere to each.

II

Constitutional protection of the woman's decision to terminate her pregnancy derives from the Due Process Clause of the Fourteenth Amendment. It declares that no State shall "deprive any person of life, liberty, or property, without due process of law." The controlling word in the cases before us is "liberty." Although a literal reading of the Clause might suggest that it governs only the procedures by which a State may deprive persons of liberty, for at least 105 years, since *Mugler v. Kansas*, 123 U.S. 623, 660-661 (1887), the Clause has been understood to contain a substantive component as well, one "barring certain government actions regardless of the fairness of the procedures used to implement them." *Daniels v. Williams*, 474 U.S. 327, 331 (1986). As Justice Brandeis (joined by Justice Holmes) observed, "[d]espite arguments to the contrary which had seemed to me persuasive, it is settled that the due process clause of the Fourteenth Amendment applies to matters of substantive law as well as to matters of procedure. Thus all fundamental rights comprised within the term liberty are protected by the

Federal Constitution from invasion by the States." *Whitney v. California*, 274 U.S. 357, 373 (1927) (concurring opinion). "[T]he guaranties of due process, though having their roots in Magna Carta's *'per legem terrae'* and considered as procedural safeguards 'against executive usurpation and tyranny', have in this country 'become bulwarks also against arbitrary legislation.'" *Poe v. Ullman*, 367 U.S. 497, 541 (1961) (Harlan, J., dissenting from dismissal on jurisdictional grounds) (quoting *Hurtado v. California*, 110 U.S. 516, 532 (1884)).

The most familiar of the substantive liberties protected by the Fourteenth Amendment are those recognized by the Bill of Rights. We have held that the Due Process Clause of the Fourteenth Amendment incorporates most of the Bill of Rights against the States. See, *e.g.*, *Duncan v. Louisiana*, 391 U.S. 145, 147-148 (1968). It is tempting, as a means of curbing the discretion of federal judges, to suppose that liberty encompasses no more than those rights already guaranteed to the individual against federal interference by the express provisions of the first eight Amendments to the Constitution. See *Adamson v. California*, 332 U.S. 46, 68-92 (1947) (Black, J., dissenting). But of course this Court has never accepted that view.

It is also tempting, for the same reason, to suppose that the Due Process Clause protects only those practices, defined at the most specific level, that were protected against government interference by other rules of law when the Fourteenth Amendment was ratified. See *Michael H. v. Gerald D.*, 491 U.S. 110, 127-128, n. 6 (1989) (opinion of SCALIA, J.). But such a view would be inconsistent with our law. It is a promise of the Constitution that there is a realm of personal liberty which the government may not enter. We have vindicated this principle before. Marriage is mentioned nowhere in the Bill of Rights and interracial marriage was illegal in most States in the 19th century, but the Court was no doubt correct in finding it to be an aspect of liberty protected against state interference by the substantive component of the Due Process Clause in *Loving v. Virginia*, 388 U.S. 1, 12 (1967) (relying, in an opinion for eight Justices, on the Due Process Clause). Similar examples may be found in *Turner v. Safley*, 482 U.S. 78, 94-99 (1987); in *Carey v. Population Services International*, 431 U.S. 678, 684-686 (1977); in *Griswold v. Connecticut*, 381 U.S. 479, 481-482 (1965), as well as in the separate opinions of a majority of the Members of the Court in that case, *id.*, at 486-488 (Goldberg, J., joined by Warren, C. J., and Brennan, J., concurring) (expressly relying on due process), *id.*, at 500-502 (Harlan, J., concurring in judgment) (same), *id.*, at 502-507 (WHITE, J., concurring in judgment) (same); in *Pierce v. Society of Sisters*, 268 U.S. 510, 534-535 (1925); and in *Meyer v. Nebraska*, 262 U.S. 390, 399-403 (1923).

Neither the Bill of Rights nor the specific practices of States at the time of the adoption of the Fourteenth Amendment marks the outer limits of the substantive sphere of liberty which the Fourteenth Amendment protects. See U.S. Const., Amdt. 9. As the second Justice Harlan recognized:

"[T]he full scope of the liberty guaranteed by the Due Process Clause cannot be found in or limited by the precise terms of the specific guarantees elsewhere provided in the Constitution. This 'liberty' is not a series of isolated points pricked out in terms of the taking of property; the freedom of speech, press, and religion; the right to keep and bear arms; the freedom from unreasonable searches and seizures; and so on. It is a rational continuum which, broadly speaking, includes a freedom from all substantial arbitrary impositions and purposeless restraints, . . . and which also recognizes, what a reasonable and sensitive judgment must, that certain interests require particularly careful scrutiny of the state needs asserted to justify their abridgment." *Poe* v. *Ullman, supra,* at 543 (opinion dissenting from dismissal on jurisdictional grounds).

Justice Harlan wrote these words in addressing an issue the full Court did not reach in *Poe v. Ullman,* but the Court adopted his position four Terms later in *Griswold v. Connecticut, supra.* In *Griswold,* we held that the Constitution does not permit a State to forbid a married couple to use contraceptives. That same freedom was later guaranteed, under the Equal Protection Clause, for unmarried couples. See *Eisenstadt v. Baird,* 405 U.S. 438 (1972). Constitutional protection was extended to the sale and distribution of contraceptives in *Carey v. Population Services International, supra.* It is settled now, as it was when the Court heard arguments in *Roe v. Wade,* that the Constitution places limits on a State's right to interfere with a person's most basic decisions about family and parenthood, see *Carey v. Population Services International, supra; Moore v. East Cleveland,* 431 U.S. 494 (1977); *Eisenstadt v. Baird, supra; Loving v. Virginia, supra; Griswold v. Connecticut, supra; Skinner v. Oklahoma ex rel. Williamson,* 316 U.S. 535 (1942); *Pierce v. Society of Sisters, supra; Meyer v. Nebraska, supra,* as well as bodily integrity, see, e. g., *Washington v. Harper,* 494 U.S. 210, 221-222 (1990); *Winston v. Lee,* 470 U.S. 753 (1985); *Rochin v. California,* 342 U.S. 165 (1952).

The inescapable fact is that adjudication of substantive due process claims may call upon the Court in interpreting the Constitution to exercise that same capacity which by tradition courts always have exercised: reasoned judgment. Its boundaries are not susceptible of expression as a simple rule. That does not mean we are free to invalidate state policy choices with which we disagree; yet neither does it permit us to shrink from the duties of our office. As Justice Harlan observed:

"Due process has not been reduced to any formula; its content cannot be determined by reference to any code. The best that can be said is that through the course of this Court's decisions it has represented the balance which our Nation, built upon postulates of respect for the liberty of the individual, has struck between that liberty and the demands of organized society. If the supplying of content to this Constitutional concept has of necessity been a rational process, it certainly has not been one where judges have felt free to roam where unguided speculation might take them. The balance of which I speak is the balance struck by this country, having regard to what history teaches are the traditions from which it developed as well as the traditions from which it broke. That tradition is a living thing. A decision of this Court which radically departs from it could not long survive, while a decision which builds on what has survived is likely to be sound. No formula could serve as a substitute, in this area, for judgment and restraint." *Poe v. Ullman*, 367 U.S., at 542 (opinion dissenting from dismissal on jurisdictional grounds).

See also *Rochin v. California, supra*, at 171-172 (Frankfurter, J., writing for the Court) ("To believe that this judicial exercise of judgment could be avoided by freezing 'due process of law' at some fixed stage of time or thought is to suggest that the most important aspect of constitutional adjudication is a function for inanimate machines and not for judges").

Men and women of good conscience can disagree, and we suppose some always shall disagree, about the profound moral and spiritual implications of terminating a pregnancy, even in its earliest stage. Some of us as individuals find abortion offensive to our most basic principles of morality, but that cannot control our decision. Our obligation is to define the liberty of all, not to mandate our own moral code. The underlying constitutional issue is whether the State can resolve these philosophic questions in such a definitive way that a woman lacks all choice in the matter, except perhaps in those rare circumstances in which the pregnancy is itself a danger to her own life or health, or is the result of rape or incest.

It is conventional constitutional doctrine that where reasonable people disagree the government can adopt one position or the other. See, *e. g.*, *Ferguson v. Skrupa*, 372 U.S. 726 (1963); *Williamson v. Lee Optical of Okla., Inc.*, 348 U.S. 483 (1955). That theorem, however, assumes a state of affairs in which the choice does not intrude upon a protected liberty. Thus, while some people might disagree about whether or not the flag should be saluted, or disagree about the proposition that it may not be defiled, we have ruled that a State may not compel or enforce one view or the other. See *West Virginia Bd. of Ed. v. Barnette*, 319 U.S. 624 (1943); *Texas v. Johnson*, 491 U.S. 397 (1989).

Our law affords constitutional protection to personal decisions relating
to marriage, procreation, contraception, family relationships, child rearing,
and education. *Carey v. Population Services International*, 431 U.S., at 685. Our
cases recognize "the right of the *individual*, married or single, to be free from
unwarranted governmental intrusion into matters so fundamentally affecting a person as the decision whether to bear or beget a child." *Eisenstadt v.
Baird, supra*, at 453 (emphasis in original). Our precedents "have respected
the private realm of family life which the state cannot enter." *Prince v. Massachusetts*, 321 U.S. 158, 166 (1944). These matters, involving the most intimate and personal choices a person may make in a lifetime, choices central
to personal dignity and autonomy, are central to the liberty protected by the
Fourteenth Amendment. At the heart of liberty is the right to define one's
own concept of existence, of meaning, of the universe, and of the mystery
of human life. Beliefs about these matters could not define the attributes of
personhood were they formed under compulsion of the State.

These considerations begin our analysis of the woman's interest in
terminating her pregnancy but cannot end it, for this reason: though the
abortion decision may originate within the zone of conscience and belief,
it is more than a philosophic exercise. Abortion is a unique act. It is an act
fraught with consequences for others: for the woman who must live with
the implications of her decision; for the persons who perform and assist
in the procedure; for the spouse, family, and society which must confront
the knowledge that these procedures exist, procedures some deem nothing
short of an act of violence against innocent human life; and, depending on
one's beliefs, for the life or potential life that is aborted. Though abortion
is conduct, it does not follow that the State is entitled to proscribe it in all
instances. That is because the liberty of the woman is at stake in a sense
unique to the human condition and so unique to the law. The mother who
carries a child to full term is subject to anxieties, to physical constraints, to
pain that only she must bear. That these sacrifices have from the beginning
of the human race been endured by woman with a pride that ennobles her
in the eyes of others and gives to the infant a bond of love cannot alone be
grounds for the State to insist she make the sacrifice. Her suffering is too
intimate and personal for the State to insist, without more, upon its own
vision of the woman's role, however dominant that vision has been in the
course of our history and our culture. The destiny of the woman must be
shaped to a large extent on her own conception of her spiritual imperatives
and her place in society.

It should be recognized, moreover, that in some critical respects the abortion decision is of the same character as the decision to use contraception,

to which *Griswold v. Connecticut, Eisenstadt v. Baird,* and *Carey v. Population Services International* afford constitutional protection. We have no doubt as to the correctness of those decisions. They support the reasoning in *Roe* relating to the woman's liberty because they involve personal decisions concerning not only the meaning of procreation but also human responsibility and respect for it. As with abortion, reasonable people will have differences of opinion about these matters. One view is based on such reverence for the wonder of creation that any pregnancy ought to be welcomed and carried to full term no matter how difficult it will be to provide for the child and ensure its well-being. Another is that the inability to provide for the nurture and care of the infant is a cruelty to the child and an anguish to the parent. These are intimate views with infinite variations, and their deep, personal character underlay our decisions in *Griswold, Eisenstadt,* and *Carey.* The same concerns are present when the woman confronts the reality that, perhaps despite her attempts to avoid it, she has become pregnant.

It was this dimension of personal liberty that *Roe* sought to protect, and its holding invoked the reasoning and the tradition of the precedents we have discussed, granting protection to substantive liberties of the person. *Roe* was, of course, an extension of those cases and, as the decision itself indicated, the separate States could act in some degree to further their own legitimate interests in protecting prenatal life. The extent to which the legislatures of the States might act to outweigh the interests of the woman in choosing to terminate her pregnancy was a subject of debate both in *Roe* itself and in decisions following it.

While we appreciate the weight of the arguments made on behalf of the State in the cases before us, arguments which in their ultimate formulation conclude that *Roe* should be overruled, the reservations any of us may have in reaffirming the central holding of *Roe* are outweighed by the explication of individual liberty we have given combined with the force of *stare decisis.* We turn now to that doctrine.

III

A

The obligation to follow precedent begins with necessity, and a contrary necessity marks its outer limit. With Cardozo, we recognize that no judicial system could do society's work if it eyed each issue afresh in every case that raised it. See B. Cardozo, The Nature of the Judicial Process 149 (1921). Indeed, the very concept of the rule of law underlying our own Constitution requires such continuity over time that a respect for precedent is, by definition, indispensable. See Powell, Stare Decisis and Judicial Restraint, 1991 Journal of Supreme Court History 13, 16. At the other extreme, a different necessity would make itself felt if a prior judicial ruling should come to be seen so clearly as error that its enforcement was for that very reason doomed.

Even when the decision to overrule a prior case is not, as in the rare, latter instance, virtually foreordained, it is common wisdom that the rule of *stare decisis* is not an "inexorable command," and certainly it is not such in every constitutional case, see *Burnet v. Coronado Oil & Gas Co.*, 285 U.S. 393, 405-411 (1932) (Brandeis, J., dissenting). See also *Payne v. Tennessee*, 501 U.S. 808, 842 (1991) (SOUTER, J., joined by KENNEDY, J., concurring); *Arizona v. Rumsey*, 467 U.S. 203, 212 (1984). Rather, when this Court reexamines a prior holding, its judgment is customarily informed by a series of prudential and pragmatic considerations designed to test the consistency of overruling a prior decision with the ideal of the rule of law, and to gauge the respective costs of reaffirming and overruling a prior case. Thus, for example, we may ask whether the rule has proven to be intolerable simply in defying practical workability, *Swift & Co. v. Wickham*, 382 U.S. 111, 116 (1965); whether the rule is subject to a kind of reliance that would lend a special hardship to the consequences of overruling and add inequity to the cost of repudiation, *e. g., United States v. Title Ins. & Trust Co.*, 265 U.S. 472, 486 (1924); whether related principles of law have so far developed as to have left the old rule no more than a remnant of abandoned doctrine, see *Patterson v. McLean Credit Union*, 491 U.S. 164, 173-174 (1989); or whether facts have so changed, or come to be seen so differently, as to have robbed the old rule of significant application or justification, *e. g., Burnet, supra,* at 412 (Brandeis, J., dissenting).

So in this case we may enquire whether *Roe*'s central rule has been found unworkable; whether the rule's limitation on state power could be removed without serious inequity to those who have relied upon it or significant damage to the stability of the society governed by it; whether the law's growth in the intervening years has left *Roe*'s central rule a doctrinal anachronism discounted by society; and whether *Roe*'s premises of fact have so far changed in the ensuing two decades as to render its central holding somehow irrelevant or unjustifiable in dealing with the issue it addressed.

1

Although *Roe* has engendered opposition, it has in no sense proven "unworkable," see *Garcia v. San Antonio Metropolitan Transit Authority,* 469

U.S. 528, 546 (1985), representing as it does a simple limitation beyond which a state law is unenforceable. While *Roe* has, of course, required judicial assessment of state laws affecting the exercise of the choice guaranteed against government infringement, and although the need for such review will remain as a consequence of today's decision, the required determinations fall within judicial competence.

2

[The discussion of "reliance" as a factor in *stare decisis* has been redacted.]

3

No evolution of legal principle has left *Roe*'s doctrinal footings weaker than they were in 1973. No development of constitutional law since the case was decided has implicitly or explicitly left *Roe* behind as a mere survivor of obsolete constitutional thinking.

It will be recognized, of course, that *Roe* stands at an intersection of two lines of decisions, but in whichever doctrinal category one reads the case, the result for present purposes will be the same. The *Roe* Court itself placed its holding in the succession of cases most prominently exemplified by *Griswold v. Connecticut*, 381 U.S. 479 (1965). See *Roe*, 410 U.S., at 152-153. When it is so seen, *Roe* is clearly in no jeopardy, since subsequent constitutional developments have neither disturbed, nor do they threaten to diminish, the scope of recognized protection accorded to the liberty relating to intimate relationships, the family, and decisions about whether or not to beget or bear a child. See, *e. g.*, *Carey v. Population Services International*, 431 U.S. 678 (1977); *Moore v. East Cleveland*, 431 U.S. 494 (1977).

Roe, however, may be seen not only as an exemplar of *Griswold* liberty but as a rule (whether or not mistaken) of personal autonomy and bodily integrity, with doctrinal affinity to cases recognizing limits on governmental power to mandate medical treatment or to bar its rejection. If so, our cases since *Roe* accord with *Roe*'s view that a State's interest in the protection of life falls short of justifying any plenary override of individual liberty claims. *Cruzan v. Director, Mo. Dept. of Health*, 497 U.S. 261, 278 (1990); cf., *e. g.*, *Riggins v. Nevada*, 504 U.S. 127, 135 (1992); *Washington v. Harper*, 494 U.S. 210 (1990); see also, *e. g.*, *Rochin v. California*, 342 U.S. 165 (1952); *Jacobson v. Massachusetts*, 197 U.S. 11, 24-30 (1905).

Finally, one could classify *Roe* as *sui generis*. If the case is so viewed, then there clearly has been no erosion of its central determination. The original holding resting on the concurrence of seven Members of the Court in 1973 was expressly affirmed by a majority of six in 1983, see *Akron v. Akron Center for Reproductive Health, Inc.*, 462 U.S. 416 *(Akron I)*, and by a majority of five in 1986, see *Thornburgh v. American College of Obstetricians and Gynecologists*, 476 U.S. 747, expressing adherence to the constitutional ruling despite legislative efforts in some States to test its limits. More recently, in *Webster v. Reproductive Health Services*, 492 U.S. 490 (1989), although two of the present authors questioned the trimester framework in a way consistent with our judgment today, see *id.*, at 518 (REHNQUIST, C. J., joined by WHITE and KENNEDY, JJ.); *id.*, at 529 (O'CONNOR, J., concurring in part and concurring in judgment), a majority of the Court either decided to reaffirm or declined to address the constitutional validity of the central holding of *Roe*. See *Webster*, 492 U.S., at 521 (REHNQUIST, C. J., joined by WHITE and KENNEDY, JJ.); *id.*, at 525-526 (O'CONNOR, J., concurring in part and concurring in judgment); *id.*, at 537, 553 (BLACKMUN, J., joined by Brennan and Marshall, JJ., concurring in part and dissenting in part); *id.*, at 561-563 (STEVENS, J., concurring in part and dissenting in part).

Nor will courts building upon *Roe* be likely to hand down erroneous decisions as a consequence. Even on the assumption that the central holding of *Roe* was in error, that error would go only to the strength of the state interest in fetal protection, not to the recognition afforded by the Constitution to the woman's liberty. The latter aspect of the decision fits comfortably within the framework of the Court's prior decisions, including *Skinner v. Oklahoma ex rel. Williamson*, 316 U.S. 535 (1942); *Griswold, supra; Loving v. Virginia*, 388 U.S. 1 (1967); and *Eisenstadt v. Baird*, 405 U.S. 438 (1972), the holdings of which are "not a series of isolated points," but mark a "rational continuum." *Poe v. Ullman*, 367 U.S., at 543 (Harlan, J., dissenting). As we described in *Carey v. Population Services International, supra*, the liberty which encompasses those decisions

> "includes 'the interest in independence in making certain kinds of important decisions.' While the outer limits of this aspect of [protected liberty] have not been marked by the Court, it is clear that among the decisions that an individual may make without unjustified government interference are personal decisions 'relating to marriage, procreation, contraception, family relationships, and child rearing and education.'" 431 U.S., at 684-685 (citations omitted).

The soundness of this prong of the *Roe* analysis is apparent from a consideration of the alternative. If indeed the woman's interest in deciding whether to bear and beget a child had not been recognized as in *Roe*, the State might as readily restrict a woman's right to choose to carry a pregnancy to term as to terminate it, to further asserted state interests in population control, or eugenics, for example. Yet *Roe* has been sensibly relied upon to counter any such suggestions. *E. g.*, *Arnold v. Board of Education of Escambia County, Ala.*, 880 F.2d 305, 311 (CA11 1989) (relying upon *Roe* and concluding that government officials violate the Constitution by coercing a minor to have an abortion); *Avery v. County of Burke*, 660 F.2d 111, 115 (CA4 1981) (county agency inducing teenage girl to undergo unwanted sterilization on the basis of misrepresentation that she had sickle cell trait); see also *In re Quinlan*, 70 N. J. 10, 355 A. 2d 647 (relying on *Roe* in finding a right to terminate medical treatment), cert. denied *sub nom. Garger v. New Jersey*, 429 U.S. 922 (1976)). In any event, because *Roe*'s scope is confined by the fact of its concern with postconception potential life, a concern otherwise likely to be implicated only by some forms of contraception protected independently under *Griswold* and later cases, any error in *Roe* is unlikely to have serious ramifications in future cases.

4

We have seen how time has overtaken some of *Roe*'s factual assumptions: advances in maternal health care allow for abortions safe to the mother later in pregnancy than was true in 1973, see *Akron I, supra*, at 429, n. 11, and advances in neonatal care have advanced viability to a point somewhat earlier. Compare *Roe*, 410 U.S., at 160, with *Webster, supra*, at 515-516 (opinion of REHNQUIST, C. J.); see *Akron I*, 462 U.S., at 457, and n. 5 (O'CONNOR, J., dissenting). But these facts go only to the scheme of time limits on the realization of competing interests, and the divergences from the factual premises of 1973 have no bearing on the validity of *Roe*'s central holding, that viability marks the earliest point at which the State's interest in fetal life is constitutionally adequate to justify a legislative ban on nontherapeutic abortions. The soundness or unsoundness of that constitutional judgment in no sense turns on whether viability occurs at approximately 28 weeks, as was usual at the time of *Roe*, at 23 to 24 weeks, as it sometimes does today, or at some moment even slightly earlier in pregnancy, as it may if fetal respiratory capacity can somehow be enhanced in the future. Whenever it may occur, the attainment of viability may continue to serve as the critical fact, just as it has done since *Roe* was decided; which is to say that no change in *Roe*'s factual underpinning has left its central holding obsolete, and none supports an argument for overruling it.

5

The sum of the precedential enquiry to this point shows *Roe*'s underpinnings unweakened in any way affecting its central holding. While it has

engendered disapproval, it has not been unworkable. An entire generation has come of age free to assume *Roe*'s concept of liberty in defining the
capacity of women to act in society, and to make reproductive decisions;
no erosion of principle going to liberty or personal autonomy has left *Roe*'s
central holding a doctrinal remnant; *Roe* portends no developments at odds
with other precedent for the analysis of personal liberty; and no changes of
fact have rendered viability more or less appropriate as the point at which
the balance of interests tips. Within the bounds of normal *stare decisis* analysis, then, and subject to the considerations on which it customarily turns,
the stronger argument is for affirming *Roe*'s central holding, with whatever
degree of personal reluctance any of us may have, not for overruling it.

B

In a less significant case, *stare decisis* analysis could, and would, stop at
the point we have reached. But the sustained and widespread debate *Roe*
has provoked calls for some comparison between that case and others of
comparable dimension that have responded to national controversies and
taken on the impress of the controversies addressed. Only two such decisional lines from the past century present themselves for examination, and
in each instance the result reached by the Court accorded with the principles we apply today.

The first example is that line of cases identified with *Lochner v. New
York*, 198 U.S. 45 (1905), which imposed substantive limitations on legislation limiting economic autonomy in favor of health and welfare regulation, adopting, in Justice Holmes's view, the theory of laissez-faire. *Id.*, at
75 (dissenting opinion). The *Lochner* decisions were exemplified by *Adkins
v. Children's Hospital of District of Columbia*, 261 U.S. 525 (1923), in which
this Court held it to be an infringement of constitutionally protected liberty
of contract to require the employers of adult women to satisfy minimum
wage standards. Fourteen years later, *West Coast Hotel Co. v. Parrish*, 300 U.S.
379 (1937), signaled the demise of *Lochner* by overruling *Adkins*. In the
meantime, the Depression had come and, with it, the lesson that seemed
unmistakable to most people by 1937, that the interpretation of contractual
freedom protected in *Adkins* rested on fundamentally false factual assumptions about the capacity of a relatively unregulated market to satisfy minimal levels of human welfare. See *West Coast Hotel Co., supra*, at 399. As Justice
Jackson wrote of the constitutional crisis of 1937 shortly before he came on
the bench: "The older world of *laissez faire* was recognized everywhere outside the Court to be dead." The Struggle for Judicial Supremacy 85 (1941).

The facts upon which the earlier case had premised a constitutional resolution of social controversy had proven to be untrue, and history's demonstration of their untruth not only justified but required the new choice of constitutional principle that *West Coast Hotel* announced. Of course, it was true that the Court lost something by its misperception, or its lack of prescience, and the Court-packing crisis only magnified the loss; but the clear demonstration that the facts of economic life were different from those previously assumed warranted the repudiation of the old law.

The second comparison that 20th century history invites is with the cases employing the separate-but-equal rule for applying the Fourteenth Amendment's equal protection guarantee. They began with *Plessy v. Ferguson*, 163 U.S. 537 (1896), holding that legislatively mandated racial segregation in public transportation works no denial of equal protection, rejecting the argument that racial separation enforced by the legal machinery of American society treats the black race as inferior. The *Plessy* Court considered "the underlying fallacy of the plaintiff's argument to consist in the assumption that the enforced separation of the two races stamps the colored race with a badge of inferiority. If this be so, it is not by reason of anything found in the act, but solely because the colored race chooses to put that construction upon it." *Id.*, at 551. Whether, as a matter of historical fact, the Justices in the *Plessy* majority believed this or not, see *id.*, at 557, 562 (Harlan, J., dissenting), this understanding of the implication of segregation was the stated justification for the Court's opinion. But this understanding of the facts and the rule it was stated to justify were repudiated in *Brown v. Board of Education*, 347 U.S. 483 (1954) *(Brown I)*. As one commentator observed, the question before the Court in *Brown* was "whether discrimination inheres in that segregation which is imposed by law in the twentieth century in certain specific states in the American Union. And that question has meaning and can find an answer only on the ground of history and of common knowledge about the facts of life in the times and places aforesaid." Black, The Lawfulness of the Segregation Decisions, 69 Yale L.J. 421, 427 (1960)

. . . .

West Coast Hotel and *Brown* each rested on facts, or an understanding of facts, changed from those which furnished the claimed justifications for the earlier constitutional resolutions. . . . In constitutional adjudication as elsewhere in life, changed circumstances may impose new obligations, and the thoughtful part of the Nation could accept each decision to overrule a prior case as a response to the Court's constitutional duty.

Because the cases before us present no such occasion it could be seen as no such response. Because neither the factual underpinnings of *Roe*'s central holding nor our understanding of it has changed (and because no other indication of weakened precedent has been shown), the Court could not pretend to be reexamining the prior law with any justification beyond a present doctrinal disposition to come out differently from the Court of 1973. To overrule prior law for no other reason than that would run counter to the view repeated in our cases, that a decision to overrule should rest on some special reason over and above the belief that a prior case was wrongly decided. See, *e. g., Mitchell v. W T. Grant Co.*, 416 U.S. 600, 636 (1974) (Stewart, J., dissenting) ("A basic change in the law upon a ground no firmer than a change in our membership invites the popular misconception that this institution is little different from the two political branches of the Government. No misconception could do more lasting injury to this Court and to the system of law which it is our abiding mission to serve"); *Mapp v. Ohio*, 367 U.S. 643, 677 (1961) (Harlan, J., dissenting).

C

The examination of the conditions justifying the repudiation of *Adkins* by *West Coast Hotel* and *Plessy* by *Brown* is enough to suggest the terrible price that would have been paid if the Court had not overruled as it did. In the present cases, however, as our analysis to this point makes clear, the terrible price would be paid for overruling. . . .

. . . .

In two circumstances, however, the Court would almost certainly fail to receive the benefit of the doubt in overruling prior cases. There is, first, a point beyond which frequent overruling would overtax the country's belief in the Court's good faith. . . . . .

. . . Where, in the performance of its judicial duties, the Court decides a case in such a way as to resolve the sort of intensely divisive controversy reflected in *Roe* and those rare, comparable cases, its decision has a dimension that the resolution of the normal case does not carry. It is the dimension present whenever the Court's interpretation of the Constitution calls the contending sides of a national controversy to end their national division by accepting a common mandate rooted in the Constitution.

The Court is not asked to do this very often, having thus addressed the Nation only twice in our lifetime, in the decisions of *Brown* and *Roe*. But when the Court does act in this way, its decision requires an equally rare precedential force to counter the inevitable efforts to overturn it and to thwart its implementation. Some of those efforts may be mere unprincipled emotional reactions; others may proceed from principles worthy of profound respect. But whatever the premises of opposition may be, only the most convincing justification under accepted standards of precedent could suffice to demonstrate that a later decision overruling the first was anything but a surrender to political pressure, and an unjustified repudiation of the principle on which the Court staked its authority in the first instance. So to overrule under fire in the absence of the most compelling reason to reexamine a watershed decision would subvert the Court's legitimacy beyond any serious question. Cf. *Brown v. Board of Education*, 349 U.S. 294, 300 (1955) (*Brown II*) ("[I]t should go without saying that the vitality of thee] constitutional principles [announced in *Brown I,]* cannot be allowed to yield simply because of disagreement with them").

The country's loss of confidence in the Judiciary would be underscored by an equally certain and equally reasonable condemnation for another failing in overruling unnecessarily and under pressure. . . . .

. . . .

The Court's duty in the present cases is clear. In 1973, it confronted the already-divisive issue of governmental power to limit personal choice to undergo abortion, for which it provided a new resolution based on the due process guaranteed by the Fourteenth Amendment. Whether or not a new social consensus is developing on that issue, its divisiveness is no less today than in 1973, and pressure to overrule the decision, like pressure to retain it, has grown only more intense. A decision to overrule *Roe*'s essential holding under the existing circumstances would address error, if error there was, at the cost of both profound and unnecessary damage to the Court's legitimacy, and to the Nation's commitment to the rule of law. It is therefore imperative to adhere to the essence of *Roe*'s original decision, and we do so today.

IV

From what we have said so far it follows that it is a constitutional liberty of the woman to have some freedom to terminate her pregnancy. We conclude that the basic decision in *Roe* was based on a constitutional analysis which we cannot now repudiate. The woman's liberty is not so unlimited, however, that from the outset the State cannot show its concern for the life of the unborn, and at a later point in fetal development the State's interest in life has sufficient force so that the right of the woman to terminate the pregnancy can be restricted.

That brings us, of course, to the point where much criticism has been directed at *Roe*, a criticism that always inheres when the Court draws a specific rule from what in the Constitution is but a general standard. We conclude, however, that the urgent claims of the woman to retain the ultimate control over her destiny and her body, claims implicit in the meaning of liberty, require us to perform that function. Liberty must not be extinguished for want of a line that is clear. And it falls to us to give some real substance to the woman's liberty to determine whether to carry her pregnancy to full term.

We conclude the line should be drawn at viability, so that before that time the woman has a right to choose to terminate her pregnancy. We adhere to this principle for two reasons. First, as we have said, is the doctrine of *stare decisis*. Any judicial act of line-drawing may seem somewhat arbitrary, but *Roe* was a reasoned statement, elaborated with great care. . . .

The second reason is that the concept of viability, as we noted in *Roe*, is the time at which there is a realistic possibility of maintaining and nourishing a life outside the womb, so that the independent existence of the second life can in reason and all fairness be the object of state protection that now overrides the rights of the woman. See *Roe v. Wade*, 410 U.S., at 163. Consistent with other constitutional norms, legislatures may draw lines which appear arbitrary without the necessity of offering a justification. But courts may not. We must justify the lines we draw. And there is no line other than viability which is more workable. To be sure, as we have said, there may be some medical developments that affect the precise point of viability, see *supra*, at 860, but this is an imprecision within tolerable limits given that the medical community and all those who must apply its discoveries will continue to explore the matter. The viability line also has, as a practical matter, an element of fairness. In some broad sense it might be said that a woman who fails to act before viability has consented to the State's intervention on behalf of the developing child.

The woman's right to terminate her pregnancy before viability is the most central principle of *Roe v. Wade*. It is a rule of law and a component of liberty we cannot renounce.

. . . .

Yet it must be remembered that *Roe v. Wade* speaks with clarity in establishing not only the woman's liberty but also the State's "important and legitimate interest in potential life." *Roe, supra*, at 163. That portion of the decision in *Roe* has been given too little acknowledgment and implementation by the Court in its subsequent cases. Those cases decided that any regulation touching upon the abortion decision must survive strict scrutiny, to be sustained only if drawn in narrow terms to further a compelling state interest. See, *e. g., Akron I, supra*, at 427. Not all of the cases decided under that formulation can be reconciled with the holding in *Roe* itself that the State has legitimate interests in the health of the woman and in protecting the potential life within her. In resolving this tension, we choose to rely upon *Roe*, as against the later cases. *Roe* established a trimester framework to govern abortion regulations. Under this elaborate but rigid construct, almost no regulation at all is permitted during the first trimester of pregnancy; regulations designed to protect the woman's health, but not to further the State's interest in potential life, are permitted during the second trimester; and during the third trimester, when the fetus is viable, prohibitions are permitted provided the life or health of the mother is not at stake. *Roe, supra,* at 163-166. Most of our cases since *Roe* have involved the application of rules derived from the trimester framework. See, *e. g., Thornburgh v. American College of Obstetricians and Gynecologists, supra; Akron I, supra.*

The trimester framework no doubt was erected to ensure that the woman's right to choose not become so subordinate to the State's interest in promoting fetal life that her choice exists in theory but not in fact. We do not agree, however, that the trimester approach is necessary to accomplish this objective. A framework of this rigidity was unnecessary and in its later interpretation sometimes contradicted the State's permissible exercise of its powers.

Though the woman has a right to choose to terminate or continue her pregnancy before viability, it does not at all follow that the State is prohibited from taking steps to ensure that this choice is thoughtful and informed. Even in the earliest stages of pregnancy, the State may enact rules and regulations designed to encourage her to know that there are philosophic and social arguments of great weight that can be brought to bear in favor of continuing the pregnancy to full term and that there are procedures and institutions to allow adoption of unwanted children as well as a certain degree of state assistance if the mother chooses to raise the child herself. "[T]he Constitution does not forbid a State or city, pursuant to democratic processes, from expressing a preference for normal childbirth." *Webster v. Reproductive Health Services,* 492 U.S., at 511 (opinion of the Court) (quoting *Poelker v. Doe,* 432 U.S. 519, 521 (1977)). It follows that States are free to enact laws to provide a reasonable framework for a woman to make a decision that has such profound and lasting meaning. This, too, we find consistent with *Roe*'s central premises, and indeed the inevitable consequence of our holding that the State has an interest in protecting the life of the unborn.

We reject the trimester framework, which we do not consider to be part of the essential holding of *Roe*. See *Webster v. Reproductive Health Services,* 492

U.S., at 518 (opinion of REHNQUIST, C. J.); *id.*, at 529 (O'CONNOR, J., concurring in part and concurring in judgment) (describing the trimester framework as "problematic"). Measures aimed at ensuring that a woman's choice contemplates the consequences for the fetus do not necessarily interfere with the right recognized in *Roe*, although those measures have been found to be inconsistent with the rigid trimester framework announced in that case. A logical reading of the central holding in *Roe* itself, and a necessary reconciliation of the liberty of the woman and the interest of the State in promoting prenatal life, require, in our view, that we abandon the trimester framework as a rigid prohibition on all previability regulation aimed at the protection of fetal life. The trimester framework suffers from these basic flaws: in its formulation it misconceives the nature of the pregnant woman's interest; and in practice it undervalues the State's interest in potential life, as recognized in *Roe*.

As our jurisprudence relating to all liberties save perhaps abortion has recognized, not every law which makes a right more difficult to exercise is, *ipso facto*, an infringement of that right. An example clarifies the point. We have held that not every ballot access limitation amounts to an infringement of the right to vote. Rather, the States are granted substantial flexibility in establishing the framework within which voters choose the candidates for whom they wish to vote. *Anderson v. Celebrezze*, 460 U.S. 780, 788 (1983); *Norman v. Reed*, 502 U.S. 279 (1992).

The abortion right is similar. Numerous forms of state regulation might have the incidental effect of increasing the cost or decreasing the availability of medical care, whether for abortion or any other medical procedure. The fact that a law which serves a valid purpose, one not designed to strike at the right itself, has the incidental effect of making it more difficult or more expensive to procure an abortion cannot be enough to invalidate it. Only where state regulation imposes an undue burden on a woman's ability to make this decision does the power of the State reach into the heart of the liberty protected by the Due Process Clause. See *Hodgson v. Minnesota*, 497 U.S. 417, 458-459 (1990) (O'CONNOR, J., concurring in part and concurring in judgment in part); *Ohio v. Akron Center for Reproductive Health*, 497 U.S. 502, 519-520 (1990) (*Akron II*) (opinion of KENNEDY, J.); *Webster v. Reproductive Health Services, supra*, at 530 (O'CONNOR, J., concurring in part and concurring in judgment); *Thornburgh v. American College of Obstetricians and Gynecologists*, 476 U.S., at 828 (O'CONNOR, J., dissenting); *Simopoulos v. Virginia*, 462 U.S. 506, 520 (1983) (O'CONNOR, J., concurring in part and concurring in judgment); *Planned Parenthood Assn. of Kansas City, Mo., Inc. v. Ashcroft*, 462 U.S. 476, 505 (1983) (O'CONNOR, J., concurring in judgment in part and dissenting in part); *Akron I*, 462 U.S., at 464 (O'CONNOR, J., joined by WHITE and REHNQUIST, JJ., dissenting); *Bellotti v. Baird*, 428 U.S. 132, 147 (1976) (*Bellotti I*).

For the most part, the Court's early abortion cases adhered to this view. In *Maher v. Roe*, 432 U.S. 464, 473-474 (1977), the Court explained: "*Roe* did not declare an unqualified 'constitutional right to an abortion,' as the District Court seemed to think. Rather, the right protects the woman from unduly burdensome interference with her freedom to decide whether to terminate her pregnancy." See also *Doe v. Bolton*, 410 U.S. 179, 198 (1973) ("[T]he interposition of the hospital abortion committee is unduly restrictive of the patient's rights"); *Bellotti I, supra*, at 147 (State may not "impose undue burdens upon a minor capable of giving an informed consent"); *Harris v. McRae*, 448 U.S. 297, 314 (1980) (citing *Maher, supra*). Cf. *Carey v. Population Services International*, 431 U.S., at 688 ("[T]he same test must be applied to state regulations that burden an individual's right to decide to prevent conception or terminate pregnancy by substantially limiting access to the means of effectuating that decision as is applied to state statutes that prohibit the decision entirely").

These considerations of the nature of the abortion right illustrate that it is an overstatement to describe it as a right to decide whether to have an abortion "without interference from the State." *Planned Parenthood of Central Mo. v. Danforth*, 428 U.S. 52, 61 (1976). All abortion regulations interfere to some degree with a woman's ability to decide whether to terminate her pregnancy. It is, as a consequence, not surprising that despite the protestations contained in the original *Roe* opinion to the effect that the Court was not recognizing an absolute right, 410 U.S., at 154-155, the Court's experience applying the trimester framework has led to the striking down of some abortion regulations which in no real sense deprived women of the ultimate decision. Those decisions went too far because the right recognized by *Roe* is a right "to be free from unwarranted governmental intrusion into matters so fundamentally affecting a person as the decision whether to bear or beget a child." *Eisenstadt v. Baird*, 405 U.S., at 453. Not all governmental intrusion is of necessity unwarranted; and that brings us to the other basic flaw in the trimester framework: even in *Roe*'s terms, in practice it undervalues the State's interest in the potential life within the woman.

Roe v. Wade was express in its recognition of the State's "important and legitimate interest[s] in preserving and protecting the health of the pregnant woman [and] in protecting the potentiality of human life." 410 U.S., at 162. The trimester framework, however, does not fulfill *Roe*'s own promise that the State has an interest in protecting fetal life or potential life.

Roe began the contradiction by using the trimester framework to forbid any regulation of abortion designed to advance that interest before viability. *Id.*, at 163. Before viability, *Roe* and subsequent cases treat all governmental attempts to influence a woman's decision on behalf of the potential life within her as unwarranted. This treatment is, in our judgment, incompatible with the recognition that there is a substantial state interest in potential life throughout pregnancy. Cf. *Webster,* 492 U.S., at 519 (opinion of REHNQUIST, C. J.); *Akron I, supra,* at 461 (O'CONNOR, J., dissenting).

The very notion that the State has a substantial interest in potential life leads to the conclusion that not all regulations must be deemed unwarranted. Not all burdens on the right to decide whether to terminate a pregnancy will be undue. In our view, the undue burden standard is the appropriate means of reconciling the State's interest with the woman's constitutionally protected liberty.

The concept of an undue burden has been utilized by the Court as well as individual Members of the Court, including two of us, in ways that could be considered inconsistent. See, *e. g., Hodgson v. Minnesota, supra,* at 459-461 (O'CONNOR, J., concurring in part and concurring in judgment); *Akron II, supra,* at 519-520 (opinion of KENNEDY, J.); *Thornburgh v. American College of Obstetricians and Gynecologists, supra,* at 828-829 (O'CONNOR, J., dissenting); *Akron I, supra,* at 461-466 (O'CONNOR, J., dissenting); *Harris v. McRae, supra,* at 314; *Maher v. Roe, supra,* at 473; *Beal v. Doe,* 432 U.S. 438, 446 (1977); *Bellotti I, supra,* at 147. Because we set forth a standard of general application to which we intend to adhere, it is important to clarify what is meant by an undue burden.

A finding of an undue burden is a shorthand for the conclusion that a state regulation has the purpose or effect of placing a substantial obstacle in the path of a woman seeking an abortion of a nonviable fetus. A statute with this purpose is invalid because the means chosen by the State to further the interest in potential life must be calculated to inform the woman's free choice, not hinder it. And a statute which, while furthering the interest in potential life or some other valid state interest, has the effect of placing a substantial obstacle in the path of a woman's choice cannot be considered a permissible means of serving its legitimate ends. To the extent that the opinions of the Court or of individual Justices use the undue burden standard in a manner that is inconsistent with this analysis, we set out what in our view should be the controlling standard. Cf. *McCleskey v. Zant,* 499 U.S. 467, 489 (1991) (attempting "to define the doctrine of abuse of the writ with more precision" after acknowledging tension among earlier cases). In our considered judgment, an undue burden is an unconstitutional burden.

See *Akron II*, 497 U.S., at 519-520 (opinion of KENNEDY, J.). Understood another way, we answer the question, left open in previous opinions discussing the undue burden formulation, whether a law designed to further the State's interest in fetal life which imposes an undue burden on the woman's decision before fetal viability could be constitutional. See, *e. g., Akron I*, 462 U.S., at 462-463 (O'CONNOR, J., dissenting). The answer is no.

Some guiding principles should emerge. What is at stake is the woman's right to make the ultimate decision, not a right to be insulated from all others in doing so. Regulations which do no more than create a structural mechanism by which the State, or the parent or guardian of a minor, may express profound respect for the life of the unborn are permitted, if they are not a substantial obstacle to the woman's exercise of the right to choose. See *infra*, at 899-900 (addressing Pennsylvania's parental consent requirement). Unless it has that effect on her right of choice, a state measure designed to persuade her to choose childbirth over abortion will be upheld if reasonably related to that goal. Regulations designed to foster the health of a woman seeking an abortion are valid if they do not constitute an undue burden.

Even when jurists reason from shared premises, some disagreement is inevitable. Compare *Hodgson*, 497 U.S., at 482-497 (KENNEDY, J., concurring in judgment in part and dissenting in part), with *id.*, at 458-460 (O'CONNOR, J., concurring in part and concurring in judgment in part). That is to be expected in the application of any legal standard which must accommodate life's complexity. We do not expect it to be otherwise with respect to the undue burden standard. We give this summary:

(a) To protect the central right recognized by *Roe v. Wade* while at the same time accommodating the State's profound interest in potential life, we will employ the undue burden analysis as explained in this opinion. An undue burden exists, and therefore a provision of law is invalid, if its purpose or effect is to place a substantial obstacle in the path of a woman seeking an abortion before the fetus attains viability.

(b) We reject the rigid trimester framework of *Roe* v. *Wade*. To promote the State's profound interest in potential life, throughout pregnancy the State may take measures to ensure that the woman's choice is informed, and measures designed to advance this interest will not be invalidated as long as their purpose is to persuade the woman to choose childbirth over abortion. These measures must not be an undue burden on the right.

(c) As with any medical procedure, the State may enact regulations to further the health or safety of a woman seeking an abortion. Unnecessary health regulations that have the purpose or effect of presenting a substantial obstacle to a woman seeking an abortion impose an undue burden on the right.

(d) Our adoption of the undue burden analysis does not disturb the central holding of *Roe v. Wade*, and we reaffirm that holding. Regardless of whether exceptions are made for particular circumstances, a State may not prohibit any woman from making the ultimate decision to terminate her pregnancy before viability.

(e) We also reaffirm *Roe*'s holding that "subsequent to viability, the State in promoting its interest in the potentiality of human life may, if it chooses, regulate, and even proscribe, abortion except where it is necessary, in appropriate medical judgment, for the preservation of the life or health of the mother." *Roe v. Wade*, 410 U.S., at 164-165.

These principles control our assessment of the Pennsylvania statute, and we now turn to the issue of the validity of its challenged provisions.

V

The Court of Appeals applied what it believed to be the undue burden standard and upheld each of the provisions except for the husband notification requirement. We agree generally with this conclusion, but refine the undue burden analysis in accordance with the principles articulated above. We now consider the separate statutory sections at issue.

A

Because it is central to the operation of various other requirements, we begin with the statute's definition of medical emergency. Under the statute, a medical emergency is

> "[t]hat condition which, on the basis of the physician's good faith clinical judgment, so complicates the medical condition of a pregnant woman as to necessitate the immediate abortion of her pregnancy to avert her death or for which a delay will create serious risk of substantial and irreversible impairment of a major bodily function." 18 Pa. Cons. Stat. § 3203 (1990).

Petitioners argue that the definition is too narrow, contending that it forecloses the possibility of an immediate abortion despite some significant health risks. If the contention were correct, we would be required to invalidate the restrictive operation of the provision, for the essential holding of *Roe* forbids a State to interfere with a woman's choice to undergo an abortion procedure if continuing her pregnancy would constitute a threat to her health. 410 U.S., at 164. See also *Harris v. McRae*, 448 U.S., at 316.

The District Court found that there were three serious conditions which would not be covered by the statute: preeclampsia, inevitable abortion, and premature ruptured membrane. 744 F. Supp., at 1378. Yet, as the Court of Appeals observed, 947 F. 2d, at 700-701, it is undisputed that under some circumstances each of these conditions could lead to an illness with substantial and irreversible consequences. While the definition could be interpreted in an unconstitutional manner, the Court of Appeals construed the phrase "serious risk" to include those circumstances. *Id.*, at 701. It stated: "[W]e read the medical emergency exception as intended by the Pennsylvania legislature to assure that compliance with its abortion regulations would not in any way pose a significant threat to the life or health of a woman." *Ibid.* As we said in *Brockett v. Spokane Arcades, Inc.*, 472 U.S. 491, 499-500 (1985): "Normally, . . . we defer to the construction of a state statute given it by the lower federal courts." Indeed, we have said that we will defer to lower court interpretations of state law unless they amount to "plain" error. *Palmer v. Hoffman*, 318 U.S. 109, 118 (1943). This "refiect[s] our belief that district courts and courts of appeals are better schooled in and more able to interpret the laws of their respective States.'" *Frisby v. Schultz*, 487 U.S. 474, 482 (1988) (citation omitted). We adhere to that course today, and conclude that, as construed by the Court of Appeals, the medical emergency definition imposes no undue burden on a woman's abortion right.

B

We next consider the informed consent requirement. 18 Pa. Cons. Stat. § 3205 (1990). Except in a medical emergency, the statute requires that at least 24 hours before performing an abortion a physician inform the woman of the nature of the procedure, the health risks of the abortion and of childbirth, and the "probable gestational age of the unborn child." The physician or a qualified nonphysician must inform the woman of the availability of printed materials published by the State describing the fetus and providing information about medical assistance for childbirth, information about child support from the father, and a list of agencies which provide adoption and other services as alternatives to abortion. An abortion may not be performed unless the woman certifies in writing that she has been informed of the availability of these printed materials and has been provided them if she chooses to view them.

Our prior decisions establish that as with any medical procedure, the State may require a woman to give her written informed consent to an abortion. See *Planned Parenthood of Central Mo. v. Danforth*, 428 U.S., at 67. In this respect, the statute is unexceptional. Petitioners challenge the statute's definition of informed consent because it includes the provision of specific information by the doctor and the mandatory 24-hour waiting period. The conclusions reached by a majority of the Justices in the separate opinions filed today and the undue burden standard adopted in this opinion require us to overrule in part some of the Court's past decisions, decisions driven by the trimester framework's prohibition of all previability regulations designed to further the State's interest in fetal life.

In *Akron I*, 462 U.S. 416 (1983), we invalidated an ordinance which required that a woman seeking an abortion be provided by her physician with specific information "designed to influence the woman's informed choice between abortion or childbirth." *Id.*, at 444. As we later described the *Akron I* holding in *Thornburgh v. American College of Obstetricians and Gynecologists*, 476 U.S., at 762, there were two purported flaws in the Akron ordinance: the information was designed to dissuade the woman from having an abortion and the ordinance imposed "a rigid requirement that a specific body of information be given in all cases, irrespective of the particular needs of the patient . . . ." *Ibid.*

To the extent *Akron I* and *Thornburgh* find a constitutional violation when the government requires, as it does here, the giving of truthful, non-misleading information about the nature of the procedure, the attendant health risks and those of childbirth, and the "probable gestational age" of the fetus, those cases go too far, are inconsistent with *Roe*'s acknowledgment of an important interest in potential life, and are overruled. This is clear even on the very terms of *Akron I* and *Thornburgh*. Those decisions, along with *Danforth*, recognize a substantial government interest justifying a requirement that a woman be apprised of the health risks of abortion and childbirth. *E. g., Danforth, supra*, at 66-67. It cannot be questioned that psychological well-being is a facet of health. Nor can it be doubted that most women considering an abortion would deem the impact on the fetus relevant, if not dispositive, to the decision. In attempting to ensure that a woman apprehend the full consequences of her decision, the State furthers the legitimate purpose of reducing the risk that a woman may elect an abortion, only to discover later, with devastating psychological consequences, that her decision was not fully informed. If the information the State requires to be made available to the woman is truthful and not misleading, the requirement may be permissible.

We also see no reason why the State may not require doctors to inform a woman seeking an abortion of the availability of materials relating to the consequences to the fetus, even when those consequences have no direct relation to her health. An example illustrates the point. We would think it constitutional for the State to require that in order for there to be informed consent to a kidney transplant operation the recipient must be supplied with information about risks to the donor as well as risks to himself or herself. A requirement that the physician make available information similar to that mandated by the statute here was described in *Thornburgh* as "an outright attempt to wedge the Commonwealth's message discouraging abortion into the privacy of the informed-consent dialogue between the woman and her physician." 476 U.S., at 762. We conclude, however, that informed choice need not be defined in such narrow terms that all considerations of the effect on the fetus are made irrelevant. As we have made clear, we depart from the holdings of *Akron I* and *Thornburgh* to the extent that we permit a State to further its legitimate goal of protecting the life of the unborn by enacting legislation aimed at ensuring a decision that is mature and informed, even when in so doing the State expresses a preference for childbirth over abortion. In short, requiring that the woman be informed of the availability of information relating to fetal development and the assistance available should she decide to carry the pregnancy to full term is a reasonable measure to ensure an informed choice, one which might cause the woman to choose childbirth over abortion. This requirement cannot be considered a substantial obstacle to obtaining an abortion, and, it follows, there is no undue burden.

Our prior cases also suggest that the "straitjacket," *Thornburgh, supra,* at 762 (quoting *Danforth, supra,* at 67, n. 8), of particular information which must be given in each case interferes with a constitutional right of privacy between a pregnant woman and her physician. As a preliminary matter, it is worth noting that the statute now before us does not require a physician to comply with the informed consent provisions "if he or she can demonstrate by a preponderance of the evidence, that he or she reasonably believed that furnishing the information would have resulted in a severely adverse effect on the physical or mental health of the patient." 18 Pa. Cons. Stat. § 3205 (1990). In this respect, the statute does not prevent the physician from exercising his or her medical judgment.

Whatever constitutional status the doctor-patient relation may have as a general matter, in the present context it is derivative of the woman's position. The doctor-patient relation does not underlie or override the two more general rights under which the abortion right is justified: the right to make family decisions and the right to physical autonomy. On its own, the doctor-patient relation here is entitled to the same solicitude it receives in other contexts. Thus, a requirement that a doctor give a woman certain information as part of obtaining her consent to an abortion is, for constitutional purposes, no different from a requirement that a doctor give certain specific information about any medical procedure.

All that is left of petitioners' argument is an asserted First Amendment right of a physician not to provide information about the risks of abortion, and childbirth, in a manner mandated by the State. To be sure, the physician's First Amendment rights not to speak are implicated, see *Wooley v. Maynard*, 430 U.S. 705 (1977), but only as part of the practice of medicine, subject to reasonable licensing and regulation by the State, cf. *Whalen v. Roe*, 429 U.S. 589, 603 (1977). We see no constitutional infirmity in the requirement that the physician provide the information mandated by the State here.

The Pennsylvania statute also requires us to reconsider the holding in *Akron I* that the State may not require that a physician, as opposed to a qualified assistant, provide information relevant to a woman's informed consent. 462 U.S., at 448. Since there is no evidence on this record that requiring a doctor to give the information as provided by the statute would amount in practical terms to a substantial obstacle to a woman seeking an abortion, we conclude that it is not an undue burden. Our cases reflect the fact that the Constitution gives the States broad latitude to decide that particular functions may be performed only by licensed professionals, even if an objective assessment might suggest that those same tasks could be performed by others. See *Williamson v. Lee Optical of Okla., Inc.*, 348 U.S. 483 (1955). Thus, we uphold the provision as a reasonable means to ensure that the woman's consent is informed.

Our analysis of Pennsylvania's 24-hour waiting period between the provision of the information deemed necessary to informed consent and the performance of an abortion under the undue burden standard requires us to reconsider the premise behind the decision in *Akron I* invalidating a parallel requirement. In *Akron I* we said: "Nor are we convinced that the State's legitimate concern that the woman's decision be informed is reasonably served by requiring a 24-hour delay as a matter of course." 462 U.S., at 450. We consider that conclusion to be wrong. The idea that important decisions will be more informed and deliberate if they follow some period of reflection does not strike us as unreasonable, particularly where the statute directs that important information become part of the background of the decision. The statute, as construed by the Court of Appeals, permits avoidance of the waiting period in the event of a medical emergency and the record evidence shows that in the vast majority of cases, a 24-hour delay does not create any appreciable health risk. In theory, at least, the waiting period is a reasonable measure to implement the State's interest in protecting the life of the unborn, a measure that does not amount to an undue burden.

Whether the mandatory 24-hour waiting period is nonetheless invalid because in practice it is a substantial obstacle to a woman's choice to terminate her pregnancy is a closer question. The findings of fact by the District Court indicate that because of the distances many women must travel to reach an abortion provider, the practical effect will often be a delay of much more than a day because the waiting period requires that a woman seeking an abortion make at least two visits to the doctor. The District Court also found that in many instances this will increase the exposure of women seeking abortions to "the harassment and hostility of antiabortion protestors demonstrating outside a clinic." 744 F. Supp., at 1351. As a result, the District Court found that for those women who have the fewest financial resources, those who must travel long distances, and those who have difficulty explaining their whereabouts to husbands, employers, or others, the 24-hour waiting period will be "particularly burdensome." *Id.*, at 1352.

These findings are troubling in some respects, but they do not demonstrate that the waiting period constitutes an undue burden. We do not doubt that, as the District Court held, the waiting period has the effect of "increasing the cost and risk of delay of abortions," *id.*, at 1378, but the District Court did not conclude that the increased costs and potential delays amount to substantial obstacles. Rather, applying the trimester framework's strict prohibition of all regulation designed to promote the State's interest in potential life before viability, see *id.*, at 1374, the District Court concluded that the waiting period does not further the state "interest in maternal health" and "infringes the physician's discretion to exercise sound medical judgment," *id.*, at 1378. Yet, as we have stated, under the undue burden standard a State is permitted to enact persuasive measures which favor childbirth over abortion, even if those measures do not further a health interest. And while the waiting period does limit a physician's discretion, that is not, standing alone, a reason to invalidate it. In light of the construction given the statute's definition of medical emergency by the Court of Appeals, and the District Court's findings, we cannot say that the waiting period imposes a real health risk.

We also disagree with the District Court's conclusion that the "particularly burdensome" effects of the waiting period on some women require its invalidation. A particular burden is not of necessity a substantial obstacle. Whether a burden falls on a particular group is a distinct inquiry from whether it is a substantial obstacle even as to the women in that group. And the District Court did not conclude that the waiting period is such an obstacle even for the women who are most burdened by it. Hence, on the record before us, and in the context of this facial challenge, we are not convinced that the 24-hour waiting period constitutes an undue burden.

We are left with the argument that the various aspects of the informed consent requirement are unconstitutional because they place barriers in the way of abortion on demand. Even the broadest reading of *Roe*, however, has not suggested that there is a constitutional right to abortion on demand. See, *e. g.*, *Doe v. Bolton*, 410 U.S., at 189. Rather, the right protected by *Roe* is a right to decide to terminate a pregnancy free of undue interference by the State. Because the informed consent requirement facilitates the wise exercise of that right, it cannot be classified as an interference with the right *Roe* protects. The informed consent requirement is not an undue burden on that right.

C

Section 3209 of Pennsylvania's abortion law provides, except in cases of medical emergency, that no physician shall perform an abortion on a married woman without receiving a signed statement from the woman that she has notified her spouse that she is about to undergo an abortion. The woman has the option of providing an alternative signed statement certifying that her husband is not the man who impregnated her; that her husband could not be located; that the pregnancy is the result of spousal sexual assault which she has reported; or that the woman believes that notifying her husband will cause him or someone else to inflict bodily injury upon her. A physician who performs an abortion on a married woman without receiving the appropriate signed statement will have his or her license revoked, and is liable to the husband for damages.

The District Court heard the testimony of numerous expert witnesses, and made detailed findings of fact regarding the effect of this statute. These included:

[The opinion here quotes detailed district court findings regarding the severity and frequency of spousal abuse; they are redacted for brevity.]

Other studies fill in the rest of this troubling picture. Physical violence is only the most visible form of abuse. Psychological abuse, particularly forced social and economic isolation of women, is also common. L. Walker, The Battered Woman Syndrome 27-28 (1984). Many victims of domestic violence remain with their abusers, perhaps because they perceive no superior alternative. Herbert, Silver, & Ellard, Coping with an Abusive Relationship: 1. How and Why do Women Stay?, 53 J. Marriage & the Family 311 (1991). Many abused women who find temporary refuge in shelters return to their husbands, in large part because they have no other source of income. . . .

This information and the District Court's findings reinforce what common sense would suggest. In well-functioning marriages, spouses discuss important intimate decisions such as whether to bear a child. But there are millions of women in this country who are the victims of regular physical and psychological abuse at the hands of their husbands. Should these women become pregnant, they may have very good reasons for not wishing to inform their husbands of their decision to obtain an abortion. Many may have justifiable fears of physical abuse, but may be no less fearful of the consequences of reporting prior abuse to the Commonwealth of Pennsylvania. Many may have a reasonable fear that notifying their husbands will provoke further instances of child abuse; these women are not exempt from § 3209's notification requirement. Many may fear devastating forms of psychological abuse from their husbands, including verbal harassment, threats of future violence, the destruction of possessions, physical confinement to the home, the withdrawal of financial support, or the disclosure of the abortion to family and friends. These methods of psychological abuse may act as even more of a deterrent to notification than the possibility of physical violence, but women who are the victims of the abuse are not exempt from § 3209's notification requirement. And many women who are pregnant as a result of sexual assaults by their husbands will be unable to avail themselves of the exception for spousal sexual assault, § 3209(b)(3), because the exception requires that the woman have notified law enforcement authorities within 90 days of the assault, and her husband will be notified of her report once an investigation begins, § 3128(c). If anything in this field is certain, it is that victims of spousal sexual assault are extremely reluctant to report the abuse to the government; hence, a great many spousal rape victims will not be exempt from the notification requirement imposed by § 3209.

The spousal notification requirement is thus likely to prevent a significant number of women from obtaining an abortion. It does not merely make abortions a little more difficult or expensive to obtain; for many women, it will impose a substantial obstacle. We must not blind ourselves to the fact that the significant number of women who fear for their safety and the safety of their children are likely to be deterred from procuring an abortion as surely as if the Commonwealth had outlawed abortion in all cases.

. . . .

. . . The unfortunate yet persisting conditions we document above will mean that in a large fraction of the cases in which § 3209 is relevant, it will operate as a substantial obstacle to a woman's choice to undergo an abortion. It is an undue burden, and therefore invalid.

This conclusion is in no way inconsistent with our decisions upholding parental notification or consent requirements. See, *e. g., Akron II*, 497 U.S., at 510-519; *Bellotti v. Baird*, 443 U.S. 622 (1979) *(Bellotti II); Planned Parenthood of Central Mo. v. Danforth*, 428 U.S., at 74. Those enactments, and our judgment that they are constitutional, are based on the quite reasonable assumption that minors will benefit from consultation with their parents and that children will often not realize that their parents have their best interests at heart. We cannot adopt a parallel assumption about adult women.

We recognize that a husband has a "deep and proper concern and interest . . . in his wife's pregnancy and in the growth and development of the fetus she is carrying." *Danforth, supra*, at 69. With regard to the children he has fathered and raised, the Court has recognized his "cognizable and substantial" interest in their custody. *Stanley v. Illinois*, 405 U.S. 645, 651-652 (1972); see also *Quilloin v. Walcott*, 434 U.S. 246 (1978); *Caban v. Mohammed*, 441 U.S. 380 *(1979); Lehr v. Robertson*, 463 U.S. 248 (1983). If these cases concerned a State's ability to require the mother to notify the father before taking some action with respect to a living child raised by both, therefore, it would be reasonable to conclude as a general matter that the father's interest in the welfare of the child and the mother's interest are equal.

Before birth, however, the issue takes on a very different cast. It is an inescapable biological fact that state regulation with respect to the child a woman is carrying will have a far greater impact on the mother's liberty than on the father's. The effect of state regulation on a woman's protected liberty is doubly deserving of scrutiny in such a case, as the State has touched not only upon the private sphere of the family but upon the very bodily integrity of the pregnant woman. Cf. *Cruzan v. Director, Mo. Dept. of Health*, 497 U.S., at 281. The Court has held that "when the wife and the husband disagree on this decision, the view of only one of the two marriage partners can prevail. Inasmuch as it is the woman who physically bears the child and who is the more directly and immediately affected by the pregnancy, as between the two, the balance weighs in her favor." *Danforth, supra*, at 71. This conclusion rests upon the basic nature of marriage and the nature of our Constitution: "[T]he marital couple is not an independent entity with a mind and heart of its own, but an association of two individuals each with a separate intellectual and emotional makeup. If the right of privacy means anything, it is the right of the *individual*, married or single, to be free from unwarranted governmental intrusion into matters so fundamentally affecting a person as the decision whether to bear or beget a child." *Eisenstadt v. Baird*, 405 U.S., at 453 (emphasis in original). The Constitution protects individuals, men and women alike, from unjustified state interference, even when that interference is enacted into law for the benefit of their spouses.

There was a time, not so long ago, when a different understanding of the family and of the Constitution prevailed. In *Bradwell v. State*, 16 Wall. 130 (1873), three Members of this Court reaffirmed the common-law principle that "a woman had no legal existence separate from her husband, who was regarded as her head and representative in the social state; and, notwithstanding some recent modifications of this civil status, many of the special rules of law flowing from and dependent upon this cardinal principle still exist in full force in most States." *Id.*, at 141 (Bradley, J., joined by Swayne and Field, JJ., concurring in judgment). Only one generation has passed since this Court observed that "woman is still regarded as the center of home and family life," with attendant "special responsibilities" that precluded full and independent legal status under the Constitution. *Hoyt v. Florida*, 368 U.S. 57, 62 (1961). These views, of course, are no longer consistent with our understanding of the family, the individual, or the Constitution.

In keeping with our rejection of the common-law understanding of a woman's role within the family, the Court held in *Danforth* that the Constitution does not permit a State to require a married woman to obtain her husband's consent before undergoing an abortion. 428 U.S., at 69. The principles that guided the Court in *Danforth* should be our guides today. For the great many women who are victims of abuse inflicted by their husbands, or whose children are the victims of such abuse, a spousal notice requirement enables the husband to wield an effective veto over his wife's decision. Whether the prospect of notification itself deters such women from seeking abortions, or whether the husband, through physical force or psychological pressure or economic coercion, prevents his wife from obtaining an abortion until it is too late, the notice requirement will often be tantamount to the veto found unconstitutional in *Danforth*. The women most affected by this law-those who most reasonably fear the consequences of notifying their husbands that they are pregnant-are in the gravest danger.

The husband's interest in the life of the child his wife is carrying does not permit the State to empower him with this troubling degree of authority over his wife. The contrary view leads to consequences reminiscent of the common law. A husband has no enforceable right to require a wife to advise him before she exercises her personal choices. If a husband's interest in the potential life of the child outweighs a wife's liberty, the State could require a married woman to notify her husband before she uses a postfertilization contraceptive. Perhaps next in line would be a statute requiring pregnant

married women to notify their husbands before engaging in conduct causing risks to the fetus. After all, if the husband's interest in the fetus' safety
is a sufficient predicate for state regulation, the State could reasonably conclude that pregnant wives should notify their husbands before drinking
alcohol or smoking. Perhaps married women should notify their husbands
before using contraceptives or before undergoing any type of surgery that
may have complications affecting the husband's interest in his wife's reproductive organs. And if a husband's interest justifies notice in any of these
cases, one might reasonably argue that it justifies exactly what the *Danforth*
Court held it did not justify-a requirement of the husband's consent as well.
A State may not give to a man the kind of dominion over his wife that parents exercise over their children.

Section 3209 embodies a view of marriage consonant with the common-
law status of married women but repugnant to our present understanding
of marriage and of the nature of the rights secured by the Constitution.
Women do not lose their constitutionally protected liberty when they
marry. The Constitution protects all individuals, male or female, married or
unmarried, from the abuse of governmental power, even where that power
is employed for the supposed benefit of a member of the individual's family. These considerations confirm our conclusion that § 3209 is invalid.

D

[Section D upheld Pennsylvania's parental consent provision based on
prior decisions.]

E

[Section E upheld Pennsylvania's recordkeeping and reporting requirements as not creating an "undue burden on a woman's choice," except
insofar as they required, in the case of a woman who had not notified her
husband of her decision, a report of her reason for not telling him.]

VI

Our Constitution is a covenant running from the first generation of
Americans to us and then to future generations. It is a coherent succession. Each generation must learn anew that the Constitution's written terms
embody ideas and aspirations that must survive more ages than one. We
accept our responsibility not to retreat from interpreting the full meaning

of the covenant in light of all of our precedents. We invoke it once again to define the freedom guaranteed by the Constitution's own promise, the promise of liberty.

***

The judgment in No. 91-902 is affirmed. The judgment in No. 91-744 is affirmed in part and reversed in part, and the case is remanded for proceedings consistent with this opinion, including consideration of the question of severability.

It is so ordered.

[Parts of the 1988 and 1989 Amendments to the Pennsylvania Abortion Control Act of 1982 were an appendix to the opinion but have not been reproduced for brevity.]

Appendix J

Opinion of Justice Blackmun[1]
— Planned Parenthood of Southeastern Pa. v. Casey (1992) —

Three years ago, in *Webster v. Reproductive Health Services*, 492 U.S. 490 (1989), four Members of this Court appeared poised to "cas[t] into darkness the hopes and visions of every woman in this country" who had come to believe that the Constitution guaranteed her the right to reproductive choice. *Id.*, at 557 (BLACKMUN, J., dissenting). See *id.*, at 499 (plurality opinion of REHNQUIST, C. J., joined by WHITE and KENNEDY, JJ.); *id.*, at 532 (SCALIA, J., concurring in part and concurring in judgment). All that remained between the promise of *Roe* and the darkness of the plurality was a single, flickering flame. Decisions since *Webster* gave little reason to hope that this flame would cast much light. See, *e.g., Ohio v. Akron Center for Reproductive Health*, 497 U.S. 502, 524 (1990) (BLACKMUN, J., dissenting). But now, just when so many expected the darkness to fall, the flame has grown bright.

I do not underestimate the significance of today's joint opinion. Yet I remain steadfast in my belief that the right to reproductive choice is entitled to the full protection afforded by this Court before *Webster*. And I fear for the darkness as four Justices anxiously await the single vote necessary to extinguish the light.

---

1. Justice Blackmun joined Parts I, II, III, V-A, V-C, and VI of the opinion of Justice O'Connor, but dissented otherwise. Some parts of Justice Blackmun's opinion have been redacted; the full opinion is available at 505 U.S. 833, 922 (1992).

I

Make no mistake, the joint opinion of JUSTICES O'CONNOR, KEN-NEDY, and SOUTER is an act of personal courage and constitutional princi-ple. In contrast to previous decisions in which JUSTICES O'CONNOR and KENNEDY postponed reconsideration of *Roe v. Wade*, 410 U.S. 113 (1973), the authors of the joint opinion today join JUSTICE STEVENS and me in concluding that "the essential holding of *Roe v. Wade* should be retained and once again reaffirmed." *Ante*, at 846. In brief, five Members of this Court today recognize that "the Constitution protects a woman's right to terminate her pregnancy in its early stages." *Ante*, at 844.

A fervent view of individual liberty and the force of *stare decisis* have led the Court to this conclusion. *Ante*, at 853. Today a majority reaffirms that the Due Process Clause of the Fourteenth Amendment establishes "a realm of personal liberty which the government may not enter," *ante*, at 847—a realm whose outer limits cannot be determined by interpretations of the Constitu-tion that focus only on the specific practices of States at the time the Four-teenth Amendment was adopted. See *ante*, at 848-849. Included within this realm of liberty is "the right of the *individual*, married or single, to be free from unwarranted governmental intrusion into matters so fundamentally affecting a person as the decision whether to bear or beget a child." *Ante*, at 851, quoting *Eisenstadt v. Baird*, 405 U.S. 438, 453 (1972) (emphasis in original). "These matters, involving the most intimate and personal choices a person may make in a lifetime, choices central to personal dignity and autonomy, are *central* to the liberty protected by the Fourteenth Amend-ment." *Ante*, at 851 (emphasis added). Finally, the Court today recognizes that in the case of abortion, "the liberty of the woman is at stake in a sense unique to the human condition and so unique to the law. The mother who carries a child to full term is subject to anxieties, to physical constraints, to pain that only she must bear." *Ante*, at 852.

. . . .

. . . [W]hile I believe that the joint opinion errs in failing to invalidate the other regulations, I am pleased that the joint opinion has not ruled out the possibility that these regulations may be shown to impose an unconsti-tutional burden. The joint opinion makes clear that its specific holdings are based on the insufficiency of the record before it. See, *e. g., ante*, at 885-886. I am confident that in the future evidence will be produced to show that "in a large fraction of the cases in which [these regulations are] relevant, [they] will operate as a substantial obstacle to a woman's choice to undergo an abortion." *Ante*, at 895.

. . . .

III

At long last, THE CHIEF JUSTICE and those who have joined him admit it. Gone are the contentions that the issue need not be (or has not been) considered. There, on the first page, for all to see, is what was expected: "We believe that *Roe* was wrongly decided, and that it can and should be overruled consistently with our traditional approach to *stare decisis* in constitutional cases." *Post*, at 944. If there is much reason to applaud the advances made by the joint opinion today, there is far more to fear from THE CHIEF JUSTICE'S opinion.

THE CHIEF JUSTICE'S criticism of *Roe* follows from his stunted conception of individual liberty. While recognizing that the Due Process Clause protects more than simple physical liberty, he then goes on to construe this Court's personal liberty cases as establishing only a laundry list of particular rights, rather than a principled account of how these particular rights are grounded in a more general right of privacy. *Post*, at 951. This constricted view is reinforced by THE CHIEF JUSTICE'S exclusive reliance on tradition as a source of fundamental rights. He argues that the record in favor of a right to abortion is no stronger than the record in *Michael H. v. Gerald D.*, 491 U.S. 110 (1989), where the plurality found no fundamental right to visitation privileges by an adulterous father, or in *Bowers v. Hardwick*, 478 U.S. 186 (1986), where the Court found no fundamental right to engage in homosexual sodomy, or in a case involving the "firing [of] a gun . . . into another person's body." *Post*, at 951-952. In THE CHIEF JUSTICE'S world, a woman considering whether to terminate a pregnancy is entitled to no more protection than adulterers, murderers, and so-called sexual deviates.[2] Given THE CHIEF JUSTICE'S exclusive reliance on tradition, people using contraceptives seem the next likely candidate for his list of outcasts.

Even more shocking than THE CHIEF JUSTICE'S cramped notion of individual liberty is his complete omission of any discussion of the effects that compelled childbirth and motherhood have on women's lives. The only expression of concern with women's health is purely instrumental—for THE CHIEF JUSTICE, only women's *psychological* health is a concern, and only to the extent that he assumes that every woman who decides to have an abortion does so without serious consideration of the moral implications of her decision. *Post*, at 967-968. In short, THE CHIEF JUSTICE'S view of the State's compelling interest in maternal health has less to do with health than it does with compelling women to be maternal.

---

2. Obviously, I do not share THE CHIEF JUSTICE'S views of homosexuality as sexual deviance. *See Bowers*, 478 U.S. at 202–03, n.2.

Nor does THE CHIEF JUSTICE give any serious consideration to the doctrine of *stare decisis*. For THE CHIEF JUSTICE, the facts that gave rise to *Roe* are surprisingly simple: "women become pregnant, there is a point somewhere, depending on medical technology, where a fetus becomes viable, and women give birth to children." *Post*, at 955. This characterization of the issue thus allows THE CHIEF JUSTICE quickly to discard the joint opinion's reliance argument by asserting that "reproductive planning could take virtually immediate account of" a decision overruling *Roe*. *Post*, at 956 (internal quotation marks omitted).

THE CHIEF JUSTICE'S narrow conception of individual liberty and *stare decisis* leads him to propose the same standard of review proposed by the plurality in *Webster*. "States may regulate abortion procedures in ways rationally related to a legitimate state interest. *Williamson v. Lee Optical of Oklahoma, Inc.*, 348 U.S. 483, 491 (1955); cf. *Stanley v. Illinois*, 405 U.S. 645, 651-653 (1972)." *Post*, at 966. THE CHIEF JUSTICE then further weakens the test by providing an insurmountable requirement for facial challenges: Petitioners must "show that no set of circumstances exists under which the [provision] would be valid." *Post*, at 973, quoting *Ohio v. Akron Center for Reproductive Health*, 497 U.S., at 514. In short, in his view, petitioners must prove that the statute cannot constitutionally be applied to *anyone*. Finally, in applying his standard to the spousal-notification provision, THE CHIEF JUSTICE contends that the record lacks any "hard evidence" to support the joint opinion's contention that a "large fraction" of women who prefer not to notify their husbands involve situations of battered women and unreported spousal assault. *Post*, at 974, n. 2. Yet throughout the explication of his standard, THE CHIEF JUSTICE never explains what hard evidence is, how large a fraction is required, or how a battered woman is supposed to pursue an as-applied challenge.

Under his standard, States can ban abortion if that ban is rationally related to a legitimate state interest—a standard which the United States calls "deferential, but not toothless." Yet when pressed at oral argument to describe the teeth, the best protection that the Solicitor General could offer to women was that a prohibition, enforced by criminal penalties, *with no exception for the life of the mother*, "could raise very serious questions." Tr. of Oral Arg. 48. Perhaps, the Solicitor General offered, the failure to include an exemption for the life of the mother would be "arbitrary and capricious." *Id.*, at 49. If, as THE CHIEF JUSTICE contends, the undue burden test is made out of whole cloth, the so-called "arbitrary and capricious" limit is the Solicitor General's "new clothes."

Even if it is somehow "irrational" for a State to require a woman to risk her life for her child, what protection is offered for women who become pregnant through rape or incest? Is there anything arbitrary or capricious about a State's prohibiting the sins of the father from being visited upon his offspring?[3]

But, we are reassured, there is always the protection of the democratic process. While there is much to be praised about our democracy, our country since its founding has recognized that there are certain fundamental liberties that are not to be left to the whims of an election. A woman's right to reproductive choice is one of those fundamental liberties. Accordingly, that liberty need not seek refuge at the ballot box.

IV

In one sense, the Court's approach is worlds apart from that of THE CHIEF JUSTICE and JUSTICE SCALIA. And yet, in another sense, the distance between the two approaches is short—the distance is but a single vote.

I am 83 years old. I cannot remain on this Court forever, and when I do step down, the confirmation process for my successor well may focus on the issue before us today. That, I regret, may be exactly where the choice between the two worlds will be made.

---

3. JUSTICE SCALIA urges the Court to "get out of this area," *post*, at 1002, and leave questions regarding abortion entirely to the States, *post*, at 999–1000. Putting aside the fact that what he advocates is nothing short of an abdication by the Court of its constitutional responsibilities, JUSTICE SCALIA is uncharacteristically naive if he thinks that overruling *Roe* and holding that restrictions on a woman's right to an abortion are subject only to rational-basis review will enable the Court henceforth to avoid reviewing abortion-related issues. State efforts to regulate and prohibit abortion in a *post-Roe* world undoubtedly would raise a host of distinct and important constitutional questions meriting review by this Court. For example, does the Eighth Amendment impose any limits on the degree or kind of punishment a State can inflict upon physicians who perform, or women who undergo, abortions? What effect would differences among States in their approaches to abortion have on a woman's right to engage in interstate travel? Does the First Amendment permit States that choose not to criminalize abortion to ban all advertising providing information about where and how to obtain abortions?

Appendix K

Dissenting Opinion of Chief Justice Rehnquist[1]
— *Planned Parenthood of Southeastern Pa. v. Casey* (1992) —

The joint opinion, following its newly minted variation on *stare decisis*, retains the outer shell of *Roe v. Wade*, 410 U.S. 113 (1973), but beats a wholesale retreat from the substance of that case. We believe that *Roe* was wrongly decided, and that it can and should be overruled consistently with our traditional approach to *stare decisis* in constitutional cases. We would adopt the approach of the plurality in *Webster v. Reproductive Health Services*, 492 U.S. 490 (1989), and uphold the challenged provisions of the Pennsylvania statute in their entirety.

I

In ruling on this litigation below, the Court of Appeals for the Third Circuit first observed that "this appeal does not directly implicate *Roe;* this case involves the regulation of abortions rather than their outright prohibition." 947 F.2d 682, 687 (1991). Accordingly, the court directed its attention to the question of the standard of review for abortion regulations. In attempting to settle on the correct standard, however, the court confronted the confused state of this Court's abortion jurisprudence. After considering the several opinions in *Webster v. Reproductive Health Services, supra*, and *Hodgson v. Minnesota*, 497 U.S. 417 (1990), the Court of Appeals concluded that JUSTICE O'CONNOR'S "undue burden" test was controlling, as that was the narrowest ground on which we had upheld recent abortion regulations. 947 F. 2d, at 693-697 ("When a fragmented court decides a case and no

---

1. The opinion was joined by Justices White, Scalia, and Thomas. The full opinion is available at 505 U.S. 833, 944 (1992).

single rationale explaining the result enjoys the assent of five Justices, the holding of the Court may be viewed as that position taken by those Members who concurred in the judgments on the narrowest grounds" (quoting *Marks v. United States*, 430 U.S. 188, 193 (1977) (internal quotation marks omitted)). Applying this standard, the Court of Appeals upheld all of the challenged regulations except the one requiring a woman to notify her spouse of an intended abortion.

In arguing that this Court should invalidate each of the provisions at issue, petitioners insist that we reaffirm our decision in *Roe v. Wade, supra*, in which we held unconstitutional a Texas statute making it a crime to procure an abortion except to save the life of the mother.[2] We agree with the Court of Appeals that our decision in *Roe* is not directly implicated by the Pennsylvania statute, which does not prohibit, but simply regulates, abortion. But, as the Court of Appeals found, the state of our *post-Roe* decisional law dealing with the regulation of abortion is confusing and uncertain, indicating that a reexamination of that line of cases is in order. Unfortunately for those who must apply this Court's decisions, the reexamination undertaken today leaves the Court no less divided than beforehand. Although they reject the trimester framework that formed the underpinning of *Roe*, JUSTICES O'CONNOR, KENNEDY, and SOUTER adopt a revised undue burden standard to analyze the challenged regulations. We conclude, however, that such an outcome is an unjustified constitutional compromise, one which leaves the Court in a position to closely scrutinize all types of abortion regulations despite the fact that it lacks the power to do so under the Constitution.

In *Roe*, the Court opined that the State "does have an important and legitimate interest in preserving and protecting the health of the pregnant woman, . . . and that it has still another important and legitimate interest in protecting the potentiality of human life." 410 U.S., at 162 (emphasis omitted). In the companion case of *Doe v. Bolton*, 410 U.S. 179 (1973), the Court referred to its conclusion in *Roe* "that a pregnant woman does not have an absolute constitutional right to an abortion on her demand." 410 U.S., at 189. But while the language and holdings of these cases appeared to leave

---

2. Two years after *Roe*, the West German constitutional court, by contrast, struck down a law liberalizing access to abortion on the grounds that life developing within the womb is constitutionally protected. *Judgment of February* 25, 1975, 39 BVerfGE 1 (translated in Jonas & Gorby, West German Abortion Decision: A Contrast to *Roe v. Wade*, 9 JOHN MARSHALL J. PRAC. & PROC. 605 (1976)). In 1988, the Canadian Supreme Court followed reasoning similar to that of *Roe* in striking down a law that restricted abortion. Morgentaler v. Queen, 1 S. C. R. 30, 44 D. L. R. 4th 385 (1988).

States free to regulate abortion procedures in a variety of ways, later decisions based on them have found considerably less latitude for such regulations than might have been expected.

For example, after *Roe*, many States have sought to protect their young citizens by requiring that a minor seeking an abortion involve her parents in the decision. Some States have simply required notification of the parents, while others have required a minor to obtain the consent of her parents. In a number of decisions, however, the Court has substantially limited the States in their ability to impose such requirements. With regard to parental *notice* requirements, we initially held that a State could require a minor to notify her parents before proceeding with an abortion. *H. L. v. Matheson*, 450 U.S. 398, 407-410 (1981). Recently, however, we indicated that a State's ability to impose a notice requirement actually depends on whether it requires notice of one or both parents. We concluded that although the Constitution might allow a State to demand that notice be given to one parent prior to an abortion, it may not require that similar notice be given to *two* parents, unless the State incorporates a judicial bypass procedure in that two-parent requirement. *Hodgson v. Minnesota, supra.*

We have treated parental *consent* provisions even more harshly. Three years after *Roe*, we invalidated a Missouri regulation requiring that an unmarried woman under the age of 18 obtain the consent of one of her parents before proceeding with an abortion. We held that our abortion jurisprudence prohibited the State from imposing such a "blanket provision . . . requiring the consent of a parent." *Planned Parenthood of Central Mo. v. Danforth*, 428 U.S. 52, 74 (1976). In *Bellotti v. Baird*, 443 U.S. 622 (1979), the Court struck down a similar Massachusetts parental consent statute. A majority of the Court indicated, however, that a State could constitutionally require parental consent, if it alternatively allowed a pregnant minor to obtain an abortion without parental consent by showing either that she was mature enough to make her own decision, or that the abortion would be in her best interests. See *id.*, at 643-644 (plurality opinion); *id.*, at 656-657 (WHITE, J., dissenting). In light of *Bellotti*, we have upheld one parental consent regulation which incorporated a judicial bypass option we viewed as sufficient, see *Planned Parenthood Assn. of Kansas City, Mo., Inc. v. Ashcroft*, 462 U.S. 476 (1983), but have invalidated another because of our belief that the judicial procedure did not satisfy the dictates of *Bellotti*, see *Akron v. Akron Center for Reproductive Health, Inc.*, 462 U.S. 416, 439-442 (1983). We have never had occasion, as we have in the parental notice context, to further parse our parental consent jurisprudence into one-parent and two-parent components.

In *Roe*, the Court observed that certain States recognized the right of the father to participate in the abortion decision in certain circumstances. Because neither *Roe* nor *Doe* involved the assertion of any paternal right, the Court expressly stated that the case did not disturb the validity of regulations that protected such a right. *Roe v. Wade, supra*, at 165, n. 67. But three years later, in *Danforth*, the Court extended its abortion jurisprudence and held that a State could not require that a woman obtain the consent of her spouse before proceeding with an abortion. *Planned Parenthood of Central Mo. v. Danforth*, 428 U.S., at 69-71.

States have also regularly tried to ensure that a woman's decision to have an abortion is an informed and well-considered one. In *Danforth*, we upheld a requirement that a woman sign a consent form prior to her abortion, and observed that "it is desirable and imperative that [the decision] be made with full knowledge of its nature and consequences." *Id.*, at 67. Since that case, however, we have twice invalidated state statutes designed to impart such knowledge to a woman seeking an abortion. In *Akron*, we held unconstitutional a regulation requiring a physician to inform a woman seeking an abortion of the status of her pregnancy, the development of her fetus, the date of possible viability, the complications that could result from an abortion, and the availability of agencies providing assistance and information with respect to adoption and childbirth. *Akron v. Akron Center for Reproductive Health, supra*, at 442-445. More recently, in *Thornburgh v. American College of Obstetricians and Gynecologists*, 476 U.S. 747 (1986), we struck down a more limited Pennsylvania regulation requiring that a woman be informed of the risks associated with the abortion procedure and the assistance available to her if she decided to proceed with her pregnancy, because we saw the compelled information as "the antithesis of informed consent." *Id.*, at 764. Even when a State has sought only to provide information that, in our view, was consistent with the *Roe* framework, we concluded that the State could not require that a physician furnish the information, but instead had to alternatively allow nonphysician counselors to provide it. *Akron v. Akron Center for Reproductive Health*, 462 U.S., at 448-449. In *Akron* as well, we went further and held that a State may not require a physician to wait 24 hours to perform an abortion after receiving the consent of a woman. Although the State sought to ensure that the woman's decision was carefully considered, the Court concluded that the Constitution forbade the State to impose any sort of delay. *Id.*, at 449-451.

We have not allowed States much leeway to regulate even the actual abortion procedure. Although a State can require that second-trimester abortions be performed in outpatient clinics, see *Simopoulos v. Virginia*,

462 U.S. 506 (1983), we concluded in *Akron* and *Ashcroft* that a State could not require that such abortions be performed only in hospitals. See *Akron v. Akron Center for Reproductive Health, supra*, at 437-439; *Planned Parenthood Assn. of Kansas City, Mo., Inc. v. Ashcroft, supra*, at 481-482. Despite the fact that *Roe* expressly allowed regulation after the first trimester in furtherance of maternal health, "present medical knowledge," in our view, could not justify such a hospitalization requirement under the trimester framework. *Akron v. Akron Center for Reproductive Health, supra*, at 437 (quoting *Roe v. Wade, supra*, at 163). And in *Danforth*, the Court held that Missouri could not outlaw the saline amniocentesis method of abortion, concluding that the Missouri Legislature had "failed to appreciate and to consider several significant facts" in making its decision. 428 U.S., at 77.

Although *Roe* allowed state regulation after the point of viability to protect the potential life of the fetus, the Court subsequently rejected attempts to regulate in this manner. In *Colautti v. Franklin*, 439 U.S. 379 (1979), the Court struck down a statute that governed the determination of viability. *Id.*, at 390-397. In the process, we made clear that the trimester framework incorporated only one definition of viability—ours—as we forbade States to decide that a certain objective indicator—"be it weeks of gestation or fetal weight or any other single factor"—should govern the definition of viability. *Id.*, at 389. In that same case, we also invalidated a regulation requiring a physician to use the abortion technique offering the best chance for fetal survival when performing postviability abortions. See *id.*, at 397-401; see also *Thornburgh v. American College of Obstetricians and Gynecologists*, 476 U.S., at 768-769 (invalidating a similar regulation). In *Thornburgh*, the Court struck down Pennsylvania's requirement that a second physician be present at postviability abortions to help preserve the health of the unborn child, on the ground that it did not incorporate a sufficient medical emergency exception. *Id.*, at 769-771. Regulations governing the treatment of aborted fetuses have met a similar fate. In *Akron*, we invalidated a provision requiring physicians performing abortions to "insure that the remains of the unborn child are disposed of in a humane and sanitary manner." 462 U.S., at 451 (internal quotation marks omitted).

Dissents in these cases expressed the view that the Court was expanding upon *Roe* in imposing ever greater restrictions on the States. See *Thornburgh v. American College of Obstetricians and Gynecologists*, 476 U.S., at 783 (Burger, C. J., dissenting) ("The extent to which the Court has departed from the limitations expressed in *Roe* is readily apparent"); *id.*, at 814 (WHITE, J., dissenting) ("[T]he majority indiscriminately strikes down statutory provisions that in no way contravene the right recognized in *Roe*"). And, when confronted with state regulations of this type in past years, the Court has become increasingly more divided: The three most recent abortion cases have not commanded a Court opinion. See *Ohio v. Akron Center for Reproductive Health*, 497 U.S. 502 (1990); *Hodgson v. Minnesota*, 497 U.S. 417 (1990); *Webster v. Reproductive Health Services*, 492 U.S. 490 (1989).

The task of the Court of Appeals in the present cases was obviously complicated by this confusion and uncertainty. Following *Marks v. United States*, 430 U.S. 188 (1977), it concluded that in light of *Webster* and *Hodgson*, the strict scrutiny standard enunciated in *Roe* was no longer applicable, and that the "undue burden" standard adopted by JUSTICE O'CONNOR was the governing principle. This state of confusion and disagreement warrants reexamination of the "fundamental right" accorded to a woman's decision to abort a fetus in *Roe*, with its concomitant requirement that any state regulation of abortion survive "strict scrutiny." See *Payne v. Tennessee*, 501 U.S. 808, 827-828 (1991) (observing that reexamination of constitutional decisions is appropriate when those decisions have generated uncertainty and failed to provide clear guidance, because "correction through legislative action is practically impossible" (internal quotation marks omitted)); *Garcia v. San Antonio Metropolitan Transit Authority*, 469 U.S. 528, 546-547, 557 (1985).

We have held that a liberty interest protected under the Due Process Clause of the Fourteenth Amendment will be deemed fundamental if it is "implicit in the concept of ordered liberty." *Palko v. Connecticut*, 302 U.S. 319, 325 (1937). Three years earlier, in *Snyder v. Massachusetts*, 291 U.S. 97 (1934), we referred to a "principle of justice so rooted in the traditions and conscience of our people as to be ranked as fundamental." *Id.*, at 105; see also *Michael H. v. Gerald D.*, 491 U.S. 110, 122 (1989) (plurality opinion) (citing the language from *Snyder*). These expressions are admittedly not precise, but our decisions implementing this notion of "fundamental" rights do not afford any more elaborate basis on which to base such a classification.

In construing the phrase "liberty" incorporated in the Due Process Clause of the Fourteenth Amendment, we have recognized that its meaning extends beyond freedom from physical restraint. In *Pierce v. Society of Sisters*, 268 U.S. 510 (1925), we held that it included a parent's right to send a child to private school; in *Meyer v. Nebraska*, 262 U.S. 390 (1923), we held that it included a right to teach a foreign language in a parochial school. Building on these cases, we have held that the term "liberty" includes a right to marry, *Loving v. Virginia*, 388 U.S. 1 (1967); a right to procreate, *Skinner v. Oklahoma ex rel. Williamson*, 316 U.S. 535 (1942); and a right to use contraceptives, *Griswold v. Connecticut*, 381 U.S. 479 (1965); *Eisenstadt v. Baird*, 405 U.S. 438 (1972). But a reading of these opinions makes clear that they do not endorse any all-encompassing "right of privacy."

In *Roe v. Wade*, the Court recognized a "guarantee of personal privacy" which "is broad enough to encompass a woman's decision whether or not to terminate her pregnancy." 410 U.S., at 152-153. We are now of the view that, in terming this right fundamental, the Court in *Roe* read the earlier opinions upon which it based its decision much too broadly. Unlike marriage, procreation, and contraception, abortion "involves the purposeful termination of a potential life." *Harris v. McRae*, 448 U.S. 297, 325 (1980). The abortion decision must therefore "be recognized as *sui generis*, different in kind from the others that the Court has protected under the rubric of personal or family privacy and autonomy." *Thornburgh v. American College of Obstetricians and Gynecologists, supra*, at 792 (WHITE, J., dissenting). One cannot ignore the fact that a woman is not isolated in her pregnancy, and that the decision to abort necessarily involves the destruction of a fetus. See *Michael H. v. Gerald D., supra*, at 124, n. 4 (To look "at the act which is assertedly the subject of a liberty interest in isolation from its effect upon other people [is] like inquiring whether there is a liberty interest in firing a gun where the case at hand happens to involve its discharge into another person's body").

Nor do the historical traditions of the American people support the view that the right to terminate one's pregnancy is "fundamental." The common law which we inherited from England made abortion after "quickening" an offense. At the time of the adoption of the Fourteenth Amendment, statutory prohibitions or restrictions on abortion were commonplace; in 1868, at least 28 of the then-37 States and 8 Territories had statutes banning or limiting abortion. J. Mohr, Abortion in America 200 (1978). By the turn of the century virtually every State had a law prohibiting or restricting abortion on its books. By the middle of the present century, a liberalization trend had set in. But 21 of the restrictive abortion laws in effect in 1868 were still in effect in 1973 when *Roe* was decided, and an overwhelming majority of the States prohibited abortion unless necessary to preserve the life or health of the mother. *Roe v. Wade*, 410 U.S., at 139-140; *id.*, at 176-177, n. 2 (REHNQUIST, J., dissenting). On this record, it can scarcely be said that any deeply rooted tradition of relatively unrestricted abortion in our history supported the classification of the right to abortion as "fundamental" under the Due Process Clause of the Fourteenth Amendment.

We think, therefore, both in view of this history and of our decided cases dealing with substantive liberty under the Due Process Clause, that the Court was mistaken in *Roe* when it classified a woman's decision to terminate her pregnancy as a "fundamental right" that could be abridged only in a manner which withstood "strict scrutiny." In so concluding, we repeat the observation made in *Bowers v. Hardwick*, 478 U.S. 186 (1986):

"Nor are we inclined to take a more expansive view of our authority to discover new fundamental rights imbedded in the Due Process Clause. The Court is most vulnerable and comes nearest to illegitimacy when it deals with judge-made constitutional law having little or no cognizable roots in the language or design of the Constitution." *Id.*, at 194.

We believe that the sort of constitutionally imposed abortion code of the type illustrated by our decisions following *Roe* is inconsistent "with the notion of a Constitution cast in general terms, as ours is, and usually speaking in general principles, as ours does." *Webster v. Reproductive Health Services*, 492 U.S., at 518 (plurality opinion). The Court in *Roe* reached too far when it analogized the right to abort a fetus to the rights involved in *Pierce, Meyer, Loving,* and *Griswold,* and thereby deemed the right to abortion fundamental.

[Section II discussing *stare decisis* has been omitted.]

III

A

Section 3205 of the Act imposes certain requirements related to the informed consent of a woman seeking an abortion. 18 Pa. Cons. Stat. § 3205 (1990). Section 3205(a)(1) requires that the referring or performing physician must inform a woman contemplating an abortion of (i) the nature of the procedure and the risks and alternatives that a reasonable patient would find material; (ii) the fetus' probable gestational age; and (iii) the medical risks involved in carrying her pregnancy to term. Section 3205(a)(2) requires a physician or a nonphysician counselor to inform the woman that (i) the state health department publishes free materials describing the fetus at different stages and listing abortion alternatives; (ii) medical assistance benefits may be available for prenatal, childbirth, and neonatal care; and (iii) the child's father is liable for child support. The Act also imposes a 24-hour waiting period between the time that the woman receives the required information and the time that the physician is allowed to perform the abortion. See Appendix to opinion of O'CONNOR, KENNEDY, and SOUTER, JJ., *ante*, at 902-904.

This Court has held that it is certainly within the province of the States to require a woman's voluntary and informed consent to an abortion. See *Thornburgh v. American College of Obstetricians and Gynecologists*, 476 U.S., at 760. Here, Pennsylvania seeks to further its legitimate interest in obtaining informed consent by ensuring that each woman "is aware not only of the reasons for having an abortion, but also of the risks associated with an abortion and the availability of assistance that might make the alternative of normal childbirth more attractive than it might otherwise appear." *Id.*, at 798-799 (WHITE, J., dissenting).

We conclude that this provision of the statute is rationally related to the State's interest in assuring that a woman's consent to an abortion be a fully informed decision.

. . . .

C

Section 3209 of the Act contains the spousal notification provision. It requires that, before a physician may perform an abortion on a married woman, the woman must sign a statement indicating that she has notified her husband of her planned abortion. A woman is not required to notify her husband if (1) her husband is not the father, (2) her husband, after diligent effort, cannot be located, (3) the pregnancy is the result of a spousal sexual assault that has been reported to the authorities, or (4) the woman has reason to believe that notifying her husband is likely to result in the infliction of bodily injury upon her by him or by another individual. In addition, a woman is exempted from the notification requirement in the case of a medical emergency. 18 Pa. Cons. Stat. § 3209 (1990). See Appendix to opinion of O'CONNOR, KENNEDY, and SOUTER, JJ., *ante*, at 908-909.

We first emphasize that Pennsylvania has not imposed a spousal *consent* requirement of the type the Court struck down in *Planned Parenthood of Central Mo. v. Danforth*, 428 U.S., at 67-72. Missouri's spousal consent provision was invalidated in that case because of the Court's view that it unconstitutionally granted to the husband "a veto power exercisable for any reason whatsoever or for no reason at all." *Id.*, at 71. But the provision here involves a much less intrusive requirement of spousal *notification*, not consent. Such a law requiring only notice to the husband "does not give any third party the legal right to make the [woman's] decision for her, or to prevent her from obtaining an abortion should she choose to have one performed." *Hodgson v. Minnesota, supra*, at 496 (KENNEDY, J., concurring in judgment in part and dissenting in part); see *H. L. v. Matheson*, 450 U.S., at 411, n. 17. *Danforth* thus does not control our analysis. . . .

The question before us is therefore whether the spousal notification requirement rationally furthers any legitimate state interests. We conclude that it does. First, a husband's interests in procreation within marriage and in the potential life of his unborn child are certainly substantial ones.

See *Planned Parenthood of Central Mo. v. Danforth,* 428 U.S., at 69 ("We are not unaware of the deep and proper concern and interest that a devoted and protective husband has in his wife's pregnancy and in the growth and development of the fetus she is carrying"); *id.,* at 93 (WHITE, J., concurring in part and dissenting in part); *Skinner v. Oklahoma ex rel. Williamson,* 316 U.S., at 541. The State itself has legitimate interests both in protecting these interests of the father and in protecting the potential life of the fetus, and the spousal notification requirement is reasonably related to advancing those state interests. . . .

The State also has a legitimate interest in promoting "the integrity of the marital relationship." 18 Pa. Cons. Stat. § 3209(a) (1990). This Court has previously recognized "the importance of the marital relationship in our society." *Planned Parenthood of Central Mo. v. Danforth, supra,* at 69. In our view, the spousal notice requirement is a rational attempt by the State to improve truthful communication between spouses and encourage collaborative decision-making, and thereby fosters marital integrity. See *Labine v. Vincent,* 401 U.S. 532, 538 (1971) ("[T]he power to make rules to establish, protect, and strengthen family life" is committed to the state legislatures). Petitioners argue that the notification requirement does not further any such interest; they assert that the majority of wives already notify their husbands of their abortion decisions, and the remainder have excellent reasons for keeping their decisions a secret. In the first case, they argue, the law is unnecessary, and in the second case it will only serve to foster marital discord and threats of harm. Thus, petitioners see the law as a totally irrational means of furthering whatever legitimate interest the State might have. But, in our view, it is unrealistic to assume that every husband-wife relationship is either (1) so perfect that this type of truthful and important communication will take place as a matter of course, or (2) so imperfect that, upon notice, the husband will react selfishly, violently, or contrary to the best interests of his wife. See *Planned Parenthood of Central Mo. v. Danforth, supra,* at 103-104 (STEVENS, J., concurring in part and dissenting in part) (making a similar point in the context of a parental consent statute). The spousal notice provision will admittedly be unnecessary in some circumstances, and possibly harmful in others, but "the existence of particular cases in which a feature of a statute performs no function (or is even counterproductive) ordinarily does not render the statute unconstitutional or even constitutionally suspect." *Thornburgh v. American College of Obstetricians and Gynecologists,* 476 U.S., at 800 (WHITE, J., dissenting). The Pennsylvania Legislature was in a position to weigh the likely benefits of the provision against its likely adverse effects, and presumably concluded, on balance, that the provision would be beneficial. Whether this was a wise decision or not, we cannot say that it was irrational. We therefore conclude that the spousal notice provision comports with the Constitution. See *Harris v. McRae*, 448 U.S., at 325-326 ("It is not the mission of this Court or any other to decide whether the balance of competing interests . . . is wise social policy").

[Sections D and E—addressing the statute's reporting requirements and the "medical emergency" provision—are omitted.]

IV

For the reasons stated, we therefore would hold that each of the challenged provisions of the Pennsylvania statute is consistent with the Constitution. It bears emphasis that our conclusion in this regard does not carry with it any necessary approval of these regulations. Our task is, as always, to decide only whether the challenged provisions of a law comport with the United States Constitution. If, as we believe, these do, their wisdom as a matter of public policy is for the people of Pennsylvania to decide.

Appendix L

Opinion of Justice Breyer for the Court[1]

— *Whole Woman's Health v. Hellerstedt* (2016) —

In *Planned Parenthood of Southeastern Pa.* v. *Casey,* 505 U.S. 833, 878 (1992), a plurality of the Court concluded that there "exists" an "undue burden" on a woman's right to decide to have an abortion, and consequently a provision of law is constitutionally invalid, if the "*purpose or effect*" of the provision "*is to place a substantial obstacle* in the path of a woman seeking an abortion before the fetus attains viability." (Emphasis added.) The plurality added that "[u]nnecessary health regulations that have the purpose or effect of presenting a substantial obstacle to a woman seeking an abortion impose an undue burden on the right." *Ibid.*

We must here decide whether two provisions of Texas' House Bill 2 violate the Federal Constitution as interpreted in *Casey.* The first provision, which we shall call the "*admitting-privileges requirement,*" says that

> "[a] physician performing or inducing an abortion . . . must, on the date the abortion is performed or induced, have active admitting privileges at a hospital that . . . is located not further than 30 miles from the location at which the abortion is performed or induced." Tex. Health & Safety Code Ann. §171.0031(a) (West Cum. Supp. 2015).

This provision amended Texas law that had previously required an abortion facility to maintain a written protocol "for managing medical emergencies and the transfer of patients requiring further emergency care to a hospital." 38 Tex. Reg. 6546 (2013).

The second provision, which we shall call the "*surgical-center requirement,*" says that

---

1. Justice Breyer delivered the opinion of the Court, in which Justices Kennedy, Ginsburg, Sotomayor, and Kagan joined. Parts of Justice Breyer's opinion have been redacted; the full opinion is available at 136 S. Ct. 2292 (2016).

"the minimum standards for an abortion facility must be equivalent to the minimum standards adopted under [the Texas Health and Safety Code section] for ambulatory surgical centers." Tex. Health & Safety Code Ann. §245.010(a).

We conclude that neither of these provisions offers medical benefits sufficient to justify the burdens upon access that each imposes. Each places a substantial obstacle in the path of women seeking a previability abortion, each constitutes an undue burden on abortion access, *Casey, supra,* at 878 (plurality opinion), and each violates the Federal Constitution. Amdt. 14, §1.

I

A

In July 2013, the Texas Legislature enacted House Bill 2 (H. B. 2 or Act). In September (before the new law took effect), a group of Texas abortion providers filed an action in Federal District Court seeking facial invalidation of the law's admitting-privileges provision. In late October, the District Court granted the injunction. *Planned Parenthood of Greater Tex. Surgical Health Servs.* v. *Abbott,* 951 F. Supp. 2d 891, 901 (WD Tex. 2013). But three days later, the Fifth Circuit vacated the injunction, thereby permitting the provision to take effect. *Planned Parenthood of Greater Tex. Surgical Health Servs.* v. *Abbott,* 734 F. 3d 406, 419 (2013).

The Fifth Circuit subsequently upheld the provision, and set forth its reasons in an opinion released late the following March. In that opinion, the Fifth Circuit pointed to evidence introduced in the District Court the previous October. It noted that Texas had offered evidence designed to show that the admitting-privileges requirement "will reduce the delay in treatment and decrease health risk for abortion patients with critical complications," and that it would "'screen out' untrained or incompetent abortion providers." *Planned Parenthood of Greater Tex. Surgical Health Servs.* v. *Abbott,* 748 F. 3d 583, 592 (2014) (*Abbott*). The opinion also explained that the plaintiffs had not provided sufficient evidence "that abortion practitioners will likely be unable to comply with the privileges requirement." *Id.,* at 598. The court said that all "of the major Texas cities, including Austin, Corpus Christi, Dallas, El Paso, Houston, and San Antonio," would "continue to have multiple clinics where many physicians will have or obtain hospital admitting privileges." *Ibid.* The *Abbott* plaintiffs did not file a petition for certiorari in this Court.

B

On April 6, one week after the Fifth Circuit's decision, petitioners, a group of abortion providers (many of whom were plaintiffs in the previous lawsuit), filed the present lawsuit in Federal District Court. They sought an injunction preventing enforcement of the admitting-privileges provision as applied to physicians at two abortion facilities, one operated by Whole Woman's Health in McAllen and the other operated by Nova Health Systems in El Paso. They also sought an injunction prohibiting enforcement of the surgical-center provision anywhere in Texas. They claimed that the admitting-privileges provision and the surgical-center provision violated the Constitution's Fourteenth Amendment, as interpreted in *Casey*.

The District Court subsequently received stipulations from the parties and depositions from the parties' experts. The court conducted a 4-day bench trial. It heard, among other testimony, the opinions from expert witnesses for both sides. On the basis of the stipulations, depositions, and testimony, that court reached the following conclusions:

1. Of Texas' population of more than 25 million people, "approximately 5.4 million" are "women" of "reproductive age," living within a geographical area of "nearly 280,000 square miles." *Whole Woman's Health* v. *Lakey*, 46 F. Supp. 3d 673, 681 (2014); see App. 244.

2. "In recent years, the number of abortions reported in Texas has stayed fairly consistent at approximately 15–16% of the reported pregnancy rate, for a total number of approximately 60,000–72,000 legal abortions performed annually." 46 F. Supp. 3d, at 681; see App. 238.

3. Prior to the enactment of H. B. 2, there were more than 40 licensed abortion facilities in Texas, which "number dropped by almost half leading up to and in the wake of enforcement of the admitting-privileges requirement that went into effect in late-October 2013." 46 F. Supp. 3d, at 681; App. 228–231.

4. If the surgical-center provision were allowed to take effect, the number of abortion facilities, after September 1, 2014, would be reduced further, so that "only seven facilities and a potential eighth will exist in Texas." 46 F. Supp. 3d, at 680; App. 182–183.

5. Abortion facilities "will remain only in Houston, Austin, San Antonio, and the Dallas/Fort Worth metropolitan region." 46 F. Supp. 3d, at 681; App. 229–230. These include "one facility in Austin, two in Dallas, one in Fort Worth, two in Houston, and either one or two in San Antonio." 46 F. Supp. 3d, at 680; App. 229–230.

6. "Based on historical data pertaining to Texas's average number of abortions, and assuming perfectly equal distribution among the remaining seven or eight providers, this would result in each facility serving between 7,500 and 10,000 patients per year. Accounting for the seasonal variations in pregnancy rates and a slightly unequal distribution of patients at each clinic, it is foreseeable that over 1,200 women per month could be vying for counseling, appointments, and follow-up visits at some of these facilities." 46 F. Supp. 3d, at 682; cf. App. 238.

7. The suggestion "that these seven or eight providers could meet the demand of the entire state stretches credulity." 46 F. Supp. 3d, at 682; see App. 238.

8. "Between November 1, 2012 and May 1, 2014," that is, before and after enforcement of the admitting-privileges requirement, "the decrease in geographical distribution of abortion facilities" has meant that the number of women of reproductive age living more than 50 miles from a clinic has doubled (from 800,000 to over 1.6 million); those living more than 100 miles has increased by 150% (from 400,000 to 1 million); those living more than 150 miles has increased by more than 350% (from 86,000 to 400,000); and those living more than 200 miles has increased by about 2,800% (from 10,000 to 290,000). After September 2014, should the surgical-center requirement go into effect, the number of women of reproductive age living significant distances from an abortion provider will increase as follows: 2 million women of reproductive age will live more than 50 miles from an abortion provider; 1.3 million will live more than 100 miles from an abortion provider; 900,000 will live more than 150 miles from an abortion provider; and 750,000 more than 200 miles from an abortion provider. 46 F. Supp. 3d, at 681–682; App. 238–242.

9. The "two requirements erect a particularly high barrier for poor, rural, or disadvantaged women." 46 F. Supp. 3d, at 683; cf. App. 363–370.

10. "The great weight of evidence demonstrates that, before the act's passage, abortion in Texas was extremely safe with particularly low rates of serious complications and virtually no deaths occurring on account of the procedure." 46 F. Supp. 3d, at 684; see, *e.g.,* App. 257–259, 538; see also *id.,* at 200–202, 253–257.

11. "Abortion, as regulated by the State before the enactment of House Bill 2, has been shown to be much safer, in terms of minor and serious complications, than many common medical procedures not subject to such intense regulation and scrutiny." 46 F. Supp. 3d, at 684; see, *e.g.,* App. 223–224 (describing risks in colonoscopies), 254 (discussing risks in vasectomy and endometrial biopsy, among others), 275–277 (discussing complication rate in plastic surgery).

12. "Additionally, risks are not appreciably lowered for patients who undergo abortions at ambulatory surgical centers as compared to nonsurgical-center facilities." 46 F. Supp. 3d, at 684; App. 202–206, 257–259.

13. "[W]omen will not obtain better care or experience more frequent positive outcomes at an ambulatory surgical center as compared to a previously licensed facility." 46 F. Supp. 3d, at 684; App. 202–206.

14. "[T]here are 433 licensed ambulatory surgical centers in Texas," of which "336 . . . are apparently either 'grandfathered' or enjo[y] the benefit of a waiver of some or all" of the surgical-center "requirements." 46 F. Supp. 3d, at 680–681; App. 184.

15. The "cost of coming into compliance" with the surgical-center requirement "for existing clinics is significant," "undisputedly approach[ing] 1 million dollars," and "most likely exceed[ing] 1.5 million dollars," with "[s]ome . . . clinics" unable to "comply due to physical size limitations of their sites." 46 F. Supp. 3d, at 682. The "cost of acquiring land and constructing a new compliant clinic will likely exceed three million dollars." *Ibid.*

On the basis of these and other related findings, the District Court determined that the surgical-center requirement "imposes an undue burden on the right of women throughout Texas to seek a previability abortion," and that the "admitting-privileges requirement, . . . in conjunction with the ambulatory-surgical-center requirement, imposes an undue burden on the right of women in the Rio Grande Valley, El Paso, and West Texas to seek a previability abortion." *Id.,* at 687. The District Court concluded that the "two provisions" would cause "the closing of almost all abortion clinics in Texas that were operating legally in the fall of 2013," and thereby create a constitutionally "impermissible obstacle as applied to all women seeking a previability abortion" by "restricting access to previously available legal facilities." *Id.,* at 687–688. On August 29, 2014, the court enjoined the enforcement of the two provisions. *Ibid.*

. . . .

[Section I C addresses details of the court of appeals decision and has been redacted. Section II addresses the procedural issue of claim preclusion and has been redacted.]

III

Undue Burden—Legal Standard

We begin with the standard, as described in *Casey.* We recognize that the "State has a legitimate interest in seeing to it that abortion, like any other medical procedure, is performed under circumstances that insure maximum safety for the patient." *Roe* v. *Wade,* 410 U.S. 113, 150 (1973). But, we added, "a statute which, while furthering [a] valid state interest, has the effect of placing a substantial obstacle in the path of a woman's choice cannot be considered a permissible means of serving its legitimate ends." *Casey,* 505 U.S., at 877 (plurality opinion). Moreover, "[u]nnecessary health regulations that have the purpose or effect of presenting a substantial obstacle to a woman seeking an abortion impose an undue burden on the right." *Id.,* at 878.

The Court of Appeals wrote that a state law is "constitutional if: (1) it does not have the purpose or effect of placing a substantial obstacle in the path of a woman seeking an abortion of a nonviable fetus; and (2) it is reasonably related to (or designed to further) a legitimate state interest." 790 F. 3d, at 572. The Court of Appeals went on to hold that "the district court erred by substituting its own judgment for that of the legislature" when it conducted its "undue burden inquiry," in part because "medical uncertainty underlying a statute is for resolution by legislatures, not the courts." *Id.,* at 587 (citing *Gonzales* v. *Carhart,* 550 U.S. 124, 163 (2007)).

The Court of Appeals' articulation of the relevant standard is incorrect. The first part of the Court of Appeals' test may be read to imply that a district court should not consider the existence or nonexistence of medical benefits when considering whether a regulation of abortion constitutes an undue burden. The rule announced in *Casey,* however, requires that courts consider the burdens a law imposes on abortion access together with the benefits those laws confer. See 505 U.S., at 887–898 (opinion of the Court) (performing this balancing with respect to a spousal notification provision); *id.,* at 899–901 (joint opinion of O'Connor, Kennedy, and Souter, JJ.) (same balancing with respect to a parental notification provision). And the second part of the test is wrong to equate the judicial review applicable to the regulation of a constitutionally protected personal liberty with the less strict review applicable where, for example, economic legislation is at issue. See, *e.g., Williamson* v. *Lee Optical of Okla., Inc.,* 348 U.S. 483, 491 (1955). The Court of Appeals' approach simply does not match the standard that this Court laid out in *Casey,* which asks courts to consider whether any burden imposed on abortion access is "undue."

The statement that legislatures, and not courts, must resolve questions of medical uncertainty is also inconsistent with this Court's case law. Instead, the Court, when determining the constitutionality of laws regulating abortion procedures, has placed considerable weight upon evidence and argument presented in judicial proceedings. In *Casey,* for example, we relied heavily on the District Court's factual findings and the research-based submissions of *amici* in declaring a portion of the law at issue unconstitutional. 505 U.S., at 888–894 (opinion of the Court) (discussing evidence related to the prevalence of spousal abuse in determining that a spousal notification provision erected an undue burden to abortion access). And, in *Gonzales* the Court, while pointing out that we must review legislative "factfinding under a deferential standard," added that we must not "place dispositive weight" on those "findings." 550 U.S., at 165. *Gonzales* went on to point out that the "*Court retains an independent constitutional duty to review factual findings where constitutional rights are at stake.*" *Ibid.* (emphasis added). Although there we upheld a statute regulating abortion, we did not do so solely on the basis of legislative findings explicitly set forth in the statute, noting that "evidence presented in the District Courts contradicts" some of the legislative findings. *Id.*, at 166. In these circumstances, we said, "[u]ncritical deference to Congress' factual findings . . . is inappropriate." *Ibid.*

Unlike in *Gonzales*, the relevant statute here does not set forth any legislative findings. Rather, one is left to infer that the legislature sought to further a constitutionally acceptable objective (namely, protecting women's health). *Id.*, at 149–150. For a district court to give significant weight to evidence in the judicial record in these circumstances is consistent with this Court's case law. As we shall describe, the District Court did so here. It did not simply substitute its own judgment for that of the legislature. It considered the evidence in the record—including expert evidence, presented in stipulations, depositions, and testimony. It then weighed the asserted benefits against the burdens. We hold that, in so doing, the District Court applied the correct legal standard.

IV

Undue Burden—Admitting-Privileges Requirement

Turning to the lower courts' evaluation of the evidence, we first consider the admitting-privileges requirement. Before the enactment of H. B. 2, doctors who provided abortions were required to "have admitting privileges *or* have a working arrangement with a physician(s) who has admitting privileges at a local hospital in order to ensure the necessary back up for medical complications." Tex. Admin. Code, tit. 25, §139.56 (2009) (emphasis added). The new law changed this requirement by requiring that a "physician performing or inducing an abortion . . . must, on the date the abortion is performed or induced, have active admitting privileges at a hospital that . . . is located not further than 30 miles from the location at which the abortion is performed or induced." Tex. Health & Safety Code Ann.

§171.0031(a). The District Court held that the legislative change imposed an "undue burden" on a woman's right to have an abortion. We conclude that there is adequate legal and factual support for the District Court's conclusion.

The purpose of the admitting-privileges requirement is to help ensure that women have easy access to a hospital should complications arise during an abortion procedure. Brief for Respondents 32–37. But the District Court found that it brought about no such health-related benefit. The court found that "[t]he great weight of evidence demonstrates that, before the act's passage, abortion in Texas was extremely safe with particularly low rates of serious complications and virtually no deaths occurring on account of the procedure." 46 F. Supp. 3d, at 684. Thus, there was no significant health-related problem that the new law helped to cure.

The evidence upon which the court based this conclusion included, among other things:

- A collection of at least five peer-reviewed studies on abortion complications in the first trimester, showing that the highest rate of major complications—including those complications requiring hospital admission—was less than one-quarter of 1%. See App. 269–270.

- Figures in three peer-reviewed studies showing that the highest complication rate found for the much rarer second trimester abortion was less than one-half of 1% (0.45% or about 1 out of about 200). *Id.*, at 270.

- Expert testimony to the effect that complications rarely require hospital admission, much less immediate transfer to a hospital from an outpatient clinic. *Id.*, at 266–267 (citing a study of complications occurring within six weeks after 54,911 abortions that had been paid for by the fee-for-service California Medicaid Program finding that the incidence of complications was 2.1%, the incidence of complications requiring hospital admission was 0.23%, and that of the 54,911 abortion patients included in the study, only 15 required immediate transfer to the hospital on the day of the abortion).

- Expert testimony stating that "it is extremely unlikely that a patient will experience a serious complication at the clinic that requires emergent hospitalization" and "in the rare case in which [one does], the quality of care that the patient receives is not affected by whether the abortion provider has admitting privileges at the hospital." *Id.*, at 381.

- Expert testimony stating that in respect to surgical abortion patients who do suffer complications requiring hospitalization, most of these complications occur in the days after the abortion, not on the spot. See *id.*, at 382; see also *id.*, at 267.

- Expert testimony stating that a delay before the onset of complications is also expected for medical abortions, as "abortifacient drugs take time to exert their effects, and thus the abortion itself almost always occurs after the patient has left the abortion facility." *Id.*, at 278.
- Some experts added that, if a patient needs a hospital in the day or week following her abortion, she will likely seek medical attention at the hospital nearest her home. See, *e.g., id.,* at 153.

We have found nothing in Texas' record evidence that shows that, compared to prior law (which required a "working arrangement" with a doctor with admitting privileges), the new law advanced Texas' legitimate interest in protecting women's health.

We add that, when directly asked at oral argument whether Texas knew of a single instance in which the new requirement would have helped even one woman obtain better treatment, Texas admitted that there was no evidence in the record of such a case. See Tr. of Oral Arg. 47. This answer is consistent with the findings of the other Federal District Courts that have considered the health benefits of other States' similar admitting-privileges laws. See *Planned Parenthood of Wis., Inc.* v. *Van Hollen,* 94 F. Supp. 3d 949, 953 (WD Wis. 2015), aff'd *sub nom. Planned Parenthood of Wis., Inc.* v. *Schimel,* 806 F. 3d 908 (CA7 2015); *Planned Parenthood Southeast, Inc.* v. *Strange,* 33 F. Supp. 3d 1330, 1378 (MD Ala. 2014).

At the same time, the record evidence indicates that the admitting-privileges requirement places a "substantial obstacle in the path of a woman's choice." *Casey,* 505 U.S., at 877 (plurality opinion). The District Court found, as of the time the admitting-privileges requirement began to be enforced, the number of facilities providing abortions dropped in half, from about 40 to about 20. 46 F. Supp. 3d, at 681. Eight abortion clinics closed in the months leading up to the requirement's effective date. See App. 229–230; cf. Brief for Planned Parenthood Federation of America et al. as *Amici Curiae* 14 (noting that abortion facilities in Waco, San Angelo, and Midland no longer operate because Planned Parenthood is "unable to find local physicians in those communities with privileges who are willing to provide abortions due to the size of those communities and the hostility that abortion providers face"). Eleven more closed on the day the admitting-privileges requirement took effect. See App. 229–230; Tr. of Oral Arg. 58.

Other evidence helps to explain why the new requirement led to the closure of clinics. We read that other evidence in light of a brief filed in this Court by the Society of Hospital Medicine. That brief describes the undisputed general fact that "hospitals often condition admitting privileges on reaching a certain number of admissions per year." Brief for Society of Hospital Medicine et al. as *Amici Curiae* 11. Returning to the District Court record, we note that, in direct testimony, the president of Nova Health Systems, implicitly relying on this general fact, pointed out that it would be difficult for doctors regularly performing abortions at the El Paso clinic to obtain admitting privileges at nearby hospitals because "[d]uring the past 10 years, over 17,000 abortion procedures were performed at the El Paso clinic [and n]ot a single one of those patients had to be transferred to a hospital for emergency treatment, much less admitted to the hospital." App. 730. In a word, doctors would be unable to maintain admitting privileges or obtain those privileges for the future, because the fact that abortions are so safe meant that providers were unlikely to have any patients to admit.

Other *amicus* briefs filed here set forth without dispute other common prerequisites to obtaining admitting privileges that have nothing to do with ability to perform medical procedures. See Brief for Medical Staff Professionals as *Amici Curiae* 20–25 (listing, for example, requirements that an applicant has treated a high number of patients in the hospital setting in the past year, clinical data requirements, residency requirements, and other discretionary factors); see also Brief for American College of Obstetricians and Gynecologists et al. as *Amici Curiae* 16 (ACOG Brief) ("[S]ome academic hospitals will only allow medical staff membership for clinicians who also . . . accept faculty appointments"). Again, returning to the District Court record, we note that Dr. Lynn of the McAllen clinic, a veteran obstetrics and gynecology doctor who estimates that he has delivered over 15,000 babies in his 38 years in practice was unable to get admitting privileges at any of the seven hospitals within 30 miles of his clinic. App. 390–394. He was refused admitting privileges at a nearby hospital for reasons, as the hospital wrote, "not based on clinical competence considerations." *Id.,* at 393–394 (emphasis deleted). The admitting-privileges requirement does not serve any relevant credentialing function.

In our view, the record contains sufficient evidence that the admitting-privileges requirement led to the closure of half of Texas' clinics, or thereabouts. Those closures meant fewer doctors, longer waiting times, and increased crowding. Record evidence also supports the finding that after the admitting-privileges provision went into effect, the "number of women of reproductive age living in a county . . . more than 150 miles from a provider increased from approximately 86,000 to 400,000 . . . and the number of women living in a county more than 200 miles from a provider from approximately 10,000 to 290,000." 46 F. Supp. 3d, at 681. We recognize that increased driving distances do not always constitute an "undue burden." See *Casey,* 505 U.S., at 885–887 (joint opinion of O'Connor, Kennedy, and Souter, JJ.). But here, those increases are but one additional burden, which, when taken together with others that the closings brought about, and when viewed in light of the virtual absence of any health benefit, lead us to conclude that the record adequately supports the District Court's "undue burden" conclusion. Cf. *id.*, at 895 (opinion of the Court) (finding burden "undue" when requirement places "substantial obstacle to a woman's choice" in "a large fraction of the cases in which" it "is relevant").

The dissent's only argument why these clinic closures, as well as the ones discussed in Part V, *infra*, may not have imposed an undue burden is this: Although "H. B. 2 caused the closure of *some* clinics," *post*, at 26 (emphasis added), other clinics may have closed for other reasons (so we should not "actually count" the burdens resulting from those closures against H. B. 2), *post*, at 30–31. But petitioners satisfied their burden to present evidence of causation by presenting direct testimony as well as plausible inferences to be drawn from the timing of the clinic closures. App. 182–183, 228–231. The District Court credited that evidence and concluded from it that H. B. 2 in factled to the clinic closures. 46 F. Supp. 3d, at 680–681. The dissent's speculation that perhaps other evidence, not presented at trial or credited by the District Court, might have shown that some clinics closed for unrelated reasons does not provide sufficient ground to disturb the District Court's factual finding on that issue.

In the same breath, the dissent suggests that one benefit of H. B. 2's requirements would be that they might "force unsafe facilities to shut down." *Post*, at 26. To support that assertion, the dissent points to the Kermit Gosnell scandal. Gosnell, a physician in Pennsylvania, was convicted of first-degree murder and manslaughter. He "staffed his facility with unlicensed and indifferent workers, and then let them practice medicine unsupervised" and had "[d]irty facilities; unsanitary instruments; an absence of functioning monitoring and resuscitation equipment; the use of cheap, but dangerous, drugs; illegal procedures; and inadequate emergency access for when things inevitably went wrong." Report of Grand Jury in No. 0009901–2008 (1st Jud. Dist. Pa., Jan. 14,2011), p. 24, online at http://www.phila.gov /districtattorney/pdfs/grandjurywomens medical.pdf (as last visited June 24, 2016). Gosnell's behavior was terribly wrong. But there is no reason to believe that an extra layer of regulation would have affected that behavior. Deter-mined wrongdoers, already ignoring existing statutes and safety measures, are unlikely to be convinced to adopt safe practices by a new overlay of regulations. Regardless, Gosnell's deplorable crimes could escape detection only because his facility went uninspected for more than 15 years. *Id.*, at 20. Pre-existing Texas law already contained numerous detailed regulations covering abortion facilities, including a requirement that facilities be inspected at least annually. See *infra,* at 28 (describing those regulations). The record contains nothing to suggest that H. B. 2 would be more effective than pre-existing Texas law at deterring wrongdoers like Gosnell from criminal behavior.

V

Undue Burden—Surgical-Center Requirement

The second challenged provision of Texas' new law sets forth the surgical-center requirement. Prior to enactment of the new requirement, Texas law required abortion facilities to meet a host of health and safety requirements. Under those pre-existing laws, facilities were subject to annual reporting and recordkeeping requirements, see Tex. Admin. Code, tit. 25, §§139.4, 139.5, 139.55, 139.58; a quality assurance program, see §139.8; personnel policies and staffing requirements, see §§139.43, 139.46; physical and environmental requirements, see §139.48; infection control standards, see §139.49; disclosure requirements, see §139.50; patient-rights standards, see §139.51; and medical- and clinical-services standards, see §139.53, including anesthesia standards, see §139.59. These requirements are policed by random and announced inspections, at least annually, see §§139.23, 139.31; Tex. Health & Safety Code Ann. §245.006(a) (West 2010), as well as administrative penalties, injunctions, civil penalties, and criminal penalties for certain violations, see Tex. Admin. Code, tit. 25, §139.33; Tex. Health & Safety Code Ann. §245.011 (criminal penalties for certain reporting violations).

H. B. 2 added the requirement that an "abortion facility" meet the "minimum standards . . . for ambulatory surgical centers" under Texas law. §245.010(a) (West Cum. Supp. 2015). The surgical-center regulations include, among other things, detailed specifications relating to the size of the nursing staff, building dimensions, and other building requirements. The nursing staff must comprise at least "an adequate number of [registered nurses] on duty to meet the following minimum staff requirements: director of the department (or designee), and supervisory and staff personnel for each service area to assure the immediate availability of [a registered nurse] for emergency care or for any patient when needed," Tex. Admin. Code, tit. 25, §135.15(a)(3) (2016), as well as "a second individual on duty on the premises who is trained and currently certified in basic cardiac life support until all patients have been discharged from the facility" for facilities that provide moderate sedation, such as most abortion facilities, §135.15(b)(2)(A). Facilities must include a full surgical suite with an operating room that has "a clear floor area of at least 240 square feet" in which "[t]he minimum clear dimension between built-in cabinets, counters, and shelves shall be 14 feet." §135.52(d)(15)(A). There must be a preoperative patient holding room and a postoperative recovery suite. The former "shall be provided and arranged in a one-way traffic pattern so that patients entering from outside the surgical suite can change, gown, and move directly into the restricted corridor of the surgical suite," §135.52(d)(10)(A), and the latter "shall be arranged to provide a one-way traffic pattern from the restricted surgical corridor to the postoperative recovery suite, and then to the extended observation rooms or discharge," §135.52(d)(9)(A). Surgical centers must meet numerous other spatial requirements, see generally §135.52, including specific corridor widths, §135.52(e)(1)(B)(iii). Surgical centers must also have an advanced heating, ventilation, and air conditioning system, §135.52(g)(5), and must satisfy particular piping system and plumbing requirements, §135.52(h). Dozens of other sections list additional requirements that apply to surgical centers. See generally §§135.1–135.56.

There is considerable evidence in the record supporting the District Court's findings indicating that the statutory provision requiring all abortion facilities to meet all surgical-center standards does not benefit patients and is not necessary. The District Court found that "risks are not appreciably lowered for patients who undergo abortions at ambulatory surgical centers as compared to nonsurgical-center facilities." 46 F. Supp. 3d, at 684. The court added that women "will not obtain better care or experience more frequent positive outcomes at an ambulatory surgical center as compared to a previously licensed facility." *Ibid.* And these findings are well supported.

The record makes clear that the surgical-center requirement provides no benefit when complications arise in the context of an abortion produced through medication. That is because, in such a case, complications would almost always arise only after the patient has left the facility. See *supra*, at 23; App. 278. The record also contains evidence indicating that abortions taking place in an abortion facility are safe—indeed, safer than numerous procedures that take place outside hospitals and to which Texas does not apply its surgical-center requirements. See, *e.g., id.,* at 223–224, 254, 275–279. The total number of deaths in Texas from abortions was five in the period from 2001 to 2012, or about one every two years (that is to say, one out of about 120,000 to 144,000 abortions). *Id.,* at 272. Nationwide, childbirth is 14 times more likely than abortion to result in death, *ibid.,* but Texas law allows a midwife to oversee childbirth in the patient's own home. Colonoscopy, a procedure that typically takes place outside a hospital (or surgical center) setting, has a mortality rate 10 times higher than an abortion. *Id.*, at 276–277; see ACOG Brief 15 (the mortality rate for liposuction, another outpatient procedure, is 28 times higher than the mortality rate for abortion). Medical treatment after an incomplete miscarriage often involves a procedure identical to that involved in a nonmedical abortion, but it often takes place outside a hospital or surgical center. App. 254; see ACOG Brief 14 (same). And Texas partly or wholly grandfathers (or waives in whole or in part the surgical-center requirement for) about two-thirds of the facilities to which the surgical-center standards apply. But it neither grandfathers nor provides waivers for any of the facilities that perform abortions. 46 F. Supp. 3d, at 680–681; see App. 184. These facts indicate that the surgical-center provision imposes "a requirement that simply is not based on differences" between abortion and other surgical procedures "that are reasonably related to" preserving women's health, the asserted "purpos[e] of the Act in which it is found." *Doe*, 410 U.S., at 194 (quoting *Morey* v. *Doud*, 354 U.S. 457, 465 (1957); internal quotation marks omitted).

Moreover, many surgical-center requirements are inappropriate as applied to surgical abortions. Requiring scrub facilities; maintaining a one-way traffic pattern through the facility; having ceiling, wall, and floor finishes; separating soiled utility and sterilization rooms; and regulating air pressure, filtration, and humidity control can help reduce infection where doctors conduct procedures that penetrate the skin. App. 304. But abortions typically involve either the administration of medicines or procedures performed through the natural opening of the birth canal, which is itself not sterile. See *id.*, at 302–303. Nor do provisions designed to safeguard heavily sedated patients (unable to help themselves) during fire emergencies, see Tex. Admin. Code, tit. 25, §135.41; App. 304, provide any help to abortion patients, as abortion facilities do not use general anesthesia or deep sedation, *id.*, at 304–305. Further, since the few instances in which serious complications do arise following an abortion almost always require hospitalization, not treatment at a surgical center, *id.*, at 255–256, surgical-center standards will not help in those instances either.

The upshot is that this record evidence, along with the absence of any evidence to the contrary, provides ample support for the District Court's conclusion that "[m]any of the building standards mandated by the act and its implementing rules have such a tangential relationship to patient safety in the context of abortion as to be nearly arbitrary." 46 F. Supp. 3d, at 684. That conclusion, along with the supporting evidence, provides sufficient support for the more general conclusion that the surgical-center requirement "will not [provide] better care or . . . more frequent positive outcomes." *Ibid.* The record evidence thus supports the ultimate legal conclusion that the surgical-center requirement is not necessary.

At the same time, the record provides adequate evidentiary support for the District Court's conclusion that the surgical-center requirement places a substantial obstacle in the path of women seeking an abortion. The parties stipulated that the requirement would further reduce the number of abortion facilities available to seven or eight facilities, located in Houston, Austin, San Antonio, and Dallas/Fort Worth. See App. 182–183. In the District Court's view, the proposition that these "seven or eight providers could meet the demand of the entire State stretches credulity." 46 F. Supp. 3d, at 682. We take this statement as a finding that these few facilities could not "meet" that "demand."

The Court of Appeals held that this finding was "clearly erroneous." 790 F. 3d, at 590. It wrote that the finding rested upon the "*ipse dixit*" of one expert, Dr. Grossman, and that there was no evidence that the current surgical centers (*i.e.,* the seven or eight) are operating at full capacity or could not increase capacity. *Ibid.* Unlike the Court of Appeals, however, we hold that the record provides adequate support for the District Court's finding.

For one thing, the record contains charts and oral testimony by Dr. Grossman, who said that, as a result of the surgical-center requirement, the number of abortions that the clinics would have to provide would rise from "14,000 abortions annually" to "60,000 to 70,000"—an increase by a factor of about five. *Id.,* at 589–590. The District Court credited Dr. Grossman as an expert witness. See 46 F. Supp. 3d, at 678–679, n. 1; *id.,* at 681, n. 4 (finding "indicia of reliability" in Dr. Grossman's conclusions). The Federal Rules of Evidence state that an expert may testify in the "form of an opinion" as long as that opinion rests upon "sufficient facts or data" and "reliable principles and methods." Rule 702. In this case Dr. Grossman's opinion rested upon his participation, along with other university researchers, in research that tracked "the number of open facilities providing abortion care in the state by . . . requesting information from the Texas Department of State Health Services . . . [, t]hrough interviews with clinic staff[,] and review of publicly available information." App. 227. The District Court acted within its legal authority in determining that Dr. Grossman's testimony was admissible. See Fed. Rule Evid. 702; see also *Daubert* v. *Merrell Dow Pharmaceuticals, Inc.,* 509 U.S. 579, 589 (1993) ("[U]nder the Rules the trial judge must ensure that any and all [expert] evidence admitted is not only relevant, but reliable"); 29 C. Wright & V. Gold, Federal Practice and Procedure: Evidence §6266, p. 302 (2016) ("Rule 702 impose[s] on the trial judge additional responsibility to determine whether that [expert] testimony is likely to promote accurate factfinding").

For another thing, common sense suggests that, more often than not, a physical facility that satisfies a certain physical demand will not be able to meet five times that demand without expanding or otherwise incurring significant costs. Suppose that we know only that a certain grocery store serves 200 customers per week, that a certain apartment building provides apartments for 200 families, that a certain train station welcomes 200 trains per day. While it is conceivable that the store, the apartment building, or the train station could just as easily provide for 1,000 customers, families, or trains at no significant additional cost, crowding, or delay, most of us would find this possibility highly improbable. The dissent takes issue with this general, intuitive point by arguing that many places operate below capacity and that in any event, facilities could simply hire additional providers. See *post*, at 32. We disagree that, according to common sense, medical facilities, well known for their wait times, operate below capacity as a general matter. And the fact that so many facilities were forced to close by the admitting-privileges requirement means that hiring more physicians would not be quite as simple as the dissent suggests. Courts are free to base their findings on commonsense inferences drawn from the evidence. And that is what the District Court did here.

The dissent now seeks to discredit Dr. Grossman by pointing out that a preliminary prediction he made in his testimony in *Abbott* about the effect of the admitting-privileges requirement on capacity was not borne out after that provision went into effect. See *post*, at 31, n. 22. If every expert who overestimated or underestimated any figure could not be credited, courts would struggle to find expert assistance. Moreover, making a hypothesis—and then attempting to verify that hypothesis with further studies, as Dr. Grossman did—is not irresponsible. It is an essential element of the scientific method. The District Court's decision to credit Dr. Grossman's testimony was sound, particularly given that Texas provided no credible experts to rebut it. See 46 F. Supp. 3d, at 680, n. 3 (declining to credit Texas' expert witnesses, in part because Vincent Rue, a nonphysician consultant for Texas, had exercised "considerable editorial and discretionary control over the contents of the experts' reports").

Texas suggests that the seven or eight remaining clinics could expand sufficiently to provide abortions for the 60,000 to 72,000 Texas women who sought them each year. Because petitioners had satisfied their burden, the obligation was on Texas, if it could, to present evidence rebutting that issue to the District Court. Texas admitted that it presented no such evidence.

Tr. of Oral Arg. 46. Instead, Texas argued before this Court that one new clinic now serves 9,000 women annually. *Ibid.* In addition to being outside the record, that example is not representative. The clinic to which Texas referred apparently cost $26 million to construct—a fact that even more clearly demonstrates that requiring seven or eight clinics to serve five times their usual number of patients does indeed represent an undue burden on abortion access. See Planned Parenthood Debuts New Building: Its $26 Million Center in Houston is Largest of Its Kind in U.S., Houston Chronicle, May 21, 2010, p. B1.

Attempting to provide the evidence that Texas did not, the dissent points to an exhibit submitted in *Abbott* showing that three Texas surgical centers, two in Dallas as well as the $26-million facility in Houston, are each capable of serving an average of 7,000 patients per year. See *post,* at 33–35. That "average" is misleading. In addition to including the Houston clinic, which does not represent most facilities, it is underinclusive. It ignores the evidence as to the Whole Woman's Health surgical-center facility in San Antonio, the capacity of which is described as "severely limited." The exhibit does nothing to rebut the commonsense inference that the dramatic decline in the number of available facilities will cause a shortfall in capacity should H. B. 2 go into effect. And facilities that were still operating after the effective date of the admitting-privileges provision were not able to accommodate increased demand. See App. 238; Tr. of Oral Arg. 30–31; Brief for National Abortion Federation et al. as *Amici Curiae* 17–20 (citing clinics' experiences since the admitting-privileges requirement went into effect of 3-week wait times, staff burnout, and waiting rooms so full, patients had to sit on the floor or wait outside).

More fundamentally, in the face of no threat to women's health, Texas seeks to force women to travel long distances to get abortions in crammed-to-capacity superfacilities. Patients seeking these services are less likely to get the kind of individualized attention, serious conversation, and emotional support that doctors at less taxed facilities may have offered. Healthcare facilities and medical professionals are not fungible commodities. Surgical centers attempting to accommodate sudden, vastly increased demand, see 46 F. Supp. 3d, at 682, may find that quality of care declines. Another commonsense inference that the District Court made is that these effects would be harmful to, not supportive of, women's health. See *id.,* at 682–683.

Finally, the District Court found that the costs that a currently licensed abortion facility would have to incur to meet the surgical-center requirements were considerable, ranging from $1 million per facility (for facilities with adequate space) to $3 million per facility (where additional land must be purchased). *Id.*, at 682. This evidence supports the conclusion that more surgical centers will not soon fill the gap when licensed facilities are forced to close.

We agree with the District Court that the surgical-center requirement, like the admitting-privileges requirement, provides few, if any, health benefits for women, poses a substantial obstacle to women seeking abortions, and constitutes an "undue burden" on their constitutional right to do so.

. . . .

[Section VI addresses procedural arguments of Texas and has been redacted].

     *   *   *

For these reasons the judgment of the Court of Appeals is reversed, and the case is remanded for further proceedings consistent with this opinion.

It is so ordered.

Appendix M

Concurring Opinion of Chief Justice Roberts[1]

— *June Medical Services LLC v. Russo* (2020) —

In July 2013, Texas enacted a law requiring a physician performing an abortion to have "active admitting privileges at a hospital . . . located not further than 30 miles from the location at which the abortion is performed." Tex. Health & Safety Code Ann. § 171.0031(a)(1)(A) (West Cum. Supp. 2019). The law caused the number of facilities providing abortions to drop in half. In *Whole Woman's Health v. Hellerstedt*, 579 U.S. ___ (2016), the Court concluded that Texas's admitting privileges requirement "places a substantial obstacle in the path of women seeking a previability abortion" and therefore violated the Due Process Clause of the Fourteenth Amendment. *Id.*, at ___ (slip op., at 2) (citing *Planned Parenthood of Southeastern Pa. v. Casey*, 505 U.S. 833, 878 (1992) (plurality opinion)).

I joined the dissent in *Whole Woman's Health* and continue to believe that the case was wrongly decided. The question today however is not whether *Whole Woman's Health* was right or wrong, but whether to adhere to it in deciding the present case. See *Moore v. Texas*, 586 U.S. ___, ___ (2019) (Roberts, C. J., concurring) (slip op., at 1).

Today's case is a challenge from several abortion clinics and providers to a Louisiana law nearly identical to the Texas law struck down four years ago in *Whole Woman's Health.* Just like the Texas law, the Louisiana law requires physicians performing abortions to have "active admitting privileges at a hospital . . . located not further than thirty miles from the location at which the abortion is performed." La. Rev. Stat. Ann. § 40:1061.10(A)(2)(a) (West Cum. Supp. 2020). Following a six-day bench trial, the District Court found that Louisiana's law would "result in a drastic reduction in the number and geographic distribution of abortion providers." *June Medical Services LLC v. Kliebert*, 250 F. Supp. 3d 27, 87 (MD La. 2017). The law would

---

1. Chief Justice Roberts' opinion is available at 140 S. Ct. 2103, 2133 (2020).

reduce the number of clinics from three to "one, or at most two," and the number of physicians providing abortions from five to "one, or at most two," and "therefore cripple women's ability to have an abortion in Louisiana." *Id.,* at 87–88.

The legal doctrine of *stare decisis* requires us, absent special circumstances, to treat like cases alike. The Louisiana law imposes a burden on access to abortion just as severe as that imposed by the Texas law, for the same reasons. Therefore Louisiana's law cannot stand under our precedents.

I

Stare decisis ("to stand by things decided") is the legal term for fidelity to precedent. Black's Law Dictionary 1696 (11th ed. 2019). It has long been "an established rule to abide by former precedents, where the same points come again in litigation; as well to keep the scale of justice even and steady, and not liable to waver with every new judge's opinion." 1 W. Blackstone, Commentaries on the Laws of England 69 (1765). This principle is grounded in a basic humility that recognizes today's legal issues are often not so different from the questions of yesterday and that we are not the first ones to try to answer them. Because the "private stock of reason . . . in each man is small, . . . individuals would do better to avail themselves of the general bank and capital of nations and of ages." 3 E. Burke, Reflections on the Revolution in France 110 (1790).

Adherence to precedent is necessary to "avoid an arbitrary discretion in the courts." The Federalist No. 78, p. 529 (J. Cooke ed. 1961) (A. Hamilton). The constraint of precedent distinguishes the judicial "method and philosophy from those of the political and legislative process." Jackson, Decisional Law and Stare Decisis, 30 A.B.A.J. 334 (1944).

The doctrine also brings pragmatic benefits. Respect for precedent "promotes the evenhanded, predictable, and consistent development of legal principles, fosters reliance on judicial decisions, and contributes to the actual and perceived integrity of the judicial process." *Payne v. Tennessee,* 501 U.S. 808, 827 (1991). It is the "means by which we ensure that the law will not merely change erratically, but will develop in a principled and intelligible fashion." *Vasquez v. Hillery,* 474 U.S. 254, 265 (1986). In that way, "*stare decisis* is an old friend of the common lawyer." Jackson, *supra,* at 334.

Stare decisis is not an "inexorable command." *Ramos v. Louisiana,* 590 U.S. ___, ___ (2020) (slip op., at 20) (internal quotation marks omitted). But for precedent to mean anything, the doctrine must give way only to a rationale that goes beyond whether the case was decided correctly. The Court accordingly considers additional factors before overruling a precedent, such as its adminstrability, its fit with subsequent factual and legal developments, and the reliance interests that the precedent has engendered. See *Janus v. State, County, and Municipal Employees*, 585 U.S. ___, ___–___ (2018) (slip op., at 34–35).

Stare decisis principles also determine how we handle a decision that itself departed from the cases that came before it. In those instances, "[r]emaining true to an 'intrinsically sounder' doctrine established in prior cases better serves the values of *stare decisis* than would following" the recent departure. *Adarand Constructors, Inc. v. Peña*, 515 U.S. 200, 231 (1995) (plurality opinion). *Stare decisis* is pragmatic and contextual, not "a mechanical formula of adherence to the latest decision." *Helvering v. Hallock*, 309 U.S. 106, 119 (1940).

II

A

Both Louisiana and the providers agree that the undue burden standard announced in *Casey* provides the appropriate framework to analyze Louisiana's law. Brief for Petitioners in No. 18–1323, pp. 45–47; Brief for Respondent in No. 18–1323, pp. 60–62. Neither party has asked us to reassess the constitutional validity of that standard.

Casey reaffirmed "the most central principle of *Roe v. Wade*," "a woman's right to terminate her pregnancy before viability." *Casey*, 505 U.S., at 871 (plurality opinion).[2] At the same time, it recognized that the State has "important and legitimate interests in . . . protecting the health of the pregnant woman and in protecting the potentiality of human life." *Id.*, at 875–876 (internal quotation marks and brackets omitted).

To serve the former interest, the State may, "[a]s with any medical procedure," enact "regulations to further the health or safety of a woman seeking an abortion." *Id.*, at 878. To serve the latter interest, the State may, among other things, "enact rules and regulations designed to encourage her to know that there are philosophic and social arguments of great weight that can be brought to bear in favor of continuing the pregnancy

---

2. Although parts of *Casey*'s joint opinion were a plurality not joined by a majority of the Court, the joint opinion is nonetheless considered the holding of the Court under *Marks v. United States*, 430 U.S. 188, 193 (1977), as the narrowest position supporting the judgment.

to full term." *Id.*, at 872. The State's freedom to enact such rules is "consistent with *Roe*'s central premises, and indeed the inevitable consequence of our holding that the State has an interest in protecting the life of the unborn." *Id.*, at 873.

Under *Casey*, the State may not impose an undue burden on the woman's ability to obtain an abortion. "A finding of an undue burden is a shorthand for the conclusion that a state regulation has the purpose or effect of placing a substantial obstacle in the path of a woman seeking an abortion of a nonviable fetus." *Id.*, at 877. Laws that do not pose a substantial obstacle to abortion access are permissible, so long as they are "reasonably related" to a legitimate state interest. *Id.*, at 878.

After faithfully reciting this standard, the Court in *Whole Woman's Health* added the following observation: "The rule announced in *Casey* . . . requires that courts consider the burdens a law imposes on abortion access together with the benefits those laws confer." 579 U.S., at ___–___ (slip op., at 19–20). The plurality repeats today that the undue burden standard requires courts "to weigh the law's asserted benefits against the burdens it imposes on abortion access." *Ante*, at 2 (internal quotation marks omitted).

Read in isolation from *Casey*, such an inquiry could invite a grand "balancing test in which unweighted factors mysteriously are weighed." *Marrs v. Motorola, Inc.*, 577 F.3d 783, 788 (CA7 2009). Under such tests, "equality of treatment is . . . impossible to achieve; predictability is destroyed; judicial arbitrariness is facilitated; judicial courage is impaired." Scalia, The Rule of Law as a Law of Rules, 56 U. Chi. L. Rev. 1175, 1182 (1989).

In this context, courts applying a balancing test would be asked in essence to weigh the State's interests in "protecting the potentiality of human life" and the health of the woman, on the one hand, against the woman's liberty interest in defining her "own concept of existence, of meaning, of the universe, and of the mystery of human life" on the other. *Casey*, 505 U.S., at 851 (opinion of the Court); *id.*, at 871 (plurality opinion) (internal quotation marks omitted). There is no plausible sense in which anyone, let alone this Court, could objectively assign weight to such imponderable values and no meaningful way to compare them if there were. Attempting to do so would be like "judging whether a particular line is longer than a particular rock is heavy," *Bendix Autolite Corp. v. Midwesco Enterprises, Inc.*, 486 U.S. 888, 897 (1988) (Scalia, J., concurring in judgment). Pretending that we could pull that off would require us to act as legislators, not judges, and would result in nothing other than an "unanalyzed exercise of judicial will" in the guise of a "neutral utilitarian calculus." *New Jersey v. T. L. O.*, 469 U.S. 325, 369 (1985) (Brennan, J., concurring in part and dissenting in part).

Nothing about *Casey* suggested that a weighing of costs and benefits of an abortion regulation was a job for the courts. On the contrary, we have explained that the "traditional rule" that "state and federal legislatures [have] wide discretion to pass legislation in areas where there is medical and scientific uncertainty" is "consistent with *Casey*." *Gonzales v. Carhart*, 550 U.S. 124, 163 (2007). *Casey* instead focuses on the existence of a substantial obstacle, the sort of inquiry familiar to judges across a variety of contexts. See, *e.g., Burwell v. Hobby Lobby Stores, Inc.*, 573 U.S. 682, 694–695 (2014) (asking whether the government "substantially burdens a person's exercise of religion" under the Religious Freedom Restoration Act); *Arizona Free Enterprise Club's Freedom Club PAC v. Bennett*, 564 U.S. 721, 748 (2011) (asking whether a law "imposes a substantial burden on the speech of privately financed candidates and independent expenditure groups"); *Murphy v. United Parcel Service, Inc.*, 527 U.S. 516, 521 (1999) (asking, in the context of the Americans with Disabilities Act, whether an individual's impairment "substantially limits one or more major life activities" (internal quotation marks omitted)).

Casey's analysis of the various restrictions that were at issue in that case is illustrative. For example, the opinion recognized that Pennsylvania's 24-hour waiting period for abortions "has the effect of increasing the cost and risk of delay of abortions," but observed that the District Court did not find that the "increased costs and potential delays amount to substantial obstacles." 505 U.S., at 886 (joint opinion of O'Connor, Kennedy, and Souter, JJ.) (internal quotation marks omitted). The opinion concluded that "given the statute's definition of medical emergency," the waiting period did not "impose[ ] a real health risk." *Ibid.* Because the law did not impose a substantial obstacle, *Casey* upheld it. And it did so notwithstanding the District Court's finding that the law did "not further the state interest in maternal health." *Ibid.* (internal quotation marks omitted).

Turning to the State's various recordkeeping and reporting requirements, *Casey* found those requirements do not "impose a substantial obstacle to a woman's choice" because "[a]t most they increase the cost of some abortions by a slight amount." *Id.,* at 901. "While at some point increased cost could become a substantial obstacle," there was "no such showing on the record" before the Court. *Ibid.* The Court did not weigh this cost against the benefits of the law.

The same was true for Pennsylvania's parental consent requirement. *Casey* held that "a State may require a minor seeking an abortion to obtain the consent of a parent or guardian, provided there is an adequate judicial bypass procedure." *Id.,* at 899 (citing, among other cases, *Ohio v. Akron*

Center for Reproductive Health, 497 U.S. 502, 510–519 (1990)). *Casey* relied on precedent establishing that judicial bypass procedures "prevent another person from having an absolute veto power over a minor's decision to have an abortion." *Akron*, 497 U.S., at 510. Without a judicial bypass, parental consent laws impose a substantial obstacle to a minor's ability to obtain an abortion and therefore constitute an undue burden. See *Casey*, 505 U.S., at 899 (joint opinion).

The opinion similarly looked to whether there was a substantial burden, not whether benefits outweighed burdens, in analyzing Pennsylvania's requirement that physicians provide certain "truthful, nonmisleading information" about the nature of the abortion procedure. *Id.*, at 882. The opinion concluded that the requirement "cannot be considered a substantial obstacle to obtaining an abortion, and, *it follows*, there is no undue burden." *Id.*, at 883 (emphasis added).

With regard to the State's requirement that a physician, as opposed to a qualified assistant, provide the woman this information, the opinion reasoned: "*Since* there is no evidence on this record that requiring a doctor to give the information as provided by the statute would amount in practical terms to a substantial obstacle to a woman seeking an abortion, we conclude that it is not an undue burden." *Id.*, at 884–885 (emphasis added). This was so "even if an objective assessment might suggest that those same tasks could be performed by others," meaning the law had little if any benefit. *Id.*, at 885.

The only restriction *Casey* found unconstitutional was Pennsylvania's spousal notification requirement. On that score, the Court recited a bevy of social science evidence demonstrating that "millions of women in this country . . . may have justifiable fears of physical abuse" or "devastating forms of psychological abuse from their husbands." *Id.*, at 893 (opinion of the Court). In addition to "physical violence" and "child abuse," women justifiably feared "verbal harassment, threats of future violence, the destruction of possessions, physical confinement to the home, the withdrawal of financial support, or the disclosure of the abortion to family and friends." *Ibid.* The spousal notification requirement was "thus likely to prevent a significant number of women from obtaining an abortion." *Ibid.* It did not "merely make abortions a little more difficult or expensive to obtain; for many women, it [imposed] a substantial obstacle." *Id.*, at 893–894. The Court emphasized that it would not "blind [itself] to the fact that the significant number of women who fear for their safety and the safety of their children are likely to be deterred from procuring an abortion as surely as if the Commonwealth had outlawed abortion in all cases." *Id.*, at 894.

The upshot of *Casey* is clear: The several restrictions that did not impose a substantial obstacle were constitutional, while the restriction that did impose a substantial obstacle was unconstitutional.

To be sure, the Court at times discussed the benefits of the regulations, including when it distinguished spousal notification from parental consent. See *Whole Woman's Health*, 579 U.S., at ___-___ (slip op., at 19–20) (citing *Casey*, 505 U.S., at 887–898 (opinion of the Court); *id.*, at 899–901 (joint opinion). But in the context of *Casey*'s governing standard, these benefits were not placed on a scale opposite the law's burdens. Rather, *Casey* discussed benefits in considering the threshold requirement that the State have a "legitimate purpose" and that the law be "reasonably related to that goal." *Id.*, at 878 (plurality opinion); *id.*, at 882 (joint opinion).

So long as that showing is made, the only question for a court is whether a law has the "effect of placing a substantial obstacle in the path of a woman seeking an abortion of a nonviable fetus." *Id.*, at 877 (plurality opinion). *Casey* repeats that "substantial obstacle" standard nearly verbatim no less than 15 times. *Id.*, at 846, 894, 895 (opinion of the Court); *id.*, at 877, 878 (plurality opinion); *id.*, at 883, 884, 885, 886, 887, 901 (joint opinion).[3]

The only place a balancing test appears in *Casey* is in Justice Stevens's partial dissent. "Weighing the State's interest in potential life and the woman's liberty interest," Justice Stevens would have gone further than the plurality to strike down portions of the State's informed consent requirements and 24-hour waiting period. *Id.*, at 916–920 (opinion concurring in part and dissenting in part). But that approach did not win the day.

Mazurek v. Armstrong places this understanding of *Casey*'s undue burden standard beyond doubt. *Mazurek* involved a challenge to a Montana law restricting the performance of abortions to licensed physicians. 520 U.S., at 969. It was "uncontested that there was insufficient evidence of a 'substantial obstacle' to abortion." *Id.*, at 972. Therefore, once the Court found that the Montana Legislature had not acted with an "unlawful motive," the

---

3. Justice Gorsuch correctly notes that *Casey* "expressly disavowed any test as strict as strict scrutiny." *Post*, at 20 (dissenting opinion). But he certainly is wrong to suggest that my position is in any way inconsistent with that disavowal. Applying strict scrutiny would require "*any* regulation touching upon the abortion decision" to be the least restrictive means to further a compelling state interest. *Casey*, 505 U.S., at 871 (plurality opinion) (emphasis added). *Casey* however recognized that such a test would give "too little acknowledgement and implementation" to the State's "legitimate interests in the health of the woman and in protecting the potential life within her." *Ibid.* Under *Casey*, abortion regulations are valid so long as they do not pose a substantial obstacle and meet the threshold requirement of being "reasonably related" to a "legitimate purpose." *Id.* at 878; *id.* at 882 (joint opinion).

Court's work was complete. *Ibid.* In fact, the Court found the challengers' argument—that the law was invalid because "all health evidence contradicts the [State's] claim that there is any health basis for the law"—to be "*squarely foreclosed* by *Casey* itself." *Id.*, at 973 (internal quotation marks omitted; emphasis added).

We should respect the statement in *Whole Woman's Health* that it was applying the undue burden standard of *Casey*. The opinion in *Whole Woman's Health* began by saying, "We must here decide whether two provisions of [the Texas law] violate the Federal Constitution as interpreted in *Casey*." 579 U.S., at ___ (slip op., at 1). Nothing more. The Court explicitly stated that it was applying "the standard, as described in *Casey*," and reversed the Court of Appeals for applying an approach that did "not match the standard that this Court laid out in *Casey*." *Id.*, at ___, ___ (slip op., at 19, 20).

Here the plurality expressly acknowledges that we are not considering how to analyze an abortion regulation that does not present a substantial obstacle. "That," the plurality explains, "is not this case." *Ante*, at 40. In this case, *Casey*'s requirement of finding a substantial obstacle before invalidating an abortion regulation is therefore a sufficient basis for the decision, as it was in *Whole Woman's Health*. In neither case, nor in *Casey* itself, was there call for consideration of a regulation's benefits, and nothing in *Casey* commands such consideration. Under principles of *stare decisis*, I agree with the plurality that the determination in *Whole Woman's Health* that Texas's law imposed a substantial obstacle requires the same determination about Louisiana's law. Under those same principles, I would adhere to the holding of *Casey*, requiring a substantial obstacle before striking down an abortion regulation.

B

Whole Woman's Health held that Texas's admitting privileges requirement placed "a substantial obstacle in the path of women seeking a previability abortion," independent of its discussion of benefits. 579 U.S., at ___ (slip op., at 2) (citing *Casey*, 505 U.S., at 878 (plurality opinion)).[4] Because Loui-

---

4. Justice Gorsuch considers this is a "nonexistent ruling" nowhere to be found in *Whole Woman's Health. Post*, at 19 (dissenting opinion). I disagree. *Whole Woman's Health* first surveyed the benefits of Texas's admitting privileges requirement. 579 U.S., at ___–___ (slip op., at 23–24). The Court then transitioned to examining the law's burdens: "*At the same time*, the record evidence indicates that the admitting-privileges requirement places a substantial obstacle in the path of a woman's choice." *Id.* at ___ (slip op., at 24) (internal quotation marks omitted; emphasis added). And the Court made clear that a law which has the purpose or effect of placing "a substantial obstacle in the path of a woman seeking an abortion before the fetus attains viability" imposes an "undue burden" and therefore violates the

siana's admitting privileges requirement would restrict women's access to abortion to the same degree as Texas's law, it also cannot stand under our precedent.[5]

To begin, the two laws are nearly identical. Prior to enactment of the Texas law, abortion providers were required either to possess local hospital admitting privileges or to have a transfer agreement with a physician who had such privileges. Tex. Admin. Code, tit. 25, § 139.56(a) (2009). The new law, adopted in 2013, eliminated the option of having a transfer agreement. Providers were required to "[h]ave active admitting privileges at a hospital . . . located not further than 30 miles from the location at which the abortion is performed." Tex. Health & Safety Code Ann. § 171.0031(a)(1)(A).

Likewise, Louisiana law previously required abortion providers to have either admitting privileges or a transfer agreement. La. Admin. Code, tit. 48, pt. I, § 4407(A)(3) (2003), 29 La. Reg. 706–707 (2003). In 2014, Louisiana removed the option of having a transfer agreement. Just like Texas, Louisiana now requires abortion providers to "[h]ave active admitting privileges at a hospital . . . located not further than thirty miles from the location at which the abortion is performed." La. Rev. Stat. § 40:1061.10(A)(2)(a).

Crucially, the District Court findings indicate that Louisiana's law would restrict access to abortion in just the same way as Texas's law, to the same degree or worse. In Texas, "as of the time the admitting-privileges requirement began to be enforced, the number of facilities providing abortions dropped in half, from about 40 to about 20." *Whole Woman's Health*, 579 U.S., at ___ (slip op., at 24). Eight abortion clinics closed in the months prior to the law's effective date. *Ibid.* Another 11 clinics closed on the day the law took effect. *Ibid.*

Similarly, the District Court found that the Louisiana law would "result in a drastic reduction in the number and geographic distribution of abortion providers." 250 F. Supp. 3d, at 87. At the time of the District Court's decision, there were three clinics and five physicians performing abortions in Louisiana. *Id.,* at 40, 41. The District Court found that the new law would reduce "the number of clinics to one, or at most two," and the number of physicians in Louisiana to "one, or at most two," as well. *Id.,* at 87. Even in the best case, "the demand for services would vastly exceed the supply." *Ibid.*

Whole Woman's Health found that the closures of the abortion clinics led to "fewer doctors, longer waiting times, and increased crowding." 579 U.S.,

---

Constitution. *Id.* at ___ (slip op., at 1) (internal quotation marks omitted; emphasis deleted). Thus the discussion of benefits in *Whole Woman's Health* was not necessary to its holding.

5. For the reasons the plurality explains, *ante,* at 11–16, I agree that the abortion providers in this case have standing to assert the constitutional rights of their patients.

at ___ (slip op., at 26). The Court also found that "the number of women of reproductive age living in a county more than 150 miles from a provider increased from approximately 86,000 to 400,000 and the number of women living in a county more than 200 miles from a provider from approximately 10,000 to 290,000." *Ibid.* (internal quotation marks and alterations omitted).

The District Court here likewise found that the Louisiana law would result in "longer waiting times for appointments, increased crowding and increased associated health risk." 250 F. Supp. 3d, at 81. The court found that Louisiana women already "have difficulty affording or arranging for transportation and childcare on the days of their clinic visits" and that "[i]ncreased travel distance" would exacerbate this difficulty. *Id.*, at 83. The law would prove "particularly burdensome for women living in northern Louisiana . . . who once could access a clinic in their own area [and] will now have to travel approximately 320 miles to New Orleans." *Ibid.*

In Texas, "common prerequisites to obtaining admitting privileges that [had] nothing to do with ability to perform medical procedures," including "clinical data requirements, residency requirements, and other discretionary factors," made it difficult for well-credentialed abortion physicians to obtain such privileges. *Whole Woman's Health*, 579 U.S., at ___ (slip op., at 25). In particular, the Court found that "hospitals often condition[ed] admitting privileges on reaching a certain number of admissions per year." *Id.*, at ___ (slip op., at 24) (internal quotation marks omitted). But because complications requiring hospitalization are relatively rare, abortion providers were "unlikely to have any patients to admit" and thus were "unable to maintain admitting privileges or obtain those privileges for the future." *Id.*, at ___ (slip op., at 25).

So too here. "While a physician's competency is a factor in assessing an applicant for admitting privileges" in Louisiana, "it is only one factor that hospitals consider in whether to grant privileges." 250 F. Supp. 3d, at 46. Louisiana hospitals "may deny privileges or decline to consider an application for privileges for myriad reasons unrelated to competency," including "the physician's expected usage of the hospital and intent to admit and treat patients there, the number of patients the physician has treated in the hospital in the recent past, the needs of the hospital, the mission of the hospital, or the business model of the hospital." *Ibid.*[6]

And the District Court found that, as in Texas, Louisiana "hospitals often grant admitting privileges to a physician because the physician plans

---

6. Justice Alito misunderstands my discussion of credentials as focusing on the law's lack of benefits. See *post*, at 4 (dissenting opinion). But my analysis, like *Casey*, is limited to the law's effect on the availability of abortion.

to provide services in the hospital" and that "[i]n general, hospital admitting privileges are not provided to physicians who never intend to provide services in a hospital." *Id.,* at 49. But "[b]ecause, by all accounts, abortion complications are rare, an abortion provider is unlikely to have a consistent need to admit patients." *Id.,* at 50 (citations omitted).[7]

Importantly, the District Court found that "since the passage of [the Louisiana law], all five remaining doctors have attempted *in good faith* to comply" with the law by applying for admitting privileges, yet have had very little success. *Id.,* at 78 (emphasis added). This finding was necessary to ensure that the physicians' inability to obtain admitting privileges was attributable to the new law rather than a halfhearted attempt to obtain privileges. Only then could the District Court accurately identify the Louisiana law's burden on abortion access.

The question is not whether we would reach the same findings from the same record. These District Court findings "entail[ed] primarily . . . factual work" and therefore are "review[ed] only for clear error." *U.S. Bank N. A.* v. *Village at Lakeridge, LLC,* 583 U.S. ___, ___, ___ (2018) (slip op., at 6, 9). Clear error review follows from a candid appraisal of the comparative advantages of trial courts and appellate courts. "While we review transcripts for a living, they listen to witnesses for a living. While we largely read briefs for a living, they largely assess the credibility of parties and witnesses for a living." *Taglieri* v. *Monasky,* 907 F.3d 404, 408 (CA6 2018) (en banc).

We accordingly will not disturb the factual conclusions of the trial court unless we are "left with the definite and firm conviction that a mistake has been committed." *United States* v. *United States Gypsum Co.,* 333 U.S. 364, 395 (1948). In my view, the District Court's work reveals no such clear error, for the reasons the plurality explains. *Ante,* at 19–35. The District Court findings therefore bind us in this case.

*   *   *

Stare decisis instructs us to treat like cases alike. The result in this case is controlled by our decision four years ago invalidating a nearly identical Texas law. The Louisiana law burdens women seeking previability abortions to the same extent as the Texas law, according to factual findings that are not clearly erroneous. For that reason, I concur in the judgment of the Court that the Louisiana law is unconstitutional.

---

7. I agree with Justice Alito that the validity of admitting privileges laws "depend[s] on numerous factors that may differ from State to State." *Post,* at 9 (dissenting opinion). And I agree with Justice Gorsuch that "[w]hen it comes to the factual record, litigants normally start the case on a clean slate." *Post,* at 14 (dissenting opinion). Appreciating that others may in good faith disagree, however, I cannot view the record here as in any pertinent respect sufficiently different from that in *Whole Woman's Health* to warrant a different outcome.

Appendix N

Opinion of Justice Bertha Wilson[1]

In the case of *Morgentaler vs. Her Majesty the Queen and the Attorney General of Canada* (1988)

At the heart of this appeal [from 52 O.R. (2d) 353, 48 C.R. (3d) 1, 22 C.C.C. (3d) 353, 22 D.L.R. (4th) 641, 17 C.R.R. 223, 11 O.A.C. 81] is the question whether a pregnant woman can, as a constitutional matter, be compelled by law to carry the foetus to term. The legislature has proceeded on the basis that she can be so compelled, and indeed has made it a criminal offence punishable by imprisonment under s. 251 of the Criminal Code, R.S.C. 1970, c. C-34, for her or her physician to terminate the pregnancy unless the procedural requirements of the section are complied with.

My colleagues the Chief Justice and Beetz J. have attacked those requirements in reasons which I have had the privilege of reading. They have found that the requirements do not comport with the principles of fundamental justice in the procedural sense and have concluded that, since they cannot be severed from the provisions creating the substantive offence, the whole of s. 251 must fall.

With all due respect, I think that the court must tackle the primary issue first. A consideration as to whether or not the procedural requirements for obtaining or performing an abortion comport with fundamental justice is purely academic if such requirements cannot as a constitutional matter be imposed at all. If a pregnant woman cannot, as a constitutional matter, be compelled by law to carry the foetus to term against her will, a review of the procedural requirements by which she may be compelled to do so seems pointless. Moreover, it would, in my opinion, be an exercise in futility for the legislature to expend its time and energy in attempting to remedy the defects in the procedural requirements unless it has some assurance that

---

1. Justice Wilson's opinion has been redacted for brevity; the full opinion is available at [1988] 1 S.C.R. 30 [Canada]. For a discussion of the several *Morgentaler* cases and the opinions of the other Justices, *see* Chapter 3 in this treatise, A. McClellan and O. O'Dell, *Abortion Law in Canada.*

this process will, at the end of the day, result in the creation of a valid criminal offence. I turn, therefore, to what I believe is the central issue that must be addressed.

1. The Right of Access to Abortion

Section 7 of the Canadian Charter of Rights and Freedoms provides:

> 7. Everyone has the right to life, liberty and security of the person and the right not to be deprived thereof except in accordance with the principles of fundamental justice.

I agree with the Chief Justice that we are not called upon in this case to delineate the full content of the right to life, liberty and security of the person. This would be an impossible task because we cannot envisage all the contexts in which such a right might be asserted. What we are asked to do, I believe, is define the content of the right in the context of the legislation under attack. Does s. 251 of the Criminal Code, which limits the pregnant woman's access to abortion, violate her right to life, liberty and security of the person within the meaning of s. 7?

Leaving aside for the moment the implications of the section for the foetus and addressing only the s. 7 right of the pregnant woman, it seems to me that we can say with a fair degree of confidence that a legislative scheme for the obtaining of an abortion which exposes the pregnant woman to a *threat* to her security of the person would violate her right under s. 7. Indeed, we have already stated in *Singh v. Can. (Min. of Employment & Immigration); Thandi v. Can. (Min. of Employment & Immigration); Mann v. Can. (Min. of Employment & Immigration)*, [1985] 1 S.C.R. 177, 12 Admin. L.R. 137, 17 D.L.R. (4th) 422, 14 C.R.R. 13, 58 N.R. 1 [Fed.], that security of the person even on the purely physical level must encompass freedom from the *threat* of physical punishment or suffering as well as freedom from the actual punishment or suffering itself. In other words, the fact of exposure is enough to violate security of the person. I agree with the Chief Justice and Beetz J., who, for differing reasons, find that pregnant women are exposed to a threat to their physical and psychological security under the legislative scheme set up in s. 251 and, since these are aspects of their security of the person, their s. 7 right is accordingly violated. But this, of course, does not answer the question whether even the ideal legislative scheme, assuming that it is one which poses no threat to the physical and psychological security of the person of the pregnant woman, would be valid under s. 7. I say this for two reasons: (1) because s. 7 encompasses more than the right to security of the person; it speaks also of the right to liberty, and (2) because security of the person may encompass more than physical and psychological security; this we have yet to decide.

It seems to me, therefore, that to commence the analysis with the premise that the s. 7 right encompasses only a right to physical and psychological security and to fail to deal with the right to liberty in the context of "life, liberty and security of the person" begs the central issue in the case. If either the right to liberty or the right to security of the person or a combination of both confers on the pregnant woman the right to decide for herself (with the guidance of her physician) whether or not to have an abortion, then we have to examine the legislative scheme from the point of view of fundamental justice not only in the procedural sense but in the substantive sense as well. I think, therefore, that we must answer the question: What is meant by the right to liberty in the context of the abortion issue? Does it, as Mr. Manning suggests, give the pregnant woman control over decisions affecting her own body? If not, does her right to security of the person give her such control? I turn first to the right to liberty.

(a) The Right to Liberty

In order to ascertain the content of the right to liberty we must, as Dickson C.J.C. stated in *R. v. Big M Drug Mart Ltd.*, [1985] 1 S.C.R. 295, [1985] 3 W.W.R. 481, 37 Alta. L.R. (2d) 97, 18 C.C.C. (3d) 385, 18 D.L.R. (4th) 321, 85 C.L.L.C. 14,023, 13 C.R.R. 64, 60 A.R. 161, 58 N.R. 81, commence with an analysis of the purpose of the right. Quoting from the Chief Justice at p. 344 [S.C.R.]:

> ... the purpose of the right or freedom in question is to be sought by reference to the character and the larger objects of the *Charter* itself, to the language chosen to articulate the specific right or freedom, to the historical origins of the concepts enshrined, and where applicable, to the meaning and purpose of the other specific rights and freedoms with which it is associated within the text of the *Charter*. The interpretation should be, as the judgment in *Southam* [supra] emphasizes, a generous rather than a legalistic one, aimed at fulfilling the purpose of the guarantee and securing for individuals the full benefit of the *Charter*'s protection.

We are invited, therefore, to consider the purpose of the Charter in general and of the right to liberty in particular.

The Charter is predicated on a particular conception of the place of the individual in society. An individual is not a totally independent entity disconnected from the society in which he or she lives. Neither, however, is the individual a mere cog in an impersonal machine in which his or her values, goals and aspirations are subordinated to those of the collectivity. The individual is a bit of both. The Charter reflects this reality by leaving a wide range of activities and decisions open to legitimate government control while at the same time placing limits on the proper scope of that control. Thus, the rights guaranteed in the Charter erect around each individual, metaphorically speaking, an invisible fence over which the state will not be allowed to trespass. The role of the courts is to map out, piece by piece, the parameters of the fence.

The Charter and the right to individual liberty guaranteed under it are inextricably tied to the concept of human dignity. Professor Neil MacCormick, Regius Professor of Public Law and the Law of Nature and Nations, University of Edinburgh, in Legal Right and Social Democracy: Essays in Legal and Political Philosophy, speaks of liberty as "a condition of human self-respect and of that contentment which resides in the ability to pursue one's own conception of a full and rewarding life" (p. 39). He says at p. 41:

> To be able to decide what to do and how to do it, to carry out one's own decisions and accept their consequences, seems to me essential to one's self-respect as a human being, and essential to the possibility of that contentment. Such self-respect and contentment are in my judgment fundamental goods for human beings, the worth of life itself being on condition of having or striving for them. If a person were deliberately denied the opportunity of self-respect and that contentment, he would suffer deprivation of his essential humanity.

Dickson C.J.C. in *R. v. Big M Drug Mart Ltd.*, supra, makes the same point at p. 346 [S.C.R.]:

> It should also be noted, however, that an emphasis on individual conscience and individual judgment also lies at the heart of our democratic political tradition. The ability of each citizen to make free and informed decisions is the absolute prerequisite for the legitimacy, acceptability, and efficacy of our system of self-government. It is because of the centrality of the rights associated with freedom of individual conscience both to basic beliefs about human worth and dignity and to a free and democratic political system that American jurisprudence has emphasized the primacy or "firstness" of the First Amendment. It is this same centrality that in my view underlies their designation in the *Canadian Charter of Rights and Freedoms* as "fundamental". They are the *sine qua non* of the political tradition underlying the *Charter*.

It was further amplified in Dickson C.J.C.'s discussion of Charter interpretation in *R. v. Oakes*, [1986] 1 S.C.R. 103 at 136, 50 C.R. (3d) 1, 24 C.C.C. (3d) 321, 26 D.L.R. (4th) 200, 19 C.R.R. 308, 14 O.A.C. 335, 65 N.R. 87:

> A second contextual element of interpretation of s. 1 is provided by the words "free and democratic society". Inclusion of these words as the final standard of justification for limits on rights and freedoms refers the Court to the very purpose for which the *Charter* was originally entrenched in the Constitution: Canadian society is to be free and democratic. The Court must be guided by the values and principles essential to a free and democratic society which I believe embody, to name but a few, respect for the inherent dignity of the human person, commitment to social justice and equality, accommodation of a wide variety of beliefs, respect for cultural and group identity, and faith in social and political institutions which enhance the participation of individuals and groups in society. The underlying values and principles of a free and democratic society are the genesis of the rights and freedoms guaranteed by the *Charter* and the ultimate standard against which a limit on a right or freedom must be shown, despite its effect, to be reasonable and demonstrably justified.

The idea of human dignity finds expression in almost every right and freedom guaranteed in the Charter. Individuals are afforded the right to choose their own religion and their own philosophy of life, the right to choose with whom they will associate and how they will express themselves, the right to choose where they will live and what occupation they will pursue. These are all examples of the basic theory underlying the Charter, namely, that the state will respect choices made by individuals and, to the greatest extent possible, will avoid subordinating these choices to any one conception of the good life.

Thus an aspect of the respect for human dignity on which the Charter is founded is the right to make fundamental personal decisions without interference from the state. This right is a critical component of the right to liberty. Liberty, as was noted in *Singh*, supra, is a phrase capable of a broad range of meaning. In my view, this right, properly construed, grants the individual a degree of autonomy in making decisions of fundamental personal importance.

This view is consistent with the position I took in the case of *R. v. Jones*, [1986] 2 S.C.R. 284, [1986] 6 W.W.R. 577, 47 Alta. L.R. (2d) 97, 28 C.C.C. (3d) 513, 31 D.L.R. (4th) 569, 25 C.R.R. 63, 73 A.R. 133, 69 N.R. 241 . One issue raised in that case was whether the right to liberty in s. 7 of the Charter included a parent's right to bring up his children in accordance with his conscientious beliefs. In concluding that it did, I stated at pp. 318–19:

I believe that the framers of the Constitution in guaranteeing "liberty" as a fundamental value in a free and democratic society had in mind the freedom of the individual to develop and realize his potential to the full, to plan his own life to suit his own character, to make his own choices for good or ill, to be non-conformist, idiosyncratic and even eccentric—to be, in today's parlance, "his own person" and accountable as such. John Stuart Mill described it as "pursuing our own good in our own way". This, he believed, we should be free to do "so long as we do not attempt to deprive others of theirs or impede their efforts to obtain it". He added:

> Each is the proper guardian of his own health, whether bodily or mental and spiritual. Mankind are greater gainers by suffering each other to live as seems good to themselves than by compelling each to live as seems good to the rest.

Liberty in a free and democratic society does not require the state to approve the personal decisions made by its citizens; it does, however, require the state to respect them.

This conception of the proper ambit of the right to liberty under our Charter is consistent with the American jurisprudence on the subject. While care must undoubtedly be taken to avoid a mechanical application of concepts developed in different cultural and constitutional contexts, I would respectfully agree with the observation of my colleague Estey J. in *Law Soc. of Upper Can. v. Skapinker*, [1984] 1 S.C.R. 357 at 366-67, 11 C.C.C. (3d) 481, 9 D.L.R. (4th) 161, 8 C.R.R. 193, 3 O.A.C. 321, 53 N.R. 169:

> With the *Constitution Act, 1982* comes a new dimension, a new yardstick of reconciliation between the individual and the community and their respective rights, a dimension which, like the balance of the Constitution, remains to be interpreted and applied by the Court.
>
> The courts in the United States have had almost two hundred years experience at this task and it is of more than passing interest to those concerned with these new developments in Canada to study the experience of the United States courts.

As early as the 1920s the American Supreme Court employed the Fifth and Fourteenth Amendments of the Bill of Rights to give parents a degree of choice in the education of their children. In *Meyer v. Nebraska*, 262 U.S. 390, 67 L. Ed. 1042, 43 S. Ct. 625, 29 A.L.R. 1446 (1923), the court struck down a law prohibiting the teaching of any subject in a language other than English. In *Pierce v. Soc. of Sisters of Holy Names of Jesus & Mary*, 268 U.S. 510, 69 L. Ed. 1070, 45 S. Ct. 571, 39 A.L.R. 468 (1925), an Oregon statute requiring all "normal children" to attend public school, and thus prohibiting private school attendance, was held to be unconstitutional. The court in *Pierce* at pp. 534–35 characterized the interest being infringed as "the liberty of parents and guardians to direct the upbringing and education of children under their control".

The sanctity of the family was underlined by the decision in *Skinner v. Oklahoma*, 316 U.S. 535, 86 L. Ed. 1655, 62 S. Ct. 1110 (1942), where the Supreme Court invalidated a state law authorizing the sterilization of individuals convicted of two or more crimes involving moral turpitude. While the law was struck down on the basis that it violated the equal protection clause of the Fourteenth Amendment, the court had this to say of the interest at stake (at p. 541): "We are dealing here with legislation which involves one of the basic civil rights of man. Marriage and procreation are fundamental to the very existence and survival of the race."

Later the Supreme Court was asked to determine the constitutionality of a Connecticut statute forbidding the use of contraceptives by married couples. In *Griswold v. Connecticut*, 381 U.S. 479, 14 L. Ed. 2d 510, 85 S. Ct. 1678 (1965), the majority held this statute to be invalid. The judges writing for the majority used various constitutional routes to arrive at this conclusion, but the common denominator seems to have been a profound concern over the invasion of the marital home required for the enforcement of the law. *Griswold* was interpreted by the Supreme Court in the later case of *Eisenstadt v. Baird*, 405 U.S. 438, 31 L. Ed. 2d 349, 92 S. Ct. 1029 (1972), where the majority stated at p. 453:

> It is true that in Griswold the right of privacy in question inhered in the marital relationship. Yet the marital couple is not an independent entity with a mind and heart of its own, but an association of two individuals each with a separate intellectual and emotional make up. If the right of privacy means anything, it is the right of the *individual*, married or single, to be free from unwarranted governmental intrusion into matters so fundamentally affecting a person as the decision whether to bear or beget a child.

In *Eisenstadt* the court struck down a Massachusetts law that prohibited the distribution of any drug for the purposes of contraception to unmarried persons on the ground that it violated the equal protection clause.

The equal protection clause was also used by the Supreme Court in *Loving v. Virginia*, 388 U.S. 1, 18 L. Ed. 2d 1010, 87 S. Ct. 1817 (1967), to strike down legislation that purported to forbid interracial marriage. The court tied its decision to the previous line of cases that protected basic choices relating to family life. It stated at p. 12:

> The freedom to marry has long been recognized as one of the "vital personal rights essential to the orderly pursuit of happiness by free men".

> Marriage is one of the "basic civil rights of man", fundamental to our
> very existence and survival . . . the freedom to marry . . . resides with the
> individual . . .

Thus by a process of accretion the scope of the right of individuals to make
fundamental decisions affecting their private lives was elaborated in the
United States on a case-by-case basis. The parameters of the fence were
being progressively defined.

For our purposes the most interesting development in this area of
American law are the decisions of the Supreme Court in *Roe v. Wade*, 410
U.S. 113, 35 L. Ed. 2d 147, 93 S. Ct. 705 (1973), and its sister case *Doe v.
Bolton*, 410 U.S. 179, 35 L. Ed. 2d 201, 93 S. Ct. 739 (1973). In *Roe v. Wade*
the court held that a pregnant woman has the right to decide whether or
not to terminate her pregnancy. This conclusion, the majority stated, was
mandated by the body of existing law ensuring that the state would not be
allowed to interfere with certain fundamental personal decisions such as
education, child-rearing, procreation, marriage and contraception. The
court concluded that the right to privacy found in the Fourteenth Amendment guarantee of liberty "is broad enough to encompass a woman's decision whether or not to terminate her pregnancy" (p. 153 [U.S.]).

This right was not, however, to be taken as absolute. At some point the
legitimate state interests in the protection of health, proper medical standards, and prenatal life would justify its qualification. Professor Tribe, Professor of Law, Harvard University, in American Constitutional Law (1978),
conveniently summarizes the limits the court found to be inherent in the
woman's right. I quote from pp. 924–25:

> Specifically, the Court held that, because the woman's right to decide
> whether or not to end a pregnancy is fundamental, only a compelling
> interest can justify state regulation impinging in any way upon that right.
> During the first trimester of pregnancy, when abortion is less hazardous
> in terms of the woman's life than carrying the child to term would be, the
> state may require only that the abortion be performed by a licensed physi-
> cian; no further regulations peculiar to abortion as such are compellingly
> justified in that period.
>
>   After the first trimester, the compelling state interest in the mother's
> health permits it to adopt reasonable regulations in order to promote safe
> abortions — but requiring abortions to be performed in hospitals, or only
> after approval of another doctor or committee in addition to the woman's
> physician, is impermissible, as is requiring that the abortion procedure
> employ a technique that, however preferable from a medical perspective, is
> not widely available.

Once the fetus is viable, in the sense that it is capable of survival outside the uterus with artificial aid, the state interest in preserving the fetus becomes compelling, and the state may thus proscribe its premature removal (i.e., its abortion) except to preserve the mother's life or health.

The decision in *Roe v. Wade* was reaffirmed by the Supreme Court in *Akron (City) v. Akron Centre for Reproductive Health Inc.*, 462 U.S. 416, 76 L. Ed. 2d 687, 103 S. Ct. 2481 (1983), and again, though by a bare majority, in *Thornburgh v. Amer. College of Obstetricians & Gynecologists*, 90 L. Ed. 2d 779, 106 S. Ct. 2169 (1986). In *Thornburgh*, Blackmun J., speaking for the majority, identifies the core value which the American courts have found to inhere in the concept of liberty. He states at pp. 2184–85:

> Our cases long have recognized that the Constitution embodies a promise that a certain private sphere of individual liberty will be kept largely beyond the reach of government . . . That promise extends to women as well as to men. Few decisions are more personal and intimate, more properly private, or more basic to individual dignity and autonomy, than a woman's decision — with the guidance of her physician and within the limits specified in *Roe* — whether to end her pregnancy. A woman's right to make that choice freely is fundamental. Any other result, in our view, would protect inadequately a central part of the sphere of liberty that our law guarantees equally to all.

In my opinion, the respect for individual decision-making in matters of fundamental personal importance reflected in the American jurisprudence also informs the Canadian Charter. Indeed, as the Chief Justice pointed out in *R. v. Big M Drug Mart Ltd.*, supra [at p. 346 (S.C.R.)], beliefs about human worth and dignity "are the *sine qua non* of the political tradition underlying the *Charter*". I would conclude, therefore, that the right to liberty contained in s. 7 guarantees to every individual a degree of personal autonomy over important decisions intimately affecting their private lives.

The question then becomes whether the decision of a woman to terminate her pregnancy falls within this class of protected decisions. I have no doubt that it does. This decision is one that will have profound psychological, economic and social consequences for the pregnant woman. The circumstances giving rise to it can be complex and varied and there may be, and usually are, powerful considerations militating in opposite directions. It is a decision that deeply reflects the way the woman thinks about herself and her relationship to others and to society at large. It is not just a medical decision; it is a profound social and ethical one as well. Her response to it will be the response of the whole person.

It is probably impossible for a man to respond, even imaginatively, to such a dilemma, not just because it is outside the realm of his personal experience (although this is of course the case) but because he can relate to it only by objectifying it, thereby eliminating the subjective elements of the female psyche which are at the heart of the dilemma. As Noreen Burrows, Lecturer in European Law, University of Glasgow, has pointed out in her essay "International Law and Human Rights: The Case of Women's Rights", in Human Rights: From Rhetoric to Reality, the history of the struggle for human rights from the 18th century on has been the history of men struggling to assert their dignity and common humanity against an overbearing state apparatus. The more recent struggle for women's rights has been a struggle to eliminate discrimination, to achieve a place for women in a man's world, to develop a set of legislative reforms in order to place women in the same position as men (pp. 81–82). It has *not* been a struggle to define the rights of women in relation to their special place in the societal structure and in relation to the biological distinction between the two sexes. Thus, women's needs and aspirations are only now being translated into protected rights. The right to reproduce or not to reproduce which is in issue in this case is one such right, and is properly perceived as an integral part of modern woman's struggle to assert *her* dignity and worth as a human being.

Given then that the right to liberty guaranteed by s. 7 of the Charter gives a woman the right to decide for herself whether or not to terminate her pregnancy, does s. 251 of the Criminal Code violate this right? Clearly it does. The purpose of the section is to take the decision away from the woman and give it to a committee. Furthermore, as the Chief Justice correctly points out, the committee bases its decision on "criteria entirely unrelated to [the pregnant woman's] priorities and aspirations" [ante, p. 21]. The fact that the decision whether a woman will be allowed to terminate her pregnancy is in the hands of a committee is just as great a violation of the woman's right to personal autonomy in decisions of an intimate and private nature as it would be if a committee were established to decide whether a woman should be allowed to continue her pregnancy. Both these arrangements violate the woman's right to liberty by deciding for her something that she has the right to decide for herself.

(b) The Right to Security of the Person

Section 7 of the Charter also guarantees everyone the right to security of the person. Does this, as Mr. Manning suggests, extend to the right of control over their own bodies?

I agree with the Chief Justice and with Beetz J. that the right to "security of the person" under s. 7 of the Charter protects both the physical and psychological integrity of the individual. State-enforced medical or surgical treatment comes readily to mind as an obvious invasion of physical integrity. Lamer J. held in *Mills v. R.*, [1986] 1 S.C.R. 863, 52 C.R. (3d) 1, 26 C.C.C. (3d) 481, 29 D.L.R. (4th) 161, 21 C.R.R. 76, 16 O.A.C. 81, 67 N.R. 241, that the right to security of the person entitled a person to be protected against psychological trauma as well — in that case the psychological trauma resulting from delays in the trial process under s. 11(*b*) of the Charter. He found that psychological trauma could take the form of "stigmatization of the accused, loss of privacy, stress and anxiety resulting from a multitude of factors, including possible disruption of family, social life and work, legal costs and uncertainty as to outcome and sanction" [p. 920]. I agree with my colleague and I think that his comments are very germane to the instant case because, as the Chief Justice and Beetz J. point out, the present legislative scheme for the obtaining of an abortion clearly subjects pregnant women to considerable emotional stress as well as to unnecessary physical risk. I believe, however, that the flaw in the present legislative scheme goes much deeper than that. In essence, what it does is assert that the woman's capacity to reproduce is not to be subject to her own control. It is to be subject to the control of the state. She may not choose whether to exercise her existing capacity or not to exercise it. This is not, in my view, just a matter of interfering with her right to liberty in the sense (already discussed) of her right to personal autonomy in decision-making, it is a direct interference with her physical "person" as well. She is truly being treated as a means — a means to an end which she does not desire but over which she has no control. She is the passive recipient of a decision made by others as to whether her body is to be used to nurture a new life. Can there be anything that comports less with human dignity and self-respect? How can a woman in this position have any sense of security with respect to her person? I believe that s. 251 of the Criminal Code deprives the pregnant woman of her right to security of the person as well as her right to liberty.

2. The Scope of the Right under S. 7

I turn now to a consideration of the degree of personal autonomy the pregnant woman has under s. 7 of the Charter when faced with a decision whether or not to have an abortion or, to put it into the legislative context, the degree to which the legislature can deny the pregnant woman access to abortion without violating her s. 7 right. This involves a consideration of the

extent to which the legislature can "deprive" her of it under the second part
of s. 7 and the extent to which it can put "limits" on it under s. 1.

(a) The Principles of Fundamental Justice

Does s. 251 deprive women of their right to liberty and to security of the
person "in accordance with the principles of fundamental justice"? I agree
with Lamer J., who stated in *Re B.C. Motor Vehicle Act*, [1985] 2 S.C.R. 486 at
513, (sub nom. *Ref. re S. 94(2) of Motor Vehicle Act*) 48 C.R. (3d) 289, [1986]
1 W.W.R. 481, 69 B.C.L.R. 145, 36 M.V.R. 240, 23 C.C.C. (3d) 289, 24 D.L.R.
(4th) 536, 18 C.R.R. 30, 63 N.R. 266, that the principles of fundamental
justice "cannot be given any exhaustive content or simple enumerative definition, but will take on concrete meaning as the courts address alleged violations of s. 7". In the same judgment Lamer J. also stated at p. 503:

> In other words, the principles of fundamental justice are to be found in
> the basic tenets of our legal system. They do not lie in the realm of general
> public policy but in the inherent domain of the judiciary as guardian of
> the justice system. Such an approach to the interpretation of "principles
> of fundamental justice" is consistent with the wording and structure of
> s. 7, the context of the section, *i.e.*, ss. 8 to 14, and the character and larger
> objects of the *Charter* itself. It provides meaningful content for the s. 7
> guarantee all the while avoiding adjudication of policy matters.

While Lamer J. draws mainly upon ss. 8 to 14 of the Charter to give substantive content to the principles of fundamental justice, he does not preclude, but seems rather to encourage, the idea that recourse may be had to
other rights guaranteed by the Charter for the same purpose. The question,
therefore, is whether the deprivation of the s. 7 right is in accordance not
only with procedural fairness (and I agree with the Chief Justice and Beetz
J., for the reasons they give, that it is not) but also with the fundamental
rights and freedoms laid down elsewhere in the Charter.

This approach to s. 7 is supported by comments made by La Forest J. in
R. v. Lyons, [1987] 2 S.C.R. 309, 61 C.R. (3d) 1, (sub nom. *R. v. L.*) 80 N.R.
161 [N.S.]. He urged that the rights enshrined in the Charter should not be
read in isolation. Rather, he states [p. 326]:

> . . . the *Charter* protects a complex of interacting values, each more or less
> fundamental to the free and democratic society that is Canada (*R. v. Oakes*,
> [1986] 1 S.C.R. 103, at 136), and the particularization of rights and freedoms
> contained in the *Charter* thus represents a somewhat artificial, if necessary
> and intrinsically worthwhile attempt to structure and focus the judicial expo-
> sition of such rights and freedoms. The necessity of structuring the discus-

sion should not, however, lead us to overlook the importance of appreciating the manner in which the amplification of the content of each enunciated right and freedom imbues and informs our understandings of the value structure sought to be protected by the *Charter* as a whole and, in particular, of the content of the other specific rights and freedoms it embodies.

I believe, therefore, that a deprivation of the s. 7 right which has the effect of infringing a right guaranteed elsewhere in the Charter cannot be in accordance with the principles of fundamental justice.

In my view, the deprivation of the s. 7 right with which we are concerned in this case offends s. 2(*a*) of the Charter. I say this because I believe that the decision whether or not to terminate a pregnancy is essentially a moral decision, a matter of conscience. I do not think there is or can be any dispute about that. The question is: whose conscience? Is the conscience of the woman to be paramount, or the conscience of the state? I believe, for the reasons I gave in discussing the right to liberty, that in a free and democratic society it must be the conscience of the individual. Indeed, s. 2(*a*) makes it clear that this freedom belongs to "everyone", i.e., to each of us individually. I quote the section for convenience:

> 2. Everyone has the following fundamental freedoms:
> (*a*) freedom of conscience and religion . . .

In *R. v. Big M Drug Mart Ltd.*, supra, Dickson C.J.C. made some very insightful comments about the nature of the right enshrined in s. 2(*a*) of the Charter, at pp. 345-47 [S.C.R.]:

> Beginning, however, with the Independent faction within the Parliamentary party during the Commonwealth or Interregnum, many, even among those who shared the basic beliefs of the ascendant religion, came to voice opposition to the use of the State's coercive power to secure obedience to religious precepts and to extirpate non-conforming beliefs. The basis of this opposition was no longer simply a conviction that the State was enforcing the wrong set of beliefs and practices but rather the perception that belief itself was not amenable to compulsion. Attempts to compel belief or practice denied the reality of individual conscience and dishonoured the God that had planted it in His creatures. It is from these antecedents that the concepts of freedom of religion and freedom of conscience became associated, to form, as they do in s. 2(*a*) of our *Charter*, the single integrated concept of "freedom of conscience and religion".
>
> What unites enunciated freedoms in the American First Amendment, in s. 2(*a*) of the *Charter* and in the provisions of other human rights documents in which they are associated *is the notion of the centrality of individual conscience and the inappropriateness of governmental intervention to compel or to*

constrain its manifestation. In *Hunter v. Southam Inc., supra,* the purpose of the Charter was identified, at p. 155, as "the unremitting protection of individual rights and liberties". It is easy to see the relationship between respect for individual conscience and the valuation of human dignity that motivates such unremitting protection.

It should also be noted, however, that an emphasis on individual conscience and individual judgment also lies at the heart of our democratic political tradition. *The ability of each citizen to make free and informed decisions is the absolute prerequisite for the legitimacy, acceptability, and efficacy of our system of self-government.* It is because of the centrality of the rights associated with freedom of individual conscience both to basic beliefs about human worth and dignity and to a free and democratic political system that American jurisprudence has emphasized the primacy or "firstness" of the First Amendment. It is this same centrality that in my view underlies their designation in the *Canadian Charter of Rights and Freedoms* as "fundamental". They are the *sine qua non* of the political tradition underlying the *Charter.*

Viewed in this context, the purpose of freedom of conscience and religion becomes clear. The values that underlie our political and philosophic traditions demand that every individual be free to hold and to manifest whatever beliefs and opinions his or her conscience dictates, provided inter alia only that such manifestations do not injure his or her neighbours or their parallel rights to hold and manifest beliefs and opinions of their own. Religious belief and practice are historically prototypical and, in many ways, paradigmatic of conscientiously-held beliefs and manifestations and are therefore protected by the Charter. Equally protected, and for the same reasons, are expressions and manifestations of religious non-belief and refusals to participate in religious practice. It may perhaps be that freedom of conscience and religion extends beyond these principles to prohibit other sorts of governmental involvement in matters having to do with religion. For the present case it is sufficient in my opinion to say that whatever else freedom of conscience and religion may mean, it must at the very least mean this: government may not coerce individuals to affirm a specific religious belief or to manifest a specific religious practice for a sectarian purpose. I leave to another case the degree, if any, to which the government may, to achieve a vital interest or objective, engage in coercive action which s. 2(a) might otherwise prohibit. [My emphasis.]

The Chief Justice sees religious belief and practice as the paradigmatic example of conscientiously-held beliefs and manifestations and, as such, protected by the Charter. But I do not think he is saying that a personal morality which is not founded in religion is outside the protection of s. 2(*a*). Certainly, it would be my view that conscientious beliefs which are not religiously motivated are equally protected by freedom of conscience in s. 2(*a*). In so saying I am not unmindful of the fact that the Charter opens with an affirmation that "Canada is founded upon principles that recognize the supremacy of God". But I am also mindful that the values entrenched in the Charter are those which characterize a free and democratic society.

As is pointed out by Professor C.E.M. Joad, then Head of Department of Philosophy and Psychology, Birkbeck College, University of London, in Guide to the Philosophy Of Morals and Politics, the role of the state in a democracy is to establish the background conditions under which individual citizens may pursue the ethical values which in their view underlie the good life. He states at p. 801:

> For the welfare of the state is nothing apart from the good of the citizens who compose it. It is no doubt true that a State whose citizens are compelled to go right is more efficient than one whose citizens are free to go wrong. But what then? To sacrifice freedom in the interests of efficiency is to sacrifice what confers upon human beings their humanity. It is no doubt easy to govern a flock of sheep; but there is no credit in the governing, and, if the sheep were born as men, no virtue in the sheep.

Professor Joad further emphasizes at p. 803 that individuals in a democratic society can never be treated "merely as means to ends beyond themselves", because:

> To the right of the individual to be treated as an end, which entails his right to the full development and expression of his personality, all other rights and claims must, the democrat holds, be subordinated. I do not know how this principle is to be defended any more than I can frame a defence for the principles of democracy and liberty.

Professor Joad stresses that the essence of a democracy is its recognition of the fact that the state is made for man and not man for the state (p. 805). He firmly rejects the notion that science provides a basis for subordinating the individual to the state. He says at pp. 805–806:

> Human beings, it is said, are important only in so far as they fit into a biological scheme or assist in the furtherance of the evolutionary process. Thus each generation of women must accept as its sole function the production of children who will constitute the next generation who, in their turn, will devote their lives and sacrifice their inclinations to the task of producing a further generation, and so on ad infinitum. This is the doctrine of eternal sacrifice — "jam yesterday, jam tomorrow, but never jam today". For, it may be asked, to what end should generations be produced, unless the individuals who compose them are valued in and for themselves, are, in fact, ends in themselves? There is no escape from the doctrine of the perpetual recurrence of generations who have value only in so far as they produce more generations, the perpetual subordination of citizens

who have value only in so far as they promote the interests of the State to which they are subordinated, except in the individualist doctrine, which is also the Christian doctrine, that the individual is an end in himself.

It seems to me, therefore, that in a free and democratic society "freedom of conscience and religion" should be broadly construed to extend to conscientiously-held beliefs, whether grounded in religion or in a secular morality. Indeed, as a matter of statutory interpretation, "conscience" and "religion" should not be treated as tautologous if capable of independent, although related, meaning. Accordingly, for the state to take sides on the issue of abortion, as it does in the impugned legislation by making it a criminal offence for the pregnant woman to exercise one of her options, is not only to endorse but also to enforce, on pain of a further loss of liberty through actual imprisonment, one conscientiously-held view at the expense of another. It is to deny freedom of conscience to some, to treat them as means to an end, to deprive them, as Professor MacCormick puts it, of their "essential humanity". Can this comport with fundamental justice? Was Blackmun J. not correct when he said in *Thornburgh*, supra, at p. 2185: "A woman's right to make that choice freely is fundamental. Any other result . . . would protect inadequately a central part of the sphere of liberty that our law guarantees equally to all."?

Legislation which violates freedom of conscience in this manner cannot, in my view, be in accordance with the principles of fundamental justice within the meaning of s. 7.

(b) Section 1 of the Charter

The majority of this court held in *Re B.C. Motor Vehicle Act*, supra, that a deprivation of the s. 7 right in violation of the principles of fundamental justice in the substantive sense could nevertheless constitute a reasonable limit under s. 1 and be justified in a free and democratic society. It is necessary therefore to consider whether s. 251 of the Criminal Code can be saved under s. 1. The section provides:

> 1. The *Canadian Charter of Rights and Freedoms* guarantees the rights and freedoms set out in it subject only to such reasonable limits prescribed by law as can be demonstrably justified in a free and democratic society.

This section received judicial scrutiny by this court in *R. v. Oakes*, supra. Dickson C.J.C., speaking for the majority, set out two criteria which must be met if the limit is to be found reasonable: (1) the objective which the legislation is designed to achieve must relate to concerns which are pressing and substantial; and (2) the means chosen must be proportional to the objective sought to be achieved. The Chief Justice identified three important components of proportionality at p. 139:

> First, the measures adopted must be carefully designed to achieve the objective in question. They must not be arbitrary, unfair or based on irrational considerations. In short, they must be rationally connected to the objective. Second, the means, even if rationally connected to the objective in the first sense, should impair "as little as possible" the right or freedom in question: *R. v. Big M Drug Mart Ltd., supra*, at p. 352. Third, there must be a proportionality between the *effects* of the measures which are responsible for limiting the *Charter* right or freedom, and the objective which has been identified as of "sufficient importance".

Does s. 251 meet this test?

In my view, the primary objective of the impugned legislation must be seen as the protection of the foetus. It undoubtedly has other ancillary objectives, such as the protection of the life and health of pregnant women, but I believe that the main objective advanced to justify a restriction on the pregnant woman's s. 7 right is the protection of the foetus. I think this is a perfectly valid legislative objective.

Miss Wein submitted on behalf of the Crown that the Court of Appeal was correct in concluding that "the situation respecting a woman's right to control her own person becomes more complex when she becomes pregnant, and that some statutory control may be appropriate" [p. 31]. I agree. I think s. 1 of the Charter authorizes reasonable limits to be put upon the woman's right having regard to the fact of the developing foetus within her body. The question is: At what point in the pregnancy does the protection of the foetus become such a pressing and substantial concern as to outweigh the fundamental right of the woman to decide whether or not to carry the foetus to term? At what point does the state's interest in the protection of the foetus become "compelling" and justify state intervention in what is otherwise a matter of purely personal and private concern?

In *Roe v. Wade*, supra, the United States Supreme Court held that the state's interest became compelling when the foetus became viable, i.e., when it could exist outside the body of the mother. As Miss Wein pointed out, no particular justification was advanced by the court for the selection of viability as the relevant criterion. The court expressly avoided the question as to when human life begins. Blackmun J. stated at p. 159:

> We need not resolve the difficult question of when life begins. When those trained in the respective disciplines of medicine, philosophy, and theol-

ogy are unable to arrive at any consensus, the judiciary, at this point in the development of man's knowledge, is not in a position to speculate as to the answer.

He referred, therefore, to the developing foetus as "potential life" and to the state's interest as "the protection of potential life".

Miss Wein submitted that it was likewise not necessary for the court in this case to decide when human life begins, although she acknowledged that the value to be placed on "potential life" was significant in assessing the importance of the legislative objective sought to be achieved by s. 251. It would be my view, and I think it is consistent with the position taken by the United States Supreme Court in *Roe v. Wade*, that the value to be placed on the foetus as potential life is directly related to the stage of its development during gestation. The undeveloped foetus starts out as a newly-fertilized ovum; the fully-developed foetus emerges ultimately as an infant. A developmental progression takes place in between these two extremes and, in my opinion, this progression has a direct bearing on the value of the foetus as potential life. It is a fact of human experience that a miscarriage or spontaneous abortion of the foetus at six months is attended by far greater sorrow and sense of loss than a miscarriage or spontaneous abortion at six days or even six weeks. This is not, of course, to deny that the foetus is potential life from the moment of conception. Indeed, I agree with the observation of O'Connor J., dissenting, in *Akron (City) v. Akron Center for Reproductive Health Inc.*, supra, at p. 461 (referred to by my colleague Beetz J. in his reasons), that the foetus is potential life from the moment of conception. It is simply to say that, in balancing the state's interest in the protection of the foetus as potential life under s. 1 of the Charter against the right of the pregnant woman under s. 7, greater weight should be given to the state's interest in the later stages of pregnancy than in the earlier. The foetus should accordingly, for purposes of s. 1, be viewed in differential and developmental terms: see Sumner, Professor of Philosophy, University of Toronto, Abortion and Moral Theory (1981), pp. 125-28.

As Professor Sumner points out, both traditional approaches to abortion, the so-called "liberal" and "conservative" approaches, fail to take account of the essentially developmental nature of the gestation process. A developmental view of the foetus, on the other hand, supports a permissive approach to abortion in the early stages of pregnancy and a restrictive approach in the later stages. In the early stages the woman's autonomy would be absolute; her decision, reached in consultation with her physician, not to carry the foetus to term would be conclusive. The state would have no business inquiring into her reasons. Her reasons for having an abortion would, however, be the proper subject of inquiry at the later stages of her pregnancy, when the state's compelling interest in the protection of the foetus would justify it in prescribing conditions. The precise point in the development of the foetus at which the state's interest in its protection becomes "compelling" I leave to the informed judgment of the legislature, which is in a position to receive guidance on the subject from all the relevant disciplines. It seems to me, however, that it might fall somewhere in the second trimester. Indeed, according to Professor Sumner (p. 159), a differential abortion policy with a time limit in the second trimester is already in operation in the United States, Great Britain, France, Italy, Sweden, the Soviet Union, China, India, Japan and most of the countries of Eastern Europe, although the time limits vary in these countries from the beginning to the end of the second trimester: cf. Stephen L. Isaacs, "Reproductive Rights 1983: An International Survey" (1983), 14 Columbia Human Rights L. Rev. 311, with respect to France and Italy.

Section 251 of the Criminal Code takes the decision away from the woman at *all* stages of her pregnancy. It is a complete denial of the woman's constitutionally-protected right under s. 7, not merely a limitation on it. It cannot, in my opinion, meet the proportionality test in *Oakes*, supra. It is not sufficiently tailored to the legislative objective and does not impair the woman's right "as little as possible". It cannot be saved under s. 1. Accordingly, even if the section were to be amended to remedy the purely procedural defects in the legislative scheme referred to by the Chief Justice and Beetz J., it would, in my opinion, still not be constitutionally valid.

One final word. I wish to emphasize that in these reasons I have dealt with the existence of the developing foetus merely as a factor to be considered in assessing the importance of the legislative objective under s. 1 of the Charter. I have not dealt with the entirely separate question whether a foetus is covered by the word "everyone" in s. 7 so as to have an independent right to life under that section. The Crown did not argue it, and it is not necessary to decide it in order to dispose of the issues on this appeal.

3. Disposition

I would allow the appeal. I would strike down s. 251 of the Criminal Code as having no force and effect under s. 52(1) of the Constitution Act,

1982. I would answer the first constitutional question in the affirmative as regards s. 7 of the Charter and the second constitutional question in the negative. I would answer QQ. 3, 4 and 5 in the negative and Q. 6 in the manner proposed by Beetz J. It is not necessary to answer Q. 7.

I endorse the Chief Justice's critical comments on Mr. Manning's concluding remarks to the jury.

Appeal allowed; acquittal restored.

Appendix O

Amicus Curiae Brief of Americans United for Life

Filed in *June Medical Services LLC v. Russo*[1]

INTEREST OF *AMICUS CURIAE*[2]

Amicus Americans United for Life (AUL) is a pro-life non-profit organization dedicated to advocating for comprehensive legal protections for human life. Founded in 1971, before this Court's decision in *Roe v. Wade*, 410 U.S. 113 (1973), AUL has nearly 50 years of experience relating to abortion jurisprudence. AUL attorneys are highly-regarded experts on the Constitution and legal issues touching on abortion and are often consulted on various bills, amendments, and ongoing litigation across the country.

SUMMARY OF ARGUMENT

The six traditional stare decisis factors weigh strongly in favor of overruling *Roe* at the earliest practical opportunity. Scholarly and judicial criticism of *Roe* have been unremitting. After abandoning the constitutional rationale for the abortion right espoused in *Roe*, a majority of the Court has not settled on a coherent rationale, and the centralization of the abortion issue in the Court has made the Court and the Justices the focus of ferocious campaigns of personal destruction. Changes in law, especially growing

---

1. Some non-substantive redactions and formatting edits have been made to the original brief as filed in *June Medical Services LLC v. Russo*, 140 S. Ct. 2103 (2020).

2. No party's counsel authored any part of this brief. No person other than *Amici* and their counsel contributed money intended to fund the preparation or submission of this brief. Counsel for all parties have filed blanket consents to the filing of *amicus* briefs in support of either or no party.

legal protection for prenatal human life, have upended major assumptions on which *Roe* was based. These and other political, legal, and social factors have kept *Roe* radically unsettled 47 years after it was decided, and call for its reexamination.

ARGUMENT

I. THE STANDARD OF REVIEW IN ABORTION CASES SET OUT IN ROE AND CASEY HAS PROVEN UNWORKABLE, AND THE COURT SHOULD RECONSIDER THOSE PRECEDENTS AT THE EARLIEST PRACTICAL OPPORTUNITY.

The lower courts' struggle to apply the Supreme Court's most recent iteration of the standard of review in abortion cases in *Whole Woman's Health v. Hellerstedt*, 136 S. Ct. 2292 (2016) was caused by the unworkable role that the Supreme Court fashioned for itself in *Roe v. Wade*, which cannot be resolved until *Roe* is reconsidered and overruled. In considering whether to adhere to precedent (*stare decisis*), the Supreme Court has traditionally examined six primary factors: 1) whether the precedent is *settled*; 2) whether the precedent was *wrongly decided*; 3) whether the prior decision is *workable*; 4) whether *factual changes* have *eroded* the original decision; 5) whether *legal changes* have *eroded* the original decision; and 6) whether *reliance interests* in the precedent are substantial. Experience and precedent demonstrate that all of the six traditional stare decisis factors weigh in favor of reconsidering *Roe* at the earliest practical opportunity.

First, *Roe* remains unsettled forty-seven years after it was decided. The original decision in *Roe* was divided, and most abortion decisions since then have been closely divided. The application of the standard of review across numerous abortion decisions has been inconsistent. Judicial criticism continues. Scholarly criticism has been frequent, repeated, intense, and continuous. The Court's abortion decisions have spawned ceaseless confusion among the lower federal courts. The search by a majority of the Court for a coherent constitutional rationale for the abortion right continues. The current presidential administration, as have numerous previous administrations, campaigned on and calls for the overruling of *Roe*. As demonstrated by the 2019 state legislative sessions, the increasing expectations—on both sides of the issue—is that the Court will eventually overturn *Roe*.[3]

Second, *Roe* is widely regarded as having been wrongly decided. Over the past forty-six years, *Roe* has been subjected to regular, severe, and continuing

---

3. *See* Clarke D. Forsythe, *A Draft Opinion Overruling* Roe v. Wade, 16 GEO. J. L. & PUB. POL. 445 (2018) (discussing the factors and their application to *Roe*).

criticism by renowned legal scholars for its lack of any constitutional foundation, including Alexander Bickel, Archibald Cox, John Hart Ely, Philip Kurland, Richard Epstein, Mary Ann Glendon, Gerald Gunther, Robert Nagel, Michael Perry, and Harry Wellington.[4] As Professor Mark Tushnet has written, "[i]t seems to be generally agreed that, as a matter of simple craft, Justice Blackmun's opinion for the Court was dreadful." Mark V. Tushnet, *Following the Rules Laid Down: A Critique of Interpretavism and Neutral Principles*, 96 Harv. L. Rev. 781, 820 (1983). That criticism continued on *Roe*'s fortieth anniversary.[5]

The unsettled status of *Roe*'s doctrine can be traced back to its creation. *Roe* and *Doe v. Bolton*, 410 U.S. 179 (1973)—the companion case to *Roe*— were originally accepted for review by this Court to decide a procedural question, the application of *Younger v. Harris*.[6] *Roe* and *Doe* were decided by lower courts on motions to dismiss or for summary judgment, without any trial or evidentiary record on abortion, its risks, or its implications. Those cases were directly appealed to the Supreme Court, with no intermediate appellate review.[7]

Consequently, all the sociological, medical, and historical premises cited in the Court's opinions in *Roe* and *Doe* were assumptions, mostly derived from interest group briefs filed for the first time in the Supreme Court. Henry J. Friendly, *The Courts and Social Policy: Substance and Procedure*, 33 U. Miami L. Rev. 21, 37 (1978) (The *Roe* Court concluded "[m]ortality rates for women undergoing early abortions, where the procedure is legal, appear to be as low as or lower than the rates for normal childbirth" but that was based on "materials not of record in the trial court, and that conclusion constituted the underpinning for the holding that the asserted interest of the state 'in protecting the woman from an inherently hazardous procedure' during the first trimester did not exist."). This error contradicted a long line of precedents, before and since *Roe*, that this Court will not decide a constitutional claim without an "adequate, full-bodied record." *Witters v. Wash. Dept. of Services for the Blind*, 474 U.S. 481, 486 n.3 (1986)

---

4. Clarke D. Forsythe & Stephen B. Presser, *Restoring Self-Government on Abortion: A Federalism Amendment*, 10 Tex. Rev. Law & Pol. 301, 313–16 nn.62–72 (2005) (citing sources).

5. Randy Beck, *Twenty-Week Abortion Statutes: Four Arguments*, 43 Hastings Const. L.Q. 187, 194 n.42 (2016) (citing symposia); Colloquium, *The Fortieth Anniversary: Roe v. Wade in the Wilds of Politics*, 74 Ohio St. L.J. 1 (2013); Symposium, Roe v. Wade *at 40*, 24 Stan. L & Pol. Rev. 1 (2013); Symposium, Roe *at 40: The Controversy Continues*, 71 Wash. & Lee L. Rev. 817 (2014).

6. 401 U.S. 37 (1971).

7. *See* Clarke D. Forsythe, Abuse of Discretion: The Inside Story of Roe v. Wade 17–24 (2013).

("Nor is it appropriate . . . for us to consider claims that have not been the subject of factual development in earlier proceedings."); *Associated Press v. Nat'l Labor Relations Bd.*, 301 U.S. 103, 132 (1937) ("Courts deal with cases upon the basis of the facts disclosed, never with nonexistent and assumed circumstances.").

Roe also lacked any support in precedent.[8] Cases preceding *Roe* did not establish a right to abortion and the Court's opinion in *Roe* conceded as much. The Court cited a string of cases for the *ipse dixit* that the "right of privacy" is "broad enough to encompass a woman's decision whether or not to terminate her pregnancy," *Roe*, 410 U.S. at 152–53, but then conceded six pages later that a woman "carries an embryo and, later, a fetus" and that "[t]he situation therefore is inherently different from marital intimacy, or bedroom possession of obscene material, or marriage, or procreation, or education, with which *Eisenstadt* and *Griswold, Stanley, Loving, Skinner,* and *Pierce* and *Meyer* were respectively concerned." *Id.* at 159. The *Roe* Court strung together a group of cases and called them "privacy" cases, even though "privacy" was not the rationale relied upon in those decisions. In fact, the Court in *Maher v. Roe* referred to them as "a group of disparate cases restricting governmental intrusion, physical coercion, and criminal prohibition of certain activities." 432 U.S. 464, 471 (1977).

Roe adopted a historical rationale for a substantive due process right to abortion that has been subjected to intense, exhaustive, and sustained criticism.[9] If the *Roe* Court had applied the proper analysis for a fundamental constitutional right, abortion would not have qualified, because there is no evidence that any right to abortion was "deeply rooted in this Nation's history and tradition." *Washington v. Glucksberg*, 521 U.S. 702, 721 (1997). Legal and historical criticisms of *Roe* have provided considerable data that the

---

8. *See* Whole Woman's Health v. Hellerstedt, 136 S. Ct. 2292, 2327 (2016) (Thomas, J., dissenting). *See also* PHILIP BOBBITT, CONSTITUTIONAL FATE 159 (1982) ("The two principal propositions on which it [*Roe*] rests are neither derived from precedent nor elaborated from larger policies that may be thought to underly such precedent. And the precedent it establishes is broader than the questions before the Court, while at the same time disclaiming having decided issues that appear logically necessary to its holding."); John Hart Ely, *The Wages of Crying Wolf: A Comment on* Roe v. Wade, 82 YALE L.J. 920 (1973); Richard A. Epstein, *Substantive Due Process by Any Other Name: The Abortion Cases*, 1973 SUP. CT. REV. 159 (1973).

9. *See, e.g.,* JOSEPH W. DELLAPENNA, DISPELLING THE MYTHS OF ABORTION HISTORY 15, nn.71–72 (citing sources), 97–110, 125–84, 687–695 (2006); John Keown, *Back to the Future of Abortion Law:* Roe*'s Rejection of America's History and Traditions*, 22 ISSUES L. & MED. 3 (2006); Paul Benjamin Linton, Planned Parenthood v. Casey: *The Flight from Reason in the Supreme Court*, 13 ST. LOUIS U. PUB. L. REV. 15, 38 (1992); Dennis J. Horan et al., *Two Ships Passing in the Night: An Interpretavist Review of the White-Stevens Colloquy on* Roe v. Wade, 6 ST. LOUIS U. PUB. L. REV. 229, 272–73 (1987) (compiling existing scholarly criticism).

English common law prohibited abortion at the earliest point that the law could detect that a developing human being was alive prenatally. Numerous English common law cases treated abortion as a crime before the crime was first codified in the English abortion statute of 1803 (Lord Ellenborough's Law).[10] As one leading scholar has noted, "the authors of the [nineteenth] century's two leading American treatises on the law of crimes (Joel Prentiss Bishop and Francis Wharton) both concluded that abortion at any stage of pregnancy was a common law crime."[11] What is more, the *Roe* Court overlooked the many State protections provided to prenatal life in tort, criminal, property, and equity law.[12] These numerous problems likely explain why the Court abandoned any historical justification for *Roe* by the time of its decision in *Webster*. Instead, the Court in *Planned Parenthood of Southeastern Pennsylvania v. Casey* relied almost exclusively on stare decisis for its reaffirmation of *Roe*, hoping that *Roe* could be fixed, as substantially modified. 505 U.S. 833, 854–69 (1992). The Court's new rationale for *Roe* switched from history to sociology and the claim of "reliance interests." *Id.* at 855.

Casey's failure to justify *Roe* as an original matter and its reliance on stare decisis was severely criticized by numerous scholars.[13] The rationale for *stare decisis* that the Court created in *Casey* was largely ad hoc and has not been followed in subsequent cases. As in *Roe*, the *Casey* Court had no record evidence by which to assess "reliance" and initially declined to hear the overruling question at the time it granted review.[14] The Court ended up citing just two pages from one book to support "reliance."[15]

---

10. *See* Dellapenna, *supra* note 9, at 127–49, n.18; John Keown, Abortion, Doctors and the Law: Some Aspects of the Legal Regulation of Abortion in England from 1803 to 1982 (1988); Eugene Quay, *Justifiable Abortion: Medical and Legal Foundations*, 49 Geo. L.J. 395 (1961).

11. Dellapenna, *supra* note 9, at 425.

12. Gregory J. Roden, *Prenatal Tort Law and the Personhood of the Unborn Child: A Separate Legal Existence*, 16 St. Thomas L. Rev. 207 (2003); James Bopp Jr. & Richard E. Coleson, *The Right to Abortion: Anomalous, Absolute, and Ripe for Reversal*, 3 BYU J. Pub. L. 181 (1989); David Kader, *The Law of Tortious Prenatal Death Since* Roe v. Wade, 45 Mo. L. Rev. 639 (1980).

13. *See, e.g.*, Steven G. Calabresi, *Text, Precedent, and the Constitution: Some Originalist and Normative Arguments for Overruling* Planned Parenthood of Southeastern Pennsylvania v. Casey, 22 Const. Comment. 311 (2005); Morton J. Horowitz, *The Constitution of Change: Legal Fundamentality Without Fundamentalism*, 107 Harv. L. Rev. 30, 71 (1993) (criticizing the plurality's characterization of *Lochner v. New York*, 198 U.S. 45 (1905) and *Plessy v. Ferguson*, 163 U.S. 537 (1896)); Linton, *supra* note 9; Earl M. Maltz, *Abortion, Precedent, and the Constitution: A Comment on* Planned Parenthood of Southeastern Pennsylvania v. Casey, 68 Notre Dame L. Rev. 11 (1992).

14. *Planned Parenthood of Se. Pa. v. Casey*, 505 U.S. 833, 1056–57 (1992).

15. *Id.* at 856 (citing Rosalind P. Petchesky, Abortion and Woman's Choice 109, 133 n.7 (rev. ed. 1990).

All of these factors demonstrate that *Roe* was not derived from text, history, tradition, structure, or precedent, which are the only sources of constitutional legitimacy that might have authorized the Court to impose *Roe* on the nation. Since abortion is not a right derived from the federal constitution, it is a matter for the people to decide through the democratic process in the States.[16]

Third, the *Roe/Casey* standard has proven *unworkable*. In spite of the fact that the practice of medicine has been regulated by the States since before the Founding,[17] this Court has prescribed a national rule and assumed a unique role of judicial administration over just one medical procedure— one never exercised before or since—"as the Nation's '*ex officio* medical board with powers to approve or disapprove medical and operative practices and standards throughout the United States.'" *City of Akron v. Akron Ctr. for Reprod. Health, Inc.*, 462 U.S. 416, 456 (1983) (O'Connor, J., dissenting).[18]

Roe announced that there were two major state interests in regulating abortion: fetal life and maternal health.[19] But there was no evidentiary record to guide the Court's recognition or understanding or definition of these state interests, or the value to be given to them, or whether any other state interests existed. The application of *Roe* to state regulations of abortion to protect the state interests in fetal life and maternal health has been difficult and haphazard. The fact that *Roe* has been unworkable was immediately demonstrated in *Doe* where the Court did not apply the same standards as the Court purported to apply in *Roe*, as Justice Powell pointed out in his concurring opinion in *Carey v. Population Services International.*[20]

As the application of *Roe* and *Doe* in many subsequent cases has demonstrated, the Court has no capacity to assume or exercise such a role as the nation's medical review board of abortion. The Court has no capacity to oversee operative procedures or to assess safety. The Court cannot regulate or monitor or intervene. It cannot anticipate medical developments or medical data. Instead, the Court, through *Roe*, *Doe*, *Casey*, and *Hellerstedt*, has tied the hands of state and local public health officials who do have the

---

16. *See* McDonald v. City of Chicago, 561 U.S. 742 (2010); Washington v. Glucksberg, 521 U.S. 702 (1997).

17. Dent v. West Virginia, 129 U.S. 114 (1889).

18. *See also Hellerstedt*, 136 S. Ct. at 2326 (Thomas, J., dissenting) (noting the significance of *Hellerstedt* resurrecting appointment as "the nation's ex officio medical board").

19. 410 U.S. at 164–65.

20. 431 U.S. 678, 704 (1977) (noting that, in contrast to what *Roe* purported to adopt, *Doe* did not refer to the "compelling interest" standard but instead used the "reasonably related" test).

capacity to create and effectively enforce adequate health and safety standards at the local level.

The five-month limits on abortion passed since *Gonzales v. Carhart*, 550 U.S. 124 (2007), by the U.S. House and twenty-one states highlight the contradictions in the *Roe* Court's construction of the so-called state interest in maternal health. The Court created the viability rule in *Roe* based largely on the mistaken factual assumption that abortion is safer than childbirth.[21] The viability rule allows abortion beyond the point where abortion is more dangerous than childbirth, at least in the vast majority of cases.[22] And yet when states have asserted their interest in maternal health to limit abortion before viability at 20 weeks, the federal courts following *Roe* and *Casey* have invalidated those limits by rigidly applying the viability rule.[23]

The enterprise of applying a standard—whether undue burden or some other standard—to a public health issue such as abortion, with all its complexity, is not suited to the federal courts. Federal courts are not public health agencies and cannot serve that role. *Roe* and *Casey* have been repeatedly criticized by numerous federal judges for standards that cannot be consistently applied.[24]

Before *Hellerstedt*, federal courts had difficulty in applying the state's interest in maternal health when it seemingly conflicted with access to abortion. Which value were federal courts to adopt? In *Planned Parenthood Southeast, Inc. v. Bentley*,[25] the court recognized that the American medical profession has largely abandoned abortion practice, that abortion providers are diminishing, that providers are often flown in from out of town, or

21. *See* Brief Amicus Curiae of the Am. Ctr. for Law and Justice and the Am. Acad. of Med. Ethics in Support of Respondent-Cross-Petitioner, *June Med. Servs. L.L.C. v. Gee*, Nos. 18-1323 & 18-1460 (2019) (demonstrating that the claim that abortion is safer than childbirth is based on no reliable medical data).

22. *See* Linda A. Bartlett et al., *Risk Factors for Legal Induced Abortion-Related Mortality in the United States*, 103 Obstetrics & Gynecology 729 (2004) ("Compared with women whose abortions were performed at or before 8 weeks of gestation, women whose abortions were performed in the second trimester were significantly more likely to die of abortion-related causes."); *see* Clarke Forsythe, *The Medical Assumption at the Foundation of* Roe v. Wade *and Its Implications for Women's Health*, 71 Wash. & Lee L. Rev. 827, 873 (2014) (containing three appendices listing over 270 international, peer-reviewed medical studies finding increased, long-term medical risks after abortion).

23. *See, e.g.*, Isaacson v. Horne, 884 F. Supp. 2d 961 (D. Ariz. 2012) (upholding state's 20-week limit), *rev'd*, Isaacson v. Horne, 716 F.3d 1213 (9th Cir. 2013) (invalidating state's 20-week limit), *cert. denied*, 571 U.S. 1127 (2014).

24. *See* Forsythe, *supra* note 3, at 491–93 for a compiled list current as of 2018.

25. 951 F. Supp. 2d 1280 (M.D. Ala. 2013) (granting temporary restraining order against challenge to Alabama law requiring local hospital admitting privileges law for abortion-performing physicians).

out of state, or out of the country to do abortions, precisely the reason to require admitting privileges to protect patient follow-up and the physician-patient relationship.

Hellerstedt exemplifies this Court's inability to administer the standards laid down in *Roe* and *Casey*.[26] Twenty-four years after *Casey*, members of the Court disputed fundamental elements of *Roe*'s abortion doctrine in *Hellerstedt*.[27] The majority in *Hellerstedt* casually endorsed the district court's findings against the regulations, although the record contained medical evidence showing that the regulations were reasonably related to protecting maternal health. The Court in *Gonzales* questioned the propriety of facial challenges to state abortion regulations,[28] but the majority in *Hellerstedt* distorted prior facial challenge doctrine to resurrect a claim that the plaintiffs did not ask for.[29] The *Hellerstedt* Court exalted an interest in unfettered "access" to abortion against the state's interest in maternal health, in a case where the generally-applicable state regulations were reasonably related to protecting maternal health.[30] The Court also did not apply normal severability principles.[31]

Hellerstedt shows that the Court cannot perform its role as the "ex officio medical review board" because it cannot scrupulously examine the "benefits and burdens" of individual regulations. When faced with the obligation to carefully review multiple regulations, the Court invalidated all of the clinic regulations without specific findings against each, even generally-applicable medical regulations that are unquestionably sound and reasonable. *Hellerstedt* exemplifies the problem that, under the Court's abortion doctrine, judges can use facial challenges to broadly sweep away abortion regulations because of the difficulty of analyzing the specific impact of regulations.

Casey conceded that *Roe* was not workable as applied, overruling *Akron* and *Thornburgh v. American College of Obstetricians and Gynecologists*, 476 U.S.

26. *Hellerstedt*, 136 S. Ct. 2292 (2016).

27. *Id.* at 2321 (Thomas, J., dissenting) (questioning level of scrutiny and third-party standing).

28. *Gonzales v. Carhart*, 550 U.S. 124, 167 (2007) ("[T]hese facial attacks should not have been entertained in the first instance. In these circumstances the proper means to consider exceptions is by as-applied challenge.").

29. *Hellerstedt*, 136 S. Ct. at 2339 (Alito, J., dissenting) ("There is simply no reason why petitioners should be allowed to relitigate their facial claim.").

30. Brief of Association of American Physicians and Surgeons, Inc. as Amicus Curiae in Support of Respondent, *June Med. Servs. L.L.C., v. Gee*, Nos. 18-1323, 18-1460 (2019) (detailing the long practice, based on objective medical standards, of physician credentialing and admitting privileges for current competence and patient health)

31. *Hellerstedt*, 136 S. Ct. at 2350 (Alito, J., dissenting).

747 (1986) and announcing a new standard. But the "undue burden" standard applied since *Casey* has not been workable, because, among other reasons, it unavoidably motivates judges to apply their policy preferences and subordinates all state interests to "access." Due to the inherent institutional limits on this Court and its inconsistent application of the abortion doctrine over forty-five years, *Roe* has been demonstrated to be unworkable. The undue burden standard has done nothing to improve predictability, consistency, or coherence. The experience since *Casey* demonstrates that *Casey*'s re-engineering of *Roe* has not made *Roe* any more workable.[32] Clearly, *Roe* has never been a "simple limitation."[33] This has been a failure in judicial administration and it does not serve the rule of law. "[T]he fact that a decision has proved 'unworkable' is a traditional ground for overruling it." *Montejo v. Louisiana*, 556 U.S. 778, 792 (2009).

Fourth, changes in fact justify a reconsideration of *Roe*. The *Casey* Court declared that no facts had changed that justified overruling *Roe*.[34] But *Roe* established no reliable baseline from which to judge a change in facts, since there was no trial or evidentiary record in *Roe*. Much, if not all, of *Roe* rested on sociological "assumptions."[35] It is those assumptions that have been seriously challenged with the passage of time.

Moreover, the *Casey* Court deferred briefing on the overruling of *Roe* when it limited the questions to be addressed and side-stepped a searching analysis of changes in *Roe*'s assumptions.[36] The *Casey* Court simply issued an *ipse dixit* that change had not occurred. However, to the objective observer, *Roe*'s assumptions have changed considerably since 1973. Biological and technological developments, including the development of in vitro fertilization since the 1970s, have reinforced the medical conclusion of the 19th century that the life of the individual human being begins at conception.[37] The states have increasingly relied on this biological evidence to increase

---

32. Paul C. Quast, *Respecting Legislators and Rejecting Baselines: Rebalancing* Casey, 90 NOTRE DAME L. REV. 913 (2014).

33. *Casey*, 505 U.S. at 855 (describing Roe as a "simple limitation beyond which a state law is unenforceable.").

34. *Id.* at 864.

35. *City of Akron v. Akron Center for Reprod. Health, Inc.*, 462 U.S. 416, 430 n.12 (1983) ("the validity of Roe's factual assumption"); *Casey*, 505 U.S. at 860 ("We have seen how time has overtaken some of Roe's factual assumptions.").

36. *Casey*, 505 U.S. at 860–61.

37. Maureen L. Condic, *When Does Human Life Begin? The Scientific Evidence and the Terminology Revisited*, 8 U. ST. THOMAS J. L. & PUB. POL'Y 44 (2013); Dellapenna, *supra* note 9, at 256–61 & nn.241, 282, 298 (describing the evolution in medical understanding that influenced judicial and legislative protection from conception in the nineteenth century).

legal protection from conception in prenatal injury, wrongful death, and fetal homicide law. The widespread clinical use of ultrasound, a technological development that the *Roe* Court did not anticipate, came to the commercial market shortly after *Roe* and substantially affected medical practice and public understanding of prenatal development.[38] *Roe* was premised on the assumption that legalization of abortion would end the "the back alley butchers"[39] and allow abortion to be treated as "a medical procedure . . . governed by the same rules as apply to other medical procedures . . . with reasonable medical safeguards."[40] Repeated and continuing scandals involving clinics and providers have contradicted that assumption.[41] And there is a growing body of international medical data involving women from dozens of countries finding increased long-term risks to women from abortion.[42]

Most abortions today are not performed by doctors from the Mayo Clinic or by a woman's "own doctor."[43] American medicine has largely

38. Malcolm Nicolson & John E. E. Fleming, Imaging and Imagining the Fetus: The Development of Obstetric Ultrasound 1–7 (2013) ("Ultrasonic imaging has also had a momentous social impact because it can visualize the fetus. Fifty years ago, the unborn human being was hidden, enveloped within the female abdomen, away from the medical gaze. . . . [T]he scanner had become widely deployed within the British hospital system by 1975. By the late 1970s, the ultrasound scanner had become a medical white good, a standardized commodity in a mass marketplace."); *id.* at 213 ("By the early 1970s, some American hospitals were beginning to equip themselves with ultrasound scanners."); Laurie Troxclair, et al., *Shades of Gray: A History of the Development of Diagnostic Ultrasound in a Large Multispecialty Clinic*, 11 Oschner J. 151 (2011) (describing introduction of ultrasound for clinical use in 1975).

39. Randy Beck, *Prioritizing Abortion Access over Abortion Safety in Pennsylvania*, 8 U. St. Thomas J.L. & Pub. Pol'y 33, 40–41 (2013).

40. *Id.* at 34 n.4 (quoting Brief for Planned Parenthood Federation of America, Inc. and American Association of Planned Parenthood Physicians as Amici Curiae supporting Respondents, in *Roe v. Wade*, 410 U.S. 113 (1973) and *Doe v. Bolton*, 410 U.S. 179 (1973) (Nos. 70-18, 70-40)).

41. Ams. United for Life, UNSAFE: AMERICA'S ABORTION INDUSTRY ENDANGERS WOMEN (2018 ed.) (documenting that 227 abortion providers in 32 states were cited for more than 1,400 health and safety deficiencies between 2008 and 2016), https://aul.org/wp-content/uploads/2018/10/AUL-Unsanfe-2018-Final-Proof.pdf; Clarke D. Forsythe & Bradley N. Kehr, *A Road Map through the Supreme Court's Back Alley*, 57 Vill. L. Rev. 45, 65–70 (2012).

42. See, *e.g.*, Erika Bachiochi, THE COST OF "CHOICE": WOMEN EVALUATE THE IMPACT OF ABORTION, 63–102 (ed., 2004); Forsythe, *The Medical Assumption at the Foundation of* Roe v. Wade *and Its Implications for Women's Health*, *supra* note 22 (citing dozens of international, peer-reviewed medical studies finding increased medical risks after abortion).

43. See, *e.g.*, Debra B. Stulberg et al., *Abortion Provision Among Practicing Obstetricians-Gynecologists*, 118 Obstetrics & Gynecology 609 (2011) ("Among practicing ob-gyns, 97% encountered patients seeking abortions, whereas 14% performed them.").

abandoned abortion, so only a small percentage of doctors perform abortions.[44] Abortion is largely separated from the rest of obstetrical and gynecological care and practice.[45] Abortion does not involve the medical judgment that *Roe* assumed; in more than 90% of cases, abortion is not a medically-indicated procedure, but an elective procedure chosen for social reasons.[46] Contraception devices and methods have expanded,[47] and the shame previously associated with non-marital childbearing and with single parenting has been largely eliminated from American life.[48] Nations face population implosion, not explosion. Population in the U.S. in 2016 "grew at its lowest rate since the Great Depression," below replacement levels (0.7%).[49] The abortion rate has fallen to its lowest level since *Roe*,[50] during the same

---

44. Steven H. Aden, *Driving Out Bad Medicine: How State Regulation Impacts the Supply and Demand of Abortion*, 8 U. St. Thomas J.L. & Pub. Pol'y 14 (2013); Planned Parenthood Se., Inc. v. Bentley, 951 F. Supp. 2d 1280 (M.D. Ala. 2013) (challenge to Alabama admitting privileges law), subsequent decision, Planned Parenthood Se., Inc. v. Strange, 9 F. Supp. 3d 1272 (M.D. Ala. 2014).

45. *See* Stenberg v. Carhart, 530 U.S. 914, 958 (2000) (Kennedy, J., dissenting) ("Dr. Carhart has no specialty certifications in a field related to childbirth or abortion and lacks admitting privileges at any hospital."); *Akron*, 462 U.S. at 473 (1983) (O'Connor, J., dissenting) ("It is certainly difficult to understand how the Court believes that the physician-patient relationship is able to accommodate any interest that the State has in maternal physical and mental well-being in light of the fact that the record in this case shows that the relationship is nonexistent.").

46. *Cf. Roe*, 410 U.S. at 165–66 ("[T]he abortion decision in all its aspects is inherently, and primarily, a medical decision. . . ."); Lawrence B. Finer et al., *Reasons U.S. Women Have Abortions: Quantitative and Qualitative Perspectives*, 37 Perspectives on Sexual & Reprod. Health 110, 113–14 (2005) (explaining that between 8% and 12% of women cited health concerns as a reason for obtaining an abortion; between 3–4% cited health reasons as the most important reason why they obtained an abortion), https://onlinelibrary.wiley.com /doi/pdf/10.1111/j.1931- 2393.2005.tb00045.x.

47. *See* John Bongaarts & Elof Johansson, *Future Trends in Contraception in the Developing World: Prevalence and Method Mix*, 33 Stud. Family Planning 24 (2002).

48. Helen M. Alvare, *Beyond the Sex-Ed Wars: Addressing Disadvantaged Single Mothers' Search for Community*, 44 Akron L. Rev. 167 (2011).

49. Janet Adamy & Paul Overberg, *Census Says U.S. Population Grew at Lowest Rate Since Great Depression This Year*, Wall St. J. (Dec. 20, 2016) https://www.wsj.com/articles/census -says-u-s-population-grew-at-lowest-rate-since-great-depression-this-year-1482262203; Brady E. Hamilton et al., Div. of Vital Statistics, Nat'l Ctr. for Health Statistics, *Births: Provisional Data for 2017*, Report No. 004 (May 2018) https://www.cdc.gov/nchs/data/vsrr/report004 .pdf ("The [Total Fertility Rate] in 2017 was again below replacement—the level at which a given generation can exactly replace itself (2,100 births per 1,000 women). The rate has generally been below replacement since 1971").

50. Rachel K. Jones & Jenna Jerman, *Abortion Incidence and Service Availability in the United States, 2014*, 49 Perspectives on Sexual & Reprod. Health 17, 20 (2017) https://doi .org/10.1363/psrh.12015 ("This is the lowest rate since abortion was legalized nationally in 1973.").

decades that the female unemployment rate has fallen to its lowest level in nearly 20 years. Clearly, there is less reliance than the *Casey* Court assumed.

Fifth, there have been significant *legal changes* which have eroded *Roe*'s assumptions. The legal roadblocks that affected pregnant women before 1970, on which the *Roe* Court placed considerable emphasis, have been repealed. That can be attributed in part to the significant growth in the number of female legislators who shape State policy—including abortion policy.[51] Employment discrimination against pregnant women is prohibited by federal statute and by most states.[52] Women's rights have expanded since the 1960s due to the protections accorded by anti-discrimination statutes, including Title VII of the Civil Rights Act, the Pregnancy Discrimination Act, and a myriad of state civil rights and human rights statutes. "Safe Haven" laws have been enacted in all fifty states and the District of Columbia, allowing a woman to leave her newborn at a safe location.[53] The Family and Medical Leave Act of 1993 has altered the situation for maternity leave in America.[54] *None* of these legislative and judicial changes are due to *Roe*.

As discussed above, the law's protection of human life, exemplified in homicide law, goes back at least eight centuries in Anglo-American law. Legal protection of human life against abortion was considerable before *Roe*, more than the *Roe* Court admitted, in areas of tort, criminal, property, and equity law. Despite *Roe*, states have expanded legal protection for the unborn child, in many states from conception. *Roe* limited what the states could do to protect fetal life in the context of abortion, but *Roe* said nothing about state protection of fetal life outside the context of abortion, in the areas of tort, criminal, property, or equity law.[55] The States have increasingly isolated *Roe* as an anomaly in the law's protection of prenatal life. Virtually all of the states now have prenatal injury laws that recognize the unborn child as an independent human being. At least thirty-seven states now have fetal homicide laws, and thirty states have fetal homicide laws that extend protection from conception. At least thirty-six states now have wrongful

---

51. Ctr. for Am. Women and Politics, *Women in State Legislatures 2018*, http://www.cawp .rutgers.edu/women-state-legislature- 2018 ("Since 1971, the number of women serving in state legislatures has more than quintupled.").

52. Nat'l Conference of State Legislatures, State Employment-Related Discrimination Statutes (July 2015), http://www.ncsl.org/documents/employ/Discrimination-Chart-2015 .pdf (citing 40 states); Young v. United Parcel Serv., Inc., 575 U.S. 206, 251 (2015).

53. Lynne Marie Kohm, Roe's *Effects on Family Law*, 71 WASH. & LEE L. REV. 1339, 1354 n.58 (2014) (citing all fifty states' and the District of Columbia's safe haven laws).

54. Family and Medical Leave Act of 1993, Pub. L. 103-3, 29 U.S.C. §§ 2601 *et seq.*

55. *Cf.* Webster v. Reprod. Health Servs., 492 U.S. 490, 506 (1989). (recognizing that "[s]tate law has offered protections to unborn children in tort and probate law.").

death laws that protect the unborn child, and at least 10 extend protection from conception. The viability rule has been expressly rejected by most states in the areas of prenatal injury law and in the area of fetal homicide, and it has been increasingly rejected in the area of wrongful death law.[56] And the states have moved ahead with legal protection of fetal life to a greater degree, creating a stark contrast between the Court's abortion doctrine and state protection for fetal life in other areas of American life.[57] *Roe* has become increasingly at odds with state tort law's treatment of the unborn child, with state criminal law's treatment of the unborn child, with limits placed on abortion by the states. This contradiction in *Roe*, and the subsequent developments in state and federal law, have created deep-seated incoherence between the Court's abortion doctrine and all other areas of law affecting prenatal protection.

Simultaneously, a growing number of states have, year after year, adopted stronger and stronger limits on abortion, consciously limited, in turn, by the federal courts. There are numerous ways in which the states discourage or limit abortion through regulations, partial prohibitions, and limits on public funding. Numerous states elected to opt-out of the abortion provisions of the Affordable Care Act: In March 2015, for example, Arizona became the twenty- fifth state to ban most abortion coverage on health care exchanges.[58]

Numerous federal statutes have been enacted to address the unintended consequences of *Roe*. In 2002, Congress passed the Born-Alive Infants Protection Act of 2002 (BAIPA), by unanimous vote in the U.S. Senate.[59] In 2003, Congress enacted the Partial-Birth Abortion Ban Act of 2003 (PBABA).[60] These acts by the People's democratically elected representatives are the most reliable means to determine whether the assumptions underlying *Roe* have come to be understood by the people differently.[61] As reflected in the democratic acts of elected representatives, over four decades, at the state and federal level, the people have supported increasing limits on abortion that contradict what *Roe* in fact enacted.

---

56. *Hamilton v. Scott*, 97 So. 3d 728, 735 (Ala. 2012) (applying state's wrongful death law from conception).

57. *See* Paul Benjamin Linton, *The Legal Status of the Unborn Child under State Law*, 6 U. St. Thomas J.L. & Pub. Pol'y 141, 141–43 (2012).

58. Caitlin Owens, *Abortion Remains Contentious Under Obamacare*, The Atlantic (Apr. 1, 2015), https://www.theatlantic.com/politics/archive/2015/04/abortion-remains-conten tious-under-obamacare/452133/.

59. 1 U.S.C. § 8.

60. 18 U.S.C. § 1531.

61. Cf. *Casey*, 505 U.S. at 864.

What is more, *Roe* has not been followed internationally. The United States is one of only four nations, of 195 around the world, which allows abortion for any reason after fetal viability, and one of only seven nations that allows abortion after twenty weeks.[62] This puts the Court at odds with both international law and domestic public opinion.

Finally, the "reliance interests" in *Roe* that *Casey* cited are unproven. *Casey* held that women had come to rely on abortion as a back-up to failed contraception:

> [F]or two decades of economic and social developments, people have organized intimate relationships and made choices that define their views of themselves and their places in society, in reliance on the availability of abortion in the event that contraception should fail. The ability of women to participate equally in the economic and social life of the Nation has been facilitated by their ability to control their reproductive lives.[63]

Casey was a singular example of reliance interests in a non-commercial context.[64]

But the notion that women had ordered their thinking and living around abortion was not documented in *Casey* or derived from the record.[65] Just as there was no record of evidence in *Roe* for its rationale for the abortion "right," there was no record of evidence in *Casey* for its switch to "reliance interests" as the rationale for keeping *Roe*. And the *Casey* Court never connected women's social or economic advancement to abortion. To support reliance, the *Casey* Court offered nothing in the case record, but merely a citation to two pages in a 1990 book, Rosalind Petchesky's *Abortion and Woman's Choice*.[66] Petchesky never made the claim for which the Court cited her.[67] The *Casey* Court simply got the facts wrong: if there is any "reliance," it is on contraception, not abortion.

62. Randy Beck, Gonzales, Casey, *and the Viability Rule*, 103 NW. U. L. REV. 249, 261–65 (2009); CTR. FOR REPROD. RIGHTS, THE WORLD'S ABORTION LAWS 1–2 (2009).

63. 505 U.S. at 856.

64. Lucas A. Powe, Jr., *Intragenerational Constitutional Overruling*, 89 NOTRE DAME L. REV. 2093, 2095 (2014) ("Thus *Roe* was deemed that rarest of situations where reliance was found outside a commercial context.").

65. *Cf. Casey*, 505 U.S. at 856. (record).

66. 505 U.S. at 856; *cf.* McCorvey v. Hill, 385 F.3d 846 (5th Cir. 2004) (Jones, J., concurring) (noting courts cannot consider evidence of impact of abortion on women unless the Court changes the standard of review or invites such evidence).

67. *See* Erika Bachiochi, *A Putative Right in Search of a Constitutional Justification: Understanding* Planned Parenthood v. Casey's *Equality Rationale and How it Undermines Women's Equality*, 35 QUINNIPIAC L. REV. 593, 630 (2017) (pointing out that Petchesky does not claim that abortion contributed to women's "increased participation in the workforce.").

Further, the *Casey* Court assumed, erroneously, that overruling *Roe* would immediately make abortion illegal.[68] This supposition was false then, and it remains false today. Overturning *Roe* will not return the country to the status quo ante. Depending on what state courts and legislatures might do, approximately 16 states have prohibitions on the books during the first trimester. The rest have no prohibitions on the books before 20 weeks or viability. Approximately twenty-one states have prohibitions at twenty weeks. This means abortion will be legal through the twentieth week of gestation unless the states enact new prohibitions. And many large, populous states, like California, Illinois, New York, will keep it legal for the foreseeable future. Reliance interests are weakened by the fact that the overturning of *Roe* would not lead to immediate prohibition of abortion in many states. A number of state courts have created their own versions of *Roe* under the state constitution.[69] Thus, there will be little immediate legal change in most states. The states will clearly adopt a pluralistic approach to abortion policy.

The *Casey* Court conceded that reliance was limited because individuals can change their behavior based on a change in the law.[70] Individuals may rely on contraception, their local pharmacy, monetary means, state law, or the local market, but there is little evidence they rely on this Court's decision in *Roe*. There is little evidence—in terms of public opinion polls, state legislation, or public actions since *Roe*—that a majority of Americans have relied on this Court retaining a right to abortion for any reason at any time of pregnancy, or on the viability rule. The consistent practice of three-fifths of our states to adopt limits on abortion contradicts the notion that the sweeping result in *Roe* has "become part of our national culture."[71]

Without a record of evidence, the Court in *Roe* nevertheless put some emphasis on assumptions about the economic and social status of women and the impact of pregnancy and abortion policies. Much has changed in the United States since 1973 due to social practices and state and federal legislation. These social and legal changes will continue even when *Roe* is overturned.

---

68. 505 U.S. at 856 (referring to "any sudden restoration of state authority to ban abortions.").

69. *See generally*, Paul Benjamin Linton, ABORTION UNDER STATE CONSTITUTIONS (2d ed. 2012); Paul Benjamin Linton, *The Legal Status of Abortion in the States if* Roe v. Wade *Is Overruled*, 27 ISSUES L. & MED. 181 (2012).

70. 505 U.S. at 856 ("[R]eproductive planning could take virtually immediate account of any sudden restoration of state authority to ban abortions.").

71. Dickerson v. United States, 530 U.S. 428, 443–44 (2000).

As *Roe, Casey,* and *Hellerstedt* have shown, this Court cannot settle the abortion issue. Even if the Court unanimously reaffirmed *Roe*, it would merely preserve the legal schizophrenia that exists between the Court's policy and state and federal law, and do nothing to change the basic social and legal factors that have made *Roe* immune to settlement.

CONCLUSION

The Court should reconsider *Roe v. Wade* at the earliest practical opportunity.

Respectfully submitted,
CATHERINE GLENN FOSTER
STEVEN H. ADEN
CLARKE D. FORSYTHE
Counsel of Record
KATIE GLENN
NATALIE M. HEJRAN
AMERICANS UNITED FOR LIFE
1150 Connecticut Ave NW Suite 500
Washington, D.C. 20036 *Clarke.Forsyth@aul.org* Tel.: (202) 289-1478
January 2, 2020

Appendix P

Abortion Surveillance
— United States 2018[1] —

By Katherine Kortsmit, PhD*,†; Tara C. Jatlaoui, MD*; Michele G. Mandel*; Jennifer A. Reeves, MD*; Titilope Oduyebo, MD*; Emily Petersen, MD*; Maura K. Whiteman, PhD*

ABSTRACT

Description of System: Each year, CDC requests abortion data from the central health agencies for 50 states, the District of Columbia, and New York City. For 2018, 49 reporting areas voluntarily provided aggregate abortion data to CDC. Of these, 48 reporting areas provided data each year during 2009–2018. Census and natality data were used to calculate abortion rates (number of abortions per 1,000 women aged 15–44 years) and ratios (number of abortions per 1,000 live births), respectively. Abortion-related deaths from 2017 were assessed as part of CDC's Pregnancy Mortality Surveillance System (PMSS).

Results: A total of 619,591 abortions for 2018 were reported to CDC from 49 reporting areas. Among 48 reporting areas with data each year during

---

* Division of Reproductive Health, National Center for Chronic Disease Prevention and Health Promotion, CDC.

† Oak Ridge Institute for Science and Education

1. Appendix P is excerpted from the November 17, 2020 Morbidity and Mortality Weekly Report of the U.S. Centers for Disease Control and Prevention (some footnote numbers changed by redaction). The unredacted report is available at https://www.cdc.gov/mmwr/volumes/69/ss/ss6907a1.htm?s_cid=ss6907a1_w. Ed. Note: The CDC uses "surgical abortion" to include dilation and curettage (aspiration curettage, suction curettage, manual vacuum aspiration, menstrual extraction, and sharp curettage) and dilation and evacuation procedures. All abortions in the report are considered by the CDC to be legally induced unless stated otherwise.

2009–2018, in 2018, a total of 614,820 abortions were reported, the abortion rate was 11.3 abortions per 1,000 women aged 15–44 years, and the abortion ratio was 189 abortions per 1,000 live births. From 2017 to 2018, the total number of abortions and abortion rate increased 1% (from 609,095 total abortions and from 11.2 abortions per 1,000 women aged 15–44 years, respectively), and the abortion ratio increased 2% (from 185 abortions per 1,000 live births). From 2009 to 2018, the total number of reported abortions, abortion rate, and abortion ratio decreased 22% (from 786,621), 24% (from 14.9 abortions per 1,000 women aged 15–44 years), and 16% (from 224 abortions per 1,000 live births), respectively.

In 2018, women in their 20s accounted for more than half of abortions (57.7%). In 2018 and during 2009–2018, women aged 20–24 and 25–29 years accounted for the highest percentages of abortions; in 2018, they accounted for 28.3% and 29.4% of abortions, respectively, and had the highest abortion rates (19.1 and 18.5 per 1,000 women aged 20–24 and 25–29 years, respectively). By contrast, adolescents aged <15 years and women aged ≥40 years accounted for the lowest percentages of abortions (0.2% and 3.6%, respectively) and had the lowest abortion rates (0.4 and 2.6 per 1,000 women aged <15 and ≥40 years, respectively). However, abortion ratios in 2018 and throughout 2009–2018 were highest among adolescents (aged ≤19 years) and lowest among women aged 25–39 years. Abortion rates decreased from 2009 to 2018 for all women, regardless of age. The decrease in abortion rate was highest among adolescents compared with women in any other age group. From 2009 to 2013, the abortion rates decreased for all age groups and from 2014 to 2018, the abortion rates decreased for all age groups, except for women aged 30–34 years and those aged ≥40 years. In addition, from 2017 to 2018, abortion rates did not change or decreased among women aged ≤24 and ≥40 years; however, the abortion rate increased among women aged 25–39 years. Abortion ratios also decreased from 2009 to 2018 among all women, except adolescents aged <15 years. The decrease in abortion ratio was highest among women aged ≥40 years compared with women in any other age group. The abortion ratio decreased for all age groups from 2009 to 2013; however, from 2014 to 2018, abortion ratios only decreased for women aged ≥35 years. From 2017 to 2018, abortion ratios increased for all age groups, except women aged ≥40 years.

In 2018, approximately three fourths (77.7%) of abortions were performed at ≤9 weeks' gestation, and nearly all (92.2%) were performed at ≤13 weeks' gestation. In 2018, and during 2009–2018, the percentage of abortions performed at >13 weeks' gestation remained consistently low

(≤9.0%). In 2018, the highest proportion of abortions were performed by surgical abortion at ≤13 weeks' gestation (52.1%), followed by early medical abortion at ≤9 weeks' gestation (38.6%), surgical abortion at >13 weeks' gestation (7.8%), and medical abortion at >9 weeks' gestation (1.4%); all other methods were uncommon (<0.1%). Among those that were eligible (≤9 weeks' gestation), 50.0% of abortions were early medical abortions. In 2017, the most recent year for which PMSS data were reviewed for pregnancy-related deaths, two women were identified to have died as a result of complications from legal induced abortion.

Interpretation: Among the 48 areas that reported data continuously during 2009–2018, decreases were observed during 2009–2017 in the total number, rate, and ratio of reported abortions, and these decreases resulted in historic lows for this period for all three measures. These decreases were followed by 1%–2% increases across all measures from 2017 to 2018.

Public Health Action: The data in this report can help program planners and policymakers identify groups of women with the highest rates of abortion. Unintended pregnancy is a major contributor to induced abortion. Increasing access to and use of effective contraception can reduce unintended pregnancies and further reduce the number of abortions performed in the United States.

Introduction

This report summarizes data on legal induced abortions for 2018 that were provided voluntarily to CDC by the central health agencies of 49 reporting areas (47 states, the District of Columbia, and New York City, excluding California, Maryland, and New Hampshire) and comparisons over time for the 48 reporting areas that reported each year during 2009–2018 (47 states and New York City). A summary of data for the 49 reporting areas that provided data voluntarily to CDC for 2017 is available (Supplementary Tables; https://stacks.cdc.gov/view/cdc/96608). This report also summarizes abortion-related deaths reported voluntarily to CDC for 2017 as part of the Pregnancy Mortality Surveillance System (PMSS). Since 1969, CDC has conducted abortion surveillance to document the number and characteristics of women obtaining legal induced abortions in the United States (1). After nationwide legalization of abortion in 1973, the total number, rate (number of abortions per 1,000 women aged 15–44 years), and ratio (number of abortions per 1,000 live births) of reported abortions increased rapidly, reaching the highest levels in the 1980s, before decreasing at a slow yet steady pace (*2–4*). During 2006–2008, a break occurred in the previously sustained pattern of decrease (*5–8*), although this break has been followed in subsequent years by even greater decreases (*9–19*). Nonetheless, throughout the years, abortion incidence continues to vary across subpopulations (*20–26*). Continued surveillance is needed to monitor changes in abortion incidence in the United States.

Methods

[The discussion of study methods and statistical methodologies has been redacted.]

Results

Total Abortions Reported to CDC by Occurrence

Among the 49 reporting areas that provided data for 2018, a total of 619,591 abortions were reported. Of these abortions, 614,820 (99.2%) were from 48 reporting areas that provided data every year for 2009–2018. In 2018, these continuously reporting areas had an abortion rate of 11.3 abortions per 1,000 women aged 15–44 years and an abortion ratio of 189 abortions per 1,000 live births (Table 1). In 2017, the total number, rate, and ratio of reported abortions decreased to historic lows for the period of analysis for all three measures. From 2017 to 2018, the total number of reported abortions and abortion rate increased 1% (from 609,095 to 614,820 total abortions and from 11.2 to 11.3 abortions per 1,000 women aged 15–44 years), and the abortion ratio increased 2% (from 185 to 189 abortions per 1,000 live births). From 2009 to 2018, the total number of reported abortions decreased 22% (from 786,621), the abortion rate decreased 24% (from 14.9 abortions per 1,000 women aged 15–44 years), and the abortion ratio decreased 16% (from 224 abortions per 1,000 live births) (Figure).

In 2018, a considerable range existed in abortion rates by reporting area of occurrence (from 2.4 to 26.8 abortions per 1,000 women aged 15–44 years in South Dakota and New York City) and abortion ratios (from 32 to 518 abortions per 1,000 live births in South Dakota and the District of Columbia)[2] (Table 2). The percentage of abortions obtained by out-of-state

---

2. Comparisons do not include Wyoming, which reported <20 abortions and therefore was excluded from this and all subsequent analyses.

residents also varied among reporting areas (from 0.4% in Arizona to 65.4% in the District of Columbia). Overall, 9.3% of abortions were reported to CDC with unknown residence.

Age Group, Race/Ethnicity, and Marital Status

Among the 48 areas that reported abortion numbers by women's age for 2018, women in their 20s accounted for the majority (57.7%) of abortions and had the highest abortion rates (19.1 and 18.5 abortions per 1,000 women aged 20–24 and 25–29 years, respectively) (Table 3). Women in the youngest (<15 years) and oldest (≥40 years) age groups accounted for the smallest percentages of abortions (0.2% and 3.6%, respectively) and had the lowest abortion rates (0.4 and 2.6 abortions per 1,000 women aged <15 and ≥40 years, respectively). In contrast, abortion ratios in 2018 were lowest among women aged 25–39 years (126–189 per 1,000 live births).

Among the 44 reporting areas that provided data each year by women's age for 2009–2018, this pattern across age groups was stable, with the majority of abortions and the highest abortion rates occurring among women aged 20–29 years and the lowest percentages of abortions and abortion rates occurring among women in the youngest and oldest age groups (Table 4). From 2009 to 2018, abortion rates decreased among all age groups, although the decreases for adolescents (64% and 55% for adolescents aged <15 and 15–19 years, respectively) were greater than the decreases for women in all older age groups. From 2009 to 2013, the abortion rates decreased for all age groups, and from 2014 to 2018, the abortion rates decreased for all age groups except women aged 30–34 years and ≥40 years. From 2017 to 2018, abortion rates did not change or decreased among women aged ≤24 and ≥40 years; however, the abortion rate increased among women aged 25–39 years. During 2009–2018, abortion ratios decreased among women in all age groups, except for adolescents aged <15 years. The abortion ratio decreased for all age groups from 2009 to 2013; however, from 2014 to 2018, abortion ratios only decreased for women aged ≥35 years. From 2017 to 2018, abortion ratios increased for all age groups, except women aged ≥40 years.

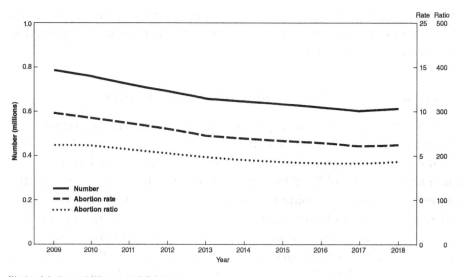

*Number of abortions per 1,000 women aged 15–44 years.
†Number of abortions per 1,000- live births
§Data are for 48 reporting areas; excludes California, District of Columbia, Maryland, and New Hampshire.

FIGURE. NUMBER, RATE,* AND RATIO† OF ABORTIONS PERFORMED, BY YEAR—SELECTED REPORTING AREAS,§ UNITED STATES, 2009-2018

Among the 46 areas[3] that reported women's age by individual year among adolescents for 2018, adolescents aged 18–19 years accounted for the majority (69.7%) of adolescent abortions and had the highest adolescent abortion rates (8.6 and 12.2 abortions per 1,000 adolescents aged 18 and 19 years, respectively). Adolescents aged <15 years accounted for the smallest percentage of adolescent abortions (2.5%) and had the lowest adolescent abortion rate (0.4 abortions per 1,000 adolescents aged 13–14 years). In 2018, the abortion ratio for adolescents was highest among adolescents aged <15 years (833 abortions per 1,000 live births) and was lowest among adolescents aged ≥17 years (336, 346, and 284 abortions per 1,000 live births among adolescents aged 17, 18, and 19 years, respectively).

Among the 31 areas that reported race/ethnicity data for 2018, non-Hispanic White women and non-Hispanic Black women accounted for the largest percentages of all abortions (38.7% and 33.6%, respectively), and Hispanic women and non-Hispanic women in the other race category accounted for smaller percentages (20.0% and 7.7%, respectively) (Table 5). Non-Hispanic White women had the lowest abortion rate (6.3 abortions per 1,000 women) and ratio (110 abortions per 1,000 live births), and

---

3. Excludes California, Connecticut, Illinois, Maryland, New Hampshire, and Wyoming.

non-Hispanic Black women had the highest abortion rate (21.2 abortions per 1,000 women) and ratio (335 abortions per 1,000 live births).

Among the 42 areas that reported by marital status for 2018, 14.8% of women who obtained an abortion were married, and 85.2% were unmarried (Table 6). The abortion ratio was 44 abortions per 1,000 live births for married women and 378 abortions per 1,000 live births for unmarried women.

Previous Live Births and Abortions

Data from the 43 areas that reported the number of previous live births for women who obtained abortions in 2018 indicate that 40.7%, 24.8%, 19.8%, and 14.7% of these women had zero, one, two, or three or more previous live births, respectively (Table 7). Data from the 40 areas that reported the number of previous abortions for women who obtained abortions in 2018 indicate that the majority (59.9%) had previously had no abortions, 23.9% had previously had one abortion, 9.9% had previously had two abortions, and 6.4% had previously had three or more abortions (Table 8).

Weeks of Gestation and Method Type

Among the 42 areas that reported gestational age[4]¶¶ at the time of abortion for 2018, approximately three fourths (77.7%) of abortions were performed at ≤9 weeks' gestation, and nearly all (92.2%) were performed at ≤13 weeks' gestation (Table 9). Fewer abortions were performed at 14–20 weeks' gestation (6.9%) or at ≥21 weeks' gestation (1.0%). Among the 34 reporting areas that provided data every year on gestational age for 2009–2018, the percentage of abortions performed at ≤13 weeks' gestation changed negligibly, from 91.8% to 91.5% (Table 10). However, within this gestational age range, a shift occurred toward earlier gestational ages, with the percentage of abortions performed at ≤6 weeks' gestation increasing 8% and the percentage of abortions performed at 7–9 weeks' and 10–13 weeks' gestation decreasing 2% and 14%, respectively. During 2009–2018, abortions performed at >13 weeks' gestation accounted for ≤9.0% of abortions. Among the 45 areas that reported by method type for 2018 and included medical abortion on their reporting form, 52.1% of abortions were surgical

---

4. Arkansas, South Carolina, and Texas collected probable postfertilization age. Two weeks were added to the probable postfertilization age to provide a corresponding measure to gestational age based on the clinician's estimate. Virginia reported clinician's estimate of gestational age based on conception; no modifications were made to these data.

abortions at ≤13 weeks' gestation, 38.6% were women accounted for the largest percentages of all abortions (38.7% and 33.6%, respectively), and Hispanic women and non-Hispanic women in the other race category accounted for early medical abortions (a nonsurgical abortion at ≤9 weeks' gestation), 7.8% were surgical abortions at >13 weeks' gestation, and 1.4% were medical abortions at >9 weeks' gestation; other methods, including intrauterine instillation and hysterectomy/hysterotomy, were both uncommon (<0.1%) (Table 11). Among the 37 reporting areas[5] that included medical abortion on their reporting form and provided these data for the relevant years of comparison, use of early medical abortion increased 9% from 2017 to 2018 (from 34.7% of abortions to 37.7%) and 120% from 2009 to 2018 (from 17.1% of abortions to 37.7%). Increases in early medical abortion occurred both from 2009 to 2013 (from 17.1% of abortions to 22.7% [33% increase]) and from 2014 to 2018 (from 23.3% of abortions to 37.7% [62% increase]).

Among the 40 areas that reported abortions categorized by individual weeks of gestation and method type, surgical abortion accounted for the largest percentage of abortions within every gestational age category, except ≤6 weeks' gestation (Table 12). At ≤6 weeks' gestation, surgical abortion accounted for 45.1% of abortions. Surgical abortion accounted for 55.3% of abortions at 7–9 weeks' gestation, 93.8%–98.4% of abortions at 10–20 weeks' gestation, and 91.9% of abortions at ≥21 weeks' gestation. In contrast, medical abortion accounted for 54.9% of abortions at ≤6 weeks' gestation, 44.7% of abortions at 7–9 weeks' gestation, 6.2% of abortions at 10–13 weeks' gestation, 1.5%–3.2% of abortions at 14–20 weeks' gestation, and 7.2% of abortions at ≥21 weeks' gestation. For each gestational age category (if applicable), abortions performed by intrauterine instillation or hysterectomy/hysterotomy were rare (<0.1%–0.8% of abortions).

Weeks of Gestation by Age Group and Race/Ethnicity

In selected reporting areas, abortions that were categorized by weeks of gestation were further categorized by age and race/ethnicity (Table 13). In every subgroup for these characteristics, the largest percentage of abortions occurred at ≤9 weeks' gestation. In 42 reporting areas, by age, 55.1% of adolescents aged <15 years and 71.5% of adolescents aged 15–19 years obtained an abortion at ≤9 weeks' gestation, compared with ≥76.8% among age

---

5. Excludes Alabama, California, Delaware, Florida, Hawaii, Illinois, Louisiana, Maryland, Nevada, New Hampshire, New Mexico, Tennessee, Vermont, Wisconsin, and Wyoming.

groups aged ≥20 years. Conversely, 21.7% of adolescents aged <15 years and 10.3% of adolescents aged 15–19 years obtained an abortion after 13 weeks' gestation, compared with 7.3%–8.0% for women in older age groups. In 30 reporting areas, by race/ethnicity, 73.3% of non-Hispanic Black women obtained an abortion at ≤9 weeks' gestation, compared with 79.6%–81.5% of women from other racial/ethnic groups. Differences in abortions after 13 weeks' gestation across race/ethnicity were minimal (8.8% for non-Hispanic Black women, compared with 6.5%–8.1% for women in the remaining racial/ethnic groups).

Abortion Mortality

Using national PMSS data (*53*), CDC identified two abortion-related deaths for 2017, the most recent year for which data were reviewed for abortion-related deaths (Table 14). Investigation of these cases indicated that two deaths were related to legal abortion.

The annual number of deaths related to legal induced abortion has fluctuated from year to year since 1973 (Table 14). Because of this variability and the relatively limited number of deaths related to legal induced abortions every year, national legal abortion case-fatality rates were calculated for consecutive 5-year periods during 1973–2017. The national legal induced abortion case-fatality rate for 2013–2017 was 0.44 legal induced abortion-related deaths per 100,000 reported legal abortions. This case-fatality rate was lower than the rates for the preceding 5-year periods.

Discussion

For 2018, a total of 619,591 abortions were reported to CDC by 49 areas. Of these reporting areas, 48 submitted data every year for 2009–2018, thus providing the information necessary for consistently reporting trends. Among these 48 areas, for 2018, the abortion rate was 11.3 abortions per 1,000 women aged 15–44 years, and the abortion ratio was 189 abortions per 1,000 live births. Although the rate of reported abortions declined overall from 2009 to 2018, from 2017 to 2018, the number and rate of reported abortions increased 1%, and the abortion ratio increased 2%.

Among areas that reported data continuously by age from 2009 to 2018, women in their 20s accounted for the majority of abortions and had the highest abortion rates, whereas adolescents aged ≤19 years had the lowest abortion rates. During 2009–2018, women aged ≥40 years accounted for a relatively small proportion of reported abortions (≤3.7%). However, the abortion ratio among women aged ≥40 years continues to be higher than among women aged 25–39 years. These data underscore important age differences in abortion measures.

The adolescent abortion trends described in this report are important for monitoring progress that has been made toward reducing adolescent pregnancies in the United States. From 2009 to 2018, national birth data indicate that the birth rate for adolescents aged 15–19 years decreased 54% (44,55), and the data in this report indicate that the abortion rate for the same age group decreased 55%. These findings highlight that decreases in adolescent births in the United States have been accompanied by large decreases in adolescent abortions (44,55). As in previous years, abortion rates and ratios differ across racial/ethnic groups. For example, in 2018, compared with non-Hispanic White women, abortion rates and ratios were 3.4 and 3.0 times higher among non-Hispanic Black women and 1.7 and 1.4 times higher among Hispanic women. Similar differences have been demonstrated in other U.S.-based research (3,4,20–26,56). The comparatively higher abortion rates and ratios among non-Hispanic Black women have been attributed to higher unintended pregnancy rates and a greater percentage of unintended pregnancies ending in abortion in this group (57). The complex factors contributing to differences to ensure equitable access to quality family planning services need to be identified (58,59).

In 2018, the majority of abortions occurred early in gestation (≤9 weeks), when the risks for complications are lowest (60–63). In addition, over the last 10 years, approximately three fourths of abortions were performed at ≤9 weeks' gestation, and this percentage increased from 74.2% in 2009 to 76.2% in 2018. Moreover, among the areas that reported abortions at ≤13 weeks' gestation by individual week, the distribution of abortions by gestational age continued to shift toward earlier weeks of gestation, with the percentage of early abortions performed at ≤6 weeks' gestation increasing from 33.6% in 2009 to 36.2% in 2018.

From 2009 to 2018, the percentage of abortions performed at >13 weeks' gestation did not change appreciably, remaining at ≤9.0%. Previous research indicates that the distribution of abortions by gestational age differs by various sociodemographic characteristics (64–66). In this report, the percentage of adolescents aged ≤19 years who obtained abortions at >13 weeks' gestation was higher than the percentage of women in older age groups who obtained abortions. Multiple factors might influence the gestational age when abortions are performed (56,60–63,65–69).

The trend of obtaining abortions earlier in pregnancy has been facilitated by changes in abortion practices. Research conducted in the United

States during the 1970s indicated that surgical abortion procedures performed at ≤6 weeks' gestation, compared with 7–12 weeks' gestation, were less likely to result in successful termination of the pregnancy (*70*). However, subsequent advances in technology (e.g., improved transvaginal ultrasonography and sensitivity of pregnancy tests) have allowed very early surgical abortions to be performed with completion rates exceeding 97% (*71–74*). Likewise, the development of early medical abortion regimens has allowed for abortions to be performed early in gestation, with completion rates for regimens that combine mifepristone and misoprostol reaching 96%–98% (*74–77*). In 2018, 77.7% of all reported abortions were ≤9 weeks' gestation thus were eligible for early medical abortion; of these, 50.0% were reported as medical abortions. Moreover, among areas that included medical abortion on their reporting form, the percentage of all abortions performed by early medical abortion increased 120% from 2009 to 2018.

Because the annual number of deaths related to legal induced abortion is small and statistically unstable, case-fatality rates were calculated for consecutive 5-year periods during 1973–2017. The national legal induced abortion case-fatality rate for 2013–2017 was fewer than 1 per 100,000 abortions, as it was for all the previous 5-year periods since the late 1970s, demonstrating the low risk for death associated with legal induced abortion.

Limitations

[The discussion of data limitations has been redacted for brevity.]

Public Health Implications

Ongoing surveillance of legal induced abortion is important for several reasons. First, abortion surveillance can be used to help evaluate programs aimed at preventing unintended pregnancies. Although pregnancy intentions can be difficult to assess (*79–84*), abortion surveillance provides an important indicator of unintended pregnancies because up to 42% of unintended pregnancies in the United States end in abortion (*57*). Efforts to help women avoid unintended pregnancies might reduce the number of abortions (*85,86*). Second, routine abortion surveillance is needed to assess trends in clinical practice patterns over time. Information in this report on the number of abortions performed through different methods (e.g., medical or surgical) and at different gestational ages provides the denominator data that are necessary for analyses of the relative safety of abortion practices (*54*). Finally, information on the number of pregnancies ending in abortion is needed in conjunction with data on births and fetal losses to estimate the number of pregnancies in the United States and determine rates for various outcomes of public health importance (e.g., adolescent pregnancies) (87).

Approximately 18% of all pregnancies in the United States end in induced abortion (19). Multiple factors influence the incidence of abortion, including access to health care services and contraception (85,86,88,89); the availability of abortion providers (8,11,16,90–93); state regulations, such as mandatory waiting periods (69,94,95), parental involvement laws (96,97), and legal restrictions on abortion providers (98–102); increasing acceptance of nonmarital childbearing (103,104); and changes in the economy and the resulting impact on fertility and contraceptive use (105).

The most recent data available indicate that the proportion of pregnancies in the United States that were unintended decreased from 51% in 2008 to 45% during 2011–2013 (57). Changing patterns of contraception use might have contributed to this decrease in unintended pregnancy. Use of long-acting reversible contraception (LARC) (i.e., intrauterine devices and hormonal implants), which are the most effective reversible contraceptive methods, has recently increased among all women (106–109), and the use of contraception overall appears to be increasing among sexually active adolescents (110). In addition, immediate postpartum and postabortion contraception provision, especially of LARC, has been shown to decrease rapid repeat pregnancy and repeat abortions (111–117). Further, providing contraception for women at low or no cost can increase use of more effective contraceptive methods for pregnancy prevention and reduce unintended pregnancy and abortion rates (85,86,88,118–120). Inadequate provider reimbursement and training, insufficient client-centered counseling, lack of youth-friendly services, and low client awareness of available contraceptive methods are reported barriers to accessing contraception (121–124). Reducing these barriers might help improve access to contraception and potentially reduce the number of unintended pregnancies and the number of abortions in the United States.

Conflicts of Interest

All authors have completed and submitted the International Committee of Medical Journal Editors form for disclosure of potential conflicts of interest. No potential conflicts of interest were disclosed.

References

1. Smith JC. Abortion surveillance report, hospital abortions, annual summary 1969. Atlanta, GA: US Department of Health, Education, and Welfare, Public Health Service, Health Services and Mental Health Administration, National Communicable Disease Center; 1970.

2. Gamble SB, Strauss LT, Parker WY, Cook DA, Zane SB, Hamdan S. Abortion surveillance—United States, 2005. MMWR Surveill Summ 2008;57(No. SS-13). PMID:19037196

3. Henshaw SK, Kost K. Trends in the characteristics of women obtaining abortions, 1974 to 2004. New York, NY: Guttmacher Institute; 2008. https://www.guttmacher.org/report/trends-characteristics-women - obtaining-abortions-1974-2004-supplemental-tables

4. Jones RK, Kost K, Singh S, Henshaw SK, Finer LB. Trends in abortion in the United States. Clin Obstet Gynecol 2009;52:119–29. PMID:19407518 https://doi.org/10.1097/GRF.0b013e3181a2af8f

5. Pazol K, Gamble SB, Parker WY, Cook DA, Zane SB, Hamdan S. Abortion surveillance—United States, 2006. MMWR Surveill Summ 2009;58(No. SS-8). PMID:19940837

6. Pazol K, Zane S, Parker WY, et al. Abortion surveillance—United States, 2007. MMWR Surveill Summ 2011;60(No. SS-1). PMID:21346710

7. Pazol K, Zane SB, Parker WY, Hall LR, Berg C, Cook DA. Abortion surveillance—United States, 2008. MMWR Surveill Summ 2011;60(No. SS-15). PMID:22108620

8. Jones RK, Kooistra K. Abortion incidence and access to services in the United States, 2008. Perspect Sex Reprod Health 2011;43:41–50. PMID:21388504 https://doi.org/10.1363/4304111

9. Pazol K, Creanga AA, Zane SB, Burley KD, Jamieson DJ. Abortion surveillance—United States, 2009. MMWR Surveill Summ 2012;61(No. SS-8). PMID:23169413

10. Pazol K, Creanga AA, Burley KD, Hayes B, Jamieson DJ. Abortion surveillance—United States, 2010. MMWR Surveill Summ 2013;62(No. SS-8). PMID:24280963

11. Jones RK, Jerman J. Abortion incidence and service availability in the United States, 2011. Perspect Sex Reprod Health 2014;46:3–14. PMID:24494995 https://doi.org/10.1363/46e0414

12. Pazol K, Creanga AA, Burley KD, Jamieson DJ. Abortion surveillance—United States, 2011. MMWR Surveill Summ 2014;63(No. SS-11). PMID:25426741

13. Pazol K, Creanga AA, Jamieson DJ. Abortion surveillance—United States, 2012. MMWR Surveill Summ 2015;64(No. SS-10). PMID:26619390 https://doi.org/10.15585/ss6410a1

14. Jatlaoui TC, Ewing A, Mandel MG, et al. Abortion surveillance—United States, 2013. MMWR Surveill Summ 2016;65(No. SS-12). PMID:27880751 https://doi.org/10.15585/mmwr.ss6512a1

15. Jatlaoui TC, Shah J, Mandel MG, et al. Abortion surveillance—United States, 2014. MMWR Surveill Summ 2017;66(No. SS-24). PMID:29166366 https://doi.org/10.15585/mmwr.ss6624a1

16. Jones RK, Jerman J. Abortion incidence and service availability in the United States, 2014. Perspect Sex Reprod Health 2017;49:17–27. PMID:28094905 https://doi.org/10.1363/psrh.12015

17. Jatlaoui TC, Boutot ME, Mandel MG, et al. Abortion surveillance—United States, 2015. MMWR Surveill Summ 2018;67(No. SS-13). PMID:30462632 https://doi.org/10.15585/mmwr.ss6713a1

18. Jatlaoui TC, Eckhaus L, Mandel MG, et al. Abortion surveillance—United States, 2016. MMWR Surveill Summ 2019;68(No. SS-11). PMID:31774741 https://doi.org/10.15585/mmwr.ss6811a1

19. Jones RK, Witwer E, Jerman J. Abortion incidence and service availability in the United States, 2017. New York, NY: Guttmacher Institute; 2019. https://www.guttmacher.org/report/abortion-incidence-service-availability-us-2017

20. Henshaw SK, Silverman J. The characteristics and prior contraceptive use of U.S. abortion patients. Fam Plann Perspect 1988;20:158–68. PMID:3243346 https://doi.org/10.2307/2135791

21. Henshaw SK, Kost K. Abortion patients in 1994–1995: characteristics and contraceptive use. Fam Plann Perspect 1996;28:140–7, 158. PMID:8853278

22. Jones RK, Darroch JE, Henshaw SK. Patterns in the socioeconomic characteristics of women obtaining abortions in 2000–2001. Perspect Sex Reprod Health 2002;34:226–35. PMID:12392215 https://doi.org/10.2307/3097821

23. Jones RK, Finer LB, Singh S. Characteristics of U.S. abortion patients, 2008. New York, NY: Guttmacher Institute; 2010. https://www.guttmacher.org/report/characteristics-us-abortion-patients-2008

24. Jones RK, Kavanaugh ML. Changes in abortion rates between 2000 and 2008 and lifetime incidence of abortion. Obstet Gynecol 2011;117:1358–66. PMID:21606746 https://doi.org/10.1097/AOG.0b013e31821c405e

26. Jones RK, Jerman J. Population group abortion rates and life-time incidence of abortion: United States, 2008–2014. Am J Public Health 2017;107:1904–9. PMID:29048970 https://doi.org/10.2105/AJPH.2017.304042

44. Martin JA, Hamilton BE, Osterman MJK. Births in the United States, 2018. NCHS Data Brief 2019;346:1–8. PMID: 31442195

53. CDC. Pregnancy mortality surveillance in the United States. Atlanta, GA: US Department of Health and Human Services, CDC; 2015. https://www.cdc.gov/reproductivehealth/maternal-mortality/pregnancy-mortality-surveillance-system.htm

54. Zane S, Creanga AA, Berg CJ, et al. Abortion-related mortality in the United States: 1998–2010. Obstet Gynecol 2015;126:258–65. PMID:26241413 https://doi.org/10.1097/AOG.0000000000000945

55. Martin JA, Hamilton BE, Osterman MJK, Driscoll AK, Mathews TJ. Births: Final data for 2015. Natl Vital Stat Rep 2017;66:1. PMID:28135188

56. Jones RK, Jerman J. Characteristics and circumstances of U.S. women who obtain very early and second-trimester abortions. PLoS One 2017;12:e0169969. PMID:28121999 https://doi.org/10.1371/journal.pone.0169969

57. Finer LB, Zolna MR. Declines in unintended pregnancy in the United States, 2008–2011. N Engl J Med 2016;374:843–52. PMID:26962904 https://doi.org/10.1056/NEJMsa1506575

58. Dehlendorf C, Rodriguez MI, Levy K, Borrero S, Steinauer J. Disparities in family planning. Am J Obstet Gynecol 2010;202:214–20. PMID:20207237 https://doi.org/10.1016/j.ajog.2009.08.022

59. Pazol K, Robbins CL, Black LI, et al. Receipt of selected preventive health services for women and men of reproductive age—United States, 2011–2013. MMWR Surveill Summ 2017;66(No. SS-20). PMID:29073129 https://doi.org/10.15585/mmwr.ss6620a1

60. Buehler JW, Schulz KF, Grimes DA, Hogue CJ. The risk of serious complications from induced abortion: do personal characteristics make a difference? Am J Obstet Gynecol 1985;153:14–20. PMID:4036997 https://doi.org/10.1016/0002-9378(85)90582-4

61. Ferris LE, McMain-Klein M, Colodny N, Fellows GF, Lamont J. Factors associated with immediate abortion complications. CMAJ 1996;154:1677–85. PMID:8646655

62. Bartlett LA, Berg CJ, Shulman HB, et al. Risk factors for legal induced abortion-related mortality in the United States. Obstet Gynecol

2004;103:729–37. PMID:15051566 https://doi.org/10.1097/01. AOG
.0000116260.81570.60

63. Lichtenberg ES, Paul M; Society of Family Planning. Surgical abortion prior to 7 weeks of gestation. Contraception 2013;88:7–17. PMID:23574709 https://doi.org/10.1016/j.contraception.2013.02.008

64. Foster DG, Kimport K. Who seeks abortions at or after 20 weeks? Perspect Sex Reprod Health 2013;45:210–8. PMID:24188634 https:// doi .org/10.1363/4521013

65. Jones RK, Finer LB. Who has second-trimester abortions in the United States? Contraception 2012;85:544–51. PMID:22176796 https://doi .org/10.1016/j.contraception.2011.10.012

66. Kiley JW, Yee LM, Niemi CM, Feinglass JM, Simon MA. Delays in request for pregnancy termination: comparison of patients in the first and second trimesters. Contraception 2010;81:446–51. PMID:20399953 https://doi.org/10.1016/j.contraception.2009.12.021

67. Drey EA, Foster DG, Jackson RA, Lee SJ, Cardenas LH, Darney PD. Risk factors associated with presenting for abortion in the second trimester. Obstet Gynecol 2006;107:128–35. PMID:16394050 https:// doi.org/10.1097/01.AOG.0000189095.32382.d0

68. Finer LB, Frohwirth LF, Dauphinee LA, Singh S, Moore AM. Timing of steps and reasons for delays in obtaining abortions in the United States. Contraception 2006;74:334–44. PMID:16982236 https://doi .org/10.1016/j.contraception.2006.04.010

69. Joyce TJ, Henshaw SK, Dennis A, Finer LB, Blanchard K. The impact of state mandatory counseling and waiting period laws on abortion: a literature review. New York, NY: Guttmacher Institute; 2009. https:// www.guttmacher.org/report/impact-state-mandatory-counseling-and -waiting-period-laws-abortion-literature-review

70. Kaunitz AM, Rovira EZ, Grimes DA, Schulz KF. Abortions that fail. Obstet Gynecol 1985;66:533–7. PMID:4047543

71. Creinin MD, Edwards J. Early abortion: surgical and medical options. Curr Probl Obstet Gynecol Fertil 1997;20:1–32.

72. Edwards J, Carson SA. New technologies permit safe abortion at less than six weeks' gestation and provide timely detection of ectopic gestation. Am J Obstet Gynecol 1997;176:1101–6. PMID:9166176 https:// doi.org/10.1016/S0002-9378(97)70410-1

73. Paul ME, Mitchell CM, Rogers AJ, Fox MC, Lackie EG. Early surgical abortion: efficacy and safety. Am J Obstet Gynecol 2002;187:407–11. PMID:12193934 https://doi.org/10.1067/mob.2002.123898

74. Baldwin MK, Bednarek PH, Russo J. Safety and effectiveness of medication and aspiration abortion before or during the sixth week of pregnancy: A retrospective multicenter study. Contraception 2020;102:13–7. PMID:32298713 https://doi.org/10.1016/j.contraception.2020.04.004

75. Nippita S, Paul M. Abortion. In: Hatcher RA, Nelson AL, Trussell J, et al, eds. Contraceptive technology, 21st ed. New York, NY: Ayer Company Publishers, Inc.; 2018:779–827.

76. Kapp N, Baldwin MK, Rodriguez MI. Efficacy of medical abortion prior to 6 gestational weeks: a systematic review. Contraception 2018;97:90–9. PMID:28935220 https://doi.org/10.1016/j.contraception.2017.09.006

77. Kapp N, Eckersberger E, Lavelanet A, Rodriguez MI. Medical abortion in the late first trimester: a systematic review. Contraception 2019;99:77–86. PMID:30444970 https://doi.org/10.1016/j.contraception.2018.11.002

79. Klerman LV. The intendedness of pregnancy: a concept in transition. Matern Child Health J 2000;4:155–62. PMID:11097502 https://doi.org/10.1023/A:1009534612388

80. Lifflander A, Gaydos LM, Hogue CJ. Circumstances of pregnancy: low income women in Georgia describe the difference between planned and unplanned pregnancies. Matern Child Health J 2007;11:81–9. PMID:17080316 https://doi.org/10.1007/s10995-006-0138-3

81. Sable MR, Wilkinson DS. Pregnancy intentions, pregnancy attitudes, and the use of prenatal care in Missouri. Matern Child Health J 1998;2:155–65. PMID:10728272 https://doi. org/10.1023/A:1021827110206

82. Santelli J, Rochat R, Hatfield-Timajchy K, et al; Unintended Pregnancy Working Group. The measurement and meaning of unintended pregnancy. Perspect Sex Reprod Health 2003;35:94–101. PMID:12729139

83. Santelli JS, Lindberg LD, Orr MG, Finer LB, Speizer I. Toward a multidimensional measure of pregnancy intentions: evidence from the United States. Stud Fam Plann 2009;40:87–100. PMID:19662801 https://doi.org/10.1111/j.1728-4465.2009.00192.x

84. Trussell J, Vaughan B, Stanford J. Are all contraceptive failures unintended pregnancies? Evidence from the 1995 National Survey of Family Growth. Fam Plann Perspect 1999;31:246–7, 260. PMID: 10723650

85. Ricketts S, Klingler G, Schwalberg R. Game change in Colorado: widespread use of long-acting reversible contraceptives and rapid decline in births among young, low-income women. Perspect Sex Reprod Health 2014;46:125–32. PMID:24961366 https://doi. org/10.1363/46e1714

86. Peipert JF, Madden T, Allsworth JE, Secura GM. Preventing unintended pregnancies by providing no-cost contraception. Obstet Gynecol 2012;120:1291–7. PMID:23168752 https://doi.org/10.1097/AOG.0b013e318273eb56

87. Kost K, Maddow-Zimet I, Arpaia A. Pregnancies, births and abortions among adolescents and young women in the United States, 2013: national and state trends by age, race and ethnicity. New York, NY: Guttmacher Institute; 2017. https://www.guttmacher.org/sites/default/files/report_pdf/us-adolescent-pregnancy-trends-2013.pdf

88. Biggs MA, Rocca CH, Brindis CD, Hirsch H, Grossman D. Did increasing use of highly effective contraception contribute to declining abortions in Iowa? Contraception 2015;91:167–73. PMID:25465890 https://doi.org/10.1016/j.contraception.2014.10.009

89. Roth LP, Sanders JN, Simmons RG, Bullock H, Jacobson E, Turok DK. Changes in uptake and cost of long-acting reversible contraceptive devices following the introduction of a new low-cost levonorgestrel IUD in Utah's Title X clinics: a retrospective review. Contraception 2018;98:63–8. PMID:29574095 https://doi.org/10.1016/j.contraception.2018.03.029

90. Finer LB, Henshaw SK. Abortion incidence and services in the United States in 2000. Perspect Sex Reprod Health 2003;35:6–15. PMID:12602752

91. Henshaw SK. Abortion incidence and services in the United States, 1995–1996. Fam Plann Perspect 1998;30:263–70, 287. PMID: 9859016

92. Jones RK, Zolna MR, Henshaw SK, Finer LB. Abortion in the United States: incidence and access to services, 2005. Perspect Sex Reprod Health 2008;40:6–16. PMID:18318867 https://doi.org/10.1363/4000608

93. Quast T, Gonzalez F, Ziemba R. Abortion facility closings and abortion rates in Texas. Inquiry 2017;54:46958017700944. PMID:28351188 https://doi.org/10.1177/0046958017700944

94. Sanders JN, Conway H, Jacobson J, Torres L, Turok DK. The longest wait: examining the impact of Utah's 72-hour waiting period for abortion. Womens Health Issues 2016;26:483–7. PMID:27502901 https://doi.org/10.1016/j.whi.2016.06.004

95. Ely G, Polmanteer RSR, Caron A. Access to abortion services in Tennessee: does distance traveled and geographic location influence return for a second appointment as required by the mandatory waiting period policy? Health Soc Work 2019;44:13–21. PMID:30561624 https://doi.org/10.1093/hsw/hly039

96. Dennis A, Henshaw SK, JoyceTJ, Finer LB, Blanchard K.The impact of laws requiring parental involvement for abortion: a literature review. New York, NY: Guttmacher Institute; 2009. https://www .guttmacher.org/report/impact-laws-requiring-parental-involvement -abortion-literature-review

97. Ramesh S, Zimmerman L, Patel A. Impact of parental notification on Illinois minors seeking abortion. J Adolesc Health 2016;58:290–4. PMID:26794433 https://doi.org/10.1016/j.jadohealth.2015.11.004

98. Grossman D, Baum S, Fuentes L, et al. Change in abortion services after implementation of a restrictive law in Texas. Contraception 2014;90:496–501. PMID:25128413 https://doi.org/10.1016/j .contraception.2014.07.006

99. Joyce T. The supply-side economics of abortion. N Engl J Med 2011;365: 1466–9. PMID:22010912 https://doi.org/10.1056/ NEJMp1109889

100. Grossman D, White K, Hopkins K, Potter JE. Change in distance to nearest facility and abortion in Texas, 2012 to 2014. JAMA 2017;317:437–9. PMID:28114666 https://doi.org/10.1001/jama.2016.17026

101. White K, Baum SE, Hopkins K, Potter JE, Grossman D. Change in second-trimester abortion after implementation of a restrictive state law. Obstet Gynecol 2019;133:771–9. PMID:30870293 https://doi .org/10.1097/AOG.0000000000003183

102. Jones RK, Ingerick M, Jerman J. Differences in abortion service delivery in hostile, middle-ground, and supportive states in 2014. Womens Health Issues 2018;28:212–8. PMID:29339010 https://doi .org/10.1016/j.whi.2017.12.003

103. Martinez GM, Chandra A, Abma JC, Jones J, Mosher WD. Fertility, contraception, and fatherhood: data on men and women from cycle 6 (2002) of the 2002 National Survey of Family Growth. Vital Health Stat 23 2006;23:1–142. PMID:16900800

104. Ventura SJ. Changing patterns of nonmarital childbearing in the United States. NCHS Data Brief 2009;18:1–8. PMID:19450389

105. Guttmacher Institute. A real-time look at the impact of the recession on women's family planning and pregnancy decisions. New York, NY: Guttmacher Institute; 2009. https://www.guttmacher.org/report/real -time-look-impact-recession-womens-family-planning-and-pregnancy -decisions

106. Kavanaugh ML, Jerman J. Contraceptive method use in the United States: trends and characteristics between 2008, 2012 and 2014. Contraception 2018;97:14–21. PMID:29038071 https://doi. org/10.1016/j .contraception.2017.10.003

107. Abma JC, Martinez GM. Sexual activity and contraceptive use among teenagers in the United States, 2011–2015. Natl Health Stat Report 2017;104:1–23. PMID:28696201

108. Kann L, McManus T, Harris WA, et al. Youth risk behavior surveillance—United States, 2015. MMWR Surveill Summ 2016;65(No. SS-6). PMID:27280474

109. Daniels K, Abma J. Current contraceptive status among women aged 15–49: United States, 2015–2017. NCHS Data Brief 2018;327:1–8.

110. Lindberg LD, Santelli JS, Desai S. Changing patterns of contraceptive use and the decline in rates of pregnancy and birth among U.S. adolescents, 2007–2014. J Adolesc Health 2018;63:253–6. PMID:30149926 https://doi.org/10.1016/j.jadohealth.2018.05.017

111. Rose SB, Lawton BA. Impact of long-acting reversible contraception on return for repeat abortion. Am J Obstet Gynecol 2012;206:37.e1–6. PMID:21944222 https://doi.org/10.1016/j.ajog.2011.06.102

112. Cameron ST, Glasier A, Chen ZE, Johnstone A, Dunlop C, Heller R. Effect of contraception provided at termination of pregnancy and incidence of subsequent termination of pregnancy. BJOG 2012;119:1074–80. PMID:22703553 https://doi.org/10.1111/j.1471-0528.2012.03407.x

113. Ames CM, Norman WV. Preventing repeat abortion in Canada: is the immediate insertion of intrauterine devices postabortion a cost-effective option associated with fewer repeat abortions? Contraception 2012;85:51–5. PMID:22067796 https://doi.org/10.1016/j.contraception.2011.05.002

114. Goodman S, Hendlish SK, Reeves MF, Foster-Rosales A. Impact of immediate postabortal insertion of intrauterine contraception on repeat abortion. Contraception 2008;78:143–8. PMID:18672116 https://doi.org/10.1016/j.contraception.2008.03.003

115. Qasba NT, Stutsman JW, Weaver GE, Jones KE, Daggy JK, Wilkinson TA. Informing policy change: a study of rapid repeat pregnancy in adolescents to increase access to immediate postpartum contraception. J Womens Health (Larchmt) 2020;29:815–8. PMID:31990605 https://doi.org/10.1089/jwh.2019.8122

116. Lichtenstein Liljeblad K, Kopp Kallner H, Brynhildsen J. Risk of abortion within 1–2 years after childbirth in relation to contraceptive choice: a retrospective cohort study. Eur J Contracept Reprod Health Care 2020;25:141–6. PMID:32083501 https://doi.org/10.1080/13625187.2020.1718091

117. Harrison MS, Zucker R, Scarbro S, Sevick C, Sheeder J, Davidson AJ. Postpartum contraceptive use among Denver-based adolescents and young adults: association with subsequent repeat delivery. J Pediatr

Adolesc Gynecol 2020;33:393–397.e1. PMID:32251837 https://doi. org/10.1016/j.jpag.2020.03.012

118. Goyal V, Canfield C, Aiken AR, Dermish A, Potter JE. Postabortion contraceptive use and continuation when long-acting reversible contraception is free. Obstet Gynecol 2017;129:655–62. PMID:28277358 https://doi.org/10.1097/AOG.0000000000001926

119. Gyllenberg FK, Saloranta TH, But A, Gissler M, Heikinheimo O. Induced abortion in a population entitled to free-of-charge long-acting reversible contraception. Obstet Gynecol 2018;132:1453–60. PMID:30399102 https://doi.org/10.1097/AOG.0000000000002966

120. Biggs MA, Taylor D, Upadhyay UD. Role of insurance coverage in contraceptive use after abortion. Obstet Gynecol 2017;130:1338–46. PMID:29112661 https://doi.org/10.1097/AOG.0000000000002361

121. Boulet SL, D'Angelo DV, Morrow B, et al. Contraceptive use among nonpregnant and postpartum women at risk for unintended pregnancy, and female high school students, in the context of Zika preparedness— United States, 2011–2013 and 2015. MMWR Morb Mortal Wkly Rep 2016;65:780–7. PMID:27490117 https://doi.org/10.15585 /mmwr. mm6530e2

122. Kumar N, Brown JD. Access barriers to long-acting reversible contraceptives for adolescents. J Adolesc Health 2016;59:248–53. PMID:27247239 https://doi.org/10.1016/j.jadohealth.2016.03.039

123. Parks C, Peipert JF. Eliminating health disparities in unintended pregnancy with long-acting reversible contraception (LARC). Am J Obstet Gynecol 2016;214:681–8. PMID:26875950 https://doi. org/10.1016/j .ajog.2016.02.017

124. Klein DA, Berry-Bibee EN, Keglovitz Baker K, Malcolm NM, Rollison JM, Frederiksen BN. Providing quality family planning services to LGBTQIA individuals: a systematic review. Contraception 2018;97:378–91. PMID:29309754 https://doi.org/10.1016/j.contraception.2017.12.016

Ed. Note: The following tables have been omitted: (1) Table 7: Reported abortions, by known number of previous live births and reporting area of occurrence—selected reporting areas, United States, 2018; (2) Table 8: Reported abortions, by known number of previous induced abortions and reporting area of occurrence—selected reporting areas, United States, 2018; and (3) Table 14: Number of deaths and case-fatality rates for abortion-related deaths reported to CDC, by type of abortion—United States, 1973–2017. The data in those tables is well summarized in the text, and in the case of mortality, the frequency is so slight that the detailed table adds little.

TABLE 1. Number, Percentage, Rate,* and Ratio† of Reported Abortions—Selected Reporting Areas, United States, 2009-2018

	Selected reporting areas§	Continuously reporting areas¶		
Year	No.	No. (%)**	Rate	Ratio
2009	789,217††	786,621 (99.7)	14.9	224
2010	765,651	762,755 (99.6)	14.4	225
2011	730,322	727,554 (99.6)	13.7	217
2012	699,202	696,587 (99.6)	13.1	208
2013	664,435	661,874 (99.6)	12.4	198
2014	652,639	649,849 (99.6)	12.1	192
2015	638,169	636,902 (99.8)	11.8	188
2016	623,471	623,471 (100.0)	11.6	186
2017	612,719	609,095 (99.4)	11.2	185
2018	619,591	614,820 (99.2)	11.3	189

* Number of abortions per 1,000 women aged 15–44 years.

† Number of abortions per 1,000 live births.

§ For each given year, excludes reporting areas that did not report that year's abortion numbers to CDC: California (2009–2018), District of Columbia (2016), Maryland (2009–2018), and New Hampshire (2009–2018).

¶ For all years, excludes reporting areas that did not report abortion numbersevery year during the period of analysis (2009–2018): California, District of Columbia, Maryland, and New Hampshire.

** Abortions from areas that reported every year during 2009–2018 as a percentage of all reported abortions for a given year.

†† This number is greater than reported in the 2009 report because of numbers subsequently provided by Delaware (**Source:** Pazol K, Creanga AA, Zane SB, Burley KD, Jamieson DJ. Abortion surveillance—United States, 2009. MMWR Surveill Summ 2012;61[No. SS-8]).

TABLE 2. Number, Rate,* and Ratio† of Reported Abortions, by Reporting Area of Occurrence and Percentage of Abortions Obtained by Out-of-State Residents^β—United States, 2018¶

State/Area	Abortions reported by area of occurrence**			Abortions obtained by out-of-state residents
	No.	Rate	Ratio	No. (%)
Alabama	6,484	6.8	112	1,029 (15.9)
Alaska	1,283	8.8	127	17 (1.3)
Arizona	12,438	9.0	154	48 (0.4)
Arkansas	3,069	5.3	83	321 (10.5)
Colorado	8,975	7.7	143	1,032 (11.5)
Connecticut	9,294	13.9	268	423 (4.6)
Delaware	1,740	9.7	164	236 (13.6)
District of Columbia††	4,771	25.3	518	3,119 (65.4)
Florida	70,239	18.1	317	2,653 (3.8)
Georgia	33,918	15.7	269	5,558 (16.4)
Hawaii	2,121	8.0	125	31 (1.5)
Idaho	1,257	3.7	59	48 (3.8)
Illinois	42,441	16.9	293	5,668 (13.4)
Indiana	8,037	6.2	98	774 (9.6)
Iowa	2,849	4.8	75	302 (10.6)
Kansas	6,972	12.4	192	3,498 (50.2)
Kentucky	3,203	3.8	59	489 (15.3)
Louisiana	8,097	8.7	136	1,315 (16.2)
Maine	1,949	8.4	158	81 (4.2)
Massachusetts	18,256	13.1	264	575 (3.1)
Michigan	26,716	14.2	243	1,158 (4.3)
Minnesota	9,910	9.2	147	1,014 (10.2)
Mississippi	3,005	5.1	81	317 (10.5)
Missouri	2,910	2.5	40	265 (9.1)
Montana	1,674	8.7	145	170 (10.2)
Nebraska	2,078	5.6	82	246 (11.8)
Nevada	8,819	14.8	247	456 (5.2)
New Jersey^{§§}	22,936	13.6	227	1,304 (5.7)
New Mexico	3,847	9.7	167	853 (22.2)
New York	77,447	19.8	342	7,514 (9.7)
New York City	49,759	26.8	457	4,308 (8.7)
New York State	27,688	13.5	236	3,206 (11.6)
North Carolina	27,581	13.5	232	4,996 (18.1)

State/Area	Abortions reported by area of occurrence**			Abortions obtained by out-of-state residents
	No.	Rate	Ratio	No. (%)
North Dakota	1,141	7.7	107	309 (27.1)
Ohio	20,425	9.2	151	1,210 (5.9)
Oklahoma	4,990	6.5	100	368 (7.4)
Oregon	8,735	10.6	207	828 (9.5)
Pennsylvania	30,364	12.7	224	2,124 (7.0)
Rhode Island	2,817	13.5	268	382 (13.6)
South Carolina	4,646	4.8	82	227 (4.9)
South Dakota	382	2.4	32	85 (22.3)
Tennessee	10,880	8.2	135	2,063 (19.0)
Texas	55,140	9.2	146	1,234 (2.2)
Utah	3,082	4.5	65	187 (6.1)
Vermont	1,204	10.5	222	215 (17.9)
Virginia	16,474	9.8	165	935 (5.7)
Washington	17,264	11.5	201	934 (5.4)
West Virginia	1,507	4.7	83	208 (13.8)
Wisconsin	6,224	5.7	97	182 (2.9)
Total	**619,591**	**NA**	**NA**	**NA**

Abbreviation: NA = not applicable.

* Number of abortions per 1,000 women aged 15–44 years.

† Number of abortions per 1,000 live births.

§ Additional details on the reporting area in which abortions were provided, cross-tabulated by the state of residence, are available at https://www.cdc.gov /reproductivehealth/data_stats/Abortion.htm.

¶ Data from 48 reporting areas; excludes four reporting areas (California, Maryland, New Hampshire, and Wyoming) that did not report or did not meet reporting standards.

** The total abortions include those with known and unknown residence status.

†† Reporting to the central health agency is not required.

§§ Reporting to the central health agency is not required. Data are requested from hospitals and licensed ambulatory care facilities only.

TABLE 3. Reported Abortions, by Known Age Group and Reporting Area of Occurrence—Selected Reporting Areas,* United States, 2018

State/Area	Age group (yrs)							Total abortions reported by known age
	<15	15–19	20–24	25–29	30–34	35–39	≥40	
	No. (%)[†]	No. (%)	No. (%)	No. (%)	No. (%)	No. (%)	No. (%)	No. (% of all reported abortions)[§]
Alabama	24 (0.4)	634 (9.8)	1,997 (30.8)	1,956 (30.2)	1,104 (17.0)	585 (9.0)	181 (2.8)	**6,481 (100.0)**
Alaska	—[¶]	154 (12.0)	365 (28.4)	355 (27.7)	233 (18.2)	131 (10.2)	—	**1,283 (100.0)**
Arizona	28 (0.2)	1,126 (9.1)	3,787 (30.4)	3,471 (27.9)	2,178 (17.5)	1,380 (11.1)	467 (3.8)	**12,437 (100.0)**
Arkansas	17 (0.6)	290 (9.4)	974 (31.7)	879 (28.6)	507 (16.5)	315 (10.3)	87 (2.8)	**3,069 (100.0)**
Colorado	26 (0.3)	850 (9.5)	2,619 (29.2)	2,566 (28.6)	1,663 (18.6)	913 (10.2)	327 (3.6)	**8,964 (99.9)**
Connecticut	24 (0.3)	845 (9.3)	2,489 (27.3)	2,697 (29.6)	1,738 (19.1)	1,003 (11.0)	305 (3.4)	**9,101 (97.9)**
Delaware	—	201 (11.6)	516 (29.7)	473 (27.2)	314 (18.0)	175 (10.1)	—	**1,740 (100.0)**
District of Columbia**	13 (0.3)	437 (9.2)	1,349 (28.3)	1,461 (30.6)	882 (18.5)	460 (9.6)	168 (3.5)	**4,770 (100.0)**
Florida	101 (0.1)	5,370 (7.7)	18,999 (27.1)	20,643 (29.5)	14,207 (20.3)	7,899 (11.3)	2,863 (4.1)	**70,082 (99.8)**
Georgia	74 (0.2)	2,717 (8.0)	9,523 (28.1)	10,454 (30.8)	6,443 (19.0)	3,554 (10.5)	1,153 (3.4)	**33,918 (100.0)**
Hawaii	—	200 (9.4)	627 (29.6)	567 (26.7)	406 (19.1)	227 (10.7)	—	**2,121 (100.0)**
Idaho	—	138 (11.0)	411 (32.7)	329 (26.2)	200 (15.9)	140 (11.1)	—	**1,256 (99.9)**
Illinois[††]	94 (0.3)	3,223 (8.8)	10,702 (29.3)	11,043 (30.2)	6,632 (18.1)	3,729 (10.2)	1,164 (3.2)	**36,587 (99.7)**
Indiana	22 (0.3)	787 (9.8)	2,513 (31.3)	2,291 (28.5)	1,381 (17.2)	771 (9.6)	272 (3.4)	**8,037 (100.0)**
Iowa	7 (0.2)	283 (10.0)	822 (28.9)	785 (27.6)	557 (19.6)	282 (9.9)	107 (3.8)	**2,843 (99.8)**
Kansas	15 (0.2)	647 (9.3)	2,221 (31.9)	1,942 (27.9)	1,152 (16.5)	741 (10.6)	254 (3.6)	**6,972 (100.0)**
Kentucky	14 (0.4)	287 (9.0)	933 (29.1)	917 (28.6)	601 (18.8)	338 (10.6)	113 (3.5)	**3,203 (100.0)**

State/Area	Age group (yrs)							Total abortions reported by known age
	<15 No. (%)[†]	15–19 No. (%)	20–24 No. (%)	25–29 No. (%)	30–34 No. (%)	35–39 No. (%)	≥40 No. (%)	No. (% of all reported abortions)[§]
Louisiana	18 (0.2)	721 (8.9)	2,400 (29.6)	2,399 (29.6)	1,508 (18.6)	786 (9.7)	265 (3.3)	8,097 (100.0)
Maine	—	194 (10.0)	581 (29.8)	527 (27.1)	337 (17.3)	228 (11.7)	—	1,947 (99.9)
Massachusetts	25 (0.1)	1,256 (6.9)	4,678 (25.6)	5,283 (28.9)	3,943 (21.6)	2,276 (12.5)	793 (4.3)	18,254 (100.0)
Michigan	54 (0.2)	2,265 (8.5)	7,719 (29.0)	8,651 (32.5)	4,652 (17.5)	2,450 (9.2)	814 (3.1)	26,605 (99.6)
Minnesota	16 (0.2)	793 (8.0)	2,713 (27.4)	2,775 (28.0)	2,037 (20.6)	1,193 (12.0)	383 (3.9)	9,910 (100.0)
Mississippi	13 (0.4)	285 (9.5)	899 (29.9)	932 (31.0)	530 (17.6)	276 (9.2)	70 (2.3)	3,005 (100.0)
Missouri	14 (0.5)	286 (9.8)	861 (29.6)	861 (29.6)	542 (18.6)	272 (9.4)	73 (2.5)	2,909 (100.0)
Montana	—	183 (11.0)	479 (28.7)	468 (28.0)	307 (18.4)	172 (10.3)	—	1,671 (99.8)
Nebraska	9 (0.4)	220 (10.6)	663 (31.9)	546 (26.3)	360 (17.3)	206 (9.9)	74 (3.6)	2,078 (100.0)
Nevada	17 (0.2)	713 (8.3)	2,356 (27.5)	2,444 (28.5)	1,704 (19.9)	982 (11.5)	353 (4.1)	8,569 (97.2)
New Jersey[§§]	69 (0.3)	2,023 (8.8)	6,167 (26.9)	6,779 (29.6)	4,479 (19.5)	2,507 (10.9)	907 (4.0)	22,931 (100.0)
New Mexico	9 (0.2)	502 (13.9)	1,066 (29.4)	932 (25.7)	651 (18.0)	328 (9.1)	134 (3.7)	3,622 (94.2)
New York	168 (0.2)	6,843 (8.9)	20,723 (26.8)	21,988 (28.5)	15,272 (19.8)	9,035 (11.7)	3,221 (4.2)	77,250 (99.7)
New York City	108 (0.2)	3,984 (8.0)	12,833 (25.8)	14,259 (28.7)	10,238 (20.6)	6,047 (12.2)	2,288 (4.6)	49,757 (100.0)
New York State	60 (0.2)	2,859 (10.4)	7,890 (28.7)	7,729 (28.1)	5,034 (18.3)	2,988 (10.9)	933 (3.4)	27,493 (99.3)
North Carolina	72 (0.3)	2,240 (8.4)	7,550 (28.3)	8,198 (30.7)	4,987 (18.7)	2,794 (10.5)	840 (3.1)	26,681 (96.7)
North Dakota	—	103 (9.0)	329 (28.8)	332 (29.1)	215 (18.8)	116 (10.2)	—	1,141 (100.0)
Ohio	54 (0.3)	1,884 (9.2)	6,128 (30.0)	6,206 (30.4)	3,639 (17.8)	1,912 (9.4)	602 (2.9)	20,425 (100.0)

State/Area	Age group (yrs)							Total abortions reported by known age
	<15	15–19	20–24	25–29	30–34	35–39	≥40	
	No. (%)[†]	No. (%)	No. (%)	No. (%)	No. (%)	No. (%)	No. (%)	No. (% of all reported abortions)[§]
Oklahoma	25 (0.5)	471 (9.4)	1,507 (30.2)	1,474 (29.6)	904 (18.1)	469 (9.4)	135 (2.7)	4,985 (99.9)
Oregon	12 (0.1)	809 (9.3)	2,462 (28.2)	2,415 (27.7)	1,650 (18.9)	1,028 (11.8)	353 (4.0)	8,729 (99.9)
Pennsylvania	72 (0.2)	2,529 (8.3)	8,644 (28.5)	9,252 (30.5)	5,753 (18.9)	3,191 (10.5)	923 (3.0)	30,364 (100.0)
Rhode Island	—	218 (7.8)	827 (29.6)	814 (29.1)	526 (18.8)	294 (10.5)	—	2,797 (99.3)
South Carolina	14 (0.3)	449 (9.7)	1,360 (29.3)	1,343 (28.9)	814 (17.5)	510 (11.0)	156 (3.4)	4,646 (100.0)
South Dakota	0 (0.0)	41 (10.7)	112 (29.3)	109 (28.5)	79 (20.7)	31 (8.1)	10 (2.6)	382 (100.0)
Tennessee	22 (0.2)	972 (9.0)	3,241 (29.9)	3,320 (30.6)	1,981 (18.3)	1,048 (9.7)	270 (2.5)	10,854 (99.8)
Texas	112 (0.2)	4,856 (8.8)	16,187 (29.4)	15,790 (28.6)	10,322 (18.7)	5,935 (10.8)	1,938 (3.5)	55,140 (100.0)
Utah	6 (0.2)	412 (13.4)	946 (30.8)	769 (25.0)	511 (16.6)	324 (10.6)	102 (3.3)	3,070 (99.6)
Vermont	—	101 (8.4)	358 (29.8)	318 (26.5)	220 (18.3)	146 (12.1)	—	1,202 (99.8)
Virginia	16 (0.1)	1,196 (7.3)	4,499 (27.3)	4,927 (29.9)	3,226 (19.6)	1,938 (11.8)	649 (3.9)	16,451 (99.9)
Washington	36 (0.2)	1,725 (10.0)	4,722 (27.4)	4,738 (27.5)	3,288 (19.1)	2,033 (11.8)	706 (4.1)	17,248 (99.9)
West Virginia	5 (0.3)	140 (9.3)	459 (30.5)	430 (28.5)	266 (17.7)	155 (10.3)	52 (3.5)	1,507 (100.0)
Wisconsin[††]	17 (0.3)	561 (9.3)	1,839 (30.4)	1,771 (29.3)	1,080 (17.9)	615 (10.2)	159 (2.6)	6,042 (100.0)
Total	1,362 (0.2)	53,180 (8.7)	173,322 (28.3)	179,620 (29.4)	115,981 (19.0)	65,893 (10.8)	22,018 (3.6)	611,376 (99.6)[¶¶]
Abortion rate[***]	0.4	6.0	19.1	18.5	12.6	7.2	2.6	—
Abortion ratio[†††]	872	334	271	189	126	142	218	—

See table footnotes on the next page.

* Data from 48 reporting areas; excludes four reporting areas (California, Maryland, New Hampshire, and Wyoming) that did not report, did not report by age, or did not meet reporting standards.

† Percentages for the individual component categories might not add to 100% because of rounding.

§ Percentage is calculated as the number of abortions reported by known age divided by the sum of abortions reported by known and unknown age. Values ≥99.95% are rounded to 100.0%.

¶ Cells with a value in the range of 1–4 or cells that would allow for calculation of these small values have been suppressed.

** Reporting to the central health agency is not required.

†† Includes residents only.

§§ Reporting to the central health agency is not required. Data are requested from hospitals and licensed ambulatory care facilities only.

¶¶ Percentage based on a total of 613,681 abortions reported among the areas that met reporting standards for age.

*** Number of abortions obtained by women in a given age group per 1,000 women in that same age group. Adolescents aged 13–14 years were used as the denominator for the group of adolescents aged <15 years, and women aged 40–44 years were used as the denominator for the group of women aged ≥40 years. For the total abortion rate only, abortions for women of unknown age were distributed according to the distribution of abortions among women of known age.

††† Number of abortions obtained by women in a given age group per 1,000 live births to women in that same age group. For the total abortion ratio only, abortions for women of unknown age were distributed according to the distribution of abortions among women of known age.

TABLE 4. Reported Abortions, by Known Age Group and Year—Selected Reporting Areas,* United States, 2009–2018

Age group (yrs)	Year										% change			
	2009	2010	2011	2012	2013	2014	2015	2016	2017	2018	2009 to 2013	2014 to 2018	2017 to 2018	2009 to 2018
Reported abortions by known age (%)														
<15	0.5	0.5	0.4	0.4	0.3	0.3	0.3	0.3	0.2	0.2	-40.0	-33.3	0.0	-60.0
15–19	15.5	14.6	13.5	12.2	11.4	10.4	9.8	9.4	9.1	8.8	-26.5	-15.4	-3.3	-43.2
20–24	32.7	32.9	32.9	32.8	32.7	32.1	31.1	30.0	29.3	28.5	0.0	-11.2	-2.7	-12.8
25–29	24.4	24.5	24.9	25.4	25.9	26.8	27.6	28.5	29.0	29.4	6.1	9.7	1.4	20.5
30–34	14.8	15.3	15.8	16.4	16.8	17.2	17.7	18.0	18.3	18.8	13.5	9.3	2.7	27.0
35–39	8.8	8.9	8.9	9.1	9.2	9.7	10.0	10.3	10.5	10.7	4.5	10.3	1.9	21.6
≥40	3.3	3.4	3.6	3.7	3.6	3.6	3.6	3.6	3.6	3.5	9.1	-2.8	-2.8	6.1
Abortion rate†														
<15	1.1	1.0	0.9	0.8	0.6	0.5	0.5	0.4	0.4	0.4	-45.5	-20.0	0.0	-63.6
15–19	12.8	11.7	10.5	9.2	8.2	7.3	6.7	6.2	5.9	5.8	-35.9	-20.5	-1.7	-54.7
20–24	27.7	26.8	25.0	23.3	21.9	20.9	19.9	19.1	18.3	18.2	-20.9	-12.9	-0.5	-34.3
25–29	20.7	20.2	19.4	18.9	18.2	18.1	17.9	17.8	17.3	17.6	-12.1	-2.8	1.7	-15.0
30–34	13.4	13.2	12.7	12.4	11.8	11.7	11.7	11.6	11.5	11.9	-11.9	1.7	3.5	-11.2
35–39	7.6	7.6	7.5	7.3	7.0	7.1	7.0	6.9	6.7	6.8	-7.9	-4.2	1.5	-10.5
≥40	2.8	2.8	2.8	2.8	2.5	2.5	2.5	2.5	2.5	2.5	-10.7	0.0	0.0	-10.7
Abortion ratio§														
<15	832	848	839	804	791	745	700	733	777	853	-4.9	14.5	9.8	2.5
15–19	328	332	325	304	299	291	289	296	301	318	-8.8	9.3	5.6	-3.0
20–24	281	290	284	272	262	256	250	250	249	256	-6.8	0.0	2.8	-8.9
25–29	183	184	178	174	168	166	167	169	171	178	-8.2	7.2	4.1	-2.7
30–34	138	138	132	128	121	116	115	113	114	119	-12.3	2.6	4.4	-13.8
35–39	172	171	165	158	147	145	140	136	134	135	-14.5	-6.9	0.7	-21.5
≥40	275	273	275	269	245	239	228	220	211	206	-10.9	-13.8	-2.4	-25.1

Age group (yrs)	Year										% change			
	2009	2010	2011	2012	2013	2014	2015	2016	2017	2018	2009 to 2013	2014 to 2018	2017 to 2018	2009 to 2018
Total (no.)	695,952	675,732	643,628	614,570	582,260	569,100	556,221	544,663	528,130	533,375	—	—	—	—

* Data from 44 reporting areas; excludes eight reporting areas (California, District of Columbia, Florida, Maine, Maryland, New Hampshire, Vermont, and Wyoming) that did not report, did not report by age, or did not meet reporting standards for ≥1 year. By year, these reporting areas represent 87%–99% of all abortions reported by age to CDC during 2009–2018.

† Number of abortions obtained by women in a given age group per 1,000 women in that same age group. Adolescents aged 13–14 years were used as the denominator for the group of adolescents aged <15 years, and women aged 40–44 years were used as the denominator for the group of women aged ≥40 years. Women aged 15–44 years were used as the denominator for the overall rate. For the total abortion rate only, abortions for women of unknown age were distributed according to the distribution of abortions among women of known age.

§ Number of abortions obtained by women in a given age group per 1,000 live births to women in that same age group. For the total abortion ratio only, abortions for women of unknown age were distributed according to the distribution of abortions among women of known age.

TABLE 5. Reported Abortions, by Known Race/Ethnicity and Reporting Area of Occurrence—Selected Reporting Areas,* United States, 2018

State/Area	Non-Hispanic White No. (%)†	Black No. (%)	Other No. (%)	Hispanic No. (%)	Total abortions reported by known race/ethnicity No. (% of all reported abortions)§
Alabama	1,986 (30.7)	3,981 (61.5)	170 (2.6)	332 (5.1)	**6,469 (99.8)**
Alaska	603 (51.1)	77 (6.5)	447 (37.9)	53 (4.5)	**1,180 (92.0)**
Arizona	4,828 (40.6)	1,237 (10.4)	1,109 (9.3)	4,714 (39.7)	**11,888 (95.6)**
Arkansas	1,380 (45.2)	1,318 (43.2)	158 (5.2)	198 (6.5)	**3,054 (99.5)**
Connecticut	3,351 (38.8)	2,809 (32.5)	449 (5.2)	2,027 (23.5)	**8,636 (92.9)**
Delaware	742 (42.9)	722 (41.8)	71 (4.1)	193 (11.2)	**1,728 (99.3)**
District of Columbia¶	883 (19.4)	2,498 (55.0)	529 (11.6)	634 (14.0)	**4,544 (95.2)**
Florida	21,215 (32.8)	21,898 (33.9)	2,814 (4.4)	18,684 (28.9)	**64,611 (92.0)**
Idaho	881 (73.0)	37 (3.1)	54 (4.5)	235 (19.5)	**1,207 (96.0)**
Indiana	4,326 (54.8)	2,422 (30.7)	463 (5.9)	687 (8.7)	**7,898 (98.3)**
Kansas	3,930 (56.5)	1,649 (23.7)	497 (7.1)	882 (12.7)	**6,958 (99.8)**
Kentucky	1,873 (58.5)	973 (30.4)	128 (4.0)	228 (7.1)	**3,202 (100.0)**
Michigan	10,731 (40.9)	13,215 (50.4)	1,309 (5.0)	985 (3.8)	**26,240 (98.2)**
Minnesota	4,488 (49.4)	2,421 (26.7)	1,396 (15.4)	774 (8.5)	**9,079 (91.6)**
Mississippi	655 (21.9)	2,147 (71.9)	104 (3.5)	79 (2.6)	**2,985 (99.3)**
Missouri	1,231 (42.6)	1,375 (47.5)	218 (7.5)	69 (2.4)	**2,893 (99.4)**
Montana	1,401 (83.7)	28 (1.7)	155 (9.3)	90 (5.4)	**1,674 (100.0)**
Nevada	3,236 (38.5)	1,466 (17.5)	1,058 (12.6)	2,635 (31.4)	**8,395 (95.2)**
New Jersey**	6,565 (30.8)	6,696 (31.4)	3,341 (15.7)	4,732 (22.2)	**21,334 (93.0)**
North Carolina	8,348 (32.4)	12,487 (48.4)	1,922 (7.5)	3,031 (11.8)	**25,788 (93.5)**

Ohio	8,028 (46.0)	7,183 (41.2)	1,226 (7.0)	1,014 (5.8)	**17,451 (85.4)**
Oregon	4,954 (65.5)	449 (5.9)	844 (11.2)	1,314 (17.4)	**7,561 (86.6)**
South Carolina	2,181 (47.0)	1,873 (40.4)	234 (5.0)	351 (7.6)	**4,639 (99.8)**
South Dakota	237 (62.2)	51 (13.4)	56 (14.7)	37 (9.7)	**381 (99.7)**
Tennessee	4,417 (41.6)	5,258 (49.5)	331 (3.1)	620 (5.8)	**10,626 (97.7)**
Texas††	14,990 (27.2)	14,759 (26.8)	3,948 (7.2)	21,408 (38.8)	**55,105 (99.9)**
Utah	2,077 (70.8)	123 (4.2)	240 (8.2)	494 (16.8)	**2,934 (95.2)**
Vermont	1,052 (89.8)	28 (2.4)	53 (4.5)	39 (3.3)	**1,172 (97.3)**
Virginia	4,943 (34.6)	6,500 (45.4)	1,361 (9.5)	1,500 (10.5)	**14,304 (86.8)**
Washington	8,468 (57.7)	1,798 (12.2)	2,266 (15.4)	2,149 (14.6)	**14,681 (85.0)**
West Virginia	1,328 (88.1)	148 (9.8)	24 (1.6)	7 (0.5)	**1,507 (100.0)**
Total	**135,328 (38.7)**	**117,626 (33.6)**	**26,975 (7.7)**	**70,195 (20.0)**	**350,124 (94.1)§§**
Abortion rate¶¶	6.3	21.2	11.9	10.9	—
Abortion ratio*	110	335	213	158	—

See table footnotes on the next page.

* Data from 31 reporting areas; excludes 21 reporting areas (California, Colorado, Georgia, Hawaii, Illinois, Iowa, Louisiana, Maine, Maryland, Massachusetts, Nebraska, New Hampshire, New Mexico, New York City, New York State, North Dakota, Oklahoma, Pennsylvania, Rhode Island, Wisconsin, and Wyoming) that did not report, did not report by race/ethnicity, or did not meet reporting standards.

† Percentages for the individual component categories might not add to 100% because of rounding.

§ Percentage is calculated as the number of abortions reported by known race/ethnicity divided by the sum of abortions reported by known and unknown race/ethnicity. Values ≥99.95% are rounded to 100.0%.

¶ Reporting to the central health agency is not required.

** Reporting to the central health agency is not required. Data are requested from hospitals and licensed ambulatory care facilities only.

†† Reporting form contains only one question for race/ethnicity; therefore, abortions reported for women of White, Black, and other races (Asian and Native American) are not explicitly identified as non-Hispanic.

§§ Percentage is based on a total of 372,077 abortions reported among the areas that met reporting standards for race/ethnicity.

¶¶ Number of abortions obtained by women in a given racial/ethnic group per 1,000 women in that same racial/ethnic group. For the total abortion rate only, abortions for women of unknown race/ethnicity were distributed according to the distribution of abortions among women of known race/ethnicity.

*** Number of abortions obtained by women in a given racial/ethnic group per 1,000 live births to women in that same racial/ethnic group. For the total abortion ratio only, abortions for women of unknown race/ethnicity were distributed according to the distribution of abortions among women of known race/ethnicity.

TABLE 6. Reported Abortions, by Known Marital Status and Reporting Area of Occurrence—Selected Reporting Areas,* United States, 2018

State/Area	Marital status		Total abortions reported by known marital status
	Married	**Unmarried**	
	No. (%)[†]	No. (%)	No. (% of all reported abortions)[§]
Alabama	711 (11.0)	5,772 (89.0)	**6,483 (100.0)**
Alaska	274 (21.9)	977 (78.1)	**1,251 (97.5)**
Arizona	1,728 (13.9)	10,710 (86.1)	**12,438 (100.0)**
Arkansas	398 (13.0)	2,657 (87.0)	**3,055 (99.5)**
Colorado	1,393 (18.2)	6,254 (81.8)	**7,647 (85.2)**
Connecticut	886 (10.7)	7,392 (89.3)	**8,278 (89.1)**
Delaware	214 (12.3)	1,526 (87.7)	**1,740 (100.0)**
Florida	9,682 (15.8)	51,725 (84.2)	**61,407 (87.4)**
Georgia	4,103 (13.9)	25,461 (86.1)	**29,564 (87.2)**
Idaho	229 (20.8)	874 (79.2)	**1,103 (87.7)**
Illinois[¶]	3,578 (10.3)	31,052 (89.7)	**34,630 (94.3)**
Indiana	1,178 (14.7)	6,858 (85.3)	**8,036 (100.0)**
Iowa	474 (16.6)	2,373 (83.4)	**2,847 (99.9)**
Kansas	1,096 (15.7)	5,871 (84.3)	**6,967 (99.9)**
Kentucky	479 (15.0)	2,724 (85.0)	**3,203 (100.0)**
Louisiana	868 (11.1)	6,939 (88.9)	**7,807 (96.4)**
Maine	310 (16.6)	1,560 (83.4)	**1,870 (95.9)**
Massachusetts	2,757 (17.1)	13,362 (82.9)	**16,119 (88.3)**
Michigan	2,806 (10.7)	23,355 (89.3)	**26,161 (97.9)**
Minnesota	1,560 (16.4)	7,936 (83.6)	**9,496 (95.8)**
Mississippi	283 (9.5)	2,686 (90.5)	**2,969 (98.8)**
Missouri	401 (14.6)	2,348 (85.4)	**2,749 (94.5)**
Montana	289 (17.3)	1,382 (82.7)	**1,671 (99.8)**
Nebraska	322 (15.6)	1,740 (84.4)	**2,062 (99.2)**
New Jersey[**]	2,720 (12.0)	19,922 (88.0)	**22,642 (98.7)**
New Mexico	559 (15.3)	3,089 (84.7)	**3,648 (94.8)**
New York City	7,888 (18.4)	34,943 (81.6)	**42,831 (86.1)**
North Carolina	3,821 (15.3)	21,142 (84.7)	**24,963 (90.5)**
North Dakota	183 (16.1)	957 (83.9)	**1,140 (99.9)**
Ohio	2,670 (14.5)	15,703 (85.5)	**18,373 (90.0)**
Oklahoma	932 (18.7)	4,052 (81.3)	**4,984 (99.9)**

| State/Area | Marital status | | Total abortions reported by known marital status |
| | Married | Unmarried | |
	No. (%)[†]	No. (%)	No. (% of all reported abortions)[§]
Oregon	1,666 (20.6)	6,411 (79.4)	**8,077 (92.5)**
Pennsylvania	3,521 (11.6)	26,832 (88.4)	**30,353 (100.0)**
South Carolina	648 (14.1)	3,956 (85.9)	**4,604 (99.1)**
South Dakota	71 (18.6)	311 (81.4)	**382 (100.0)**
Tennessee	1,448 (13.6)	9,199 (86.4)	**10,647 (97.9)**
Texas	9,656 (17.5)	45,484 (82.5)	**55,140 (100.0)**
Utah	761 (24.9)	2,297 (75.1)	**3,058 (99.2)**
Vermont	227 (20.4)	887 (79.6)	**1,114 (92.5)**
Virginia	2,492 (15.1)	13,982 (84.9)	**16,474 (100.0)**
West Virginia	283 (18.8)	1,223 (81.2)	**1,506 (99.9)**
Wisconsin[¶]	830 (13.8)	5,198 (86.2)	**6,028 (99.8)**
Total	**76,395 (14.8)**	**439,122 (85.2)**	**515,517 (93.7)[††]**
Abortion ratio[§§]	**44**	**378**	—

* Data from 42 reporting areas; excludes 10 areas (California, District of Columbia, Hawaii, Maryland, Nevada, New Hampshire, New York State, Rhode Island, Washington, and Wyoming) that did not report, did not report by marital status, or did not meet reporting standards.

† Percentages for the individual component categories might not add to 100% because of rounding.

§ Percentage is calculated as the number of abortions reported by known marital status divided by the sum of abortions reported by known and unknown marital status. Values ≥99.95% are rounded to 100.0%.

¶ Includes residents only.

** Reporting to the central health agency is not required. Data are requested from hospitals and licensed ambulatory care facilities only.

†† Percentage is based on a total of 550,201 abortions reported among the areas that met reporting standards for marital status.

§§ Number of abortions obtained by women by marital status per 1,000 live births to women of the same marital status. For the total abortion ratio only, abortions for women of unknown marital status were distributed according to the distribution of abortions among women of known marital status.

TABLE 9. Reported Abortions, by Known Weeks of Gestation* and Reporting Area of Occurrence—Selected Reporting Areas,† United States, 2018

State/Area	Weeks of gestation							Total abortions reported by known gestational age
	≤6	7–9	10–13	14–15	16–17	18–20	≥21	
	No. (%)§	No. (%)	No. (%)	No. (%)	No. (%)	No. (%)	No. (%)	No. (% of all reported abortions)¶
Alabama	1,135 (17.5)	3,219 (49.7)	1,382 (21.3)	326 (5.0)	169 (2.6)	175 (2.7)	77 (1.2)	6,483 (100.0)
Alaska	323 (25.2)	653 (51.0)	252 (19.7)	52 (4.1)	—††	—	0 (0.0)	1,281 (99.8)
Arizona	3,685 (29.6)	5,704 (45.9)	1,921 (15.4)	469 (3.8)	254 (2.0)	266 (2.1)	139 (1.1)	12,438 (100.0)
Arkansas**	639 (20.8)	1,506 (49.1)	524 (17.1)	120 (3.9)	110 (3.6)	149 (4.9)	21 (0.7)	3,069 (100.0)
Colorado	3,000 (33.4)	3,986 (44.4)	1,172 (13.1)	218 (2.4)	161 (1.8)	109 (1.2)	323 (3.6)	8,969 (99.9)
Connecticut	4,196 (46.3)	3,257 (36.0)	952 (10.5)	257 (2.8)	158 (1.7)	147 (1.6)	89 (1.0)	9,056 (97.4)
Delaware	314 (18.1)	853 (49.1)	437 (25.1)	94 (5.4)	17 (1.0)	14 (0.8)	9 (0.5)	1,738 (99.9)
Florida	50,863 (72.4)	11,934 (17.0)	4,885 (7.0)	983 (1.4)	662 (0.9)	697 (1.0)	215 (0.3)	70,239 (100.0)
Georgia	13,352 (39.4)	12,805 (37.8)	4,892 (14.4)	1,009 (3.0)	775 (2.3)	826 (2.4)	259 (0.8)	33,918 (100.0)
Hawaii	580 (27.4)	955 (45.1)	366 (17.3)	75 (3.5)	56 (2.6)	64 (3.0)	23 (1.1)	2,119 (99.9)
Idaho	310 (24.7)	650 (51.8)	251 (20.0)	36 (2.9)	8 (0.6)	0 (0.0)	0 (0.0)	1,255 (99.8)
Indiana	1,401 (17.4)	4,619 (57.5)	1,983 (24.7)	7 (0.1)	7 (0.1)	9 (0.1)	9 (0.1)	8,035 (100.0)
Iowa	1,298 (45.6)	1,094 (38.4)	296 (10.4)	62 (2.2)	45 (1.6)	47 (1.6)	7 (0.2)	2,849 (100.0)
Kansas	2,829 (40.6)	2,680 (38.4)	983 (14.1)	192 (2.8)	121 (1.7)	142 (2.0)	25 (0.4)	6,972 (100.0)
Kentucky	1,160 (36.2)	1,250 (39.0)	487 (15.2)	126 (3.9)	64 (2.0)	85 (2.7)	31 (1.0)	3,203 (100.0)
Louisiana	2,663 (32.9)	3,525 (43.6)	1,405 (17.4)	322 (4.0)	139 (1.7)	40 (0.5)	0 (0.0)	8,094 (100.0)
Maine	622 (31.9)	907 (46.5)	305 (15.6)	52 (2.7)	36 (1.8)	27 (1.4)	0 (0.0)	1,949 (100.0)

State/Area	Weeks of gestation							Total abortions reported by known gestational age
	≤6 No. (%)§	7–9 No. (%)	10–13 No. (%)	14–15 No. (%)	16–17 No. (%)	18–20 No. (%)	≥21 No. (%)	No. (% of all reported abortions)¶
Michigan	8,502 (31.8)	11,348 (42.5)	4,105 (15.4)	1,112 (4.2)	680 (2.5)	583 (2.2)	365 (1.4)	26,695 (99.9)
Minnesota	4,135 (42.4)	3,463 (35.5)	1,246 (12.8)	336 (3.4)	203 (2.1)	210 (2.2)	165 (1.7)	9,758 (98.5)
Mississippi	892 (29.7)	1,366 (45.5)	544 (18.1)	177 (5.9)	22 (0.7)	—	—	3,005 (100.0)
Missouri	267 (9.2)	1,302 (44.7)	814 (28.0)	191 (6.6)	146 (5.0)	133 (4.6)	57 (2.0)	2,910 (100.0)
Montana	576 (34.5)	707 (42.3)	256 (15.3)	55 (3.3)	33 (2.0)	34 (2.0)	10 (0.6)	1,671 (99.8)
Nebraska	945 (45.5)	691 (33.3)	317 (15.3)	71 (3.4)	30 (1.4)	21 (1.0)	0 (0.0)	2,075 (99.9)
Nevada	3,379 (38.7)	3,650 (41.8)	1,114 (12.7)	285 (3.3)	161 (1.8)	114 (1.3)	39 (0.4)	8,742 (99.1)
New Jersey§§	9,062 (40.2)	7,674 (34.0)	2,936 (13.0)	1,026 (4.6)	693 (3.1)	595 (2.6)	552 (2.4)	22,538 (98.3)
New Mexico	1,654 (46.2)	940 (26.2)	370 (10.3)	105 (2.9)	68 (1.9)	111 (3.1)	335 (9.3)	3,583 (93.1)
New York	24,546 (33.1)	30,973 (41.8)	11,713 (15.8)	2,370 (3.2)	1,490 (2.0)	1,515 (2.0)	1,507 (2.0)	74,114 (95.7)
New York City	21,637 (43.6)	17,714 (35.7)	5,813 (11.7)	1,310 (2.6)	950 (1.9)	1,083 (2.2)	1,171 (2.4)	49,678 (99.8)
New York State	2,909 (11.9)	13,259 (54.3)	5,900 (24.1)	1,060 (4.3)	540 (2.2)	432 (1.8)	336 (1.4)	24,436 (88.3)
North Carolina	9,029 (33.0)	11,675 (42.7)	4,458 (16.3)	1,001 (3.7)	705 (2.6)	450 (1.6)	7 (0.0)	27,325 (99.1)
North Dakota	390 (34.2)	496 (43.5)	191 (16.7)	54 (4.7)	9 (0.8)	—	—	1,141 (100.0)
Ohio	4,806 (23.5)	8,939 (43.8)	4,356 (21.3)	994 (4.9)	590 (2.9)	634 (3.1)	106 (0.5)	20,425 (100.0)
Oklahoma	2,369 (47.8)	1,671 (33.7)	621 (12.5)	120 (2.4)	84 (1.7)	72 (1.5)	16 (0.3)	4,953 (99.3)
Oregon	3,777 (43.5)	3,204 (36.9)	1,066 (12.3)	217 (2.5)	117 (1.3)	153 (1.8)	153 (1.8)	8,687 (99.5)
South Carolina**	960 (20.7)	1,635 (35.2)	1,750 (37.7)	284 (6.1)	—	—	8 (0.2)	4,646 (100.0)
South Dakota	44 (11.6)	232 (61.2)	100 (26.4)	—	0 (0.0)	—	0 (0.0)	379 (99.2)

	Weeks of gestation							Total abortions reported by known gestational age
	≤6	7–9	10–13	14–15	16–17	18–20	≥21	
State/Area	No. (%)§	No. (%)	No. (%)	No. (%)	No. (%)	No. (%)	No. (%)	No. (% of all reported abortions)¶
Tennessee	1,680 (15.6)	5,582 (51.7)	2,519 (23.3)	607 (5.6)	280 (2.6)	120 (1.1)	9 (0.1)	10,797 (99.2)
Texas**	21,299 (38.6)	21,635 (39.2)	8,124 (14.7)	1,930 (3.5)	1,083 (2.0)	813 (1.5)	256 (0.5)	55,140 (100.0)
Utah	1,103 (35.8)	1,274 (41.3)	446 (14.5)	97 (3.1)	62 (2.0)	58 (1.9)	42 (1.4)	3,082 (100.0)
Vermont	509 (42.3)	471 (39.1)	131 (10.9)	33 (2.7)	15 (1.2)	25 (2.1)	20 (1.7)	1,204 (100.0)
Virginia	8,783 (53.6)	5,228 (31.9)	1,935 (11.8)	66 (0.4)	91 (0.6)	203 (1.2)	93 (0.6)	16,399 (99.5)
Washington	7,310 (42.5)	6,637 (38.5)	1,960 (11.4)	399 (2.3)	260 (1.5)	283 (1.6)	370 (2.1)	17,219 (99.7)
West Virginia	383 (25.4)	669 (44.4)	289 (19.2)	126 (8.4)	34 (2.3)	—	—	1,507 (100.0)
Total	204,770 (40.2)	191,059 (37.5)	73,854 (14.5)	16,058 (3.2)	9,644 (1.9)	8,936 (1.8)	5,341 (1.0)	509,662 (99.0)¶¶

* Gestational age based on clinician's estimate (Alabama, Alaska, Arizona, Connecticut, Colorado, Delaware, Florida, Georgia, Hawaii, Idaho, Indiana, Iowa, Kansas, Kentucky, Louisiana, Maine, Michigan, Minnesota, Mississippi, Missouri, Montana, Nebraska, Nevada, New Jersey, New Mexico, New York City, North Carolina, North Dakota, Ohio, Oregon, Rhode Island, South Dakota, Tennessee, Vermont, Washington, and West Virginia); gestational age calculated from the last normal menstrual period (Oklahoma and Utah); clinician's estimate of gestation based on estimated date of conception (Virginia); probable postfertilization age (Arkansas, South Carolina, and Texas).

† Data from 42 reporting areas; excludes 10 areas (California, District of Columbia, Illinois, Maryland, Massachusetts, New Hampshire, Pennsylvania, Rhode Island, Wisconsin, and Wyoming) that did not report, did not report by gestational age, or did not meet reporting standards.

§ Percentages for the individual component categories might not add to 100% because of rounding.

¶ Percentage is calculated as the number of abortions reported by known gestational age divided by the sum of abortions reported by known and unknown gestational age. Values ≥99.95% are rounded to 100.0%.

†† Cells with a value in the range of 1–4 or cells that would allow for calculation of these small values have been suppressed.

** Two weeks were added to the probable postfertilization age to provide a corresponding measure to gestational age based on the clinician's estimate.

§§ Reporting to the central health agency is not required. Data are requested from hospitals and licensed ambulatory care facilities only.

¶¶ Percentage based on a total of 514,718 abortions reported among the areas that met reporting standards for gestational age.

TABLE 10. Reported Abortions, by Known Weeks of Gestation and Year—Selected Reporting Areas,* United States, 2009-2018

Weeks of gestation	Year										% change			
	2009	2010	2011	2012	2013	2014	2015	2016	2017	2018	2009 to 2013	2014 to 2018	2017 to 2018	2009 to 2018
≤13 weeks' gestation (%)	**91.8**	**91.9**	**91.5**	**91.4**	**91.6**	**91.0**	**91.0**	**91.0**	**91.1**	**91.5**	**-0.2**	**0.5**	**0.4**	**-0.3**
≤6	33.6	34.7	34.3	35.1	34.7	33.8	34.3	34.2	35.1	36.2	3.3	7.1	3.1	7.7
7-9	40.6	40.1	40.1	39.4	39.9	40.0	40.0	40.3	40.4	40.0	-1.7	0.0	-1.0	-1.5
10-13	17.6	17.0	17.1	16.9	17.0	17.2	16.7	16.4	15.7	15.2	-3.4	-11.6	-3.2	-13.6
>13 weeks' gestation (%)	**8.2**	**8.1**	**8.5**	**8.6**	**8.4**	**9.0**	**9.0**	**9.0**	**8.9**	**8.5**	**2.4**	**-5.6**	**-4.5**	**3.7**
14-15	3.3	3.3	3.4	3.5	3.4	3.5	3.5	3.6	3.4	3.4	3.0	-2.9	0.0	3.0
16-17	1.8	1.8	1.9	1.9	1.9	2.2	2.1	2.1	2.2	2.1	5.6	-4.5	-4.5	16.7
18-20	1.8	1.8	1.9	1.9	1.8	1.9	2.0	2.0	2.0	1.9	0.0	0.0	-5.0	5.6
≥21	**1.3**	**1.2**	**1.4**	**1.3**	**1.3**	**1.3**	**1.3**	**1.3**	**1.3**	**1.2**	**0.0**	**-7.7**	**-7.7**	**-7.7**
Total (no.)	**519,164**	**508,841**	**481,667**	**457,201**	**435,881**	**426,636**	**414,914**	**408,903**	**394,181**	**395,960**	—	—	—	—

* Data from 34 reporting areas; excludes 18 areas (California, Connecticut, Delaware, District of Columbia, Florida, Illinois, Maine, Maryland, Massachusetts, Mississippi, Nebraska, New Hampshire, New York State, Pennsylvania, Rhode Island, Vermont, Wisconsin, and Wyoming) that did not report, did not report by gestational age, or did not meet reporting standards for ≥1 year. By year, these reporting areas represent 78%–98% of the abortions reported by gestational age to CDC during 2009–2018.

TABLE 11. Reported Abortions, by Known Method Type and Reporting Area of Occurrence—Selected Reporting Areas,* United States, 2018

| State/Area | Surgical† | | | Medical | | | Intrauterine instillation§ | Hysterectomy/ Hysterotomy | Total abortions reported by known method type |
	Surgical, ≤13 weeks' gestation No. (%)¶	Surgical, >13 weeks' gestation No. (%)	Surgical, unknown gestational age No. (%)	Medical, ≤9 weeks' gestation No. (%)	Medical, >9 weeks' gestation No. (%)	Medical, unknown gestational age No. (%)	No. (%)	No. (%)	No. (% of all reported abortions)**
Alabama	3,719 (57.4)	735 (11.3)	0 (0.0)	1,967 (30.4)	53 (0.8)	—††	0 (0.0)	—	6,478 (99.9)
Alaska	863 (67.3)	52 (4.1)	—	362 (28.2)	—	0 (0.0)	—	0 (0.0)	1,283 (100.0)
Arizona	6,345 (51.0)	972 (7.8)	0 (0.0)	4,890 (39.3)	112 (0.9)	0 (0.0)	112 (0.9)	0 (0.0)	12,431 (99.9)
Arkansas§§	1,691 (55.1)	399 (13.0)	0 (0.0)	920 (30.0)	59 (1.9)	0 (0.0)	0 (0.0)	0 (0.0)	3,069 (100.0)
Colorado	3,134 (38.3)	425 (5.2)	—	4,519 (55.2)	109 (1.3)	—	—	0 (0.0)	8,193 (91.3)
Connecticut	4,460 (48.0)	648 (7.0)	169 (1.8)	3,923 (42.2)	23 (0.2)	69 (0.7)	—	—	9,294 (100.0)
Delaware	776 (44.7)	129 (7.4)	0 (0.0)	781 (45.0)	49 (2.8)	—	0 (0.0)	—	1,737 (99.8)
District of Columbia¶¶	2,520 (53.0)	511 (10.8)	0 (0.0)	1,701 (35.8)	19 (0.4)	0 (0.0)	0 (0.0)	0 (0.0)	4,751 (99.6)
Florida	33,565 (50.1)	2,438 (3.6)	0 (0.0)	30,567 (45.7)	356 (0.5)	0 (0.0)	0 (0.0)	5 (0.0)	66,931 (95.3)
Georgia	16,418 (48.6)	2,864 (8.5)	0 (0.0)	14,328 (42.4)	204 (0.6)	0 (0.0)	0 (0.0)	0 (0.0)	33,814 (99.7)

| State/Area | Surgical† | | | Medical | | | Intrauterine instillation§ | Hysterectomy/ Hysterotomy | Total abortions reported by known method type |
| | Surgical, ≤13 weeks' gestation | Surgical, >13 weeks' gestation | Surgical, unknown gestational age | Medical, ≤9 weeks' gestation | Medical, >9 weeks' gestation | Medical, unknown gestational age | | | No. (% of all reported abortions)** |
	No. (%)¶	No. (%)	No. (%)	No. (%)	No. (%)	No. (%)	No. (%)	No. (%)	
Hawaii	1,154 (54.4)	218 (10.3)	—	744 (35.1)	—	0 (0.0)	0 (0.0)	0 (0.0)	2,121 (100.0)
Idaho	694 (55.3)	44 (3.5)	—	509 (40.6)	5 (0.4)	—	0 (0.0)	0 (0.0)	1,254 (99.8)
Indiana	4,709 (58.6)	31 (0.4)	—	3,229 (40.2)	66 (0.8)	—	0 (0.0)	0 (0.0)	8,037 (100.0)
Iowa	748 (26.3)	155 (5.4)	0 (0.0)	1,896 (66.6)	49 (1.7)	0 (0.0)	0 (0.0)	0 (0.0)	2,848 (100.0)
Kansas	2,205 (31.6)	472 (6.8)	0 (0.0)	4,240 (60.8)	53 (0.8)	0 (0.0)	0 (0.0)	0 (0.0)	6,970 (100.0)
Kentucky	1,356 (42.3)	297 (9.3)	—	1,540 (48.1)	9 (0.3)	0 (0.0)	—	0 (0.0)	3,203 (100.0)
Maine	936 (48.0)	112 (5.7)	0 (0.0)	879 (45.1)	22 (1.1)	0 (0.0)	0 (0.0)	0 (0.0)	1,949 (100.0)
Massachusetts***	NA	NA	10,826 (59.8)	NA	NA	7,257 (40.1)	8 (0.0)	0 (0.0)	18,091 (99.1)
Michigan	13,761 (51.6)	2,681 (10.0)	13 (0.0)	9,999 (37.5)	213 (0.8)	8 (0.0)	—	—	26,677 (99.9)
Minnesota	5,284 (53.3)	889 (9.0)	59 (0.6)	3,532 (35.6)	52 (0.5)	93 (0.9)	—	—	9,910 (100.0)
Mississippi	758 (25.2)	195 (6.5)	—	1,994 (66.4)	55 (1.8)	0 (0.0)	0 (0.0)	—	3,004 (100.0)
Missouri	2,039 (70.1)	509 (17.5)	0 (0.0)	340 (11.7)	19 (0.7)	0 (0.0)	—	—	2,909 (100.0)
Montana	606 (36.2)	132 (7.9)	—	912 (54.5)	19 (1.1)	—	0 (0.0)	0 (0.0)	1,672 (99.9)

State/Area	Surgical†			Medical			Intrauterine instillation§	Hysterectomy/ Hysterotomy	Total abortions reported by known method type
	Surgical, ≤13 weeks' gestation	Surgical, >13 weeks' gestation	Surgical, unknown gestational age	Medical, ≤9 weeks' gestation	Medical, >9 weeks' gestation	Medical, unknown gestational age			No. (% of all reported abortions)**
	No. (%)¶	No. (%)	No. (%)	No. (%)	No. (%)	No. (%)	No. (%)	No. (%)	
Nebraska	730 (35.1)	121 (5.8)	—	1,211 (58.3)	13 (0.6)	—	0 (0.0)	0 (0.0)	2,078 (100.0)
Nevada	5,252 (61.4)	583 (6.8)	41 (0.5)	2,639 (30.9)	14 (0.2)	21 (0.2)	—	—	8,553 (97.0)
New Jersey†††	12,593 (54.9)	2,682 (11.7)	219 (1.0)	6,891 (30.0)	367 (1.6)	179 (0.8)	—	—	22,933 (100.0)
New York	43,279 (57.3)	6,243 (8.3)	1,141 (1.5)	21,472 (28.4)	1,887 (2.5)	1,443 (1.9)	72 (0.1)	15 (0.0)	75,552 (97.6)
New York City	31,443 (63.4)	4,295 (8.7)	24 (0.0)	13,390 (27.0)	438 (0.9)	8 (0.0)	18 (0.0)	15 (0.0)	49,631 (99.7)
New York State	11,836 (45.7)	1,948 (7.5)	1,117 (4.3)	8,082 (31.2)	1,449 (5.6)	1,435 (5.5)	54 (0.2)	0 (0.0)	25,921 (93.6)
North Carolina	12,241 (47.1)	2,030 (7.8)	48 (0.2)	11,410 (43.9)	200 (0.8)	41 (0.2)	—	—	25,972 (94.2)
North Dakota	762 (66.8)	63 (5.5)	0 (0.0)	307 (26.9)	9 (0.8)	0 (0.0)	0 (0.0)	0 (0.0)	1,141 (100.0)
Ohio	11,940 (58.5)	2,300 (11.3)	—	6,103 (29.9)	80 (0.4)	0 (0.0)	0 (0.0)	—	20,425 (100.0)
Oklahoma	2,021 (40.8)	288 (5.8)	17 (0.3)	2,587 (52.2)	19 (0.4)	20 (0.4)	0 (0.0)	0 (0.0)	4,952 (99.2)
Oregon	3,848 (44.1)	595 (6.8)	17 (0.2)	4,137 (47.4)	100 (1.1)	31 (0.4)	—	—	8,731 (100.0)

State/Area	Surgical[†]			Medical			Intrauterine instillation[§]	Hysterectomy/Hysterotomy	Total abortions reported by known method type
	Surgical, ≤13 weeks' gestation No. (%)[¶]	Surgical, >13 weeks' gestation No. (%)	Surgical, unknown gestational age No. (%)	Medical, ≤9 weeks' gestation No. (%)	Medical, >9 weeks' gestation No. (%)	Medical, unknown gestational age No. (%)	No. (%)	No. (%)	No. (% of all reported abortions)[**]
Pennsylvania[§§§]	14,056 (46.3)	3,840 (12.6)	—	10,564 (34.8)	1,902 (6.3)	0 (0.0)	0 (0.0)	—	30,363 (100.0)
Rhode Island	1,071 (41.8)	185 (7.2)	—	499 (19.5)	5 (0.2)	800 (31.2)	—	0 (0.0)	2,562 (90.9)
South Carolina[§§]	1,772 (38.1)	290 (6.2)	0 (0.0)	1,919 (41.3)	665 (14.3)	0 (0.0)	0 (0.0)	0 (0.0)	4,646 (100.0)
South Dakota	243 (63.6)	—	—	129 (33.8)	5 (1.3)	—	0 (0.0)	0 (0.0)	382 (100.0)
Tennessee	4,702 (43.5)	984 (9.1)	22 (0.2)	4,915 (45.5)	124 (1.1)	43 (0.4)	—	—	10,808 (99.3)
Texas[§§]	31,966 (58.0)	4,033 (7.3)	0 (0.0)	18,891 (34.3)	243 (0.4)	0 (0.0)	—	—	55,138 (100.0)
Utah	1,552 (51.3)	230 (7.6)	0 (0.0)	1,209 (40.0)	32 (1.1)	0 (0.0)	0 (0.0)	0 (0.0)	3,023 (98.1)
Vermont	436 (36.2)	86 (7.1)	0 (0.0)	670 (55.7)	11 (0.9)	0 (0.0)	0 (0.0)	0 (0.0)	1,203 (99.9)
Virginia	10,241 (62.4)	433 (2.6)	46 (0.3)	5,647 (34.4)	38 (0.2)	—	—	0 (0.0)	16,407 (99.6)
Washington	7,892 (45.8)	1,304 (7.6)	20 (0.1)	7,963 (46.2)	46 (0.3)	25 (0.1)	0 (0.0)	0 (0.0)	17,250 (99.9)
West Virginia	852 (56.5)	161 (10.7)	0 (0.0)	473 (31.4)	21 (1.4)	0 (0.0)	0 (0.0)	0 (0.0)	1,507 (100.0)
Wisconsin[***,¶¶¶]	NA	NA	4,302 (71.2)	NA	NA	1,739 (28.8)	—	—	6,042 (100.0)
Total	289,931 (52.1)	43,576 (7.8)	—[****]	214,779 (38.6)	7,743 (1.4)	—[†††]	219 (0.0)	46 (0.0)	556,294 (98.5)[§§§§]

See table footnotes on the next page.

802

Whose Choice Is It?

TABLE 11. *(Continued)* Reported Abortions, by Known Method Type and Reporting Area of Occurrence—Selected Reporting Areas,* United States, 2018

Abbreviation: NA = not available.

* Data from 45 reporting areas; excludes seven reporting areas (California, Illinois, Louisiana, Maryland, New Hampshire, New Mexico, and Wyoming) that did not report, did not report by method type, or did not meet reporting standards. Areas reporting by method type with unknown gestational age are included.

† Includes aspiration curettage, suction curettage, manual vacuum aspiration, menstrual extraction, sharp curettage, and dilation and evacuation procedures.

§ Intrauterine instillations reported at ≤12 weeks' gestation were considered as unknown for method type.

¶ Percentages for the individual component categories might not add to 100% because of rounding.

** Percentage is calculated as the number of abortions reported by known method type divided by the sum of abortions reported by known and unknown method type. Values ≥99.95% are rounded to 100.0%.

†† Cells with a value in the range of 1–4 or cells that would allow for calculation of these small values have been suppressed.

§§ Two weeks were added to the probable postfertilization age to provide a corresponding measure to gestational age based on the clinician's estimate.

¶¶ Reporting to the central health agency is not required.

*** Numbers for surgical procedures at ≤13 weeks versus >13 weeks and for medical abortions at ≤9 weeks versus >9 weeks are not presented because gestational age data were not provided by method type.

††† Reporting to the central health agency is not required. Data are requested from hospitals and licensed ambulatory care facilities only.

§§§ Gestational age reported in this table as ≤9 weeks includes ≤8 weeks; >9 weeks includes ≥9 weeks; ≤13 weeks includes ≤12 weeks; >13 weeks includes ≥13 weeks.

¶¶¶ Includes residents only. Wisconsin reports as surgical, unspecified and does not differentiate surgical procedures from hysterectomy/hysterotomy. All abortions were reported as surgical or chemically induced. For this report, all surgical abortions were classified as surgical and all chemical abortions as medical.

**** For the total only, surgical abortions reported without a gestational age were distributed among the surgical abortion categories according to the distribution of surgical abortions at known gestational age.

†††† For the total only, medical abortions reported without a gestational age were distributed among the medical abortion categories according to the distribution of medical abortions at known gestational age.

§§§§ Percentage is based on a total of 565,024 abortions reported among the areas that met reporting standards for method type.

TABLE 12. Reported Abortions, by Known Weeks of Gestation and Method Type—Selected Reporting Areas,* United States, 2018

Method type	Weeks of gestation							
	≤6 No. (%)†	7–9 No. (%)	10–13 No. (%)	14–15 No. (%)	16–17 No. (%)	18–20 No. (%)	≥21 No. (%)	Total No. (%)
Surgical§								
≤13 weeks' gestation	88,854 (45.1)	101,978 (55.3)	66,711 (93.8)	NA	NA	NA	NA	257,543 (52.5)
>13 weeks' gestation	NA	NA	NA	15,180 (98.4)	9,086 (97.7)	8,287 (95.9)	4,272 (91.9)	36,825 (7.5)
Medical¶								
≤9 weeks" gestation	108,305 (54.9)	82,339 (44.7)	NA	NA	NA	NA	NA	190,644 (38.9)
>9 weeks' gestation	NA	NA	4,399 (6.2)	232 (1.5)	168 (1.8)	274 (3.2)	334 (7.2)	5,407 (1.1)
Intrauterine instillation	—**	—	4 (0.0)	8 (0.1)	44 (0.5)	70 (0.8)	38 (0.8)	164 (0.0)
Hysterectomy/ Hysterotomy	13 (0.0)	9 (0.0)	3 (0.0)	4 (0.0)	4 (0.0)	7 (0.1)	4 (0.1)	44 (0.0)
Total	**197,172 (100.0)**	**184,326 (100.0)**	**71,117 (100.0)**	**15,424 (100.0)**	**9,302 (100.0)**	**8,638 (100.0)**	**4,648 (100.0)**	**490,627 (100.0)**

Abbreviation: NA = not applicable.

* Data from 40 reporting areas; excludes 12 areas (California, District of Columbia, Illinois, Louisiana, Maryland, Massachusetts, New Hampshire, New Mexico, Pennsylvania, Rhode Island, Wisconsin, and Wyoming) that did not report, did not report method type by weeks of gestation, did not meet reporting standards, or did not have medical abortion as a specific category on their reporting form.

† For each gestational age category, percentages of all method types might not add to 100% because of rounding.

§ Includes aspiration curettage, suction curettage, manual vacuum aspiration, menstrual extraction, sharp curettage, and dilation and evacuation procedures.

¶ The administration of medication or medications to induce an abortion; at ≤9 weeks' gestation, typically involves the use of mifepristone and misoprostol; at >9 weeks' gestation, typically involves the use of vaginal prostaglandins.

** Intrauterine instillations reported at ≤12 weeks' gestation have not been included with known values.

TABLE 13. Reported Abortions, by Known Weeks of Gestation, Age Group, and Race/Ethnicity—Selected Reporting Areas, United States, 2018

	Weeks of gestation						
	≤6	7–9	10–13	14–15	16–17	18–20	≥21
Characteristic	No. (%)	No. (%)	No. (%)	No. (%)	No. (%)	No. (%)	No. (%)
Age group (yrs)[*,†]							
<15	258 (22.9)	363 (32.2)	261 (23.2)	80 (7.1)	61 (5.4)	56 (5.0)	47 (4.2)
15–19	14,520 (32.6)	17,284 (38.9)	8,090 (18.2)	1,805 (4.1)	1,089 (2.4)	1,038 (2.3)	653 (1.5)
20–24	55,059 (38.3)	55,392 (38.5)	22,029 (15.3)	4,706 (3.3)	2,765 (1.9)	2,556 (1.8)	1,417 (1.0)
25–29	60,885 (41.0)	55,796 (37.5)	21,179 (14.2)	4,394 (3.0)	2,654 (1.8)	2,406 (1.6)	1,329 (0.9)
30–34	40,940 (42.5)	35,299 (36.7)	12,760 (13.3)	2,841 (3.0)	1,758 (1.8)	1,592 (1.7)	1,046 (1.1)
35–39	23,700 (43.3)	19,756 (36.1)	7,169 (13.1)	1,630 (3.0)	926 (1.7)	924 (1.7)	638 (1.2)
≥40	8,674 (46.9)	6,339 (34.3)	2,105 (11.4)	526 (2.8)	349 (1.9)	321 (1.7)	185 (1.0)
Total	**204,036 (40.2)**	**190,229 (37.5)**	**73,593 (14.5)**	**15,982 (3.1)**	**9,602 (1.9)**	**8,893 (1.8)**	**5,315 (1.0)**
Race/Ethnicity[*,§]							
Non-Hispanic							
White	56,901 (42.5)	49,684 (37.1)	17,888 (13.4)	3,796 (2.8)	2,297 (1.7)	2,214 (1.7)	1,128 (0.8)
Black	39,809 (34.7)	44,253 (38.6)	20,530 (17.9)	4,481 (3.9)	2,635 (2.3)	2,215 (1.9)	781 (0.7)
Other	11,894 (45.1)	9,210 (35.0)	3,115 (11.8)	888 (3.4)	454 (1.7)	473 (1.8)	315 (1.2)
Hispanic	33,522 (48.3)	23,022 (33.2)	8,257 (11.9)	1,948 (2.8)	1,127 (1.6)	980 (1.4)	477 (0.7)
Total	**142,126 (41.3)**	**126,169 (36.6)**	**49,790 (14.5)**	**11,113 (3.2)**	**6,513 (1.9)**	**5,882 (1.7)**	**2,701 (0.8)**

* Percentages for the individual component categories might not add to 100% because of rounding.

† Data from 42 reporting areas; excludes 10 reporting areas (California, District of Columbia, Illinois, Maryland, Massachusetts, New Hampshire, Pennsylvania, Rhode Island, Wisconsin, and Wyoming) that did not report, did not report weeks of gestation by age, or did not meet reporting standards.

§ Data from 30 reporting areas; excludes 22 reporting areas (California, Colorado, District of Columbia, Georgia, Hawaii, Illinois, Iowa, Louisiana, Maine, Maryland, Massachusetts, Nebraska, New Hampshire, New Mexico, New York City, New York State, North Dakota, Oklahoma, Pennsylvania, Rhode Island, Wisconsin, and Wyoming) that did not report, did not report weeks of gestation by race/ethnicity, or did not meet reporting standards.

Appendix Q

Excerpts from CDC Guidance for the Prenatal Diagnosis of Zika Infection and the Management of Infants with Zika[1]

The Centers for Disease Control and Prevention (CDC) has updated its interim guidance for U.S. health care providers caring for infants with possible congenital Zika virus infection (*1*) in response to recently published updated guidance for health care providers caring for pregnant women with possible Zika virus exposure (*2*), unknown sensitivity and specificity of currently available diagnostic tests for congenital Zika virus infection, and recognition of additional clinical findings associated with congenital Zika virus infection. All infants born to mothers with possible Zika virus exposure[2] during pregnancy should receive a standard evaluation at birth and at each subsequent well-child visit including a comprehensive physical examination, age-appropriate vision screening and developmental monitoring and screening using validated tools (*3–5*), and newborn hearing screen at birth, preferably using auditory brainstem response (ABR) methodology (*6*). Specific guidance for laboratory testing and clinical evaluation are provided for three clinical scenarios in the setting of possible maternal Zika virus exposure: 1) infants with clinical findings consistent with congenital Zika syndrome regardless of maternal testing results, 2) infants without

---

1. On Oct. 20, 2017, the U.S. Centers for Disease Control and Prevention published *Interim Guidance for the Diagnosis, Evaluation, and Management of Infants with Possible Congenital Zika Virus Infection—United States, October 2017* at 66 MOBILITY AND MORTALITY WEEKLY REPORT 1089 (2017), https://www.cdc.gov/mmwr/volumes/66/wr/mm6641a1.htm?s_cid=mm6641a1_e#contribAff. The excerpts printed here pertain to prenatal diagnosis of Zika infection in fetuses and the management of and diagnosis of Zika in infants.

2. Possible Zika virus exposure includes travel to, or residence in an area with mosquitoborne Zika virus transmission or sex without the use of condoms with a partner who has traveled to or resides in an area with mosquitoborne Zika virus transmission.

clinical findings consistent with congenital Zika syndrome who were born to mothers with laboratory evidence of possible Zika virus infection,[3] and 3) infants without clinical findings consistent with congenital Zika syndrome who were born to mothers without laboratory evidence of possible Zika virus infection. Infants in the first two scenarios should receive further testing and evaluation for Zika virus, whereas for the third group, further testing and clinical evaluation for Zika virus are not recommended. Health care providers should remain alert for abnormal findings (e.g., postnatal-onset microcephaly and eye abnormalities without microcephaly) in infants with possible congenital Zika virus exposure without apparent abnormalities at birth.

Congenital Zika Virus Infection

Zika virus infection during pregnancy can cause serious fetal brain anomalies and microcephaly (7). Among infants with substantial loss of brain volume, severe microcephaly and partial collapse of the bones of the upper skull or cranium produce a distinctive physical appearance. Characteristic findings in the brain and spinal cord include thin cerebral cortices with enlarged ventricles and increased extra-axial fluid collections, intracranial calcifications particularly between the cortex and subcortex, abnormal gyral patterns, absent or hypoplastic corpus callosum, hypoplasia of the cerebellum or cerebellar vermis, and hypoplasia of the ventral cord (8–10). Reported anomalies of the anterior and posterior eye include microphthalmia, coloboma, intraocular calcifications, optic nerve hypoplasia and atrophy, and macular scarring with focal pigmentary retinal mottling (11–13). Some infants with suspected congenital Zika virus infection without structural eye lesions have cortical visual impairment, attributable to abnormalities in the visual system of the brain (13). Other reported neurologic sequelae include congenital limb contractures, dysphagia, sensorineural hearing loss, epilepsy, and abnormalities of tone or movement, including marked hypertonia and signs of extrapyramidal involvement (14,15). Currently, there is no evidence suggesting that delayed-onset hearing loss occurs following congenital Zika virus infection. Since publication of the previous interim guidance in August 2016 (1), additional clinical findings have been reported in the setting of laboratory evidence of Zika virus infection in the mother or infant, including eye findings in infants without microcephaly or

---

3. A detailed definition of laboratory evidence of possible Zika virus infection during pregnancy is presented in the unredacted CDC guidance document.

other brain anomalies (*16*), postnatal-onset microcephaly in infants born with normal head circumferences (*17*), postnatal-onset hydrocephalus in infants born with microcephaly (*18*), abnormalities on sleep electroencephalogram (EEG) in some infants with microcephaly who did not have recognized seizures (*19*), and diaphragmatic paralysis in infants born with microcephaly and arthrogryposis (*20–22*).

Zika Virus Laboratory Testing

Laboratory testing for Zika virus has a number of limitations. Zika virus RNA is only transiently present in body fluids; thus, negative nucleic acid testing (NAT) does not rule out infection. Serologic testing is affected by timing of sample collection: a negative immunoglobulin M (IgM) serologic test result does not rule out infection because the serum specimen might have been collected before the development of IgM antibodies, or after these antibodies have waned. Conversely, IgM antibodies might be detectable for months after the initial infection; for pregnant women, this can make it difficult to determine if infection occurred before or during a current pregnancy. In addition, cross-reactivity of the Zika virus IgM antibody tests with other flaviviruses can result in a false-positive test result, especially in persons previously infected with or vaccinated against a related flavivirus, further complicating interpretation (*23,24*). Limitations of Zika virus IgM antibody assays that were approved under an Emergency Use Authorization have been recognized; both false-positive and false-negative test results have occurred. CDC is updating the Emergency Use Authorization to improve assay performance and develop more standardized methods to improve precision (*25*). Recent epidemiologic data indicate a declining prevalence of Zika virus infection in the Americas; lower prevalence results in a lower pretest probability of infection and a higher probability of false-positive test results.

Updated Guidance for Testing of Pregnant Women with Possible Zika Virus Exposure

Given the decreasing prevalence of Zika virus infection cases in the Americas and emerging data regarding Zika virus laboratory testing, on July 24, 2017, CDC published updated guidance for testing of pregnant women with possible Zika virus exposure (*2*). Zika virus NAT testing should be offered as part of routine obstetric care to asymptomatic pregnant women with ongoing possible Zika virus exposure (residing in or frequently traveling to an area with risk for Zika virus transmission); serologic testing is no longer routinely recommended because of the limitations of IgM tests, specifically the potential persistence of IgM antibodies from an infection before conception and the potential for false-positive results. Zika virus testing is not routinely recommended for asymptomatic pregnant women who have possible recent, but not ongoing, Zika virus exposure; however, guidance might vary among jurisdictions (2). The updated guidance for maternal testing (2) is intended to reduce the possibility of false-positive results in the setting of the lower pretest probability; however, there is a possibility that the lack of routine testing might delay identification of some infants without clinical findings apparent at birth, but who may have complications from congenital Zika virus infection. Communication regarding possible maternal exposures between pediatric health care providers and obstetric care providers is critical, and strategies to enhance coordination of care and communication of health information are being developed. For families of infants with possible congenital Zika virus infection, health care providers should ensure that psychosocial support is in place and that families have access to care. The long-term prognosis for infants with congenital Zika virus infection is not yet known; health care providers should strive to address families' concerns, facilitate early identification of abnormal findings, and refer infants for neurodevelopmental follow-up and therapy when indicated.

* * * * * * * * * * * * * * *

Special Considerations for the Prenatal Diagnosis of Congenital Zika Virus Infection

While much has been learned about congenital Zika syndrome, limitations of laboratory testing exist and the full spectrum of congenital Zika virus infection is not yet known. Similar to other congenital infections, prenatal diagnostic evaluation can inform the clinical evaluation of infants with possible Zika virus exposure. Current CDC guidance regarding prenatal diagnosis is reviewed below (2); as more data become available, understanding of the diagnostic role of prenatal ultrasound and amniocentesis in the clinical evaluation of congenital Zika syndrome will improve and guidance will be updated.

Ultrasound. Routine screening for fetal abnormalities is a component of prenatal care in the United States. Comprehensive ultrasound examination to evaluate fetal anatomy is recommended for all women at 18–22 weeks' gestation (36). However, for the detection of abnormalities associated with congenital Zika virus infection, the sensitivity, specificity, and positive and negative predictive values of ultrasound are unknown. Prenatal ultrasound findings associated with congenital Zika virus infection include intracranial calcifications at the gray-white matter junction, ventriculomegaly, abnormalities of the corpus callosum, microcephaly, and limb anomalies (10,37). The reliability of ultrasound detection for each of these abnormalities as isolated findings is unknown (37,38). Limited data suggest that a constellation of ultrasound abnormalities (e.g., microcephaly, ventriculomegaly, or abnormalities of the corpus callosum) identified prenatally in the context of maternal Zika virus exposure correlates with reported structural abnormalities in infants at birth (20,21,39–43).

Questions remain about optimal timing of ultrasound among pregnant women with possible maternal Zika virus exposure. Abnormalities have been detected anywhere from 2 to 29 weeks after symptom onset (39,41,43,44); therefore, insufficient data are available to define the optimal timing between exposure and initial sonographic screening. Brain abnormalities associated with congenital Zika syndrome have been identified by ultrasound in the second and third trimesters in published case reports (20,39,41,43,44). Currently, the negative predictive value of serial normal prenatal ultrasounds is unknown. Serial ultrasound monitoring can detect changes in fetal anatomy, particularly neuroanatomy, and growth patterns (39,41,44). CDC previously recommended serial ultrasounds every 3–4 weeks for women exposed during pregnancy with laboratory evidence of Zika virus infection, based upon existing fetal growth monitoring for other maternal conditions (e.g., hypertension or diabetes) (2). However, there are no data specific to congenital Zika virus infection to guide these timing recommendations; clinicians may consider extending the time interval between ultrasounds in accordance with patient preferences and clinical judgment. Women with possible exposure but without laboratory evidence of Zika virus infection during pregnancy should receive ultrasound screening as recommended for routine prenatal care. Future data will be used to inform the optimal timing and frequency of ultrasound in pregnant women with possible Zika virus infection.

Amniocentesis. The role of amniocentesis for the detection of congenital Zika virus infection is unknown. Data regarding the positive and negative predictive values and optimal timing for amniocentesis are not available. Reports of the correlation between positive Zika test results in amniotic fluid and clinical phenotype or confirmatory infant laboratory testing are inconsistent (20,42,45,46). Zika virus RNA has been detected in amniotic fluid specimens; however, serial amniocenteses have demonstrated that

Zika virus RNA might only be present transiently (*45*). Therefore, a negative test result on amniotic fluid cannot rule out congenital Zika virus infection. However, if amniocentesis is indicated as part of the evaluation for abnormal prenatal findings, NAT testing for Zika virus should be considered to assist with the diagnosis of fetal infection.

Summary of prenatal diagnosis of congenital Zika virus infection. Given the limitations in the available screening modalities and the absence of effective interventions to prevent and treat congenital Zika virus infection, a shared decision-making model is essential to ensure that pregnant women and their families understand the risks and benefits of screening in the context of the patient's preferences and values. For example, serial ultrasound examinations might be inconvenient, unpleasant, and expensive, and might prompt unnecessary interventions; amniocentesis carries additional known risks such as fetal loss. These potential harms of prenatal screening for congenital Zika syndrome might outweigh the clinical benefits for some patients; therefore, these decisions should be individualized (*47*).

References

1. K. Russell et al., Update: Interim Guidance for the Evaluation and Management of Infants with Possible Congenital Zika Virus Infection—United States, 65 M.M.W.R. Morb. Mortal Wkly Rep. 870–78 (2016), https://dx.doi.org/10.15585/mmwr.mm6533e2.

2. T. Oduyebo et al., *Update: Interim Guidance for Health Care Providers Caring for Pregnant Women with Possible Zika Virus Exposure—United States (Including U.S. Territories)*, 66 M.M.W.R. Morb. Mortal Wkly Rep. 781–93 (2017), https://dx.doi.org/10.15585/mmwr.mm6629e1.

3. American Academy of Pediatrics, Committee on Practice and Ambulatory Medicine, Section on Ophthalmology, American Association of Certified Orthoptists, American Association for Pediatric Ophthalmology and Strabismus, American Academy of Ophthalmology, *Visual System Assessment in Infants, Children, and Young Adults by Pediatricians*, 137 Pediatrics e20153596 (2016), https://dx.doi.org/10.1542/peds.2015-3596.

4. R.J. Scharf, G. Scharf & A. Stroustrup, *Developmental Milestones*, 37 Pediatr. Rev. 25–37 (2016), https://dx.doi.org/10.1542/pir.2014-0103.

5. Council on Children with Disabilities; Section on Developmental Behavioral Pediatrics; Bright Futures Steering Committee; Medical Home Initiatives for Children with Special Needs Project Advisory Committee, *Identifying Infants and Young Children with Developmental Disorders in the Medical Home: An Algorithm for Developmental Surveillance and*

Screening, 118 PEDIATRICS 405–20 (2006), https://dx.doi.org/10.1542/peds.2006-1231.

6. American Academy of Pediatrics, Joint Committee on Infant Hearing, *Year 2007 Position Statement: Principles and Guidelines for Early Hearing Detection and Intervention Programs*, 120 PEDIATRICS 898–921 (2007), https://dx.doi.org/10.1542/peds.2007-2333.

7. S.A. Rasmussen et al, *Zika Virus and Birth Defects—Reviewing the Evidence for Causality*, 374 NEW ENG. J. MED. 1981–87 (2016), https://dx.doi.org/10.1056/NEJMsr1604338.

8. A.N. Hazin et al., *Microcephaly Epidemic Research Group, Computed Tomographic Findings in Microcephaly Associated with Zika Virus*, 374 NEW ENG. J. MED. 2193–95 (2016), https://dx.doi.org/10.1056/NEJMc1603617.

9. M. de Fatima Vasco Aragao et al., *Clinical Features and Neuroimaging (CT and MRI) Findings in Presumed Zika Virus Related Congenital Infection and Microcephaly: Retrospective Case Series Study*, 353 B.M.J. i1901 (2016), https://dx.doi.org/10.1136/bmj.i1901.

10. P. Soares de Oliveira-Szejnfeld et al., *Congenital Brain Abnormalities and Zika Virus: What the Radiologist Can Expect to See Prenatally and Postnatally*, 281 RADIOLOGY 203–18 (2016), https://dx.doi.org/10.1148/radiol.2016161584.

11. B. de Paula Freitas et al., *Ocular Findings in Infants with Microcephaly Associated with Presumed Zika Virus Congenital Infection in Salvador, Brazil*, 134 J.A.M.A. OPHTHALMOL. 529–35 (2016), https://dx.doi.org/10.1001/jamaophthalmol.2016.0267.

12. C.V. Ventura et al., *Ophthalmological Findings in Infants with Microcephaly and Presumable Intra-uterus Zika Virus Infection*, 79 ARQ. BRAS. OFTALMOL.1–3 (2016), https://dx.doi.org/10.5935/0004-2749.20160002.

13. I. Verçosa et al., *The Visual System in Infants with Microcephaly rRlated to Presumed Congenital Zika Syndrome*, 21 J. AAPOS 300–304.e1 (2017), https://dx.doi.org/10.1016/j.jaapos.2017.05.024.

14. C.A. Moore et al., *Characterizing the Pattern of Anomalies in Congenital Zika Syndrome for Pediatric Clinicians*, 171 J.A.M.A. PEDIATR. 288–95 (2017), https://dx.doi.org/10.1001/jamapediatrics.2016.3982.

15. M.C. Leal et al., *Hearing Loss in Infants with Microcephaly and Evidence of Congenital Zika Virus Infection—Brazil, November 2015–May 2016*, 65 M.M.W.R. MORB. MORTAL WKLY REP. 917–19 (2016), https://dx.doi.org/10.15585/mmwr.mm6534e3.

16. A.A. Zin et al., *Screening Criteria for Ophthalmic Manifestations of Congenital Zika Virus Infection*, 171 J.A.M.A. PEDIATR. 847–54 (2017), https://dx.doi.org/10.1001/jamapediatrics.2017.1474.

17. V. van der Linden et al., *Description of 13 Infants Born during October 2015–January 2016 with Congenital Zika Virus Infection without Microcephaly at Birth—Brazil*, 65 M.M.W.R. Morb. Mortal Wkly Rep. 1343–48 (2016), https://dx.doi.org/10.15585/mmwr.mm6547e2.

18. V. van der Linden, E.L.R. Filho & A. van der Linden, *Congenital Zika Syndrome: Clinical Aspects, in* Zika in Focus: Postnatal Clinical, Laboratorial and Radiological Aspects 33–46 (M. Vasco Aragão ed., 2017).

19. M.D. Carvalho et al., *Sleep EEG Patterns in Infants with Congenital Zika Virus Syndrome*, 128 Clin. Neurophys. 204–14 (2017), https://dx.doi.org/10.1016/j.clinph.2016.11.004.

20. A.S. Melo et al., *Congenital Zika Virus Infection: Beyond Neonatal Microcephaly*, 73 J.A.M.A. Neurol. 1407–16 (2016), https://dx.doi.org/10.1001/jamaneurol.2016.3720.

21. J.D.A. Meneses et al., *Lessons Learned at the Epicenter of Brazil's Congenital Zika Epidemic: Evidence from 87 Confirmed Cases*, 64 Clin. Infect. Dis. 1302–08 (2017), https:dx.doi.org/10.1093/cid/cix166.

22. A.S.R. Souza ASR et al., *Clinical and Laboratory Diagnosis of Congenital Zika Virus Syndrome and Diaphragmatic Unilateral Palsy: Case Report*, 16 Rev. Bras. Saude Mater. Infant 467–73 (2016), https://dx.doi.org/10.1590/1806-93042016000400007.

23. I.B. Rabe et al., *MTS. Interim Guidance for Interpretation of Zika Virus Antibody Test Results*, 65 M.M.W.R. Morb. Mortal Wkly Rep. 543–46 (2016), https://dx.doi.org/10.15585/mmwr.mm6521e1.

24. C.H. Calisher et al., *Antigenic Relationships between Flaviviruses as Determined by Cross-neutralization Tests with Polyclonal Antisera*, 70 J. Gen. Virol. 37–43 (1989), https://dx.doi.org/10.1099/0022-1317-70-1-37.

25. U.S. Dep't of Health & Human Services, Food & Drug Admin., *Zika Virus Response Updates from FDA* (2017), https://www.fda.gov/EmergencyPreparedness/Counterterrorism/MedicalCountermeasures/MCMIssues/ucm485199.htm.

[References 26–35 are omitted because they pertain only to parts of the CDC Guidance that are not included here.]

36. Committee on Practice Bulletins—Obstetrics and the American Institute of Ultrasound in Medicine, *Practice bulletin no. 175: Ultrasound in Pregnancy*, 128 Obstet. Gynecol. e241–56 (2016), https://dx.doi.org/10.1097/AOG.0000000000001815.

37. M. Vouga & D. Baud, *Imaging of Congenital Zika Virus Infection: The Route to Identification of Prognostic Factors*, 36 PRENAT. DIAGN. 799–811 (2016), https://dx.doi.org/10.1002/pd.4880.

38. E.C. Chibueze et al., *Diagnostic Accuracy of Ultrasound Scanning for Prenatal Microcephaly in the Context of Zika Virus Infection: A Systematic Review and Meta-analysis*, 7 SCI. REP. 2310 (2017), https://dx.doi.org/10.1038/s41598-017-01991-y.

39. P. Brasil et al., *Zika Virus Infection in Pregnant Women in Rio de Janeiro*, 375 NEW ENG. J. MED. 2321–34 (2016), https://dx.doi.org/10.1056/NEJMoa1602412.

40. M. Sarno et al., *Progressive Lesions of Central Nervous System in Microcephalic Fetuses with Suspected Congenital Zika Virus Syndrome*, ULTRASOUND OBSTET. GYNECOL. (2016), https://dx.doi.org/10.1002/uog.17303.

41. M. Parra-Saavedra et al., *Serial Head and Brain Imaging of 17 Fetuses with Confirmed Zika Virus Infection in Colombia, South America*, 130 OBSTET. GYNECOL. 207–12 (2017), https://dx.doi.org/10.1097/AOG.0000000000002105.

42. M. Besnard et al., *Congenital Cerebral Malformations and Dysfunction in Fetuses and Newborns Following the 2013 to 2014 Zika Virus Epidemic in French Polynesia*, 21 EURO. SURVEILL. 30181 (2016), https://dx.doi.org/10.2807/1560-7917.ES.2016.21.13.30181.

43. F.H. Carvalho et al., *Associated Ultrasonographic Findings in Fetuses with Microcephaly Because of Suspected Zika Virus (ZIKV) Infection during Pregnancy*, 36 PRENAT. DIAGN. 882–87 (2016), https://dx.doi.org/10.1002/pd.4882.

44. B. Schaub et al., *Ultrasound Imaging for Identification of Cerebral Damage in Congenital Zika Virus Syndrome: A Case Series*, 1 LANCET CHILD ADOLESC. HEALTH 45–55 (2017), https://dx.doi.org/10.1016/S2352-4642(17)30001-9.

45. B. Schaub et al., *Analysis of Blood from Zika Virus-Infected Fetuses: A Prospective Case Series*, 17 LANCET INFECT. DIS. 520–27 (2017), https://dx.doi.org/10.1016/S1473-3099(17)30102-0.

46. K. Herrera et al., *Vertical Transmission of Zika Virus (ZIKV) in Early Pregnancy: Two Cases, Two Different Courses*, 5 CASE REP. PERINATAL MED. 131–33 (2016), https://dx.doi.org/10.1515/crpm-2016-0027.

47. D.A. Grimes & K.F. Schulz, *Uses and Abuses of Screening Tests*, 359 LANCET 881–84 (2002), https://home.kku.ac.th/sompong/pdf/lancet/10.pdf.

Table of Cases